D1195508

Twentieth-Century Literary Criticism

Guide to Gale Literary Criticism Series

For criticism on	Consult these Gale series
Authors now living or who died after December 31, 1959	*CONTEMPORARY LITERARY CRITICISM (CLC)*
Authors who died between 1900 and 1959	*TWENTIETH-CENTURY LITERARY CRITICISM (TCLC)*
Authors who died between 1800 and 1899	*NINETEENTH-CENTURY LITERATURE CRITICISM (NCLC)*
Authors who died between 1400 and 1799 .	*LITERATURE CRITICISM FROM 1400 TO 1800 (LC)* *SHAKESPEAREAN CRITICISM (SC)*
Authors who died before 1400	*CLASSICAL AND MEDIEVAL LITERATURE CRITICISM (CMLC)*
Authors of books for children and young adults	*CHILDREN'S LITERATURE REVIEW (CLR)*
Dramatists	*DRAMA CRITICISM (DC)*
Poets	*POETRY CRITICISM (PC)*
Short story writers	*SHORT STORY CRITICISM (SSC)*
Black writers of the past two hundred years	*BLACK LITERATURE CRITICISM (BLC)*
Hispanic writers of the late nineteenth and twentieth centuries	*HISPANIC LITERATURE CRITICISM (HLC)*
Native North American writers and orators of the eighteenth, nineteenth, and twentieth centuries	*NATIVE NORTH AMERICAN LITERATURE (NNAL)*
Major authors from the Renaissance to the present	*WORLD LITERATURE CRITICISM, 1500 TO THE PRESENT (WLC)*

ISSN 0276-8178

Volume 89

Twentieth-Century Literary Criticism

**Criticism of the
Works of Novelists, Poets, Playwrights,
Short Story Writers, and Other Creative Writers
Who Lived between 1900 and 1960,
from the First Published Critical
Appraisals to Current Evaluations**

Jennifer Baise
Editor

Thomas Ligotti
Associate Editor

GALE GROUP

Detroit
San Francisco
London
Boston
Woodbridge, CT

STAFF

Jennifer Baise, *Editor*

Thomas Ligotti, *Associate Editor*

Maria Franklin, *Permissions Manager*
Kimberly F. Smilay, *Permissions Specialist*
Kelly A. Quin, *Permissions Associates*
Sandy Gore, *Permissions Assistant*

Victoria B. Cariappa, *Research Manager*
Andrew Guy Malonis, Barbara McNeil, Gary J. Oudersluys, Maureen Richards, Cheryl L. Warnock, *Research Specialists*
Patricia T. Ballard, Tamara C. Nott, Tracie A. Richardson, *Research Associates*
Phyllis Blackman, Corrine Stocker, *Research Assistant*

Mary Beth Trimper, *Production Director*
Cindy Range, *Buyer*

Gary Leach, *Graphic Artist*
Randy Bassett, *Image Database Supervisor*
Robert Duncan, Michael Logusz, *Imaging Specialists*
Pamela Reed, *Imaging Coordinator*

Library of Congress Catalog Card Number 76-46132
ISBN 0-7876-2745-3
ISSN 0276-8178

Printed in the United States of America
10 9 8 7 6 5 4 3 2 1

Contents

Preface   vii

Acknowledgments   xi

Preface

Since its inception more than fifteen years ago, *Twentieth-Century Literary Criticism* has been purchased and used by nearly 10,000 school, public, and college or university libraries. *TCLC* has covered more than 500 authors, representing 58 nationalities, and over 25,000 titles. No other reference source has surveyed the critical response to twentieth-century authors and literature as thoroughly as *TCLC*. In the words of one reviewer, "there is nothing comparable available." *TCLC* "is a gold mine of information—dates, pseudonyms, biographical information, and criticism from books and periodicals—which many libraries would have difficulty assembling on their own."

Scope of the Series

TCLC is designed to serve as an introduction to authors who died between 1900 and 1960 and to the most significant interpretations of these author's works. The great poets, novelists, short story writers, playwrights, and philosophers of this period are frequently studied in high school and college literature courses. In organizing and reprinting the vast amount of critical material written on these authors, *TCLC* helps students develop valuable insight into literary history, promotes a better understanding of the texts, and sparks ideas for papers and assignments. Each entry in *TCLC* presents a comprehensive survey of an author's career or an individual work of literature and provides the user with a multiplicity of interpretations and assessments. Such variety allows students to pursue their own interests; furthermore, it fosters an awareness that literature is dynamic and responsive to many different opinions.

Every fourth volume of *TCLC* is devoted to literary topics. These topic entries widen the focus of the series from individual authors to such broader subjects as literary movements, prominent themes in twentieth-century literature, literary reaction to political and historical events, significant eras in literary history, prominent literary anniversaries, and the literatures of cultures that are often overlooked by English-speaking readers.

TCLC is designed as a companion series to Gale's *Contemporary Literary Criticism,* which reprints commentary on authors now living or who have died since 1960. Because of the different periods under consideration, there is no duplication of material between *CLC* and *TCLC*. For additional information about *CLC* and Gale's other criticism titles, users should consult the Guide to Gale Literary Criticism Series preceding the title page in this volume.

Coverage

Each volume of *TCLC* is carefully compiled to present:

- criticism of authors, or literary topics, representing a variety of genres and nationalities

- both major and lesser-known writers and literary works of the period

- 6-12 authors or 3-6 topics per volume

- individual entries that survey critical response to each author's work or each topic in literary history, including early criticism to reflect initial reactions; later criticism to represent any rise or decline in reputation; and current retrospective analyses.

Organization of This Book

An author entry consists of the following elements: author heading, biographical and critical introduction, list of principal works, reprints of criticism (each preceded by an annotation and a bibliographic citation), and a bibliography of further reading.

- The **Author Heading** consists of the name under which the author most commonly wrote, followed by birth and death dates. If an author wrote consistently under a pseudonym, the pseudonym will be listed in the author heading and the real name given in parentheses on the first line of the biographical and critical introduction. Also located at the beginning of the introduction to the author entry are any name variations under which an author wrote, including transliterated forms for authors whose languages use nonroman alphabets.

- The **Biographical and Critical Introduction** outlines the author's life and career, as well as the critical issues surrounding his or her work. References to past volumes of *TCLC* are provided at the beginning of the introduction. Additional sources of information in other biographical and critical reference series published by Gale, including *Short Story Criticism, Children's Literature Review, Contemporary Authors, Dictionary of Literary Biography,* and *Something about the Author,* are listed in a box at the end of the entry.

- Some *TCLC* entries include **Portraits** of the author. Entries also may contain reproductions of materials pertinent to an author's career, including manuscript pages, title pages, dust jackets, letters, and drawings, as well as photographs of important people, places, and events in an author's life.

- The **List of Principal Works** is chronological by date of first book publication and identifies the genre of each work. In the case of foreign authors with both foreign-language publications and English translations, the title and date of the first English-language edition are given in brackets. Unless otherwise indicated, dramas are dated by first performance, not first publication.

- Critical essays are prefaced by **Annotations** providing the reader with information about both the critic and the criticism that follows. Included are the critic's reputation, individual approach to literary criticism, and particular expertise in an author's works. Also noted are the relative importance of a work of criticism, the scope of the essay, and the growth of critical controversy or changes in critical trends regarding an author. In some cases, these annotations cross-reference essays by critics who discuss each other's commentary.

- A complete **Bibliographic Citation** designed to facilitate location of the original essay or book precedes each piece of criticism.

- Criticism is arranged chronologically in each author entry to provide a perspective on changes in critical evaluation over the years. All titles of works by the author featured in the entry are printed in boldface type to enable the user to easily locate discussion of particular works. Also for purposes of easier identification, the critic's name and the publication date of the essay are given at the beginning of each piece of criticism. Unsigned criticism is preceded by the title of the journal in which it appeared. Some of the essays in *TCLC* also contain translated material. Unless otherwise noted, translations in brackets are by the editors; translations in parentheses or continuous with the text are by the critic. Publication information (such as footnotes or page and line references to specific editions of works) have been deleted at the editor's discretion to provide smoother reading of the text.

- An annotated list of **Further Reading** appearing at the end of each author entry suggests secondary sources on the author. In some cases it includes essays for which the editors could not obtain reprint rights.

Cumulative Indexes

- Each volume of *TCLC* contains a cumulative **Author Index** listing all authors who have appeared in Gale's Literary Criticism Series, along with cross references to such biographical series as *Contemporary Authors* and *Dictionary of Literary Biography*. For readers' convenience, a complete list of Gale titles included appears on the first page of the author index. Useful for locating authors within the various series, this index is particularly valuable for those authors who are identified by a certain period but who, because of their death dates, are placed in another, or for those authors whose careers span two periods. For example, F. Scott Fitzgerald is found in *TCLC,* yet a writer often associated with him, Ernest Hemingway, is found in *CLC.*

- Each *TCLC* volume includes a cumulative **Nationality Index** which lists all authors who have appeared in *TCLC* volumes, arranged alphabetically under their respective nationalities, as well as Topics volume entries devoted to particular national literatures.

- Each new volume in Gale's Literary Criticism Series includes a cumulative **Topic Index,** which lists all literary topics treated in *NCLC, TCLC, LC 1400-1800,* and the *CLC* yearbook.

- Each new volume of *TCLC,* with the exception of the Topics volumes, includes a **Title Index** listing the titles of all literary works discussed in the volume. In response to numerous suggestions from librarians, Gale has also produced a **Special Paperbound Edition** of the *TCLC* title index. This annual cumulation lists all titles discussed in the series since its inception and is issued with the first volume of *TCLC* published each year. Additional copies of the index are available on request. Librarians and patrons will welcome this separate index; it saves shelf space, is easy to use, and is recyclable upon receipt of the following year's cumulation. Titles discussed in the Topics volume entries are not included *TCLC* cumulative index.

Citing Twentieth-Century Literary Criticism

When writing papers, students who quote directly from any volume in Gale's literary Criticism Series may use the following general forms to footnote reprinted criticism. The first example pertains to materials drawn from periodicals, the second to material reprinted from books.

[1]William H. Slavick, "Going to School to DuBose Heyward," *The Harlem Renaissance Re-examined,* (AMS Press, 1987); reprinted in *Twentieth-Century Literary Criticism,* Vol. 59, ed. Jennifer Gariepy (Detroit: Gale Research, 1995), pp. 94-105.

[2]George Orwell, "Reflections on Gandhi," *Partisan Review,* 6 (Winter 1949), pp. 85-92; reprinted in *Twentieth-Century Literary Criticism,* Vol. 59, ed. Jennifer Gariepy (Detroit: Gale Research, 1995), pp. 40-3.

Suggestions Are Welcome

In response to suggestions, several features have been added to *TCLC* since the series began, including annotations to critical essays, a cumulative index to authors in all Gale literary criticism series, entries devoted to criticism on a single work by a major author, more extensive illustrations, and a title index listing all literary works discussed in the series since its inception.

Readers who wish to suggest authors or topics to appear in future volumes, or who have other suggestions, are cordially invited to write the editors.

Acknowledgments

The editors wish to thank the copyright holders of the criticism included in this volume and the permissions managers of many book and magazine publishing companies for assisting us in securing reproduction rights. We are also grateful to the staffs of the Detroit Public Library, the Library of Congress, the University of Detroit Mercy Library, Wayne State University Purdy/Kresge Library Complex, and the University of Michigan Libraries for making their resources available to us. Following is a list of the copyright holders who have granted us permission to reproduce material in this volume of *TCLC*. Every effort has been made to trace copyright, but if omissions have been made, please let us know.

Producer" in *The First Film Makers.* Edited by Richard Dyer MacCann. The Scarecrow Press, Inc., 1989. © Copyright 1989 by Richard Dyer MacCann. All rights reserved. Reproduced by permission.—Jacobsen, Sally A. From *Virginia Woolf: Themes and Variations.* Pace University Press, 1993. Copyright © 1993 by Pace University Press. All rights reserved. Reproduced by permission of the author.

PHOTOGRAPHS AND ILLUSTRATIONS APPEARING IN *TCLC,* VOLUME 89, WERE RECEIVED FROM THE FOLLOWING SOURCES:

Mead, George Herbert, photograph. The Library of Congress. Thomas, Martha Carey, photograph. UPI/Corbis-Bettmann. Reproduced by permission.Williams, Ben Ames, photograph. The Library of Congress.

Thomas H. Ince

1882-1924

(Full name Thomas Harper Ince) American filmmaker.

INTRODUCTION

A prolific director and producer of the silent film era, Ince is regarded as a pioneer in the motion picture industry and generally credited with streamlining the modern method of studio filmmaking. He is principally noted for his introduction of very detailed, written "continuities"—later known as shooting scripts—into the filmmaking process, an innovation that greatly improved efficiency and quality in Hollywood films. Also among his accomplishments, Ince is thought to have elevated the film genre of the Western to the level of true art with his production of *The Aryan*. While Ince personally directed many of his features at the beginning of his career, including his early triumph *The Battle of Gettysburg,* and produced hundreds more, he is generally remembered for his work as the executive producer and creative force behind a multitude of motion pictures, including the antiwar film *Civilization.*

Biographical Information

Ince was born in Newport, Rhode Island on 6 November 1882. His father was a comedian, and from his youth Ince took acting jobs in vaudeville and stage dramas. Later he defected to the new medium of film, performing for Carl Laemmle's Independent Motion Pictures (IMP) Company and others. Ince directed his first motion picture, entitled *Little Nell's Tobacco,* for IMP in 1910. After completing several more films for Laemmle and agreeing to direct a series of movies starring Mary Pickford, Ince signed on with the New York Motion Picture Company in late 1911, and began making pictures, mostly Westerns, in Los Angeles. With some hundred shorter films to his credit, Ince began work on his first full-length feature, *The Battle of Gettysburg.* After completing the film in 1913, Ince ceased the work of direction himself for all but a few projects, delegating this responsibility to such notables as Reginald Barker, Fred Niblo, Lambert Hillyer, William S. Hart, Roland Lee, and Frank Borzage. In 1915, Ince and his business associates formed their own production company, Triangle. The success of his works with Triangle, including *Civilization,* allowed Ince to build a large studio complex at Culver City in 1916. Ince departed Triangle in 1918 to form his own production company. He eventually joined Associated Producers, Inc. in 1919 and continued to produce a great number of films for the next several years after Associated Producers was absorbed by First National in 1922. In November of 1924, Ince attended a party on the yacht of newspaper mogul William Randolph Hearst. He was carried off the boat and died of heart failure two days later amid unsubstantiated rumors of scandal and foul play.

Major Works

Critics have found Ince's contribution to the motion picture industry somewhat difficult to evaluate. From 1910 to 1913, when he was still directing his films, he created a series of popularly successful, realistic Westerns, most notably *War on the Plains* and the well-regarded Civil War picture *The Battle of Gettysburg,* a film that no longer exists. A collaborator for the majority of his career, Ince's credit on most of his later films is as executive producer. Fulfilling this role, Ince insisted that his directors follow strict shooting scripts, which included detailed commentary on sets, costumes, camera angles, and the various other minutiae of filmmaking, factors which are generally left in the hands of individual directors. Ince is also generally credited with the technical innovations of such films as *The Bargain,* which features a series of powerful exterior shots of a picturesque Arizona canyon. Again as a producer, Ince is said to have infused the genre of the Western with the grandeur of legend in *The Aryan.* Considered Ince's greatest production, the propaganda film *Civilization* dramatizes the evils of war in grandiose spectacle. A submarine commander unwilling to torpedo a passenger ship, the hero of *Civilization* opens the way to mutiny and precipitates the destruction of his sub. Following his death, his soul travels to Purgatory and to Heaven, where he is redeemed by Christ.

Critical Reception

In the early days of film, many of Ince's motion pictures were immensely successful and lucrative ventures. In the years since his death, critical speculation as to Ince's legacy in the history of film has been the source of considerable contention. Scholars in America have generally acknowledged Ince's business acumen, eye for talent, and innovative systemization of the filmmaking process. A contingent of European film historians, however, have taken a broader view. Led by the influential French critic Jean Mitry, European commentators have viewed Ince as an original artist whose influence rivals that of filmmaker D. W. Griffith. Mitry has remarked, "If Griffith was the first poet of an art whose basic syntax he created, one could say that Ince was its first dramaturgist. His experiments, in fact, were based on the composition of original themes, on the expression of ideas. . . . He was able to guide and discipline his collaborators only because, like them, he was a director, and superior to them."

*PRINCIPAL WORKS

Little Nell's Tobacco (film) 1910
A Manly Man (film) 1911
The Aggressor (film) 1911
Artful Kate (film) 1911
Behind the Stockade (film) 1911
The Dream (film) 1911
The Fisher-Maid (film) 1911
For Her Brother's Sake (film) 1911
Her Darkest Hour (film) 1911
In Old Madrid (film) 1911
In the Sultan's Garden (film) 1911
Maid or Man (film) 1911
The Message in the Bottle (film) 1911
The New Cook (film) 1911
The New Cowboy (film) 1911
The Silver Dollar (film) 1911
Sweet Memories of Yesterday (film) 1911
Their First Misunderstanding (film) 1911
The Winning of Wonega (film) 1911
A Double Reward (film) 1912
Across the Plains (film) 1912
The Battle of the Red Men (film) 1912
The Colonel's Ward (film) 1912
The Crisis (film) 1912
Custer's Last Fight (film) 1912
The Deserter (film) 1912
For Freedom of Cuba (film) 1912
The Hidden Trail (film) 1912
The Indian Massacre (film) 1912
The Invaders (film) 1912
The Law of the West (film) 1912
Lieutenant's Last Fight (film) 1912
On the Firing Line (film) 1912
Renegade (film) 1912
War on the Plains (film) 1912
When Lee Surrenders (film) 1912
A Shadow of the Past (film) 1913
The Ambassador's Envoy (film) 1913
The Battle of Gettysburg (film) 1913
Bread Cast upon the Water (film) 1913
The Boomerang (film) 1913
Days of '49 (film) 1913
The Drummer of the Eighth (film) 1913
The Mosaic Law (film) 1913
The Pride of the South (film) 1913
The Seal of Silence (film) 1913
With Lee in Virginia (film) 1913
A Relic of Old Japan (film) 1914
The Golden Goose (film) 1914
The Last of the Line (film) 1914
Love's Sacrifice (film) 1914
One of the Discard (film) 1914
The Despoiler (film) 1915
The Aryan [producer] (film) 1916
Civilization [producer] (film) 1916

*Ince collaborated to some degree on nearly all of his films. The Principal Works list includes only those works (except for *Civilization* and *The Aryan*) for which he is named as the principal director.

CRITICISM

Peter Milne (essay date 1922)

SOURCE: Chapter XV and Chapter XVI, in *Motion Picture Directing: The Facts and Theories of the Newest Art*, Falk Publishing Co., Inc., 1922, pp. 136-51.

[*In the following excerpt, Milne describes Ince's strict film production process and lists several studio directors who successfully used his methods.*]

As a general rule there is no love lost between directors and scenario writers. This is particularly the case in the big producing companies where directors work more or less on a schedule, an elastic schedule to be sure, but nevertheless a schedule. In these companies a director seldom has a chance to co-operate with the scenario writer on the construction of a continuity. Sometimes he has complaints on it which are never taken up and discussed due to lack of time. As a result the director blames the scenario writer for the mistakes in the finished picture.

With the case of the directors who have proven themselves in an artistic way, it will be found that the majority of them have much to say about the handling of their stories in continuity form. They either actually co-operate on the writing of the continuity from which they are to work or they claim to discard continuities altogether and work from notes, a brief synopsis or—from the head.

Both the De Milles have much to say about the writing of continuities from which they work. As a consequence when it comes to the actual task of directing they are dealing with their own ideas. It has been related how D. W. Griffith prefers to work without a continuity and his reasons therefore. Frank Borzage is a champion for the continuity synopsis, a running account of the plot, undivided into scenes. Many other directors prefer this method, dividing their pictures into the desired and natural number of scenes during actual work. All such directors claim that to follow a scene numbered continuity through directly results in a mechanical picture. Like the De Milles they claim that to produce such a picture well, they must also have a hand in the writing of the mechanical continuity.

On the face of it the arguments of these directors seem sound. But it is easy enough to take the other side of the question and riddle the arguments completely. The stand can be taken that the motion picture director performs no other functions than those performed by the stage director. And many and many a stage director has turned out productions of artistic worth by merely following the author's manuscript. Few stage directors decline to direct a Shakespearean production for the reason that they didn't have a hand in the writing of the play.

Which brings up the methods employed by Thomas H. Ince, probably the most successful producing-director in the entire field of motion pictures. Mr. Ince is at the head of a number of producing units. He has a certain number of directors making pictures for him. Over the work of these men he exercises an actual supervision. And when a director works for Mr. Ince he does what Mr. Ince tells him to do.

Mr. Ince is one of the veterans of the picture producing craft. He has developed more stars, perhaps, than any other man in the field today. William S. Hart, Charles Ray, Dorothy Dalton and Louise Glaum are the brightest of those he has brought out. And the secret of Thomas H. Ince's greatness, whether he admits it himself or not, is the minute attention he pays to the matter of preparing the continuities of the pictures from which his directors work.

Probably Mr. Ince pays more attention to this preparation of a continuity than does any other producer. In his opinion the greater part of the work of producing a picture has been completed when the continuity is in final shape to hand to the director.

Equipped with the power of visualization to a remarkable degree Mr. Ince and his production manager thoroughly scrutinize the continuity when it is handed them by a member of the scenario department. Every point in the story, and every point in its development at the hands of the continuity writer is discussed. As a rule when the continuity is returned to its author there are a number of alterations and changes to be made. And when these are made Mr. Ince goes over the script again. Sometimes this interchange of ideas is carried on between Mr. Ince and his scenario department for six or eight times before the continuity is in final shape for the director.

Then when the director finally does receive the manuscript he finds some such order as this stamped across its face: "Produce this exactly as written!" This, however, is not the arbitrary demand of an autocrat. If the director sees a place where a change will work some good to the story he has the privilege of placing the matter before Mr. Ince himself. But for the most part the Ince continuities are so thoroughly gone over before placing them in the hands of the directors that few if any changes for the better suggest themselves.

Therefore when the Ince director starts to work on the picture he is carrying out the ideas of the continuity writer and his chief to the most minute detail. His is the business of directing the picture, not of creating it in the broadest sense of the words.

Now according to other directors who insist that such a method of procedure produces mechanical results, is responsible for a work lacking in inspiration and all the finer qualities that go to make a picture, and degrades the director into the position of a mere clerk, Mr. Ince's pictures would be the worst the art has to offer. The fact that they are the most consistently meritorious that the art has to offer would seem to refute the arguments brought up by these others completely.

So what is the answer? Griffith produces good pictures after his method. Borzage and a number of others produce good pictures after the same methods, or methods practically the same. And Mr. Ince, hands his director a continuity divided strictly into scenes, each camera angle is numbered and for a purpose, for the director to go out and make all these camera angles, these scenes, just as Mr. Ince ordered him to.

The answer is, after all, quite simple. Mr. Ince has capabilities matched by no other director in the producing art. One of his capabilities may be matched here and there but never all of them by another individual. Thus Mr. Ince and his scenario department are the creators of Ince pictures. The directors he employs carry out his ideas. And these directors, while the above argument may prove them mere automatons, are in reality skilled men, artists for the most part, versed in all the niceties of picture producing. The fact that the majority of them, when they have left Mr. Ince's fold, have succeeded on their own separate accounts, is proof of that.

The matter, therefore, simmers down to this simple problem. Can a producing organization turn out better pictures than an individual director? The solution of the problem is in the following qualified statement: Yes, when the producing organization is headed by Thomas H. Ince.

Mr. Ince's qualifications for such leadership are manifold. To begin with, he is, naturally, a born leader of men. If chance had led him into the business world instead of the art of motion picture producing he might well be a bank director or a railroad official. He would know his business thoroughly whatever it was and then would proceed with the utmost confidence in his own knowledge. Of course he would make mistakes even as he has made some few mistakes in picture producing but more often the reverse from mistakes would be the case.

Anyone familiar with Mr. Ince will talk for hours on his magnetic personality. It is a personality that few, if any, seem able to resist. Thus he is able to give orders and have them carried out to the letter without giving offense. It seems that giving orders without accompanying them by a modicum of offense is a pretty hard thing to do. Dozens of men in the craft of picture producing would trade almost anything they've got for this ability of Mr. Ince's.

On top of these qualities, invaluable from whatever angle of business or art that they are approached is Mr. Ince's thorough knowledge of making pictures. This knowledge is not confined to one department of production, nor does he specialize in a single department of production. He is conversant with every department and is able to consider each one in its proper light, to value it properly, particularly with its relation to the others.

Still there are the individualists that oppose Mr. Ince and belittle his methods. He doesn't bother about them often as he employs directors who are willing to work into his scheme of production and these for the most part have been richly rewarded.

There is an interesting story in connection with one individualistic director, whose name shall be kept a secret for his own sake, and the Ince organization. It appears that Mr. Ince had signed this director to a contract without inquiring into his willingness to work along the prescribed Ince lines.

The continuity of a comedy-drama was handed him shortly after his arrival at the studio and he was told that everything was in readiness for him to begin work.

The director read the continuity and addressed himself to Mr. Ince somewhat as follows: "You don't expect me to produce this, do you? Why this continuity is so bad that it couldn't possibly turn out to be a good picture. I won't make it!"

Mr. Ince, with the director's name fastened on the end of a contract, is alleged to have replied with a certain degree of forcefulness: "You will produce it."

The argument went back and forth. The director wanted to work but he didn't want to work in the Ince manner. Mr. Ince's pride and temper were undoubtedly stirred and he insisted that the director produce the picture along the lines prescribed by him.

Finally an agreement was reached. The director condescended to produce the picture on condition that when it was produced his name was to be left off it as director. Mr. Ince acceded to this demand.

To do the director credit he then went about his work sincerely. Mr. Ince watched him carefully and realized that he was doing his best, though still believing the cause was hopeless. The director, when he finished work, was dismissed from whatever further terms were contained in the contract.

And so the picture was put before the public without the individualistic director's name upon it. It was one of the most successful pictures ever released. It was an irresistible comedy-drama and everyone who saw it fairly revelled in it.

The director when he realized how he had talked himself out of credit for one of the art's best pictures must have fretted and fumed considerably. Equally galling must have been the large advertising bills he received for pointing out the fact to the motion picture trade in large announcements that he had directed the picture. For Mr. Ince had lived up to the agreement to the letter. He had not only left the director's name off the picture but had removed it from all advertising as well.

Mr. Ince had his little joke.

And probably the director doesn't care much now anyway. He is a success with another company and is still saying that he can't make good pictures from a continuity on which he didn't work himself.

. . . . .

Those who cry down the methods employed by Thomas H. Ince with respect to the directors who work in his studio often state that the Ince school of directing snuffs out any original ideas that a director may possess and makes him a mere picture mechanic, capable only of turning out mechanical and uninteresting pictures.

And lest it be thought that sufficient proof hasn't been offered to counteract this argument some few of the directors who started under the early Ince regime and left to make their marks as individualists elsewhere are mentioned here.

There is Reginald Barker, long on the Ince staff, who until recently was employed at the Goldwyn studios and who was entrusted with the direction of many of their most important stories and stars. The facts and records point to only one conclusion, that Mr. Barker has directed some of the most successful pictures made by the Goldwyn company and is one of the most reliable men in the field today.

There is Fred Niblo who after a short session at the Ince studio turned his energy elsewhere. Mr. Niblo happens to be the man who directed Douglas Fairbanks in the highly successful *Three Musketeers*. No one, within or without the field of motion pictures, has once stated that *The Three Musketeers* appears to be the work of an automaton.

There is R. William Neill, who, since he left the Ince school some several years ago has been hard put to it to accept all the positions he has had offered him. Other picture producers are not in the habit of seeking a man to fill the responsible position of director when he can only carry out the definite orders of his superior.

There is Jerome Storm who while with the Ince organization made a big name for himself by directing many of the pictures in which Charles Ray appeared. Mr. Storm left Mr. Ince when Mr. Ray left him. Mr. Storm directed Mr. Ray's first independent picture. Mr. Ray, since he has been directing his own pictures, shows sadly the lack of Mr. Storm's guiding hand. And Mr. Storm has had various positions since leaving Mr. Ray—in fact, has had quite as many as he could well take care of.

There is Victor Shertzinger who while with Mr. Ince also made some very good Charles Ray pictures. With the Goldwyn company he made an enviable reputation for himself as a director of light comedy and proved more successful in handling Mabel Normand than any other director with the sole exception of Mack Sennett himself. Mr. Shertzinger is now at the head of his own producing company. A difficult post for a man to achieve who is no more than a mere mechanic taking orders from a producing genius such as Mr. Ince!

There is Lambert Hillyer, who with this writing is back with Mr. Ince after several years in the service of William S. Hart, directing and writing the majority of that star's pictures. Mr. Hart would hardly pick a mechanical nincompoop to direct his screen efforts which are considerably important both to Mr. Hart and the public at large.

There is Frank Borzage himself who was with Mr. Ince a long time as an actor and who had ample opportunity to absorb his system of directing. And Mr. Borzage, as has been previously stated, is quite a worthy director.

There is Roland Lee, one of the younger directors, developed by Mr. Ince who only recently left him and who immediately made a name for himself directing some Hobart Bosworth pictures and who at this writing is with the Goldwyn company handling the directorial end of some of that company's most important pictures.

This is an array of directors rather difficult to match. And if it was tried to match it from a list of directors turned out by any other producing-director or any other producing organization, the poor fellow who tried would find himself in for a life's job.

To work in the Ince school of directing is, indeed, the luckiest thing that can befall a director. Instead of making him an insignificant employe, merely carrying out the work mapped out by the man higher up, it teaches him thoroughly all branches of picture directing so that when he strikes out for himself he is far better able to approach the excellence achieved by his former superior than he would be without such schooling.

Thomas H. Ince (essay date 1925)

SOURCE: "The Challenge for the Motion Picture Producer," in *The First Film Makers*, edited by Richard Dyer MacCann, The Scarecrow Press, Inc., 1989, pp. 110-14.

[*In the following essay, originally published in 1925, Ince expresses his desire for clarity, continuity, intensity, and above all realism in motion pictures.*]

We are living in an age when the white light of criticism is turned upon accepted and established standards in all phases of life. The old order of things has passed, and all over the world worn-out traditions and methods are toppling. We are in the grip of another renaissance, a revolution of ideals. Like the phoenix of mythology, the new world order is rising out of the ashes of the old.

The picture of yesterday fulfilled its mission, giving way to the newer and higher standards demanded of the picture of today. And because some of the modern productions are now reaching such a high standard, the public has learned to expect even greater achievements. Picturegoers have shown their faith in us, and by that very faith they have thrown us a challenge to produce bigger and

better pictures. Are we going to accept that challenge and make the picture of tomorrow take its rightful place in the onward march of progress? I, for one, pledge myself to this task.

The demand for better pictures is universal. On that point we all agree. But that demand brings up the question, 'What constitutes better pictures?' This question must be answered first by the producer and finally by the public itself, for in the final analysis it is the public who is the court of last appeal on the merits of a picture. It is in their hands to make it or break it.

But the producer with insight and a real desire to perfect his art, can and must feel the pulse of the vast American audience, and anticipate its desires and demands.

I hold it not only a duty but a privilege to study carefully the reactions of various types of pictures on the average audience, for only in that way can I reach my conclusions and give my interpretation of what constitutes better pictures.

The really successful photodrama of today, and I believe tomorrow, is one that catches the interest and holds the eager attention through sheer force of HUMANNESS AND FIDELITY TO DETAIL OF LIFE. The day has long since passed when our characters move like marionettes across the screen.

The public demands, and justly so, the faithful portrayal of life as it is lived by real flesh and blood people in all its various walks. They demand true characterizations, that they may see themselves reflected on the screen. The problems of human existence vary only in degree. Basically they are identical and fundamental. Therefore a picture with forced dramatic situations and emotions does not ring true. It is based upon a false premise and the audience leaves the theatre unsatisfied and unconvinced.

But a picture that is written and produced by those who are close students of human nature—and who portray faithfully the problems and desires of the human family—holds up the mirror of life to us and we see ourselves in circumstances and surroundings that are familiar to us. But that is not all. Seeing those everyday things of life worked out on the screen to successful or non-successful issues, as the case may be, we will get a new angle, perhaps, on how to handle our particular problems. Seeing real characters with real problems to solve, which parallel our own, we will get reactions that, in many instances, will give us courage to meet our own problems, our own successes and our own heartaches, and to handle them to our own satisfaction.

Nor do I mean by that, that the screen must preach. That is not its mission. It must entertain and give us the form of amusement that relaxes and at the same time stimulates. But it must do this through the portrayal of life as we know it, and it must give us something that will enhance the value of our own lives, which are too often drab and colorless.

It makes no difference whether the story is a comedy, a tragedy, or a straight dramatic exposition of life, so long as it rings true and gives us life as we know it, and something to take away with us that is finer and bigger than what we may have had before.

A striking instance of this comes to mind which had just that result. A play was put on the stage several years ago which was a brilliant comedy. I use that term in its finest sense. It was not a frothy farce. It was a story which dealt with one of the accepted tragedies of life, and would have been treated as such by nine playwrights out of ten. But this particular playwright chose to treat his theme as a comedy.

The principal character was played by a woman of perhaps forty who had been jilted by her lover on the eve of her wedding, twenty years before. Instead of accepting this condition as a tragedy and allowing it to cloud her life, she overcame it and developed into a woman of poise, charm, and power, handling her life with that light touch that laughs at grim tragedy, and handling all whom she contacted as she would handle pawns on a chessboard, bringing them all to her feet as willing victims of her charm and beauty of nature.

It is not the story that I wish to dwell upon in this instance, but the effect that it had upon the audience. At the end of the first act, the middle-aged people in the audience were sitting up with a new sense of their own power and importance. At the end of the second act there was a sparkle in the eyes of those who had felt that life was slipping into the background. When the curtain fell on the last act, which was the final triumph of the jilted lady, there was a tumultuous applause, and in the faces of the audience that left the theater, old and young, men and women, there was a look that bespoke a new lease on life and a courage to handle each individual problem that was uppermost in their own lives.

That play was a slice of life, faithfully portrayed. There was not one action that did not ring true, not one characterization that was false, and its effect crashed across the footlights and found a response in the hearts of all who saw it.

When pictures were in their infancy, which was but a few short years ago, the one idea seemed to be to make something happen on the screen. Action, and more action, with little thought of making that action portray the emotions and true experiences of life.

Action is absolutely essential to the successful photoplay. Without it there would be no screen drama. But it must be action which conveys the coordination of mind, heart, and body, rather than meaningless action alone. Because of this a distinct technique of creating screen material has developed and is in the process of larger and fuller development.

In the last few years there has been an enormous demand for rights to the published story and the successful play, but the field for that type of material is becoming exhausted. Furthermore, producers are realizing that the published story and play are not always adapted to the screen.

Stripped of the brilliant, intense, and humorous lines which have put a play over, or the literary style of a published story, there is, in many cases, very little left to carry five reels of plot and action on the screen. In other words there is not enough meat in the plot itself.

Therefore the producer is compelled to pad it, or to entirely rebuild the story, and when it is finished it has either lost its spontaneity or is so unlike the original that the public is disappointed. It is not a new story and it is not the one that they know and love. It is neither fish nor fowl nor good red herring.

This is not necessarily true of every published story or play, however. It is the exception that proves the rule, and in some instances a producer procures the rights to a Broadway hit or a best seller which is admirably adapted to the screen and then we have a double hit.

But for a sustained and consistent source of photoplay material the screen must develop its own writers, men and women who possess insight into the lives and emotions of their fellow beings, and who are able to depict the characterizations about them with sincerity and simplicity.

The theme or keynote of the story must be REAL. It must be based upon a fundamental principle of life, something which every man and woman knows in common with his neighbor—some underlying basis of human existence which touches the lives of the laborer or the capitalist, the show girl or the queen. The theme must be a universal language—love, greed, sacrifice, fear, or any emotion which is generally known to the human family.

Building on the theme, the plot should be no less one of sincerity and simplicity. It should have one clearly defined logical plot thread running unbroken through the story, with the counter plots converging to the main thread of the story and never distracting the attention from it.

Plots should be constructed UP, not DOWN. Situations and episodes should be gauged to lead to a climax that will accentuate all preceding scenes. The climax should be strong, virile, picturesque, colorful—redolent of life's passions.

Sequences should be arranged with strict attention to coherency and continuity of action. Each situation should be better and stronger than its predecessor, almost independent of its forerunner, so far as quality and story values are concerned.

Many writers have fallen short of their mark because they opened their plot with a crash, so to speak, and depending on this intensity at the start, allowed interest to lag, through failure to provide subsequent situations and climaxes of real dramatic merit. The successful photoplay is one that is well balanced throughout, always leading on and on, stimulating imagination and preparing for the ultimate finale which appeases and satisfies the expectant spectator.

It is a mistake to pile in many complications to force the action. This distracts the mind of the audience from the main story plot and is confusing. After such a picture has been viewed, it is almost impossible for the average person to relate the story in any logical sequence, and the result is that their brains are muddled and the reactions they get are a hodge-podge of complications and forced action.

The situations which carry the plot to its climax must be the everyday experiences that happen in the lives of the human family. Nor does that destroy the dramatic values of the story.

A dramatic scene portrayed on the screen will thrill an audience with its intensity even though that same scene lived in a Harlem flat or on a Texas ranch would impress those who were living the episode as commonplace or at least pleasant or unpleasant as the case may be. They would fail to realize the dramatic value of their own lives.

That is the art of the screen, as I see it, and the secret of better pictures: to hold up the mirror of life and show us to ourselves.

The stories that are going to lead to better pictures must be deeply human, expressed in such a way that every ounce of pathos, humor, characterization, and dramatic quality is felt by the audience, without forcing these elements to an illogical point or permitting imagination to make inroads upon truth.

George Mitchell (essay date 1960)

SOURCE: "Thomas H. Ince Was the Pioneer Producer Who Systematized the Making of a Movie," in *Films in Review*, Vol. XI, No. 8, October, 1960, pp. 464-84.

[*In the following essay, Mitchell details Ince's life and career as a film director-producer.*]

Thomas H. Ince, one of the more important of the pioneer filmmakers and one of the most interesting of the early producers, was only 43 when he died, suddenly, in 1924.

Today film historians are divided in their estimates of him. Some dismiss him as merely a *commercial* producer, who contributed nothing of lasting significance. Some praise his contributions to scenario construction and film editing, which, they say, did much to elevate the motion

picture in its formative years. In France Ince has even been called "the equal, if not the master" of D. W. Griffith.

He was neither, but he nonetheless deserves a prominent place in film history. It was he who systematized the production methods, inaugurated by J. Stuart Blackton, which are the standard operating procedures of the motion picture industry today. In doing this Ince made his greatest contribution to motion picture technique: he proved that filmmaking is better, as well as more economical, when a scenario is complete to the last detail before shooting begins.

Ince was a demanding man, but he could do, and often did, the things he demanded of others, including altering a script, directing a scene, and editing a final negative. Indeed, in his heyday he was often called "the doctor of sick film." For he was also a showman, and his flair for ballyhooing a picture, and himself, accounted for much of his commercial success, and for much of the reclame which still attaches to the pictures that bear the legend: "Thomas H. Ince Presents."

He was born on November 16, 1882, in Newport, R.I., but not in one of the millionaire mansions of that famous resort. He was christened Thomas Harper Ince by parents who earned a precarious living on the stage. His father enjoyed something of a reputation for his ability to "impersonate Chinese," and later became a theatrical agent in New York, where he was known as "Pop" Ince. Sidney Olcott, one of the important early motion picture directors (see *Films in Review*, April '54) was one of the young actors placed by "Pop" Ince.

There were two other Ince boys—John, three years older than Tom, and Ralph, five years younger. [Both acted in, and directed, many motion pictures. John entered the movies in '13, directed for most of the early companies, notably Pathe, Lubin and Metro, returned to acting in the '30s, and was often used by Warners, Columbia, Mascot and Fox. I believe he is still alive. Ralph impersonated Lincoln in Vitagraph's *Battle Hymn of the Republic* ('12), and in '15 directed one of that company's finest films, *The Juggernaut*, starring Earl Williams and Anita Stewart. He was well thought of as both actor and director at the time of his death in '37.] All three went on the stage early—Tom at the age of six. At 15 he appeared with Leo Ditrichstein, and shortly thereafter had a part in the Broadway production of *Shore Acres*. He barnstormed through Canada with the Beryl Hope Stock Company, and worked in vaudeville as a song-&-dance man.

In the summer of 1902, while working as a lifeguard at Atlantic Highlands, New Jersey, which was more fashionable then than now, he became convinced money could be made by staging vaudeville acts in the Highlands' seaside pavilion on summer nights. He saved enough the following winter from his salary as the half-wit in *The Ninety and Nine* to lease the pavilion. But the venture was not lucrative.

He returned to Broadway, in both drama and musical comedy, and while appearing in *Hearts Courageous*, a drama of the American Revolutionary War starring Orrin Johnson, he became friends with William S. Hart, who had the Patrick Henry role. After *Hearts Courageous* closed he and Hart and Frank Stammers, an actor-musician, roomed together in the old Hotel Harrington on Broadway at 44th street. They were on short rations and often out of work and for recreation in the winter of 1903-04 Stammers would play his cello and Hart would tell stories of the Old West, especially of the Sioux Indians, whom he had known as a boy in the Dakota Territories. The Ince-Hart friendship was to last for many years.

In 1905 Ince promoted a stock company of his own, but it was not successful. Then, after appearing with William Thompson in *The Bishop*, he got a featured part in a musical comedy success, *For Love's Sweet Sake*, which lasted two years. During the run of this show, on October 19, 1907, he married a member of its cast, Eleanor Kershaw.

The next few years were precarious and in the fall of 1910 Ince was standing on Times Square "trying to figure out how to keep the proverbial wolf from the door of my Harlem flat," when a big, flashy automobile pulled up to the curb. He was surprised to see descend from it an actor named Joseph Smiley, with whom he had worked in vaudeville. Smiley greeted Ince warmly, invited him to lunch, and revealed that his prosperity was the result of working "in the movies—for the IMP Company." Although Ince had always thought only actors who couldn't make the grade on the stage went into the movies, he asked if there was any chance for him at IMP. Smiley replied: "Why, yes, there should be. You're an actor, aren't you? There may be something there this afternoon."

The IMP studio was then on 56th Street and resembled, according to Ince's later recollection, "the dreadful tank-town theatres I had played in on tour." However, a 1-reeler was being directed that afternoon by Harry Salter, whom Ince had known on the stage. Salter gave him a small part and paid him $5. A few days later IMP offered him a job as a stock actor.

After several weeks at IMP Ince accepted the part of the heavy in Biograph's *His New Lid*, starring Lucille Lee Stewart, the wife of his brother Ralph. It was a 1-reeler and was directed by Frank Powell, formerly an actor in Griffith's stock company at Biograph. *His New Lid* was released on November 24, 1910.

By this time Ince had become interested in directing movies, and believing there was no chance of doing so at Biograph, he returned to act for IMP when Tom Cochrane, the studio manager there, promised to make him a director at the first opportunity.

This happened sooner than either expected. One of IMP's regular directors suddenly quit and Cochrane handed Ince an amateurish script based on an old poem called "Little Nell's Tobacco." Ince rewrote the script and shot the 1-reeler in record time. Cochrane was impressed, but to make Ince a permanent director he needed the OK of Carl Laemmle, the head of IMP. Laemmle agreed to look at the picture and did so in a nearby nickelodeon, where it was playing. Ince accompanied him and called each favorable manifestation by the audience to Laemmle's attention. Result: Ince was hired as a permanent director, to the chagrin of jealous IMP actors and technicians.

Laemmle, who had originally operated movie theatres and a film exchange in Chicago, was at that time embattled with the Motion Pictures Patents Co., which, he charged, was a "trust". In 1910 he had lured Mary Pickford from Biograph to his Independent Motion Picture Co. (IMP) and had been sued by the MPP Co., of which Biograph was a part, for patent infringement. In '11 he had sent Ben Turpin, later famous as the cross-eyed comedian in Mack Sennett comedies, to scout out a location in California free from the reach of the "trust". Turpin reported there was no such place. So Laemmle decided to make movies in Cuba.

He sent a company of 72 there under the supervision of his production chief, C. A. ("Doc") Willat, who, curiously, was the son-in-law of W. R. Rock, of Vitagraph, one of the companies licensed to use the Edison patents controlled by the MPP Co. Among the 72 were Mary Pickford, Owen Moore, King Baggott, Jack Pickford, Mrs. Charlotte Pickford, Lotte Pickford, Hayward Mack, Charles Westen (property master), Tony Gaudio (cameraman), Joseph Smiley, and Ince, who was put in charge of the films starring Mary Pickford. Smiley headed the unit that made the films starring King Baggott.

The Cuban hegira was a series of misadventures. Trouble began when Mrs. Pickford discovered that Mary had secretly married Owen Moore. The MPP Co. did what it could to gum things up. Willat couldn't get enough raw film. The climate didn't agree with some of the key technicians. An irreconcilable personality clash developed between Ince and Owen Moore. In her autobiography Mary Pickford says the climax was reached when an assistant of Ince's, a man named North, insulted her and Moore beat him up and North called the police. To prevent Moore's arrest Mrs. Pickford got him and Mary out of Cuba.

Despite the misadventures, movies *were* produced and Ince gained valuable experience. So much so that he soon tired of making for Laemmle such 1-reel chromos as *Their First Misunderstanding, Artful Kate, Her Darkest Hour, The Empty Shell, Message in the Bottle, The Dream* and *Sweet Memories*. When he heard that Adam Kessel, Jr., and Charles O. Bauman, the heads of the New York Motion Picture Co., were looking for a director to take charge of their West Coast studio, Ince went to see them.

Kessel and Bauman were an interesting pair. They were former bookmakers who, in 1909, promoted themselves into the motion picture business after New York's Governor Charles Evans Hughes banned horse racing. At first they operated a film exchange in New York City, and they got into the production of films when "the trust" cut off their supply of pictures. At the time Ince visited them they had a production unit called Bison Life Motion Pictures which made Westerns at Edendale, a suburb of Los Angeles, and a producing company in New York called Reliance, and had agreed to finance Mack Sennett's Keystone comedy unit. Ince later described his meeting with K & B as follows:

> I was entirely ignorant of the fact that Kessel and Bauman were considering me. . . . I decided to apply for the job feeling I would have greater opportunities in this new field than in New York. A little strategy was necessary, I felt, to impress my prospective employers with my importance, so I allowed a mustache to grow and, on the day of my interview with Bauman, I borrowed a large, sparkling diamond ring from Doc Willat. This, I figured, would give the impression that I was a man of means who did not have to work for the paltry $60 a week which was my munificent salary at IMP.

This ruse worked. When Bauman offered him $100 a week, Ince "hesitated" and Bauman raised it to $150—with a three-month guarantee—and gave Ince some stock in the Sennett Keystone comedy unit to boot.

When Ince left IMP he took actress Ethel Grandin and property-master Charles Weston along with him. They arrived in Los Angeles, together with Mrs. Ince and Ray C. Smallwood, a cameraman, in October 1911.

The "studio" in Edendale had been a grocery store and consisted of a small office and laboratory, and, in the back yard, a crude open-air stage without even a muslin overhead sunlight diffuser. A shed served as a scene dock and a nearby bungalow—rented—as a dressing room. "The sets," Ince said later, "consisted of a few pieces of very bad furniture and one backdrop with a flock of birds supposedly in flight. The furniture was bad enough, but when I thought of stationary birds poised in mid-air as the backdrop for a moving picture, I gave way to a moment of discouragement."

But he began a picture almost immediately. It was called *The New Cook* and starred Ethel Grandin. When it got so cold that the actors' breath was visible, Ince made the actors smoke throughout the scene and the actresses keep their mouths shut.

Ince knew he would have to do something spectacular if he were to establish himself on more solid terms with K & B, and by chance he discovered that the Miller Brothers' 101 Ranch Wild West Show, which was wintering in nearby Venice, could be hired for $2500 a week *on an annual basis*. Kessel and Bauman agreed, and thereby acquired a complete company of cowboys, Indians, longhorn cattle, buffalo, tepees, stage-coaches, wagons and other equipment for the making of large-scale Westerns.

They were also smart enough to transfer their production activities from Edendale to 18,000 acres of land along the Pacific Coast north of Santa Monica. The Edendale lot continued to serve as a processing laboratory and was turned over to Mack Sennett upon his arrival on the Coast, and ultimately became the Keystone Studio.

The first film made with the 101 Ranch troupe was *War on the Plains,* a 2-reeler also called *Across the Plains*. It was released in January 1912. William Eagleshirt, a full-blooded Sioux, and Ray Myers, who had collaborated with Ince on the script, played the principal roles. It got good reviews, was liked by the public, and encouraged Ince to make more 2-reelers of the same sort: *Battle of the Red Men, Blazing the Trail, Indian Massacre,* and *The Lieutenant's Last Fight.*

In the summer of '12 Ince directed and produced his most ambitious film to date, a 3-reeler called *Custer's Last Fight,* which depicted the events leading up to the battle of the Little Big Horn, and the battle itself. Francis Ford, brother of John Ford, played Custer, and the supporting cast included William Eagleshirt, Ann Little, J. Barney Sherry, Grace Cunard and Charles K. French. The large-scale action used hundreds of extras—Indians and soldiers. The script was by Richard V. Spencer, then Ince's principal writer, and the camerawork was Ray Smallwood's. *Custer's Last Fight* was re-issued in '25 by an independent distributor who "built" it up to 5 reels.

Using real Sioux Indians brought Ince some unforeseen problems. Since they were wards of the US government, he had to arrange with the local Indian agent not only for their care, but also for their schooling. Though docile, the Indians were averse to work, and they "appropriated" such brightly colored props as rugs, blankets, etc. They also got drunk, and local saloon keepers would call Ince in the middle of the night and complain that some of his "wards" were disturbing the peace.

"I left the house every morning at 7.30 for my day's work," Ince wrote years later. "I would direct and shoot all day and return home at seven in the evening, eat a hurried dinner, and start preparing for the activities of the next day. The result of each day's work had to be carefully inspected. My projection room was the kitchen of my small Hollywood bungalow, and, with Mrs. Ince's assistance, I would cut and assemble scenes taken the day before. As she unwound the reel I examined the negative, and, as it ran through my fingers, it was caught in a clothes basket on the floor.

"When the film was cut and assembled I would turn my attention to stories and would work until midnight writing scenarios for the following day. With my wife's help I managed to keep my production up to par. . . . Life was fraught with many discouragements and anxieties for those who were engaged in the early motion picture industry. There were many disheartening problems and set backs. Each step of the way had to be tried, mistakes in judgment and execution, the results of experimentation, had to be corrected, and new ideas tried out."

To meet the ever increasing demand for more pictures, Ince made Francis Ford a director of a second production unit. Ford, an experienced actor on both stage and screen, had previously directed movies for Gaston Melies in Texas. He was an independent fellow with definite ideas of how pictures should be made, and Ince, to make sure Ford did as he was told, had Richard Spencer prepare a detailed continuity—in fact, a shooting script—in which each scene was carefully outlined, and camera placements, props, costumes, make-up and special effects, were specified. Ince screened the scenes after Ford staged them and edited the final prints.

Not long before his death several years ago, Francis Ford wryly remarked that if one of the pictures he had made turned out better than expected, Ince had no scruples about claiming the credit for the direction, and often for the story as well.

In June '12 Kessel and Bauman had merged their holding company—the New York Motion Picture Co.—with Carl Laemmle's IMP to form the Universal Film Mfg. Co. Personalities clashed at once and open war began, with both sides claiming breach of contract and attempting to invade the other's territory and upset production. While making one picture Ince strapped on a six-shooter and posted a prop Civil War cannon loaded with scrap iron at the mouth of the Santa Ynez canyon to ward off Laemmle's men.

An agreement was finally reached. Laemmle was awarded $17,000 damages and the "101 Bison" trademark, and obtained Francis Ford's services as actor and director. Whereupon Kessel and Bauman aligned their NYMP Co. with Mutual Film Exchanges, Inc., headed by John R. Freuler and Harry M. Aitken. Following the break with Laemmle, Ince issued his pictures under such trade names as Broncho, Domino and Kay-Bee.

To replace Francis Ford, Kessel and Bauman sent out Charles Giblyn and Scott Sidney, who had been directing Reliance pictures in New York City. Ince also increased the directing staff by hiring Reginald Barker, Raymond B. West, Burton King, Walter Edwards, Jay Hunt and Richard Stanton (the last three also appeared as actors). Most of these men had acted on the stage, and West had worked in films for several years as a cameraman and assistant director. Barker was the only one who had directed (Broncho Billy Anderson Westerns for Essanay). A Scotsman, he became Ince's best and most prolific director. His forte was action stories with tough virile characters.

Ince's most important acquisition around this time was C. Gardner Sullivan, whom many still regard as one of the finest scriptwriters ever in the business. He hailed from Minnesota, had worked on newspapers in St. Paul and New York City, and became a scenario writer by accident after he sold a story to the old Edison Company and discovered he could make more money that way than by pounding a newspaper typewriter. Ince bought some of his early stories, and was smart enough to get Sullivan to work for him exclusively. It was one of Ince's most fortunate moves.

By '13 Ince was producing, in addition to Westerns, stories about the Civil War and the American melting pot. Their titles indicate the contents: *The Sharpshooter, Widow Maloney's Faith, The Banshee, Eileen of Erin, Banzai, For Love of the Flag, A Military Judas, The Witch of Salem, A Child of War, A Highland Romance.* Ince made more than 150 films in '13. A fairly representative group of them have survived (and were recently shown on the Movie Museum tv program). From such 2-reelers as *The Drummer of the Eighth, Little Dove's Romance, In the Tennessee Hills, The Quakeress, The Woman, Past Redemption, With Lee in Virginia, Blazing the Trail* and *Silent Heroes* it is possible to gain an insight into the American public Ince was making movies for. Each of those little films had a definite story line; clear characterization; spectacular action; good production values; and clear, sharp photography.

Ince's most creative period was from 1912 to '14. Unfortunately, some of his best work in this period has been lost. There are no known prints of his first feature, **The Battle of Gettysburg,** but a copy of its script is still in existence in New York. The *detail* in **The Battle of Gettysburg** scenario is noteworthy—*dialogue* is even written in for the principal characters. Instructions to the director are specific down to the facial expressions of the actors. The script for **The Battle of Gettysburg** has an exact breakdown of the battle scenes and instructions to the cameraman for the angles to be covered by no less than eight cameras.

It will be remembered that Bauman gave Ince some stock in Sennett's Keystone Company. Ince and Sennett became good friends, and Ince was always more than willing to do Mack a favor. When Ince shot big action spectacles he'd invite Sennett to come to the Santa Ynez canyon and take advantage of the props, sets and mobs of extras. Sennett did so while **The Battle of Gettysburg** was shooting and on its sets put Ford Sterling, Mabel Normand et al through their paces in *Cohen Saves the Flag,* an interesting 1-reeler that is still available.

The large-scale action shown in this Sennett film proves **The Battle of Gettysburg** must have been an impressive picture. It was released in 5 reels in December '13 by Mutual. It is possibly the only feature picture Ince ever directed. Charles Giblyn and Raymond B. West assisted him.

Ince's next 5-reel feature was *The Wrath of the Gods.* It was begun in January '14 and completed in about three weeks. The story, by C. Gardner Sullivan, centered around a shipwreck and volcanic eruption in Japan which required a number of special effects. Sessue Hayakawa made his screen debut in this picture, as did his wife, Tsuru Aoki. Frank Borzage, now a prominent Hollywood director, played the American hero. Reginald Barker directed and Raymond B. West handled the special effects. A print of *The Wrath of the Gods* was recently acquired by Don Malkames, a cinematographer who is also a cinema collector. Ince is said to have considered *The Wrath of the Gods* one of his best films.

Ince's next feature, *The Typhoon* ('14), also starred Hayakawa. It was an adaptation, by Charles Swickard, of the stage melodrama in which Hayakawa had been appearing when Ince "discovered" him. Reginald Barker directed. Vachel Lindsay thought Hayakawa should have been more effectively used—"dooming a talent like Mr. Hayakawa to the task of interpreting the Japanese spy does not conduce to accord with Japan, however the technique may move us to admiration." There is a print of *The Typhoon* at the George Eastman House in Rochester.

Sessue Hayakawa was Ince's first important star, and the only Ince star who is still prominent in motion pictures. But he was not properly developed by Ince, who, after *The Wrath of the Gods* and *The Typhoon*, relegated him to a series of 2-reelers. After nine months of them Hayakawa left Ince and joined Lasky (now Paramount), where his career flourished.

Some of the Japanese actors in *The Wrath of the Gods*, *The Typhoon* and other Ince films later became prominent in the Japanese film industry. Thomas Kurihara, Yutake (Jack) Abe and Henry Kotani became directors (Abe still directs). Until recently Kotani was employed as a cameraman by the US Army Signal Corps in Tokyo. Among the American directors Ince trained, or helped to develop, were Fred Niblo, Henry King, Lambert Hillyer, Victor Schertzinger, Jerome Storm, Irvin V. Willat, John Griffith Wray, Roy William Neill, Rowland V. Lee and Frank Borzage.

Meanwhile the sprawling movie lot at the mouth of the Santa Ynez canyon was growing into what was properly known as "Inceville." It resembled a rough construction camp, for the 101 Ranch Show's cowboys and Indians lived in tents and cabins up and down the canyon. Stables and corrals had been hastily erected for the livestock. The permanent residents had planted vegetable gardens.

Interiors were photographed on an open air stage over which hung muslin cloth to diffuse the sunlight. On rainy days tarpaulins were suspended over the sets (they were also used to shut out sunlight during the photographing of night scenes). Several pictures were usually being shot on this stage simultaneously and care had to be taken to avoid mixing the companies.

Robert Brunton, formerly a scenic artist with Sir Henry Irving and with Oliver Morosco, was the art director and production manager. Up and down the canyon, and along the beach, he had erected sets depicting a New York street, a frontier fort, a Western town, and what have you. Charles Weston, the property master, had assembled a varied collection of props especially rich in Civil War cannons, muskets, rifles, pistols, sabers, flags, guidons,

drums, etc., most of which were authentic relics purchased from Francis Bannerman's military surplus store, and some of which are still being used in Hollywood productions.

Ince's films were noted for clear photography and technological innovation. The newly developed Bell and Howell turret camera was used on almost all Ince films after 1912. Under the aegis of Chief Cameraman Ray Smallwood and Irvin V. Willat some good cinematographers were trained, including Chester Lyons, Robert Doeran, James Crosby, Charles Kaufman, Robert S. Newhard, Otis Cove, J. D. (Dev) Jennings, Joseph H. August, Paul E. Eagler and Clyde de Vinna. August, later William S. Hart's cameraman, is best remembered today for the photography in Ford's *The Informer*. Eagler currently operates a company that does special photographic effects for independent Hollywood producers.

William S. Hart, Ince's most lucrative "property," was not discovered by Tom Ince (see *Films in Review*, April '55). Nor did Ince have much to do with the development of Hart's screen personality. In fact, it was with considerable misgiving that Ince agreed to put Hart in a picture at all. But it is to his credit that he *did* give Hart his opportunity, and he certainly deserves *some* credit for the *initial* success of Hart's wonderful films. However, as time passed and Hart became more experienced, Ince had less and less to do with Hart's pictures, even though he is credited as producer, or supervisor, on all of them between 1914 and '18.

The Italian, another of Ince's most notable early films, was produced and released early in '15. It was a realistic study of immigrant life in the slums of New York City. George Beban had the title role, and Barker directed from a script by Sullivan. There is a paper print of *The Italian* in the Library of Congress. Also of *The Cup of Life* ('15), and *Rumplestiltskin* ('15), with Clyde Tracy and Betty Burbridge.

On July 20, '15, Kessel, Bauman and Harry M. Aitken, met secretly with Ince, Mack Sennett and D. W. Griffith, in the Harvey House, La Junta, Colorado, and arranged for the formation of the Triangle Film Corporation. The name evolved from the three production units to be run by Ince, Griffith and Sennett. Their prime purpose was to stop the growing monopoly of Adolph Zukor. Triangle quickly contracted with such stage stars as Sir Herbert Beerbohm Tree, DeWolf Hopper, Constance Collier, Frank Kennan, Willie Collier, Dustin Farnum, Billie Burke, Raymond Hitchcock, Orrin Johnson and Willard Mack. Also a stage actor named Douglas Fairbanks. Ince, of course, brought William S. Hart to Triangle.

On September 23, '15, a program of Triangle's first films opened, at a $2 top, in the Knickerbocker Theater in New York City. The pictures were *My Valet*, starring Raymond Hitchcock and directed by Sennett; *The Lamb*, starring Douglas Fairbanks, directed by Christy Cabanne, and supervised by Griffith; and *The Iron Strain*, starring

Dustin Farnum, Louise Glaum and Enid Markey, directed by Reginald Barker, and supervised by Ince.

Alas, Triangle's high-salaried stage stars were unknown in the US hinterland and had little or no box office pull. For example, Billie Burke was paid $40,000 for eight weeks' work on Ince's *Peggy* (early '16 and directed by Charles Giblyn). That was the largest salary ever paid a screen artist for a single performance up to that time. On the other hand, William S. Hart continued to receive a relatively small salary even though his pictures were bringing in most of Triangle's revenue. Ince, who owned Hart's contract, did nothing about raising his salary and this was one of the factors that led to the break between them.

It was also in '15 that a real estate promoter named Harry Culver offered free land to anyone who would build a motion picture studio in a development he was sponsoring between Venice and Los Angeles and calling Culver City. Ince took him up on it and was given some acreage off Washington Boulevard (he wanted to get out of Santa Ynez canyon because of the fog from the ocean, the constant hazard of brush fires, and the sand which blew into the lab and ruined prints). Ince was in the process of building a studio on Culver's gift site at the time Triangle was formed and Triangle took over the new studio. But Ince retained the deed to the land. The new studio, completed in January '16, consisted of five large glass enclosed stages and supporting buildings spread over some 16 acres of land. This studio is now the main part of the great MGM lot.

Although the bulk of Triangle's production, and most of Ince's films, were made there, Hart continued making his films at Inceville, Griffith worked in his Fine Arts Studio at 4500 Sunset Boulevard in Hollywood, and Sennett still used the old, but greatly expanded and improved, Edendale lot.

In 1916 Woodrow Wilson's re-election campaign slogan, "He kept us out of war," gave Ince the idea for a special production he called *Civilization.* It was written by C. Gardner Sullivan and revolved around a devastating war between two mythical countries. Avowedly anti-war in theme, the foreword to *Civilization* stated: "This is an allegorical story about war—it does not concern itself about which side is right or wrong, but deals with those ranks which are paying the grim penalty—the ranks of humanity. . . ." The foreword was signed by Ince, who expressed his "thanks" to Raymond B. West, Reginald Barker, J. Parker Read Jr., Scot Sidney et al for their "assistance" in producing *Civilization.* The film is said to have been directed mainly by West. Irvin Willat and Robert Newhard were the cinematographers.

Ince took an active part in selling and promoting *Civilization.* He personally showed the film to President Wilson, who, it was alleged, praised it highly. [President Wilson appeared with Ince in the foreword. They were photographed in '16 at Wilson's summer home "Shadow Lawn," by Lambert Hillyer.] When it opened in New York City on June 2, '16, Billie Burke, then working for Ince, "fainted" in the audience to create publicity.

Civilization does not hold up well today and is actually a very unimportant film. It is naive and almost ludicrous in both conception and execution. But at the time it was well received and made money. It also had an interesting aftermath: William Cochrane, press representative of the Democratic National Convention, claimed the picture contributed to Wilson's victory over Charles Evans Hughes.

. . . . .

What sort of a man was Tom Ince?

He seems to have been different things to many people. He has been described as ambitious, aggressive, dynamic, egotistical, emotional, irascible and intractable. If we can believe Bill Hart, he was ruthless, conniving and selfish (Hart also says in his autobiography Ince had considerable personal charm and that they resolved their differences not long before Ince died). Mack Sennett liked Ince and hints in his book, *King of Comedy,* that he was something of a philanderer. Lambert Hillyer, who directed many films for Ince, thinks "Ince was a good organizer who knew how to pick capable men and to use them correctly . . . men like C. Gardner Sullivan, for example."

Harry C. Carr, writing in the July '15 issue of *Photoplay,* described Ince this way: "His face is round and strong with a small restless mouth and penetrating gray eyes. His voice is quick, sharp, clear and incisive. The secret of Ince's big stuff is very simple. He has the unusual ability to *visualize* a scenario. He can see what things are going to look like. He doesn't figure things out; he thinks in mental pictures. He has one of the peculiar minds that think in terms of photography."

Ince often worked far into the night, in his private projection room, editing and re-editing film. He would frequently change the original story in order to evolve something more logical and convincing. John B. Richie, one of his associates, described him at work: "Something of his own vital personality is recognizable in every one of his pictures. While sitting as a silent spectator watching the evolution of a picture on the screen he will suddenly start up, gesticulate, emotionalize, blurt out subtitles and corrections faster than a stenographer could record them and in one live instant change the fate of a picture. . . . He was one of the first to perceive that screen drama must consist of vivid, flashing incidents, hurrying restlessly on to a logical and cumulative crisis."

Ince made a few revealing comments about himself: "Personally, I count the years I spent on the stage before I became a director and then a producer as the greatest single factor contributing toward whatever measure of success I may have achieved. No one except the public orator knows the glow that comes to the actor who is 'pulling his house' with him. That taste of crowd psychology taught me to recognize to a hair-breadth what shades of emotional acting most appeal to people in the orchestra seats and those up top in the peanut gallery; taught me just when to strike for a 'big laugh' or when to tone down a 'gag' which was dragging; taught me how to judge story values."

Here is what he had to say about direction: "The ideal director is one who, having pictured a scene in his mind, having tested it by putting himself into the various roles and getting reactions natural to those characters, still allows his cast enough scope to bring out additional touches that will add spontaneity to the interpretation and dramatic upbuilding. . . . Primarily the director must know life, but he must know, too, how to project life, not in narrative form, but by selected dramatic moments, each of which builds towards a definite crisis or climax that will bring a burst of emotional response from every audience. . . . He is the personification of every character in his drama as he directs each scene, carrying the story development so closely in his consciousness that he is a dozen persons at once. . . . But, above all else, a director must excel in coaxing, cajoling and spurring his actors on to heights of artistry. . . . He must teach them the a-b-c of movement: that bodily positions bring definite emotional reactions (this is the reason for 'walking' parts before thinking them) just as emotions and thought result in physical postures. Exhilaration of spirit brings the out-thrown chest, the outspread arms and open, welcoming hands. The reception of a new unwelcome thought is an unconscious backward movement or recession, perhaps a fending-off gesture with the hands to protect the mind and body from what may be unwelcome."

On movie pantomime:

"Do any but those who are intimately familiar with the stage world and its art realize the tremendous loss of power the actor of the silent drama suffers because his voice is stilled? After all, is there any ability more remarkable than that of the gifted actor who, without the aid of the emotion-arousing voice and the power of flesh and blood presence, can so project a characterization that the figments of some author's brain come to life for audiences gathered from every walk of life and numbering millions? Thought becomes reality—that is the world's greatest marvel.

To act a part an actor must feel it deeply, and so carry this feeling in his consciousness that, when he plays the scene, his reactions are instinctive. The pantomime of eyes, mouth, hands and bodily movement will seem unconscious if the actor is thinking and feeling the part. . . . It is only when the screen actor has become a past master of the art of pantomime that the audience is lulled into the oblivion of illusion."

Typical of the films Ince made during World War I for Triangle were: *The Beggar of Cawnpore,* a story of the

Sepoy mutiny of 1857 in India, starring H. B. Warner and directed by Charles Swickard; *D'Artagnan,* with Orrin Johnson, Dorothy Dalton, Arthur Maude and Louise Glaum, also directed by Swickard; *Wolf Woman,* with Louise Glaum, directed by Walter Edwards; *Happiness,* with Enid Bennett, directed by Reginald Barker; *Not My Sister,* with Bessie Barriscale; *Flame of the Yukon,* with Dorothy Dalton, directed by Charles Miller; and *The Pinch Hitter* and *The Clodhopper,* starring Charles Ray and directed by Victor Schertzinger.

The Coward, one of Triangle's '15 releases, is sometimes revived by film societies, but except for fine performances by Frank Keenan and Charles Ray, it is not really impressive. Film historian Lewis Jacobs called it one of Ince's "soul fights!"

Charles Ray was one of the most interesting and successful players Ince ever developed. Before joining Ince as a stock actor in '12, Ray had played in road companies and vaudeville on the West Coast. He worked in all types of films until Ince hit on the innocent Ray played so well. Ray was one of the few true interpreters of rural America there have been on the screen. His work was neither satire, nor a glorification. One of the main titles in *The Pinch Hitter* aptly illustrates the character Ray portrayed: "Joel Parker of Turkey Creek, Vermont—Orfull bashful and sorta dummified. . . ." Ray's popularity was extinguished in the jazz-mad '20s. His films stand up very well, and even today are an entertaining bit of Americana.

Victor Schertzinger, who directed Ray's first rural dramas, was another talent Ince used successfully. He had been born in the Pennsylvania-Dutch region and was a concert violinist with John Philip Sousa, Marcella Sembrich and Emma Calve, before he attained a measure of success by writing arrangements for Broadway musical comedies. Ince noticed him leading the Belasco Theater orchestra in Los Angeles and hired him to write scores for *Peggy,* **Civilization** and other films.

Schertzinger was one of the most gifted directors ever developed by Ince and is best remembered as the director of Grace Moore's *One Night of Love* ('34), *The Mikado* ('39), and the highly successful Bob Hope-Bing Crosby *Road to Singapore* ('40). Despite his concentration on directing films, Schertzinger never completely abandoned music, and often wrote scores and original music for his own productions.

However successful Ince was in bringing out the talent of others, he was not successful in his relations with Kessel, Bauman and Aitken. He resented it when they tried to tell him what to do, and once, when they threatened to fire him, he secreted in safe deposit vaults throughout Los Angeles the negatives of films he was working on. Finally Aitken discovered a loophole in Triangle's contract with him. But Ince had two aces up his sleeve.

He owned the land the Triangle studio was on, and he owned William S. Hart's contract.

The upshot was that Triangle paid Ince $250,000, and Ince, using his contract with Hart as bait, contracted with Adolph Zukor to produce for Paramount-Artcraft. There were really three separate contracts: the first stipulated that Hart would make 16 pictures for at least $150,000 each; the second that Ince would himself produce two "special productions" a year for at least $50,000 each; and the third that Charles Ray, Dorothy Dalton and Enid Bennett would each make a series of films for $35,000 each. The second and third contracts were to be null and void if Hart were not delivered to Paramount-Artcraft within 30 days of their signing.

After Ince broke with Triangle he leased Biograph's West Coast lot while he constructed a new studio in Culver City down the street from Triangle. He moved there in the Fall of '18. Its main administration building was designed to resemble Washington's home, Mount Vernon. After Ince's death Cecil B. De Mille made *King of Kings* there, and Pathe and RKO Radio subsequently owned it. For many years David O. Selznick rented space in it, and made *Gone With the Wind* there, and used the "Mt. Vernon" front as his trade mark. Desilu Productions is the present owner.

Ince turned pictures out in quick succession for Zukor—most of them topical films capitalizing on World War I, then in progress. They included: *The Kaiser's Shadow,* directed by Roy William Niell; *The Zepplin's Last Raid,* directed by Irvin V. Willat; *Viva la France,* with Dorothy Dalton, directed by Neill; *False Faces* with Lon Chaney and Henry B. Walthall, directed by Willat; *Claws of the Hun,* with Charles Ray, directed by Willat; *23½ Hours Leave,* a successful wartime comedy with Douglas MacLean, directed by Henry King; *Carmen of the Klondyke,* with Dorothy Dalton, directed by Barker; *Behind the Door,* with Wallace Beery and Hobart Bosworth, directed by Willat; and such Charles Ray vehicles as *String Beans,* directed by Schertzinger, and *Hayfoot Strawfoot, Homer Comes Home,* and *The Busher,* all directed by Jerome Storm.

William S. Hart continued to work in a separate studio and turned out some of his finest films: *The Narrow Trail, Blue Blazes Rawden, Wolves of the Rail, The Border Wireless, Branding Broadway* and *Riddle Gawne*— all directed by Lambert Hillyer. Although Ince was an equal partner in these pictures and is credited on the screen as the "producer," both Hart and Hillyer have said that Ince had nothing to do with their production. Ince and Hart no longer spoke to each other.

Their basic differences derived from Ince's refusal to share with Hart the tremendous profits he reaped from Hart's films. But they parted after a quarrel over Hart's horse Fritz, to which Ince had taken a violent dislike. When Hart completed his 16 pictures for Artcraft he formed his own company, and, with Hart gone, Ince had no club over Zukor. As everyone expected, those two ambitious men were soon at loggerheads, and by the middle of '19 Zukor had forced Ince out of Paramount-Artcraft.

Whereupon Ince distributed his pictures through Metro. But in October of '19 he formed a distribution company—Associated Producers, Inc.—with Mack Sennett, Marshall Neilan, Allan Dwan, George Loane Tucker, Maurice Tourneur, and his long time associate, J. Parker Read, Jr. [Read was selling advertising in Havana when Laemmle sent a company to Cuba and was hired by Doc Willat as an interpreter. After which Read went to work for Ince.] An advertisement in Wid's "Year Book" for 1920 read in part: "Associated Producers are seven men of definitive, achieved reputations and accomplishments in motion picture production. These seven men decided after long years of paying toll and tribute to distributors to cut beyond those distributors who used them to bolster up weak directors and trivial stars. They own their own personal organization for the production, release and sale of their pictures directly to the exhibitors of the country. . . ." By September '22 Associated Producers was forced to merge with First National and Ince then became an independent producer releasing through that company. His pictures did well at the box office.

Ince had wealth, and a position in the motion picture industry, but his best filmmaking was behind him. Very few of his films in the '20s were of more than passing interest. *Hail the Woman,* a "special production" of '21, was called old fashioned by most of the critics. Its large cast included Florence Vidor, Madge Bellamy, Theodore Roberts, Lloyd Hughes and Tully Marshall. John Griffith Wray, whom Ince recruited from the theatre and made his favorite, directed from a script by C. Gardner Sullivan. *The Cup of Life* ('21), directed by Rowland V. Lee, was a re-make of Ince's old '15 success. *The Hottentot* ('22), a racing comedy adapted from the Willie Collier stage success, could not, via sub-titles, convey the wit of the play. *Skin Deep* ('22), directed by Lambert Hillyer, and starring Milton Sills and Florence Vidor, a melodrama about a convict escaping from prison only to discover it was engineered by his wife and her lover so they could frame him for murder, had an excellent sequence in which a stunt man (doubling Milton Sills) leapt from the wall of the prison to the top of a moving train and then to an airplane by means of a rope ladder hung from the cockpit.

In '22 Mrs. Wallace Reid (Dorothy Davenport), widow of the actor who had died from the effects of dope addiction, supplied the idea for one of Ince's most unusual films, *Human Wreckage* ('23). It is one of the few American films influenced by *The Cabinet of Dr. Caligari.* To show the harmful effects of narcotics it had a surrealistic sequence to depict an addict under the influence of drugs. Bizarre settings and distorted, diffused camera work were used to heighten the overall atmosphere. John Griffith Wray directed, C. Gardner Sullivan wrote the scenario, and Henry Sharp did the imaginative photography. Such public figures as Dr. R. B. von Klein Smid, President of the University of Southern California; Mayor George E. Cryer of Los Angeles; Judge Beryl Bledsoe of the 12th Federal District Court; and John P. Carver, a former US Internal Revenue Collector, not only endorsed the film but played small parts in it.

Anna Christie ('23) was the first Eugene O'Neill play to reach the screen (see *Films in Review,* June-July '58). It received laudatory reviews from virtually all of the critics. Robert E. Sherwood said it was "a credit to Mr. Ince and to the movies," and "Variety" reported that "*Anna Christie* has the honor of being the first picture of the 1923-24 season to be chosen for a special showing before the National Board of Review, which makes a specialty of picking the exceptional photoplays of the year. *Anna Christie* proved worthy of the honor." Blanche Sweet was praised for her forthright portrayal of Anna, and William Russell for his of Matt Burke, and George Marion, Sr., for his Chris, a role he had created on the stage. John Griffith Wray directed and Henry Sharp photographed.

Ince is supposed to have said: "I made that one for the highbrow critics who say Tom Ince can't make anything but box office pictures."

Two comedies, *Galloping Fish,* directed by Del Andrews, and *Ten Ton Love,* directed by John Griffith Wray, were released at the beginning of '24. The first featured some of the old Keystone Comedy players—Ford Sterling, Louise Fazenda, Syd Chaplin and Chester Conklin. The "big Ince scene" was a great flood, adroitly filmed on the Colorado River, in which a circus full of animals was washed away. *Ten Ton Love* was about an elephant with uncanny intelligence and its climax was the destruction of a circus big top by a cyclone. Next came a melodrama, *Those Who Dance,* directed by Lambert Hillyer, a good gangster story with Blanche Sweet, Warner Baxter, Bessie Love, and Matthew Betz.

Charles Ray, who had left Ince to form his own producing company in '20, and had failed after an expensive and financially disastrous version of *The Courtship of Miles Standish,* returned to Ince in '24. His first picture under his new contract, *Dynamite Smith,* was directed by Ralph Ince, and had Ray in his familiar country-boy role. Ray's next picture, *Percy,* directed by Roy William Neill, was released after Ince's death.

During the summer of '24 Ince sent his brother John, and B. Reeves (Breezy) Easen, to Canada to film a buffalo stampede for the climax of a large scale Western to be called *The Vanishing Frontier.* They brought back such disjointed and unsatisfactory material that Lambert Hillyer, at that time directing *Barbara Frietchie* for Ince, was asked to take over. Hillyer did not think he could salvage anything from the footage and declined. The picture was never completed by Ince. However, the material was sold for stock shots and has been used in several films made by other producers.

Barbara Frietchie and a picture called *Enticement* were Ince's last. The former, released a few weeks before his death, was expertly directed by Lambert Hillyer, and starred Florence Vidor and Edmund Lowe. It was based on the old Clyde Fitch play and was notable for some well-staged and beautifully photographed—by Henry Sharp—Civil War battle scenes. *Enticement,* released

several months after Ince's death, was a triangle story set in the French Alps (it was shot at Lake Louise in Canada), with a well-staged avalanche sequence for a climax. Mary Astor, Clive Brook and Ian Keith starred under George Archainbaud's direction. According to Mary Astor, in her recent autobiography, she attended a showing of *Enticement* in NYC with her then romantic interest, John Barrymore, and he upbraided her for appearing in such "trash."

Late in '24 there were rumors that Ince was about to conclude a very lucrative deal with William Randolph Hearst to produce the Marion Davies-Cosmopolitan films.

It was probably this prospective association with Hearst, plus the fact that Hearst was with Ince when he was fatally stricken, that gave rise to many misleading and inaccurate stories about Ince's so-called "mysterious death." A few sensation-seeking writers have even gone so far as to claim that Ince was murdered.

This story was started by a rival of Hearst's Los Angeles newspaper which published a number of suppositions and innuendoes immediately following Ince's death. These irresponsible charges were never substantiated, nor was any evidence ever presented to the authorities to prove that Ince's death was the result of foul play. In view of the number of persons involved, it is difficult to believe a giant cover-up could have occurred and been perpetuated for 35 years.

Ince was fatally stricken while on a weekend cruise to San Diego on his yacht "Oneida." Hearst, Marion Davies, and other celebrities were guests.

The San Diego "Union" of Nov. 21, '24, reported Ince's death as follows: "[the] illness . . . began on his yacht in San Diego harbor Sunday night [November 16] when celebrities gathered to help him celebrate his 43rd birthday with a party that sent him to his berth racked with pain. Marion Davies, Seena Owen and lesser lights were in the gay party . . . William Randolph Hearst is mentioned as one of those present . . . Dr. Daniel Carson Goodman, West Coast Manager of Cosmopolitan Productions, said to have the backing of Hearst, was another. . . . Monday morning a tender from the "Oneida" landed at the West Santa Fe dock and Ince and two others got out. They went to the railroad station where Ince and Goodman, as his companion, boarded the train. The other member of the party did not go with Ince and Goodman. When the train reached Del Mar the porter summoned a car to take the sick producer to the Stratford Inn. It was hinted that he had suffered an attack of indigestion while on a hunting trip in Mexico.

At the Stratford Inn a physician [Dr. Truman Parker and later Dr. Horace Lazelle, both of La Jolla] was called and when he responded Ince told him he had been on a party in a yacht in San Diego harbor. Ince, it is reported, told the doctor that he had eaten heavily and smoked a great deal. He complained of terrific pains in the abdomen. He is also understood to have said there was plenty of liquor and that the man who furnished it could well afford to get the best.

The doctor called again Monday night and found Ince greatly improved. There was no evidence of food or liquor poisoning, he said, but he advised the producer to stay and rest several days. The doctor then left saying he would call Tuesday [November 18] morning.

But in the meantime Mrs. Ince had arrived by motor car with her 15-year-old son, William, and went to the bedside of her husband. Later Monday evening Dr. Ida C. Glasgow, said to be the Ince family physician, came to Del Mar in response to a call and the local physician was told his services were no longer needed. . . .

Despite the [local] doctor's advice to rest for several days, arrangements were made to take him North. A special car was attached to the train leaving here [San Diego] and an ambulance was dispatched. The ambulance took Ince to the special car which arrived . . . attached to the Santa Fe train.

On this car Ince made the trip to Los Angeles Tuesday and reached home early in the afternoon.

He died at five o'clock in the morning of November 19, '24, in his home, "Dias Dorados" (Golden Days), in Benedict Canyon, Beverly Hills. At his bedside were his wife, his three sons—William 15, Thomas Jr. 11, and Richard 9—and his two brothers. According to his own physician, death was due to angina pectoris induced by acute indigestion.

A small street in the rear of his old studio in Culver City has been named Ince Avenue.

Jean Mitry (essay date 1965)

SOURCE: "Thomas H. Ince: His Esthetic, His Films, His Legacy," in *Cinema Journal,* Vol. 22, No. 2, Winter, 1983, pp. 2-17.

[*In the following essay, which was first published in 1965, Mitry evaluates Ince as an artist rather than as a businessman or technical innovator.*]

> *If D. W. Griffith can be called the earliest poet of an art whose basic syntax he elaborated, then Ince can be said to be its earliest dramatist.*
>
> *Indeed, his explorations of the medium dealt far more with plot construction, with original subject matter and with the expression of ideas— allowances being made for the means at his disposal—than with technical innovation.*

I

Unlike Griffith, staging for Ince was a secondary concern and consequently his personal touch is to be found else-

where. It would thus be incorrect to speak of his "style" if indeed style subsists more in a work's outward form than in its spirit. It would, however, be quite legitimate to speak of an esthetic, of a certain concept of what a movie is which runs throughout his films, making them so many diverse instances of a single underlying intention.

His primary concern was to establish an equilibrium between form and content, between the means of expression and the dramatic exigencies of the theme, imposing on the latter values and requirements similar to those of classic dramaturgy.

While careful to distinguish the formal attributes of theatrical construction from those of filmic construction, Ince nevertheless came to form a bridge, however shaky and precarious, between two apparently antithetic art forms which, through a reversal of their respective means, had too often been confused on the screen.

In other words, in addition to taking full advantage of the possibility of shooting anywhere which had freed him from theatrical staging, Ince drew upon dramaturgy for a construction which avoids every semblance of theatrical representation.

His work, which can be seen as complementing Griffith's, seems thus a kind of "dramatization" of the real by means of a certain way of representing reality.

Griffith almost by need created a language which allowed him to express himself to the full measure of his genius. If at the beginning of his career his themes were simplistic and rudimentary, they were so only to the same extent as were the forms he had to work with. As he continued to enlarge these forms he gradually heightened his tone and expressed—at least until his apogee in 1919—ideas of increasing ambitiousness, his weakness being his oversimplified and rather old-fashioned ideas, a weakness attributable as much to the straightening of an ungrown medium as it was to the receptive capacities of his audience at that time. Nevertheless precisely because he was still shaping his own language, it tended, by very reason of its newness, to fall short of the ideas for whose expression he had brought it into being. With the possible exception of *Broken Blossoms* and *True Heart Susie,* his two most polished works, the richest and most complex of his films, not excluding *The Birth of a Nation* and *Intolerance,* suffer from the lack of a steady balance between form and content. Splendid as they are, those great wobbling structures are often unable to contend with the mighty subjects they were supposed to be expressing.

Availing himself of Griffith's discoveries and content to apply them with discrimination, Ince proceeded, as it were, from the opposite direction. Accepting acquired form and uninterested in perfecting it, he valued the means at his disposal only for what they allowed him to express clearly through the sole resource of the moving image.

Despite an already extensive vocabulary and an eloquent syntax, it was still impossible to delineate characters of any complexity or to suggest fine shades of meaning. The slightest twinge of conscience necessitated a battery of titles. But to use images to illustrate titles as the only way of advancing the action hardly qualifies as cinema.

In bad films intertitles so abounded that it was quite meaningless to speak of their continuity. But in films that were less bad, it was found that intertitles were needed to render dialog. In such cases the titles were cut right into the action and inserted *into a continuing shot.* Since the film had been shot before it was titled, the image which followed the title did not coincide with the image that preceded it. This was necessary because the title took the place of events presumed to be happening while it was being flashed on the screen. It was thus impossible to remove a title without leaving a gap in the action. Ince and his collaborators, on the other hand, consistently placed their titles *between* shots, with the result that suppressing them would signal no more than a simple change of shot. Yet to keep them from proliferating Ince had to be content to develop unambiguous situations and ideas that were sometimes generalized to the point of being cryptic. His titles performed a strictly *indicative* function, serving only to bind sequences together and to set the stage for the action. While never underestimating the importance of psychological considerations, he tried to put his characters into situations where nuances were unnecessary for understanding their predicaments. Development he suggested by means of an accumulation of vignettes, leaving the audience to infer its causes while showing only its effects. His preference, however, was to choose characters sufficiently explained by their actions in brief and clear-cut conflicts.

The challenge was in letting the story unfold with enough freedom to give the audience the impression that it was watching a document taken directly from life—an "image," at very least, of real life—rather than a dramatic contrivance with a predictable ending. While giving the film its indispensable structure, it was important to lose none of the advantages of cinema, none of its ability to capture life "in the very heart of life."

But since psychological development was desirable only to the extent that it made the motivations of the characters comprehensible, and since analysis was out of the question, Ince chose to apply his efforts to stripping the facts down to their bare essentials. He concentrated the action around a few dramatic mainsprings, leaving in shadow—ambiguous or suggested by a few sufficient hints—the background events and the dragging moments, mercilessly cutting away anything that would impede the forward thrust of the action. By this means he achieved extreme leanness, but also, perforce, excessive oversimplification in his social dramas.

But to insure that the staging would meet these prescribed conditions it was necessary to specify it beforehand.

Scenarios had been written since 1908. A general outline would be jotted down in a few pages to serve the director as a guide, but the film was still composed on the spot according to the inspiration of the moment. The "line" of the work, its rhythm and modeling (insofar as these terms are applicable to films made prior to 1912) were left to the editing. Griffith himself never worked from a script. When one considers that *Intolerance,* with all its vast complexity, was shot with nothing more to go on than a sheaf of some thirty pages of notes to jog his memory, one is staggered at the immensity of his labor on the set.

Seconded by Gardner Sullivan, a scenarist of key importance in the development of the story film, Ince was the first to construct a film on paper, foreseeing all the contingencies of shooting to make what would today be called a shot-breakdown of the action. There is no doubt whatsoever that he was forced to do this by the fact of having personally directed so few of the films for which he was responsible. These blueprints guaranteed that the execution of his films would conform with his intentions. Indeed, one could say, grosso modo, that if it was Griffith who first gave cinema the notion of editing in its fullest sense of symbolic significance arrived at through the intercutting of shots, it was Ince who introduced the notion of the script as a breakdown and detailing of shots.

The whole of his output can be divided into historical propaganda films (***Custer's Last Fight, The Battle of Gettysburg***), thesis films (*The Painted Soul, The Moral Fabric, Those Who Pay*), comedy dramas (*Peggy, Plain Jane, Paddy O'Hara*), and Westerns in which he established concepts and patterns that would culminate in the films of William S. Hart.

II

His personal work can strictly be said to comprise only the first two of those categories.

In *The Wrath of the Gods* (1914) action was for the first time paralleled with a natural phenomenon (a volcano's eruption) which stood in for it, simplistically but very effectively, as its outsize symbolic projection: a husband kills his unfaithful wife and then commits ritual suicide while the oncoming cataclysm steadily sweeps all before it, destroying the city of Sakurajima.

This device, which became so identified with Ince, of intercutting a natural phenomenon into a dramatic event, was somewhat later to be adopted by Griffith in *Way Down East* in the sequence of the break up of the ice. The construction of these Ince films seems no less deliberated than that systematic arousal of the audience which Eisenstein described as *the mounting of attractions;* in any case they are the earliest instances on record of the kind of parallel editing the latter would eventually define in his essay "Nature Is Not Indifferent."

The Battle of Gettysburg (1914) is a big spectacular fresco. Griffith was then preparing *The Birth of a Nation.*

Ince wanted to try his own hand at a broad canvas, even though his temperament was not especially suited to the epic form. Even so, thanks to a sensitive feeling for the life of crowds, thanks to breakneck pacing, to a narrative thrust which is at first held back and then released on a downward course of gathering speed, the film's rhythm at times transforms it into something that all but equals Griffith. In it Ince consistently employs the measured power, the chastened line and the directness he had already evinced in *Custer's Last Fight* (1912). It is without a doubt his grandest achievement.

His most violent, however, was *The Typhoon* (1914). This was simply an emotional drama whose governing sentiment might be described as a deviant variety of classical passion. Yet the forward motion of the narrative, together with the headstrong nature of the characters, made for a visual schematization which, without prejudice to the film's psychology, powerfully reinforced its action. The somewhat banal turns of plot, while serving no other purpose, portray a morality and a psychology that is unabashedly stunted: it is not hard to see in it a forecast of Naziism. The drama revolves around such mainsprings as the victimizing of the innocent, the grim will to become the tool of a narrow nationalism, the contempt for weakness and the destruction of anyone who lets himself succumb to it (which can all the more easily happen if he begins by feeling contempt for it). Cecil B. De Mille's success *The Cheat,* released some fifteen months later, was little more than a melodramatic elaboration of the same ideas, a rehash of techniques—cutting, lighting, acting style—that Ince had already used.

The Despoiler (1915) and **Civilization** (1916) are anti-German propaganda films. The first deals with atrocities to prisoners: "In the Near East a German colonel hands over to the Kurdish troops under his command a convent of Catholic nuns to slake their lust upon. As it happens, his own daughter has taken refuge in the cloister. Raped by the chief of the Kurds, she kills him, but the colonel, enraged when this is reported to him, orders the execution of the girl who did it. The order is carried out, whereupon the colonel receives word that his daughter is hiding among the nuns. He has a search made for her and learns, too late, that she is the very one whose execution he had ordered."

An arbitrary and conventional tale, to be sure. Yet thanks to precise and economical plot development, it has impact. With some truth it could be called a *psychological Grand Guignol.*

With **Civilization** Ince tried to uplift his tone to the level of *philosophical Grand Guignol.* The philosophy, alas, is nothing to rave about, purveyed as it is through a rudimentary symbolism which cheapens it and at moments lends it to ridicule. Thanks to the device still prevalent at the time of "picturing" literary symbols and of "representing" metaphysical entities, this film, which created a furor when it was first released, is one of the most badly dated of the Ince films.

Gardner Sullivan's theme might have breathed life into a work conceived as a fable in which the tragedy was transposed into the realm of fantasy. As it is, fancy is superimposed on a realist framework which cannot support it: the image of the Nazarene looms large in the foreground of the universal conflict. Crucifixions are juxtaposed with tanks and cannons. Entering the remains of Count Ferdinand, who was killed while torpedoing a luxury liner, the reincarnated Christ proceeds to preach peace to the German people, tries to get the Kaiser to see reason, etc.

It must be emphasized, however, that the naivete of this symbolism was peculiar neither to Ince nor to the cinema in which he was working. Indeed, just as it did here, that cinema often made use of an outmoded pictorial art which the middlebrow culture of the day still considered the last word in artistic expression. It was nothing worse than a lapse into those stock ideas which often define an era. We have only to glance at the newspapers, the occasional poetry produced by the favorite versifiers of the epoch, and at the official painting and statuary of 1914!

A realism whose intentions were less grandiose and less grandiloquent would have been more moving, and would certainly have given rise to a more durable piece of work, for there are numerous moments where the film is redeemed by its visual power, and never more so than when it is not trying to preach or convince but just to describe, to reveal in all its horror a reality whose meaning is itself. Yet despite its breathless rhythm and the broad sweep of its scenes of spectacle—such as the sinking of an ocean liner one must still look to its details to see the style of its maker: "Only an artist," wrote Colette, "could have composed those groupings, such as the one of the stricken mother pressing her three children to her while there files before them an off-camera army the shadows of whose spiked helmets and slanted bayonets rake their trembling knees."

Among his films of social criticism, *The Painted Soul* (1915) was one of the first to successfully develop its argument within a visually cinematic form. Careful lighting, the authenticity of the settings and especially the naturalness of its actors gave it a particular truth. It concerned a young painter who falls in love with a girl he picked up in a bar. She becomes his model and, tired of a life on the streets, tries to live down her past. But the young man's upright family oppose their union and the girl returns to her old life. Free living arrangements were still so far in the future that they could not be countenanced by the official morality of the day, which condemned them as an affront to virtue. The subject may well seem trite and melodramatic to us now, but in their films Ince and Sullivan regularly castigated middle-class narrow-mindedness and hypocrisy, just as, in films like *The Hateful God* (1914), they pilloried puritanism and religious bigotry.

The Sons of Toil (1915) defended the right of laborers to take collective action against exploitive employers.

The Moral Fabric (1916) developed the argument that advocates of the new morality are wont to put their theories into practice only to the extent that they serve their passions and self-interest. As soon as they themselves might be threatened by the emancipation they preach, they raise an outcry and take refuge behind respect for the usages of modern civilization and for established principles.

The Sorrows of Love (1916) strove to assert the rights of women and young girls in a man's world where they are often victims of their trust and credulity.

The Corner (1916) compared and contrasted the deeds of an unscrupulous financier with a jobless man jailed for stealing food to feed his family.

Those Who Pay (1917) insisted on the rights of abandoned mothers and of natural children vis-a-vis society. And so on.

The influence of the "thesis play" whose heyday in the theatre was the opening years of the century is obvious. So much so indeed that in 1918, one French reviewer, dazzled by the revelation which these films were to Europeans at the time, exclaimed, "It might almost have been written by Bernstein!"

And it certainly is true that the influence of such French playwrights as Henri Bernstein, Henri Bataille, Eugene Brieux, Georges de Porto-Riche, and even Pierre Frondaie, Charles Mere, and Henry Kistemaeckers, and of their American counterparts and emulators David Belasco, Edward Sheldon, and Clyde Fitch pervades Ince's films of this period.

These films would still have the power to move us had their characters been drawn with greater subtlety. As it is, they are all too often far-fetched, the situations exaggerated and their consequences blown out of all proportion. Their implausibilities are less often matters of fact than of how facts are presented. Everything is raised to the pitch of melodrama with the sole purpose of giving greater weight to the argument, but that very process robs it of its credibility. The author, overly eager to prove his point, is no longer led by his characters, he *coaches* them. He assigns them a line of conduct so specific that, however well-drawn they may be, they appear to be *embodiments of ideas* acting in accordance with the demands of the thesis, rather than characters who are free to work out their own solutions to their dramas.

It is important to keep in mind, however, that in 1915 the movie public was hardly accustomed to films like these—to images like these and above all to words like these. Anything therefore that could render the ideas more compelling had to be squeezed in and given heavy emphasis. Not only was the plot pared down to the fundamental but also, perforce, the very substance of the story itself.

Quite different, however, were his Westerns, his films inspired by the Civil War and certain dramas whose documentary character is striking even today. One such is

The Italian (dir. Reginald Barker, 1915). This film tells the story of an immigrant just off the boat who struggles to support his family and who, despite the repeated efforts to fleece him by one of the American characters, succeeds in establishing his rights and in finding a small place for himself among the pushcart vendors of Brooklyn. The prologue, which is set among the gondoliers of Venice, is redolent of pasteboard, hokum, the masquerades of early cinema, despite some touches which do not lack humor. But as soon as we get to New York and the streets of Brooklyn, it all changes. What we then find is truth, the unmistakable authenticity of life "caught unawares." Some scenes already anticipate Stroheim's *Greed,* while others, especially those of the immigrant wandering the streets looking for the man who has cheated him, bring to mind a *Bicycle Thief* made some thirty years before De Sica's.

In his Westerns he stays away from conflicts between men of different social backgrounds, or their opposition to laws which oppress them—situations in which nuances are unavoidable—but rather he establishes individual characters in some brief, violent, savage drama, highlighting their relationship to their geographical and social environments and exalting raw but powerful feelings by means of the exemplifying act.

It could be said, therefore, that whereas his social dramas showed similarities to his thesis plays, his Westerns and his Civil War pieces resembled nothing so much as the short story, or even the poem. It has been observed that unlike the novel, the poem—and I speak here of the narrative poem—must limit itself to specific acts, to linear action, and must deal with highly typified heroes (Masferer, Roland, Siegfried, et al.), and that its lyric value lies outside the plot itself, in the way the action is presented, in the nature of the diction, in the prosodic rhythm. These are *formal* attributes whose equivalents here are the registering of detail, the dramatic movement and the rhythm of images.

The drama serves as the pretext for the evocation of a "climate." It seeks to bring to life characters to whom the brevity of the action, the conciseness of the story give a special glamor, characters who would be uninteresting in themselves. The film deals in tragic circumstances only. The individuals are less interesting than their dilemmas and attain to consciousness through them alone.

Thus, by stressing the conditioning role of a character's environment, by making the setting the drama's chief protagonist, Ince achieved a sobriety which confers a tragic grandeur on some of his Westerns. From this arose a poetry whose likes the screen had never seen, such as no one could have thought it capable of, a lyric power due most often to the way a thing was expressed or suggested, to a vigilant care to make the most of the telling detail, to an approach which became established as the foundation of a language.

The particular excellence of these films which so happily combine myth and reality, the imaginary and the real, and of which it may be said that some have remained ageless, consists mainly of registerings or notations which take on a singular resonance like words in a poem. These might be tiny details pointed out in passing, or subsidiary events which illuminate the action, and plot seems at times to have no other point than to elicit these images which transfigure it. As Louis Delluc observed at the time: "It is not just that visual notations are placed alongside psychological notations; it is that this is done in such a way that each becomes enhanced by a vibrancy which is poetry itself."

It may be said that instead of the prefabricated moral intentions of the thesis films, we find something here which was not *intended* exactly but which gradually emerges in the course of these films, a thing of which the author is fully aware and *which his composition takes into account* but which has not been artificially contrived. It is in this way that that dimension of aliveness, that immediate and palpable truth which is a part of his intentions but which is denied his other films, appears in these in all its power and in all its novel splendor.

It is, for instance, a stream flashing in the sunlight at the bottom of a quiet and majestic valley, while on its banks, a little way off, we *know* that two men are struggling, locked in mortal combat. After the fight, whose outcome is carefully kept from us, the horse of one of them moves off alone. There hangs from its trailing saddle a drinking gourd, a revolver jutting from a half-open holster—and the bag of gold which caused the fatal struggle.

Some of these films—the finest of them—contain a sort of somber and desperate idealism. All feelings are laid bare; it is drama reduced to stark savagery, senseless tragedy, life given a vigorous shake so that its most tempting fruits can be gathered but yielding only uselessness and extinction.

Of William S. Hart's earliest Westerns, the most impressive are *The Passing of Two-Gun Hicks* (1914) and *The Taking of Luke McVane* (1915), both directed by Hart assisted by Clifford S. Smith, and both based on stories by Bret Harte.

The first tells the story of the leader of a gang of outlaws who rides down from the mountains with his men. They hold up a stagecoach, shoot up a small town, rob its saloon, commit rape on its girls, and leave as unopposed as they came, going on to an extended raid on the ranches of the vicinity. The Hart character—we'll call him Rio Jim—brings away the memory of a woman, the wife of the town drunkard, who gave herself to him in part to save her husband and in part to put a stop to the pillage of the town.

The second already has the earmarks of some poetic short story. "Rio Jim, this time a tough gambler, is taken with a dance-hall girl. He comes to her aid when she is molested by some drunken Mexicans. Surprised and touched by this unexpected bit of chivalry, she offers him

the rose she wears over her breast. Then, during a card game, a man cheats. A fight ensues and Rio Jim shoots him. With the girl's help he makes a getaway but, feeling guilty of no crime, he doubles back and waits for the sheriff in his office. The latter comes and places him under arrest. The two of them set off on horseback for the next town, where the sheriff must hand him over to the authorities. As they cross the desert they are attacked by Indians. Both defend their lives dearly. The next day the two men are found dead. Rio Jim is smiling, the rose entwined in his fingers."

These sketches inevitably culminated in *The Aryan* (1916), the first masterpiece of its type:

> Rio Jim, a frontiersman, is on his way home with a money-belt full of gold dust. In the first saloon in the first little town he comes to, he is sized up as an easy mark by some cardsharps. A female decoy plays up to the guileless man of the prairies, gets him drunk and persuades him to gamble. Waking the next morning with a hangover, Rio Jim discovers that he has been victimized and at the same moment learns of the death of his mother, the news of which had been kept from him the night before in order to get him to the roulette table. Blind with rage, he dashes to the room of the girl who has duped him, kills her lover, gives her a beating and then, throwing her across his saddle, spurs his horse and gallops into the desert.
>
> The years pass. Rio Jim, who has reduced the former casino belle to working as his slave, has nurtured in his simple and hasty heart a distrust not only of women but of the entire white race. Now the leader of a gang of racially mixed outlaws, he preys upon the wagon trains of the white settlers and lives by robbing and spreading havoc.
>
> One day, the leader of a wagon train of immigrants and gold seekers which has lost its way comes to him and appeals for help and protection. Nursing his grudge, Rio Jim refuses to help his blood brothers, denying them water for their children and taking the women captive in order to hand them over to his brutish men. But one girl, hardly more than a child, dares to come all alone to the outlaw camp and plead for her companions. At first, the leader repulses her, ridicules her, refuses to be swayed. But the girl is not discouraged. She persists, appealing to the badman in the name of his own race and of simple humanity. Rio Jim, surrounded as he is by cutthroats, suddenly realizes where his duty lies. At the risk of his own life, he rescues the women, provisions the wagon train and personally leads it back to the right road. Then, rejecting their thanks but with a last goodbye, the frontiersman rides back into the desert alone.

It is easy to see how cleverly the authors have turned everything to account in this tale. There are innumerable touches which suddenly acquire a tragic meaning, such as the water bucket from which Rio Jim drinks with a dipper in the scene where he refuses to help the thirsting wagon train. The girl's glance, the glittering water, Rio Jim's manner, these together compose a tragedy condensed into a single image with the water in the foreground. At each moment some similar detail is registered and enriches the impressionistic synthesis of an *essentially descriptive* gesture.

The Coward (1915) is one of the Civil War stories. Frank, son of a Southern colonel, enlists against his will. On sentry duty he is seized with panic, deserts his post and flees to his parents' home. The colonel, despite his advanced age, goes off to take his son's place in order to eradicate the dishonor incurred by his behavior. The advancing Union army arrives, however, and sets up its headquarters in Frank's house. Through a series of lucky circumstances Frank succeeds in laying hands on the Union battle plan. At the risk of his life he brings it through the Union lines to the field headquarters of the Confederates who, that same day, use it to score an important victory.

Obviously, the theme itself is not strikingly original, but the feelings delineated in it are extraordinarily understated, except those of the old colonel, which finally become irritating. The important thing is the manner in which the characters behave, the truth with which the incidents are presented, the *factual* authenticity of a story which is plausible, albeit conventional and arbitrary. In short, it is not the anecdote that matters but its presentation. And from that standpoint it is masterly.

Among his films of social criticism, many of them semi-documentaries which, in the same way as *The Italian,* paved the way for all the usages of contemporary social realism, a representative sampling might include *The Gangsters and the Girl* (1914), a sort of realist *Three-Penny Opera,* which pictured, in a quasi-documentary manner, the life of the reprobates, the indigent and the outcasts of society. A slender plot-line serves as the guide-wire for this intrusion of the camera into the poorest and most squalid haunts of the big American cities.

The brutalizing tendency of poverty is vividly delineated in *Not of the Flock* (1914), while *Civilization's Child* (1916), whose action takes place among the poorest Ukranian immigrants, depicts the hardships of a girl who is seduced and abandoned and who, in time, is stripped of her hard-earned possessions and her modicum of well-being when her husband and son incur the wrath of a pair of socially prominent individuals. Many other examples could be cited.

While certain *esthetic constants* identify each Ince production as unmistakably his, at the same time his contributing directors inevitably left the marks of their own personalities on the films Ince assigned to them. Reginald Barker, Raymond B. West, Walter Edwards and Charles Miller can be mentioned as representative.

One of the most interesting directors of the Kay-Bee Westerns, Reginald Barker, a Scot who had directed some Broncho Billy films at Essanay, infuses his films with a kind of epic power. While his William S. Hart films are especially notable, his other films are impressive in different ways. In *Jim Grimsby's Boy* (1916), the development of the young girl's personality—from child to woman—is achieved by a number of small touches which are rudimentary yet exactly right. Furthermore the old man's crankiness and the untamed wildness of the natural setting form a climate which is harsh, brutal, illuminated with ingenuousness as if by sunlight breaking through foliage and glistening on clear water.

A cameraman and assistant director before joining the Ince organization, Raymond B. West brings to his films a turbulent vigor along with a tendency to sentimentality and sermonizing which mar such otherwise interesting films of social criticism as *Those Who Pay.*

A performer in the 101 Wild West Show and an actor in Ince's early Westerns, Walter Edwards has certain traits in common with Barker. His violence comes more easily and he is sometimes brutal, but his films can equal Barker's in power, and they too benefit from the sobriety and conciseness which were characteristic of all the Ince films. Of Edwards's films, the one most often cited is *The Dividend* (1916), a rather free adaptation of Octave Mirbeau's satire *Les affaires sont les affaires.* It has on the whole the same weaknesses as Raymond West's pictures while exhibiting a more objective outlook which is careful to give each happening its proper weight. Edwards's *Lieutenant Danny, U.S.A.* (1916) also deserves mention. A humorous episode of the border raids during the Mexican Revolution, its truculent good humor would twenty years later find their culmination in Jack Conway's *Viva Villa.*

As tough and violent as were these directors, defenders of heavy-handed theses and makers of crude poems, so Charles Miller, if less powerful, is far more subtle and restrained. A theatre director before coming to Ince, his films—romantic comedies for the most part—are not free of either sentimentality or cloyingness but they almost invariably radiate a charm which is as reserved as it is winning. They rarely exploit melodramatic possibilities. They depict the small pleasures and pains of everyday life, going visiting in one's Sunday best, a girl's pleasure in silk stockings, getting off work at the end of the day, shy avowals exchanged in the shade of an elm tree, soon-forgotten desires, thwarted longings, a stream of delicate and flowing sentiment (albeit at times a bit saccharine) which is held back, timorous, full of youth and spontaneity, and has withal a lambent kind of grace which, since Dickens, only Anglo-Saxon literature, and women's literature especially, has exemplified and which here reaches the screen for the first time. What we later encounter in Griffith's *True Heart Susie*—with a different kind of mastery to be sure—in the Joseph de Grasse/Charles Ray *The Girl I Loved* (1923) or, to name only sound films, in George Cukor's *Little Women* and *David Copperfield,* in Henry Hathaway's *Peter Ibbetson,* in Clarence Brown's *Ah, Wilderness,* or even in Michael Curtiz's *Four Daughters,* is already present in the sensitive and radiant *Plain Jane* (1916), one of Miller's most attractive films.

Of Jack Conway, as of Frank Borzage, young beginners at this period working under the aegis of Ince and Griffith, most often in collaboration with more experienced men, and whose real careers would not get under way until several years later, nothing can be said in this connection that would contribute to an appreciation of their real worth.

Fred Niblo, Victor Schertzinger and Jerome Storm, like Lambert Hillyer, belong more to the final period of Ince's production, the post-Triangle phase during which he released his films through Paramount and First National. Joining the organization at a time when Ince's achievements as an innovator had already given way to a blander commercialism, they were primarily conscientious appliers of formulas which had been established by their predecessors.

Schertzinger, also known as a composer, and Jerome Storm, whose main claim to fame were as directors of the Charles Ray films, helped to establish that actor as the definitive type of the shy and awkward juvenile lead. Some of their films, *The Clodhopper* (1917), *String Beans* (1918), *His Own Home Town* (1918), *Alarm Clock Andy* (1920), *An Old-Fashioned Boy* (1920) were, thanks especially to that actor, imbued with a kind of light-hearted mocking poetry.

Schertzinger, moreover, of all the Ince directors, was the only one, along with Reginald Barker, who went on to do respectable work in the sound era. He made most of the Grace Moore films and many other musicals.

As for Fred Niblo, who rose to fame with *The Mark of Zorro* (thanks to Douglas Fairbanks), with *Blood and Sand* (thanks to Rudolph Valentino) and with the 1925 version of *Ben-Hur,* that precarious monument of dubious taste which however contained one estimable gem, the famous chariot race, he then lapsed into the run-of-the-mill and oblivion. After directing the William S. Hart films of the Paramount period—notably *Wagon Tracks* (1919), which in some ways equals **The Aryan**—Lambert Hillyer likewise after 1930 directed only films of the "B" category.

III

In reviewing Ince's work as a whole there is one point that is particularly important for evaluating his legacy and his originality. In an Ince film the telling detail is never insisted on as it is in Griffith. The close-up which isolates a detail in order to extract nothing but its value as a transitory *sign* can be used effectively only in the epic or in subjective analysis, in any situation, in fact, which tends more or less to transfigure reality symbolically. Ince, by contrast, never loses his objectivity. In an Ince film, when it comes to emphasizing acts rather than ideas, he uses *what things say in themselves* rather than *what they are made to say.* The telling detail is grasped within the totality it forms a part of. It gets emphasis only from the special placement it is given.

Which is not to say that, in his view of it, the signifier is identical with the thing signified; but merely that the meaning is inherent in the things themselves and that he "dislodges" it from them spontaneously. To put it plainly, Ince does not *signify,* he *expresses.*

Indeed, "signification" gives rise to concepts, not to things; ideas *signify,* things express. So, with Ince, when any object acquires the value of a sign it is always that of an immediately perceivable concrete reality understood within the limits of the narrative itself. The symbol never transcends the apparent facts of the case. It may rise to the level of concept only insofar as the empirical world of the drama can justify its doing so.

It has long been established that filmic signification—unlike that of verbal expression—is not based on convention. It is fleeting, constantly differentiating, but always and necessarily *implicational.* It attaches to a detail (usually isolated), returns it to the work in its entirety, and operates through discrimination and assimilation (i.e. the eyeglasses in *Potemkin*).

In this case, the concrete fact will give rise to an *idea* which somehow transcends the presented act or object. It follows, then, that "signification" is basic to a type of language which seeks to magnify or aggrandize events: the language of epic, the language of Griffith and Eisenstein.

"Expression," on the other hand, is usually part of a flow, a continuum. It particularizes things as themselves, transcending their immediate sense only to enhance the drama of which they form a part. In *this* case, their implication is always concrete; they are things concerning things, actions concerning actions, facts concerning facts, but never things, actions or facts concerning ideas.

When William S. Hart drinks from the dipper in front of the young girl whom he is refusing to help, the meaning that attaches to the act does not go beyond the exact one which was motivating his behavior at that instant, a bit of behavior which sums up and expresses it. Instead of constantly moving, as the epic does, from the particular to the general, we stay within what particularizes a unique and carefully defined drama. Nothing outstrips the concrete fact. The concept is inherent in the things themselves; they are characterized but never transcended.

Which, in a nutshell, is the language of the short story teller, if not the novelist. Whatever lyricism accrues to it consists of just such facts or their immediate repercussions, not of any ethical or metaphysical extrapolation.

With Ince, then, film veers decisively away from *theatricality* as it does also from theatrical *construction* of drama. Rejecting the dramatic construction that goes with stage production, he uses a kind of construction more in tune with filmic expression. In this sense he can be called the true founder of cinematic dramaturgy.

With certain rare exceptions, in fact, all the truly great silent films were constructed and developed along the lines of the short story. And until quite recently, most sound films were constructed the same way. The recent growth of the notion of novelistic time has resulted in significant developments, giving film a new sense, the sense of *narrative* which is apparently to be the ultimate outcome of the audio-visual means of expression. Yet this has been made possible only by lengthening the average film's running time from ninety minutes to two, three, and even four hours. One can no more build up novelistic continuity in ninety minutes than one could write a cycle of novels in thirty pages. As long as the length of a film could not exceed that arbitrary limit, the short story structure was the only one in which it could achieve anything like perfection.

Unfortunately, when speaking of the clarity and conciseness of Thomas Ince's films, one must do so from memory. To speak personally, I have not been able to see again any of the films of which I have written here (and whose negatives were scattered when the Triangle Company was dissolved). The last time I saw **The Aryan** was in 1925. I was quite young then and cannot say to what extent that work may have aged. But happily some negatives were recovered in the past ten years and I was fortunate enough to see for the first time, in Germany two years ago, an excellent print of *The Coward,* which Reginald Barker directed, with Charles Ray in the leading role. If one keeps in mind the kind of thing that was being done in 1915, it is an extraordinary film which might have been produced at the end of the silent era and which has dated no more than, say, *The Wind* or *Sunrise,* except for such features as the sometimes broad over-playing of Frank Keenan. It is as beautiful as *Broken Blossoms* and of such starkness that, even if Ince's place in the history of forms and of a new language's means of expression is, in all truth, less than Griffith's, it still places him on a par with the latter in the history of art. Alongside the manifest authenticity of its finest sequences, certain Italian neo-realist works of the 1950s seem like mere fustian. The discovery of this film in 1963 was a momentous event for me. It is possibly Thomas Ince's masterpiece (yet how many of his other films would have to be seen before one could say for certain!). The least that can be said of it, however, is that if it lacks the brio, the flight, the epic power of *The Birth of a Nation,* it is infinitely more limpid, and in any case much closer to us now and to contemporary cinema. In place of the art of editing and of rhythm it sets the art of narration, description and suggestion. One cannot help being struck by the foresight of Louis Delluc who wrote in 1920: "Griffith is the man of the past, Ince the man of today. . . . That Griffith's fame should outshine Ince's is as it should be and of no great consequence. Griffith is the cinema's first great achiever, Ince its first prophet. . . ."

Certainly all of the many contributors to Ince's productions left the imprint of their personalities upon the films they directed.

Yet, in a multiplicity of ways, the concepts stayed the same and the esthetic intentions remained recognizable. They were nothing but the accidental variables of a cinematurgy whose initiator and creator was Ince.

It is important to emphasize that with only one or two exceptions, once freed from his tutelage none of his collaborators achieved anything much above average.

For Ince was not only a remarkable theoretician, a great director and a producer of seminal influence: in the entire history of the cinema he was and remains the only true leader of a school.

He cannot be compared with the best of contemporary producers—who are businessmen and impressarios first and foremost. First and foremost Ince was an artist. He was able to supervise, guide and shape his contributors only because he was, like them, a director, though greater than any of them.

Janet Staiger (essay date 1979)

SOURCE: "Dividing Labor for Production Control: Thomas Ince and the Rise of the Studio System," in *Cinema Journal,* Vol. XVIII, No. 2, Spring, 1979, pp. 16-25.

[*In the following essay, Staiger argues that although Ince may be seen as an innovator in the film industry his improvements generally reflect the adoption of scientific management and the division of labor to the process of filmmaking.*]

Thomas Ince was a classic case of a stage actor who, during a brief period of unemployment in 1910, turned to the fledgling movies as a source of income.[1] Yet his long-term impact on filmmaking would be very great indeed. Working first for IMP and then Biograph, he returned to IMP when promised a chance to direct. He completed his first film in December 1910. Ince soon tired of the one-reel format, however, and accepted a position in the fall of 1911 to direct for Kessel and Bauman's New York Motion Picture Company. He headed to Edendale, California, where a small group of people were already making films. The studio at that time was a converted grocery store: one stage (without even a muslin overhang), a scene dock, a small lab and office, and a bungalow which served as a dressing room. Ince wrote, directed, and cut his first film within one week.[2] From these beginnings, by 1913 he had a fully developed continuity script procedure; by 1916 a one-half million dollar studio on 43 acres of land with concrete buildings. There were a 165-foot electrically lit building (which was unique), eight stages 60 by 150 feet, an administration building for the executive and scenario departments, property, carpenter, plumbing, and costume rooms, a restaurant and commissary, 300 dressing rooms, a hothouse, and a natatorium—and 1,000 employees and a studio structure which was essentially that associated with the big studio period of later years.[3] Why?

Previous historians have provided only partial answers. Lewis Jacobs attributes Ince's innovations to the need to standardize large-scale productions through "formula" pictures and publicity: "Essentially a businessman, he [Ince] conducted himself and his film making in businesslike fashion. . . . Planning in advance meant better unity of structure, less chance of uneven quality, and economy of expression." Kalton Lahue, in *Dreams for Sale,* writes, "Ince kept [his studio] functioning at peak efficiency by holding a tight rein on everything that was done." Eric Rhode notes that Ince "was among the first film-makers to adapt his craft to the latest ideas in industrial management and to set up the assembly-line type of production."[4]

What historians describe without outlining structure is the division of labor under the control of a corporate manager. Nor do they indicate the steps Ince took in progressing to his final system. Using Paul A. Baran and Paul M. Sweezy's monograph *Monopoly Capital* as a large framework, Harry Braverman, in *Labor and Monopoly Capital,* sets up a model and explanation of how and why labor is divided. As a model it is stochastic rather than deterministic—some amount of variation may occur, but on the whole, the model should account for an individual instance of the historical change and development of a labor structure.

BRAVERMAN'S MODEL OF LABOR IN MONOPOLY CAPITAL

According to Braverman, in the most basic capitalistic situation, humans have a potential labor power which they sell to the capitalist who, in turn, hopes to derive from their labor power the greatest possible surplus. But this potential labor power is affected by: 1) "the organization of the process" and 2) "the forms of supervision over it."[5] By selling his/her labor power, the worker is no longer in control of his/her labor time; that control is ceded to the capitalist who has purchased the labor time and the potential of labor power. Naturally, given the profit maximization motive, the capitalist will seek to gain as much as possible from that potential in time and power.

However, unlike physical capital, the results of this purchase are uncertain. The original method of the capitalist was to "[utilize] labor as it [came] to him from prior forms of production," which usually was the craft or domestic system of labor.[6] The capitalist subcontracted for the work he wanted accomplished. But certain problems arose with this system: "irregularity of production, loss of materials in transit and through embezzlement, slowness of manufacture, lack of uniformity and uncertainty of the quality of production."[7]

The first means of striving for control of these variables was to centralize the employment, which provided some control over the irregularity of production through the threat of loss of employment. This initial step, however, had no effect on the other problems. It is here that division of the labor process develops as a second means of solving the other areas of uncertainty.

The division of labor process "begins with the *analysis of the labor process* . . . the separation of the work of production into its constituent elements."[8] Assigning a worker to repeat a single segment of a total task produces three advantages according to Adam Smith: 1) increase in dexterity, 2) saving time, and 3) "the invention of a great number of machines which facilitate and abridge labor."[9] A fourth advantage, saving costs, was pointed out by Charles Babbage. Since the task was segmented, only the worker who was doing the most difficult part of the work had to be paid for his/her skill rather than paying all the workers for the most difficult part—which was what happened under the older craft system. Braverman asserts that these principles have led to separating the worker's brain from his/her hands and that division of labor promotes an almost systematic elimination of skills required for a person to work.

This division of labor was the second of three steps in monopoly capital's quest for organizing and supervising the potential for labor time and power. The third was "scientific management" which was "the control over work through the control over the *decisions that are made in the course of work.*"[10] This advancement in management was initiated, in particular, by Frederick Winslow Taylor, whose work (often called "Taylorism" and typified by the efficiency experts of the first part of the twentieth century) began to be widely disseminated after 1890.

The effects of division of labor and scientific management were multiple—all leading to the separation of the planning phase and the execution phase. This separation destroys an ideal of the whole person, both the creator and the producer of his/her ideas.[11] Practically, this results in certain characteristics which appear consistently in divided labor.

First, there is a physical separation between the conception and production phases.

> The concept of control adopted by modern management requires that every activity in production have its several parallel activities in the management center: each must be devised, precalculated, tested, laid out, assigned and ordered, checked and inspected, and recorded throughout its duration and upon completion. The result is that the process of production is replicated in paper form before, as, and after it takes place in physical form.[12]

Second, not only is conception and execution divided, but specialization results in both planning and producing. Thus there develops the modern corporation which is characterized by: 1) corporate managers, 2) "producing activities which are subdivided among functional departments, each having a specific aspect of the process for its domain,"[13] and 3) extensive development of the marketing process.

Ince had several models of organizing work available to him. He had worked in the theater and might have chosen a labor structure similar to that. Or he might have followed Griffith's (and most of the rest of the industry's) lead: group units which shot from a brief outline.[14] Instead, he seems to have followed the lead of modern industry. Ince, however, is not unique. He is an innovator, perhaps ahead of others in some respects but not by much. His contributions to the production structure of the film industry need to be placed in perspective by examining the conception/execution process and the labor division in his production unit.

THE SEPARATION OF CONCEPTION AND EXECUTION

The first part of this structure is Ince's separation of the conception and production phases of filmmaking. To repeat Braverman's observation:

> The concept of control adopted by modern management requires that every activity in production have its several parallel activities in the management center. . . . The result is that the process of production is replicated in paper form before, as, and after it takes place in physical form.[15]

For Ince and filmmaking, this replication is in the continuity script. The framework for the continuity script already existed in the scenarios of the period. In nearly every issue of *The Moving Picture World* descriptions of how to write scenarios are given budding screenwriters. Even as Ince was beginning to direct, an article in 1911 advises:

> Follow the cast of characters with the scenario proper. Divide the scenario into scenes, giving each change in the location of the action a separate scene—that is, whenever the plot renders it necessary for the operator to change the position of his camera, as from an interior to an exterior view, begin a new scene. Number the scenes consecutively to the end of the play. At the beginning of each scene, give a brief but clear word picture of the settings of the scene; also the position and action of the characters introduced when the picture first flashes on the screen. . . . Now carefully study out the needed action for each scene; and then describe it briefly, being careful to cut out every act that does not have a direct bearing on the development of the plot.[16]

The article continues to describe many of the characteristics we now associate with classical Hollywood cinema.

Ince had traveled to Edendale in October 1911. According to a trade paper, in June 1912 Ince split his studio into two production units because his staff was increasing in size and becoming unwieldy. At this time Ince was writing scenarios, shooting footage, and editing the films, and the company was averaging one two-reel film per week. Under this new system Ince would direct the two- and three-reel Western dramas and Francis Ford, John's older brother, would shoot Western comedies and smaller-cast dramas.[17] A later commentator, George Mitchell, attributes the detailed continuity script to Ince's desire for control over what Ford did.[18] This speculation

seems plausible: if management desires to control uniformity and quality of product, some means of supervising the individual work tasks must be devised. But there may be more to it than that. The continuity script also provides efficiency and regularity of production. Describing the Ince studio eighteen months later, W. E. Wing wrote:

> To the writer the most striking feature of Inceville . . . was its system. Although housing an army of actors, directors and subordinates, there is not a working hour lapses in which all the various companies are not at work producing results. We failed to see actors made up and dressed for their various roles, loafing about the stages or on locations; perturbed directors running here and there attempting to bring order out of chaos, while locations waited and cameramen idly smoked their cigarettes, waiting for the "next scene."
>
> With preparations laid out in detail from finished photoplays to the last prop, superintended by Mr. Ince himself, far in advance of action, each of the numerous directors on the job at Santa Ynez canyon is given his working script three weeks ahead of time.[19]

Ince's scenarios had, by 1913, become what are now labeled continuity scripts. A good number of these scripts, as well as scenarios for Griffith and Sennett films, are available in the Aitken Brothers Papers at Madison, Wisconsin.[20] The earliest Ince script available is for *The Raiders,* which was shot in late 1913. This one is as fully developed as later ones, containing the constituent parts of all of his continuities.

Each script has a number assigned to it which provides a method of tracing the film even though its title might shift. A cover page indicates who wrote the scenario, who directed the shooting, when shooting began and ended, when the film was shipped to the distributors, and when the film was released. This entire history on paper records the production process for efficiency and waste control.

The next part is a list of all intertitles and an indication as to where they are to be inserted in the final print. The location page follows that. It lists all exterior and interior sites along with their scene numbers, providing efficiency and preventing waste in time and labor. These continuities were apparently used during the filming process since pencil lines are drawn through the typed information.

The cast of characters follows. The typed portions list the roles for the story and penciled in are the names of the people assigned to play each part.

A one-page synopsis follows and then the script itself. Each scene is numbered consecutively and its location is given. Intertitles are typed in, often in red ink, where they are to be inserted in the final version. The description of mise-en-scène and action is detailed. Penciled over each scene is a scribble (presumably marking the completion of shooting), and sometimes on the side is a handwritten number—possibly the footage length of the scene. Production stills for advertising often accompany the script.

Occasionally there is the typed injunction: "It is earnestly requested by Mr. Ince that no change of any nature be made in the scenario either by elimination of any scenes or the addition of any scenes or changing any of the action as described, or titles, without first consulting him." The usual anecdotes of a stamped phrase "shoot as written" or "produce this exactly as written" were not confirmed by any of these scripts.[21] Rather, contemporary accounts suggest that Ince, his production manager, the scenarist, and the director discussed and revised the script until it was in final shape for shooting.[22] The continuities include detailed instructions such as special effects and tinting directions for the intertitles. Later, when Ince gave up cutting the films, notes to the editors are added.

Finally, and very significantly, attached to the continuity is the entire cost of the film, which is analyzed in a standard accounting format. The first section is labor costs, which account for eighty to ninety percentage of the direct costs of production. The second part is costs for expendables such as props, scenery, rentals, and music. In addition, the precise number of feet of negative and positive film is indicated along with a breakdown of cost per reel and per foot.[23]

All of this demonstrates that Ince's use of the continuity script resulted in a two-stage labor process—the work's preparation on paper by management followed by its execution by the workers. The five problems associated with optional systems—irregularity of production, loss of materials, slowness of manufacture, lack of uniformity, and uncertainty of quality—are controlled by that management. This standardization of the work process was used by Ince's publicity department as a mark of quality and uniformity of the film product: "Ince" becomes a brand name through its advertising.

THE DIVISION OF LABOR

The second major part of this structure is the growth of division of labor as planning becomes specialized in the hands of the corporate managers. When Ince began directing, some division of labor already existed for certain tasks, but the jobs were still flexible. Often the scenario might come from any one of the group.[24] Ince himself performed several of the functions which were to be separated out and bracketed as specific tasks: he was the organizer of the work (the producer), the controller of the final script (the scenario editor), the head of shooting (the director), and the film cutter (the editor). As the company expanded operations, he relinquished parts of his work and became a supervisor, utilizing control methods through middle management heads to maintain operations as he wanted them.

The first function to be transferred was the basic writing of the script. By Spring 1912 Richard Spencer was in charge of writing the scenarios, and *The Moving Picture World* called the Edendale scenario department the "most highbrow motion picture institution in town."[25] Ince, of course, still worked on the scripts with Spencer. C. Gardner Sullivan, who was to write many of the scenarios, was hired during this period. By 1915, the writing had been split: Spencer was chief story editor and Sullivan headed the scenario department which included six writers.[26]

The next of Ince's functions to go was the actual direction of the films. After Francis Ford was placed in charge of a second unit in 1912, the direction staff increased rapidly, and INCE GRADUALLY STOPPED DIRECTING. By 1914, Inceville had eight directors, and by 1915, Reginald Barker headed a group of nine with five or six production units shooting simultaneously. Ince was now titled "Director-General" for the company.[27] The third function which Ince relinquished direct control of was that of actually cutting the films, a task he had delegated to others by 1915.[28] Ince still retained final control through continuity script directions and final examination of each produced film.

The division of labor did not involve Ince's work alone; the steady growth in studio facilities and in scale of production concurrently resulted in additional segmenting of other film production functions. The management of such a complex organization required more professional abilities and, in the Spring of 1913, George B. Stout became Ince's financial head. After reorganizing the administrative system, Stout turned over the controls to Gene Allen and then transferred to Mack Sennett's studio which Ince nominally controlled as West Coast head for Kessel and Bauman. There, Stout also proceeded to divide Sennett's labor by breaking his studio into ten departments based on work functions.[29] Ince's photography unit expanded rapidly, and set and construction demanded an art supervisor. In 1915, the New York Motion Picture Company aligned with the newly formed Triangle Film Corporation, and Ince, as well as Griffith and Sennett, became vice-president of the corporation. An expansion period followed, and more specialists were hired: a former chief cameraman from Universal was employed "to superintend the development of negative films"; Victor Schertzinger began writing musical scores to accompany the films; and Melville Ellis, described as a "designer and fashion expert of International reputation," was hired for the costume department.[30]

One aspect has been left out of this description of the growth of division of labor and that is the situation of the actors and actresses. Stunt people and stock players were replaceable workers. But what about the stars? At an exhibitors' convention both the stars and Ince's control as a mark of quality and uniformity were the central advertising themes. So the stars were not as interchangeable as were the other players.[31] Instead they seemed to serve a function similar in nature to Ince's: product differentiation. For that reason, it would be important that a star be tied to a particular studio so that the star's "unique" qualities would be associated only with that studio's films. At the time of Triangle's formation, Ince disclosed that his idea was "to get stars, teach them the tricks of the camera and then keep them at salaries high enough to restrain them so that they cannot work first for one company and then for another."[32] Even at this time the star as worker was often "bound" to the studio through multiple-year contracts in order to reduce fluctuation in the studio's image. Although a worker, in the sense of being an interchangeable part in the script, the star is also a quality or substance in the product itself and fulfills the function of a means to differentiate the pictures of one company from another.

One way to comprehend the growth of the entire studio structure is to recall the initial description of the new studio that Ince built in Culver City in late 1915, at the same time that he was renovating Inceville in Santa Monica: the 165-foot electrically lit building, the eight stages 60 by 150 feet, an administration building for executive and scenario offices, property, carpenter, and costume buildings, 300 dressing rooms, a hothouse, a natatorium, and so forth. But as impressive as that description is, Ince does not seem to have been unique. While he had the best scenario department, others also had them; Keystone, too, was divided into task sections. A special issue of *The Moving Picture World* in 1915 describes the growth of the West Coast production companies and lists the New York Motion Picture Company as just one of many whose facilities were expanding.[33] The highly mobile employment patterns in the industry, the widespread publicity, and evidence of the organization of other studios make it clear that Ince was not unusual; that, in fact, most studios were structured somewhat like his.[34]

A REVISED PERSPECTIVE

By 1915 the major divisions of labor had been segmented. A pyramid of labor was the dominant structure with a top manager, middle-management department heads, and workers. This fulfills Braverman's description of a fully organized modern corporation in which "the producing activities are subdivided among functional departments, each having a specific aspect of the process for its domain. . . ."[35]

This development was more important to the long-term structure of the film industry and to the development of the form and the style of the films that industry was to produce than was the impact of any individual film or director. In the 1910s several models for organizing motion picture labor competed for acceptance, but the model based on a well organized factory, brought to its fruition by Ince, eventually succeeded in dominating. While his system was attacked as potentially producing "mechanical picture[s]," [36] its economical advantages seem to have won over any artistic fears.

Yet we should not create in Ince another great man of history. While he was an innovator of the continuity script, the industry as a whole was departmentalizing its

production units. Earlier historians' comments that the continuity script led to economical and efficient production are correct, but the script is only part of the system of the creation of the product. The continuity script works because it is an external manifestation of a more fundamental structure inextricable from modern corporate business—the separation of the conception and production phases of work and the pyramid of divided labor. It is this fundamental structure which explains Ince's production organization, a structure which earlier historians have failed to foreground.

A question that derives from this is, was there a simultaneous standardization of the product? To answer this question would require an extensive analysis of Ince's films—both the well-known and the lesser works. But it is clear that in the broader model of division of labor and scientific management, the film industry by 1915 had the structure it was to follow for the next fifty years.

NOTES

[1] This paper is a result of a seminar in social and economic problems in American film history conducted by Douglas Gomery, Fall 1977, at the University of Wisconsin-Madison. I would like to thank the members of the seminar for their suggestions and help in formalizing these ideas. I also appreciate further research leads given me by members of the Society for Cinema Studies at the 1978 conference where a draft of this paper was read.

[2] George Mitchell, "Thomas H. Ince," *Films in Review,* 11 (October 1960), 464-68; "The 'IMP' Company Invades Cuba," *The Moving Picture World,* 8, no. 3 (21 January 1911), 146. (*The Moving Picture World* will be abbreviated *MPW* hereafter.)

[3] Kalton C. Lahue, *Dreams for Sale: The Rise and Fall of the Triangle Film Corporation* (South Brunswick and New York: A. S. Barnes, 1971), pp. 61, 65-6, 71; "Los Angeles Letter," *MPW,* 25, no. 8 (21 August 1915), 1301; "Forty-Three Acres for Incity," *MPW,* 27, no. 6 (12 February 1916), 958.

[4] Lewis Jacobs, *The Rise of the American Film: A Critical History* (New York: Harcourt, Brace, 1939), pp. 162, 205-6; Lahue, *Dreams for Sale,* p. 46; Eric Rhode, *A History of the Cinema: From Its Origins to 1970* (New York: Hill and Wang, 1976), p. 58.

[5] Harry Braverman, *Labor and Monopoly Capital: The Degradation of Work in the Twentieth Century* (New York: Monthly Review Press, 1974), p. 54.

[6] Braverman, p. 59.

[7] Braverman, p. 63.

[8] Braverman, p. 75.

[9] Adam Smith quoted by Braverman, pp. 76-7.

[10] Braverman, p. 107.

[11] For a Marxist analysis of these effects, also see Ernst Fischer, *The Essential Marxist,* trans. Anna Bostock (New York: The Seabury Press, 1970), pp. 15-51.

[12] Braverman, p. 125.

[13] Braverman, p. 260.

[14] Peter Milne, *Motion Picture Directing* (New York: Falk, 1922), p. 136.

[15] Braverman, p. 125.

[16] Everett McNeil, "Outline of How to Write a Photoplay," *MPW,* 9, no. 1 (15 July 1911), 27.

[17] "Doings in Los Angeles," *MPW,* 12, no. 10 (8 June 1912), 913; "Doings in Los Angeles," *MPW,* 14, no. 1 (5 October 1912), 32.

[18] Mitchell, pp. 469-70.

[19] W. E. Wing, "Tom Ince, of Inceville," *The New York Dramatic Mirror,* 70, no. 1827 (24 December 1913), 34 [also in George C. Pratt, *Spellbound in Darkness,* revised ed. (Greenwich, Connecticut: New York Graphic Society, 1973), pp. 144-45].

[20] Aitken Brothers Papers, Scenarios, Manuscript Collection (Wisconsin Center for Film and Theater Research, Madison, Wisconsin), Boxes 1-9.

[21] Milne, p. 140; Jacobs, p. 204; Arthur Knight, *The Liveliest Art: A Panoramic History of the Movies* (New York: Macmillan, 1957), p. 38; Edward Wagenknecht, *The Movies in the Age of Innocence* (Norman: University of Oklahoma Press, 1962), p. 175; Lahue, *Dreams for Sale,* p. 45; Rhode, p. 58.

[22] Wing, p. 34; Milne, p. 140; William S. Hart, *My Life East and West* (Boston and New York: Houghton Mifflin, 1929), pp. 206-7.

[23] For example, *The Iron Strain* (1915) costs were $2737.56 per reel (six reels) and $2.73 per foot.

[24] Mitchell, p. 468.

[25] "Doings in Los Angeles," *MPW,* 15, no. 7 (15 February 1913), 668.

[26] Wing, p. 34; Jean Mitry, *Histoire du cinéma: Art et Industrie, Vol. I: 1895-1914* (Paris: Editions Universitaires, 1967), p. 440; Mitry, *Vol. II: 1915-1925,* pp. 88-9; Hart, p. 213; Lahue, *Dreams for Sale,* p. 40.

[27] "William S. Hart," *MPW,* 22, no. 7 (14 November 1914), 920; Mitry, *II,* pp. 88-9; Lahue, *Dreams for Sale,* p. 40; Ad, *MPW,* 25, no. 2 (10 July 1915), 333.

[28] Lahue, *Dreams for Sale,* p. 45.

[29] Kalton C. Lahue, *Mack Sennett's Keystone: The Man, the Myth, and the Comedies* (Cranbury, New Jersey: A. S. Barnes, 1971), p. 244.

[30] Mitchell, pp. 472-3; Mitry, *I,* p. 440; "Los Angeles Letter," *MPW,* 25, no. 9 (28 August 1915), 1466; "Ince's Big Picture Completed," *MPW,* 27, no. 10 (11 March 1916), 1638; "Los Angeles Letter," *MPW,* 25, no. 8 (21 August 1915), 1301; "Triangle Appoints a General Manager," *MPW,* 25, no. 8 (21 August 1915), 1303; "Triangle Opening Announced," *MPW* 25, no. 10 (4 September 1915), 1622; "Manufacturers' Exposition," *MPW,* 25, no. 5 (31 July 1915), 820.

[31] "Manufacturers' Exposition," *MPW,* 25, no. 5 (31 July 1915), 820; Aitken Brothers Papers, Scenarios, Boxes 1-9.

[32] "Los Angeles Letter," *MPW,* 25, no. 7 (14 August 1915), 1144.

[33] George Blaisdell, "Mecca of the Motion Picture," *MPW,* 25, no. 2 (10 July 1915), 216.

[34] Aitken Brothers Papers, Correspondence, Boxes 10-14.

[35] Braverman, p. 260.

[36] Milne, p. 136.

FURTHER READING

Criticism

MacCann, Richard Dyer. "Ince and Hart." In *The First Film Makers,* pp. 61-114. Metuchen, N. J.: The Scarecrow Press, Inc., 1989.
> Collection of essays on Ince's filmmaking technique by various contributors, including the actor-director William S. Hart.

Pratt, George C. "Thomas H. Ince." In *Spellbound in Darkness: A History of the Silent Film,* pp. 143-75. Greenwich, Conn.: New York Graphic Society Ltd., 1973.
> Includes a brief biographical sketch of Ince, along with commentary on the films *The Bargain* and *Satan McAllister's Heir* produced by Ince. The balance of the article reproduces a detailed shooting scenario for *Satan McAllister's Heir.*

George Herbert Mead

1863–1931

American philosopher and social scientist.

INTRODUCTION

Mead is acclaimed as one of the most influential social psychologists of the early twentieth century. Although his theories were never published during his lifetime, they were preserved and posthumously published from his lecture notes and the transcriptions of his students. Mead is best known for his interpretation of the self and the role of language and social interaction in its development. Over several years he developed a system of thought that demonstrates how social behaviorism is related to the disciplines of cosmology and metaphysics.

Biographical Information

Mead was born in 1863 in South Hadley, Massachusetts. In 1883 he graduated from Oberlin College and a few years later, attended Harvard University. After leaving Harvard in 1888, he studied psychology and philosophy in Leipzig and Berlin, where he was influenced by the work of physiological psychologist Wilhelm Wundt. He returned to the United States in 1891 and taught philosophy at the University of Michigan. In 1894 he began teaching at the University of Chicago, where he would remain until his death three decades later. During this time he would become a prominent member of the pragmatist movement in philosophy, along with another University of Chicago philosopher, John Dewey. A school of thought founded by Charles S. Peirce and William James, pragmatism holds that meaning should be sought in practical ways; the function of thought is to guide action; and the scientific method is superior to all other methods of gaining knowledge. Mead died in Chicago on April 26, 1931.

Major Works

Mead's first collection of lectures, *The Philosophy of the Act*, explores the concepts of sociality and perspective. In *Mind, Self, and Society from the Standpoint of a Social Behaviorist* Mead develops the notions of self and society, contending that human beings can understand the idea of self only when the individual can perceive his or her own behavior from the perspective of another. It is when the individual gains this perspective that they have achieved a sense of self. Central to this theory is the doctrine that mind and self are not inborn, but evolve through social interaction. Regarded as a useful historical study, Mead's *Movements of Thought in the Nineteenth Century* traces important scientific and revolutionary trends since the Renaissance. In his final work, *The*

Philosophy of the Present, Mead analyzes how organisms adjust to their social environment and determines how these adaptations affect the process of evolution. Moreover, he examines the different phases of adjustment—emergence, novelty, creativity, thinking, communication, and continuous adjustment—and explains how these concepts are interrelated.

Critical Reception

Mead has been consistently praised for his contribution to social psychology and philosophy. His theories of mind, self, and society have supported a wide variety of interests, from linguistics through experimental psychology to metaphysics and educational theory and practice. Yet some critics have deemed aspects of Mead's philosophy as dense, muddled, and sometimes ambiguous. His work has therefore inspired many critical studies that interpret and explore these areas of his doctrine. Many commentators have discussed the influence of Mead's ideas on a number of prominent psychologists and sociologists, such as Talcott Parsons and Robert Merton. The central doctrine of his work, the concept of self, has been contrasted with Jean-Paul Sartre's theory of man and critics have found similarities between Mead's scientific method and that of B. F. Skinner. Yet many scholars continue to note that despite the scope and influence of his work, he is still relatively unknown compared to other important early twentieth-century pragmatists—such as John Dewey and Charles S. Peirce—and urge further critical reassessment and analysis of Mead's philosophy.

PRINCIPAL WORKS

The Philosophy of the Present [edited by Arthur E. Murphy] (lectures) 1932

Mind, Self, and Society from the Standpoint of a Social Behaviorist [edited by Charles W. Morris] (lectures) 1934

Movements of Thought in the Nineteenth Century [edited by Merritt H. Moore] (lectures) 1936

The Philosophy of the Act [edited by Charles W. Morris] (lectures) 1938

The Social Psychology of George Herbert Mead [edited by Anselm Strauss] (essays and lectures) 1956

Selected Writings [edited by Andrew J. Reck] (essays and lectures) 1964

The Individual and the Social Self: Unpublished Work of George Herbert Mead [edited by David L. Miller] (essays and lectures) 1982

CRITICISM

John Dewey (essay date 1931)

SOURCE: "George Herbert Mead," in *The Journal of Philosophy,* Vol. XXVIII, No. 12, June 4, 1931, pp. 309-14.

[*In the following essay, Dewey discusses Mead's influence on social psychology and reflects on their personal relationship.*]

As I look back over the years of George Mead's life, and try to sum up the impression which his personality left upon me, I seem to find running through everything a sense of energy, of vigor, of a vigor unified, outgoing and outgiving. Yet as I say this I am aware that perhaps only those who knew him best have a similar impression. For there was nothing about him of the bustle and ado, the impatient hurry, we often associate with vigor. On the contrary he was rather remarkably free from the usual external signs of busy activity. He was not one to rush about breathless with the conviction that he must somehow convince others of his activity. It was rather that he threw himself completely into whatever he had to do in all the circumstances and relations which life brought to him. He gave himself with a single heart to whatever the day and the moment brought. When anything needed to be done, there was no distinction in his life between the important and the unimportant; not that he was careless and undiscriminating, but that whatever really needed to be done, whatever made a demand upon him, was important enough to call out his full vigor. If he did not give the impression of bustling energy, it was precisely because in all that he did his energy was so completely engaged and so unified from within. He faced everything as it came along; incidents were opportunities for reflection to terminate in decision. One can fancy him perplexed temporarily in thought by the complexities of some issue; one can not imagine him hesitant to meet the issue or shillyshallying in meeting it. His consciousness never sicklied over the scene of decision and action; it completely and inwardly identified itself with it. It might be household duties, it might be the needs of a friend, or of the physical and mental needs of the many young persons that he and Mrs. Mead gathered about them! It might be his reading, his study, his reflection, his recreations, tramps, and travels. In each occasion as it arose there was found the natural opportunity for the free and vital release of his powers.

For his vigor was unified from within, by and from the fullness of his own being. More, I think, than any man I have ever known, his original nature and what he acquired and learned, were one and the same thing. It is the tendency of philosophic study to create a separation between what is native, spontaneous, and unconscious and the results of reading and reflection. That split never existed in George Mead. His study, his ideas, his never ceasing reflection and theory were the manifestation of his large and varied natural being. He was extraordinarily free from not only inner suppressions and the divisions they produce, but from all the artificialities of culture. Doubtless like the rest of us he had his inner doubts, perplexities, and depressions. But the unconscious and spontaneous vigor of his personality consumed and assimilated these things in the buoyant and nevertheless tranquil outgivings of thought and action.

He experienced great difficulty in finding adequate verbal expression for his philosophical ideas. His philosophy often found utterance in technical form. In the early years especially it was often not easy to follow his thought; he gained clarity of verbal expression of his philosophy gradually and through constant effort. Yet this fact is evidence of the unity of his philosophy and his own native being. For him philosophy was less acquired from without, a more genuine development from within, than in the case of any thinker I have known. If he had borrowed his ideas from without, he could have borrowed his language from the same source, and in uttering ideas that were already current, saying with some different emphasis what was already in other persons' minds, he would easily have been understood. But his mind was deeply original—in my contacts and my judgment the most original mind in philosophy in the America of the last generation. From some cause of which we have no knowledge concerning genuinely original minds, he had early in life an intuition, an insight in advance of his day. Of necessity, there was not ready and waiting for him any language in which to express it. Only as the thoughts of others gradually caught up with what he felt and saw could he articulate himself. Yet his native vigor was such that he never thought of ceasing the effort. He was of such a sociable nature that he must have been disappointed by the failure of others to understand him, but he never allowed it to discourage his efforts to make his ideas intelligible to others. And while in recent years his efforts were crowned with success, there was no time in which his mind was not so creative that anyone in contact with it failed to get stimulation; there was a new outlook upon life and the world that continued to stir and bring forth fruit in one's own thought. His mind was germinative and seminal. One would have to go far to find a teacher of our own day who started in others so many fruitful lines of thought; I dislike to think what my own thinking might have been were it not for the seminal ideas which I derived from him. For his ideas were always genuinely original; they started one thinking in directions where it had never occurred to one that it was worth while even to look.

There was a certain diffidence which restrained George Mead from much publication. But even more than that there was the constant activity of his mind as it moved out into new fields; there were always new phases of his own ideas germinating within him. More than any one I have known he maintained a continuity of ideas with constant development. In my earliest days of contact with him, as he returned from his studies in Berlin forty years ago, his mind was full of the problem which has always occupied him, the problem of individual mind and consciousness in relation to the world and society. His psychological and philosophical thinking during the intervening years never got far from the central push of his mind. But his mind was so rich and so fruitful that he was always discovering new phases and relations. He combined in a remarkable way traits usually separated—a central idea and unceasing growth. In consequence he was always dissatisfied with what he had done; always outgrowing his former expressions, and in consequence so reluctant to fix his ideas in the printed word that for many years it was his students and his immediate colleagues who were aware of the tremendous reach and force of his philosophic mind. His abounding vigor manifested itself in transcending his past self and in immediate communication with those about him. His mind was a forum of discussion with itself and of sharing discussion with those with whom he had personal contact. I can not think of him without seeing him engaged in untired discussion with himself and others, turning over and over his ideas and uncovering their hitherto unsuspected aspects and relations. Unlike, however, most minds of intense vigor, he had no interest in imposing his mind on others—it was discussion and discovery that interested him, not the creation of his own mental image in others.

No reference to his abounding and outgoing energy would be anything like adequate that did not allude to the range and breadth of his intellectual interests. His grasp and learning were encyclopedic. When I first knew him he was reading and absorbing biological literature in its connection with mind and the self. If he had published more, his influence in giving a different turn to psychological theory would be universally recognized. I attribute to him the chief force in this country in turning psychology away from mere introspection and aligning it with biological and social facts and conceptions. Others drew freely upon his new insights and reaped the reward in reputation which he was too interested in subject-matter for its own sake to claim for himself. From biology he went on to sociology, history, the religious literature of the world, and physical science. General literature was always his companion. His learning without exaggeration may be termed encyclopedic. But perhaps only a few are aware of his intense love of poetry. It is only within the last few days that I became aware from members of his immediate family of not only his appreciation of poetry, but his capacious retentive memory. He knew large parts of Milton by heart, and has been known to repeat it for two hours without flagging. Wordsworth and Keats and Shakespeare, especially the sonnets, were equally familiar to him. Those who have accompanied him on his walks through mountains, where his physical energy and courage never flagged, have told me how naturally and spontaneously any turn of the landscape evoked from him a memory of English poetry that associated itself with what he saw and deeply felt in nature. An accurate and almost photographic memory is rarely associated with a mind that assimilates, digests, and reconstructs; in his combination as in so many others, Mr. Mead was so rare that his personality does not lend itself to analysis and classification.

George Mead's generosity of mind was the embodiment of his generosity of character. Everything in the ordinary and extraordinary duties of life claimed him and he gave himself completely. I am sure it never occurred to him that he was sacrificing himself; the entire ethics of self-sacrifice was alien to his thought. He gave himself so spontaneously and so naturally that only those close to him could be aware that he was spending his energy so freely. So, too, while he was extraordinarily tolerant and charitable in his judgments of persons and events, I am confident it never occurred to him that he was so. His tolerance was not a cultivated and self-conscious matter; it grew out of the abundant generosity of his nature. He had the liveliest interest in every social problem and issue of the day. If at times he tended to idealize, to find more meaning and better meaning in movements about him than less generous eyes could see, it was because of the same outgoing abundance of his nature. While his insight was keen and shrewd, one can not associate anything of the nature of cynicism with him. Henry Mead has told me that the phrase which he most associates with his father when any social problem was under discussion is, "It ought to be possible to do so and so," and having seen the vision of possibility his mind at once turned to considering how the possibility could be realized. His extraordinary faith in possibilities was the source of his idealism.

I shall not try to give any idea, even an inadequate one, of his philosophical conceptions; this is not the time nor place. But there are three phases of it which are so intimately associated with his own natural being, his instinctive response to the world about him, that I can not forego mentioning them. Every one who knew him philosophically at all is aware of his interest in the immediate aspect of human experience—an interest not new in literature, but new in the form which it took in his philosophy. I am sure I am not wrong in connecting this interest, so central in his whole philosophy, with his own immediate sensibility to all the scenes of nature and humanity. He wrote little, I believe, on esthetics, but in many ways the key to his thought seems to me to be his own intense and immediate appreciation of life and nature and literature—and if we do not call this appreciation esthetic, it is because it includes so much more than is contained in the conventional meaning that word has taken on.

All who have intellectual association with Mr. Mead, directly or indirectly, also know how central was his conception of the "complete act"—the source of whatever is sound in the behavioristic psychology and active philosophy of our day. In the integrated act there is found the union of doing, of thought, and of emotion which traditional psychologies and philosophies have sundered and set against one another. This renovating, this regenerating, idea also had its source in George Mead's own personality. There was no division in his philosophy between doing, reflection, and feeling, because there was none in himself.

Again every one who knows anything about Mr. Mead knows of his vital interest in social psychology, and in a social interpretation of life and the world. It is perhaps here that his influence is already most widely felt; I know that his ideas on this subject worked a revolution in my own thinking, though I was slow in grasping anything like its full implications. The individual mind, the conscious self, was to him the world of nature first taken up into social relations and then dissolved to form a new self which then went forth to recreate the world of nature and social institutions. He would never have felt this idea so deeply and so centrally if it had not been such a complete embodiment of the depth and fullness of his own personality in all its human and social relations to others. The integrity and the continuing development of George Mead's philosophy is the natural and unforced expression of his own native being.

One feels not only a sense of tragic personal loss in the death of George Mead, but a philosophical calamity in that he was not able to extend and fill out his recently delivered Carus lectures. But if the publication of his ideas is incomplete and cut short, one has no such sense in connection with George Mead's own life and personality. In all relationships, it stands forth as a complete

because integral thing. Would that he might have lived longer with his family, his friends, his students, his books, and his studies. But no added length of years could have added to the completeness of his personal being; it could not have added even to the fullness with which he continues to live in the lives of those who knew him.

NOTES

[1] This article is the greater part of what Professor Dewey said at the funeral of Professor Mead in Chicago, April 30, 1931.

C. J. Bittner (essay date 1931)

SOURCE: "G. H. Mead's Social Concept of the Self," in *Sociology and Social Research,* Vol. XVI, September-October, 1931, pp. 6-22.

[*In the following essay, Bittner explores the most notable features of Mead's theory of self.*]

The death of Dr. George Herbert Mead of the Department of Philosophy of the University of Chicago is a great loss to modern philosophy and contemporary social thought. In him the academic world has lost one of its most profound thinkers. Though his writings are not numerous, he has exercised, nevertheless, a profound and lasting influence upon American social thought. During the long years of his professorial career Dr. Mead has been instrumental in shaping and moulding the philosophical point of view of a large number of the present leaders of American social thought. If it is said of Machiavelli that he had marched into the hall of fame with only a small volume under his arm, it might equally well be said of Dr. Mead that he has attained wide recognition with only a few short essays in social psychology. It is quality, and not quantity, that counts. The unique character of Dr. Mead's mind enabled him to embody in a few short essays a larger amount of information than could be found in several volumes written by less gifted men and dealing with the same subject-matter. Each one of Dr. Mead's essays is a masterpiece in logic and exposition. The merit of his work is widely recognized. Of all modern social philosophers he is, perhaps, most quoted and least criticized. Few books in social psychology of real merit have appeared in which Dr. Mead is not quoted. This is particularly true of those books which are dealing with the problem of the 'self'. Narrow and trivial as this topic may appear to some, it constitutes, nevertheless, the most abstruse, the most subtle, and the most difficult problem in philosophy and social psychology.

The eternal problem of the self has been studied by the philosophers of all ages and no satisfactory solution has been found. To this problem Dr. Mead had devoted his life work, and he has, apparently, succeeded in formulating a theory of the nature and function of the self which has received wide acceptance.

Possessing a rare capacity for generalization, Professor Mead has developed what one might call a "functional" theory of the self, which represents the culmination of modern philosophical thought on this particular topic.

Recognizing the great influence which the writings of Professor Mead have had upon social theory in the United States, the present writer will attempt to make a brief examination of the most salient features of Professor Mead's theory of the self. The chief aim of this cursory survey is to show the nature of the main conceptual hypotheses upon which his theory of the self rests, and to indicate the points of contact that these concepts make with the philosophical thought in general.

THE CONCEPT OF THE PSYCHICAL

Professor Mead's theory of the self cannot be understood very well without getting first a clear and definite knowledge of his concept of the 'psychical', and of the fundamental philosophical principles, in terms of which the nature and function of the self is defined.

Professor Mead's concept of the mind is similar to that of William James, F. Woodbridge, and John Dewey. Consciousness is teleological or purposive; it serves as a tool in the adjustment of the individual to his environment. It is also selective; previous experience serves to determine the nature of the stimuli attended to. Professor Mead rejected the concept of the mind as a "spiritual stuff" and returned the contents of the mind to things experienced.

"The natures of the objects are in the objects, they are of the very essence of the objects. . . . Sensuous qualities exist also in the objects, but only in their relations to the sensitive organism whose environments they form."[1] The objective content of consciousness, such as memory images, are dependent upon the conditions of the organism, especially those of the central nervous system, "but they are not mental or spiritual stuff."

Professor Mead defines sensation in terms of *act* and not in terms of *content,* and thus aligns himself with functional psychology. Objects exist in nature as patterns of action. Environment arises for the organism through the selective power of attention that is determined by its impulses seeking expression. The stream of ongoing activities of the organism defines its world for the organism. The physical object is a mental construct, and a percept is a "collapsed act."[2] Concepts, according to Professor Mead, have the character of actions which are directed toward the attainment of an end. The same point of view is voiced by Professor J. Royce, according to whom "Ideas are like tools, they are there for an end."[3] Professor Stout also thinks that "Ideas are plans of action."[4] Professor Mead appears to be accepting the pragmatic point of view that ideas are not true in themselves, but represent labor-saving devices or abbreviating schemes for dealing with the vast and chaotic manifold of sensations.

From the pragmatic point of view also things are real only in so far as they constitute the objects of our desires. Objects are defined in terms of conduct, hence the doctrine that social consciousness must antedate physical consciousness. Thus, according to Professor Mead, "Whatever our theory may be as to the history of things, social consciousness must antedate physical consciousness. A more correct statement would be that experience in its original form became reflective in the recognition of selves, and only gradually was there differentiated a reflective experience of things which are purely physical."[5] In this connection Professor Mead is in line with the teachings of Hegel and Royce.[6]

It is of interest here to note that Professor Cooley advocated a point of view which is diametrically opposed to that of Profesor Mead. According to Professor Cooley, our rational and conceptual knowledge develops in dealing with the material world, while for the purpose of understanding social facts and the "internal contacts" we are in possession of "a vast and obscure outfit of human susceptibilities, known as instincts, sentiments, emotions, drives, and the like" which furnish personal and social knowledge.[7] This, of course, is in line with Bergson's argument to the effect that intellect "feels itself at home among inanimate objects, more especially among solids, where our action finds its fulcrum and our industry its tools."[8]

For Professor Mead the 'psychical' is not the content of consciousness, but the cognitive act of the mind.[9] Sensations are not psychical. They are parts of the data which define the conditions under which the immediate problem is to be solved. The 'psychical' is the synthetic activity of the mind. In his theory of reality Professor Mead seems to stand on the middle ground between Idealism and Materialism. His philosophy is that of 'immediate experience'; reality is composed of a 'neutral stuff', which is neither physical nor psychical. In conflicting situations "mutually contradicting attitudes toward an object cause the disintegration of the object; the subject and object, the ego and alter, disappear from the field of consciousness which becomes protoplasmic." In this protoplasmic state of consciousness *content* and *process* cannot be distinguished.

Disintegration is followed by reconstruction. Judgment is the process of reconstruction. Disintegration and reconstruction of the object necessitate a definition of the problem. The solution of the problem takes place within the field of subjectivity, which is a 'neutral stuff', neither '*me*' nor other, neither mind nor body. The world provides the data and the self provides the hypothesis for the solution of the problem. But it is not the individual as '*me*' that can perform this solution. Such an empirical self belongs to the world which it is the function of this phase of consciousness to reconstruct.[10] It is the Ego or the '*I*' that effects the reconstruction. The result of the reconstruction will be a new individual (a new empirical self), as well as a new social environment. In the process of reconstruction "the consciousness of the new object, its values and meaning, seem to come earlier to consciousness than the new self that answers to the new object.[11] The self is not a content but an activity, and is defined in terms of the laws of analysis and construction.

Briefly stated, Professor Mead's theory of the 'psychical' rests upon the following propositions: The self is central to all so-called mental experiences; the *'I'* or the Ego is identical with the analytic and synthetic processes of cognition, which in conflicting situations reconstruct out of the 'protoplasmic' states of consciousness both the empirical self (the *'me'*) and the world of objects; the objective world is a mental construct and is defined in terms of the needs of the *'I'* or the Ego.

Professor Mead retains the concept of the Ego or *'I'* in his psychological system. He deplores the fact that William James has so harshly dealt with it. "There is nothing," says Mead, "that has suffered more through loss of dignity of content in modern positivistic psychology than the *'I'*. The *'me'* has been most honorably dealt with. It has waxed in diameter and interest, not to speak of number, with continued analysis, while the *'I'* has been forced from its metaphysical throne, and robbed of all its ontological garments; and the rags of 'feeling of effort about the head and chest', of the 'focalization of sense-organs', the 'furrowings of the eyebrows' seems but a sorry return for the antique dogmas."[12]

Professor Mead accepts the distinction between the *'I'* and the *'me'* found in the philosophy of Kant and in post-Kantian Idealism. He agrees with Kant that "the self cannot appear in consciousness as an *'I'*, and that it is always an object, i.e., a *'me'*, and that the *'me'* is inconceivable without an *'I'*." He also maintains the Kantian point of view "that such an *'I'* is a presupposition, but never a presentation of conscious experience."[13] The *'I'* is thus the result of cognitive inference. "The *'I'* therefore can never exist as an object in consciousness, but the very conversational character of our inner experience, the very process of replying to one's own talk, implies an *'I'* behind the scenes who answers to the gestures, the symbols, that arise in consciousness. The *'I'* is the transcendental self of Kant, the soul that James conceived behind the scene holding on to the skirts of an idea to give it an added increment of emphasis."[14]

For Professor Mead the Ego is an *act*. "It is an act that makes use of all the data that reflection can present, but used them merely as the conditions of the new world that cannot possibly be foretold from them."[15] The *'I'* appears to be unconditioned and free; it is an *activity* and not a *content*. "It is the self of unconditioned choice, of undreamt hypotheses, of inventions that change the whole face of nature."[16] The *'I'* is the active agent in the solution of problems and in the reconstruction of experience. As the *'I'* is always "out of sight of himself" the empirical self or the *'me'* becomes the object of scientific investigation.[17]

THE CATEGORIES OF 'FORM' AND 'CONTENT' IN THE GENESIS OF THE SELF

The concepts of 'form' and 'content' are important categories in Professor Mead's theory of the genesis of the self. The concept of the *'form of social object'* is basic in his explanation of the nature of self-consciousness. The role of the 'form of the social object' in Professor Mead's theory of the genesis of self-consciousness can best be understood if we examine it in the light of idealistic philosophy. Idealism assumes substance as being the synthesis of the categories of 'form' and 'matter', the latter being *ab initio* formless and chaotic. According to Kant the 'manifold of the senses' is formless, chaotic, to which the mind applies its categories of form, space, time, etc., in synthesizing objective reality. For Hegel the 'form' is the active principle. His 'concrete universals' are logical forms from which all reality is deduced in the same manner as a conclusion is deduced from its premises. His highest category, the Notion, is a free and infinite form.

Professor Mead regards sense-experience as protoplasmic, amorphous and unorganized. It will not become a self unless it assumes the 'form of a social object' which is derived in the experience of other selves. In the process of the development of self-consciousness, "the mere presence of experience of pleasure and pain, together with organic sensations, will not form an object unless this material can fall into the scheme of an object."[18] The scheme or form into which the amorphous experience is poured, is furnished by other social beings. Even in the case of objective consciousness of one's own body, "The form of the object is given in the experience of things, which are not his physical self.". . . "The appearance of his (the child's) body as a unitary thing, as an object, will be relatively late and must follow up the structure of the objects of his environment. This is as true of the object that appears in social conduct, the self.". . . "The form of the social object must be found first of all in the experience of other selves."[19]

Professor Mead's theory of self-consciousness consists thus of the assumption that the empirical self, or *'me'*, is the synthesis of the amorphous subjective experience with the objective 'form' furnished by the social object, or another self. His theory of self-consciousness is stated as follows: "It (the form) is rather an importation from the field of social objects into an amorphous unorganized field of what we call inner experience. Through the organization of this object, the self, this material is itself organized and brought under control of the individual in the form of so-called self-consciousness."[20]

TRANSFERENCE OF THE FORM OF THE SOCIAL OBJECT TO INNER EXPERIENCE

According to Professor Mead the transference of the 'form of the social object' from the environment to one's inner experience takes place in the use of vocal gestures. By means of vocal gestures the individual stimulates himself in the same manner as he stimulates others. Self-stimulation and response create the form of the social object to which the amorphous subjective experience is referred. This gives rise to the self as an object. "What is there in human social conduct," asks Mead, "that gives rise to 'me', as a self which is an object? Why does the human animal transfer the form of a social object from his environment to an inner experience?"

To these questions he replies in the following manner: "The fact that the human animal can stimulate himself as he stimulates others and can respond to his stimulations as he responds to the stimulations of others, places in his conduct the form of social object out of which may arise a 'me' to which can be referred so-called subjective experiences."[21] In stimulating himself as others would do, the individual becomes an object to himself. "This takes place when the individual assumes the attitude or uses the gesture which other individuals would use, and responds to it himself, or tends to respond.". . . "It arises in the life of the infant through what is unfortunately called imitation, and finds expression in the normal play life of young children."[22] The consciousness of the self arises when the individual in imitation takes the attitude of another toward himself. In acting out his role of another, the individual discovers that the activities belong to his own nature. "We must be others before we are ourselves."[23]

Now, it stands to reason that the meaning of the term 'self' cannot be learned by imitation of other individuals, because each individual attaches to it a different meaning; the contents of each individual self are uniquely organized in conformity with his own perspective upon the world. According to Professor Mead himself, "the ongoing activity of the individual form marks and defines its world for the form, which thus exists for it as it does not for any other form."[24] The importation of the 'form of the social object' into one's inner consciousness involves comparison, and comparison is a relation which cannot take place unless both terms, the self and the other, are present in consciousness. We cannot consciously be others unless we know what we are ourselves. And to be a 'generalized other' means to be an abstraction, a nonentity. Imitation as such cannot generate self-consciousness; it may only intensify it if it exists at the outset. Psychologists usually distinguish two kinds of imitation, conscious or voluntary, and unconscious imitation. Now if the child imitates voluntarily by performing acts set before him by social examples, then the act of imitation represents an activity which presupposes self-consciousness at the outset as a motive to bring his own self into conformity with social patterns of behavior. But if the imitative act is unconscious or 'subcortical', then no consciousness of the self will ever arise in the imitative process. No parrot has ever become self-conscious, but many "self-conscious" individuals have become parrots.

THE CONCEPT OF THE 'GENERALIZED OTHER'

In his theory of the genesis of self-consciousness Professor Mead has developed another concept, namely, the 'generalized other', which is closely related to the 'form of the social object'. According to Mead we sympathetically assume the roles of others and find in our own experiences the responses of others. The 'generalized other' develops in the process of communication. "Communication," says Mead, "is the mechanism by means of which the individual enters the perspective of the community."[25] In games or in other organized group activities the individual is able then to become a 'generalized other' in addressing himself in the attitude of the group, or the community. In this situation he has become a definite self over against the social whole to which he belongs.[26] In the process of communication, the self, which is revealed, is not the 'I', but the empirical self, or the 'me'. The 'I' is an activity, and as such it cannot appear at the same time as subject and object. "We can be conscious of our acts only through the sensory process set up after the act has begun."

The notion of the 'generalized other' rests upon the assumption that originally the self is only objectively conscious, and that the child is consciously affected by others before he is conscious of being affected by himself, and that we naturally interpret ourselves in terms of others. In the opinion of the present writer there is no such stage of pure objective consciousness; the interpretation of the self in terms of others implies reasoning by analogy; it involves the consciousness of both terms of the subject-object relationship. It is rather doubtful whether a young child can ever arrive at the notion of the 'generalized other', which is a conceptual abstraction derived from mature experience.

THE SOCIAL SELF

For Professor Mead the content of consciousness is of social origin. "Inner consciousness is socially organized by the importation of the social organization of the outer world." The consciousness of others precedes self-consciousness. The 'I' can never appear immediately in consciousness and can never be conscious of itself. The self appearing as 'I' is the memory image of the self who acted toward himself and is the same self who acts toward other selves. The stuff that goes to make up the 'me' is the experience which is induced by this action of the 'I'. "The 'me' consciousness is of the same character as that which arises from the action of the other upon him. That is, it is only as the individual finds himself acting with reference to himself as he acts towards others, that he becomes a subject to himself rather than object, and only as he is affected by his own social conduct in the same manner in which he is affected by that of others, that he becomes an object to his own social conduct."[27]

In his analysis of the social self, Professor Mead calls our attention to the fact that there is a "constant factor" of awareness of what we do, say, or think, in the field of our consciousness. It is a sort of inner response to our activities. This 'inner observer' is not to be confused with the 'I', or the implied object of our actions. "The observer," says Mead, "who accompanies all our self-conscious conduct is then not the actual 'I' who is responsible for the conduct in *propria persona*—he is rather the response which one makes to his own conduct."[28] This response of the individual to his own stimulations is due to the fact that one "cannot hear himself speak without assuming in a measure the attitude which he would have assumed if he had been addressed in the same words by another."[29] There is, then, another empirical self, another *'me'* which Professor Mead calls the *'reflective self'*.

THOUGHT AND THE MEANING OF VOCAL GESTURES

According to Professor Mead, thought is an inner conversation in which the self becomes an object to himself; he hears himself talk and replies. Mead thinks that "the mechanism of introspection is therefore given in the social attitude which man necessarily assumes toward himself, and the mechanism of thought, in so far as thought uses symbols which are used in social intercourse, is but an inner conversation."[30] Thought, then, is an inner conversation, and develops in connection with the development of the self in experience. It is a sublimated conversation between the self and the imagined specific other or the 'generalized other'.

Reflective consciousness presupposes a social situation, and language is the outgrowth of vocal gestures. Gestures are instrumental in the development of the consciousness of meaning. The meaning of a gesture arises when one imagines the social consequences of a gesture. "One's own gestures could not take on meaning directly. The gestures aroused by them in others would be that upon which attention is centered. And these gestures become identified with the content of one's own emotional attitude."[31]

There is much truth in this statement. But the present writer thinks that the meaning of gestures is not wholly determined from without, particularly in regard to one's emotional gestures. It was previously assumed by Professor Mead that human consciousness is teleological, or purposive, serving as a tool in the adjustment process. It was also assumed that consciousness is selective, determining the direction of attention, and the nature of the stimuli attended to. If this is true, the meaning of one's gestures is not wholly determined from without. An action cannot be conscious and purposive without having at the same time a meaning. My gesture consciously directed toward others has a meaning for me as calculated to arouse certain anticipated reactions and attitudes in others. The meaning of my own act or gesture is not always the same as the responding gesture or attitude of my neighbor. My gesture does not always arouse an identical gesture and emotion in the other fellow. The meaning of my vocal gesture is not, for instance, determined by the gestures provoked in an insane person, or in a child, or animal.

Language gestures are symbols of things, attributes, relations, and meanings. Though they are social products, their meaning is determined in one's subjective experience. A vocal gesture has the same relation to an idea, or mental image, as a label on a package has to the contents of the package. Thought is not sublimated conversation, but that which makes the sublimated conversation possible. There is no natural and unalterable connection between a concept and its verbal symbol. Symbols do not determine the meaning of mental images, but mental images determine the meaning of symbols conditioned to the meaning. One can hardly agree with Professor Mead that all meanings are socially determined, and that social consciousness antedates physical consciousness. However, there are passages in Professor Mead's writings which indicate that meaning can be explained as a consciousness of an attitude of an individual toward an object to which he is responding. The latter point of view has been widely accepted.

SUMMARY AND CONCLUSIONS

Professor Mead assumes that social relations are internal: they modify the attitudes of the interacting individuals. The consciousness of meaning presupposes the existence of self-consciousness. The subjective aspect of the self is identified with psychic activity. In his later writings Professor Mead developed the relational theory of the mind resembling that of Woodbridge and Montague.[32]

His theory of the self represents a logical deduction from certain fundamental propositions. Some of these propositions, such as the analytic and constructive activity of the self; the doctrine of the social form; the amorphous nature of sense-experience; the centered position of the self, indicate plainly the idealistic antecedents of his theory of the self.

The concept of the 'generalized other' is a word-hypothesis, rather than an empirical fact obtained by observation. The point of view that we must be others if we are to be ourselves, and that other selves in social environment logically antedate the consciousness of self, has not been consistently maintained throughout all his essays, and the hypothesis has been advanced that "the self arises in consciousness *pari passu* with the recognition and definition of other selves."[33] The latter view is more plausible than the former. Social situations no doubt promote the development of self-consciousness, but to maintain the idea that we are 'generalized others' before we are ourselves, is a sheer metaphysical speculation. No less fantastic is the assumption that "we cannot use our responses to others as the materials for construction of the self,—this imagery goes to make up the other selves."[34]

In one connection Professor Mead speaks of the *'me'* as the real self, which is an importation into the inner consciousness of the social organization of the outer world. In another connection the *'me'* is only a presentation to the *'I'*, an objective datum, like any other presentation, which disintegrates in conflicting situations, and has to be reconstructed by the real self, the *'I'* which is defined "in terms of the laws of analysis and construction."[35]

For Professor Mead, then, the real attitude of subjectivity (self-consciousness) resides in the *'I'*, and the conflicting impulses of the *'I'* constitute the subject-matter of functional psychology.[36] The '*I*' is an activity, a process; the '*me*' is the content. But, according to Mead, "what the content of the function is going to be is dependent upon the character of the process."[37] Thus, Professor Mead's point of view appears to be that the '*me*', or the empirical self, is constructed in conformity with the impulses and needs of the '*I*'. To contend then, as Professor Mead does, that the empirical self is exclusively a social product, is to use the term in a narrow sense following the tradition of idealistic philosophy. Social facts are not the only conditioning factors in the genesis of self-consciousness; one's contact with the physical world must have a share in arousing self-consciousness. An individual need not assume the role of a 'generalized other' in order to realize that he is self-conscious.

Professor Mead has given us what one might call a logical explanation of the nature of the self. The idealistic assumption, namely, that self-consciousness arises only in the presence of other selves, is the main theme of his essays. He has not availed himself of the data furnished by genetic and abnormal psychology bearing upon the problem of the self. However, the most promising sources of data as to the nature and function of the self lie undoubtedly in these fields.

NOTES

[1] G. H. Mead, "A Behavioristic Account of the Significant Symbol," *Journal of Philosophy*, XIX:157 ff.

[2] G. H. Mead, "The Mechanism of Social Consciousness," *Journal of Philosophy*, IX (1912), 401.

[3] J. Royce, *The World and the Individual*, I:308.

[4] Stout, *Analytic Psychology*, II:114, 124.

[5] G. H. Mead, "What Social Objects Must Psychology Presuppose?" *Journal of Philosophy*, VII:180 f.

[6] J. Royce, "External World and the Social Consciousness," *Philos. Review*, III:513-45; *see also* J. Royce, "Self-consciousness, Social Consciousness and Nature," *Philos. Review*, IV:473.

[7] C. H. Cooley, "The Roots of Social Knowledge," *American Journal of Sociology*, XXXII:66 ff.

[8] *L'Evolution creatrice*, English translation, p. ix.

[9] G. H. Mead, "What Social Objects Must Psychology Presuppose?" *Journal of Philosophy*, VII:180 ff.

[10] G. H. Mead, *The Definition of the Psychical*, p. 34.

[11] G. H. Mead, "The Social Self," *Journal of Philosophy*, X:378.

[12] G. H. Mead, *The Definition of the Psychical* (University of Chicago Press, 1903), p. 30.

[13] G. H. Mead, "The Social Self," *Journal of Philosophy*, X:374.

[14] G. H. Mead, "The Mechanism of Social Consciousness," *Journal of Philosophy*, IX (1912), 406.

[15] G. H. Mead, *The Definition of the Psychical*, p. 35.

[16] *Ibid.*, pp. 35 f.

[17] G. H. Mead, "The Mechanism of the Social Consciousness," *Journal of Philosophy*, IX (1912), 406.

[18] G. H. Mead, "The Mechanism of Social Consciousness," *Journal of Philosophy*, IX (1912), 404

[19] *Ibid.*, p. 404.

[20] *Ibid.*, p. 405.

[21] *Ibid.*, p. 405.

[22] G. H. Mead, "A Behavioristic Account of the Significant Symbol," *Journal of Philosophy*, XIX (1922), 160.

[23] G. H. Mead, "Genesis of Self and Social Control," *International Journal of Ethics*, XXXV: 276. The same doctrine is expressed by J. W. Scott as follows: "For as conscious I *am* others; I am many men in one," *Proceedings Aristotle Society*, XX (1919-1920), 130.

[24] *Ibid.*, pp. 256-57; 259-60.

[25] G. H. Mead, "The Objective Reality of Perspectives," in the *Proceedings of the Sixth International Congress of Philosophy*, 1926, p. 80.

[26] *Ibid.*, p. 80.

[27] G. H. Mead, "The Social Self," *Journal of Philosophy*, X (1913), 374-75.

[28] *Ibid.*, p. 376.

[29] *Ibid.*, pp. 376-77.

[30] *Ibid.*, pp. 377-78.

[31] G. H. Mead, "Social Psychology, as Counterpart of Physiological Psychology," *Psychology Bulletin*, VI (1909), 406-407.

[32] G. H. Mead, "A Behavioristic Account of the Significant Symbol," *Journal of Philosophy*, XIX:157-63.

[33] G. H. Mead, "Psychology of Social Consciousness Implied in Instruction," *Science*, XXXI:691-92. *See also* his article, "The Objective Reality of Perspectives," *Proceedings of the Sixth International Congress of Philosophy*, 1926, p. 81.

[34] G. H. Mead, "The Mechanism of Social Consciousness," *Journal of Philosophy*, IX (1912), 406.

[35] G. H. Mead, *The Definition of the Psychical*, p. 34.

[36] *Ibid.*, p. 35.

[37] *Ibid.*, p. 36.

T. V. Smith (essay date 1932)

SOURCE: "George Herbert Mead and the Philosophy of Philanthropy," in *The Social Service Review,* Vol. VI, No. 1, March, 1932, pp. 37-54.

[*In the following essay, Smith elucidates Mead's theory of philanthropy in light of his ideas on the individual, community, and socialization.*]

Next to the highly satisfying romanticism of an idealism that identifies what is with what ought to be, would come the pragmatic claim that what is *implies* what ought to be. Success or failure in vindicating such a claim would reverberate far in the social sciences. Almost a quarter of a century ago George Herbert Mead was already so sensitive to the crucial significance, for the social sciences, of this relation between the ideal and the real that he declared that "the evolutionary social science which shall describe and explain the origins of human society, and the social sciences which shall finally determine what are the laws of social growth and organization, will be as essential for determining the objective conditions of social consciousness as the biological sciences are to determine the conditions of consciousness in the biological world."[1] Indeed, the attempt to relate science and ideals is crucial for social service, as that term is currently used. For such relief work is not only "social" but is also "service." Now the service motif in philanthropy is so idealistic that it has drawn, perhaps still draws, its major sustenance from supernatural religion.[2] The generous outgiving, which in the nineteenth century loaded the white man's shoulders with the burdens of all those not white, and dotted—some are beginning to say spotted—the whole world with European and American missionaries, transpired in the name of God and for the sake of human salvation. Social movements, like physical motion, acquire a momentum that outruns the original impetus; but neither they nor it will continue indefinitely when the source of energy dries up. The deep inner wonder, not to say skepticism, and the widespread outer questioning, not to say distrust, of the Christian missionary movement already jointly betoken a failing source;[1] and whatever the specific results of such a dramatic precipitate of this spirit as the body of American experts now engaged in a far-flung assessment of the missionary movement, no one doubts what it reflects; and few doubt that it will deepen the crisis of Christianity conceived as a service organization.

In a word, the "service" that was of old Christian has already become as among equals, and is becoming as between civilized and simpler peoples, "social," i.e., secular. The settlement movement, the community-chest movement, the dole system abroad, and at home the municipal, state, and national relief organizations (functioning through Red Cross or voluntary committees), not to mention the purely medical and educational aspects of the foreign missionary enterprise—all undertake in the name of the natural community what would so short a time ago have been done, if done at all, in the name of the divine. Now if the term "social" reveals a new unfailing spring whose life-giving energy may be tapped onto the mains that have heretofore carried energy from religious sources, it is well to know it, and reassuring to be able to depend upon it. If this be not so, to know it in time may happily stimulate our search elsewhere and perchance forearm us for a sterner way of life. But before dealing with this problem on its merits, it will be well to remark and evaluate Professor Mead's attempt to furnish a scientific sanction for the ends once cherished as Christian. It is hardly necessary to say that, his mind and influence being what they were, whatever light this article sheds will be light borrowed in no small degree from Mead himself. Heavy reliance will hereafter be put upon his splendid article entitled **"Philanthropy from the Point of View of Ethics."**[4]

I

What I have suggested elsewhere[5] regarding the adequacy of Mead's social philosophy, is that the ameliorative thrust does not borrow efficacy from his scientific analysis of human nature. His analysis indicates that individuality is derived from the social process through a describable technique. Ignoring here the technique, we remark only that the process in question breaks up under analysis into processes, and that these processes are in conflict. Not only are they objectively in conflict, but Mead makes it unmistakably clear that the conflict runs deeper than the empirical field. The emotions that water the processes are themselves naturally divisive. Social conflicts being thus doubly based, a self created by and from them, unless it has undisclosed access to alien energy, cannot but perpetuate the conflicts that produce it. In a word, then, as we have elsewhere concluded,[6] an empirically social derivation of personality is not enough to guarantee a humane social order when such personalities are thrown together in society. Nor can the corrective fact that they have grown rather than been thrown together itself obviate the easy observation that the growth has ugly seams. We have seemed to detect in Mead some remnant of the general philosophic predilection to count "isness" for "oughtness" in operative efficacy.

Social service as a conspicuous branch of social philosophy furnishes a sobering approach for any philosopher. It at least keeps his eye fastened upon the difficulty, and thus tends to anchor his attention. For social service starts with the admission that things are not as they should be—starts, indeed, from the feeling of obligation to do something about the unideal conditions. Moreover, such anchored interest necessitates a study of ways and means for overcoming the inertia of others that thwarts, unless remedied, one's own ameliorative concern. Mead's lifelong interest in the settlement movement[7] and in every form of community relief indicates a mind extraordinarily sensitive to suffering; and his profound speculative bent guarantees that whatever deeper or fresher insight the philosophic mind can bring to bear upon practical concerns will be suggested, if not developed, in his analysis of philanthropy.

He seems to have started his intellectual career, as I have elsewhere indicated,[8] with a declaration of independence on behalf of himself and of his world. Deep in his philosophy lies the confidence that reality at large and in its separate sections is autonomous; it is a process that can and does run itself. But the social process, like a river bedded in unevenness, develops by its own momentum, eddies, shallows, falls. Indeed, the very emotions upon which sociality naturally depends thwart the farther reaches of social aspiration. Charity is itself as natural a gesture as is eating. Traceable as it is back to animals lower than man, "the kindliness that expresses itself in charity is as fundamental an element in human nature as are any in our original endowment. The man without a generous impulse is abnormal and abhorrent."[9] Not only is it indigenous but it is also private: "it implies both an attitude and a type of conduct which may not be demanded of him who exercises it. Whatever the donor's inner obligation may be, the recipient on his side can make no claim upon it."[10] Here we have briefly indicated both the assets and the debits of instinctive kindness, the earliest and deepest basis of social service. Its very naturalness and privateness constitute a kind of sanctionless sanction that alone guarantees perpetuity. Onto this ancient trunk must be grafted every form of social service if the ideal itself is to be implemented. But the privacy of the sanction constitutes on its inner side—for, note that "it cannot be demanded"—as serious a limitation upon natural charity as does upon the outer side the unexpected baneful eventuation of much impulsive giving. The discovery that impulsive kindness calls for further charity until dependence becomes chronic and almsgiving a source of spiritual pride—this has itself been adequate to impugn native benevolence.

Through the work of reason, however, charity organizes itself in order to become itself more reasonable. The self-frustrating nature of impulsive generosity becomes in this way self-fulfilling, if it can become self-sustaining. The latter condition constitutes the rub; for as impulsive kindness suffers from initial blindness so charity as such suffers from chronic impotence. Since by nature the claim of charity cannot be demanded of the one who feels it, it ceases to be available for relief whenever the call outreaches the feeling. Now, modern humanitarianism has pretty clearly outgrown its glands. The need for social service is so great that there is not enough feeling to fulfil it. It is easy for the isolated farm wife to gratify her charitable impulse by feeding every tramp that comes to her back door, if tramps come infrequently enough. It may be possible to organize this impulse in most urban

communities in normal times so as both to preserve it and to render it adequate. But in abnormal times—that is, practically all times in a thoroughly industrialized community—the need for relief outruns the willingness, and sometimes the ability, to pay. For, "the donor," as Mead observes, "cannot fail in his other commitments because he has answered the appeals of charity with too great a generosity."[11] When this felt obligation which "cannot be demanded" of one meets felt obligations that can be legally exacted and can also be socially debited against one's business reputation, a private feeling has met a public force; and power has its usual way with impotence.

When charity, in its pilgrim's progress, comes to this crossroads, it has certain alternatives: (1) it may seek to maintain the feeling of obligation while withholding the concrete support; (2) it may reduce the feeling to make it commensurate with relief contribution; (3) it may undertake to raise practice up to the level of the feeling of obligation to relieve. Down the first road, one meets sentimentalism and later hypocrisy; down the next road a lowered self-respect awaits one at first, then, with the growth of habit, social insensitivity, and eventually barbarism; up the next road—for it will be uphill all the way—there awaits one—who knows whether communism or capitalism, whether utopia or disaster, awaits one?

II

Though we do not know for certain what awaits us if we undertake fully to implement the conscience that animates social service today, it is our business to inquire. The philosophical basis of social service awaits this inquiry. But before we inquire let us see more clearly why we cannot really elect to take either of the easier roads confronting us. Sentimentalism is an easy, tawdry virtue. There is enough of spontaneous fellow-feeling in every human being to make of him an ideological humanitarian. There is enough of this quality at large in humanity to build utopian literatures and get them read; there has been enough to construct the heavens of religion and build on earth sacred institutions to lower for men the thresholds of these transcendental asylums. X-ray the imagination of any passer-by and you will find enough of kindness in his reveries to build Jerusalem in this green and sunny land—if it could be built of air, on air. The inquiring reporter of the enterprising press elicits from all subjects, in answer to the question, "What would you do with a million dollars?" variegated but splendid schemes of social improvement. But with our actual incomes we cannot do the grand thing; and it would be a kind of treason to our dreams to do the paltry little thing that can be done. So we sentimentalize the vision into a sacred ideal and proceed to let the needy need. For a time one may be sincere and still harbor this discrepancy; but there are few men who do not eventually suspect themselves of hypocrisy in holding their conduct to a course far below the mounting curve of their ideals; and hypocrisy robs even sentimentalism of its thrill. What begins as sentimentalism and develops as hypocrisy eventuates as the kind of hardness that enjoys what it has in plain sight of the suffering of those who may then easily be thought unworthy merely because they are unfortunate. This all too common rationalization marks the logical degradation of ethical perfectionism.[12] It is this easy understanding of the natural evolution of sentimentalism that makes it really impossible for the sensitive man self-consciously to elect to take this proffered way at the present crossroads.

And if it is psychologically impossible to take this path, it certainly is not probable that we can take the other indicated course, i.e., divest ourselves of the kindly feelings that transcend our actual practice. If we are not to acknowledge and treasure the fact that our reach exceeds our grasp, we shall progressively find ourselves to be grasping less and less.

> Such feasting ended, then
> As sure an end to men.

If we hold unimplemented idealism a vice, and pride ourselves upon a realism that is content with the might-makes-right principle, we shall not only sink again into barbarism, ethically speaking, but shall find that power and privilege slip away from us as we shed our moral discontents. The ledgers of industrialism do not disclose all sources of industrial profit. There must be at last some accounting for

> All instincts immature
> All purposes unsure,
> That weighed not as his work, yet swelled
>   the man's amount.

While it is not impossible as a matter of heavy-footed fact, it is impossible as a matter of conscious intention for civilized men wholeheartedly to will themselves back to barbarism. And so we shall dismiss from our discussion as a critical alternative this second way of retrogression.

But if we cannot content ourselves with either cultural sentimentalism or ethical nihilism, neither can we stand gazing at the crossroads. We are on a moving stairs that whisks us on whether we will or no. If we cannot will to go down that way or down this, then let us step upon the ascending stairs and see what exhibits are on the floor above. Upon this platform we are again in the company of Mead, our present mentor.

It is indeed from our inability to will either the hypocritic or the complacent way that, negatively, Mead derives his philosophy of philanthropy. What is implied, he seems early to have asked himself, by the fact that we cannot keep from seeing life through other people's eyes? Certainly it implies that we are at least in part social. We cannot but to some extent sympathize with misfortune (any more than we can fail to some extent to lighten our countenances in the presence of another's good fortune). But this is an old observation of common sense and furnishes the basis for a philosophical tradition that was already hoary when Aristotle coined it into an aphorism. Put in Aristotle's form, however, it cannot outrun the fact. We are merely as social and as sympathetic as we

are observed to be. But it is clear that this observation is not enough to furnish a basis for improvement; it merely celebrates a fortunate discovery, but not fortunate enough to take as disclosing all the potentiality of the actual. Mead thought he saw in the discovery, however, some assurance that our partical sociality is promissory of further sociality without limit. His resolution of individual to social psychology was the scientific form this conviction took. If, in our very texture we are products of community forces, then do we not need only to become self-consciously what we unconsciously are in order to guarantee complete socialization? His uncompromising emphasis, therefore, upon the self-conscious life as alone worthy of man had as its motif not merely the enjoyment of our human estate but, even more the improvement thereby of our animal inheritance.

If, as according to his social psychology, we become selves only by assuming the rôles of others, the cultivation of our personality is dependent upon the possibility of our participating in the community's affairs, upon our promotion of communal welfare. Since, however—as is indicated by the unideal need that necessitates social service—we start with a community that must be greatly improved before it can be greatly enjoyed, the prospect of our own self-realization is limited by the possibility of social amelioration. Let us now inquire more in detail what, both negatively and positively, this implies for social service. Negatively, it implies that the enemies of those whose rôles we take are our enemies. Moreover, enmity will be aroused by whatever persons or conditions thwart or restrict the full out-working of human capacity. No other conception of evil is needed than this simple one of frustration. But what attitude on our part does the feeling of enmity imply? It clearly implies a gesture of destruction. "The immediate effect," Mead admits, "of sympathetic identification with the other is to call out the other's response in attempting to ward off or alleviate suffering, and this calls out at once resentment or criticism against the individuals or institutions which may seem to be responsible for it."[13] This negative implication of the other-assuming rôle Mead makes unmistakably clear by declaring that

> it is a mistake, however, to assume that putting one's self in the place of the other is confined to the kindly or charitable attitude. Even in a hostile attack one feels in his own muscles the response of the other, but this only arouses still further one's own attack and directs the response to the attack of the opponent; and in the consciousness of one's rights one places himself in the attitude of others who acknowledge that right in so far as he recognizes this right as inhering in them.[14]

One sees this destructiveness of sympathetic identification writ large in the current desire of communism to foment world-revolution; for, in the ideology at issue, it is only through the destruction of the enemies of the proletariat that the proletariat may come fruitfully into its own.

There is, however, in communism, as elsewhere, the positive implication of the function of sympathy. Sinners must perish that saints may flourish. It is upon this more positive implication of the rôle-assuming technique that Mead lays heaviest stress. "The identification of ourselves with Lazarus," as he says, "puts in motion those immediate defensive reactions which give rise not only to efforts of amelioration but also to judgments of value and plans for social reform."[15] This transition from the destructive gesture of sympathy aimed at enemies to the constructive counterpart on behalf of friends is not as clearly indicated as one might wish. But Mead not only assumes the presence of both, but goes so far as to say that the step from the destructive attitude "to the ideal of social conditions under which this evil would not exist is *inevitable*. Out of these ideas arise plans, possibly practical, for remedying at the source the misfortunes of those in distress." Indeed, it is the actual presence of this dual response, which arises from putting ourselves in another's place, that constitutes for Mead the philosophical basis of social service: "In any case it must be in our reactions against evils, and with its victims, with whom we sympathize, that the ethics of charity must lie." We have here laid in the very nature of man, even in the unpromising shadow of his antipathetic responses, a promise of sociality greater than exists at any given time and place; for, to feel for others is to thrust away from them the menacing evil and to withdraw them to a safer position.

III

With this psychological foundation laid, we are prepared to advance to sociological and political considerations. We should march inevitably to utopia, it appears, if there were not one insuperable obstacle in the way. I have commented elsewhere[16] upon the psychological obstacle that arises, according to Mead, from the fact that the very emotions upon which we depend for advance are themselves divisive. Though this is not the inhibition upon which I here focus attention, it may prove to be the secret source of our halting advance. The obstacle here seems to be that there is not adequate motivation to furnish the necessary sinews for indispensably needed relief. The natural emotions are dismissed by Mead in this connection not because they are in themselves divisive but because they turn out badly. "The bare impulse to help is on the same level with that of the dogs that licked the sores on Lazarus' body."[17] Not only so, but it may pass from canine tenderness to feline indirection: "The kindly impulses that lead us to help those in distress. . . . may breed beggars."[18]

> We may condemn such impulsive action [continues Mead], but the condemnation is based upon the fact that a sense of values, with the consequent possibility of reasoned choice, did not play its proper part in the action. . . . Oganized charity has arisen to bring reason into their exercise. Bringing reason into charity consists, on the one hand, in definitely tracing out the consequences of impulsive giving, and, on the other hand, of so marking out the distress and misery of the community that constructive remedial work may take the place of haphazard giving.[19]

But the obstacle now appears in full force: Where are we to get the means for organized charity to do the necessary work which social sentiments envisage in times of adversity? The answer to this question will thrust us as far beyond social service as social service is beyond Christian charity. It will project us bodily beyond both onto the plane of justice.

It is high time that we make definitely clear the boundary line between the charity-service motif and the justice motif. The one leaves off and the other begins precisely where what is privately acknowledged becomes publicly enforceable. When conscience is threatened with either sentimentalism or complacency, taxation comes to the rescue; and there arises a public impersonal conscience to displace the ineffective private one. Mead combines into a single statement a fine appreciation and a splendid illustration of this metamorphosis:

> When a man feels not simply an impulse to assist another in distress, but also an obligation, he always implies a social order in which this distress would make a claim upon the community that could be morally enforced, as, for example, in a community where employees in industry are insured, the distresses incident to old age, sickness, and unemployment must be relieved.[20]

Before canvassing the further practical significance of this derivation of justice, it is well to indicate again that Mead sees in the evolution of charity into social service and social service into some form of commonwealth a logical development for which he uses the notion of "implication." Though he uses the term "inevitable" to describe the implication, we are not, I think, to understand anything like a Marxian dialectics that plunges willy-nilly to some certain goal. Rather, Mead means that if a man is both humane and consistent he will, if he thinks at all, be forced to the *conclusion*, though not, alas, to the *action*, which the analysis indicates. If Mead errs here, it is in the direction of now and then forgetting this distinction and making logical implication play, in a pinch, the part of a social force.

To return, then, to the process of implication itself. It is certainly morally reassuring to believe, with Mead, that the same impulse which leads us to give at all will lead us to regulate our giving so as to make it effective, once we discover that generosity breeds impecuniousness. This implication, however, itself is conditioned by one crucial fact; and that is that we are more interested in the receiver than in the giver. It is to counteract the age-old suspicion that this is basically not so that Mead has elaborated his social psychology. Whatever weakness attaches to his social psychology will show itself here as invalidating the first stage of that implication whereby Mead proceeds from impulse to justice. It is commendable caution to put alongside the fact that this transition has here and there taken place, the memory that there were centuries when charity was more prized for self-salvation than for social relief and the recognition that social service is still in some communities hardly more than an artificial island scientifically fabricated, as it were, in an ocean of primitive impulsiveness. But the manner in which, and the extent to which, social service is implied by elemental tenderness, mark also the implication of justice by social service. For, when generous impulses enlist our aid in behalf of a sufferer, and scientific inspection reveals that he can be relieved in such manner as permanently to be helped, and this without eventual sacrifice to ourselves, then justice appears to us just as much the indicated step beyond service as cautious service was beyond reckless impulsiveness. But to say that each stage is implied by the other assumes a growth in both thoughtfulness and benevolence which the earlier stage does not appear wholly to explain. There is, as in emergent evolution theories, a surplus unexplained but gratefully acknowledged. This interstitial contingency resolved only by individual audacity at individual risk renders all progress (Mead's "implication") purely hypothetical. Moreover, the growth that causes one to acknowledge as inevitable a next step in thought frequently fails to activate an advance in conduct. It is this latter observation upon which I wish now to dwell.

Thought can admit as inevitable a next step which for action is impossible, because the conditions which render logically inevitable a next step may be so different from the conditions that actually confront conduct as to leave the one out of the question while making the other appear necessary. And yet these conditions may operate so subconsciously as to permit one consciously to argue that because the thought follows, the action must match it. Mead himself furnishes a clear illustration of both the fact and its violation when, in a brilliant article on internationalism, he proceeds from the true observation that we can no longer *think* our international relations in terms of war (since war is in very essence their invalidation) to the contrary-to-fact conclusion that "we can no longer depend upon war for the fusion of disparate and opposing elements in the nation."[21] Now is not so to conclude clearly to substitute an ideal for a fact? We can and do still depend upon just that—taking the chance, of course, that we may one day destroy ourselves as well as our enemies. We ought not, but we do. The very impotence of ideals breeds in the most sensitive natures an urgency peculiarly likely to claim as effected what, alas, is only yet desired. Ideals do not have the potency to heave themselves by fiat into full-bodied being. Nowhere does our imagination run more riot than with reference to benevolence. We start our mental activity, observation of children proves, not easily able to distinguish the ideal and the actual; we find the ideal more to our liking; and all our lives we are likely to slip the cog of actuality in pursuit of uncriticized eidola. That Mead draws hope for the march of events from his delineation of the course of logic seems clear. Nor is this wholly to be deprecated; but it is certainly to be watched to the extent of emphasizing the fact that implication is a term in logic rather than a fact in nature. There is a logic of events, and it may differ sadly from any known logic of thought. This caution, however, should not inhibit, rather it should encourage, the getting of our thoughts clear, even when

conduct does not follow the clarification. He who will not do the minimum when estopped from the maximum is not likely to achieve the maximum when the opportunity arises. The least we can do is to understand. The latter, Mead believed to be a great step, perhaps he believed it too great a step, in the direction of social amelioration.

Even if Mead's generous mind did sometimes over-play ideals, he has himself indicated clearly the limitation that actuality puts upon generosity. His illustration takes the form of showing how a benevolence which might be actual on one level—a level, too, which is implied by a lower level—is impossible upon that lower level itself. The principle of progression upon which he relies is, he says, "an implication that can become explicit only when the social structure and the ideas behind it make it possible."[22] In the present order of society, Mead goes on to observe, "those who have advantages cannot share them with the rest of the community. This could only be possible in a community more highly organized, otherwise bred and trained."[23] But turning to a radical thought of self-sacrifice which has found lodgment in every generous mind, Mead declares, "To sell all we have and give to the poor would not change this situation." Indeed, "so far as this community is concerned, we can morally enjoy what from one standpoint is an exploitation of those whose submerged life has given us economic and spiritual wealth which our peculiar situations have enabled us to inherit." While we enjoy our differential privileges, however, "we feel," he concludes, "the adventitious nature of our advantages, and still more do we feel that the intelligence which makes society possible carries within itself the demand for further development in order that the implications of life may be realized."[24]

IV

We have now before us the two sides of Mead's philosophy of philanthropy: on the one side, we are obligated to relieve suffering and underprivilege inside a social system which normally perpetuates gross injustices and in doing so makes impossible an effective discharge of the generosity which we feel; on the other side, we are obligated to work for a social order in which full justice would supplant service as service is supplanting charity. We may now finally summarize the distinctions involved in these contrasts. Charity remains purely voluntary, justifies itself in terms of satisfaction to the giver, and hopes for the best consequences in the receiver.[25] Social service resembles charity in that it cannot be exacted of us, but transcends charity by regulation of the generous impulse in terms of consequences, and finally justifies itself not in terms of personal feeling but of social good. Justice removes the last trace of charity by exacting what is required for the needs of others. The common nerve that nourishes all these forms of generosity is the elemental impulse to put ourselves in the place of others and react for their sake rather than for our own. Indeed, Mead's social psychology means by postulating a common matrix for all minds so completely at bottom to obliterate the very distinction between *meum* and *teum* that it will seem anomalous wherever it thereafter occurs.

Even if not wholly successful in this attempt, he does give new vigor to the attempt to render rational the sentiment of benevolence. What is more, he parades a principle of progression which challenges continuous growth on the part of our generous natures. The sap is always elemental impulse, but the trunk proliferates into professional and economic and political and religious branches. Impulse liberated and enlarged through understanding the consequences of impulse—this is the key principle. Charity stands face to face with need, and justifies itself in terms of the good feeling to the giver that accompanies the gift. But there are consequences of all gestures, whether recked or not. To discover these consequences, to prize them as indications for further diagnosis, and to be generous for the sake of the foreseen good effects upon others is to practice or support social service. Understanding transports us from the level of the generous dog before the sores of Lazarus to the level of the critical intelligence at work today in organized charity. But a further recognition of consequences will mark a more advanced stage in the evolution of altruism. Social service has, as a result of its success, the perpetuation of a social order to which the most generous mind can never give its thoroughgoing approval. How discrepant indeed our social order is from the highly desirable may be seen, not only in the fact that charity is necessary, but in the further fact that the necessary is impossible of performance upon a voluntary basis. The need for social service visibly outruns the effective general will to render it. When that which we feel we ought to, but do not voluntarily, give can be effectively demanded of us by another because of his needs, social service will have given way to more effective organization supporting ameliorative programs by taxation.

This seems to imply political organization and, indeed, to make the state the final goal of ethical aspiration. While Mead apparently never shared the American mania for the political principle of brittle individualism or the common phobia of his environment against socialism,[26] he was more interested in bases for reform and methods of procedure than in programs. If business privately undertook through its own organization—*à la* the Swope proposal at the moment in the public eye—to do in America what governments in Europe ordinarily do, Mead's principle would be illustrated, so far forth. The qualification is added because, though such regional agreements would supplant the ineffective voluntary with the enforceable, yet they would not remedy another weakness in our social structure. Legislation by any group that is not ubiquitous leaves somebody exposed to the consequences of the legislation itself; for, to right wrong is not infrequently to wrong somebody else. Now, the only group that is completely ubiquitous, even though it be not in the same sense omnicompetent, is the political. Indeed, the attempt to deal with the unforeseen evil consequences of impulsive charity which led to scientific social service and Mead's attempt to deal constructively with the farthest and therefore generally unforeseen consequences of social service, isolates for inspection the very principle upon which John Dewey, in *The Public and Its Problems*,

attempts to found the state. All actions have consequences. The consequences foreseen by interested parties will be good if the parties be intelligent. But not all persons are equally intelligent; and even if they were, they are not on the lookout for all consequences to the end of time but only for those that are relevant to the purpose embodied in specific conduct. The state, Dewey plausibly argues, arose and exists precisely to acknowledge and to administer these indirect consequences of conduct which otherwise, in being nobody's business, impair everybody's business. On such a theory—and enough has been said to show that Mead shares the general point of view[27]—political action would be the logical result and state regulation of common affairs the normal goal of our ameliorative interest. Mead's preoccupation is so much centered, however, upon the common affairs that he always sees the political process as itself highly socialized, which of course it not always is in practice. As external, it can get nowhere; as internalized, it is no longer merely political.

> We must recognize [as Mead astutely remarks] that the most concrete and most fully realized society is not that which is presented in institutions as such, but that which is found in the interplay of social habits and customs, in the readjustments of personal interests that have come into conflict and which take place outside of court, in the change of social attitude that is not dependent upon an act of legislature.[28]

V

The director of organized relief is so strategically placed in an industrial society that she must become a social engineer to guarantee her efforts larger eventuation than her job requires her to acknowledge. If she sinks herself in the job, content to perpetuate the society she relieves, she loses her soul to a society that is not worthy of the sacrifice. Unless she sees as among the consequences of her work a human order more just than any yet achieved, she denies a better through slavish devotion to a good. To serve with efficiency and high morale a present good without losing contact—yea because of contact—with a better-growing-toward-a-best—this is for her to become a priestess whose mind redeems her service from the taint of sacrifice. She serves, willy-nilly, larger ends than are set before her. The only possible guarantee—and it is not enough, for there is no adequate guarantee of the ideal save its actualization—that these larger ends will also be better ends is for her to become wise in the ways of science, scenting causal connections and clairvoyant of remote consequences of action. If she sets out from a democratic background, she may wisely remember that democracy early emphasized three goals—equality and fraternity, as well as liberty. If through an overweening devotion to liberty our industrial civilization has so overemphasized the voluntary element as to deprive millions of men of the efficacy even of the will to work, it is acting in the true spirit of democracy to correct that error by a new emphasis upon equality of opportunity. If she sets out from a religious background, she may truly remember the democratic fraternity motif was meant to implement, more fully than religion had been able to do, the ideal of human brotherhood. God works in secular ways man's blunders to transform. If she be liberal, she may well draw her secret morale from a vision of a socialistic commonwealth. If she be radical, she may foresee, as implied in the philosophy of her work, a classless society arising magically on earth through the turmoil of a dictatorship of the proletariat.

The point I wish here to emphasize is not the details of the case but the general fact that the wise social worker will see as the goal of her service some general social reconstruction. This, following Mead, we have seen to be implied, not only by the nisus toward enlargement on the part of the generous impulse, but by the impossibility of adequately meeting the minimum needs of men where and when the resources from which to meet them cannot be demanded of those who have them. A purely voluntaristic humanitarianism is a travesty when adversity becomes chronic, as it does when society is fully industrialized. It throws an undue burden upon the most sensitive; it rewards the relatively insensitive; and it permits far too many men, women, and children to live their lives below the level of their minimum needs. When men come to feel of privileges hitherto voluntarily granted to them that they are theirs by right, then peaceably or violently they will have their rights. And when what one feels himself obligated to give, another feels himself privileged to demand, social or political organization has strengthened free will, and the principle of justice—whether actual justice follows or not—supplants the principle of service. Dewey's account of the origin and function of the state converges with Mead's account of the upward implication of impulsive kindness to indicate organized justice effectively administered as the goal of moral striving. "It is this feel," says Mead, "for a social structure which is implicit in what is present that haunts the generous nature, and carries a sense of obligation which transcends any claim that his actual social order fastens upon him. It is an ideal world that lays the claim upon him, but it is an ideal world which grows out of this world and its undeniable implications."[29]

NOTES

[1] "Social Psychology as Counterpart to Physiological Psychology," *Psychological Bulletin*, VI (1909), 408.

[2] Apologetic theologians, like Professor R. A. Millikan, believe that "about 95 per cent of all altruistic and humanitarian work in the world has come and is coming directly or indirectly from the influence of organized religion" (*Homiletic Review*, December, 1929).

[3] The Federal Council of the Churches of Christ in America, immediately after quoting the foregoing extravagance from Professor Millikan, is able to trace, and that vaguely, less than 30 per cent of the money spent in relief in America last winter to religious sources (editorial bulletin on *Churches and Unemployment*).

[4] Faris *et al.*, *Intelligent Philanthropy*, pp. 133-48.

[5] *American Journal of Sociology*, XXXVII (1931), 368-85.

[6] *Ibid.* p. 381.

[7] "The Social Settlement: Its Basis and Function," *University* [of Chicago] *Record*, XII, 108.

[8] *American, Journal of Sociology*, XXXVII (1931), p. 371.

[9] Faris, *et al.*, *op. cit.*, p. 133.

[10] *Ibid.*

[11] *Ibid.*, p. 133.

[12] Mead has a fine illustration in an early article, "Suggestions toward a Theory of the Philosophical Disciplines," *Philosophical Review*, IX (1900), 4.

[13] *Op. cit.*, p. 140.

[14] *Ibid.*

[15] *Ibid.*, p. 140. Italics are mine.

[16] *American Journal of Sociology*, XXXVII (1931), 375.

[17] Faris *et al.*, *op. cit.*, p. 140.

[18] *Ibid.*, p. 134.

[19] *Ibid.*

[20] *Ibid.*, p. 138.

[21] *International Journal of Ethics*, XXXIX (1929), 400.

[22] Faris *et al.*, p. 142.

[23] *Ibid.*, p. 145.

[24] *Ibid.*, p. 145.

[25] Cf. one of Mead's examples: "The author of a mediaeval tréatise on charity considering the lepers as a field for good works contemplated the possibility of their disappearance with the ejaculation 'which may God forbid'" (*American Journal of Sociology*, XXIII [1918], 596).

[26] "Socialism, in one form or another," he early saw and declared, "lies back of the thought directing and inspiring reform" (*ibid.*, V [1899], 367).

[27] Mead was not, it may be remarked, very hopeful of our ability so "to forecast any future condition that depends upon the evolution of society as to be able to govern our conduct by such a forecast." He more modestly contents

himself in such cases with "a method and a control in application, not an ideal to work toward" (*ibid.*, p. 369).

[28] "Natural Rights and the Theory of the Political Institution," *Journal of Philosophy,* XII (1915) 152. This entire article should be required reading for every serious student of the social sciences.

[29] Faris *et al., op. cit.,* p. 145.

T. V. Smith (essay date 1932)

SOURCE: "The Religious Bearings of a Secular Mind: George Herbert Mead," in *The Journal of Religion,* Vol. XII, No. 2, April, 1932, pp. 200-13.

[*In the following essay, Smith relates Mead's religious background to his philosophical ideas.*]

George Herbert Mead built upon secular foundations a mind and personality and philosophy so wholesomely virile as constantly to seem to exemplify and celebrate in daily living the finest human emotions. To religious men who are at the same time statesmen of the modern spirit he has therefore more to offer than a substantial reminder of what as thinkers and teachers they are up against. He has a formula of life prepotent to engender such emotions as he celebrated in theory and practice. Moreover, he has a doctrine to accompany his formula, a doctrine of altruistic potentiality not unlikely more intelligible to this generation than any yet presented in the name of religion.[1] But before articulating his formula or indicating his doctrine, let me take up, conjecturally where I cannot do it more substantially, the slack between his religious childhood and his secular, unscarred maturity.

I

Even as before college days were over he had achieved independence from the dogmas of the church and had joyously set out to direct his own course in life,[2] so he was later to project cosmically his own early competence. German idealism had absolutized the autonomy which he ascribed to nature, and in doing so had made it impossible to find, as Mead has it, any "such intelligent process within ourselves as would enable us to take the helm into our hands and direct the course of our own conduct, either in thought or action."[3] He needed only to drop the absolutistic basis of the romanticism supporting idealism in order to find empirically what others sought transcendentally. This he early and, it appears, easily did, though not without being first endued by it with a "vision," as he says of Royce's influence upon him at Harvard, "that followed me for many years."[4]

That vision, indeed, appears to have borne fruit throughout his whole life of speculation, though it was sublimated into scientific modesty by kindly time and maturing insight. Mead appears never to have doubted that the universe is itself an active process, coming to conscious-

ness in man, and receiving increments of meaning as well as direction from man's resolution of his own perplexities. Science, indeed, appears as but man's systematic attempt to orient in nature the exceptions which nature's spontaneity breeds; and in the scientific process the human individual plays the directive rôle.[5]

To this supreme confidence in science as a technique and in man as its agent, Mead came by a process which critically and overtly, though always graciously, eliminated religion from any primary rôle in his life. He came to it by discovering that problem-solving is the most intellectually interesting and the most spiritually rewarding thing in life and that problem-solving transpires in terms of the resources of the problem itself rather than in borrowed terms. In publicly calling attention once to the work of the University of Chicago Settlement, he told of his friendly conversations with a scientist who was to immure himself with the same leper settlement on the island of Molokai to which Father Damien (whose heroism was celebrated by Robert Louis Stevenson's spirited and eloquent defense of him) had been attached as a self-sacrificing missionary. Mead remarks upon this incident with the freshness of which he was capable: "it never occurred to me till long after these conversations not to look upon him as a very lucky fellow, as he indeed regarded himself."[6]

This incident will help to make clear why Mead could never regard the alleged heroism, the self-sacrifice, the borrowed wisdom, the adventitious sanctions, which make up so large a part of religious morale, as hardly more than pathological, morally if not psychologically so. Any justifiable "self-sacrifice" would not merely become but would be and seem self-realizational, if one had the right kind of self. The more strictly religious element of the great religions, Mead habitually thought of as arising from some frustration rather than as some fulfilment of human life. I do not mean that he did not see a positive and beneficent rôle sometimes played by them. I shall speak of this in course. But their inception and genius he seemed to see as life gone awry rather than as life come to fruition. Indeed, in one of the last and best articles Mead wrote he says, by way of celebrating man's benevolent tendencies: "Universal religions have issued from their frustration—New Jerusalems where all tears are wiped away, Nirvanas where all wants have ceased."[7] Whether commenting upon the negative side or the positive aspect of historic religions, Mead could be relied upon to see their implication for human welfare and yet to keep straight, as he in one place puts it, the fact that "human experience, especially in recent times, has abundantly proved that the implication lies in social attitudes, which religious doctrines have formulated but for which they are not responsible."[8]

This borrowed nature of its insight, this rôle secondary to any creation of values, made religion unavailable because inapplicable in the adventurous realm where Mead lived. Not only in invidiously[9] contrasting the church with the social settlement as an agency of betterment but also in a more seasoned assessment, he puts tellingly the limitations of institutionalized religion. "The pulpit," he says, "is committed to a right and wrong which are unquestioned, and from its point of view unquestionable. Its function then is not the intellectual one of finding out what in the new situation is right, but in inspiring to a right conduct which is supposed to be so plain that he who runs may read."[10] This assessment cannot be dismissed, even from our vantage-point of a quarter of a century later, as an indictment growing out of an identification of religion as a whole with Christian fundamentalism. It is a basic attitude hardly less characteristic of modernism than of fundamentalism of which Mead here speaks, as his subsequent illustrations make clear: "The result has been that in the great moral issues of recent industrial history, such as the child labor, woman's labor, protection of machinery, and a multitude more, the pulpit has been necessarily silent. It had not the means nor the technique for finding out what was the right thing to do."[11] Not unction but penetration, as he makes clear in the article on the social settlement, is what sensitive men need. For such men to know is ordinarily for them to do; but to assume knowledge available in situations that are genuinely doubtful—as are most of the situations that challenge us—is to be worse than useless; it is to raise false confidence where what we need is not confidence but light. It is only after issues have been fairly settled on economic or moral or more broadly social grounds by other than religious methods that religious men can fruitfully take sides, and that is too late for any logical aid. The best that Mead can say of the church in the really crucial situations of life is that "it holds its peace, for it must give no uncertain sound to the battle." Indeed, as he concludes, "the only overt social issues with which the pulpit in recent times has identified itself have been temperance and chastity."[12] Deferring his evaluation of religious insight, we may summarize his weighed judgment of religious institutions: What we most poignantly need is not exhortation to do our duty, but, as Mead puts it, light "to enable us to form new moral judgments as to what is right and wrong, where we have been in such painful doubt."[13]

II

Science carried for Mead all the fine connotation that religion lacked. Indeed, science is but a name we give to the attitude most opposed to what Mead had delineated as religious impotence. It is intelligence at work; "once it has been set to work it can only be dismissed by dismissing the intelligence itself."[13] The attitude is the same wherever, though the difficulties increase with the metamorphosis from nature to man; and Mead is unfaltering in his trust of the attitude which expects to get its light for darkness from inspecting the darkened situations themselves. He rings the changes on the necessity of rendering scientific the social field and of identifying morality with science become effective in the social field. In his philosophy of the social settlement, he sings the praises of "an identification of moral consciousness with our modern scientific consciousness"; and in the sequel adjudges that if the social settlement "did nothing else it illustrates concretely how the community ought to form a new

moral judgment," i.e., by open-mindedly living with the difficulties themselves. "The same interest," he avers, "which the scientific observer of social phenomena takes to his investigations takes possession of the genuine settlement resident, for his first task is to comprehend his social environment. His most important virtue is not blind devotion but intelligence."[14] Mead elsewhere generalizes this belief in such a fashion as to make clear its larger bearings: "Moral advance," he says, "consists not in adapting individual natures to the fixed realities of a moral universe, but in constantly reconstructing and recreating the world as the individuals evolve";[15] for, as he elsewhere concludes, "the order of the universe that we live in is the moral order."[16] What he wars against here as elsewhere is not religion as such, of course, but against every form of externalism. Whatever transcends the situation in question is suspect. It may be useful to and for the situation, but this must be decided by mobile intelligence in the presence of the situation as itself the test and measure. The moralist is as guilty here as is the theologian: "the besetting assumption of the moralist that a moral reconstruction can be made intelligible only by a perfect moral order from which we have departed, or toward which we are moving, has very grave practical consequences."[17] If the moralist in the long run proves more fruitful than the theologian, it is because the former can without complete loss of cast transcend (though with what difficulty let the history of ethics bear witness) his intuitionalism and formalism and accept the scientific method as his only reliance. The religious, when he undertakes such metamorphosis, falls naturally into mysticism. Not that there is anything wrong with mysticism— save only that it lacks even more flagrantly than does formal religion a technique for validating its presumed insight. It sees so much in its moment of illumination that it cannot later prove that it saw anything. Such experience may reveal to one, as a contemporary mystic has it, "the anatomy of the body of God"; but it cannot elucidate even the simplest human perplexity. This does not mean that moral insight must be itself mere awareness of consequences; but it does mean that sensitivity to and respect for consequences is the only validation of moral insight—or of any other kind of insight, for that matter.[18]

Indeed, it is this implied continuity of all kinds of insight which constitutes Mead's major emphasis. Freudianism he appraises as making functionally continuous with consciousness what is popularly supposed to be outside the pale. Behaviorism he espouses as uniting through the act the psychical and the physical. Pragmatism he preaches as being the best generalized account of this pervasive and functional continuity, "the unity of the object and of the world in our own activity."[19] It is mind, everywhere mind, that transforms temporary contradictions into abiding continuities. This is Mead's legacy from idealism, but it is a legacy which he puts out at a high rate of interest. Mind does not discover merely what seems to be contradictory and then by true seeing resolve the false seeming. It discovers real contradictions but, by a more careful inspection of their possibilities, transforms through action the discrepant into the accordant. This function ascribed to the finite intelligence guarantees from Mead an amazingly high estimate of the significance of human individuality; but his conception of the conditions of this function of mind guarantees at the same time the most confirmed suspicion of any attempt to set off from curiosity and inspection and manipulation any segment of experience. To him there can be nothing sacred except the shared. More blamable by far than impotence, through lack of a technique for assisting intelligence in this high vocation, is the constant tendency of religion and transcendental ethics to thwart the realization of a growing better by emotional fixation—piously called devotion, invidiously phrased as loyalty to a cause—upon an absolute good inaccessible in its sterile fixity. "Society gets ahead," Mead thunders in many keys, "not by fastening its vision upon a clearly outlined distant goal, but by bringing about the immediate adjustment of itself to its surroundings, which the immediate problem demands."[20] The memorable article of Mead's on **"The Philosophical Basis of Ethics"** is crammed with fine insights. I must content myself here with its concluding gem: "not only does an external moral ideal rob immediate moral conduct of its most important values, but it robs human nature of the most profound solace which can come to those who suffer—the knowledge that the loss and the suffering, with its subjective poignancy, has served to evaluate conduct, to determine what is and what is not worth while."[21] We are now prepared to state the formula of life already foreshadowed: "The imperative necessity . . . is that responsibility should be tested by the consequences of an act; that the moral judgment should find its criterion in the mutual determination of the individual and the situation."[22] The psychological foundation for this formula is furnished by Mead's conviction that "the motive is the recognition of the end as it arises in consciousness."[23]

More important, however, than the formula is the doctrine that implements it. The confidence in human nature to find its own best way by trusting as good the fulfilment of its own impulses and as right what occurs to it to do when confronted by problematic situations constitutes Mead's substitute for religion. Mead could treat as secondary all religious claims because he had found to have primary significance insights that were not religious. Secular insights must be secularly discerned. It is correct to say that he started at the bottom, for he makes no initial assumption of a human soul.[24] Since, indeed, there is no source from which a soul could be borrowed, man must navigate without one or manage to construct one as he voyages. Honestly and diligently Mead undertook and consummated in his social psychology no less a task than that of elaborating a natural history of the soul. Important as this is, I must content myself with a reference to available articles for Mead's own elaboration of the view that starting as animal organisms we achieve by an empirical assuming of the rôles of others the self-consciousness of which personality consists.[25]

III

Suppose that, assuming Mead's sociological derivation of the self, we admit with him that religion is but a name for

values already achieved, that it has no technique for the achieving, that at worst it stands in the way of the birth of new values, but that at best it loves the child born of the poignancy of another and regularly celebrates its birthdays. Forgetting our former dispraise, suppose we have adequate motivation for wanting to know what at the best could be said in praise of religion. The best that could be said is, I believe, to be found in the work of George Herbert Mead. Let us see what it is.

The first observation would concern the moral significance of the cult as such. Mead has made clear in an article upon **"Scientific Method and Moral Sciences"** that "though an institution should arise and be kept alive by its own function," nevertheless "in so far as it does not function, the ideal of it can be kept alive only by some cult, whose aim is not the functioning of the institution, but the continued presence of the idea of it in the minds of those who cherish it."[26] The church Mead proceeds to single out as the "outstanding illustration of such an institution. Its most important function has been the preservation in the minds of the community of the faith in a social order which did not exist."[27] He goes on to show that the cult makes its values sacred, stands in the way of their realization, and should give way to "functional value" in so far as the institution "approaches realization." But in periods when idealism is wholly impotent, Mead seems to feel that they also serve who only kneel to worship. His most explicit word upon this point is this: "The cult value of the institution is legitimate only when the social order for which it stands is hopelessly ideal."[28]

The second observation favorable to religion is closely connected with the first. One may celebrate the actual as well as the "hopelessly ideal." Mead does not himself seem to see why one should call religious this celebration of the desirable actual, but the rôle he assigns to the aesthetic in human experience is clearly appropriable by religious persons who seek a substantial (non-theological) content for religion, as not a few contemporaries appear to do. Modern life has made it increasingly impossible for the majority of men to combine the ends for which they work with the work itself as means. Only "the artist, the research scientist, and the skilled artisan" enjoy vocations where normally "something of the delight of consummation can crown all intermediate processes."[29] For most the reward is distant; drudgery is at hand. Only imagination can pole vault one from the dreary here into the shining there. Consequently the not astonishing popularity of the two institutions—the cinema and the yellow press—which can support the imagination in its will to escape by spreading before it for two pennies or fifteen cents the rich substance of reverie. What the picture paper and the movie do consummately, other institutions, including the church, do haltingly. That is to say, the significance of a cult is not exhausted by keeping a hopeless ideal alive until a more fortunate day for its realization. It also imports into the otherwise arid present a semi-substantial experience filched from the yet-to-be. In Mead's fine phrase, "it has been the inspiration of universal religions . . . to bring something of the universal achievement, of the solemn festival, of common delight into the isolated and dreary activities which all together make possible the blessed community. . . ."[30] In so far as religion can transubstantiate the prospective into the aesthetic, not to say kinaesthetic, it plays an evidently enriching rôle. Moreover, these actualized escape values perform a wholesome therapy of catharsis in what Mead so happily calls "the economy of keeping house with oneself."

The third indicated observation in praise of religion follows hard upon if not indeed from the second. The value of values is the having of the desirable in common. Approving Professor Dewey's saying that "shared experience is the greatest of human goods," Mead in the foregoing article gives a new definition to isolation: "the isolated man is the one who belongs to a whole that he yet fails to realize."[31] "We have become bound up in a vast society," as he continues, "all of which is essential to the existence of each one, but we are without the shared experience which this should entail." While we wait and work for such social inventions as will remedy "man's isolation in society," religion as well as art can help us, in Mead's phrase, "to taste in Whitmanesque manner the commonalty of existence."

IV

If we drop for a moment, however, the rôle of the expositor for that of a most kindly critic, there is a point of view from which it might appear that Mead was more Christian than he intended. That the preponderant social solicitude in the Christian tradition appealed to Mead profoundly, as to so many sensitive thinkers, may be passed as a simple fact. But the assumption so easy as to make its opposite unthought, if not almost unthinkable, that the sharing of experience is the greatest good—this assumption by Mead provokes and rewards questioning. That which is private is "therefore subject to disintegration" and in fact exists only "because of the incompleteness of social organization."[32] It is the goal of science and the burden of morality, as Mead thinks, to complete this organization of society. This passion for solidarity is a veritable *idola tribus* of our time, and Mead is its secular prophet. "In the society which is closest to that of the primitive man," we hear him saying, "we find the reality of all that is prefigured and set out in . . . institutions."[33] And yet it is not really unthinkable that individuality in the most subjective and private sense, the unsharable, is a great virtue to be treasured and fought for rather than bartered away in a passion for gregariousness. That even more than this mild demurrer is thinkable, remember Nietzsche, who set the life-work of more sensitive modern thinkers than perhaps any other single man, and this because he called in question the rightful ubiquity of the Christian emphasis upon thoroughgoing community.[34] Wise men in other cultures have sometimes shown a high regard for antipathetic tendencies in human nature. The brotherhood of man as a cult has challenged loyalty longer than its complementary cult, the fatherhood of God. But anyone who has pondered realistically Mark

Twain's account of Captain Stormfield's visit to heaven, or who has observed the practices of his neighbors friendlily gossiping at the dinner table, which latter, at least, Mead had realistically remarked,[35] may be forgiven a doubt as to whether, down below the level of talk, we actually do want such social solidarity as the brotherhood of man implies and as Mead's social philosophy seems constantly to assume as norm. It is so uncharacteristic of Mead's cautious curiosity to make a cause of what really is not uncontestably good that it arouses the suspicion that he but carried on uncritically in this regard the Christian tradition. Would a Mohammedan thinker, not to mention a classic Greek mind, of Mead's acumen have assumed that all human experience implies enlargement and intensification of community without limit? If not, it is certainly a high tribute to the strength of the Christian leaven that it could so raise the threshold of even Mead's tough mind as to bring curiosity to its knees before the sacred altar of brotherhood.

If Mead unconsciously owed this basic assumption to the Christian religion, then he consciously paid back the debt in liberal measure. For his social psychology, which I have elsewhere described as his prizepole to budge charity toward reform and to heave social service on to the plane of justice, may equally truly be described as his corrective for the most fatal weakness of religion. This weakness, as the foregoing discussion has led us to see, is perfectionism. If Mead had been consciously and proudly Christian, he might well have said to himself: "I will scientifically implement this Golden Rule by showing that man to his very marrow is adapted to practice what some who do not understand his nature have scouted as utopian." Has he not indeed shown, or sought to show, that we are actually members one of another? Have we not acquired, by his account, our very souls by putting ourselves in one another's place until what arises in us as psyche is really socius? We are made of one sociological stock, and our being can do no better than to perpetuate the process of our becoming. Without the habit of taking the rôle of others, we ourselves should never have come to be; and this habit once established easily implements the injunction for us to do unto others as we would have them do unto us. In fact, and this would be indeed an eventuation so curious as to mock while it comforts, has not Mead implemented the Golden Rule so thoroughly by his social psychology that it is no longer a prescription at all but now a description of how we do inevitably act?

So to query is covertly to charge Mead with being romantic even after his transcending of romanticism. His, however, is the romance of man. How profoundly he did believe in man! The strength of our hands is not yet disclosed, because our hands move as yet to cross purposes. We do in small groups exemplify the Golden Rule by the very technique of our being; but it remains a mere prescription across group lines, which is to say in most of the areas of life. But Mead's philosophy of prescriptions, of ideals, renders them always ingratiating candidates for actuality. *Man can if he will; and he will if he knows; but he can know only through the concrete technique called science.* This profound confidence in man's indigenous power to know what he needs to know and in his natural willingness to follow his knowledge all the way might itself be called Mead's final capitulation to religion—if it did not in its first element contradict most religions and in its second element transcend them.

NOTES

[1] Other aspects of his philosophy I have noted in two articles. The one, "The Social Philosophy of George Herbert Mead," *American Journal of Sociology*, XXXVII (1931), 368-85; the other, "George Herbert Mead and the Philosophy of Philanthropy," *Social Service Review*, Vol. VI, No. 1 (March 1922).

[2] *George Herbert Mead* (Memorial Addresses and a Biographical Note by His Son), p. 34.

[3] *International Journal of Ethics*, XL (1930), 217.

[4] The entire sentence summarizing Royce's influence is worth quoting. "I received an impression from him of freedom of mind, and of dominance of thought in the universe, of a clear unclouded landscape of spiritual reality where we sat like gods together—but not careless of mankind—and it was a vision that followed me for many years" (*ibid.*, XXVII [1917], 170).

[5] See his contribution to *Creative Intelligence*, perhaps Mead's most systematic and profound essay.

[6] "The Social Settlement: Its Basis and Function," *University of Chicago Record*, XII (1908), 109-10.

[7] "Philanthropy from the Point of View of Ethics," *Intelligent Philanthropy*, p. 140.

[8] *Ibid.*, p. 144.

[9] The university of course partakes of the merit of the settlement; for it too "is the community organized to find out what culture is as well as to give it; . . . to find out what is right and what is wrong as well as to teach them . . . that is, to be continually redefining education as well as administering it" (*Survey*, XXXV [1915], 351).

[10] *International Journal of Ethics*, XVIII (1908), 321-22.

[11] *Ibid.*

[12] *University of Chicago Record*, XII (1908), 110.

[13] *International Journal of Ethics*, XXXIII (1925), 236.

[14] *University of Chicago Record*, XII (1908), 110.

[15] *International Journal of Ethics*, XVIII (1908), 318.

[16] *Ibid.*, XXXIII (1923), 247.

[17] *Ibid.*, XVIII (1908), 319.

[18] The basic use Mead makes of this utilitarian principle in promoting philanthropy to the plane of justice may be seen in his article for the symposium, *Intelligent Philanthrophy*, edited by Ellsworth Faris *et al.*

[19] *Philosophical Review*, IX (1900), 5.

[20] *International Journal of Ethics*, XXXIII (1923), 247.

[21] *Ibid.*, XVIII (1908), 323.

[22] *Ibid.*, p. 322.

[23] *Ibid.*, p. 315.

[24] Mead of course normally uses the term "self."

[25] For the more systematic presentation of the bases of Mead's social psychology, see his articles in the *Journal of Philosophy*, Vols. IX, X, and XIX; and in the *International Journal of Ethics*, Vols. XXXIII and XXXV. A volume is now being edited by Professor Charles W. Morris, perhaps under the title, *Mind, Self and Society*, containing, in addition to the articles upon social-psychological problems, stenographic reports upon Mead's justly famous course at the University of Chicago on "Social Psychology." For suggestions as to the content of his social psychology as it appears from the vantage of other social preoccupations than religion, see my two articles referred to in n. 1.

[26] *International Journal of Ethics*, XXXIII (1923), 240.

[27] *Ibid.* Elsewhere and much earlier he had already defined "the religious object as one which, while transcending through its universality the particular situations of life, still is felt to be representative of its meaning and value" (*Philosophical Review*, IX [1900], 17).

[28] *Ibid.*, p. 243.

[29] "The Nature of the Aesthetic Experience," *ibid.*, XXXVI (1926), 382-93.

[30] *Ibid.*, p. 384.

[31] *Ibid.*, p. 389.

[32] *Ibid.*, p. 393. Cf. his early article (*Philosophical Review*, IX [1900], 5), where he makes clear the logical basis of this ethical assumption: the subjective, the private, the psychical, arises only as a result of disintegration and exists for the sake of reintegration. Subjectivity is the homeless sprite of that which is no more and of that which is not yet.

[33] *Journal of Philosophy*, XII (1915), 152-53. Indeed, where this is not assumed, Mead sometimes seems to make its discovery the goal of science. "We assume," he

says in an early article, "that human society is governed by laws that involve its solidarity, and we seek to find these out that they may be used" (*American Journal of Sociology,* V [1899], 370).

[34] Cf. W. M. Urban's feeling remarks: "I shall never forget the long night in which I read through the *Genealogy of Morals.* It was, I believe, the greatest single spiritual adventure of my life. In the grey light of the morning I found myself surveying the wreckage of my beliefs in a curious mood. . . . Enough that I knew from that moment that, not only was the problem of values my problem, but also that it was destined to be the key problem of the epoch in which I was to live" (*Contemporary American Philosophy,* II, 359).

[35] See the delightful quotation from Mead, *American Journal of Sociology,* XXXVII (1931), 375 n.

Ellsworth Faris (essay date 1936)

SOURCE: A review of *Mind, Self, and Society,* in *American Journal of Sociology,* Vol. XLI, No. 6, May, 1936, pp. 809-13.

[*In the following essay, Faris praises Mead's significant contribution to social psychology as evinced in* Mind, Self, and Society.]

Few men of his day lived life more fully than George Mead and fewer still were better qualified to write about it. He was an active participant in civic organizations, took his duties as a citizen seriously, and had traveled far and often so that nothing human was alien. He had read and remembered the books—all the important books in every department of philosophy, the social sciences, and mathematics, not excluding fiction and poetry. And besides all this, his was "a seminal mind of the very first order" which enabled him to see relations and gain insights which gave to familiar facts an undiscovered significance. This above all—he lectured on social psychology for nearly forty years, even before the term became current, and hundreds of scholars now teaching and writing gratefully acknowledge him as their most stimulating teacher.

But Mead never wrote his book on social psychology. The present volume [*Mind, Self, and Society*] was assembled from the notebooks of students who heard him in the latter part of his career. The editor has, unfortunately, seen fit to give it another title and has taken the liberty to rearrange the material in a fashion that will be deprecated by many who knew Mead and thought they understood him. The task of the editor under such circumstances is one of unusual difficulty; and disappointment over the imperfections of the result yields to the feeling of gratitude to those men who did the best they could, according to their lights, and all who are interested in social psychology should be thankful for even this much.

The work in sociology at the University of Chicago has been greatly influenced by Mead's conceptions and conclusions, and for many years there has been a relationship of the closest sort. The course in social psychology is considered basic to the work of the Department of Sociology and has been offered for the past sixteen years, having been introduced at the request of Mead himself. It was at first planned as an introduction to Mead and served also to give to him an opportunity to discuss in his own course the growing body of controversial literature. That the course was thus in fact divided will explain the absence in the notes of the latter period of certain topics to which the editor calls attention, such as the detailed treatment of integration.

Mind, self, and society is the reverse order to that which the structure of Mead's thought would seem to make appropriate. Not mind and then society; but society first and then minds arising within that society—such would probably have been the preference of him who spoke these words. For societies exist in which neither minds nor selves are found, and it is only in human societies that a subject is its own object—only in these is there consciousness of self. Man, he held, is not born human; the biological accident becomes a personality through social experience.

The position taken is that man's personality is derived from nature without residue, that is to say, with no forces or influences that do not appear in the emerging development of the form itself, and this view is extensively elaborated. The organism is assumed to be originally acting and for this action no cause need be sought. But the acts are always within a society, and the ongoing social process with its habits, customs, language, and institutions is a pre-existent organization into which every child is born. The immature member of a society acts, but his acts are social acts at first, social because helpless and prolonged infancy limits him to contacts with social beings. The social objects have this essential character that they respond and change, and therefore adjustment must be made to them. Thus gestures arise, for the initial movements are acts that are parts of a whole, acts that mean larger acts; and the meaning of these gestures arises in the experience of response. In redintegration the incomplete picture is filled out in the imagination with material that has once been the complement, and thus meaning is brought into experience. In this way the doctrine is developed that ideas, the meaning aspect of symbols, are derived from the consequences of gestures performed by a participant in a social act. Ideas are not private and mental but social and motor.

Intelligence cannot be denied to the lower animals and the presence of symbols among them seems demonstrable. But *significant* symbols and reflective intelligence belong only to man, and it is in the effort to account for this crucial difference that Mead has made his most original contribution. That it has not had wider influence in contemporary sociology and psychology is due to the fact that it has not been readily accessible to scholars, a lack which this book ought to do something to supply.

It is in the phenomenon of human speech that Mead finds his most important clue. Speech is sometimes "the expression of thought in words" but this is only a secondary function. Speech is vocal gesture, it is behavior with meaning, and the meaning is a result of the social effects of the speech. In detail it is shown that the acquisition of language cannot be explained as the result of imitation, but that the elements, all of them, appear in the developing activity of spontaneous vocalization. The importance of the vocal gesture is that the one who stimulates another stimulates himself at the same time, since he hears his own voice. The self-stimulation makes possible self-response and this response is influenced by the response of the other. The result is the ability to take the rôle of the other which becomes sometimes "sympathetic introspection" but, what is even more important, leads the self to take the attitude of the other to himself; thus becoming an object to himself, with all that this implies.

Why man alone can achieve significant symbols and why he always does so in communication is assumed to be due to some complication in the central nervous system, the nature of which is as yet unknown, for we know more about our minds than we do about our brains. The neurology of speech is only partly explored and the neurology of attention is still a dark continent. But this phenomenon is observable in all normally developing human beings and cannot be found occurring in any other animal.

Once this standpoint has been taken, there are numerous other problems that arise as corollaries. The self is a rôle but there are too many "others" for us to adopt the thousand rôles that would seem to be necessary. There arises the "generalized other," in which occurs a synthesis of group attitudes which men hold in common. And to the voice of this generalized other we hearken when the failure of habit forces reflection.

Human conduct does not become a matter of adaptation to environment, for the conscious act is not a response to a stimulus. Mead does not conceive of the human form as an infinitely complex slot machine; action is rather the resultant of an impulse seeking expression and the "stimulus" is not only selected, it is sought for. The stimulus is the occasion for the release of the impulse. When the situation is problematic, there is an inability for conduct to go on, an uncertainty about the object and a vagueness and inefficiency about the impulse. When the broken whole is redintegrated the response is *into* the stimulus and *constitutes* the stimulus. Thus the organism creates its environment.

The psychology of perception receives welcome illumination. Perception becomes neither the passive awareness of an object nor a bundle of sensations united by some synthesizing mental power, but rather one kind of action. The perception of a physical object he calls a collapsed or "telescoped" act in which there is immediate experience of what would result did we go through a series of movements. Ice looks cold because it would produce certain effects were we to go toward it and touch it. The imagery of the past fuses with the excitation of the present and objects that have been organized are thus perceived.

Social objects require adjustment, for they are responding and changing, and thus they demand that attention be fastened on the beginning of the act thus giving rise to the gesture. Physical objects are non-responding, the attention being on the last of a series of movements rather than on the first, and, therefore, though the size, shape, and color may apparently change, these changes are neglected since the attention is on the end. If a physical object occasions surprise or any emotion, there is a tendency to regress to the social acts with which experience began. This occurs in such varied circumstances as the irritation at a chair into which we bump in the dark, the magical incantations of the rainmaker, and the sophisticated poetry of nature. Objects are not passively apprehended, they arise inside experience, and are constructed, organized, created.

The relation of the body and especially the central nervous system to mind and consciousness is a problem that still exercises us all. To locate it inside the brain as is often done with uncritical naïveté, or to put it inside the head with all the solipsistic consequences as Russell does, is to raise the insuperable difficulties of interactionism. Mead's view is that consciousness must be considered as functional, not substantive, objective and not subjective, and that what takes place in the brain are the processes which make it possible. The grounds for this position cannot be given in the scope of this review.

Whether the material in the book as here presented places an undue emphasis on the effort of Mead to redeem the word "behaviorism" from the connotation given to it by its inventor is a question on which his former students may differ. But all will agree that Mead considered the human self as a resultant of action and communication in society, and that the concepts of consciousness and imagination were necessary. The explanation of new organizations in experience as a result of the "conditioning" of reflexes or responses he found inadequate.

It is not only in the assumption of the priority of culture and of the primacy of impulses to action that the mechanical consequences of orthodox behaviorism are found wanting. In the passages where the "I" and the "me" are discussed, there is set forth another ground for assuming a spontaneity and creativeness which transcend the mechanical.

Many other aspects of the collective life receive attention but the material available does not always permit adequate development. Other posthumous volumes of Mead's work are promised and these will help to bring to the attention of scholars the work of one of the most original men of our generation.

Charles Hartshorne (essay date 1937)

SOURCE: "Mead and Alexander on Time," in *Beyond Humanism: Essays in the Philosophy of Nature*, University of Nebraska Press, 1968, pp. 242-52.

[*In the following essay, which was originally published in 1937, Hartshorne contrasts Mead's philosophy of time with that of S. Alexander, concluding that Alexander's theory is "the only carefully elaborated, honest attempt . . . to work out a non-psychic metaphysics which the twentieth century has so far witnessed."*]

George Herbert Mead was a great philosopher and certainly a humanist. Until his *Philosophy of the Act* has been published it will be too soon to pass judgment on his philosophy. But there are some aspects of his system which seem fairly well defined by his extant writings, and these aspects suggest the following criticisms. In his *Philosophy of the Present* Mead declares that each age creates its own past—not its own image of the past, for Mead seems to deny the validity of this distinction. The past *is* the best image we can construct on the basis of present experience in its past-pointing characteristics. The question then arises of how the past which we infer in this manner differs from the future which we may also infer. What is the direction of pastness? To this question Mead's writings seem to give only a cloudy answer. And in any case, it seems contradictory to assert that our efforts to know the past create the past we wish to know. In Mead's own discussion we can feel the unwished-for but really inescapable naïve meaning of past as the "irrevocable," the settled and done for, contrasted with the future, the unsettled, which can be more and more settled in this way or in that as it comes closer and closer to the present. Mead admits that an absolutely fixed past is possible only theistically, but he considers only the old type of theism according to which the future is fixed also, and he rightly objects that in that case past and future lose their distinctness and time is explained away, not explained. But then is this not also the result if we make both past and future unsettled? The point is to distinguish them, and both old theism and Mead's humanism seem, though in opposite ways, to confuse them together. Is it not striking that Mead's paradoxical view was expressly adopted under the conviction that the only alternative was the medieval or Roycean absolute (which Mead mistakenly supposed was also Whitehead's doctrine)?

In theory of value Mead was a great thinker. But his view of the social nature of mind is dangerously unprotected against the conclusion that society is the only real locus of value. His sympathetic critic, Professor T. V. Smith, has warned against this danger.[1]

In any case, Mead's social psychology is compatible with organic sympathy, since the "mind" which, according to him, is generated by relations to other human organisms is mind as reflective consciousness, as understanding of "significant symbols," not mind as merely feeling and striving, and the embracing of these factors in a unity of awareness with its element of meaning as awareness "of" an environment. Or did Mead really think that *all* sense of meaning, including that involved in simple memory and desire and emotional attitudes, is due to "taking the role of the other" in the fashion which is achieved only by man? (That all life whatsoever is "social" in a broad sense Mead fully grants.)

Again, in *Movements of Thought in the Nineteenth Century,* Mead says that a physical object really is, in the perspective of the beholding organism, what it looks to be—colored, etc.[2] But the question between psychism and its critics concerns what the object is when *not* in the perspective of human perception, e.g., before animals existed on earth, or today when we are all asleep. Mead says the world is the totality of perspectives.[3] Then we must ask, What is the perspective that belongs individually to a molecule as a man's perceptions belong to the man? Does the molecule's perspective possess quality, and if so how can it lack feeling or sensation? Does it possess the past as real in the present, and then how can it lack memory? Is it subject to order, and then how can it lack some germ of purpose, i.e., of present pattern binding upon the future? Only if the *Philosophy of the Act* illuminates these questions will Mead's philosophy present a significant alternative to psychic naturalism.

Perhaps the most important of all recent efforts to interpret the world without resort to the cosmic psychic variables is that of S. Alexander in *Space, Time, and Deity.* Alexander's view is that the only cosmic principle is space-time or, as he expresses it, pure motion. If one asks, Motion of what? Alexander replies, in effect at least, that there need be nothing to move except bits of motion themselves. In other words change of position can take place even though there is nothing at any position except change of position. This frank assertion of a paradox seems to me more honest intellectually than Santayana's pretense to possess in the term "matter" a key to what it is that has locus and that changes.

Out of pure motion "emerge" certain special properties ("local variables" in our terminology) such as quality, life, mind. But there are no cosmic variables, except bare space-time or motion, by which these local variables may be described.

In cosmic terms this system differs from older materialisms in three ways. First, space is held to be essentially temporal. Second, "matter" is given up as a cosmic principle except in so far as it means simply what is spatio-temporal. (This of course is the only positive meaning it ever did have.) Third, really new, unpredictable qualities perpetually appear in the universe. (The quality now emerging is deity, nascent divinity.) Because of these differences Alexander greatly objects to being called a materialist. When this charge is brought, he points out with great earnestness that he has described time as "the mind of space." But if asked what this means, and whether or not, by virtue of time, space thinks or feels, he replies that his metaphor must not be taken too seriously. The psychist cannot but suspect that Alexander has an intuition of the cosmic range of memory and expectation as essential to time, but has not clarified this intuition.

So far as I know, Alexander's is the only carefully elaborated, honest attempt (unless we should except Nicolai Hartmann's) to work out a non-psychic metaphysics which the twentieth century has so far witnessed. By virtue of his thoroughness and honesty the following difficulties appear plainly enough. First, pure structure is made independent of qualities. For space-time is nothing definite except a changing pattern of relations. "Relations of what?" remains unanswered. Second, the fact that space-time does in fact produce qualities is not explained. Third, there is in the system no ground of order in change.

It is also interesting that Alexander, writing a third of a century after Boutroux and Peirce had exploded the pretensions of determinism, tried to combine the absoluteness of law in physics with the absolute unpredictability of emergent properties.[4] Both absolutes are groundless obstacles to any understanding of time. It is also interesting that Alexander's quasi-materialism was not deliberately chosen as an alternative to a temporalistic panpsychism, but as an alternative to absolute idealism and ordinary materialism.

Alexander's point that space is inconceivable apart from time is an improvement over older materialisms, yet a weakness. For it is easier to overlook the emptiness of the concept of non-psychic reality in a static than in a dynamic context. That psychic reality is essentially dynamic is obvious, since thinking, feeling, striving, loving, hating, are all acts and since novelty and surprise are aesthetically valuable, and the very thought of their total absence is unbearable if we really strive to imagine it. But the blank notion of lifeless, insentient existence suggests no activity, for it suggests nothing definite, except, as Alexander says, the bare stuff of motion itself, and then it throws no light on what it is that moves. Becoming is a richer notion than being, and hence it reveals even more clearly the poverty of "matter" or of "non-psychic reality." If there is becoming, *something* must become which is not just a bit of becoming. Alexander's error is the universal one of all dualisms and materialisms, that of trying to explain the concrete by the abstract, "the fallacy of misplaced concreteness."

Alexander gives a very interesting argument for his rejection of quality as a cosmic variable.[5] He says that there is no "plan," or principle of variability, in quality similar to the plan of "humanity" as varied in Caucasian, Mongolian, and other races. He even doubts that there is any plan to color, and is confident that there is none uniting red and hard and sweet—all the sense qualities.

Strangely, he says nothing about the continuity of colors, and of course nothing about the possibility that discontinuities among the different senses are due to the fact that human sense-feelings are not all possible feelings, but a restricted realization of these possibilities, even by comparison with other existent animals. Hence Alexander's conclusion that "quality" is only a collective name for red, sour, hard, etc., is hastily arrived at. Nor can it be justified, since no observation can prove the impossibility of qualities intermediate between red and sweet, or sweet and warm, or in general any discontinuity of this type. And the only plan of variability any universal can have is dimensionality, a continuous spread of values (admitting various discontinuous spreads as special cases).

Starting, as Alexander does, from motion as an ultimate, one cannot interpret quality and qualitative change. But if we start from the notion of qualitative changes as socially interlocked, sympathetically interacting with one another, motion becomes readily explicable.[6] For motion is change of relative position and position is determined by the principle: "My neighbor is he with whom I intimately interact" (Peirce). Hence motion is simply the changes in the degrees of interaction among qualitative changes. Furthermore, it is explicable why there should be such changes in interaction. For, given a certain feeling-quality in *A*, then the degree to which this quality is compatible with intimate relationship to a given quality in *B* is determined. To take an example on the human plane: If I am melancholy in such a settled way that it conflicts with my mood to be vividly aware of a cheerful neighbor, I shall tend to keep at a certain distance from cheerful persons and to seek out intimate relations with persons in a melancholy mood. But if I pass from this state to one of feeling cheerless in a restless, painful way that makes me wish to be "cheered up," I shall seek out the society of happy people. The aesthetic unity of contrasting feelings which is necessary if feeling is not to be indefinitely destroyed by boredom or intolerable discord thus implies that changes in feeling-quality should be accompanied by changes in degree of relationship to other feeling-qualities, that is, by motion. And it matters not how simple the feelings may be, how subhuman or superhuman, for this law of unity in contrast is perfectly general and implies no higher degree of complexity than an electron may enjoy. Thus there is no riddle in the fact that our human feelings may produce motions in the human brain and muscles, for the parts of these organs sympathize with our changing feelings to such a degree as to involve sharp changes in their internal qualities, and from this their motion follows necessarily. The reverse process is equally explicable. Motion in the brain particles necessarily involves changes in their qualities, hence, by sympathy, qualitative changes in us. It also involves shifts in our relative intimacy with different parts of the brain (shifts of attention), so that one can truly say that consciousness moves.

It is easy to see why it is that science deals with motion as the causative factor rather than with qualitative change.

All motion involves qualitative changes, but these are usually inaccessible to us by ordinary practical or scientific means. Only with animals a great deal like ourselves can we rather easily infer something about the feelings involved in their "behavior." With inorganic bodies, which do not as wholes feel, since the feelings of their parts are not pooled into a single aesthetic pattern, we find it much easier to infer analogy to ourselves in terms of mere behavior than in terms of feeling-quality. And the behavioristic analogy serves our purposes. Why does it do so? How can we know the shapes of things whose feelings we do not know? How can we separate what in our sensations is due to motion in the environment from what is due to qualitative change? It seems almost a sufficient explanation to say that the aesthetic unity of the world is such that when we take the motions by themselves, we find them characterized by a very definite quantitative pattern. Doubtless the complete aesthetic pattern involves qualities also. But these qualities evidently change in such a way as to involve motions (changes in the relations between qualitative changes) which, considered in abstraction from the qualitative side, yield fairly definite patterns of their own, somewhat as the pattern of a poem is relatively independent of the meanings of its words. Thus the final proof of the atomic theory of matter was the proof that if there is a definite law of heat, heat must be a mode of motion, whatever else it may be. In other words, our sensations can be predicted if we suppose changes in them to be correlated with motional changes in the environment and in ourselves and if we suppose these changes to follow certain patterns. Not that it does not matter what qualities there may be in the environment, but that it does not matter to us whether or not we *know* these qualities. For we do know this about them, that they are such as to be compatible with the patterns of motion which explain our sensations, and this is all we need to know. We get the results of the qualities in terms of motions and of the qualities of our sensations, and that satisfies us.

But the fact is that we do not in reality know the precise motions in nature, nor even anything much like them. We know statistical patterns and certain *limits* of motions, but the course of behavior of an individual electron inside these limits escapes us. We have positive grounds for denying that this behavior follows an absolute law by which it could be precisely predicted; but if we really knew the individual behavior of an electron up to a given moment, it might well be that we should be able to make a fairly close estimate of what it would do next. But also we should have some sympathy for it as an individual. We should know how long it has endured a given energy-state, how likely it is, by the general tolerance of electrons for given types of monotony, that it is "tired" of this state and ready to "react" away from it to something affording the relief of novelty. But the wonderful fact is that this knowledge would not for practical purposes tell us anything we need to know unless we could simultaneously observe millions of electrons in this individual fashion; and we should then have to have superhuman intelligence to put the facts together into a significant story. For we live on the macroscopic plane, where individual particles are insignificant.

It seems to come to this, that motion is decisive because, in abstraction from qualities, it yields the statistical patterns needed for our type of prediction and control of ourselves through control of the environment. The pattern of motions which is abstractable from the real but elusive changes of quality in the environment is continued into the body (not without some modifications no doubt, but to a significant extent), so that physiology is in a measure a mere complication of physics. But here motions and qualities begin to seem inseparable even for our knowledge. There is in a bright color a sense of exhilaration and in the sensation of black a "dead" quality which correspond to the fact that in one case the given part of the retina is stimulated, and in the other is merely left to its own internal energy or lack of it. And the cells or molecules concerned may be supposed to share (with appropriate qualifications) in such feelings of excitement or calm. Many other examples could be given (see the author's *The Philosophy and Psychology of Sensation*).

The facts on the whole seem entirely in agreement with the assumption that the ultimate or complete pattern of nature is a pattern in which qualities and motions are inseparable, but that the motion-patterns can be abstracted and, in statistical aspects, yield all the law we human beings can for most practical or scientific purposes desire; while, on the other hand, there is evidence that behind the statistical behavioristic laws there are patterns of individual behavior which could not be fully grasped apart from qualitative sympathy with the individuals. The study in which this double point of view enters even into scientific contexts is psychophysics. But here we must note the difficulty that quality, in the strict sense of the non-structural properties of things, seems inevitably to elude reason, for reason deals with patterns, structures. In the book mentioned above I have tried to deal with this question, essentially by pointing out that qualities are similar to one another, and that similarity is a relationship subject to exact—in fact, geometrical—patterns. Starting with one's own sense qualities as origin, such relationships might conceivably lead to an insight even into the qualities of microscopic entities. But the problem will hardly be adequately formulated in our generation, one reason being that the advanced psychophysical knowledge which would make such a formulation useful is not yet at hand.

It is quite different with internal properties of a structural character, such as memory or purpose or complexity of feeling. It should be possible to make rapid progress in ascertaining how long on the average an electron vividly remembers or how far ahead it effectively anticipates. Physics can in this regard pass easily into a branch of comparative psychology, hindered indeed only by the fact that we do not deal directly with individuals. This psychology of structural properties is the only kind that is generally admitted to be possible even for animals, nay even for human beings, if we believe the behaviorists.

Alexander is right in choosing continuous dimensions for his cosmic variables; but variables of feeling-quality and of thought and volition may be continuous as well as those of space and time, and for philosophy may be even more important. Of course we have to abstract from any one set of particular thoughts or feelings or strivings, just as we do from any one set of space-time patterns. But to abstract from a whole infinite dimension such as the variables of thought or feeling are, is precisely the indefensible process of explaining concreteness by the merely abstract, that which is not even potentially concrete. Space-time is potentially all that particular patterns of motion are concretely, but it is not even potentially concrete particularizations of quality or thinking. It requires these latter particularizations for the particularization of its own dimensions, but the dimensions of qualitative particularization, for instance, are additional to the physical dimensions. The opponents of psychism have yet to explain what they take to be the relation of abstractions to the concrete. Peirce and Whitehead and Bergson have explained this most carefully. For them, to generalize the results of experience is to generalize experience itself. The variability of experience is itself experienced, by virtue of the sociability and the flexibility or freedom of the latter. Variability of a "reality" held to be distinguishable from all experience is, on the other hand, experientially meaningless. "Pure motion" is unimaginable not relatively but absolutely; it is a *contradiction* of the empirical variability—which is irreducibly more than four-dimensional—upon which the idea of motion and every idea must be based. The totality of irreducible dimensions of the experienceable variability of experience is the totality of irreducible dimensions of existence. The narrowness or provincial character of human experience, both with respect to what is "below" and what is "above" it, lies not in its dimensions, but in the limits of the "slice" of values humanly realized along these dimensions. If this statement is true, philosophical understanding is possible; otherwise it is not possible.

NOTES

[1] Cf. T. V. Smith, *Beyond Conscience* (McGraw-Hill Book Co., 1934).

[2] Mead, *Movements of Thought in the Nineteenth Century* (University of Chicago Press, 1935), p. 414.

[3] *Ibid.,* p. 315.

[4] Alexander, *Space, Time, and Deity* (The Macmillan Co., 1920), I, 326 ff.

[5] *Ibid.,* II, 328.

[6] On space as a pattern of sympathetic interconnection see Whitehead, *Adventures of Ideas*, pp. 226, 258-60; and *Process and Reality* (The Macmillan Co., 1929), Part IV.

Charles W. Morris (essay date 1938)

SOURCE: "Peirce, Mead, and Pragmatism," in *The Philosophical Review*, Vol. XLVII, No. 278, March, 1938, pp. 109-27.

[*In the following essay, Morris traces the progression of pragmatism by comparing the early metaphysical idealism of Charles Pierce to Mead's later empirical naturalist approach.*]

I

In recent years we have had spread before us the results of the intellectual labors of Charles S. Peirce and George H. Mead. In the same period John Dewey has rounded out the implications of his views for esthetics, religion, and political theory, and has given us a glimpse of the reformulation and systematization of his logical doctrine. William James' mode of thought has been kept before us by Ferdinand Schiller's collection of his own later cosmological essays, and by the full length portrait of James' life and thought painted in words by Ralph Barton Perry. C. I. Lewis has devoted himself to the theory of knowledge from the point of view which he calls "conceptualistic pragmatism". And a number of characteristic pragmatic theses have begun to show their familiar faces in the writings of American and European philosophers of science—especially among the logical empiricists and the defenders of operationalism.

In terms of this deluge of new material, representing as it does the main interests and the main thinkers in the pragmatic movement, the task of appraising America's most distinctive philosophic expression is rendered at once more easy and more difficult. It is more difficult because the very richness of the material makes impossible the facile explanations, acceptances, and damnations which ran riot during the futile decades in which discussion centered almost exclusively around the concept of truth. Those decades are happily past, and the phoenix which has arisen from the ashes reveals herself as a much more luxuriant creature. We find ourselves confronted with the task of assessing a distinctive version of empiricism, an extensive logical tradition, a developed theory of value, a comprehensive formulation of ethics and social philosophy, a detailed theory of mind, and a minutely elaborated cosmology. And this is a more difficult task than either the friends or the enemies of the pragmatic movement have hitherto set themselves. Indeed, the relevant critical task has hardly been envisaged, to say nothing of being performed.

Yet in another sense, the recent literature has made the task of assessment easier. It becomes clearer than ever before that there is a sustained unity to the pragmatic movement. Pragmatism reveals itself in all its phases as a series of constantly deepening analyses of a single set of theses. The differences between the leading representatives are primarily variations on a common theme, variations in part dictated by differences in fields of interest and application. There are genuine differences to be sure, but these too are often merely differences as to the permissible range of extension of a doctrine otherwise held in common. Pragmatism comes thus to take on an integrated character. One has the sense of a complex philosophic tapestry which has been woven through coöperative enterprise. The movement has in our day achieved something of an esthetic culmination, like a fine conversation which has worked itself out to its natural termination.

It is not of course possible on this occasion to attempt either of the tasks which the pragmatic movement makes imperative. We can neither try to show the systematic contours of pragmatism nor critically to estimate it as a whole. But as a step in these directions, it has seemed worth while to compare and contrast Peirce and Mead in certain selected respects. The American philosophical public is now at work digesting the published results of these thinkers, but as yet little has been written on the men individually, and nothing, so far as I know, of a comparative sort. The selection to be made also has the advantage of drawing attention to the somewhat neglected cosmological theories of the pragmatists in relation to the constant consideration by such thinkers of the general theory of signs. The fact that no obvious influence of Peirce on Mead is discernible, coupled with the fact that Peirce approached his problems as a logician while Mead approached his as a social psychologist, makes more significant their convergences and their differences. It is believed, further, that this comparison of the earliest and the latest stage of pragmatism makes the continuity and the discontinuity of the development stand out vividly, and provides a basis for evaluating the change that has taken place from the metaphysical idealism of Peirce through the radical empiricism of James to the empirical naturalism of Dewey and Mead. The lines of this evolution likewise throw light on the possible future of the pragmatic movement.

II

Even the most superficial sampling of the writings of Peirce and Mead reveals certain striking similarities between the thought of the two men. Mead held that "philosophy is concerned with the import and presence in the universe of human reflective intelligence". Peirce and Mead, in common with all pragmatists, were led to their views by a consideration of the phenomenon of reflective intelligence—as perhaps was Aristotle in an earlier age. This is in a sense the center with reference to which all pragmatic doctrines form an ever-expanding series of circumferences. A consideration of reflective intelligence suggests a number of important consequences: it leads to attaching central importance to the theory of signs—and both Peirce and Mead spent a large part of their life in the elaboration of this discipline; it inevitably raises questions as to the relation of signs and thought—and both men shared the view that there is no thought without signs; it demands an answer in post-Darwinian days as to the relation of thought and organic action—and both men insisted that thinking functions in the context of interested action as an instrument in the realization of sought values. The consideration of reflective thinking provokes queries as to the relation of thought to empirical data— and the common answer was given that all thought must find its ultimate validation in terms of such data; such

consideration sensitizes the inquirer to the phenomenon of universality—and both Peirce and Mead aim adequately to take account of the objectivity of universality, generality, law; it seems to indicate that the envisagement of ends is a genuine factor in the attainment of these ends—and both philosophers insisted upon the reality of final causes, defending the objectivity of teleology, chance, and novelty against any type of mechanistic theory which would take from mind its rôle as an active agent. The study of reflective thinking inevitably draws attention to the social aspect of thought—and both men held in high respect the category of the social, discerning in the universe wider social processes of which the sociality of the human mind is a particular manifestation; finally, such study raises doubts as to the validity of any form of dualistic separation of mind and the world—and both Peirce and Mead chop at the roots of the lingering traces of Cartesianism and present a universe unfractured by the dichotomies of subjective experience and external nature, quality and quantity, mind and matter, mechanism and purpose.

So it is that the earliest and latest phases of pragmatism show significant agreement on basic issues. There is presented an expanded and renovated empiricism which has relinquished the individualistic, subjectivistic, sensationalistic, and nominalistic extremes of late British empiricism; linked with this empiricism is an evolutionary cosmology, constructed with minute fidelity to modern physical and biological science, but in which mechanical law has not squeezed out novelty, chance, or purpose; while the keystone of the arch is found in a theory of mind in terms of which mind is at once set in the framework of interested action and yet linked with things in such a way that envisaged ends are concretized into embodied actualities.

Nevertheless, in spite of these basic convergences, the same superficial sampling also discloses profound divergences which at first glance perhaps obscure the fact that the differences are more as to the range of applicability of a doctrine than as to the doctrine itself. Peirce shows more the mentality of the traditional metaphysician; Mead writes more as a scientist. Peirce discusses fully the doctrines of pragmatism and the empirical theory of meaning, but often fails to live up to his own methodological precepts; Mead does not write much concerning these topics, but his thinking moves more firmly within a pragmatic and empirical orbit. One characteristic of the metaphysical type of mind—perhaps the dominant characteristic—is to note the existence of series and then to affirm the existence of the limits of these series. Some things are better than other things—hence there must be an absolute best; one theory is truer than another—hence there is one absolutely true theory; one perspective is more embracing than another—hence there is an absolute perspective; there are purposes which include subordinated purposes—hence there is one final purpose to which all things move. Peirce's writings show strongly this metaphysical tendency: truth, reality, meaning, probability, value are all defined in terms of the "long run".

Mead's thinking is by contrast contextual or situational; he defines all of these terms in reference to specific contexts and situations. He agrees more with the attitude of the mathematician that the existence of a series in itself gives no assurance that the series has a limit. He stresses the point that while science approximates to the conception of the world at an instant, the existence of such a limit cannot be reached without rendering meaningless the very concepts which science employs. And while Mead sets no practical bound to the degree to which thought may symbolically embrace common features of a plurality of existential perspectives, the very nature of a perspective as he conceives it makes impossible an actual single all-inclusive perspective, so that the metaphysics of absolute idealism is closed to him as it was not to Peirce. Mead's system accounts in various ways for the organization of nature, but not at the expense of the fundamental pluralism which is characteristic of his thought.

The mention of idealism furnishes another way to bring out the contrast. We are all familiar with Peirce's dictum that "the one intelligible theory of the universe is that of objective idealism, that matter is effete mind, inveterate habits becoming physical laws".[2] Thinking of mind as the operation of final causes, and making liberal use of the principle of continuity, Peirce extends the operation of mind to the cosmic scale, so that mind becomes "the fountain of existence" (VI.61). Mead, on the contrary, while admitting that mind is a particular form of processes which everywhere occur, insists more sharply on the biological, social, and linguistic preconditions of mind, with the result that the term 'mind' is not extended so widely: mental processes are not assigned throughout nature, and mind, though one active factor in the organization of nature, can in no sense be said to be the general source of existence. Mead's account is thus more naturalistic than Peirce's, and the principle of discontinuity is treated with as much respect as the principle of continuity.

Peirce's statement that mind is the fountain of existence recalls another characteristic feature of his cosmology, namely, his tendency to conceive of possibility, existence, and law as constituting three "Realms of Being" or "Universes of Experience" parallel to the three categories (Firstness, Secondness, Thirdness) and the three kinds of signs (Icon, Index and Symbol). Although Peirce often stresses the interdependence of the three categories, yet in practice his cosmology tends to fall apart into realms, and we are presented with a description of the world as a process by which mind (as Thirdness) converts possibility (Firstness) into determinate forms of existence (Secondness). There is thus a decided tendency to hypostatize the eternal possibilities, the laws which control the characters and relations of existences, and the final causes which direct the process into an embodiment of "concrete Reasonableness". No such tendency is found in Mead. The reality of possibility, law, and the efficacy of mind are admitted, but as we shall see later, they are integrated by Mead's distinctive concept of the act and his resulting objective relativistic cosmology.

As a final way of exhibiting relevant differences, attention may be called to the place of pragmatism in the two philosophies. Peirce to be sure speaks of his proof of pragmatism as "the one contribution of value that he has to make to philosophy" (V.415). And yet it is clear that the importance of pragmatism for Peirce lay primarily in its metaphysical implications and only secondarily in its contribution to the method of determining the meaning of any concept. He thought that the establishment of pragmatism carried with it the establishment of critical common-sensism, the reality of laws, and the doctrine of continuity—and these were the philosophical treasures which Peirce sought. For when the pragmatic maxim seemed to conflict with these and other prized results he drew back: thus in spite of his analysis which would make the meaning of any concept ultimately identical with a habit (V.494), he continually raised doubts "whether belief is a mere nullity so far as it does not influence conduct" (V.32); he feared certain applications of the doctrine to mathematical concepts (V.3); and he even came to add a fourth stage of the clearness of ideas over and above the third or pragmatic stage: the meaning of a concept is then found in the contributions of the reaction it produces to "concrete Reasonableness" (V.3). Such tendencies are absent in Mead's account; in his writings the instrumentalist position is never compromised, and meaning remains embedded to the end in its empirical and behavioristic context. Pragmatism is peripheral in Peirce, but focal in Mead; to the one it is a step in the establishment of certain metaphysical and religious beliefs, while to the other it becomes the persistent center for detailed analysis of philosophic and scientific concepts.

Thus we see that while Peirce and Mead have much in common, Mead in every case gives a more restricted validity to doctrines accepted by both, and the restriction always tends toward a more empirical, pluralistic, behavioristic, and naturalistic formulation. We must now attempt to see the sources of this difference, and then note their effect in determining the cosmological formulations of the two men.

III

It is my suggestion that the source of the differences should be most evident in the analyses of signs which Peirce and Mead gave, for both men very early singled out the field of semiotic as of central importance, and in a life-time of devotion to this ancient philosophical discipline made contributions second to none in the modern period.

First we must note in a summary fashion the striking convergence of the two analyses. In both cases the sign is held to function within a triadic situation. The members of this triad are called by Peirce the Representamen, Interpretant, and Object. Something becomes a representamen by functioning as a substitute for some object in virtue of being interpreted as indicating that object. Two further qualifications are needed, and these must be discussed separately. The first qualification is that for Peirce not all representamens are signs: a representamen becomes a sign if the interpretant is a cognition of a mind (II.242). Thus the concept of representamen is not restricted to situations involving minds or even living beings. Nevertheless, it is characteristic of Peirce to maintain that even in such situations something akin to mind is involved, and he occasionally speaks in this connection of a "quasi-mind". He not merely holds that "meaning is obviously a triadic relation", but also that "every genuine triadic relation involves thought or meaning" (I.345). Since Thirdness is taken to be a categorical character of reality, the fact that Peirce makes the sign situation a special case of triadic relations and ascribes thought or meaning to all such relations constitutes one of the essential sources for his idealism, and the ground for the view that the universe is a vast representamen working out God's purposes. It is this aspect of Peirce's thought that Royce could so easily turn to the service of absolute idealism.

At this point we find one source of Mead's divergence. Mead does not ground his analysis of signs on a general theory of triadic relations, but there is no incompatibility between his position and such a formulation. He too holds that signs involve a triadic relation, and distinguishes non-significant from significant symbols, the latter corresponding to Peirce's genuine sign. Using a terminology developed by Brewster[3] to make more explicit what is involved in Mead's analysis we may say that Mead's non-significant symbol includes two sorts of signs: physical signs and gesture signs. A physical sign is any property of an object interpreted by a reacting organism as an indication of further properties of the object which are to be encountered in a later stage of the act: thus the bone as seen is a physical sign to the dog of the bone to be snatched and chewed. A gesture sign is an early phase of the act of one living form which is interpreted by another living form as an indication of the later stage of the act of the first form: thus the clenched fist of *A* may serve as a sign to *B* of *A's* coming blow. As contrasted with both physical signs and gesture signs, the significant symbol (or language sign) is a sign common to a number of living beings, so that what it designates to one is designated to all alike. We shall not consider in detail Mead's analysis of the origin and nature of such signs, but merely state that in his opinion it is through the spoken word connected with common reactions in a number of organisms engaged in coöperative activity that the gesture-sign situation becomes transformed into a situation involving genuine language signs or significant symbols. It is essential to note, however, that the transformation from one level of sign to another is not explained by introducing the term 'mind' for higher levels in contrast to 'quasi-mind' for lower ones. Rather the different situations are taken to characterize the concept of mind: to have a mind and to take cognizance of objects by the mediation of significant symbols are in Mead's terminology one and the same thing. Signs do not therefore presuppose a previously existent mind; mind is rather a characteristic of behavior involving a unique kind of sign—

the language sign. The result is that by the genetic differentiation of levels of signs, Mead is able to isolate features distinctive of these levels, and the recognition of common features offers no temptation to read down into the lower levels features distinctive of the upper levels. Mind is not extended throughout nature and no idealistic conclusions are drawn. It may perhaps be said that this difference is only terminological, since 'mind' can be defined as distinctive of certain levels of signs or as a common factor involved in all sign situations. Nevertheless, however the term is used, the actual differences of various levels of triadic situations must not be neglected, and the danger of a wide use of the term 'mind' lies precisely in the emotional temptation surreptitiously to extend the distinctive characteristics of higher levels to the lower, stressing continuities and disregarding the equally basic discontinuities. The avoidance of this temptation may be taken as one advantage of Mead's genetic approach over the purely logical analysis of Peirce, for the latter approach in isolation contains no check against a too-wide extension of its results.

This line of argument may become clearer if we introduce the second qualification to Peirce's view that a sign involves a representamen functioning as a substitute for some object in virtue of its being interpreted as indicating that object. For Peirce it is characteristic of a genuine sign that the interpretant of a representamen in turn becomes a representamen indicating for a successive interpretant the same object indicated by the first representamen (I.541, II.242, V.138). Peirce is impressed by this situation because it seems to make evident the doctrine of continuity in the realm of mind and meaning, and to support the contention of idealism that the world process is a continuous expansion and interpretation of meaning. Mead admits the fact in regard to language signs,[4] but once again his explanation involves no such metaphysics. The fact is explained in terms of the social character of the significant symbol. Since at the level of mind (the level of the functioning of significant symbols) the thinking individual has internalized the social process of communication, he tends to reply to his own symbols as another would reply. He thus progressively interprets the meaning of his symbols in terms of further symbols, and so amplifies and extends his response to the object indicated by the symbols at the initiation of the process. Mead thus gives the background which makes intelligible such statements of Peirce as the following: "I call this putting of oneself in another's place *retroconsciousness*" (I.586); "the inner world, apparently derived from the outer . . ." (V.493); "all thinking is dialogic in form. Your self of one instant appeals to your deeper self for his assent" (VI.338); "we become aware of ourself in becoming aware of the not-self" (I.324). Dozens of statements of this sort might be quoted, and could have been written by Mead as well as by Peirce; they indicate the remarkable degree of convergence of the two analyses of signs and their relation to thought. The point important for our purpose is that these statements of Peirce attain a consistent explanation when interpreted in terms of Mead's social behavioristic approach, but when so interpreted the recognition of the distinctive preconditions for the appearance of mind and significant symbols removes the warrant for regarding nature as a great mind interpreting itself by the ever-unfolding chain of signs. If it be said that such an extension is justified by the principle of continuity, it must be answered that Peirce himself occasionally admits that this is a methodological rather than a metaphysical principle, and certainly the triumphs of the atomic theory and quantum mechanics in our own day indicate that the principle of discontinuity is methodologically of equal importance to its much overworked complementary principle.

So much by way of substantiating the hypothesis that the significant differences between Mead and Peirce center in their interpretation of the phenomena of signs. We have seen how Mead's social behavioristic approach permits of a theory of signs which concurs with Peirce's results obtained by logical analysis, and yet furnishes a principle of limitation which does not require that these results be interpreted in the idealistic manner. We now wish to explore in more detail the resulting cosmological differences, concentrating our attention especially upon the treatment of possibility, existence, and generality, and upon the relation of mind to nature.

IV

We have been contrasting the metaphysical aspect of Peirce's thought with Mead's more constant scientific temper. In one sense this is unfair. It is possible to pick from Peirce's writings many passages in which he insists that philosophy is to be scientific, never passing beyond probable statements based on empirical evidence; that metaphysics is to be grounded on formal logic and this in turn upon semiotic; that metaphysical principles are simply logical principles accepted "by a figure of speech" as "truths of being"; that metaphysics consists primarily in "thoughts about words, or thoughts about thought" (V.244, 343). And such passages would make possible an interpretation of Peirce as primarily a logician, reducing metaphysics to a somewhat literary and metaphorical extension of logical results. This is clearly not a false interpretation, but it can hardly be regarded as the full story. Peirce certainly permits himself many statements that from this point of view would have to be regarded as sentences which are really about signs but are wrongly interpreted as being about non-symbolic objects. Peirce however could hardly accept this correction, for it is clear that he is congenial to the typical rationalistic belief in an isomorphism between signs and things that are not signs; he expressly holds that thought is "the mirror of being" (I.487). The issues here are complex and not to be resolved by a word. Nevertheless, one can admit that there are some propositions true both about signs, and things that are not signs, without holding that the isomorphism is complete: not merely is a reference to the conventional factors in language relevant, but the introduction of special signs in a language to indicate the relation between signs in the language makes it impossible to find ontological significance for all signs. It follows that one

must exercise great caution in reading out logical principles metaphysically. Peirce's Scotist affiliations occasionally cause him to transgress such caution.

However, it is not the general issue that occupies our attention at this point, but rather the special form of the problem presented by the Peircean categories. Firstness, Secondness, Thirdness, isolated by attention to iconic, indexical, and symbolic types of signs, are given metaphysical validity as the generalized expression of the "realms" or "universes" of possibility, existence, and mind. We have already remarked that Peirce tends often to talk metaphorically about these realms, as if mind works on possibility to direct existence into the form of embodied lawfulness. Now in terms of the general thesis that the difference between Peirce and Mead is rather upon the extension of certain doctrines than in the doctrines themselves, our problem is not to deny the Peircean doctrine of "realms" and their interactions, but to see how in Mead's formulation the somewhat hypostatized and metaphorical description drops away. This requires that we comprehend Mead's concept of the act and the objective relativistic cosmology which results from its application.[5]

Keeping for the moment to the level of biological existences, we may say roughly that for Mead an act is a process of adjustment of a living form to an environing world, the process moving from an initial want or interest through stages of perception and manipulation of objects to the satisfaction of the want or interest by a suitable object. The act may be relatively simple, as in the case of satisfying hunger, or very complex, as in the social act by which a nation realizes such a complex end as victory in war. The act is an instance of "natural teleology" in that its statement involves reference to the goal to which the early stages of the act tend; it does not however necessarily involve "psychical states" nor consciousness of the goal or deliberation concerning the steps to be taken in reaching the goal. Now the important point is that the complex behavior-object circuit can be considered from the point of view of behavior, or with reference to the object, and a significant parallelism of statements results. In terms of the agent the process may be analyzed into the stages of perception, manipulation, and consummation; in terms of the object the object may be said to manifest in this process corresponding distance, manipulatory, and value properties. This is the clue to the most significant feature of Mead's objective relativistic cosmology, for it involves the view that secondary, primary, and tertiary qualities are genuine properties of the object relative to the appropriate stage of the act. The food object is odorous at the perceptual stage of the act, it is a physical object as revealed at the manipulatory stage, and it is a value object relative to the consummatory goal of the act. Thus objects in nature have qualitative, quantitative, and value characters relative to certain situations, and these situations must be stated if the sentences which ascribe these characters are to be complete. Mead's thought is in harmony with the growing recognition that objects have properties only in virtue of existing within one or more systemic contexts; his position is a generalized objective relativism in that nature is regarded as the organization of such contexts (situations, systems, perspectives, presents).

Mind appears within the act when the later stages of the act are controlled by the intervention of significant symbols which indicate these stages and the corresponding properties of objects. With the appearance of mind, itself a phenomenon in nature, the agent is able to transform the end or goal of the act into an end-in-view and to take account of the conditions set by the object which must be met if the act is to pass to its culmination. "Final causes" in this way gain reality, but not in a wholesale and speculative fashion: the term either refers to the objective purposiveness of the act, or, preferably, to the fact that a symbolically indicated future is made available for the control of the ongoing act. The tendency to hypostatize mind loses its excuse for being and the metaphysical statements often made in terms of 'control by the future' or 'the interaction of the realm of final causation with the realm of existence' are replaced by their empirical equivalents.

The same transformation occurs with respect to the concept of mechanism. The world which physical science presents is primarily the world as it reveals itself at the level of manipulation. This physical world assumes great importance since the passage from the stage of perception to the stage of consummation of all or most acts involves passing through the stage of manipulation. Hence in isolating the most constant physical features of objects, physical science gives the conditions necessary for the completion of all or most acts. This central importance of the world presented by science does not however render any less real the status of distance and consummatory qualities in nature, nor permit of an all-embracing generalization of the concept of the mechanical. For the mechanical, conceived as the conditions of the completion of the act, coincides with the predictable, and the completion of the act is not predictable in terms of the conditions it must meet. Science presents at the best the conditions necessary for the successful termination of the act, but not the sufficient conditions. What possible characters of objects will be realized depends on how the agent will react to and use those objects, and this depends in turn upon the purposes of the agent. Even when the biological sciences present accounts of the act, of how symbols operate, and of what purposes agents normally have under certain conditions, these accounts are still theoretical constructions within still more complex acts whose termination will utilize those accounts without being uniquely determined by them. A completely generalized mechanical account, if meant as more than a methodological precept, reveals itself as another instance of the metaphysical passage to the existence of a limit of a serial process. I think it is a fair interpretation of Mead's results to say that they render the generalized opposition of the mechanical and the teleological a false formulation and the problem of their reconciliation a pseudo-problem. For on the one hand there is no limit to the attempt

of science to isolate what is predictable, and yet on the other hand the results of science, however much they may interact upon purposes actually held, never uniquely determine the terminations of the wider acts within which scientific theories function.

The implications of Mead's approach for the status of possibility, law, and mind in nature are clear and need no extended discussion. Possibilities are objective in that the properties which objects manifest depend on the interaction of these objects with other objects within determinate systems. There is no temptation to erect possibilities into "eternal objects" in the sense of Peirce and Whitehead. Possibilities are objective, but not as entities; statements of possibility are statements of the behavior of objects within various systemic contexts. It is evident that this account does not minimize Secondness or existence. That there are physical things with characteristic modes of interaction under stipulated conditions is simply a fact, and the laws of science are statements of these modes of behavior in a form suitable for prediction. As for Thirdness, Mead admits its objective character through his insistence upon the occurrence of acts in nature, and in his recognition that the eventuation of these acts may be directed by the symbolic indication of a hypothetical future. In all three cases Mead is able to take account of what is vaguely and ambiguously referred to under the term 'universality'. Many objects persist through many contexts and exhibit common properties in these contexts; the same laws are applicable to many situations and entities; some signs have a common meaning to a number of persons. Signs are universal (or general) to the degree that they apply to diverse entities and occasions; entities and occasions are universal (or general) to the degree that they may be designated by the same signs. But in neither case do universals constitute a class of entities in addition to the domain of natural processes and acts of symbolization. Mead's account implements more thoroughly than Peirce had done the latter's thesis that the being of universals "consists in the truth of an ordinary predication".

Hence in Mead's cosmology all of Peirce's characteristic emphases are satisfied, but with the important difference that possibility, existence, and mind do not fall apart into realms: they remain as distinguishable but mutually implicative aspects of nature, and their predication in propositional form is valid only under definite and specific conditions. In this way, unless I am mistaken, the ambiguities and difficulties which many readers have found in the Peircean categories are resolved. Just as Mead's social behaviorism avoids the idealistic consequences inherent in Peirce's theory of signs, so does Mead's objective relativism provide the basis for the integration of Peirce's three Realms of Being.

One remark may be added at this point, though it cannot be given the importance it warrants. In our account of Mead's cosmology we limited ourselves to the biological aspect of the concept of the act. It must now be pointed out that the concept of act is only a form of a wider category of process, just as the biological concept of the social is only a particular form of a wider concept of the social. In places Mead used the Whiteheadian term 'organism' for what we called process or act, and then distinguished inanimate and animate organisms.[6] Regardless of the suitability of the terms, the intent is clear: Mead wishes to assert the reality of processes or "acts" at all levels of nature. To this extent natural teleology, Thirdness, chance, and novelty are extended throughout nature. Nature then consists of interrelated social systems or perspectives—nature is social both in the sense that its basic constituents are systems in which the nature of the members is determined by the relationship to other members of the system, and in the sense that these systems are integrated by members which are social in virtue of their inclusion in a number of systems. There is, however, on Mead's analysis no possibility of one all-embracing system of the type found in the absolutistic philosophies. There are sub-biological, biological, and mental levels of nature, and the later levels are interpreted as emergents from the other levels and integrated with them by emergent entities common to all. The terms 'process (or 'act'), 'social', 'emergent', and 'possibility' apply at all levels and in the interconnection of levels, but recognition of continuity is accompanied by an equal recognition of discontinuity, so that Mead, unlike Peirce, Whitehead, and certain contemporary philosophers of science, does not apply throughout nature the concepts of thought, feeling, mind, self, end-in-view, final cause, deliberative self-control—for the good reason that the conditions necessary for the appearance of the phenomena in question are not found throughout nature. Once again we see how Mead's analysis, while agreeing with certain general theses of Peirce, interprets these theses in a more empirical and restricted manner, so that in place of a metaphysical idealism there results a thorough-going naturalistic cosmology.

V

If our account has been reasonably accurate it should allow us to discern both the historical continuity of the pragmatic movement and the possible direction of its future development. We have noticed on the one hand the tendency to submit certain general and metaphorical expressions to a more critical analysis—and in this sense pragmatism has become increasingly less metaphysical and increasingly more empirical and naturalistic; on the other hand, provided we bring Dewey's work within the range of our attention, we noticed a tendency for pragmatism to round itself out by giving its version of all the traditional philosophic interests (logic, ethics, esthetics, social philosophy, cosmology)—and in this sense pragmatism moves in the direction of systematization. More careful analysis and wider attention to fields subject to such analysis: this is the twofold direction which pragmatism has gained from its past and the probable twofold direction of its future.

While pragmatism has been becoming at once more critical and more ambitious, a new flower has come to bloom in the philosophical garden—logical empiricism. Its roots are as deep historically, and its growths have already assumed a sturdy size. Are these flowers of the same or different stock? Can they grow in a common soil? Schiller seems to think not; he apparently finds in the logical empiricist's striving for careful logical analysis the seeds of a new dogmatic absolutism.[7] Schiller's protest at least makes us aware of the persistence of the Jamesean tradition within pragmatism, but since he makes the same criticism of Peirce it is possible that his interpretation is as wrong in the one case as in the other. It is no doubt true that the biological orientation of most pragmatists after Peirce is unmistakably different from the analytic orientation of the logical empiricists. Nevertheless it seems possible to regard the two traditions as complementary and convergent components within a wider and more inclusive movement which I have called scientific empiricism.[8] It must not be forgotten that Peirce's version of pragmatism in no sense weakened his interest in logical analysis or in a theory of meaning stated in terms of the criterion of verifiability. There is evidence in C. I. Lewis and others of the possibility of regaining this wide orientation of Peirce without sacrificing the contributions of James, Dewey, and Mead. From this point of view the logical empiricist's refinement of the techniques of logical analysis and of the empirical criteria of the meaningful are further steps in the direction which Peirce indicated. Thus Peirce's distinction of logical and material leading principles comes to sharper formulation in Carnap's treatment of logical and physical rules; Peirce's stress on the "strata of signs" is developed in the concept of meta-language and in the theory of types; Peirce's stress on the importance of probability inferences is amplified in Reichenbach's theory of probability and induction. In incorporating into itself the attitude of Peirce, contemporary pragmatism is thus moving into the circle of interests which characterize the logical empiricists.

It is also true that the logical empiricists have in their own way been moving with remarkable rapidity in the direction of typical pragmatic emphases. Hahn and Carnap have stressed the instrumental significance of formal structures within the total scientific enterprise; the earlier tendency to regard judgments of perception as indubitable has given way to the recognition that the verification of all propositions is in varying degrees only partial; the empirical theory of meaning has been widened by Carnap[9] and Reichenbach in a way which obviates the main criticisms often raised by pragmatists against positivism; Reichenbach[10] has recently written that "there is as much meaning in a proposition as can be utilized for action", and has himself seen the connection of his views with pragmatism; the earlier somewhat Machian sensationalism has been replaced by a behavioristically oriented psychology; the term logical empiricism is now generally preferred to the term logical positivism, and an empirical realism is explicitly defended by Reichenbach, Feigl, and Schlick; the tendency to neglect the category of the social has attained partial correction in Neurath's conception of social behaviorism;

the growing stress upon the concept of convention, the relativity of logical propositions to a specific language, and the dependence of formal linguistic structures upon rules of operation would all seem inevitably to lead to a more conscious consideration of the pragmatic aspect of thought and language.

In the light of such convergences—and many more might be mentioned on both sides—it does not seem unreasonable to think of pragmatism and logical empiricism as different emphases within a common movement. Peirce was at once formal logician, empiricist, and pragmatist, and all of these points of view are integrated in scientific empiricism just as they are all incorporated in the scientific enterprise itself. In working within this wider perspective, pragmatism will remain faithful to its founder and will avoid a one-sided emphasis upon the biological which has at times hindered the recognition, and led to the distortion, of some of its most central insights. It is true that the logical empiricists have done little with judgments of value or with assessing the cultural implications of science or with the systematization of a cosmology. Here the work of Dewey and Mead may offer stimulation towards a more exact and systematic formulation of their insights which the newer techniques of analysis make possible. That the unity of science movement, with the *International Encyclopaedia of Unified Science*[11] as one of its organs, will in its development enlarge its considerations to include such matters seems certain. Within the framework of the larger movement—whether called scientific empiricism or by some other name—there is manifest the striving for a coöperative intellectual synthesis which would bear to our day the relation which the thought of Aristotle and Leibniz bore to theirs. Within this modern form of the Great Tradition the impulses which have carried the pragmatic movement to its present culmination will be preserved and amplified.

NOTES

[1] Presidential address to the western division of the American Philosophical Association, Knox College, April 23, 1937. Footnotes have been added.

[2] *Collected Papers*, VI. 25 (Harvard University Press).

[3] John M. Brewster, "A Behavioristic Account of the Logical Function of Universals", *Journal of Philosophy*, vol. 33, 1936.

[4] *Mind, Self, and Society*, 181 (University of Chicago Press, 1934).

[5] See Mead's *The Philosophy of the Act* (University of Chicago Press, 1938).

[6] *Philosophy of the Present*, 175 (Open Court Publishing Co., 1932).

[7] See his discussion with the author in the *Personalist*, Vol. 17, 1936, pp. 56-63; 294-306.

[8] C. W. Morris, *Logical Positivism, Pragmatism, and Scientific Empiricism* (Hermann et Cie, Paris, 1937).

[9] R. Carnap, "Meaning and Testability," *Philosophy of Science*, 1936, 1937.

[10] H. Reichenbach, *Experience and Prediction*, 80 (University of Chicago Press, 1938).

[11] To be published by the University of Chicago Press, beginning March, 1938.

Arthur E. Murphy (essay date 1939)

SOURCE: "Concerning Mead's *The Philosophy of the Act*," in *The Journal of Philosophy*, Vol. XXXVI, No. 4, February 16, 1939, pp. 85-103.

[*In the following essay, Murphy attempts to explicate ambiguous areas in Mead's The Philosophy of the Act.*]

With the appearance of this important volume [*The Philosophy of the Act*] one major phase in the task of making Mead's philosophic doctrines accessible to a wider public than that of his own colleagues and pupils is completed. The editors tell us that "except for a large body of student notes, which contain much of interest on Mr. Mead's interpretation of the history of ideas, the present material exhausts all the known literary remains deemed worthy of publication" (pp. v, vi). "Practically all the material from Mr. Mead's own hand was used" and this, consisting in considerable part of alternative statements of a theory which Mead himself never brought to a final formulation, includes much that is repetitive and much that, as it stands, was probably not intended for publication. For students of this original philosophy there is none of this material which will not prove enlightening, and the more difficult and fragmentary passages are frequently the most illuminating. The editors were doubtless well advised, therefore, in presenting so inclusive a selection and, with its presentation, the philosophic inquirer outside the Chicago School and its immediate circle of influence has available the full substance of a theory for which great claims have recently been made and from which, as many of us believe, there is much of primary philosophical importance to be learned.

The theory thus presented remains, however, extraordinarily difficult to understand. This is not due merely or even mainly to the incomplete and fragmentary character of the material. The editors have provided a very full and faithful Introduction, in which the various strands in Mead's doctrine are brought together within the outlines of an "empirical-pragmatic-naturalistic cosmology" (p. lxxiii) which is both comprehensive and systematically articulated. Yet the Introduction is philosophically at least as puzzling as is the text. The difficulty appears rather to arise from an essential ambiguity in this theory itself, which invites and at times even requires us to interpret it in a way consistent neither with its primary intent nor with the facts to which it appeals for confirmation. Many of its most important tenets must be taken in one sense if the philosophical claims of the doctrine are to be made good, and in a quite different sense if they are to have any genuine empirical basis or accurately to describe the processes which they purport initially to be about. The result is that even the reader who is wholly sympathetic with Mead's aim to describe mental behavior as an emergent phase of natural process and "so to state the universe that what we call our conscious life can be recognized as a phase of its creative advance" (p. 515), and who is most anxious to understand his description of the "bio-social" environment within which such mental behavior occurs, is likely to find himself confused and ultimately baffled. He will encounter, for instance, an account of the "emergence" of objects "within the Act" which seems at once to reduce the history of physical objects to that of our ideas of or theories about them and at the same time to assume that these theories can retain their ordinary sense as an account of events and processes which antedate and extend beyond the situation in which theories and hypotheses arise and are reconstructed. He will find statements to the effect that "the interior of the scientific physical object" is or is experienced as "the spatially bounded content of effort in the organism" (p. 438) and be compelled to wonder whether this description is speculative psychology, an analysis of the meaning of scientific statements, or, as the Introduction puts it, an account of "the process by which the enduring thing, the categories and the cosmos implicated by science arise within the act" (p. x). And when this last interpretation is offered as the philosophic dividend of the whole inquiry, he may well be inclined to suspect that "the act" referred to is as dubious a pretender to philosophical ultimacy as its traditional metaphysical rivals, and that the attempt to describe all aspects of the experienced world in terms literally adequate only to some fairly elementary types of biological and social adjustment will have its fruits, as have similar reductive experiments in the past, chiefly in an esoteric language, a systematic confusion in contextual reference, and an interminable controversy with alternative and equally inadequate "isms."

If this should be the result it would be a genuine misfortune. For Mead's philosophy is far more than this, and it provides, in at least some of its implications, the basis for a contextual analysis by means of which confusions of this unhappy type can be eliminated. But it does have this aspect as well, and so long as this is made central, as it is in the present volume both by Mead himself and by his editors, the original and constructive elements in this theory will be far less useful and enlightening than they ought to be, and an important contribution to our knowledge of the mind and its working will be confused with a puzzling speculative reduction of the meaning of statements about physical objects to their function within the empirically insufficient context of "the act."

It is my purpose in the following discussion to show that the confusion I have indicated is present throughout *The Philosophy of the Act,* that it is due to the illicit substitution of "the act" as a pretender to philosophic ultimacy, providing *the* context in which all statements about perceptual and physical objects have their final meaning, for the several specific contexts in which such statements do in fact have their meaning in use, and that its elimination would render more accessible and secure the very considerable contributions that Mead has made to our knowledge of mental behavior. For this purpose it will be necessary to stress the difficulties of the theory and to leave unemphasized many valuable insights included in it. These latter, however, are very fully expounded in the Introduction. That Mead's philosophy offers a pioneer charting of a region of great importance and that we all have much to learn from it is now, I believe, fairly generally agreed. It is, however, a chart that requires critical examination and revision. And it is not a service to the philosophic exploration it is intended to direct to ignore its inadequacies or to treat a blur in its outline as a sign of buried treasure.

II

What, then, is "the philosophy of the act"? Of one of its primary aims there can be but little question. Mental behavior is to be understood as a phase of the creative advance of nature. The meanings appropriate to reflective thought, to scientific description, and to philosophical inquiry develop within the situation in which a bio-social organism adjusts itself to its environment, and are to be interpreted in terms of their rôle in such adaptive behavior. "The act" is in the first place this process of adjustment, and the *philosophy* of the act is an exhibition of reference to such process as both necessary and sufficient for an adequate interpretation of "mind" and its characteristic activities, of the objects, perceptual and physical, with which it purports to deal, and of the meaning and value of its ideas.

But if mental behavior is to be referred to "nature," its distinctive environment, so Mead argues, must go with it. And an adequate account of this environment must recognize its essentially "perspective" character. "Things are what they are in the relationship between the individual and his environment, and this relationship is that of conduct" (p. 218). An object has the distinctive status of "food" only in relation to the wants and digestive capacities of an organism. Similarly the distance qualities of perceived objects are really "there" as directing organic response though they are not normally included in a statement of the "reality" of the physical object. "These characters have actually emerged in the objects and not simply in the individuals, and our statement must include them as actually belonging to the object in the perspective of the individual where they exist" (p. 225). Hence the "objective reality" of perspectives is a necessary correlate of "social behaviorism" as a theory of mind. For mental behavior can only be interpreted as activity in a natural world if the special environment or perspective determined by its adaptive relations is accepted as a part of nature.

There is, however, a rival account of nature and mind which would exclude this interpretation and, in consequence, read mind out of the natural world. This theory has its basis in the mechanical conception of the world fostered and encouraged by "Renaissance science," and is the parent of those dualisms and idealisms which Mead believes have rendered an adequate theory of mind impossible. The root of the trouble "lies in an implication—that this scientific analysis reveals the reality of nature, not only as it was but as it remains in experience, to the exclusion from the same field of reality of all from which this mechanical statement abstracts" (p. 439). Nor is this implication easy to avoid. "It is evident that as long as we assume the existence of a world of given physical particles in motion with given masses, velocities, accelerations, and directions in a fixed space and time, this world will always constitute a noumenal reality of which experience with its objects (including living forms and their environments) will be but appearances, for we shall always refer experience with its novelties to this physical world as providing its structure and necessary conditions" (p. 422).

If, however, the world of experience, with its perspective characters, is extruded from nature it can only be located in a "mind," now thought of not in terms of social behavior but as the locus of "subjectivity" in this wider and more dubious sense. And from such a non-natural mind to the self as an emergent in social interaction there is no intelligible transition. Hence, if Mead's theory of mind is to stand, some alternative account of the status and "reality" of physical objects must be given which finds a place for the validity of perceptual and scientific knowledge but does not involve any such "bifurcation" of nature as that here objected to.

It is at this point that the specific problem and method of *The Philosophy of the Act* emerge. The material contained in this volume is not primarily concerned with the nature of mental behavior on the specifically social level, as was *Mind, Self, and Society*.[2] Nor does it develop, though it does foreshadow, the ambitious speculations about the "sociality" of evolution presented in *The Philosophy of the Present*.[3] Its chief concern is with the status of perceptual and physical objects, as these "emerge" with the anticipatory response of an organism to hypothetical consequences of alternative ways of acting, in the "reconstruction" of accepted theories about the perceptual and physical world in order to remove conflicts and difficulties that block on-going activity and, at considerable length, in that organization of alternative time-systems which Mead takes to be the philosophical meaning of Einstein's theory of relativity. The discussion of each of these issues is ingenious and endlessly painstaking. But the reader who treats these analyses primarily as accounts of the specific subjects with which they purport to deal will miss their philosophical import in Mead's theory. The objects described are brought "within the act" not merely in order to clarify the contextual reference of statements which concern them, but in order to show that they have a derivative and instrumental status

relative to the completion of delayed responses, and are hence not prior or independent "realities" which are entitled to set up in their own right and to exclude organic process and its correlative environment from the natural world. If such objects, philosophically considered, arise "within the act," indeed within the very perspective adjustments previously relegated to mind, then no philosophical rival to these perspective situations for the status of "reality" remains and Mead can claim, with epistemological and cosmological justification:

> The reflective experience, the world, and the things within it exist in the form of situations. These situations are fundamentally characterized by the relation of an organic individual to his environment or world. The world, things, and the individual are what they are in this relation. . . . The peculiarities of the different situations are not those of appearances or phenomena which inadequately reflect an absolute reality. These situations are the reality. [P. 215.]

Viewed in the light of its philosophical antecedents and rivals, this theory is comprehensible enough. Its aim is "to present an unfractured universe, qualitied as well as quantitied, together with all its meanings, and overcome the bifurcation of nature which arose from scientific measurement and philosophic dogma" (p. 516). It is assumed that so long as statements concerning perceptual and scientific objects appear to have a reference beyond the context in which they are used to reconstruct a problematic situation for the sake of "on-going activity" and future consummatory satisfaction, such bifurcation will be inevitable. But "If one regards knowledge as the process of establishing a hypothetical field of conduct in the presence of the conflicts of alternative terminations of acts which are already initiated, thinking is simply the indication of a possible plan of conduct, an extension of the manipulatory area, by placing the content of resistance into the distance characters and thus making them into hypothetical things. The meanings of things are their relationships within this present insofar as these can be indicated" (p. 539). In such a theory "bifurcation" is simply avoided by identifying the context of meaning with that in which no such ulterior reference arises, and that, in its fullest sense, is the philosophical significance of the philosophy of the act. It leaves as "the reality" the sort of situation which Mead regards as of primary philosophic importance, and it reduces to a phase of this reality the "transcendent" objects that appeared to dispute its claim.

Novel as the resulting system is in its content and particular analyses, the philosophical pattern it follows is a very familiar one. A rising philosophy discerns some specific sort of situation which it holds to be indispensable to an adequate view of the world. In this case it is the adaptive "perspective" relation of organism and environment which is thus, and rightly, held to be essential. The new philosophy finds the field of "reality" preëmpted by a rival claimant which would reduce this basic "situation" to a mere appearance. But how better or more effectively remove this rival than by showing the perspective situation itself to be "the reality" and developing within this situation all the meanings and references which were alleged to transcend it? It is instructive to see how naturally the Introduction falls into this "ism" pattern. If we are not to have a philosophy of mechanism, or of idealism as its compensatory outcome, then surely we must have "within the sociobiological framework of pragmatic thought" (p. xi) a place for all major philosophic interests and be able to say that "in the last analysis the entire world of scientific objects is an elaborate instrumentation functioning in the service of social values" (p. lxvii).

A theory of this sort is bound to operate on two rather different levels. As one "ism" among others it shares their common assumption that there must be some primary context to which, "in the last analysis," all meaningful statements must refer. If "the world of scientific objects" were given such a status it would constitute a noumenal reality, a non-natural mind would then be presupposed as the locus for perspective characters excluded from it, and we should not be able to understand reflective thought in its essential and constructive function in human behavior. To this view the philosophy of the act offers an attractive alternative. It is empirical, for it refers statements about scientific objects to a context within experience; it is naturalistic, for it treats reflective thought as an emergent from "bio-social" behavior, and it is able to accomplish these results because, as a pragmatic or instrumentalist theory, it claims to test the validity of ideas by their meaning and use in the activities in which thought justifies itself in operation. Such an account is liberal and constructive in intent. It fits the temper of science and allows the philosopher to use, for his own purposes, the language of biology and social psychology in a very up-to-date and frequently enlightening way. As compared with its rivals, it has much to recommend it.

But there is a different level of philosophical inquiry than this, and a more important one. It is that in which a theory is used to clarify the empirical situations to which it claims "ultimately" to refer. It is to Mead's abiding credit that he was not content, as his disciples have sometimes been, to celebrate the merits of the "isms" in question, but sought also, and primarily, to exhibit its contextual application. Unhappily, however, the very characteristics which, on the controversial level, seem so persuasive, operate here to confuse and frustrate the analysis. The "act" is an impressive philosophical pretender, but it is an extremely unsatisfactory contextual referent. The fact appears to be that there *is* no "basic" activity in terms of which all meaning can be defined, and the attempt to construct one is a source not of philosophical enlightenment but of analytic confusion. Its controversial motivation is wholly understandable, but its results are not. There are many activities in which a reflective thinker is engaged and what he means by his statements is, of course, to be understood by the way in which he uses them and the kind of validation which, in practice, he claims for them. To discriminate such meanings and

refer each to its appropriate context is a work of considerable merit. But it can only be empirically fruitful if the context of reference is that in which the statements do in fact function in their primary and non-philosophical use, *not* one constructed *ad hoc* to eliminate references which, on metaphysical or epistemological grounds, have been found objectionable, and to justify the claims of something or other to be of social significance or objective "reality."

There is no doubt that Mead intended his account to be empirically applicable, and for his insistence on the need of reference to specific situations we can hardly be grateful enough. But it is none the less true that he combined with this intention a philosophical commitment that tended to defeat its purpose. "The act," as required to justify the claims of "instrumentalism," is simply not the activity, nor any one among the activities, in terms of which the rôle of "ideas" in perception and scientific inquiry can be understood. And the difficulty that arises from its illicit substitution for such activities is a systematic inability to deal with these situations on their own terms. This may seem to be a paradoxical charge to bring against this philosophy, but it is one which the evidence, I believe, will substantiate. And an emphasis upon it may serve to center attention on those features of the theory which require an empirical examination which they have so far simply not received. The primary objection to be made against *The Philosophy of the Act,* is not that it robs us of belief in a "transcendent" reality, or brings philosophy down from its "ivory tower" into the world of "life," but that it so confuses the reference of empirical statements that we are never able to keep our eyes on the objects we are supposed to be describing. "By their fruits ye shall know them," and for all its admirable intentions one of the principal products of this philosophy is intellectual confusion, systematically perpetuated for the sake of a theory of knowledge devised to avoid a reference to objects with which, on metaphysical grounds, the author is unwilling to deal.

The consequence of such a confusion of reference ought, if this hypothesis is correct, to show itself in the following way. One aim of the theory is to specify the status of "objects" as they are referred to in perception, or physical theory, or historical inquiry. In each of these fields Mead has an excellent knowledge of the subject and much that is valuable to say. But in no case can he take statements about such objects on their own terms, for that would involve a reference beyond the "situation" in which, in his philosophical theory, all meaning is "finally" to be found. Hence we shall constantly find that he is not talking about such statements in their own proper usage but is reducing them to, or deriving them from, another to which they are contextually inappropriate. This reduction must be made if the philosophy is to work, and it can not be made if the analysis is to apply literally and meaningfully to the situations it purports to describe. Hence the statements in question must *both* retain their ordinary sense *and also* be used in a way with which that ordinary sense is incompatible. It will not be surprising if such a philosophy, even in the hands of as outstanding a thinker as Mead, remains frustrated, esoteric, and incomplete. That the difficulties of *The Philosophy of the Act* arise in this fashion has now to be shown.

III

The relativity of objects, as objects of inquiry, to their place within the activity of research, has long been one of Mead's primary themes. He returns to it in the present volume. The world within which scientific investigation proceeds is a world that is "there" not as infallibly known but simply as the assured basis for action. Objects of inquiry belong to the world that is "there" so long as they are assumed to be actual, and so long as this assumption does not give rise to difficulties. When problems arise, however, within this world, the task of research is to reconstruct it in such fashion that activity may continue to a satisfactory consummation. In this reconstruction objects may lose their objective status and lapse into subjectivity. They are then accounted mere ideas which have failed to justify themselves. But as long as they were accepted as genuine, so long they were genuine objects in the world within which inquiry occurs, though they were "there," of course, only in relation to the activity which treated them as there (cf. 71 ff.).

Now there is a sense in which a description of this sort can be true and enlightening. A change in men's ideas about the world is a change in an objective situation, namely, the situation in which they respond to their environment in terms of what they take it to be. An account of such changes can be an important contribution to the history of ideas. But it can not, without serious confusion, be taken as indicating the context in which our references to the objects of inquiry have their ultimate meaning. For there is presupposed in such inquiry a reference to objects as "there" or not "there" in a physical medium, and as having in this medium a history which is not merely that of what they are *taken to be* for the purpose of on-going activity, but of what in their own nature and physical relations they are. A man may "emerge" as the murderer wanted by the police only several days after the crime has been committed. He becomes "the guilty man," so far as the investigation is concerned only at that time, and his status is notably and objectively changed by this fact. But the whole warrant for his identification is that he was in fact the murderer before he was so identified, and was there when the crime was committed when he was not yet "there" as an object of suspicion.

The paradoxical feature of Mead's contribution to the history of ideas is that in it the derivative status which an object acquires through social acknowledgment defines its primary meaning. Only thus can the objectionable reference to the past as it was, and not as it will come to have been when history is satisfactorily rewritten, be eliminated. Only thus, in other words, can the objects of historical inquiry be reduced to a metaphysically innocuous status within the act of bio-social adjustment. But an historical inquiry whose primary object is simply its own

on-going process is not the inquiry that historians are engaged in when they try to find out what actually happened in the past. To treat it as though it were is to rob it of its primary reference and justification. The transformation that ensues is controversially required if the philosophy of the act is to maintain itself. It is not, however, an adequate basis for the contextual analysis of the meaning of historical statements. And when it is taken as such, the result is a confusion of the sort already described.

In the present volume, however, "the act" is not, for the most part, that of historical research, but the more elementary bio-social adjustment which occurs when the organism by attributing an "inside" to distant stimuli is able to bring the future of its own possible action into the range of its present response. Mead's theory here is in the first place an account of the manner in which an organism comes to treat stimuli not merely as incitements to action but as characters of objects which now possess the "reality" they would be found to have if one were in contact with them, and whose "future" can now be used to organize anticipatory responses for on-going activity. It is made abundantly plain that the object, thus described, has its meaning within an activity which begins with the perception of distance characters and has its end in a satisfying consummatory experience. "By placing the perception of physical things within the act, we find that such perception is not the final character in experience. This is commonly termed 'consummation'" (p. 136). The object thus considered is simply an organization of present responses for the sake of future satisfaction, and is essentially instrumental to such satisfaction. It is a "collapsed act."

Viewed in this light the following statements about physical objects and their status are intelligible. "The physical thing, then, as distinct from a stimulus, is a hypothetical, hence future, accomplishment of an initiated process, to be tested by the contact experience" (p. 25). "The act, then, is antecedent to the appearance of things and of the organism as objects" (p. 147). And especially, "the physical object has an interior in the same sense that the social object, or the other, has an interior. It is one which is provided by the organism tending to act toward itself as the physical or social object acts toward the organism. Indeed the physical object is but an abstraction from the social object. It is this inner content of the physical object which constitutes its matter, its effective occupation of space" (p. 430).

But, in the second place, Mead intends to use "the object" *thus identified* as the ultimate referent for perceptual and scientific statements. It is *this* content which is isolated first in ordinary perception and later in "Renaissance science" as the "reality" of the physical thing, and when relativity physics shows that imputed contact values vary with the motion or rest of the measured object, it rescues the "reality" of the object from this supposititious independence and brings it back within the "perspectives" which, in their present organization for the sake of future action, really constitute "the reality." When a physicist, therefore, talks about the relative motion of measured objects, it is this imputed content of effort or resistance to which he is "ultimately" referring, and the equations he uses express the sociality in terms of which one can pass from one "perspective" to another by "taking the rôle of the other," and in this fashion so represent alternative "futures" of present action as to enable a choice between them to be made and blocked activity to continue. The basis of physical relativity is thus "bio-social."

It is this claim which must be kept in the foreground of attention if Mead's theory is to be understood. I shall examine it on three levels: first, the situation in which external objects are alleged to "arise" within the act when an anticipated future functions (through the organism's capacity to resist its own responses as the object if present would resist) to resolve a blocked or problematic situation and to enable activity to proceed to its consummatory phase. Here the object simply *is* what it contributes to the ongoing act, and to speak of it as a "collapsed act," a future operating in the present and the like, has a literal meaning. The second level is the situation in which objects are perceived as external to the organism, in which a distinction is made between what such objects appear to be and what (in terms of contact values) they "really" are. This is the situation to which, as Mead holds, "the scientist" always returns and in which his statements get their confirmation or confutation. The third level is the situation described by relativity physics (at least in Whitehead's version of it) in which alternative reference systems or "perspectives" are acknowledged and the laws of physics employed for the transformation of the results obtained in one such system into those obtainable in any other. Mead's theory consists in considerable part in an attempt to show that the distinctive traits of the object in (2) and (3) follow from its function in (1) and that the reference involved in statements of these latter types is identical with that of type (1).

The characteristic traits of the first type of situation, in so far as they are relevant to the subsequent derivation, are the following: Reflection, and with it "the object," arise when on-going activity is blocked, and a choice between alternative possible actions is required. The mechanism for the accomplishment of this choice is the representation as present of consequences which are actually future relative to the situation of the organism. This representation can be made only in so far as the organism now plays the part of the future object by acting as that object would act if present. It is able to do this because it has in its repertory a response which is the same in kind as that of the future object. It can resist its own responses as the thing if present for manipulation would resist. This resistance, referable either to the organism's present or the object's future, *is* the inner reality of the object as a physical thing. It provides the basis for the contrast between perspective characters which are "there" for the organism at a distance and control its approach to the object, and the contact values which define the object's reality "where it is." From this the scientific distinction

between primary and secondary qualities follows. This response brings the future into the present, thus providing an object that is "spatially but not spatio-temporally distant from the organism" and defines a timeless space over against the "passage" of the organism's own activity. And it provides the material for that organization of possible futures between which a choice is to be made which has its more developed expression in the space-time of relativity. And since the separation of such contact values from both the distance characters of the object and the final consummatory experience for which the organism is headed is obviously provisional and instrumental, this account removes all appearance of independent "reality" for the objects in question or of external reference for statements about them. Such is the theory.

This theory, even on the bio-social level, requires an empirical confirmation it has not so far offered. That the resolution of a problematic situation involves an anticipatory response in which the organism may be said to stimulate itself as the object if present would stimulate it, and that this anticipatory response is an essential condition for our perception of objects (as distinct from a mere response to stimuli) is a plausible claim. But Mead's theory involves more than this. It claims that this anticipatory response takes the form of an enactment by the organism of the behavior which the object if present would manifest. That is why it seems so clear to Mead that "resistance" must be the "inner content" of the object. "I am prepared to seize the object, and then in the rôle of the thing I resist this grasp, pushing, we will say, the protuberances of the thing into the hand and arousing more effort in the hand by the leverage which the extended portion of the object will exercise, and through these responses of the thing I reach not only the final attitude of prepared manipulation but also a physical object with an inside and an inherent nature" (p. 110). Thus "one pushes from the inside of the thing against the effort one is preparing to exert against it" (p. 195) and this of course while the thing is still at a distance and only pushing through its behavioral deputy.

How is this theory to be understood? It may be that such histrionic pushing is in fact an essential part of the organism's bodily adjustment to the objects to which it is responding. The question is one for a psychologist or physiologist to settle if he can, and in so far as Mead's hypothesis is a contribution to these sciences, its critical assessment must be left to qualified practitioners. To say that in this sense a content of effort "constitutes" the object is to say that it is its behavioral deputy. If this should prove to be true it would be a useful contribution to our knowledge of organic behavior. But it would be wholly insufficient as an account of what we mean by a perceptual or physical object when we are not merely mimicking its behavior in an anticipatory bodily adjustment, but are making judgments that claim to be true about it and in many cases can be verifiably proved to be so. That we *then* represent it as an "inner content of effort," identify its present with its anticipated resistant future, or refer to it merely for the sake of completing a blocked activity does not in the least follow, and is not empirically true. Yet it must be assumed if "the act" to which objects are relative is to be identified with the bio-social drama so far described. The peculiarity of Mead's description is that it must be all of these things at once and yet can be none specifically, since its precise specification in any one context would exclude its use, in the same sense, in a different context, while such use is the basis of its philosophical pretensions.

This at once becomes apparent when we turn explicitly to the analysis of perceptual judgments. A chair is a perceptual object, and perceptually verifiable statements can be made about it. But the object of which these verifiably true statements are made is not a collapsed act, an inner content of effort, or an anticipated future enacted in present behavior. It is a material object. I can sit down in a chair, but I can not sit down in a collapsed act. The inside of a chair is what one finds when it is cut open and this (barring surprises) is solid wood. This chair did not arise in the process in which I organize blocked responses; it was manufactured by a familiar physical process long before I ever saw it. And its use as a means to the consummatory phase of the act depends on its physical relations to other objects, my body among them, relations in which an anticipated future contact experience functioning in a present physiological drama could not stand.

It is true, of course, that all these statements have a contextual meaning which is relative to the perceptually guided activities in which they function. But this context is that in which material objects are seen and handled and described, and the "object" that is here referred to is that of which such statements as "it is solid," "it is the book I was reading yesterday," and the like, are true in their ordinary sense. To say of *this* object that it "arises" within the act, that its "reality" consists in contact values alone, or that I identify its present reality with what it will (or would) be if my present response to it were completed is simply not to describe the object here referred to, but to reduce it to the assumed psychological and physiological conditions of its perception. Such reductions have not been uncommon in the history of epistemology, but they have proved on the whole more productive of confusion than of accurate analysis and description.

Such is the case in the present instance. Mead's theory will work only if "the object" on both the perceptual and scientific level can be literally and adequately described in terms of the alleged process of "bio-social" behavior which constitutes "the act." Hence, as has been seen, the insistence on "resistance" as the "inner" reality of the object and hence the contrast between temporal characters which change their value as the organism approaches the object and an ultimate "spatial" content whose temporal distance from the organism is cancelled since it is now as responded to what a later contact experience would present. If it could be shown that the distinction between primary and secondary qualities is simply an extension of the principle that "the ultimate reality of the

distance experience is to be found in that of contact experience" (p. 16), and if the "timeless" space in which motion and rest have a physical meaning could be equated with that of the "collapsed act" in which a future response is brought into present adjustment and functions as constant while distance characters change, this reduction would be measurably justified. It is in the interest of this reduction that Mead's analysis is made. In terms of it he is led to say that "the 'what a perceptual object is,' is found in contact experience alone" (p. 13) and to speak of a type of ultimate contact experience "in which all the other qualities of the object are lost" (p. 297). But this surely is incorrect. The "reality" of a perceptual object is what in perception it is found to be, and in perceptual judgments color belongs to its "reality" quite as much as shape or weight. It is, of course, true that contact experience has a primary rôle in determining what perceptual objects *are,* as distinct from what they merely appear to be, but this is due to its superior constancy and reliability for ordinary purposes, not to the representation of an inner content defined in terms of contact experience alone. The ground for denying secondary qualities to the objects of physical analysis is found not in the primacy of an ultimate contact experience as defining the "reality" of an object, but in the success of mechanical physics, the development of the modern physiological theory of perception, and the discovery of the finite velocity of light. The qualitative physics of Aristotle did not find the "reality" of a physical thing in its primary qualities alone, nor was it any consideration arising out of such attribution that led to the overthrow of qualitative theories in chemistry. The properties attributed to physical objects are not those which enable the organism to enact their future in its own anticipatory behavior, but those that explain observed physical events. So long as a qualitative physics was found satisfactory for purposes of explanation and prediction, physical reality was described in qualitative terms. And when recent physics found it convenient to treat such "ultimate" contact values as themselves variable for physical measurement, the "reality" of physical objects was not thereby called in question. This matter has been fully discussed by Meyerson[4] and does not need elaboration here. Enough has perhaps been said to indicate that the claim that in physical theory the "reality" of the physical object need be that of an anticipated contact value alone is unwarranted. That as competent an historian of science as Mead should have overlooked this fact is explicable only in terms of his philosophical preconceptions.

Nor does it appear to be true that in either perceptual judgment or scientific description an object's anticipated future is identified with its present reality. If I observe a distant object to be changing I do not take it now to be what it will be when I reach it and thus bring its future into its present. Its present is what it is perceived to be now, and its future is estimated in terms of this present, not vice versa. It may be that I should not thus observe objects unless I were now acting out their futures in the process of my present response to them. But what I observe is not this process (if it occurs) but the object as, by such means, it is now perceived. It is also true that a knowledge of the finite velocity of light may lead me to say that objects now observed are not "now" what or where they are perceived to be, and thus to distinguish physical from perceptual simultaneity. But it ought not to lead me *first* to give the presently perceived object the date of the future response my body is now enacting, thus identifying the future of the response with the present of the object, and *second* to identify this temporal oddity with the relativity of physical simultaneity as determined by physical clocks, time signals, and the like, to motion. Yet it is only when both these steps are taken that the presence of the future in the "collapsed act" becomes the basis for a timeless space in which the future of the object is simultaneous with a present response to it (thus eliminating temporal distance) and such timeless spaces are equated with the alternative time-systems which physical relativity presupposes. In this fashion objects of different types can indeed be brought "within the act," but it is not clear that their status is a really satisfactory one.

It is necessary, finally, to consider the situation described in relativity physics. For it is here that Mead finds clearly established that reduction of the apparently external object to its status "within the act" which is the burden of his own philosophy. The implications of the theory (which he derives chiefly from Whitehead's account of it) are mainly two. First, discovery of the variability of contact values as measured for objects in relative motion is held to reveal the essential "perspectivity" even of those characters which were used to define the inner "reality" of the object. So long as these values were thought to be absolute, a divorce of the physical reality from its place within the act seemed plausible. But "with the analysis of relativity the object that is there returns to its normal position in the situation determined by the individual and his environment" (p. 254). Such perspective characters are objectively real, for they "arise" in the delayed response of an organism which, on Mead's view, defines the timeless space in which the distinction between rest and motion has its meaning, but they are "there" only for such organisms and can not be regarded as transcending such empirical situations. And, in the second place, the space-time organization of such perspectives does not imply an ulterior reality which *is* space-time, but finds its verifiable meaning in the ability of an observer in one time-system to "take the rôle of the other" and interpret his results, by means of physical transformation formulae, in terms that will be valid for any alternative perspective. Hence, as the Introduction tells us, "the world which science presents is disclosed as the inter-subjective world common to various perspectives and the condition for the completion of various acts" (p. lxxiii). It will be seen that space-time, thus interpreted, corresponds to that present organization of possible futures for the sake of conduct which is the meaning of the object "within the act." For alternative definitions of simultaneity there will be alternative futures (and pasts) and these will be really in nature, but only in the situations that involve organic behavior (p.

611). The "sociality" of the organization of such perspectives exhibits their place in bio-social activity and removes any vestige of suggestion of a reality that is "there" behind perspective situations themselves (pp. 251 ff.).

This fits together neatly with Mead's preconceptions, but it does not at all follow from the theory of relativity in its rôle in physical science. If the "reality" of the physical object is identified with its contact (measured) value, then the "perspectivity" of such characters robs the object of any independent status. And if the space-time structure of the physical world depends on the selective interest of the organism bent on securing a presently delayed consummatory satisfaction, then physical theory has indeed been brought "within the act."

But neither of these assumptions is warranted by the theory itself. Presumably, if philosophers are to interpret a physical theory they should know what its statements are about, and this is to be discovered by an examination of the context in which it has an independently ascertainable meaning in use. That context, in the present instance, is a subtle and intricate inquiry into the structure of the physical world on a level somewhat remote from that of ordinary bio-social adjustment. The properties attributed to objects on this level are not those which the organism can enact in its own person, nor those which are found reliable in ordinary perception. They are those which explain the sequence of observable events and direct further inquiry to a fruitful and verifiably accurate result. That measured space and time will vary with the reference system selected is a consequence not of the manner in which an organism selects its future but of the physical properties of the objects in question. It can hardly be this "choice of futures" with which an organism is confronted "within the act," unless, indeed, the activity be that of investigation in theoretical physics and its consummatory goal, an adequate knowledge of the physical world, and for this activity the "futures" as alternatives make no difference to the result achieved, since the laws of nature will be the same whichever is chosen.

Nor is the "sociality" of the result understandable in terms of any other "bio-social" interest than that in discovering invariant laws of nature. If physicists had been concerned primarily in "taking the rôle of the other" they need hardly, for purposes of sociality, have gone so far as to see themselves through the eyes of an imaginary observer leaving the earth with a velocity approaching that of light. That, perhaps, is carrying sociality a little far. The introduction of such an observer becomes intelligible when we see its relevence to a particular development in physics, but apart from this, and the light it sheds on the nature of measured space and time, its value as an extended instance of sociality is not great.

The point is, of course, that the "reality" of the physical object as represented and the "sociality" of the knowledge we have of it depend on what we have good reason to believe that the physical world is like, and are to be accounted for in terms of the inquiry which provides such information. And the considerations that explain both the form the laws of nature have taken in Einstein's theory and the specific properties attributed to physical objects in its terms, are so remote from "the act" and its bio-social objectives that to describe them in terms of it is not to reduce "abstract" theory to empirical reality but to translate its results into the incongruous terminology of social psychology.

Of the philosophical relevance of the social consequences and perceptual basis of even the most abstract physical theory there can be no serious question. But this perceptual basis is essential just in so far as it does verify the theory, that is, gives reason for believing it to be in substantial accord with the actual structure of the physical world, though doubtless capable of endless revision and refinement. And the social consequences that are of primary importance are those that follow from the use to which reliable knowledge of the physical world can be put, in so far as it is knowledge of physical objects and events and thus not merely an organization of bio-social perspectives for the sake of an anticipated satisfaction. If this is made explicit, the "sociality" of scientific inquiry, and its service to social values, can be made intelligible without compromising its primary reference to the discovery of the nature of the physical world. But this would not be sufficient for Mead's theory; it would not bring the objects referred to within the act as previously described. We must, once more, substitute for the specific activity of inquiry a more primitive adjustment in which no such reference is discernible. And thus is a philosophical reduction purchased at the price of contextual confusion.

IV

The conclusions which this analysis has sought to justify are the following. The fundamental difficulty in *The Philosophy of the Act* arises from the attempt to specify the philosophical meaning of statements about perceptual and physical objects by referring them to a context which is incongruous with their actual meaning in use. The choice of this context is determined not by an independent survey of the situations described, but by a desire to avoid certain theories about "reality" and to establish another. It can be controversially defended so long as all parties assume that some philosophically ultimate context must be discovered and that if it is not "the act" it will be a trans-empirical and non-actual reality in which intelligent adaptive behavior will have no philosophical standing. This assumption, however, is quite unwarranted and is in fact incompatible with the contextual theory of meaning whose importance Mead and Dewey have taught us. To abandon it, and to turn attention specifically to the inquiries in which ideas that require philosophical analysis have their meaning, is but to continue that enterprise of making our ideas clear to which pragmatism, in its early days, was committed. It is because that enterprise seems to me a uniquely valuable one that I have here attempted to distinguish it as clearly as possible from the questionable philosophy with which, in this volume, it remains entangled.

NOTES

[2] Chicago: The University of Chicago Press. 1934.

[3] Chicago: Open Court Publishing Co., 1932.

[4] *La déduction relativiste,* Paris, 1925, *passim.*

Kenneth Burke (essay date 1941)

SOURCE: "George Herbert Mead," in *The Philosophy of Literary Form: Studies in Symbolic Action,* Revised Edition, University of California Press, 1973, pp. 379-82.

[*In the following essay, which originally appeared in* The New Republic *in 1941,* Burke offers a mixed review of Movements of Thought in the Nineteenth Century.]

The publishers of these posthumous documents [***Movements of Thought in the Nineteenth Century***] print Whitehead's endorsement as follows: "I regard the publication of the volumes containing the late Professor George Herbert Mead's researches as of the highest importance for philosophy. I entirely agree with Professor John Dewey's estimate, 'A seminal mind of the very first order.'" The editors rank Mead, in the pragmatist movement, "as a thinker of the magnitude of Peirce, James and Dewey." And though the reader will probably feel that a philosophy is here mulled over, rather than formed, I cannot see why he should want to disagree with the above testimonials. Anyone who would cherish with gratitude what of great value may have been piled up in this country, must study these books (the journalistic remaining, as always, for those who prefer the like-water-off-a-duck's-back mode of reading, and will not work over the printed page except when doing puzzles, rebuses and cryptograms).

In search of a text, as a handy way of getting at the gist of these 1,700 or so pages, I should select from the good book, under "Voice—middle":

> Middle voice (*Gram.*), that form of the verb by which its subject is represented as both the agent, or doer, and the object of the action, that is, as performing some act to or for his advantage.

Mead's philosophy of the act, in other words, takes its start in the idealist's concern with the identity of subject and object. The concept of the Self is pivotal, the very word "Self" suggesting the reflexive form, a subject that is its own object. The strategy of romantic philosophy (which Mead likens to the beginnings of self-consciousness at adolescence) was to identify the individual Self metaphysically with an Absolute Self, thereby making the reflexive act the very essence of the universe, a state of affairs that is open to lewd caricature. But Mead, turning from a metaphysical emphasis to a sociological one, substitutes for the notion of an Absolute Self the notion of mind as a social product, stressing the sociality of action and reflection, and viewing thought as the internalization of objective relationships.

Mead calls his social psychology behavioristic, while distinguishing clearly between his brand of behaviorism and that of Watson. The individual's responses are matured by such processes of complication and revision as arise from coöperative and communicative factors. The communicative, in turn, is formed by language, out of which arises the "universe of discourse," and rational self-consciousness is framed with reference to this universe of discourse.

We have been hearing much of "democracy" and much of "dialectics"—and surely Mead's approach helps us to understand the integral relationship between these concepts. For dialectics deals with the converse, the conversational, while democracy is the ideal of expression in the market place, the dramatics of the forum. The truth of the debate arises from the combat of the debaters, which would transform the competitive into the coöperative (somewhat as competitors in a game "coöperate" to make it a good game).

So Mead would envisage the act of reflection as the holding of conversation with oneself—of seeking to contain within oneself, dialectically, the entire drama—of asserting in the form of an incipient act, which is delayed, to be corrected from the standpoint of the "generalized other" ("the attitude of the generalized other is the attitude of the whole community")—and of thus waging this internal dialogue back and forth, in search of truth matured by the checking of an imaginary opponent. It is by this ability (implemented by the character of language) to put oneself in the rôle of the other, that human consciousness is made identical with self-consciousness, that the subject can see itself as object (an "I" beholding its "me"), and that the subject can mature by encompassing the maximum complexity of rôles.

The metaphor of the conversation (uniting "democratic" and "dialectical" by the *forensic* element common to both) is systematically carried throughout Mead's view of human relations. "The parry is an interpretation of the thrust," as one even "converses" with objects, coöperating with them to his benefit only in so far as he allows them to have their say, takes their rôle by telling himself what their modes of assertion are, and corrects his own assertions on the basis of their claims. To "silence" them by the use of one's dictatorial opportunities is to deny oneself the opportunity to gauge their resistances correctly, an imposing of the quietus that would take its vengeance upon him by restricting his available knowledge of reality. Or again, when discussing two phases of universal societies (the religious, which are treated as extensions of neighborliness, and the economic, which are treated in the spirit of Adam Smith's apologetics, as the exchange of surpluses to the mutual advantage of the exchangers), he writes: "One cannot complete the process of bringing goods into a market except by developing means of communication. The language in which that is expressed is the language of money"—where the philosopher presumably so carries out his conversational metaphor as to say, without irony, that "money talks."

The general tenor of Mead's social psychology is in keeping with the promissory mood that went with the happier days of progressive evolution. Here man the problem-solver looks with Whitmanesque delight upon the state of affairs wherein each solution is the basis of a new problem. Mead considers the possibility that, in seeking to encompass the total conversation, one might make of oneself an internal wrangle, with more of heckling than discussion (particularly where he would identify himself with a society in which subgroups are at odds)—but characteristically, he treats this as a complicating factor, as something to look out for and try to guard against, rather than as a basic element of discord in his picture.

The books covers a vast range of material. *Mind, Self and Society* is the volume in which Mead's sociological pattern is developed. *The Philosophy of the Act* deals with his devices for transferring his concepts of sociality and perspective into cosmological interpretations, wherein he uses the physicist's theories of relativity to his purposes. And *Movements of Thought in the Nineteenth Century* is a highly serviceable historical treatment of trends since the Renaissance, mainly centered upon matters of science and revolution. It is a great loss to the quality of discussion in America that the volumes were not publicly available during the period of upheaval and recasting that went with our attempts to refurbish our individualism for collective necessities after 1929. One might conceivably sometimes want to put pluses where Mead put minuses, and vice versa, particularly where Mead considers social developments, in promissory fashion, as a straight line towards a kind of ideal League of Nations. Again and again, one misses Veblen. But particularly in his remarks on attitudes as incipient acts, on modes of identification, on personality and abstraction, on the relations between the biological and the social, and on thought as gesture, his writings seem to map out the field of discussion for forthcoming years.

Unfortunately, the piety of Mead's disciples has worked against him somewhat, as they sought to preserve for us his every word rather than to seek condensation and saliency. For there is another sense in which these books hinge about the metaphor of the conversation. They are composed mainly of transcripts from classroom discussion, so that much is repeated, and is said loosely. As a result, there are many paragraphs, but no sentences.

Grace A. de Laguna (essay date 1946)

SOURCE: "Communication, The Act, and The Object with Reference to Mead," in *The Journal of Philosophy,* Vol. XLIII, No. 9, April 25, 1946, pp. 225-38.

[*In the following essay, de Laguna provides a critical analysis of a few of the central ideas of Mead's philosophy that she deems confused and inadequate, such as human acts, cooperation, and communication.*]

Whether John Dewey's estimate of George H. Mead as a seminal mind of the first order is acceptable or not, few will deny the importance of his thought or its continuing influence. It is because I have found his writings stimulating and provocative, and at the same time confusing if not confused, that I have been led to attempt a critical analysis of some of the central ideas of his philosophy.

The most fundamental concept is that of the "act." The analysis of this is the central theme of Mead's philosophy, and it is as specialized developments and variations of this central theme that his theories of the physical object of science with the separation of space and time from spatio-temporal order, of emergence, of self and mind, language and reflective thought, are all treated. Whether his treatment of these topics as they appear in his three published works, *The Philosophy of the Present, Mind, Self and Society,* and *The Philosophy of the Act,* actually constitutes a systematic body of internally consistent doctrine, I am not concerned to consider. My purpose is rather to inquire whether his formulated doctrines do justice to his own insights and make adequate use of his own fundamental concepts.

Acts, as conceived by Mead, occur in nature wherever there are living organisms.[1] An act is not a mere temporal series of passing events, but it is a process directed toward an end, in which the consummation is functionally present in the beginning, controlling the process. Even the twining of a plant is not a mere senseless series of movements in different directions, but is a continuous activity of turning toward the light. It is this constant fixity of end that gives unity to the series and constitutes it an act. At a higher level the act occurs in a more complex but fundamentally similar fashion. The animal which sights or smells its prey at a distance stalks it in anticipation of eating it. The stalking is not merely locomotion toward the distant object, but is itself preparation for the final spring, as the spring, when it occurs, is preparatory for the seizure by the jaws and the consummation of chewing and swallowing. As his mouth may water and his digestive juices begin to flow from the first smell of the distant prey, so the end is present to the active organism from the beginning.

Human acts, from perception to reflective thinking, emerge from such behavior as this, and exhibit the same fundamental structure along with new and distinctive features. Human acts are essentially social. The human being, even in the securing of food, does not act merely as an individual, but as a member of a group engaged in concerted action for a common end. His individual acts, at least so far as they exhibit mind and intelligence, are "abstracted fragments" (Charles Morris, ed., *Philosophy of the Act,* p. ix) from such a complex social act. The human individual, indeed, has a mind in so far as he has internalized symbolically the social act.

"Sociality" is thus in Mead's philosophy a concept almost, if not quite, equal in importance to that of the "act" itself. Like the act, sociality occurs at different levels. Its most general definition is given by Mead in *Philosophy of the Present* as "the capacity for being many things at once." Thus at the highest level organized society depends on the capacity of men to be at once fathers and husbands, citizens, philosophers and rulers, officials of a political party and patriotic citizens, and, above all, complete individuals and members of society. If these claims conflict, such conflict marks the limits of the sociality achieved. At the human level sociality appears also in the objects of men's acts. The gold in the eternal hills becomes a wedding ring, a king's treasure, or a prisoner's bribe. So a book may be at once achievement of an author's ambition, a publisher's remainder, and an evening's delight to a reader. At a lower level, sociality is found in the flower of the plant which is at once a means of propagation for the plant and a source of food to the fertilizing bee. Taken in its widest generality, indeed, sociality appears even within the act, in that like a melody it must have the end present in the beginning and the whole in the part. Even so the specious present is social in that it includes within itself as integral to it past and future.

If this concept of "sociality" is illuminating, affording opportunity for wide and fruitful application, it is not without danger. For in being generalized it may become so abstract that its application in particular cases, especially the more complex cases, may lose its significance. For example, it might well be urged that inanimate objects are also social. A cloud casts a shadow and contains particles of moisture; water dissolves sugar and precipitates lime; the same body is part of the crust of the earth and of the bed of the Pacific Ocean. If to be social is to have the capacity for being many things at once, then everything existent is social.

That Mead does not always escape this danger is perhaps more evident in his treatment of the concept of "coöperation." Yet no one has done more than he to distinguish coöperation as it occurs at the human level from the simpler form of coöperative action among the lower animals.

I do not find any general definition of coöperation given by Mead such as he gives of sociality, but we may gather its meaning from his usage of the term. A favorite illustration of coöperative action is a dog fight. It not only takes two to make a fight, but for the fight to continue it is necessary that the acts or gestures of each dog should stimulate the other to a response, which in turn serves as a reciprocal stimulus to the first. It is the rôle played by the behavior of one individual in stimulating the response of another that Mead treats as the significant feature of coöperative action. If it seems ridiculous to us to call a dog fight coöperation, that is because the dogs have no common end. The result of their reciprocal behavior, the continuation of the fighting, is not indeed what either dog wants; on the contrary each is trying to end the fight, although in opposed ways. Mead's failure to consider a community of end to be essential to coöperation, as evinced by his use of this illustration, is even more evident in his extending the concept to include responses to physical objects. One could not walk, Mead points out, unless the ground resisted the pressure of our feet; so also our handling of objects involves a reaction of resistance on their part which is the counterpart to the pressure exerted by our hands. It is owing to this mutual resistance that we are led to attribute a dynamic "inside" to objects and become aware of our own bodies. In manipulation, as in the dog fight, the pressure of the hand against the object calls out the resistance on the part of the object, and this in turn excites the organism to further manipulatory exploration and response. Perception of the object (which I wish to consider in more detail later) occurs in so far as the organism responds to the distance stimulus (vision) by anticipatory preparation of manipulatory response, thus, as Mead says, playing the rôle of the object in stimulating itself as the object would if it were "at hand." All manipulatory action, like walking, or indeed any bodily movement, thus is essentially coöperative in that it can be maintained only through reciprocal action and reaction between the organism and physical objects. But this extension of the concept is possible only if the "end" of the action is identified with physical effect. The walking organism may indeed be directed toward an end and so perform a genuine "act," as Mead has defined it, but to impute this to the inanimate object in its mechanical resistance, is to rob the concepts of both "coöperation" and of "act" of all theoretical significance.

Mead's emphasis on the reciprocal stimulation of one another by coöperating individuals and his neglect of the end as an essential factor in coöperation has further consequences of great theoretic importance, both in his analysis of communication through significant symbols, and in his analysis of the physical object of common sense. In order to show this let us make certain distinctions.

A number of individuals may be said to be engaged in "composite" action when each contributes independently to a joint result. An example of "composite" action would be the accumulation of a pile of stones by a number of individuals each of whom deposits a stone whenever he passes a certain sacred spot. Here the end is merely individual or private.

A group of individuals engage in what we may call "concerted" action when, on the other hand, the movements of each are controlled and adjusted to the movements of others. The movements of a grazing herd would be an example, and so also would be the hunting of a pack of wolves, or the behavior of ants or bees.

The end of concerted action may be "shared," but it is not a "common" end. The end of the concerted hunt, for example, is shared in that the kill is made and the food secured through joint acts. The food is there for all but for each severally, since each eats only his own individual food. Each wolf may be said to hunt only *for* himself, although he hunts *with* others in concerted action.

Genuinely coöperative action is to be distinguished from this in that it is directed toward a *common* end. An end

is common when its being an end for one individual is integral to its constituting an end for the other. Most distinctively human ends, the "goods" of life, are of this sort. The housewife will not usually cook a dinner for herself alone, nor can any of us enjoy a feast in solitude, much less if the food disgusts or nauseates a companion. Let us, following Mead's example, indulge in a little social psychology to discover what is involved in this fact.

A human being is so constituted that the expression of emotion in another individual calls out an answering emotion in himself. Sometimes this is reciprocal, as when your angry looks directed at me rouse my anger toward you, or my fear of you. If your emotion or your obvious feeling is not directed toward me, but toward a third person or object, I may also be roused to emotion directed either toward you, as when a child's fear of a dog arouses the tender reassurance of his older companion, or toward the third person or object, as when the child's fear arouses the mother's anger toward the threatening dog. A man naturally loves at least some other human beings not merely in the sense of entertaining tender emotions toward them, but in the sense of cherishing them and making their welfare and happiness his own end. But this involves more than a mere emotional response toward others; it involves the apprehension of others as acting for ends, as directed upon objects, and of objects as matters of concern for others. It also involves the distinguishing of living conscious beings from inanimate objects, first, as acting in pursuit of ends, and, second, as hostile or friendly both to ourselves and to others. Furthermore it is through the apprehension of others as friendly or hostile, and thus as acting toward ourselves as ends, that we become aware of ourselves as selves and of others as other selves. It is only individuals who are selves who can have genuinely common ends and who can coöperate for these ends. Such ends are sought by each individual because they are apprehended as ends for others. Such ends must first be apprehended in their relationship to others as well as simply "there" and secondly this relationship of being ends for others is intrinsic to their being an end for the self.

Now I do not intend to assert that this psychological analysis is foreign to Mead or even that every point just made is not to be found in his writings. It is rather that he does not make adequate use of the distinctions involved in such analysis in his treatment.

What I wish to emphasize is this: as common ends can be sought as common only in being apprehended as ends for others, so others can be apprehended as selves with whom one may coöperate only so far as they are recognized as acting towards ends in relation to oneself. Being selves is never a merely reciprocal affair between two individuals, in which they are mutually ends and means for each other. There must always be involved the relation of each to a third factor, an end objective to each, which is integral to their reciprocal relationship to each other. It is this which Mead neglects in his treatment of human coöperation and communication through significant symbols.

Animals coöperate, he tells us, in so far as the behavior of one acts as a stimulus to the other to carry on its part in a composite enterprise. Human coöperation differs from this in that the vocal gesture uttered by one individual not only acts as a stimulus to the other to an appropriate response but *stimulates the speaker to the same response.* Along with his own response he arouses in his hearer sociality. The essential feature of the development of communication, writes Mead,

> is the stimulation in one organism that is exciting another to the same response that it arouses in the other. The vocal gesture is pre-eminently adapted to this function because it affects the auditory apparatus of the form that produces it as it does the others. The final outcome in human social conduct is that the individual, in exciting through the vocal gesture the response of another, initiates the same response in himself and, in the attitude of the other, comes to address himself, that is, he appears as an object to himself in his own conduct [*The Philosophy of the Act,* pp. 189-190].

Now Mead is led to make this formulation because of the very depth of his insight into the nature of communication. He points out as no other writer has done the conditions which must obtain if communication is to take place. If I criticize his treatment for its inadequacy in certain fundamental respects, it is because I recognize the importance and value of his contribution. The importance of his analysis of language lies in this: The utterance of sounds does not become language from the fact that it stimulates the individual who hears them to respond in such a way that an end for both is secured. The dog who obeys the command: "Fetch the ball!" has enjoyed no communication of meaning; he has heard a signal, if you please, but he has not heard what Mead calls a significant symbol, even though the man has himself uttered sounds which for him are such symbols. They would become significant for the dog only if he were able to play the part of the man and himself use the words to elicit a similar response from another. To use sounds or other gestures as significant symbols one must be able to play both the rôle of the speaker and that of the hearer. One must, in Mead's terms, "play the role of the particular other and the role of the generalized other." We may find an illustration of Mead's meaning in the playing of any organized game. Such a game must have rules and the individual in playing it must act as any other player in his position would act. Thus a football "tackle" must play the rôle of a particular other ("tackle" and not "center") and he must also play the rôle of a generalized other in that he must play tackle as any "tackle" would play. Moreover, he is playing against individuals who are themselves playing particular rôles in a generalized way. Using a language is playing such an organized game. To speak intelligibly one must use standardized sounds in a standardized way, one must speak, for example, in the first person using the form of the verb to agree with the

first person singular. Convention may establish, to be sure, that on occasion, perhaps in some forms of literary composition, one avoids this usage and uses the editorial "we," or even speaks in the third person, as "the present writer." But whether I use "I" or "we" or the impersonal form, I must speak or write as any user of the English language would do under similar conditions. It is this unique individual, indeed, who speaks, but I, who speak to be understood, must speak as any "I," and you, my intelligent listeners, must hear as any "you's." If you and I could not do this, we could not cooperate as citizens of a state in its essential democracy, nor could we be moral beings, subject to a self-imposed categorical imperative; we would not, in short, be rational beings at all. Mead thus exhibits the use of significant symbols as constituting the very essence of rationality, the ability to play the rôle of the generalized other. It is the use of such symbols which is the fundamental manifestation of rational intelligence, upon which all other forms of rational activity are dependent.

If rational thought, like virtue, is essentially ideal and a function or character of the soul within, rather than of the individual as a natural creature in his public dealings with his fellows in an external world, as Mead himself would urge, that is because the rational and moral individual is one who has attained selfhood in becoming another to himself. Man may be born with a soul, as no animal is, if you please, an intrinsically rational being; but his soul remains dormant, his rationality merely potential unless he is aroused by his fellows to coöperative action and the achievement of language. It is only when the give and take of reciprocal stimulation and response to others has become internalized in the form of inner conversation, when one has learned to address oneself as another and to respond to such address as to another that one has become a self or achieved rationality. One thinks reflectively in order to find answers to the questions one asks oneself. But one asks and answers such questions as any self or any other, in short, as a rational being. Such is the ideal function of language as Mead's profound insight has disclosed it. But this ideal inner function is correlative with its natural public function in controlling coöperative action toward distant ends. The analysis of the one function must yield a corresponding analysis of the other function.

Let us return to Mead's formulation. The use of significant symbols involves genuine communication, says Mead, in so far as the speaker not only stimulates the hearer to a response toward a distant end, but in so doing stimulates himself to the same response he elicits from the other. The meaning of what is said, Mead states, is to the hearer the response he makes, and the identity of meaning for speaker and hearer, essential to communication, lies in an identity of response on the part of each.

> We must be constantly responding to the gesture we make if we are to carry on successful vocal conversation. The meaning of what we are saying is the tendency to respond to it. You ask somebody to bring a visitor a chair. You arouse the tendency to get the chair in the other, but if he is slow to act you get the chair yourself. The response to the

vocal gesture is the doing of a certain thing, and you arouse that same tendency in yourself. You are always replying to yourself, just as other people reply. You assume that in some degree there must be identity in the reply. It is action on a common basis. [*Mind, Self and Society,* p. 67.]

The reader of this passage (and there are many such passages in Mead's writings) is torn between appreciation of the point Mead wishes to make, and repudiation of what he has actually said. The difficulties are so many and so obvious that it is hard to decide where to begin criticism. If one takes it at its face value it seems to involve the absurdity that it is only in being stimulated by the sound of our own voices that we come to understand what we say, in which case the problem of how we are able to formulate significant remarks would be insoluble. But leaving this obvious absurdity, we are still faced with the difficulty of equating the meaning of what is said with the response made to it. Even in a case where it might most plausibly be urged, for example of a command which "to hear is to obey," the obedience is a response to the command as uttered by the proper person under proper circumstances and not to the symbolic expression itself. This may retain a constant meaning while eliciting the most diverse responses on different occasions. The naughty child evinces his understanding of his mother's command, "Come in and do your homework!" as much by running away, or by pleading a headache, as by obedience. Nor is the mother's understanding of her own command to be found in any incipient tendency on her part to play the particular rôle to which she tries to incite her child. An incidental, if important, weakness of Mead's formulation is its failure to make any distinction between the three fundamental forms of speech, the command, the declaration, and the question, in their relation to responsive behavior. The command is, of course, intended by the speaker to elicit a particular response, even though its meaning can not be equated with this response. A declaration has a far less direct relation to response, and the response may be symbolic reply or an act of primary behavior. A question demands a symbolic reply, and if by its meaning and form it prescribes a range of possible answers its meaning is not to be equated with any particular response. A question may, indeed, like any form of speech, express a *double entendre;* it may be used to convey a threat, or an insult, or a compliment, and one may reply to the intention thus conveyed. But, and this is essential to the significance of symbolic utterance, it could not convey the intended threat or insult unless it had a symbolic significance independent of this particular use.

Yet Mead is right so far as he is contending for an organic relation between meaning and response. One who speaks to us in a foreign tongue which we do not understand leaves us blank and baffled. On the other hand we test the understanding of our students by the replies they make to our expositions or to the statements of the text. We may even devise a cunning examination such that an affirmative answer to a question is conclusive evidence of the student's understanding a given proposition and a negative answer equally conclusive evidence of his failure to understand. And in asking such a question the examiner has certainly prepared the answer, his own answer, in advance. Test of communication, of identity of meaning as between teacher and student, would surely seem to lie here in identity of response on the part of the two communicants. But this would be a hasty and ill-judged conclusion. For the reply of the student is to the *question* primarily rather than to the statement the question is designed to test. And it may happen, as we professional examiners know only too well, that the student may have misunderstood the question when quite clear about the statement at issue. To discover this, we must ask a second critical question about the first, and assume that this is understood if we would test the understanding of the first question.

If I have labored an obvious point, it is in order to emphasize the all-important fact that speech as a symbolic act is only a *conditional* determinant of response. This is equally true whether the response be an act of primary behavior, or a reply in symbolic terms. The statement "Your house is on fire!" may be made with the intention of rousing you to suitable action, but it does not prescribe what this action is to be in the particular case. The significance of the statement is not to be identified with your actual response, nor is it exhausted in any list of possible alternative responses you might make. It has a universality which is not reducible to any number of alternative particulars. Similarly, if a remark is made in conversation with the intention of eliciting a reply, its symbolic significance is not to be identified with the rejoinder, however relevant such rejoinder may be. Actually, of course, one replies to what one takes to be the intention of the other in making the remark; one interprets the remark as made by the particular conditions. In this sense conversation involves a playing the rôle of the particular other. The first speaker "adapts" his remarks to his particular hearer, and the hearer "interprets" the remarks addressed to him by the particular speaker. In some sense language is always *used,* is *directed* to some audience or special public for some purpose. Whether like the radio speaker skillfully conducting political propaganda, or the scholar reading a Platonic dialogue, one must adapt and interpret and thus play the rôle of the particular other. Apart from such directed use it may well be urged that language has no meaning, symbols no significance. But the propagandist could not make the particular use of language that he does make if the words and phrases he utters did not have a universality of significance which makes them usable for other purposes and on other occasions. Nor could the scholar begin to interpret Plato without an understanding of the terms of his discourse; he must interpret what Plato means in terms of what Plato says. Both speaker and hearer must, in short, play the rôle of the universal other in order to play the rôle of the particular other, and neither can play this rôle unless the other is playing it also. There is indeed an identity of action between communicants, but it is not an identity expressible in terms of particular acts. Playing the rôle of the universal other must necessarily be carried on, actualized in a particular rôle. It is like an essence which can exist only as the form of a concrete individual along with accidents. The particular accidents may vary but the essence remains the same.

The fundamental fallacy of Mead's treatment of communication is thus akin to that of the English empiricists. It lies in his reduction of the shared universality of symbolic significance to a mere identity of particulars.

If we now turn to his treatment of the act and the object we may find a complementary inadequacy in his analysis of the object. We have already seen that he analyzes coöperation in terms of the reciprocal control of one another's acts, neglecting to analyze the nature of the common end to which such acts are directed. The community of end recognized by Mead seems to consist in its being the end of identical responses on the part of the coöperating individuals. Its status as the end thus lies in its place in the act of each as a particular response. Now coöperation, it must be acknowledged, can take place only in a world not only of common ends but of common objects. A common end is an objective end and any object, as such, must be intrinsically capable of being common either as potential end or potential means. An object must be intelligible, knowable by intelligent rational beings. Even if we distinguish the object of perception from the object of judgment, we must recognize that the objects perceived are such as can be judged. So the objects constituting the field of action of a rationally perceiving individual must be such as may be constituents of the field of another's action.

The object of human perception, as Mead analyzes it, is the spatio-temporal or physical object. ("Physical" object here does not mean the object of physical science but that of ordinary human experience.) It is the colored, fragrant, substantial, resistant thing, large or small, hard or soft, round or square or pointed, now existing at a distance and enduring in its self-sameness as I move toward it or away from it, and while handling it at arm's length. That it is such as this, Mead explains, is due to the fact that it is the manipulatory object of an organism with visual distance receptors, the object of man uniquely endowed with mutually adjusted eyes and human hands. It is not the consummatory end of a human act, as is food, for example, for manipulation is not a consummation, but a halfway stage in the completed act. A human being perceives an object because he sees something not only to be reached presently by taking so many steps toward it, but something he can handle and look at simultaneously, seeing what he touches and touching what he sees. From his first glimpse of the distant vision he is preparing his manipulatory response, incited by the vision to stimulate himself as the thing would if within his grasp, thus playing, in Mead's phrase, the rôle of the other and so generating both object and his own bodily self. He thus organizes in advance, by a sort of preliminary ideal trial and error of tentative alternative manipulatory movements, the completed act which leads through prepared manipulation to final consummation. It is because the human act is thus broken by the intervening manipulation

while still remaining a single continuous act directed to a constant end, that primitive passage is bifurcated into exactly and permanently simultaneous spatial positions on the one hand and a succession of discrete temporal instants on the other.

I am not concerned to discuss here the subtleties of Mead's treatment of space and time. Leaving this aspect of his philosophy aside, let us consider quite naturalistically and naïvely Mead's analysis of the object in terms of manipulation. As he pictures it, handling an object is (appears as) a preparation for consummation, a halfway house between seeing and eating, for example, in which man may peel his fruit or dismember his prey before putting it into his less efficient human mouth. That human manipulation is more and other than this, Mead is, of course, as well aware as you and I. But he does not take account of this in his analysis. The object of human perception, as he analyzes it, is the object one handles directly; its hardness and resistance lie in its reaction to direct pressure, its shape and size are perceived in terms of the stretching and flexing of fingers and hand moving in contact with its contours. But the simple and all important fact is that man's hand is a tool-using hand. He perceives objects in perceiving them as possible tools, or as things to be reached and poked and pounded and shaped by means of tools. He perceives a tool, to be sure, as a thing he must grasp with a certain strength of fingers and hand, but also as long enough to reach one object and not another, of a shape and size to fit one aperture and not another, as heavy enough to smash a given object when thrown, sharp enough to cut with, etc., etc. Manipulation is no mere transition between distant vision and final consummation, not a stage in a single act, but a focal center from which radiate out an interlacing network of possible acts.

If manipulation is considered as it is in itself, as a handling and moving of fingers, hand, and arm in relation to the body, it falls into a limited range of possible movements and combinations of movements. There are alternative ways of grasping and handling any object by itself. The organism has a repertoire of possible alternative direct responses, and, as Mead analyzes it, it is in the anticipatory selection and organization of these that the perceived object emerges. The object is thus essentially a factor, or element, within the particular act, sharing the limitations and particularity of the act. But such a limited and particular object could have no identity with itself from act to act, nor could it belong to a world, as common to other individuals. If, however, manipulation be considered not merely as grasping and direct handling, but as the manipulation of a tool in dealing with a third thing, it is no longer restricted to a limited repertoire of manual movements. It is not that the engraver or the woodsman or the baseball pitcher acquires an increased manual dexterity, a great range and fineness of movement, but that the manipulation of a tool-user may enter as a factor into an indefinite number of possible acts; they belong within a system which may be extended, complicated, and organized without limit.

Being an object is not merely an affair between itself and the human individual. One does not perceive an object merely as so far away from oneself, but as above or below, behind or in front of, or beside other objects and at roughly determinate distances from them. So one does not find its physical massiveness merely in its direct resistance to the pressure of the hand, but through the blows of the axe on the tree, the crushing of the glass, the thrown stone, or the rebound of the volleyed tennis ball. An object can appear as an object only within a field containing other objects and immersed in a continuum bringing them together with one and other and with the percipient individual.

It must be recognized, however, that it is only as moments of directed activity that objects are perceived or cognized. To see, one's gaze must be focused and one's attention be directed, and it is only through such directed focusing that a field is organized in which objects appear. Such directed activity determines a perspective, not merely visual, but dynamic. As visual perspective selects or determines aspects, in their particularity uniquely characterizing the perspective, so the directed act determines dynamic aspects. One perceives what is relevant to one's end and is blind to the irrelevant. But these perspective aspects do not themselves constitute the visual field, nor do the perspectives of nature constitute a world, as Mead maintains in his ontology. We do not constitute the objects of our perception and thought by what Mead terms "the fitting together of perspectives." Nor do we, while in one perspective, include another within it. If in some sense we are limited to aspects, we see them as aspects of the objects we perceive. Perspectivity is not merely a fact of perception for the percipient. Thus the object is perceived as more than the visible aspect; it is cognized as more than it is apprehended as. Nor is this "more" a limited more, to be exhausted in the aspects of other familiar perspectives or such as have been experienced in the past. There is, indeed, in all cognition, a limitation by negation, but if certain possibles are excluded, there remains an inexhaustible potentiality. In short an object of perception is an individual and not a mere particular exhausted in confinement to a particular act.

So far as perception is cognitive, however, one perceives an individual object as a particular case of some universal. Thus the stick of wood I pick up to put on the fire is an individual object but I perceive and pick it up as a stick, of appropriate size and shape, to be laid in its place in the fireplace. So any tool is such through its shape, its size, and other universal properties, which it may share with innumerable others. It is at once an individual and a particular case of a universal. It is as a particular case that one deals with it on any given occasion; one selects, for example, a pencil from the number of objects lying on one's desk, and one selects it and uses it with a view to the sharpness of its point, the color and hardness of its lead. One is immediately concerned with it only in respect to its relevant aspects, as a factor in the act in which one is engaged. But one is prepared for the interruption of one's writing by the breaking of the lead; the pencil now becomes an object to be sharpened and other aspects spring into view. If in the process of sharpening we suddenly discovered that the lead did not go the whole length of the wooden cylinder, or if it explode in our hands, we should be surprised, and we should then recognize that what we had taken for a pencil was only a fake or something mysterious. But even though we found it was not the pencil we had mistakenly perceived it as, we should still perceive it to be the same individual object. The original object has not disappeared and another taken its place as we cease one act and begin another. In fact we perceived the pencil all along as an individual which was more than it was perceived as (to adapt a familiar locution of Dewey). We perceived it not only as a pencil to write with but as one in need of frequent sharpening, but if we did not perceive it as the fake incapable of being sharpened or as an infernal machine, we did perceive it all along as an individual and as such charged with potentialities. We are constantly surprised and often meet the unexpected, but we are nevertheless prepared for the surprising and we expect the unexpected. Otherwise we should be incapable of learning anything new or recognizing a mistake as a mistake. It is because the objects of perception are genuine individuals that they can be objects of knowledge about which judgments can be made. And it is also because they are perceived as individuals, inexhaustible in their reactions to the act in progress, that they may be objects for the acts of others, genuinely common objects concerning which we may discourse significantly to others.

Nor is the act which determines the perspective in which objects must appear to be known (since all our knowing is in some perspective) merely a particular act. Mead truly asserts that the acts of thinking human beings are fragments of social acts embracing other acting individuals, even though he fails to make adequate application of this conception. But an act must also be an incident in, or a phase of, the life of an enduring and becoming individual, who lives in and through the living of others. As an incident, each act passes, and as a phase it is complete. Nevertheless as the act of a conscious intelligent being it is experienced as belonging within the broken continuum of living. The range of my action like the range of my vision is limited to an environment determined by my actualized powers and in turn determining me in my possession of them. But the environment in which I act, like the scene which I see, I recognize as belonging within the wider continuum of a world, beyond the range of my action, but merging into it as into the unseen distance beyond my vision's range. Only an act which belongs to the continuous living of an individual and is carried on within a world can yield either a self or an object known.

NOTES

[1] It may be of interest to compare the author's own discussion of "the complete act" in *Speech: Its Function and Development*, chap. viii.

David L. Miller (essay date 1947)

SOURCE: "Comments and Criticism: De Laguna's Interpretation of G. H. Mead," in *The Journal of Philosophy*, Vol. XLIV, No. 6, March 13, 1947, pp. 158-62.

[*In the following essay, Miller responds to de Laguna's criticism of Mead's philosophy, asserting de Laguna's analysis is irrelevant, trivial, and lacks perspective.*]

It would be surprising indeed if Mead's immediate students would allow Professor de Laguna's interpretation of Mead to pass without further comment. She speaks of Mead's failures, inadequacies, and fundamental fallacies without, I think, having Mead's broader perspective and problems in mind. Mrs. de Laguna says she is "not concerned to discuss here the subtleties of Mead's treatment of space and time." And she makes what I consider to be a false statement, namely, "'Physical' object here [for Mead] does not mean the object of physical science but that of ordinary human experience."

What I am suggesting is that without an appreciation of Mead's physical theory it is impossible to understand his doctrine of sociality at all, and if one does understand Mead's broader problem, as stated more fully in *The Philosophy of the Act* and especially in *The Philosophy of the Present,* Mrs. de Laguna's criticisms seem trivial if not altogether irrelevant. Let us consider some of the points she makes.

"Mead's failure to consider a community of end to be essential to coöperation, . . . is even more evident in his extending the concept to include responses to physical objects" (p. 227). Mrs. de Laguna's argument is that "coöperation" should not refer to acts beyond the human level and to human acts only when the persons engaged have a "common end" clearly conscious to all engaged in the act. Obviously this is a matter of definition of "coöperation" as Mrs. de Laguna will recognize, but I suppose she would contend that Mead's definition (at least his use of it) is insignificant. This I want to deny. What Mead wants to explain is that there are different kinds of coöperation even as there are different kinds of sociality, but that fundamentally all kinds involve some sort of interaction. Mead wants to get at the genetic and biological basis of the more complicated and historically later kinds of coöperation by starting with the simple type. He uses the "dog fight" as a simple type of coöperation in order to explain exactly the difference between that kind of interaction and the kind that is possible when "one can call out in himself the same response that is called out in the other." Since Mead does this, it is consistent for him to take the *act* as a primitive concept or as a metaphysical basis with reference to which all types of *interaction* are made intelligible. If Mrs. de Laguna wants to substitute the word "interaction" for "cooperation," that is legitimate provided it is used in a significant way and is used consistently. But we would still have the problem of explaining the qualitative difference between types of interaction from a naturalistic point of view.

Apparently Mrs. de Laguna wants to reserve the word "coöperation" for acts in which communication by way of significant symbols is involved. Mead did not choose to so use that word and, therefore, any criticism of his use of it must be from the standpoint of his consistency in the use of it. That is the challenge he presents to his readers. I do not think Mrs. de Laguna has found any inconsistency. Rather, as any reader will find, Mead's general use of "coöperation" enables him to develop a theory of universal sociality in *The Philosophy of the Present.* There he writes: "The social character of the universe we find in the situation in which the novel event is in both the old order and the new which its advent heralds. Sociality is the capacity of being several things at once" (p. 49).

Obviously if one starts with social psychology, as Mead did (and one must start somewhere), and if one assumes that the universe hangs together in an intelligible manner, then it would be easier to carry the fundamental concepts into related fields and finally into a general metaphysical system. It is not only easier for Mead to generalize the concept of coöperation and sociality, but it is a significant part of his philosophy in the sense that he believes the logical structure of nature, in so far as it is intelligible, must have its basis in the structure of the social psychological process of interacting, communicating social selves. Mead's problem is not: Which is fundamental or primary, the self or society? Rather it is: What is the functional relationship between selves and society? And although Mead is able to state the qualitative differences between the *I* and the me (the subjective and the objective) his main problem is to show how communication takes place. Here it is important to note that adjustment due to the novel (the emergent) is the central issue in Mead's philosophy[2] and that, just as communication takes place between and among selves because of novel situations and just as the novel is the stimulus for reflective thinking, so in all non-human interaction the novel is the basis for adjustment and for sociality. He writes:

> The social nature of the present arises out of emergence. I am referring to the process of readjustment that emergence involves. . . . I am here using the term "social" with reference, not to the new system, but to the process of readjustment.[3]

It is not practical at this time to go further into a discussion of Mead's use of "coöperation" and "sociality." But let us proceed to what Mrs. de Laguna considers a fundamental weakness in Mead's conception of "communication"; namely, communication takes place when one, through significant symbols, calls out in himself the same response that he calls out in the other. Mrs. de Laguna cites the common case (p. 232) in which "The naughty child evinces his understanding of his mother's command, 'Come in and do your homework!' as much by running away, or by pleading a headache, as by obedience." Certainly Mrs. de Laguna misses the point here. It is simply this: In so far as the mother calls out the same response in the child as she calls out in herself, there has been communication. Mead does not say "calling out the same response in the other as one calls out in himself'' means both listener and speaker must perform the act overtly! The response usually takes place only covertly in the one who gives the command and must take place covertly in the listener *before* it can take place overtly. But it may not and need not take place overtly in either speaker or listener. Nevertheless communication does not take place unless the response in both communicants takes place covertly. It may also, and often does, take place overtly in the listener. The *attitude,* the tendency to respond (the idea of the act—the internalization of the act—the collapse act), must be alike in at least two persons before communication is possible, and if that tendency to respond alike has been effected through symbols, there is communication. The child must first have the attitude of doing homework or the implicit response of doing it *before excuses for not doing it can be made.* In turn, in so far as the mother responds implicitly to the excuses there is further communication between the two. But without these implicit responses, there could be no communication, and they constitute the nerve of communication.

We must remember, further, that Mead defends the proposition that men condition themselves (through significant symbols and reflective thinking) and, therefore, *select* the stimuli to which they respond. Consequently if it were the case that every person always carried out the command of another person, there would be no selection. But nevertheless selection implies alternative possible courses of action, the rejection of some, and the acceptance of others. Mrs. de Laguna leaves us with the impression that communication requires an immediate explicit fixed response to the symbols of the speaker. Communication can not require that sort of response necessarily. That would be more like conditioned response in which there is no communication necessarily.

Mrs. de Laguna writes further:

> Being selves is never a merely reciprocal affair between two individuals, in which they are mutually ends and means for each other. There must be involved the relation of each to a third factor, an end objective to each, which is integral to their reciprocal relationship to each other. It is this which Mead neglects in his treatment of human coöperation and communication through significant symbols. [P. 229.]

I do not think Mead would subscribe in full to the above quotation. If Mrs. de Laguna means that coöperation and communication can take place only when the communicants have the *same end,* then I believe she is mistaken. I do not understand Mead to say this and furthermore, I believe he denies that this is necessarily the case. It could be set up as an ideal, and possibly Mrs. de Laguna intends it to be so, but in fact it is not always so and need not be so in order to have both communication and coöperation. Whether it is desirable is another question. We find that Mead does treat this problem carefully in his article **"The Genesis of the Self,"** and elsewhere. He writes:

> A social act may be defined as one in which the

occasion or stimulus which sets free an impulse is found in the character or conduct of a living form that belongs to the proper environment of the living form whose impulse it is. I wish, however, to restrict the social act to the class of acts which involve the cooperation of more than one individual, and whose object as defined by the act, in the sense of Bergson, is a social object. I mean by a social object one that answers to all the parts of the complex act though these parts are found in the conduct of different individuals. The objective of the act is then found in the life-process of the group, not in those of the separate individuals alone.[4]

> If the social object is to appear in his experience, it must be that the stimuli which set free the responses of the others involved in the act should be present in his experience, not as stimuli to his response, but as stimuli for the responses of others; and this implies that the social situation which arises after the completion of one phase of the act, which serves as the stimulus for the next participant in the complex procedure, shall in some sense be in the experience of the first actor, tending to call out, not his own response, but that of the succeeding actor.[5]

The mother and the child may have different purposes or ends when the child "does her homework." Yet there is coöperation and communication. The buyer and the seller may have different motives for a business transaction; yet there is communication and coöperation. Is it possible to have absolutely common motives and still have individual selves? This is the question to which Mrs. de Laguna must address herself in her criticism of Mead's "neglect." Mead never intended to suggest that the self can or should identify itself with society. Rather communication and coöperation can take place in a world in which selves maintain their peculiar identity. As we have indicated above, his problem is this: What is the functional relationship between selves in a community of selves? But Mead could never subscribe to the rationalistic, idealistic tendency to sacrifice the individual to the "whole."

NOTES

[1] See "Communication, the Act, and the Object with Reference to Mead," *Journal of Philosophy,* Vol. XLIII, (1946), pp. 225-238.

[2] See the writer's "G. H. Mead's Conception of 'Present,'" *Philosophy of Science,* Vol. 10 (1943), pp. 40-46.

[3] *The Philosophy of the Present,* p. 47.

Van Meter Ames (essay date 1956)

SOURCE: "Mead and Sartre on Man," in *The Journal of Philosophy,* Vol. LIII, No. 6, March 15, 1956, pp. 205-19.

[In the following essay, Ames contrasts Mead's view of man with that of Jean-Paul Sartre.]

Mead and Sartre have much in common. Both think of life as process and transition, taking time and moving into a future that requires constant revision of the past, so that nothing is ever settled and anything can be thrown into question. But Mead relies on the life-sciences; Sartre would like to reject them in favor of a supposed higher outlook. The reason is that his nineteenth or seventeenth century notion of science, including psychology, is mechanistic and deterministic. So he feels obliged to get away from science to make room for freedom, whereas for Mead science is the great means of increasing freedom. Sartre almost prefers magic to science, and apparently would if he did not believe that he can rise above science and magic to Husserl's transcendental grasp of consciousness as its own pure source.

Beginning with his dissertation, *L'Imagination* (1936), he accepts a mysterious unbridgeable chasm between the existence *in itself* (*en soi*) of things, and consciousness, which can never be a thing because it exists in a way that is *being for itself* (*l'être pour soi*). Consciousness is pure spontaneity over against a world of things in sheer inertia. This is simply a reassertion of the Cartesian dualism between thought and extension. Sartre inveighs against traditional psychology for treating psychical facts as things—particularly for not distinguishing, except in degree, between image and perception. He contends that an image is radically different from an object, concluding that an image is an act and not a thing.

Mead would agree that imagination is an act, if not that an image is, and would locate the image within an act. He says: "Imagery may be found at any place in the act, playing the same part that is played by objects and their characteristics." He explains that the image differs from an object in being "the continued presence of the content of an object which is no longer present."[1] Sartre also says that what appears as image appears as absent, and that this accounts for the relative poverty of what is imagined, as compared with what is perceived: the latter lending itself to endless observation and discovery, whereas the image is limited to what is retained from the past.[2] Mead seems to differ from Sartre in seeing that imagery and perception are intermingled instead of regarding them as dichotomous. Mead notes that images "may merge into immediate perceptions, giving the organism the benefit of past experience in filling out the object of perception; or they may serve to extend the field of experience beyond the range of immediate perception, in space or time or both. . . ."[3] Sartre's closest approach to Mead on this point is in *L'Imaginaire: Psychologie phénoménologique de l'imagination* (1940), where he notes that "each affective quality is so profoundly incorporated in the object that it is impossible to distinguish what is felt and what is perceived." But even here Sartre does not intend to recognize a fusion of perception and imagination, for he goes on to say that in "the constitution of the unreal object, the part of perception is played by knowledge

(*savoir* as learning from past experience), and it is with the latter that sentiment is incorporated."[4] Instead of admitting a coöperation of perception and imagination in the object, which might then be called both given and imagined, he sets up two kinds of object: one real, which is perceived, albeit with an admixture of feeling for it; and one that is unreal, imagined, again with feeling, though on the basis of experience (*savoir*) of such an object in past reality. Before long, however, Sartre abandons his dichotomy enough to grant "a liaison between the unreal and the real," inasmuch as "every apprehension of the real as world tends to complete itself through the production of unreal objects. . . ." This is because such apprehension involves "a free reduction of the world to nought, and this *from a particular point of view.*" He says further that the correlative of free consciousness "must be a world carrying within it the possibility of negation . . . by an image. On the other hand, an image, being a negation of the world from a particular point of view, can never appear except *on the basis of a world* and in connection with that basis." Thus "being in the world . . . is the necessary condition of imagination."[5] It comes through Sartre's mysterious language that he cannot after all avoid agreeing with Mead that imagination mixes with perception.

Both men speak of the act as central to an interpretation of human life, but Mead's assumption that the act is the act of an organism is in contrast to Sartre's squeamish separation of the human from the animal or the physical. Charles Morris has remarked: "Perhaps the most important single contribution of pragmatism has been the development of a general theory of mind upon an empirical basis." Also: "The tendency to individualistic subjectivism is the accompaniment of an inadequate theory of mind."[6] It is for lack of such a theory that Sartre's often acute insights are vitiated. He sees no way to acknowledge free creative intelligence short of lifting mind or consciousness above the facts accessible to science, because he thinks of these as simply physical and hence mechanistic. That the nature of the physical is altered when it enters into a living organism has not dawned on him; much less that activity on the level of mind could arise within the interrelations of organisms, as they act and interact in their environment, and come to respond to events as signs. Sartre's shortcoming here is in the limitation of his reading in philosophy and psychology, which is almost confined to French and German and some classical British writers. Although he makes a few references to William James, these seem to rest upon quotations he has come across here and there, and show no real appreciation of his work. So empiricism means Hume and the associationists to Sartre. Darwin is lost on him, with all that Darwin has meant to Mead. The result is that Sartre, although he thinks he rejects idealism, is pretty much of an idealist, in holding that the psychical must be kept out of the meshes of the physical—as if here were two disparate realms rather than two levels of reality.

In *L'Imaginaire*, as in *L'Imagination*, he finds the act to be the key to imagination, rather than little images of things out in the world. But he still supposes that the act of imagining is distinct from the act of realizing or perceiving—instead of being part of the latter, or a remembrance or anticipation of it. He must say that memory and anticipation differ from imagination, in focusing upon what is there in retrospect or on the way to being there ahead. Yet in *L'Imaginaire* he comes close to Mead's account of gesture as the beginning of an act, warning of what is to follow if the act is carried out. Sartre speaks of the future as the *real* development of the form begun by the stroke of a tennis racket. He speaks of the arabesque hidden by a chair as the complement of the act of moving the chair. Again, in *L'Etre et le Néant,* he has something like Mead's conception of the unity of the act, in speaking of the present as receiving from the future the feel of a beginning.[7] But Sartre cannot speak of imagination as foreseeing what is about to happen, because this would destroy his dichotomy between the real and the imagined. He does, to be sure, say that an image is based on or borrowed from past acquaintance (*savoir*); but he does not, like Mead, see that, regardless of the origin of imagery in past experience, "its reference to the future is as genuine as to the past," though "it may be there without immediate reference to either future or to past."[8]

Mead would say that the future is genuinely future in not yet being set in its course, because not yet existing. How could even infinite intelligence previse what is not there to be observed ahead of time? For Mead the future always arrives with some unforeseeable aspect, whether negligible or quite surprising, even though some broad features can be predicted with high probability. Sartre, on the contrary, has to regard the future as already real, so far as it can be prevised at all, since otherwise he would have to say with Mead that it is extrapolated from the present through imagination; and the imagined for Sartre is only imaginary, in a dimension that cannot become real. He is obliged to say: "To posit an image is to constitute an object outside the totality of the real; it is to hold the real at a distance; to be emancipated from it; in a word, to contradict it."[9] This is important to Sartre because he requires it to refute the determinism he identifies with science. He says: "We need not fear to affirm that, if consciousness were a succession of determined psychic facts, it would be totally impossible for it ever to produce anything but the real. For a consciousness to be able to imagine, it must, by its very nature, escape from the world . . . it must be free."[10]

For Mead it is not necessary to escape from the world in order to be free. The world is there, with its past, as formulated by science and culture, through laws and institutions which establish lines of responsibility; but the world and its past are being made over by men, as individuals and as members of society. Indeed men become whole, as Mead sees it, in the degree to which they can enter fully into the process of reconstruction that they find going on and help to guide. No man calls everything into question or tries to change everything at once. The world is accepted as given except where a problem is felt. There the creative intelligence freely goes to work, especially in research science.

What Sartre says about techniques and projects is in the Promethean spirit of science, though he does not appreciate science. Mead has the advantage of interest in various sciences, where he sees the actual and practical functioning of human freedom, overcoming obstacles and distances. For him the sciences are the great example and explanation of progress. Sartre shares his view of the past as what must be left behind to make the future realizable,[11] and notes that it would be only an honorary past that had no connection with the present. Though there is no indication that he ever heard of Mead, he comes near Mead's ***Philosophy of the Present*** in saying that, instead of merely receiving our past, we have to choose it in relation to the end we choose.[12]

Men could scarcely have had this idea of the past before the modern development of research science and its technological applications. Now the idea is becoming accepted and even taken for granted. But Sartre's statement picturesquely exaggerates the obsolescence of the past, as if it could be sloughed off completely. Mead has more piety, in not forgetting that what we are is determined by what we were as well as by what we do. For him, when we emerge into or bring about a new state of affairs, it comes with its own temporal scheme; that is, with its own past, present, and future, within which what happens is determined. Thus there is a new past for each new situation, fitting it as much as its future does. The emergent novelty is explained as conditioned by and resulting from a chain of events which could not have been prevised—could only be seen by hindsight from a subsequent present. In retrospect any new departure can be traced back to what preceded. The foundation is found, afterwards, solid as need be. With its support a further transformation can be wrought, which in turn makes it possible to reach back to somewhat different and hitherto undiscoverable antecedents. Psychologists have long recognized the selectivity of memory in relation to ends in view, but have assumed a fixed absolute single past within which what was relevant to a new occasion was picked out. They did not see that each new present calls for a new past to fit new specifications—before Bergson, Einstein, Whitehead, Dewey, and Mead, with their sense of time's creative edge and relation to the surge of life into a future that is future in breaking loose from the past, until the past is recast to obliterate the break.

Sartre is too much imbued with the age he lives in not to feel the increasing speed with which his generation rushes into the unforeseen, which cannot be foreseen before it is settled, however much what is in the offing can be anticipated or dreaded. He has pointed out how the contemporary novel, especially American, in contrast to the Victorian type, which comfortably chronicled what had already taken place, in the past tense, now plunges the reader into all the uncertainty of the unfinished. In his own novel of our mid-century he even outdoes the American writers he admits learning from, in giving the intensity of the moment, which is momentous because loaded with an outcome that depends on what is still undecided, what is yet to be done, by a character identified with oneself, and by others over against him, while it is painfully brought home that in an actual situation a person may find himself doing something he thought he had rejected. The future hanging on what may or may not be touched off in the present, Mead reads in the sciences, biological, social, physical, as they increase control of choices and release chances harder to control. But one must read Mead, or what Mead has read, to appreciate the kinship between serious fiction of our time and his philosophy. Sartre as novelist has done his homework, not as philosopher; at least not for today. His being thoroughly of today in his very makeup gives him a grasp that no amount of study might equal, though it might prevent some of his intellectual distortions or exaggerations. At any rate, not only as novelist but as philosopher, he is in accord with Mead that the significance of what is past depends much upon what is coming, which in turn may depend upon what we do. "It is the America of 1917 which decides the value and significance of La Fayette's undertakings."[13]

The old problem of free will versus determinism, as a question of man's being entirely free or not free at all, is left behind by Sartre as well as by Mead. Both see man as at the same time free and unfree, though Sartre inconsistently speaks of absolute freedom. He sees the ambiguity of any situation as partly resisting and partly yielding or helpful, in relation to a project. He notes that the world is not simply there unalterably, since man can act upon it through freely chosen ends and techniques.[14] He says that, while we may feel confined by the place we are in, aside from human presence there would be no space or place. The original and absurd fact is my being here rather than there.[15] It is my projected action which makes my place a help or hindrance; and what would be an obstacle for one person is not for another. So it is free choice that creates obstacles and distances, to overcome them in progress toward the future. We must recall, however, when Sartre omits it, the fact that the world is there and we are in it, in one situation or another. What we make of it is our own making. But if we are to live we must make something favorable of what we are up against, and it may not be easy. Sartre plays down the odds when he is playing up freedom; but when he dwells on them he lets freedom dwindle to a metaphysical nothing.

He forfeits the effective aid to freedom that Mead finds in science. Sartre regards it rather as establishing merely external relations which suppress potentiality; as Aldous Huxley in *Brave New World* and George Orwell in *1984* have presented science as fatal to creative human living. Mead, to be sure, notes that the research scientist works at reducing novelty to determinism by reconstructing the past to account for emergence. But for Mead science discovers and produces genuine novelty. The new is always the head and front, and it wags the tail of the past, which must follow each new lead in order to fit to it. If there is paradox here, it is not at the expense of a free future, always freshly escaping reduction to the past. Sartre turns the apparent contradiction between the fixed

and the free against freedom. He makes being so Eleatic that potentiality can be nothing more than a kind of nothing.[16] If what is is static and solid, becoming must be something that is not. Then if man can act he must do it by negating what is, what is there; must introduce lack into the world, the incompleteness that leaves room for possibility.[17] To act is to have a future; that is, to unveil the possibilities of things. So Sartre says that if man were a pure present a match would be just a white splinter of wood with a black head. It is through and for him, as an agent moving into the future, that it becomes a match, or that an inkwell becomes an inkwell. Almost like James here, Sartre sees things as utensils in view of the uses found for them. Yet he persists in thinking of the scientists as reducing things finally to mere external thereness, despoiled of implication of any creative transforming activity. One wonders how, except through a too literary education and reading unscientific philosophy, he could so completely miss the freedom that Mead equates with research science. Sartre walks right up to this insight without seeing it when he says it is through action that man projects his possibilities into the *en soi,* the bare thereness, giving it the potentializing structure of perception.[18] For Sartre science is not, as for Mead, the enhancement of human activity but an inhuman abstraction from man's actions, in search of a manless world. Granted that objectivity in this sense is part of science, and may still fascinate some men of science, it is an outdated and emptied-out notion compared with the actual practice of research as it brings human operations to bear upon nature, to find out what will happen *if* a certain apparatus is set up and a certain procedure followed. This involves knowing, so far as possible, what is there apart from human intervention; but theoretical no less than practical investigation hinges more and more upon the question of what will happen *if* certain steps are taken. And if knowledge and doing are indissoluble, then the *en soi* and the *pour soi* must be inseparable. The Cartesian dualism in Sartre's thinking is incompatible with the methodology of science.

Dualism is also irreconcilable with Sartre's own sense of the continuity of experience. But as a dualist, in spite of treating the fixed and the free as actually mixed up, he tries to separate them. His theory of emotion depends on separating them. Emotion is for him the shock of shifting from the world as fixed by mechanistic determinism, which he associates with science, to a sudden freedom from it, which for him is magic. In his *Esquisse d'une Théorie des Emotions* (1947) he elaborates this idea of emotion as a break from the rational fitting together of means and ends to a realm of wonder and horror where distance is abolished and action does away with mediation. Physiological phenomena do not cause or constitute emotion but show the seriousness of the emotional transformation of the world. Emotional conduct and the emotional state form a synthesis, in Sartre's view. So he feels that he has advanced beyond what he calls the physiological explanation of James to a theory of emotion as signification; as referring to what it signifies, which is nothing less than the totality of human relations with the world. But he says that his phenomenological psychology of emotion calls for an *a priori* intuition of human reality which could be given only by a pure phenomenology. The trouble is that "while phenomenology can prove that emotion is a realization of the essence of human reality so far as it is *affection,* it is impossible for it to show that human reality must necessarily manifest itself in any particular emotions." This is a factual matter that must be referred to the empirical approach, which "will probably prevent forever a joining of the psychological working back and the phenomenological working down."[19]

There could scarcely be a more revealing confession from Sartre. In the same breath he discounts scientific empiricism for not rising to a transcendental vision, and admits that this vision is blind to the facts. His forte and his undoing are melodramatic dichotomies which no sooner make the bold impression of flouting sense and science than he has to go back on them. As *en soi* and *pour soi* are ranged against and outside each other, as consciousness is pitted against thing, so is freedom set against mechanism, until a liaison is uncovered to mitigate the absurdity. An evolutionary view of grades of being, with new levels emerging from previous ones, through a new organization and relation of what had been merely physical or physiological, is beyond his philosophy. Thus freedom for him must be mysteriously introduced as a kind of nothingness into a being that is too solidly what it is to make a place for anything but a nothing. Personality as conscious must be other than what it is, in order to be free. Yet Sartre is constrained to admit that free acts always take place within situations, which have a "coefficient of adversity." He contends that something can always be done about any adversity whatsoever. It may be observed, however, that if a situation pains a person or weighs on him at all, so that he needs to do something about it, he is far from going scot free. Merleau-Ponty is clear that the idea of situation, the admission that we are inextricably mixed up with the world and other people, "excludes absolute liberty at the very base of our entanglements."[20] Sartre's own assertions and admissions, taken together, come down to something like a sensible view of freedom as relative. Yet he continues to speak of freedom as absolute. Mead avoids such obfuscation by considering the organism free when it "enters entirely into the act as a whole," and deprived of freedom so far as disintegrated by compulsion. Thus "there are degrees of freedom in proportion to the extent to which the individual becomes organized as a whole." It follows that people become more free as they are able to reconstruct their situation into an order that "is more adequate."[21]

Mead and Sartre both see man as free to make his way and make himself. Sartre puts this in terms of man's being such a being that he can "understand more or less obscurely his human reality, which means that I make myself man in understanding myself as such."[22] But, for lack of an empirical account of the self as a natural process, he is obliged in his main work, *L'Etre et le Néant* (1943), to say that selfhood is characterized by separation from what it is, by all it is not, which means that the self must emerge in nothingness in order to get away from what simply is and hence is foreign to self. For a self to appear; it must appear in nothingness; the world itself must be suspended in nothingness, and the realization of this is anguish.[23] Mead not only can account for the emergence of the self without such hocus pocus, but can welcome it as an advance to enjoy. For Sartre it is something to suffer; and man's being somehow free of the determinism of all that just is, Sartre regards as a terrible burden. He says man is "condemned to be free."

Mead and Sartre agree that human freedom needs an independent reality to work on and work over. Mead sees that the mechanical causations and connections in nature enable man to make plans and carry them out. Sartre does too, though he takes Heidegger's attitude toward means and ends as utterly uninteresting. At any rate Sartre recognizes the value of *given* circumstances as fitting together in relationships that human activity can turn into techniques. He notes that planned action could not take place if not for the indifference of the field of action provided by the *en soi*; also that the independence of things makes for a "margin of the unforeseen."[24] This calls for the readiness of intelligence to swerve and try another tack, which Mead honors as creative. Thus both thinkers focus on the act, and refuse to consider it as determined by the past. For both, the act is a project guided by its goal. Sartre generalizes that man "decides upon his past under the form of tradition in the light of his future,"[25] and practically says with Mead that we organize our world through our acts. For Sartre an act is not only to be understood as a project of the self toward one of its possibilities; he speaks of a correspondence between my possibilities and my world somewhat as Mead speaks of the close relation between organism and environment.[26]

Mead would sympathize with Sartre's delight in the heightened sense of freedom (contrary to his pessimistic expression of being "condemned to liberty") in "those marvelous and extraordinary moments when the earlier project founders in the past in the light of a new project which surges upon its ruins and so far is only sketched; when humiliation, anguish, joy, hope, are closely knit; when we let go to seize and seize to let go. . . ." It is after this zestful passage that Sartre compliments the behaviorists for considering that "the only positive psychological study should be that of conduct in rigorously defined situations." He thinks, however, that the behaviorist idea of conduct destroys itself, since the determination to act is itself an action, of a sort that is not a movement but an intention—which cannot be explained by anything given but only by a goal breaking with the given. Mead's behaviorism is modified enough to allow for guidance by anticipation of a goal. So he would agree that the given cannot become a motive except in relation to something not yet there in actuality. Obviously he could not accept the fantastic twist which Sartre gives to this account in saying: "it is in the light of non-being that being is lighted up" and "nothing-ized."[27]

The deep difference between the two thinkers is that Mead's outlook is social as well as scientific. Sartre thinks of the person or *pour-soi* as somehow there alone, living his life in freedom, then suddenly being disagreeably limited in discovering the presence of others. He has to grant that being with the other is perhaps the original fact, but could not accept Mead's biological and social explanation of the genesis of the self: from the give and take of the organism with its fellows, when it reaches the level of communication. The human and humanizing factor is for Mead the significant symbol: the sign with the same import for user and receiver. Thus a man can tell something to another and tell it to himself at the same time. Hearing and understanding his own words as the other does puts him in genuine communication. Sartre does note that a man can see his own sentence as another does.[28] He also sees with Mead that a sentence is always to be understood with reference to a situation; and that words get their meaning from their use, as a hammer is revealed by hammering.[29] He even assumes that the use and setting of words must be social; as the individual must find his way in a world that is a world for others. Yet he regards their presence as just part of the given complex of means and ends which can be employed as techniques. Sartre's individual thinks of other men as means rather than ends; and as diabolically transcending the status of *his* means to reduce him to *their* means, for their ends, if they can. This is for the most part true of Sartre's fictional characters. The hero of *La Nausée* is presented in such isolation that he scarcely has the problem of relating to other people. In the long novel, *Les Chemins de la Liberté,* almost without exception, each person sees the human condition through the author's eyes: sees it as social only in the sense that the individual is up against other individuals.[30] Sartre's world is practically devoid of anything like Mead's notion of sharing with others, caring about them, merging with them in a "generalized other." Sartre's claim to humanism may seem to lie in this direction. But he is driven to it by desperation, as the soldiers are driven to it in the third volume of *Les Chemins,* when they have been defeated and are waiting to be captured. This kind of humanism still fits the anti-social philosophy of *L'Etre et le Néant.*

Some of Sartre's insights are anticipated by Mead, as when he says that the most powerful stimulus is that of another's gaze. Mead does not find it Medusa-like, but feels the need of guarding privacy; noting that the forms of politeness serve to keep others off as well as to promote intercourse. For him, however, annoyance with social relations, avoidance of them, even attack upon them, does not mean that they seldom or never exist in deep and heartfelt fashion; but is owing to excess of them, to maladjustment or some abnormal condition. For him, contrary to Sartre, men turn against fellow-feeling only when driven from it. They do not have to be driven toward it. In fairness to Sartre, Miss Murdoch points out that in his *Situations,* and in his pamphlet *L'Existentialisme est un Humanisme,* while he may feel forced toward "a kingdom of harmonising ends wherein human wills are to be united,"[31] he also seems to yearn toward the remote possibility of such a kingdom as what ought to replace the actual and utter loneliness of the individual which he takes to be the common lot. Loneliness is the plight of the individual almost throughout his long novel, *Les Chemins de la Liberté.* Miss Murdoch finds in the fourth volume "one hint . . . of real emotion, in the personal sphere . . . in the relationship of Brunet and Schneider." But she observes that the author appears embarrassed about it and that it "remains unanalyzed."[32] If she is right that "Sartre wishes to affirm the preciousness of the individual and the possibility of a society which is free and democratic," she recognizes that he has no foundation in his philosophy to justify such values. "The universe of *L'Etre et le Néant* is solipsistic."[33]

It is desperately hard for Sartre to make room even for solipsism in his universe. To do it he feels obliged to defy nature and science. He presents the human individual as an anomaly, an impossible set of possibilities, a kind of nothing coming about through a weird rotting of reality. In turn, man's discovery of being is through the irrational revelation of an *a priori* insight which owes nothing to experience. Sartre leans on Husserl's transcendental teaching that the ego constitutes not only itself but all objectivity, including that of other selves.[34] This is the line of Sartre's attempt to refute the charge of solipsism. He declares that "the characteristic of the being of human reality is that it is its being *with* others." Yet he comes right back to solipsism in saying, "I discover the transcendent relation to others as constituting my own being." I do not grasp "being with others" first of all in the world, in a way that would be "indispensable to my own existence, since I existed before the meeting." I come upon "existence with others" through "making explicit the pre-ontological comprehension which I have of myself."[35] Having my being made up before surveying the world or meeting other people, is intended to keep the self free of any determining influence. And Sartre has been equally afraid of forfeiting the freedom of the self by allowing it to have any original structure such as Husserl's transcendental Ego would have. In his article on *La Transcendance de l'Ego*[36] Sartre repudiated the ego as anything more than the spontaneous fitting together of states and acts. But he has kept the intimate sense of being a self. Though he has felt obliged to consider it a kind of nothingness, to avoid a defining essence, the self retains for him what he calls "human reality." And he refers to it in *L'Etre et le Néant,* if not by the term "ego," by many other designations: man, self (*soi* and *pour soi*), ipseity or *selbtstheit,* one (*on*), *Dasein,* I (*je*), my own being (*mon être propre*), and myself (*moi-même*).[37] Still his attempt to deny the self any original nature, or any biological or social genesis, is a barricade of big words against genuine inquiry, beside Mead's account of a self arising naturally and understandably as the give and take of organisms gradually arrives at communication.

Lack of any such evolutionary and social view of the self is the reason for Sartre's violent theory of value. He bases value on what he considers to be the unlimited liberty of the individual, and draws the corollary that *nothing* justifies any choice. To him it is anguish to realize this; for then any value, any scale of values, can be questioned or overthrown. He feels: If we do not usually worry about this, it is because we do not think about it. Each of us is involved in a world of values, always in a situation with its exigencies in connection with projects under way, in a course of conduct with its corresponding honesty and taboos. We are kept in line by "alarm clocks, signboards, tax notices, policemen, as so many guard rails against anguish." But when one of us thinks about it, "all the fences, all the railings collapse, destroyed by the consciousness of my freedom: I have and can have no recourse to any value aside from the fact that it is I who maintain the being of values; nothing can reassure me against myself. . . . I must realize the meaning of the world and of my essence: I decide it, alone, unjustifiably, and without excuse."[38] This is the note on which Sartre ends his big book. He says it will take another book to deal with the moral questions raised here. But, so far, the last word of his basic writing is the anguish of discovering that the moral agent is "the only source of value,"[39] with the consequence that the world as world rests upon his nothingness.

Aside from the verbal trick of reducing man's footing to zero by calling him nothing because he is not something immovably inhuman, the pessimism here derives what plausibility it has from Sartre's mechanical habit of dichotomy. For him either man has nothing to decide concerning values or they are utterly and unbearably up to him, and up to him all by himself as an isolated individual, with no support from society or tradition or reason. There is, at least so far in Sartre's intellectual development, no middle ground between absolute standards, which he rejects, and the moral chaos he plunges into, as his hero Mathieu finally asserts his freedom in suicidal violence.

Mead can dismiss absolutes without taking this plunge. He agrees with Sartre: "You cannot lay down in advance fixed rules as to just what should be done." But Mead adds: "You can find out what are the values involved in the actual problem and act rationally with reference to them. That is what we ask, and all we ask, of anyone. . . . The only rule that an ethics can present is that an individual should rationally deal with all the values that are found in a specific problem."[40] Mead does not pretend that this is always easy, or that there may be no disagreement about values. But he can dissolve much of the difficulty conjured up by Sartre, by recognizing the social nature of the self, so far as it is constituted by social relations. We may fail to appreciate our wider interests "and then to bring them into some sort of rational relationship with the more immediate ones. There is room for mistakes. . . ."[41] For sense and science no method is foolproof. But for Mead there is a method of morality. It accounts for what harmony there is in human relations, so far as not explained by custom and tradition. As the latter become inadequate to cope with new problems posed by new ways of life introduced by science and technology, a method of morality is more clearly the only alternative to moral anarchism that is indeed anguish.

Moral method for Mead is akin to scientific method: resting upon and taking off from what has been reliable in the past, with confidence in the human capacity to find new directions and plan ahead. This is a common venture which should be concerned for the good of all; and must include, as long as we cherish practical and political freedom, room for differences of initiative and satisfaction. Thus Mead says: "there is no scientist who can instruct us in remaking our hearts' desires when we are burdened with the mystery of all this weary and unintelligible world. So there is no definitive scientific statement of what sort of men, or in other words, what sort of life, ought to be bred upon this earth. . . ."[42] Man for Mead is men, free in being able to make something of their togetherness. Man for Sartre is the lonely individual, condemned to the freedom of making nothing of himself but Nothing.

NOTES

[1] George H. Mead, *The Philosophy of the Act*, pp. 223-224.

[2] Jean-Paul Sartre, *L'Imaginaire: Psychologie phénoménologique de l'imagination*, p. 229, p. 189.

[3] George H. Mead, *Mind, Self, and Society*, p. 340.

[4] *L'Imaginaire*, p. 180.

[5] *Ibid.*, pp. 235-236.

[6] Charles Morris, *Logical Positivism, Pragmatism and Scientific Empiricism*, pp. 62-63, 68.

[7] Jean-Paul Sartre, *L'Etre et le Néant*, pp. 544-545.

[8] *Mind, Self, and Society*, p. 344.

[9] *L'Imaginaire*, p. 233.

[10] *Ibid.*, p. 234.

[11] *L'Etre et le Néant*, p. 578.

[12] *Ibid.*, p. 578.

[13] *Ibid.*, p. 627.

[14] *Ibid.*, p. 569.

[15] *Ibid.*, pp. 571-572.

[16] *Ibid.*, p. 247.

[17] *Ibid.*, p. 246.

[18] *Ibid.*, pp. 246-251.

[19] Jean-Paul Sartre, *Esquisse d'une Théorie des Emotions*, p. 52.

[20] M. Merleau-Ponty, *Phénoménologie de la perception*, p. 518.

[21] *The Philosophy of the Act*, p. 663.

[22] *Esquisse d'une Théorie des Emotions*, p. 9.

[23] *L'Etre et le Néant*, p. 53.

[24] *Ibid.*, p. 588.

[25] *Ibid.*, p. 530.

[26] *Ibid.*, pp. 537, 538.

[27] *Ibid.*, pp. 555, 556-557.

[28] *Ibid.*, p. 599, footnote.

[29] *Ibid.*, p. 601.

[30] *Ibid.*, p. 602.

[31] Iris Murdoch, *Sartre: Romantic Rationalist* (New Haven, 1953), p. 48.

[32] *Ibid.*, p. 24.

[33] *Ibid.*, pp. 50-51.

[34] E. Husserl, *Méditations Cartésiennes*, see. 41.

[35] *L'Etre et le Néant*, p. 301.

[36] In *Recherches Philosophiques*, No. VI, 1936-37, pp. 85 ff.

[37] Cf. *L'Etre et le Néant*, pp. 53, 301.

[38] *Ibid.*, p. 77.

[39] *Ibid.*, p. 722.

[40] *Mind, Self, and Society*, p. 388.

[41] *Ibid.*, pp. 388-389.

[42] *The Philosophy of the Act*, p. 501.

Paul Tibbetts (essay date 1974)

SOURCE: "Mead's Theory of the Act and Perception: Some Empirical Confirmations," in *The Personalist*, Vol. LV, No. 2, Spring, 1974, pp. 115-38.

[*In the following essay, Tibbetts explores Mead's theory of the act and suggests how it can be used to interpret recent findings in experimental psychology.*]

INTRODUCTION

To students of recent American philosophy George Herbert Mead presents a paradox, for whereas Dewey and Whitehead recognized Mead as perhaps this country's most profound and original thinker, his writings largely continue to be ignored by most philosophers today. Though substantial work has been done on Mead's place in the history of ideas[1-5], his social psychology[6-9], and his theory of knowledge[10-13], little has appeared on his theory of the act[14-17]. This is highly unfortunate since this was Mead's most distinctive and suggestive contribution to philosophy. Certainly no attempts have been made to my knowledge to relate Mead's theory of the act and action to recent findings in the experimental study of human behavior.

Mead was a seminal thinker of the first caliber. On this basis alone an account of his thought would prove interesting from the point of view of the history of ideas. However, once it is seen the great extent to which his theory of human action provides a viable explanatory framework for integrating numerous behavioral and perceptual studies, then his thought has more than a merely historical interest. With this in mind, the first half of this paper will present Mead's theory of the act. In the second half I will then go on to suggest how his theory can be used to interpret certain much discussed findings in recent experimental psychology. Especially in its later stages, Mead's philosophy became quite complex and comprehensive. For the purposes of this paper I will only focus on that portion of his thought directly bearing on the theme being developed here. This should account for the omission of other, equally important doctrines in Mead's philosophy.

A. MEAD'S THEORY OF THE ACT

The simplest way of understanding Mead's theory of the act is to see how within a pragmatic theory of knowledge objects first arise in experience. Mead, as all pragmatists, rejects the view that experience is of objects which are formed independently of human action. Dewey somewhere defined an object as "an event with meaning." Mead's position largely centers around the various ways in which events attain meaning in terms of human perceptual, manipulatory and evaluative activity. In line with this, Mead recognized with James and Dewey that the realist-idealist issue with regard to meanings is based on one uncritically accepted presupposition: that objects are extra-experiential entities. To reject this presupposition has historically entailed solipsism. However, by redefining experience in terms of organism-environment transactions rather than as a purely *psychological* affair, the pragmatists hoped to by-pass the subjective connotations usually associated with the concept of experience. In fact the functionalist account of perception outlined by Angell, Moore, Mead and Dewey at Chicago even rejected the view that the subject-object relation is essentially or even primarily a *cognitive* relation. To use Dewey as an example, in *Knowing and the Known* (1949) he suggested that philosophers discard the term "knower" in favor of "knowings," with the latter expression being defined in terms of ". . . organic phases of transactionally observed behaviors"[17] rather than by reference to cognitive states or other non-behavioral events. This for the reason that for Dewey and the other functionalists the organism-environment relation was preferable because less intellectualized than the traditional distinction between knowing subject and known object. With the shift toward a more biological/behavioral model of the subject-object relation there was in turn a corresponding interest in explicating the concept of behavior or the "act," to use Mead's expression. It is not of course accidental that Mead and the other functionalists were greatly influenced by the conceptual framework of the biological sciences, an explanatory framework which even today largely converges with the functionalist point of view.[18]

Following Dewey, Mead also saw that to reject the traditional conception of the subject as a *knower* entailed that we also discard the sort of object associated with this sort of subject. This would be the conception of an object as an extra-mental, external reality in which our perceptions and representations somehow terminated; the object in this sense functioned as "that to which our percepts and linguistic descripta corresponded," in some not clearly understood way. Hence, where James had earlier attacked the theory of truth associated with this account of the relation between propositions and their designata, Mead questioned the entire representative theory of perception and theory of cognition upon which the dualistic account rested. Rather than think of ideas and things, the knower and the known, as independent entities (which assumption historically gave rise to the 'problem of knowledge'), Mead's alternative was to take the act as primary and to define both perceiver and perceived, subject and object, in terms of phases or dimensions within the act. As we will see, Mead will not only interpret the distinction between subjectivity and objectivity within the context of the act but also the distinction between what is perceptually veridical and non-veridical, real and imaginary. Given such an interpretation, Mead felt that his position could avoid the entire realism-idealism controversy regarding the logical and existential priority of material objects to ideas and concepts about such objects. The attempt to avoid this issue is not of course unique with Mead. For example, in Mach's *Analysis of Sensation,* James' *Essays in Radical Empiricism,* Russell's *Analysis of Mind,* Carnap's *Logische Aufbau,* and Dewey's *Experience and Nature* we find five systematic attempts to construct both mental and physical reality out of a neutral material, variously termed "elements," "pure experience," "phenomena," or "primary experience."[19-20] By beginning with a neutral datum which was neither mental nor physical, thought nor thing, it was believed that the idealism-realism controversy could be shown to be more a conceptual matter than a genuine ontological issue.

It is interesting to note in this context that with the exception of James[21] and, less obviously, Dewey[22] none of the other above theorists ever placed any emphasis on the role of bodily acts in their respective accounts of empirical knowledge and the knower-known relation. It was Mead who most clearly recognized that the "neutral datum" these writers referred to must be concretely situated within and defined in terms of the act rather than being allowed to float free. Otherwise it would be impossible to account for the limiting conditions imposed on present experience by bodily, biological and environmental factors, by previous experience, and by intentional and evaluative considerations. Mead felt that through his account of the act it was possible to recognize the interrelations between thought, bodily activity and the environment. This requires, though, that we reject the Cartesian and Lockean dualism between thoughts and things, knowers and knowns, as anything other than a methodological or functional distinction between intra- and extra organic events. To do otherwise would be to take a distinction which arises within the context of the act and reify it into an unbridgeable gap between two mutually exclusive sorts of things.

With the above discussion as a general background let us now turn to Mead's account of the act and how he manages to build an entire theory of perception, knowledge and reality around the act.

THE SENSES: RE-ESTABLISHING PRIORITIES

Within the historical context of empiricism from Locke and Hartley to Russell and Ayer, sensation was almost exclusively identified with the process of seeing and hearing. Accordingly the external referent of a sensation was thought of as something spatially separated from the perceiver's visual and auditory sensory organs (or sensory receptors). The emphasis on these two receptors is understandable. The chemical senses of taste and smell, for example, though anatomically distinct from the other senses do not easily lend themselves to exact study by either phenomenological (descriptive) or physiological (scientific) techniques. In fact until fairly recently the sensitivity and range of discrimination of the smell and taste receptors were only qualitatively expressable. With regard to the sense of equilibrium and the kinaesthetic sense a different problem occurs: these senses only inform us as to the position of our own body rather than of objects in the external physical environment. Being concerned with the perceiver-perceived relation rather than with intra-organic events, philosophers have accordingly devoted few pages to these two sensory modalities in their discussion of the so-called "problem of knowledge." One of the few exceptions I know of is Mach's *Space and Geometry* (1906), one of his more infrequently discussed works. With regard to the tactual sense an additional difficulty arises. Being coextensive with the skin or membrane covering the entire body this sensory system is so voluminous as to be practically unlimited in extent thus making extremely difficult the sort of analyses the visual and auditory senses lend themselves to. It is for these reasons that sensory psychologists and philosophers interested in perception have considered the eye and the ear as *the* paradigm sensory modalities.

Even granted these practical difficulties in the study of the senses, it now appears that Aristotle, for example, was essentially correct in regarding the tactual sense as the primary sensory organ, for the following reasons. It is now theorized in neurophysiology that the retina and the cochlea (respectively, the light and pressure sensitive cells in the eye and ear) are biologically descendent from cells originally composing the skin, though Aristotle could not have known this. Nor could he have known that by far the largest amount of sensory cortex in the human brain is devoted to the sense of touch. Following Aristotle, however, it is not upon considerations of evolutionary biology that Mead will similarly emphasize the tactual over the visual and auditory senses. Mead's argument will be that in the order in which experience of the external environment is conceptually built up by the perceiver, the tactual sense is epistemically prior to the distance receptors since it is the only sensory modality which brings us into direct bodily contact with the surfaces of objects. Even allowing that contact sensations together with visual and auditory experiences are contemporary with one another in both the infant and adult, Mead will maintain that due to their greater reliability contact and tactual sensations constitute the evidential ground for verifying knowledge claims concerning distance objects. We will return to this important point later, though let me suggest for now that the experimental literature in part two will substantially support Mead's position regarding contact experience.[23]

MEAD'S ANALYSIS OF THE ACT

The functionalist movement in American thought is usually dated from Dewey's classic paper, "The Reflex Arc Concept in Psychology" (*Psychological Review,* 1896). This paper largely centered around the question, "Does the stimulus object define the perceptual response or vice versa?" The functionalist's reply is that this begs the question, assuming as it does that the stimulus object (that is, that object in the environment which elicits a response by the organism) is something which exists prior to and independently of the organism's responses to it. For Dewey as for Mead, a stimulus is to be defined relative to the biological structure and behavior of a given organism; for example, ultra-violet light is a visual stimulus to certain insect life but not to primates. In addition, what will count as a stimulus is also determined by the behavior and intentions of the organism, including its previous behavior and anticipated goals; for example, food is not a stimulus to an animal being pursued whereas a possible hiding place may be. To argue that the stimulus object continues to function as a *potential* stimulus independently of the organism, even when it is not being attended to or actually stimulating the organism, is to assume that there is some essential property which characterizes the stimulus apart from the response of an organism to it. But what would this property or quality be? If a stimulus is always stimulus-under-such-and-such-conditions or relative to-a-given-organic-and-intentional-state then stimuli are no more separable from a particular organism-behavior-environment context than

are buyers and sellers definable apart from an economic context. The important point for the functionalist is that stimulus and response are equally to be defined in terms of intentional factors, biological structure, organic needs, and the behavioral situation.

With this in mind, along with the brief discussion of the importance of tactual and manipulatory activity over the other sensory modalities, we are now ready to appreciate Mead's account of the act. He begins by analyzing the act into four stages: impulse, perception, manipulation, and consummation. The stage of impulse is the antecedent motivating condition underlying the other three stages or levels of animal (including human) behavior. It is that level of organic activity which motivates or drives the animal to move about in its physical and social environment to satisfy its biological needs and psychological needs (e.g., elimination of boredom, curiosity interests, and in the case of men the need to understand and explain). Obviously this is a greatly condensed statement of the range of animal and human needs in contrast, for example, with Maslow's more expanded account of a "hierarchy of needs" in the *Psychology of Being.* In any case, an impulse is terminated and a need satisfied when the organism succeeds in reestablishing a "balanced relationship" with its environment. However, to bring itself into a condition where its needs and values are consummated, the animal must first perceive then manipulate its environment. Let us now examine in some detail how these second and third stages of the act transform felt needs into consummated experiences.

On the level of impulse the behavioral response immediately follows the presentation of the stimulus, as in the case of a frog diving into the water when any large object passes into its visual field, or the dog barking at a strange noise. On the perceptual level, on the other hand, there is a delayed response between the reception of the stimulus and the resulting response. Such a delay in response requires "the conscious attitude [on the part of the organism] of the response, and the imagery of the response."[24] That is to say, various alternative responses are weighed prior to actually responding to the stimulus in question. The response of the organism is now evaluated in terms of its *appropriateness* to the situation which first occasioned the response. By "conscious attitude" Mead does not mean anything at all like Descartes' "reflecting Cogito" but simply that decision-making and sign-using process which occurs whenever an organism's response is dictated neither by internal reflexive mechanisms (which applies to the behavior of the frog) nor by previous conditioning (as in the case of the dog trained to retrieve ducks). To use a different example, the selecting of a proper site to build a nest probably occurs on the perceptual level since the consequences of building it in an unprotected area are anticipated and avoided, whereas the actual construction of the nest (including its design and materials) may very well be genetically conditioned and therefore independent of conditions in the external environment. In other words, the perceptual stage of the act is marked by conscious anticipation of the appropriateness of a particular behavioral response to a given stimulus. Hence, between the response and the stimulus which originally acted on the animal there is a temporal delay during which occurs the sign-mediated process of deliberation and the weighing of the appropriateness of this or that response. If the response immediately follows given the stimulus then the behavior is instinctive or conditioned, not consciously controlled through the mediation of signs. As humans we have available to us innumerable means for anticipating the appropriateness or inappropriateness of our responses, in contrast with other forms of life. The guinea pig, the experimental scale model, and the computor simulation program are increasingly sophisticated means for anticipating the consequences of possible courses of action and for determining the variables which will increase the success of our actions. The important point in all of this is that to the extent animal behavior is ordered and goal-directed then for Mead it is rule-governed and sign-mediated behavior.

It is important to recall here that the perceptual field is not only determined by the structure and function of an organism's sensory systems but also by its needs, expectations, and behavioral responses. As such, the perceptual field could be said to be a field or perspective which radiates outward from the organism as a pattern of actual and potential responses. If we also remember that stimuli and responses are interdependent and mutually defining, we can then derive the following formula: no organism, no perceptual field; no perceptual field no stimulus objects. As Mead remarks,

> There is a mutual interdependence [of organism and perceptual field]. This is expressed in the term "perspective." In biology the dependence of the organism upon its field has been the dominant standpoint, . . . However, this overlooks the fact that the environment is a selection which is dependent upon the living form.[25]

He then draws the conclusion that

> The conception of a world that is independent of any organism is one that is without perspectives. There would be no environments.[26]

It follows that *the basic reality for Mead is the organism in a behavioral situation* which confronts the organism with obstacles, resistances, and Challenges. Nor is the organism simply one perceptual object among others for then there would be no center to the perceptual field. On the basis of its biological structure, needs, and intentions, the organism selectively discriminates and then assigns significance to the objects and events in the perceptual field. As it moves through its behavioral environment, then, not only the perceptual field but also the significance of the elements constituting the field are continually shifting, not unlike the way in which a spotlight illuminates now this and now that region of a visual field. (The analogy is of course misleading if the reader thinks of the illuminated objects as having a value or significance independently of their being illuminated!) In the

final analysis, behavioral responses, intentions, perceptual objects, and the perceptual field stand in a complex interlocking relation or "transaction" (to use Dewey's term), where each of these factors is but one element of the total organism-environment situation. Consequently, for Mead as for Dewey no explication of any one of these factors is possible in isolation from all the other elements.

The third and most important stage of the act for our purposes is that of manipulation. This is where an organism comes into actual contact with perceptual objects. In contrast with the visual and auditory characteristics of objects, which vary with movement of either the organism or the object, contact features are invariable with respect to spatial position or motion. As one moves around a stick partially immersed in water, its visual appearance changes until in one plane (that perpendicular to the surface of the water) it appears straight. When touched the stick is straight from any perspective. (It should be remarked, though, that straightness for the hand and for the eye may not be the same. Whether we call it 'straightness' or something else, the point still holds that contact experiences are invariable with respect to movement.) Mead goes so far as to argue that *what a thing is is found in contact experiences alone.*[27] By contact Mead simply means the active grasping and manipulation of an object by an organism. It should come as no surprise then that rather than define manipulation in terms of the physical object and stimuli in the external environment, Mead reverses the conceptual order and defines the physical object as "that [which] retains the same character of the effective occupation of space within the range of manipulation."[28] Within the sphere or range of manipulatory activity the hand is the basic contact organ (at least for the primate), though through practice other portions of the body could serve the same function. More will be said on this in part two.

Let us now compare perceptual space with manipulatory space. For Mead when we perceive a distant object we anticipate a possible manipulation of that object; as we reach for the hammer our fingers and thumb become formed in a certain way, the muscles in our arm become tense, the hand and forearm rotate relative to our shoulder, and so on. "We are ready to grasp the hammer before we reach it, and the attitude of manipulatory response directs the approach. What we are going to do determines the line of approach and in some sense its manner."[29] The perception of a distant object can therefore be termed *a collapsed (because anticipated) contact experience.* Visual illusions can be explained in terms of our tendency to project onto the distant object the dimensions it would have if close at hand and manipulated.

> When we see things in the dimensions and form of the manipulatory area, we are in a measure seeing the distant object in terms of a space which is the extension of the . . . space of the manipulatory area, . . .
>
> Thus we see the elliptical top of the table as round and the corners of the ceiling as right angles. Seeing

the ellipse as round and the angle greater than a right angle is the control of the visualization by the attitudes of the response belonging to the manipulatory area. . . . We are ready to act toward the shorter diameter of the ellipse as if it were equal to the longer diameter. The extent to which the sensuous content of the percent may be affected by this control is shown in various psychological illusions.[30]

The resistance features of an object are for Mead more fundamental than its visual characteristics. In fact Mead will argue that it is in the experience of the resistance features of manipulatory objects that the organism first comes to perceive itself as a "physical thing", that is, as a thing which exhibits resistance qualities and which has an "inside". (For further discussion of this point I refer the interested reader to Mead's **"The Physical Thing"** in his *The Philosophy of the Present*.)

To return to the point above, it could even be argued that it is when visual and contact experiences fail to coincide that perceptual illusions first arise (disregarding of course those illusions which result from some intra-organic factor, such as the influence on perception of certain drugs). Unlike the visual experiences of either near or distant objects, there is no intervening medium in contact experiences. For this reason, then, Mead can argue that "The ultimate experience of contact is not subject to the divergencies of distance experience. It is that into which every perspective can be translated. The round solid coin in the hand is the ultimate fact of every oval of vision."[31] As it is due to variables in the intervening medium which are responsible for the bent-stick illusion or the seeing of water in the distance while driving on a summer's day, the elimination of an intervening medium (in these cases, the water and the atmosphere) would minimize if not eliminate these visual illusions. Following Mead, I would go so far as to maintain that within the tactual and manipulatory sphere there are no illusions; it is only when the tactual experience of an object is contrasted with a visual experience of that same object that perceptual illusions first arise. Hence, if we were creatures not capable of receiving distance perceptions, and all our knowledge of the surrounding environment were based solely on actual contact and manipulatory experiences, there would be no category in our language corresponding to "perceptual illusion". More will be said in part two on the great difference between distance and contact experience.

On the level of consummation, the fourth and last stage of the act, objects are possessed, enjoyed, rejected, or satisfying; that is, they take on a *value*. Though this stage of the act is not central to the purposes of this paper, it should be noted that for Mead the ultimate *telos* and natural fulfillment of every act is the consummation or enjoyment of physical objects in immediate experience; apart from this an act would remain truncated because incomplete. He remarks for example that beyond the perceptual and the manipulatory field of objects lies "the ultimate completion of the act in consummation, which is

an experience that is referred to these objects but transcends their physical character." It was Mead's conviction that of all those who participate in the act, it is the primary function of the artist to make explicit the values that remain implicit or even hidden in objects, values which at times are eclipsed by purely practical considerations. To perceive an object aesthetically for Mead is therefore to abstract it from its immediate utility.

> . . . in appreciation we contemplate, and abide, and rest in our presentations. The artisan who stops to sense the nice perfection of a tool or machine has interrupted its use to appreciate it and is in an aesthetic mood. He is not interested in its employment; he is enjoying it.
>
> To so construct the object that it shall catch this joy of consummation is the achievement of the artist.[32]

THE DISTINCTION BETWEEN PERCEPTUAL AND SCIENTIFIC OBJECTS

On both the perceptual and the manipulatory levels of the act Mead wants to distinguish between the immediate experience of objects as against reflective analysis of that experience. In immediate experience the object-as-seen and the object-as-felt are simply *there;* their meaning is exhausted by their perceptual or manipulatory qualities. When the object takes on a representative function, such that it now serves to signify something not immediately present, it thereby acquires connotations not originally present in immediate experience. In other words, the object now functions as a sign. Being abstracted from the context of immediate experience and therefore from the perceptual or manipulatory spheres, the object of reflection (or, as Mead sometimes calls it, the "scientific object") becomes infused with meanings of increasing generality. In turn, the object of reflection remains ambiguous to the extent that its empirical significance is not securely defined in terms of one or another stage of the act and, consequently, in terms of organism-environment transactions. This conclusion also follows given Mead's instrumentalism, according to which the abstract entities of reflective analysis are simply logical fictions postulated within the context of a theoretical explanatory framework to account for directly observed phenomena in the physical and behavioral environment. As Mead remarks,

> The whole tendency of the natural sciences, as exhibited especially in physics and chemistry, is to replace the objects of immediate experience by hypothetical objects which lie beyond the range of possible experience. As I have pointed out above, an experimental science must bring any theory to the test of an experience which is immediate, which lies within the "now." [It] must be possible to regard the hypothetical subexperiential objects as the statements of the methods and formulas for the control of objects in the world of actual experience, in other words, that so-called objects which lie beyond the range of possible experiences are in reality complex procedures in the control of actual experience.[33]

Though it is not important in the present context, it is highly unfortunate that Mead, unlike Peirce and Morris (at one time Mead's student), never developed a sophisticated theory of signs or semiotics for specifying the empirical significance of any given sign or symbol within the context of the act.[34] With regard to this distinction between the act and *reflection on* the act, Mead's entire project in *The Philosophy of the Act* is of course occurring on the reflective level, as is the case with all conceptual analysis. Mead never forgot, though, that the ultimate rationale for distinctions and knowledge claims made on the reflective level is the act. As Mead notes,

> . . . reflective analysis, does resolve the whole field, including the organism, into physical elements which could conceivable be the objects in a hypothetical perception; that is, their characters of location, effective occupation of space, inertia, and motion are those characters which appear in actual contact experience as the ultimate reality of objects in perception. This analysis [on the reflective level] substitutes for the color, sound, odor, taste, temperature, and even the feel of the object, structures and motions which cannot be any of the characters which they undertake to account for.[35]

Again, it is important to note that this distinction within experience between what is part of the act as such and what is inferential or postulated occurs on both the perceptual and manipulatory levels. This distinction between immediate and reflective experience is absolutely fundamental to Mead's entire theory of knowledge. It also provides him with a criterion for distinguishing between the real and the imaginary, a distinction which must be drawn within the context of the act, there being no other epistemological point of reference for Mead to resort to. Accordingly, the "real" is defined as "that which controls our responses." This is in keeping with the definition of the stimulus or perceptual object in terms of our responses rather than in terms of some antecedently existing entity.[36]

Mead is thus rejecting those accounts of the real and reality which resort to either logical or metaphysical considerations (as with Plato and the British idealists), to transcendental arguments (as in Kant), or even to what is immediately given in sensory observation (as with Mach). With regard to the first two positions, Mead was in my estimation rightly critical of the *a priori* method employed by both British and post-Kantian idealism; for Mead both approaches end by reducing reality to what is logically deducible from intuitively-given first principles. Mead was too much of an empiricist to be attracted to deductive metaphysics; just as importantly, he was highly suspicious of any position which employed criteria other than the act in formulating and evaluating empirical knowledge claims. He was also highly critical of phenomenalism, or that form of empiricism which equated the real with an atomic-like sensory given. For Mead, the phenomenalist's characterization of perceptual experience was not dictated by experience *per se* but was rather a consequence of a particular theory *about* such experi-

ence, a theory influenced by late nineteenth century views concerning artistic perception. Most importantly of all for Mead, with the exception of Berkeley traditional empiricism and idealism had equally ignored the importance of action and bodily activity in their respective theories of knowledge and perception. This was a significant omission for it had the effect of creating a dualism between a perceiving subject and an external reality (with this reality either being conceived as something transcendent or as that which is perceived through the senses). By emphasizing the role of the body and action in his theory of knowledge, Mead felt that he was thereby able to by-pass both epistemological and metaphysical dualism. In turn, he was able to redefine the real with reference to bodily activity and the stages of the act rather than simply with reference to intellectual or cognitive activity, an approach which Merleau-Ponty has referred to as "intellectualism."

Thus Mead's theory of knowledge and perception was explicitly formulated in direct opposition to those positions which postulated as the outset a dualism between subject and object, mind and an external reality, knower and known. Given these three variations on the same dualistic hypothesis, one then had to resort to a host of essentially artificial devices such as impressions, sensations, sense data and, more recently, neural impulses and sensory information to account for the relation between the two poles of this dualism. By interpreting both the notion of a "perceiving subject" and a "perceived object" as abstractions relative to the context of the act and the on-going organism-environment transaction, Mead avoids in my opinion the dilemmas regarding knowledge and the external world traditionally entailed by both epistemological and metaphysical dualism. Accordingly, Mead's rejection of "reality" as something set over against "mind" is quite consistent with his definition of a perceptual or stimulus object in terms of the act and bodily activity rather than by reference to a world of objects and events, the significance of which is determined independently of the act. Though Mead does talk about a "world that is there" prior to the act, this is not a "world" in the usual sense of that word, that is, designating a world of perceptual and manipulatory objects in space and time. (For further discussion of epistemological dualism and its implications for the theory of perception, see reference[37].)

Returning to our discussion of signs above, when perceptual or manipulatory objects take on a representative character there frequently occurs a temporary suspension of action such that our usual behavioral responses to that object are interrupted. For example, if when reaching for a wooden match we suddenly see (or conceive) this object as symbolic of man's partial control over his environment, or if we recall the story of Prometheus and what his giving of fire to men symbolized for Aeschylus and Greek culture, our hand is momentarily arrested in its movement. A tool as immediately experienced on the manipulatory level, to take another example, is simply a weight in one's hand, having a certain shape and surface texture, a specific function, and so on; taken symbolically it represents human creativity. The axe bound by rods in Roman culture is no longer literally an axe but a symbol of consular power and the unity of the Italian tribes.

Symbols on the reflective level thus come to function as "conceptual substitutes" or "short-hand devices" for the objects of immediate experience. Through conceptual manipulation of these symbols future patterns of action can be projected and anticipated. The experiential and the reflective realms thus come for Mead to compliment one another. It is quite false therefore to accuse the pragmatist of emphasizing action and *praxis* at the expense of human reflection and contemplation. What Mead and the other pragmatists do stress, however, is that the primary function of thought is the directing of action to consummatory objects adequate to anticipated goals. As the editor of *The Philosophy of the Act* rightly notes, for Mead thinking is not instrumental to action as such but to consummation, to

> . . . the attainment of the value characters of objects. What are wanted are objects of such character that they not merely release but satisfy the blocked impulse or interest, and the whole context of Mead's thought makes it clear that action does not normally stop with the manipulation of objects but passes on to their consummatory use: in the last analysis the entire world of scientific objects is an elaborate instrumentation functioning in the service of social values.[38]

In summary we have seen that the meaning of a perceptual object is to be defined in terms of consummatory experience, that is in terms of as satisfaction or frustration of real or imagined needs. We have also seen that the *reality* of an object is determined by manipulatory experiences, whereas the *meaning* of that object is ultimately defined by the consummations it subserves.[39] Though Mead would certainly want to recognize a hierarchy of needs (biological, social, intellectual, religious, and aesthetic), he does insist that such needs, to be satisfied and realized, must eventually be translated into experiences grounded in the act and therefore within the organism-environment transaction. It is not to be assumed from this that Mead was insensitive to the demands of reflection and abstract thinking. On the contrary, Mead did recognize the importance of reflective activity in human expression for it is on this level that we first postulate then imaginatively inhabit various conceptually possible "worlds." In fact, for all the pragmatists this is one of the primary functions of reflective intelligence: the creation in one's imagination of alternative conceptual possibilities regarding reality.[40] To expand upon this feature of Mead's philosophy would take us too far a field from our more immediate purpose.

With this discussion of the four stages of the act, of the organism-environment transaction, the epistemological priority of manipulatory over perceptual/distance experiences, and the distinction between immediate experience and reflective analysis, let us now turn to some experi-

mental studies which in my estimation provide strong empirical support for Mead's position on these matters.

B. SOME EXPERIMENTAL STUDIES ON HUMAN PERCEPTUAL BEHAVIOR: THE IMPORTANCE OF THE TACTUAL FEATURES OF OBJECTS

Philosophers have long theorized as to whether a blind man upon receiving sight would be able to recognize the visual shapes of objects with which he had only previously had tactual experience. Two psychologists were recently able to document such a situation with a cornea-transplant patient. The subject was in his fifties and had been totally blind. Within a few days of the operation, the subject could easily distinguish different objects on the ground when looking out his upper-story window, though he was totally unable to estimate their distance; in fact he thought that he could easily lower himself to the ground. Even the moon appeared to be only a short distance away. On the whole, though, his early estimates of the size and distance of objects ". . . seem to have been quite accurate *providing they were objects already familiar to him by touch.*"[41]

In three drawings of a bus, done at forty eight days, six months, and one year after the operation, there was a marked increase in detail. His first drawing of the bus, which was exclusively based on tactual experience, came to be gradually supplemented with visual details, such as advertisement on the side of the bus and even the design of the hubcaps. Eventually he could even draw the faces of persons. Both of these examples illustrate his increasing ability to employ specifically visual information and would seem to argue against the primacy of tactual experience thesis. However, though he could *see* objects he had great difficulty in *recognizing* them unless he could touch them. "His vision [alone] did not serve to give him recognition of individuals from their faces or of the *significance* of facial expression." ([42]; my italics)

The most interesting and certainly the most spectacular finding of this case study for our purposes was the following incident. The subject was taken to a science museum which had tools like those he had used for many years while blind. He was then confronted with a lathe similar to one he was familiar with before his operation.

> He was quite unable to say anything about it, except that he thought the nearest part was a handle . . . We then asked a museum attendant for the case to be opened, and S. B. (the subject) was allowed to touch the lathe. The result was startling; he ran his hands deftly over the machine, touching first the transverse feed handle and confidently naming it as "a handle," and then on to the saddle, the bed and the head-stock of the lathe. He ran his hands eagerly over the lathe, with his eyes tight shut. Then he stood back a little and opened his eyes and said: "Now that I've felt it I can see it."[43]

The crucial passage is of course the last one: "Now that I've felt it I can see (recognize) it." Let us assume that we can draw a distinction between *seeing* and *recogniz-*

ing (and the above and other experimental literature strongly suggests we should). It could then be argued that visual *recognition* requires either present or previous tactual experience of the object. Gregory and Wallace do not draw this conclusion though it is I feel empirically justified on the basis of their study. Even as normal subjects we distinguish between what is seen and what is recognized; why not then for the subject of the above study? Though the findings of this case study are certainly open to alternative interpretations, the study does in my estimation lend some support to Mead's position that tactual experience is to some extent a factor intentionally present in all perceptual recognition and perceptual objectivity. This conclusion was also arrived at by Dewey in his *Psychology*. "Ultimately visual perception rests on tactual . . . Spatial perceptions are not originally perceived by the eye, but are the result of the association of visual sensations with previous muscular and tactual experiences."[44]

However, it should be noted that this thesis would appear to directly conflict with the conclusion drawn by two other perceptual psychologists. On the basis of their studies, Rock and Harris maintain that "The sense of touch does not educate vision; that vision is totally dominant over touch," and that "Our experiments all show . . . that when a subject's sense of touch conveys information that disagrees with what he is seeing, the visual information determines his perception."[45] Elsewhere Rock does admit that "If, early in life, vision had been educated by touch, it [vision] may nevertheless have become dominant thereafter by virtue of its greater ability to give information about distance and its over-all versatility."[46]

There are, however, two different ways in which touch could educate vision. First, in the way Rock suggests in this last quoted statement, namely, as being perhaps more fundamental in early childhood experience, though becoming of secondary importance later in life. Secondly, there is the possibility (defended by Mead and Dewey) that touch continues to inform and educate sight *throughout* a person's life. Not informing in the sense of providing direct sensory information (which it obviously does not in the case of distance perception), but in the sense of providing a sort of "intentional background or framework" within which visual perception is situated. According to this last suggestion, the meaning we assign to a given visual image in perceptual recognition is *to some extent* influenced by the anticipated and possible contact or manipulatory experiences we could in principle have of the visually perceived object. In other words, we visually perceive a distant object as-a-chair, that is, as something to sit in, as an obstacle to walk around, as something to stand on to reach a shelf, and so on. In all three cases we integrate the visual object with future bodily activity (sitting in, walking around, and standing on). In defense of Mead, then, bodily and behavioral activity would continue to exercise no little influence over our adult visual perceptions in the way of providing an intentional context for recognizing and interpreting visual objects. This suggestion is not only reinforced by the

Gregory-Wallace case study but also receives independent support from the following experiments.

In the early fifties a classic experiment was performed by Adelbert Ames which produced results at odds with those found by Rock and Harris, a discrepancy they fail to note. In Ames' experiment as reported by his colleagues Ittelson and Kilpatrick, a distorted room is used in which the rear wall slopes away from the subject from right to left, the floor and ceilings also slope, and the windows are trapezoidal in shape and of different sizes. The subject views this distroted room from a point where the room appears normal, as if

> . . . the floor were level, the rear wall at right angles to the line of sight and the windows rectangular and of the same size. . . . If he now takes a long stick and tries to touch the various parts of the room, he will be unsuccessful, even though he has gone into the situation knowing the true shape of the room.

> With practice, however, he becomes more and more successful in touching what he wants to touch with the stick. *More important, he sees the room more and more in its true shape,* even though the stimulus pattern on his retina has remained unchanged. ([47]; my italics)

It is the tactual rather than the visual experience which provides the subject with the correct shape of the room, that is, with its distortions. This finding is in line with a conclusion Kilpatrick drew elsewhere: "The most effective way of accomplishing perceptual reorganization is through *action* by the perceiver."[48]

It is sometimes overlooked, however, that the *only* means we have at our disposal for acting on our environment is by moving some part of our body over or around the objects in the perceptual field. Mead might add that it is also through movements and tactual perceptions that a number of the properties of the external environment are first experienced and given objective status within the experiences of the perceiver; for example, the resistance features of objects, the three-dimensional character of our perceived world and the objects which compose it, and even the element of perceptual depth. It is therefore no accident that when a subject is placed in Ames' distorted room he will employ his body to determine the "true shape" of the room. (The stick held by Ames' subjects is of course an extension of the hand and therefore of the body.) The behavior of the subjects in this experiment would seem to reinforce Mead's recognition of the importance of bodily movements and contact experiences for ascertaining both the true shape and true size of objects in the environment. Though further work is currently being done in this area, it is indeed questionable whether the findings obtained by Ames and others could be accounted for in any model which ignored or even minimized the role of manipulatory and contact perceptions. I propose that Mead has provided us with at least the basic framework for an adequate model for understanding perceptual behavior and the means we employ for separating the objective from the distorted, unreliable factors in the external environment.

THE EFFECT OF MOVEMENT OF VISUAL PERCEPTION

A number of years ago the psychologist George Stratton discovered that by wearing prisms in place of his usual eye glasses the visual environment was completely inverted. In a series of experiments extending over a period of a few years, Stratton wore these prisms and recorded their influence on his visual experience. As Stratton's inquiries have formed the starting point for a number of more recent inquiries into the effects of inversion of perception[49], his studies and findings will briefly be discussed. Stratton began by wearing the prisms for three days. At first objects

> . . . seemed upside down. The hands when stretched out from below into the visual field seemed to enter from above . . . The present perceptions were for some time translated involuntarily into the language of normal vision; the present visual perceptions were used simply as signs to determine how and where the object would appear if it could be seen with restored normal vision. Things were thus *seen* in one way and *thought of* in a far different way.
>
> All movements of the body at this time were awkward, uncertain, and full of surprises. Only when the movement was made regardless of visual images, by aid of touch and memory alone—as when one moves in the dark—could walking or movements of the hand be performed with reasonable security and directness. . . . The vivid connection of tactual and visual perceptions began to take away the overpowering force of the localization lasting over from normal vision.[50]

By the third day the room appeared to be more integrated, with "floors and walls . . . getting into a constant relation to one another, so that during a movement of the head I could more or less accurately anticipate the order in which things would enter the visual field."[51] He then concluded that the inversion of the image on the retina at the back of the eye is not a necessary condition for normal, upright vision, otherwise the room would not have righted itself when wearing the prisms, no matter how long the prisms were worn. In other words, the room appeared upright regardless of whether the room were perceived through regular eye glasses or through inverting prisms.

Just as important for our purposes is the great stress Stratton placed on the role of tactual activity and movement in these studies. He notes, for example, that of those parts of the body which were visible when wearing the inverting prisms, their new appearance and location were able to "drive the old from the field, because the new localization by sight showed a perfect and constant relation to the reports by *muscular and tactual perception.*" ([52]; my italics) He also expressed little doubt that tactual experience would eventually bring even the unseen parts of the body into conjunction with the new framework.

On the basis of these findings, Stratton then concluded that

> Any visual field in which the relations of the seen parts to one another would always correspond to the relations found by touch and muscular movement would give us "upright" vision, whether the optic image lay upright, inverted, or at any intermediate angle whatever on the retina.[53]

In a later experiment[54] Stratton wore the inverting prisms over a period of eight days. On the fifth day he made a crucial observation:

> . . . the most harmonious experiences were obtained during *active* operations on the scene before me. [Conversely,] during a *passive* observation I still involuntarily represented my head, shoulders, and chest in the old preexperimental relation to the actual things in sight.[55]

He also experimented with touch experiments on his fingers. When two of Stratton's fingers remained stationary and were simultaneously touched with two different types of stimuli (a pencil point on one and the assistant's finger tip on the other), the contacts could be voluntarily felt as coming from one finger or the other, or even from the same finger. On the other hand,

> A movement of one of the fingers, such as a slight bending and straightening of it, while the other remained passive, produced a marked difference between the two fingers, both as to their visual appearance and as to the character of the tactual sensations just mentioned; and this movement rendered the arbitrary reference of the two contacts impossible. Each contact could then be felt only in the place where it was seen to be.[56]

We will return to this distinction between active and passive movements of the body when discussing the experiments of Held.

While wearing the inverting prisms Stratton discovered that his tactual perceptions were unaffected: ". . . they never changed their place. They simply got a new visual translation."[57] In other words, any given tactual or manipulatory perception was always associated with a specific region of the body, and though the left hand, for example, now *visually* appeared (when wearing the prisms) at the right side of the body, movements of the left hand were always *felt* on the left side of the body. Again this would seem to support Mead's claim that tactual and manipulatory perceptions are more fundamental *due to their greater consistency and reliability,* whether under the unusual conditions described by Stratton or by Ames.[58] Let us now turn to the important distinction between active and passive movements mentioned above, a distinction of great relevance for Mead's position.

In a more recent series of experimental studies by Richard Held, Stratton's findings received additional support. Concentrating on the role of voluntary or self-induced movement in perception, Held found that a subject wearing inverting prisms could adapt to visual distortions provided that during the experiment ". . . he has been allowed to make voluntary use of his muscles in a more or less normal vay."[59]

In one series of experiments, for example, Held employed kittens which had been raised in complete darkness from birth. He placed these subjects in a circular-shaped enclosure which had alternate patterns of grey, black, and white stripes painted on the enclosing surface. This provided the only visual input to the test animals. One animal was allowed to walk freely around the enclosure while the other animal was carried in a gondola so as to prevent movement on this animal's part. Both animals received identical visual input, except that with one subject this input was accompanied by motor activity (walking) while in the other subject it was not. Held found that the active animal developed normal coordination between its visual perceptions and body movements while the other subject failed to do so. The ability of the former animal to make visual discriminations and reasonably accurate distance perceptions was also found to be significantly superior to those of the passively-moved subject.

> After an average of about 30 hours in the apparatus the active member of each pair showed normal behavior in several visually guided tasks. It blinked at an approaching object; it put out its forepaws as if to ward off collision when gently carried downward toward a surface, and it avoided the deep side of a visual cliff—an apparatus in which two depths, one shallow and the other a sharp drop, appear beneath a sheet of glass. After the same period of exposure each of the passive kittens failed to show these types of behavior. The passive kittens did, however, develop such types of behavior within days after they were allowed to run about in a normal environment.[60]

The same experiment was then performed with human subjects, though in this case both the active and the passively-moved participants wore distorting prisms similar to those worn by Stratton. (A passively-moved subject is one whose movement is not self-produced or self-originating; in the present experiment the subject was moved about in a wheelchair.) When the normal correlation between movement and visual perception was altered under these experimental conditions, there was a marked difference between the actual visual experiences of the two human subjects. This difference was made evident by a series of perceptual tests which were administrated after the subjects left the enclosure. As both participants had identical visual input, the differences in their visual experiences was attributable to the presence or absence of active movement on the subject's part. To Held this demonstrated a "close, one-to-one correlation between movement and visual feedback and . . . further evidence of a link between motor and visual mechanisms in the central nervous system. . . [These] experiments have uncovered a fundamental role of the motor-sensory feedback loop."[61]

The findings of these studies thus converge with the conclusions drawn by Stration regarding the central contribu-

tion made by bodily movements to perceptual recognition. However, Held's experiments on the distinction between active and passive movement do take us one step further than did Ames and Stratton's studies. Mead would certainly want to draw a distinction between movement done *by* and movement done *on* the body, and that from the point of view of perceptual activity only active movement is movement in the strictest sense. This last point is well documented by the following studies of the effects on perception of complete cessation of movement. These studies will complete our examination of empirical support for Mead's position.

THE EFFECT OF IMMOBILITY ON VISUAL EXPERIENCE

The effect of immobility on perception is perhaps best illustrated by sensory deprivation studies. In these experiments a subject was voluntarily confined himself to a bed in a small cubicle twenty four hours a day up to seven days, during which time the subject wore translucent goggles which prevented patterned vision of objects and shapes in the cubicle. The arms and hands of the subjects were then fitted with cardboard tubes to minimize movement and, in turn, tactual perceptions. The only bodily movement the subjects were permitted was to periodically eat and use the toilet.

Two main findings were obtained from these studies, both of which were unexpected. First of all, after a dozen hours or so, during which most subjects slept, they began to have blank periods when they either thought of nothing at all or else could not control their experiences. All of the subjects then went on to have hallucinatory experiences so severe that a number of the subjects were forced to conclude the experiment. With regard to this first finding, the experimenters concluded that

> Prolonged exposure to a monotonous environment, then, has definitely deleterious effects. The individual's thinking is impaired; he shows childish emotional responses; his visual perception becomes disturbed; he suffers from hallucinations; his brainwave pattern changes. It appears that, aside from their specific functions, sensory stimuli have the general function of maintaining this arousal and they rapidly lose their power to do so if they are restricted to the monotonously repeated stimulation of an unchanging environment.[62]

In another article they reported the second finding, which concerns the subject's perception of objects in the visual environment after leaving the cubicle and after a period of tactual and kinaesthetic deprivation.[63] When the goggles were removed there was at first a large amount of random movement and drifting of objects in the visual field. The experimenter and the room appeared to the subject to rapidly become taller and wider, then bulge toward or away from the observer. One subject reported that, "The wall is waving all over the place—a horrifying sight, as a matter of fact. I find it difficult to keep my eyes open for any length of time, the visual field is in such a state of chaos."[64] There was also an apparent movement of the visual field associated with the head and eye movement of the subject, with a subsequent loss of position constancy: an object appeared to approach or retreat as the subject moved his head toward or away from the object. One participant even reported a tendency for perceptual lag to occur

> . . . when objects were moved across the visual field, [with] part of the moving figure appearing to trail behind the rest. Thus, when a thin black line was rotated against a dimly illuminated screen in a darkened room, the line seemed S-shaped because the ends "lagged" behind the center part.[65]

The experimenters concluded the study with the remark that ". . . exposing the subject to a monotonous sensory environment can cause disorganization of brain function similar to, and in some respects as great as, that produced by drugs or lesions."[66] They also noted that the effects recorded above are usually avoided under conditions of normal sensory stimulation, tactual feedback, and bodily movement. This is of course the conclusion most relevant to the purposes of this paper.

In conclusion the studies discussed in the last few pages of this paper should suggest to the reader the largely negative effects immobility has on visual (and auditory) perception. When the findings from these sensory deprivation studies are conjoined with the results obtained by Ames, Stratton, and Held, the dependence of normal (that is, non-hallucinatory and non-distorted) visual experiences on tactual, manipulatory, and bodily activity is further confirmed. In everyday experience we are seldom aware of the extent of this dependence. In the situation created in the psychological laboratory, though, where the variables affecting perceptual experience can be more easily isolated and controlled, the importance of such factors as manipulation and movement become more and more pronounced.

As we have seen, Mead's conceptual model is most concretely expressed in terms of his analysis of the act into three stages (perceptual, manipulatory, and consummatory), and the corresponding relation between the acting organism and the physical environment within each of these stages. This model thus functions as an interpretation of Mead's theory of the relation between perception and action, with a number of the postulates of the theory being built into the model. This complex theory of perception and action should not, however, be equated with the particular model developed in the first part of this paper; the model outlined there expresses but *one* aspect of Mead's overall theory of knowledge and theory of mind. His account of the interrelation (or transaction) between mind, self, and society, for example, is not easily interpretable in terms of the three stages of the act, so that an additional model must be employed with regard to his social psychology.[67] Additionally, unlike the model of the kinetic theory of gases or Bohr's model of the atom, Mead's model (of the three stages) is neither visualizable nor substantial in character. This follows given that the analysis of the act into three stages, along with the distinction between organism and environment, are purely

methodological distinctions, introduced for the purpose of analysis. To take either of these distinctions as substantial would be completely foreign to Mead's instrumental interpretation of both models and theories.

Mead's theory of the act and perception is in my estimation highly attractive on both conceptual and empirical grounds for the following reasons. First, of the competing theories of perception in the current epistemological literature, only in the case of Mead and a few other positions (such as those of Piaget and Merleau-Ponty) do we find any *systematic* attempt to integrate perceptual and bodily activity within a single explanatory framework. Secondly, Mead's recognition of the central and indispensable role played by touch and manipulation in perceptual recognition, is highly confirmed by numerous experimental studies, a number of which were discussed in part two. Thirdly, Mead's position in contrast with a number of others allows the experimentalist to anticipate and predict what empirical findings he will obtain regarding visual recognition if the subject is denied manipulatory and bodily feedback. To recall a few, Ames' subjects could recognize the true geometrical shape of the room only after touching the corners and walls with a stick; Held's passively-moved subjects experienced great difficulty in perceptual recognition tasks after having worn inverting prisms; and Heron's sensory deprivation studies revealed the negative effects of sustained immobility on perceptual experience. Lastly, there is the epistemological thesis that veridical or non-illusory, non-distorted perceptual experience rests on a transaction between *what is contributed by the experiencing subject* (e.g., previous perceptual experience, recognition and knowledge of the object being perceived, intentions, and bodily activity), *along with environmental conditions* (e.g., the geometrical features of objects in the perceptual field, their size and distance from the observer, etc.). This is in sharp contrast with those dualistic accounts of the subject-object relation where the subject supposedly constructs his interpretations of reality independently of previously acquired and presupposed environmental cues, and where the characteristics of the perceptual object are thought to be totally independent of the intentions and bodily activity of the subject.

The theory which eventually emerged in Mead's writings concerning the organism-environment transaction was therefore not only coordinated with empirical findings but, perhaps as importantly, served to integrate such findings within a theoretical framework that was at once both comprehensive and suggestive. For these reasons, Mead's position does merit the sustained attention of both epistemologists and behavioral scientists. Hopefully, the recent upsurge of interest among philosophers in the theory of action, and among psychologists in the role of bodily activity in perceptual recognition, will signal further research into Mead's position, surely one of the more extensive accounts of perception and action to be found in Western philosophy.

NOTES

[1] D. Rucker, *The Chicago Pragmatists* (Minneapolis: University of Minnesota Press, 1969).

[2] J. Dewey, "George Herbert Mead," *Journal of Philosophy,* 28 (1931), pp. 309-314.

[3] H. Schneider, *A History of American Philosophy,* second edition (New York: Columbia University Press, 1962).

[4] H. S. Thayer, "George Herbert Mead," in his *Meaning and Action: A Critical History of Pragmatism* (Indianapolis: Bobbs-Merrill Co., 1968).

[5] A. J. Reck, "The Constructive Pragmatism of George Herbert Mead," in his *Recent American Philosophy* (New York: Random House, 1962).

[6] M. H. Kuhn, "Major Trends in Symbolic Interaction Theory in the Past Twenty-Five Years," *Sociological Quarterly,* V (1964), pp. 61-84.

[7] T. V. Smith, "The Social Philosophy of George Herbert Mead," *American Journal of Sociology,* 37 (1932), pp. 368-385.

[8] P. E. Pfuetze, *Self, Society, Existence: Human Nature and Dialogue in the Thought of G. H. Mead and Martin Buber* (New York: Harper Torchbooks, 1954).

[9] P. Tibbetts, "Mead and Symbolic Interaction Theory on the Self, Behavior, and the Social Environment," to appear in *Pragmatism Reconsidered,* ed. by E. Freeman and J. Smith, Open Court (late 1974).

[10] C. W. Morris, "Peirce, Mead, and Pragmatism," *Philosophical Review,* 47 (1938), pp. 109-127.

[11] M. Natanson, "The Concept of the Given in Peirce and Mead," *The Modern Schoolman,* 32 (1955), pp. 143-157.

[12] G. A. DeLaguna, "Communication, the Act and the Object with Reference to Mead," *Journal of Philosophy,* 43 (1946), pp. 225-238.

[13] S. Rosenthal, "Peirce, Mead, and the Logic of Concepts," *Transactions of the C. S. Peirce Society,* 5 (1969), pp. 173-187.

[14] W. H. Werkmeister, "Mead's Philosophy of the Act," in his *A History of Philosophical Ideas in America* (New York: The Ronald Press, 1949).

[15] A. E. Murphy, "Concerning Mead's *Philosophy of the Act,*" *Journal of Philosophy,* 36 (1939), pp. 85-103.

[16] C. W. Morris, Introductory Remarks to Mead's *Philosophy of the Act* (Chicago: Chicago University Press, 1938), pp. vii-lxxiii.

[17]_____, *The Pragmatic Movement in American Philosophy* (New York: George Braziller, Inc., 1970).

[18] P. Tibbetts, "A Philosopher Examines the Organism-Environment Relation in Modern Ecology and Ethology," *Man-Environment Systems,* P4 (1971), pp. 1-20.

[19]_____, "William James and the Doctrine of 'Pure Experience'," *Journal of the History of the Behavioral Sciences* (to appear in August, 1974).

[20]_____, "The 'Levels of Experience' Doctrine in Modern Philosophy of Mind," *Dialectica,* 25 (1971), pp. 131-151.

[21] Cf. James's "The Experience of Activity," in his *Essays in Radical Empiricism* (New York: Longmans, Green and Co., 1912), where he writes that

> . . . The world experienced (otherwise called the 'field of consciousness') comes at all times with our body at its centre, centre of vision, centre of action, centre of interest. Where the body is is 'here'; when the body acts is 'now'; what the body touches is 'this'; all other things are 'there' and 'then' and 'that'. These words of emphasized position imply a systematization of things with reference to a focus of action and interest which lies in the body; and the systematization is now so instinctive (was it ever so?) that no developed or active experience exists for us at all except in that ordered form. (p. 170)

This statement reveals James's recognition of the importance of the body in experience, a factor which only James and Mead of all the pragmatists placed at the center of their respective theories of knowledge.

[22] P. Tibbetts, "John Dewey and Contemporary Phenomenology on Experience and the Subject-Object Relation," *Philosophy Today,* 15 (1971), pp. 250-275.

[23] On Dewey's similar emphasis on the tactual modality over the visual, Herbert Schneider relates the following interesting incident.

> . . . I remember very vividly a dinner party that [Frederick] Woodbridge gave, and Dewey was there; and Woodbridge began talking about the visible world and the importance of vision for the theory of understanding. Dewey listened to it all; but then he said rather quietly, "I think this whole problem of understanding should be approached not from the point of view of the eyes, but from the point of view of the hands. It's what we grasp that matters." The next day Woodbridge said to me, "Is Dewey serious about this?" And I said, "Very serious; this is very important to him." He said, "Well, I guess I don't understand this." And I really believe that was the basic contrast in their whole conception of knowledge—Dewey took manipulation very seriously, *whereas Woodbridge took the more Platonic visual approach.* (my italics)

—from *Dialogue on John Dewey,* edited by C. Lamont (New York: Horizon Press, 1959), pp. 95-96.

For further discussion on this see H. Schneider's "The Prospect for Empirical Philosophy," in *John Dewey, The Man and His Philosophy* (Cambridge: Harvard University Press, 1930), esp. pp. 120-121.

24 G. H. Mead, *The Philosophy of the Act,* edited by C. W. Morris et. al. (Chicago: University of Chicago Press, 1938), p. 3. It should be noted that this book consists of essays from the last period of Mead's career and were not intended for publication. They were collected by Morris and others and published in their present form after Mead's death in 1931. This also applies to Mead's other posthumous writings: *The Philosophy of the Present* (1932), *Mind, Self, and Society* (1934), and *Movements of Thought in the Nineteenth Century* (1936). A number of Mead's articles in periodicals have been edited and published by A. J. Reck, *G. H. Mead, Selected Writings* (1964).

25 *Ibid.,* p. 164.

26 *Ibid.,* p. 165. It is instructive to compare this with Merleau-Ponty's remark that there can be no "perspectiveless perspective".

27 *Ibid.,* p. 13.

28 *Ibid.,* p. 166.

29 *Ibid.,* p. 24. In a later essay Mead adds that "In the content of resistance which goes into the chair seen at a distance the organism is inviting itself to sit down in the chair. . . . In some fashion the organism must be in the attitude of reacting in contact fashion to the distant stimulus if it is to be brought into the now." (pp. 162-163)

30 *Ibid.,* p. 212.

31 *Ibid.,* p. 284.

32 *Ibid.,* p. 454-455.

33 *Ibid.,* pp. 291-292. For further discussion of this point see P. Tibbetts, "Observable Versus Inferred Entities: Pragmatic and Phenomenological Considerations," *Studium Generale,* 24 (1971), pp. 1067-1078.

34 For further discussion of the relation between a general theory of signs (or "semiotics") and Mead's theory of the act, see C. W. Morris, "Peirce, Mead, and Pragmatism," *Philosophical Review,* 47 (1938), pp. 109-127, and S. Rosenthal, "Peirce, Mead, and the Logic of Concepts," *Transactions of the C. S. Peirce Society,* 5 (1969), pp. 173-187.

35 G. H. Mead, *The Philosophy of the Act,* op. cit., p. 14.

36 Mead later distinguishes three relatively distinct qualities of stimulus objects in terms of the responses of the perceiver and the stages of the act; respectively, those qualities which mediate locomotion, manipulation, and consummation.

37 P. Tibbetts, "Perceptual Theory and Epistemological Dualism: Some Examples from Experimental Psychology," *Psychological Record,* 22 (1972), pp. 401-411.

38 C. W. Morris, in the Introduction to *The Philosophy of the Act,* op. cit., p. lxviii.

39 The "meaning" of a thing may at times be determined by its function, as with the case of an object primarily designed with utility in mind. This is not always the case though. Art objects, for example, are not generally thought of in terms of utility, nor are religious icons, poems, or even manuscripts by philosophers. The meaning of these latter objects is established by the cultural context and, in the final analysis, by the aspirations which gave rise to them and the ideals they subserve.

40 Cf. William James's *The Principles of Psychology* (New York: Dover Books, 1890). Especially see vol. II, "The Perception of Reality," where James discusses the various 'sub-universes' postulated by theoretical reflection: the magical, the religious, the aesthetic, the scientific, and so forth.

41 R. L. Gregory and J. G. Wallace, "Recovery From Early Blindness: A Case Study," Monograph No. 2 of the *Experimental Psychology Society* (1963). Reprinted in and quoted from *Perception: Selected Readings From Science and Phenomenology,* edited by P. Tibbetts (Chicago: Quadrangle Books, 1969), p. 367.

42 *Ibid.,* p. 382.

43 *Ibid.,* p. 383.

44 J. Dewey, *Psychology* (New York: American Book Co., third edition, 1891), p. 165.

45 I. Rock and C. S. Harris, "Vision and Touch," *Scientific American,* 216 (May, 1967), p. 104. Somewhat different conclusions are reached by M. A. Souder in "Visual and Proprioceptive Determinants of Space Perception and Movement", *Journal of Motor Behavior,* 4 (1972), pp. 13-22.

46 I. Rock, *The Nature of Perceptual Adaptation* (New York: Basic Books, 1966), pp. 225-226.

47 W. H. Ittelson and F. P. Kilpatrick, "Experiments in Perception," *Scientific American,* 185 (August, 1951), p. 55.

48 F. P. Kilpatrick, "Perception in Critical Situations," in *Explorations in Transactional Psychology,* edited by F. P. Kilpatrick (New York: New York University Press, 1961), p. 319.

The reader may be interested in knowing that a correspondence took place during the forties between some of the pragmatists and the transactional school of psychology. Adelbert Ames was the founder of this movement, with Ittelson and Kilpatrick important later contributors. The correspondence was initiated and sustained by the common interests of the transactionalists and the pragmatists, especially over the interrelation between perception, meaning, and action. For a further account of this correspondence see *The Morning Notes of Adelbert Ames*, edited by H. Cantril (New Brunswick: Rutgers Univ. Press, 1960), and *J. Dewey and A. Bentley: A Philosophical Correspondence, 1932-1951*, edited by S. Ratner et. al. (New Brunswick: Rutgers University Press, 1964). Also see, P. Tibbetts, "The Transactional Theory of Human Knowledge and Action: Notes Toward a 'Behavioral Ecology'," *Man-Environment Systems*, 2, P2 (1972), pp. 37-59.

[49] G. M. Stratton, "Some Preliminary Experiments on Vision Without Inversion of the Retinal Image," *Psychological Review*, 3 (1896), pp. 611-617.

[50] *Ibid.*, pp. 613-615.

[51] *Ibid.*, p. 615.

[52] *Ibid.*, p. 617.

[53] *Ibid.*, p. 617.

[53] *Ibid.*, p. 617.

[54] _____, "Vision Without Inversion of the Retinal Image," *Psychological Review*, 4 (1897), pp. 341-360 and 463-481.

[55] *Ibid.*, p. 356.

[56] *Ibid.*, p. 359.

[57] *Ibid.*, p. 476.

[58] For further studies related to Stratton's work see Ivo Kohler, "Experiments With Goggles," *Scientific American* (May, 1962), pp. 63-72. Kohler's studies were designed to explore ". . . the unconscious learning process that goes on in normal vision [by investigating] how the visual system responds to images that are systematically distorted."

[59] R. Held, "Plasticity in Sensory-Motor Systems," *Scientific American*, 213 (Nov., 1965), pp. 84-94.

[60] *Ibid.*, p. 84.

[61] *Ibid.*, p. 94. For further research into the distinction between active and passive movement, along with a theory as to the neurological significance of this distinction, I refer the reader to a much discussed article by Eduard von Holst, "Relations Between the Central Nervous System and the Peripheral Organs," *Animal Behavior*, II (1954), pp. 89-94. Reprinted in *Perception: Selected Readings From Science and Phenomenology*, edited by P. Tibbetts, op. cit., pp. 104-116.

[62] W. Heron, "The Pathology of Boredom," *Scientific American*, 196 (Jan., 1957), pp. 53-56.

[63] The following account is from W. Heron, B. K. Doane, and T. H. Scott, "Visual Disturbances After Prolonged Perceptual Isolation," *Canadian Journal of Psychology*, X (1956), pp. 13-18. Reprinted in and quoted from *Perception*, edited by P. Tibbetts, op. cit., pp. 389-397.

[64] *Ibid.*, p. 392.

[65] *Ibid.*, p. 395.

[66] *Ibid.*, p. 397. For additional studies on perceptual isolation see P. Solomon, et al., editors, *Sensory Deprivation* (Cambridge: Harvard University Press, 1961).

[67] P. Tibbetts, "Mead and Recent Symbolic Interaction Theory on the Self, Behavior, and the Social Environment," in *Pragmatism Reconsidered*, op. cit.

William P. Nye (essay date 1977)

SOURCE: "George Herbert Mead and the Paradox of Prediction," in *Sociological Analysis*, Vol. 38, No. 2, Summer, 1977, pp. 91-105.

[*In the following essay, Nye discusses the more obscure ideas of Mead's philosophy, and places them in context with Mead's better known work.*]

It has been stated and reiterated that George Herbert Mead has become the captive of his interpreters (Natanson, 1956:2; Douglas, 1970:17). The purpose of this essay is to initiate a metaphorical liberation of Mead from his social psychological captivity. However, this is not another attempt to unearth what Mead "really meant" when he speaks of the social self, the "I," the "me," the "generalized other" or the like. This has already been done repeatedly with the net result of establishing two schools of interpreters, the determinists and the non-determinists (Kuhn, 1964; Abbott, *et al.*, 1973; Singlemann, 1973). I wish instead to employ an approach which attempts to understand Mead's "social psychology" in the context of his work considered as a whole. The need for such an approach has been noted indirectly by Nisbet (1974: 110-13) and more directly by Friedrichs (1970:185) in stating that "American sociologists, although acknowledging Mead as perhaps their most creative theorist, appeared to extract from his larger pragmatic humanism only those portions that would fit into the mold of an epistemology borrowed from natural science."

Friedrichs does not, however, explicitly develop what this "larger pragmatic humanism" entails, nor does he trace its implications for sociological thought. It is my purpose, then, to examine this remaining problem by attempting to grasp the *pragmatic* significance of Mead's thought for anyone, but particularly any sociologist, who seriously considers this thought *in its entirety*.

One way to grasp the problem at hand is by employing Friedrich's (1970:177-89) notion of the "paradox of prediction." This concept is not entirely original as it is closely connected with Thomas' "definition of the situation" (Thomas, 1920:584; McHugh, 1968) and Merton's "self-fulfilling prophecy" (Merton, 1948). The paradox of prediction adds a new twist, however, in that it self-consciously focuses its meaning on social scientific research and is encapsulated in the dictum, "All social research is in principle action research" (Friedrichs, 1970:181). More specifically, it holds that

> The social scientist's perception of uniformities represents *a new and unique event* that by its very appearance must to some degree in the shorter or longer run operate to deny the full validity of the perceived sequence when he seeks to reconfirm at a later time the order apprehended earlier (Friedrichs, 1970:180).

The relation of the paradox of prediction to the work of George H. Mead is both striking and ironic. Mead was well aware of the power of language to influence, indeed to form, the minds and behavior of men, and, as I will now attempt to show, he was equally well aware (or at least convinced) that his own scientifically-oriented system of thought, his own truth as it were, contained the means within itself to bring itself to full realization. To put this hypothesis more plainly, the main contention of this essay is that Mead's thought exhibits all the earmarks of a grand scale, self-fulfilling prophecy; that his view of social and psychological man contains the potential, once it has been communicated, internalized and acted upon, *to bring itself into being* in an ongoing, processual manner. The irony contained in this view of Mead will also be brought out by suggesting how Mead's better known interpreters have perhaps unwittingly stood in the way of what can be aptly described as Mead's self-fulfillment as a thinker and agent of social change.

MEAD'S PROJECT

The first point to be established is that Mead's so-called social psychology loses its importance as a self-fulfilling prophecy or program of action when it is extracted from the setting of his larger philosophical concerns. The means I have devised to accomplish this utilizes his best known, most widely quoted and read book, *Mind, Self, and Society.* Although this work was compiled posthumously on the basis of students' notes, it is still largely consistent with articles and books which Mead did write. This is at least true at the general level of analysis I intend to pursue. Moreover, given my concern with the effect Mead had on his sociologically-oriented contemporaries and subsequent generations of students, the great popularity of the book—seventeen printings as of 1970— is a point in favor of using it as a general reflection of Mead's thought. The importance of this book as an accurate and inclusive summary of Mead's thought has been duly noted by the book's knowledgeable editor, Charles W. Morris. He informs us in the Preface that the work is based on Mead's famous course called "Social Psychology" which "gave the foundation of Mead's thought. It was in effect Mead as scientist; it was upon this foundation that his philosophical elaboration and social participation rested" (Mead, 1934:5).

The truth of this assessment can be confirmed through a careful and thorough reading of the book and by comparison with Mead's other published works though as Natanson's cogent analysis shows, Mead's more sophisticated philosophical analyses are to be located elsewhere (Natanson, 1956). The fact that *Mind, Self, and Society* is essentially the transcript of a lecture course invites one to adopt something of a student's attitude toward its analysis, and for heuristic purposes this is precisely the approach I shall employ. "Let us pretend," as they say, that we are taking Mead's course in "Social Psychology" and let us further pretend that, as students, we wish to understand the course as one which states its premises, develops them and gets "somewhere" in the sense that it contains conclusions. I believe it is quite common for those of us who teach to have a "point" or "set of points" to our courses. It is considered good form to develop a course in such a way that we deliver our most general and most important and meaningful points toward the end. If this principle can be accepted, and I think it applies particularly well to Mead's course, then the final lectures should represent the culmination of Mead's thought on his given topic of inquiry. I believe this principle holds especially true for introductory or survey courses and Mead's "Social Psychology" appears to have been just this. It makes little sense, then, to follow the lead of others and lift the middle section of Mead's course, that on "Self," and consider this the "guts" of the course or the most important body of thought contained in the integrated set of lectures. On the contrary, one should prefer to look at the midsection as a means to the end, or the way toward the more important conclusions. Moreover, Mead's final lectures show this to be the case, for it is there that he brings home the lessons to be derived from his theory of the social self. In fact, in order to demonstrate partially that the conventional interpretational emphasis on self is misleading, I will deliberately omit any reference to the "self" part of the course which the editors block off as lectures 18-29 (Mead, 1934:135-226). In a certain sense, what Mead has to say is more clearly understood without these refinements.

However, before analyzing the final lectures of Mead's course on Social Psychology I feel it is necessary to at least make some reference to a central theme developed in the opening lectures. This theme is Mead's unequivocal insistence on the "reflexive" character of "mind" or intelligence:

> The evolutionary appearance of mind or intelligence takes place when the whole social process of experience and behavior is brought within the experience of any one of the separate individuals implicated therein, and when the individual's adjustment to the process is modified and refined by the awareness or consciousness which he thus has of it. It is by means of reflexiveness—the turning-back of the experience of the individual upon himself—that the whole social process is thus brought into the experience of the individuals involved in it, it is by such means, which enable the individual to take the

attitude of the other toward himself, that the individual is able consciously to adjust himself to that process in any given social act in terms of his adjustment to it. Reflexiveness, then, is the essential condition, within the social process, for the development of mind (Mead, 1934:134).[1]

Consideration of reflexiveness is an "essential condition" for any thorough understanding of Mead, for reflexiveness constitutes the key mechanism through which his prophecies are to be fulfilled. Without reflexiveness man becomes incapable of voluntary action which for Mead is largely synonymous with intelligence (Mead, 1934:95).

This theme of voluntarism is central to Mead's prophetic thought in that it permits social evolution toward "higher" or "better" forms of social organization through intelligence. Intelligence in this sense finds its origins in that most basic social institution of language as clearly indicated in these quotations drawn from lecture 13:

> Language is a process of indicating certain stimuli and changing the response to them in the system of behavior. Language as a social process has made it possible for us to pick out responses and hold them in the organism of the individual, so that they are there in relation to that which we indicate. . . . Ideas as distinct from acts, or as failing to issue in over behavior, are simply what we do not do; they are possibilities of overt responses which we test out implicitly in the central nervous system and then reject in favor of those which we do in fact act upon or carry into effect. The process of intelligent conduct is essentially a process of selection from among various alternatives; intelligence is largely a matter of selectivity (Mead, 1934:97, 99).

In lecture 16, entitled **"Mind and the Symbol,"** Mead reiterates the theme of voluntarism and gives it biological grounding by positing it as a feature of the human being's central nervous system. In this way he makes freedom, in the sense of being able to form and actively choose from a number of linguistically organized alternatives, a biological potential which is realizable through the social process.

Having expressed Mead's position on the issue of voluntary action I now wish to move directly to his concluding lectures on "Society" where he develops this Romantic theme of freedom in social context into a prophetic vision. In the concluding thought of lecture 32 called **"Organism, Community, and Environment,"** Mead finally makes perfectly clear where his views on the social process lead: ". . . human society presents an end of the process of organic development. It is needless to say that, so far as the development of human society is concerned, the process itself is a long way from its goal" (Mead, 1934:252). From here Mead presents a series of lectures which serve to elucidate the components of his developmental or evolutionary view of human society, the goal of this process and finally, how this goal is continuously being realized. Lecture 34 or, **"The Community and the Institution"** gives schematic attention to these matters

and the remaining lectures serve to fill in the details. Mead starts this lecture by introducing one of his most significant units of social structure or what he calls the "institution." Its importance can be seen in that it represents the social embodiment, as it were, of both self and mind, or, to use Mead's words:

> There are what we have termed "generalized social attitudes" which make an organized self possible. In the community there are certain ways of acting under situations which are essentially identical, and these ways of acting on the part of anyone are those which we excite in others when we take certain steps. . . . There are then, whole series of such common responses in the community in which we live, and such responses are what we term "institutions." The institution represents a common response on the part of all members of the community to a particular situation. . . . Without social institutions of some sort, without the organized social attitudes and activities by which social institutions are constituted, there could be no fully mature individual selves or personalities at all. . . . Social institutions, like individual selves, are developments within, or particular and formalized manifestations of, the social life-process at its human evolutionary level (Mead, 1934: 260-62).

And then Mead follows this with a clear statement as to how reflexiveness or voluntarism fits into this dialectic of self and society.[2]

> Human society, we have insisted, does not merely stamp the pattern of its organized social behavior upon any one of its individual numbers, so that this pattern becomes likewise the pattern of the individual's self; it also, at the same time, gives him a mind, as the means or ability of consciously conversing with himself in terms of the social attitudes which constitute the structure of his self and which embody the pattern of human society's organized behavior as reflected in that structure. And his mind enables him in turn to stamp the pattern of his further developing self (further developing through his mental activity) upon the structure or organization of human society, and thus in a degree to reconstruct and modify in terms of his self the general pattern of social group behavior in terms of which his self was originally constituted (Mead, 1934:263n).

What this shows above all else is that Mead's view of society (perhaps more properly called the social process) was open-ended. Mead was against dogmatism both in the context of religious beliefs in particular, and social values in general. The questioning and ongoing reconstruction of values through reflective intelligence was an essential aspect of Mead's view of social process. Moreover, he saw this continual reconstructive process moving in a predictable direction, that of the universal. That is, he believed that attitudes changed as institutions changed and believed as well that both were moving, historically and "rationally," toward the realization of ever larger communities.

Barry (1968) has noted this orientation in Mead's practical involvement with the multi-ethnic sociopolitical realities of Chicago but Mead's larger view prophesied a more or less inevitable evolution toward a universal social order. It was also Mead's position that reflective intelligence as an interactional process would simultaneously become ever more fully realized and developed. One could even say that Mead looked upon human history as one long and collective socialization process wherein the mind set he labeled the generalized other and the mean human capacity for reflective intelligence were continually expanding in a way which reflexively constructed and embraced increasingly larger collectivities of social actors.

It is part and parcel of conventional sociological knowledge about Mead to state the following: "Primary socialization ends with the formation of the generalized other within the mind of the child. With this formation the child has internalized both a sense of society, identity and reality, etc . . ." (P. Berger and B. Berger, 1972: 55-65). Any such view, however, represents a funneling or narrowing of Mead, for if we closely examine *Mind, Self, and Society,* we find that in Mead's view primary socialization in the above sense was a process which should never stop if society was to achieve its goal. All of this can be seen in the following passage which derogatorily likens anything less than an internationally oriented conception of the generalized other to the sense of community possessed by a juvenile delinquent.

> Education is definitely the process of taking over a certain organized set of responses to one's own stimulation; and until one can respond to himself as the community responds to him, he does not genuinely belong to the community, as the small boy belongs to a gang rather than to the city in which he lives. We all belong to small cliques and we may remain simply inside of them. The "organized other" present in ourselves is then a community of narrow diameter. We are struggling now to get a certain amount of international mindedness. We are realizing ourselves as members of a larger community. The situation is analogous to that of the boy and the gang; the boy gets a larger self in proportion as he enters into this larger community. In general, the self has answered definitely to that organization of the social response which constitutes the community as such; the degree to which the self is developed depends upon the community, upon the degree to which the individual calls out that institutionalized group of responses in himself (Mead, 1934:265).

To understand the implications of what Mead is getting at here, it is necessary to refer to a point brought out in the early lectures, the idea of the "universal." Lecture 12 centers about this concept and Mead's fundamental definition locates the universal as an essential and inescapable aspect of language:

> Thinking takes place in terms of universals, and a universal is an entity that is distinguishable from the object by means of which we think it. When we think of a spade we are not confined in our thought to any particular spade. Now if we think

of the universal spade there must be something that we think about, and that is confessedly not given in the particular occurrence which is the occasion of the thought. The thought transcends all occurrences (Mead, 1934:88).

Without much distortion one can equate this concept with what we now think of as the generic, or, with that kind of concept which is of prime importance in scientific research. Mead does not pay further direct attention to universals until lecture 34, the point at which we left off, but here the term re-enters the discussion as an essential component of his prophecy. It may well be that Mead's lack of attention to universals in the "Self" part of *Mind, Self, and Society* has had a deleterious effect on the fate of his intellectual legacy. In any event, lecture 34 shows Mead paying extended and detailed attention to the idea of universal communities, particularly those involving linguistic discourse. The following passage clearly and unequivocally gives Mead's views on the subject:

> We are apt to assume that our estimate of the value of the community should depend upon its size. The American worships bigness as over against qualitative social content. A little community such as that of Athens produced some of the greatest spiritual products which the world has ever seen. . . . I wish to bring out the implicit universality of the highly developed, highly organized community. Now, Athens as the home of Socrates, Plato, and Aristotle, the seat of a great metaphysical development in the same period, the birthplace of political theorists and great dramatists, actually belongs to the whole world. The qualitative achievements which we ascribe to a little community belong to it only in so far as it has the organization that makes it universal. The Athenian community rested upon slave labor and upon a political situation which was narrow and contracted, and that part of its social organization was not universal and could not be made the basis for a large community. The Roman Empire disintegrated very largely because its whole economic structure was laid on the basis of slave labor. It was not organized on a universal basis. From the legal standpoint and administrative organization it was universal, and just as Greek philosophy has come down to us so has Roman law. To the degree that any achievement of organization of a community is successful it is universal, and makes possible a bigger community. In one sense there cannot be a community which is larger than that represented by rationality, and the Greek brought rationality to its self-conscious expression. In that same sense the gospel of Jesus brought definitely to expression the attitude of neighborliness to which anyone would appeal, and provided the soil out of which could arise a universal religion. That which is fine and admirable is universal—although it may be true that the actual society in which the universality can get its expression has not arisen (Mead, 1934:266-67).

Here we have it: "That which is fine and admirable is universal" and "To the degree that any achievement or organization of a community is successful it is universal and makes possible a bigger community." Thus, that which is social organization or community is universal and therefore fine and admirable, with rationality forming the largest of all possible communities. At this point one is tempted to call Mead an American prophet of world community and as we continue on, Mead gives us even more reason to do so. When Mead looks about him to find evidence that universal communities are being formed out of the evolutionary social process, he finds and discusses at length the significant examples of international economic relations, universal religious movements of a missionary nature, and the social phenomenon of sympathy (Mead, 1934:282-310).

In these final or culminating lectures Mead frequently draws from the more properly social psychological sections of his course, most particularly his discussions of reflective intelligence in the context of self-other relations. But what comes through most clearly is his eloquent and extended insistence that the reflective and reflexive social selves, characterizing all socialized members of the human species, act in historical concert, as it were, to achieve the "inevitable" goal of human progress: a universal brotherhood of man engaged in ongoing communication. He speaks, for example, of how nationalism is but a transitional stage toward the achievement of international-mindedness and discusses some surmountable obstacles that remain in the path of the "Ideal Society." For the sake of brevity, however, I would like to quote just one further passage from lecture 41 which I believe summarizes Mead's pragmatic vision:

> The ideal of human society is one which does bring people so closely together in their interrelationships, so fully develops the necessary system of communication, that the individuals who exercise their own peculiar functions can take the attitude of those whom they affect. The development of communication is not simply a matter of abstract ideas, but is a process of putting one's self in the place of the other person's attitude, communicating through significant symbols. Remember that what is essential to a significant symbol is that the gesture which affects others should affect the individual himself in the same way. It is only when the stimulus which one gives another arouses in himself the same or like response that the symbol is a significant symbol. Human communication takes place through such significant symbols, and the problem is one of organizing a community which makes this possible. If that system of communication could be made theoretically perfect, the individual would affect himself as he affects others in every way. That would be the ideal of communication, an ideal attained in logical discourse wherever it is understood. The meaning of that which is said is here the same to one as it is to everybody else. Universal discourse is then the formal ideal of communication. If communication can be carried through and made perfect, then there would exist that kind of democracy to which we have referred, in which each individual would carry just the response in himself that he knows he calls out in the community (Mead, 1934: 327).

What remains to be seen, however, is how this social ideal is to be realized at the level of practice as opposed to theory. It is at this point that we believe the paradox of prediction alluded to above takes on importance. If one, that is *any one,* looks upon mind, self and society in the manner of Mead—i.e., if one adopts Mead's scientifically-oriented view of social process—then one's own self has been automatically opened to the possibility of consciously realizing universal communities of discourse. That is, if a social actor conceives of his own self as a process which develops or grows or realizes itself only in so far as it reflexively enlarges its notion of the generalized other to incorporate all of mankind, then it follows that this same self tends toward achieving Mead's social ideal. The paradox of prediction is thus implicitly contained in Mead's social philosophy: *Realization of the social ideal of universal selfhood is dependent upon the internalization of a rational* (i.e., scientific) *view of self as a relative, emergent,*[3] and dynamic product of social process in the manner described by Mead.

MEAD'S SOCIOLOGY

At this point the reader may ask what does all this have to do with the alleged narrowing of Mead's thought by his sociological interpreters? How, for example, have they deflected the prophetic element of Mead's thought? Several possible answers exist but the most important can be discovered by examining a frequently reiterated sociological criticism of Mead to the effect that he developed no extended theory of social structures and their relations. Herbert Blumer, for example, as Mead's best known sociological student and interpreter, has lauded Mead for reversing "the traditional assumptions underlying philosophical, psychological, and sociological thought to the effect that human beings possess minds and consciousness as original givens . . . ," but he goes on to say that, "in making his brilliant contributions along this line he did not map out a theoretical scheme of human society" (Blumer, 1969:61-62). This apparently apt criticism of Mead, however, serves as a significant factor in the "sociological retardation" of Mead's predictive thought and may quite possibly stem from an "occupational myopia" common to many sociologists. This is the sociologist's tendency to reify his own categorical depictions of social structure. What I mean by this is that many sociologists possess, or at least sometimes write as if they possess, something of a vested interest in the existence and perpetuation of group divisions. Is it not true, for instance, that class, caste, political party, sex and religious affiliation constitute but a few of the sociologist's most treasured and useful independent variables for the purposes of description and analysis? We tend to take such "things" very seriously and many of us would be professionally lost, in a cognitive sense, without them. But as Blumer states above, a problem arises in the sociological use of Mead's thought in that he pays little close attention to such variables as significant social entities. It is my opposing belief, however, that it has done and continues to do serious damage to the prophetic nature of the Meadian system for the sociologist (usually from the standpoint of symbolic interactionism) to attempt to affix his preferred collection of social structural realities as an appendage to Mead's thought. I do not think the sociologist's perceived need to do this can be legitimated by pointing to an oversight, or lack of concern for such structures, on the part of Mead. I believe instead that Mead looked upon such group categories as historically transient impediments to the realization of his formulated social ideal. Evidence for this can be gleaned from *Mind, Self, and Society,* by examining his comments on caste divisions in lecture 41 (Mead, 1934:318-19), but more directly applicable statements can be found elsewhere in his published writings. For instance, in a remarkable essay written near the end of his career under the title, **"National-Mindedness and International-Mindedness"** (Mead, 1929), Mead showed direct concern for the divisive nature which group divisions—particularly those associated with nationalism—tend to create. In expressing this concern Mead spells out why he did not place what can be called long-range, positive significance on such "variables" in his scientific and philosophical description of evolutionary social process. In this article Mead rightly discerns how there is nothing quite as effective as a "just war" to create moral unity and communal solidarity in a given society. A common enemy serves as a wondrous remedy for waning societal morale. But he could not conclude that war was a moral good because of its apparent functionality. Instead, Mead speaks from the perspective of his own thought to suggest that the problem of nationalism, i.e., the ceaseless bellicosity and recurrence of wars, be replaced with international-mindedness as an ethically more desirable functional equivalent.

In explaining this position Mead clearly elaborates the conclusions to be drawn from his course on social psychology, and he does so with considerable eloquence and passion. Mead continually points to components of social structure in a manner which underscores their immanently social nature, describes their contribution to our apperceived individuality as social actors, and most importantly, demonstrates their existence as historically produced obstacles in the way of attaining his evolutionary social ideal of universal selfhood. He writes, for example, that:

> Civilization is not an affair of reasonableness; it is an affair of social organization. The selfhood of a community depends upon such an organization that common goods do become the ends of the individuals of the community. . . . But there are still great gaps in our social organization, notably between our producers and the social service which they perform. Here there are groups that have to assure themselves of their self-respect by fighting on occasions. The labor unions and the employers as well preserve their solidarity, that is their sense of common selfhood, by the mechanisms of hostility, that is by the threats of strikes and lockouts. Back of it lies the inability of the laborer to realize himself in the social process in which he is engaged. Where such a situation becomes acute, men, if they can, will always bind themselves together by hostile organizations to realize their

common purposes and ends and thus assure themselves the selfhood which society denies them. Men will always jealously maintain and guard this mechanism to assure themselves to themselves. We will get rid of the mechanism of warfare only as our common life permits the individual to identify his own ends and purposes with those of the community of which he is a part and which has endowed him with a self (Mead, 1929:406-507).

This last quotation should give clear indication of the role our more conventional notions of social structure were to play in Mead's visionary system. Group affiliations were important in the short run but in evolutionary historical perspective they were to be viewed as temporary and transitional associations of incomplete selves, much as adolescent peer groups, or the "near groups" which delinquent gangs have been observed to form (Yablonsky, 1966), serve as stepping stones to membership in the larger adult community. In Mead's mind most of us remain socially and personally incomplete because of our various gang-like allegiances. To possess a fully realized self in the Meadian sense means to affirm and actively strengthen one's membership in the ideal community; where selves exist in an ever expanding nexus of isomorphic discourse; where international-mindedness is involved in the reflexive consciousness of all, and where "moral advance consists not in adapting individual natures to the fixed realities of a moral universe, but in constantly reconstructing and re-creating the world as the individuals evolve" (Mead, 1908:318).

One justifiable interpretation of the sociological import of Mead's message is that social progress is to go hand-in-hand with the disappearance of subject matter for a good deal of the "sociological enterprise" as it is presently constituted. Mead would have it that group divisions and interests would give way, through greater self-realization, to more universal collectivities and patterns of thought. Thus, elaborate theories of social structures and their influence are neither necessary nor actually compatible with Mead's action-centered social philosophy. Mead urged that men seek, embrace and further that which they had in common; that men make themselves more fully human by transcending that which divided them through the creative and reconstructive process of reflective intelligence. But this is not to say that Mead's thought is therefore useless for contemporary sociology. On the contrary, Mead's vision is profoundly sociological and deserves conscious and due consideration by sociologists for its uncommon success in handling the problem of reification. But this is not all, for the direction and purpose of Mead's thought demonstrates striking similarity to the later work and legacy of the acknowledged master of sociological thought, Emile Durkheim. I am not referring here to the Durkheim of the "social facts" fame but to the Durkheim who wrote *The Elementary Forms . . .* and founded the *Année Sociologique* School of French sociology. This is not the place to explicate the commonalities between Durkheim and Mead[4] except to say that the mature views of both thinkers converged on the idea that the scientifically-oriented student of human (i.e., social) behavior could not escape the revelation that, to quote Mead once more, "the isolated man is the one who belongs to a whole that he yet fails to realize" (Mead, 1926:389).

A somewhat indirect indication of this convergence can be gleaned from the work of Louis Dumont, a prominent French anthropologist who writes in the latter Durkheimian tradition. Dumont's apparent ability to represent this tradition is probably due to the fact that his mentor was Durkheim's famous nephew and chief collaborator in the *Année Sociologique* studies, Professor Marcel Mauss.[5] Dumont has encapsulated this tradition in what he calls the "sociological apperception," a phrase which he describes in this manner:

> . . . While sociology as such is found in egalitarian society (e.g., society ideologically based on doctrines of individualism), while it is immersed in it, while it even expresses it—in a sense to be seen—it has its roots in something quite different: the apperception of the social nature of man. To the self-sufficient individual it opposes man as a social being; it considers each man no longer as a particular incarnation of abstract humanity, but as a more or less autonomous point of emergence of a particular collective humanity, of a *society*. To be real, this way of seeing things must, in the individualistic universe, take the form of a revelation, and this is why I speak of *"sociological apperception"* (Dumont, 1970:5).

I believe there can be little doubt that the work of George Herbert Mead is deeply imbued with "sociological apperception." Indeed, I believe he carried it one step further in a philosophic sense and urged us to actively extend this apperception to include all mankind. If Mead can be faulted for anything it is for being overly optimistic about contemporary man's capacity for reflective intelligence. He may also have been unrealistic or naive in regard to the tenacity with which divisive categories and habits of thought hold and constrain the self-realization process of the ordinary man. We live in a world of racism, sexism, nationalism and a hundred other "isms" which serve to retard Mead's apocalyptic prophecy. Yet, to return to where we began, to the paradox of prediction, we, as sociologists, teachers and as proselytizers of the sociological apperception, could aid the prophetic legacy of Mead by internalizing and communicating the whole of his work and not just those segments which lend themselves to the research interests of a specialized group of social psychologists.

The discipline of sociology has done admirably well in meeting Weber's criterion that a properly scientific study of society must limit itself to the empirical investigation of the "Is," and leave all consideration of the "Ought" to theologians, metaphysicians and moral philosophers. To this end, sociologists have constructed an intellectual edifice which chronicles, catalogues and analyzes the social structural objectivations of man's past and present, cultural activity. Sociologists have traditionally devoted the bulk of their efforts to the explication of social structures and their interrelationships. Were one to count, for example, the number of empirical studies which sociologists have done on the purely structural aspects of stratification, kinship systems and organizations of varying size and complexity, I am sure the total would be quite impressive. The irony of this approach, however, is that it has served to create a body of knowledge which has diverted sociology from another of its traditionally received goals: the ascertainment of basic commonalities, or recurrent patterns in human behavior. Sociology's emphasis on extant social structures describes a world order composed of antagonistic collectivities of people which behave and interact in ways which make them appear singularly different from one another, at least when considered on a group level. Sociologists tend to speak and write quite objectively about categorical and statistically significant separations between groups of people. The irony manifests itself in a corpus of knowledge which purports to be the study of mankind but appears, on closer examination, to be the study of *mankinds*.

It is because of this, that I find the prophetic, indeed the teleological, elements in Mead's work so potentially important for the discipline of sociology. A more complete understanding of Mead by sociologists would aid in reorienting sociological inquiry and the dissemination of sociological knowledge, toward an examination and strengthening of the ties that bind as opposed to describing those social relations which presently divide. I wish to suggest that the view of social *process* (as opposed to structure) advocated by Mead poses a challenge which should direct at least some of our efforts beyond the sober and objective analysis of contemporary, social structural realities. In a qualified sense, Mead imparted a mystical vision to us, but one which emerged from a context of precise, empirical observation and analysis. Mead began from, and continually returned to, a scientific consideration of man's biologic nature. Upon this substratum he built a scientifically informed theory of the superorganic; of how the social structural realities of language, mind, self and society emerge, sustain themselves and change, in a context of historical evolution. The mystical element in Mead's thought tells us that man can use his reflective intelligence to transcend the antagonisms, animosities and open hostilities which presently characterize his collectively organized existence. Mead's position even goes beyond this, for he posits a personal faith in the *inevitable* nature of this transcendence toward achieving the mystical ideal of universal selfhood. Putting aside questions concerning the efficacy and validity of Mead's faith in the inevitability of this process, it must be emphasized in his favor that he describes how his prophecy shall come to pass by making continual reference to the scientific reality of man's biologically given capacity to symbolize. Socialized human beings possess the ability to create and employ symbols in a manner which far surpasses even the most remarkable feats of communication accomplished by those chimpanzees having had the dubious privilege of being raised in the homes of various psychologists and linguists. Man's exceptional ability to symbolize has meant that he lives in a world of linguistically formed values, ideas, intentions, motives, goals, alternatives and the like. Man, in effect, resides in a symbolic universe which is collectively maintained and changed through everyday discourse. In this sense, Mead was very much a "constructivist" in the manner described by Sampson (1975:8-20), for his mysticism emerged through a contemplation of how man's power to symbolize has increased through historical time. Mead observed that certain clusters of symbols, most notably those associated with scientific rationality, logic and the forms of economic and religious activity mentioned above, served the purpose of making the modern world an increasingly smaller place. Simultaneously, Mead observed that man possessed the potential to push this process to its logical conclusion; to transcend the multitude of symbol-encrusted identities which have historically divided the world's people by creating ever-widening, universal communities of discourse; to achieve the mystical ideal of a universal community of human kind, an ideal which in itself could not exist were it not for man's potent ability to symbolize.

Once the larger contours of Mead's thought are viewed from this perspective, it is possible to conclude that his work contains two important messages for the creators and communicators of sociological knowledge. In the first instance he urges us to retain our scientific approach to the study of social phenomena. Mead strongly believed in the merits of scientific rationality as a truth-seeking, self-correcting mode of inquiry. But he also exhorts us to utilize our scientifically produced knowledge in a manner which draws us beyond the traditional limits of empirical inquiry and bring us into the value-ladened realm of everyday, practical activity as willing participants and symbolizers. Mead demonstrates, by the example of his own work, how we should examine and actively communicate those products of our researches which promise to facilitate the human reconstruction of a more desirable world order. Mead tells us to actively discover and promote these traits, attributes, ideas and capabilities which all socialized human beings do have, or can have, in common. He instructs us to appreciate the historical transience of the bulk of our myriad cultural differences, and to see how we can become a unified species on a social level in a manner which parallels our biological unity. In this way, Mead asks us to engage in a ceaseless process of self-development, both to our own selves and the selves of others—to make maximal and optimal use of the non-polluting, human resource called symbolic communication—in an effort to realize an international community where each person's generalized other incorporates the rest of mankind.

SOCIOLOGY OF RELIGION

Mead's intellectual legacy possesses particular relevance for the sociology of religion. His potential contributions to this specialty exist as implications contained in much of what has been stated above. The more important of these implications can be explicated and discussed by dividing them into two categories. One set of Mead's insights can be grouped and characterized as a boldly empirical view of religious phenomena, and another second set is describable as a humanistic and Christian-derived vision of the future society.

As an empiricist, or more specifically as a radical empiricist of the school established by William James (Wild, 1969), Mead offers many valuable insights into the nature of religious experience which make no appeal to metaphysical entities for their intelligibility. For example, in *Mind, Self, and Society,* he explained religious exaltation in this-worldly terms by describing it as a fusion of the "I" and the "Me" (Mead, 1934:273-81). Elsewhere, he described aesthetic experience in a manner which cast it as an interaction between selves and concrete physical objects (Mead, 1926; Miller, 1973:218-27). Mead's investigations, regardless of whether they tended more toward the social psychological or the philosophical, always began and ended with the concrete. This was true whether his topic was baseball, democracy or religion, and it is this fact which constitutes Mead's basic utility for the scientifically-minded student of religion.

Simultaneously, and more importantly within the context of this paper, Mead offers the more humanistically-minded student of religious phenomena an empirically grounded vision of how the Kingdom of God—the idea which Niebuhr (1959) holds to be central to American religion—can be established through action. T. V. Smith made the comment that "Mead was more Christian than he intended" (1932:206), for he kept Royce's ideal of the "Blessed Community" before his mind's eye in whatever he said, did or wrote (Barry, 1968:188). At the risk of coining a potentially discrediting phrase, this aspect of Mead offers us a nascent "sociology for religion." This may seem a contradiction in terms to some, or a dangerous or perhaps pompous suggestion to others. Yet Mead's scientific social psychology is conducive to an ethics that is compatible with a core value common to most, if not all, of the world's religions.

In a remarkable little essay entitled **"Science and Religion"** (1938:466-74), Mead states that a basic assumption of Christianity "is that all men should belong to a universal society in which the interests of each would be the interest of all. This assumption Christianity has in common with the other universal religions" (1938:466). But Mead possessed little faith that the organized religions of his day were capable of accomplishing much toward this end. He chided the churches on more than one occasion, either for their tendency to emphasize preaching at the expense of practice or for having reduced universal ideals to dogmatic beliefs and cultic rituals (Mead, 1908a; 1908b; 1934:296). Mead's faith resposed elsewhere, for he sincerely believed that science and the social process could provide the "salvation of the self as a social being" (1938:476).

Mead exhorts us to act as scientists with a religiously informed mission. This does not mean, however, that accepting his invitation will cause us to be unscientific. Mead, like Weber (1958), saw science as an open-ended means for the clarification of given ends or values; neither conceived of science as a source of such values. What Mead asks is that we utilize the scientific method to continually redefine the means by which the universal value of world community can be organized. Moreover, he urges us to consider his social psychology, particularly the ideas of role-taking and the social self, as seriously as possible by actively seeking their ongoing realization toward the final end of universal brotherhood; an end contained within Mead's social psychology as an implicit self-fulfilling prophecy.

And who would seem better suited to take up Mead's invitation than those whose chosen profession is the scientific investigation of religious phenomena in societal context? Given his special interests and expertise, the sociologist of religion would seem a likely candidate for Mead's call to sociology for, or in behalf of, a scientifically informed religion.

Yet, as was argued above, the sociologists of religion need not stand alone, for all sociologists and all of humankind would have much to gain by rediscovering and embracing the whole Mead. As the philosopher T. V. Smith put it: ". . . . Mead's philosophy of prescriptions, of ideals, renders them always ingratiating candidates for actuality. *Man can if he will; and he will if he knows; but he can know only through the concrete technique called science*" (Smith, 1932:213). The only remaining question is are we, as human beings and as social scientists, willing?

NOTES

[1] An explanation may be in order for the relatively extravagant use of quotations in this essay. My reason for doing so is that I believe the common practice of quoting just a phrase or sentence from Mead has done much to obscure his thought. Mead's concepts and ideas are complex and interrelated and when a sentence or two are lifted out of context for the purpose of establishing a concise definition, it becomes quite easy to lose sight of the important intricacies and qualifications normally involved. An example would be the recurrent practice of defining Mead's "I" by quoting Mead's dictum, "The 'I' is the response of the organism to the attitude of the others" (Mead, 1934:175), but such a short definition is open to varying interpretations going far afield from what Mead intended. A prime illustration of this is given in Arnold Rose's (1962) depiction of Mead's "I" as an ordered and all-inclusive set of "me's"; a far cry from anything my investigations of Mead's thought on the subject have turned up. It is my hope that the generous use of quotations will alleviate the tendency to distort Mead's ideas by letting him speak for himself as much as possible.

[2] It is of some interest to ask in passing, why this superb passage was relegated to the status of a footnote by the editor of *Mind, Self, and Society*? It is surely not a minor digression on the part of Mead.

[3] The meanings of relativity and emergence are given in the final lecture of *Mind, Self, and Society*. These terms are important to and consistent with the interpretation of Mead presented here but I have omitted discussing them because of the amount of space required. See Mead (1938:1934) or Natanson (1956) for explication.

[4] This has already been done to a certain extent by Robert Nisbet (1974).

[5] A brief but excellent account of the work of the *Année Sociologique* school and of Mauss' intellectual indebtedness to Durkheim is given in Mauss (1968).

REFERENCES

Abbott, Carrell W., Charles R. Brown and Paul V. Crosbie. 1973. "Exchange as symbolic interaction for what?" *American Sociological Review* 40:504-06.

Barry, Robert M. 1968. "A man and a city: George Herbert Mead in Chicago." pp. 173-92 in M. Novak (ed.), *American Philosophy and the Future Essays of a New Generation.* New York: Scribner's.

Berger, Peter L. and Brigitte Berger. 1972. Sociology: A Biographical Approach. New York: Basic Books.

Blumer, Herbert. 1969. "Sociological implications of the thought of George Herbert Mead." Pp. 61-77 in Herbert Blumer, *Symbolic Interactionism.* Englewood Cliffs, N.J.: Prentice-Hall.

Coser, Lewis A. 1971. Masters of Sociological Thought: Ideas in Historical and Social Context. New York: Harcourt, Brace Jovanovich.

Crane, Diana. 1967. "The gatekeepers of science: some factors affecting the selection of articles for scientific journals." *American Sociologist* 2:195-201.

Douglas, Jack D. 1970. "Understanding everyday life." Pp. 3-44 in Jack D. Douglas (ed.), *Understanding Everyday Life: Toward the Reconstruction of Sociological Knowledge.* Chicago: Aldine.

Dumont, Louis. 1970. Homo Hierarchicus: An Essay on the Caste System. Tr. by Mark Sainsbury. Chicago: University of Chicago.

Friedrichs, Robert W. 1970. A Sociology of Sociology. New York: Free Press.

McHugh, Peter. 1968. Defining the Situation: The Organization of Meaning in Social Interaction. Indianapolis: Bobbs-Merrill.

Mannheim, Kark. 1936. Ideology and Utopia. New York: Harcourt Brace.

Mauss, Marcel. 1968. "A category of the human spirit." *Psychoanalytic Review* 55: 457-81.

Mead, George Herbert. 1908a. "The philosophical basis of ethics." *International Journal of Ethics* 18:311-23.

⸻. 1908b. "The social settlement: its basis and function." *University of Chicago Record* 12:108-10.

⸻. 1926. "The nature of the aesthetic experience." *International Journal of Ethics* 37:382-92.

⸻. 1929. "National-mindedness and international-mindedness." *International Journal of Ethics* 39:382-407.

⸻. 1934. *Mind, Self, and Society: From the Standpoint of a Social Behaviorist.* Ed. and Intro. Charles W. Morris. Chicago: University of Chicago Press.

⸻. 1936. *Movements of Thought in the Nineteenth Century.* Ed. Merritt H. Moore. Chicago: University of Chicago.

⸻. 1938. *The Philosophy of the Act.* Ed. and Intro. Charles W. Morris. Chicago: University of Chicago.

Merton, Robert K. 1948. "The self-fulfilling prophecy." *Antioch Review* 8:192-210.

Miller, David L. 1973. George Herbert Mead: Self, Language, and the World. Austin: University of Texas.

Natanson, Maurice. 1958. The Social Dynamics of George H. Mead. Intro. Horace M. Kallen. Washington, D.C.: Public Affairs.

Niebuhr, H. Richard. 1959. The Kingdom of God in America. New York: Harper and Row.

Nisbet, Robert A. 1974. The Sociology of Emile Durkheim. New York: Oxford.

Rose, Arnold. 1972. "A systematic summary of symbolic interaction theory." Pp. 3-19 in A. Rose (ed.), *Human Behavior and Social Processes: An Interactionist Approach.* Boston: Houghton Mifflin.

Sampson, Edward E. 1975. Ego at the Threshold: In Search of Man's Freedom. New York: Dell.

Singelmann, Peter. 1973. "On the reification of paradigms: reply to Abbott, Brown, and Crosbie." *American Sociological Review* 40:506-09.

Smith, T. V. 1932. "The religious bearings of a secular mind: George Herbert Mead." *Journal of Religion* 12:200-13.

Thomas, W. I. 1920. The Child in America. New York: Knopf.

Weber, Max. 1958. "Science as a vocation." Pp. 129-56 in H. H. Gerth and C. W. Mills (eds.), *From Max Weber: Essays in Sociology.* New York: Oxford.

Wild, John. 1969. The Radical Empiricism of William James. Garden City, N.Y.: Doubleday.

Yablonsky, Lewis. 1966. The Violent Gang. Baltimore: Penguin.

Clarence J. Karier (essay date 1984)

SOURCE: "In Search of Self in a Moral Universe: Notes on George Herbert Mead's Functionalist Theory of Morality," in *Journal of the History of Ideas,* Vol. XLV, No. 1, January-March, 1984, pp. 153-61.

[*In the following essay, Karier maintains that despite Mead's secular outlook, "he nonetheless depended heavily on certain key assumptions from his Christian past with which to fashion his new secular liberal reformist view of the world."*]

George Herbert Mead was born and reared in a heavily saturated Christian environment. His father was a clergyman who taught homiletics at the Theological Seminary at Oberlin College, and his mother was educated at the Seminary at Ipswich, Massachusetts. His best friend during his adolescent years was Henry Castle, the son of American missionary parents in the Hawaiian Islands. In 1891, when Mead gave up his student life and joined John Dewey at the University of Michigan, he married Henry's sister, Helen Castle. In spite of this strong Christian influence, Mead moved away from the faith of his parents. Shortly after the death of his father and his own graduation from Oberlin College, Mead seemed to undergo a severe religious crisis which was intimately tied, not only to both parents, but also to a choice of careers. Mead's decision against going into the ministry and for adopting the life of an academic philosopher meant far more than a mere occupational decision. It meant most of all a movement away from a Christian world view to that of a secular liberal humanist. Mead's experiences with William James at Harvard, followed by his German university experience, further helped him become one of America's leading secular social psychologists.

The purpose of this essay is to suggest that, although Mead appeared to shed many of his early Christian beliefs, he nonetheless depended heavily on certain key assumptions from his Christian past with which to fashion his new secular liberal reformist view of the world. In this sense his secular humanism required a Christian past, indeed, a moral capital of the past upon which to build. However, Mead lived very much in his present, and as he did so he sensitively touched on problems which became part of his emerging future. Thus, in this way, his ahistorical view of the past, his sense of the moral community, the role of the self in that community, as well as his functionalist theory of value, all have peculiar relevance for our age.

Working with John Dewey at the University of Michigan and then at the University of Chicago from 1894 to 1904,

Mead progressively developed and refined his conception of psychology. Even though Dewey left the University of Chicago for Columbia University in 1904, the close intellectual alliance between the two continued unabated until Mead's death in 1931. Dewey's instrumentalism and Mead's social psychology evolved out of the searching dialogue that took place between the two. Mead provided the psychology which was a basis for Dewey's instrumentalism, while Dewey provided the practical philosophy which steadied Mead's psychology. Dewey often expressed his indebtedness to Mead. Dewey saw Mead's contribution to philosophy as the development of an evolutionary conception of nature and man which made man neither a pawn of the universal forces of nature nor a victim of individual subjectivism.

His identification of the process of evolution with that of continuous reconstruction by which nature and man (as a part of nature that has become conscious) solve the problem of the relations of the universal and the individual, the regular and the novel—this identification is his own outstanding contribution to philosophy.[1]

Although Mead had been influenced by his reading of Aristotle, he rejected Aristotle's conception that human nature was fixed. Mead viewed human nature as emerging within a social context. Man, in the course of evolution, became human when he began to think reflectively. He began to think when, in a social context, he advanced from gestures to language which could be symbolically internalized. In contrast to Freud, who saw the original development of culture as the loss of some portion of one's happiness in order to attain security, Mead saw the development of culture as the origin of intelligence which increased man's chance for happiness. Indeed, while there was continuity between the mind of man and that of the animal, there remained a qualitative difference in the ability of man to symbolize his past, present, and future reflectively and to direct his actions accordingly. To Mead, stimulus-response psychology could explain how animals and humans learned certain habitual kinds of behavior, but it failed to explain adequately purposive behavior which was symbolically generated. In his view, mind, self, and society were functionally related in a transactional, continuous, and emerging process.

The child is born a physiological organism with undifferentiated tendencies to act. Through verbal gestures in a social context the child learns the meaning of the symbols held in common by the group. Once he learns language, the child can internalize conversation, and he becomes a thinking being. Through various kinds of social activities, the child learns to symbolically take the role of the other, and there gradually emerges a conception of self in which he sees himself as others see him. As the individual takes the role of the other, and sees himself as others see him, there develops the "generalized other," which includes society's values, attitudes, and beliefs which are then internalized in the individual in the form of the "me." Thus far, one has substantially a picture of the "organization man." This, however, is not all. There

is another side to the self—the "I"—which, unlike the "generalized other" or the "me," represents the novel, creative, impulsive side of the self which repeatedly surprises the "me." The "I's" behavior is never completely predictable.[2]

In keeping with his mentor, William James, who opposed determinism, Mead's social behaviorism also rejected the notion of complete determinism. Mead suggested that the ability of the self to introduce novel behavior in the social group forever confounds attempts at prediction of individual behavior, as well as at complete standardization of group control. The group undergoes continuous change as individuals change within the group. To Mead, social institutions are basically made up of neither "I's" nor "me's" but of whole individuals with emerging selves behaving cooperatively to achieve greater freedom. This socialized individualism assumes that freedom is gained through society and not from society. Alienation of man from society can, in this context, only dehumanize man.

Although Mead did much creative work in analyzing the self in an increasingly alienated society, his major focus was not so much on the "self" nor on the society, but on the transactional relationship that took place between them. It was in that arena that he found intelligence at work and the possibility that science as a kind of creative questioning intelligence might prove to be the real redeemer of humanity. All this was possible within a community, a moral community. Mead's writings are laced with moral questions which emerged as he translated key assumptions drawn from his Christian background.[3] For Mead, the social order was a moral order:

> It is that the intelligible order of the world implies a determined moral order—and for a moral order we may substitute a social order, for morality has to do with the relations of intelligent beings with each other—and that this determined moral or social order is a world as it should be and will be. . . . Whatever the conception of this moral order Kantian, Utilitarian or Christian, definite or vague, it always has implied that the process of the universe in which we live in a real sense is akin to and favorable to the most admirable order in human society.[4]

There exists an implicit moral ideal in every society. This ideal takes on living reality as it becomes a functional part of institutional life. Because some ideals are not functionally alive, they are usually kept alive only by the activities of some form of cult. As Mead puts it:

> The cult value of the institution is legitimate only when the social order for which it stands is hopelessly ideal. In so far as it approaches realization, its functional value must supercede its ideal value in our conduct. It is to this task that a scientifically trained intelligence must insistently devote itself, that of stating, just as far as possible, our institutions, our social habits and customs, in terms of what they are to do, in terms of their function. (*Ibid.,* 243)

Our values which we have inherited from our past "possess and control us," while the values which we "discover and invent" help us to "possess and control the world." (*Ibid.*, 247)

Mead had developed a pragmatic functionalist theory of value in which the appeal was not to fixed codes external to the individual, but, rather, to the "actual problem" out of which the functional values could be wrought. If "the intelligible order of the world implies a moral or social order, i.e., a world as it should be and may be," what form, then, does this take, Mead asked, if we apply scientific method to social conduct?

> Scientific method has no vision given in the mount, of a perfected order of society, but it does carry with it the assumption that the intelligence which exhibits itself in the solution of problems in natural science is of the same character as that which we apply or should apply in dealing with our social and moral problems. . . . Not only is man as an animal and as an inquirer into nature at home in the world but the society of men is equally a part of the order of the universe. What is called for in the perfection of this society is the same intelligence which he uses in becoming more completely a part of his physical environment and so controlling that environment. (*Ibid.*, 243, 245)

Mead's functionalist theory of value was premised upon the necessity of social control in order to perfect society. The older Judeo-Christian moral system pictured men as pilgrims and strangers on this earth seeking an abiding city of God in another world. Mead, on the other hand, pictured his scientific humanism as "a great secular adventure" where society got ahead, not by "fastening its vision upon a clearly outlined distant goal, but by bringing about the immediate adjustment of itself to its surroundings, which the immediate problem demands." (*Ibid.*, 247)

Through the process of interaction within the problematic situation, both the individual and society are changed. The human social animal cannot see great distances into the future, but he has a mind and can test for solutions in his present problematic world: "He does not know what the solution will be, but he does know the method of the solution. We, none of us, know where we are going, but we do know that we are on the way." (*Ibid.*)

Rejecting, then, the Christian dualism of his youth, he embraced a functionalist theory of value in his mature years, with a reformist faith of a missionary carrying forth the social gospel of scientific redemption. His was a neo-enlightenment faith, perhaps no better expressed than when he concluded his essay on **"Scientific Method and Moral Sciences"** by saying:

> The order of the universe that we live in *is* the moral order. It has become the moral order by becoming the self-conscious method of the members of a human society. We are not pilgrims and strangers. We are at home in our own world,

but it is not ours by inheritance but by conquest. The world that comes to us from the past possesses and controls us. We possess and control the world that we discover and invent. And this is the world of the moral order. It is a splendid adventure if we can rise to it. (*Ibid.*)

Although Mead saw himself as thoroughly endorsing a humanist faith, and would, if he had lived, have endorsed John Dewey's *Common Faith,* it is also clear that he never completely broke with certain key assumptions he derived from his Christian background. The first of these involved the desirability of the common brotherhood of man. T. V. Smith suggested that this was one of Mead's supreme values: "The sharing of experience is the greatest good."[5] This assumption, which he seems to have carried over from his Christian past, appears largely unexamined. He saw the private as subjective and disintegrative, and much of Christianity perpetuated as a cult. It was perpetuated, he believed, because of the incompleteness of the "organization of society." He thought scientific intelligence might help build a society where the ideal values imbedded in Christianity as cult values might ultimately become functional values of society.

God had died for Mead as well as for Nietzsche. For Nietzsche, however, the Christian brotherhood was a fraudulent conception. Moving beyond good and evil, Nietzsche espoused the individualism of the superman. Mead, on the other hand, still assumed a Christian article of faith in the brotherhood of man. T. V. Smith put it well when he said:

> It is so uncharacteristic of Mead's cautious curiosity to make a cause of what really is not uncontestably good that it arouses the suspicion that he but carried on uncritically in this regard the Christian tradition. Would a Mohammedan thinker, not to mention a classic Greek mind, of Mead's acumen have assumed that all human experience implies enlargement and intensification of community without limit? If not, it is certainly a high tribute to the strength of the Christian leaven that it could so raise the threshold of even Mead's tough mind as to bring curiosity to its knees before the sacred altar of brotherhood.[6]

Mead's functionally moral community was not far removed from the Christian ideal which appeared to underwrite Josiah Royce's "blessed community" as well. Fundamental to Mead's ethics was the Christian secularized doctrine of enlightened self-interest which was not far removed from the Golden Rule. For Mead, the danger was that this rule would be preached from the pulpit as, indeed, his father might have preached it. So preached, it depended on its cult value rather than on its functional value to survive. It must rather be recognized as a functioning part of the moral structure of community life itself. Mead suggested:

> The most grandiose of these community ideals is that which lies behind the structure of what was called Christendom, and found its historic expression

in the Sermon on the Mount, in the parable of the Good Samaritan, and in the Golden Rule. These affirm that the interests of all men are so identical, that the man who acts in the interest of his neighbors will act in his own interest.[7]

Mead's social psychology, which described the process of the emergence of "self," taking the role of the other and the idea of the generalized other, made possible the functional acceptance, rather than the cultist acceptance of the Golden Rule. Smith suggested as much when he asked:

> . . . has not Mead implemented the Golden Rule so thoroughly by his social psychology that it is no longer a prescription at all but now a description of how we do inevitably act?[8]

As we pass from cult to function, or prescription to description, or what ought to be to what is, we move from moral choice to an "inevitable act." There is slippage here between a prescriptive and a descriptive view of the world and it is found in the precise nature of the transactional relationship between the individual and his social environment. Smith summed up Mead's faith best when he said: *"Man can if he will; and he will if he knows; but he can know only through the concrete technique called science."* (Ibid.)

In these ways, Mead's social psychology, at least with respect to unexamined assumptions about the brotherhood of man, the nature of the Golden Rule, as well as the perfectibility of society rested in some abbreviated form on the moral capital of the past. For many in modern day society, this capital has long since run out.

A powerful ambivalence runs throughout Mead's work between the subjective and the objective side of personality. At times he seemed to treat the "I" and the "me" as somewhat equal, while at other times he would treat the "I" and all the subjective emotional elements that went with it as something to be avoided. He treated the "private," the "mystic," the "sentimental," and the "emotional" as personal phenomena which some day, perhaps through better social institutions, might be controlled. One might recognize that through his early religious crisis years he associated his own attachment to Christianity as emotional, while his growing interest in philosophy he associated as rationally intelligent. The "I" as well as the "me" were clearly in evidence in those early years. This ambivalence seems to have remained throughout his life. His reluctance to commit his social behaviorism to an environmental determinism may have been due to his personal psychological makeup, or perhaps it was due to his lingering Christian values. For whatever the reason, it still was to his credit that his social behaviorism did not take the path of eliminating the "I" and thus producing a social psychology like Mao Tse Tung's, which utilized the group to scientifically work to control and predict the "me" and eliminate, as far as possible, the "I."

Some years after studying the effectiveness of Mao's social behaviorism for the United States Air Force, Robert Jay Lifton, following in the footsteps of Erik Erikson, wrote the "Protean Man." In that essay, he argued that since World War II modern man has been undergoing what appeared to him to be a continuous identity crisis where one's inner and outer world remain unconnected, and every kind of faith and loyalty remains a tentative proposition of the passing present. He attributed this phenomenon to two things:

> The first is the worldwide sense of what I have called *historical* (or *psychohistorical*) *dislocation,* the break in the sense of connection which men have long felt with the vital and nourishing symbols of their cultural tradition—symbols revolving around family, idea-systems, religions, and the life cycle in general. . . . The second large historical tendency is the flooding of imagery produced by the extraordinary flow of postmodern cultural influences over mass-communication networks.[9]

Lifton argued that we were entering a new era in which a new kind of person was being produced, a person with relatively weak loyalties, nonideological, with the ability to survive in a world of rapid change without too much psyche damage. As he peered into the alienated consciousness of modern men, he thought he saw the historical events which marked the break in his consciousness. For Lifton, World War II was the turning point.

In the postwar period, psychiatrists and sociologists sought to describe what was happening to modern man. Whether it was sociologists speaking of anomie, psychiatrists speaking of identity diffusion, David Reisman writing about the other directed person, Erikson writing about identity crisis, or Lifton about the "Protean Man," all seemed to be dealing with the same growing phenomenon of alienated man in the post World War II society.

Earlier in this century, Mead had sensitively analyzed a similar phenomenon of the alienated self. In retrospect, however, the phenomenon appeared as a gentle stream kept within the bounds of tradition, whereas, in the post World War II period, it became a raging torrent which swept aside cherished values for many. Thus, the condition of the alienated self appears even more desperate than it was in Mead's lifetime. Although this phenomenon appeared earlier at the turn of the century in European art, literature, music, and youth culture (in a somewhat abbreviated fashion in America's Greenwich Village and among our expatriot artists on the Left Bank), nevertheless, the major groundswell appeared in America after World War II.

Mead, in those earlier years, had perceptively analyzed the cult value of religion in modern society. More than most, Mead understood the relationship of religion, self, and community. His analysis of cults as working in terms of the increasing reification of ideal values in a functionally alienating social system helps to explain, in part at least, the modern quest for cult worship, as evidenced from the modern day experience with such cults as Jim Jones, Synanon, the Moonies, and many others.

Mead did yeoman work in analyzing the modern alienated self. In so doing, he perceptively described the ontological perceptions of such a person. The ontological nature of the thoroughly alienated person is essentially ahistorical. For such a person, the world is no longer made up of pasts, presents, and futures. Rather, it contains only significant presents. Mead's analysis of history very well describes the ahistorical sense of reality for many twentieth-century thinkers. For Mead, there was only one reality and that was the present. Similar to Dewey's later view of history was Mead's view of the past as "that conditioning phase of the passing present which enables us to determine conduct with reference to the future which is also arising in the present."[10] To Mead, the past is dead and has meaning only as we ascribe meaning to it from the present context. In this sense, we actually read history backward but create the illusion that we read it forward. For instance, the historical perspectives of Hegel, Marx, Comte, and Freud were all interpretations of the past derived from the present perspective of their individual lives. Mead went on to assert that: "Every great social movement has flashed back its light to discover a new past."[11] There are, in this sense, as many pasts as there are futures demanding a new past. Mead said: "The novelty of every future demands a novel past."[12] He summarized his conception of history when he said:

> The long and short of it is that the only reality of the past open to our reflective research is the implication of the present, that the only reason for research into the past is the present problem of understanding a problematic world, and the only test of the truth of what we have discovered is our ability to so state the past that we can continue the conduct whose inhibition has set the problem to us. (*Ibid.,* 324)

The thoroughly alienated man exists in a problematic present without a history, other than that which he can make out of his past today.

Although Mead did creative work in describing the modern person's dilemma, he also, along with Dewey, was practically involved in helping shape new liberal reforms. Active in both city and school politics in Chicago, he served as chairman of the Chicago City Club in 1912 and later retired as President in 1920. In education, Mead worked with Dewey on his laboratory school, served as a trustee of Jane Addams' Settlement House, edited *The Elementary School Teacher,* and became deeply involved in the vocational educational movement.

While his influence on practical reform politics and on education in Chicago in the early days of the century, was considerable, and in line with his youthful dreams, his most important impact was his influence on the field of sociology, social psychology, and, in general, the social sciences. He was one of the early creators of the sociological functionalist theory of value, just as he has rightly been hailed, along with C. H. Cooley, as the co-founder of social psychology. Mead's ideas on human nature

were carried into educational thought by John Dewey,[13] into the mental hygiene movement by Adolph Meyer,[14] into the therapeutic psychology by Harry Stack Sullivan,[15] and into social science theory by Talcott Parsons, Kingsley Davis, Robert K. Merton, and others. Many social scientists in the twentieth century who thought in terms of social psychology, moral values, community, communication, and transactional relationships, thought in terms which Mead had previously laid out. Most social science theorists today would agree with Dewey that Mead was "deeply original."

Interestingly, however, in a world of publish or perish, George Herbert Mead would have perished. In the forty years of his academic work, Mead did not publish a single book. He was first and foremost a teacher, creating and recreating ideas with students, which left little time for publication. in comparison with the massive publication lists of Hall, Thorndike, or Dewey, Mead's few articles look sparse indeed. Consequently, his influence on American thought cannot be gauged by his publication list but rather by the many influential people who were either formally or informally his students. The fact that Mead was at the University of Chicago, one of the leading institutions in the field of sociology during the first half of the twentieth century, no doubt contributed to his influence. As students from the new fields of sociology and social psychology flocked to his philosophy course, it was clear that Mead had something significant to offer. After his death in 1931, dedicated students compiled his notes and articles into three volumes: *Mind, Self and Society*; *The Philosophy of the Present*; and *The Philosophy of the Act.*

Mead's preference for teaching over writing may have been due to the subjective versus objective split which appears not only in his thinking, but also in his writing. His professional writing is best characterized as highly rationalized and devoid of emotion, while his personal correspondence is heavily laced with evidence of the poetic. Mead once defined freedom as the "expression of the whole self."

> But in freedom the personality as a whole passes into the act. Compulsion disintegrates the individual into his different elements; hence there are degrees of freedom in proportion to the extent to which the individual becomes organized as a whole. It is not often that the whole of us goes into any act so that we face the situation as an entire personality.[16]

In an earlier age, freedom was defined in terms of capability to act or not to act; but in the alienated world of modern men and women, freedom is more often defined in Mead's terms of "getting one's act together" as a "whole person." For Mead, this was no easy task, and it would be safe to suggest he was not often free. Mead was the philosopher of the alienated self *par excellence.* He was, from his identity crisis of younger years in his "dreams and plans to design and construct in new ways," to use an Erik Erikson phrase, always seeking ways to overcome that alienation, always in search of self in a moral universe. In 1901 he wrote to his wife, Helen:

> The world is strange and it gets stranger as I get older. The infinitesimal shifts of a day or an hour make the things that had the solidity of the everlasting hills and the dull grey of the unquestioned commonplace become like dreams and opalescent as the Hawaiian Sea. The iridescence of youth and its imagination is unstable and lacks the assurance which makes real poetry of life. There is always the dualism of the untried world which is not yet one's own that the youth cannot surmount. He must be romantic. But to be at home in one's world and yet be able to see it shift and change and feel the movement with no question of its reality and therefore: no discord upon its appreciation. It's a process of going into one's self and finding the world there. As one grows older he gets deeper and nearer the creator. But for all emotion, reflection from one's other self is necessary even if that self has to be built up. The Lord in his great mercy grant that we may continue to be the other selves to each other's experience.[17]

Later in life he seemed to have overcome his alienation and to have found his way through that labyrinth of emotional self-analysis through discovery and invention of the moral universe:

> We are not pilgrims and strangers. We are at home in our own world, but it is not ours by inheritance but by conquest. The world that comes to us from the past possesses and controls us. We possess and control the world that we discover and invent. And this is the world of the moral order. It is a splendid adventure if we can rise to it.[18]

NOTES

[1] John Dewey, "The Work of George Mead," *The New Republic*, 87 (1936), 329.

[2] In direct contrast to John B. Watson and B. F. Skinner, Mead assumed that an important part of human behavior would remain unpredictable. See Anselm Strauss, ed., "The Process of Mind in Nature" in *George Herbert Mead on Social Psychology* (Chicago, 1964), 105. See also Herbert W. Schneider, *History of American Philosophy*, (New York, 1946).

[3] See T. V. Smith, "The Religious Bearings of a Secular Mind: George Herbert Mead," *The Journal of Religion*, 12, 2 (April 1932), 201. For many of the insights involving the moral thrust of Mead's mature thought and its religious bearing, I am indebted to the work of T. V. Smith.

[4] George Herbert Mead, "Scientific Method and Moral Sciences," *The International Journal of Ethics*, XXXIII (April 1923), 229-30.

[5] T. V. Smith, *loc. cit.* (note 3 above), 211.

[6] *Ibid.*, 212.

[7] Mead, "Scientific Method and Moral Sciences," 239.

[8] T. V. Smith, *loc. cit.* (note 3 above), 213.

[9] Robert Jay Lifton, *History and Human Survival* (New York, 1970), 318.

[10] Anselm Strauss, *George Herbert Mead on Social Psychology: Selected Papers*, 335.

[11] *Ibid.*, 321.

[12] *Ibid.*, xxv.

[13] See Anselm Strauss, *The Social Psychology of George Herbert Mead* (Chicago, 1959).

[14] See Christine Mary Shea, "The Ideology of Mental Health and the Emergence of the Therapeutic Liberal State: The American Mental Hygiene Movement, 1900-1930," unpublished Ph.D. Dissertation, University of Illinois, Champaign, 1980.

[15] Sullivan traced his own thinking from the social psychology of Mead. See Ernest Becker, *The Birth and Death of Meaning* (New York, 1962), 48.

[16] George Herbert Mead, *The Philosophy of the Act*, ed. Charles W. Morris (Chicago, 1938), 663.

[17] Letter to Helen Castle from G. H. Mead, June 12, 1901. George Herbert Mead Papers, University of Chicago Archives.

[18] Mead, "Scientific Method and Moral Sciences," (*loc. cit.*, note 4 above), 247.

Thomas Natsoulas (essay date 1985)

SOURCE: "George Herbert Mead's Conception of Consciousness," in *Journal for the Theory of Social Behavior*, Vol. 15, No. 1, March, 1985, pp. 60-75.

[*In the following essay, Natsoulas provides an analysis of Mead's two main concepts of consciousness and their relation to one another.*]

Efforts have been underway for some time to integrate into social science George Herbert Mead's contributions to our understanding of mind, self, and society. Such efforts have not yet ended for excellent reasons pertaining to the depth, richness, and repeatedly renewed relevance of Mead's theories. However, a currently relevant approach to Mead's contributions has not been exploited due to the well-known reaction early this century against mentalism. In Mead's own writings, this reaction is discussed and the methodological merits of behaviorism acknowledged. Yet, Mead's agreement with some behaviorist proscriptions did not prevent his addressing the forbidden subject matter of consciousness (e.g. Mead, 1934, p. 10). Therefore, his conception of consciousness may contribute some needed theoretical underpinnings to the current revival of scientific interest in "the problem" (Natsoulas, 1978a, 1981, 1983a, 1983b).

Throughout his long attempt to comprehend man, society, and nature itself, Mead had consciousness in the forefront of his thinking. Any somewhat extended segment from his writings or lectures confirms that he did. Dewey's (1932) interpretation of Mead's journey of discovery goes even further. Dewey believed Mead's preoccupation with the nature of consciousness can explain the specific directions in which Mead's work developed (cf. Dewey, 1931). The importance of consciousness to Mead ensures that I do no injustice to his thought simply by focusing on those parts of it that bear directly on the nature of consciousness.

My discussion of Mead's conception of consciousness considers in turn his two main concepts of consciousness. For a better understanding, these need to be addressed in relation to each other as well. The second of his two concepts refers to phenomena that arise in human conduct from a context provided by the first kind of consciousness, which I call "consciousness qua experience", "the presence of objects in experience", or simply "experience". And in discussing Mead's concept of experience, I consider as well the hypothesized influence on its referent of the second kind of consciousness, which I call "consciousness qua awareness" or simply "awareness".

Mead's concept of consciousness qua awareness corresponds to the third definition of *consciousness* listed in the *Oxford English Dictionary* (OED). Consciousness$_3$ is "the state or faculty of being mentally conscious or aware *of* anything" (cf. James's, 1904, function of knowing). We can be conscious of an endless list of things; and involved in each instance is an occurrent cognition, an act of awareness. Mead's concept of consciousness qua experience might also be thought to refer to a form of awareness, but this would be incorrect because, according to Mead, the concept's referent lacks any necessary cognitive dimension (see below).

I give some attention as well to two further important concepts, which refer to reflexive kinds of consciousness and are related to Mead's two main concepts. (a) One reflexive concept is implicated in consciousness qua awareness, which "always has implicitly, at least, the reference to an 'I' in it" (Mead, 1934, p. 165). Awareness "only belongs to selves" (Mead, 1924-1925/1964, p. 278), and to be "a self" a human being must respond to himself or herself in a certain way (to be discussed). Although awareness can be of anything, it has involved in it from the start consciousness qua self-awareness (Mead, 1938, p. 75). (b) Mead also had something to say about a second reflexive concept of consciousness, which I refer to here as the concept of conscious experience. This concept applies to the presence of objects in experience when their presence is combined with awareness of the experience's occurrence.

These two kinds of reflexive consciousness correspond, respectively, to the second and fourth OED definitions of consciousness. (a) Consciousness$_2$ is "internal knowledge or conviction; knowledge as to which one has the testimony within oneself; esp. of one's own innocence, guilt, deficiencies, etc". That is, one stands to oneself in a certain cognitive relation, being the witness to one's conduct and able to give testimony about it (cf. Natsoulas, 1983b). (b) The second reflexive concept from Mead corresponds to the OED's consciousness$_4$, which is "the state or faculty of being conscious, as a condition or concomitant of all thought, feeling, and volition; 'the recognition by the thinking subject of its own acts or affections' (Hamilton)". Mead would revise this definition, since consciousness$_4$ is not a necessary condition or concomitant, in his view, of consciousness qua experience: "What is implied in [the concept of] experience is that things and events are stated in terms of their values for the individual as revealed in his conduct—and values here do not imply what would ordinarily be called consciousness of the values" (Mead, 1938, p. 406; cf. pp 411-412; Natsoulas, 1978c).

THE CONCEPT OF CONSCIOUSNESS QUA EXPERIENCE

To those familiar only with Mead's theory of the social origins of what is in fact another kind of consciousness (Mead, 1934, p. 18) the following point may be, at first, somewhat surprising. Consciousness qua experience does not depend on social interaction to get going:

> Earlier psychologists—and many psychologists of the present time, for that matter—assume that at a certain point in the development of the organism consciousness as such arises. . . . The suggestion I have made is that consciousness, as such, does not represent a separate substance or a separate something that is superinduced upon [an animal] form, but rather that the term "consciousness" (in one of its basic usages) represents a certain sort of an environment in its relation to sensitive organisms. . . . Consciousness, in the widest sense, is not simply an emergent at a certain point, but a set of characters that is dependent upon the relationship of a thing to an organism. . . . The objects are colored, odorous, pleasant or painful, hideous or beautiful, in their relationship to the organism. . . . In one sense of the term, such characters constitute the field of consciousness. (Mead, 1934, pp 329-330)

Awareness develops from a noncognitive state of affairs containing certain necessary conditions. Broadly speaking, these are (a) an adequately functioning nervous system that provides the ability to take the other's role and (b) a pattern of interaction that produces the individual's social experiential field. In order to take the role of another person and to develop an "other" with which to interact in thought, the individual must already have a field of experience that includes the presence of another human being. Yet, *emergence* is the right word for what takes place when awareness first occurs in a human being's mental life, because the matrix from which awareness develops is the presence of objects in experience, which "does not carry the implication of cognition with it" (Mead, 1938, p. 657; cf. Mead, 1932, pp 4-5).

In trying to grasp Mead's two main concepts of consciousness, the concept of experience presents perhaps the greater difficulty because it refers to occurrences that (a) are not instances of being conscious of something (Mead, 1932, p. 4) and (b) are often not themselves objects or contents of consciousness (Mead, 1938, p. 656). This should lead someone to ask whether the word *experience* was not applied beyond its proper domain to a kind of occurrence (of being affected by something) no more psychical than a stimulus-presentation.

Freud's (e.g., 1895, 1915, 1923, 1938) thinking about consciousness and unconsciousness provides us with a useful contrast. He argued that there are unconscious psychical processes in the form of wishes for something, activated unconscious memories, unconscious thoughts, and the like. Each of these involves "being mentally conscious of" something (as the OED defines consciousness$_3$ or awareness). That is, there is something other than itself with which an unconscious (or conscious) psychical process is occupied. Other psychical processes are intrinsically conscious, according to Freud; all experiences fit here. They all have a "subjective side"—are self-intimationally conscious by their own nature. States of feeling and emotion are cases in point; these are always conscious states, in Freud's view, by virtue of being the special kind of process that they are. Feelings and emotions were admitted to at times occur without the person's awareness of their ideational content. The latter belongs to an associated thought process, according to Freud, that may be unconscious even though the respective feeling or emotion is perforce conscious by its intrinsic nature.

Mead went further by postulating experiences that possess neither ideational content nor are themselves objects of direct (reflective) consciousness. Nevertheless, Mead (e.g., 1934, p. 329) believed that he was putting to use a common meaning of the word *consciousness*. We can make sense of this as follows. In the first place, Mead applied his concept to experiences that he and we directly know of through having them. We may suppose with Mead that unconscious experiences also occur in us, that one need not be aware of all the occurrences of one's experiences. Our attitudes toward very young children (and animals) are consistent with this. We normally suppose that those children also undergo experiences who have not yet acquired consciousness qua awareness, according to Mead, and are not in a position, therefore, to have conscious experiences in his view. They, too, exemplify the presence of objects in experience though they cannot, according to Mead, be aware of those objects or of experiencing them.

Mead's claim was not a merely methodological one, namely, that young children cannot report on their experiences, and therefore we need to infer their experiences from their circumstances, behaviors, and physical resemblance and continuity with adult human beings. Other adult human beings present us with a similar problem, since we cannot verify the occurrence of their particular experiences, what they say or do serves as evidence for the latter whether the experiences are conscious ones or not. A postulation of experiences may be a postulation of conscious or unconscious experiences or both. Mead postulated the occurrence of unconscious experiences as well as conscious ones.

Mead's conception of conscious experience (i.e., what makes experiences conscious) is an "appendage" type of theory (Freud's, 1895, term). That is, conscious experiences involve a distinct act of awareness of them; which occurred this time, say, and might not occur next time the same intrinsically unconscious experience occurs (cf. Skinner, 1945, 1953, 1957, 1974; Natsoulas, 1978b). Conscious experiences thus derive their consciousness from something that, as it were, focuses upon them, namely, from consciousness qua awareness in a specific form that directly refers to them. In young children, this "appendage" has not yet been acquired, and so they have a kind of (unconscious) experience unlike the experiences of which we more commonly speak.

Also, we tend to believe as Mead did that creatures who cannot, according to Mead, acquire the ability to be aware of their experiences also exemplify consciousness qua experience. In defining *experience*, Mead quite deliberately excluded the necessary involvement in the animal's experience of any other kind of consciousness, including an innate or intrinsic direct access to the experiences: "'Experience', in the sense in which it is used in this paper, refers to the portion of the life-process of an [animal] form which includes the actions of the form as a whole with reference to an environment" (Mead, 1983, p. 405). The environment in which an animal form experientially lives results from the actions of the form, as a whole, in response to the stimulation of its sense organs and receptors:

> The nature of the environment of the biological form is its relationship to the form, what we term the logical determination of the environment by the form. . . . The logical determination of the field by the individual, of the environment by the biological form . . . results in the appearance of objects, which would not otherwise exist. (Mead, 1938, p. 20)

Whereas the actions of the animal form as a whole do not include, for example, its processes of blood circulation, they do include the form's perceptual activities. Mead (1938) conceived these activities to be a part of the total act that starts from impulse and stimulation and ends with consummation. And it is the total act, extended over time, that determines the specific qualities and values of the habitat as experienced.

This "environment", about which Mead always had something systematically relevant to say, was understood not simply as the animal's habitat: "We pick out an organized environment in relationship to our response, so that these attitudes, as such, not only represent our organized responses but they also represent what exists for us in the world; the particular phase of reality that is there for us is picked out for us by our response" (Mead, 1934, p. 128). Whereas the habitat (or world) does not depend for its existence on being experienced, the organism's environment does so depend because it is a certain perspective on the habitat and is determined by the organism's acts. Mead often explicitly identified consciousness qua experience with the organism's environment: "What we refer to as consciousness as such is really the character of the object" (Mead, 1936, p. 393).

Of course, in Mead's view, an organism experiencing an environment that is constituted by the organism's acts need not be, thereby, *aware* of its experienced environment. The implications of the organism's not being aware of its environment do not include that it cannot have further experiences of its environment, consistent with those it already has had, nor that it cannot continue to engage in further acts, which continue to constitute a continuous environment. Having a rich and detailed experienced environment is compatible, according to Mead, with the absence of consciousness qua awareness.

Mead's concept of experience goes about as far as a theorist can go in treating of psychological processes without becoming occupied instead with purely physiological or physical occurrences: "The experienced world is conceived by Mead as a realm of natural events, emergent through the sensitivity of organisms, events no more a property of the organism than of the thing observed" (Morris, 1934, p. xix; cf. Mead's, 1934, pp 10-11, statements concerning the explanation of "mental behavior" in terms of "non-mental behavior"). However, Mead had no intention of defining the presence of objects in experience in terms of physical descriptions and measurements, of either the organism's habitat or the stimulational patterns produced at the organism's receptors by the interaction of the organism and its habitat. Depending on the sensitivities and responsivities of the particular animal species, objects may be present in experience as, for example, colored, odorous, pleasant or unpleasant, hideous or beautiful, among other ways.

However, Mead held it possible and desirable to define in (what he believed to be) an objective way the traditional secondary qualities (e.g., colors, odors), primary qualities (e.g., forms, solidity), and values (e.g., aversiveness, beauty) of the objects in experience. This would be done in relation to the behavior (i.e., to the complete act, which includes a perceptual stage, a manipulatory stage, and a consummatory stage) of the kind of organism whose experiences have those qualities and values. This "behavioristic" approach to defining the organism's experiential environment was considered by Mead a major advance over previous attempts to address the nature of experience and its relation to the world: "It remained for pragmatism to take the still more radical

position that in immediate experience the percept stands over against the individual, not in the relation of awareness, but simply in that of conduct" (Mead, 1924-1925/1964, p. 271). The meaning of "more radical" here pertains to pragmatism's return of qualities and values back to the things experienced, thus taking them out of the mind where they were lodged by other theorists: "When one goes back to such a conception of consciousness as early psychologists used, and everything experienced is lodged in consciousness, then one has to create another world outside and say that there is something out there answering to these experiences" (Mead, 1934, p. 333).

Hence, Mead's position has been described as an "objective relativism". There is, in his view, only one world. This world is variously experienced depending on the organism's behavior in the total sense (cf. Mead, 1938, p. 107). Objects have qualities and values in relation to the stages of the total act. But being relationally defined, qualities and values do not belong any less to the experienced objects that possess them. This applies, in Mead's view, even to characteristics that, from a different perspective (e.g., that of physical science), we would not consider the object literally to possess.

Mead believed pragmatism to be more radical than previous approaches to the treatment of experience and its relation to the world, because pragmatism abandoned the attempt to treat of perceptual experience in cognitive, representational terms. No longer was the experiencing of things to be understood on the model of belief or knowledge: "Knowledge is an undertaking that always takes place within a situation that is not itself involved in the ignorance or uncertainty that knowledge seeks to dissipate" (Mead, 1932, p. 342). Consciousness qua experience precedes the (added) process of knowledge and is essentially different from this process, as the facts we develop about the world differ from the world itself (cf. Mead, 1938, p. 50).

We have a hand in producing those facts by a process that involves inference. In no sense do we simply find them in the world, merely available for our perceptual systems to pick up. Experience provides us with "a world that is there"; for it to be there, however, we need do no self-conscious work: "If knowledge is discovery of the unknown, this world [that is there] is not known—it is simply there" (Mead, 1938, p. 45). When an error is claimed to have taken place in perceptual experience, this is "an abstraction from its former objective character" (Mead, 1938, p. 156). Truth (and knowledge) pertains to the further, cognitive process and not to the immediate experience itself.

Perceiving includes, in Mead's view, not only the functioning of a perceptual system, but also "attitudes", the internal beginnings of overt acts that occurred previously in response to the same stimulation, and imagery from previous similar situations in which such acts occurred and had certain results now imagined (Mead, 1938, p. 3). Mead emphasized the determinative contribution of the perceiver. Our perceptual experiences have their source as much in perceptual activity and behavior as in the immediate stimulation from the habitat. Thus, we may properly speak of the animal's (perceived) environment not as a spatiotemporal complex of stimulation nor the cause of this complex's occurrence, but as *the world that is there* for the animal, that is, the presence in experience of the animal's habitat. However, for Mead, there is no world beyond the world that is experienced, no world beyond to which experience "answers" echoically. There is only the one world in which all animals exist though they may experience this world differently, from different "perspectives".

While it is wrong, therefore, to construe what is perceived as something internal to our nervous system, Mead's theory implies that perceptual experience is dependent on the animal's nervous system for the properties of the objects present in experience. The qualities and values experienced depend on the organism's acts, which include those activities of the nervous system that determine how the habitat appears: "A conscious form is one that can make phases of its own life-processes parts of its environment" (Mead, 1932, p. 70; cf. p. 73). If the properties of objects are not independent of the organism, and come into existence with its responses to stimulation, then one is forced to locate experience as taking place *after* at least some of the relevant act has occurred, perhaps after a part of the neural portion.

Although this temporal placement of experience was acceptable to Mead (1934), he opposed locating experience or the experienced environment in the brain:

> Consciousness is functional; not substantive; and in either of the main senses of the term it must be located in the objective world rather than in the brain—it belongs to, or is characteristic of, the environment in which we find ourselves. What is located, what does take place in the brain, however, is the physiological process whereby we lose and regain consciousness: a process which is somewhat analogous to that of pulling down and raising a window shade. (p. 112; cf. Mead, 1938, p. 225)

This does not fully state Mead's position; he referred to "the whole act of the organism" as being "parallel to" the organism's experience (Mead, 1934, p. 111). Mead considered this "parallelism" not to be an ontological one (according to which our experiences are nonphysical) but a "practical" one. Thus, nervous systems themselves are objects in our experience when we study them scientifically: "The statement that perception takes place through the nervous system is ambiguous. The nervous system is itself a percept" (Mead, 1938, p. 103; cf. p. 411). The parallel relation of act to experience allows for the control of experience through affecting the corresponding act (e.g., altering the stimulus conditions): "Just as in so far as we present ourselves as biological mechanisms we are better able to control a correspondingly greater field of conditions which determine conduct [and the parallel experience]. On the other hand, this statement in me-

chanical terms abstracts from all purposes and all ends of conduct" (Mead, 1934, p. 352; cf. Mead, 1938, p. 226). For other purposes, one does not perform this abstraction which interprets us as biological mechanisms.

In sum, experience is what it is concretely, and we may respond to experience or treat it in different ways depending on our purposes (which will alter subsequent experience). The fact that, for certain purposes, the reality of a part of experience is brought into question does not make the doubted part any less objective, any less environmental, any more private or internal, particularly when what is experienced is shared with others: "That vibrating molecules are not yellow surfaces is true. But that vibrating molecules may not exist as colored surfaces for animals with certain retinal apparatuses is not rendered impossible by that fact" (Mead, 1932, p. 74). In fact, nature itself is perspectival (Mead, 1927/1964, p. 315; cf. Mead, 1932, p. 80). There is not the one ultimate description of it on which some forms of scientific realism insist.

THE CONCEPT OF CONSCIOUSNESS QUA AWARENESS

Suppose (a) that, as a result of learning, new acts replace those previously performed under the same conditions of stimulation and (b) the individual is again unreflectively immersed in his or her environment; that is, no more consciousness occurs than consciousness qua experience (Mead, 1938, p. 73). The new unreflective acts would mean (due to "parallelism") a change in the world that is "there". Despite sameness of stimulation, different qualities and values would be present in experience: "Any essential change in the organism brings with it a corresponding change in the environment" (Mead, 1932, p. 85). New characters and new meanings emerge with the development of new sensitivities and responsivities.

Consciousness qua awareness is a kind of conduct that develops out of social interaction within a world that is already there in experience and is determined in its immediate continuation by the behavior that occurs. Awareness, too, is an act of the whole individual and determines the experiential environment. It may be for humans the greatest source of novelty because awareness makes possible a large number of different conceptualizations of what there is in the world that is there. These conceptualizations affect how one further responds to the world that is there, and they affect through this newly acquired behavior what experience itself will be like.

Social experience makes awareness possible, and social experience must be understood theoretically in terms of the parallel social act:

> Consciousness is an emergent from such behavior; that so far from being a precondition of the social act, the social act is the precondition of it. The mechanism of the social act can be traced out without introducing into it the conception of consciousness as a separable element within the act; hence the social act, in its more elementary

states or forms, is possible without, or apart from, some form of consciousness. (Mead, 1934, p. 18; cf. Mead, 1938, p. 411)

Mead must mean consciousness qua awareness here, since consciousness qua experience in the form of the organism's environment is produced by the organism's acts. In performing a social act, the individual experiences some social object.

The concept of a social act refers "simply to that [act] which is mediated by the stimulations of other animals belonging to the same group of living forms, which lead to responses which again affect these other forms" (Mead, 1912/1964, p. 135). The other animals are social objects in that their acts produce acts in the animal that put it "en rapport" with them. The individual's acts are instinctive to begin with, but they soon come to be comprised as well of imagery of the acts' previous occurrences and of their consequences, including the responses to his or her behavior of other individuals. The social object is constituted in experience by the social act of the young child including these imaginal components.

This treatment of the social object would seem to be consistent with Mead's thinking about perception; that is, the social act is a special case of acts in general. Thus, aside from the specific instinctive responses produced by the other in the child, the concept of a social act does not introduce anything psychologically new. Compare: "A perception has in it . . . all the elements of an act—the stimulation, the response represented by the attitude [i.e., the first stage in the performance of the relevant response or responses], and the ultimate experience which follows upon the reaction, represented by the imagery arising out of past reactions" (Mead, 1938, p. 3). The schema of the act is filled in by the social act in a characteristic way, but the psychological source of consciousness qua awareness is consciousness qua experience of a certain social kind. The cognitive emerges from the noncognitive.

THE INDIVIDUAL AS SOCIAL OBJECT

As the individual's social acts are performed, he or she is a social object in the experience of others. Therefore, the individual is constituted by those social acts of others for which the individual provides stimulation by his or her social acts. The individual is part of the other's respective experiential environments, which are due as much to their total acts as to the stimulation they receive. Such an "objective relativist" concept of oneself will surely produce opposition from the many people who think of themselves in absolute terms. They will oppose the idea that one's nature is relative to the perspectives taken upon one, that one has no absolute nature distinct from these perspectives. But their opposition would mean that they had come to grips with Mead's radical concept of reality including the individual. The nature of reality (of which one is a part) is ultimately perspectival. There is no getting behind the many perspectives (which are at least as many as the individuals who have a perspective

on any part of the world) to some thing in itself, since the thing in itself does not have a single, perspective-free nature. It follows that one's nature is not of an absolute kind, and does not belong to one independently of the perspectives taken upon one.

But then who or what am I? If I am a social object, what social object am I? The answer can be inferred from Mead's (1924-1925/1964) statements about social objects in general: "I mean by a social object one that answers to all the parts of the complex act, though these parts are found in the conduct of different individuals. The objective of the act is then found in the life-process of the group, not in those of the separate individuals alone" (pp. 280-281). This statement qualifies the remarks of a previous paragraph in the present article. The social object is constituted by *a generalized group perspective* rather than by individual perspectives. It follows that what one is, one's own nature, depends on the group to which one belongs—although what one is remains open-ended, because (a) there are possible perspectives provided by other groups that one might join and (b) a change in how one is constituted as a social object may take place in one's original group.

Notice that it is not simply the individual's social conduct that makes the individual a social object or "a self". According to Mead (e.g., 1938, p. 411), social conduct does not require that the individual already be a self. For the individual to be a social object, a certain group perspective on the individual and his or her conduct must exist, and the individual must adopt this group perspective on himself or herself in order to become a self and be capable of consciousness qua self-awareness and awareness generally.

Equally applicable to the individual as a self is the following statement about the social object: "The social object can exist for the individual only if the various parts of the whole social act carried out by other members of the society are in some fashion present in the conduct of the individual" (Mead, 1924-1925/1964, p. 284). One can only be a self if one exists for oneself as a social object in the way that one exists for the group. Mead insisted that simply responding to one's responding as another would (i.e., simply taking the individual other's role) does not suffice for emergence of self. This requires that one adopt the role of the generalized other, which is a more complete, consistent group attitude. Otherwise, if there occurs only the simplest form of taking the role of another one after another, as by the child, there is lacking the stable, singular character of being a self over time (Mead, 1934, p. 152). Mead went on to speak of the individual's developing as a self in "the fullest sense". He was referring to locating oneself within the large social process, that is, taking the group's attitude towards the large-scale social projects in which one is engaged through being a member of the group, which is so engaged.

ONLY SELVES AWARE

Why does an individual need to be a self in order to be aware? As it turns out, the better question is: Why are only selves aware? Selfhood does not precede awareness. Why is application of the concept of consciousness qua awareness "a use of consciousness which always has, implicitly at least, the reference to an 'I' in it" (Mead, 1934, p. 165)? The answer is that an individual who becomes capable of being aware of things (which is more than merely experiencing them) also becomes a self. And the individual becomes capable of being aware by becoming a self. That is, the emergence of awareness and self is one process and not two.

An individual who becomes a self is in a position to engage in interaction with himself or herself of the sort that he or she engages in with others and that involves rules which the members of the group obey. In order for the individual thus to be engaged, the individual must take the role of the generalized other relative to himself or herself. And this means becoming for himself or herself, through taking this special role, a social object and self. The specific social conduct that comprises being aware is *indicating to oneself (and to another or alone) something about something else or about oneself.* Thus, in being aware of anything, one must be to oneself as though one were another—but another who is a member of the group to which one belongs and who addresses one according to the group's rules, in the way that any member would or could. Awareness is, as stated, a social act in Mead's view; and it is a social act even when what one is aware of is not a social object: "This process of indication . . . is primarily a piece of behavior toward another individual which the human individual comes to use toward himself" (Mead, 1938, p. 65). It is a social act because there is in it, implicitly at least, a reference to a social object, namely, to oneself as the one indicated to or addressed.

An individual who is being aware of a nonsocial object takes, anyway, the attitude of the generalized other to the object: "We put ourselves in the attitude of all, and that which we all see is that which is expressed in universal terms" (Mead, 1934, p. 331). In perception, the act of awareness is mediated by one's responses to the object, by the total act constituting one's experience of the object. One's experiencing of the object is not universal; there is much variation between people even when they are stimulated in common, for example, by light reflected from a surface under identical external conditions: "Each has a different sensitivity, and one color is different to me from what it is to you. These are differences which are due to the peculiar character of the organism as over against that which answers to universality" (Mead, 1934, p. 331; cf. Mead, 1938, p. 64). In contrast, consciousness qua awareness abstracts from the world that is there for each individual, and we share an abstractive perspective on it.

Awareness does not substitute for experience in perceptual instances but is added to it. In being aware of the object that is there by virtue of one's total act, one addresses oneself qua experiencer of the object, pointing out to oneself something about it that may be already present in one's experience. Accordingly, Mead (1938, p. 65) distinguished between "what the individual indicates to himself" and "the process of indication" (as he refused to distinguish between environment and experience).

This pointing out, in turn, stimulates one to respond to the awareness as one would respond to another person who was indicating to one the nature of the object. One's response to the indication may amount simply to an attitude that constitutes its meaning, that is, a set of incipient responses to the words addressed by oneself to oneself. Or, an inner dialogue may develop, in which case the kind of responses involved in responding to one's responses are obviously of a special kind. It is through the latter process of communicating with oneself about things that one becomes a self and aware: "I know of no other form of behavior than the linguistic one in which the individual is an object to himself" (Mead, 1934, p. 142). One does not only take the role of the generalized other in the communicative exchange, pointing something out to oneself from that perspective, one is also a generalized audience for it. This behavior, for which one is one's own audience, being directed to oneself, makes implicit and sometimes explicit reference to oneself and is linguistic:

> The vocal gesture is pre-eminently adapted to this function because it affects the auditory apparatus of the form that produces it as it does the others. The final outcome in human social conduct is that the individual, in exciting through the vocal gesture the response of another, initiates the same response in himself and, in that attitude of the other, comes to address himself, that is, he appears as an object to himself in his own conduct. It is this attitude which is commonly denoted as "consciousness" when this term carries with it the implication of awareness over and above the mere presence of the perceptual object in the perspective or experience of the organism. (Mead, 1938, pp. 189-190).

AWARENESS AS SELF-ADDRESS

Consciousness qua awareness of experienced objects is a form of self-address by means of significant symbols that one acquired initially from others who addressed one. In using symbols for this purpose, one must also respond to one's use of them. One responds to oneself as others would, with reference to the object whose nature one has indicated. This way of responding gives to the symbols their significance as indications of something about the object. Otherwise, if such responding (as the inner audience of one's indications) did not occur, and one simply uttered (overtly or covertly) the same pattern of words, the symbols uttered would have no significance to one.

Speaking of the idea of *dog* that one arouses in oneself and others when one indicates that something experienced is a dog, Mead (1934, p. 71) identified the idea (or meaning) with "an organization of responses which can be called out by the term 'dog'". When one conveys the meaning to oneself or to another, not all of these responses, or perhaps any of them, need be actualized. What must be produced (constituting the immediate meaning of the word), however, are very transient episodic propensities to produce a certain group of responses. This group of responses is shared among the members of the group who use the word in the same way.

Thus, in order for one's use of symbols to be significant and for an actual awareness to be thereby instantiated, one's behavior or experience must serve not only as a stimulus for their use in a generalized other-perspectival utterance directed to oneself, but one must be at the same time one's own audience for the utterance. But this double role does not amount to a "conversation" from two different perspectives. Although two perspectives are involved, they are not different; the "conversation" is analogous to an interaction occurring between two like-minded people who are fully understanding each other. For them, disagreement reflects doubt or uncertainty rather than different generalized attitudes. The meaning of the addressor's use of an utterance does not differ from the meaning of the addressee's reception of it.

THE GENERALIZED OTHER AS AUDIENCE

In being aware of something, the one to whom one is indicating is not onself in some presocial, biological sense. One is indicating to oneself as a self—as someone, therefore, who is taking the role of the generalized other relative to oneself, including one's use of significant symbols in awareness. The particular relevance of this to awareness is the importance of *who one's internalized audience is* to the character of the awareness that one has. According to Mead, this audience is of extreme importance because how one indicates depends on the effects one anticipates that one's indications will have on this audience (just as how one addresses others depends on what one anticipates their reactions will be). The inner audience guides one in one's selection, formulation, and emphasis of awarenesses according to the meanings that would be assigned to them by such an audience. What limitations, therefore, does the generalized other place on consciousness qua awareness?

It seems fair to Mead's view to say that the generalized other is not simply thrust upon the individual by the group or by virtue of membership in the group. The person should not be interpreted as a passive recipient of the groups' attitudes. He or she does not make these attitudes his or her own without exercising choices. In synthesizing a generalized other (who will serve as the individual's audience for his or her awarenesses), the individual may exercise creativity and exhibit the individuality that all people possess. As it is, the generalized other "quickly passes the bounds of the specific group. It is the *vox populi, vox dei,* the 'voice of men and of angels'. Education and varied experience refine out of it what is provincial, and leave 'what is true for all men at all times'" (Mead, 1922/1964, p. 245).

Mead (1934) spoke, therefore, of a self determined not only by the immediate group but also from the perspective of reflective thought:

> He is a member of the community of the thinkers whose literature he reads and to which he may contribute by his own published thought. He belongs to a society of all rational beings. . . . The widest community in which the individual finds himself, that which is everywhere, through and for everybody, is the thought world as such. He is a member of such a community and he is what he is as such a member. (p. 201)

One would not be a self except for one's interactions with the members of one's community, but the process by which a self and its correlative generalized other is constituted is one that moves readily beyond that immediate community. Moreover, Mead (1934) argued that the common social-interactive origin of self and generalized other does not preclude wide individual differences among people: "The structure of each is differently constituted by this [common] pattern from the way in which the structure of any other is so constituted" (p. 202).

Mead also saw the individual as a source of social change. Specifically, as applied to consciousness qua awareness, Mead's view holds that one who speaks with the voice of men and of angels (to an inner audience of the same) may speak otherwise than he or she has learned. The individual's responses do not neatly reflect the social interactions in which he or she has engaged. There is an element of unpredictability in awareness as in all other conduct. Even the individual under control of his or her generalized other in what he or she is indicating may respond unpredictably with unusual awarenesses (cf. Mead, 1934, p. 203). Also, the individual's generalized other, which exercises control of the individual's behavior including awarenesses, depends for its characteristics on the group with which the individual identifies. And this group may not be the present one in which he or she lives. It may be, instead, an ideal community from whose (synthesized) perspective one is enabled to criticize present social arrangements (Mead, 1934, p. 168). The reference community, as synthesized uniquely by the individual from materials that are available to all members of the society, may make it possible for him or her to act to produce change in the present community's practices in the direction of the reference community.

It follows that the development of consciousness qua awareness is open-ended. We can keep noticing new things about the world and about ourselves throughout our lives. We may even change radically our awareness of the world and self, depending on how we constitute the inner audience of our awareness. A truly new conception of things (such as the one that Mead himself proposed) would mean that there existed an inner audience for awareness even before other people could learn to understand.

REFERENCES

Dewey, J. George Herbert Mead. *Journal of Philosophy*, 1931, 28, 309-314.

Dewey, J. Prefatory remarks, in Mead, G. H., *The Philosophy of the Present*. Chicago: University of Chicago Press, 1932.

Freud, S. "Project for a scientific psychology," in *Standard Edition*, Vol. 1. London: Hogarth, 1966. (Composed 1895).

Freud, S. "The unconscious," in *Standard Edition*, Vol. 14. London: Hogarth, 1957. (Originally published, 1915).

Freud, S. "The ego and the id," in *Standard Edition*, Vol. 19. London: Hogarth, 1961. (Originally published, 1923).

Freud, S. "An outline of psycho-analysis," in *Standard Edition*, Vol. 23. London: Hogarth, 1964. (Composed, 1938).

James, W. "Does "consciousness" exist?" *Journal of Philosophy, Psychology, and Scientific Methods*, 1904, 1, 477-491.

Mead, G. H. "The mechanism of social consciousness," in Reck, A. J. (ed.), *Selected Writings: George Herbert Mead*. Chicago: University of Chicago Press, 1964. (Originally published, 1912).

Mead, G. H. "The genesis of the self and social control," in Reck, A. J. (ed.), *Selected Writings: George Herbert Mead*. Chicago: University of Chicago Press, 1964. (Originally published, 1924-1925).

Mead, G. H. "The objective reality of perspectives," in Reck, A. J. (ed.), *Selected Writings: George Herbert Mead*. Chicago: University of Chicago Press, 1964. (Originally published, 1927).

Mead, G. H. *The Philosophy of the Present*. Chicago: University of Chicago Press, 1932.

Mead, G. H. *Mind, Self, and Society*. Chicago: University of Chicago Press, 1934.

Mead, G. H. *Movements of Thought in the Nineteenth Century*. Chicago: University of Chicago Press, 1936.

Mead, G. H. *The Philosophy of the Act*. Chicago: University of Chicago Press, 1938.

Morris, C. W. "Introduction: George H. Mead as a social psychologist and social philosopher," in G. H. Mead, *Mind, Self, and Society*. Chicago: University of Chicago Press, 1934.

Natsoulas, T. "Consciousness." *American Psychologist*, 1978, 33, 906-914 (a).

Natsoulas, T. "Toward a model for consciousness in the light of B. F. Skinner's contribution." *Behaviorism*, 1978, 6, 139-175 (b).

Natsoulas, T. "Basic problems of consciousness." *Journal of Personality and Social Psychology*, 1981, 41, 132-178.

Natsoulas, T. Addendum to "Consciousness". *American Psychologist*, 1983, 38, 171-172 (a).

Natsoulas, T. "Concepts of consciousness." *Journal of Mind and Behavior*, 1983, 4, 13-59 (b).

Skinner, B. F. "The operational analysis of psychological terms." *Psychological Review*, 1945, 52, 270-277.

Skinner, B. F. *Science and Human Behaviour*. New York: Macmillan, 1953.

Skinner, B. F. *Verbal Behavior*. New York: Appleton-Century-Crofts, 1957.

Skinner, B. F. *About Behaviorism*. New York: Knopf, 1974.

John D. Baldwin (essay date 1988)

SOURCE: "Mead's Solution to the Problem of Agency," in *Sociological Inquiry*, Vol. 58, No. 2, Spring, 1988, pp. 139-62.

[*In the following essay, Baldwin investigates Mead's idea of agency, and explores his analytical method.*]

The thesis of this paper is that George Herbert Mead's pragmatism provides a valuable approach to the topic of agency, avoiding many of the problems that typically surround this issue. The question of agency—do human actors have autonomy and the ability to exercise free and creative choices—is at the center of several important controversies in sociology, such as the stand-off between the positivists and antipositivists, the disputes over structural and astructural theories, and the debates over action and order (Alexander 1984; Skinner 1985; Bosworth and Kreps 1986). For example, interpretive and constructionist sociologists often charge that structural and macro sociologists develop overly deterministic models that leave little or no room for human agency (Blumer 1969; Morrione 1985). But constructionist and interpretive models are often criticized for being overly voluntaristic, neglecting the structure and regularities of the social world (Collins 1981; Turner 1984, 1986). Since deterministic and voluntaristic models are usually conceived of as opposites and mutually exclusive, it is easy for people to polarize arguments about agency; and this often divides sociologists into two camps—those defending agency and those defending science.

Although scientists are often grouped together under the label "positivists," Mead's (1917) analysis of science demonstrates that scientific research does not actually conform to the model developed by the positivists. Mead was critical of positivism for several reasons, and his pragmatic model of science does not include the highly rational and deterministic assumptions associated with positivism. Mead's theory of science provides a middle course between the extreme positions based on either free will or determinism, demonstrating how sociology can construct a scientific (though not positivistic) study of human conduct and society that deals effectively with agency. There are both metaphysical and practical aspects of the problems of agency, and Mead developed methods for solving both types of problems. These methods may help resolve the apparent impasse between positivistic and voluntaristic theories in sociology. Compared with Parsons's vague definitions of voluntaristic action and the unclear implications of his theory for empirical research (Sciulli 1987), Mead's theory is notable for its precise definitions of action in terms of behavior and its unambiguous implications for a program of scientific research.

BEYOND METAPHYSICS

There are several ways of conceptualizing agency. One is to equate agency with free will. Since free will is a metaphysical construct, the debate over the ultimate nature of free will and determinism is based more on belief than on data. Although people may experience a certainty of free will, "[f]reedom is not empirically availableu . . . it is not open to demonstration by any scientific methods" (Berger 1963, p. 122).

Mead (1917, 1929, 1932) argued that we can never answer metaphysical questions about the ultimate nature of "reality," thus we can never know whether people "really" have free will or not. Many ancient Greek philosophers and mathematically oriented thinkers assumed the presence of some preexistent ultimate truths beyond the range of our fallible perceptual organs (Mead 1917), and for centuries various influential philosophers sought to reach those transcendental truths through contemplation and logic (Mead 1938, p. 513-514). However, the pragmatists noted that despite thousands of years of contemplation, philosophers had made no more net advance than the mythical figure Sisyphus did in repeatedly rolling his stone up the same hill. In contrast, science—by abandoning metaphysical puzzles and focusing on careful observation and experimentation—has made enormous advances in understanding the world in the past few centuries. The pragmatists advocated abandoning contemplation and applying the scientific method to all areas of human knowledge, including philosophy. When we do this, the "despairing sense of the philosophic Sisyphus vainly striving to roll the heavily weighted world of his reflection up into a preexistent reality" drops "away and the philosopher can face about toward the future and join in the scientist's adventure" (Mead 1964, p. 389-390).

Much of Mead's work was devoted to reconstructing philosophy and social phychology using the methods of modern science, with no reference to contemplative philosophy or metaphysics. "I have endeavored to present the world which is an implication of the scientific method of discovery with entire abstraction from any epistemological or metaphysical presuppositions or complications" (Mead 1964, p. 210). Among the metaphysical issues to be forgotten is the debate over free will and determinism.

Modern science has both deterministic and voluntaristic aspects, and Mead dealt with these in his discussions of *mechanism* and *teleology*. Newtonian physics produced mechanistic, deterministic models of the world that leave no room for purpose, freedom or choice (Mead 1936, p. 250-281). The great success of the mechanistic sciences in developing deterministic laws reinforced the notion that everything might fit such models. "Seemingly, the whole world would be absolutely fixed and determined" (p. 250). However, Mead (1932, p. 101-102; 1936, p. 259, 266, 275; 1964, p. 201-202) pointed out that mechanistic, deterministic assumptions are merely postulates or working hypotheses, and science can never prove them to be absolute truths. In addition, Mead emphasized that mechanistic laws do not adequately deal with certain important aspects of the universe, especially "with the characters which belong to living organisms" (1936, p. 260). Namely, mechanistic theories fail to treat living things as adapting organisms, with purposive qualities (p. 269). For example, a purely mechanistic analysis of the digestive process omits the issue of the function—or purpose—of digestion in maintaining life. "The complete mechanical statement would not take account of the end, of the purpose . . ." that is seen in living systems; "[a]nd that seems to be necessary to our comprehension of the world" (p. 272).

Mead used the term "teleology" to describe the purposeful, life-sustaining processes that were overlooked by purely mechanical analyses of living systems (1936, p. 268ff; 1982b, p. 108ff). However, he clearly dissociated himself from the nonscientific form of teleology espoused by vitalists (1936, p. 292-325). "Sometimes, like the vitalists, we abuse [mechanistic] science because it ignores life. But there is only a short distance we can go on the teleological program" (1982b, p. 171). That short distance is to make the point that life is more than mechanism alone: science needs to have postulates for explaining the self-organizing, purposive qualities of living systems, not just postulates about the mechanical aspects of the universe.

Both mechanism and teleology are postulates, not absolute dogmatic statements about the ultimate nature of "reality" (Mead 1936, p. 264-291). In addition, *both* mechanistic and teleological accounts can be useful: they are not mutually exclusive and they can complement each other. "In biological science you bring in both these points of view" (p. 269). Mead demonstrated their compatibility with an example of a physician and district attorney analyzing a murder (p. 268-269). The physician explains the mechanism of the murder, how the "bullet entered the body in a certain way and led to a given result" (p. 269). In contrast, the district attorney explains the motives and purposes of the murderer: "That is, he gives a teleological explanation, while the doctor who performs the autopsy gives a mechanical explanation" (p. 269). Since neither teleology or mechanism is a dogma in science, it is easy to see that "[t]here is, then, no real conflict between a mechanical and a teleological account of the world or of the facts of life" (p. 271). "Thus we see that science has gotten away from metaphysical dogma as to what the nature of things is. . . . " (p. 275). Mechanistic, deterministic hypotheses are useful in describing some aspects of nature; and purposive, teleological models are useful in describing other aspects. Neither type of hypothesis warrants conclusions about ultimate metaphysical truths, including issues of free will and determinism.

If we agree with Mead that we can never resolve metaphysical questions about the ultimate nature of "reality," we can put aside the metaphysical issue of whether or not humans have free will and ask if there is any other way to evaluate the concept of agency. Mead's pragmatism can again be of help. Mead (1936, p. 351) stated that pragmatism is based on two sources: "behavioristic psychology" and "the scientific technique, which comes back to the testing of a hypothesis by its working." Rather than attempting to reach transcendental "truths," modern psychology has "its sympathies . . . with the presuppositions and method of the natural sciences. . . . Psychology . . . has not been interested in these epistemological and metaphysical riddles, it has been simply irritated by them" (Mead 1964, p. 269). "The behavioristic psychology has tried to get rid of the more or less metaphysical complications involved in the setting-up of the psychical over against the world, mind over against body, consciousness over against matter. That was felt to lead into a blind alley" (Mead 1934, p. 105). Instead, behavioristic psychology seeks to develop a unified science of mind and body in which all facets of conduct are open to scientific investigation (Mead 1922, 1924-25). "But if mind is simply an emergent character of certain organisms in their so-called intelligent responses to their environments, mind can never transcend the environment within which it operates" (1932, p. 118). "Mind can no longer be put outside of nature" (p. 152).

A basic principle of behavioristic psychology is that abstract concepts—such as agency—should be reconceptualized in terms of the actual behaviors from which we infer the abstraction. Topics such as agency—which in the past were treated as abstract, metaphysical concepts—can be reformulated in purely scientific terms, thereby removing them from the arena of metaphysics and pure speculation and allowing them to be studied scientifically.

Mead's type of scientific approach is not a veiled attempt to create deterministic models of human conduct. Mead (1917, 1932) did not anticipate that scientists would ever succeed at constructing fully deterministic theories. All sciences repeatedly confront novel and emergent events that are not completely predictable (Mead 1932, p. 14ff, 35ff, 96-97; 1964, p. 346-347). Although it is true that in the sciences "the emergent has no sooner appeared than we set about rationalizing it . . ." (1932, p. 14), these rationalizations and theories usually have to be modified and reconstructed as later emergents arise. Thus, while science's ability to locate regularities and patterns has allowed the development of increasingly sophisticated empirical generalizations and laws, scientific laws can never become completely finalized and deterministic. "[T]he scientist's procedure and method contemplate no such finality. On the contrary, they contemplate continued reconstruction in the face of events emerging in ceaseless novelty" (p. 101-102).

Mead's rejection of fully deterministic scientific theories is not to be confused with a position on the metaphysical question of free will and determinism. Mead (1917, 1924-25, 1929, 1929-30, 1932, 1934) approved of the scientist's goal of constructing propositions and laws to explain the regularities in our experienced world. In his own approach to psychology, Mead (1934, p. 39) stated: "We are interested in finding the most general laws of correlation we can find." This process builds toward a scientific psychology in which "all the distinctions must be explained by the same general laws as those which are appealed to to account for animal organs and functions" (1964, p. 82). However, he recognized that no theory that we can craft—even in the physical sciences—is likely to ever become completely finalized, fully accurate, or totally deterministic, since novel and unpredictable events continually emerge (1929, 1932).[1] Instead, Mead anticipated only probabilistic theories of emergent events. "[W]hatever does happen, even the emergent . . ." happens under conditions that "lie within probability only" and "these conditions never determine completely the 'what it is' that will happen" (1932, p. 15). "[T]here is also the indeterminateness of what occurs" (p. 96). "And the indeterminate 'what' involves always a possibly new situation with a new complex of relationships" (p. 97). In an indeterminant universe, scientists construct probabilistic laws to explicate the regularities identified to date, without the illusion of describing an ultimate reality. In the social sciences, the development of probabilistic laws allows for general forecasting but not for precise predictions about the future of human conduct and society.

In order to clarify the pragmatic approach to agency, the following sections briefly review Mead's analysis of those behaviors that are generally considered to be central to agency. Mead defined choice and action in terms of their neural and behavioral components—which are open to empirical study—and not in terms of "free will," as metaphysically conceived. Mead's analyses of human conduct never involved hidden assumptions about or attempts to prove any metaphysical position about free will or determinism.

PRECONDITIONS FOR THE EMERGENCE OF MIND AND SELF

Mead (1924-25, 1932, 1934) took an evolutionary approach to the emergence of consciousness and deliberate action. By comparing the behavior of animals at different phyletic levels, Mead clarified the evolutionary and physiological preconditions for the emergence of the higher forms of human cognition and planned behavior. His evolutionary approach also underscores the fact that human consciousness is part of nature, not transcendental. "The genesis of mind in human society . . . is a natural development within the world of living organisms and their environment" (1932, p. 84). "I have wished to present mind as an evolution in nature . . ." (p. 85). Although some sociologists may question the relevance of biological data in discussions of agency, Mead's entire theoretical system was based on biological data and theories (Baldwin 1986).

Mead (1924-25, 1932, 1934) related the emergence of deliberate choice and self-control to the encephalon during the evolution of the advanced vertebrate cortex. "But the great advance comes with the development of the encephalon" (1932, p. 70). The vertebrate cerebral cortex provides a mechanism that makes possible more reflective and deliberate responses than do the simpler neural systems of lower species. "The mechanism by which this is accomplished is the cerebrum" (p. 126).

Mead discussed several important properties of the advanced vertebrate cortex, clearly revealing his concern for approaching choice, deliberate action and agency from a biological point of view. First, the encephalon "is primarily the nerve center of the important distance senses" (1932, p. 70-71), hence its development makes possible the detailed processing of distant stimuli. Primitive species cannot perceive or respond well to distant stimuli, and they tend to respond without delay to stimuli once they have contact experience with them. With the evolution of the cortex and increased sophistication of the distance senses, "the contact experiences to which [the distance senses] respond are delayed, and possibilities of adjustment and of choice in response are thus increased" (p. 71). Sensing a stimulus at a distance, before contact is made, allows for a time period before a contact response is required; and this time is essential for the reflective processes involved in deliberate choice.

The advanced cortex has neural pathways that "connect every response potentially with every other response in the organism" (1932, p. 125)—which enhances behavioral flexibility and the capacity to select among a variety of alternative responses. "The cerebrum . . . is an organ which integrates a vast variety of responses, including the lower reflexes . . ." (p. 126). Thus, seeing a distant stimulus calls up numerous relevant responses, including reflexes and related emotions, which are integrated into a variety of possible acts that can mutually facilitate or inhibit each other. "In a sense all responses are so interconnected by way of interrelated innervation and inhibition" (p. 125). And inhibition is a second mechanism for creating delay in response. "In the integrative process there are different alternative combinations and corresponding alternatives also for the inhibitions that integration necessarily involves. This introduces delay in re-

sponse, and adjustment by way of selection of type of response, i.e., choice" (p. 126). Inhibition is not only important in producing the delay needed for selection and choice but also for assuring that inappropriate acts are not performed. "If certain responses are prepotent they *ipso facto* inhibit all the others" (p. 127).

Third, during the delay period, the organism feels its own incipient responses to the distant stimuli. "In the innervations of the attitudes that distant objects call out the animal feels the invitation or threat they carry with them" (Mead 1932, p. 71). For example, seeing food may call up motor feelings associated with an invitation to approach, but seeing a predator may call up motor feelings associated with avoidance of threat. Thus, the animal feels its own tendencies to approach or withdraw. "His responses to his own tendencies to act provide the control that organizes all his responses into a coordinated act, so that these inner feelings wax in importance in the development of the mechanism [of the encephalon]. . . . It is here that we first meet the stuff of ideation" (p. 71). Rather than the organism's responding in an immediate, undeliberated manner when contacting external stimuli, "[i]ts own [internal] condition determines the objects and influences to which it will respond" (p. 71). Its own internal feelings influence the stimuli it selects to attend to, and in this way they influence its final response. "In this case the animal has become conscious" (p. 72).

Fourth, as the cortex evolved, simple internal feelings of incipient responses became more sophisticated forms of "response imagery" (p. 74). And in advanced species, both "sense imagery" and "motor imagery" play an important role in the performance of the act: ". . . sense imagery . . . controls the selection of stimuli and motor imagery . . . facilitates the response" (1982a, p. 28). Sense imagery makes the organism aware of the stimuli it needs to hunt for or avoid, and motor imagery both reveals the variety of possible motor responses available to choose from and helps the organism prepare for performing the response that is selected. "[T]his imagery arises from past experience . . ." (1964, p. 134). Images of past actions and their results help in anticipating the future consequences of similar actions. "This imagery gives us the result of the act before we carry it out" (1982a, p. 29). Because the cerebrum allows the organism to anticipate the results of the act, the cerebrum has "introduced the future into the mechanism of the act . . ." (1932, p. 132). Imagery of the future phases of various alternative acts and their results allows the organism to select among them and make "purposive responses" (p. 74). "In this manner temporal distance can be organized in the central nervous system. . . . [And] the central nervous system can affect the organism at present with this future act. . . . It is the ability of later responses to play back into immediate responses that gives us our flexibility and power of choice" (1982b, p. 158).

By tracing several important preconditions of choice to the central nervous system, Mead clearly showed an interest in a scientific analysis of choice and related processes. He also demonstrated how to construct biosocial theories that integrate relevant biological data into sociologically important analyses—which is something that few sociologists do as well as Mead did.

SYMBOLIC THOUGHT AND CONSCIOUSNESS

Although Mead often discussed the central nervous system as the mechanism for delayed response and choice, he was interested in more than neural mechanisms. "[T]he cortex is not simply a mechanism. It is an organ that exists in fulfilling its function" (1964, p. 282), namely it is "an organ of social conduct" (p. 283). The full emergence of mind and self can occur only through social interaction, especially through the social use of language.

Language provides "word images" (1932, p. 75) that enrich the sensory and motor images used in making choices. "Ideas are closely related to images. . . . Since the symbols with which we think are largely recognized as word images, ideas and images have a very close consanguinity" (p. 75). Words allow us to call up symbolic images of all phases of our acts, along with the interplay of our acts with the environment and other people. They also bring images of the past and the future into our present, and this "[i]deation extends spatially and temporally the field within which activity takes place," leading to an "extended present" that reaches far beyond our immediate perceptual present (p. 88).

The meanings that words carry are a central component of the extended present and the deliberate actions we take in it. By analyzing meaning from a behavioristic perspective, Mead was able to avoid the metaphysical problems associated with traditional views of "ideas" and "meanings." In discussing "the meaning of things," Mead (1934, p. 127) stated: "We are are here avoiding logical and metaphysical problems, just as modern psychology does." Mead explained meaning in terms of his theory of the act, and showed how words can come to stand for the meanings that emerge from the act. First, objects and actions take on meanings based on completions of the acts in which they are involved. "The completions that need to occur before the act is completed are behavioristic meanings" (1982b, p. 143). For example, "the ultimate act of driving a nail is for us the meaning of the hammer" (p. 130). The hammer's capacity for driving the nail establishes its meaning. "When we indicate this pattern of final manipulation we indicate the meaning of the act" (p. 143). Second, words such as "hammer" are symbols that come to stand for the meanings that are based on people's actions, such as using hammers to drive nails.

Beginning in childhood, even before we can talk, our understanding of meaning arises through our behaving and interacting with the physical and social environment, hence meaning can be studied by observing the relevant behaviors and interactions. When parents give a ball to a child and show the child how to play with it, they are helping the child learn the uses—and meanings—of the ball.

The adult, in this process, is constantly indicating to the child the results of his own motions: the ball is something to get hold of and throw. Things done with the object are referred to the child, so that when the child plays he will see the end and learn to pick out the object's ultimate use (Mead 1982b, p. 134).

It is "the results of his own motions" that convey to the child the "ultimate use" of the ball *and* its meaning. "Through all this the child is busy getting the meaning of things" (p. 134). When the parents couple the word "ball" with the child's activities with balls, the child learns to attach the word "ball" to the meanings that arise from the acts of rolling, bouncing, and playing games with balls.

Not only physical objects, but also social gestures—such as a wink or a smile—take on meanings, based on the results of the acts involving them. "If that gesture does so indicate to another organism the subsequent (or resultant) behavior of the given organism, then it has meaning. In other words, the relationship between a given stimulus—as a gesture—and the later phases of the social act of which it is an early . . . phase constitutes the field within which meaning originates and exists. Meaning is thus a development of something objectively there as a relation between certain phases of the social act; it is not a psychical addition to that act and it is not an 'idea' as traditionally conceived" (e.g., by metaphysical or idealist philosophers). Rather, "[t]he gesture stands for a certain resultant of the social act, . . . so that meaning is given or stated in terms of response" (Mead 1934, p. 76). More specifically, Mead stated that social meaning involves a "three-fold relation among phases of the social act," namely, the "relation of the *gesture* of one organism to the adjustive *response* of another organism . . . and to the *completion* of the given act . . ." (p. 76, emphasis added). "The basis of meaning is thus objectively there in social conduct, or in nature in its relation to such conduct" (p. 80). As such it is amenable to scientific study.

"Awareness or consciousness is not necessary to the presence of meaning in the process of social experience" (p. 77). Two snarling dogs are exchanging and responding to meaningful signals in their conversation of gestures, but are not consciously aware of the meanings. "The mechanism of meaning is thus present in the social act before the emergence of consciousness or awareness of meaning occurs" (p. 77). Awareness of meaning emerges only when the "gesture becomes a symbol, a significant symbol" (p. 78), namely a symbol that people use in a conventional manner so that it calls up the same meaning for those users. Meaning "is not essentially or primarily a psychical content (a content of mind or consciousness), for it need not be conscious at all, and is not in fact until significant symbols are evolved in the process of human social experience. Only when it becomes identified with such symbols does meaning become conscious" (p. 80).

"In language, what we have reached is the consciousness of meaning attached to a gesture" (1982a, p. 43). "We do not have the consciousness of meaning except when we can indicate the stimuli, the symbols, to ourselves" (p. 44). Both a human and an animal can see and be perceptually aware of a hammer on the ground; but humans can gain the additional awareness of the meaning of the hammer by verbally describing it and its use. "Mentality on our approach simply comes in when the organism is able to point out meanings to others and to himself. This is the point at which mind appears, or if you like, emerges" (1934, p. 132). This approach to mind introduces none of the mysterious elements present in idealist and metaphysical conceptions of meaning and mind.

We can use words either out loud or quietly to ourselves in the inner conversation we call mind. "[T]he mechanism of thought, insofar as thought uses symbols which are used in social intercourse, is but an inner conversation" (1964, p. 146). The inner conversation can be with ourselves, with specific individuals we imagine to be talking with, or with some generalized "they"—as occurs when we ask ourselves "What would *they* think if I did such and such?" This generalized "they" is what Mead called the "generalized other" (p. 284).

How does Mead's behavioristic approach deal with highly abstract and generalized meanings? In metaphysical and idealistic world views, highly abstract meanings seem to refer to universals at a Platonic or transcendental level. An idealist might think that "this meaning or universal character [is something] with which a behavioristic psychology is supposed to have difficulty in dealing" (1934, p. 82). However Mead disagreed: "It is the possibility of such a behavioristic statement that I endeavor to sketch" (p. 83).

Mead explained "universals" in terms of the behavior seen when any of a variety of different stimuli can call up the same response. When we have to write a brief note, we recognize that many types of pens, pencils or markers will suffice: All members of a certain class of stimuli can call up the response of picking up the object and writing. "[R]ecognition can be stated in terms of a response that may answer to any one of a certain group of stimuli" (p. 83). If a person is attempting to drive a nail and cannot find a hammer, the individual may recognize that "a brick or a stone" will also serve the same function (p. 83). "Anything that he can get hold of that will serve the purpose will be a hammer. That sort of response which involves the grasping of a heavy object is a universal" (p. 83). The brick or stone can function *as if* it were a hammer; hence all three fall into the same class of objects because they—as hard, heavy objects—are functionally similar in carrying out the behavior of hammering the nail. The recognition of functional equivalence allows the universal "response that answers to a whole set of particulars" (p. 84). "It is this which has been supposed to be beyond the behavioristic explanation or statement. What behavioristic psychology does is to state that character of the experience in terms of response" (p. 84).

Mead attempted to explain the capacity for universal responding in terms of the central nervous system (p. 83ff)

and the social practices of the language community (p. 88ff). Although his data on the central nervous system were limited and his argumentation indirect, he concluded: "I see no reason why one should not find, then, in the organization of the attitude as presented in the central nervous system, what it is we refer to as the meaning of the object, that which is universal" (p. 87). In addition, Mead traced the development of universals to the social nature of language use. Verbal communication involves a "co-operative process:" In order to understand each other, we must share in the same "universe of discourse" in which "gestures and symbols have the same or common meanings for all members of that group . . ." (p. 89). Because language use allows an individual to hear his or her own words as if from the perspective of others, it makes possible the "individual taking the attitudes of others toward himself, and of his finally crystallizing all these particular attitudes into a single attitude or standpoint which may be called that of the 'generalized other'" (p. 90). This generalized attitude enhances our capacity to grasp universals and abstractions based on the perspectives of the broader community.

Our membership in a verbal community—a culture with symbolic knowledge—helps us acquire a broad range of knowledge about things experienced first by others. We do not have to be swept away by a raging river to learn about the strength and danger of a powerful torrent. "[I]n the community of those who communicate with each other, the force of the torrent has taken on a meaning insofar as each is wont to indicate this to others and so to himself" (1964, p. 336). The consequences of stepping into a powerful torrent establish its meaning as "something to be avoided"; and experienced people can communicate those meanings to individuals who have never had first-hand experience with the torrent and its consequences. This cooperative social process allows individuals to expand their understanding of universals—e.g., adding "the torrent" to the class of stimuli that carry the universal meaning of "something to be avoided"—based on the experience of others.

REFLECTIVE INTELLIGENCE

Mead's (1934, p. 90-100) analysis of reflective intelligence reveals his scientific approach to yet another important aspect of agency. When we have several alternative responses open to us in a given situation, we can use significant symbols to heighten our awareness of and reflect on our choices of possible actions before acting. "[R]eflective behavior arises only under the conditions of self-consciousness and makes possible the purposive control . . . of its conduct . . ." (p. 91). Words make us aware of the details of each alternative action and the likely future consequences of each one. People are especially likely to use this type of intelligence in problematic situations (p. 122ff). "This [reflective intelligence] is the most effective means of adjustment to the social environment, and indeed to the environment in general, that the individual has at his disposal" (p. 100).

Mead identified several components of reflective intelligence, all of which are amenable to scientific investigation. "Intelligence is essentially the ability to solve the problems of present behavior in terms of its possible future consequences as implicated on the basis of past experience . . ." (p. 100). When we confront a problem, we can use symbols to imagine several possible solutions to the problem and to evaluate the anticipated consequences of each alternative, based on past experience, before choosing a course of action. People do this when they—either out loud or in their inner conversation—talk themselves through several alternative solutions to a problem and use their memories of past experiences to evaluate the possible future consequences of each alternative.

Mead (p. 91) stated that "[i]t is essential that such reflective intelligence be dealt with from the point of view of social behaviorism." By conceptualizing the components of reflective intelligence in terms of behavior, Mead avoided the metaphysical notions of free will that arise from nonempirical approaches to choice and agency. "What the behaviorist is occupied with, what we have to come back to, is the actual reaction itself, and it is only in so far as we can translate the content of introspection over into response that we can get any satisfactory psychological doctrine" (p. 105).

Mead avoided introspective methods by analyzing reflective intelligence in terms of objective variables, such as neural mechanisms and overt social symbolic interaction. Not only did he demonstrate the role of meaningful words, inner conversation, and taking the role of others in his analysis of reflective processes, he also indicated the importance of the physiological mechanisms that mediate reflective intelligence (1934, p. 98-100). He stressed the fact that "the purposive element in behavior has a physiological seat . . ." (p. 100). "Human intelligence, by means of the physiological mechanism of the human central nervous system, deliberately selects one from among the several alternative responses . . ." (p. 98), and that selection is based on the neural mechanisms that allow future phases of the act to be activated early in an act and influence the performance of the whole act. "[T]he central nervous system can affect the organism at present with this future act. . . . It is the ability of later responses to play back into immediate responses that gives us our flexibility and power of choice" (1982b, p. 158).

Although reflective intelligence is mediated by the mechanisms of the central nervous system, it is not a totally mechanical activity that produces completely predictable outcomes. Rather it is an organic, creative process.

> That which takes place in present organic behavior is always in some sense an emergent from the past, and never could have been precisely predicted in advance . . . and in the case of organic behavior which is intelligently controlled, this element of spontaneity is especially prominent by virtue of the present influence exercised over such behavior by the possible future results or consequences which it may have (1934, p. 98-99).

The spontaneous, creative qualities of the organic processes seen in reflective intelligence are important fea-tures of agency. Problem solving processes—such as those seen in reflective intelligence—are an especially important stimulant for creativity (Weisberg 1986): As we reflect on the possible solutions of problems, we become aware of novel and unexpected alternatives, reevaluate and reconstruct our memories of past experiences, and reassess the possible future outcomes of the alternatives. From the complicated interaction of the perceptual present with images of the past and future, complex decisions and actions emerge.

Since Mead's time, psychologists have studied the various and complex ways in which people lay out alternative solutions to their problems, draw upon memory resources, apply rational, emotional and intuitive procedures to evaluate each alternative, allocate different amounts of time and effort to problems of differing levels of complexity and import, and so forth (Chase and Simon 1973; Anderson 1982; Dreyfus and Dreyfus 1986). These and related studies have facilitated the development of guidelines and training programs for helping people to improve their skills at reflective intelligence (Meichenbaum 1977; Baron and Steinberg 1986). Rather than devaluing reflective intelligence and creativity by "explaining them away," the scientific study of these activities can help us become more reflective and creative.

THE SOCIAL SELF

As children acquire language and culture, they develop not only minds and reflective intelligence but also selves. "The self is not so much a substance as a process" (1934, p. 178) involving self-observation and self-regulation. Mead's theory of the self—which is perfectly amenable to scientific evaluation and development—helps illuminate several additional features of agency. We will first note the social origins of the self then deal with the contribution of the self to both creativity and self-control.

Mead's theory of self is a social theory. Without a social self, the individual would be isolated in a solipsistic world,[2] confronted with insurmountable problems of intersubjectivity. "Shut up within his own world . . . he would have no entrance into possibilities other than those which his own organized act involved" (1932, p. 83). Mead rejected the theories of the isolated self that derive from introspective philosophy, Cartesian doubting, and individualistic psychology. He developed a social theory of self that avoided the problems of intersubjectivity that arise when one assumes that thinking and self are primary, arising before or independent of social interaction. "[W]e do not assume that there is a self to begin with. Self is not presupposed as a stuff out of which the world arises. Rather the self arises in the world," especially in the social world (1982b, p. 107). "What I want particularly to emphasize is the temporal and logical preexistence of the social process to the self-conscious individual that arises in it" (1934, p. 186).

Babies are not born with selves. "The self is not present in the early months of life" (1982b, p. 107). Only through symbolic social interaction does the self emerge. "[I]n infancy we can see the beginning of the self arising" (p. 144). "The self is something which has a development; it is not initially there, at birth, but arises in the process of social experience and activity" (1934, p. 135). As such, the emergence of self is open to scientific studies of child development; and Mead (1934, p. 144-164; 1964, p. 283-288; 1982b) himself provided the outlines of a behavioristic theory of the origins of the self as the child engages in increasingly complex forms of role taking during language development, play, and games.

Mead stressed that the self is empirically available, and not otherworldly (as metaphysical and idealist theories imply). "[T]he self arises out of the world. . . . [T]hat self is not made up from physical stuff" (1982b, p. 107). "The self is not so much a substance as a process in which the conversation of gestures has been internalized within an organic form" (1934, p. 178). "We are thus tied to the body insofar as we have a self" (1982b. p. 148). In the past half century, the scientific study of child development and socialization has advanced considerably; and empirical research on the development of self during socialization helps assure that the self is not conceptualized in metaphysical or idealist terms.

Mead (1934, p. 173-222) divided the self into the "I" and the "me," which allowed him to explain two complementary facets of agency: creativity and control. The "I" and "me" merely reflect two different perspectives on the human actor: The "I" is the subject; the "me" is the object. The "I" is the self that acts; the "me" is the self that we see as an object when we observe ourselves from the role of the other. When we talk, it is the "I" who does the talking. When we hear our own words, we perceive those vocal actions as an object, as a "me." The relationship between the "I" and the "me" can be conceived of as a serial process: The "I" of one moment is perceived the next moment as a "me" and the information about the "me" can influence the next action of the "I"—which is seen as the next "me," which can influence the next "I," and so forth.

We can never directly observe the "I" because every time we attempt to observe the "I," we perceive a "me." "[I]t is only the 'me'—the empirical self—that can be brought into the focus of attention—that can be perceived. The 'I' lies beyond the range of immediate experience" (1964, p. 140). "The 'I' does not get into the limelight; we talk to ourselves, but do not see ourselves" (1934, p. 174). The "I" creates the act of the moment; and as soon as we perceive ourselves acting, we perceive ourselves as an object, therefore as a "me." "The 'I' of this moment is present in the 'me' of the next moment. There again I cannot turn around quick enough to catch myself. I become a 'me' in so far as I remember what I said" (p. 174). "The 'I' appears in our experience in memory" as a "me" (p. 196), but it is not something the person can directly observe. Nevertheless, the "I" is not beyond scientific analysis: The goal of Mead's behavioristic psychology was to explain the processes of the act, including its conscious, unconscious, habitual, and creative facets

(1934, p. 7-8, 22-23, 36-41, 126, 163, 214ff; 1964, p. 127ff; 1982a, p. 31), along with the actors own perception of that act—as a "me."

THE "I" AND CREATIVITY

Creativity is an important aspect of agency. The "I" is a facet of the self that is the source of actions—be they creative and unpredictable actions, or habitual and predictable responses.[3] Most adults know their own response patterns well enough to predict part of their next actions; but people can never directly observe or fully understand the source of their actions well enough to completely predict their next acts. Thus, the "I" always remains at least partially unpredictable: "[T]he 'I' is something that is more or less uncertain" (1934, p. 176). "[T]he 'I' is something that is never entirely calculable" (p. 178).

Because the "I" is at least partly unpredictable, it is the source of spontaneity and innovation. "The novelty comes in the action of the 'I' . . ." (p. 209). "That action of the 'I' is something the nature of which we cannot tell in advance" (p. 177). "[E]xactly how we will act never gets into experience until after the action takes place" (p. 177-178). Therefore, "[t]he 'I' gives the sense of freedom, of initiative" (p. 177). (This "sense of freedom" leads some people to a metaphysical belief in free will.)

Even if a person tries to be totally predictable in a given situation and "has rehearsed the situation in his own mind," his actual acts may turn out to be different from those he rehearsed (p. 197). As a consequence, the person "astonishes himself by his conduct as much as he astonishes other people" (p. 204).

> However carefully we plan the future it always is different from that which we can previse, and this something that we are continually bringing in and adding to is what we identify with the self that comes into the level of our experience only in the completion of the act (p. 203).

Mead (1934, p. 324ff; 1936, p. 405-417; 1964, p. 341, 357) stated that the unique, creative contributions of the individual are the most precious qualities of the individual, both for the individual and the society. "[T]he possibilities of the 'I'" are "in some sense the most fascinating part of our experience. It is there that novelty arises and it is there that our most important values are located" (1934, p. 204). Not only are people fascinated by their own novel, unpredicted and creative acts, these creative acts can be valuable contributions to their own personal experience and to the development of society (p. 324ff).

Although scientific studies may help explain some of the causes of creative and innovative behavior, creativity is one of those emergent aspects of behavior that can never be explained completely. For example, empirical studies on problem solving and creativity help explain some of the preconditions and skills needed for creative activity (Adams 1974; Weisberg 1986); but these theories can make only probabilistic statements about people's future creative acts. Even though scientists cannot develop complete and deterministic models of the creative components of human conduct, creativity is open to empirical investigation; and modern empirical studies of creativity are identifying increasing numbers of the precursors and predictors of creativity.

THE "ME" AND SELF-CONTROL

Although it might be tempting to focus on the unexpected, creative elements of human action—from the "I"—as the essence of agency, such a strategy could make agency seem to be little more than the unpredictable variations in human behavior. The ramblings of a backward psychotic might contain more random and unpredictable elements than the carefully weighed decisions of a Supreme Court justice. Agency is a complex concept that entails more than unpredictable behavior. Agency involves a balance between creativity and responsible self-control—between the freedom to make choices and the responsibility to choose wisely. Whereas the "I" is the source of creativity and a "sense of freedom" (1934, p. 177), the "me" makes possible the exercise of responsible self-control (p. 210, 214).

The "me" is the object we perceive when we observe ourselves from the role of others. Our self-observations of the "me" provide information that can be useful in evaluating our behavior from the perspective of others and deciding how to act in the future. Because we see the "me" from a social perspective, we gain information that can be useful in helping us to reflect on the social consequences of our actions and decide how to act in a socially responsible manner. Although young children have only a rudimentary capacity to understand social values, they acquire broader perspectives of the "me"—reflecting the perspectives of increasing numbers of people—as they grow up and gain social experience. By adulthood, "[t]he 'me' is essentially a member of a social group, and represents, therefore, the value of the group . . ." (1934, p. 214).

Mead (1913; 1924-25; 1934, p. 135-226; 1982a; 1982b) outlined an empirically testable theory to explain the ways in which people acquire the capacity to evaluate the "me" in a socially responsible manner. His theory is compatible with several of the empirically grounded modern theories of moral development. In the early years of life, "little children play at being a parent, at being a teacher. . . . These are personalities which they take, roles they play, and in so far control the development of their own personality" (1934, p. 153). Children often take the role of a parent and either praise or scold their dolls or imaginary playmates, much as they have heard their own parents talk to children. "The child fashions his own self on the model of other selves. . . . The child's consciousness of its own self is quite largely the reflection of the attitudes of others toward him" (1982a, p. 54). The social judgments of adults provide the child with his or her first criteria for self-evaluation and judgment. "At first, the child accepts the judgment of others about himself . . ." (p. 62). Young

children (who have had adequate parental contact) are likely to evaluate themselves, then praise or blame themselves, according to the same general criteria that their parents apply to them. "Thus the child can think about his conduct as good or bad only as he reacts to his own acts in the remembered words of his parents" (1964, p. 146).

As they grow up, children spend increasing time playing games and participating in various social institutions (such as schools and churches), which helps them learn to organize their actions to fit into larger groups. "The game is then an illustration of the situation out of which an organized personality arises." While playing games, the child "is becoming an organic member of society" (1934, p. 159). Games have rules that help children learn to structure their behavior to synchronize with others. "For in a game there is a regulated procedure, and rules" (1964, p. 285). "[I]n the game he sees himself in terms of the group or the gang and speaks with a passion for rules and standards" (p. 246).

When playing games, children must learn how all the team players will respond to their actions and adjust their behavior accordingly. "The child must not only take the role of the other, as he does in the play, but he must assume the various roles of all the participants in the game, and govern his action accordingly. . . . Their organized reactions to him" become organized into "what I have called the 'generalized other' that accompanies and controls his conduct" (p. 285). Games help children move beyond taking the role of specific individuals—such as mother or father—and acquire an awareness of the views of the larger group. "In the game we get an organized other, a generalized other . . ." (1934, p. 160).

The generalized other emerges not only in games, but whenever children engage in structured social interactions. "What goes on in the game goes on in the life of the child all the time. He is continually taking the attitudes of those about him, especially the roles of those who in some sense control him and on whom he depends" (p. 160). Through all of this, "[h]e becomes something which can function in the organized whole . . ." (p. 160). As the child learns to take the role of the group—the generalized other—the child sees a "'me' representing that group of attitudes which stands for others in the community, especially that organized group of responses which we have detailed in discussing the game on the one hand and social institutions on the other" (p. 194).

Over the years, the individual may learn to take the roles of increasing numbers of people, from ever larger portions of society. This broadens the person's conceptualization of the generalized other and allows the person to judge his or her actions from an ever broader perspective. Naturally, some individuals acquire a broader and more accurate conception of the generalized social perspective than others do.

To the degree that we learn to observe and evaluate—e.g., approve of or condemn—ourselves from the group's point of view, we develop socially responsible selves. "We are in possession of selves just insofar as we can and do take the attitudes of others toward ourselves and respond to those attitudes We approve of ourselves and condemn ourselves. We pat ourselves on the back and in blind fury attack ourselves. We assume the generalized attitude of the group, in the censor that stands at the door of our imagery and inner conversations . . ." (1964, p. 288). "[T]his organized reaction becomes what I have called the 'generalized other' that accompanies and controls his conduct" (p. 285). Namely, seeing our own actions from the perspective of the generalized other provides us with the data needed to regulate our behavior the way that society would. "Social control, then, will depend upon the degree to which the individual does assume the attitudes of those in the group who are involved with him in his social activities" (p. 290), and some people control their behavior in this way more than others do.

When the "me" is perceived from the role of the generalized other, it provides us with society's perspective on our own behavior, which helps us practice socially responsible self-control. "Social control is the expression of the 'me' over against the expression of the 'I'. It sets the limits, it gives the determination that enables the 'I,' so to speak, to use the 'me' as the means of carrying out what is the undertaking that all are interested in" (1934, p. 210). In the practice of reflective intelligence, we can use the information about the "me" to make carefully weighed decisions about future actions; and the social perspective increases the likelihood the choices will be socially responsible.

It must be pointed out that Mead's view of social control did not imply that people act in blind obedience to the generalized other: It is "not simply the social control that results from blind habit . . ." (1936, p. 377). Responsible decisions are arrived at through the organic and creative processes of reflective intelligence; and in these processes, the social values and control functions of the "me" are counterbalanced by the innovative functions of the "I" (1934, p. 199-200, 214-217). Mead described the "I" and the "me" as functioning smoothly together in the fully developed social self. "Both aspects of the 'I' and 'me' are essential to the self in its full expression" (1934, p. 199). Although emphasis on the "me" alone might make a person "a conventional and habitual individual" (p. 197), the "I" provides the creative and sometimes nonconformist inputs that allow each individual to be a unique contributor, "a definite personality" (p. 200). The "I" provides the source of activity needed for the "reconstruction of the society" (p. 214), for leadership (p. 216), and for accomplishing "important social changes" (p. 217). It is sometimes identified with "genius," as in the work of "the great artist, scientist, statesman, religious leader" and so forth (p. 217).

Mead's views on ethical decision making also help clarify how social responsibility (from the "me") and creative reflective intelligence (from the "I") function together. Ethical problems arise when different values conflict in a particular undertaking. To make a socially responsible ethical choice, a person "must take into account and do justice to all of the values that prove to be involved in the enterprise . . ." (1964, p. 256). A careful decision requires the use of reflective intelligence to evaluate all the possible alternative solutions to the problem, drawing upon the creative capacities of the "I" *and* the social values available from observing the "me" (from the perspective of the generalized other) as we imagine ourselves carrying out the different alternative acts. Such a complex decision-making process is far from "blind habit." It is, in fact, more akin to the creative and systematic application of the scientific method to moral questions (Mead 1923; 1938, p. 460-465). For example, when two values are in conflict, "[w]e may be able to get both of the values by rearranging our conduct. We can state our ends in that sense in terms of means in reflective thinking" (1938, p. 463). Of course, in reality, there are many values to consider. "In the solution of the problem we must take all relevant values into account." Then "we want to reconstruct our lives so as to take in all the values involved" (p. 461). The moral process involves not only wise decisions, but also changing our behavior—reconstructing our lives.

Mead also saw the individual as active in attempting to reconstruct society. Although Eastern societies suppress the self and social criticism, "we, on the contrary, attack society and try to produce a better society instead of suppressing the self . . ." (1982b, p. 151). When social conditions are problematic, people can reflect "critically . . . upon the organized social structure of the society . . . and . . . reorganize or reconstruct or modify that social structure . . ." (1934, p. 308). "We can reform the order of things; we can insist on making the community standards better standards. We are not simply bound by the community. . . . That is the way, of course, in which society gets ahead . . ." (p. 168). The degree to which people have the political freedom to modify and reconstruct their societies is, of course, open to empirical research.

Modern social psychology has made significant progress in the scientific study of the origins of moral, responsible, and socially constructive behavior, though many details are still unresolved. Researchers working within several different traditions—based on the work of Piaget, Kohlberg, Bandura, Mischel, and others—have established numerous ways in which parents, teachers, media, and other social sources influence the acquisition and practice of creative social responsibility; and this work demonstrates that moral conduct is open to empirical investigation, much as the other facets of agency discussed in this paper are. This lends support to Mead's thesis that we can avoid metaphysical problems and solve both the philosophical and psychological problems regarding creative and morally responsible choice by the scientific study of the relevant social and personal practices.

CONCLUSIONS

The question of agency is central to several important debates in contemporary sociology. Discussions of agency can become embroiled with issues related to free will and determinism. For example, the debate over whether or not we can develop a science of human conduct and society can be linked to issues of free will, since science's goals of prediction and control are not appropriate if people have free will.

Because metaphysical problems (such as those of free will and determinism) have never been shown to be resolvable by any form of logic or empirical study, and because scientific studies (which neglect metaphysics and focus on observables) have proven very successful at establishing pragmatically useful knowledge about countless facets of our world, Mead advocated avoiding metaphysical debates by stating all problems in terms that are amenable to study via scientific method. This paper presents Mead's work relevant to agency, revealing both Mead's method and the details of his theory. First, it shows how Mead followed the basic methods of behavioristic psychology, which require abstract philosophical and psychological concepts to be defined in terms of the actual behaviors involved. A strict focus on behavior helps in avoiding metaphysical impasses when dealing with such "loaded" topics as decision making and choice. Second, the paper presents an overview of Mead's specific theories about awareness, meaning, decision making, choice, creativity, and social responsibility, showing how he analyzed these concepts in terms of the central nervous system, language, inner conversation, taking the role of others, reflective intelligence, the "I" and the "me," and related concepts.

For those who agree that metaphysical questions such as those related to free will and determinism are inherently unanswerable, Mead's approach offers an escape from endless wrangling over unprovable metaphysical beliefs; and it provides a productive way to conceptualize and empirically study the actual behaviors that are the referents of the word "agency." Perhaps Mead's work can help resolve some of the current sociological debate over agency and allow us to move on to more fruitful analyses of human conduct and society.

If Mead's theories are found to be useful, the next task is to modify and modernize Mead's work in light of contemporary data. Mead's writings indicate that he would approve of—and be excited by—the prospects of such a reconstruction of his work. In various places, Mead (1917, 1923, 1929, 1932, 1936, 1938) described how all sciences advance through the process of reconstruction, and he argued that this is the best way to advance our knowledge about any topic. "Research is ready to find a problem at any point in the structure of scientific doctrine, a problem which may invalidate any theory. Indeed it welcomes such outbreaks, and lives its exciting life in their midst" (1964, p. 324). Although metaphysical philosophers sought unchanging eternal truths about the ultimate realities of the world, neither scientific data nor method promise such finality.

> It is customary to interpret the independence of data as a metaphysical affirmation of a real world independent of all observation and speculation. There is no necessary implication of this in the scientist's methodology. For the metaphysical affirmation is of a reality that is final, while the scientist's procedure and method contemplate no such finality. On the contrary, they contemplate continued reconstruction in the face of events emerging in ceaseless novelty (1932, p. 101-102).

The attempt to do a scientific analysis of the behavioral components of agency does not raise the specter of a deterministic, mechanical model of agency. No science ever reaches the finalized state needed for deterministic predictions about the future. Novel and unpredictable events continue to emerge and require reconstruction of our best theories (Mead 1932). Thus, the empirical approach to agency should not raise fears that Mead's approach is a method for introducing determinism into sociological theories of agency.

In the decades since Mead wrote, there has been considerable scientific research on cognition, reflective intelligence, creativity, moral processes and other components of Mead's theory. Important empirical contributions have been made from several intellectual traditions. At present it is premature to judge which facets of each tradition will eventually prove most useful; and careful attention to details is warranted in drawing upon the contributions of each.

Although the behavioral tradition has not been well represented in sociology, modern behavioral studies of humans—including social learning theory and cognitive behaviorism—are more similar to Mead's social behaviorism than most sociologists recognize (Baldwin 1981, 1985). In the past several decades, behaviorism has grown to be one of the strongest empirically-based fields within psychology; and it has much to offer contemporary sociology. For example, Bandura (1986) presents the contemporary behavioral data on numerous components of agency, such as cognitive development, self-reflective capacity, goal setting, self-regulation, self-efficacy, perceived self-efficacy, cognitive strategies of problem solving, moral judgment, reciprocal determinism, and more. Bandura's basic behavioristic position is quite similar to Mead's. The major differences between the two theories result from the fact that modern behaviorists have access to more data and empirically grounded theories than were available to Mead. Although I urge sociologists to give serious consideration to modern behaviorism, differences of opinion on behaviorism must not obscure Mead's contribution as a pragmatist philosopher in showing how to escape the impasses of metaphysical philosophy.

NOTES

* I would like to thank Tamotsu Shibutani, Otis Dudley Duncan, and three anonymous reviewers for constructively critical comments on a draft of this manuscript.

[1] "I wish, however, to insist that the essential fallacy in this materialism, lies . . . in the assumption that it is possible to give an exhaustive account of any event that

takes place in terms of the conditions of its occurrence" (1932, p. 38). Mead (p. 8, 26, 29, 31) clearly recognized that absolute, perfect and final accounts are beyond human reach.

[2] From Mead's social point of view, "[s]olipsism is an absurdity" (1982a, p. 55). Also see Mead (1910; 1936, p. 413; 1938, p. 150-153; 1982b, p. 162).

[3] Although some psychodynamic and ethological theories suggest that the unconscious part of the self is selfish, hostile or antisocial (Freud 1925; Lorenz 1963), Mead's theory did not describe the "I" as wild or antisocial. It is merely the source of actions—some of which are expected, others not.

REFERENCES

Adams, J. L. 1974. *Conceptual Blockbusting: A Guide to Better Ideas.* New York: W. H. Freeman.

Alexander, J. C. 1984. "Social-Structural Analysis: Some Notes on Its History and Prospects." *Sociological Quarterly* 25:5-26.

Anderson, J. R. 1982. "Acquisition of Cognitive Skill." *Psychological Review* 89:369-406.

Baldwin, J. D. 1981. "George Herbert Mead and Modern Behaviorism." *Pacific Sociological Review* 24:410-440.

———. 1985. "Social Behaviorism on Emotions: Mead and Modern Behaviorism Compared." *Symbolic Interaction* 8:263-289.

———. 1986. *George Herbert Mead: A Unifying Theory for Sociology.* Beverly Hills: Sage.

Bandura, A. 1986. *Social Foundations of Thought and Action: A Social Cognitive Theory.* Englewood Cliffs, NJ: Prentice-Hall.

Baron, J. B., and R. J. Steinberg. 1986. *Teaching Thinking Skills: Theory and Practice.* New York: W. H. Freeman.

Berger, P. L. 1963. *Invitation to Sociology: A Humanistic Perspective.* Garden City, NY: Anchor.

Blumer, H. 1969. "The Methodological Position of Symbolic Interactionism." Pp. 1-60 in *Symbolic Interactionism: Perspective and Method,* edited by H. Blumer. Englewood Cliffs, NJ: Prentice-Hall.

Bosworth, S. L., and G. A. Kreps. 1986. "Structure as Process: Organization and Role." *American Sociological Review* 51:699-716.

Chase, W. G., and H. A. Simon. 1973. "Perception in Chess." *Cognitive Psychology* 4:55-81.

Collins, R. 1981. "On the Microfoundations of Macrosociology." *American Journal of Sociology* 86:984-1014.

Dreyfus, H. L., and S. E. Dreyfus. 1986. *Mind Over Machine: The Power of Human Intuition and Experience in the Era of the Computer.* New York: Macmillan/Free Press.

Freud, S. 1925. "Instincts and Their Vicissitudes." *Collected Papers,* Vol. 4, edited by S. Freud. London: Institute for Psychoanalysis and Hogarth Press.

Lorenz, K. 1963. *On Aggression.* New York: Harcourt, Brace and World.

Mead, G. H. 1910. "What Social Objects Must Psychology Presuppose?" *Journal of Philosophy, Psychology, and Scientific Methods* 7:174-180.

———. 1913. "The Social Self." *Journal of Philosophy, Psychology, and Scientific Methods* 10:374-380.

———. 1917. "Scientific Method and Individual Thinker." Pp. 176-227 in *Creative Intelligence: Essays in the Pragmatic Attitude.* New York: Henry Holt & Co.

———. 1922. "A Behavioristic Account of the Significant Symbol." *Journal of Philosophy* 19:157-163.

———. 1923. "Scientific Method and the Moral Sciences." *International Journal of Ethics* 33:229-247.

———. 1924-25. "The Genesis of the Self and Social Control." *International Journal of Ethics* 35:251-277.

———. 1929. "A Pragmatic Theory of Truth." Pp. 65-88 in *Studies in the Nature of Truth.* Vol 11. University of California Publications in Philosophy.

———. 1929-30. "The Philosophies of Royce, James, and Dewey in Their American Setting." *International Journal of Ethics* 40:211-231.

———. 1932. *The Philosophy of the Present,* edited by A. E. Murphy. Chicago: Open Court.

———. 1934. *Mind, Self, and Society,* edited by C. W. Morris. Chicago: University of Chicago Press.

———. 1936. *Movements of Thought in the Nineteenth Century,* edited by M. H. Moore. Chicago: University of Chicago Press.

———. 1938. *The Philosophy of the Act,* edited by C. W. Morris. Chicago: University of Chicago Press.

———. 1964. *Selected Writings,* edited by A. J. Reck. New York: Bobbs-Merrill.

———. 1982a. "1914 Class Lectures in Social Psychology." Pp. 27-105 in *The Individual and Social Self,* edited by D. L. Miller. Chicago: University of Chicago Press. (Original, published in 1914.)

———. 1982b. "1927 Class Lectures in Social Psychology." Pp. 106-175 in *The Individual and the Social Self,* edited by D. L. Miller. Chicago: University of Chicago Press. (Original, published in 1927.)

Meichenbaum, D. 1977. *Cognitive Behavior Modification: An Integrative Approach.* New York: Plenum.

Morrione, T. J. 1985. "Situated Interaction." Pp. 161-192 in *Studies in Symbolic Interaction, Supplement 1.*

Sciulli, D. 1987. "Voluntaristic Action as a Distinct Concept: Theoretical Foundations of Societal Constitutionalism." *American Sociological Review* 51:743-766.

Skinner, Q. 1985. *The Return of Grand Theory in the Human Sciences.* New York: Cambridge University Press.

Turner, J. H. 1984. *Societal Stratification: A Theoretical Analysis.* New York: Columbia University Press.

———. 1986. "The Theory of Structuration." *American Journal of Sociology* 91:969-977.

Weisberg, R. W. 1986. *Creativity: Genius and Other Myths.* New York: W. H. Freeman.

John D. Baldwin (essay date 1988)

SOURCE: "Mead and Skinner: Agency and Determinism," in *Behaviorism: A Forum for Critical Discussion,* Vol. 16, No. 2, Fall, 1988, pp. 109-62.

[*In the following essay, Baldwin compares Mead's ideas on agency and determinism to B. F. Skinner's, and finds considerable similarities in their scientific reasoning.*]

With some behaviorists heeding the "call to cognition" (Deitz & Arrington, 1984; Morris, 1985), behaviorists are raising increasing numbers of questions about the role of thought, deliberate action, agency and determinism in behavioral theories. Most methodological behaviorists and radical behaviorists equate agency with free will, which they reject (Zuriff, 1985), or with inner causes that can be explained with behavior principles (Zuriff, 1975, 1979, 1985). In contrast, social learning theorists and cognitive behaviorists emphasize the importance of cognitive processes in the construction of deliberate action, and criticize the more traditional behaviorists for assuming that self-determined behavior can be completely predicted from genetic and environmental data (Bandura, 1986; Pierce & Epling, 1984;).

Is this polarization within behaviorism necessary? George Herbert Mead's behavioral theory demonstrates how one can avoid these conflicts about agency. Although it is often recognized that behaviorism has its roots in pragmatism, little attention has been given to Mead (1863-1931), who was one of the original pragmatists and social behaviorists. As a Chicago school philosopher, Mead developed a form of pragmatism and social behaviorism that clarifies philosophical questions related to determinism, agency, and other issues of importance to behaviorists; yet Mead is seldom cited in the contemporary behavioral literature. For example, Zuriff's (1985) excellent summary of the philosophical foundations of behaviorism (with over eleven hundred references) makes no mention of Mead. Boakes's (1984) historical analysis of the emergence of behaviorism from 1870 to 1930 contains only passing references to Mead (pp. 145f, 162). Although Staats (1975), Powell and Still (1979) and a few others discuss *parts* of Mead's work, most behaviorists show little awareness of the full breadth of Mead's contributions.

Mead's ideas have been lost due, in part, to his being misinterpreted by his most outspoken followers in sociology and symbolic interactionism. Herbert Blumer (1955, 1962, 1966) and other interactionists selectively drew upon one subset of Mead's work—on mind and the self—to create a mentalistic model of the human actor. Citing Mead's lectures, Blumer and other students of Mead created a secondary literature on Mead's theory; and for decades, knowledge of Mead's work was transmitted by the secondary literature or by an "oral tradition" (Kuhn, 1964), with little serious attention to Mead's written work. As Mead's name became identified with a mentalistic theory of the self and interpretive processes, it is quite understandable that many behaviorists did not turn to his work for ideas.

Recent studies of Mead's original writings—that carefully document his views with numerous quotations and references—reveal that he has been seriously misinterpreted (Baldwin, 1986; McPhail & Rexroat, 1979, 1980; Wood & Wardell, 1983). The goals of this paper are (1) to demonstrate the relevance and utility of Mead's pragmatic and behavioristic philosophy for contemporary behaviorists, (2) to do so by showing how Mead dealt with the problems of agency and determinism, and (3) to show the similarities and differences between Mead and Skinner. The contrast of Mead's and Skinner's positions reveals only one small, nonscientific assumption that impedes a rapprochement between cognitive and more traditional behaviorism.

GEORGE HERBERT MEAD

Mead and the other pragmatists argued that the scientific method was superior to all other methods of acquiring knowledge and should be extended to deal with every area of inquiry. All ideas and theories—even philosophical and theoretical ones—should be treated as hypotheses that can be tested by their ability to solve problems and provide useful information. Any idea can be evaluated in terms of the type of consequences that result from it (Mead, 1900; 1908; 1913; 1923; 1925-26; 1938, pp. 454ff). In philosophical debates, the scientific method was to replace the methods of contemplation and idealistic thinking that were common before the development of pragmatism (Mead, 1938, pp. 513ff).

One of Mead's (1922, 1924-25, 1927, 1929-30) central goals was to use the scientific method to create a unifying theory that would synthesize empirical findings on all aspects of human behavior—including its inner and outer aspects—in a nondualistic manner. "We must consider inside and outside together, and the world cannot be divided into inside and outside" (Mead, 1927, p. 107). "Mind and body are not to be separated on the basis of our present physical science" (p. 167). Whereas Watson attempted to avoid dualism by excluding mental events from his theory, Mead (1934, pp. 10f, 101f) faulted this strategy and argued that the mind can be studied behaviorally. Although Mead and Watson were friends, Mead (1934, p. 10) criticized Watson's approach to mind as "misguided and unsuccessful, for the existence as such of mind or consciousness, in some sense or other, must be admitted—the denial of it leads inevitably to obvious absurdities." Using an argument similar to Skinner's (1969, pp. 227f; 1971, pp. 190f), Mead stated that "it is not possible to deny the existence of mind or consciousness or mental phenomena, nor is it desirable to do so; but it is possible to account for them or deal with them in behavioristic terms which are precisely similar to those which Watson employs in dealing with non-mental psychological phenomena" (1934, p. 10).

Mead developed a thoroughly nondualistic approach to mind and cognitive processes, tracing the emergence of cognitive processes first during the evolutionary process and second, in humans, during socialization. Biological evolution helps explain the emergence of the brain structures that establish the potential for language; and language provides the mechanism for the symbolic processes that make human consciousness different from the consciousness of other species. "The mechanism of thinking [is] that of inward conversation" (1932, p. 84). "An objective psychology is not trying to get rid of consciousness, but trying to state the intelligence of the individual in terms which will enable us to see how that intelligence is exercised, and how it may be improved" (1934, p. 39). Describing mind in terms of neural mechanisms and "inward" verbal behavior clearly places mind in nature, available for empirical study. "But if mind is simply an emergent character of certain organisms in their so-called intelligent responses to their environments, mind can never transcend the environment within which it operates" (1932, p. 118). "Mind can no longer be put outside of nature" (p. 152).

Mind and self are not inborn, but arise in social interaction. "What I want particularly to emphasize is the temporal and logical pre-existence of the social process to the self-conscious individual that arises in it" (1934, p. 186). Mead advocated studying self-conscious behavior by tracing it's development, working from the outside social environment to the emergence of inside events. This strategy "works from the outside to the inside instead of from the inside to the outside, so to speak, in its endeavor to determine how such [inner] experience does arise within the [social] process" (p. 8). This approach allowed Mead (1927, p. 106) to "avoid introspection . . . We do not approach the organism from within. . . . The actual process begins at the periphery and goes to the center"

(p. 156). "Just as there is a functional relationship between the organism and its environment, so there is one between what is 'in the mind' and what is 'outside'" (1936, p. 307). In numerous ways, Mead traced the structure of the mind and the self back to the structure of the environment. Nevertheless, this approach did not lead him to develop a deterministic model of the human actor, as can be understood by examining Mead's views on metaphysics and decision making.

BEYOND METAPHYSICS

Mead's approach to agency can be useful to contemporary behaviorists. There are several ways of conceptualizing agency. One is to equate agency with free will. However, free will is a metaphysical construct, and as such can never be evaluated empirically. Mead (1917, 1929, 1932) argued that we can never resolve metaphysical questions about the ultimate nature of "reality"; thus we can never know whether people "really" have free will or not.

Some ancient Greek philosophers and mathematically oriented thinkers assumed the presence of some preexistent ultimate truths beyond the range of our fallible perceptual organs (Mead, 1917); and for centuries various influential philosophers sought to reach those transcendental truths through contemplation and logic (1938, pp. 513f). However, the pragmatists noted that despite thousands of years of contemplation, philosophers had made no more net advance than the mythical figure Sisyphus had in repeatedly rolling his stone up the same hill. In contrast, science—by abandoning metaphysical puzzles and focusing on careful observation and experimentation—has made enormous advances in understanding the world in the past few centuries. The pragmatists advocated abandoning contemplation and metaphysics, to rely solely on the scientific method as our means of inquiry. When we do this, the "despairing sense of the philosophic Sisyphus vainly striving to roll the heavily weighted world of his reflection up into a preexistent reality" drops "away and the philosopher can face about toward the future and join in the scientist's adventure" (1964, pp. 389f). A belief in transcendental truths creates a problematic dualism between ideal knowledge and earthly knowledge; but a strong adherence to the scientific method and empirical data helps avoid the problem. "The solution of the problem carries with it the disappearance of the problem and the metaphysical system at the same time" (1964, p. 10).

Much of Mead's work was devoted to reconstructing philosophy and psychology using the methods of modern science, with no reference to contemplative philosophy or metaphysics. Relevant to philosophy, Mead (1964, p. 210) stated: "I have endeavored to present the world which is an implication of the scientific method of discovery with entire abstraction from any epistemological or metaphysical presuppositions or complications." Relevant to behavioristic psychology, Mead stated: "Psychology . . . has not been interested in these epistemological and metaphysical riddles, it has been simply irritated by them" (p. 269). "The behavioristic psychology has tried to get rid of the more or less metaphysical complications involved in the setting-up of the psychical over against the world, mind over against body, consciousness over against matter. That was felt to lead into a blind alley" (1934, p. 105). Among the metaphysical issues to be dropped is the debate over free will and determinism.

Nevertheless, some branches of science have deterministic qualities, and Mead dealt with these in his discussions of mechanism. Newtonian physics produced mechanistic, deterministic models of the world that left no room for purpose, freedom or choice (1936, pp. 250-281). The great success of the mechanistic sciences in developing deterministic laws reinforced the notion that everything might fit such models. "Seemingly, the whole world would be absolutely fixed and determined" (p. 250). However, Mead pointed out that mechanistic, deterministic assumptions are merely "postulates" or "working hypotheses," and science can never prove them to be absolute truths.

In the mechanistic disciplines, scientists often espouse *methodological determinism* as a perspective that focuses their efforts on uncovering regularities in nature (Kaplan, 1964, pp. 124f), and taking this perspective is often reinforced by the discovery of empirical generalizations, basic principles or laws. However, "Methodological determinism states only that laws are worth looking for here, not that they surely *exist* here, and surely not that they necessarily exist always and everywhere" (Kaplan, 1964, p. 124). Mead approved of methodologies that focus our efforts on constructing propositions and laws to explain the regularities in behavior. He stated that behavioral psychology has "its sympathies . . . with the presuppositions and method of the natural sciences" (1964, p. 269). "We are interested in finding the most general laws of correlation we can find" (1934, p. 39). This process builds toward a scientific psychology in which "All the distinctions must be explained by the same general laws as those which are appealed to to account for animal organs and functions" (1964, p. 82).

However, Mead recognized that no theory that we can craft—even in the physical sciences—is likely to ever become completely finalized, fully accurate, or totally deterministic: novel and unpredictable events continually emerge that force us to revise and reconstruct our theories (1917, 1929, 1932). As fallible organisms, humans are not likely to ever develop such perfect models that all future events could be predicted; hence all sciences repeatedly confront novel and emergent events that are not completely predictable. When scientists use methodological determinism, "the emergent has no sooner appeared than we set about rationalizing it . . ." (1932, p. 14); however, these rationalizations and theories usually have to be modified and reconstructed as later unexpected events emerge. Thus, while science's ability to locate regularities and patterns has allowed the development of increasingly sophisticated empirical generaliza-

tions and laws, scientific laws are unlikely to ever become completely finalized and totally deterministic. In fact, "the scientist's procedure and method contemplate no such finality. On the contrary, they contemplate continued reconstruction in the face of events emerging in ceaseless novelty" (pp. 101f). After constructing any theory or doctrine, "the scientist himself expects this doctrine to be reconstructed just as other scientific doctrines have been reconstructed" in the past (p. 105).

Instead of deterministic laws, Mead anticipated only probabilistic theories of our world of emergent events. "[W]hatever does happen, even the emergent . . ." happens under conditions that "lie within probability only" and "these conditions never determine completely the 'what it is' that will happen" (p. 15). "[T]here is also the indeterminateness of what occurs" (p. 96). "And the indeterminate 'what' involves always a possibly new situation with a new complex of relationships" (p. 97). In an indeterminant universe, scientists construct probabilistic laws to explicate the regularities identified to date, without the illusion of attaining the perfect knowledge needed to construct totally deterministic laws.

Finally, Mead emphasized that mechanistic laws do not adequately deal "with the characters which belong to living organisms" (1936, p. 260). Namely, mechanistic theories fail to treat living things as adapting organisms, with qualities captured by the vocabulary of design and purpose (p. 269). For example, a purely mechanistic analysis of the digestive process omits the issue of the function—or purpose—of digestion in maintaining life. "The complete mechanical statement would not take account of the end, of the purpose . . ." that is seen in living systems; "[a]nd that seems to be necessary to our comprehension of the world" (p. 272).

Mead used the term "teleology" to describe the purposeful, life-sustaining processes that were overlooked by purely mechanical analyses of living systems (1927, pp. 108ff; 1936, pp. 268ff). However, he clearly dissociated himself from the nonscientific form of teleology espoused by vitalists (1936, pp. 292-325). "Sometimes, like the vitalists, we abuse [mechanistic] science because it ignores life. But there is only a short distance we can go on the teleological program" (1927, p. 171). That short distance is to make the point that life is not fully described by mechanistic terms alone: Science needs to have concepts for explaining the self-organizing, purposive qualities of living systems, not just concepts about the mechanical aspects of the universe.

Both mechanism and teleology are postulates, not metaphysical dogma about the ultimate nature of "reality" (1936, pp. 264-291). They provide two different languages—mechanistic and action languages—that help us describe different aspects of living systems. *Both of these languages can be useful in behavioral sciences; and they are not mutually exclusive:* They can complement each other. "In biological science you bring in both these points of view" (p. 269). Consider the example of a physician and district attorney analyzing a murder (pp. 268f). The physician explains the mechanism of the murder, how the "bullet entered the body in a certain way and led to a given result" (p. 269). In contrast, the district attorney explains the motives and purposes of the murderer: "That is, he gives a teleological explanation, while the doctor who performs the autopsy gives a mechanical explanation" (p. 269). Since neither teleology nor mechanism is a dogma in science, it is easy to see that "[t]here is, then, no real conflict between a mechanical and a teleological account of the world or of the facts of life" (p. 271). "Thus we see that science has gotten away from metaphysical dogma as to what the nature of things is . . ." (p. 275). Mechanistic, deterministic hypotheses are useful in describing some aspects of nature; and purposive, teleological models are useful in describing other aspects. Neither type of hypothesis warrants conclusions about ultimate metaphysical questions, including those concerning free will and determinism.

If we agree with Mead that we can never resolve metaphysical questions about the ultimate nature of "reality," we can put aside the metaphysical issue of whether or not humans have free will and ask if there is any other way to conceptualize and evaluate agency. Mead followed the behavioral strategy of analyzing the *behaviors* that are the referents of the abstract term agency. When concepts such as agency—which in the past have been treated as abstract, metaphysical concepts—are reformulated in purely behavioral terms, they are clearly removed from the arena of metaphysics and contemplative philosophy.

DECISION MAKING

In order to clarify Mead's pragmatic approach to agency, the following sections briefly review Mead's analysis of those behaviors—such as choice and decision making—that are generally considered to be central to agency. Mead analyzed choice, planning, and decision making in terms of their neural and behavioral components—which are open to empirical study—and not in terms of "free will," as metaphysically conceived. Mead's analyses of human conduct never involved hidden assumptions about or attempts to prove any metaphysical position about free will or determinism.

Mead (1924-25, 1932, 1934) took an evolutionary approach to the emergence of consciousness and deliberate action. By comparing the behavior of animals at different phyletic levels, Mead outlined the evolutionary preconditions for the emergence of the higher forms of human cognition and planned behavior. His evolutionary approach also underscores the fact that human consciousness is part of nature, not transcendental. "The genesis of mind in human society . . . is a natural development within the world of living organisms and their environment" (1932, p. 84). "I have wished to present mind as an evolution in nature . . ." (p. 85). As such, Mead attempted to identify the biological and psychosocial precursors of human mental capacities, with special attention to neurophysiological and social factors.

NEUROPHYSIOLOGY

Mead (1924-25, 1932, 1934) related the development of deliberate choice and self-control to the evolution of the encephalon during the emergence of the advanced vertebrate species. He discussed several cortical mechanisms that allow delay and inhibition of response, imagery of possible future responses, and the capacity for choice between various possible alternative responses (1932, pp. 68-76, 89ff, 124-136; 1934, pp. 98-100, 109-118).

First, the encephalon "is primarily the nerve center of the important distance senses" (pp. 70f), hence its development makes possible the detailed processing of distant stimuli before contact is made. With the evolution of the cortex and increased sophistication of the distance senses, "the contact experiences to which [the distance senses] respond are delayed, and possibilities of adjustment and of choice in response are thus increased" (p. 71). Sensing a stimulus at a distance, before contact is made, allows for a time period before a contact response is required; and this time allows for the selective processes involved in deliberate choice.

"The cerebrum . . . is an organ which integrates a vast variety of responses including the lower reflexes . . ." (p. 126). "In a sense all responses are so interconnected by way of interrelated innervation and inhibition" (p. 125). Integration and inhibition provide a second mechanism for creating delay in response. "This introduces delay in response, and adjustment by way of selection of type of response, i.e., choice" (p. 126).

Third, during the delay period, the organism feels its own incipient responses to the distant stimuli. "In the innervations of the attitudes that distant objects call out the animal feels the invitation or threat they carry with them" (p. 71). Invitation or threat call up response tendencies to act. "His responses to his own tendencies to act provide the control that organizes all his responses into a coördinated act, so that these inner feelings wax in importance in the development of the mechanism" of the encephalon (p. 71). "It is here that we first meet the stuff of ideation" (p. 71).

Fourth, as the cortex evolved, simple internal feelings of incipient responses became more sophisticated forms of "response imagery" (p. 74). Images of past actions and their results help in anticipating the future results—or consequences—of similar actions. "This imagery gives us the result of the act before we carry it out" (1914, p. 29). Because the cerebrum allows the organism to anticipate the results of the act, the cerebrum has "introduced the future into the mechanism of the act . . ." (1932, p. 132). Imagery of the future consequences of various alternative acts allows the organism to select among them and make "purposive responses" (p. 74). "It is the ability of later responses to play back into immediate responses that gives us our flexibility and power of choice" (1927, p. 158). Note that choice and purposive responses are defined behaviorally—as behaviors controlled by anticipated future consequences, which are established from past experience.

Although neural mechanisms provide part of Mead's explanation of choice, language and verbal behavior have allowed the emergence of advanced levels of deliberate action in humans.

SYMBOLIC THOUGHT AND CONSCIOUSNESS

The full emergence of mind and deliberative processes can occur only through social interaction, especially through the social use of language (Mead, 1924-25, 1934). As children interact socially and acquire language, they gain the tools for symbolic thought and increasing self-determination. Language provides "word images" (1932, p. 75) that enrich the more primitive response imagery used in making choices. "Ideas are closely related to images . . . Since the symbols with which we think are largely recognized as word images, ideas and images have a very close consanguinity" (p. 75). Words allow us to call up symbolic images of all phases of our acts, along with the consequences of those acts. They also bring images of the past and anticipated future into our present, and this "[i]deation extends spatially and temporally the field within which activity takes place," leading to an "extended present" that reaches far beyond our immediate perceptual present (p. 88).

The meanings that words carry are a central component of the extended present and the deliberate actions we take in it. By analyzing meaning from a behavioristic perspective, Mead was able to avoid the metaphysical problems associated with traditional views of "ideas" and "meanings." In discussing "the meaning of things," Mead (1934, p. 127) stated: "We are here avoiding logical and metaphysical problems, just as modern psychology does." First, objects and actions take on meanings based on the results or completions of the acts in which they are involved. "The completions that need to occur before the act is completed are behavioristic meanings" (1927, p. 143). For example, "the ultimate act of driving a nail is for us the meaning of the hammer" (p. 130). The hammer's capacity for driving the nail establishes its meaning. "When we indicate this pattern of final manipulation we indicate the meaning of the act" (p. 143). Second, words such as "hammer" are symbols that come to stand for the meanings that are based on people's actions, such as using hammers to drive nails.

Not only physical objects, but also social gestures—such as a wink or a smile—take on meanings, based on the results of the acts involving them. "If that gesture does so indicate to another organism the subsequent (or resultant) behavior of the given organism, then it has meaning. In other words, the relationship between a given stimulus—as a gesture—and the later phases of the social act of which it is an early . . . phase constitutes the field within which meaning originates and exists" (1934, p. 76). The meaning of a smile is established by the results of the acts following the smile, which of course can vary across different contexts. In those contexts where smiles have been followed by cheerful and kind behavior in the past, a person will tend to perceive smiles as indicating cheerfulness and kindness; but the meaning of smiles can be quite different when context cues are present that in the past indicated that smiles might be followed by insincere or manipulative behavior. Thus, the meaning of the social gesture is based on the phases of the social act that follow it. "Meaning is thus a development of something objectively there as a relation between certain phases of the social act; it is not a psychical addition to that act and it is not an 'idea' as traditionally conceived" (e.g., by metaphysical or idealist philosophers). Rather. "[t]he gesture stands for a certain resultant of the social act, . . . so that meaning is given or stated in terms of response" (p. 76). "The basis of meaning is thus objectively there in social conduct, or in nature in its relation to such conduct" (p. 80). As such it is amenable to scientific study.

"Awareness or consciousness is not necessary to the presence of meaning in the process of social experience" (p. 77). Two snarling dogs are exchanging and responding to meaningful signals in their exchange of gestures, but are not consciously aware of the meanings. "The mechanism of meaning is thus present in the social act before the emergence of consciousness or awareness of meaning occurs" (p. 77). Meaning becomes aware only when the "gesture becomes a symbol, a significant symbol" (p. 78), namely a symbol that people use in a conventional manner, so that it calls up the same meaning for those users. Meaning "is not essentially or primarily a psychical content (a content of mind or consciousness), for it need not be conscious at all, and is not in fact until significant symbols are evolved in the process of human social experience. Only when it becomes identified with such symbols does meaning become conscious" (p. 80). Both a human and an animal can see and be perceptually aware of a hammer on the ground; but humans can gain the additional awareness of the meaning of the hammer by verbally describing it and its use. "Mentality on our approach simply comes in when the organism is able to point out meanings to others and to himself. This is the point at which mind appears, or if you like, emerges" (p. 132). This approach to mind introduces none of the mysterious elements present in idealist and metaphysical conceptions of meaning and mind.

How does Mead's behavioristic approach deal with highly abstract and generalized meanings? In metaphysical and idealistic world views, highly abstract meanings seem to refer to universals at a Platonic or transcendental level. An idealist might think that "this meaning or universal character [is something] with which a behavioristic psychology is supposed to have difficulty in dealing" (1934, p. 82). However Mead disagreed: "It is the possibility of such a behavioristic statement that I endeavor to sketch" (p. 83).

Mead explained "universals" in terms of the behavior seen when any of a variety of different stimuli can call up the same response. When we have to write a brief note, we recognize that many types of pens, pencils or markers will suffice: All members of a certain class of stimuli can call up the response of picking up the object and writing. "[R]ecognition can be stated in terms of a response that may answer to any one of a certain group of stimuli" (p. 83). If a person is attempting to drive a nail and cannot find a hammer, the individual may recognize that "a brick or a stone" will also serve the same function (p. 83). "Anything that he can get hold of that will serve the purpose will be a hammer. That sort of response which involves the grasping of a heavy object is a universal" (p. 83). The brick or stone can function *as if* it were a hammer; hence all three fall into the same class of objects because they—as hard, heavy objects—are functionally similar in carrying out the behavior of hammering the nail. The recognition of functional equivalence allows the universal "response that answers to a whole set of particulars" (p. 84). "It is this which has been supposed to be beyond the behavioristic explanation or statement. What behavioristic psychology does is to state that character of the experience in terms of response" (p. 84).

Our membership in a verbal community—a culture with symbolic knowledge—helps us acquire a broad range of knowledge about things experienced first by others. We do not have to be swept away by a raging river to learn about the strength and danger of a powerful torrent. "[I]n the community of those who communicate with each other, the force of the torrent has taken on a meaning insofar as each is wont to indicate this to others and so to himself" (1964, p. 336). The consequences of stepping into a powerful torrent establish its meaning as "something to be avoided"; and experienced people can communicate those meanings to individuals who have never had first-hand experience with the torrent and its consequences. This cooperative social process allows individuals to expand their understanding of universals—e.g., adding "the torrent" to the class of stimuli that carry the universal meaning of "something to be avoided"—based on the experience of others.

REFLECTIVE INTELLIGENCE

Mead's (1934, pp. 90-100) analysis of reflective intelligence reveals his scientific approach to yet another important aspect of agency. When we have several alternative responses open to us in a given situation, we can use significant symbols to heighten our awareness of and reflect on our choices of possible actions before acting. "[R]eflective behavior arises only under the conditions of self-consciousness and makes possible the purposive control . . . of its conduct . . ." (p. 91). Words make us aware of the details of each alternative action and the likely future consequences of each one. People are especially likely to use this type of intelligence in problematic situations (pp. 122ff). "This [reflective intelligence] is the most effective means of adjustment to the social environment, and indeed to the environment in general, that the individual has at his disposal" (p. 100).

Mead identified several components of reflective intelligence, all of which are amenable to scientific investigation. "Intelligence is essentially the ability to solve the problems of present behavior in terms of its possible future consequences as implicated on the basis of past experience . . ." (p. 100). When we confront a problem, we can use symbols to imagine several possible solutions to the problem and to evaluate the anticipated consequences of each alternative, based on past experience, before choosing a course of action. People do this when they—either out loud or in their inner conversation— talk themselves through several alternative solutions to a problem and use their memories of past experiences to anticipate the possible future consequences of each alternative.

Mead (p. 91) stated that "[i]t is essential that such reflective intelligence be dealt with from the point of view of social behaviorism." By conceptualizing the components of reflective intelligence in behavioral terms, Mead avoided the metaphysical notions of free will that arise from nonempirical approaches to choice and agency. "What the behaviorist is occupied with, what we have to come back to, is the actual reaction itself, and it is only in so far as we can translate the content of introspection over into response that we can get any satisfactory psychological doctrine" (p. 105).

Although reflective intelligence is mediated by the mechanisms of the central nervous system and inner conversation, it is not a totally mechanical activity that produces completely predictable outcomes. Rather it is an organic, creative process.

> That which takes place in present organic behavior is always in some sense an emergent from the past, and never could have been precisely predicted in advance . . . and in the case of organic behavior which is intelligently controlled, this element of spontaneity is especially prominent by virtue of the present influence exercised over such behavior by the possible future results or consequences which it may have. (Mead, 1934, pp. 98f)

The spontaneous, creative qualities of the organic processes seen in reflective intelligence are important features of agency. Problem solving processes—such as those seen in reflective intelligence—are an especially important stimulant for creativity (Weisberg, 1986): As we reflect on the possible solutions of problems, we become aware of novel and unexpected alternatives, re-evaluate and reconstruct our memories of past experiences, and reassess the possible future outcomes of the alternatives. From the complicated interaction of the perceptual present with images of the past and future, complex decisions and actions emerge. Like all emergents, these events are not completely predictable from data on preceding events (Mead, 1932, pp. 14ff, 35ff, 96f; 1964, pp. 346f).

Although Mead traced the contents of mind and the methods of reflective intelligence back to the central nervous system and society, he did not believe that the empirical data on physiology and social structure were adequate to make perfect predictions about the decisions that people would make. This is most obvious when we have to predict the exact outcome of a complex choice made by a person who has an extensive repertoire of decision making skills, ponders a large number of possible alternatives, and takes creative approaches to the problem solving process. A precise prediction would require an enormous amount of data on all aspects of the person's genetics, physiology, prior learning experience, and current stimuli. Since it is unlikely that humans can ever attain enough knowledge about all the controlling variables, it is more feasible to expect probabilistic forecasts than deterministic predictions. Mead's rejection of fully deterministic scientific theories is not to be confused with a position on the metaphysical question of free will and determinism. Mead merely stated that complex processes are not likely to be predicted with total precision, hence the behavior that emerges from reflective intelligence and other complex mediational processes is likely to have a spontaneous, creative quality that is difficult to predict completely.

Since Mead's time, psychologists have studied the various and complex ways in which people lay out alternative solutions to their problems, draw upon memory resources, apply rational, emotional and intuitive procedures to evaluate each alternative, allocate different amounts of time and effort to problems of differing levels of complexity and import, and so forth (Anderson, 1982; Chase & Simon, 1973; Dreyfus & Dreyfus, 1986). These and related studies have facilitated the development of guidelines and training programs for helping people to improve their skills at reflective intelligence (Baron & Steinberg, 1986; Meichenbaum, 1977). Rather than devaluing reflective intelligence and creativity by "explaining them away" with purely mechanistic and deterministic models, the scientific study of these activities can help us become more reflective and creative.

SKINNER

How does Skinner's position on cognition, choice and agency compare with Mead's? Skinner appears to have vacillated in his arguments about the "causal efficacy of events that occur inside the skin" (Killeen, 1984, p. 25). He has also taken positions on determinism that can easily *appear* to be inconsistent and confusing. After examining the ways in which Skinner's analysis of choice and indeterminism is compatible with Mead's work, we will turn to the central differences between these two behaviorists.

First, Skinner's position on the nature of consciousness and inner experience is similar to Mead's. Although methodological behaviorists have refused to analyze events inside the skin, Skinner and other radical behaviorists have argued that this position is unwise and unnecessary. Speaking of methodological behaviorists, Skinner (1969, pp. 227f) stated that "the charge is justified that they have neglected the facts of consciousness. The strategy is, however, quite unwise. It is particularly important

that a science of behavior face the problem of privacy. It may do so without abandoning the basic position of behaviorism," by treating inner events "as part of behavior itself." Skinner (1953, 1974) has done a skillful job of behaviorally conceptualizing and analyzing many types of private experiences—including perception, thinking, memory, emotions, problem solving, the self, and self-control—explaining how they are shaped by the external contingencies.

Second, Skinner not only treats inner events as stimuli and responses that can be traced to environmental causes, he has recognized at least ten types of inner causes (Zuriff, 1979). Although Skinner has long been critical of hypothetical inner causes that are not amenable to scientific analyses, he has dealt with inner causes that can be stated in behavioral terms and analyzed in traditional behavioral manners. "In the ten examples . . . covert variables control overt behavior in all the ways that external environmental variables do. . . . Thus, if the external environment may be said to 'cause' behavior, then in the examples presented, inner events may also be said to 'cause' behavior" (Zuriff, 1979, p. 1). These inner causes are different from nonscientific inner causes because "they are acquired in overt form, obey the same laws and have the same dimensions as overt responses, and are ultimately controlled by environmental variables" (p. 8). However, Zuriff points out that, "as the present discussion clearly demonstrates, these inner activities often play an important role in the causation of overt behavior" (p. 8). The same could be said of Mead's treatment of inner causes.

Thus, Skinner's (1969, 1971) numerous attacks on mentalistic psychology, hypothetical mental way stations, and autonomous inner man must not be confused as a criticism of all inner causes. Mead (1910, 1913, 1927, 1934) also was critical of the theories based on introspective psychologies, and was careful to describe his inner causes of choice and reflective intelligence in terms of stimuli and responses amenable to behavioral analysis.

These first two points clearly indicate that Skinner is not adverse to analyzing inner experiences and causes, working from the outside to the inside, much as Mead did. The next four points demonstrate that Skinner's behavioral analysis of external and internal responses does not produce a completely deterministic theory, but rather is compatible with Mead's model of an indeterminate science of behavior.

Third, Skinner's (1938, 1953) analysis of operant behavior clearly reveals that operants are more unpredictable than reflexes. In both unconditioned and conditioned reflexes, an antecedent stimulus elicits a respondent in a rather automatic manner than can suggest mechanistic and deterministic models. Skinner (1938, pp. 19f, 178; 1953, p. 107) was careful to point out that operants are performed much less automatically and predictably than are respondents. In describing the "spontaneity" of operants, Skinner (1938) stated: "I do not mean that there are not originating forces in spontaneous behavior but simply that they are not located in the environment. We are not in a position to see them, and we have no need to. This kind of behavior might be said to be *emitted* by the organism . . ." (p. 20). "The prior stimulus does not elicit the response; it merely sets the *occasion* upon which the response will be reinforced" (1938, p. 178). Skinner contrasted the "static laws" of respondent behavior with the "dynamic laws" needed to describe operant behavior, which is "an event appearing spontaneously with a given frequency" (p. 21). Since it is difficult to predict exactly when an operant will occur in the presence of its controlling S^D's, operants do not fit deterministic models as well as they fit the probabilistic models that Mead advocated. "Both prediction and control are inherent in operant conditioning, but the notion is always probabilistic . . ." (Skinner, 1974, p. 226).

According to Skinner (1969, p. 227f): "The skin is not that important as a boundary. Private and public events have the same kind of physical dimensions." Thus, covert operants involved in thought and choice would be expected to fit probabilistic models as much as overt operants do.

Fourth, Skinner (1953, 1957, 1968, 1969) has analyzed various types of verbal problem-solving behavior, one of which—the self-probe—is quite similar to Mead's description of reflective intelligence. In the self-probe, we probe ourselves for data and arguments needed to solve a problem, much as others probe us for information when helping us decide what to do. "Tentative solutions, perhaps assembled for this purpose, are systematically reviewed" (1953, p. 250). "We facilitate choosing or making a decision in various ways—for example, by 'reviewing the facts.' If we are working with external materials, verbal or otherwise, we may indeed re-view them in the sense of looking at them again. . . . In reviewing an argument we simply argue again" (1974, p. 112). A culture can help people learn to verbalize about their behaviors and related consequences. "As a culture evolves, it encourages running comment of this sort and thus prepares its members to solve problems most effectively" (1969, p. 143). "A crude description may contribute to a more exact one, and a final characterization which supports a quite unambiguous response brings problem solving to an end" (p. 142). Cultures also help people learn rules for problem solving. "Many rules which help in solving the problem of solving problems are familiar. 'Ask yourself "What is the unknown?"'" (p. 145). In the *Technology of Teaching*, Skinner (1968) suggested ways to teach thinking, problem solving, and creativity.

Skinner provided more detail than Mead did on the ways in which people learn reflective intelligence and other methods of problem solving. However, Skinner's type of behavioral analysis does not allow us to predict exactly when and how an individual will solve most kinds of problems. In discussing problem solving behavior, Skinner (1968, pp. 138f) stated: "The behavior is not unlawful, but we lack the information needed to predict the moment of its occurrence with certainty." In fact, it is not

only *the timing* of the response, but also the topography of the behavior and its effects on the environment that can be difficult to predict with complete certainty. We could never gain enough knowledge about people's genetics, prior conditioning history, and current stimulus inputs to predict in perfect detail the solutions to novel problems, such as a scientist's solution to a complex problem at the frontier of research. Novel problems confront people with numerous S^D's—many of which do not have strong stimulus control over specific operants—mixed in unfamiliar patterns, making it unlikely that a rote or easily predicted response will emerge. When problem solving involves the interaction of numerous complex behavioral skills, the interaction effects increase the probability of unexpected results. Since problem solving often involves lengthy chains of verbal and nonverbal operants (each link of which provides the S^D's for the next link), the probabilistic nature of each operant in the chain makes it difficult to predict which operant and which S^D's will emerge to set the occasion for the next operant. Thus, as a chain is performed, the uncertainties of predicting each link of the chain are amplified at each step; and such amplification mechanisms sometimes lead to highly unpredictable outcomes (cf, Crutchfield et al., 1986, p. 49). Clearly, probabilistic models are more appropriate than deterministic models.

Fifth, problems present S^D's that can set the occasion for creative thinking. In his early work, Skinner (1953, p. 255) traced novel and original behavior to novel environmental conditions: "Novel contingencies generate novel forms of behavior. . . . The question of originality can be disposed of . . . by providing plausible accounts of the way in which a given idea might have occurred." Later, Skinner (1968, pp. 169-184) recognized that original, unpredictable behavior could be explained in other ways. For example, the reinforcement of novel behavior or punishment of commonplace behavior can produce original and creative behavior (pp. 181-184). Experimental studies have documented that creativity can, in fact, be enhanced by this type of reinforcement (Goetz & Baer, 1973; Maloney & Hopkins, 1973). Since the response class being reinforced is very broadly defined—as behavior that is novel and/or not commonplace—it is very hard to predict precisely *what* behavior will be emitted next (aside from the fact that it may be novel). In fact, Skinner (1974, p. 114) compared creative thought with mutations in biology, which he described as "random." Creative operants "are, if not random, at least not necessarily related to the contingencies under which they will be selected" (p. 114). Namely, they are not determined by the controlling variables. This is the stuff of indeterminacy.

Behaviorists have good reason to believe that behavioral analysis is quite well suited for explaining how people acquire creative skills; but this knowledge is not sufficient to allow us to predict the precise timing and topography of the behavior generated from a creative repertoire. Creative actions are among the events "emerging in ceaseless novelty" that prevent sciences from ever reaching finality (Mead, 1932, p. 102). Mead's form of behaviorism and Killeen's (1984) "emergent behavior-ism" provide a more appropriate treatment of emergent behavior than does a behaviorism that purports to be totally deterministic.

Sixth, concepts such as purpose and intentional design are also related to the topic of agency. Broadly defined, all operant behavior is future oriented, hence purposive. Skinner (1974, p. 55) states: "Possibly no charge is more often leveled against behaviorism or a science of behavior than that it cannot deal with purpose or intention. A stimulus-response formula has no answer, but operant behavior is the very field of purpose and intention. By its nature it is directed toward the future: a person acts *in order that* something will happen, and the order is temporal." Although all operants can be seen as purposive, this definition of purpose is not likely to coincide with the lay person's uses of the word. Skinner's treatment of intentional behavior and design comes closer to lay definitions of purposive action.

All through *Beyond Freedom and Dignity,* Skinner (1971) was critical of nonscientific conceptions of autonomous inner man; however, near the end, he concluded: "What is needed is more 'intentional' control, not less, and this is an important engineering problem" (p. 177). The intentional design of environmental controlling variables—hence of behavior—is possible; and Skinner (1953, 1968, 1971) frequently advocated intentional design at both the individual and cultural levels. He argued that our increasingly detailed knowledge of behavior principles can be used in designing and engineering the environmental conditions needed to produce intentionally designed behaviors. When intentionality is defined and analyzed behaviorally, it is not off limits to behavioral theory. Even the intentional behavior commonly seen in everyday life—whether effectively designed and implemented or not—can be analyzed behaviorally. "[T]he behavior from which we infer choice, intention, and originality is within reach of behavioral analysis . . ." (1974, p. 239).

THE DIFFERENCES

There are numerous other facets of Skinner's writings that parallel Mead's theories (Baldwin, 1981). In these areas of commonality, the most conspicuous difference between Mead's and Skinner's work arises from Skinner's having access to a much larger and more modern body of empirical data and theories than Mead had. For example, both Mead and Skinner analyzed reflective intelligence and problem solving in terms of verbally reviewing each possible solution and its consequences, but Skinner has a much more precise theory of the role of social and natural contingencies in the acquisition and modification of verbal skills and reflective processes.

Probably the most important basic difference between Mead's and Skinner's versions of behaviorism lies in their different treatment of determinism. Much as Mead had, Skinner has recognized the probabilistic nature of

behavior and the impossibility of metaphysical certainty about issues of free will and determinism. Speaking of methodological determinism, Skinner (1968, p. 171) stated: "Determinism is a useful assumption because it encourages a search for causes." In a similar vein, Mead (1932, 1936) had described methodological determinism as a "postulate" that has been useful in the pursuit of mechanistic laws. Nevertheless, Skinner emphasized determinism more than Mead did. Whereas Mead counterbalanced his discussion of methodological determinism with discussions of the emergence of unpredictable events, Skinner emphasized methodological determinism much more than probability or emergence.

In addition, Skinner developed a technique never found in Mead's work. He extrapolated from methodological determinism to develop *interpretive analyses* in which he examined complex behaviors *as if* methodological determinism might someday produce a totally deterministic science of them. Skinner (1973, p. 261) explained his strategy: "My *Verbal Behavior* was an exercise in interpretation . . . *Beyond Freedom and Dignity* is also an exercise in interpretation. It is not science as such, but it is not metaphysics, either." Skinner is aware of the limits of deterministic interpretations. "[A]lthough a science of behavior permits a person to interpret what he sees more effectively, it will never tell him the whole story about the individual case" (1974, p. 242).

In spite of an awareness of the limitations of deterministic interpretations, Skinner has at times taken them to the extreme, making statements that sometimes sound like pronouncements about complete determinism. For example, from the observation that there is "new evidence of the predictability of human behavior," Skinner concluded: "Personal exemption from a *complete determinism* is revoked as a scientific analysis progresses . . ." (1971, p. 21, emphasis added). "*All* behavior is determined, directly or indirectly, by consequences . . ." (1974, p. 127, emphasis added). When such statements are not understood as interpretive analyses, they sound like statements about absolute metaphysical truths—*or* naive assertions about the power of a science of behavior.

Skinner's defense of deterministic interpretations reveals a penchant for deterministic thinking: "We cannot prove, of course, that human behavior as a whole is fully determined, but the proposition becomes more plausible as facts accumulate . . ." (p. 189). Advances in the science of behavior might suggest the plausibility of determinism to some, but a serious recognition of the probabilistic and unpredictable nature of many types of behavior has the opposite effect, undermining the assumption "that human behavior as a whole is fully determined." Although Skinner frequently focused on determinism and overlooked sources of indeterminacy, Mead (1932, p. 14), in contrast, saw that his task was "to bring into congruence with each other this universality of determination which is the text of modern science, and the emergence of the novel. . . ." Mead advocated looking for "the most general laws" possible

(1934, p. 39), but he expected the laws to be probabilistic, not deterministic (1932, pp. 14f, 32f).

Is it wise for behaviorists to take the extreme position on determinism that Skinner does in his interpretive analyses? One answer lies in the consequences of the behavior. On the positive side, exercises in deterministic interpretations may encourage behaviorists to apply methodological determinism to all types of behavior—including thinking, problem solving, self-control, teaching, and culture—in search for causes. Skinner's deterministic analyses provide behaviorists with models that show how such analyses might be done, and reading them can provide reinforcement for expanding the domain of behavioral study by demonstrating that behavior principles can deal successfully with issues once thought to be beyond the range of the discipline.

In addition, deterministic interpretations provide a vivid contrast between accounts of behavior based on free will and those based on methodological determinism. This contrast helps behaviorists learn to identify prescientific intellectual baggage and problems that have their roots in the metaphysics of free will. For example, in *Beyond Freedom and Dignity,* this exercise revealed important points about the literature of freedom, including its lack of attention to the dangers of weak control and positive control (Skinner, 1973). Such exercises may hasten the demise of prescientific interpretations of behavior. "When I question the supposed residual freedom of autonomous man, I am not debating the issue of free will. I am simply describing the slow demise of a prescientific explanatory device . . . The argument is, I believe, quite similar to that against vital forces in biology" (1973, p. 261). Is it true that the demise of prescientific causal explanations will leave only determinism as an interpretive tool? Skinner appears to have underestimated the importance of emergence, probability, and indeterminacy in developing scientific theories that introduce no metaphysical assumptions of free will. Mead did not.

Not all the consequences of Skinner's deterministic interpretations have been positive. His extreme positions have caused many serious scientists and scholars to reject behaviorism, much as Watson's extremes did. Skinner's attempts to explain—or explain away—all mental causes as fully determined by environmental contingencies have generated numerous criticisms of behaviorism (Black, 1973; Chomsky, 1959; Lefcourt, 1973; Ritchie-Calder, 1973; Toynbee, 1973). Even though the actual scientific contributions of behavioral research are proving to be quite valuable in child rearing, education, various branches of therapy, and so forth, many people dislike or fear the brave new deterministic world they identify with behaviorism. Even behaviorists, such as Mahoney (1974), Schwartz and Lacy (1982), and Bandura (1986) have reacted against Skinner's extreme positions on determinism and the environmental determination of inner cognitions, introducing serious schisms into the discipline.

Do the benefits of deterministic interpretations outweigh the costs of alienating serious scientists and scholars who otherwise might profit from knowledge of behavior principles? Perhaps only history can tell. Even though Watson has been severely criticized outside the field of behavioral psychology (Broadbent, 1961; Gould, 1982; Harrell & Harrison, 1938), he is still viewed with respect by behaviorists for his contributions to the growth of our discipline (Boakes, 1984; Bolles, 1979). Perhaps Skinner's effectiveness in inspiring behaviorists to pursue methodological determinism is more important than his alienating nonbehaviorists. Nevertheless, we may still wish to ask if behaviorism would be better served by indeterminant and probabilistic models such as those advocated by Mead.

INDETERMINISM

In his careful analysis and critical restructuring of the philosophical tenets of behaviorism, Zuriff (1985, p. 177) states: "Determinism . . . is a methodological working assumption for the behaviorist, rather than a metaphysical commitment." This working assumption derives in part from behaviorists' commitment to the natural sciences. "Because behaviorists generally subscribe to the world view of the natural sciences, they profess grave philosophical doubts about the possibility of a free agent operating in behavior" (p. 177). However, doubting free will does not necessarily lead the natural scientist to espouse determinism or take positions similar to Skinner's deterministic interpretations.

Although earlier, mechanistic physics portrayed a deterministic world, contemporary physicist have moved to a more probabilistic view. Research on radiation along with the development of theories of relativity and Heisenberg's uncertainty principle led physicists to withdraw from completely mechanistic and deterministic theories. Mead (1932, 1938) discussed the theory of relativity as part of his argument for recognizing the importance of emergence and probabilistic theories. By 1936, both physicists and philosophers of science were questioning the old "deterministic methods which have brought such great success to the physical sciences. . . . And now we are witnessing physical science itself not only raising doubt as to the adequacy of Newtonian mechanics and the laws of the conservation of energy, but also challenging the entire classical conception of physical causation" (Cohen, 1936, p. 327).

Skinner's response to these developments in physics was different from Mead's. Speaking of the principle of indeterminacy, Skinner (1953, p. 17) stated: "In our present state of knowledge, certain events therefore appear to be unpredictable. It does not follow that these events are free or capricious." It is true that the indeterminacy principle does not introduce a free agent, but it does not support Skinner's interpretations in terms of complete determinism. It reinforces arguments for probabilism and indeterminant models.

More recently, the theory of chaos has lent even stronger support to the position that numerous phenomena—including Brownian motion, fluid turbulence, weather, genetic variability, behavior, and society—have random, chaotic, and capricious elements (Crutchfield et al., 1986; Mayer-Kress, 1986). In systems that involve complex chains of events operating over time, minor variations in initial conditions can influence subsequent events such that small errors in original measurements are amplified as events proceed, sometimes leading to highly unpredictable outcomes, i.e., to chaos. For example, it would be impossible to make accurate predictions about the position of billiard balls on a table under frictionless conditions one minute after they have been hit by the cue ball. "The large growth in uncertainty comes about because the balls are curved, and small differences at the point of impact are amplified with each collision. The amplification is exponential: it is compounded at every collision. . . . Any effect, no matter how small, quickly reaches macroscopic proportions. . . . With chaos, predictions are rapidly doomed to gross inaccuracy" (Crutchfield et al., 1986, p. 49). As a result, "long-term predictions are intrinsically impossible" (p. 56). The same is true for complex human behavior and cognition. In a twenty link chain of cognitive operants, we can make much better predictions of the final outcome if we have knowledge about as many links of the chain as possible, rather than having data only about the original environmental conditions, as one would if using Skinner's deterministic interpretive approach to trace inner causes back to environmental contingencies rather than studying them in process. The less deterministic types of behaviorism advocated by Mead, Mahoney, Killeen, Bandura, and others recognize the utility of studying all links of cognitive chains as they function together for increasing the accuracy of prediction, control, and therapy.

Finally, there are questions about the wisdom of Skinner's (1953, 1971) applying his deterministic interpretations to society and social evolution. Random processes appear to be important features of social interaction and cultural evolution (Brenner, 1983; Duncan, 1986; Kaufman, 1985). Since social systems are influenced by so many controlling variables that are difficult to measure and model precisely, they often change in random and chaotic manners. Deterministic interpretations of social processes may lead us to overestimate our capacity for prediction, control, planned change, and the minimization of human error. A healthy recognition of the indeterminacy of social systems tempers ones confidence about long-term or extremely accurate predictions and sensitizes one to the need to monitor the countless unpredictable events that affect the next occurrences in social systems. Methodological determinism remains the best approach we have for studying social systems; but it can be expected to produce only probabilistic propositions, not completely deterministic laws.

CONCLUSIONS

G. H. Mead was a philosopher who developed sophisticated theories of pragmatism and behavioral psychology that avoid the deterministic and "empty organism" mod-

els that so many scholars find objectionable in some versions of behaviorism. Unfortunately, many contemporary behaviorists are not aware of Mead's contributions, which could be useful in remedying some of the problems in modern behaviorism and providing a strong philosophical position that could unite radical and cognitive behaviorists. This paper has attempted to show that Skinner the scientist has taken a position quite similar to Mead's. Skinner's awareness of the importance of inner causes—along with the spontaneous and probabilistic nature of operants, problem solving and creativity—makes it clear that Skinner, the scientist, did not anticipate a completely deterministic or empty-headed science of behavior. It is primarily his deterministic interpretations, which he explained were neither science nor metaphysics (1973, p. 261), that deviate from Mead's position. Since these deterministic interpretations are not scientific, they can be separated from the science of behavior, in which case, Skinner's position becomes even closer to Mead's and is compatible with cognitive and emergent behaviorism.

Mead attempted to create a unified world view that integrated data on biology, psychology and society in order to explain overt behavior and inner processes. His theory can be useful in helping contemporary behaviorists overcome some of the problems and schisms within our discipline. This paper has focused on agency because of its central importance to a science of behavior that has significant deterministic proclivities; but there is much more in Mead's work that warrants attention (Baldwin, 1986).

REFERENCES

Anderson, J. R. (1982). Acquisition of cognitive skill. *Psychological Review, 89,* 369-406.

Baldwin, J. D. (1981). George Herbert Mead and modern behaviorism. *Pacific Sociological Review, 24,* 411-440.

Baldwin, J. D. (1986). *George Herbert Mead: A unifying theory for sociology.* Beverly Hills, CA: Sage.

Bandura. A. (1986). *Social foundations of thought and action: A social cognitive theory.* Englewood Cliffs, NJ: Prentice-Hall.

Baron, J. B., & Steinberg. R. J. (1986). *Teaching thinking skills: Theory and practice.* New York: W.H. Freeman.

Black, M. (1973). Some aversive responses to a would-be reinforcer. In H. Wheeler (Ed.), *Beyond the punitive society* (pp. 125-134). San Francisco. CA: W.H. Freeman.

Blumer, H. (1955). Attitudes and the social act. *Social Problems, 3,* 59-65.

Blumer, H. (1962). Society as symbolic interaction. In A. Rose (Ed.), *Human behavior and social processes* (pp. 179-192). Boston, MA: Houghton Mifflin.

Blumer, H. (1966). Sociological implications of the thought of George Herbert Mead. *American Journal of Sociology, 71*, 535-544.

Boakes, R. (1984). *From Darwin to behaviorism: Psychology and the minds of animals.* New York: Cambridge University Press.

Bolles, R. C. (1979). *Learning theory* (2nd ed.). New York: Holt, Rinehart and Winston.

Brenner, R. (1983). *History—the human gamble.* Chicago, IL: University of Chicago Press.

Broadbent, D. E. (1961). *Behaviour.* New York: Basic Books.

Chase, W. G., & Simon, H. A. (1973). Perception in chess. *Cognitive Psychology, 4*, 55-81.

Chomsky, N. (1959). A review of B.F. Skinner's *Verbal behavior. Language, 35*, 26-58.

Cohen, M. R. (1936). The statistical view of nature. *Journal of the American Statistical Association, 31*, 327-347.

Crutchfield, J. P., Farmer, J. D., & Packard N. H. (1986). Chaos. *Scientific American, 255*(6), 46-57.

Deitz, S. M. & Arrington, R. L. (1984). Wittgenstein's language-games and the call to cognition. *Behaviorism, 12*, 1-14.

Dreyfus, H. L., & Dreyfus, S. E. (1986). *Mind over machine: The power of human intuition and experience in the era of the computer.* New York: Macmillan/Free Press.

Duncan, O. D. (1986). Probability, disposition, and the inconsistency of attitudes and behavior. *Synthese, 68*, 65-98.

Goetz, E. M., & Baer, D. M. (1973). Social control of form diversity and the emergence of new forms in children's block building. *Journal of Applied Behavior Analysis, 6*, 209-217.

Gould, J. L. (1982). *Ethology: The mechanisms and evolution of behavior.* New York: W.W. Norton.

Harrell, W., & Harrison, R. (1938). The rise and fall of behaviorism. *The Journal of General Psychology, 18*, 367-421.

Kaplan, A. (1964). *The conduct of inquiry: Methodology for behavioral science.* New York: Harper & Row.

Kaufman, H. (1985). *Time, chance and organizations.* Chatham, NJ: Chatham House.

Killeen, P. R. (1984). Emergent behaviorism. *Behaviorism, 12*, 25-39.

Kuhn, M. H. (1964). Major trends in symbolic interaction theory in the past twenty-five years. *Sociological Quarterly, 5*, 61-84.

Lefcourt, H. M. (1973). The function of the illusions of control and freedom. *American Psychologist, 28*, 417-425.

Mahoney, M. J. (1974). *Cognition and behavior modification.* Cambridge, MA: Ballinger.

Maloney, K. B. & Hopkins, B. L. (1973). The modification of sentence structure and its relationship to subjective judgements of creative writing. *Journal of Applied Behavior Analysis, 6*, 425-433.

Mayer-Kress, G. (Ed.). (1986). *Dimensions and entropies in chaotic systems.* New York: Springer-Verlag.

McPhail, C., & Rexroat, C. (1979). Mead vs. Blumer: The divergent methodological perspectives of social behaviorism and symbolic interactionism. *American Sociological Review, 44*, 449-467.

McPhail, C., & Rexroat, C. (1980). *Ex cathedra* Blumer or *ex libris* Mead. *American Sociological Review, 45*, 420-430.

Mead, G. H. (1900). "Suggestions toward a theory of philosophical disciplines." *The Philosophical Review, 9*, 1-17.

Mead, G. H. (1908). "The philosophical basis of ethics." *International Journal of Ethics, 18*, 311-323.

Mead, G. H. (1913). "The social self." *Journal of Philosophy, Psychology, and Scientific Methods, 10*, 374-380.

Mead, G. H. (1914). "1914 class lectures in social psychology." In D. L. Miller (Ed., 1982). *The individual and the social self* (pp. 27-105). Chicago, IL: University of Chicago Press.

Mead, G. H. (1917). "Scientific method and individual thinker." In *Creative intelligence: Essays in the pragmatic attitude* (pp. 176-227). New York: Henry Holt.

Mead, G. H. (1922). "A behavioristic account of the significant symbol." *Journal of Philosophy, 19*, 157-163.

Mead, G. H. (1923). "Scientific method and the moral sciences." *International Journal of Ethics, 33*, 229-247.

Mead, G. H. (1924-1925). "The genesis of the self and social control." *International Journal of Ethics, 35*, 251-277.

Mead, G. H. (1925-1926). "The nature of aesthetic experience." *International Journal of Ethics, 36*, 382-393.

Mead, G. H. (1927). "1927 class lectures in social psychology." In D. L. Miller (Ed.), *The individual and the social self* (pp. 106-175). Chicago, IL: University of Chicago Press.

Mead, G. H. (1929). "A pragmatic theory of truth." In *Studies in the nature of truth*, vol. 11 (pp. 65-88). University of California, Publications in Philosophy.

Mead, G. H. (1929-1930). "The philosophies of Royce, James, and Dewey in their American setting." *International Journal of Ethics*, 40, 211-231.

Mead, G. H. (1932). *The philosophy of the present*. A. E. Murphy (Ed.). Chicago, IL: Open Court.

Mead, G. H. (1934). *Mind, self and society*, C. W. Morris (Ed.). Chicago, IL: University of Chicago Press.

Mead, G. H. (1936). *Movements of thought in the nineteenth century*, M. H. Moore (Ed.). Chicago, IL: University of Chicago Press.

Mead, G. H. (1938). *The philosophy of the act*, C. W. Morris (Ed.). Chicago, IL: University of Chicago Press.

Mead, G. H. (1964). *Selected writings*, A. J. Reck (Ed.). New York: Bobbs-Merrill.

Meichenbaum, D. (1977). *Cognitive behavior modification: An integrative approach*. New York: Plenum.

Morris, E. K. (1985). "Wittgenstein's language-games and the call to cognition:" Comments on Deitz and Arrington. *Behaviorism, 13*, 137-146.

Pierce, W. D., & Epling, W. F. (1984). On the persistence of cognitive explanation: Implications for behavior analysis. *Behaviorism, 12*, 15-27.

Powell, R. P., & Still, A. W. (1979). Behaviorism and the psychology of language: An historical reassessment. *Behaviorism, 1*, 71-89.

Ritchie-Calder, L. (1973). Beyond B.F. Skinner. In H. Wheeler (Ed.), *Beyond the punitive society* (pp. 212-216). San Francisco, CA: W.H. Freeman.

Schwartz, B., & Lacey, H. (1982). *Behaviorism, science, and human nature*. New York: W.W. Norton.

Skinner, B. F. (1938). *The behavior of organisms*. New York: Appleton-Century-Crofts.

Skinner, B. F. (1953). *Science and human behavior*. New York: Macmillan.

Skinner, B. F. (1957). *Verbal behavior*. New York: Appleton-Century-Crofts.

Skinner, B. F. (1968). *The technology of teaching*. Englewood Cliffs, NJ: Prentice-Hall.

Skinner, B. F. (1969). *Contingencies of reinforcement*. New York: Appleton-Century-Crofts.

Skinner, B. F. (1971). *Beyond freedom and dignity*. New York: Knopf.

Skinner, B. F. (1973). Answers for my critics. In H. Wheeler (Ed.), *Beyond the punitive society* (pp. 256-266). San Francisco, CA: W.H. Freeman.

Skinner, B.F. (1974). *About behaviorism*. New York: Knopf.

Stoats, A.W. (1975). *Social behaviorism*. Homewood, IL: Dorsey.

Toynbee, A. (1973). Great expectations. In H. Wheeler (Ed.), *Beyond the punitive society* (pp. 113-120). San Francisco, CA: W.H. Freeman.

Weisberg, R. W. (1986). *Creativity: Genius and other myths*. New York: W.H. Freeman.

Wood, M., & Wardell, M. L. (1983). G.H. Mead's social behaviorism vs. the astructural bias of symbolic interactionism. *Symbolic Interaction, 6*, 85-96.

Zuriff, G. E. (1975). Where is the agent in behavior? *Behaviorism, 3*, 1-21.

Zuriff, G. E. (1979). Ten inner causes. *Behaviorism, 7*, 1-8.

Zuriff, G. E. (1985). *Behaviorism: A conceptual reconstruction*. New York: Columbia University Press.

Andrew Feffer (essay date 1990)

SOURCE: "Sociability and Social Conflict in George Herbert Mead's Interactionism, 1900-1919," in *Journal of the History of Ideas*, Vol. 51, No. 2, April-June, 1990, pp. 233-54.

[*In the following essay, Feffer places Mead's philosophy in the political and cultural context of the Chicago reform culture at the turn of the twentieth century.*]

During the 1970s and 80s philosophers, psychologists, and intellectual historians revived the Pragmatist tradition in American philosophy. They devoted the greater share of study to the work of Charles S. Peirce and John Dewey. A number of scholars, however, also participated in a minor but persistent revival of interest in the work of George Herbert Mead, Dewey's partner and collaborator at the University of Chicago and one of the founders of social psychology in the United States.

One generally welcomes renewed attention to a thinker and writer of such unappreciated brilliance as Mead. This renaissance would be no different were it not for the fact that it yielded relatively little in the way of historical study. While many scholars have established Mead's intellectual credentials, only a few have spent much time investigating the genesis of Mead's ideas or determining what his writing meant in the context of American intellectual, social, and political history. A thorough intellectual biography (not to mention *any* sort of biography) of Mead still waits to be written.[1]

I would like to use this essay to begin deepening our historical knowledge of Mead's work, and to do so in a particular manner. Historian Daniel Rodgers argues that one of the limits to our understanding of political concepts is our reluctance to view them as rhetorical tools used in contentious political environments. Political language at various times has become the object of dispute between identifiable political factions and contending social groups. Those fighting over territory and power also fought over the meaning of words, over their use, over their reference, even over their rightful ownership. And because control of words and the discourses of political power were so important in determining the outcome of more tangible conflicts, political language played a key role in mapping out the political terrain of American history.[2]

The problems Rodgers identifies in the general history of American political ideas can be found in our more particular history of Mead's intellectual development. Even as a philosopher Mead addressed politically freighted issues. For Mead both theoretical and applied psychology functioned as social practice, guiding and inspiring social and political activism, in which he was personally involved. The activist nature of Mead's writing presents us (as readers in the present) with a problem of clearly identifying both the intended and unintended meanings of his key terminology, which, like the political language of any era, is subject (if viewed in context) to just those contentions Rodgers describes. Did Mead's frequently used term "social control," for example, refer to greater state power or to more just forms of social organization? There is ample room for both interpretations in the context of social and political dispute during Mead's lifetime. What did Mead and his contemporaries mean by "democracy"? Did Mead genuinely embrace a radically participatory democracy? Or shall we accept the more established condemnation that Mead's generation simply used democratic rhetoric in the pursuit of middle-class professional power?[3]

To answer these questions we need to place Mead's philosophy in a clear historical context, viewing it against the Chicago reform culture of the turn of the century, which Mead and his colleagues helped create. While I do not want to argue that Mead's psychology is entirely bound to that political and cultural context, it is essential to study his words and ideas against the terrain of significant events, institutions, and people. Like Rodgers, I would like to focus on several "keywords," used by Mead, his colleagues and his generation, and begin to uncover their political and historical nuances. Most of these terms cluster about the notion of a "social self" that formed the core of Mead's interactive social psychology: "sociability," "sociality," "social consciousness," and

"the social self" are a few. Other terms linked Mead's concept of the social self to broader political issues; for example, the physiological and psychological notion of "coordination" and its political equivalent "cooperation." Mead referred these terms to each other and intended them to share common meanings, as did John Dewey and the lesser-known members of the University of Chicago faculty, on which Mead spent most of his career.

Mead generalized from these interrelated terms with a reformist political intent. He tried to form a critical vocabulary and a set of theories that would emphasize human qualities incompatible with free-market capitalism. To achieve "cooperation" in the new century, he tried to demonstrate that social reciprocity (a more fundamental form of cooperation) is a natural part of human character. This goal motivated much of the philosophical and psychological studies in Mead's department. Resulting theories in turn laid the groundwork for moderate social reform that emerged in Chicago between 1890 and 1910, a reformism preferred by Mead and his circle. The political significance of Mead's philosophy, however, was not as clear as the above statement implies. As I hope to show, Mead and his colleagues did not always control the significance of their words and theories. Their contentious political environment also shaped their philosophy. The theory thus followed the contours of actual social change and political dispute in Chicago between 1894 and 1919.

Dewey and Mead. Mead began writing about the social self around 1900. By that time John Dewey already had been exploring the philosophical implications of cooperation for over fifteen years.[4] In the 1890s Dewey refined earlier arguments about the evolution of human action into his mature theory of the reflex circuit or "coordination," which was presented in his famous 1896 article criticizing reductionist stimulus-response models of human behavior (or, as Dewey called them, "reflex-arc" psychologies). By this time Dewey had abandoned much of his early theological language for the terminology of scientific psychology, but he did not change substantially his overall argument. In his reflex-arc critique Dewey characterized action as a form of "reconstruction," in which the agent constantly constitutes an object world (as well as a subjective identity) out of his problematic encounter with his biological and social environment.

Dewey addressed this argument to fellow philosophers, psychologists, and theologians, but ethical and political concerns also strongly motivated him. He wrote the reflex-arc critique just two years after wandering into the midst of the Pullman strike, Chicago's worst social conflagration of the century. In this unfolding historical context Dewey wanted, in developing his theoretical alternatives to reductionist psychology, to demonstrate two things.

First, like the German idealists and liberal theologians who inspired him, Dewey hoped to show that the rational was immanent in experience. Rational consciousness and spirituality emerged out of the struggle for survival, transforming it into "intelligent" and ethical "action," that is, behavior with a rational goal. As a fully integrated circuit of "coordination," human action remained habitual and automatic until the individual encountered a problem in its environment, interfering with habitual fulfillment of needs. Ideas, beginning with the most primitive impulsive intention and ending with the most abstract philosophical theory, served in the circuit as plans for the adjustment of behavior to new problematic situations. A successful adjustment would lead to a new, provisionally successful habit, and the circuit would begin again. Rational consciousness evolved in a continuous fashion from fundamental psychological and biological functions, such as neural reaction responses to stimuli, or impulses. "Reflex-arc" responses, then, contained a kernel of human rationality and constructive intelligence. An organic continuity existed between the elements of human action: the rational was immanent in the impulse.[5]

Second, Dewey, influenced by the Social Gospel of the 1880s, hoped to show that a cooperative rather than prudential rationality emerged from human impulse, based on socially constructive reciprocity rather than individual pecuniary gain. The inclination of many Darwinists (including physiological psychologists) to align evolutionary theory with some kind of utilitarianism threatened to strengthen philosophical justifications of a market-oriented and individualistic capitalism. Dewey tried to escape the utilitarian implications of the most mechanistic and reductionist psychologies then emerging out of the post-Darwinian controversy.[6] That which is most lofty in human nature, he argued, *does* emerge from the material struggle. "Reconstruction" (meaning reform), cooperation, and reciprocity are, argued Dewey, psychologically and therefore biologically natural to humans. Thus, the reflex-arc critique made an important political as well as philosophical point, which many hoped would lead to a stronger concept of reciprocity or cooperation specially applicable to the social problems of the late nineteenth century. If purpose and spirituality could be shown to emerge naturally in human evolution, then a major hurdle could be overcome in justifying a more humane social ethic, one which stressed Christian harmony in historical development rather than the tooth-and-nail struggle for survival.[7]

Dewey, however, encountered serious philosophical obstacles to his effort to reconstruct psychology and society. An evolutionist like most of his contemporaries, Dewey argued that an individual achieved social and ethical "conduct" because in the broadest sense one *had* to for the purposes of survival. It was not particularly convincing, however, to argue that social consciousness developed as an adaptation to individual need. This obviously was not Dewey's intent. Yet he could not adequately distinguish his understanding of sociality and its origins from a Utilitarian calculus or Darwinian prudence. Dewey did not demonstrate that the prudent "intelligence" by which an individual discovered the means to achieve the goals of ongoing action necessarily (and psychologically) involved recognizing the significance and autonomy of others.[8]

Mead and the problem of sociability. George H. Mead joined Dewey at the University of Michigan in 1891 and followed the older philosopher to Chicago in 1894. During the 1890s Mead, picking up where Dewey left off, tried to establish the natural origins of social cooperation in human evolution without relying on Darwinian or Utilitarian notions of individual prudence. By 1909, as the result of this effort, Mead had laid the foundation of his interactionist social psychology.[9] He refined his theory in a series of articles on the social nature of the self and of consciousness between 1909 and 1913. By 1914 a fairly complete outline of Mead's mature social psychology, such as is usually taken from his later lectures, *Mind, Self and Society,* could be found in lectures given that year at the University.

Around 1900 Mead began exploring how and why humans evolved into social beings, trying, like Dewey, to demonstrate the social nature of ethical conduct, using the terms of experimental psychology. It was with the later work of Wilhelm Wundt that Mead began a psychological argument for the social nature of man. Wundt appealed to Mead for two reasons. First, Wundt argued that language begins with the gesture, initially an impulsive act, or near act, which becomes, in a social context, a sign of emotion and intention. Because language is an act rather than a reflection of ideas or transcendent meanings, its content, rather than being the subject matter of logic and philology, instead should be the subject matter of a functionalist psychology that studies voluntary acts. Mead found Wundt's study particularly appealing because the German philosopher interpreted communication and sociality in psychological terms. The community "mind" or *Volkseele* inhered in the common language which emerged from the psychological processes of social interaction.[10]

Second, Wundt's language theory seemed to confirm Dewey's belief in the continuity between reason and impulse. Wundt's notion that the primitive "gesture" led to fully developed language linked the individual's irrational, biological nature with the socially ordered world of communication, suggesting the continuity between impulsive, unreflective behavior and rational socialized conduct. Unlike traditional philologists, wrote Mead, Wundt "is able to refer the beginning of language to the primitive impulse to expression. The sound is at first but a gesture" (*Lautgeberde*). Wundt, according to Mead, could move fluidly from the physical gestures to sound gestures to articulate language, demonstrating the origins of language in the primitive act (that is, in human and animal biology) "instead of being forced to build it up out of intellectual elements."[11]

Building on a critical interpretation of Wundt's theory, Mead speculated that social consciousness emerged as an interaction between individuals (or "forms," as Mead called them) through the interplay of gestures. The key to social organization and to the origin of social attitudes would then be in communication, the way in which "the conduct of one form is a stimulus to another." This "stimulus" is for the other to perform a certain act, which in turn becomes "a stimulus to [the] first to a certain reaction, and so on in ceaseless interaction." It was not the similarity of acts that constituted or encouraged social interaction but the meaning each act had, in terms of the act's consequences, for the other "form." Thus, "[t]he probable beginning of human communication was in cooperation . . . where conduct differed and yet where the act of the one answered to and called out the act of the other." This seemed the solution to Dewey's dilemma. Communication did not begin in prudence or competition nor in imitation but in constructive cooperation. This suggested that sociability likewise did not emerge as a prudent strategy for individual adaptation, but was present with the appearance of language.[12]

Mead, however, needed to extend Wundt's theory to address fully the problems raised by Dewey. Mead believed that Wundt's theory of language still did not adequately explain the emergence of sociability or communication from individual gestures and impulses. Wundt, like most of his contemporaries in laboratory psychology, began with the individual as a unit of analysis, explaining sociability as something added on to that individual identity.[13] Mead wanted to explain that individual identity, in fact all aspects of individual psychology, with sociability as a starting point. "Until the social sciences are able to state the social individual in terms of social processes, as the physical sciences define their objects in terms of physical change, they will not have risen to the point at which they can force their object upon an introspective psychology."[14] He wanted not just a theory of communication but a scientifically convincing genetic psychology of human cooperation. In other words Mead hoped to convince his readers that people could not be human, in any sense of the term, *unless* they were social (that is, cooperative).

Mead particularly found fault with Wundt's explanation of the meaning of gestures. Gestures are acts that signal something to another individual. What they signal, however, was a matter of some dispute. Wundt argued that gestures signalled emotional states and that those emotions constituted the meaning of the gestures. In the broadest sense Mead agreed. But according to the prevailing psychologies, emotions were reactions to stimuli. Wundt accepted this prevailing view, and it was on this count that Mead considered Wundt's explanation mechanistic, based upon individualistic reflex psychology. Mead preferred Dewey's theory, which paralleled his critique of the reflex-arc, that the emotions are "truncated acts," acts which do not achieve their purpose because they are inhibited either by circumstances or by the actor. Emotions signify the inhibition of the act, and spur the actor to find a solution to the problem.[15] A gesture, by expressing an emotional state, then, expresses an intended or an inhibited act. An animal gnashes its teeth when it wants to tear at the throat of another animal but has not yet done so, expressing the emotional state which reflects the unsatisfied desire, the uncompleted response to the combative "situation."

The gesture, thus, does not express simply an emotional state but also signifies to the other the possible consequences of the emotional state, of the truncated act which constitutes the emotion—the "value of the act for the other individual." As the other responded "in terms of another syncopated act" a "field of social signification" was born, within which communication and social interaction would take place. Gestures had meanings "when they reflected possible acts," i.e., possible consequences for another individual who could see in that gesture a repressed yet still latent act.[16]

Upon Wundt's theory of the gesture Mead grafted a conception of meaning adopted from Dewey and Josiah Royce—that for a sentient being the meaning of an object is the purpose that object will serve in some foreseeable future or the role it will play in some action that culminates desire or need. Like Dewey and Royce, Mead argued that meaning involved the reference, through signs (that is, ideas, emotions, and "attitudes"), to future acts and experiences. But that meaning, continued Mead, could only be constituted as an intention conveyed to some "other" through gestures and language. According to Mead, therefore, meaning was actional (as Dewey argued), but it was also fundamentally social. In this way the play of gestures represented "the birth of the symbol, and the possibility of thought," a form of "sublimated conversation." Thus, Mead argued, "reflective consciousness implies a social situation which has been its precondition."[17]

Mead believed he had added two things to Wundt's theory of the gesture. First, by referring the meaning of gestures entirely to social acts, Mead believed he had eliminated a main vestige of individualistic psychology that referred psychological events in the other direction to internal states of mind (in this case internal emotions). Second, by externalizing and socializing emotional states, Mead laid the groundwork for socializing even more fundamental psychological concepts. In 1910 Mead expanded this second line of argument. In two articles Mead tried to demonstrate that consciousness of the self and of objects also had cooperative social origins.

Arguing from the principle that "meaning is consciousness of attitude," Mead concluded that one cannot be *self*-conscious without a consciousness of others because the self is no more than an awareness of one's own attitude. It is only through the responses of others to one's actions, especially to one's gestures, that one becomes conscious of one's own attitudes, including one's self-identity. Thus, "[o]ther selves in a social environment logically antedate the consciousness of self which introspection analyzes. They must be admitted as there, as given, in the same sense in which psychology accepts the given reality of physical organisms as a condition of individual consciousness." The self is not "an attitude which we assume . . . toward our inner feelings," (i.e., private introspection), but one directed "toward other individuals whose reality was implied even in the inhibitions and reorganizations which characterize this inner consciousness."[18]

Two years later Mead described two kinds of self that evolved from the primary interpersonal interaction. There is no true self in the philosophical meaning of the term, argued Mead. We do not identify ourselves first as "knowers" that precede the experience, physical or social, of the world. We are primarily object rather than subject, "me" rather than "I." Our self identity follows rather than precedes conversation whether it is the actual conversation of language or the "inner conversation" that Mead argued constituted thought. The self is a constant product of an imagination striving to see itself as others see it. The absolute subject, the "I," the self of Descartes, of idealism, of Kant's transcendental apperception, is never accessible to us. It is forever immanent in our conversations with others and ourselves, the sum total of our social experience.[19]

Sociality, however, penetrates consciousness and perception even more deeply. Not only can we not know ourselves without first being enmeshed in some form of symbolic social interaction, but our consciousness of things, of physical objects, post-dates our entrance into the conversation of gestures. For us an object can only be an object if it retains some meaning in the course of our practical activity. Since Mead argued that consciousness of meaning emerges from the play of gestures, then it would follow that consciousness of objects themselves depends upon social interaction. So Mead contended that "[w]hatever our theory may be as to the history of things, social consciousness must antedate physical consciousness" and that "experience in its original form became reflective in the recognition of selves, and only gradually was there differentiated a reflective experience of things which were purely physical."[20]

Thus, by 1910 Mead had demonstrated (to his *own* satisfaction) that consciousness is social and that the objects of our consciousness (including the self) are socially constructed. Sociability, concluded Mead, is not just grafted onto the experience of fully conscious, rational individuals already capable of prudent decisions (including the decision to recognize other people). Sociability developmentally precedes conscious rationality, individual self-identity, and even the objects between which individuals rationally or prudentially choose.

The Cloud of Witnesses. When providing an account of Mead's philosophical development, one should not willingly stop here. My purpose is not to defend or dress up Mead's theory but to show its contextual significance. As Dewey proclaimed in 1896, "the point of this story is in its application." It was no coincidence that Mead developed these theories while he was occupied with mediating conflicts between Chicago industrialists and their workers. Mead's discourse on social psychology was inaccessible to most participants in Chicago's class struggle, but Mead addressed his writing to the problems raised in that conflict as much as to the inadequacy of earlier social psychologies.[21]

Virtually all of the department's members participated in the social reform movements that flourished in Chicago after the 1890s. Dewey came to Chicago not only to head the department but also to establish his University Laboratory School from which to "reconstruct" society by fostering "democratic" education. Mead continued the struggle for democratic schools after Dewey's departure from Chicago in 1904. Mead's primary involvement in educational reform came through his membership in the City Club, a fraternal organization of Chicago professionals and small businessmen interested in progressive reform. Mead sat on and eventually chaired the club's educational committee, for which Mead directed an influential study on vocational and industrial education. Mead's involvement in social and labor reform, however, went far beyond school politics. Through the City Club Mead, together with his colleague James H. Tufts, also directly mediated labor-management conflicts in the city's industries. Mead helped negotiate a settlement to the garment strike of 1910; and although the agreement fell through, its principles became the basis for the model arbitration agreement of 1915 between the clothing workers and Hart, Schaffner, and Marx, the city's largest clothing manufacturer. Several years later Tufts sat on the arbitration board that supervised that agreement, which soon was extended to cover most of the major clothing firms in the city. As part of their crusade for the peaceful mediation of labor disputes, both Tufts and Mead earned reputations as consistent advocates for union recognition.[22]

As the struggled in the pages of learned journals to demonstrate the cooperative origins of all consciousness, Mead preached to Chicagoans the need for industrial cooperation and reciprocity between capital and labor. The key common term in Mead's psychology and his reform was "cooperation," or reciprocity. Mead called for cooperation between classes and opposing social groups, which would be based upon the reciprocity natural to human interaction and communication: "[T]he recognition of the given character of other selves" (i.e., the recognition of others as significant) comes "from psychology itself, and arises out of the psychological theory of the origin of language and its relation to meaning."[23]

Such a synthesis of psychology and social analysis became the hall-mark of Chicago's activist social psychology and a linchpin of later liberal political discourse. For Dewey the organic continuity of human action had suggested that the social conflict tearing Chicago apart, caused by the inadequate social organization of modern industrial society in general, reflected a break in the coherence of human psychology. The factory system and the market place had divided the psychological functions between different classes, thereby creating opponents in the political arena as well. Mead agreed. Industrial leaders controlled the "intellectual" functions of production, such as planning and evaluation. Their employees participated only as the hands, the final executors of social action.

Dewey and Mead depicted the social conflicts of their day in the psychological terms of the reflex-arc critique.

Labor and capital acted out on a social and political scale the circuit of psychological coordination that Dewey had proposed as an alternative to reflexology. Owners and managers pursued a conservative politics of a class unaffected by social ills, expressing a psychology of "rational" managerial planning. The responsibilities of management inclined them habitually to perpetuate hitherto successful forms of social conduct and organization, even when it was to the detriment of the city's manual workers.[24] Social problems, however, emerged from the habitual practice of a society run by an intellectual and economic elite. The working class responded to these problems as a class that experienced the injustices and hardships of industrialism directly. Having been denied intellectual training and control, workers (especially the unskilled) tended toward politics that expressed the essentially impulsive nature of manual activity, to the exclusion of political foresight. They haphazardly experimented with and projected, in radically utopian and revolutionary form, new social practices. This, according to both philosophers, was the nature of the "radicalism" that flourished in the working class districts of "red" Chicago, and that periodically enflamed (as the middle class saw it) social conflagrations such as the Haymarket incident or the Pullman strike. Yet this could be a functional relationship. Industrial management and political leadership conservatively protected social habits but conceded new, provisional practices under the demand of impulsive "radicalism." New practices that dealt with a problem successfully would be implemented as new habits. As Dewey argued in 1897, the two sides psychologically and socially needed each other and needed to resolve social conflict through reconciliation because it was only through the interpenetration of impulse and habit that psychological and social development could occur.[25]

Mead considered it especially urgent "to establish a theory of social reform among inductive science" that would mediate between "conservatism" and "utopian" revolution.[26] Without changing Dewey's political or philosophical assumptions, Mead deepened the elder philosopher's psychological explanation of social conflict. Not only is social reciprocity psychologically necessary to social order, but without it even human consciousness would be impossible. The thought which makes us human, what Mead called the "inner conversation," depends upon social cooperation and reciprocity even if it is only implicit in the evolution of human capacities.

In applying this psychology to politics, Mead and Dewey tried to balance impulse against reason, radical vision against conservative habit. The central feature of their social psychology was cooperation between social classes, each of which articulated a partially developed facet of human psychology. The goal for Mead and Dewey was "social control," but by that they meant a form of cooperative self-control through reciprocal agreements, such as the arbitration agreement that governed Chicago's garment industry in the teens. Such agreements required that opposing classes take the roles of their opponents, recognizing the other's perspective in

order to be able to find a new social practice acceptable to all and beneficial to a reconstructed social order. They should not, just as all social interactions should not, involve the imposition of authority or the imitation by subordinates of prescribed habits. "The important character of social organization of conduct or behavior through instincts is not that one form [i.e., one individual] in a social group does what the others do, but that the conduct of one form is a stimulus to another to a certain act, and that this act again becomes a stimulus to [the] first to a certain reaction, and so on in ceaseless interaction."[27] Social control, argued Mead, is the process of "constantly carrying about with us this self which is seen through the eyes of others" and subjecting that self-image to criticism.[28] As Mead's colleague, Edward S. Ames, declared, we live in a "cloud of witnesses." Our self-identities are determined by our interaction with people of different social stations, different ethical and political viewpoints, different personal needs, and, through literature, different eras.[29]

The world according to Mead was a Greek drama of roles and choruses, interacting, readjusting, and responding. Social life and language, maintained Mead, involve the "continued readjustment of one individual to another." So do social reconstruction and individual growth, the "play back and forth between the selves," between impulsive tendencies embodied in real individuals or in the imaginary voices of one's inner conversation, the real or imaginary cloud of witnesses.[30] Individual intellectual and moral development, in fact, is a form of social reconstruction; for while "the organization of this inner social consciousness is a reflex of the organization of the outer world," the individual nonetheless strains to "reconstruct" the conflicting chorus of his consciousness. As the individual comes to terms with his conflicting social roles, he proposes a new order to the society as well.[31]

Mead's social conception of the "self" and his commitment to social reconstruction have led historians to link Mead's theory with European social democracy. Like the European socialists, Mead insisted that the labor movement and its social democratic leaders most effectively contributed to "reconstructing" society. Social democratic labor, guided by theorists such as Ferdinand Lasalle, created a situation "in which people *had* to put themselves in the place of others." Labor *demanded* reciprocity, a voice in the chorus, and therefore, through the constructive expression of worker demands, "forced communities to think in social terms" and individuals to "put themselves into other people's places."[32]

Labor's demands encouraged constructive social reform in yet another manner peculiar to the role workers played in industrial society. A capitalist economy, Mead argued, distorted human social psychology by forcing everyone to enter practical, industrial relations through the exchange of money, as wages and profits, on the marketplace. Consequently, the industrialist who does not actually work in the factory he owns can no longer understand the actual social relations involved in manufacturing, nor can he grasp the "human products of the process," the hardships and injustices of industrialism. Rather than put himself in the place of others, the industrialist calculates the bottom line of his ledger book.

The industrialist's pecuniary narrowmindedness, his inability to understand the factory system in social rather than merely economic terms, leads him to adopt a narrow and abstract philosophy of life, hedonism, the calculation of one's own pleasure and pain without regard to others and without a real understanding of the objects he finds pleasurable.[33] While the industrialist may have a practical understanding of the economy and of money, he has little understanding of the practicalities of life in the concrete. This side of experience is reserved in limited form for the industrialist's workers, who produce society's goods. In such a situation a barrier is erected between people, deep within the social psychology of industrial life. Mead had argued that the natural form of practical activity involves the coordination of present experience and future possibility. In perception this coordination occurs, Mead continued, between the "contact stimuli" of touch and ingestion and the "distance stimuli" of seeing and hearing. For animals this coordination is fairly primitive and immediate, involving little inhibition of impulse or delay of gratification. For humans the coordination of distance and contact stimuli occurs within the matrix of social communication by means of linguistic signs. Objects originally took form in the consciousness of primitive men (and children) because of this social "situation."[34]

Mead did not present this last facet of his theory directly as a social psychological critique of industrialism, but one can piece together some of its political implications without too much conjecture. Through history the experience of contact and distance stimuli became divided between classes or castes or, in the best of times, between people occupying different functional roles. Workers handled the concrete objects of social existence, while elite castes and intellectuals understood the world in abstract terms. To the latter the calculation of the future came easy. But the exigencies of the present, the direct contact with industrial life, lay beyond their experience. So in order to become perceptually and psychologically whole, the rationality of the businessman had to be united through communication and reciprocal cooperation with the manual practicality of the industrial worker.[35]

While championing the labor movement, however, Mead rejected European socialist theories of revolutionary class conflict. If the occupation of separate roles amounted to a significant or enduring conflict, something would be socially and psychologically wrong. If we should perceive ourselves as members of a class or caste, then our efforts (to pursue radical social change or promote a limited social interest) would defy the natural development of social relations. For Mead and his colleagues class conflict was a vestige of primitive societies governed by military practices in which people identified themselves exclusively as members of a clan, caste, or nation.[36]

Going even further than this historical condemnation, Mead held class consciousness disrupted our natural social and psychological growth. When an individual belongs to a caste, he is unable to take the role of someone from another caste, for that is precluded by the rules of caste membership: "Where there is a fixed, stratified society, a person does not present himself in the form of another. . . ." This inability to assume another's role prevents the caste member from reconciling conflicts in the caste system. One can no longer reform the social order because "there is no social problem" to reform (that is, it is not recognized) and because one is not able to reconcile unassumed roles. Nor does one hear an inner conversation between opposing selves because that ability requires assuming the roles of socially significant "others." Thus, personal development is also limited. Someone who is unable to "enter into the place of the other" is, Mead insisted, "intellectually deficient." "Inability to put yourself in the place of another puts up a barrier, prevents grasping of the social situation at all. The process of clear and adequate thinking is the process of putting one's self completely in the place of the other. The process of thought is simply the abstraction of this social procedure."[37] The object of constructive social conflict is "such a reconstruction of the situation that different and enlarged and more adequate personalities may emerge." The new social situation is truly reconstructed only if "all the personal interests are adequately recognized" and if one has a "new world harmonizing the conflicting interests into which enters the new self." It is only under the conditions in which individuals assume roles integrated in a harmonious social whole that truly "democratic consciousness" occurs.[38]

In a normally developing social "situation," opposing social roles simply represented conflicting but reconcilable social functions. This ability to achieve consensus in any conflict, Mead believed, existed on the most fundamental psychological and linguistic level. Humans form their conceptions of the world through the reconciliation of conflicting stimuli. An example from Dewey's 1896 essay illustrated Mead's point. A child confronted with a flame, Dewey had argued, "reconstructs" his understanding of the flame by playing with it. At first the child is attracted by the flame, as if it were a toy. The child fits the flame into a set of perceptions that do not distinguish flames from toys. More importantly, habitually *behaving* as though the flame were a toy, the child grabs the flame and is burned. Now at this point (or after a few more attempts) the child has learned that the flame is a flame, that is to say, a bright, shiny, but dangerous and painful object. But, Dewey asked, what *exactly* has the child learned? Dewey analyzed the problem as a process of adjusting habitual behavior to new, problematic stimuli. The child can treat the flame as a toy until interacting with it as if it were a toy, and this makes painfully problematic the *habit* of playing with all bright objects. The child deals with that problem by coming up with a new set of ideas and habits that distinguish *behaviorally* between toys and flames.[39]

Mead looked at the problem from a slightly different angle, as a situation in which the child is trying to reconcile two opposing perceptions or conceptions (of the object as plaything and of the object as dangerous) and therefore two different *roles.* After initially being burned the child now has two objects in the field of consciousness, the flame as bright shiny toy-like object and the flame as dangerous. When the child comes up with a new habit of dealing with flames and similar objects, he or she is learning to perceive the object in a more complete way by finding an object that combines the earlier two: the flame looks like a toy but burns like a flame. In this way the child reconciles contradictions faced in his or her experience. Up to here Mead did not significantly expand Dewey's theory. But Mead, dissatisfied, asked, how does this happen? How can the child do this but not, say, a dog? Animals could not perceive objects as men do. "[T]here is a conscious construction which men carry out that we do not find in the lower animals," contended Mead. "There is an ability to hold in consciousness the conflicting stimulations and tendencies to respond in a conflicting fashion."

We can perceive objects clearly because we are able to see ourselves from more perspectives than one. Our conflicting versions of the object before us, our conflicting sets of raw data, our hypotheses, really represent conflicting responses we might make to given stimuli. Our ability to see those responses comes from our ability to view ourselves in different roles, the role, for example, of the child avoiding flames or, alternatively, the role of the child burning his fingers. Our process of reflection, of forming hypotheses (and habits), argued Mead, amounts to "our own responses to our own replies to these conflicting stimuli." Thought is a "field of discourse, a social field." But it is a process in which we reconcile all opposing tendencies, all roles. It is a process of achieving agreement between the conflicting voices.[40] Our ability to reason and act rationally, then, depends upon our natural ability to reconcile opposing voices within the cloud of witnesses that constitutes our consciousness. This "self" construction, the creation of new roles out of old conflicting ones, is fundamentally human. It is also naturally "cooperative," conciliatory, and social, in the manner Mead prescribed for opposing social groups.

The Twilight of Cooperation. Mead's manner of naturalizing social reconciliation, of course, presented serious problems. First, the changing context of Chicago's political and social conflicts clouded the notions of cooperation and reciprocity employed by Mead and his colleagues. Early in the reform movement the demand for reciprocity implied a radical change in the relationship between the city's economic elite and the laboring poor. "Cooperation," as Mead saw it, in fact all normal human interaction, required giving a voice (in the social chorus and the inner conversation) to the as yet voiceless victims of the factory system. In the context of the 1890s giving workers a voice would have been liberating. More substantially, industrial mediation and workplace cooperation entailed, at the very least, union recognition and suggested that employees should participate in the management of their workplaces. However conservative many unions actually were, calling for open recognition

of their right to bargain collectively for industrial workers was still a fairly radical proposal.[41]

But times changed, and as the business leaders of Chicago realized that new forms of industrial organization would be necessary to maintain social order and economic stability, the meaning of "cooperation" shifted in a conservative direction. Gradually, reformers succeeded in making the political system more responsive to the demands of the city's poor. Such was the case in the arbitration of labor disputes and in the regulation of housing and public utilities. These improvements, however, were limited in scope and on terms set by the city's business leaders. To the extent that "cooperation" began to govern industrial and urban relations, it confined working class aspirations as much as it gave voice to their demands for a true industrial and urban democracy.

This result, however, should not have surprised anyone. The ambiguous legacy of cooperative social reform was latent in reform ideology and rhetoric as expressed in the general political discourse and in the more specific writings of intellectuals like Mead. From the start Chicago's social groups contested the notions of industrial democracy and social cooperation employed by Mead and others. The working class used "cooperation" to promote workers' power in various workplaces. The city's industrial leaders, on the other hand, used "cooperation" and similar words to demand greater responsibility from Chicago's working class.

Nowhere was this clearer than in the city school system, where the militant Chicago Teachers Federation (CTF) demanded teachers' councils that would control curriculum and administration of the schools. The initial dispute arose over the dispensation of tax money and the level of teachers' salaries, issues raised by the fledgling CTF led by union activist and political radical Margaret Haley. Haley and the union, however, soon broadened their movement. Haley considered the Chicago school board's perennial campaigns for teaching efficiency and centralization of authority part of a broader attack by a corporate elite on democratic institutions. The school, Haley argued, is the training ground of future citizens. Unless they are taught by autonomous teachers, those students will simply be groomed for roles as factory operatives and servants. A truly democratic school system should remain under the control of teachers and the lower level district superintendents, who, unlike the central administrators, were usually former teachers. Workplace and educational reciprocity, from Haley's point of view, involved genuinely participatory and democratic control of work and schooling.[42]

More conservative reformers, however, often allied with commercial and business organizations, spoke differently of educational democracy and cooperation. The city's civic and business leaders had to contend with an educational system unsuited to the needs of a city rapidly growing in population and territory. Their solution, centralization, suited the ideological predilections of the business elite. A powerful school super-intendent during the first decade of the century, Edwin Cooley, promoted the centralization program. Like the teachers, Cooley used the rhetoric of reciprocity and cooperation. But for Cooley cooperation meant responsibility and the submission to the larger and more centralized plans of the community, represented by Chicago's Commercial Club. Teachers had to cooperate with the school board, cease irresponsible demands (such as teachers' councils), and recognize the rational forms of social and educational administration which civic leaders thought right and just. Not surprisingly, an essential part of Cooley's, the Commercial Club's and the school board's program was removing the teachers' union, and this was successfully achieved with the passage in 1916 of the notorious "Loeb rule" outlawing teachers' organizations.[43]

By no means did Dewey and his colleagues attack corporate leaders with Haley's vehemence or invective, but they made common cause with Haley, the CTF, and the local labor movement in several important educational disputes. In 1908 Chicago's business leaders began, as part of their effort to centralize decisions over public school curriculum, to promote public vocational education. Ironically, vocationalism built upon an already existing movement led by Dewey and Mead calling for education relevant to the needs and interests of the laboring poor. Industrial education and manual training, Mead and Dewey believed, would foster reciprocity between classes by engaging the interests of working-class children more effectively and by mediating in a common school system between the children of conflicting classes. Business vocationalism, however, strove to construct a school system divided into intellectual and industrial tracks, an unacceptable arrangement for the Chicago philosophers, teachers, and the city's labor movement. From 1908 until 1917, when federal statutes made the issue moot, Mead and his colleagues lobbied against the vocational education promoted by Chicago's industrial elite.[44] They also frequently argued for teachers' autonomy from administration and from commercial interests (including textbook publishers). The only educators sensitive enough to devise a truly child-centered common school curriculum, argued Dewey, were those in close daily contact with the students.[45] Mead supported the right of the teachers' union to bargain collectively for its members as well as for the principle of teachers' control and even advocated (provisionally) the creation of teachers' councils. But like Cooley, Mead expected a level of responsibility from the teachers that they were not willing or able to give, particularly in the political context of the 'teens, when the school board's assault on teachers' autonomy was most intense. In 1907 Margaret Haley did not cooperate fully with a temporarily liberal (but still centralizing) school board, and this indicated to Mead that the Chicago Teachers' Federation was not holding up its end of the bargain. The teachers, of course, saw it differently.[46]

Similarly, both Mead and colleague James Tufts expected of labor leaders and their union members an un-

reasonable level of social and economic responsibility. Even though in 1908 Mead advocated moderate forms of workers' self-management, it was contingent upon proper education to the responsibilities of "social control" and rational self-control. Later, Mead bitterly criticized labor's unwillingness to cooperatively forgo wage increases while their employers profited heavily from war production. He was equally unhappy with labor's heightened demands after the war, when it was clear that corporations had enriched themselves in the previous two years, while wages and benefits had stagnated. Mead could only complain that American labor had not reached the level of responsibility or political awareness of their British counterparts.[47]

Oddly, Mead left little room in his social psychology for the persistent and irreconcilable conflicts that characterized the Chicago context. As a result, his expectations for cooperative reforms were unrealistic, psychologically as well as politically. As critics have pointed out, while Mead tried to explain the emergence of rationality, he presumed an already rational individual subject as a starting point. Why was it necessarily the case that individuals would be able to reconcile opposing voices in their inner conversation or in the outer cloud of witnesses, in their consciousnesses or in the social environment? Why not the persistence of psychological conflict or psychosis? The persistent social disorder of modern America might be better explained by a theory that assumed a fundamentally irrational and coercive self rather than a rational conciliatory one.[48]

Mead's social psychology only explained a limited set of social relations, those in which parties agree beforehand that rational and amicable resolutions of conflict shall be reached. Knowledge of the other's role is no guarantee of ethical reciprocity, which insures that the knower will act for that other's benefit. The knower may, if he is a confidence man or a thief who is skilled at sizing up his mark, use that knowledge to gain a selfish advantage. The same principle applied to advertising (emerging at the time Mead wrote), especially that which used knowledge of consumer desires and needs to manipulate buying.

A more pertinent case for Mead involved the managers of Chicago industry with whom he negotiated on behalf of the city's working class. By the 1920s many industrialists, repudiating the hedonism of classical economics, tried more sophisticated, "corporate" personnel policies, enlisting the expertise of men and women educated or influenced by professors at the University of Chicago (for example, Earl Dean Howard, one of Tufts' former students and Hart, Schaffner, and Marx's spokesman in the clothing arbitration agreement of 1915). By the 1920s, a form of capitalist relations within the corporation developed that applied some of the notions (though not necessarily self-consciously) of reciprocity and cooperation championed by Mead and his colleagues. The rise of welfare capitalism, which incorporated social psychology into workplace management, did not truly involve the kind of "expanded self" Mead had in mind but rather allowed factory managers to control workplace relations in the pursuit of higher profits.[49]

The relevance of Mead's psychology to the political context was its strong suit, but paradoxically it was at that intersection of politics and psychology that we find its greatest weakness. We can find part of its failure in the fact that by 1917 the Chicago philosophers had been beguiled by the success of progressive reform institutions. That success, in the case of labor arbitration for example, was limited only to opening dialogue between the leaders of opposing social groups and classes. Dialogue gave a voice to the previously voiceless, but it was not enough. Unfortunately, the outcome of social conflict was usually decided not reciprocally but by the unbalance of power in favor of dominant classes and groups. The laboring poor and others could only exert limited influence over their own future.

In the specific political context of Chicago at the end of the Gilded Age, Mead and his colleagues found themselves in a dilemma. Their political universe rapidly polarized between conflicting social forces, each interpreting America's political heritage and political lexicon differently. While the Chicago philosophers preached some form of liberation for those suffering the worst excesses and restrictions of the industrial system, they also preached restraint and tried, whenever possible, to mediate class differences rather than take "sides" in industrial conflicts. So although they criticized unrestricted capitalism, Mead and his colleagues cautiously avoided the radical socialism and anarchism of the urban working class. Their centrist position in the political sphere worked its way into the Chicago philosophy as a broader political and philosophical ambivalence. This ambivalence shaped their theory.

We can find another source of Mead's failure, however, in the philosophy itself. Mead and his colleagues believed that a rational social order based on cooperation and reciprocity lay immanent in the present, in the actual social and political relations of late nineteenth-century America. Since the days when Dewey wrote apologetics for the liberal churches, the Chicago philosophers had argued that values are immanent in what exists. This meant that scientific study could elucidate values, goals latent in a factual present—more specifically, that Mead could indeed find, through the exploration of biologically based psychology, the seeds of social cooperation in the necessary conditions for human consciousness.

The philosophical immanence of values also meant, however, that the ethical goals of social reform could only be found by determining what ideals were realistic. Thus, Mead and his colleagues demanded that no utopia guide the politics of the present, that radically "impulsive" visions of the future should not dictate terms to the habits of the past. And yet their own belief in cooperation and reciprocity hardly conformed to the reality of social relations. The gradual improvement of society through cooperation and reciprocity did not lie within the grasp of the

present. It needed some kind of vision as a guide to dialogue, a greater witness above the cloud of witnesses, a conversationalist outside the inner and outer conversation.

Paradoxically this dilemma led Mead simultaneously to embrace and deny utopian advocacy. Almost in desperation Mead and his colleagues continually sought guidance from institutions and political leadership that stood above the fray, whether from labor leaders sufficiently "responsible" or political "visionaries" like Woodrow Wilson, who preached something resembling Christian reciprocity but meant something quite different. In 1917, showing remarkable naiveté about the behavior of the politically powerful, the entire department supported the war effort. They actively contributed to a propaganda machine that squelched criticism and rationalized the widespread suspension of civil liberties.[50] Consistently, Mead and his colleagues turned to the state as the source of "cooperative" authority despite the fact that the state and its subsidiary institutions usually lay in the control of one party to a dispute and, as the behavior of Wilson's Justice Department in 1919 demonstrated, were far from sensitive to the needs and desires of its critics.

When viewed in the context of turn-of-the-century political and social conflict, then, one sees in Mead's writing two "souls" created by the contradictions of the theory and of the moment. On the one hand Mead demanded a dialogue, democratically freeing the voices immanent in industrial Chicago. On the other hand he advocated stifling those voices that tried to rise above the dialogue when it became fruitless to continue discussion. The fact that the dialogue could not continue fit neither with Mead's original intention nor with the theory he constructed to solve the problems of social conflict and injustice.

NOTES

[1] Two published biographical studies known to me as of this writing have contributed greatly to our understanding of Mead but focus primarily on the explication of his published works. David Miller, *George Herbert Mead: Self, Language and the World* (Austin, 1973); Hans Joas, *G. H. Mead: A Contemporary Reexamination of his Thought* (Cambridge, 1985), has done the most to place Meadian theory in social context; and see his introduction for a survey of the literature. For a very different interpretation from the one presented in this essay, see Stephen Diner, *A City and its Universities* (Chapel Hill, 1980), 5, 36-43, 86-129, 149-50; and "George Herbert Mead and Reform in Chicago" (unpublished 1973 manuscript at Chicago Historical Society).

[2] Daniel Rodgers, *Contested Truths* (New York, 1987), Prologue.

[3] Joas, 10; Diner, *A City and its Universities*, 25, 59, 89; Dmitri Shalin, "G. H. Mead, Socialism and the Progressive Agenda," *American Journal of Sociology*, 93 (1988), 913-51.

[4] For a fuller account see my "Between Head and Hand: Chicago Pragmatism and social reform, 1886-1919" (Ph.D. diss., University of Pennsylvania, 1987), chapters 4 and 6.

[5] Dewey, "The Reflex-Arc Concept in Psychology," *Psychological Review,* 3 (1896), repr. in Jo Ann Boydston et al. (eds.), *John Dewey, The Early Works* (5 vols.; Carbondale, 1973), (hereafter referred to as *EW* with volume number), V, 96-109; Dewey, *Psychology* (New York, 1891), reprinted as *EW* II, *passim;* Dewey, "Soul and Body," *Bibliotheca Sacra,* 43 (1886), reprinted in *EW* I, 96-98.

[6] Dewey argued this case in many essays. A few are: John Dewey, "Evolution and Ethics," *Monist,* 8 (1898), repr. in *EW* IV, 3-11; Dewey, *The Ethics of Democracy* (Ann Arbor, 1888), repr. in *EW* I, 227-52; Dewey, *Outlines of a Critical Theory of Ethics* (Ann Arbor, 1891), repr. in *EW* III, 239-338. For a full discussion of Dewey's interest in liberal theology and the Social Gospel see Daniel Day Williams, *The Andover Liberals* (New York, 1941), passim; Bruce Kuklick, *Churchmen and Philosophers* (New Haven, 1985), 191-98; Feffer, chapters 2-4.

[7] Dewey, "The Reflex-arc Concept in Psychology," 109.

[8] Thus Dewey opened his philosophy to the long prevailing interpretation of it as a form of utilitarian Darwinism. See, e.g., Gail Kennedy, "The Pragmatic Naturalism of Chauncey Wright," *Studies in the History of Ideas,* III (3 vols.; New York, 1935), 486, 503; also Philip Wiener, "Chauncey Wright's Defense of Darwin and the Neutrality of Science," *JHI,* 6 (1945), 27; Dewey, *The Study of Ethics: a Syllabus* (Ann Arbor, 1894), repr. in *EW* IV, 338-39.

[9] For some reason Joas does not trace Mead's interest in sociability to Dewey, Joas, Chapter 3. Mead's personal odyssey from devout but troubled son of a Congregationalist minister reveals much about the roots of his social theory in late-nineteenth century religious conflict. See Robert Crunden, *Ministers of Reform* (New York, 1982), chapter 1; Feffer, 55-75.

[10] Wilhelm Wundt, *Völkerpsychologie* (2 vols.; Leipzig, 1900), I, Einleitung; Mead, "The Relations of Psychology and Philology," *Psychological Bulletin,* 1 (1904), 377.

[11] *Ibid,* 380, 382.

[12] Mead, "Social Psychology as Counterpart to Physiological Psychology," *Psychological Bulletin,* 6 (1909), 406.

[13] Mead, "1914 Class Lectures in Social Psychology," *The Individual and the Social Self* (Chicago, 1982), 37.

[14] Mead, "What Social Objects Must Psychology Presuppose?," *Journal of Philosophy,* 7 (1910), 176.

[15] Mead, "1914 Class Lectures in Social Psychology," 40; Dewey, "A Theory of Emotion," *Psychological Review,* 1 (1894), 2 (1895), reprinted in *EW* IV, 152-88.

[16] Mead, "Social Psychology as a Counterpart to Physiological Psychology," 407.

[17] Mead, "Social Consciousness and the Consciousness of Meaning," *Psychological Bulletin,* 7 (1910), 399; Mead, "Social Psychology as Counterpart to Physiological Psychology," 407.

[18] Mead, "What Social Objects Must Psychology Presuppose?," 179. "We are conscious of our attitudes because they are responsible for the changes in the conduct of other individuals," wrote Mead: "Social Consciousness and the Consciousness of Meaning," 403; see also "1914 Lectures on Social Psychology," 46.

[19] Mead, "The Mechanism of Social Consciousness," *Journal of Philosophy,* 9 (1912), 405-6.

[20] Mead, "What Social Objects Must Psychology Presuppose?," 180.

[21] Dewey, "The Reflex-arc Concept in Psychology," 109.

[22] Feffer, chapter 8; Shalin, 924.

[23] Mead, "What Social Objects Must Psychology Presuppose?," 177.

[24] Mead, "Industrial Education, the Working Man and the School," *Elementary-School Teacher,* 9 (1908-9), 369-83; Mead, "1914 Class Lectures in Social Psychology," 86-93; James H. Tufts and John Dewey, *Ethics* (New York, 1908), ch. 12 (written by Tufts).

[25] Dewey, *The Significance of the Problem of Knowledge* (Chicago, 1897), repr. in *EW* V, 4-24.

[26] Mead, "The Working Hypothesis in Social Reform," *American Journal of Sociology,* 5 (1899), 367.

[27] Mead, "Social Psychology as Counterpart to Physiological Psychology," 406.

[28] Mead, "1914 Class Lectures on Social Psychology," 72.

[29] Edward S. Ames, *The Higher Individualism* (Boston, 1915), 67-71.

[30] Mead, "1914 Class Lectures on Social Psychology," 43, 75.

[31] *Ibid.,* 74; Mead, "The Social Self," *Journal of Philosophy,* 10 (1913), 377.

[32] Mead, "1914 Class Lectures on Social Psychology," 98.

[33] *Ibid.,* 96-97, 100.

[34] Mead, "Concerning Animal Perception," *Psychological Review,* 14 (1907), 383-90.

[35] Mead, "1914 Class Lectures on Social Psychology," 100.

[36] Tufts and Dewey, *Ethics,* 500; Mead, "1914 Class Lectures on Social Psychology," 87.

[37] *Ibid.,* 68, 95.

[38] Mead, "The Social Self," 379; Mead, "1914 Class Lectures on Social Psychology," 95.

[39] Dewey, "The Reflex-arc Concept in Philosophy," 97-99.

[40] Mead, "1914 Class Lectures on Social Psychology," 52-53, 77.

[41] Edwin Witte, *Historical Survey of Labor Arbitration* (Philadelphia, 1952), 3-4.

[42] Margaret Haley to Jane Addams, May 4, 1906, Anita McCormick Blaine Papers, Wisconsin Historical Society; *Bulletin* of the Chicago Teachers' Federation, number 35, September 25, 1903, 4.

[43] Marjorie Murphy, "From Artisan to Semi-professional: White Collar Unionism Among Chicago Public School Teachers, 1870-1930," (Ph.D. diss., University of California, Davis, 1981), passim; Edwin G. Cooley, *Vocational Education in Europe* (Chicago, 1912); Minutes for November 23, 1908 of City Club Committee on Education (City Club Papers, Chicago Historical Society).

[44] Mead, "Introduction," *A Report on Vocational Training in Chicago* (Chicago, 1912); Feffer, 294-316; Sol Cohen, "The Industrial Education Movement, 1906-17," *American Quarterly,* 20 (1968), 95-110.

[45] Dewey, "The Educational Situation," *School Journal* (1901), repr. in *John Dewey, The Middle Works* (Carbondale, 1977), 272; see also Ella Flagg Young, *Isolation in the Schools* (Chicago, 1901), 75 and passim, for a classic and often cited statement of the Deweyan position; also Young, untitled article in the *Bulletin* of the Chicago Teachers' Federation, vol. II, no. 32, May 22, 1903.

[46] Mead, "The Educational Situation in the Chicago Public Schools," City Club *Bulletin,* 1 (1907), 132-35; George H. Mead to Helen Castle Mead, July, 1906 (Mead Papers, Regenstein Library, University of Chicago).

[47] Mead, "Industrial Education, the Working-man and the School," 380-83. "Labor is being difficult," Mead wrote to his daughter-in-law, Irene Tufts Mead, about labor demands for higher wages, George H. Mead to Irene Tufts Mead, July 18, 1919; see also Mead's correspondence to Irene T. Mead for August 26, 27, and 29 and for September 6, 1919 (Mead Papers, Regenstein Library, University of Chicago).

[48] Julian Henriques, et al, *Changing the Subject* (London, 1984), 17-19, 23.

[49] Richard Edwards, *Contested Terrain* (New York, 1979), passim; Dewey was indirectly involved in an early experiment in such welfare capitalism, one which management approached with little sincerity and which degenerated into a means of breaking a later strike. Robert Ozanne, *A Century of Labor-Management Relations at McCormick and International Harvester* (Madison, 1967), 41-43; also James Weinstein, *The Corporate Ideal in the Liberal State* (Boston, 1968), ch. 1.

[50] See, for example, Mead, *The Conscientious Objector* (New York, 1918); Tufts recounted his war activities in a letter to Ralph Ricker, October 31, 1937 (Tufts Papers, Frost Library, Amherst College).

Sandra B. Rosenthal (essay date 1992)

SOURCE: "Free Selves, Enriched Values, and Experimental Method: Mead's Pragmatic Synthesis," in *International Philosophical Quarterly,* Vol. XXXII, No. 1, March, 1992, pp. 79-93.

[*In the following essay, Rosenthal views the intertwining of Mead's notions of individuality, freedom, and creativity with biological activity and experimental method as imperative for a full understanding of his concept of self.*]

The philosophy of G. H. Mead is firmly rooted within the mainstream of classical American pragmatism. He maintained an ongoing philosophic exchange with John Dewey over a period of many years, and as part of the Chicago school of pragmatism was influenced from various directions by scholars working in the context of this tradition. His appropriation of pragmatism, however, took it in new directions, and the originality of his ideas contributed greatly to its further development. His writings on the nature of the self have been an important focus of interest not just for philosophers but for sociologists and social psychologists as well.

The characterization of Mead as a behavioral and social psychologist, combined with his strong pragmatic emphasis on the importance of scientific method and the biological approach to human activity, has too often led to interpretive tendencies which involve an inadequate grasp of the role of individuality, freedom, and creativity in his concept of the self as cognitive and social. And, along with this there is the concomitant inadequate grasp of the nature of the value situation and of his understanding of scientific method itself. Yet, if the biological dimension and the import of scientific method are ignored in the attempt to grasp his cognitive, social self, then the status of individuality, freedom, and creativity, as well as the adequacy of his understanding of the value situation, are again brought into question, though from a different direction. Oddly, both lines of criticism stem from a peculiar separation of the cognitive self from its biological aspects. The following integration is intended to explore Mead's understanding of freely developing selves and the expansion and enrichment of values by utilizing the full import of the inseparable intertwining of these features with biological activity and experimental method.

For Mead, all knowledge and experience are infused with interpretive aspects, funded with past experience. This interpretive dimension of human activity involves a creative organization of experience which directs the way we focus on experience and which is tested by its workability in directing the ongoing course of future activities. Experience is experimental for Mead in that the very nature of human activity involves selective creative activity guided by direction and noetically transformative of its environment. Truth emerges in the process of experimental activity within a common world when problematic situations are resolved by restructuring a part of the world that is there in ways that work, that allow ongoing conduct, which had been stopped by a conflict of meanings, to continue.[1] In this sense, "truth is synonymous with the solution of the problem."[2] The adequacy of the application of any hypothesis, of any bestowing of meaning within experience, from the most abstract articulations of science to the most prereflective behavioral grasp of things in the world, lies in the ongoing conduct of the biological organism immersed in the natural world. In this way, when we act in a certain manner, what we expect to happen does in fact occur. The achievement of this, Mead stresses, is the function of scientific method.[3]

The very emergence of rudimentary intelligent activity embodies the pragmatic understanding of experience as experimental, as incorporating the rudimentary dynamics of experimental or scientific or instrumental method, for it involves "a continual meeting and solving of problems," and thus "we can find in this intelligence, even in its lowest expression, an instance of what we call 'scientific method.'"[4] Mead's focus on behavior in the context of scientific method is not an attempt to reduce human behavior to the second level objectifications of the contents of science but to show that the lived experience of scientific activity is continuous with, and emerges from, the behavioral dynamics embedded within the very structure of human activity.[5]

The anticipatory nature of experience as experimental leads to the interplay of gestures among interacting organisms in dealing with problematic situations. And, in this interplay of gestures and the taking of the role of the other which this involves, minds and selves emerge. Mind, thinking, and selfhood are not aspects of some mental substance. Neither, however, are they reducible to the material functioning of the brain and the nervous system. Mind, thinking, and selfhood are emergent levels of activity of organisms within nature. Meaning emerges in the interactions among conscious organisms, in the adjustments and coordinations needed for cooperative action in the social context. Mental processes are part of a process that is going on between organism and environment, and language itself is possible because of the communicative interactions on which the existence of meaning is based. In communicative interaction, individuals take the perspective of the other in the development of their conduct, and in this way there develops the common content which provides community of meaning. To have a self is to have a particular type of ability, the ability to be aware of one's behavior as part of the social process of adjustment, to be aware of oneself as a social object, as an acting agent within the context of other acting agents. Not only can selves exist only in relationship to other selves, but no absolute line can be drawn between our own selves and the selves of others, since our own selves are there for and in our experience only in so far as others exist and enter into our experience. The origins and foundation of the self, like those of mind, are social or intersubjective.

In incorporating the perspective of, or taking the role of, the other, the developing self comes to take the perspective of others in the group as a whole. In this way the self comes to incorporate the standards and authority of the group, the organization or system of attitudes and responses which Mead terms "the generalized other"; there is a passive dimension to the self, that aspect of the self Mead refers to as the "me." Yet, in responding to the perspective of the other, it is this individual as a unique center of activity that responds; there is a creative dimension to the self, which Mead refers to as the "I." Any self thus incorporates, by its very nature, both the conformity of the group perspective and the creativity of its unique individual perspective. The "me," then, represents the conformity of the self to the past and to the norms and practices of society, while the "I" represents the unique, creative dimension of the self as it operates in a funded present, rich with possibilities emerging from a sedimented past and oriented toward an indefinite future. Thus, the tensions between tradition and change, conformity and individuality, conservative and liberating forces, emerge as two dynamically interacting poles constitutive of the very nature of selfhood. Mead's understanding of the self as dialogical, as consisting of an ongoing internal dialogue between the "I" and the "me," incorporates these bi-polar dynamics into the very nature of reflective awareness. Not only is experience inherently perspectival, creatively interpretive, but this perspectival creativity is built into the very nature of selfhood. The self consists of a creative ongoing interpretive interplay between the individual and social perspective, and it can thus be anticipated that freedom of the self will be found, in a general sense, to lie in the proper relation between these two poles.

It is precisely here, however, that the adequacy of Mead's understanding of creativity and freedom begins to be questioned, and from two diverse directions. First, there are the widely accepted claims that Mead is, in spite of his talk about freedom, a social determinist because of his emphasis on the generalized other, the "me" component of the self. This type of criticism comes often from interpreters of Mead in the areas of psychology and sociology, but it is also to be found in the interpretations of philosophers.[6] And, coming from a different direction, Mead's understanding of creativity and freedom are found lacking because, as one recent critic has concisely stated the supposed problem, on the one hand Mead views the "I" as merely a functional or fictional distinction, while on the other hand he views it as the source of real novelty and as rescuing us from determinism.[7] There is, however, no problem if one takes seriously Mead's claim that the distinction between the "I" and the "me" is functional in that it is made "from the point of view of conduct itself."[8] The "I" and the "me" represent "two distinguishable phases" (*MSS* 177) of the ongoing conduct of a concrete organism. The "I" and the "me" emerge as two dimensions of the concrete subject which, in its vital functioning as creativity passing into sedimentation, provides the ontological grounding for the sense of the cognitive or dialogical stretch. It is perhaps the very pervasiveness of the functioning of corporeal activity in Mead's understanding of the self that causes it to be so often and so oddly overlooked. The following discussion will briefly explore this too often overlooked ontological grounding of the dialogical nature of the self.

Mead holds that the social aspect of the self, "the me," the incorporation of the generalized other, arises before the "I" aspect can emerge. One has an "I" only over against or in relation to the "me." The "I" pole emerges subsequent to the "me" pole as its correlate, and the internal conversation between the "I" and the "me" that is the voice of the other becomes possible. As Mead carefully points out, however, "though the voice is the voice of another, the source of it all is one's self—the organized group of impulses which I have called the biologic individual" (*MSS* 372). As he states, "I have termed it 'biologic' because the term lays emphasis on the living reality which may be distinguished from reflection" (*MSS* 353). And, as he characterizes the biologic individual, "this self adjusted to its social environment, and through this to the world at large, is the object" (*MSS* 371).

The term "biologic individual" then, as used by Mead in the above context, is the self in its primordial biological dimension, the concrete, decentered subject in its living reality as the source of reflective awareness and hence of the I-me poles of internal dialogue. It is prior to and the source of the cognitive I-me distinction, prior to its appropriation of itself as an object of reflection, as both knower and known. It is the lived body as intentional and social, the concrete decentered subject which is prior to reflection but which, once reflection has arisen, is appropriated as a "me" by an "I." Mead's reference to the *source of* the cognitive relation as in any sense a self may appear somewhat strange, for the self, for Mead, is essentially cognitive,[9] consisting of the nature of a dialogue between the "I" and the "me." Yet, this label is in another sense most appropriate, for the functioning of the con-

crete subject which gives rise to the I-me cognitive dynamics of the self is not discarded when the reflective self arises in experience. It is never discarded but subtends such dynamics; it is not just genetically prior to the cognitive self but logically prior in its ongoing dynamics. Thus, the concrete subject, as that which underlies the I-me distinction, is a dimension of the self, the "living reality" which pervades reflection, and it partakes of the general features of temporality which Mead attributes to the universe in general, the features of creativity passing into sedimentation, of adjustments which render the novel emergent continuous with the past out of which it has arisen. The past both conditions and adjusts to the emergent novelty of the present, while what is taking place in the present adjusts to the future as the oncoming event.[10]

Here it is important to distinguish between ambiguous uses of "the body" in Mead's writings. Mead holds, that "we can distinguish very definitely between the self and the body. . . . It is perfectly true that the eye can see the foot, but it does not see the body as a whole. . . . The parts of the body are quite distinguishable from the self. . . . The body does not experience itself as a whole, in the sense in which the self in some way enters into the experience of the self" (*MSS* 136). The phenomenological sense of the lived body, however, is not something partially grasped by sight, the body as something that I have. Rather it is something that is a lived unity grasped as a whole in experience, the body that I am, the body that is an expression of selfhood. This is what Mead intends when he stresses that the self "must be related to the entire body."[11] Mead's focus on the body in these two different ways leads to his diverse treatments of the body in relation to the self, and it is the latter focus that leads to his most important, though often brief, indications of the biological dimensions of the self.

The omission of the temporal dynamics of this lived body which subtends the dialogical nature of the self is the source of Tugendhat's objection that the exercise of roles cannot handle the question "Who do I want to be?" not in the sense of "a good teacher" or a "good parent," but in the sense of "What kind of a person do I want to be?"[12] Habermas has attempted to capture this sense of concreteness which goes beyond particular roles through the distinction between role identity and ego identity, with the claim that this lies in the distinction between past and future: what kind of a person I have become as opposed to what kind of person I want to be.[13] These accounts of Mead may at first seem merely to involve a somewhat more restricted sense of role taking than is intended by him, for it may be held that the kind of person I want to be is handled by the kind of integration of roles I want to achieve. The very sense of the question as to "the kind of person I want to be," or "the kind of integration of roles I want to achieve," however, seems to require not only more than the exercise of a series of specific roles but also more than any integration of roles.

The sense of what has been called "ego identity" as opposed to role identity would seem to lie not in a distinction between the past and the future, but in the sense of the decentered self as the source of the role taking, the ontological "thickness" or living reality which takes, integrates, and changes roles but which can never be exhausted through this expression. Mead's brief focus on the biological dimension of the self which is never lost is the implicit focus on this concrete creativity which can never be exhausted by any number of roles. From this backdrop of the ontological grounding of the dialogical self in bodily behavior manifesting the creative temporal dynamics of a processive universe, the ensuing discussion can turn more directly to the constitution of free selves.

The "I," it has been seen, represents the novel, the emergent, the unexpected. Freedom, however, does not lie in unbridled novelty or wild or impulsive behavior. Impulsive conduct is uncontrolled conduct (*MSS* 211-12). Mead holds that to act freely is to be governed by one's self rather than by external causes, but here it must be remembered that without the social dimension, the internalized generalized other, the "me," there is no self. Freedom, then, does not lie in opposition to the restrictions of norms and authority, but in a self-direction which requires the proper dynamic interaction of these two poles within the self. For Mead, freedom requires control over one's actions, self-determination. This is possible only through the use of reflective intelligence, which involves the dialogical relation between the novel actions and choices of the "I" and the social dimension, the generalized other, the past, the "me." Thus, freedom does not lie in being unaffected by others[14] and by one's past, but in the way the "I" uses the "me" in its novel decisions and actions.

The "me" calls for a certain sort of an "I." The me is in a sense a censor, "but the 'I' is always something different from what the situation itself calls for. . . . The 'I' both calls out the 'me' and responds to it" (*MSS* 178). The "me" evaluates the acts of the "I," and the self-evaluations of the "me" embody social values which are incorporated into the self through its ability to take the role of the other or the attitude of the other. The significance of this interrelationship is that without these two phases of the self there would be no conscious responsibility (ibid.). This interrelationship incorporates one's ability to "talk to himself in terms of the community to which he belongs and lay upon himself the responsibilities that belong to the community"; the ability to "admonish himself as others would," the ability to "recognize what are his duties as well as what are his rights" (*MTNC* 375-77). The "me" represents the social controls internally operative within the self. For Mead, self-criticism is fundamentally social criticism.

Here it must be noted, however, that these controls have themselves resulted not just from the internalization of the attitudes of the other but from the effect on these attitudes of the past responses of the "I." Not only is the "I" not enslaved by or determined by the "me," but the "me" has itself been formed in part from the past creative

acts or perspectives of the "I." The "me" represents the constraints not just of society but also of one's own past creative acts. The "I" as agent enters into the organization of attitudes which constitutes the generalized other. Further, it determines what roles it takes, and how they are appropriated and organized, and hence altered. It also selects that upon which it directs its interests and concerns, and chooses its mode of response. The "me" represents present possibilities for future activities which limit but do not determine the choice to be made. Thus, what yields the possibilities for present choice is a product of the conditions into which individuals are thrown: their past, their traditions, the generalized other with which they interact, and also their own creative responses to these conditions, responses which in turn have reshaped them. My freedom is limited by the constraints of my past and by the generalized other into which I am thrown, for these limit the range of possibilities open for my choosing. Yet, this range has been partially shaped by previous free acts. The response of the "I" changes the organization of attitudes of the "me," which in turn resituates or alters the possibilities for future choices.

Mead's concept of freedom is intimately interrelated with the concepts of reflective intelligence and moral agency. Freedom originates from the self and involves self-determination based on reflective intelligence. It is tied to the sense of the moral as responsibility to rational action. The temporal foundations of freedom can best be approached via Mead's concept of moral necessity. He holds that while the "me" involves an organization of the community incorporated in our own attitudes and to which we respond, yet the response that occurs "is something that just happens. There is no certainty in regard to it. There is a moral necessity but no mechanical necessity for the act" (*MSS* 178). Mead's understanding of moral necessity can be seen in his characterization of, and agreement with, a particular aspect of the way Bergson "rescues freedom." As Mead characterizes this rescue, "The coming of the future into our conduct is the very nature of our freedom. We may be able to get the reason for everything we do after the act, according to the mechanical statement; but to see conduct as selective, as free, we must take account of that which is not yet in position to be expressed in terms of a mechanical statement" (*MTNC* 317). Or, as he states in discussing his own position, "At the future edge of experience we project the causal mechanism into the future, but always as the condition of the future that has been selected, not as the condition of the selection."[15] Thus, the selection made is not determined by the causal structure which is elicited (*PA* 348).

Moral necessity involves precisely that which is not necessitated. We can look back, give reasons, say why we acted as we did, view the act in its continuity with the past, though in its occurrence it was a novel event, the "I's" movement into the future" which "we cannot tell in advance" (*MSS* 176). Moral necessity occurs in a passing present oriented toward the future, while mechanical necessity involves the statement of the past.[16] Moral necessity is the self-controlled step into the future in a world full of present possibilities emerging from a past. As Mead states,

> The moral necessity lies not in the end acting from without, nor in the push of inclination from within, but in the relation of the conditions of action to the impulses to action. The motive is neither a purely rational, external end, nor a private inclination, but the impulse presented in terms of its consequences over against the consequences of these other impulses. The impulse so conditioned, so interpreted becomes a motive to conduct.[17]

Moral necessity thus involves the free play of rational choice rooted in the vital drives of the lived body.[18] Such rational choice, in weighing consequences, must take into account the environment, the social dimension, the "me." Freedom, then, lies in the contextually set selection of an oncoming future. Freedom is always situated freedom. Freedom is not capricious; nor is moral necessity conformity to the past. Freedom and moral necessity are two sides of the same coin. They each involve the creativity of choice within a concrete or existential context set by present possibilities emerging from a past.

Freedom at its fullest involves rational choice in the actualization of possibilities, but this is precisely moral conduct at its fullest. Mead holds that moral awareness is the most concrete awareness in that there is no phase of life that may not become a condition or phase of conduct. Thus moral conduct reaches its highest expression by incorporating into evaluations all aspects of the self and of the situation which can possibly be included.[19] Moral awareness permeates experience, and all experience is value laden to some degree, for the consummatory phase of anticipatory activity is partially constitutive of the very nature of human experience. Human experience as anticipatory, is also ultimately consummatory, and as rationally organized, is, for Mead, the foundation of happiness (*PA* 136). The moral dictum implies that individuals fully recognize the conflict between the consequences of an impulse and the consequences of all the other social processes that go to make them up,[20] and thus, to live according to the moral dictum "is simply to live as fully and consciously and as determinedly as possible."[21] The "I" can make a rational choice, a choice not stemming from blind compulsion or outmoded ideals because it is aware of the possible consequences of the choice. This involves, ultimately, the fullness of the interrelationship of the self and the situational context.[22] Thus, moral action is rational action in terms of an estimation of consequences within a situation constituted by organism-environment interaction, a situation which provides the matrix of possibilities for intelligent choice.

The estimation of conflicting consequences leads to the reconstruction of a situation which resolves the conflicting demands. Mead holds that the immediate statement of the end appears through the reconstruction of the conflict and the awareness of the consequences such reconstruction involves.[23] The motive itself arises within this con-

text of reconstruction, for, as was seen above from the perspective of the discussion of moral necessity, antecedently given ends of activities do not give rise to motives. Rather, the recognition of the end as it comes to conscious awareness is the motive.[24] The motive and end arise together in the reconstructive act. For this reason, if abstract valuations are used instead of concrete valuations, they are usually inadequate, "as the abstract external valuations are always the precipitations of earlier conduct."[25] As Mead states this in more general terms, "We cannot interpret the meaning of our present through the history of the past because we must reconstruct that history through the study of the present" (*PA* 486).

External fixed ends do not provide incentives to moral action, but rather the reservoir of moral power lies in the vitality of the impulses behind the various interests. Because the power of moral action comes from the vitality of the purposive organism, not from the activities which serve as the occasion of their expression, and even more so not from static ideals, Mead can claim that "The good reasons for which we act and by which we account for our actions are not the real reasons" (*PA* 480). At times it is not necessary to distinguish these different aspects, for they work in harmony. At times, however, our underlying attitudes change enough that they cannot connect with former occasions for conduct or with accepted ideals, and "uneasiness and friction" arise within the individual. At these times, Mead states, "Our minds[26] . . . fall behind the profound development that is taking place underneath" (*PA* 480). Indeed, Mead holds that profound social reconstruction can take place "back of our minds" before our minds can analyze the situation in terms of the new attitudes. There is a "mental lag" (*PA* 480ff.). For Mead corporeal intentions are lived, at times without our being explicitly conscious of them, before being brought to explicit formulation as an object of choice through the I-me dialogue of reflective awareness.

Too much of a mental lag between underlying changing attitudes and awareness of needed changes in ideals and occasions for expression of attitudes can lead to complexes and compulsions (*PA* 480). These disintegrate the individual into fragmented elements, thereby diminishing free activity. As Mead states, "We cannot gather ourselves together when we do not feel free" (*PA* 663). Thus, there are degrees of freedom in proportion to the extent to which the individual becomes organized as a whole (ibid.). The "felt" fragmentation or unification operative in non-reflective awareness, "underneath" reflection, underlies the degrees of freedom expressible through consciously directed choice; and in authentic freedom, explicit choices must be in harmony with the changes, often profound, "taking place underneath."

Mead's stress on the "I" in the exercise of freedom may seem to indicate that habitual behavior, behavior which manifests the "me" as a "conventional, habitual individual" (*PA* 197), cannot be free. This, however, is not the case. The "me" is a structure of habits that are at once a sedimentation of one's past[27] and an orientation toward the future. It is "the self we refer to as character."[28] These habits define how one would probably act in specific types of situations with the consequences they imply. In the area of value, this can be understood as general tendencies to act in specific types of situations when one is motivated by particular types of ends, as well as general tendencies for one to be motivated by particular types of ends. If the network of habits which constitute the sedimented dimension of the lived body provides an integrative unification, then non-reflective habitual behavior is free. Thus, Mead holds that while "in freedom the personality as a whole passes into the act . . . [t]his does not necessarily spell creation, spontaneity" (**PA** 663). It does, however, involve previous reflective reconstructive activity (ibid.).

Further, even the most ingrained habits of response involve minimal novelty and reconstructive activity, for they not only reflect previous creative activity but also involve, in their step toward the future, the reintegration of possibilities constitutive of the present. Thus, Mead can claim that the need for moral action "is simply the necessity of action at all."[29] Networks of habits are partially sedimentations of one's own past reconstructive acts and, to the extent and for the time that they work in providing an integrative function, they are expressions of an individual's achievement of freedom. The self, it has been seen, is both an "I" and a "me." The self has the dimensions of creativity and conformity. And, freedom lies neither in the "I" nor in the "me," in the creativity or in the conformity, but in the proper relation between the two; and while both aspects are essential to the self in its full expression, the relative importance of the "me" and the "I" depends upon the situation. Sometimes it is important to act in a habitual or a socially conforming way, sometimes it is important to be highly creative.[30]

The "I," as the creative dimension of the lived body, gives the sense of freedom, of agency (**MSS** 177). This experiential sense of freedom and agency in its relation to the experience of temporality is indicated in Mead's claim that at the future edge of experience there is readiness to accept control of what is taking place, and *this itself is "a datum of experience"* (**PA** 343-44). It is the sense of the "living act which never gets directly into reflective experience" as an object (**MSS** 203). With the development of selfhood, the sense of the temporal present becomes the sense of one's own agency. The sense of freedom in the passing present is the sense of agency, not a grasp of any particular content. The sense of the novelty of the "I" is the sense of its passing from an old "me," out of which its novelty has arisen, into a new "me," which accommodates it and renders it continuous with what came before, the sense of novelty arising out of a context of past conditions and passing into a context of new conditions. Thus, though the "I," as representing the creative dimension of the self, represents the sense of freedom, of agency, yet such a sense ultimately involves the sense of the entire self. The very sense of freedom in the passing present, then, is the sense of situated freedom, founded in the bi-polar dynamics of

selfhood. The temporal dynamics which permeate the dynamics of the lived body provide the conditions for freedom. We are, ontologically, free. But, authentic freedom must be won through the integrative function of rational self-control.

In the breakdown of the workable value situation, in the reconstruction and reintegration of values, the sense of creativity functioning comes to the fore.[31] Thus, there is the opportunity for a new integration which more adequately fulfills the demand for self fulfillment. Rational reconstruction becomes permeated with an enhanced sense of the vital drives of the concrete subject which must fit into the reconstructed situation. It is this sense of the vital concrete subject that we are continually trying to realize through conduct and that we can never get fully before ourselves in reflection (**MSS** 203-204). It is that which is never exhausted in the exercise of roles and which cannot be totally confined within role identity.[32] In the functioning of concrete, corporeal subjectivity[33] "novelty arises and it is there that our most important values are located. It is the realization in some sense of this self that we are continually seeking," and we do not know just what its energy possibilities are (**MSS** 204). We surprise ourselves by our actions and choices because of the novelty of the "I," but the "I" as the dimension of creativity operates within a present rich with the possibilities presented by the past, by the "me" as the social and sedimented dimension of the decentered subject. Not only can we not know in advance the novel choices to be made by the "I," but neither can we exhaustively grasp in its concrete entirety the range of possibilities open to it in even the most limited of circumstances, because we can never exhaustively grasp the richness of the intentional possibilities of the lived body, of corporeal subjectivity functioning in its temporal dynamics, through any number of objectifications of it as an object "me" to an observing "I." The "me" as representing the object pole of the cognitive relation is by definition always the object, never the subject, but an object which can never be exhaustively grasped, just as no object can be exhaustively grasped. As Mead stresses, "Many of the aspects or features of this entire pattern do not enter into consciousness" (**MSS** 144, n.).

In an objection which again evinces a lack of focus on the biological self, the decentered corporeal subject underlying the dialogical nature of the self, Tugendhat claims that Mead's understanding of freedom in the sense of self-determination is one-sided, recognizing the explicit or implicit process of deliberation aiming for an objectively justified preference, but not recognizing that "the process of adducing grounds must come to an end when decisions about one's life are at issue; thus the decision retains an irreducibly volitional or subjective aspect."[34] Yet, Mead recognizes this aspect not just for decisions about one's life but in a more general sense, since no amount of deliberation can determine the exact form which any decision will take. Nor can deliberation necessarily determine the general nature of the decision, since, as has been seen, the explicit decision may stem from possibilities latent in the present which have never been brought to conscious awareness, possibilities which may lead to a non-reflective commitment toward a particular line of action which explicit choice appropriates but which reflection cannot exhaust.

This is precisely what lies implicit in Mead's understanding of moral necessity, discussed above. The "essential determination" of action by self reflection does not exhaust the process of choosing, though after the choice one can look back and provide the "deliberative reasons" for the choice. The response of the "I" is rooted in the vital intentionality of corporeal subjectivity, and this concrete functioning can never be exhausted by deliberative awareness. The sense of the temporal flow of corporeal intentionality functioning provides a non-reflective sense of workable adjustment in the decision process which underlies and overflows deliberative reasoning, thus bringing rationality down to its foundation in existence, the "development taking place underneath," the reconstructive activity "back of our minds," the well-spring of concrete creativity and adjustment which eludes explicit breakdown and is inexhaustible by any amount of self-reflective or deliberative activity. Freedom, like selfhood, involves self-conscious deliberation, but freedom, selfhood, and rationality itself are ultimately rooted in the non-reflective[35] sense of the temporal, corporeal subject functioning within the dynamics of experience as experimental.

While Mead rejects the notion of fixed, absolute values and moral norms, yet he opposes relativism as well. The energies of the self cannot successfully be confined within the constraints of a generalized other which stifle its development. As Mead states, "The individual in a certain sense is not willing to live under certain conditions which would involve a sort of suicide of the self in its process of realization." At these times the "I" reconstructs the society, and hence the "me" which belongs to that society (*MSS* 214). Yet, one never stands as a pure "I" in opposition to the generalized other,[36] for,

> The only way in which we can react against the disapproval of the entire community is by setting up a higher sort of community which in a certain sense outvotes the one we find. A person may reach a point of going against the whole world about him; he may stand out by himself over against it. But to do that he has to speak with the voice of reason to himself. He has to comprehend the voices of the past and of the future. (*MSS* 167-68)

In brief, he has remained in the most inclusive generalized other, the universe of discourse (*MSS* 157-58), and must use this to comprehend what possibly can be in the light of what has been. For Mead, there is always novelty and change, but novelty and change within the context of tradition and continuity.

Mead views the demand for freedom always as the demand to move from a narrow or restricted community to one that is larger in the sense of having less restricted

rights (*MSS* 199). And, growth of community involves growth of self. When we allow value conflicts and their possible resolution to be stated in terms of old selves, the moral problem takes on the character of a necessary sacrifice either of one's self or of the others. A proper consideration of the problem, however, should involve a reconstruction of the situation in such a way that there is no conflict among selves, but rather the emergence of enlarged and more adequate selves. "Solution is reached by the construction of a new world harmonizing the conflicting interests into which enters the new self."[37]

This process Mead sees as "logically identical" with the replacement of an inadequate scientific hypothesis by a new one which overcomes previous problems and conflicts. There is a "complete parallel" holding between the social situation and the situation of the scientist. "The scientist has his own hypothesis, and the question is, Is it the one on which the community as a whole can act or work? The individual is trying to restate his community in such a way that what he does can be a natural function in the community" (*PA* 663). The difference lies in the fact that moral situations deal with concrete human interests in which there is a restructuring of the entire self in its interrelation with other selves essential for its development.[38] The expansion of the self involves the larger incorporation of other selves, an expanded generalized other which becomes a part of one's own self, for as has been seen, the self is distinguishable but not separable from other selves. Thus Mead claims that freedom is the expression of the whole self which has become entire through the reconstruction which has taken place (*MSS* 162-63). In this way, "Freedom lies definitely in a reconstruction which is not in the nature of a rebellion but in the nature of presenting an order which is more adequate than the order which has been there" (*PA* 663).

The importance of scientific method in the moral situation can be indicated through two claims made by Mead. The first involves the universalizing dimension of ideals:

> To the degree that any achievement of organization of a community is successful it is universal, and makes possible a bigger community. In one sense there cannot be a community which is larger than that represented by rationality. . . . That which is fine and admirable is universal—although it may be true that the actual society in which the universality can get its expression has not arisen. (*MSS* 266-67)

As Mead relates this to science.

> Now there is nothing so social as science, nothing so universal. Nothing so rigorously oversteps the points that separate man from man and groups from groups as does science. There cannot be any narrow provincialism or patriotism in science. Scientific method makes that impossible. Science is inevitably a universal discipline which takes in all who think. It speaks with the voice of all rational beings. It must be true everywhere; otherwise it is not scientific. But science is evolutionary . . . there is

a continuous process which is taking on successively different forms. (*MTNC* 168)

The ongoing reconstruction of the social situation in terms of a more encompassing perspective which works in integrating previously conflicting segments, providing an enlargement of self corresponding to the new ideal, is precisely the operation, within the sphere of values, of scientific method. This represents the fullest expression of freedom (*PA* 663) through the universalizing dimension of rationality. Freedom is tied to the sense of the moral as responsibility to rational action, and this is precisely responsibility to the method of science, for the operation of scientific method is the operation of impartial intelligence.[39] Scientific method can be dismissed only by dismissing intelligence itself,[40] though "unfortunately, men have committed this sin against their intelligence again and again."[41]

Scientific endeavor best reflects creative reconstruction, impartial intelligence[42] and the ideal of universality—not universality as a "philosophical abstraction," a final completion, a metaphysical assumption, or a fixed form of the understanding,[43] but as the "working character" of its claims, claims which are always subject to reconstructive change (*MSS* 289). These features of free activity manifest in scientific method provide, for Mead, the basis for a doctrine of rights which can be natural rights,[44] without the traditional entanglement with notions of atomic individuals or natural law.[45] And, these features of free activity are also the ingredients of Mead's understanding of democracy as the political expression of the functioning of experimental method. Any social structure or institution[46] can be brought into question through the use of social intelligence guided by universalizing ideals, leading to reconstructive activity which enlarges the situation and the selves involved, providing at once a greater degree of authentic self expression and a greater degree of social participation. Democracy, for Mead, involves not a particular form of government but a particular type of self and a particular type of method (*MSS* 286). In this way, democracy provides for a society which controls its own evolution. Any organization of roles involves a shared value or goal, and the overreaching goal of a human society, according to Mead, is precisely "this control of its own evolution" (*MSS* 251).

Thus, the ultimate "goal" involving the working character of universality is growth or development, not final completion. This in turn indicates that neither democracy nor the working ideal of universality can imply that differences should be eliminated or melted down (*MSS* 352), for these differences provide the necessary materials by which a society can continue to grow. Though the generalized other indeed represents social meanings and social norms, yet social development is possible only through the dynamic interrelation of the unique, creative individual and the generalized other. Thus Mead holds that the value "is the contribution of the individual to the situation, even though it is only in the social situation that the value obtains" (*MSS* 212). Moral intelligence is social intelligence, though social intelligence is not possible without individual creativity. As can be seen from Mead's entire analysis of the self, the freedom of the individual and the constraints of the generalized other are not two isolatable entities, but rather two poles in a dynamic temporal process which become manifest as two poles within the self and two poles within the society. The proper functioning of these two inseparable, dynamically interrelated poles results in authentic freedom. Thus Mead can hold that freedom can thrive only in a society characterized by the reign of law and the sense of responsibility (*PA* 496-97). Freedom is the ability to regulate and reconstruct conduct through the creative development of universalizing norms and ideals. Mead's strong emphasis on the activity of the scientists in relation to the exercise of freedom and moral responsibility lies in the fact that in both areas "the individual functions in his full particularity, and yet in organic relationship with the society that is responsible for him."[47]

Nowhere in Mead's writings is the method of the scientist as the model for understanding human activity more prominent than in his study of freedom and values, yet nowhere can the contents of the respective fields be found to be more disparate. Thus, Mead's understanding of the reconstruction of values points out perhaps more clearly than any other area of his thought the way in which for Mead, the pragmatist, scientific method, as the method of experimental inquiry, is a method which takes experience on its own terms, so to speak, refusing to reduce away any area of lived experience to the second level objectifications of any particular science. The method of science is, for Mead, the pragmatist, operative in all arenas of life because it is expressive of the dynamics of life itself. It has been seen that these dynamics involve an organizing creativity which is embodied in or directs one's anticipatory activity, the fulfillment of which in the ongoing course of experience constitutes truth as workability. Only through the proper functioning of this method can free selves work toward the enrichment of values. And, the adequacy of this interrelation can be grasped only when it is recognized that the bi-polar dynamics of the dialogical or cognitive self are rooted in the temporal dynamics of the corporeal intentionality of the biological dimension of the self, and, via this, rooted ultimately in the temporal dynamics of a processive universe in which this "body that I am" is embedded.

NOTES

[1] "A Pragmatic Theory of Truth," *Mead: Selected Writings,* ed. Andrew Reck (New York: Bobbs-Merrill, 1964), p. 328.

[2] Ibid.

[3] Scientific Method and the Individual Thinker," *Selected Writings,* p. 210.

[4] G. H. Mead, *Movements of Thought in the Nineteenth Century,* ed. Merritt Moore (Chicago: Univ. of Chicago Press, 1936), p. 346. Hereafter, MTNC.

5 For an in-depth discussion of the significance of scientific method within classical American pragmatism in general, see my *Speculative Pragmatism* (Amherst: Univ. of Massachusetts Press, 1986); paperback edition (La Salle, IL: Open Court, 1990).

6 Andrew Reck indicates the potential problem in *Persons and Community in American Philosophy*, ed. Konstantin Korea (Rice University Studies, Vol. 66, 1980).

7 Mitchell Aboulafia, *The Mediating Self: Mead, Sartre, and Self-Determination* (New Haven: Yale Univ. Press, 1986), p. 25. Abdoulafia seems to identify functional and fictional. Abdoulafia's generally keenly perceptive analysis runs into this kind of problem with Mead because his way of focusing on Mead in relation to Sartre draws him away from any concern with the centrality of the lived body. See also Paul Pfuetze, *The Social Self* (New York: Bookman Associates, 1954), pp. 94-96.

8 *Mind, Self, and Society*, ed. Charles Morris (Chicago: Univ. of Chicago Press, 1934), p. 173. Hereafter, MSS.

9 See, for example, MSS 173: "The essence of the self is cognitive."

10 These are the general features of Mead's temporalist pragmatic "metaphysics of sociality," a further development of which lies beyond the scope of this paper. See *The Philosophy of the Present*, ed. Arthur Murphy (La Salle, IL: Open Court, 1959).

11 *The Individual and the Social Self*, ed. David Miller (Chicago: Univ. of Chicago Press, 1982), p. 148.

12 Ernst Tugendhat, *Self-Consciousness and Self-Determination*, trans. Paul Stern (Cambridge, MA: MIT Press, 1986), pp. 234-48.

13 Jürgen Habermas, *The Theory of Communicative Action*, II, trans. Thomas Mccoy (Boston: Beacon Press, 1987), p. 106.

14 In the area of value, this may seem to take on the overtones of "sympathy" or "empathy," but Mead stresses that what is involved is not "feeling the other's joys and sorrows." And, Mead in fact defines sympathy in terms of the dialogical relation involved in taking the role of the other. See MSS 298-99.

15 *The Philosophy of the Act*, ed. Charles Morris (Chicago: Univ. of Chicago Press, 1938), p. 348. Hereafter, PA.

16 "Scientific Method and the Individual Thinker," p. 256.

17 "The Philosophical Basis of Ethics," *Selected Writings*, p. 87.

18 David Miller analyzes Mead's position in terms of what he calls three levels of morality: the level of impulsive behavior, springing from such instincts as involved in food, shelter, companionship, etc.; the level of conformity to the restraining force of the "me"; and the reconstructive creativity of the "I," noting that freedom enters at this third level. David Miller, *George Herbert Mead: Self, Language, and the World* (Austin: Univ. of Texas Press, 1973), p. 238.

Hans Joas, on the other hand, seems not only to detach what Miller calls the first level from the sphere of morality, but also to claim that for Mead, morality has no biological roots. *G. H. Mead: A Contemporary Re-examination of His Thought* (Cambridge, MA: MIT Press, 1985), p. 133.

Although Mead's range of instincts may well be unacceptable, yet the biological roots of morality would seem to be rightfully essential to Mead's position.

19 "The Philosophical Basis of Ethics," p. 84.

20 Ibid., p. 87.

21 Ibid.

22 Ibid.

23 Ibid.

24 Ibid., pp. 85-86.

25 Ibid., p. 93. This discussion interrelates with his understanding of moral necessity discussed above.

26 As he states, "I am not now using the term 'mind' in a technical sense. I refer to the meanings and values which things have for us and the responses they call out" (PA 479).

27 Here it must be remembered that this sedimentation of one's past includes both past creativity and past social conformity, past "I's" and past "me's."

28 "The Social Self," *Selected Writings*, p. 147.

29 "The Philosophical Basis of Ethics," p. 85.

30 Ibid., p. 199.

31 See, for example, "The Definition of the Psychical," *Selected Writings*, pp. 25-59.

32 See the above discussion of Ernst Tugendhat and Jürgen Habermas.

33 Mead's refers here to the "I," but it is the "I" as representative of the creative dimension of the body that I am, rather than as representative of subject over against an object.

34 Tugendhat, *Self Consciousness and Self Determination*, p. 265. He concludes that an adequate concept of

responsibility and autonomy "consists in a specific way of choosing that is not exhausted in the reflective self-relation, but is essentially determined by it" (ibid., p. 313).

[35] The non-reflective is at once pre-reflective as regards what is to come, but post reflective in that it incorporates past reflective activity.

[36] As David L. Miller so well states, "No individual, short of insanity, can, as an 'I,' stand over against the entire generalized other. That would mean the loss of one's mind and resorting to sheer unsocialized impulses." "The Meaning of Freedom From the Perspective of G. H. Mead's Theory of the Self," *The Southern Journal of Philosophy* 20 (1982), 453-63.

[37] "The Social Self," *Selected Writings,* pp. 148-49.

[38] Ibid., p. 149.

[39] "Scientific Method and the Moral Sciences," *Selected Writings,* p. 256.

[40] Ibid., p. 255.

[41] Ibid., p. 156.

[42] Ibid., pp. 248-66.

[43] "Scientific Method and the Individual Thinker," p. 201.

[44] "Natural Rights and the Theory of the Political Institution," *Selected Writings,* p. 163.

[45] As Mead states, "If you can make your demand universal, if your right is one that carries with it a corresponding obligation, then you recognize the same right in everyone else, and you can give a law, so to speak, in the terms of all the community" (*MSS* 287, n. 17).

[46] Institutions are social habits. See, for example, *MTNC* 377.

[47] "Scientific Method and the Individual Thinker," p. 211. Thus Mead illustrates the sense of felt creativity by reference to the creative effort involved in the scientist's search for an hypothesis. "The Definition of the Psychical," *Selected Writings,* p. 43.

Gary A. Cook (essay date 1993)

SOURCE: "The Development of Mead's Social Psychology," in *George Herbert Mead: The Making of a Social Pragmatist,* University of Illinois Press, 1993, pp. 48-66.

[In the following essay, Cook traces the origins of Mead's social psychological work and urges a fuller appreciation of his innovative ideas in the field of human social conduct.]

The least neglected facet of Mead's much neglected contribution to American thought has been his social psychology. Even here, however, interest has generally been restricted to certain portions of the posthumously published *Mind, Self and Society.* This volume, which is based primarily upon stenographic student notes taken in Mead's 1928 advanced social psychology course at the University of Chicago,[1] provides a readable account of the conclusions at which Mead had arrived in this field near the end of his career. But there is little in it that helps the reader trace the roots of Mead's social psychological work in the psychological functionalism of the early Chicago School or locate this work in the larger framework of his thought as a whole. For a fuller appreciation of Mead's contributions to the study of human social conduct we must look beyond *Mind, Self and Society* to selected portions of his other writings, particularly to the best of those periodical articles he wrote during the first half of his career at Chicago.

A careful examination of selected essays Mead published between 1900 and 1913, the years when he was working out his key social psychological ideas, confirms an observation John Dewey made in his prefatory remarks for the 1932 publication of Mead's *The Philosophy of the Present*: "When I first came to know Mr. Mead, well over forty years ago, the dominant problem in his mind concerned the nature of consciousness as personal and private. . . . I fancy that if one had a sufficiently consecutive knowledge of Mr. Mead's intellectual biography during the intervening years, one could discover how practically all his inquiries and problems developed out of his original haunting question."[2] Mead's struggle with this "original haunting question" led him to a growing emphasis upon the social dimensions of human conduct. And his consequent analysis of sociality as a dominant feature of conduct greatly enriched the organic model of action initially set forth by Dewey, thus providing the conceptual framework within which Mead's mature social psychology was to develop.

MEAD'S EARLY FUNCTIONALISM

As Darnell Rucker has pointed out in his excellent study, *The Chicago Pragmatists,* Dewey and Mead were primarily responsible for the creation of the functionalist approach to psychology that constituted the basis for much that was distinctive in the philosophy of the Chicago School.[3] At the heart of their functionalism was a new organic concept of action, whose most celebrated articulation is to be found in Dewey's 1896 essay, "The Reflex Arc Concept in Psychology."[4] Since Mead's earliest published attempts to deal with the nature of human consciousness "as personal and private" involve extensive references to Dewey's essay, it is worthwhile to summarize its central points.

In this essay Mead's more famous colleague strongly criticized the stimulus-response model of action (the "reflex arc concept") as being based upon a serious conceptual confusion. The advocates of this model had failed to see that "stimulus and response are not distinctions of existence, but teleological distinctions, that is, distinctions of function, or part played, with reference to reaching or maintaining an end." Dewey argued persuasively that stimulus and response were to be understood as functional moments within an ongoing process of coordination, which "is more truly termed organic than reflex, because the motor response determines the stimulus just as truly as sensory stimulus determines movement." Dewey's analysis of the mutual adjustment involved in concrete action is well illustrated by the example of a child reaching for a flickering candle: in this reaching the act of vision must not only stimulate but also continue to control the movement of the child's arm. "The eye must be kept upon the candle if the arm is to do its work; let it wander and the arm takes up another task." The movement of the arm must, in turn, control the act of seeing; if it does not, the eye wanders and the reaching is without guidance. What most requires emphasis here is that the coordinated acts of seeing and reaching continually exchange functional roles within the complex act of which they are phases. What is at one moment a guided response may at the next moment become a guiding stimulus. Furthermore, not only does the stimulus guide the response, but the response shapes the quality of what is experienced. As Dewey put it, the response is not simply *to* the stimulus; it is *into* it. The response does not merely replace the sensory content of the stimulus with another sort of experience; rather it mediates, transforms, enlarges, or interprets that initial content in terms of its significance for ongoing conduct. When a child responds to the act of seeing a flickering candle, the mere seeing is transformed into, for example, a seeing-of-a-light-that-means-pain-when-contact-occurs.[5]

As long as such conduct proceeds smoothly, Dewey contended, it involves no conscious distinction of stimulus and response. But suppose that the child is torn between a tendency to grasp the candle and a tendency to avoid it as a possible source of pain. In this type of situation doubt as to the proper completion of the act gives rise to an analysis whose purpose is to resolve the inhibiting conflict. "The initiated activities of reaching, . . . inhibited by the conflict in the coordination, turn round, as it were, upon the seeing, and hold it from passing over into further act until its quality is determined. Just here the act as objective stimulus becomes transformed into sensation as possible, as conscious, stimulus. Just here also, motion as conscious response emerges." Thus we see that the reflective isolation of stimulus and response as components of action has a particular genesis and function. It is the failure to note this genesis and function, Dewey held, that lies behind the mechanical conjunction of stimulus and response characteristic of the reflex arc model of action.[6]

Dewey concluded this now classical statement of psychological functionalism with the observation that the real significance of the organic conception of action would be seen only in its application to fundamental problems of psychology and philosophy. And it was just such applica-

tion that Mead undertook in two essays published in 1900 and 1903. The first of these essays, **"Suggestions Toward a Theory of the Philosophical Disciplines,"** was an ambitious neo-Hegelian attempt to characterize the respective provinces of metaphysics, psychology, deductive and inductive logics, ethics, aesthetics, and the general theory of logic in terms of the "dialectic within the act" as organically understood. The second essay, **"The Definition of the Psychical,"** was less ambitious in scope, although more obscure in development; here Mead narrowed his focus to the discipline of psychology, seeking to delineate more fully its distinctive subject matter as a phase of "psychical consciousness" or "subjectivity" within conduct. It is the considerable space both essays devote to this latter topic that makes them important for the present purpose.

In **"Suggestions Toward a Theory of the Philosophical Disciplines,"** Mead presented his discussion of subjectivity as an extension of Dewey's remarks concerning the genesis and function of our awareness of sensation as a distinct element in experience: "Professor Dewey maintains in his discussion of the Reflex Arc that the sensation appears always in consciousness as a problem; that attention could not be centered upon a so-called element of consciousness unless the individual were abstracting from the former meaning of the object, and in his effort to reach a new meaning had fixed this feature of the former object as a problem to be solved" (*SW* 6).[7] Holding with Dewey and William James that the content or meaning of the objects we experience is derived from their roles in our conduct, Mead pointed out that as long as action with respect to objects proceeds without a hitch, their meanings typically remain unquestioned. But when an object calls out conflicting reactions, its content is to that extent ambiguous and in need of examination. In such situations "our conscious activity finds itself unable to pass into an objective world on account of the clash between different tendencies to action," and "we are thrown back upon an analysis of these spontaneous acts and therefore upon the objects which get their content from them" (*SW* 8). Our experience takes a subjective turn, Mead suggested, when such conflict or ambiguity cannot be adequately resolved by a simple reshuffling of already existing meanings. For in these cases the conscious solution of our problem requires an abandonment of old universals and a quest for new meanings or objects to which we can more successfully relate. During the period when this quest is underway, our attention must turn from the temporarily impoverished world of objects to the flux of immediate and personal consciousness. Subjectivity thus enters conduct as "a position midway between the old universals, whose validity is abandoned, and the new universal, which has not yet appeared" (*SW* 12).

Subjective or psychical consciousness takes as its starting point whatever unproblematic meanings can be abstracted from the conflicting elements of the problem to be solved. For instance, the child who hesitates when faced by the flickering candle has before him "neither the object which burned nor yet the plaything," for both of these meanings are in question. But he does have "something behind each and true of each—a bright moving object we will say" (*SW* 13). This latter meaning is objective (i.e., it is part of the world of unproblematic objects) but not sufficient by itself to give direction to the conduct that has been inhibited. The task of subjectivity or the psychical phase of experience is to take conduct beyond this stage of abstraction to a stage of synthesis in which the abstracted meanings find their places in a reconstructed world of objects. This is accomplished by giving free play to conflicting tendencies to respond, tendencies that must for the time being be regarded merely as elements peculiar to the immediate consciousness of the individual attempting to solve the problem at hand. It is this "constructive power proportional to the freedom with which the forces abstracted from their customary objects can be combined with each other into a new whole . . . that comes nearer answering to what we term genius than anything else" (*SW* 20). The problem is solved to the extent that these tendencies find a harmonious expression in terms of new objective meanings. When a solution is found, the subjective phase of conduct has done its work, and attention is once again focused on a realm of unproblematic objects.

Mead thus proposed that we construe the distinction between subjective and objective elements of experience as functional, rather than metaphysical. The marks of the subjective or psychical state are to be understood in terms of "their position in the act, the when and the how of their appearance" rather than as characteristics of an entity that exists independently of conduct (*SW* 16). Failure to appreciate the functional nature of subjectivity, Mead maintained, has characteristically led either to an untenable psychophysical parallelism or to a kind of idealism in which all experience is reduced to states of individual consciousness. In either case, the mistake lies in the attempt to "objectify the psychical state, and deprive it of the very elements that have rendered it psychical" (*SW* 16).

Mead continued his attack on traditional conceptions of subjectivity and also further articulated his own view in **"The Definition of the Psychical."** In the constructive portion of this essay, he again took as his point of departure a suggestion attributable to Dewey: that when an object loses its validity because of a conflict in our activity, it also loses its form and organization. According to this view, the meanings abandoned in such cases are not simply transferred intact to the subjective realm. Rather, the psychical character of the situation is due precisely to the disintegration of the problematic objects and the whole effort of the individual toward reconstructing them (*SW* 40-42). In what form then, Mead asked, do the meanings or objects that have become problematic enter into psychical consciousness? He found the clue to his answer in the same source that had provided Dewey with much of his inspiration, James's *The Principles of Psychology.* No better description of psychical consciousness can be found, Mead suggested, than that supplied by James in his famous chapter on "The Stream of Con-

sciousness." For all of the characteristics James attributes to the stream of consciousness are unmistakably present in the psychical phase of problem-solving:

> The kaleidoscopic flash of suggestion, and intrusion of the inapt, the unceasing flow of odds and ends of possible objects that will not fit, together with the continuous collision with the hard, unshakable objective conditions of the problem, the transitive feelings of effort and anticipation when we feel that we are on the right track and substantive points of rest, as the idea becomes definite, the welcoming and rejecting, especially the identification of the meaning of the whole idea with the different steps in its coming to consciousness—there are none of these that are not almost oppressively present on the surface of consciousness during just the periods which Dewey describes as those of disintegration and reconstitution of the stimulus—the object. (*SW* 42-43)

Psychical consciousness as here described is clearly concerned with the immediate, with that which is peculiar to the individual and a moment of his existence. It is just these characteristics, Mead maintained, that enable it to perform its functional role in the reconstruction of conduct (*SW* 36). For the task of subjective consciousness is to introduce novelty into a situation in which the old has broken down, and this can be accomplished only by a consciousness that is not essentially tied to the world of accepted meanings and objects. Inspection of the old world can supply us with data, with conditions for the solution of the problem that has arisen, but it cannot be expected to supply us with the new meanings required for the reconstruction of that world. New meanings must arise from the reflecting individual's immediate awareness of his own activities and shifting attention as he seeks to harmonize the habitual tendencies that have come into conflict within his conduct (*SW* 52, 45). It is here "in the construction of the hypotheses of the new world, that the individual qua individual has his functional expression or rather is that function" (*SW* 52).

INTRODUCTION OF "I" AND "ME"

Mead argued in **"The Definition of the Psychical"** not only for the functional importance of personal and private consciousness as the locus of cognitive reconstruction but also for the suggestion that the human individual qua individual could be defined in terms of this reconstructive function. But herein lies a problem that Mead himself was quick to see. The human individual or self as ordinarily construed is an object, and as such it belongs to the world that it is the task of subjectivity to reconstruct. To the extent that the self as object is not infected with the problem at hand it may, of course, enter into the statement of the conditions to be met by any possible solution of that problem, but it cannot be expected to provide that solution (*SW* 53). How then can it be said that the task of reconstruction is performed by the human individual?

It was in his attempt to deal with this problem that Mead first employed the terms "I" and "me" to refer to the self functioning as subject and the self functioning as object, respectively. These terms had been given popular currency by James in a chapter of his *The Principles of Psychology* that dealt with "The Consciousness of Self," and Mead borrowed them for his own purposes. In speaking of an "I" and a "me" Mead sought to make the point that, according to the functionalist view, the human individual or self may enter into conduct in two distinguishable senses. On the one hand, the self may enter into conduct as a meaningful stimulus for the intelligent control of action. In this case the self functions as an object; this is what Mead had in mind when he spoke of the "me." The "me" is thus a *presentation* that performs a mediating role within an ongoing process of experience or action (*SW* 53-54). On the other hand, as Mead's discussion of subjectivity makes clear, the human individual may also enter into conduct as an agent of reconstruction. Here the immediate and direct experience of the individual qua individual functions as a source from which spring suggestions for new ways of ordering the process of conduct when habitual actions and meanings have become problematic. The self functioning in this latter sense is what Mead meant by the "I": it is "the self in the disintegration and reconstruction of its universe, the self functioning, the point of immediacy that must exist within a mediate process" (*SW* 53-54).

This distinction does not, however, appear to provide a wholly adequate solution to the problem that was its occasion. For if the objective status of the "me" renders it an unacceptable candidate for the functional role of reconstructor, then a similar reservation must apply to the qualifications of the "human individual" with whom Mead wished to link psychical consciousness. More generally, it would seem that any attempt to identify psychical consciousness as belonging to a finite self must inevitably tie that consciousness to an item in the world of experienced objects. Thus Mead's introduction of the term "I" in this context appears to be either a misleading use of the personal pronoun to refer to immediately felt action (as opposed to objects that may arise within it) or a device for bringing in through the back door an implicit reference to the same object self he has thrown out the front. The former interpretation seems most consistent with Mead's descriptions of subjectivity and with his reference to the subject self as "the act that makes use of all the data that reflection can present, but uses them merely as the conditions of a new world that cannot possibly be foretold from them" (*SW* 54). Unhappily, **"The Definition of the Psychical"** leaves much room for doubt concerning Mead's precise view on this matter. Perhaps this is one of the reasons he was to refer to this essay some years later as one in which his position had been developed "somewhat obscurely and ineffectually, I am afraid" (*SW* 106).

PERCEPTUAL OBJECTS AND THE SOCIAL GENESIS OF CONSCIOUSNESS

While the two essays we have considered emphasize the self functioning as subject, Mead's subsequent early publications show a dominant concern with the self as object.

His initial inquiries into the reconstructive role of subjectivity seem to have led to a greater interest in the functional nature of those objects to which subjectivity stands in contrast. And this latter interest came, in turn, to be focused in his social psychological work upon questions concerning the social and functional nature of the object self.

The first step in this line of development is seen in Mead's contributions to the functionalist view of perceptual objects in his 1907 essay, **"Concerning Animal Perception."** Here, as in his earlier articles, he carried on the articulation of the organic model of action advocated by Dewey in 1896. But now Mead turned his constructive efforts to the task of locating human perceptual consciousness of physical objects within conduct and distinguishing it from so-called animal perception. Two of the basic ingredients of perceptual consciousness, he pointed out, are readily found in animal conduct. These are the two classes of sensory experiences involving, respectively, the "distance" sense organs (e.g., the visual, olfactory, and auditory organs) and those of "contact" (e.g., touch, taste). But although animal behavior contains a coordination of these two types of experiences, Mead was inclined to doubt that it involved any perceptual consciousness of physical things as these are encountered in human experience. The grounds for this doubt are revealed in his examination of the prerequisites for the appearance of physical objects within the act.

Physical objects are to be understood as presentations arising through a particular kind of mediation within conduct. More specifically, they take shape within conduct only insofar as the contact experience that is likely to be encountered in responding to a particular distance stimulus is presented along with that stimulus (*SW* 79). Mead expressed this point best when he said several years later (in the introductory paragraphs of **"The Mechanism of Social Consciousness"**) that the physical object is "a collapsed act" in which immediate sensuous content is merged with imagery drawn from previous responses to similar stimuli (*SW* 134). Now the presentation of such objects can take place only if the appropriate elements within experience are consciously isolated and the relational connections between them attended to. But Mead found no convincing evidence that non-human animals possess the capacities required to accomplish these tasks. Consequently, he believed it likely that animal conduct proceeds without any awareness of perceptual relations: its modification presumably takes place in the unconscious manner typical of certain kinds of human learning—for instance, the development of finer sensory discrimination and related muscular adjustments involved in improving one's tennis game through practice (*SW* 74).

Furthermore, Mead held that if physical objects are to appear within the field of stimulation, then that field must be organized around enduring substrates with which varying sensory qualities can be associated. The experiential basis for such substrates, he suggested, had been correctly located by G. F. Stout in what the latter termed "manipulation," the actual contact experience or handling to which distance experience characteristically leads (*SW* 77). "Our perception of physical objects always refers color, sound, odor, to a possibly handled substrate," which is reflected in the familiar philosophical distinction between primary and secondary qualities (*SW* 78). Here again humans have a clear advantage over nonhuman animals in that their hands provide them with a wealth of manipulatory contents that can be isolated from the culminations of their activities. In nonhuman animals, however, "the organs of manipulation are not as well adapted in form and function for manipulation itself, and, in the second place, the contact experiences of lower animals are, to a large extent determined, not by the process of manipulation, but are so immediately a part of eating, fighting, repose, etc., that it is hard to believe that a consciousness of a 'thing' can be segregated from these instinctive activities" (*SW* 79).

These early suggestions outlining a functional view of perceptual objects were to be greatly elaborated in Mead's later philosophical writings. Indeed, well over 150 pages of the posthumously published *The Philosophy of the Act* and almost half of *The Philosophy of the Present* are devoted to the further working out of this view, especially with reference to the nest of epistemological and ontological problems raised by the impact upon philosophy of the twentieth-century revolution in physics. But of more immediate interest for our present purpose is Mead's extension of his earlier discussion, in a series of articles published between 1909 and 1913, to include the *social* dimension of perceptual consciousness. An examination of these articles discloses the sources of several of his most important social-psychological ideas and reveals the manner in which he employed these to greatly enrich the functionalist understanding of human conduct and consciousness.

Beginning with **"Social Psychology as a Counterpart to Physiological Psychology"** (1909), Mead's thought is less dependent upon Dewey's work than had previously been the case. Mead continued to maintain the functionalist orientation of Dewey's paper on the reflex arc concept, but he now came to believe that an adequate functionalism had to emphasize not only the organic nature of human conduct but also its fundamentally social character. Whereas his earlier discussions had sought to clarify the manner in which perceptual objects and subjective consciousness function in the control and reconstruction of conduct, his emphasis now fell upon the objective social conditions that make these developments within conduct possible. He moved, in short, toward a genetic and increasingly social functionalism.

Following the lead of such thinkers as William McDougall, Josiah Royce, James Mark Baldwin, and Charles Horton Cooley, he began to maintain that human conduct was shaped from the outset by social instincts— in which the term "social instinct" meant "a well defined tendency to act under the stimulation of another individual of the same species" (*SW* 98).[8] Mead found in this idea, first, an important suggestion bearing upon his discussion of perceptual objects. An adequate recognition of the social dimension of human action, he now realized, would allow one to enlarge that discussion by pointing out how social objects, particularly human selves, arise within the process of conduct. If objects are to be functionally understood as meaningful presentations that guide action, and if human action is characteristically social, then clearly it becomes reasonable to speak of selves as social objects. The content of such objects is implicit in those social instincts that sensitize us to social stimuli; their structure and meaning are implicit in the organized responses we make to these social stimuli. "The implication of an organized group of social instincts is the implicit presence in undeveloped human consciousness of both the matter and form of a social object" (*SW* 98).

But how do the social objects that are "implicit" in our organized social instincts become explicit elements of consciousness? The problem here, as Mead saw it, was to explain in terms of a functional conception of the social act how human individuals might come to analyze the relations within their social experience and thereby grasp the meaning of what they and others were doing. Baldwin and Royce had earlier suggested that the solution to this problem was to be found in instinctive human tendencies to imitate and then oppose the responses of others. Through such imitation and opposition, individuals come to differentiate between self and other, thus making it possible for them to grasp the social meaning of their own conduct. Mead, however, found this theory implausible. The idea of an imitative instinct, he pointed out, does not fit well with the observed nature of social conduct: "The important character of social organization of conduct or behavior through instincts is not that one form in a social group does what the others do, but that the conduct of one form is a stimulus to another to a certain act, and that this act again becomes a stimulus at first to a certain reaction, and so on in ceaseless interaction" (*SW* 101). Moreover, if we mean by "imitation" what is usually meant by that term, then this theory puts the cart before the horse. It attempts to account for the rise of human consciousness by means of a mechanism that itself presupposes such consciousness. "Imitation becomes comprehensible when there is a consciousness of other selves, and not before" (*SW* 100). The notion of imitation as it has been employed in social psychology, Mead concluded, must be replaced by a fully developed "theory of social stimulation and response and of the social situations which these stimulations and responses create" (*SW* 101). Baldwin and Royce were correct in arguing that mature human consciousness is of social origin, but they erred in giving undue emphasis to those social situations in which one individual does what others are doing. The social foundations of consciousness are rather to be found in conduct where the action of one individual calls out an appropriate (and usually dissimilar) response in another individual, and where this response becomes, in turn, a social stimulus to the first individual.

Mead's own social psychological theory concerning the genesis of consciousness was only briefly sketched in his 1909 article, but he sought to supply the needed details almost immediately in three subsequent essays: **"What Social Objects Must Psychology Presuppose?"** (1910), **"Social Consciousness and the Consciousness of Meaning"** (1910), and **"The Mechanism of Social Consciousness"** (1912). The central concept of the theory developed in these essays was that of "gesture," which had first been spelled out in Wilhelm Wundt's *Völkerpsychologie*. The gesture, as Mead understood it, is a preparatory stage of social response—a bracing for movement or an overflowing of nervous excitement that might reinforce the agent and indirectly prepare one for action. Examples include changes of posture and facial expression, flushing of the skin, audible changes in the rhythm of breathing, and certain vocal outbursts (*SW* 110, 123). These early indications of incipient conduct acquire their status as gestures through their functional role in social interaction, for they quite naturally come to serve as stimuli calling out anticipatory responses from the other individuals involved in the social act. The initial phases of these latter responses serve as gestures that may call out a modified social response from the first individual, and so on. In this manner there is set up a "conversation of gesture," a "field of palaver" consisting of "truncated acts" (*SW* 109, 124). Unlike the imitative conduct emphasized by Baldwin and Royce, such conversations of gesture presuppose no consciousness of meaning or of social objects. Consider, for instance, the familiar preliminaries of a dog fight. Here is a palaver of mutual bristling, growling, pacing, and maneuvering for position. The two animals appear to communicate quite effectively, yet it is highly doubtful that either has any consciousness of self or is able to assess the significance of its own actions.

The importance Mead attributed to the conversation of gesture as a social condition for the emergence of human consciousness derives from his Jamesian view regarding the behavioral basis of meaning, a view he shared with such thinkers as Royce, Dewey, and James Rowland Angell (*SW* 111). The contents of meanings in our consciousness of objects, he held, are supplied by our consciousness of our own "generalized habitual responses." "These contents are the consciousness of attitudes, of muscular tensions and the feels of readiness to act in the presence of certain stimulations" (*SW* 129). But if we are to appropriate these contents in a genuine consciousness of meaning, we must isolate them from the stimuli that call them forth and then grasp the relation between these two elements of experience. Only in this manner is it possible to understand the one as meaning the other. The importance of the conversation of gesture, Mead argued, is that apart from this type of conduct there is no functional basis for such an analysis within the act: "There is nothing in the economy of the act itself which tends to bring these contents above the threshold, nor distinguishes them as separable elements in a process of relation, such as is implied in the consciousness of meaning" (*SW* 129). Only in the conversation of gesture do we find

a situation in which attention is naturally directed toward one's own attitudes; here alone do we find conduct in which "the very attention given to stimulation, may throw one's attention back upon the attitude he will assume toward the challenging attitude of another, since this attitude will change the stimulation." Moreover, the conflicting acts and consequent inhibitions inherent in the conversation of gesture are ideally suited to bring about within the act the continual analysis of stimuli from which consciousness of relation may eventually arise (*SW* 131).

The apparent failure of the conversation of gesture to produce consciousness in nonhuman animals, Mead suggested, can be traced in part to the relatively low level of inhibition found in their behavior. The higher level of inhibition present in human conduct is "an essential phase of voluntary attention" and leads to an abundance of gesture not found in other animals (*SW* 110). Furthermore, the nonhuman conversation of gesture lacks the diversity of *vocal* gesture to be found in even the most primitive human social interaction. Such vocal gestures, which may have originated in the sudden changes of breathing and circulation rhythms associated with preparation for violent action, have come to "elaborate and immensely complicate" the human conversation of gesture (*SW* 136). The vocal gesture, moreover, is of particular importance in the development of consciousness because it, more than any other kind of gesture, presents to its author the same stimulus content as it presents to the other individuals involved in the social act. It thus provides an ideal mechanism through which the individual can become conscious of his own tendencies to respond (*SW* 137).

It should be noted here that Mead had little to say concerning the physical basis of the consciousness whose development he sought to describe. The determination of the physiological conditions necessary for the rise of consciousness, he held, is a task for physiological psychology. As the title of an earlier essay (**"Social Psychology as a Counterpart to Physiological Psychology"**) suggests, he viewed his own social psychological work as complementing the physiological approach by providing an account of the equally important social conditions for the genesis of consciousness. It was a cause of considerable dismay to Mead that many psychologists of his day acknowledged the physical foundation of consciousness but were apparently oblivious to its social basis. They spoke of introspective self-consciousness as if it were the source of all experience, and they maintained that one could only hypothesize concerning the existence of selves other than the one present to introspection. A proper understanding of the role played by the conversation of gesture in the genesis of consciousness, Mead argued, reveals how profoundly mistaken this kind of psychology is. For from the social psychological standpoint introspective consciousness is a relative latecomer to the field of experience. It is a subjective phase of human conduct ("subjective" in the functional sense explained previously) that is preceded and continually conditioned by experience in an objective world of social objects (*SW* 112).

The first steps in the child's development of introspective self-consciousness, Mead pointed out, are to be found in his instinctive social responses to the gestures of those about him. Gradually, through the conversation of gesture, the child comes to attend to his own responses and begins to merge the imagery of past responses with the stimulus content provided by the gestures of others. It is through the merging of these two components that the child "builds up the social objects that form the most important part of his environment" (*SW* 137). The social consciousness of other selves achieved in this manner precedes consciousness of the self that is analyzed in introspection. The self of introspective consciousness, the "me," is constituted by the merging of imagery drawn from the remembered responses of others with the gestures by which the child stimulates himself. But this merging takes place only after other selves have arisen as social objects in the child's environment. The child acquires his consciousness of himself as object by transferring the form of these earlier social objects to his inner experience (*SW* 139). The "me" of introspection is thus "an importation from the field of social objects into an amorphous, unorganized field of what we call inner experience. Through the organization of this object, the self, this material is itself organized and brought under the control of the individual in the form of so-called consciousness" (*SW* 140). The child's social consciousness of other selves antedates even his consciousness of physical objects. Or, more accurately, his experience becomes reflective—becomes perceptual in the fullest sense—in the recognition of selves, and only gradually does he arrive at a reflective experience of things that are purely physical (*SW* 112-13). The physical form of the "me," like its social structure, is an importation from the child's environment. The form of the physical object is given first in things other than his physical self. "When he has synthesized his various bodily parts with the organic sensations and affective experiences, it will be upon the model of objects about him" (*SW* 138).

THE SOCIAL SELF

Having thus traced the social genesis of introspective self-consciousness, Mead returned in the concluding paragraphs of **"The Mechanism of Social Consciousness"** and in **"The Social Self"** (1913) to a topic he had briefly discussed ten years earlier: his functional understanding of the sense in which the self is both subject and object. A comparison of these two discussions is worthwhile not only for what it reveals about the development of Mead's thought but also for the light it throws on his subsequent employment of the terms "I" and "me."

Recall that Mead's initial emphasis upon the distinction between a subject and object self was dictated by his functionalist treatment of psychical consciousness. In the context of that early discussion, the "me" was taken to be a meaningful object serving to guide ongoing conduct,

while the "I" was identified with the immediate flow of experience as distinguished from the objects that ordinarily control it. The "I" becomes available to introspective consciousness, Mead held, only in the presence of a situation in which old objects have broken down and new ones adequate to guide conduct have not yet appeared; here the "I" takes the form of an immediately experienced interplay of conflicting suggestions, from which arise novel meanings allowing for the reconstruction of problematic elements in the world of objects.

Such, in outline, was Mead's position in 1903. In the essays of 1912 and 1913 his approach to these matters had modified in accordance with the genetic and social orientation he had increasingly adopted in the intervening years. There is no indication that he had changed his earlier view of the reconstructive function of psychical consciousness, but his emphasis now fell primarily upon its social origin and structure. Instead of involving merely an interplay of conflicting suggestions, inner consciousness is said to possess a dramatic or dialogic structure imported from the individual's social experience. The "I" and the "me" are understood in terms of their functional roles within this process.

The "me," as has been remarked previously, becomes an object of consciousness through a development of the conversation of gestures. The crucial mechanism is the individual's capacity to respond to his own gestures. In thus responding, an individual tends to bring to bear upon his conduct memory images of responses made by others to similar gestures. These images are merged with the stimulus content of the gesture to constitute the "me" as a social object (*SW* 140, 146). This object self remains, as in Mead's earliest essays, a presentation within conduct; but its functional role is now understood in terms of the thoroughgoing sociality of human conduct. The "I," on the other hand, is the response the individual makes to the "me." Or, better, it is the immediate act within which the "me" functions as a meaningful presentation. This identification of the "I" is the same as that somewhat dimly articulated in Mead's 1903 essay, **"The Definition of the Psychical,"** but in his essays of 1912 and 1913 Mead avoided any suggestion that the "I" could appear in immediate awareness. Rather, he held that the "I" always remains "behind the scenes" (*SW* 141); it is "a presupposition, but never a presentation of conscious experience" (*SW* 142). The elusiveness of the "I" is to be explained by the fact that "we can be conscious of our acts only through the sensory processes set up after the act has begun" (*SW* 143). Our acts or responses can, of course, become presentations within a subsequent act, but they are then parts of a "me" and no longer an "I."

This last point is amplified by Mead's attempt, in **"The Social Self,"** to do justice to the full complexity of the self as presented in introspective consciousness. Analysis of such consciousness, he pointed out, does reveal moments in which we are aware of the self as both subject and object. "To be concrete, one remembers asking how he could undertake to do this, that, or the other, chiding himself for his shortcomings or pluming himself upon his achievements" (*SW* 142). But the subject self thus presented is not the "I." It is rather another "me" standing alongside of, evaluating or making suggestions to, the first "me." Just as one can respond to one's own actions with respect to another self and thereby be presented with a "me" standing over against that self, so one can respond to one's action with respect to the "me" and thereby be presented with a second "me" standing over against the first. Confusion of this second "me" or reflective self with the "I" is what leads to the mistaken assumption that one can be directly conscious of oneself as acting and acted upon (*SW* 145).

Since we tend to respond to ourselves in the roles of others in the social environment, sometimes even assuming their characteristic intonations and facial expressions, both the structure of inner consciousness and the content of the "me's" there presented are largely importations from objective social experience. In the young child such inner consciousness is loosely organized and quite personal; it involves an obviously social interplay between the remembered "me" who acts and the response of an "accompanying chorus" of others who figure prominently in the child's social experience. Later this drama becomes more abstract, and we have in its place an inner process of symbolic thought. "The features and intonations of the *dramatis personae* fade out and the emphasis falls upon the meaning of inner speech, the imagery becomes merely the barely necessary cues" (*SW* 147).

We may note in this connection that Mead's view concerning the relation of this dialogic structure of inner consciousness to the "I" and "me" is easily misunderstood. Consider, for instance, the problems of interpretation posed by the following typical passage: "The self-conscious, actual self in social intercourse is the objective 'me' or 'me's' with the process of response continually going on and implying a fictitious 'I' always out of sight of himself" (*SW* 141).[9] Now it is natural, perhaps, to think of this as meaning that the "I" first responds to the "me," then the "me" responds to the "I," and so on. But this line of interpretation must surely be incorrect. For Mead's functional definitions of the "I" and "me" rule out this kind of interaction by placing the two on different ontological levels. We may, consistent with Mead's view, speak of the "me" as an agent in relation to other *objects*; but in relation to the "I" it can be no more than a presentation. This being the case, the correct interpretation of Mead's meaning here must be as follows: the "I" of one moment functions as a gesture calling out the "I" of the next moment, which, in turn, functions as a gesture for the "I" of a succeeding moment, and so on. Any or all of these "I's" may carry memory images of previous social responses, these images merging with the immediate stimulus content of the gesture to yield a corresponding presentation of a "me." And since the memory images involved in different acts may be as various as the social roles we play (*SW* 146), we may have a plurality of "me's."

Because Mead was primarily concerned with the social character of inner consciousness in his essays of 1912-

13, he did not emphasize the factor of novelty as he had done in **"The Definition of the Psychical."** But this omission was not indicative of any loss of interest in that topic, for the claim that novel elements are continually emerging within conduct appears again and again in his later works. Moreover, in the 1928 lectures, later published as *Mind, Self and Society,* he attributes the introduction of novelty in human conduct to the "I," just as he had in 1903. This attribution is perfectly consistent with the interpretation of the "I" and "me" sketched above. To say, as Mead does in his 1928 lectures, that the "I" is responsible for the fact that "we are never fully aware of what we are, . . . we surprise ourselves by our own action"[10] is simply another way of making the point that the living act is always something more than the presentations that arise within it.[11]

Unfortunately, the lectures recorded in *Mind, Self and Society* do not provide any clear discussion of the functionalist conception of conduct that underlies the whole of Mead's thought. And, consequently, his treatment of the "I" in this context seems unduly arbitrary and mysterious. Indeed, at least one able critic has gone so far as to argue that in these lectures Mead employed the "I" primarily as a residual category for a group of "heterogeneous phenomena" that could not conveniently be explained in terms of the social structure attributed to the "me."[12] But if my reading of Mead's early essays is correct, his later use of the terms "I" and "me" is a consistent outgrowth of his early functionalism, and, viewed in this light, the phenomena he identifies with the "I" are not at all "heterogeneous."

CONCLUDING REMARKS

By the time he published **"The Social Self"** in 1913, Mead's struggles with that "original haunting question" of which Dewey spoke had led him to almost all the major ideas of his mature social psychology. His later essays and lectures extend and refine these ideas in important ways, but they involve no significant departure from the genetic and social functionalism developed in the essays just examined. That this continuity of Mead's social psychological work has been so often overlooked is due in part to his tendency in later years to refer to his position as a form of behaviorism. Mead's thought was indeed always concerned with conduct or behavior, but never in quite the sense now suggested by the term behaviorism. Rather, his work remained rooted in that organic model of conduct he had embraced in the early years of the Chicago School. It is their testimony to this fact that makes his publications of 1900-1913 valuable documents for any student of Mead's social psychology.

NOTES

[1] Charles W. Morris, the editor of Mead's *Mind, Self and Society,* claims in his preface that stenographic student notes of Mead's "1927 course in social psychology" were used as the basis for this volume (vi). But the date Morris mentions here appears to be inaccurate. An examination

of the materials from which Morris constructed the book reveals that the basic set of notes was taken by W. T. Lillie in Mead's course philosophy 321, advanced social psychology, during the winter quarter of 1928. See Mead Papers, box II, folders 4-13.

[2] PP xxxvi-xxxvii.

[3] Rucker, *Chicago Pragmatists,* 59-60.

[4] Dewey, "The Reflex Arc Concept in Psychology," reprinted in *John Dewey: The Early Works,* 5:96-109.

[5] *John Dewey: The Early Works,* 5:104, 102, 98-99.

[6] Ibid., 107, 108-9.

[7] All of the Mead essays discussed in this chapter are reprinted in sw, and the page references indicated in the text are to this book.

[8] In later years Mead preferred the term "impulse" when referring to the root tendencies of human conduct. "They are best termed 'impulses' and not 'instincts,' because they are subject to extensive modifications in the life-history of individuals." *MSS* 337.

[9] Mead's use of the term "fictitious" in this passage is puzzling, but it may suggest that he himself was aware of the somewhat misleading character of the term "I" as applied to the immediate act. The "I," he says several lines earlier, is the transcendental self of Kant. But this remark does nothing to render the use of a personal pronoun here less questionable.

[10] *MSS* 174.

[11] "Now, it is this living act which never gets directly into reflective experience. . . . It is that 'I' which we may be said to be continually trying to realize, and to realize through the actual conduct itself." Ibid., 203. Also, "The act itself which I have spoken of as the 'I' in the social situation is a source of unity of the whole, while the 'me' is the social situation in which the act can express itself." Ibid., 279.

[12] Kolb, "A Critical Evaluation of Mead's 'I' and 'me' Concepts," reprinted in *Symbolic Interaction: A Reader in Social Psychology,* ed. Manis and Meltzer, 241-50.

FURTHER READING

Criticism

Aboulafia, Mitchell. *The Mediating Self: Mead, Sartre, and Self-Determination.* New Haven: Yale University Press, 1986, 139 p.
   Contrasts Mead's concept of self with that of Jean-Paul Sartre.

————, ed. *Philosophy, Social Theory, and the Thought of George Herbert Mead.* Albany: State University of New York Press, 1991, 319 p.
   Collection of critical essays on Mead.

Baldwin, John D. *George Herbert Mead: A Unifying Theory for Sociology.* Newbury Park, Calif.: Sage Publications, 1986, 168 p.
   Provides an original analysis of Mead's philosophy, viewing it as a potentially unifying theory of social philosophy.

Barry, Robert M. "A Man and a City: George Herbert Mead in Chicago." In *American Philosophy and the Future: Essays for a New Generation*, edited by Michael Novak, pp. 173-92. New York: Charles Scribner's Sons, 1968.
   Explores the influence of social and political forces on Mead's conception of self and society.

Bourgeois, Patrick L. and Sandra B. Rosenthal. "Scientific Time and the Temporal Sense of Human Existence: Merleau-Ponty and Mead." *Research in Phenomenology* XX (1990): 152-63.
   Asserts that "in rejecting the ultimacy of the derived time of science in favor of the priority of lived time in which such derivations are rooted, Merleau-Ponty and Mead belie the attempts to interpret them as taking, respectively, a negative or a naïve philosophical stance toward science."

————. "Role Taking, Corporeal Intersubjectivity, and Self: Mead and Merleau-Ponty." *Philosophy Today* 34, No. 2 (Summer 1990): 117-28.
   Compares Mead's and Maurice Merleau-Ponty's interpretation of self.

Cronk, George. *The Philosophical Anthropology of George Herbert Mead.* New York: Peter Lang, 1987, 153 p.
   Offers an analysis of Mead's central philosophical concepts.

Farrell, James T. "George Herbert Mead's Philosophy of the Present." In *Literature and Morality*, pp. 177-81. New York: Vanguard Press, 1945.
   Positive assessment of Mead's *The Philosophy of the Present.*

Frings, Manfred S. "Social Temporality in George Herbert Mead and Scheler." *Philosophy Today* XXVII, No. 4 (Winter 1983): 281-89.
   Elucidates Mead's theory of the past and its relation to society.

Gunter, Pete A., ed. *Creativity in George Herbert Mead.* Lanham, MD: University Press of America, 1990, 110 p.

Collection of papers presented at the 1969 Society of Philosophy of Creativity sponsored program of the American Philosophical Association.

Hamilton, Peter, ed. *George Herbert Mead: Critical Assessments*. 4 vols. London & New York: Routledge.
Comprehensive collection of critical essays examining Mead's philosophical work.

Joas, Hans. *G. H. Mead: A Contemporary Re-examination of His Thought*. Translated by Raymond Meyer. Cambridge: Polity Press, 1980, 266 p.
Offers a thorough philological study of Mead's work.

Kang, W. *G. H. Mead's Concept of Rationality: A Study of the Use of Symbols and Other Implements*. The Hague: Mouton, 1976, 219 p.
Examines Mead's theory of rationality.

Leys, Ruth. "Mead's Voices: Imitation as Foundation, or, The Struggle against Mimesis." *Critical Inquiry* 19, No. 2 (Winter 1993): 277-307.
Explores the concepts of imitation and sympathy in Mead's philosophy of self.

Natanson, Maurice. *The Social Dynamics of George H. Mead*. Washington, D. C.: Public Affairs Press, 1956, 102 p.
Explicates the major elements of Mead's philosophical work, particularly time, emergence, perspective, sociality, and the act.

Stryker, Sheldon. "Conditions of Accurate Role-Taking: A Test of Mead's Theory." In *Human Behavior and Social Processes: An Interactionist Approach*, edited by Arnold M. Rose, pp. 41-62. Boston: Houghton Mifflin, 1962.
Provides empirical data on Mead's theory of role-taking.

Tillman, Mary Katherine. "Temporality and Role-Taking in G. H. Mead." *Social Research* 37, No. 4 (Winter 1970): 533-46.
Investigates the role of temporality in Mead's theory of social interactionism.

Werkmeister, W. H. "Mead's Philosophy of the Act." *A History of Philosophical Ideas in America*, pp. 521-40. New York: Ronald Press, 1949.
Traces the development of Mead's concept of the act.

G. E. Moore

1873-1958

(Full name George Edward Moore) English philosopher and editor.

INTRODUCTION

With Bertrand Russell, Moore is considered one of the two most important English philosophers of the first half of the twentieth century. Moore, Russell, and Austrian-born Ludwig Wittgenstein constituted the influential trio of analytical and phenomenological philosophers residing at Cambridge's Trinity College. From their respective academic positions, the philosophers formulated the tenets of New Realism, derived in part from German phenomenologist Alexius Meinong's theory of objects, which postulated the difference between objectives and objects. Moore also concerned himself with moral philosophy, as evidenced by his major work *Principia Ethica*. In this work Moore expressed that, in attempting to define the concept of good, an individual commits the "naturalistic fallacy," which is the assumption that good is capable of being defined inasmuch as definitions require their objects to comprise parts, but good abjures definition because of its simple nature. The work is also notable for its impact on the Bloomsbury Group, which included Moore, Clive Bell, Desmond MacCarthy, John Maynard Keynes, Virginia Woolf, Leonard Woolf, and E. M. Forster.

Biographical Information

Moore was born in Upper Norwood, an affluent suburb of London, the fifth of eight children. In 1892 he was awarded an academic scholarship to Trinity College, Cambridge, where he met classmate Bertrand Russell. The two men were to share ideas and inspire each other throughout their respective careers. Moore completed his degree and earned a fellowship prize for his essay on Immanuel Kant's views on ethics. The prize enabled him to spend the next six years reading philosophy and formulating the ideas that became *Principia Ethica*. A sizeable inheritance afforded Moore the opportunity to spend the next several years refining his philosophy. In 1911 Cambridge installed him as a professor of psychology. In 1925 he was made Professor of Philosophy, a position he held until his retirement in 1939. Moore took over as editor of the philosophical journal *Mind* in 1921. After his retirement and through the duration of World War II, Moore lectured in the United States.

Major Works

Moore's essay "Refutation of Idealism" appeared in a 1903 issue of *Mind*. This essay is credited as the opening salvo of the British New Realism, a branch of philosophy

with which Bertrand Russell was closely aligned. New Realism responded to the metaphysical idealism advocated by F. H. Bradley and George Berkeley, which maintained that, as Berkeley wrote, "To be is to be perceived," meaning an object's existence depends upon its being perceived. Berkeley used the fact that objects persist in their being even when creatures are not present to perceive them to postulate the existence of God, a supreme being who perceives all objects at all times, thus ensuring their continued existence. Moore's argument, echoing that of Meinong, was that common sense (i.e. objectivity) provided proof positive that objects exist whether or not a being is present to perceive them. In other words, New Realism distinguishes between the act of awareness and the object of awareness. Supporting this argument, in his essay "A Defense of Common Sense," Moore employed "two distinct elements, one which I call consciousness, and the other which I call the object of consciousness." In this essay Moore proposed that there is no basis for the belief that physical reality relies on mental reality; nor is there an inherent causality between physical reality and mental perception. In "A Defense of Common Sense" Moore also argued that the true function of philosophy lay in its analysis of reality, not its definition of it. For example, when it is said that the sky is blue, the veracity of the comment cannot be denied because common sense tells the listener that the statement is true. Philosophy exists to analyze such true statements because listeners' understanding that a statement is true does not necessarily imply that they understand the speaker's full meaning. In *Principia Ethica* Moore continued to emphasize reason over idealism, but allowed that individuals should enjoy every experience through the cultivation of friendships and a thorough appreciation of the arts: "By far the most valuable things, which we know or can imagine, are certain states of consciousness, which may be roughly described as the pleasures of human intercourse and the enjoyment of beautiful objects," which became the credo of The Bloomsbury Group.

PRINCIPAL WORKS

Principia Ethica (philosophy) 1903; revised 1922
Ethics (philosophy) 1912
Philosophical Studies (philosophy) 1922
The Philosophy of G. E. Moore (philosophy) 1942
Some Main Problems of Philosophy (philosophy) 1953
Philosophical Papers (philosophy) 1959
Commonplace Book 1919-1935 (philosophy) 1967

CRITICISM

C. D. Broad (essay date 1942)

SOURCE: "Certain Features in Moore's Ethical Doctrines," in *The Philosophy of G. E. Moore,* edited by Paul Arthur Schlipp, Northwestern University, 1942, pp. 41-68.

[*In the following essay, Broad, the author of the "Compound Theory of Materialistic Emergency," argues against the validity of Moore's* Principia Ethica.]

From the many topics in Moore's ethical writings which might profitably be discussed I am going to choose two in the present paper. They are (1) his attempted refutation of Ethical Egoism, and (2) his distinction between "Natural" and "Non-natural" characteristics, and his doctrine that the word "good" (in one very important use of it) is a name for a certain non-natural characteristic.

(I) ETHICAL EGOISM

I shall begin by defining three opposed terms, viz., "Ethical Egoism," "Ethical Neutralism," and "Ethical Altruism." The second of these is the doctrine which Moore accepts in **Principia Ethica**; the other two are extreme deviations from it in opposite directions. It will therefore be best to start with ethical neutralism.

The neutralist theory is that no-one has any special duty to himself *as such,* and that no-one has any special duty to others *as such.* The fundamental duty of each of us *is* simply to maximise, so far as he can, the balance of good over bad experiences throughout the whole aggregate of contemporary and future conscious beings. Suppose that A, by giving to B a good experience at the cost of foregoing a good experience or incurring a bad one himself, can increase this balance more than by any other means; then it is A's duty to do so. Suppose, on the other hand, that A, by getting a good experience for himself at the cost of depriving B of a good experience or giving him a bad one, can increase this balance more than by any other means; then it is equally A's duty to do so.

Ethical Egoism is the doctrine that each man has a predominant obligation towards himself as such. Ethical Altruism is the doctrine that each man has a predominant obligation towards others as such. These doctrines might be held in milder or more rigid forms according to the degree of predominance which they ascribe to the egoistic or the altruistic obligation respectively. The extreme form of Ethical Egoism would hold that each man has an ultimate obligation *only* towards himself. The extreme form of Ethical Altruism would hold that each man has an ultimate obligation *only* towards others. According to the former extreme each man's only duty is to develop *his own* nature and dispositions to the utmost and to give *himself* the most favourable balance that he can of good over bad experiences. He will be concerned with the development and the experiences of other persons only in so far as these may affect, favourably or unfavourably, his own development and his own experience. This doctrine seems to have been held by Spinoza. The extreme form of Ethical Altruism would hold that each man's only duty is to develop to the utmost the natures and the dispositions of all other persons whom he can affect and to give them the most favourable balance that he can of good over bad experiences. He will be concerned with his own experiences only in so far as they may affect, favourably or unfavourably, the development and experiences of other persons.

Now Moore professes to show in **Principia Ethica** (96-105) that Ethical Egoism is self-contradictory; and, if his argument were valid, a very similar argument could be used to refute Ethical Altruism. He alleges that Ethical Egoism involves the absurdity that *each* man's good is the *sole* good, although each man's good is different from any other man's good. In my opinion it involves nothing of the kind; and I will now try to justify that opinion.

First of all, what do we mean by such phrases as "Smith's good" or "Jones' evil?" The good of Smith is just those good experiences, dispositions, etc., which are Smith's; and the evil of Jones is just those bad experiences, dispositions, etc., which are Jones'.

Suppose now that A is an ethical egoist. He can admit that, if a certain experience or disposition of his is good, a precisely similar experience or disposition of B's will be also and equally good. But he will assert that it is not his duty to produce good experiences and dispositions as such, without regard to the question of who will have them. A has an obligation to produce good experiences and dispositions in *himself,* and no such direct obligation to produce them in B or in anyone else. A recognises that B has no such direct obligation to produce them in A or in anyone else. This doctrine does not contradict itself in any way.

What it does contradict is Sidgwick's second axiom about goodness and our obligations in respect of producing it. This is stated as follows in Book III, Chapter XIII of Sidgwick's *Methods of Ethics* (382, in the sixth edition):—" . . . as a rational being I am bound to aim at good generally—so far as it is attainable by my efforts—not merely at a particular part of it." Since Sidgwick was an ethical hedonist, he held that nothing is intrinsically good or bad except experiences. Therefore, to "aim at good" will mean to try to produce good experiences and to avert or diminish bad experiences. Therefore this axiom means that it is each person's duty to try to produce the greatest possible net balance of good over bad experiences among all the conscious beings whom he can affect, and that he has no *direct* obligation to produce such experiences in one rather than in another person or set of persons, e.g., in himself as such or in others as such. Suppose he confines his efforts to himself or to his family or to his social class or to his countrymen, or even to that very extended but still restricted group which consists of everyone but himself; then he will always need some positive justification for this restriction. And the only admissible justification is that, owing to his special limitations or their special relations to him, he can produce more good on the whole by confining his efforts to a certain restricted set of conscious beings. Any restriction in the range of one's beneficent activities needs ethical justification, and this is the only valid ethical justification for it.

It is evident, then, that Sidgwick's axiom is equivalent to the assertion of ethical neutralism, and that ethical egoism is inconsistent with it. But this does not make ethical egoism *self*-contradictory; and, unless Sidgwick's axiom be self-evidently true, the inconsistency of ethical egoism with it does not refute that doctrine.

Precisely similar remarks would apply to any argument against ethical altruism on the same lines as Moore's argument against ethical egoism. Suppose that *A* is an ethical altruist. He can admit that, if a certain experience or disposition of *B*'s is good, a precisely similar experience or disposition of his own will be also and equally good. But he asserts that it is not his duty to produce good experiences and dispositions as such, without regard to the question of who will have them. *A* has an obligation to produce good experiences and dispositions in *others,* and no such direct obligation to produce them in himself. *A* recognises that *B* has an obligation to produce good experiences and dispositions in *A* and in everyone except *B*, and that *B* has no obligation to produce them in *B*. This doctrine, again, contradicts Sidgwick's second axiom about goodness and our obligations in producing it. But it is not *self*-contradictory, and, unless Sidgwick's axiom be self-evident, the inconsistency of ethical altruism with it does not refute the latter doctrine.

An illuminating way of putting the difference between ethical neutralism and the other two theories is the following. Ethical neutralism assumes that there is a certain *one* state of affairs—"the sole good"—at which *everyone* ought to aim as an *ultimate* end. Differences in the proximate ends of different persons can be justified only in so far as the one ultimate end is best secured in practice by different persons aiming, not directly at it, but at different proximate ends of a more limited kind. The other two theories deny that there is any *one* state of affairs at which *everyone* ought to aim even as an ultimate end. In fact each theory holds that there are as many ultimate ends as there are agents. On the egoistic theory the ultimate end at which *A* should aim is the maximum balance of good over evil in *A*'s experiences and dispositions. The ultimate end at which *B* should aim is the maximum balance of good over evil in *B*'s experiences and dispositions. And so on for *C, D,* etc. On the altruistic theory the ultimate end at which *A* should aim is the maximum balance of good over evil in the experiences and dispositions of all *others-than-A*. The ultimate end at which *B* should aim is the maximum balance of good over evil in the experiences and dispositions of all *others-than-B*. And so on for *C, D,* etc. The main difference between the

two theories is that for egoism the various ultimate ends are mutually exclusive, whilst for altruism any two of them have a very large field in common.

Now there is nothing self-contradictory in the doctrine that, corresponding to each different person, there is a different state of affairs at which he and he only ought to aim as an ultimate end. And there is nothing self-contradictory in the doctrine, which is entailed by this, that there is no one state of affairs at which everyone ought to aim as an ultimate end. Moore simply assumes, in common with Sidgwick, that there must be a certain state of affairs which is *the* ultimate end at which *everyone* ought to aim; shows that ethical egoism is inconsistent with this assumption; and then unjustifiably accuses ethical egoism of being *self*-contradictory.

Granted that even the extreme forms of ethical egoism and ethical altruism are internally consistent, is there any reason to accept or to reject either of them?

(1) If ethical neutralism were true, they could both be rejected. Now the following argument can be produced in favour of ethical neutralism. On any theory except this it will sometimes be right for a person to do an act which will obviously produce less good or more evil than some other alternative act which is open to him at the time. E.g., it is often the case that *A* could either (i) do an act which would add something to his well-being at the cost of diminishing *B*'s by a certain amount, or (ii) do another act which would increase his own well-being *rather less* at the cost of diminishing *B*'s *very much less.* Plainly *A* would in general be producing more good by doing the latter act than by doing the former. But, if ethical egoism be true, it would be his duty to do the former and to avoid doing the latter. Again, it is often the case that *A* could either (i) do an act which would add something to *B*'s well-being at the cost of diminishing his own by a certain amount, or (ii) do another act which would increase *B*'s well-being *rather less* and diminish his own *very much less.* Plainly *A* would in general be producing more good by doing the latter act than by doing the former. But, if ethical altruism be true, it would be his duty to do the former and to avoid doing the latter. I think, therefore, that ethical neutralism is the only one of the three types of theory which can be combined with the doctrine that the right act in any situation will always coincide with the optimific act in that situation. Since Utilitarians hold the latter view, they ought to hold the former; and so Sidgwick was right, as a Utilitarian, to lay down an axiom which is equivalent to ethical neutralism.

It is possible, however, to distinguish between what I call an "optim*ising*" act, and what I have called an "optim*ific*" act; and it might be possible to combine ethical altruism with the doctrine that the right act always coincides with the optimising act. I will now explain this distinction and justify this assertion. Suppose that a certain act *á* is done in a certain situation S, and that the amount of value in the universe is thereby changed. It is possible to distinguish two quite different contributions which this act may make to the amount of value in the world. They may be called its *direct* and its *consequential* contributions. The act may have qualities which make it intrinsically good or bad. Even if it has not, it will have non-causal relations to other factors in the contemporary and the past situation which forms its context; and in virtue of these the whole composed of the act and the situation may be better or worse than the situation by itself or the situation combined with a different act. Any value, positive or negative, which accrues in this way to the universe through the occurrence of this act may be called its "direct" contribution. Again, the act co-operates as a cause-factor with other factors in the contemporary situation and thus leads to a train of consequences which are different from those which would have followed if no act or a different act had been done. Any value or disvalue which accrues to the universe through the values or disvalues of the consequences of an act may be called its "consequential" contribution. The "total" contribution of an act consists of its direct and its consequential contributions. An "optim*ific*" act in a given situation may be defined as one whose *consequential* contribution to the value in the universe is at least as great as that of any alternative act open to the agent. An "optim*ising*" act in a given situation is one whose *total* contribution to the value in the universe is at least as great as that of any alternative act open to the agent.

Let us now apply these notions. Suppose that there is a situation in which *A* can either (i) do an act which will increase *B*'s well-being at the cost of considerably diminishing his own, or (ii) do an act which would add rather less to *B*'s well-being and diminish his own very much less. Suppose further that an act of self-sacrifice has, as such, a certain amount of moral value. Then it might be that the direct contribution which the former act would make, as an act of self-sacrifice, more than counter-balances the consequential diminution which it causes by decreasing the agent's own well-being. So an altruistic act might be the optimising act even when it is not the optimific act.

Now common-sense does ascribe considerable positive value to acts of voluntary self-sacrifice as such. It is therefore conceivable that the right act, on the extreme altruistic view, might always coincide with the optimising act. But it is not necessary that it should, and it seems most unlikely that it always would. For it seems easy to conceive situations in which the most altruistic act possible would increase the well-being of others very slightly and would diminish that of the agent very much, whilst some other possible act would increase the well-being of others only a little less and would positively increase that of the agent. In such a situation it is most unlikely that the most altruistic act would be an optimising act, even when its direct contribution to the goodness in the universe, as an act of self-sacrifice, was taken into account.

It is quite plain that no attempt on these lines to reconcile ethical *egoism* with the doctrine that the right act coincides with the optimising act would be plausible. For common-sense attaches no positive value to an act of sacrificing others for one's own benefit, as such. Therefore, when what would be the right act on the extreme egoistic view fails to coincide with the optimific act, it is impossible that it should coincide with the optimising act.

The upshot of this discussion is as follows. Many people find it self-evident that the right act in any situation must coincide with the optimific act. Anyone who does so can safely reject pure ethical egoism and pure ethical altruism, and will almost be forced to accept ethical neutralism. When the distinction between an optimising and an optimific act is pointed out to them many of those who thought it evident that the right act must coincide with the optimific act would be inclined to amend their doctrine by substituting "optimising" for "optimific." Such people could safely reject pure egoism. It is not impossible that the most altruistic act should coincide with the optimising act even when it fails to coincide with the optimific act. But, even if it always did so, this would be a merely contingent fact; whilst they hold that the coincidence between the right act and the optimising act is necessary, since they find it self-evident. And it is very unlikely that the most altruistic act would in fact always coincide with the optimising act. Therefore the substitution of "optimising" for "optimific" would make no difference in the end. Those who find the coincidence of the right act with the optimising act self-evident could safely reject both pure altruism and pure egoism, and would have to accept ethical neutralism as the only principle of distribution which is compatible with their axiom.

(2) So far we have considered the grounds for accepting ethical neutralism, and therefore the indirect reasons for rejecting ethical egoism and ethical altruism. We will now consider the attitude of common-sense towards each of the three alternatives when judged on its own merits. (i) Common-sense would reject pure ethical egoism out of hand as grossly immoral. It is, I think, doubtful whether anyone would accept *ethical* egoism unless, like Spinoza, he had already accepted *psychological* egoism. If a person is persuaded that it is psychologically impossible for anyone to act non-egoistically, he will have to hold that each man's duties are confined within the sphere which this psychological impossibility marks out. But common-sense does not accept psychological egoism, though many philosophers have done so; and on this point common-sense is right and these philosophers are tricked by certain rather subtle ambiguities of language.

(ii) The attitude of common-sense (at any rate in countries where there is a Christian tradition) towards pure ethical altruism is different. It would, with an uncomfortable recollection of some rather disturbing passages in the Sermon on the Mount, be inclined to describe the doctrine as quixotic or impracticable but hardly as immoral. Apart from the embarrassment which persons in a Christian country feel at saying or implying that Christ sometimes talked nonsense, there is a sound practical reason for this attitude. We realise that most people are far more likely to err on the egoistic than on the altruistic side; that in a world where so many people are too egoistic it is as well that some people should be too altruistic; and that there is something heroic in the power to sacrifice one's own happiness for the good of others. We therefore hesitate to condemn publicly even exhibitions of altruism which we privately regard as excessive.

(iii) Although common-sense rejects pure egoism and does not really accept pure altruism, I do not think that it is prepared to admit neutralism without a struggle. It would regard neutralism as in some directions immorally selfish and in other directions immorally universalistic. It undoubtedly holds that each of us has more urgent obligations to benefit certain persons who are specially related to him, e.g., his parents, his children, his fellow-countrymen, his benefactors, etc., than to benefit others who are not thus related to him. And it would hold that the special urgency of these obligations is founded *directly* on these special relations.

(iv) The ideal of common-sense then is neither pure egoism nor pure altruism nor neutralism. I think it may be best described as "Self-referential Altruism." I will now explain what I mean by this. Each of us is born as a member of a family, a citizen of a country, and so on. In the course of his life he voluntarily or involuntarily becomes a member of many other social groups, e.g., a school, a college, a church, a trades-union, etc. Again, he gets into special relations of love and friendship with certain individuals who are not blood-relations of his. Now the view of common-sense is roughly as follows.

Each of us has a certain obligation to himself, as such. I do not think that common-sense considers that a person is under *any* obligation to make himself *happy*, i.e., to "give himself a good time." Possibly this is because most people have so strong a natural tendency to aim at getting the experiences which they expect to like and at avoiding those which they expect to dislike. On the other hand, the obligation to develop one's own powers and capabilities to the utmost, and to organise one's various dispositions into a good pattern is considered to be a strong one. This kind of action often goes very much against the grain, since it conflicts with natural laziness and a natural tendency to aim at the easier and more passive kinds of good experience. The obligation to make others happy and to prevent or alleviate their unhappiness is held to vary in urgency according to the nature of their relation to oneself. It is weakest when the others stand in no relation to the agent except that of being fellow sentient beings. It is strongest when the others are the agent's parents or his children, or non-relatives whom he loves and by whom he is loved, or persons from whom he has received special benefits deliberately bestowed at some cost to the giver.

A person's obligation towards *A* is more urgent than his obligation towards *B* if it would be right for him to aim at the well-being of *A* before considering that of *B*, and to begin to consider that of *B* only after he had secured

a certain minimum for *A*. The greater this minimum is, the greater is the relative urgency of his obligation towards *A* as compared with his obligation towards *B*.

Now common-sense holds that it is one's duty to be prepared to sacrifice a considerable amount of one's own well-being to secure a quite moderate addition to the net well-being of one's parents or children or benefactors, if this be the only way in which one can secure it. But it does not consider that a person has a duty to sacrifice much of his own well-being in order to secure even a substantial addition to the net well-being of others who stand in no specially intimate relations to him.

Common-sense draws a sharp distinction between making oneself happy, and developing one's own powers and capacities to the utmost and organising one's disposition into a good pattern. The obligation to make oneself happy is held to be vanishingly feeble, whilst the obligation to develop and organise oneself is held to be very urgent. Hence it is felt to be doubtful how far a person ought to sacrifice self-development and self-culture, as distinct from his own happiness, in order to add to the happiness of others. It is only when the claim is very strong, as in the case of a child on its parents or of aged and infirm parents on a grown-up son or daughter, that common-sense approves of this kind of self-sacrifice. Even here it feels considerable hesitation; and, apart from such cases, it is extremely embarrassed. It realises that it is a good thing on the whole that a certain proportion of people should voluntarily forego the development of a great many valuable aspects of their personality in order to live in the slums and add to the well-being of other persons who have no specially urgent claims on them. But, whilst it admires those who make the sacrifice, it regrets the waste of talent; and it is relieved to think that there is no great danger of too many gifted persons following their example. On the whole it favours a kind of ethical "division of labour." A certain minimum of self-sacrifice and of self-culture is demanded of everyone; but, when this minimum has been reached, common-sense approves of certain persons specialising in self-culture and others in beneficent self-sacrifice.

Lastly, common-sense considers that each of us has direct obligations to certain groups of persons of which he is a member, considered as collective wholes. The most obvious case is one's nation, taken as a collective unity. It is held that an Englishman, as such, is under an urgent obligation in certain circumstances to sacrifice his happiness, his development, and his life for England, and is under no such obligation to Germany; and that a German is under an obligation in similar circumstances to make a similar sacrifice for Germany, and is under no such obligation to England. And so on. It should be noticed that Germans, as well as Englishmen, admit that Englishmen have this peculiar obligation towards England; and that Englishmen, as well as Germans, admit that Germans have this peculiar obligation towards Germany. This is clearly recognised by the saner citizens of both countries even when they are at war with each other.

It seems to me that the fact that an Englishman considers that a German should sacrifice himself for Germany, even when his doing so is detrimental to England, and that a German considers that an Englishman should sacrifice himself for England, even when his doing so is detrimental to Germany, is of some theoretical importance. It certainly suggests that we are concerned here with a genuine and objective, though limited, obligation; and not with a mere psychological prejudice in favour of one's own nation. Opinion has varied from time to time and from place to place as to what *kind* of group has the most urgent obligation on its members. At present, among most Western peoples and in Japan, the nation is put in this supreme position. Among the Greeks and Romans it was the city. It may be that in future it will be a class rather than a nation or a city. But common-sense has always held that there is *some* group for which all its members, and only they, were bound in certain circumstances to sacrifice their happiness, their chances of culture and development, and their lives.

I said that common-sense accepts a kind of "Self-referential Altruism." My meaning should now be clear. Common-sense is altruistic in so far as it considers that each of us is often under an obligation to sacrifice his own happiness, and sometimes to sacrifice his own development and life, for the benefit of certain other persons and groups, even when it is doubtful whether more good will be produced by doing so than by not doing so. It tends to admire these acts, as such, even when it regrets the necessity for them, and even when it thinks that on the whole they had better not have been done. It has no such admiration for the attempt to make oneself happy, as such, even when it does no harm to others. And, although it admires acts directed towards self-development and self-culture, as such, especially when they are done in face of external obstacles and internal hindrances, its admiration for them is not usually very intense.

On the other hand, the altruism of common-sense is always limited in scope. It does not hold that any of us has an equally strong obligation to benefit everyone whom he can affect by his actions. According to it, each of us has specially strong obligations to benefit certain persons and groups of persons who stand in certain special relations to *himself*. And these special relations to himself are the ultimate and sufficient ground of these specially urgent obligations. Each person may be regarded as a centre of a number of concentric circles. The persons and the groups to whom he has the most urgent obligations may be regarded as forming the innermost circle. Then comes a circle of persons and groups to whom his obligations are moderately urgent. Finally there is the outermost circle of persons (and animals) to whom he has only the obligation of "common humanity." This is what I mean by saying that the altruism which common-sense accepts is "self-referential."

If this be a fair account of the beliefs of common-sense, what line could a person take who found neutralism self-evident? And, again, what line could a person take who found it self-evident that the right act must coincide with the optimising act and was therefore committed at the second move to neutralism? The problem is the same for both. He would have to do three things.

(i) He would have to hold that common-sense is mistaken in thinking that these special obligations are founded *directly* on these special relations. (ii) He would have to show that all these special obligations, so far as they are valid at all, are derivable from the one fundamental obligation to maximise the balance of good over evil among contemporary and subsequent conscious beings as a whole. He will try to do this by pointing out that each of us is limited in his power of helping or harming others, in the range of his natural sympathies and affections, and in his knowledge of the needs of others. He will argue that, in consequence of this, the maximum balance of good over evil among conscious beings as a whole is most likely to be secured if people do not aim directly at it. It is most likely to be secured if each aims primarily at the maximum balance of good over evil in the members of a limited group consisting of himself and those who stand in more or less intimate relations to him. The best that the neutralist could hope to achieve on these lines would be to reach a system of *derived* obligations which agreed roughly, both in scope and in relative urgency, with that system of obligations which common-sense mistakenly thinks to be founded *directly* upon various special relationships. In so far as this result was achieved he might claim to accept in outline the same set of obligations as common-sense does; to correct common-sense morality in matters of detail; and to substitute a single coherent system of obligations, deduced from a single self-evident ethical principle and a number of admitted psychological facts, for a mere heap of unrelated obligations. (iii) To complete his case he would have to try to explain, by reference to admitted psychological facts and plausible historical hypotheses, how common-sense came to make the fundamental mistakes which, according to him, it does make. For common-sense rejects the neutralistic principle which he finds self-evident, and it regards as *ultimate* those special obligations of an agent towards certain persons and groups which *he* regards as derivative.

How, if at all, could this last *desideratum* be fulfilled? It seems to me that it might be attempted along the following lines. It must be admitted that any society in which each member was prepared to make sacrifices for the benefit of the group as a collective whole would be more likely to flourish and persist than a society whose members were not prepared to make such sacrifices. It must also be admitted that egoistic and anti-social motives are extremely strong in everyone. Suppose, then, that there were a society in which, by any means, there had arisen a strong additional motive (however mistaken and superstitious) in support of self-sacrifice, and that this motive were conveyed from generation to generation by example and precept and were supported by the sanctions of social praise and blame. Such a society would be likely to flourish and to overcome other societies in which no such additional motive existed. Its ways of thinking on these subjects and its sentiments of approval and disapproval would tend to spread, both directly through conquest and indirectly through the prestige which its success would give to it.

On the other hand, a society in which each member was prepared to sacrifice himself just as much for other societies and for their members as for his own society and its members would be most unlikely to flourish and persist. So, if there were a society in which, by any means, a strong additional motive for *unlimited* altruism or for neutralism had arisen and been propagated, that society would be likely to go under in conflict with one in which a more restricted self-referential altruism was practised. It therefore seems likely that the societies which would still persist and flourish after a long period of conflict would be those in which there had somehow arisen, in the remote past, a superstitious approval of altruism within certain limits and a superstitious disapproval of extending it beyond those limits. These are exactly the kind of societies which we do find. If one were asked what is the most formidable society which now exists and the one which seems to have the best chance of spreading its ideals throughout the world directly by conquest and indirectly by the prestige of its success, the answer would be Germany. And, if one were asked what is the nation whose citizens combine the most intense spirit of self-sacrifice within the group with the most rigid refusal to extend that spirit beyond the group, the answer would be the same. *Non est potestas super terram quae comparetur ei.*

It seems then that, even if neutralism be true and be self-evident to the philosopher in his study, there are powerful causes which would make it likely that certain forms of self-referential altruism would appear to be true and self-evident to most unreflective persons at all times and even to reflective persons at most times. Therefore the fact that common-sense rejects neutralism and accepts certain forms of self-referential altruism as self-evident is not a conclusive objection to the *truth,* or even to the *necessary* truth, of neutralism.

(2) "NATURAL" AND "NON-NATURAL" CHARACTERISTICS[1]

It is a fundamental doctrine of Moore's ethical theory that the word "good," in its most fundamental sense, is a name for a characteristic which is simple and "non-natural." He compares it in the first respect, and contrasts it in the second, with the word "yellow."

A complete discussion of this doctrine would have to begin by raising a question which Moore never did raise but which has become acute in recent years. Is "good" a name of a characteristic at all? Or do sentences like "This is good," though grammatically similar to sentences like "This is yellow" which undoubtedly ascribe a certain characteristic to a subject, really need an entirely different kind of analysis? Is it not possible that the function of such sentences is to express or to stimulate certain kinds of emotion, or to command or forbid certain kinds of action, and not to state certain kinds of fact? There is a vast amount to be said for and against this suggestion, but I do not propose to discuss it here. I shall assume, for the sake of argument, that "good" is a name for a characteristic, and that sentences like "This is good" ascribe this characteristic to a subject.

On this assumption the next topic which would have to be discussed in any full treatment of the theory would be Moore's contention that the characteristic of which "good" is a name is simple and unanalysable. This, of course, implies that it is a pure quality and not a relational property. I do not consider that Moore has produced any conclusive reasons for this opinion, and I am very doubtful whether such an opinion *could* be established. But I propose to waive this point also, and to assume that "good" is a name for a simple characteristic.

If we make these assumptions two questions remain. (1) What exactly is meant by the distinction between a "natural" and a "non-natural" characteristic? (2) What connexion, if any, is there between the doctrine that "good," in its primary sense, denotes a characteristic which is simple and unanalysable, and the doctrine that it denotes a characteristic which is non-natural? We will take these two questions in turn.

(1) Let us begin with complex characteristics. A complex characteristic is natural if it can be analysed without remainder into a set of simple characteristics each of which is natural. A complex characteristic is non-natural if its analysis involves at least one simple characteristic which is non-natural. Suppose, e.g., that "This is good" where "good" is used in the primary sense, could be analysed into "This is something which it would be *right* to desire as an end." And suppose that "right," as applied to desires, were a name for a non-natural characteristic. Then goodness, in this sense, would be a complex non-natural characteristic. So we are eventually faced with the question: "What is meant by calling a simple characteristic *natural* or *non-natural*?"

Unfortunately we shall get very little light on this question from Moore's published works. The only place, so far as I know, in which it is explicitly discussed is *Principia Ethica,* 40 to 41. We are told there that a "natural object" is any object that is capable of existing in time, e.g., a stone, a mind, an explosion, an experience, etc. All natural objects have natural characteristics, and some of them have also non-natural characteristics. We are told that each natural characteristic of a natural object could be conceived as existing in time all by itself, and that every natural object is a whole whose parts are its natural characteristics. We are told that a non-natural characteristic of a natural object is one which *cannot* be conceived as existing in time all by itself. It can be conceived as existing only as the property of some natural object.

Now it seems to me that *every* characteristic of a natural object answers to Moore's criterion of non-naturalness, and that *no* characteristic could possibly be natural in his sense. I do not believe for a moment that a penny is a whole of which brownness and roundness are parts, nor do I believe that the brownness or roundness of a penny could exist in time all by itself. Hence, if I accepted Moore's account, I should have to reckon brownness, roundness, pleasantness, etc., as *non-natural* characteristics. Yet he certainly counts them as *natural* characteristics.

I think that Moore is intending to explain the distinction between natural and non-natural characteristics in the very difficult essay in his ***Philosophical Studies*** which is entitled **"The Conception of Intrinsic Value."** So far as I can understand his doctrine in that essay it may be summarised as follows.

(i) The characteristics of any thing T may be first divided into two great classes, viz., those which do, and those which do not, "depend solely on the *intrinsic nature* of" T. (ii) Those characteristics of a thing T which depend solely on its intrinsic nature may then be subdivided into those which are, and those which are not, "intrinsic characteristics" of T. Consider, e.g., an experience which has a certain perfectly determinate kind and degree of pleasantness. Suppose that it also has a certain perfectly determinate kind and degree of goodness. Then, if I understand him aright, Moore would say that both its pleasantness and its goodness are characteristics which depend solely on its intrinsic nature. He would say that its pleasantness is an intrinsic characteristic of it. And he would say that its goodness is not an intrinsic characteristic of it. (iii) Although he does not explicitly say so, I think that he would identify the *non-natural* characteristics of a thing with those which *are* determined solely by its intrinsic nature and yet *are not* intrinsic. The *natural* characteristics of a thing would be those which are either (a) intrinsic, or (b) not determined solely by its intrinsic nature.

Unfortunately Moore gives no clear account of this distinction between the intrinsic and the non-intrinsic varieties of the characteristics which depend on the intrinsic nature of a thing. All that he says is this. A complete enumeration of the *intrinsic* characteristics of a thing would constitute a *complete* description of it. But a description of a thing can be complete even if it omits those characteristics of it which, though determined solely by its intrinsic nature, are not intrinsic. E.g., a pleasant experience, which is also good, could not be completely described unless its pleasantness was mentioned. But it could be completely described without its goodness being mentioned.

I find it most difficult to follow or to accept this. I am inclined to think that the fact which Moore has in mind here is that goodness, in the primary sense, is always dependent on the presence of certain non-ethical characteristics which I should call "good-making." If an experience is good (or if it is bad), this is never an ultimate fact. It is always reasonable to ask: "What *makes* it

good?" or "What *makes* it bad?" as the case may be. And the sort of answer that we should expect to get is that it is made good by its pleasantness, or by the fact that it is a sorrowfully toned awareness of another's distress, or by some other such non-ethical characteristic of it. We might, therefore, distinguish the characteristics of a thing into the following two classes, viz., *ultimate* and *derivative*. Goodness would certainly fall into the class of derivative characteristics.

Now there is a sense in which one might say that a thing could not be completely described if any of its ultimate characteristics were omitted, but that it could be completely described without mentioning all its derivative characteristics. In describing a circle, e.g., it is not necessary to mention explicitly any of the innumerable properties of circles which follow of necessity from their definition together with the axioms of Euclidean geometry.

But, although this analogy may throw some light on what Moore had in mind, it certainly does not help us much towards understanding what he means by calling goodness a non-natural characteristic, and pleasantness, e.g., a natural characteristic. In the first place, the way in which the ethical properties of a thing depend on its non-ethical properties seems to be quite unlike the way in which the remaining properties of a circle depend on its defining properties. In the latter case the dependence is equivalent to the fact that the possession of the remaining properties can be *inferred deductively* from the axioms of Euclid and the presence of the defining properties. But the connexion between the non-ethical bad-making characteristic of being an emotion of delight at another's pain and the ethical characteristic of being morally evil is certainly not of this nature.

Moreover, it is surely quite as evident that pleasantness and unpleasantness are derivative characteristics of an experience as that goodness and badness are. If an experience is pleasant, it is always reasonable to ask: "What *makes* it pleasant?" And the answer will always be to mention some non-hedonic "pleasant-making" characteristic of the experience. E.g., if it is a sensation of taste, the answer might be that it is made pleasant by its sweetness; if it is an auditory experience, the answer might be that it is made pleasant by the way in which various simultaneous and closely successive sounds are combined in it; and so on. Now Moore counts pleasantness as a *natural* characteristic. If he is right in doing so, it is impossible to identify the non-natural characteristics of a thing with the derivative sub-class of those of its characteristics which depend solely on its intrinsic nature. For by that criterion pleasantness would be a non-natural characteristic just as much as goodness.

It seems impossible then to extract from Moore's writings any satisfactory account of the distinction between "natural" and "non-natural" characteristics. Yet one seems to recognize fairly well what is the extension of these two terms, even if the attempts to define them are not successful. I propose now to try a different line of approach, and to suggest an *epistemological description,* as distinct from a logical definition, of the term "natural characteristic." That is to say, I shall try to delimit the class of natural characteristics, not by stating their intrinsic peculiarities, but by stating how we come to form our ideas of them.

I propose to describe a "natural characteristic" as any characteristic which either (a) we become aware of by inspecting our sense-data or introspecting our experiences, or (b) is definable wholly in terms of characteristics of the former kind together with the notions of cause and substance. I think that this covers every characteristic which would be universally admitted to be natural. It would, e.g., cover yellowness, both in the primary non-dispositional sense in which we use the word when we say, e.g., "That looks yellow to me from here now," and in the secondary dispositional sense in which we use it when we say, e.g., "Gold is yellow." It would also cover psychological characteristics, whether non-dispositional or dispositional. We know, e.g., what is meant by the fear-quality, the anger-quality, etc., through having felt afraid, angry, etc., and having introspected such experiences. And we know, e.g., what is meant by timidity, irascibility, etc., because these dispositional properties are definable in terms of the fear-quality, the anger-quality, etc., together with the notions of cause and substance.

A "non-natural" characteristic would be described epistemologically in negative terms derived from the above-mentioned epistemological description of "natural" characteristics. A characteristic would be non-natural if (a) *no-one* could become aware of it by inspecting his sense-data or introspecting his experiences, and (b) it is *not* definable in terms of characteristics of which one could become aware in those ways together with the notions of cause and substance. These epistemological descriptions of the two kinds of characteristic leave open the question whether goodness is of the natural or the non-natural kind and provide us with a criterion for answering it.

(2) We are now in a position to deal with our second question. What connexion, if any, is there between the doctrine that "good," in its primary sense, denotes a characteristic which is *simple,* and the doctrine that it denotes one which is *non-natural*?

It is plain that our epistemological criteria at once plunge us into certain questions which are important in themselves and are never, so far as I am aware, raised in Moore's writings. If "goodness" is a name for a characteristic, how do we become aware of the characteristic for which it is a name? There is lamentably little discussion on this point in works on ethics.

It seems to me evident that goodness is not a characteristic which we can become aware of by inspecting any of our sense-data; so that in this respect it is utterly unlike yellowness, sweetness, squeakiness, etc., when used in the non-dispositional sense. It is plain that, when "good"

is used in its primary sense, it does not denote a characteristic whose presence is revealed to us by sight or touch or taste or hearing or smell, or any other sense that we do have or conceivably might have. It is doubtful whether goodness, in this sense, could belong to sense-data or to physical objects. And, even if it can, it is certain that we do not sense or perceive with our senses the goodness of such objects. At most we perceive with our senses certain natural characteristics which are good-*making,* e.g., certain combinations of colour, of sound, etc., which make the object which possesses them intrinsically good.

It seems equally clear that no simple psychological characteristic, such as we could discover by introspecting our experiences, can be identified with goodness. By introspection we become aware of experiences which are pleasant or unpleasant, toned with desire or with aversion, fearful, hopeful, and so on. Now it is true that goodness, in the primary sense, *can* belong to experiences. Indeed, some people would hold that, in this sense, it can belong to nothing else. Yet I think that a moment's reflexion will show that by calling an experience "good" we do not *mean* that it is pleasant, or that it is an experience of desire or of fear or of hope, or that it has any of the simple psychological qualities which we become aware of through introspecting our experiences.

If anyone were tempted to identify goodness with one of these simple psychological characteristics, I think that he would be doing so through the following confusion. What he really believes is that there is one and only one good-*making* quality of experiences, e.g., pleasantness. He then fails to notice the distinction between *goodness itself* and the one and only *good-making quality* which he recognizes. And so he thinks he believes that "good" and "pleasant," e.g., are just two names for a single characteristic. Since pleasantness certainly is a natural characteristic, he will thus think he believes that "good" is a name for a natural characteristic. But I do not think that the belief that "good" and "pleasant" (e.g.) are two names for one characteristic would survive after the distinction between goodness itself and a good-making characteristic had been pointed out. And similar remarks would apply to any other simple psychological quality which one might be tempted to identify with the characteristic denoted by "good."

So we come to the following conditional conclusion. *If* the word "good," when used in its primary sense, denotes a simple quality, then that quality is almost certainly *not* one which a person could become aware of either by inspecting his sense-data or introspecting his experiences. And, if the characteristic which it denotes be simple, it will not be definable at all, and therefore will not be definable in terms of characteristics which a person might have become aware of in one or other of those ways. Therefore it will be a non-natural characteristic, according to our criterion. So, with our criteria, there *is* an important connexion between the doctrine that "good" is the name of a *simple quality* and the doctrine that it is the name of a *non-natural* characteristic.

This, however, does not settle the question whether "good" is in fact the name of a non-natural characteristic. For it is by no means certain that it is the name of a characteristic at all; and, even if it is so, it is by no means certain that this characteristic is simple. Suppose "good," in the primary sense, were a name for a characteristic which is complex. Would there then be any reason to think it non-natural? I believe that there would. I know of no proposed definition of goodness in purely natural terms which is in the least plausible. But there are definitions of goodness, containing terms which appear to be non-natural, which are not without plausibility. E.g., it would not be unplausible to suggest that "x is intrinsically good" means that x is something which it would be *right* or *fitting* to desire as an end. And it would appear that "right" or "fitting," when used in this sense, answer to our criterion of being non-natural.

The legitimate conclusion then would seem to be that, if "good" in its primary sense be the name of a characteristic, that characteristic, whether simple or complex, is non-natural. Anyone who saw reason to doubt the existence of characteristics answering to our description of "non-natural" might fairly use this conclusion as the basis of an argument to show that "good" is *not* a name of a characteristic at all.

It will be worth while to develop this line of argument a little further. Is there any way of becoming aware of a simple quality belonging to particulars except by inspecting sense-data or introspecting experiences which have that quality? Many people would say that there plainly is no other way. If they are right, it follows that we could not possibly have an idea of goodness if goodness were a non-natural characteristic. For, if "good" denotes a characteristic at all, it certainly denotes one that belongs to particulars and only to them. If goodness were a simple characteristic and were non-natural, the conclusion that we could not have an idea of it would follow at once from the epistemological principle which these people find self-evident. If goodness were a complex characteristic and were non-natural, the same conclusion would follow, at the second move, from the same principle. We could not have an idea of such a complex characteristic unless we had ideas of all its simple components. By hypothesis one at least of these would be non-natural; and, if the epistemological principle be accepted, we could have no ideas of any such components.

Now, although this epistemological principle does seem to me highly plausible, I am not prepared to accept it (or any other) as self-evident. Therefore I am not prepared to assert dogmatically that no characteristic of which any-one could have an idea could be non-natural. But I do think it important to point out the following conditional conclusion. *If* goodness be a non-natural characteristic, then anyone's idea of it must be an *a priori* notion or contain *a priori* notions as elements. For an *a priori* notion just is an idea of a characteristic which is not manifested to us in sensation or introspection and is not definable wholly in terms of characteristics which

are so manifested. Anyone who holds that goodness is a non-natural characteristic and that he has an idea of it is therefore committed to the belief that there are *a priori* notions and that his idea of goodness is one of them. Now as we have seen, if "good" denotes a characteristic at all, the characteristic which it denotes is almost certainly non-natural. Therefore anyone who holds that "good" denotes a characteristic, and that he has an idea of the characteristic which it denotes, will be almost compelled to hold that there are *a priori* notions, and that his idea of goodness is or contains one of them.

There is one other epistemological point to be noticed in conclusion. Suppose a person regards goodness as a non-natural characteristic, and admits that its presence is always dependent on the presence of certain natural characteristics which are good-making. Suppose, further, that he holds that the connexion between a good-making characteristic and the goodness which it confers is *necessary*. Then he will be obliged to hold that there are *synthetically necessary* facts, and that he knows some of them. He will therefore be obliged to admit that he can make *synthetically a priori* judgments. The necessary connexion between those natural characteristics of a thing which are good-making and the goodness which they confer on it could not possibly be analytic. For this would involve the absurdity that the *non-natural* characteristic of goodness is contained as a factor in the analysis of the purely *natural* good-making characteristics.

Now it is fashionable at present to hold that all necessary connexion must be analytic and that there can be no synthetic *a priori* judgments. I do not find this principle in the least self-evident myself, though I think that it has enough plausibility and interest to justify a strenuous attempt to see whether it can be successfully applied in detail. Anyone who does accept it, and also holds that "good" is a name for a characteristic, will be compelled to draw one or other of the following conclusions. Either (a) goodness is a *natural* characteristic, or (b) the connexion between the good-making characteristics of a thing and the goodness which they confer on it is purely *contingent* and can be known only empirically. He might, of course, consistently combine both these conclusions, as Hume did. For Hume's doctrine, stated very roughly, was (a) that to be good means to be an object of emotions of approval in all or most men, and (b) that it is a contingent and empirically known fact that such emotions are called forth by what is believed to be pleasant or useful and only by objects which have that property.

NOTES

[1] This (second) part of this paper is extracted, with some additions and modifications, from a paper by the author in the Aristotelian Society's *Proceedings* for 1934, entitled "Is 'Goodness' a Name of a Simple Non-natural Quality?" C.D.B.

C. J. Ducasse (essay date 1942)

SOURCE: "Moore's 'The Refutation of Idealism'," in *The Philosophy of G. E. Moore*, edited by Paul Arthur Schlipp, Northwestern University, 1942, pp. 225-52.

[*In the following essay, Ducasse challenges Moore's belief that* esse *(to be) is not necessarily* percipi *(to be perceived).*]

Professor Moore's **"The Refutation of Idealism,"** published in 1903, is still one of the most famous articles written in philosophy since the turn of the century. Its acute and searching criticism of the proposition that esse is percipi has been widely held to have finally proved its falsity and thus to have robbed of their basis the idealistic philosophies which in one way or another had been built upon it. It is true that in the preface to his *Philosophical Studies*—in which the article was reprinted in 1922—Professor Moore writes that "this paper now appears to me to be very confused, as well as to embody a good many down-right mistakes." These, however, are not specified, and, since he does not repudiate the article as a whole, it may be presumed that he still adheres at least to its essential contention. In any case, because of the influence the wide acceptance of its argument has had on the course of subsequent philosophical thought, the article as published is now a classic and commensurate in importance with the celebrated proposition it attacks. This is enough to justify a critical examination of it on the present occasion.

As against Professor Moore, I believe there is a certain class of cases concerning which it is true that *esse* is *percipi.* This class, moreover, is the very one in terms of an instance of which his discussion is worded. I think it can be definitely proved that, so far as this class is concerned, Professor Moore's argument does not prove, as it claims to do—or even render more probable than not—that *esse* is *percipi* is false. I shall, however, try to show not only this but also that, for this class of cases, *esse* is *percipi* is true. The latter will be more difficult to demonstrate conclusively, but I believe I shall be able to show at least that the burden of proof definitely rests on those who would deny that even in these cases *esse* is *percipi.*

The considerations I shall set forth, however, will not constitute an argument for idealism, for I believe that there is also another class of cases concerning which it is false that *esse* is *percipi.* Accordingly, even if my argument is successful, its effect will not be to open the way for idealism; but only, on the one hand, to rob of its basis the kind of realism Professor Moore's article has been used to support, and on the other and chiefly, to make clear that certain facts do belong to Mind, which that realism rejects from Mind.

1. *Professor Moore's argument.*—In what I shall say, familiarity on the reader's part with the text of Professor Moore's article will be assumed, but I may state here briefly what I understand to be the essence of its argument. Using the sensation of blue as example, Professor Moore points out that the sensation of blue admittedly differs from the sensation of green, but that both are nevertheless sensations. Therefore they have 1) something in common, which he proposes to call "consciousness," and 2) something else, in respect of which one differs from the other; and he proposes to call this the "object" of each sensation. We have then, he says, "in every sensation two distinct elements;" and therefore assertion that one of them exists, assertion that the other exists, and assertion that both exist, are three different assertions. From this it follows that "if any one tells us that to say 'Blue exists' is the *same* thing as to say that 'Both blue and consciousness exist', he makes a mistake and a self-contradictory mistake."[1] Just because the *esse* of blue is something distinct from the *esse* of the *percipi* of blue, there is no logical difficulty in supposing blue to exist without consciousness of blue.

The point on which turns the validity or invalidity of this argument is of course what sort of distinctness is to be granted between the sensation or consciousness and the blue; for existential independence is not a corollary of every sort of distinctness. Existential independence is entailed by distinctness of the sort we admit when we say that for instance cat and dog or green and sweet are distinct; but not by the sort of distinctness we admit when we say that cat and spinal cord or blue and color are distinct.

Professor Moore believes that blue and the *percipi* of blue are "as distinct as 'green' and 'sweet'"[2]; and if existential independence is to follow from this, "as distinct" must be taken to mean here that the distinctness is of the same logical sort as that of green from sweet. To show that it is of the same sort Professor Moore advances both destructive and constructive considerations. The destructive consist of his criticism (which I do not pause here to summarize) of the hypothesis that blue is "content" of the sensation of blue; the constructive, of the positive account he himself offers of the relation of sensation to blue or, more generally, of awareness or experience to its "objects." This account is substantially as follows. A sensation is a case of "knowing" or "experiencing" or "being aware of" something; and this awareness is not merely

> something distinct and unique, utterly different from blue: it also has a perfectly distinct and unique relation to blue. . . . This relation is just that which we mean in every case by 'knowing'[3] . . . the relation of a sensation to its object is certainly the same as that of any other instance of experience to its object[4] . . . the awareness is and must be in all cases of such a nature that its object, when we are aware of it, is precisely what it would be, if we were not aware.[5]

As against these contentions, I shall argue that if "knowing" is taken as the name of a unique relation, then this relation is a generic one and two species of it have to be distinguished; that one of these allows the object known to exist independently of the knowing of it, but the other forbids it; that in the case of the latter relation the known is "content" of the knowing in a sense not disposed of by Professor Moore's criticism of that term; and that in this very sense blue is "content" of the sensation of blue and therefore cannot exist independently of it.

2. Cognate vs. objective accusative.—I shall lay the basis for my argument by calling attention to a certain distinction mentioned and used by S. Alexander. It is the distinction between what is expressed in language by, respectively, the cognate accusative and the objective accusative—between, for instance, striking a stroke and striking a man, or waving a farewell and waving a flag.[6]

There is not, I believe, any word in the language to denote *that in general* (or perhaps *that ambiguously*) which has, to the activity a verb names, the same relation that *a noun in the accusative in general*—i.e., in the accusative no matter whether cognate or objective—has to the verb. I shall, however, need a word for this and will therefore borrow for the purpose from grammar the word "accusative" itself—as W. E. Johnson, similarly, borrows from grammar the word "adjective" to refer to the sort of entity which any word grammar calls an adjective stands for.[7] Thus, for example, I would speak of a stroke struck as cognate accusative, but of a man struck as objective accusative, of the sort of activity called "striking." But, for reasons of euphony which will appear later, I shall, instead of "cognate," use the synonymous form "connate." Also, since the relation of "objects" of awareness to the awareness thereof is what we shall ultimately be concerned with, and we must not allow our terminology to prejudge for us surreptitiously the nature of that relation, I shall use the term "alien accusative" for what would otherwise be called "objective accusative." That is, I shall say that an accusative of an activity may be connate with or alien to—homogeneous with or heterogeneous to—the activity. For example, in what is expressed by the phrase "jumping a jump," the jump is *connate accusative* of the activity called "jumping"; whereas in what is expressed by "jumping a ditch," the ditch is *alien accusative* of the jumping.

3. Accusatives coördinate or subordinate in generality to a given activity.—Let us next notice that the relations "connate with" and "alien to" (as they concern an activity and an accusative of it) may each be either symmetrical or unsymmetrical. Each is symmetrical when its terms are of strictly *coördinate* generality as for instance "jumping" and "jump" (connate accusative), or "jumping" and "obstacle" (alien accusative). An activity and an accusative of it, which, like these, are coördinate in generality I shall call respectively *connately coördinate* (or coördinately connate), and *alienly coördinate* (or coördinately alien).

On the other hand, the relations "connate with" and "alien to" are unsymmetrical when the accusative of the activity concerned is *subordinate* in generality to the

activity. Accordingly I shall say that an accusative—for instance a leap—which is subordinate in generality to an activity which—like jumping—is connate with it, is *connately subordinate to* (or subordinately connate with) that activity. And similarly I shall say that an accusative—for instance a fence—which is subordinate in generality to an activity which—like jumping—is alien to it, is *alienly subordinate* (or subordinately alien) to that activity.

4. An accusative connate with a given activity exists only in occurrence of that activity.—Close attention must now be given to the implications as to existence which go, or do not go, with connate and alien coördinateness and subordinateness. There will be four cases. I list and illustrate all four but the last two will be the ones of special interest for the purposes of my argument.

(1) When an accusative, e.g., an obstacle, is *alienly coördinate* with an activity, e.g., jumping, then obviously this accusative may exist independently of existence, i.e., of occurrence, of the activity: obstacles exist which are not being jumped, have not been jumped, and will not be jumped. On the other hand, in so far as the activity is of the kind represented by a transitive verb, it cannot occur independently of existence of an accusative alienly coördinate with it: jumping, in so far as transitive, obviously cannot occur without existence of some obstacle—some distance or thing—being jumped. Similarly striking, in so far as transitive, cannot occur without existence of some object—be it only empty air—being struck.

(2) When an accusative, e.g., a fence, is *alienly subordinate* to an activity, e.g., jumping, then again this accusative may exist independently of occurrence of the activity: a fence, for instance, which is a species of obstacle, may exist which is not jumped at any time. But here the activity, even when it is of a transitive kind, can occur independently of existence of a *given* accusative alienly subordinate to it: transitive jumping could occur even if for instance no fences existed but ditches did.

We now come to the two cases of special interest for the purposes of this paper—the two where the accusative is connate with the activity.

(3) When an accusative, e.g., a jump, is *connately coördinate* with an activity, viz., jumping, then this accusative cannot exist independently of existence, i.e., of occurrence, of the activity: a jump exists only in the jumping, a stroke in the striking, a dance in the dancing, etc.—the *esse* of a *saltus* is its *saltari*. But, although this obviously is true, it may be well nevertheless to pause here a moment to point out why it is true.

To do so, we must ask what exactly is the logical relation between jump and jumping, between the dance and dancing, etc., i.e., between the connately coördinate accusative of an activity and the occurrences of that activity. The answer is that the *nouns* "jump," "dance," "stroke," name each a *kind,* viz., a kind of activity, considered independently of occurrence of cases of it; whereas the *verbs* "jumping," "dancing," "striking," are the linguistic entities which not only likewise name the kind but in addition allude to *existence, i.e., occurrence, of a case* of the kind of activity they name. The various tenses of which the verb admits express the various possible time-relations between the time *of discourse about* a particular occurrence of an event of the given kind, and the time ascribed *by discourse* to that particular occurrence: the time of that occurrence may be earlier or later than, or the same as, the time of our discourse about it. The noun-form, on the other hand, wholly ignores these temporal relations because it denotes a *kind* of event—not a *case,* i.e., not an occurrence, of that kind—and kinds as such have no dates. Yet the kinds we are here considering are kinds *of events,* i.e., they are kinds the existence of a case of which consists in an *occurrence*—a particular event—at a particular time. Attention to these considerations enables us to answer our question: The reason why no jump, for instance, can exist except in the jumping, and why jumping, at whatever time, is always and necessarily the jumping of a jump, is that *jump stands to jumping as kind stands to existence of a case thereof.*

(4) Let us now finally consider an accusative, e.g., a leap, *connately subordinate* to an activity, e.g., jumping. It is obvious that the activity can exist, i.e., can occur, at dates when *the given* accusative does not: jumping may be of a jump of some species other than a leap; dancing may be of a dance of some species other than the waltz; striking, of a sort of stroke other than a jab; etc.

On the other hand, *an accusative connately subordinate to a given activity cannot exist independently of that activity:* a leap exists only in the jumping thereof, a waltz only in the dancing, a jab only in the striking. That this is true is again evident even without explicit mention of the reason why it is true; but in any event the reason is that leap, waltz, jab, etc., respectively, stand to jump, dance, stroke, etc., each as species to genus; that a case of the species cannot exist unless a case of the genus exists; and that, as pointed out above, existence of a case of the genera, jump, dance, stroke, etc., consists in, respectively, jumping, dancing, striking, etc., at some time.

(5) *A cognitum connate with the cognizing thereof exists only in the cognizing.*—So much being now clear, it may next be emphasized that although the activities so far used as examples were activities both motor and voluntary, the distinctions pointed out—between connate and alien accusatives and between accusatives coördinate and subordinate in generality to a given activity—in no way depend on the activities' being motor and voluntary ones; and therefore that the implications as to existence which we found rooted in these distinctions do not depend upon these characters either. Rather, the distinctions and their existential implications are perfectly general: any sort of activity whatever has a connate accusative, and any sort of activity which is transitive has in addition an alien accusative; and further, *whatever the nature of the activity, an accusative connate with it (whether coördinately*

or subordinately) exists only in the occurrences of the activity. Because this is true universally, it is true, in particular, of the sort of activity which is of special interest to us in these pages—viz., the one called "cognizing" or "experiencing"—notwithstanding that it is not like jumping a motor activity and notwithstanding that some species of it, e.g., sensing, are involuntary instead of, like jumping, voluntary. If we now agree to call any accusative of the cognitive activity a *cognitum,* then, in the light of the considerations that precede, it will, I believe, be admitted as evident that *any cognitum connate with a cognitive activity exists only in the occurrences of that activity.*

(6) *Nature of the hypothesis I shall oppose to Professor Moore's.*—The question we now face, however, is whether such cognita as blue or bitter or sweet are connate with the species of experiencing called "sensing," or on the contrary are alien to it; for on the answer to this depends, as we have now seen, the answer to the question whether the *esse* of blue or bitter or sweet is their *percipi.* Professor Moore believes they are what I have called alien cognita of the experiencing. My contention will be on the contrary that they are cognita connate with the experiencing. At this point, however, I shall not attempt to prove this contention but only, first, to explain more fully what it means, and second, to dispose of two *prima facie* plausible objections to it. This will make evident that there does exist a genuine alternative to Professor Moore's contention regarding the relation of blue to the sensing of blue; and will enable me to show that it is an alternative he neither disposes of nor considers. To show this, however, will only be to show that his argument does not prove what it claims to prove, i.e., does not prove that the blue can exist independently of the sensing of blue. Only after this has been done shall I give the positive evidence I have to offer in support of my own contention that the blue cannot exist independently of the sensing of blue.

The hypothesis, then, which I present as alternative to Professor Moore's is that "blue," "bitter," "sweet," etc., are names not of objects of experience nor of species of objects of experience but of *species of experience itself.* What this means is perhaps made clearest by saying that to sense blue is then to sense *bluely,* just as to dance the waltz is to dance "waltzily" (i.e., in the manner called "to waltz") to jump a leap is to jump "leapily" (i.e., in the manner called "to leap") etc. Sensing blue, that is to say, is I hold a species of sensing—a specific variety of the sort of activity generically called "sensing" which, however, (unlike dancing or jumping) is an involuntary and non-motor kind of activity. In this as in all cases where the known is connate with the knowing, what is known by the knowing activity is then *its own determinate nature on the given occasion.*

With regard to the relation between blue and sensing blue, I further contend that the same remarks apply that were made above concerning the relation of jump and leap to jumping: the noun "blue" is the word we use to mention merely a certain *kind* of activity (just as are the nouns "waltz," "leap," etc.); whereas the verb "to sense blue" is the linguistic form we use when we wish not only to mention that same kind of activity but also at the same time to mention some *case,* i.e., some *occurrence,* of that kind of activity—the various tenses of the verb expressing the various possible temporal relations between the *time at which we mention* some case of that kind of activity and the time we mention as *time of that case itself.*

(7) *The objection that what is sensed is not "blue" but a case of "blue."*—It might be urged, however—perhaps under the belief that it constitutes a difficulty precluding acceptance of my hypothesis—that what we sense is never blue or bitter in general, i.e., a *kind,* but always *a* blue or *a* bitter, i.e., (it would then be alleged) some *case* of blue or bitter.

To this I reply that "blue" and "bitter" are the names of certain *determinable* kinds, and that "*a* blue" or "*a* bitter" are expressions by which we refer *not to cases but to determinates,* i.e., to *infimae species,* of that determinable kind.[8] That a determinate shade of blue is logically not a case but a species, viz., an infima species, of blue is shown by the fact that even a perfectly determinate shade of blue is susceptible of existing many times, or no times, or only once, etc. That is, *qualitative determinateness neither constitutes existence nor entails existence.* Existence of qualitatively determinate blue, bitter, etc., is a matter of presence of them *at some determinate place in time.*

On the basis of these considerations, my reply to the objection mentioned above is then that we do not *sense a case* of blue, but that our sensing blue of a determinate species, i.e., our sensing bluely-in-some-completely-specific-manner, *constitutes occurrence of a case* of blue. That is, it constitutes *presence at a determinate time* of blue of that determinate shade, and therefore of course, of blue; just as our waltzing—which if we do it at all we do in some completely determinate manner—constitutes presence at a determinate time (and place) of that determinate species of waltz, and therefore automatically also of its genus, the waltz.

(8) *The objection that one may be aware without being aware that one is aware.*—If in any case of awareness of blue what one is aware of is, as I contend, the determinate nature of one's awareness on that occasion, then, it may be objected, it would follow that being aware of blue would be one and the same thing with being aware that one is aware of blue; whereas obviously they are not the same thing. To meet this objection, I shall first analyze the nature of the difference which is felt and which I acknowledge exists; and then I shall point out why this difference leaves untouched the essence of my contention.

If on an occasion when one has asserted "I am aware of blue" one is asked or asks oneself whether this is really so, one then makes an additional judgment which (if af-

firmative) one formulates by saying "I am aware that I am aware of blue." I submit, however, that *this* judgment concerns the *appropriateness* of the concept, "being aware" to the fact one is attempting to describe by saying "I am aware of blue." Or similarly, if I have asserted "I know that Mary is eight years old" and I am asked or ask myself whether I "really know" it and conclude "I know that I know that Mary is eight years old," the question this answers is whether the concept labelled "knowing" fits the status conferred upon my belief that Mary is eight years old by the grounds I have for the belief. I compare the particular sort of relation between grounds and belief, called "knowing," with the actually existing relation between my grounds and my belief in the case of Mary's age, and ask myself whether this actually existing relation is a case of that sort of relation. This comparison—and not the examining of additional evidence as to Mary's age—is the ground of my assertion that I know that I know that Mary is eight years old. Just this sort of difference, I submit, is the difference between knowing and knowing that one knows, or being aware and being aware that one is aware.

But the statement "I am aware that I am aware," which is a correct formulation of the sort of fact just illustrated, would not be a correct formulation of the fact—of a quite different nature—that whenever I am aware at all I am "aware of an awareness" *in the same sense of the accusative* in which it is true that whenever I strike at all I strike a stroke, or that whenever I know at all I know a knowledge, or that whenever I dance at all I dance a dance. To express this sort of accusative of a given verb no *verb form* can correctly be used but only a *noun;* that is, for this sort of accusative of "being aware" we cannot, except misleadingly, use the verb forms "that I am aware" or "of being aware," but must use "of an awareness." In this sense of the accusative, moreover, it is true not only that whenever I dance at all I dance a dance, but also that I dance in some specific manner, e.g., "waltzily." Similarly in this sense of the accusative, it is true not only that whenever I am aware at all I am aware (intuitively, not discursively) of an awareness, but also that I am aware in some specific manner, e.g., bluely.

Having now made clear the nature of my hypothesis as to the relation of blue to sensing blue, and defended that hypothesis from two *prima facie* plausible objections to it, I may add that the relation the hypothesis describes is the one I shall mean whenever I say that blue is *content* of sensing blue. That is, when I so use this term I shall mean that blue stands to sensing blue (or more generally, that any given species of experience or awareness stands to experiencing or being aware) as kind stands to occurrence of a case thereof. With this understood, let us now turn to Professor Moore's criticism of what he calls the "content" hypothesis.

(9) *Professor Moore's criticism of the hypothesis that blue is "content" of the sensing of blue.*—The only place at which Professor Moore's criticism of the contention that blue is content of the sensing or awareness of blue

could be considered relevant to the meaning of "content" I have stated to be mine is the place where he raises the question "whether or not, when I have the sensation of blue, my consciousness or awareness is . . . blue."[9] He acknowledges that offence may be taken at the expression "a blue awareness," but asserts that it nevertheless "expresses just what should be and is meant by saying that blue is, in this case, a *content* of consciousness or experience."

As to this, I can only reply that what I mean (as defined above) when I say that blue is the content of my awareness of blue is not properly expressible by saying that my awareness is then blue *unless blue be taken as the name, instead of as an adjective,* of my awareness at the moment. That is, what I mean when I refer to blue as content of my awareness of blue is that my awareness is at the moment of the determinate sort *called "blue,"* and not that it has, like *lapis lazuli,* the property of being blue; for when I assert, *of lapis lazuli,* that it is blue, what I mean is that it is such that, whenever I turn my eyes upon it in daylight, it causes me to experience something called "blue"; whereas I mean nothing like this when I say, *of my awareness,* that at a given moment it is of the particular sort called "blue."

To speak of a blue awareness, I would insist, is improper in the same way it would be improper to speak of an iron metal. We can properly speak of a species of metal called "iron," but if we wish to use "iron" as an *adjective,* we have to apply it to something—for instance a kettle or a door—which stands to iron *not,* like "metal," *as genus to species, but as substance to property.*

I conclude here, then, that Professor Moore's criticism of the contention that blue is content of the awareness of blue is not a criticism of the contention that blue is a species of awareness—which is what I mean when I assert that blue is content of the awareness of blue. His criticism does not consider *this* contention at all and therefore does not refute it.

(10) *Does existential independence follow from the fact that the awareness is* OF *blue?*—It is only because Professor Moore does not in his paper consider as a possible meaning of "blue awareness" the hypothesis that blue is a species of awareness rather than a property of it, that he is able to dismiss the possibility that "awareness is blue" as unimportant even if true—saying that, in any case, the awareness is *of* blue, and "has to blue the simple and unique relation the existence of which alone justifies us in distinguishing knowledge of a thing from the thing known."[10] For he believes this relation entails in all cases that the known may exist independently of the knowing of it. But we have seen that this is so only in some cases. We do indeed speak of the tasting *of* a taste—e.g., of the taste called "bitter"—and also of the tasting *of* quinine; but although "tasting" in each case denotes a species of knowing, it obviously does not denote the same species in both cases: the relation of tasting to taste (or to bitter) is not the same as the relation of tasting to quinine or to

cheese, etc. Similarly, when we speak of the smelling *of* a smell and of the smelling *of* a rose, of the hearing *of* a tone and of the hearing *of* a bell, or—as Professor Moore himself points out elsewhere[11]—of the seeing *of* a color, e.g., brown, and of the seeing *of* a coin, we are obviously using "smelling," "hearing," "seeing," each in *two* senses notwithstanding that in each sense it is a species of knowing, and notwithstanding that in each sense the knowing is *of* something. Were any proof needed that the senses are two, it would be provided by the following consideration.

The two sentences "I see red" and "I see a rose" each represent an attempt to describe in English a judgment made by the utterer—something he believes. Now it is possible that "red" or "a rose" are not the right words to describe in English what he believes he sees; that is, either sentence may be an *incorrect wording* of his belief. But in the case of the sentence "I see red" the belief itself, which he uses that sentence to describe, cannot possibly be a mistaken belief. It cannot be erroneous because that which he believes is not anything more at all than is actually and literally seen by him at the moment. In the case of the sentence "I see a rose," on the other hand, not only as before may the sentence be an incorrect wording of his belief, but now in addition *his belief itself may be mistaken:* that, which he believes he sees, may not be what he believes it to be. It may be something else which *looks* the same as what he believes to be there, but the other characters of which are very different; for these other characters, e.g., tactual, olfactory, gustatory ones, etc., of course cannot literally be *seen.* Odor, taste, hardness, can be "seen" only in the elliptical sense that the colors literally seen *predict* to us a certain odor, taste, etc. But whenever what we believe is something the nature of which is predicted or signified even in part instead of literally and totally observed at the moment, error is possible.

The relation between seeing and seen or more generally between knowing and known is thus not as Professor Moore's paper asserts "a simple and unique relation" (unless considered generically only) but is of at least the two kinds just illustrated. Moreover if, as I contend, the first of these two relations between knowing and known is the very relation between cognizing and a cognitum *connate* therewith, then in *no* case of that first relation is the known existentially independent of the knowing thereof. Therefore, from the fact that in *all* cases of knowing the knowing is *of* something, *nothing general* follows as to the existential independence or dependence of the known upon the knowing.

To prove such independence in a given case it would be necessary to show that when we speak of, e.g., the tasting of bitter or the seeing of blue, the tasting is existentially related to the bitter or the seeing to the blue not (as I contend) as cognizing is to cognitum (subordinately) connate therewith, but on the contrary, as, for instance, green is existentially related to sweet. But this is not shown by anything in Professor Moore's paper. As just pointed out, the fact that the sensing or seeing is *of* blue does nothing to show it and, as I shall now make clear, neither does a certain additional fact to which Professor Moore appeals.

(11) *Does existential independence follow from the introspective distinguishability of the awareness from the blue?*—Professor Moore asserts that in any case of awareness of blue it is possible (even if not easy) to distinguish by careful introspective observation the awareness from the blue. This I readily grant, but I deny that it constitutes any evidence at all of the existential independence it is adduced to prove, for the fact that the awareness is observationally distinguishable from the blue leaves wholly open the question which is crucial here. This question is whether the awareness is distinguishable from the blue as for instance green is from sweet—i.e., as a case of one species from a case of a logically independent species—or on the contrary (as I contend) as a case of a genus is distinguishable (by abstractive observation) within a case of any one of its species—for instance, as a case of the generic activity, "to dance," is by abstractive observation distinguishable within any case of the species of that genus called "to waltz." That is, we can observe that a person is moving with the specific rhythm and steps called "waltzing"; and then we can abstract our attention from the specific nature of the rhythm and steps and notice only the fact (common to the waltz, polka, one-step, fox trot, etc.) that he takes steps in a rhythmical manner, i.e., that he is "dancing." Indeed, observation *merely* that the genus "dance" is the one to which belongs a case of activity concretely before us is what would normally occur if—perhaps through the rapid opening and shutting of a door—we had only a brief glimpse of the dancing going on in a room.

To prove that blue and awareness are distinct in the manner which entails existential independence, we should have to have the same sort of evidence on which is based our knowledge that green and sweet are existentially independent: we have observed, for instance, that some apples are green and not sweet, and that some are sweet and not green. That is, we should have to observe—i.e., to be aware—that at a certain time blue exists but awareness does not, and that at a certain other time awareness exists but blue does not. Of the latter we have a case whenever what we are aware of is something other than blue, for instance, sweet or green, etc.; but of the *former* it is impossible that we should ever have a case, for to be aware that one is not at the time aware is a contradiction.

This situation, it is true, does not prove that blue is existentially *dependent* on awareness of blue; yet just that sort of situation is what would confront us if blue *were* existentially dependent on awareness of blue; therefore that the situation we do confront *is* of that sort is circumstantial evidence, so far as it goes, of such dependence.

(12) *Comment on some relevant remarks of Dr. Broad's.*—It might be claimed, however, that the intro-

spective observation by which, in awareness of blue, we distinguish the awareness from the blue is not of the abstractive kind I have described, but on the contrary of the same "total" kind for the awareness as for the blue. This is perhaps what Professor Moore means to assert when he says that "to be aware of the sensation of blue is . . . to be aware of an awareness of blue; awareness being used, in both cases, in exactly the same sense."[12]

Some light will perhaps be thrown on the issue by examination of certain remarks made by Dr. C. D. Broad. He observes that a sensation of red (the case would of course be the same with blue) seems obviously to involve an act of sensing and a red "object." But it is of particular interest to note his further remark that it does not seem similarly obvious "that a sensation of headache involves an act of sensing and a 'headachy' object."[13]

To me also it is evident that there is a difference between the two cases; and the important point is that, on Professor Moore's view, there ought not to be any. *Both* cases ought to be introspectively analyzable alike into an awareness—a sensing—and an "object," viz., respectively, red and headache. The explanation of the difference is, I submit, as follows.

The eye, which is the sense organ with which the sensation of red is connected, is an organ susceptible of being oriented and focussed. That is, the eye is capable of *looking;* and it does look in this sense whenever any color is seen or even imaged, for the eye always has *some* orientation and *some* accommodation. But with any orientation and accommodation of the eye there goes a certain sort of kinaesthetic sensa (the sort connected with the muscles of the eyeball and of the lens). And these *kinaesthetic sensa,* I submit, are what Dr. Broad finds present in the sensation of red but absent in that of headache; for the latter is not, like the former, connected with an organ susceptible of orientation and accommodation and is therefore not, like the former, accompanied by characteristic kinaesthetic sensa. The difference Dr. Broad notices is really present, but it is not rightly described as presence in the one case of an "act of sensing" absent in the other. What he calls an "act of sensing" (or we can say more specifically, of "seeing") is in fact only the kinaesthetic sensa which accompany the physical act of *looking.* Similarly one must distinguish between acts of *hearing, smelling,* etc., and the kinaesthetic sensa which always accompany the physical acts of *listening, sniffing,* etc.

The red, indeed, is existentially independent of the accompanying ocular kinaesthetic sensa for, on the one hand, a completely blind person (who of course does not see even black) has them and, on the other hand, if the eye muscles of a normal person were anaesthetized he could undoubtedly nevertheless sense red. But kinaesthetic sensa are not an "act of sensing" the red. The genuine act of sensing, on the contrary, is distinguishable in the sensation of headache as well as in that of red; but it is not distinguishable from the red and the headache *as* red is from kinaesthetic sensa or from sweet, but, I now urge again in the light provided by removal of the confusion just discussed, *as a case of the dance is distinguishable within any case of the waltz.*

The point is now reached where I believe that the first part of the task I undertook has been accomplished. I submit, namely, that the preceding pages have shown that Professor Moore's argument to prove that blue can exist independently of the sensing or the being aware of blue neither proves this nor proves it to be more probable than not. I now therefore turn to the second part of my task, which is to show that blue, bitter, or any other "sensa" cannot exist independently of the experiencing thereof. This will be proved if I prove that blue, bitter, etc., are, as I have claimed, species, not objects, of experiencing.

(13) *The hypothesis that bitter, blue, etc. are "directly present" to the mind.*—For this positive attempt I shall take as starting point a fact already mentioned. It is that if, in answer to the question "What do you taste?" we answer at one time "I taste bitter" and at another time "I taste quinine," the relation of the tasting to bitter is *different* from that of the tasting to quinine. Or, to take another example, if, having been asked "What do you see?" we answer at one time "I see blue" and at another "I see some *lapis lazuli*," it is obvious that the relation of the blue to the seeing of it is not the same as that of the *lapis lazuli* to the seeing of it. Or again, if to the question "What do you hear?" we answer "I hear middle C," and at another time "I hear a bell," it is evident that the relation of middle C to the hearing of it is different from that of a bell to the hearing of it.

That it is different is obvious, but if it needed any proof it would be found in the fact that the judgment expressed by "I hear a bell" is the judgment that the cause of my hearing the tone I hear at the moment is a thing of the kind called a bell; or that the judgment "I see *lapis lazuli*" is the judgment that the cause of my seeing the blue I see is a substance of the kind called *lapis lazuli;* or that the judgment "I taste quinine" is the judgment that the substance, presence of which on my tongue is causing me to taste the bitter taste I am tasting, is a substance of the kind called quinine. That is, in these examples, to taste or see or hear an "object" is to take a taste or color or tone one is experiencing as *sign* that the cause of the experiencing of it is, respectively, something of the kind called quinine, *lapis lazuli,* a bell. To have *this* relation to one's experiencing of a taste, color, or tone is, in these examples, what being "object" tasted, seen, or heard consists of.

Therefore if bitter, blue, and middle C are also to be spoken of as "objects" respectively tasted, seen, and heard, it can be only in some *other* sense, not yet considered, of the word "object"; for obviously it could not be maintained that "I taste bitter" means (as in the case of quinine) that the cause of my tasting the bitter I taste is presence on my tongue of a substance called bitter taste, for "bitter" is not the name of any kind of substance but of a kind of taste.

Our situation is then this. We have considered so far two sorts of relation a cognitum may have to the cognizing of it: one, the relation I have called "content of," and the other, the relation ordinarily called "object of," illustrated by the example of quinine as cognitum of tasting. *This* sense of "object of" I shall label *sense A,* for convenience of reference. Now our problem was: is bitter (or blue, etc.) *content of,* or *object of,* the tasting (or the seeing, etc.) thereof? Admittedly, it is not "object of" the tasting *in sense A.* But this does not force us to conclude that bitter is (as I maintain) content of the tasting if there happens to be some *third* sort of relation, which a cognitum could have to the cognizing of it, and which is also called "object of" but constitutes what we shall now label *sense B* of "object of." The question therefore now is whether there is such a third sort of possible relation, and if so what exactly it is. The epistemologists who believe there is, usually describe it as "direct presence" of the blue or bitter to, or "immediate apprehension" of these by, the mind or consciousness. As against them I maintain that either these phrases are only other names for what I have called "content of," or else they are figures of speech for which no literal meaning that is not absurd is available. I shall now attempt to make the latter evident.

The facts which, without our noticing it, suggest to us the employment of the words "direct" or "immediate" in the phrases mentioned consist of examples of directness or immediacy such as the direct contact of quinine with the tongue, or the immediate presence of a piece of *lapis lazuli* before the eyes. The presence is in these cases "direct" or "immediate" in the sense that *there is nothing discernible between* the object and the sense organ—no medium or instrument discernible at the time between them. And when these same words—"direct" or "immediate" presence—are used to describe also the relation between bitter or blue and the mind, the only *literal* meaning they can have there is that the latter relation *resembles* that of the *lapis* to the eye or the quinine to the tongue in the respect that, in both relations, *there is nothing discernible between* the terms they relate.

But if (as of course we must where blue or bitter and the mind are the terms) we divest the word "between" of the only sense, viz., the *spatial,* which it had when quinine and the tongue or *lapis* and the eye were the terms, then, I submit, the words "nothing between" describe *no hypothesis at all* as to the nature of the relation of the blue or bitter to the mind. This means that when one of the terms of a certain relation is the mind, then—since the mind is not, like the head or sense organs, an entity having a place in space—nothing whatever is being said as to the nature of that relation by employing the words "direct presence" to describe it unless some definite meaning *other than the spatial one* is explicitly provided for those words. But everybody seems either to have assumed their meaning to be obvious and not incongruous to the cases concerned, or else to have defined the words ostensively only, as meaning the sort of relation there is between blue or bitter, etc. and consciousness of these. But of course to define "direct presence" thus only ostensively is not in the least to *analyze* the sort of relation the words apply to. In particular, it is not to offer the least evidence that analysis would not reveal it to be the very relation I have called "content of."

Aside from this, however, even if one supposes that bitter tastes are entities which would exist even if no minds existed, and one should be willing to accept the absurdity that not only minds but also bitter tastes (and likewise, of course, nauseas, dizzinesses, fears, etc.) have like tongues and quinine places in space and can move about or be moved about independently of each other so that a bitter taste or a nausea could become "present" to a mind in the sense of travelling to its spatial neighborhood until nothing remained spatially between them—even then, I submit, one would have to accept the further absurdity that this mere spatial juxtaposition *without that mind's being in any way affected by it,* i.e., *without any change being caused in that mind by it,* would constitute cognition of bitter by that mind. For if one were to say that the juxtaposition does cause in the mind a specific change, viz., one to be called not "smelling" or "hearing" etc., but "tasting," this would amount to erecting bitter taste into as strictly a physical substance as quinine, and therefore to saying that tasting bitter taste and tasting quinine are both "tasting" in essentially the same (causal) sense. Yet it was obvious and admitted from the start that "tasting" does not have the same sense in both cases.

But further still, even if "presence of bitter taste in the spatial neighborhood of a mind" were not an absurdity, and even if such "presence" did cause in that mind a change called "tasting," even then there would still remain to give an account of that minds' *intuitive cognition of its own tasting at the time it occurs,* i.e., of the event *in that mind itself* caused to occur by the advent of the bitter taste in the spatial neighborhood of that mind. And this would face us then anyway with the need for my hypothesis that "tasting bitter taste" is the name of a specific variety of the activity called "tasting," viz., the variety called "tasting *bitterly*" (in the literal not the figurative sense of this adverb), and that what the activity cognizes on every such occasion is its own specific nature on the occasion.

But everything for the doing of which we need a relation of a kind other than that of quinine to tasting is, I submit, adequately done for us by the relation just described, which I maintain is the one of bitter to tasting; and this relation does not entail the absurdities required to give a literal sense B (distinct from both "content of" and sense A of "object of") to the "direct presence" hypothesis. Moreover, because the two relations "content of" and "object of" in sense A adequately account for every case, Occam's razor enables us to dismiss the still other nominal supposition—which might be resorted to *in extremis,* that bitter is "object of" tasting in some unique and indefinable other sense C of the words.

(14) *Taste is a species, not an object, of experience.*—If the discussion in the preceding section has succeeded in what it attempted, it has shown that the phrase "direct presence to a mind" either is but another name for the relation between cognitive activity and the cognita connate therewith, or else is only a figure of speech for which no literal meaning not ultimately involving absurdities is forthcoming. If this has been shown, then the allegedly third hypothesis, which *prima facie* seemed meaningful and was the only one seeming to offer an acceptable alternative to mine, has been disposed of. I shall not rest my case here, however, but will now attempt to show that when the issues are sharply presented my assertion that blue, bitter, etc., are not objects of experience, nor species of objects of experience, but species *of experience itself,* is the very assertion common sense then finds itself ready to make. What is needed for this is only to put the question in a manner making it impossible for our judgment to be confused by the ambiguity which may still cling to the phrase "object of" in spite of what was said in the preceding section. To make the meaning of the question unmistakably clear, I then ask first what would be indubitable examples of the four possible kinds of accusatives (viz., of cognita), of "experiencing." I submit the following:

The *alienly coördinate* cognitum of "experiencing" is "object" or "objective event."

The *connately coördinate* cognitum of "experiencing" is "experience."

An *alienly subordinate* cognitum of "experiencing" is "quinine," or "a rose," etc.

A *connately subordinate* cognitum of "experiencing" is "taste," or "smell," etc.

I believe the first three examples will be readily accepted as correct; but the fourth might be disputed, for if it is accepted my case is won.

"Taste," "smell," etc., I may be told, are not, as the above would imply, *species* of experience but *"objects"* of experience. If this is said, however, I ask what then would be right examples of *connately* subordinate cognita of experiencing; or—which is equivalent since experience is the connately coördinate cognitum of experiencing—what then would be right examples of *species* of experience? I believe it would not be disputed that tasting, smelling, etc., are species of experiencing; and I submit it is equally natural and proper and indeed unavoidable to say that taste and smell are species of experience, or that there is a species of experience called "taste." For the only alternative to this is to say that taste is an "object" of experience in the same sense that quinine is an object of experience; and this is plainly false.

Moreover, one who would deny that taste is a species of experience is called upon to say what then would be the cognitum coördinately connate with the species of experiencing called "tasting." If it is not taste, what then might it be? I for one can no more think of an answer than if I were asked what would be the coördinately connate accusative of striking if it were not stroke.

(15) *Bitter is a species, not an object, of taste.*—To emphasize the point of the considerations just advanced, they will now be reiterated, but at the more determinate level where the relation of bitter to tasting is in question instead of that of taste to experiencing. Again I ask, what would be indubitable examples of the four possible sorts of cognita of tasting, and I submit the following:

The *alienly coördinate* cognitum of "tasting" is "physical substance."

The *connately coördinate* cognitum of "tasting" is "taste."

An *alienly subordinate* cognitum of "tasting" is "quinine."

A *connately subordinate* cognitum of "tasting" is "bitter."

Here again, to say that bitter is not a species but an "object" of taste is to say that bitter is related to tasting in essentially the same manner as quinine is to tasting; and this is patently false. Moreover, one who would deny that when bitter is tasted what is tasted is a species of taste is called upon to say what then would be a cognitum *connately* subordinate to tasting. If bitter is not such a cognitum, what then might be one? Again here, I can no more think of an answer than I could to the question what might be a subordinately connate accusative of striking if jab were not one.

(16) *Linguistic inertia is responsible for the error that taste is object of experience.*—It is easy to see how one is led into the error that taste is an object of experience or bitter an object of taste. What leads one into it is the tendency—which we may call linguistic inertia or linguistic optimism—to believe that when a word is the same it means the same, and that when it is not the same it does not mean the same. The sameness in this case is that of the word "of," which occurs equally and in grammatically similar positions when we speak of the experiencing *of* taste and of the experiencing *of* quinine; or of the tasting *of* bitter and of the tasting *of* quinine. The temptation to believe that "of" means the same in both halves of each pair is likely to vanish only when we realize that we likewise speak of the striking *of* a jab and of the striking *of* a man—in which case it is quite obvious that the two "of's" do not mean the same relation.

On the other hand, because the two words "experiencing" and "taste," or "tasting" and "bitter," are not *linguistically* connate, linguistic inertia tempts us to believe that the cognitive activity and the cognitum in each case, for which those words stand, are not connate either. And this temptation again is likely to vanish only when we realize that "dancing" and "waltz," or "striking" and "jab," or "jumping" and "leap," etc., are not *linguistically* connate

either, but that in each case the accusative nevertheless is obviously connate (subordinately) with the activity.

(17) *"Bitter" as name of a species of taste vs. of a property of some substances.*—The adjective "bitter" can be applied both to tastes and to substances: we speak both of a bitter taste and of a bitter substance. Owing to linguistic inertia, this tempts us to believe that the relation between what the adjective and the noun stand for in the one and in the other case is the same relation. But that the relation is on the contrary very different in the two cases becomes obvious if we note that the expression "bitter taste" expands into "taste of the species called 'bitter'," whereas the expression "bitter substance" cannot similarly be expanded into "substance of the species called 'bitter'" (since "bitter" is not the name of any species of substance), but only into "substance having the *property* 'being bitter'." In the case of "bitter taste" the relation of bitter to taste is that of *species to genus;* whereas in the case of "bitter substance" the relation of bitter to substance is that of *property to substance.* The various properties of a substance are mutually conjunct; the various (coördinate) species of a genus on the contrary mutually disjunct. A property, moreover, is essentially of the nature of a law: to say that a substance has the property "being bitter" is to say the substance is such that, if placed on the tongue, then the sort of taste called "bitter taste" occurs. But when one speaks of "bitter taste," the adjective "bitter" is not here similarly the name of a certain law but the name of a certain quality.

(18) *Special sources of confusion when visual sensa are taken as examples.*—My argument has been formulated at most places in terms of gustatory sensa, but if it is valid for them it obviously is equally so for sensa of any other kinds. The reason for having presented the argument in terms of an example from the realm of taste rather than from the favorite one of sight was that the question at issue being a very difficult one, its exact nature could be exhibited more clearly by a simple example than by one where—as in the case of sight—special risks of confusion are present. The chief of these arises from the fact that the organ of sight, viz., the eye, yields to us not only color intuitions but also place and shape intuitions. This fact means that when our eye is focussed upon, for instance, an apple, we see not only a color (say, green) but also "see" a *place* at which the color is. But simultaneously (because our own nose as well as the apple is in front of our eye) we see, although inattentively, also another color (say, pink) and a place at which it is, different from the place of the green. And the fact that the place at which the green is seen and that at which the pink is seen are *literally,* i.e., spatially, *external* to each other seems to provide for some philosophers an irresistible temptation to believe that the green attended to (and the pink too if attention is called to it) are "external" also in the *metaphorical* sense the word has when we speak of externality *to the mind,* i.e., are existentially independent of their being experienced. Obviously, however, spatial externality to each other of the places at which two colors are seen, or of the places of

two physical things such as our own eye and an apple, is something totally irrelevant to the question whether the colors, (or, for that matter, the physical things,) are "external to the mind" in the sense of existing independently of their being experienced.

(19) *Summary and conclusion.*—The essential steps of the argument of this paper may now in conclusion briefly be reviewed. First, attention was called to the distinction between accusatives connate with and alien to a given activity, and to the fact that an accusative of either sort may in point of generality, be either coördinate with or subordinate to the corresponding activity. It was then pointed out that any accusative connate with a given activity exists only in the performances of that activity and therefore in particular that any cognitum connate with a given cognitive activity exists only in the performances of it. That is, the *esse* of any cognitum connate with the cognizing is its *cognosci*. The question as to whether a sensum, e.g., blue or bitter, can or cannot exist independently of the *percipi* of it then reduces to the question whether the blue or bitter is a cognitum (subordinately) connate with or on the contrary alien to the cognizing thereof. My contention, I then stated, is that the sensum is a cognitum (subordinately) connate with the cognizing of it, i.e., that what is cognized (intuitively not discursively) in cognition of it is the specific nature the sensing activity has on the given occasion; and that, in just this sense, blue or bitter are "contents" of sensing and not "objects," i.e., not alien cognita, of sensing. It was next pointed out that Professor Moore's criticism of the "content" hypothesis concerns a hypothesis *other* than the one just described, which therefore remains a possible alternative to his own hypothesis that blue or bitter are "objects" of sensing. But since Professor Moore's paper does not disprove or even consider that alternative hypothesis, and that hypothesis entails that the blue or bitter would exist only in the sensing thereof, his paper does not prove what it seeks to prove, viz., that there is no cognitum of which it is true that its *esse* is its *percipi*. I then passed to the attempt to show that blue, bitter, etc., *are* cognita connate with the sensing thereof, and therefore that their *esse* is their *percipi*. To do so, I first pointed to the fact—stated by Professor Moore himself in another paper—that seeing brown and seeing a coin, hearing middle C and hearing a bell, tasting bitter and tasting quinine, are not "seeing," "hearing" and "tasting" in the same sense in both cases; and therefore that if the coin, the bell, and the quinine have to the seeing, hearing, and tasting the relation "object of," then brown, middle C and bitter either are not "objects of" these activities at all, or else are "objects of" them in some *other* sense of the term. The allegation that "direct presence to the mind" describes such an other sense was then examined and shown to be false; and this left as the only answer in sight concerning the relation of sensa to the sensing of them, the one I had advanced. I then further attempted to show that it is the very answer common sense renders when the question is thoroughly freed of its ordinary ambiguity. Finally, some explanations were added to show how the error that sensa are "objects" of cognition

arises. The upshot of the argument is that the distinction between sensing and sensum, to which appeal is commonly made nowadays and for which Professor Moore's paper is generally regarded as the warrant, is an *invalid* distinction, if it is taken as the one from which would follow the possibility of existential independence of the sensum from the sensing. On the other hand, there *is* a valid distinction between sensum and sensing, but it is the one I have described, and from it what follows is that the existence of the sensum consists in the sensing thereof.

Whether my argument, of which this is but a brief summary, succeeds in the two tasks it undertook to perform is something that must now be left to the decision of the reader.

NOTES

[1] *Philosophical Studies,* Harcourt Brace & Co. (1922), 17-18.

[2] *Ibid.,* 16.

[3] *Ibid.,* 26-27.

[4] *Ibid.,* 28.

[5] *Ibid.,* 29.

[6] *Space, Time, and Deity,* Vol. I, 12.

[7] *Logic,* Vol. I. 9.

[8] W. E. Johnson, in his chapter on "The Determinable" (*Logic,* Vol. I, Ch. XI) misleadingly uses the names of the various colors as illustrations of names of determinates; whereas the fact obviously is that blue, for instance, is a determinable having as sub-determinables cerulaean blue, prussian blue, etc.; and that no names exist in the language for the truly determinate colors—for instance for cerulaean blue completely determinate as to hue and as to degree of brightness and of saturation. But we could, if we wished, assign names to the various infimae species of cerulaean blue—calling a certain one, perhaps, Anna cerulaean, another, Bertha cerulaean, etc.

[9] Moore, *op. cit.,* 26.

[10] *Ibid.,* 26.

[11] *Philosophical Studies,* 187.

[12] *Ibid.,* 25.

[13] *Scientific Thought,* 254.

Norman Malcolm (essay date 1963)

SOURCE: "George Edward Moore," in *Knowledge and Certainty: Essays and Lectures,* Prentice-Hall, Inc., 1963, pp. 163-86.

[*In the following essay, Malcolm recalls his personal interaction with Moore, finding him less imaginative than Bertrand Russell and less profound than Ludwig Wittgenstein but admiring his essay "Defence of Common Sense."*]

I

I should like to say something about the character of G. E. Moore, the man and philosopher, whom I knew for the last twenty years of his life. He was a very gentle and sweet-natured human being, as anyone acquainted with him would testify. For one thing, he had a wonderful way with children. When he read or told a story or explained something to a child, the scene was so delightful that the adults within hearing were enthralled, as well as the child. He liked to spend time with children. To one son, Moore gave a music lesson every day from his third year until he went away to prep school; and that son is now a music teacher and composer. Moore loved to sing and play the piano. He also took great joy in flowers and plants, and was anxious to learn their names.

Moore was himself a childlike person. One thing that contributed to this quality in him was an extreme modesty. It was as if the thought had never occurred to Moore that he was an eminent philosopher. I recall that once when lecturing before a small class he had occasion to refer to an article that he had published some years before, and he went on to remark, without embarrassment, that it was a *good* article. I was much struck by this. Most men would be prevented by false modesty from saying a thing of this sort in public. Moore's modesty was so genuine that he could say it without any implication of self-satisfaction. How many times, both in public and private, did he declare that some previous work of his was a "dreadful muddle" or "utterly mistaken"!

Another aspect of the childlike in him was the constant freshness of his interest, his eager curiosity. This was manifest in all things, but was particularly surprising and impressive in his philosophical work. During the approximately two and a half years I spent in Cambridge at two different periods, I had regular weekly discussions with him; also I went to his weekly "at-homes," which were given over to discussion with whomever showed up. I was amazed at the way he reacted whenever anyone proposed a problem for discussion. He was all eagerness: never casual, never bored, never suggesting in his manner, "Oh, yes, I have heard of that problem before." His reaction was rather as if he had not known of it before and was anxious to look into it at once! This was so even if the topic was one that the others and himself had been thinking about together for many months. In the course of a discussion he would listen to everyone's remarks with breathless attention, as if what they were saying was entirely new and extraordinarily exciting. His younger son, who was then about seventeen years of age and a freshman at Cambridge, began to attend Moore's lectures, and I recall how in the course of a discussion that occurred after the lecture, Moore listened with this same intensity to a comment made by the young man, a beginner in philosophy and his own offspring! This continuously fresh interest and eager desire to learn was certainly one of Moore's most remarkable qualities as a philosopher.

Another aspect of the childlike in Moore was his simplicity. This was exhibited in both his speech and his writing. Although he had a mastery of the classical languages, as well as of French and German, he did not ever adorn his prose with phrases from those languages. And his writing is largely free of the jargon that philosophers typically fall into. He wrote in the plainest possible English, employing no elegant variation but rather continuous repetition. Rarely did he ever use any of the technical phrases or terms of art of philosophy; and when he did, he went to great pains to explain their meaning in the common language of everyday life.

Moore wrote an **"Autobiography,"** which is printed in the volume entitled *The Philosophy of G. E. Moore.*[1] In it he describes a striking episode of his youth. When he was eleven or twelve years old, he was converted by a group of young men whose evangelical views were similar to those of the Salvation Army. Moore says he felt it to be his duty to try to convert others as he had been converted, but that he "had to fight against a very strong feeling of reluctance." He did, however, drive himself to do various things which he "positively hated"—for example, to distribute religious tracts. "But I constantly felt," he says, "that I was not doing nearly as much as I ought to do. I discovered that I was very deficient in moral courage."[2] The three features of Moore's childlike quality that I have mentioned, his modesty, freshness, and simplicity, present themselves very clearly in his account of this incident, which I will not quote in full.

As a philosopher he was not very imaginative. He was not fertile in ideas, as was Russell. He was not a profound thinker, as was Wittgenstein. I believe that what gave Moore stature as a philosopher was his *integrity,* an attribute of character rather than of intellect. He had the depth of seriousness. When he addressed himself to a philosophical difficulty what he said about it had to be *exactly* right. Philosophical problems vexed him: but it was impossible for him to get one out of the way by ignoring some aspect of it with which he did not know how to deal. His lectures at Cambridge were always freshly written, and during a course of lectures he would continuously revise or take back what he had previously said. His lecturing was always new research, which is perhaps one reason why he never availed himself of sabbatical leave. His labor on any piece of philosophical writing was intensive and prolonged. To one paper, **"Four Forms of Scepticism,"**[3] he applied himself for some fifteen years. He gave the Tarner Lectures in Cambridge, but could not bring himself to publish them and therefore received no fee for the lectures.

The address that Moore delivered to the British Academy, entitled **"Proof of an External World,"** caused him a great deal of torment in its preparation. He worked hard at it, but the concluding portion displeased him, and he could not get it right as the time approached for his appearance before the Academy. On the day of the lecture he was still distressed about the ending of the paper. As he was about to leave the house to take the train to London, Mrs. Moore said, in order to comfort him, "Cheer up! I'm sure they will like it." To which Moore made this emphatic reply: "If they *do*, they'll be *wrong!*"

The anecdote is entirely typical of Moore. It is not what people *believe* that matters, but the truth and only the truth. When I dwell in my mind on this true love of the truth, it disturbs me. A thinker with that kind of devotion to truth must go it alone, and this is awesome and frightening.

Moore's steady, immovable integrity was exhibited in every lecture, every discussion, everything he wrote. He had a stubbornness, not of pride, but of honesty.

Along with his perfect honesty there was another thing that contributed to Moore's stature, namely, his utter absorption in philosophy. He worked at it the better part of each day. He worked very slowly with intense concentration, and he came back to the same topics again and again. The philosophical problems stayed with him; they were part of his nature; for Moore to have given up philosophy would have been inconceivable.

Let me relate another anecdote which helps to point up this side of Moore. He was awarded the Order of Merit, the highest honor that a man of letters can receive in the British Empire. The presentation was to be made by King George VI, in a private audience. Moore and his wife went to London on the day appointed and took a cab to Buckingham Palace. Mrs. Moore waited in the cab while Moore went into the palace. There he was met by the King's secretary and taken to the King's library. The secretary was a man of culture and also a Cambridge man, and while they waited for the King, he and Moore chatted about Cambridge. The King entered. He invited Moore to sit down and they talked for a while. Then the King presented the medal to Moore. After some further conversation the King arose, indicating that the audience was at an end. They shook hands and Moore was taken back to the gates of the palace. He reentered the cab and, leaning over excitedly, said to Mrs. Moore: "Do you know that the King had never heard of *Wittgenstein!*"

This exclamation of Moore's illustrates not only his naïveté, but also his complete preoccupation with philosophy. Here is philosophy, the most exciting thing in the world; here is Wittgenstein, the most exciting figure in philosophy; and here is the King, who had not even heard of Wittgenstein!

Finally, Moore had an acute and energetic mind. He could hold together all of the strands of a long, complex, and subtle discussion. As he pushed deeper and deeper into a topic he would always know what the road behind had been, how he had got to the place he was in the argument.

Thus the qualities that contributed to Moore's philosophical eminence (and by eminence I do not mean fame, but rather the quality of being first-rate) were, I think, these: complete modesty and simplicity, saving him from the dangers of jargon and pomposity; thorough absorption in philosophy, which he found endlessly exciting; strong mental powers; and a pure integrity that accounted for his solidity and his passion for clarity. These were the primary ingredients in the nature of this remarkable philosopher.

II

Let us turn now to Moore's philosophical work. He made interesting contributions on many topics: perception, knowledge, facts and propositions, the reality of time, hedonism, idealism, universals and particulars; whether goodness is a quality, whether existence is a predicate; the proof of an external world, the nature of philosophical analysis: these are some of the topics on which Moore wrote. But as I reflect on his writings, his lectures, and his oral discussions, the thing that stands out most prominently for me is his so-called **"Defence of Common Sense."** I suspect that if Moore is remembered in the history of philosophy it will be because of this theme embedded in his philosophical thought. It was not there merely as an implicit assumption. He made it an explicit principle of his philosophy, so much so that in 1925 when he published an essay intended to describe his philosophical position he actually entitled it **"A Defence of Common Sense."**

Now what did Moore mean by "Common Sense" and what is its importance in relation to philosophy? Writing in 1910, Moore said the following: "There are, it seems to me, certain views about the nature of the Universe, which are held, now-a-days, by almost everybody. They are so universally held that they may, I think, fairly be called the views of Common Sense."[4] He goes on to say: "It seems to me that what is most amazing and most interesting about the views of many philosophers is the way in which they go beyond or positively contradict the views of Common Sense."

He proceeds to mention some of these "views of Common Sense." For example: "We certainly believe that there are in the Universe enormous numbers of material objects, of one kind or another. We know, for instance, that there are upon the surface of the earth, besides our own bodies, the bodies of millions of other men; we know that there are the bodies of millions of other animals; millions of plants too; and, besides all these, an even greater number of inanimate objects—mountains, and all the stones upon them, grains of sand, different sorts of minerals and soils, all the drops of water in rivers and in the sea, and moreover ever so many different objects manufactured by men; houses and chairs and tables and railway engines, etc., etc."[5] "All this we now believe about the material Universe," he says; "It is surely Common Sense to believe it all." Another "Common Sense belief" is this: "We believe that we men, besides having bodies, also have minds."[6] And another belief of Common Sense is that we *know* all of the things that have just been mentioned.[7]

In his essay **"A Defence of Common Sense,"** published fifteen years later,[8] Moore put down another list of "Common Sense beliefs." Among the sentences on this list are the following: "I am a human being"; "There exists at present a living human body, which is my body"; "This body was born at a certain time in the past, and has existed continuously ever since." He declares that each of us *knows* these things to be true of himself, and that it would be "the height of absurdity" for any philosopher "to speak with contempt" of these Common Sense beliefs.

It might be useful to stop for a moment to examine this phrase "common sense." To me it sounds odd to speak of "a common sense belief," whereas the phrases "common belief" and "common knowledge" are quite familiar. It is, for example, a common belief that colds can be transmitted from one person to another. I doubt that we should call it a "common sense belief" or a "common sense view." How do we actually use this expression "common sense"? I can imagine one person saying to another: "If you want so very much to enter the Civil Service, then it is common sense that you have to start preparing yourself for the examination." "It is common sense" means here "It is the obvious conclusion." I am inclined to think that this is how we commonly use the phrase "common sense." Something falls under that heading if it is an obvious conclusion from information at hand. In this common use of "common sense," common sense has nothing to do with views about the universe, nor with the so-called "belief" that there are enormous numbers of material objects in the world. We say of one person that he is lacking in common sense, and of another that he has lots of common sense. What this means is that the former has a tendency to arrive at conclusions which ignore obvious facts, and that the latter does not have this tendency. In general, the expression "lacking in common sense" means "lacking in good judgment." Thomas Reid, the eighteenth-century Scotsman, who, like Moore, made "an appeal to common sense" a foundation of his philosophical work, connected "common sense" quite explicitly with good judgment:

> A man of sense is a man of judgment. Good sense is good judgment. Nonsense is what is evidently contrary to right judgment. Common sense is that degree of judgment which is common to men with whom we can converse and transact business.[9]

A man of common sense is a *sensible* man—one who makes sensible judgments. He is not to be identified as a man who holds a certain set of *views*—about the world or anything else.

Suppose that a mother has a daughter, sixteen years of age, who takes singing lessons and is said by her teacher and others to have a pretty voice. Suppose this lady tries to persuade her husband to sell his prosperous business in the small town where they live and move to New York City, so that their daughter can study in a famous school of music. Her idea is that after six months of training, during which time they will live on savings, their daughter will become an opera and concert singer, and support them for the rest of their lives. This mother's proposal could be said to be extravagant and unrealistic on a number of counts. It could also be said to show a complete lack of common sense. Her husband, in arguing against this proposal and pointing out various objections, is showing common sense. He takes a common sense view of the matter. This is a faithful example of the actual use of the expression "a common sense view" whereas to say that it is "a common sense view" that there are an enormous number of material objects in the universe is to violate the ordinary use of the expression "common sense." It is not a matter of common sense at all. Common sense has nothing to do with it.

III

Since, as I hold, the examples that Moore gives of alleged "common sense views of the world" actually are not examples of common sense, let us ask whether they are "common beliefs," or "widespread beliefs," or "universal beliefs," or "things which we all commonly assume to be true," as Moore says they are. There is one item on Moore's list of which some, at least, of the above things are true: namely, the belief that "the sun and moon and the visible stars are great masses of matter, most of them many times larger than the earth."[10] This might even be said to be common knowledge, whereas at one time it was not. But consider the following examples: "There are enormous numbers of material objects"; "Acts of consciousness are quite definitely *attached* in a particular way to some material objects";[11] "Our acts of consciousness . . . occur *in the same places* in which our bodies are";[12] "There exists at present a living human body, which is my body"; "I am a human being." Is it right to say that nearly everyone assumes these things to be true, and even knows them to be true?

If you stop to think about the things on this list you will begin to see that all of them are queer sentences. Their queerness is brought out if we ask of each of them a question that Wittgenstein taught us to ask, namely, "What is supposed to be the *use* of the sentence?" When would you seriously say it to someone? What would the circumstances be? What would be the purpose of saying it? Would it be to give someone information, or to admonish or warn him, or to remind him of something, or to teach him the meaning of a word, or what?

Let us try out this kind of inquiry with the sentence "I am a human being." When would you say this to someone or to yourself? If you think about it a bit, certain ways in which this sentence might be used will occur to you: *a.* The first example that I think of is this: Suppose we lived in a region where there were beings who looked like bears but who talked our language, so that if you heard someone talking in the next room, you often could not tell whether it was a human being or a bear. If I were to knock on someone's door he might ask me through the door, "Are you a bear?" and I could reply, "I am a human being." *b*. Second example: A child might ask me, "What is a human being?" and I could reply, "I am a human being; you are a human being; the cat there is not a human being; the baby is a human being, but the dog is not." Here I should be trying to teach him, by examples, to master the range of application of the expression "human being." *c*. Third example: Suppose that someone had been falsely informed of my death. When I appear before him he exclaims in terror, "Are you a ghost?" I reply: "I am a human being."

Those are three sorts of cases in which you could seriously say the sentence "I am a human being" and if we tried we could think of still others. Now when Moore wrote and spoke the sentence "I am a human being," in which of these circumstances was he using it? In none of them, of course. Did he believe that someone somewhere supposed he might be a bear? No. Was he trying to teach someone the application of the expression "human being"? No.

There is an inclination to think that if anyone were to utter the sentence "I am a human being," he would be stating an *obvious fact.* But there is something wrong with this. I should not know whether he was stating an obvious fact until I knew how he was using the sentence: to what question he was addressing himself or what doubt he was trying to remove. I do not think this is overly sophisticated. If some stranger should come up to me and say, "I am a human being," I should probably be at a loss as to what he meant. (Is he complaining of unfair treatment?) I should not know whether or not he was stating an obvious fact.

I am not holding, of course, that the sentence "I am a human being" is meaningless. On the contrary, it is a sentence for which we can, without much effort, imagine various contexts of use. But if I hear or see that sentence and it is not clear to me what the context of its use is, then it is not clear to me what the person meant by that sentence on that occasion. It would be useless for him to reply, "I meant that I am a human being!" That would be repeating the sentence without explaining what he meant by it.

One is strongly tempted to make something like the following reply: "There is a certain assertion that a person normally makes when he speaks or writes the sentence 'I am a human being.' The sentence is ordinarily used to make that assertion. You may not know what the speaker's *purpose* is (Moore's, for example) in making the assertion in question. But you know that Moore used the sentence in its *ordinary sense* to make the assertion that it is normally used to make."

Let us leave aside the cases in which one would not have made *any* assertion at all by saying that sentence. (For example, alone in my study, thinking about the **"Defence of Common Sense,"** I say aloud, "I am a human being." Have I made an assertion?) Why should we suppose that

when the sentence is used to make an assertion, there is some *one and the same* assertion that is "normally" made? How does one tell whether it is the same assertion that is made in different cases? Does not the particular doubt, the particular question at issue, have some bearing on this? In one of our examples the speaker *informed* someone that he was *not a bear;* in another, that he was *not a ghost;* in another, that he is *called* "a human being" (in contrast to a dog or a cat). If these differences in what is in doubt, in what comparisons are made, in what information is given, do not make for differences in *what is asserted,* then it will have no definite meaning to speak of one assertion as being "different" or the "same" as another one.

When Moore says "I am a human being," I do not wish to agree or to disagree. It is not clear to me what he is saying. Of course he is addressing himself to philosophers, and it would be reasonable to assume that his utterance is relevant to some philosophical view. But what view? Could it be some thesis of Cartesian philosophy? But which one? What philosophical thesis has the implication that Moore is not a human being? When Moore's sentence is, instead, "I *know* I am a human being," it is much easier to supply philosophical surroundings for it.

My general point is that not only does the famous **"Defence of Common Sense"** have no clear relationship to *common sense* but, furthermore, if we go through Moore's list of so-called "Common Sense views" it is far from clear, with regard to some at least, either what assertions he was making or that he was making any at all.

IV

So far I have not succeeded in explaining why the **"Defence of Common Sense"** was an important development in philosophy. I do not doubt that it was. I was strongly influenced by it, and so were many others. *Prima facie* it is not easy to understand what philosophical interest it has. Of what possible interest could it be to remind us that it is a universal or widespread belief that the sun is many times larger than the earth? Moore's list of "common sense views" is an odd assortment. Some of the items in it, like the one just mentioned, are genuine common beliefs—but they have no apparent philosophical relevance. Some, like "I am a human being," cannot be said to express common beliefs, nor am I certain that they have any philosophical relevance.

But there are some that are of real philosophical interest, although they are neither "common sense views" nor "common beliefs." An example in this category is the following statement from **"A Defence of Common Sense"**:

> I have often perceived both my own body and other things which formed part of its environment, including other human bodies; I have not only perceived things of this kind, but have also observed facts about them, such as, for instance,

the fact which I am now observing, that that mantel-piece is at present nearer to my body than that book-case.[13]

Considering that some philosophers have said that it is impossible for a person to perceive a material thing, this statement of Moore's has philosophical interest. In another work Moore discusses what he calls "judgments of perception," and his examples are seeing an inkstand, or a door, or a finger. He makes this remark:

> Some people may no doubt think that it is very unphilosophical in me to say that we ever can perceive such things as these. But it seems to me that we do, in ordinary life, constantly talk of seeing such things, and that, when we do so, we are neither using language incorrectly, nor making any mistake about the facts—supposing something to occur which never does in fact occur. The truth seems to me to be that we are using the term "perceive" in a way which is both perfectly correct and expresses a kind of thing which constantly does occur. . . . I am not, therefore, afraid to say that I do now perceive that that is a door, and that that is a finger.[14]

In still another work Moore was commenting on a feature of Hume's philosophy, which has the consequence that no person can ever know of the existence of any material thing. He says:

> If Hume's principles are true, then, I have admitted, I do *not* know *now* that this pencil—the material object—exists. If, therefore, I am to prove that I *do* know that this pencil exists, I must prove, somehow, that Hume's principles, one or both of them, are *not* true. In what sort of way, by what sort of argument, can I prove this?
>
> It seems to me that, in fact, there really is no stronger and better argument than the following. I *do* know that this pencil exists; I could not know this, if Hume's principles were true; *therefore,* Hume's principles, one or both of them, are false. I think this argument really is as strong and good a one as any that could be used; and I think it really is conclusive.[15]

Here there appears to be some sort of issue joined between Moore and some other philosophers. But I expect that some will be puzzled as to how anyone in his right mind can *deny* that we see doors and know that pencils exist. Others, who feel no difficulty about this, will be perplexed as to how Moore could think of himself as *disproving* these views; for all he does is to declare that he *does* see a door and does know that there is a pencil in front of him; so he appears to be begging the question. I should like to say something on both of these points.

With regard to the first point, anyone who begins to study problems in the philosophy of perception will soon come upon a number of arguments which appear to prove that it is impossible to see a material thing. For example, H. A. Prichard, who held a chair at Oxford and wrote and lec-

tured from about 1910 to 1940, produced various arguments to prove that it is impossible to see bodies. Prichard accepted these arguments, and I expect he had many followers. Speaking of the "view" that we do see such things as chairs, tables, and boats going downstream, he remarked: "It need hardly be said that this view, much as we should all like to be able to vindicate it, will not stand examination."[16] He said that the "consideration of any so-called illusion of sight . . . is enough to destroy this view."[17]

I will not try to give a detailed account of how he thought that the occurrence of "illusions of sight" proves that we do not see bodies, but the gist of the argument is something like this: If you are to really see a body then "the whole fact of seeing must include the thing seen,"[18] and furthermore the body cannot "look other than what it is."[19] "A body, if it be really seen and seen along with other bodies, can only present to us just that appearance which its relations to the other bodies really require."[20] For example, if a body were really seen it could not "present the appearance which a body similar but reversed as regards right and left can present," as happens when we "see" something in a mirror.[21] When it seems to us that we see a man moving in front of us (we are looking in a mirror), if "that state, activity, or process which really only seems to us to be seeing a man move across in front of us had an intrinsic character of its own, in virtue of which it was only *like,* without *being,* seeing a man move thus, then that character ought to be recognizable at the time, in an act of self-consciousness, and if so it need not be true, as in fact it always is, that we can still have the illusion even though we are not taken in by it."[22] "If the state had a character other than being just like seeing a man move across, we ought to be able while in this state to recognize that it has this character, and if we did we should no longer have the illusion."[23] There is no difference in "intrinsic character," Prichard is saying, between what is ordinarily *called* seeing a body and the cases in which we are under an illusion of seeing a body. If there is no difference in "intrinsic character" between two "states," then if one of them is not seeing a body neither is the other. "No one doubts that in certain cases we have or are under an illusion, and all I have been doing is to contend that all so-called seeing involves an illusion just as much as that so-called seeing which everyone admits to involve an illusion."[24]

The argument may be briefly recapitulated as follows: Suppose there are two "states," or "states of mind,"[25] A and B. They are states of either seeing or seeming to see a man in front of us. When state A occurs there actually is a man in front of us; state B is an illusion produced by a mirror. States A and B have the *same intrinsic character*—that is, if we considered state B "in itself we could not say that it was not a state of seeing" a man in front of us.[26] State A, therefore, which is ordinarily *called* "seeing a man in front of us" is not actually seeing a man in front of us, any more than is the admittedly illusory state B.

The reasoning is undoubtedly obscure; but at the same time it is extremely persuasive, and it is extremely difficult to put one's finger on any serious error in it. It is one of a number of attractive arguments that Prichard and others have used to prove, to the satisfaction of many philosophers, that we do not see bodies, and that what we really see are "sense-data" or "sensations." Those arguments and that conclusion, in one form or another, dominated the philosophy of perception for centuries. If you consider Moore's remark, "I am not . . . afraid to say that I do now perceive that that is a door and that that is a finger," and view it against this background of the history of philosophy, you will appreciate it as being a bold line to take.

This brings us to the second point, namely, what does Moore *achieve* by insisting that he does see material things? Is not this merely a stubborn refusal to accept the various arguments against it? Distinguished philosophers have given ingenious and persuasive proofs that we do not see material things. Moore says that we do, and that the proofs are wrong. But he does not say *how* they are wrong; so is he not begging the question?

It must be admitted that Moore never gave a satisfactory account of what he was doing; and so we ourselves must supply some explanation of this particular feature of the so-called "defence of common sense," if we are to attribute any cogency to it. In the following I will attempt an explanation.

Prichard and the others must admit that we use such sentences as "See my finger," "Now you see the dog," "Now you don't see him," every day of our lives; and furthermore that we are taught to use such sentences and teach their use to others. We are taught and do teach that the correct way to speak, in certain circumstances, is to say "I see the dog," and in other circumstances to say "I don't see him now," and in still other circumstances to say "I think I see him," and so on. Undoubtedly Prichard used such forms of speech every day (and taught them to his children, if he had any) and would have acknowledged in various ways in practical life that they are correct forms of speech.

His philosophical position, however, stands in opposition to this obvious fact. I believe that Prichard was contending that we *cannot* see bodies, not merely that we do not. He says: "I, of course, take it for granted that if it can be shown in certain cases that what we see cannot be a body, the same thing must be true of all cases."[27] He implies, I believe, that if there is just *one* case in which someone is under the illusion of seeing a certain body in front of him then no one ever sees a body. As we noted, he offers the example of seeing something in a mirror as an instance of illusion.[28] I do not believe, however, that Prichard's real point could have been that visual illusions do occur *in point of fact*. Suppose that they should cease to occur (e.g., there are no more mirrors or reflecting surfaces): would Prichard be willing to admit then that we see bodies? Obviously not. The "state" that we call "seeing a body" would not have changed its "intrinsic character" and could not do so. Visual illusions would be logically

possible, and this would be enough to prove that we do not see bodies. Prichard says: "A body, if it be really seen and seen along with other bodies, can only present to us just that appearance which its relations to the other bodies really require."[29] It cannot cease to be a logical possibility that a body should present an appearance "different from what its relations to the other bodies really require." Prichard is holding that if we could see bodies then visual illusions could not occur. The actual occurrence of illusions is not necessary for his position. The logical possibility of illusions suffices. The logical possibility of visual illusions is an a priori truth. When Prichard's view is drawn out in the only direction it can go, it turns out to be the claim that it is an a priori truth that we cannot see bodies. He is holding that the very notion of *seeing a body* is absurd. It contains a requirement that *could not* be satisfied, namely, that visual illusion should be logically impossible. In order for this requirement to be satisfied the concept of seeing a body would have to be identical with the concept of seeing an after-image—which is an impossibility of an a priori sort.[30] Prichard is holding that there is a conceptual absurdity in saying such a thing as "I see a raccoon in your corn patch," or in making *any* affirmative statement expressed by a sentence whose main verb is some form of the verb "see," used in a visual sense and taking for its object the name of a body.

If those sentences embodied some conceptual absurdity then they would not have a correct use. They could never express true statements. But those sentences do have a correct use. A child is taught that he is wrong when he says "I see pussy cat" while he is looking the wrong way, but that he is right when his eyes are following the cat's movements. If the sentence involved a conceptual absurdity he would never be right and he would not be told that he was. The language has the use that we give it.

To come back to Moore: When he said, against the skeptics, such a thing as "I now see that door," it did not matter whether he was actually looking at a *door*. He did not have to produce an example of a *true* perceptual statement. In order to refute the claim that there is an absurdity in the concept of seeing a body, Moore did not have to present a *paradigm* of seeing a body, as I once thought.[31] He only had to remind his listeners and readers that the sentence "I see a door over there" has a correct use and, therefore, *can* express a true statement. On one famous occasion Moore was actually in error in his example. This delighted his skeptical opponents in the audience. On my view he was right even when he was wrong.

I believe that Moore himself was confused about what he was doing, as is often so when one makes a philosophical advance. He always *tried* to present his audiences with examples of *true* perceptual statements. And he made a point of remarking that sentences such as "I have often seen pennies" or "I have often seen the moon" "are correct ways of expressing propositions which are true. I, personally, have in fact often seen pennies and often seen the moon, and so have many other people."[32] Why does he have this interest in giving examples of perceptual statements which are *true,* if it is irrelevant whether they are true? Part of the explanation (perhaps all of it) is Moore's mistaken idea that when he is dealing with a proposition put forward by a philosophical skeptic he is dealing with an *empirical* proposition. That Moore has this idea is shown, for one thing, by his famous "proof" of the existence of external things.[33] In **"A Reply to My Critics,"** he states explicitly that a philosopher who holds that there are no external objects is "making a false empirical statement."[34] Undoubtedly he would be inclined to say the same thing about Prichard's proposition that we do not see bodies, or about the common philosophical view that no one has absolutely certain knowledge of any empirical fact. But the examination of a typical argument for the latter view makes it plain that what is being held is that it is *logically* impossible for anyone to know with certainty the truth of any empirical statement.[35] Our brief study of Prichard's claim shows that, on his view, we could not see bodies unless something which is a logical possibility (visual illusion) were to become a logical impossibility—which is itself a logical impossibility. In replying to Prichard, therefore, it is both unnecessary and misleading for Moore to assert that he has often seen the moon. It does not matter whether he has. What is necessary and sufficient, and also puts the view he is attacking in its true light, is to point out that the sentence "I see the moon" has a correct use. It is surprising that anyone should think it has not: but philosophical reasoning has a peculiar power to blind one to the obvious.

It has been claimed that in previous writings I identified Moore's "appeal to common sense" with his "appeal to ordinary language," and that this is a mistake because they are different.[36] I want to insist, however, that if Moore's so-called "defence of common sense" has any cogency, then it is not really about *common sense* or *common beliefs,* for neither of these things is relevant to the philosophical issues in which Moore is involved. I take the philosophers with whom he is engaged to be asserting that the notion of seeing a body (or of having absolutely certain knowledge of an empirical truth, and so on) contains a logical absurdity. The actual efficacy of Moore's reply, his misnamed "defence of common sense," consists in reminding us that there is a proper use for sentences like "I see the broom under the bed" or "It is known for certain that he drowned in the lake." As Moore remarks, when we say such things we are not "using language incorrectly."[37] We should be *if* those sentences did embody some logical absurdity. The philosophical positions that Moore opposes can, therefore, be seen to be false *in advance* of an examination of the arguments adduced in support of them. We can know that something is wrong with Prichard's reasoning before we study it.

We are able to see now why Moore was not begging the question against Prichard: for when we understand the latter's position we realize that he was contending for something that is, beyond question, false. That is just the point that Moore made. He was not begging the question because the point he made (without fully realizing it) was that it is *not even a question* whether those sentences of ordinary language have a correct use.

Here there comes to light a genuine connection with common sense. Prichard showed a lack of common sense, in the ordinary meaning of the words. He was led by persuasive reasoning into losing sight of the obvious fact that it is correct to speak of seeing bodies. He was blind to something that was right before his eyes. In contrast, Moore resisted that temptation. In tenaciously keeping sight of the obvious he showed common sense.[38] And also he "appealed to common sense," in the common meaning of the words, when he reminded other philosophers of the plain facts of language.

Why should we not say that what Prichard was blind to was the fact that we do see bodies? Because, as I tried to show, his denial that we see bodies is really the claim that it is logically impossible to see bodies. Moore's assertion that we do see the moon and pennies and doors can be taken as a *reply* to Prichard only if it is understood as the assertion that there is no logical absurdity in the notion of seeing a body. But is it a "common sense view" or a "common belief" that it is logically possible to see bodies? No. It is the kind of observation that only a philosopher makes or understands.

v

I believe that Moore's misnamed "defence of common sense" was a philosophical step of first importance. Its effect is to alter one's conception of the nature of philosophy and thereby to change one's philosophical practice. Clearly Prichard would have looked at what he was doing in an entirely different way had he seen the soundness of Moore's position. He would have realized that he could not possibly prove that it is impossible to see bodies! He might have been unable to detect anything wrong in his reasoning. But he would have known that *something* was wrong in it. His attitude toward his own philosophical work would have been different.

Wittgenstein says: "A philosophical problem has the form: 'I don't know my way about.'"[39] That is: "I am confused"; "I am in a muddle." But I think a philosophical problem can take this form only if one sees the soundness of Moore's defence of ordinary language. One is tempted to hold that certain ordinary expressions *cannot* have a correct use: at the same time one realizes that of course they *do.* Then one knows that one is in a muddle.

Prichard did not have that attitude toward this view of his about seeing. If that had been his attitude he would have thought: "Here I am inclined to hold something absurdly false, namely, that we cannot see bodies. Where in my thinking do I go *wrong?*" Instead, he said that the "common view" that we see bodies "will not stand examination." He really thought that our ordinary language of perception needs to be corrected.

Wittgenstein says: "Philosophy may in no way interfere with the actual use of language; it can in the end only describe it."[40] This conception of philosophy is entirely different from Prichard's. He thought that philosophy *could* "interfere with the actual use of language." To think of philosophy as Prichard did is enormously different from thinking of a philosophical problem as a confusion. Philosophy has a different *feel* in the two conceptions, and the actual steps one will take in conducting one's philosophical inquiry will be different.

I believe that in order to grasp Wittgenstein's idea that a philosophical problem is essentially a confusion in our thinking, and that philosophical work cannot interfere with the actual use of language but must "leave everything as it is" (that is, leave our actual use of language as it is, not leave everything in philosophy as it is)—in order to grasp this idea, one must understand what is right in Moore's defence of ordinary language. The latter was an advance in philosophy because it brought us nearer to a true understanding of philosophy itself.

NOTES

[1] P. A. Schilpp, ed. (Evanston: Northwestern, 1942).

[2] *Op. cit.,* pp. 10-11.

[3] Published posthumously in G. E. Moore, *Philosophical Papers* (New York: The Macmillan Company, 1959).

[4] G. E. Moore, *Some Main Problems of Philosophy* (New York: The Macmillan Company, 1953), p. 2.

[5] *Ibid.,* pp. 2-3.

[6] *Ibid.,* p. 4.

[7] *Ibid.,* p. 12.

[8] Republished in *Philosophical Papers.*

[9] *Reid's Essays on the Intellectual Powers of Man,* A. D. Woozley, ed. (New York: The Macmillan Company, 1941), pp. 330-331.

[10] *Some Main Problems,* p. 3.

[11] *Ibid.,* p. 6.

[12] *Ibid.*

[13] *Philosophical Papers,* p. 33.

[14] *Philosophical Studies* (New York: Harcourt, Brace & World, Inc., 1922), pp. 226-227.

[15] *Some Main Problems,* pp. 119-120.

[16] *Knowledge and Perception* (New York: Oxford University Press, 1950), p. 53.

[17] *Ibid.*

[18] *Ibid.,* p. 53.

[19] *Ibid.,* p. 54.

[20] *Ibid.,* p. 53.

[21] *Ibid.*

[22] *Ibid.,* p. 50.

[23] *Ibid.*

[24] *Ibid.*

[25] *Ibid.,* p. 49.

[26] *Ibid.*

[27] *Ibid.,* p. 54.

[28] J. L. Austin justly remarks that, normally, seeing something in a mirror is *not* an illusion (*Sense and Sensibilia* [New York: Oxford University Press, 1962], p. 26).

[29] Prichard, *Knowledge and Perception,* p. 53.

[30] The two concepts are compared in "Direct Perception," pp. 85-87.

[31] I misunderstood this point when I first wrote on Moore. In "Moore and Ordinary Language," I said that Moore's replies to various skeptical assertions consist in presenting *paradigms* of knowing something for certain, seeing bodies, and so on. *The Philosophy of G. E. Moore,* p. 354.

[32] "Visual Sense-Data," *British Philosophy in the Mid-Century,* C. A. Mace, ed. (New York: The Macmillan Company, 1957), p. 205.

[33] "Proof of an External World," *Philosophical Papers,* pp. 145-146.

[34] *The Philosophy of G. E. Moore,* p. 672.

[35] See "The Verification Argument," especially p. 56.

[36] Alan R. White, *G. E. Moore* (Oxford: Basil Blackwell & Mott, 1958): see Chapters 1-3. V. C. Chappell has an interesting discussion of various interpretations of Moore's "defence of common sense" in his article "Malcolm on Moore" (*Mind,* LXX, No. 279, July 1961, 417-425). Chappell mentions two interpretations that differ from the one put forward here. One is ascribed to Moore himself. Its principal feature is the assertion that Moore's opponents are maintaining empirical theses. But in order to find out what kind of thesis a philosopher is maintaining, we have to consider the kind of support he offers for it. Prichard's reasoning, for example, clearly

implies that his thesis is nonempirical. The other interpretation, put forward by A. Ambrose and M. Lazerowitz in their essays in *The Philosophy of G. E. Moore,* contains the claim that Moore's opponents are essentially making "verbal recommendations." But there is no natural sense of "recommend" in which Prichard, for example, can be said to have *recommended* that we should no longer *speak* of seeing bodies.

[37] *Philosophical Studies,* p. 226.

[38] I owe this observation to Professor G. H. von Wright. (I would not be thought to be extolling common sense as the supreme virtue of a philosopher. Many first-rate contributions to philosophy have been made by thinkers who developed their ideas in disregard of absurd consequences. They would rather be rigorous than right. As Austin remarks: "In philosophy, there are many mistakes that it is no disgrace to have made: to make a first-water, ground-floor mistake, so far from being easy, takes one [*one*] form of philosophical genius." J. L. Austin, *Philosophical Papers,* J. O. Urmson and G. J. Warnock, eds. [New York: Oxford University Press, 1961], p. 153.)

[39] Ludwig Wittgenstein, *Philosophical Investigations,* tr. G. E. M. Anscombe (New York: The Macmillan Company, 1953), sec. 123.

[40] *Ibid.,* sec. 124.

W. D. Falk (essay date 1986)

SOURCE: "Fact, Value, and Nonnatural Predication," in *Ought, Reasons, and Morality: The Collected Papers of W. D. Falk,* Cornell University Press, 1986, pp. 99-122.

[*In the following essay, Falk attempts to clarify Moore's distinction between "good" and natural properties.*]

I

Twentieth-century views on value are broadly divided between non-naturalism and noncognitivism. The choice is between saying that '*x* is good' ('is good as such', 'good to experience', 'have', 'behold', 'ought to be', 'ought to be done') asserts some fact or truth, but one which is knowable only in some extraordinary and unique way; and saying that '*x* is good', and so forth, does not primarily assert anything at all, but is a way of speaking commendingly or directively. These are opposed views, but they share a common bond. They agree that if '*x* is good', and so on, stated any fact or truth, it could *only* be one ascertainable by some nonsensuous apprehension. What is taken to be ruled out, as involving the patent error of committing the naturalistic fallacy, is that '*x* is good' could be making a truth-claim which, for confirmation, turned in any way on the testimony of sense, or feeling, or of a reviewer's responses of favor or disfavor. Intuitionism and noncognitivism, of one sort or other, are thus presented as the only serious alternatives.

This situation may seem disconcerting. One does not part readily with the commonsense conviction that '*x* is good' is used to make some testable claim, that both 'this claret is good' and 'this claret is mild' have enough in common to be regarded as cases of predication. One may have bought the claret because it was mild and because it was good. One may take trouble to make sure whether this claret really is mild and be rash or careful in judging whether it is good. One may ask to have the mild claret brought to one, or the good claret, adding each time, "Just try and see for yourself which one I mean"; and both times one's instructions may lead to the right object's being picked out. So far, then, '*x* is mild' and '*x* is good' seem to do the same job, that of ascribing to *x* some ascertainable mark by which *x* may be picked out from among other things. And hence one hankers after some account of '*x* is good' as expressing a propositional truth. One may equally feel, however, that such an account is too dearly bought if it has to commit one to the notion of goodness as the object of a nonsensuous intuition sui generis. Rather than let oneself be driven to accept this notion, one may accept, even with qualms, the alternative view that '*x* is good', whether addressed to others or to oneself, is not primarily truth-claiming at all. The situation may be thought to have the makings of a dilemma, which raises the question, "Is this dilemma really necessary?"

II

The crux of the matter lies in two convictions which it has become common to treat as one. The one is that if '*x* is good' is, *like* '*x* is mild', a truth-claiming statement, it is also *patently unlike* '*x* is mild' or '*x* is sweet' or '*x* is digestible' or '*x* is pleasant' or any statement of the latter sort, by being a statement of quite a *different sort.* The other is that what makes '*x* is mild' and the like all statements of one type is that their truth is known in some ordinary empirical way and that, by contrast, if '*x* is good' were truth-claiming as well, this could be only as its truth was known in some extraordinary nonempirical way.

There are some striking features of value-language which make one insist on the first. '*X* is mild', 'sweet', 'digestible', or 'pleasant' are statements by which one enumerates the facts about *x.* But '*x* is good', one feels, does not state just another fact about *x* along with the rest. One cannot say that this claret is mild and smooth *and* good into the bargain; its goodness is not another feather in its cap in addition to its mildness and its smoothness. One says that things are good because of the facts about them, but their goodness does not count as just another fact about them. On the contrary, one learns that in answer to "Just give me the facts," one does not say, "*x* is good." In some sense '*x* is good' is no longer a statement of fact just by being a judgment of value. And if, nonetheless, '*x* is good' did affirm some fact or truth, this would have to be one manifestly different in type from '*x* is mild', '*x* is sweet', and so on, in the sense in which the latter count as ordinary statements of fact about *x.* The puzzle is that on the propositional view one seems to be forced to say *that the goodness of x is a fact which is not among the facts about x.* And this was G. E. Moore's point in insisting that the goodness or value of a thing must not be identified with any one of its 'natural' properties.

It has become almost axiomatic that, in acknowledging the difference in type between 'x is mild' and so on and 'x is good', one is also committed to holding that 'x is good', if propositional, must be the assertion of some nonsensuously intuitable, and in this sense 'non-natural', fact or truth. This is held on the understanding that what makes mildness and the like members of the class of natural properties or facts is an epistemological criterion: what counts as a 'natural property' or 'fact about a thing' is anything that is known in some sensibly testable way. And from this it would follow that if goodness is by contrast not among the natural properties or facts about a thing, it must be something knowable in some epistemologically nonsensuous way and so must constitute some extraordinary, nonnatural matter of fact. This conclusion is inevitable if what is common and peculiar to anything that counts as a 'natural' property is that it is known in an ordinary empirical way and that it is because of the difference between goodness and the 'natural properties' or 'facts' about things *in this respect* that 'x is good' must be treated as a statement of another type.

But that any of this really is so may be questioned. One might hold that what is common and peculiar to anything that will count as a fact in the case is not that it relates to something empirically known and that what forces the exclusion of the goodness or value of a thing from the 'facts' about it is not that it is known in some extraordinary way. Value judgments may be in some important sense 'fact-super-venient' and no longer contributive to a clarification of the 'facts in the case'. But the sense in which one is made to say this may be such that it does not directly bear one way or another on the question of how goodness or value would be *known* if it were a 'fact'.

III

It is usual to cite Moore as the father of the view I wish to query. Moore insisted that 'x is good' must be recognized as a statement different in type from 'x is mild', 'x is sweet', and the like. Although the latter are statements about the natural properties of x, 'x is good' is no longer such a statement. Moreover, by a statement about a natural property, Moore is taken to mean a statement about some empirically known matter of fact; and by a statement which is no longer about a natural property he is taken to mean one about some matter no longer testable in the way natural properties are, but in some other way. The distinction between goodness and the class of 'natural' properties, of which mildness or sweetness or pleasantness are members, is thus taken to turn on the very difference in the way goodness, as distinct from any member of the class of natural properties, is *known;* and it is in virtue of this epistemological difference that one is driven to speak of a difference in *type.*

It is noteworthy, however, that this is a misrepresentation of what Moore himself had to say. Admittedly there are difficulties in disentangling what Moore actually did want to say. These difficulties exist on his own admission. He avows in the **"Reply to My Critics"**[1] that in **Principia**[2] "I did not give any tenable explanation of what I meant by saying that 'good' was not a natural property." For an authentic account of his meaning he refers to **Philosophical Studies**[3] and to his comments on this account in the **"Reply"** itself. There is no doubt that a reading of **Principia** alone, without the light thrown on it by **Philosophical Studies** and the **"Reply,"** may create confusion. Even so, not even **Principia,** especially if read in the light of Moore's later views, makes it *definitive* of the distinction between goodness and the class of natural properties that the latter are properties known in a way in which goodness is not. Still less can such a view be extracted from Moore's later statements. Nor again does the principle of distinction between properties which are natural and those which are not, which Moore primarily employs in **Principia** and unreservedly in his later statements, entail that goodness as a 'fact' *must* be the object of a nonsensuous intuition. It is true that in **Principia** Moore at least seems to suggest that he thought it *was,* though even here it is doubtful how much he wished to commit himself to this position. For he also says that when he calls propositions about goodness "intuitions" he means "*merely* to assert that they are incapable of proof" and that he is implying "nothing whatsoever as to the manner or origin of our cognition of them."[4] But in any case, whether or not Moore wanted to say that goodness was in fact the object of a nonempirical intuition is not the point at issue. The issue is whether his distinction between goodness and the class of natural properties necessarily implied such a view.

IV

Moore says in the **"Reply"** that the way he tried to characterize the distinction between goodness and the natural properties of a thing in **Principia** seems to him "now to be utterly silly and preposterous."[5] But he also says that what he had in mind was "the very same distinction" which he described in **Philosophical Studies** as between goodness and the natural intrinsic properties of a thing. And in spite of the odd formulations which he employs in **Principia,** there is a plain continuity between the two accounts.

According to **Principia,** goodness differs from the natural properties in two ways.[6] (1) Goodness is a property which cannot *"exist by itself in time."* It depends on the object to which it is ascribed in a way in which natural properties do not. (2) Goodness, unlike the natural properties of objects, is not *among the parts of which the object is made up.* Natural properties "are in themselves substantial and give to the object all the substance that it has." And "this is not so with good." Moreover, Moore treats these two features not as separate but as if entailed by each other. Because natural properties can exist by themselves in a way in which goodness cannot they are also 'substantial'. And goodness is no longer 'substantial' for the *same reason* for which it can also not exist 'by itself'.

Obscure as this was, one can see what Moore was trying to express. There is a sense in which the goodness of this claret could not be conceived to 'exist by itself' in the way its mildness or smoothness can, for one cannot conceive how the claret could be good except through its mildness or smoothness or some other already given property. Nor can one easily conceive how its goodness could be perceived except by way of the perception of what else it is like. But the same does not apply to mildness or smoothness. One can conceive of them as features of the wine which could exist in it independent of what other properties it has, whereas there is something essentially parasitic about the way the value of a thing is always dependent on its other properties. At the same time there is also a sense in which the value of a thing seems unlike its other properties in being no longer among, as it were, its 'body-building' characteristics. Moore expresses this notion misleadingly by saying of natural properties that "if they were all taken away, no object would be left, not even a bare substance: for they are in themselves substantial and give to the object all the substance that it has," and "this is not so with good" (ibid.). But he plainly means that, while ordinary properties are constitutive of the particular nature or specifications of a thing as the object of experience or discourse in question, the same is no longer true of its value.

In *Philosophical Studies,* Moore makes much the same points in different language. He no longer says that goodness, unlike ordinary properties, "cannot exist by itself in time," but he emphasizes once more that it is typical of goodness to be a *dependent* characteristic.[7] This idea is now expressed by saying that the intrinsic (noninstrumental) goodness or value of a thing 'inheres' in its nature in the sense that what goodness or value a thing has is conditioned by that thing's intrinsic properties. He means by the 'intrinsic properties' of a thing any and all which one would enumerate in answer to the question "What exactly is or would x be like?" (ibid., p. 263); "What exactly are or would be its characteristics as the object of experience or discourse in question?" And he takes the dependence of value on intrinsic properties to entail that for any change in a thing's value there must be some change in its properties otherwise (ibid., p. 265). Moore also no longer says that goodness, unlike ordinary properties, is no longer among the "parts of which the object is made up," or that, unlike them, it is not "in itself substantial"; but he says that goodness no longer counts as another intrinsic characteristic of that to which it is ascribed (ibid., p. 273). The intrinsic properties of a thing are its 'natural' properties: those which between them serve to specify its nature. But goodness, which depends on the intrinsic properties, is such that it cannot itself count as still another one.

This last is the feature of goodness which Moore now takes as the most crucial and distinguishing: 'x is good' is *not an ordinary case of predication,* in the way in which 'x is mild', 'x is sweet', and so on are, so much so that one does not know whether to call goodness a '*property'* or not. One takes properties to belong to a thing, to be its very own, its very specifications as 'this' sort of thing. But goodness, although it is *ascribed* to things, turns out not to function in the ordinary way properties do. It does not add to the distinguishing marks of the thing as the object in question. This is why, in *Philosophical Studies,* Moore distinguishes between the intrinsic properties of a thing and its goodness, which, though an attribute that depends on its intrinsic properties, is not itself another intrinsic property, but rather a 'predicate' to which the word 'property' does not properly apply (ibid.). In the **"Reply"** he distinguishes the *natural intrinsic properties* of a thing from goodness as a *nonnatural intrinsic property,* while suggesting that by 'nonnatural intrinsic property' he means one which, when it is ascribed to an object, is "not describing that object to any extent at all."[8] The puzzle about goodness to which Moore was trying to draw attention is not unlike the puzzle concerning whether existence is a 'real' predicate or not. In both cases one seems confronted with a case of predication such that the ascription of the predicate to an object no longer adds to that object's description.

It seems plain that the distinction in type between natural properties and goodness as a 'property' which is no longer natural is not made to rest on a difference in the way natural properties, as distinct from goodness, are *known.* Admittedly, in *Principia,* Moore calls ethical theories 'naturalistic' which take goodness to be known by "empirical observation and induction."[9] He also warns that "our knowledge is not confined to the things which we can touch and see and feel" (ibid., p. 110), and hints that the knowledge of what is good is not knowledge of this sort, not of an 'object of perception'. But even in *Principia* these scant remarks seem designed to say something further about non-natural properties rather than to *define* the distinction. In *Philosophical Studies* and in the **"Reply,"** the distinction between 'natural' and 'non-natural' is drawn exclusively on logical rather than on epistemological grounds. It does not turn on the manner in which these different types of property are known but on a difference in their roles as qualifying characteristics.

It is illuminating in this connection to recall Moore's answer to Broad in the **"Reply."** Broad, being dissatisfied with Moore's attempts to distinguish between natural and non-natural properties, offers a distinction in terms of what is sensibly, as opposed to what is nonsensibly, knowable. Moore, in reply, reiterates his own account as given above and adds in conclusion:

> Having failed to find either in *Principia* or in *Philosophical Studies* any account of the distinction between "natural" and "non-natural" intrinsic properties which he considers to be tenable, Mr. Broad goes on (p. 62) to offer an account of the distinction which he does consider to be tenable. And on the account which he gives I have no criticism to offer: it seems to me quite

possible that it may be true. He insists that, in giving this account, he is only *describing* natural characteristics, not *defining* "natural"; and it is quite possible that the description which he thus gives of natural intrinsic characteristics, and the description which I suggested in *Philosophical Studies* when I suggested that natural intrinsic properties *describe* what possesses them in a sense in which non-natural ones don't, could, though different, *both* of them be true: it may be that both of these descriptions (and others as well) do apply to all *natural* intrinsic characteristics, and to none that are not natural.[10]

This reply deserves further comment. Here we have it from Moore himself that what defines the difference in type between value and the natural properties of a thing is that the latter are constitutive of the 'nature' of the thing but its value is not. Only after having stressed this point does Moore allow, what he takes to be quite another point, that it *might* also be correct to say that properties which are natural in *his* sense are coextensive with those that are epistemologically 'natural' in Broad's sense, and that value, which is first and foremost non-natural in his sense, may also be epistemologically non-natural in Broad's sense. It is plain that Moore does not wish to make epistemological non-naturalness the foundation of the distinction here in question. For in saying that 'natural' and 'non-natural' *might* be coextensive with 'empirical' and 'nonempirical' he is allowing it to be conceivable that this might not be so, i.e., that there would still be as much reason as before for distinguishing the value of a thing from its natural properties even if it turned out that not all of the latter were known 'by observation and induction' or that goodness were not known by some 'nonsensuous intuition'.

On Moore's own showing, however, there are some residual problems. One of them is that he is baffled by his own main conclusion. It is odd that value, as dependent on intrinsic properties, should not be just another intrinsic property. Ordinarily, when one fact about a thing depends on another, the consequent will count as a further fact about this thing, as being another specification of its prior specifications. And if this seemed to be not so with value, it was counterintuitive enough to need an explanation. Moore felt that there ought to be something to show why value properties are not, and cannot be, intrinsic to the nature of their object; there should be "some characteristic of intrinsic properties which predicates of value never possess." Moore, however, can only add: "And it seems to me quite obvious that there is; only I cannot see what it is."[11]

There is another, and related, problem. Finding it impossible to explain *why* value properties should be nonintrinsic, Moore claims that he can at least 'describe' *what it comes to saying that they are*. But with this project, too, he is only partially successful.

His device here was to say that intrinsic properties differ from value in that their ascription to an object always adds to its description, whereas the ascription of value to it never does; and this might be read as meaning that value ascriptions are in no way whatever descriptively contributive. But this is not Moore's view. His formula in *Philosophical Studies* is to say that intrinsic properties "describe their object *in a sense in which predicates of value never do*" (ibid., p. 274), which suggests that value ascriptions, rather than being in no way descriptively contributive, are not so only *in a sense* in which intrinsic property ascriptions are. And this notion is confirmed in the **"Reply."** There is, he says there, "a sense of the word 'describe'," "*one* of the senses in which the word is ordinarily used," in which the ascription of an intrinsic property to a thing always adds to its description, whereas the ascription of value to it never adds to its description "*in that same sense.*"[12] The implication is plain: value ascriptions are not different because they have no descriptive role but because they have no such role in *one* ordinary sense of 'describe'.

It is plain why Moore has to draw the distinction with this qualification. His object is to describe what is special about value as a property; and a property is nothing if it is not a mark that characterizes its object. Hence if the difference between value and ordinary properties were to turn on their role in characterizing their object, it could turn only on some difference in the sense in which either performs this role.

In fact, some such distinction as Moore here draws is implicit in ordinary thought. If, say, of two clarets, one is judged good to drink and the other not, one is characterizing them in some way; one ascribes to them a feature by which, at a pinch, they could be identified and distinguished from each other. This is why one may think of their 'being good' or 'poor' as a property. All the same, if asked to 'describe' them, using the term in its ordinary sense, one will not reply that they are good or poor, but that they are mild, or fruity, or acid, or other such terms. One will take these features of the wines and not their degrees of goodness to be constitutive of their ordinary description.

Moore is therefore pointing to a distinction of which ordinary usage has an intuitive comprehension and which is convincing to that extent. But the sense of this intuition is still unexplained. One wants the description spelled out in its ordinary sense: by what principle properties like 'being mild', or 'fruity', or an indefinite host of others are part of it, and how, by the same token, value ascriptions are excluded. Short of such an explanation, whatever rational grounds there are for distinguishing ordinary properties from value will still be unresolved. But here, once again, Moore stops short of an answer. His position in the **"Reply"** is summed up by saying that the account he has finally been offering is "still vague and not clear." And he adds: "To make it clear it would have been necessary to specify the sense of 'describe' in question; and I am no more able to do this now as I was then" (ibid.).

In the end, therefore, Moore can no more explain how exactly value properties are not 'ordinarily descriptive' than he can explain what precludes them from being so. And this problem raises new questions.

v

We saw that Moore resisted Broad's suggestion that 'natural' and 'nonnatural' should be identified with 'empirical' and 'nonempirical'. But Moore's difficulties in explaining his own view may make it appear that Broad had been right after all. The difference between ordinary description and what is not ordinary is explained by the difference between description in empirical and nonempirical terms.

Such a view is not infrequently though to be entailed by the common meaning of terms such as 'descriptive' or 'factual'. What makes '*x* is good' nondescriptive must be the absence of the very same feature that makes natural properties descriptive, or ordinary 'facts in the case'; and what makes a property, in the ordinary sense, descriptive of a thing, or makes it count as a 'fact' about it, is precisely that it is known in an ordinary empirical way. 'Descriptive' or 'factual' are here taken in a way in which 'being fattening' would be part of the description of, or among the facts about, eating pork, whereas 'being counter to the will of God' would not. The reason why '*x* is good' may not count as an ordinary descriptive characteristic is that only empirical characteristics count as such.

But such a view could not resolve Moore's problem. Possibly, one may mean an 'ordinary description' to be one in empirical terms, or 'a matter of fact' to be a 'matter of empirical fact'. But this would not be conclusive. 'Descriptive' and 'factual' may also be used in other ways, according to the contrast to which one is drawing attention. 'Describing' may be contrasted with 'explaining'; 'stating a fact' with 'conjecturing' or 'predicting'; a 'point of fact' with a 'point of law'; a 'matter of fact' with a 'matter of opinion' or 'of religious belief'. Each time, what will count as 'descriptive' or 'factual' will vary with the context.

Nor does any of this correspond to the sense in which what is part of the ordinary description of a thing, or what counts as the 'facts' about it, is contrasted with its goodness or value. For Moore, the value of a thing contrasts with its 'intrinsic nature', which is with all that goes to make it what it is as the object for evaluation in question. And it is in the sense in which all these features are part of the ordinary object description that the value no longer is.

Now, quite evidently, what in this context counts as ordinarily descriptive, or as fact in the case, is not confined to what can be empirically known. True, such matters will bulk large among value-determining characteristics. Whether this wine is good to drink will depend in part on whether it is mild or acid; whether I ought to eat pork will depend on whether pork is digestible. What here counts as 'fact' is either what is actually the case and

directly verifiable by experience or, as is typical in the case of actions, what can be conjectured with reasonable certainty.

But judgments of another sort may bear on the complexion of the case as well. 'To put this in writing would be to enter into a contract' would add to the 'facts' although making a point of law rather than a point of fact; 'because you would die in the attempt, the consequences would not be for you to face' would make a logical point rather than a factual one; 'employing him would cost that much, given the time and rate of pay' would be to state the result of arithmetical calculation. Nor again would it be any less to refer to a fact in the case (in the required sense) whether one said that this picture was painted on canvas, with oils, mainly in blues and reds, or that the colors were intricately balanced, the design firm and harmonious, the shapes expressive and symbolic. The list, though not scientifically descriptive, would contain the very 'facts' on which the aesthetic value of the picture would largely depend. Likewise, it would be no less to refer to the facts in the case whether one said that this action would destroy the vegetation or the beauty of the countryside or that eating pork leads to indigestion or will be punished by God. All these would be contributions toward the description of the case in the sense in which evaluation is founded on the facts about it, though the specifying claims may express facts or conjectures, empirical or logical truths, symbolic interpretations, or supposedly revealed truths.

All this shows that if '*x* is good' is, by contrast with '*x* is mild', '*x* is sweet', and so on, no longer ordinarily descriptive of *x*, or a fact about it, in the way these are, this is not because only what is empirically verifiable counts as descriptive or as properly a fact about *x*. 'Eating pork will be punished by God' is no longer part of a 'factual' (here empirical) description of eating pork. Yet it *is* part of a description of the action on which one could base the claim that it would be bad or ought not to be done. 'Will be punished by God' still counts as another *fact in the case* even though it details a 'fact' in some nonempirical order of discourse. But 'eating pork is bad' or 'ought not to be done' is debarred from counting as *still another* fact about eating pork, in the sense in which even 'will be punished by God' is not. What prevents the value of *x* from straightforwardly counting as another fact about it cannot therefore be that value is a fact in some nonempirical order of discourse. The crucial ground of the contrast between value and ordinary fact must still lie in something else; and what this is, provided that '*x* is good' is not merely prescriptive but affirms some fact or truth, remains to be explained.

vi

It is well to note here that prescriptivists can deal more successfully with this problem than cognitivists. Given that their view is otherwise acceptable, they can explain why '*x* is good' is felt not to state another fact about *x* even in the tenuous sense in which '*x* is willed by God' would. The characteristic function of value judgments is to be choice-guiding, to direct affective or conative attitudes; and value judgments perform this job by way of making commendations to others and of making choices for oneself. 'This wine is good' supervenes on 'this wine is mild', 'you ought not to eat pork' on 'pork is fattening' not by way of making a further truth-claim but by way of making an exhortative or otherwise direction-giving noise; and, if so, it is plain that these are utterances which are over and above the facts in the case. The least that all descriptive statements have in common is that they make some truth-claim: '*x* is good' is no longer descriptive by being unlike any descriptive statement in no longer doing this. If the non-cognitivist premise is correct, it would explain why 'good' is a misfit as a predicate term. But it is well to note that this explanation implies that the original form of the problem had been misconceived. The question was why 'good' is not an ordinary descriptive term, but that is not really the question. 'Good' is not an *ordinary* descriptive term only because it is not a *descriptive term* at all. Noncognitivism preserves the logical gap between value and fact by reinterpreting it as a hiatus. On the other hand, if there are or seem to be reasons for thinking that 'good' is used in asserting some fact or truth, then the puzzle remains as to what makes it not an 'ordinarily descriptive' fact or truth. If no anser can be found consistent with the assumption that '*x* is good' is propositional, this would heavily count in favor of prescriptivism.

VII

I believe, however, that such an answer can be found and that Moore failed to grasp it, though it was before him all along. He was always aware that value predication had two salient features: that value is, on the one hand, essentially resultant, depending on the prior existence of other properties of its object; and that, on the other, it is nonconstitutive, no longer directly adding to the object another qualifying property. *What he failed to see was that the special manner in which value results from the other properties of a thing also makes it nonconstitutive.*

The last was certainly not Moore's view. In the **"Reply,"** he says, in answer to an objection of Broad's, that he would never have suggested that 'good was non-natural' if he had not supposed it to be 'derivative', but that he did not think that it was non-natural for that reason. That goodness is 'derivative' is to say "if a thing is good, then, that it is so, *follows from the fact that* it possesses certain natural intrinsic properties"; and there are properties other than goodness which are also derivative but are not non-natural (ibid., p. 588). The assumption here is that the property dependence of value is not as such different from that of other resultant properties. Moore is aware that goodness does not depend on what a thing is like in any ordinary sense 'of depending on'; that 'this claret is good' does not follow from the fact that it is mild by ordinary material, or formal, implication. The connection, he thought, was, somewhat mysteriously, synthetic and necessary. Nevertheless, he takes it that the fact that

this claret is good is as directly a consequence of the fact that it is mild as the fact that it is intoxicating is directly a consequence of the fact that it is alcoholic. Hence the reason why value was not among the natural properties could not be that it was property-dependent.

There is difficulty in presenting the dependence relation in this way. For Moore the dependence of value on the object is on its 'intrinsic nature', and this means on *all* that makes it what it is like as the object in question. But it seems impossible to say that anything *further* follows from the fact that a thing has *all* the properties it has. It is possible to say only that something further follows from the fact that a thing has *all the other* properties it has. And it is plain why. One cannot count the specifications of a thing as *complete* and also say that something further *follows from the fact that* it has these specifications, for in affirming the last one would be denying the first. And yet this is what Moore finds himself committed to saying about goodness. It therefore seems that the crucial point about the fact-dependence of goodness cannot be made by saying that the goodness of a thing is a consequence of *the fact that* the thing has *all* the properties it has. And if one has to say, as one does, that the value of a thing turns on *all* its properties (and not only on all its *other* properties), then there must be something very special about the dependence of value on fact, such that it would allow one even as much as to state this relation without contradiction.

I think that Moore went wrong, however, in not seeing that value, though essentially a resultant characteristic, is not a resultant characteristic in the ordinary way. The goodness of the wine does not depend on its mildness in the way the indigestibility of pork depends on its fat content. The indigestibility of pork depends directly on the *fact that* pork is fat, but the goodness of a wine does not depend directly on the *fact that* the wine is mild. This point is crucial, and, although language may conceal it, it can also illuminate it. One may say that pork is indigestible *because* it is fat, as one may say that this wine is good *because* it is mild. So it may seem that both times one is saying the same sort of thing: the indigestibility of pork is a consequence of the fact that pork is fat, and the goodness of the wine a consequence of the fact that it is mild. Language also suggests a difference, however. One may say that the wine is good both *because* it is mild and *on account* of its mildness, *on the strength* or *on the score* of it; one may also say that one ought not to do this both *because* it would cause hurt and *on account of,* or *in view of* the fact that it would. This language is not applicable to the indigestibility of pork. One may indeed *judge* or *claim* that pork is indigestible on account of the evidence, as one may also judge or claim on account of the evidence that this wine is good. But the difference is that the wine not only is *judged* good but also *is* good on account of its mildness; pork, however, may be judged to be indigestible only on account of its fatness but *is* indigestible because and not on account of it. One may likewise say that it is its fatness that *causes* pork to be indigestible, while one will refer to the mildness of the wine not as the cause of its goodness, but as a *reason* why it is good and to the facts about an action as the reasons or grounds that render it obligatory. 'Reason' figures here like 'reason' for a judgment or belief, as something of which one is cognizant and on which something further depends. But what depends on the reason is not a conclusion or belief but the goodness of a thing or the obligation to do an action. Value is such that things *have* it for reasons, and they are judged to have value by reason of the reasons that confer value on them.

The difference between saying that the wine is good on account of its mildness and that it is intoxicating because it is alcoholic is radical. 'On account of', 'on the score of' suggest 'on taking account', 'on a computation of', 'on a reckoning with'. For something to be good on account of what it is like is thus to say that it is good through what it is like, by way of being correctly accounted for, computed, or reckoned with. Its value is conceived to depend on its properties, but on them as disclosed in experience or beheld in contemplation or anticipation. What makes the wine good is that, as experienced, it would be experienced as mild and so on, on a truly discriminating perception of its properties. What makes a novel good are its content and form as they would disclose themselves to a perceptive reader. What makes the death penalty bad is what is involved in inflicting it as correctly understood and contemplated by someone. What makes it that one ought not to inflict it is what would be involved in inflicting it as correctly and imaginatively anticipated. Every time the goodness or the obligation is conceived to arise from the properties of the thing or action as the object of a true perception, computation, or anticipation.

The dependence of value on fact is therefore unlike the ordinary dependence of one fact about a thing on another. If the wine is intoxicating because it is alcoholic, then that it is intoxicating will be the *direct* consequence of its being alcoholic. But if it is good because it is mild, its goodness will not result directly from its being mild but only *mediately* so, by way of the effect of its recognition. Of course, if the wine were not mild, it could not be experienced as mild, in a discriminating perception. What a thing is like entails what having a true comprehension of what it is like would be. Hence one may say that the goodness of the wine follows from what it is like, from the existence of certain properties in the wine, but still not directly so but only mediately so, by way of the mildness being correctly appraised. This is why things are good both *because* and on *account* of what they are like.

The difference in the dependence shows up clearly *in how the consequent comes to be known.* If the wine is intoxicating because it is alcoholic, the consequent will be the case whenever the antecedent is the case, and it will be *perceptible all by itself, whether the* antecedent *is known or thought of or not.* But if the wine is good because it is mild, the consequent will be *perceptible only* when the antecedent is not only the case but is *also known and attended to.* It is a basic truth about the judg-ment of value that value cannot be judged of except when the facts from which it results are before one. Only then will the value that belongs to an object *come to be in evidence.* The cognitive object-dependence of value entails that it is discerned only by some cognitively object-dependent perception. Moore did not notice this point, but it was stressed by later intuitionists such as W. D. Ross. Whatever it is, he says, that causes a noise to be loud, "I can perceive it to be loud without knowing anything of the causes which account for this"; but "it is only by knowing or thinking my act to have a particular character . . . that I know, or think, it to be right."[13]

Moore should therefore have allowed that the dependence of value on fact is as distinctive a feature as its noninclusion among the facts. For such dependence is uniquely different from the ordinary dependence of one fact about a thing on another. Actually, Moore was groping for this point in **Principia,** when he said of goodness that it could not be *'imagined'* otherwise than property-dependent. The natural properties of things may or may not depend on the prior existence of other properties of them. But the value of a thing could not be conceived at all except as depending on the features it otherwise possessed; and this follows from its cognitive dependence. As resulting by way of the comprehension of its object, value cannot be conceived to exist without dependence on what is featured in such a comprehension. This is why nothing *can* be good without something further about its object to make it so.

Here is also the reason why the value of a thing can be said to depend on *all* the facts about it. If value depended directly *on the facts,* it could not depend on *all* of them but only on all the *others;* for anything that depends on the fact that a thing has a certain characteristic will add to it a further characteristic. But value can depend on *all* the facts since it does not directly, but only mediately, depend on *any* of them.

Here also is the reason why the value of things should be a fact which is not among the ordinary facts about them. This is implied by the very dependence of value on these facts. In counting the properties of a thing one will count any feature that would qualify it as the object of discourse in question, including any feature it would have as a direct consequence of its having certain other features. Let us call these the object's *first-order properties:* the ones which between them constitute the nature of the object as the object in question and, through its nature, as the possible bearer of its value. It will then be a truism that its value will not be among them. That a thing has value *presupposes* that it has a constituted nature already; and it has value by virtue of its nature, as a property that supervenes on what it is like, instead of being part of what it is like. In relation to the object properties on which it depends, value is a *second-order property,* one which emerges only when its antecedent first-order properties are correctly and fully taken into account.

It is only as depending on first-order properties, however, that value will be a second-order property. It may also be a third-order property depending on a second-order property. Thus one may say that these oak trees ought to be preserved because they are beautiful. That they are beautiful may here be represented as a second-order feature, one depending on account being taken of other features which are first-order features; and 'ought to be preserved' would thus be a third-order feature depending on account being taken of a second-order feature. The general point is simply that value, on whatever grounds it is ascribed, is never on the same level of discourse with these grounds themselves. That the trees ought to be preserved is no longer part of their nature as aesthetic objects for the same reason for which that they have aesthetic value is no longer part of their nature as 'natural' objects. That they have aesthetic value depends on their nature as 'natural' objects; that they ought to be preserved on their aesthetic value as comprehended. Both times what *depends* on some prior nature or description of the object *as comprehended* cannot be part of the comprehension of that very nature or description on which it depends. It can add nothing to the first-order nature of the trees that, if their first-order nature is taken note of, they are something good to see; and it adds nothing to their second-order nature as something good to see that on taking this into account they ought to be preserved.

Here, then, is the principal reason for speaking of value as a 'non-natural' property, as a 'fact' that is no longer an 'ordinary' fact, as a predicate that can be ascribed to things without further specifying their distinctive character as the sort of things they are. It is part of the ordinary description of this wine as a beverage that it is mild, alcoholic, and so on, but no longer that it is good; and part of the ordinary description of eating pork that it is fattening and, maybe, frowned upon by God, but no longer that it ought not to be eaten. That the former are properties which are part of the ordinary description of the wine or of eating pork is to say that they are part of their description in the first instance; and to say that '*x* is good' and '*x* ought to be done' is no longer ordinarily descriptive of *x* is to say that they are no longer part of the description of *x* or of its description in the first instance.

The reason why one speaks like this is patent. That anything can be good or ought to be done presupposes that it can be conceived as possessing a distinctive nature in the first place, fully accountable in itself and distinct from anything that would follow from it only as taken account of. This is what forces the apartheid of value from ordinary fact. Value, which as fact or truth turns on correctly beholding the nature of things, cannot be a fact or truth in the same order of discourse as is the nature of these things themselves. As a 'fact' that is not among 'the facts in the case' it is not necessarily esoteric but essentially supervenient.

As mentioned, Moore sometimes hesitated whether value may strictly be called a 'property'. The role of property terms is to ascribe to things a mark by which they can be identified and distinguished from others; and value performs this role, but not in the standard way. It is not that '*x* is good' in no way characterizes *x*. 'Bring the good wine' is no less a workable instruction than 'bring the mild wine'. It also characterizes the wine, not in terms of its first-order nature but of an implication of beholding it in this nature. Though their value properties can make objects distinguishable, however, that is not their most characteristic role. This remains reserved for the first-order properties on which value supervenes. The reason is partly that things of different natures can share the same value properties, so that 'bring the wine which is mild and dry' will distinguish the object more unambiguously than 'bring the good one'. But, more essentially, characterization in value terms is logically secondary to it in first-order terms. To recognize the object as good, one must first recognize it in the character which would be the ground of its goodness; and, for purposes of identification, instruction in terms of this character would suffice, without need for also drawing the evaluative conclusion. Value therefore plays the part of a property term, but not all the way. It *can* serve as an identification mark, but broadly it is *supernumerary* in this role.

VIII

It is well here to note the implications of these reflections for the notion of the naturalistic fallacy. When Moore uses this term in its specific sense (rather than in the generic sense of the patent miselucidation of any term, whether a value term or not) he means by it the patent error of trying to elucidate the meaning of 'good' in terms of some 'natural' characteristic, whether complex or simple. '*X* is good' cannot mean the same as '*x* is desired', or 'pleasant', or 'conducive to survival', because these are not properties which, like goodness, are distinct in being both object-dependent and nonintrinsic. By this standard all such attempted elucidations would be ruled out on a point of principle.

But all that this standard implies, on Moore's own showing, is that any elucidation of 'good' would have to satisfy these formal requirements; and there is nothing *in them* to justify the wider claims often made for the naturalistic fallacy argument. As far as Moore's own characterization of these requirements goes, there is nothing in them to entail that goodness must be a simple quality and could not be defined in more complex terms; or that, if a property, it could only be one apprehended by some nonsensuous intuition and not possibly one apprehended by the testimony of feeling or a reviewer's responses. All of this may or may not be so; but none of it, one way or the other, follows directly from Moore's attempts to clarify the logical role of value as a property term.

IX

How this conclusion may offer release from the deadlock between intuitionism and prescriptivism I shall briefly indicate in the rest of this essay. It has been noted that for '*x* is good' one may substitute '*x* is such that it would be rightly desired', 'x would be the fitting object of a pro-attitude'; and there are other substitutions: 'x deserves favor', 'x would justify favor', and 'there is a case for favoring x'. One may interpret these sentences as expressing the claim that x has the power to evoke favor by way of a true comprehension of what it is like; that it would justify favor in the sense that it would sustain, on a true comprehension of its properties, the favor of those who are for it already; or would deserve favor, in the sense that it would command, on a true comprehension of its properties, the favor of those who are not yet for it. It is presupposed here that certain properties of things, like mildness in wines, contrasts or harmonies in pictures or music, will evoke favor in those who experience them or will come to evoke it once they have become familiar with them; or that certain properties or states of affairs, for example concerning the contribution they would make to the life or well-being of sentient beings, would evoke approval in those who contemplate them, or would come to evoke it if those beings used their imagination on them. It would follow that what favor is *actually* bestowed on things or states of affairs is corrigible by what may be broadly termed 'rational methods'. One may learn to bestow on things greater favor than before by becoming more discerning or discriminating about their properties, and one may conceive of this process of learning as approximating or as reaching an ideal limit. This limit would have been reached when the favor bestowed on something would no longer be corrigible by any more discriminating and sustained experience of its properties or by any more knowledgeable and imaginative assessment of them. One may speak of such favor as well founded and distinguish it from other value attitudes which, by contrast, might be described as misplaced, cockeyed, capricious, biased, compulsive, or plain stupid; and one might speak of things or states of affairs as being such that they have it 'in' them to evoke such well-founded favor. That something is good, that it would be rightly or fittingly favored, would here be taken as entailing precisely these points. 'Rightness' and 'fittingness' are relational terms commonly used to express that one thing is in agreement or in line with another in a certain respect. That an object would be rightly or fittingly favored would here entail that an attitude of favor toward it would be in line with *all* its favor-evoking capacities, that it would be supported by a true and sustained appraisal of the properties of the object.

Goodness or value on this showing would be a *dispositional property* of things as truly comprehended, and it would be defined in terms partly psychological and partly not: in terms of a power to evoke responses, but responses as they ultimately would be in the ideal case of a *perfect*, no-further-corrigible, comprehension of the things in question. Value judgments would therefore be only weakly verifiable and in principle all corrigible, for the ideal limit of a perfect comprehension may always turn out to have not yet been reached.

The support for the claim that something is good or has value would, on such a view, be empirical. Judiciously conducted experiment would be the method of settling questions of value for oneself. It would be the method for others to use in verifying one's claims about the value of things. In trying to settle such questions for oneself one would seek to determine what favor something would evoke in one on a sincere attempt to comprehend it perceptively and patiently; and in trying to convince others, one would invite them to engage in such experimentation, while aiding them as far as possible in acquiring the necessary discrimination or information. Judgments of value require one to seek *acquaintance as a responding being* with what can be tasted in foods or wines, seen in pictures, read in novels, heard in music, experienced in love or friendship, in exercise or cogitation, in a free or dependent form of life. In trying to judge what is good in this way one will come to learn how to favor things in accordance with the favor they have it 'in' them to evoke. But there need never be anything finite about learning well-founded appreciation. There may always be more to be learned about things through greater discrimination and familiarity that may still modify what favor one has toward them at any point prior to the ideal case of perfect comprehension.

This view has its antecedents jointly in Hume and Kant and differs from emotivist views, as well as from Moore's, while incorporating features from each. Emotivists view 'x is good', 'x deserves favor', and the like as utterances whose primary use is to express commendations, not involving any testable objective claim. They also allow that such commendations may be supported by 'rational methods', or indeed that it is a feature of commendations using 'good' or 'ought' to make the *implicit* claim that they are so supportable. But once this last is admitted, there seems little point in persisting with the emotivist approach. This approach had been devised on the assumption that no cognitive meaning could be given to 'x is good', 'x deserves favor', 'x is commendable'. But the very assumption that favor for x can be supported by rational means implies that one may also *say* and *judge* that favor for x is so supportable; and, if taken as affirming this, 'x is commendable' and 'x is deserving of favor' turn again into statements that make some objectively testable claim. It thus becomes possible to reverse the emotivist approach by saying that it is the primary and explicit function of 'x is good' to stake out the claim *that* favor for x would be supportable by appropriate rational procedures in a broad sense. And this could be held without prejudice to the point that in using 'x is good' in speaking to others, one uses it with characteristic emotive or prescriptive overtones. 'This wine is good', when said to another, is typically said commendingly, with a view to promoting his 'agreement in attitude'. But in thus *speaking* commendingly, one seeks to achieve one's aim by way of gaining assent to the claim one is making, namely, that what is commended is also commendable, that a case for favoring the thing in question will be found by those who will look for it. At the same time one can now treat the commendatory use of value language as the special case it really is. Emotivists must say that someone who is judging or thinking to himself that something is good is engaged in commending it to himself, or exhorting himself to be for it, or resolving to be for it in the future, all of which is decidedly odd. On our showing one would be free to say that he was simply engaged in judging or thinking, for example, that the wine before him has got what it takes.

That '*x* is good' makes an objective claim brings this point of view into line with Moore's in that on both accounts the value of things is essentially dependent on what they are like. At the same time it becomes clear why their value depends only *indirectly* on their properties; for it is only by way of being comprehended, and not simply through being existent, that the properties of things can arouse responses of favor or disfavor. Moore also insisted, however, that if value depends on what things are like, it must be conceived as depending on this *solely.*[14] The dependence is such as to entail that if two things are exactly alike, and one is good, then the other *must* also be good *in every conceivable universe.* There is therefore mutual exclusiveness between the view that the value of things depends on their nature and the view that it depends on their being an object of interest. If the value of things depends to any extent on the last, one could no longer say of two things exactly alike that if one is good the other *must* be good *in every conceivable universe,* but only that it *must* be good among members, as it were, of the *same psychological universe.*

The view suggested departs from Moore on this point. That something has the power to evoke favor on a true comprehension of what it is like would depend partly on what it is like and partly on the affectivity of those who experience it or contemplate it for what it is like. The value of things, on our showing, would always hold in relation to beings or to a class of beings with a nature receptive to what is disclosed in experience or contemplation. Nothing could conceivably have value except for those who can love or hate. Nor is there anything necessarily noxious in such a view. That the value of things depends on the facts about them does not entail that it depends *solely* on them. This would be entailed only by a further assumption which Moore in fact makes, namely, that when A says that *x* is good and B denies this, A and B must *always* be contradicting each other. True enough, this assumption is supported by the fact that in ordinary discourses we tend to act on it. One takes disagreements about value between human beings as primarily a result of differences in comprehension. One's approach is regulated by the initial assumption that if one is right in thinking that there really is a case for favoring *x,* others too could be brought to favor *x* if only they came to be as comprehending about it as one is oneself. But one is also prepared reluctantly to treat this assumption as defeasible. If one were to contend that taking exercise was good on its own account, and someone else denied this, one would first inquire when he had last taken it. Only when he had assured us that he had been taking it every day and been loathing it all the time would one feel forced to fall back on saying, "Well, then, it really isn't good as far as you are concerned." Many cases are such

that, unlike this one, there is no reasonably sure way of deciding whether or not the difference in value judgments might still be caused by a difference in comprehension. In such cases, one is neither inclined nor compelled to treat the general working assumption as defeated.

One should not therefore be misled by the fact that in ordinary speech one claims that things are good or have value without adding the qualifying clause "at least as far as I or all or most humans are concerned." For that such a qualifying clause is not normally *mentioned* does not imply that it is not *logically presupposed* or that it may not sometimes be in place to bring it into the open. The situation here is not so different from that which applies to the logic of dispositional properties otherwise. When A says '*x* is digestible' and B denies this, they will normally be taken to be contradicting each other; nor will one expect them to add each time, "I mean, of course, only as far as I or all or most humans, and not necessarily as far as Martians or koala bears or anteaters are concerned." Nevertheless, these are qualifications which are presupposed and so '*x* is not digestible' is sometimes not the contradictory of '*x* is digestible'. '*X* is good', '*x* would command favor on a true comprehension of what it is like', are similar. That one here means that it is the favor of *humans* that *x* would command goes without saying; and that one can speak of humans per se rests on a working assumption in which, more often than not, it makes sense to persist.

My principal contention in this essay is that a view of this sort cannot be ruled out as just another instance of committing the naturalistic fallacy. One may call such a view a naturalistic, as distinct from a metaempirical, account of value on the ground that it makes value a natural fact or characteristic: there is nothing epistemologically or ontologically 'non-natural' about the fact that some things are, in virtue of their nature, more fitted than others to command the favor of human beings. But to *call* a view naturalistic is not yet to *brand* it, unless its 'naturalism' involves some patent error; and the patent error of 'naturalism' in any account of goodness or value lies in another dimension. It relates to the confusion of goodness or value with anything that could still count as part of the nature or description of the thing evaluated. And this error cannot be imputed to the view that the value of things consists of their power to justify or to command favor on a true comprehension of what they are like. On the contrary, the necessary apartheid of 'fact' from 'value' would, on such a view, be patently clear. To conceive of human responses to a world of objects or states of affairs as these responses would be on a true comprehension of these things, one has to conceive of such objects or states of affairs as already fully describable in themselves. Value predication must be in a separate order of discourse because it relates to *noetic* responses, that is, to responses *to* things *on account of* the character which is conceived to *be* theirs whether taken account of or not. There is thus a logical bar to including the world of value in the world of fact, if 'the world of fact' means anything that in turn can become an object of evaluation.

That value is no part of fact in this sense does not mean, however, that it cannot be fact in any sense, or only some odd 'non-natural' fact. It simply means that the logic of discourse requires a distinction between the world of things comprehended in the character they have or would have and a world of human responses in full face of the character of things so comprehended. That value affirmations relating to such responses are also in a characteristic way normative or direction-giving is implied rather than contradicted by this account. The enterprise of judging the power of a thing to evoke favor on a true comprehension is in the service of learning to appreciate that thing with the aid of such judgments and in accordance with the ideal canon of sufficiency implied in them.

NOTES

[1] P. A. Schlipp, ed., *The Philosophy of G. E. Moore* (New York: Tudor, 1952).

[2] G. E. Moore, *Principia Ethica* (Cambridge: Cambridge University Press, 1922).

[3] G. E. Moore, *Philosophical Studies* (London: Kegan Paul, 1922).

[4] Moore, *Principia*, p. x.

[5] Schlipp, ed., *Philosophy of G. E. Moore*, "Reply," p. 582.

[6] Moore, *Principia*, p. 41.

[7] Moore, *Philosophical Studies*, p. 260.

[8] "Reply," pp. 590-91.

[9] Moore, *Principia*, p. 39.

[10] Moore, "Reply," p. 592.

[11] Moore, *Philosophical Studies*, p. 274.

[12] "Reply," p. 591.

[13] W. D. Ross, *The Foundations of Ethics* (Oxford: Clarendon Press, 1939), p. 168.

[14] Moore, *Philosophical Studies*, p. 260.

Stuart Hampshire (essay date 1987)

SOURCE: "Liberator, Up to a Point," in *The New York Review of Books*, Vol. 34, March 26, 1987, pp. 37-9.

[*In the following review of Tom Regan's* Bloomsbury Prophet: G. E. Moore and the Development of His Moral Philosophy *and a collection of Moore's early essays, Hampshire agrees with Regan's assessment that Moore's methodology was Platonic.*]

G. E. Moore was a dominant figure in British philosophy from 1903 until his death at eighty-five in 1958. In 1958 many British philosophers would have named Russell, Wittgenstein, and Moore as the three great English-speaking philosophers of the twentieth century. During the last twenty-five years Moore has slowly ceased to be at the center of interest in the way Russell and Wittgenstein are, except for the early chapters of his still famous book on moral philosophy, *Principia Ethica*, first published in 1903.

Tom Regan, a professor of philosophy at North Carolina State University, argues that the true significance of this book, and of Moore himself, have been largely misinterpreted by academic commentators. They have studied him as the founding father of that peculiar and productive movement in the recent history of thought, the philosophy of ordinary language. They have overlooked, Regan argues, the history of his early moral beliefs and metaphysical doubts and despairs, from which the argument of *Principia Ethica* developed. Even more important, they have not accounted for the extraordinary effect which his moral philosophy had among the men and women of genius and of talent who were his admiring friends around 1900 and who later formed the Bloomsbury Group. Regan recalls again the sense of liberation and enlightenment, the anticipation of new beginnings in conduct and in social relations, that *Principia Ethica* suggested to Keynes, to Lytton Strachey, and to Leonard Woolf among others. In "My Early Beliefs" Keynes wrote:

> [*Principia Ethica*] was not only overwhelming; . . . it was the extreme opposite of what Strachey used to call *funeste;* it was exciting, exhilarating, the beginning of a new renaissance, the opening of a new heaven on a new earth. We were the fore-runners of a new dispensation, we were not afraid of anything.

This has to be taken seriously, because Keynes was not easily deceived in philosophical matters; he was to write a classical treatise on the theory of probability himself and he was born and educated among Cambridge philosophers. Tom Regan intends his book to set the record straight, and to correct the emphasis on analytical philosophy which he thinks has largely concealed the real, historical Moore.

I think he has certainly succeeded in at least supplementing the conventional picture of Moore. He shows that around the turn of the century Moore was passing through a phase of moral despair, a *fin de siècle* sense of the vanity of vanities, because he could not find a rational basis for attributing objective value to anything, either in the natural order or in human experience. In 1901 he writes to his most intimate friend, the literary critic Desmond MacCarthy: "I seem to find it increasingly difficult to satisfy myself with anything, which sometimes makes me feel very desperate."

The guarded and honest "seem" and "sometimes" are typical of Moore at all times, but this crisis was genuine and intense. A year earlier he had written a paper on moral conversion, a state of mind not connected with ideas of God, but which he described as "a new birth, leading to a new life, an awakening of conscience, a conviction of sin." This is said to be the state of mind of the Wordsworthian happy warrior, and Moore himself had once or twice experienced this exalted state, as he had experienced also the vanity of vanities, complete despair. How can the moral conversion, which is perfect knowledge of what is good combined with the ability always to pursue it, be made permanent? This is the heavy question he asked himself for several years.

Without this background of urgent moral concern *Principia Ethica* would have lacked the power to change the lives and the thought of his clever and skeptical friends. On this point Professor Regan is convincing. Moore was passionate and polemical in the book. But more has to be said about Moore's peculiar personality, the impression made by his physical appearance and manners in any gathering, before his civilizing and genial influence can be fully understood. George Eliot and many others had represented the agonies of an earnest morality without a secure foundation in God's designs; and around 1900 this was still a well-known late Victorian theme. Moore was wholly different, of our time and not of theirs.

For late Victorian and Edwardian Cambridge the distinctive change, the beginning of the new life, is marked in philosophy by the transition from Henry Sidgwick to Moore, and this is as much a matter of their human characters, and of their styles of feeling and of writing, as of philosophical doctrine. Sidgwick was one of Moore's teachers at Cambridge, and his *Method of Ethics* is the one undisputed classic of utilitarian philosophy since Mill, a great, if sometimes tedious, work still alive in its careful arguments and still actively studied by moral philosophers. Sidgwick had nobly refused to assent to the Thirty-nine Articles of the Church of England as was required of college fellows, and he resigned his Trinity fellowship in consequence; he was a model of high-mindedness, integrity, and social responsibility in all his activities.

And yet a deadly pall of Victorian bourgeois stuffiness hangs over him, the atmosphere of those solid Cambridge houses with damp, laureled gardens in which good citizens and learned academics, heavily cultured, experimented with spiritualism, parapsychology, and self-improvement before 1914. As usual, Keynes and Strachey have the right words to re-create the period and to make the history live. In a letter Keynes wrote:

> Sidgwick never did anything but wonder whether Christianity was true and prove that it wasn't and hope that it was. . . . There is no doubt of his moral goodness. And yet it is all so dreadfully depressing, no intimacy, no clear-cut boldness.

Strachey, like Keynes reflecting on Sidgwick's *A Memoir*, writes, "What an appalling time to have lived. It was the Glass Case Age. Themselves as well as their orna-

ments were left under glass cases." He goes on typically to write of the impotence common among Victorian sages. It is an often unwelcome truth that, ever since philosophy separated itself decisively from the natural sciences, the lasting influence of a philosopher has typically not been independent of his dramatic or engaging personality, except perhaps for logicians; and many good, and even great, philosophers have themselves recognized this disturbing fact. Certainly Russell, Wittgenstein, and Moore all knew that their philosophical vision was closely linked to their idiosyncrasies and intellectual mannerisms and literary styles. In addition they each cultivated over the years distinctive and constrasting styles of argument, and styles of vivid assertion, which they knew would fit their visible and public selves. They were far from being innocent or deceived in this respect.

Moore was a man of immense natural charm, and the mere sight of him smoking his pipe and listening to a philosophical discussion was an incitement to happiness. He seemed in his later years sedentary and serene, yet fiercely alert, and, in an abstract manner, passionate, following the spoken words in a discussion rather as a predator stalks its prey, ready to pounce if any of the words or phrases used dropped out of their logical place, as they nearly always do in any philosophical argument. In argument he somehow combined ruthless and destructive criticism with obvious disinterestedness and with the unforced assumption of a common interest in squashing error. He seemed a pure intellectual, completely free of any respect for conventional opinion and of any pious attitudes toward past philosophies and religions.

Unlike the comparable academic moral philosophers of his time in England, H. A. Pichard and David Ross at Oxford, and unlike Sidgwick, no one could have supposed him to be even normally inclined to moral disapproval, or that he felt any special reverence for duty or for moral virtue or for the moral law. On the contrary he seemed to find the notions of duty and of obligation rather disagreeable and in any case of marginal interest. They are "tedious and worthless necessities." He was looking in music and in the enjoyment of nature and in friendship for the experiences that make life seem worth living, and no longer empty and trivial. That he believed that the positive teaching of the truth should be the center of moral philosophy was suggested by his intensely civilized and accurate speech, his powerful and selfish silences, his quiet determination to go his own way in thought and to ignore established opinion of all kinds.

Professor Regan shows the unity of Moore's theory and practice in this determination to go his own way, his independence of the past, and he attributes the exhilarating influence of *Principia Ethica* on the Bloomsbury Group partly to the suppression of the claims of duty and moral virtue, except insofar as they are necessary means to the realization of good states of mind. Aesthetic emotion and personal affection are "obviously" (Moore's word) the only things that are intrinsically good and the only things that, in various combinations, render one state of affairs better than another. All our efforts both in private life and in social policy should be directed to the realization of these intrinsic goods; we should calculate the effects of our actions as best we can, without regard to any other features of conduct that in the past have been thought to be important from a moral point of view.

This is indeed liberating, and from more than Victorian constraints. For example, traditional moralists, and this reviewer, have believed that the prohibition that bans murder is one of the foundations of morality itself, and one may believe this, even if one is not entirely sure that respect for moral necessities is inconceivable without a peculiar respect for the life of individual persons. Careful reflection and a study of different literatures and of history would for most people lead to the same conclusion: namely, that the prohibition of murder is acceptable as a prohibition even in the perhaps exceptional case where a projected murder cannot be shown to have bad effects on the propagation of aesthetic enjoyment and personal affection. Moore's goals, types of intrinsic goodness, seem irrelevant to the case of murder. It would not in general be right, the "unliberated" believe, secretly to poison a friendless vandal in peacetime.

Lytton Strachey and Keynes felt in 1903 that a new world was opening up for them and for the enlightened everywhere, Stendhal's "happy few," because Moore seemed to have given utterly respectable reasons for not taking too seriously the negative aspects of morality as a set of universal commandments and absolute prohibitions. Moore's argument was utterly respectable because he was not a skeptic who saw moral distinctions as subjective and as human inventions, nor did he follow Bentham and Mill in making moral distinctions dependent on the vagaries of human feeling. On the contrary: throughout *Principia Ethica* and in all his early writings, and until he "wobbled" toward the end of his life, he often repeated that our actual opinions about what is intrinsically good are one thing and intrinsic goodness itself is another. Our feelings, attitudes, and opinions do not determine the truth in the question of goodness, which is for each of us the most important of all questions. Professor Regan quotes many passages in Moore's writing to this effect. Real moral distinctions are absolutely objective. Morality ought not to be thought of as primarily the prevention of evil, oppression, and injustice, but only and exclusively as the means to preserve and extend the things that we ought to love and to want, because they are good in themselves. This was the new beginning, even if a delusive one.

What path then must we and the Bloomsbury Group follow in order to arrive at the truth about the ends of life, the final values, the intrinsically good states of affairs, and how clearly did Moore mark the path? The answer, which may seem preposterous or at least implausible, had large effects in the history of thought. We must sit down and think steadily about the meaning of the word "good," what it stands for in its various senses, about the notions that it represents, and we must distinguish the primary

notion of the intrinsically good from all others with which it has commonly been confused; for instance, from the notion of the useful or the desirable. The path leading to discovery of the ends of life is the habit of, and the passion for, drawing exact distinctions, distinctions between the meanings of words, distinctions that are easily overlooked and meanings that have been fatally confused in all past philosophies. This philosophical method of Moore's came later to be called the method of analysis, because it involved separating confused or complex notions, or meanings, into their simple components, a kind of chemistry of ideas: hence the familiar label "analytical philosophy."

Professor Regan calls Moore's method of discovery in *Principia Ethica* a form of Platonism, and this seems to me a correct characterization and an illuminating one. First, like Plato, Moore treated concepts or ideas as constituting a real world of their own, independent of varying human habits of thought; second, he represented pure thought in a study or academy as sufficient for attaining truth in morals as well as in metaphysics, provided the thinkers were to think clearly. Third, and most important, Moore, being resolved on a new beginning in philosophy, as his title implies, and despising past philosophies, overlooked the fact that Aristotle, arguing against Plato, had decisively shown that the word "good" is not used to stand for a single identifiable quality, whether of states of affairs or of anything else.

Keynes memorably spoke of the beauty of the literalness of Moore's mind, and remarked that concepts and propositions seemed to him as solid and real and independent in their existence as chairs and tables; more so in fact, since Moore came to doubt the independent existence of chairs and tables as solid objects, and sometimes thought that the world consisted of propositions. To explain this Platonic realism about abstract entities as an error in the philosophy of language is not adequate; much more is involved, both in Moore's thought and whenever the objectivity of goodness and of moral values is discussed, as it still is. There is a historical and an emotional dimension to the perennial appeal of Platonism and to the craving to believe that our moral notions correspond to solid objects, or definite features, in a world independent of us. After Sidgwick's agonizing over the reality of a Christian God as the source of Christian moral law, a passion for moral truth as correspondence with the nature of things seemed to Moore the only acceptable redemption from egoism and from triviality and insignificance.

Moral distinctions had to be built into the representation of the deep structure of things, like scientific truths: hence the title *Principia* with its splendid Cambridge resonances. If moral distinctions were not built into the unperceived structure of things, the moral quest could never be taken seriously as the successor of religious worship. The communion of intimate friends dedicated to fearless and uninhibited discussion is a free church and yields a shared meaning to life, with argument substituted for Quaker inspirations. But there has to be an intelligible forward movement, as in the natural sciences, a convergence upon independent truth through intense discussion. Seen in this historical context, moral realism is, as a belief, something like a semantic variant of belief in a Last Judgment. Reality must resist us and strike back when we deny a moral distinction that exists and when we identify one that does not.

But it is surely unrealistic to claim that the best way, and in the last resort the only way, to discover what makes life worth living and what the ends of life should be is to remain in the academy or in Chesterton Road, Cambridge, Moore's home for many years, talking to other philosophers and to a few intellectual friends, and all the time thinking intensely and without distraction about the meanings of words. If there were an entirely general answer to a question about what is intrinsically good and what ought to exist for its own sake, this eternal truth would surely not be found by reflection on meanings, as if our inherited vocabulary, rightly interpreted, was the ultimate oracle and the final guide to life. Aristotle reasonably claimed that experience is a necessary, though not sufficient, condition for having intelligent opinions about moral and political issues; and experience is in this context to be contrasted with innocence. Professor Regan's quotations from Bloomsbury writings clearly show that it was precisely the evident purity and innocence of Moore's personality, the unworldliness, that made his revelations doubly impressive as secular prophecy.

It seems to me that they were wrong to count Moore's purity of intention and unworldliness as virtues in a moral philosopher. They are virtues in a certain kind of person but not in a moral philosopher. Moore confessed to an excited interest in the First World War, which did not immediately horrify him as it horrified Russell. But he had no evident curiosity about tryanny, massacres, genocide, torture, treachery and patriotism, political contrivance, and other obvious features of reality outside universities which any moralist needs to think about. Despising moral theories of the past was no advantage to him here, as it may have been in metaphysics.

Professor Regan's interpretation of Moore is at one point inconsistent, I think. He represents Moore as both stating clearly and dogmatically the eternal truth about the ends of life and also as proclaiming the freedom of the individual to make his own moral discoveries. It is true that Moore urged people to reflect on the meanings of "good" and on similar distinctions of meaning, but their reflection inevitably leads to one "obvious" conclusion, when it is not a botched analysis. The individual is indeed free to choose his own specifications and realizations of the good, but only under the two known headings: principally the enjoyment of beauty and of love and friendship.

Given these objections, a reader may wonder why Moore has for so long been considered an important philosopher, even if Professor Regan has quite clearly explained why Keynes and Strachey, his friends in 1903, were at

that time delighted and encouraged by his new morality. In two classic essays, **"The Refutation of Idealism"** (1903) and **"A Defense of Common Sense"** (1923), Moore had convinced many philosophers in Britain and America that they must attend with scrupulous and unremitting care to distinctions embedded in the prose of ordinary speech and ordinary writing if there is to be any secure progress in metaphysics and the theory of knowledge. They must not rush ahead, as Russell always did, with grand theories of the external world and the nature of knowledge and of belief, without having first examined, very slowly and with excruciating patience, all the idioms with which we ordinarily convey our perceptions, our beliefs, and our freedom to choose and to act. For instance, Moore asked why we cannot possibly say something as simple as "The cat is on the mat, but I do not believe that it is," although there is no logical incompatibility between the cat being on the mat and my not believing that it is—at least as "logic" is ordinarily understood. Reflection on this impossibility, apparently trivial, leads to discoveries both about the concept of belief and about the nonlogical features of languages. Nietzsche wrote, in *Human All Too Human:* "It is the mark of a higher culture to value the small unpretentious truths which have been discovered by means of rigorous method more highly than the errors handed down by metaphysical and artistic ages." Bloomsbury certainly knew this. Moore was the effective inventor of the Emperor's New Clothes approach to grand metaphysical theories which might assert or imply, for example, that time is unreal or that I cannot know that any physical thing exists.

Moore had another kind of greatness and originality, which is linked to his influence on Bloomsbury, but which has had far wider consequences. He invented and propagated a style of philosophical talking which has become one of the most useful and attractive models of rationality that we have, and which is still a prop to liberal values, having penetrated far beyond philosophical circles and far beyond Bloomsbury circles; it is also a source of continuing enjoyment, once one has acquired the habit among friends who have a passion for slow argument on both abstract and personal topics. When I look back to the Thirties and call on memories, it even seems that Moore invented a new moral virtue, a virtue of high civilization admittedly, which has its ancestor in Socrates' famous following of an argument wherever it may lead, but still with a quite distinctive modern and Moorean accent. Open-mindedness in discussion is to be associated with extreme literal clarity, with no rhetoric and the least possible use of metaphor, with an avoidance of technical terms wherever possible, and with extreme patience in step-by-step unfolding of the reasons that support any assertion made, together with all the qualifications that need to be added to preserve literal truth, however commonplace and disappointing the outcome. It is a style and a discipline that wring philosophical insights from the English language, pressed hard and repeatedly; as far as I know, the style has no counterpart in French or German. As Nietzsche suggested, cultivated caution and modesty in assertion are incompatible with the bold egotism of most German philosophy after Kant. This style of talking, particularly when applied to emotionally charged personal issues, was a gift to the world, not only to Bloomsbury, and it is still useful a long way away from Cambridge.

The group of friends who thought of themselves, and presented themselves to posterity, as Bloomsbury saved historians a lot of work by fully documenting in advance their aims and beliefs, their love affairs and their friendships, and the original and expanding constitution of the group itself. Since the Pre-Raphaelites there has been no more fully visible set of historical actors upon a self-constructed stage in England. Professor Regan tells again some of the well-known stories about them and describes some of the now familiar personalities. The world outside England has reason to be interested in Virginia Woolf and perhaps also in Lytton Strachey, but their imaginations in their later work showed few traces of Moore. Moore's substantial influence was on Keynes's liberalism, which started with a Moorean scheme supplying the ends of action and with Keynes's own theory of probability supplying rationality in the calculation of means. But the story of Keynes's political thought must be a long and very complex one, and Moore was only the beginning; for Keynes he was the acid that at the turn of the century dissolved classical utilitarianism and all forms of idealism, and also simple-minded relativism, in social theory. That was certainly an achievement that had consequences in many places.

The early essays printed by Professor Regan altogether lack the "clear-cut boldness" of *Principia Ethica* and **"A Defense of Common Sense,"** although Moore's famous serpentine style, replete with qualifications and caution, distinguish them from the good run-of-the-mill academic philosophy of the time. But how can one interpret Wittgenstein's amazing remark to F. R. Leavis, quoted by Professor Regan: "[Moore] shows you how far a man can get with absolutely no intelligence whatever"? By "intelligence" did Wittgenstein mean cleverness? Perhaps he meant to imply that Moore's triumph was a moral one—a matter, once again, of purity of mind.

Charles E. Caton (essay date 1987)

SOURCE: "Moore's Paradox, Sincerity Conditions, and Epistemic Qualification," in *On Being and Saying: Essays for Richard Cartwright,* edited by Judith Jarvis Thomson, The MIT Press, 1987, pp. 133-50.

[*In the following essay, Caton attempts an epistemological examination of Moore's paradox.*]

I

This is not a scholarly paper on Moore's paradox. Many of the points I make have been made by others (long ago in some cases), and I hope they will acquiesce in my

putting them in the present context without further acknowledgment. I want to suggest in this paper that a Moore paradox of the statemental type has to do with epistemic force rather than merely with sincerity conditions of illocutionary acts (if with them at all). Although something like a sufficient condition for an utterance to be odd in the Moore-paradoxical way will emerge, I do not try to say what conditions it is *necessary* to have to have a paradox of this type. The main reason for this is that the original paradigms primarily dealt with in connection with Moore's paradox have involved two forms of sentence that are (supposedly) suited for making statements, viz.

(A) *p,* but I don't believe that *p*

and

(B) Not-*p,* but I believe that *p*

although it is a feature of the account of Moore's paradox to be given here that the utterance of many other forms of sentence can involve what is apparently the same sort of oddity, that of sentences whose use is somehow impossible or ruled out although they do not involve self-contradiction.

In fact, I have no evidence, other than that of linguistic intuition and the plausibility of my descriptions of them, that the original paradigms of Moore's paradox and the other examples of odd utterances I deal with exhibit one and the same sort of oddity. But because it appears that a unified account of all of them can be given, I conduct my discussion under the assumption that just one kind of oddity is in question. (For further remarks on the larger picture, see section V.)

When statemental utterances are in question, the present account falls under the type of account of Moore's paradox sometimes called the "saying and disbelieving" line. Although popular, it is not particularly well named, because even paradoxes using sentences of form (A) have to do not with disbelieving things but with saying that one does; nor does this name mention implying (or indicating, etc.) what one believes, reference to which is essential. According to this account, the statemental conjunctive utterances that are Moore paradoxical are so because what is said in uttering one of the conjuncts (its propositional content) is logically incompatible with what is merely implied by uttering the other conjunct. Actually, it is a matter here of what *would* be the case if these utterances were made in the normal assertive way, because in fact they are in a sense impossible utterances (or things that one cannot say) and probably never actually get uttered in this way. Interchanging assertion and denial, as in cases of form (B), gives rise to an analogous type of utterance that we might call the "denying and believing" form of Moore's paradox and make similar comments about.

Thus, as examples of the original paradigms of Moore's paradox, we have such utterances as

(1) It is raining, but I don't believe that it is

and

(2) It is not raining, but I believe that it is.

Actually, completeness requires dealing with a third form, as a result of an ambiguity in (A), as a result of a phenomenon known to linguists as "raising" and resulting in a difference in the scope of the negation with respect to "believe." Let "(A1)" stand for the sentence form (A) interpreted as involving narrow scope of the negation (with respect to "believe"), and let "(A2)" stand for (A) with the wider scope. (The "not" in (A), understood this way, was said to have been "raised" (transformationally) from the complement clause; the one in sentence (A2) was not raised.) (A) on interpretation (A1) thus means

(A1) p, but I believe that it is not the case that p

whereas on interpretation (A2) it means

(A2) p, but it is not the case that I believe that p.

The "saying and disbelieving" line on Moore paradoxes of this form can still be construed as holding that what uttering the first conjunct implies (in the sense in question) is explicitly denied by the second conjunct, because the second conjunct (like that of an utterance of the same form disambiguated the other way) is still logically contrary to the implicatum of uttering the first conjunct.

A "denying and believing" line would be the analogue of those just mentioned, holding instead that uttering the first conjunct of a Moore-paradoxical utterance of form (B) implied (in the sense in question) that the speaker did not believe what the second conjunct explicitly says the speaker believes.

The account of Moore's paradox that I try to develop in what follows belongs, broadly, to the saying-and-disbelieving, denying-and-believing type of account, but I try to pursue systematically the suggestion (implicit in some of the earlier literature) that the conflict involved is one involving epistemic force or what I have elsewhere (Caton 1966, 1981) called epistemic qualifiers.

II

In this section I explain what I take to be the broad outlines of the system of epistemic qualification, starting with some discussion of the kind of pragmatic relations that I believe define these broad outlines, and then try to locate belief (important in connection with Moore's paradox) within it.

Discourse Relations

As I use the term, a *remark* is any illocutionary act in the most complete sense, including content, of Austin (1962), Alston (1964), or Searle (1969). Where convenient, I talk about the *content* of a remark, its *illocutionary*

force (= what type of illocutionary act was performed in issuing it), the *sentence* used or that could be used to make it, a *clause* that could be used to express it, etc.

By a *discourse* (or *d-*) *relation,* I mean a relation between remarks in a discourse. One example of a discourse relation is *d-commitment:* if making a certain remark in a discourse commits one to making another remark in that discourse, there is a certain relation between the two remarks involved; it is sometimes even ordinarily called commitment (although of course other things are also) and may be called d-commitment. A special case of d-commitment is the relation deriving from the fact that the propositional content of a certain remark one makes logically entails that of a certain other remark. Another example of a d-relation is the relation holding between two remarks as a result of the fact that making one of them in a certain discourse *excludes* making the other, on pain of incoherence (uninterpretability) of that discourse; this relation between remarks may be called *d-exclusion* or *d-incompatibility.*

These two d-relations may be related definitionally, because if one is d-committed to making a certain remark $R2$ by what one has already said $R1$, surely $R1$ is d-incompatible with agreeing with the negation of $R2$. This must be the case at least when statemental remarks are in question.

Epistemic Qualification

Three further concepts are useful in expounding the nature of our system of epistemic qualification. The fundamental one is that of an epistemic state, and deriving from it are those of an epistemic qualifier and of an epistemic qualifying expression.

By an *epistemic state* here I refer to knowledge (in the propositional sense of knowing that p, for some proposition p), its various species or types, such as remembering and realizing, and the various states that are contrary to it, in the sense that it cannot be at one and the same time that one is in one of those states and also knows that p. For example, if one just thinks that p (and does not know that p), then obviously one cannot also know that p. (I think here of responding to the question of whether one *knows* that p or (just) *thinks* that p.) But also, if one suspects that p, then equally, I think, one cannot also then know that p.

Just referring to knowledge, its types, and its competitors might not, I think, delimit a complete natural class of epistemic states, for it might be that there are states functioning in the same sort of linguistic and conceptual way that are compatible with knowledge without being types of it. In particular, belief may be of this sort; yet the epistemic qualifier 'I believe'[1] correlated with it is plainly in the same business as those related to the epistemic states mentioned: By itself, it is a qualifier of middling strength, competing on the one hand, for example, with those related to knowing and being certain and on the other with, for example, those related to inclination to believe, suspicion, and thinking it possible that *p*. So I must confess that up to this point I do not have a satisfactory definition of epistemic states nor therefore of epistemic qualifiers or epistemic qualifying expressions.

By an *epistemic qualifier* I mean a qualification or modification of a proposition occurring in one's discourse so as to indicate what one takes one's epistemic state to be with regard to that proposition at the time it occurs, so qualified, in the discourse.

By an *epistemic qualifying expression* I mean a linguistic expression (or other linguistic device) that is used to express an epistemic qualifier, that is, to indicate what epistemic state the speaker takes her/himself to be in with respect to an indicated proposition. Examples of epistemic qualifying expressions are "I know," "I think," "I believe," "I'm certain," "I feel certain," "It seems to me," "I incline to think." Those in this group may be called *personal epistemic qualifiers* because they explicitly mention the speaker. Ones that may be called *impersonal*, because they do not explicitly mention the speaker, include "It is certain," "It is virtually certain," "It is definite," "It must be" (or the auxiliary " . . . must . . ."), "It is overwhelmingly probable," "It is likely," "There is a good chance," "It is possible," and "It may be" (or the auxiliary " . . . may . . ."). I also call the epistemic qualifier expressed by a certain epistemic qualifying expression a personal or impersonal epistemic qualifier, according as the epistemic qualifying expression is personal or impersonal.

Because epistemic qualifying expressions usually have other uses besides their use to express a certain epistemic qualification of an indicated proposition, where necessary I speak of an epistemic qualifying expression "functioning to express an epistemic qualifier." For example, in the conditional statement

> (3) When it is certain that she has left, the desk clerk will use his pass key to let the officers in

the epistemic qualifying expression "it is certain" is not being used to indicate what epistemic state the speaker takes her/himself to be in at the time of utterance with respect to some proposition (notably not with respect to the proposition that the person referred to has left); that is, the epistemic qualifying expression is not there functioning to express an epistemic qualifier, as it would be (for example) in the statement that

> (4) It is certain that she has left

given, say, in answer to the question of whether it is certain that the person referred to has left.

Personal epistemic qualifying expressions containing one of the verbs that denote epistemic states seem to tend to function to express epistemic qualifiers when in what one might call the Austinian position in their conjugation, viz. the first-person singular present indicative active. This is, of course, the position in which performative (or

illocutionary act) verbs have their striking performative force. If there is some reason why there should be this coincidence, it is not known to me. (It may be noted that Austin included as (possible) performative verbs some that might, perhaps, have been better regarded as epistemic qualifying expressions; these were "doubt," "believe," and "know" (Austin 1962, p. 161). Note, though, that not even all personal epistemic qualifying expressions function to express epistemic qualifiers only in the Austinian position, at least not if "It seems to me that *p*" counts as a personal one.)

One epistemic qualifying device important in connection with Moore paradoxes (and illocutionary acts) is not in English and other familiar languages a word or phrase but rather a device linguists might call a *zero-form*, that is, the absence of any other indication of the speaker's epistemic state. Because a person who uses this device can often be said to have made a "flat statement," I appropriate this term and call the epistemic qualifier thus expressed the *flat-statement epistemic qualifier,* denoting it by Qfs. (I see no reason to suppose that there is more than one.) Epistemic qualifying expressions do not appear to be ambiguous as to what epistemic state they denote, although what they convey in a particular application may well be what Toulmin (1958, ch. 1) calls "field-dependent." It thus seems legitimate to refer to a mapping from epistemic qualifying devices into epistemic states and of a one-to-one correlation between sets of equivalent epistemic qualifying devices and epistemic states.

Epistemic states, epistemic qualifiers, and epistemic qualifying expressions exhibit what may be termed *epistemic strength:* epistemic states, in that some of them are preferable to others if one wants to be in as evidentially good a state with respect to some matter as one can; epistemic qualifiers, in that they are associated with this epistemic preferability through being correlated with epistemic states; and epistemic qualifying devices, in that they express these so correlated epistemic qualifiers. A number of conversational moves reflect this ordering of epistemic qualifiers, for example, those involving remarks of the form "It's not just that $Q1(p)$; (but also/rather) $Q2(p)$," as in "I don't just believe that *p;* I know that *p*."

Three broad strength groups of epistemic qualifiers can be distinguished, using the relation of d-incompatibility, as follows: a *strong* epistemic qualifier Qs may be defined as one such that saying that Qs(p) is d-incompatible with saying that it may be that not-*p*; for example, "I know," "I'm certain," "It is certain." The flat-statement qualifier is among these. A *moderate* epistemic qualifier Qm may be defined as one such that saying that Qm(p) is d-compatible with saying that it may be that not-*p*, but is d-incompatible with saying that Qm(not-*p*); for example, "I am almost certain," "I believe," "It is likely." And a *weak* epistemic qualifier Qw may be defined as one such that saying that Qw(p) is d-compatible with saying that not-*p*; for example, "There is some evidence," "It is possible," " . . . may . . . ".

Two epistemic qualifiers Q1 and Q2 can be incompatible in the sense that for no proposition p is any discourse coherent that contains both the remark that $Q1(p)$ and the remark that $Q2(p)$, neither having been withdrawn. (I refer to serious literal remarks here.) For example, the epistemic qualifiers 'I know' and 'I guess' are, I believe, incompatible in this sense.

I have reference throughout to the system expressible in English, which is I believe similar to that expressed in other familiar languages. This overall system of epistemic qualification seems to be largely constituted by relations of the various sorts that have so far been mentioned, together with further ones, some of which are mentioned later.

My epistemic qualification line on Moore's paradox is that these paradoxical utterances arise from epistemically qualifying propositional factors in an utterance in ways that are not consistent with the system of epistemic qualification.

Belief and Epistemic Qualification

"I think" and "I believe" do not allow all the same completions and constructions, but in the part of their use that I am concerned with here they seem to be synonymous, and I refer to them interchangeably. In particular, either can be used to formulate the original examples of Moore's paradox. Because they can also be so used for many of the additional examples dealt with here, it is important to clarify how the epistemic qualifier 'I believe' functions in the system of epistemic qualification.

But the epistemic qualifying expression "I believe" is problematical in that it appears to correlate both with a less and also with a more comprehensive epistemic state. (By "more comprehensive" I mean that a given subject will almost always be in the more comprehensive state with respect to more propositions than he or she will be with respect to the other.) For example, it seems to have a broad sense in a question such as

(5) Did Aristotle believe that the earth was round?

where the fact that Aristotle regarded the matter as quite certain does not mean that sentence (5) should be answered in the negative; on the contrary, it would mean that it should be answered in the affirmative. Yet with respect to the question

(6) Did Aristotle *know* that the earth was round or just *believe* that it was?

that Aristotle knew or was certain that the earth was round would mean that the second alternative was a factually incorrect answer.

Thus, in the epistemic qualifier-epistemic state correlation, the narrow use of "I believe" seems not to correlate with the epistemic state referred to in historical belief reports but rather (if it correlates with any at all) with a

narrower epistemic state. Yet we do not, I think, feel that "believe" has changed its meaning from the one case to the other or that we must ask for disambiguation of a sentence such as

(7) Aristotle believed that the earth was round.

I do not say that the string (7) is not, in context, associated with two different meanings (or propositional types), I think it is: one related to question (5), expressing an affirmative answer to it, and the other to a question such as question (6), giving the second alternative in answer. But I do not think these derive from two different lexical meanings of "believe."

We seem, then, to confront a puzzle about "I believe": How can it exhibit linguistic behavior of kinds associated with an ambiguous expression but apparently without being ambiguous?

Since Grice (1975), good method dictates that in analyzing conversational phenomena we try to explain as many effects as we can in terms of his maxims of conversation, rather than postulating a multiplicity of meanings of the expressions involved; this is vulgarly called "gricing" the use of the expression in question.

Let me try to do that here. Suppose that the actual lexical meaning of the verb "to believe" is that associated with the broader use. Then its curious behavior in Austinian position may be griced using the maxim of quality (or quantity), as follows. This epistemic qualifying expression functions to express an epistemic qualifier in situations in which it would be appropriate (according to this maxim) to say that $Q'(p)$, with a stronger epistemic qualifier Q', if one candidly could (that is, if one was in a position to do so); because one does not, the inference is that one can not. So the force of "I believe that p" is (unless explicitly canceled) that of "I merely/just believe that p." The "merely/just" fits the case because the unused alternative is "I know" or "I'm certain," which involves stronger epistemic qualifiers. Because this sort of situation is often faced, what Grice calls a *generalized conversational implicature* would develop, so that the phrase would be regularly understood in the way inferred here, unless explicitly canceled. For the implicature to be a conversational (or generalized conversational) one, it does need to be cancelable; and it apparently can be canceled, as in "Aristotle not only *believed* that the earth was round; he was absolutely *certain* that it was."

(It is hard to know which of Grice's maxims is involved because he does not relate evidence and information to the epistemic qualification of the remarks involved. If epistemic qualification is included—and how can it not be?—then the maxim of quantity is presumably the maxim involved: "I believe that p" would convey less (purported) information than "I know that p," for example. If, somehow, the epistemic qualification is not included, then the maxim of quality would presumably be the one involved: The quality of "I believe that p," in the sense of the evidential basis for conveying that *p* (epistemic qualified that way) would not be as high as that of "I know that *p*." If the maxims were revised so as to deal explicitly with epistemic qualification, this problem would, I imagine, solve itself.)

If "I believe" can be griced in this way (or some other), it remains an open question whether or not knowledge entails belief. For simplicity, let us suppose that it does. Then personal epistemic qualifiers, at least, can be divided into those that entail belief (the *doxastic epistemic qualifiers,* as they may be called) and those that do not (although they are, perhaps, not incompatible with belief, for example, thinking it possible that *p*). There would be a broad epistemic state denoted by "believe," which, when its correlated epistemic qualifying expression occurred in Austinian position, would by the Gricean implicature (unless canceled) narrow down to the epistemic state correlated with just/merely believing, that is, to believing without (putatively) knowing. "I believe" would be correlated with the epistemic state of being in some doxastic epistemic state or other, which would be compatible (we are supposing) with knowing and also with not knowing but would be incompatible with not believing, whether in the sense of (A1) or in that of (A2).

III

John Searle's account of Moore's paradox is that, in a Moore-paradoxical utterance, such as

(1) It is raining, but I don't believe that it is

in the assertive utterance of the first conjunct, one does not *say* but rather *expresses* the putative fact that a certain "sincerity condition" holds, which the second conjunct explicitly denies. In the case of utterance (1), the sincerity condition is that the speaker believes that it is raining, and the denial of this condition is that the speaker does not believe it is raining. Thus Searle's account of Moore's paradox is explicitly tied to a speech act, the illocutionary act that would be performed in a normal assertive utterance of "It is raining" (and to the saying-and-disbelieving form of Moore's paradox).

Searle's account as he gives it cannot be correct, because his statement of sincerity conditions for assertive utterances is not correct. That it is not is not made especially salient by examples such as utterance (1), because "I don't believe that it is raining" expresses either disbelief (in the sense of believing that it is not the case that it is raining) or a denial of belief (its not being the case that one believes that it is raining), the utterance of either of which is d-incompatible with "it is raining." What one expresses by saying that it is raining is, however, not, as Searle says, that one believes that it is raining, if "believes" is taken in the narrow way, but rather the flat-statement epistemic qualifier, something similar to one's (not just thinking but) *knowing* that it is raining.

Others have said that what is implied or expressed by a speaker who says that *p* is either that the speaker believes or that the speaker knows that *p*, but I think this is pretty clearly wrong, because a Moore paradox of the given form (1) is forthcoming in any case. That something with this epistemic force is what is expressed is clear from the fact that, if what the speaker would express as

(8) I believe that it is raining

were what was expressed, that is, was the epistemically strongest thing expressed (as opposed to said, in a strict sense), then one could follow the utterance of "It is raining" with that of

(9) It may not be raining

without withdrawing or qualifying remark (8), just as one can follow an utterance of sentence (8) with an utterance of sentence (9) (linked with "but," say). But one cannot, just as one cannot follow an utterance of

(10) I know that it is raining

with an utterance of sentence (9), without withdrawing or qualifying remark (10).

If, on the other hand, it is the broader use of "believe" that Searle has in mind in connection with his sincerity condition, one that would cover claims to know that *p,* unadorned flat statements that *p,* saying that one believes that *p,* etc., then there is a problem about the sincerity condition of epistemically qualified statements. In the case of a statement such as (10), the sincerity condition would be (what the speaker could express as)

(11) I believe that I know that it is raining.

Similarly, for a statement such as

(12) I am certain that it is raining

the sincerity condition would be

(13) I believe that I am certain that it is raining.

That is, the epistemic qualifying expression of whatever qualifier was explicit in the original statement would turn up within the scope of "I believe" in the statement of the sincerity condition of the original statement. Now, although statements such as (11) and (13) have interpretations, they are not the right things to be sincerity conditions; rather, they are, as far as I can see, either metalinguistic statements (in the context equivalent to "I believe the right word to describe the situation is that I *know* that it is raining") or statements expressing uncertainty about the state one is in ("Yes, on further consideration it *is certainty* that I feel"), neither of which is necessarily present in sincere utterances of sentences (10) and (12) and certainly not as their sincerity conditions.

The correct sincerity condition in the case of utterance (12), surely, is just that the speaker *is* certain that it is raining. In the case of (10), where truth of the proposition said to be known is (presumably) logically entailed, the sincerity condition (which of course can be satisfied without entailing it) may be described as being that the speaker *takes* it that (or perhaps that the speaker *assumes* that) he or she knows that it is raining. In neither the case of statement (10) nor statement (12) is belief involved in the way Searle describes. Perhaps knowing and being certain that *p* are doxastic epistemic qualifiers. If so, then denying that one believes that *p* would be as Moore paradoxical as if believing that *p* were the sincerity condition of saying that it is raining. But "believe" taken broadly cannot, apparently, be used to state accurately an overall pattern of sincerity conditions of the kind Searle gives (1983, p. 9) for statemental utterances. The uniformity he finds in their sincerity conditions does not exist. These conditions are more specific and are relative to the epistemic qualifiers involved.

IV

According to the account of Moore's paradox that I wish to present here, Moore paradoxes are one kind of epistemic qualifier conflict, in the sense (already described) of d-incompatibility of epistemically qualified utterances. That is, Moore paradoxes are, on this account, cases in which epistemic qualifiers are so applied to propositional contents that d-incompatible (but not contradictory) illocutionary acts result. I now try to spell out what the conflict is in the case of Moore's original paradigms of the paradox. Their particular case is complicated by their involving the problematical concept of belief.

The system of epistemic qualification is constituted by various d-relations among epistemically qualified utterances; it is these relations that define the several roles of the epistemic qualifiers in the system. In some cases these relationships can be encapsulated in general principles or rules. I state several of these and use them in the explanations of Moore paradoxicality.

It appears to be the case that one of the general principles of the sort just mentioned is, briefly, that an epistemic qualifier d-incompatible with a given epistemic qualifier is d-incompatible with any stronger epistemic qualifier. More precisely stated:

(I) If saying that $Q1(p)$ is d-incompatible with saying that $Q2(q)$ and if $Q3$ is stronger than $Q1$, then saying that $Q3(p)$ is also d-incompatible with saying that $Q2(q)$.

Suppose that this is, in fact, a principle constitutive of or derivative from the system of epistemic qualifiers. Then one particular instance of principle (I) is that involved in a Moore paradox of form (A1), that is, the kind of case in which q = not-p, $Q1 = Q2$ = 'I believe', and $Q3 = Q$fs. 'I believe' is a moderately strong epistemic qualifier, so that (by definition of that strength) saying that $Q1(p)$ is d-

incompatible with saying that $Q1$(not-p), that is (in this case), with saying that $Q2(q)$. Thus the first condition in the antecedent of (I) is satisfied for these choices of epistemic qualifiers and contents. Because Qfs is plainly stronger than 'I believe', the second condition is also satisfied, so that by (I) it follows that saying that Qfs(p) is d-incompatible with saying that one believes that not-p, which in form (A1) is what "I don't believe that p" means. Thus the two conjuncts in an instance of form (A1) are d-incompatible, and a fluent speaker is able to see right off that the utterance as a whole is something that in the relevant sense one cannot say. Furthermore, an instance of form (A1) satisfies the defining condition on Moore paradoxes that the utterance is not self-contradictory. As usual, we verify that such an instance is not self-contradictory by putting it into a non-Austinian position in its conjugation and finding that what it then expresses might well have been true; for example, it might well have been true that it was raining but I did not believe that it was.

Principle (I) may also be invoked to explain the paradoxicality of Moore paradoxes of the form (B). Because d-incompatibility is (presumably) a symmetric relation, the same choice of epistemic qualifiers, rewriting p as not-p and q as p, suffices.

Moore paradoxes of form (A2) require a more complicated treatment, because the scope of the negation in the second conjunct is here to be understood as wider than that of the epistemic qualifier 'I believe'. However, a minimal assumption from epistemic qualification-enriched speech-act theory seems to suffice, for there seems to be some such principle as

(II) Saying that Qfs(p) is d-incompatible with denying that Qm(p).

To take the case at hand, saying that it is raining (with flat-statement epistemic qualification) seems clearly d-incompatible with denying that one believes it is raining; thus the following conversation becomes odd at the point where such a denial would occur:

(C1) X: It is raining.

Y: You think it is raining?

X: No, it is not true that I think it is raining.

I mean, of course, ordinary or regular denying rather than metalinguistic denying, as in "It is not true that I *think* it is raining; I *know* it is." The almost overwhelming temptation to take X's second remark in dialogue (C1) to involve withdrawal of X's first remark would be explained by (C1)'s otherwise being counter to principle (I). And a Moore paradox of form (A2) is an instance of principle (II), its two conjuncts being the incompatible utterances in question.

There is a problem inherent in trying to make plausible the postulation of principles such as (I) and (II), viz. that they must be (i) simple, familiar, and obvious, so as to make it plausible to impute knowledge of and obedience to them to speakers generally, and yet that (ii) they must fit the examples in question fairly simply, so that it may plausibly be supposed that their quick application is automatically made by a fluent speaker. Conditions (i) and (ii) operating together tend to make the principles look ad hoc. A methodological antidote is to show that there are many cases that can be explained by the principles, not just the ones one is working on. I do believe that their postulation will be borne out by such further consideration, although I cannot undertake it here.

As we saw and as Searle points out, his account of Moore's paradox would generalize to any illocutionary act with a sincerity condition, that is (if Searle is right (1969, p. 65, under 2)), to almost any illocutionary act whatever. But, unfortunately, his account is defective in at least the way indicated. However, some Moore-paradoxical-looking utterances do seem to be explicable in terms of his account but not mine, for example, his "I promise that p but I do not intend that p" (1979, p. 5). It may be that the propositional contents of these nonstatemental utterances are not epistemically qualified. If so, a different sort of explanation of their oddity than the present one is required. But even this sort of utterance can be odd in the way the present account claims that statemental Moore paradoxes are, for the present account of Moore's paradox generalizes not just to other sorts of illocutionary act (and not to them just because of their sincerity conditions, where, however, epistemic qualification may figure), but to utterances involving epistemic qualifier conflicts generally, which can manifest themselves in a variety of ways that are independent of illocutionary force, as I try to illustrate in a moment.

The question is, What exactly is necessary in order to have a paradoxical utterance resembling a Moore paradox (besides its being noncontradictory as a whole)? Because weak epistemic strength is not defined in terms of a d-incompatibility (but rather a d-compatibility), it might be thought that Moore-paradoxical utterances (in this perhaps extended sense) have to involve a pair of epistemically qualified propositions, at least one of which is at least moderately epistemically qualified. However, the following seems to be a counterinstance:

> (14) It may be that his sister has gone, but it may be that he does not have a sister

where the first conjunct may (perfectly ordinarily and indeed as usual) be taken in a sense that accepts the presupposition (the denial of which is the proposition epistemically qualified in the second conjunct) that he has a sister, in which case the two conjuncts are d-incompatible.

I am not, in fact, at all sure what, in general, is necessary in order to have a Moore paradox. As we have seen and in the list to be given, a variety of features involved in or suggested by the original paradigms or by Searle's (or

others') account of Moore's paradox are *not,* apparently, required in order to have what seems similar paradoxicality.

But let me say first what it is that on the present line is characteristic of these utterances: a conflict between two epistemically qualified propositions somehow or other involved in them. (The problem is to see *how* they must be involved in them.) Three things seem to figure in this, viz. (1) the unqualified content of the propositions, (2) their epistemic qualification (that is, how they are epistemically qualified, what epistemic force they are propounded with), and (3) the logical form, in a broad sense, of the utterance overall.

The following general remarks may be made concerning these factors: As to point 1, the contents may be contrary to one another in the familiar content-logical sense, that is, the truth-value-possibilities sense in which propositions not epistemically qualified may stand. This contrariety might, when these contents are epistemically qualified, make the overall utterance self-contradictory (in an utterance-logical sense, that is, in a sense appropriate to utterances involving epistemic qualification, rather than simply content-logical relationships), in which case it would (by definition) not be a Moore paradox. But the particular epistemic qualifiers involved might be personal epistemic qualifiers, in which case Moore's paradox could result, as in the original paradigms of forms (A) and (B). The statement "It is raining, but it is not raining" is just self-contradictory (content- and utterance-wise); but "It is raining, but I don't believe that it is" is a Moore paradox. "It is raining, but it may not be raining," with the impersonal epistemic qualifier '. . . may . . .' (= 'it may be') is perhaps problematic (because of its peculiar indirect-discourse properties), although maybe either a contradiction or a Moore paradox.

However, as to point 2, their epistemic qualification, the contents of two epistemically qualified propositions, may be consistent in the content-logical sense and yet produce a paradoxical utterance because of the relationship between the epistemic qualifiers (this being one constituent part of the system of epistemic qualifiers). The example in item (iii) on the following list, viz.

> (15) It is raining, and/but it may be raining

involves one and the same self-consistent proposition as the contents involved, for example. The problem is with the epistemic qualifiers, the strong flat-statement qualifier and a weak epistemic qualifier, there being (to encapsulate this little part of the system) some principle, constitutive of these respective epistemic qualifiers, to the effect that

> (III) One cannot say that $Q\text{fs}(p)$ and $Q\text{w}(p)$.

So another sort of conflict between epistemically qualified propositions derives not from a conflict between their contents but rather from the ways those contents are there epistemically qualified.

But, to bring in point 3, the epistemically qualified propositions involved in the conflict need to occur in certain ways in the overall utterance; the kind of occurrence I call a matter of the "logical form" of the utterance, including semantic presupposition (if any) as one facet thereof. To illustrate, look at the logical form (in this sense) of an utterance of sentence (14); as there glossed, this form needs to be distinguished from that of an utterance involving the same sentence, but, as we may assume has been made clear by a different sort of context, *not* presupposing that the person referred to has a sister. More generally, the logical form of an utterance that is a conjunction or disjunction obviously needs to be distinguished from one that is a conditional or a generalization. As another illustration of how logical form can affect paradoxicality or the lack of it in an utterance, consider disjunctive utterances. The epistemic qualification of the disjuncts in such an utterance will, I believe, often not be epistemically qualified (although the disjunctive content as a whole will) and so a fortiori will not give rise to Moore's paradox in the ways discussed concerning points 1 and 2, whereas of course it was the epistemic qualification of the conjuncts of a conjuctive utterance that gave rise to the original paradigms of Moore paradoxicality.

Thus various restrictions on the form and/or the content of Moore-paradoxical utterances that, from the original paradigms and early exemplars, might have been expected to hold apparently do not do so universally. The following list contains at least some of these restrictions, with some illustrative examples. In such an utterance:

(i) there is no restriction on the propositional content epistemically qualified;

(ii) it is not required that one conjunct be a flat statement and the other be explicitly epistemically qualified; for example, "It is certain that it is raining, but it may not be";

(iii) it is not required that one conjunct be negative and the other affirmative; for example, "It is raining, and/but it may be raining";

(iv) it is not required that one propositional content be logically incompatible with the other—take the last example;

(v) it is not required that both conjuncts be statements, for example, "I realize that it is raining, but may it not be?";

(vi) it is not required that the speaker, in one conjunct, *say* something conflicting with what saying the other only *implies* or *expresses;* compare the example in (iii);

and, in fact:

(vii) neither conjunct need be a statement; for example (assuming a bequest is not a statement), "To my only son I bequeath my gold watch and to my third son, if it turns out that there is such a person, the rest of my estate";

(viii) the utterance need not be conjunctive in form; for example, "If, as is likely, her second child is a boy, she must regret having had only one child";

and of course:

(ix) sincerity conditions of illocutionary acts need not be involved.

v

What if the component parts of an odd utterance are separated, as they might be in a speaker's contributions to a conversation, say, or in a one-speaker discourse? It seems clear from the sorts of example we have been considering that the two components would still be related in the way they were in the paradox. But of course the conflict is not perceived as a single, impossible, paradoxical, odd utterance but rather as a kind of inconsistency in one's remarks, as a situation in which, typically, not both of a certain pair of things can be said, because incoherence in the total discourse would result. Or perhaps the person is not speaking honestly or candidly; or perhaps one has fogotten what one said earlier or has changed one's mind about what one wants to say. There may be many interpretations of the situation. Whatever the cause of the incoherence, the speaker cannot rest with saying both of the things which, placed together, would be Moore paradoxical; the speaker must withdraw at least one of them. The speaker must, or his or her discourse, in this part, will be rendered incoherent; we will not be able to understand it or perhaps the speaker.

But now, despite the apparent fact that the requisite relationships between the components still hold, the present dimension is, for some reason, not one along which Moore paradoxicality is apparently preserved. For some reason utterances of this type are not perceived as odd or paradoxical but rather as rendering the discourse incoherent or inconsistent. Unless it is simply the fact that two bursts of speech are involved, I do not know why this is, but I suspect that it has to do with the fact that there has (typically) been time in the discourse for the speaker to forget or revise what s/he said earlier (as of course we often do without much if any notice).

Also, up to now, it has been a question of epistemic qualifier conflict in just a single speaker's discourse, whether compressed into a Moore paradox or similar odd utterance or (as just discussed) spread out across an inconsistent or incoherent discourse. Allowing more than one speaker to be involved—one making one of the component remarks and one making the other, results in more than just a pair of speakers taking turns giving their opinions to each other. Nor do we get incoherent discourse (necessarily). What we get is *disagreement.* I believe that the situation is, in fact, that any Moore-paradoxical utterance, including the odd utterances of various sorts considered, will, if one speaker illocutes one component and another speaker illocutes the other, constitute their disagreeing with each other, either of the direct confrontation variety or (for example) of the kind where one disagrees with something the other is assuming, or perhaps some other. Note, for example, that

(16) I think it is, but/and I think it is not

(not taken in the sense in which it is used to introduce a distinction or a hedge) is a Moore-paradoxical utterance and that in the two-person conversation

(C2) X: I think it is.

Y: I think it is not.

the speakers disagree despite the apparent fact that each is referring to himself, to what he himself thinks. Yet in the single utterance

(17) It may be and it may not be

there is no oddity; nor is there disagreement (but only a reminder) in the conversation

(C3) X: It may be.

Y: And it may not be.

Thus there are different sorts of discourse relations, among which are discourse incompatibilities. A particular case of the latter are epistemic qualifier conflicts. When epistemic qualifier conflicts occur at their minimal limits along any of several lines, one reaches hypothetical utterances that resemble the original paradigms of Moore's paradox. Thus what may be (or may be regarded as) linguistic oddity of the same sort they exhibit spreads out over language as a whole, appearing in different guises as it goes: sometimes as Moore paradoxicality, sometimes as self-contradiction, and finally as incoherence or inconsistency in one's discourse and as interpersonal disagreement.

NOTE

[1] Single quotes will be used to form names of what will be called epistemic qualifiers (for example, 'I know'); double quotes, to refer to linguistic expression (for example, "I know").

REFERENCES

Alston, W. P. 1964. *Philosophy of Language.* Englewood Cliffs, N.J.: Prentice-Hall.

Austin, J. L. 1962. *How to Do Things with Words.* Cambridge, Mass.: Harvard University Press.

Caton, C. E. 1966. "On the general structure of the epistemic qualification of things said in English." *Foundations of Language* 2: 37-66.

Caton, C. E. 1981. "Stalnaker on pragmatic presupposition," in *Radical Pragmatics,* Peter Cole, ed. New York: Academic Press, 83-100.

Grice, H. P. 1975. "Logic and conversation," in *The Logic of Grammar,* G. Harman and D. Davidson, eds. Encino, Calif.: Dickenson, 64-75. Also in *Syntax and Semantics 3: Speech Acts,* J. L. Morgan and P. Cole, eds. (New York: Academic Press, 1975), 41-58.

Searle, John R. 1969. *Speech Acts.* Cambridge, England: Cambridge University Press.

Searle, John R. 1979. *Expression and Meaning.* Cambridge England: Cambridge University Press.

Searle, John R. 1983. *Intentionality.* Cambridge, England: Cambridge University Press.

Toulmin, S. E. 1958. *The Uses of Argument.* Cambridge, England: Cambridge University Press.

James C. Klagge (essay date 1988)

SOURCE: A review of 'Principia Ethica', in *Ethics,* Vol. 98, No. 3, April, 1988, pp. 582-84.

[*In the following review, Klagge confesses to disagreeing with Moore's theories but commends Regan for explaining them more clearly than Moore.*]

G. E. Moore's **Principia Ethica** was the culmination of nearly a decade of personal turmoil and philosophical progress. Through the books under review, Tom Regan hopes to force a reconsideration of **Principia Ethica,** and of Moore, by attending to this decade. He should be successful.

This task was begun by Paul Levy in *Moore: G. E. Moore and the Cambridge Apostles* (London: Weidenfeld & Nicolson, 1979), but Levy is not a philosopher. Regan is a very good philosopher, and he illuminates very many philosophical issues ignored or obscured by Levy. Just as translations are best done by native speakers of the readers' language, so philosophers are best served by biographical work done by other philosophers.

Moore suffered great personal turmoil because of his inability to see religious belief as rational. Regan recounts Moore's pilgrimage from the melancholy of religious unbelief to the sense of meaningfulness gained through belief in the intrinsic value of beauty and friendship. Art and morality provide the consolation of religion without its existential commitments. **Principia Ethica** becomes Moore's defense of the meaningfulness of life.

Moore's philosophical evolution explains the form that his views take in **Principia.** Regan shows how **Principia** is Moore's development of and reaction to Kant's moral philosophy. The non-natural status of Goodness and the synthetic nature of moral judgments, for example, are accommodations to problems Moore inherited from Kant's notion of transcendental freedom. Unfortunately, Regan says little about how Moore's consequentialism emerges. Here Moore seems most at odds with Kant.

Regan helpfully illuminates the progress of Moore's moral philosophy by extracting six criteria that Moore seems implicitly to be using in evaluating his own, and others', views. In essence, they are: (1) Intrinsic value is an objective quality. (2) Intrinsic value is a diachronically supervenient quality—in the sense that if a thing ever has (or lacks) intrinsic value, it always must have (or lack) it as long as it does not change in any naturalistic respects. (To this, Regan might also have added a related criterion, that intrinsic value is a synchronically supervenient quality—in the sense that if a thing has intrinsic value, any other thing must have it too as long as it does not differ in naturalistic respects.) (3) Intrinsic value must be possessed by at least some natural objects. (4) We must be able to conceive of states of affairs that have more intrinsic value than any state of affairs that actually exists. (The motivation for the third and fourth criteria is unclear. Why must the actual world be neither the worst nor the best of all possible worlds?) (5) We must have some way of deciding whether actions are right or wrong. And, (6), we must have some way of deciding whether a natural object has intrinsic value.

Regan explains developments in Moore's moral philosophy by showing how they better satisfy these criteria. While all Moore's earlier positions fail one or more of these criteria, *Principia* turns out to satisfy all six.

Regan's collection of Moore's early essays, originally published between 1897 and 1904, helps to remind us of the evidence for the formative influences on *Principia,* as well as others of his early concerns.

Actually, though, Regan's discussion draws at least as heavily on unpublished material as it does on previously published material. For one who published relatively little in his lifetime, Moore was impressively prolific in the decade before *Principia.* As a member of the Apostles, Moore presented at least twenty-one papers for discussion between 1894 and 1900. Regan refers to ten of these papers, four of them extensively. As a member of the Trinity Sunday Essay Society, Moore presented at least seven papers between 1895 and 1902. Regan refers to six of them, two extensively. Moore wrote two dissertations at Cambridge—the first in 1897, the second in 1898. And in the fall of 1898 he gave a series of ten lectures in London, entitled **"The Elements of Ethics, with a View to an Appreciation of Kant's Moral Philosophy."** Moore's notes for the lectures, as well as both dissertations, have been preserved, and Regan makes extensive use of all three.

Although I have no idea what difficulties would attend editing and publishing all or part of this mass of material,

it seems odd that it was all passed over in favor of collecting already published material (two pieces having appeared in this journal [*Ethics*]). Presumably serious scholars of Moore already knew of these published papers, or will learn of them by reading Regan's book. While gaining access to old journals is difficult, it is far less difficult than gaining access to unpublished material. A much greater service to serious scholars of Moore would be the publication of at least some of the unpublished material.

In the course of explaining the background for *Principia,* Regan also explains its importance for the Bloomsbury Group. While philosophers have traditionally seen *Principia* as embodying a commonsense, conservative morality, the Bloomsbury Group saw it as morally liberating. Someone seems to have misread *Principia,* and it is Regan's contention that it is the philosophers. According to Regan, "Moore . . . offer[s] a moral philosophy that . . . is a radical defense of the freedom of the individual to judge and choose" (p. xii). Regan spends many pages explaining and emphasizing Moore's defense of individual moral autonomy. I found these portions of the book rather puzzling.

No objective theory, such as Moore's, can grant individuals the ability to make certain actions right. That could only be allowed by some form of subjectivism. (Regan unaccountably seems to suggest [p. 214] that Stevenson's emotivism would threaten autonomy.) So the autonomy Regan has in mind must be epistemological: Moore defends individuals' freedom to figure out for themselves whether an action is right (though, due to objectivity, they might figure incorrectly). The defense relies on Moore's rejection of naturalism: If naturalism were true, then morality would be analytically reducible to some natural or metaphysical science. The determination of moral truths would be the privilege of specialists. But Moore is concerned to establish that there can be no experts about morality. All people (with adequate knowledge of nonmoral facts) are equally qualified to make moral judgments—though they may be wrong.

This defense seems faulty in two respects. First, the rejection of naturalism does not ensure that there can be no moral experts, since reductions can be synthetic. Moore in fact confronts this issue in his later years. Second, it is not clear how the existence of experts would endanger autonomy. Freedom is only endangered by laws, not science or moral philosophy.

Regan needs to explain exactly what kind of autonomy is endangered and how naturalism, but not objectivism, is a threat to that kind of autonomy. Perhaps it is really Moore's pluralism, and not his antinaturalism, that ensures that there is no nonautonomous science of morals. Sciences seem to require a kind of systematization that Moore's moral philosophy strongly resists.

To conclude, *Bloomsbury's Prophet* is a well-written and provocative book, the main virtue of which is that it makes *Principia Ethica* and the early Moore much more understandable and interesting to us than they have been until now.

Stephen W. Ball (essay date 1988)

SOURCE: "Reductionism in Ethics and Science: A Contemporary Look at G. E. Moore's Open-Question Argument," in *American Philosophical Quarterly,* Vol. 25, No. 3, July, 1988, pp. 197-213.

[*In the following essay, Ball argues that Moore's "open-question" against ethical naturalism is flawed but, ultimately, valid.*]

The so-called "open question" argument is an argument against a general meta-ethical theory, or group of theories, known as ethical naturalism, according to which statements about what is morally right or wrong are reducible or equivalent in meaning to certain statements about empirical facts of nature. The standard objection to Moore's argument is that it is question-begging or circular. While this objection is currently accepted by ethicists, it has been recently objected that Moore's argument is in fact *logically invalid,* since it would yield inaccurate results if applied to established reductionist identities in science. Part I of the present essay examines, and rejects, the version of this objection given by Gilbert Harman. Part II examines, and again rejects, Putnam's version of the objection, which relies also on an analogy to science but goes on to apply Kripke's theory in philosophy of language. Part III attempts to show that the analogy between ethics and science, assumed by both Harman and Putnam, is incorrect. Finally, Part IV formulates and defends an interpretation of Moore's argument which is neither invalid nor circular. The conclusion is that the open-question argument provides relevant *evidence* against the usual forms of naturalist reductionism which Moore, as well as emotivists or moral non-cognitivists today, are concerned to refute.

I

Ethical naturalists have offered a variety of definitions to specify exactly which natural facts are being asserted by ethical statements. It has been suggested, for instance, that statements of the form "*X* is good" or "*X* is morally obligatory" just mean that "*X* is desired" or "is approved of" (by the speaker, the speaker's society, or mankind generally, etc.). Such definitions have been criticized individually as having strange implications which render them implausible accounts of what ethical statements really do mean. The purpose of G. E. Moore's open-question argument, however, is to show that any naturalistic analysis of moral terms must be implausible, regardless of any more specific objections to the particular proposals. Such proposals will have the form:

"*x* is good or ought to be done" = *df.* "*x* (or doing *x*) has natural property *P*."

The insight of Moore's argument is that no matter what a naturalist takes *P* to be, one can recognize that a given *x* has *P* and yet still reasonably ask whether *x* is good or morally right—that is, this remains an "open question." Even if the answer is yes, or if being good/right is always *correlated* with having *P*, the fact that this question nevertheless makes sense shows that the correlated statements don't *mean* the same, as naturalists allege. Responding to Russell's proposal that "good" be defined as what we "desire to desire," Moore himself puts it this way in the *locus classicus* which premiers the open-question argument:

> . . . [W]hatever definition is offered, it may always be asked, with significance, of the complex so defined, whether it is itself good . . . It may indeed be that what we desire to desire is always good; perhaps, even the converse may be true: but it is very doubtful that this is the case, and the mere fact that we understand what is meant by doubting it, shows clearly that we have two different notions before our minds.[1]

Harman raises two objections to this argument. On the one hand, he suggests that the argument is *circular* or question-begging. This is the rather standard objection that if "good" or "right" really means what the naturalist says it does, then the question indicated above is not really "open," and to assert that it is amounts simply to assuming, rather than arguing, that naturalism is false.[2] We will return to this objection in Part IV. The second objection, which appears to be new, is that the open-question argument is *logically invalid,* since the same sort of argument could be used to "refute" established results of physical science:

> More important, perhaps, is the fact that as it stands the open-question argument could be used on someone who was ignorant of the chemical composition of water to 'prove' to him that water is not H_2O. This person will agree that it is not an open question whether water is water but it is an open question, at least for him, whether water is H_2O. Since this argument would not show that water is not H_2O, the open-question argument cannot be used as it stands to show that for an act to be an act that ought to be done is not for it to have some natural characteristic C.[3]

This objection to the open-question argument (hereafter "OQ") is not, as it stands, very convincing. One's initial reaction to it is that Moore's argument against ethical naturalism is an attempt to refute a theory of *meaning,* and that a parallel argument in the water/H_2O case could not yield the conclusion that water *is not* H_2O, as Harman indicates, but only the conclusion that the terms "water" and "H_2O" do not mean the same, or that, as Moore puts it in the quoted passage, there are "two different *notions*" involved here. On this view, the proposed application of Moore's argument would indicate only that it is an "open question" or a "significant question," whether water is H_2O, and Moore would surely say that it is such a question—and one which has been significantly answered by science. What Moore would presumably deny here is not the truth of "Water is H2O" but rather the status of this truth as analytic, or as one of definition.

There are two supports for the above interpretation of *OQ* and for rejecting Harman's argument against it. The first is that, historically, the main tradition of ethical naturalism has in fact presented itself as a semantic theory which gives a *reportive* definition of the actual meanings of ethical terms in ordinary language.[4] The second is that this at any rate is clearly the sort of theory that Moore himself, and others who have endorsed his argument, have intended to refute with *OQ*, and it is the only view consistent with Moore's own position in ethics. In holding the meta-ethical position that "good" is indefinable, Moore does not deny the truth of all statements about what activities or experiences *are* good; the claim is only that all such statements are "synthetic and never analytic," or can never give "the very meaning of the word."[5] Part of Moore's position in meta-ethics is in fact the thesis that some such synthetic statements connecting "good" with empirical states of affairs are known to be true by a cognitive faculty of intuition. Specifically, as an act-utilitarian in normative ethics, Moore holds that right actions *are* those which maximize happiness, though again he rejects the attempts which he finds exemplified in Bentham and Mill, respectively, to treat these statements as *definitions* of what "right" and "good" *mean.*[6] Moore's using *OQ* to refute such a definition is consistent, then, with his recognizing that statement as synthetically true. Analogously, in response to Harman's counterexample, Moore can deny that "water" and "H2O" have the same meaning without denying that water is H2O, since he clearly—and explicitly in the passage cited—is construing "meaning" in such a way that two expressions can have different meanings even though their *extensions* are synthetically the same.

It may appear that this defense of *OQ* against the objection of invalidity can be rebutted on the basis of recent challenges to the analytic-synthetic distinction itself, but this appearance is deceptive. Admittedly, Moore would have trouble establishing that the putative definitions of ethical naturalists are "synthetic and never analytic" if there is no such distinction; he cannot prove, by posing the "open question," that a statement like "*X* ought to be done if and only if *x* has natural property *P*" is not analytic, if there exist no criteria for analyticity to begin with. In the Preface to his text, Harman seems sympathetic to this view as he comments on what he takes to be its historical influence in ethics, suggesting that the arguments of Quine and others "undermined the distinction between meta-ethics and normative ethics by showing that there can be no real separation between questions of substance and questions of meaning."[7] There are, however, several points in response to this line of criticism that may be made on behalf of Moore. First of all, it is of course not obvious that the arguments of Quine and others conclusively establish that there is no analytic-synthetic distinction. Even if one has no general counter-

arguments, such as those offered by Grice and Strawson, much less an articulated account of the criteria for distinguishing analytic from synthetic statements, one may still reasonably take the position—which has a certain G. E. Moore ring to it—that there is nonetheless an obvious difference in kind (i.e., of *some* kind) between statements like "All bachelors are unmarried" and those like "My hat is on the table."[8] Similarly, in ethics, one might contend that, Quine notwithstanding, some such distinction between "meaning" and "substance" does in fact differentiate importantly distinct kinds of questions.[9] In any event, if one rejects the analytic-synthetic distinction altogether, this would seem to undermine the objection that *OQ* is invalid. If the object of *OQ* is, as just seen, to show that certain statements about "good" or "ought" are not analytic, or true by definition or in virtue of meanings, and so on, then rejecting the analytic-synthetic distinction would presumably imply that the problem with the argument is not its logic, but rather the *unintelligibility* of its conclusion.

II

A more recent version of Harman's objection has been presented by Putnam which more explicitly connects Moore's argument against naturalism with the theme of concepts (or "notions") and linguistic meaning that is salient in Moore's own characterization.[10] Putnam does not explicitly discuss *OQ* by name, but focuses instead on Moore's closely related idea of the "naturalistic fallacy": an expression coined by Moore which initially suggests the mistake of *inferring* normative statements from statements of natural fact, though Moore applies this label also to attempts by naturalists at bridging Hume's gap between "is" and "ought" with a premise *defining* the latter in terms of the former. *OQ*, then, is Moore's argument for the claim that the naturalist's "definist fallacy" (as Frankena calls it) really is fallacious or mistaken.[11] Putnam agrees with Harman's assessment (which he evidently arrives at independently) that *OQ* is logically invalid. As Putnam observes, Moore is arguing that if ethical naturalism was true then some statement such as

> *S:* This action is not good even though it is conducive to maximizing utility.

is *self-contradictory.* Moore presumably demonstrates that it is not self-contradictory by observing that "This action maximizes utility, but is it good?" is an open question. Putnam argues, however, that even if *S* is not contradictory, it does not follow, as Moore must claim, that "although being Good and being conducive to maximizing total utility might be *correlated* properties, they could not be the same *identical* property."[12] According to Putnam, *OQ* rests on assumptions which he and other contemporary philosophers of language reject, the first being Moore's implicit denial of the *synthetic identity of properties*. This mistake makes *OQ* subject to the same type of criticism waged by Harman:

> One could use Moore's 'proof' to show that temperature must be a 'non-natural property,' in

fact. For one is not *contradicting oneself* when one says '*x* has temperature *T* but *x* does not have mean molecular energy *E*', where *E* is the value of the kinetic energy that corresponds to temperature *T,* even if the statement is always false as a matter of empirical fact. So, Moore would have to conclude, Temperature is only correlated with Mean Molecular Kinetic Energy; the two properties cannot literally be *identical.*[13]

Moore's mistake of assuming that an indentity of properties cannot be asserted by a synthetic statement is presumably generated by another more fundamental mistake, namely that of confusing *properties* with *concepts:*

> The *concept* 'good' may not be synonymous with any physicalistic concept (after all, moral-descriptive language and physicalistic language are extremely different 'versions', in Goodman's sense), but it does not follow that *being good* is not the same property as *being P,* for some suitable physicalistic (or, better, *functionalistic*) *P*. In general, an ostensively learned term for a property (e.g., 'has high temperature') is not synonymous with a theoretical definition of that property; it takes empirical and theoretical research, not linguistic analysis, to find out what temperature is (and, some philosopher might suggest, what *goodness* is), not reflections on meanings."[14]

Putnam further suggests that this criticism of Moore may be seen as an application of Kripke's theory of names.[15] According to Kripke, scientific identity statements like "Temperature is mean molecular kinetic energy" or "Water is H2O" are metaphysically *necessary,* since the terms "temperature" and "mean molecular energy", or "water" and "H2O," *rigidly designate,* that is, in all possible worlds, the same physicalistic property, even though we cannot know the truth of such statements a priori. Since these statements are not known to be true a priori, it is presumably an "open question" whether they are true, and consequently Moore's argument would seem to commit him here to the false conclusion that they must be *contingently* true, that is, that the properties in question cannot really be identical. Similarly, Moore argues that for any natural property *N,* goodness cannot be identical to *N*-ness since it is an open question whether *N* is good, but for Kripke goodness *is N*-ness just in case that "is good" and "has *N*" rigidly designate the same property, whether or not this identity can be known a priori, or can be "significantly questioned." On this view of the objection, then, the logical invalidity of *OQ* is due to the fact that it sets up an *epistemic* test for *metaphysical* necessity or essence, and Kripke generally denies that a-priority can be so conflated with necessity.[16] As Putnam concludes:

> These ideas of Kripke's have had widespread impact on philosophy of language, metaphysics, and philosophy of mathematics; applied to Moore's argument they are devastating. Moore argued from the fact that [S] *can only be false contingently,* that *P* (for some natural property *P*) could not be an essential property of goodness; this is what the new theory of necessity blocks. All that one can validly infer from the fact that [S] is not self-contradictory is that 'good' is not synonymous with 'conducive to maximizing utility' (not synonymous with *P,* for any term *P* in the physicalistic version of the world). From this non-synonymy of *words* nothing follows about non-identity of *properties.* Nothing follows about the essence of goodness.[17]

In an earlier writing, Putnam acknowledges Moore's insistence that he is illuminating concepts, not words, but Putnam argues that this comes to much the same thing.[18]

This criticism of Moore again raises the issue of what *OQ* is supposed to prove (or disprove). If the argument is an attempt to refute an ethical naturalist's claim about *analyticity,* or the *meanings* of the terms "good" and "ought," and so on, then it has not been shown that Kripke's ideas are so devastating. In general, Kripke's rigid-designator theory of necessity does not settle the issue of what terms mean (or the meaning of "meaning," as it has been referred to in the literature) and in fact some of what he says conveniently suggests that an epistemic criterion is appropriate for testing meanings. Kripke disassociates the qualities used to "fix the reference" of a term from the meaning of the term. Various descriptions involving accidental or contingent properties may be used to "define" a term in this reference-fixing sense—as when "gold" is defined as a yellow metal, a "meter" is defined as the length of a stick in Paris, or terms like "water," "temperature," "Hesperus" and "Phosphorus," and so on, are defined with respect to certain overt phenomenological qualities—even though, according to Kripke, such descriptions do not give the meanings of, or become *synonymous* with, these terms.[19] In the case of natural-kind terms, Kripke notes that it is not self-contradictory to suppose that a thing so described should lack the qualities paradigmatically used to pick it out, or to give a standard dictionary "definition" of it: such as, to suppose that a given tiger is three-legged, or that all "cats" might turn out to be automata or demons instead of animals.[20] Analogously, in the present meta-ethical debate, then, one might argue that ethical naturalists have confused the reference-fixing qualities of being desired, pleasurable, conducive to happiness, and so on, with the *meaning* of "good" or "obligatory," or have attempted to give "definitions" which, as Kripke puts it, *could turn out* to be false. If so, it is not clear why the test of *contradiction* posed by *OQ,* as Putnam construes it, would be irrelevant to exposing their mistake. It is not implausible to suppose that native speakers can test the meanings of their own concepts or words by asking themselves whether certain exceptions are epistemically possible, and in fact this is not obviously so different from Kripke's arguing for his theory by asking readers to consider what *name* they would apply to an object under certain hypothetical circumstances.

It is true, as Putnam points out, that an epistemic contradiction-test will not tell one what natural properties a term *refers* to, but this again appears irrelevant to the issue of meaning which Moore uses *OQ* to decide. While

Kripke distinguishes meaning and reference-fixing, he does not say (or imply) that the meaning of a term is entirely referential, or a matter of what it rigidly designates. Even if it were, Putnam's objection would still be incorrect. On this view, if "good" and "happiness-maximizing" ("pleasurable," "desired," etc.) do in fact designate the same properties, then the statement that something is good if and only if it is pleasurable, desirable, etc. becomes analytic, or true in virtue of the "meanings" of terms. The objection to *OQ*, then, should presumably be not that it is logically invalid, but that it is question-begging in its assumption that "*X* is happiness-maximizing but not good" is non-contradictory, or that the question of whether this statement can be true is really "open." Kripke, in any case, wants to say that scientifically discovered identities like "Hesperus is Phosphorus," "Gold has an atomic number of 79," or "Water is H2O" are metaphysically *necessary,* not that they are *analytic,* that the terms involved are synonyms or that this is what "gold" or "water" *means.*[21]

On Putnam's own view, the meaning of a term is not merely the same as its *extension,* though he is concerned also to refute the view that "meanings are in our heads" or are to be equated with intensional concepts. As Putnam sees it, the meaning of a term like "water" has several components, including extension and stereotypic qualities, and though the latter are part of the "meaning" of any natural-kind term, it is not analytic that all things of that kind exhibit all such qualities (e.g., a tiger may lack stripes, four legs, etc . . .).[22] Since *OQ* is supposed to establish that "good" is a "simple" notion unlike "complex" natural kinds, Putnam's latter point will not vitiate Moore's conclusion, from the non-analyticity of *S,* that "maximizes utility" is not even *part* of the *meaning* of "good." More importantly, however, as an argument against the *analyticity* of naturalistic definitions, *OQ* itself need not involve any further conclusion about this referential or extensional component of meaning. According to Putnam and Kripke, "Water is H2O" is, though necessarily true, still "a *synthetic* identity of properties," and if *OQ* is supposed to establish only the conceptual point that naturalistic definitions are synthetic, then its validity is compatible with the Putnam-Kripke result in philosophy of language.

III

These considerations prompt a closer look at the prospect of a synthetic identity in ethics, between moral and natural properties, of the same kind established by science in the analogy on which Harman and Putnam base their objection. In defense of the objection, it may be argued that Moore and other anti-naturalists using *OQ* are, after all, interested in establishing something about moral *properties,* in addition to any point about the *meaning* of moral terms. The initial force of the objection derives from the fact that Moore himself does hold a metaphysical view about what goodness is, and he does appear to deny that "good" and "conducive to happiness" are *identical* properties, even synthetically. It may also be noted

that Harman, having presented the above objection to *OQ,* goes on to suggest that this argument from the analogy between ethics and science works only against what he calls "naturalism in general," and not against "definitional naturalism."[23] Though, as seen below in Part IV, there in some equivocation in Herman's treatment of these, the former is evidently the thesis that moral properties can be *reduced* to natural ones, in the same way that science produces reductionist identities, such as that reducing color to physical and optical properties, while only the latter "definitional" variants of naturalism assert that "moral judgments [statements?] are definitionally equivalent to natural judgments," that is, yielding a synonymy of *meaning.*[24] The suggestion, then, is that *OQ* is indeed logically invalid when applied at least to "general" or (non-definitional) reductionist naturalism.

Since *OQ* is originally Moore's argument, we might begin again by inquiring whether Moore can plausibly be charged with having given a logically invalid argument against this form of naturalism. Several points should be kept in mind here. First, the invalidity objection depends crucially on the assumption that *OQ* must be an attempt to show that "good" cannot be, as Putnam puts it, a "physicalistic property"; however, if Moore in fact does not clearly delineate *properties* from *concepts,* or from *word-meaning*—as we've seen Putnam himself concedes—then presumably Moore's use of the term "property" cannot be read unambiguously as supporting this interpretation. The passage cited earlier which presents *OQ* is phrased interchangeably in terms of "predicates," "meaning," and the distinctness of "notions before our minds"—that is, which would seem to make an *epistemic* test relevant. Again, Putnam himself, earlier in the text containing his objection and elsewhere, has distinguished two senses of *property:* one pertaining to physicalistic magnitudes, and the like, in science, and an older usage which is merely an equivalent expression for "concept" or "predicate," where the principle of individuation is synonymy.[25] Thus, it is odd that Putnam or Harman should suppose that Moore must be addressing the newer, scientific sense of property required by their objection.

The foregoing point is related to a second: Moore's argument *against* naturalism need not be construed as establishing, by itself, any view about what kind of property goodness *is.* Here there is an important disanalogy between the application of *OQ* in ethics, and this style of argument as applied to "temperature" and "mean molecular energy" in science, for in ethics a popular alternative to naturalism is the emotivist or non-cognitivist view that moral language does not ascribe any properties at all, natural or non-natural. Since *OQ* does not establish non-natural properties in ethics, then, it is misleading for Putnam to criticize *OQ* on grounds that, applied in science, it would yield the conclusion that temperature is a non-natural property. According to Moore, one cannot conclude that "good" is a simple and indefinable *non-natural* property until one has eliminated *both* naturalistic theories of meaning as well as the possibility that good "means nothing at all, and there is no subject of Ethics."[26]

Admittedly, Moore thought that a second application of *OQ* could establish that "good," as compared with "pleasant," denotes a "unique property of things"—but again, in the sense of a "distinct meaning" or "unique object before the mind."[27] Writing in 1903, Moore clearly underestimates the prospect of non-cognitivist alternatives to naturalism, that is, the possibility of providing some type of subjective, emotivist (prescriptive, etc.) "meaning" for ethical terms; however, the oversight in this second argument *for* non-natural properties does not vindicate the charge that Moore's first argument *against* ethical naturalism is logically invalid, and indeed emotivists themselves have found *OQ* a persuasive argument against naturalism.[28]

It may be replied that *OQ* would still be invalid in science, even when limited to a conclusion about what "temperature" is *not;* however, the objection is otiose if there is a more fundamental disanalogy between ethics and science: namely, if there is, in ethics, no further basis, beyond conceptual or linguistic considerations, for so identifying moral properties with, or "reducing" them synthetically to, natural or physicalistic ones. The guiding spirit of naturalism in ethics is a modern, scientifically-minded quest to make moral statements confirmable by an empirical method, so as to obviate problems of the older tradition of intuitionism. The latter type of theory would make ethics most closely *analogous* to science (or at least to a prevalent picture of *that* side of the analogy) by postulating a special realm of *meta*physical moral properties and a special *extra*sensory faculty to perceive them, and this would in any case be the most obvious way to get an objective ontology of properties which moral terms might *synthetically* denote. Naturalists themselves, however, reject such properties, and Harman too denies this analogy between ethics and science, on grounds that it is not the *best explanation* of moral experience, a claim which presumably encapsulates standard empiricist arguments that have been around since Hume: 1) the non-verifiability of moral statements by the five senses, the uniqueness of a putative moral sense, disanalogies with ordinary perception, and so on; 2) the degree of moral disagreement in the world, its emotional character, systematic differences between cultures, etc.; and 3) alternative Humean accounts of the origin and function of moral belief, and so on.[29] Whether or not one accepts this line of argumentation, the point is that it is accepted by those whom *OQ* is designed to refute, and if accepted, it would tend to eliminate the prospect of synthetic identities in ethics of the sort to which Harman and Putnam call attention in science. Moreover, this prospect in ethics, which is supposed to make *OQ* invalid, is eliminated by the same type of argumentation as establishes such identities in science. Another way to put the point is to say that *OQ* may be supported by supplementary argumentation, such that the combined argument is not logically invalid, even on the Harman-Putnam interpretation. The upshot is that Moore's emphasis, then, on an epistemic or linguistic instrument of analysis should be more useful in ethics than the objection allows.

Admittedly, Moore himself could not avail himself or empiricist arguments against intuitionist or metaphysical theories of morality. On the one hand, Moore's own position is intuitionist. On the other hand, he suggests that *OQ* is sufficient against other systems of what he calls "metaphysical ethics"—exemplified in the Stoics, Spinoza, Kant or Hegel—which attempt to "reduce" (Moore's term) normative statements to, or *infer* them from, metaphysical propositions about what is real or rational, etc. Moore rejects these as committing the "naturalistic fallacy," the motor of which, as we have seen, is *OQ*.[30] Certainly *OQ* by itself, as a semantic test, does not directly refute the existence of metaphysical moral properties. This would suggest that Harman's objection to *OQ* as invalid against "general naturalism" is more applicable with respect to metaphysical theories of morality like Spinoza's or Hegel's, where the meaning of moral language is not the central issue. Such theories, however, are hardly what *OQ* is designed to refute, and in fact Moore explicitly applies *OQ* only against modern, definitional theories of meaning, not against metaphysical property-theories. Even in the latter case, *OQ* may be helpful in pointing out that an inferential move from metaphysical to moral propositions is not analytic, and therefore requires some additional, extra-semantic basis. Construed in this way, *OQ* would establish at least a *burden of proof* which shifts to the moral metaphysician. In terms of Harman's and Putnam's argument, the moral metaphysician must prove a synthetic identity, and if Moore cannot deny such an identity on empiricist grounds, neither can the metaphysician assert the identity on these grounds. Again, then, *OQ* figures to be at least an important part of an argument against a moral-to-metaphysical reductionist program.

Putnam is critical of the foregoing empiricist argumentation, but his criticism is unconvincing. Part of the argument in (3) has been recently developed by J. L. Mackie in his contention that the apparent objective status of moral values is best explained as the result of a psychological process whereby values are "projected" out into reality in order to enhance their effectiveness as a means of social control.[31] Putnam rejects this view, according to which moral experience is "mislocated subjective feeling," arguing that a theory which postulates an innate sense of justice is "simpler and more sophisticated" than the projection theory, and that a cognitive moral sense is analogous to intuition in logic, or the perception of colors.[32] In rebuttal, one might first point out that traditional moral-sense or "perception" theories are, at any rate, not *ontologically* simpler than non-cognitivism, and that a full-scale projection theory, which must give an account of the specific psychological mechanisms involved in conditioning various types of moral motivation, can get quite "sophisticated." Secondly, since intuition in logic and mathematics enters into scientific explanations, it is indirectly confirmed in a way that the putative moral sense is not, and this is still more obvious in the case of colors: One's eyesight, unlike moral insight, fits into an explanatory scheme corroborated by the other empirical senses, and it is implausible to try to *explain* colors as projected attitudes conditioned in the same way by social factors. This is not to deny the point—popular since

Kuhn, and developed also by Putnam—that *values* enter into our determination of *facts,* but even the statement of this thesis recognizes some conceptual distinction, and there appears to be an obvious difference, or asymmetry, in the *way* that facts and values characteristically arise or interrelate.[33]

A final consideration in favor of a projection theory, when fully developed, is its explanation of the psychological phenomenon of moral emotions (associated with [2] above), and the solution it offers to Hume's problem of why moral judgments motivate actions. The property theory suggested by Putnam appears explanatorily redundant, insofar as it must presumably include the same type of theory about how moral emotions evolve, or why social behavior coordinates with moral cognition. But after this psychological, or sociobiological story is told, then, ontologically objective moral properties appear to play no explanatory role. Thus, the Ockham's-razor principle of theoretical simplicity in science favors the projection theory as being not only *ontologically* simpler, but as fitting into a simpler and more coherent explanation of moral experience. The projection theory should be especially attractive to the extent that one regards even the perception of physical "facts" as functionally determined by their survival value, or human interests in adapting to or dealing conveniently with the world. Here the projection theory, which provides a similar, functionalist account of moral values, would fit into a larger, *unified* explanatory scheme, part of which would be the value of theoretical simplicity itself.

The preceding motivation argument is not self-contained, but rather connects to another empiricist argument often thought to be independent, and which Putnam independently rejects. Thus, another of Mackie's arguments against intuitionism, this one falling under the rubric of (1) above, is his contention that moral values, conceived as objective qualities in the world, be rejected as both metaphysically and epistemologically "queer" from an empiricist standpoint: that is, requiring an ontology of invisible value-entities unlike any natural objects, an imperatival element of to-be-done-ness as somehow built into certain goals or actions, invisible moral suction pipes between creditors and debtors, or invisible hooks linking individuals with objects to which they have a right, and so on.[34] The existence of such prescriptive properties, whose cognition somehow automatically motivates action, would presumably provide a response to the foregoing suggestion that an objectivist moral-property theory must be supplemented by an account of moral psychology, but if the queerness argument works, this avenue of response is unavailable. Putnam rejects the queerness argument:

> Mackie defends his claim that goodness is ontologically 'queer' by introducing as a premiss that one cannot *know* that something is good *without* having a "pro" attitude towards that something. This amounts to assuming *emotivism* in order to prove emotivism. The devils in hell are frequently depicted as using "good" with *negative*

emotive force . . . ; contrary to Mackie, I do not find such uses to be linguistically improper or to involve any contradiction.[35]

This response to the queerness argument has problems. If pro-attitudes are separated from moral cognition as Putnam asserts, then this reinstates the objection that a separate account must be given for the evolution of moral attitudes, and there is the problem again that moral properties and the moral sense become explanatorily superfluous. In any event, Putnam's agrument is off target, since the point about queerness is that the moral sense theory implies weird properties, containing an objective, cognizable imperative element, whether or not a given moral observer has the usual attitude, or has decided to act contrary to the norm. Putnam's *linguistic* argument against this fails on two grounds. First, language does, in general, reflect this imperative quality which would make moral properties strange. The uses indicated by Putnam are non-standard, and Putnam himself goes on in the above passage to observe that moral terms do, in general, have *commending* force.[36] Secondly, Putnam's argument seems to overlook the same basic point that he uses against Moore. Even if a speaker may, without *contradiction,* use moral terms without commending, a moral property may still be *synthetically* identified as prescriptive. Such a property, exemplified by Plato's form of justice, would indeed be "queer" from an empiricist perspective. The uniqueness of metaphysically objective value enities must itself be at least a factor *weighing* against their acceptance from that standpoint, but part of their "queerness" is also their lack of any explanatory function in an empiricist scheme. Of course, this entire line of argument presupposes an empiricist scheme, or what Putnam later refers to as "the assumption that the physicalistic version of the world is the Old True Theory."[37] Since the plausibility of this theory, however, connects to many issues outside of ethics, on which empiricists like Mackie give further argument, this position in ethics is in an important sense not merely an assumption.[38] The full argument is certainly not "assuming emotivism in order to prove emotivism."

Despite the traditional contrast between intuitionist and modern naturalistic theories, much of the same empiricist argumentation may be applied against a synthetic identification of moral properties with objective ones, whether physical or metaphysical. In fact both types of reduction may be viewed as forms of "naturalism": While moral-to-physical reductionism is the standard sense of naturalism (hereafter *EN*1) which *OQ* is supposed to refute, intuitionism is naturalistic in a broad sense (*EN*2), insofar as it also conceives of moral values as somehow built into "nature." Indeed, Moore implicitly suggests this similarity in his above charge that "metaphysical ethics" likewise, along with *EN*1-theories, commits the "naturalistic fallacy."[39] Though *EN*1 appears more congenial to the modern outlook than *EN*2, since the former does not postulate any metaphysical pipes or hooks in the universe, *EN*1 still implies a kind of "objective" ontology of values (goodness, justice, etc.) as *mysteriously connected* to physicalistic properties of actions (their being desired, pleasant, etc . . .).[40] As with *EN*2, then, there is a queerness argument also against *EN*1, and if there is not the same epistemic oddity about "intuiting" *EN*1 properties, there is a corresponding difficulty as to how one is supposed to "see" that moral properties are *identical* with empirically observable qualities. Putnam's own remarks above suggest that moral properties in fact cannot be so identified with any of the simple physical properties indicated in standard naturalistic definitions, such as the first-person approval theory. Putnam notes that one may intelligibly say that *X* is good without approving of it, while Moore's *OQ* makes the same point in reverse: Given that *X* is *approved,* one may still intelligibly ask "But is *X* good?" Similarly, goodness does not appear to be identifiable with any simple natural property of being approved by *others,* that is by one's society, or with promoting the general welfare (in one's society), and so on. Though the origin and function of morality may be best explained in terms of socially accepted norms which generally promote human well-being—Harman, for instance, goes on to develop such a theory—there appears to be no *single descriptive meaning* of this sort which statements about goodness or rightness must always have. If so, this would support the validity of the *OQ* test by explaining why the open question should be open; namely, that *OQ* may implicitly operate on the fact that the defect of any particular naturalistic definition is its descriptive *inflexibility.*[41] The objection by Putnam and Harman *would* work if there were *extra-linguistic* reasons to assert synthetic identities in ethics, as there are in science; however, the foregoing argumentation undermines this analogy, and again from a perspective which naturalists themselves endorse. As indicated earlier, naturalists regard their definitions as theories of *meaning,* and these considerations indicate why naturalistic theories *must* be viewed in this way, rather than as synthetic reductions.

Putnam's subsequent reaction to ethical naturalism inadvertently suggests a stronger argument for *OQ:*

> . . . We have built a certain *neutrality,* a certain *mindlessness,* into our very notion of Nature. Nature is supposed to have no interests, intentions, or point of view . . . It is this same mindlessness of Nature that makes the action-guiding [predicate] 'is right' . . . seem 'queer.' If one physicalistic property *P* were *identical* with moral rightness . . . that *would* be queer . . . It would be as if Nature itself had values.[42]

As noted above, there are presumably broad, Quinean grounds for supposing nature to be value-neutral, and while rejecting Mackie's version of the queerness argument, Putnam evidently concurs in rejecting a picture of the world as having moral values truly *built-in.* This suggests, however, that *OQ,* as a *linguistic* test, may be relevant even against a *synthetic* identity of values with natural facts. If nature really did come equipped with values, we would expect pro-attitudinal meaning to become infused into moral language, to the extent that statements identifying value and nature should indeed begin to feel *analytic.* Moore's observation that it obviously is not, then, should be relevant linguistic *evidence*

against the moral-property identity theory even in Putnam's sense. On the other hand, if value-*neutrality* is built into *our very notion* of "nature," then such fact/value identity statements can never be analytic, which is exactly what Moore's *OQ* confirms.

IV

As seen earlier, Harman raises two objections to *OQ:* 1) that it is circular, since the so-called "open question" must simply assume that moral statements are not equivalent to assertions of natural fact; and 2) that *OQ* is logically invalid, since one cannot infer the falsity of naturalism even if the open question is really open. Clearly, however, Moore cannot be making both alleged mistakes in the same argument. If *OQ* does assume as a premise the very conclusion it is trying to prove, namely, the falsity of naturalism, then at least *OQ* must be logically valid. Conversely, if the Harman-Putnam invalidity objection is correct, then Moore's desired conclusion does not follow from his premise, which assures that he has not already logically presupposed the conclusion. Thus, the new invalidity objection, based on an analogy to science, contains some good news for Moore, for if *OQ* is logically invalid, then at least the usual circularity objection must be incorrect. On the other hand, if the invalidity objection fails, as argued above, *OQ* is still vulnerable to the charge of circularity. We will see that there is also an alternative way to formulate the invalidity objection so as to accommodate the analysis of Part III. Further examination is needed, then, to determine which, if either, mistake Moore makes.

The conflict between the objections may be removed by saying that *OQ* is circular when applied to some types of naturalism, and invalid when applied to others. We have already seen that ethical naturalisms can be classified in terms of the kind of "natural facts" to which morality is reduced, and there are additionally different kinds of "reduction"—scientific or explanatory reduction, as contrasted to the semantic type with which Moore is primarily concerned. It may be argued, then, that *OQ* is *circular* against *semantic* naturalistic definitions, and *invalid* only against non-semantic reductions. Harman *suggests* this when, having presented the invalidity objection, he remarks, "The open question argument is often put forward as a refutation, not of ethical naturalism in general, but of a more particular version, which we might call definitional naturalism"; however, he goes on to argue that *OQ* is invalid also against at least some "definitional" forms of naturalism:

> There are, however, various kinds of definitions and the open question argument is not relevant to most of them. For example, a scientist defines water as H2O and, as we have seen, the open question argument applied to this definition does not refute it.[43]

It is misleading for Harman to pick scientific "definitions" as illustrative of definitional naturalism in ethics. Though Harman never explicitly formulates what "general" naturalism is, the general idea seems to be a type of reduction which depends on *explanation* rather than "word meanings," and on this characterization scientific reductions are "general" rather than "definitional."[44] In any case, as has been argued, the definitions of science are established by a type of non-semantic reduction which is disanalogous to anything available in ethics, due to the sort of arguments that Harman himself elsewhere acknowledges. Consequently, "most definitions," including those of science, are simply irrelevant to appraising *OQ* in ethics; the appropriate conclusion would seem to be not that *OQ* is invalid against, but that it is merely *inapplicable* to, non-semantic definitions. As to the application of *OQ* to semantic definitions, Harman appears to fall back on the circularity objection:

> Presumably the open question argument is aimed at someone who claims that a naturalistic definition captures the meaning of a moral term in the sense that moral judgments as we ordinarily use them are synonymous with judgments that describe natural facts. If it really is an open question whether an act that is *C* is an act that ought to be done—an open question even to someone who knows the meanings of "C" and "ought to be done," how can "C" and "ought to be done" be synonymous? It must be shown, not just assumed, however, that the relevant question is always open, no matter what the natural characteristics *C*.[45]

The circularity objection, then, is that Moore, and subsequent theorists who use his argument, have merely *assumed* that the open question is open, which is precisely what ethical naturalism denies.

Contrary to this traditional view, I wish to argue that *OQ*, properly construed, can provide a helpful type of ethical argument which is neither logically invalid nor circular, even against semantic definitions. Whether proponents of *OQ* merely assume the falsity of naturalism depends in the first instance on what the test for an "open question" is. In the passage quoted at the outset, Moore says that a question is "open" if it can be *significantly asked,* that is, if we understand what it means to *doubt* or to deny an affirmative answer. Clearly, then, for a question to be "significant" it is not a sufficient condition that it be merely *intelligible* in the sense of being capable of an answer, as is a ("closed") question trivially answered in the affirmative, such as, "Is the Pope Catholic?"; nor is it a necessary condition of "significance" that a question be meaningful in the sense that its answer is *informative,* i.e., adding to one's present knowledge, as exemplified by the (usually) pointless (but "open") question "Is radioactivity harmful?"[46] These examples suggest another interpretation, namely that a question is open/significant if it is *logically possible* or not self-contradictory to answer it in the negative. If this is the criterion of an "open question," then Frankena and others who have waged the standard objection are right: Moore's argument appears circular.[47] Where "C" is a natural term and "M" is a moral expression such as "ought to be done," the very thesis of naturalism is that some substitutions of "C" and

"M" *mean* the same, that is, that it is *not* logically possible to answer negatively some question of the form Q, "Are all C's also M's?" On a fourth interpretation, however, the open-question test is based not on *logical* possibility, but rather on the *psychological* possibility of being in *doubt,* or of *thinking* that one *understands* such doubt. This comports with the pervasive emphasis in Moore's remarks indicating that the *OQ* test is essentially *subjective*—based on "what we are thinking," what is "before our minds," or what we *think* is before our minds.[48] Oddly, this construal also squares with what appears to be Putnam's and Harman's own view that the *OQ* test is basically *epistemic* in some sense. But when Moore's argument is so construed, and applied against semantic naturalism, the argument must be at least *non-circular,* since a premise purporting to state only a psychological fact, about what one thinks could be doubted, is not itself merely a statement about what terms mean, what is logically possible, or what ethical naturalism says about this.

On the other hand, the argument is not obviously invalid, either. When applied against semantic definitions, the type of "epistemic" test involved in this version of Moore's argument operates, more specifically, on the basis of pre-philosophic *linguistic* intuitions. Moore is suggesting that the *mere fact,* as he puts it, that we ordinarily find at least "questionable" or doubtable a proposition equating a pair of *C* and *M* terms in ordinary language, is relevant to determining whether such a theory is correct. There is no reason to suppose that what people *think* they can imagine, or "have before their minds," cannot be useful in testing theories of *meaning*—if not theories of *metaphysics,* as discussed in Part III. There is something common-sensical, after all, about testing theories of word meaning by the linguistic behavior and attitudes of native speakers; indeed, there is otherwise some problem as to the sense in which "theories" of meaning are to be tested at all.

Before subjecting this version of Moore's argument to further critical analysis, it should be noted that the argument thus far is incomplete. Fully elaborated, the main strategy is to use *openness* as a test for *synonymy,* and various formulations of this link are available. In the above passage, apart from the point about doubtability, Moore makes *three* observations in reaction against Russell's definition of "good" as what we "desire to desire": i) that $Q1$, "Is it good to desire to desire [action] *A?*", is open (intelligible, informative, etc.); ii) that if Russell's alleged synonymy were correct, $Q1$ would be equivalent to $Q2$, "Do we desire to desire that we desire *A?*", but clearly $Q1$ and $Q2$ are not equivalent, Moore says, for when we think of $Q1$ "we have not before our minds anything so *complicated . . .*" as $Q2$ (italics added); and iii) that "moreover" it is obvious by inspection that an affirmative answer to $Q1$ (viz., "It is good that we desire to desire *A*") is not equivalent to "It is good that *A* is good," as presumably it would be if Russell's definition were correct.[49] In the above notation, then, the main *OQ* test for synonymy, as suggested by (i), is the following:

*T*1 A *C*-term is *not synonymous* with an *M*-term if the corresponding question of form *Q* is *open* (in the psychological sense).

Perhaps in (iii) Moore's point is that *Q*3, "Is it good that *A* is good?", is not open; whereas *Q*1 is—indicating that the terms exchanged are not synonymous. This is not merely a reiteration of the first argument, since *Q*3 is not a *Q*-type question in terms of *C*'s and *M*'s. There must be an additional synonymy test:

*T*2 A *C*-term is synonymous with an *M*-term if the result of replacing an occurrence of either by the other in the corresponding *Q*-question does not change *Q*'s open/closed status.

On the other hand, the preceding argument does not add much in practice, since it requires that one already know the original question, *Q*1, to be open, which would seem more obviously to settle the issue under *T*1. Perhaps in (iii), then, Moore is merely dramatizing the fact that *Q*1 is indeed open—that is, by contrasting it to an obviously closed question whose answer is a tautology. Alternatively, the point in (iii) may be merely to rework (ii), the point being that *Q*3 is obviously *simpler* than *Q*1. The complexity (or simplicity) argument in (ii) suggests several direct tests for synonymy which do not really involve an "open question":

*T*3 A *C*-term is synonymous with an *M*-term if the result of replacing one for the other in a statement (question) does not change the complexity of that statement (question), or its practical function.

The latter idea of the practical use of a statement (or question), though not explicitly in Moore, is illustrated in Hare's adaptation of *OQ* where it is observed that the statement "An *A* which is *C* is good" can *commend* or *guide choices*, while "An *A* which is *C* is *C*" cannot.[50] Again, however, it is plausible that Moore intends (ii) not as a separate line of argument, but as reinforcing the first argument: that is, variation in the complexity of terms may be a factor which dramatizes the openness of a question, *makes* the question open or explains *why* native speakers so regard it. Similarly, in Hare's argument, the prescriptive or emotive meaning of *M*-terms, but not *C*-terms, would be—for contemporary theorists, if not for Moore—an additional factor explaining the psychological "feel" of openness in questions of the form "Are all *C*'s also *M*'s?"

If nothing further were said, the foregoing linguistic interpretation of *OQ* would be unlikely to impress many of Moore's contemporary critics, though the appropriate objection is neither circularity nor the new type of invalidity objection waged by Harman and Putnam. The latter objection is in fact compatible with at least the essential insight of the circularity objection. Harman's and Putnam's point was that even if a naturalistic definition is not *analytic*, Moore cannot *validly infer* that the definition (i.e., as stating a synthetic identity) is false, but one might argue at the same time that the *OQ* test fails, in the

first step, to show the non-analyticity of such definitions. The central difficulty is that native speakers may simply be wrong about what terms *mean*. The precise character of this fallibility problem may be put in perspective by considering Moore's replacement arguments, which begin to look much like the infamous intentional fallacy:

1. Descartes knows that his body is spatially extended and divisible.

2. Descartes does not know that his mind is spatially extended and divisible.

3. Leibniz's Law (ranging over intentional properties).

4. Therefore, mind and body cannot be identical.

Compare:

1'. Moore knows (does not doubt) that *X* is desired.

2'. Moore does not know (can doubt) that *X* is good.

3'. *LL*

4'. Therefore, being desired is not identical with being good.

When we apply the stock objection that has been given to the Cartesian mind-body argument, this formulation of Moore's nature-morality argument is *either* logically invalid, i.e., if (2') is read *de dicto*, or circular, where (2') is taken *de re* and where one *assumes* that it is true. (Another standard objection, that intentional properties do not exist, or are not subsumed under Leibniz's Law, would generate a different kind of invalidity objection.) The above formulation of *OQ*, however, is not exactly Moore's argument, since Moore does not appear to rely in this way on intentional properties, and as argued in Part III above, *OQ* does not have to be an epistemic test of the *referential* meaning of terms. Moreover, the comparison of Descartes and Moore underscores the fact that, as just seen, the *OQ* test is subjective or psychological—that is, Moore's "significantly asks" is not a *de re* intentional verb. When construed *de dicto*, Moore's argument is again plausible, since presumably even the Cartesian argument, read *de dicto*, may validly and non-circularly establish that the *terms* "mind" and "body" differ in connotative, if not denotative, meaning. Still, critics may reasonably contend that Moore's argument for non-analyticity commits a similar, less circuitous form of *argumentum ignoratium*.[51] This is suggested especially by Moore's remarks on complexity—to wit: Native speakers do *not know* that *X* and *Y* are synonymous, possibly because *Y* is more complicated; therefore, they are not. The appropriate objection to *OQ*, then, is that it is *logically invalid* after all, but on grounds entirely different from what Harman and Putnam indicate in their analogy to science.

Though more plausible than the standard circularity objection, the foregoing objection to *OQ* is unsuccessful.

Admittedly, native speakers are not experts at judging philosophic theories of meaning; on the other hand, neither does the above argumentation establish that prephilosophic linguistic intuitions are *irrelevant* to testing such theories. In general, this charge of invalidity derives much of its strength from interpreting *OQ* as i) the claim that linguistic intuitions are a *conclusive* refutation of ethical naturalism, rather than merely relevant *evidence* against it, and as ii) an attempt to refute all naturalistic definitions *in toto*, without the need to apply the test *seriatum* to particular definitions so as to accumulate the evidence. Moore can deny both, and even if he did hold (i) or (ii), those who use *OQ* today need not. It is true that Moore himself concludes that no naturalistic definition works, but he has no doubt considered all of the prominent proposals by naturalists, against which *OQ* has seemed effective, and he may simply be drawing a good *inductive* inference that it will continue to be effective against any other definitions of the same sort. Having presented *OQ,* as applied to Russell's definition, Moore does explicitly say that one must continue to apply the test, for example, against a hedonistic definition:

> But whoever will attentively consider with himself what is actually before his mind when he asks the question 'Is pleasure (or whatever it may be) after all good?' can easily satisfy himself that he is not merely wondering whether pleasure is pleasant. *And if he will try this experiment with each suggested definition in succession,* he may become expert enough to recognize that in every case he has before his mind a unique object, with regard to the connection of which with any other object, a distinct question may be asked. (italics added)[52]

While it is clear that Moore does not think one should infer the falsity of all naturalistic theories from one linguistic experiment, he also does not contend that native speakers are automatically "experts" here without "attentively considering" their linguistic intuitions, or (as he puts it on the previous page) exercising some "reflection."

These considerations raise larger issues, concerning the relationship of ethics to linguistics, which cannot be explored in the present essay; however, the initial plausibility of the above argument is in fact *supported* by contemporary reflection related to science. The argument has been that Moore's test at least focuses on relevant data, having evidentiary weight for (dis)confirming naturalistic theories of meaning. Here one must additionally observe that the format of Moore's test is at any rate not merely to treat native speakers as linguistic experts who pass judgment directly on a given naturalistic theory of meaning—they are not simply asked whether they think a given definition is correct. Instead, the point of posing a question to speakers, and asking them whether they *seem* to understand its denial, is presumably to "catch them in the act," so to speak, of actual linguistic behavior, *not* of meta-linguistic theorizing. Surely, this first-order linguistic behavior should have some general relevance to testing a theory of synonymy or analyticity. Thus, from a Quinean point of view, the analyticity of statements is determined by a behavioristic test that gauges the degree of one's *reluctance to deny or revise* them, as determined ultimately by the overall fit of one's conceptual scheme with experience.[53] Similarly, Moore's test measures the intuitive reluctance of speakers to deny, for instance, that a pleasant thing is good. Whether or not one finds the argument compelling in every instance, reliance upon this sort of linguistic data, as a general test of semantic definitions, appears to be neither circular nor invalid.

NOTES

[1] G. E. Moore, *Principia Ethica* (Cambridge: Cambridge University Press, 1980), pp. 15 ff. First published in 1903.

[2] Gilbert Harman, *The Nature of Morality* (Oxford: Oxford University Press, 1977), p. 19. Cf. W. K. Frankena, *Ethics* (Englewood Cliffs: Prentice-Hall, 1973), pp. 99 ff.

[3] Harman, *loc. cit.*

[4] Naturalistic definitions may also be proposed as *stipulative* or *reformative*, and admittedly ethical naturalists themselves may not always distinguish these; however, historical naturalists characteristically claim that their definitions capture at least the substantial content of what ethical terms mean in everyday usage. Cf. Richard B. Brandt, *Ethical Theory* (Prentice-Hall, 1959), pp. 156 ff.

[5] Moore, *op. cit.,* p. 7.

[6] *Ibid.,* pp. 17-19, 66 ff.

[7] Harman, *op. cit.,* p. viii.

[8] See Hilary Putnam, *Mind, Language and Reality in Philosophical Papers,* Vol. 2 (Cambridge: Cambridge University Press, 1975), pp. 14, 36. On the reaction to Quine's arguments, cf. also Roderick Chisholm, *Theory of Knowledge,* 2nd edition (Englewood Cliffs: Prentice-Hall, 1977, 2nd edition), p. 61.

[9] If the meta/normative distinction has been "undermined" at all, surely ethical theorists like Hare have had more to do with this than Quine. Actually, however, even if one agrees (with Hare) that substantive normative conclusions are to be founded on linguistic intuitions, this would presumably show only that there are interesting connections *between* "meta-ethics" and "normative ethics," not that a useful schema for separating (or so relating) ethical issues has been undermined. It is perhaps still less plausible, as Harman also suggests in the cited passage, that Quine's attack on the analytic-synthetic distinction is what precipitated the shift away from *linguistic* meta-ethics toward "substantive" normative concerns in the 60's and 70's. Oddly enough, having expressed his dissatisfaction with the older linguistic tradition of meta-ethics (c. 1930-1960—cf. *op. cit.,* pp. vii, ix), Harman

proceeds to develop a theory of moral relativism which relies upon linguistic arguments: cf. Chs. 9 and 10.

[10] Hilary Putnam, *Reason, Truth and History* (Cambridge: Cambridge University Press, 1981), pp. 205 ff.

[11] The classic piece on this is W. K. Frankena's "Naturalistic Fallacy," reprinted in the collection of his essays ed. by Kenneth E. Goodpaster, *Perspectives in Morality* (Notre Dame: University of Notre Dame Press, 1976). Frankena makes four major points: (1) that any such inference from *is* to *ought* can be made logically valid simply by adding a naturalistic definition as a premise (p. 4); (2) that if this premise is regarded as an "ought" proposition, then Moore is not merely endorsing Hume's is/ought bifurcation (p. 5); (3) that, in any case, if Moore is objecting to a type of definition, then the term "fallacy" is a misnomer (*loc. cit*); and (4) that Moore has no real argument against such definitions (pp. 8f). Though (1)-(3) are technically correct and conceptually illuminating, it is reasonable to view Moore's "naturalistic fallacy" as being essentially in the spirit of Hume's reaction against the "imperceptible" inferential move from *is* to *ought* in "vulgar morality." Moore reinforces Hume's bifurcation by also disallowing any "perceptible" or overt definitional connections between "is" and "ought" in less vulgar systems of ethics, and as Frankena later saw (cf. *Ibid.*, p. 210), *OQ* is the argument at work behind the scenes here.

[12] Putnam, *Reason, Truth and History, op. cit.* p. 206.

[13] *Ibid.*, pp. 206-7.

[14] *Ibid.*, p. 207.

[15] *Ibid.*, pp. 207-8.

[16] Putnam explicitly discusses neither Moore's concept of an "open question" nor Kripke's concept of "rigid designation." See Saul Kripke, *Naming and Necessity* (Cambridge, MA: Harvard University Press, 1980), pp. 34-39. (Putnam does not cite specific pages.) Cf. also *id.*, "Identity and Necessity," *Identity and Individuation*, ed. by Milton K. Munitz (New York: New York University Press, 1971), pp. 149 ff.

[17] *Ibid.*, p. 208.

[18] Putnam, *Mind, Language and Reality*, pp. 3, 8 ff.

[19] Cf. *Naming and Necessity*, pp. 26, 54 ff., 116 ff., 135 ff.

[20] *Ibid.*, pp. 119 ff, 122, 125-26.

[21] Cf. *ibid.*, pp. 103 ff., 125, 128, 141 ff. Kripke does not try to explicate the concept of analyticity. He *stipulates* an "analytic" truth to be "one which depends on *meanings* in the strict sense and therefore is necessary as well as a priori": pp. 56, n. 21; 122f, n. 63; and cf. pp. 39,

56n. Since the above truths are not known *a priori*, then, this presumably indicates that the terms do not "mean" the same even though they refer to the same objects. In the p. 122 note Kripke also recognizes a sense of analyticity whereby a statement can be known a priori due to its being true by "definition" in the reference-fixing sense. This would make some analytic truths contingent, but they still do not involve *synonyms* for Kripke: cf. pp. 14 ff. 63.

[22] Addressing the example of the "twin earth" in which what is called "water" turns out to be not H2O but rather some other chemical composition *XYZ*, Putnam sees two options for a theory of meaning to go with Kripke's theory that names of natural kinds are rigid designators: 1) to say that the word "water" in the two worlds (our earth and the "twin") has the same meaning but different extensions, i.e., to identify meanings with concepts, or ii) to say, as Putnam prefers, that "meaning determines extension," so that different extensions automatically indicate different meanings: cf. *Mind, Language and Reality*, pp. 223 ff., 234, 245 ff; "water" is defined at p. 269; for the point about meaning and ambiguity, cf. pp. 140 ff., 250, 256.

[23] Harman, *op. cit.*, p. 19.

[24] *Ibid.*, pp. 19-20; ethical "reduction" is discussed on the previous page, and is introduced at pp. 13-14 in connection with the idea of explanation.

[25] Cf. *Reason, Truth and History*, p. 84, and "On Properties," reprinted in *Mathematics, Matter and Method* in *Philosophical Papers*, Vol. 1 (Cambridge: Cambridge University Press, 1979), pp. 305 ff. Putnam illustrates what "predicates" are with the timely example of "Is existence a predicate?" (i.e., one of Moore's famous titles), though observing that this is not merely a syntactical issue.

[26] Moore, *op. cit.*, p. 15. Harman echoes the same point where he notes that moral "nihilism" is an alternative to naturalism: *Ibid.*, p. 17. Oddly, he refers to nihilism here as a form of naturalism, though "extreme nihilism," as Harman conceives it (i.e., moral skepticism) appears neither to "reduce" morality *to* anything, nor to be a "definitional" theory of morality.

[27] *Ibid.*, p. 17. The arguments against naturalistic meaning, and against the meaninglessness of 'good', are given in paragraphs (1) and (2), respectively.

[28] For example, with "emotivist" being used here in a broad sense: R. M. Hare, *The Language of Morals* (Oxford: Clarendon Press, 1963), pp. 90 ff. An emotivist theory of what moral terms *do* mean would provide a type of argument, other than *OQ*, for criticizing all naturalistic definitions. Cf. C. L. Stevenson, *Ethics and Language* (New Haven: Yale University Press, 1944).

[29] Harman discusses the problem of observation in *The Nature of Morality*, pp. 6-9. He does not explicitly ad-

dress "intuitionism," nor does he articulate this auxiliary argumentation, which however is needed to make good the claim that intuitionism is not the "best explanation." Accordingly, it should be understood that empiricists need not regard any single argument in the above categories as conclusive. Instead, the arguments may be regarded as cumulatively constituting a *case* against intuitionist or rationalistic ethics. This case also connects to arguments beyond ethics—cf. n. 38 below.

[30] Moore, *op. cit.*, pp. 114 ff. In Moore's terminology, the "metaphysical" is "supersensible," or what does not exist in time (pp. 110 ff.). By contrast, Moore's intuited "non-natural" quality of goodness attaches to natural objects which are perceptible by the senses. See Hasna Begum, "Moore on Goodness and the Naturalistic Fallacy" *Australasian Journal of Philosophy,* vol. 57 (1979), pp. 251 ff.

[31] J. L. Mackie, *Ethics: Inventing Right and Wrong* (Harmondsworth: Penguin Books, 1977), pp. 42 ff. Cf. C. L. Stevenson's characterization of non-natural qualities as "an invisible shadow cast by confusion and emotive meaning": *Ethics and Language, op. cit.*), p. 109.

[32] *Reason, Truth and History, op. cit.*, pp. 142, 144-47. Mackie is not explicitly addressed here.

[33] As one commentator recently suggests, our beliefs about the injustice of slavery are not *forced* on us by the physical properties of objects, i.e., in the same way as our belief that fire engines are red is forced on us: Dworkin in *Ronald Dworkin and Contemporary Jurisprudence,* ed. by Marshall Cohen (Totowa: Rowman & Allanheld, 1984), p. 277. Putnam is concerned here to deny that belief in justice is like belief in ghosts, a view which he associates with the projection theory; however, Hume too distinguished belief in justice from mere superstition without postulating moral properties: *An Enquiry Concerning the Principles of Morals* (Indianapolis: Hackett Publishing Co., 1983), Sec. III, p. 31. On the comparison of ethics and mathematics, cf. Harman, *The Nature of Morality*, pp. 9 ff.

[34] Mackie, *op. cit.*, pp. 40, 74.

[35] *Reason, Truth and History, op. cit.*, p. 209.

[36] *Ibid.*, pp. 209-10. Putnam observes (p. 210) that "good" is *more* often used without personal approval than are "should," "ought," "right," etc.; but even the latter have intelligible non-standard, non-approving usages: Cf. Harman, *The Nature of Morality*, pp. 47 ff., 122-24. Nor does Mackie say that *all* uses of "good" imply personal approval: Cf. p. 55.

[37] *Reason, Truth and History, op. cit.*, p. 210.

[38] Thus, an intuitionist or moral objectivist, who does not merely *assume* that the physicalist version of the world is *false,* might go on to argue that empiricism is implausible

in other areas of philosophy, and therefore unreliable in ethics—an argument which empiricists may go on to rebut: Cf. Mackie, *Ethics, op. cit.*, p. 39. A more modest argument would be that empiricism—presumably no less than rationalism—rests on an "assumption" in the sense that the choice, or "success," of any ultimate principle of knowledge depends at least partly on one's initial, common-sense judgement as to what metaphysical objects exist, or what obviously *is known* (i.e., another G. E. Moore shift, writ large). Thus, the games of metaphysics and epistemology must be played simultaneously, with ethics as one, of many, substantive application areas. Chisholm has argued that the epistemological problems of morality, other minds, and God are interrelated in this way: *Theory of Knowledge, op. cit.*, pp. 3, 119 ff. Contrary to Chisholm's own "choice" here, one might conclude that there is no ethical knowledge of the kind commonly supposed, if a non-cognitivist explanation can be given for that supposition, and on the basis of empiricist principles (Quinean rather than positivist) which have acceptable implications in other areas. This much broader claim, at any rate, underlies the foregoing arguments in ethics.

[39] See n. 30 above. Cf. R. L. Franklin, "Recent Work in Ethical Naturalism" in *American Philosophical Quarterly Studies in Ethics,* (1973), p. 55, distinguishing naturalism in the first sense (*EN*1), according to which moral statements express empirically or scientifically ascertainable facts, apart from the will of God or intuition, from the second, broader sense (*EN*2), according to which moral statements express facts, even if non-natural or metaphysical ones. *EN*2, then, includes what might be called "ethical super-naturalism," where moral properties are intuited and revealed by God, and perhaps it would have been more accurate had Moore characterized the fallacy of (non-theistic) metaphysical ethics as committing the "super-naturalistic fallacy."

[40] Cf. Mackie, *Ethics, op. cit.*, pp. 38, 41. Of course, desires, pleasant experiences, etc., are "subjective" in a sense, and Mackie so labels a naturalistic approval definition as denying the metaphysical brand of moral "objectivity" in Plato's forms: Cf. pp. 17, 23 ff. Still, the psychological or social phenomena involved in *EN*1 definitions constitute a type of "objective" fact which moral statements may *describe,* and to which values attach.

[41] Cf. *ibid.*, pp. 50, 60-61.

[42] *Reason, Truth and History, op. cit.*, p. 211.

[43] Harman, *The Nature of Morality, op. cit.*, p. 19.

[44] Cf. p. 18, and nn. 23f above. Earlier Harman characterizes naturalism as the "general view" that "*all* facts are facts of nature" (p. 17), and subsequently observes that the "general naturalist" abandons religion (p. 21). Thus, a "general naturalist" need not subscribe to *ethical* naturalism, which in turn comes in "general" and "definitional" variants. Harman thus

appears to exclude from the ambit of "naturalism" the EN2 theories discussed in Part III.

[45] *Ibid.*, pp. 19 ff.

[46] Cf. *Principia Ethica, op. cit.,* pp. 15f. Moore associates the notion of an "open" question both with its "intelligibility" and the "information" it calls for; however, as just seen, these latter notions are overly broad. Of course, a question may "call for information" which one already has, and this broader sense of an answer's being "informative" does seem to be central to the notion of "openness." Cf. Brandt's discussion, which mentions this only as indicating the difficulty of equating open (or intelligible) questions with those that are not "pointless": *Ethical Theory, op. cit.,* pp. 164-65. But Moore presumably has in mind *non-linguistic* "information," and the more basic test of when a question calls for any such information appears to be *doubtability,* the idea with which Moore concludes the passage, and on which the circularity objection focuses.

[47] Cf. note 2 above, and Roger Hancock, "The Refutation of Naturalism in Moore and Hare," *The Journal of Philosophy,* vol. 58 (1960), pp. 328 ff.

[48] *Principia Ethica, op. cit.,* p. 16. Cf. Frank Snare, "The Open Question as a Linguistic Test," *Ratio,* vol. 17 (1975), p. 126. This essay contains the basic move for defending Moore, though without regarding this as Moore's own view of *OQ* (p. 129), and more importantly, without supplying the needed argumentation developed below. When this argument is supplied, it is not at all obvious that Moore himself—who was clearly cognizant of the fact that he was trying to refute a certain type of *linguistic* theory—did not view the *OQ* argument as involving a linguistic test.

[49] *Ibid.*, pp. 15 ff.

[50] R. M. Hare, *The Language of Morals, op. cit.,* pp. 82 ff., 89 ff., 145, 195. Compare also Fred Feldman, *Introductory Ethics* (Prentice-Hall, 1978), pp. 199-203. Feldman formulates two versions of *OQ,* the first being roughly a restricted "complexity" version of *T3* (p. 200), and a second corresponding to *T1* (p. 203). This discussion is typical of the literature in that the operative notion of 'openness' is left unanalyzed, and consequently something like the *T1*-variant is charged with circularity.

[51] The intentional fallacy may be viewed as merely a fancy type of argument from ignorance.

[52] *Principia Ethica, op. cit.,* p. 16.

[53] W. V. O. Quine, "Two Dogmas of Empiricism" in *From a Logical Point of View* (Harvard, 1953), pp. 24, 27, 31, 37 ff., 41. In the Quinean chain of analysis, *synonymy* for *single terms* is defined as interchangeability in truth-functionally synonymous *statements,* which in turn are characterized by *analyticity*—the latter resting finally on a behavioristic criterion. Cf. M. White, "The Analytic and the Synthetic: An Untenable Dualism" in *Semantics and Philosophy of Language,* ed. by Leonard Linsky (Urbana-Champaign: University of Illinois Press, 1952): the notion of "self-contradiction" characterized by "a certain feeling of horror or queerness" which native speakers have, or their "degree of discomfort" (p. 325).

Erwin R. Steinberg (essay date 1988)

SOURCE: "G. E. Moore's Table and Chair in 'To The Lighthouse'," in *Journal of Modern Literature,* Vol. 15, No. 1, Summer, 1988, pp. 161-68.

[*In the following excerpt, Steinberg examines elements of Moore's philosophy in the text of Virginia Woolf's novel* To the Lighthouse.]

Over the years critics have argued that Virginia Woolf's fiction echoes the philosophy of, variously, Henri Bergson, Plato, G. E. Moore, John McTaggart, Bertrand Russell, Friedrich Nietzsche, Sigmund Freud, and C. G. Jung. Since many of these men professed widely differing philosophies, the only conclusion that can be drawn from all of these mutually contradictory claims and counterclaims is that, in her novels, Virginia Woolf does not espouse, adhere to, instantiate, or even reflect the ideas of any particular philosopher or philosophy.[1]

In her writing, Virginia Woolf treats philosophy gingerly. In *A Room of One's Own,* for example, after encouraging women "to write books of travel and adventure, and research and scholarship, and history and biography, and criticism and philosophy and science," she comments, "Thus when I ask you to write more books I am urging you to do what will be for your good and for the good of the world at large. How to justify this instinct or belief I do not know, for philosophic words, if one has not been educated at a university, are apt to play one false." Virginia Woolf, of course, had not been educated at a university.[2]

It is not surprising, therefore, that in "A Sketch of the Past," a memoir that she wrote a year and a half before her death, Woolf is diffident about claiming to have "a philosophy." In that memoir she describes instances of what she calls "exceptional moments," moments much like what James Joyce called "epiphanies." Each such moment is a shock, a moment of insight, which is "followed by the desire to explain it." The "shock-receiving capacity," she believes, and presumably the attendant desire to write about it, "is what makes me a writer." Each shock "is a token of some real thing behind appearances; and I make it real by putting it into words. . . . make it whole":

> Perhaps this is the strongest pleasure known to me. . . . From this I reach what I might call a philosophy; at any rate it is a constant idea of mine; that behind the cotton wool is hidden a pattern; that we—I mean all human beings—are connected with this; that the whole world is a work of art; that we are parts of that work of art. . . .

This intuition of mine—it is so instinctive that it seems given to me, not made by me—has certainly given its scale to my life ever since I saw the flower in the bed by the front door at St. Ives [the occasion of the first shock that Woolf remembers]. . . . And this conception affects me every day.[3]

A philosophy? Well, perhaps only a constant idea—intuitive at that—"given" to her and not carefully developed the way a philosopher develops and thinks through a philosophy: perhaps a (mere?) conception.

In the index to *Moments of Being,* the collection of Woolf's autobiographical writings, there are no references to Bergson, McTaggart, Nietzsche, or Wittgenstein. There is a single reference to Moore and the influence of ***Principia Ethica*** on the Thursday evening meetings of "Old Bloomsbury" and two mentions of social situations in which Woolf found herself in a group with Russell. Woolf's five references to Plato are incidental comments about Plato, not discussions of his philosophy.

Three of the pieces in *Moments of Being* were papers which Woolf delivered, as Jeanne Schulkind reports, "to the Memoir Club, a group of close friends of long standing who gathered at intervals to read memoirs in which they were committed to complete candour. The intimate character of the Memoir Club is evident in the tone that pervades the three papers. . . ."[4] Certainly if Woolf had been aware of the influence of any philosopher on her thinking or writing or of her respect for a particular philosopher or even of her awareness of parallel themes in her writings and the writings of a particular philosopher, she would, in an atmosphere of complete candor, speaking intimately to a group of close friends, have noted it.

Woolf shows elsewhere a similar lack of interest in philosophy. In "On Not Knowing Greek," for example, when she discusses Plato, she notes how he sets an indoor scene and lists the questions that Socrates, Protagoras, Alcibiades, and others discuss. But it is "the dramatic genius" of Plato that interests her rather than any particular philosophical idea beyond what she learned from him of the variousness of truth.[5]

Much earlier—in August of 1908—she had complained to Clive Bell and Sydney Saxon-Turner of the difficulty she was having reading Moore's ***Principia Ethica.*** Ten years later, in her diary, Woolf notes that she is not as impressed with "the moral eminence of Moore" as her husband and others are; and two years after that she notes, again in her diary, that she is "too muddled" to follow Moore's attempt to explain Berkeley to her and comments that "he has grown grey, sunken. . . . a lack of mass somewhere." Thus she had to struggle with Moore's ethics and concluded by deprecating the philosopher. There is no record that she tried to understand or even read anything else that he wrote.[6]

All of this suggests not only a lack of interest in any particular philosophy and, indeed, in philosophy as a study in general, but also an inability to grapple with many of the basic concepts of philosophy. I say this not to deprecate Woolf; being able to follow Moore's explanation of Berkeleyean idealism, for example, is not necessarily a test of intelligence. The conclusion does, however, speak to the likelihood that Woolf had a well-thought through or even a consistent "philosophy"—and to whether she was a disciple of any philosopher or whether her ideas consistently "paralleled" those of any philosopher.

In his essay on "The Philosophical Realism of Virginia Woolf," however, S. P. Rosenbaum suggests two ways in which Moore as a person and his ideas figure in *To the Lighthouse*—neither of them necessarily contradicted by the conclusion above. But there is stronger evidence than Rosenbaum offers that Woolf probably at least glanced through Moore's ***Philosophical Studies.*** First, Rosenbaum quotes Andrew's statement to Lily on what his father's books were about:

> "Subject and object and the nature of reality," Andrew had said. And when she said Heavens, she had no notion what that meant. "Think of a kitchen table then," he told her, "when you're not there." (38)

Rosenbaum comments,

> Brief, vague, and fanciful as it is, this is an account not of Leslie Stephen's empiricism but of G. E. Moore's realism, where kitchen tables exist apart from our perceptions of them. **"The Refutation of Idealism"** is on this very subject. It even has an example of a table existing in space.

The second point which Rosenbaum makes is that "certain features of Ramsay's career resemble Moore's."[7]

"The Refutation of Idealism" was first printed in *Mind* in 1903. More important, however, it was republished in Moore's ***Philosophical Studies*** in 1922, about three years before Woolf began thinking about *To The Lighthouse.*[8] Given the high esteem in which some of the men in the Bloomsbury group held Moore, the book must have caused considerable discussion among them over a period of time and thus must have been quite visible to Woolf over that same period. It would be reasonable to hypothesize, therefore, that even if she did not read the book, she might have browsed through it and noticed various surface features, such as the fact that, as Rosenbaum mentions, it is about the nature of reality and that one of Moore's examples is a kitchen table. Indeed, the correspondence is even a little better than that. Towards the end of the novel, Lily thinks as she works on her painting:

> One must hold the scene—so—in a vise and let nothing come in and spoil it. One wanted, she thought, dipping her brush deliberately, to be on a level with ordinary experience, to feel simply that's a chair, that's a table, and yet at the same time, It's a miracle, it's an ecstasy. (299-300)

If Woolf had opened Moore's book to the first page, she would have read, "Chairs and tables and mountains *seem* to be very different from us; but when the whole universe is declared to be spiritual, it is certainly meant to assert that they are far more like us than we think." If she had read the table of contents or turned to the second essay in the book, she would have discovered further that it was entitled **"The Nature and Reality of Objects of Perception."**[9] Thus there is in both books not only a table but a table and chair; and while Moore writes about the perception of reality, Lily fights to perceive reality and translate it to the canvas.

A few lines after Lily deliberately dips her brush, she has what can quite properly be called a "spiritual" experience—an "exceptional moment." Mrs. Ramsay, ten years dead, "appears" to her:

> "Mrs. Ramsay! Mrs. Ramsay!" [Lily] cried, feeling the old horror come back—to want and want and not to have. Could she inflict that still? And then, quietly, as if she refrained, that too became part of ordinary experience, was on a level with the chair, with the table. Mrs. Ramsay—it was part of her perfect goodness—sat there quite simply, in the chair, flicked her needles to and fro, knitted her reddish-brown stocking, cast her shadow on the step. There she sat. (300)

Thus, not far apart in Moore's book and in two pages of the Woolf novel such matters as table, chair, perception, the nature of reality, mental images, and spirituality all appear together.

Similarly, in Moore's book there appears the sentence, "And so, if I say 'It will rain tomorrow,' these words have a different meaning today from what they would have if I used them tomorrow." The clause "It will rain tomorrow," again in quotation marks, is repeated again a few pages later.[10] In *To the Lighthouse,* an important theme of the opening scene is Mr. Ramsay's insistence that there will be no trip to the lighthouse on the morrow because "it won't be fine. . . . Not with the barometer falling, and the wind due west. . . . It must rain" (10, 50, 51). And Charles Tansley repeatedly reinforces Mr. Ramsay's diagnosis (12, 15, 26).

Again, later in the Moore volume, in a paper on **"External and Internal Relations,"** one reads about terms A, B, C, and D; then terms P and Q; and, finally, R. In the next thirteen pages of the paper there is no term higher than R (*i.e.,* no S, T, U . . . Z).[11] In *To the Lighthouse* one reads:

> It was a splendid mind [Mr. Ramsay's]. For if thought is like the keyboard of a piano, divided into so many notes, or like the alphabet is ranged in twenty-six letters, all in order, then his splendid mind had no sort of difficulty in running over those letters one by one, firmly and accurately, until it had reached, say, the letter Q. He reached Q. Very few people in the whole of England ever reach Q. . . . But after Q? . . . Z is only reached once by one man in a generation. Still, if he could reach R it would be something. (53-54)

And a page later: "He would never reach R" (55). It is appropriate, of course, that although the discussion in Moore's book reaches R, Mr. Ramsay cannot take that final step; for the name Ramsay begins with R. Perhaps the reader is meant to understand that Mr. Ramsay will never reach an understanding of himself. Or perhaps Woolf is just being puckish.

Rosenbaum also supports his claim that "certain features of Mr. Ramsay's career resemble Moore's":

> Mr. Ramsay is described by Mr. Banks as "'one of those men who do their best before they are forty'"; his definite contribution had been a little book when he was twenty-five, and "what came after more or less amplification, repetition" [39]. Moore was thirty when ***Principia Ethica*** appeared, and his subsequent career was an anticlimax for some of his friends. Ramsay also suggests Moore rather than [Leslie] Stephen [Virginia Woolf's father, after whom she said she modeled Mr. Ramsay] in his method of thought. His attempts "to arrive at a perfectly clear understanding of the problem" [53] is like the method of no philosopher Virginia Woolf ever read or knew of so much as Moore. The similarities have perhaps been obscured by the recurrent misunderstanding of the symbolization of Mr. Ramsay's futile struggle to get from Q to R. . . .[12]

The suggestion for that "futile struggle" could easily have come from Moore's ***Philosophical Studies.***

Many of the personality characteristics ascribed to Moore by his biographers are also shared by Mr. Ramsay. For example, Paul Levy lists "the striking traits of character that he continued to demonstrate all life long: integrity, incorruptibility, thoroughness and shining innocence."[13] In the novel Lily says of Mr. Ramsay, "the most sincere of men, the truest . . . , the best" (72). Bankes remembers Ramsay's "simplicity, his sympathy with humble things" (35). Ramsay has "a fiery unworldliness" and "a child-like resentment of interruption" (40, 41).

Sir Roy Harrod ascribed to Moore "a passion to confute error and expose confusion," and Sir Alfred Ayer said that Moore had "a passion for argument."[14] Those characteristics are abundantly evident in Mr. Ramsay's insistence that rain will not allow a trip to the lighthouse the following day and his anger at his wife's attempt to alleviate James's disappointment by saying, "'But it may be fine—I expect it will be fine'" (11).

Moore's biographers are very clear about Moore's limitations. He "was not very imaginative. He was not fertile in ideas, as was Russell. He was not a profound thinker, as was Wittgenstein." "He was not, and never had the least idea he was, a much cleverer man than McTaggart, for example, or Bradley."[15] In short, he was not a genius. Mr. Ramsay's limitations and self-knowledge are similarly clear. He thinks that his was "a splendid mind. [But he] had not genius. . . . He would never reach R" (53, 55).

Levy reports that "many have said (and written) that the most striking aspect of Moore's character was his childlike nature [, his] *naïveté.*"[16] Leonard Woolf wrote that Moore

> resembled Socrates in possessing a profound simplicity, a simplicity which Tolstoy and some other Russian writers consider to produce the finest human beings. These human beings are "simples" or even "sillies"; they are absurd in ordinary life and by the standards of sensible and practical men. . . . In many ways Moore was one of these divine "sillies." It shows itself perhaps in such simple, unrestrained, passionate gestures as when, if told something particularly astonishing or confronted by some absurd statement at the crisis of an argument, his eyes would open wide, his eyebrows shoot up, and his tongue shoot out of his mouth.[17]

Mr. Ramsay, similarly, is given to "screwing his face up. . . . scowling. . . . Why could he never conceal his feelings?" (143-45). "Such a gift he had for gesture" (222).

Because of his childlike nature, Moore was generally forgiven his "bad temper—which it must be admitted sometimes amounted to rage."[18] Mr. Ramsay's bad temper is evident throughout the first section of *To the Lighthouse;* and, generally, he is similarly forgiven—by the adults: it takes Cam and James ten years to forgive him. Early on, marching back and forth in the garden, he is "outraged and anguished" (49). Contradicted by his wife, he shouts, "'Damn you'" (50-51). Other times

> The bedroom door would slam violently early in the morning. He would start from the table in a temper. He would whizz a plate through the window [because he had found an earwig in his milk]. Other people might find centipedes. They had laughed and laughed. (296)

Sometimes "it tired Mrs. Ramsay, it cowed her a little—the plates whizzing and the doors slamming" (296). But at the slightest sign of his repentance after an outburst, ". . . she reverenced him. . . . There was nobody she reverenced more. She was not good enough to tie his shoe strings, she felt" (51).

Of the virtues "which people in the 1920s derived from Moore," said Nöel Annan, "'above all [was] ruthless honesty about oneself.'"[19] Mr. Ramsay is very honest with himself: "He had not genius; he laid no claim to that. . . . He would never reach R" (55). He knew that he was not that "one in a generation" to "reach Z" (55-56), even that "he had not done the thing he might have done" (70). Mr. Ramsay "was always uneasy about himself . . . about his own books—will they be read, are they good, why aren't they better, what do people think of me?" "That troubled [Mrs. Ramsay]. [W]ho could tell? She knew nothing about it. But it was his way with him, his truthfulness . . ." (177).

Virginia Woolf reported, of course, that she wrote *To the Lighthouse* to exorcise her memory of her parents. And,

as she said, she clearly gave Mr. Ramsay many of the characteristics of Leslie Stephen, her father.[20] Perhaps so much of Moore can be seen in Mr. Ramsay because Leslie Stephen and G. E. Moore both reflect an important Victorian male stereotype, and in using her father as a model Woolf instantiated characteristics not only of her father but also of Moore and of many other males who matured before the turn of the century. On the other hand, as Ernest and Ina Wolf comment, "a novelist as skilled, competent, and creative as Virginia Woolf fashions complex personages who combine aspects of multiple historical models."[21]

Furthermore, Mr. Ramsay's professional interests are like Moore's, not like Leslie Stephen's; and *To the Lighthouse* does reflect some of the surface features of Moore's ***Philosophical Studies.*** In reporting that her father was the model for Mr. Ramsay but not reporting that G. E. Moore also sat for that portrait, Virginia Woolf may have been having her private fun, waiting for her male friends, many of whom were devoted to Moore, to discover the likeness. That no one seems to have mentioned it (we do not know if anyone *noticed* it) may have increased her enjoyment with her little joke.

Or she may have been demonstrating the superiority of the artist over the philosopher. Thus, for example, Moore argues that "*some* of the sensible qualities which we perceive as being in certain places, really exist in the places in which we perceive them to be . . ."—in lay terms, that many of the things we see are really there.[22] One could argue that, in an episode that I have described above, Woolf gives that claim an ironic twist. After Lily thinks that "One wanted . . . to be on a level with ordinary experience, to feel simply that's a chair, that's a table" (299-300), she evokes an image of Mrs. Ramsay, long since dead (300). Thus if "on the level with ordinary experience" some of the objects we see are really present, an artist, at least (perhaps on the level with extraordinary experience), can see objects that are not present at all.

Again, in his philosophical writings, when Moore looked at nature, he saw concrete instances of philosophical problems; or perhaps he looked at nature to find occurrences which raise philosophical problems. Take one of his discussions of color:

> What then is meant by saying that one thing is the "content" of another? First of all I wish to point out that "blue" is rightly and properly said to be the content of a blue flower. If, therefore, we also assert that it is part of the content of the sensation of blue, we assert that it has to the other parts (if any) of this whole the same relation which it has to the other parts of a blue flower—and we assert only this: we cannot mean to assert that it has to the sensation of blue any relation which it does not have to the blue flower.[23]

Lily's awareness of color in nature is quite different. She sees it not with a philosopher's eye, but with an artist's. She celebrates it:

The jacmanna was bright violet; the wall staring white. She would not have considered it honest to tamper with the bright violet and the staring white, since she saw them like that, fashionable though it was, since Mr. Paunceforte's visit, to see everything pale, elegant, semitransparent. . . . So off they strolled down the garden . . . to that break in the thick hedge, guarded by red hot pokers like braisers of clear burning coal, between which the blue waters of the bay looked bluer than ever. . . . [T]he pulse of colour flooded the bay with blue, and the heart expanded with it and the body swam, only the next instant to be checked and chilled by the prickly blackness on the ruffled waves. (31-33)

The difference in the use of "blue" demonstrates how far apart for Woolf were the world of G. E. Moore and the world of the artist and, perhaps, why she was committed to recording intuitions, "exceptional moments," rather than "philosophical words, [which] are apt to play one false."

NOTES

[1] Proposing Bergson: Floris Delattre, *Le Roman Psychologique de Virginia Woolf* (Paris: Librairie Philosophique J. Vrin, 1932), pp. 127-42.

Proposing Moore: Leonard Woolf, *Beginning Again* (London: Hogarth Press, 1964), pp. 24-25; Woolf also discusses Moore's influence on himself and his friends in *Sowing* (Harcourt, Brace, 1960), pp. 144-64. Gabriel Franks, "Virginia Woolf and the Philosophy of G. E. Moore," *The Personalist* (California), L (Spring 1969), 230. S. P. Rosenbaum, "The Philosophical Realism of Virginia Woolf," in S. P. Rosenbaum, ed., *English Literature and British Philosophy* (University of Chicago Press, 1971), pp. 341-42, 319.

Proposing McTaggart: Avrom Fleishman, "Woolf and McTaggart," *ELH*, XXXVI (December 1969). 719-38.

Proposing Plato: A. C. Hoffman, "Subject and Object and the Nature of Reality: The Dialectic of *To the Lighthouse*," *Texas Studies in Literature and Language*, XIII (Winter 1972), 702.

Proposing Russell: Jaakko Hintikka, "Virginia Woolf and Our Knowledge of the External World," *Journal of Aesthetics and Art Criticism*, XXXVIII (Fall 1979), 12-13, 5.

Proposing Nietzsche and Bergson: Jan Heinemann, "The Revolt Against Language: A Critical Note on Twentieth-Century Irrationalism with Special Reference to the Aesthetico-philosophical Views of Virginia Woolf and Clive Bell," *Orbis Litterarum*, XXXII (1977), 214, 221-26.

Proposing Nietzsche, Freud, Jung, Plato: Graham Parkes, "Imagining Reality in *To the Lighthouse*," *Philosophy and Literature*, VI (1982), 36, 43, 44 (fn. 13).

[2] Virginia Woolf, *A Room of One's Own* (1929; rpt. Harvest/Harcourt Brace Jovanovich, n.d.), p. 113.

[3] Virginia Woolf, *Moments of Being*, ed. Jeanne Schulkind, sec. ed. (Harvest/Harcourt Brace Jovanovich, 1985), pp. 72-73.

[4] Jeanne Schulkind, "Introduction," *Moments of Being*, p. 11.

[5] Indeed, she notes (confesses?) that "The tired or feeble mind may easily lapse as the remorseless questioning proceeds; but no one, however weak, can fail, even if he does not learn more from Plato, to love knowledge better." Virginia Woolf, "On Not Knowing Greek," *The Common Reader* (Harcourt, Brace, 1925), pp. 33-34.

[6] Virginia Woolf, *The Letters of Virginia Woolf*, eds. Nigel Nicolson and Joanne Trautmann (Harcourt Brace Jovanovich, 1975), I, 347, 352-53, 357; Virginia Woolf, *The Diary of Virginia Woolf*, eds. Anne Olivier Bell and Andrew McNeillie (Harcourt Brace Jovanovich, 1978), II, 231.

[7] Rosenbaum, p. 339; Virginia Woolf, *To the Lighthouse* (Harcourt, Brace & World, n.d.), p. 38; hereafter cited in the text.

[8] Quentin Bell, *Virginia Woolf* (Harcourt Brace Jovanovich, 1972), II, 105, 237.

[9] G. E. Moore, "The Refutation of Idealism" and "The Nature and Reality of Objects of Perception," *Philosophical Studies* (London: Routledge & Kegan Paul, 1922), pp. 1, 31. "The Refutation of Idealism" also deals with perception and the nature of reality; but if I am right in thinking that Woolf gave the volume only a superficial reading, she may not have read deeply enough to have understood that.

[10] Moore, "William James' 'Pragmatism,'" *Philosophical Studies*, pp. 136, 141.

[11] Moore, "External Relations," *Philosophical Studies*, pp. 277, 284, 295.

[12] Rosenbaum, p. 339.

[13] Paul Levy, *Moore—G. E. Moore and the Cambridge Apostles* (Oxford: Oxford University Press, 1981), p. 8. Throughout the biography, Levy regularly refers to Moore's "childlike nature" and his *naïveté* (pp. 8, 11, 12, 293, 297).

[14] Levy, pp. 10, 12.

[15] Levy, pp. 11, 294.

[16] Levy, pp. 11, 293.

[17] Leonard Woolf, *Sowing*, p. 151; see also Levy, pp. 12, 244.

[18] Levy, pp. 12-13, 182, 272.

[19] Levy, pp. 296-97.

[20] Virginia Woolf, "Sketch of the Past," pp. 108-11.

[21] Ernest S. Wolf and Ina Wolf, "'We Perished Each Alone': A Psychoanalytic Commentary on Virginia Woolf's *To the Lighthouse,*" in Lynne Layton and Barbara Ann Schapiro, eds., *Narcissism and the Text* (New York University Press, 1986), p. 264. See also Marianna Torgovnick, who argues that Mrs. Ramsay reflects aspects not only of Virginia Woolf's mother, but also of her sister Vanessa and that Lily reflects aspects of both Virginia and Vanessa: "each fictional woman . . . is a composite of autobiographical imperatives, *the remembered attributes of more than one person,* and sheer invention" (italics added). *The Visual Arts, Pictorialism and the Novel* (Princeton University Press, 1985), p. 118.

[22] Moore, "The Nature and Reality of Objects of Perception," *Philosophical Studies,* p. 95.

[23] Moore, "The Refutation of Idealism," *Philosophical Studies,* p. 21

Paul Grice (essay date 1989)

SOURCE: "G. E. Moore and Philosphers's Paradoxes," in *Studies in the Way of Words,* Harvard University Press, 1989, pp. 154-70.

[*In the following essay, Grice applies Moore's paradoxes to other philosophical questions.*]

I shall begin by discussing two linked parts of Moore's philosophy, one of which is his method of dealing with certain philosophical paradoxes, the other his attitude toward Common Sense. These are particularly characteristic elements in Moore's thought and have exerted great influence upon, and yet at the same time perplexed other British philosophers. Later in this paper I shall pass from explicit discussion of Moore's views to a consideration of ways of treating philosophical paradoxes which might properly be deemed to be either interpretations or developments of Moore's own position.

First, Moore's way of dealing with philosopher's paradoxes. By "philosopher's paradoxes" I mean (roughly) the kind of philosophical utterances which a layman might be expected to find at first absurd, shocking, and repugnant. Malcolm[1] gives a number of examples of such paradoxes and in each case specifies the kind of reason or proof which he thinks Moore would offer to justify his rejection of these paradoxical statements; Moore, moreover, in his **"Reply to My Critics"** in the same volume, gives his approval, with one qualification, to Malcolm's procedure. I quote three of Malcolm's examples, together with Moore's supposed replies:

Example 1

Philosopher: "There are no material things."

Moore: "You are certainly wrong, for here's one hand and here's another; and so there are at least two material things."

Example 2

Philosopher: "Time is unreal."

Moore: "If you mean that no event can follow or precede another event, you are certainly wrong: for after lunch I went for a walk, and after that I took a bath, and after that I had tea."

Example 3

Philosopher: "We do not know for certain the truth of any statement about material things."

Moore: "Both of us know for certain that there are several chairs in this room, and how absurd it would be to suggest that we do not know it, but only believe it, and that perhaps it is not the case!"

Example 1 is an abbreviated version of perhaps the most famous application of Moore's technique (for dealing with paradoxes), that contained in his British Academy lecture **"Proof of an External World."** There he makes what amounts to the claim that the reply in Example 1 contains a rigorous proof of the existence of material things; for it fulfills the three conditions he lays down as being required of a rigorous proof: (a) its premise ("here's one hand and here's another") is different from the conclusion ("there are at least two material things"); (b) the speaker (Moore), at the time of speaking, knows for certain that the premise is true; and (c) the conclusion follows from the premise. Moore of course would have admitted that condition (c) is fulfilled only if "there are material things" is given one particular possible interpretation; he is aware that some philosophers, in denying the existence of material things, have not meant to deny, for example, that Moore has two hands; but he claims (quite rightly, I think) that the sentence "material things do not exist" has sometimes been used by philosophers to say something incompatible with its being true to say that Moore has two hands.

Now the technique embodied in the examples I have just quoted is sometimes regarded as being an appeal to Common Sense. Though it may, no doubt, be correctly so regarded in some sense of "Common Sense," I am quite sure that it is not an appeal to Common Sense as *Moore* uses the expression "Common Sense." In **"A Defense of Common Sense"**[2] Moore claims to know for certain the truth of a range of propositions about himself, similar in character to those asserted in the replies contained in my three examples, except that the propositions mentioned in the article are less specific than those asserted in the replies; and he further claims to know for certain that very many other persons have known for certain propositions about themselves corresponding to these propositions about himself. It is true that Moore rejects certain philosopher's paradoxes because they conflict with some of the propositions which Moore claims to know with certainty, and it is further true that Moore describes his position, in general terms, as being "that the 'Common Sense view of the world' is, in certain fundamental features, wholly true." But it is also clear that when Moore talks about Common Sense, he is thinking of a set of very generally accepted beliefs, and, for him, to "go against Common Sense" would be to contradict one or more of the members of this set of beliefs. Two points are here relevant. (1) Most of the propositions which serve as the premises of Moore's disproofs of paradoxical views are not themselves propositions of Common Sense (objects of Common Sense belief), for they are, standardly, propositions about individual people and things (e.g. Moore and hands), and obviously too few people have heard of Moore for there to be any *very* generally accepted beliefs about him. Of course, Moore's premises may justify some Common Sense beliefs, but that is not the point here. (2) In any case, it is quite clear that for Moore there is nothing sacrosanct about Common Sense beliefs as such; in the **"Defense"** he says (p. 207), "for all I know, there may be many propositions which may be properly called features in 'the Common Sense view of the world' or 'Common Sense belief' which are not true, and which deserve to be mentioned with the contempt with which some philosophers speak of 'Common Sense beliefs.'" And in *Some Main Problems* he cites propositions which were once, but have since ceased to be, Common Sense beliefs, and are now rejected altogether. So, if to describe Moore's technique as an appeal to Common Sense is to imply that in his view philosopher's paradoxes are to be rejected *because* they violate Common Sense (in Moore's sense of the term), then such a description is quite incorrect (it is, I think, fair to maintain that Moore's use of the term "Common Sense" is not the ordinary one, in which a person who lacks Common Sense is someone who is silly or absurd; and this suggests a sense in which Moore does "appeal to Common Sense" in dealing with paradoxes, for he does often say or imply that the adoption of a paradoxical view commits one to some absurdity).

Now it is time to turn to the perplexity which Moore's technique has engendered. A quite common reaction to Moore's way with paradoxes has, I think, been to feel that it really can't be as easy as that, that Moore counters philosophical theses with what amounts to just a blunt denial, and that his "disproofs" fail therefore to carry conviction. As Malcolm observes, we tend to feel that the question has been begged, that a philosopher who denies that there are material objects is well aware that he is committed to denying the truth of such propositions as that Moore has two hands and so cannot be expected to accept the premise of Moore's proof of an external world. For Moore's technique to convince a philosophical rival, something more would have to be said about the *point* of Moore's characteristic maneuver; some account will have to be given of the nature of the absurdity to which a philosophical paradox allegedly commits its propounder. Malcolm himself (loc. cit.) argues that such an account can be given; he represents Moore's technique as being a (concealed) way of showing that philosophical paradoxes "go against ordinary language" (say or imply

that such ordinary expressions are absurd or meaningless), and argues that to do this is to commit an absurdity, indeed to involve oneself in contradiction. I shall enter into the details of this thesis later; at the moment I am only concerned with the question how far Moore's own work can properly be understood on the general lines which Malcolm suggests. I must confess it seems very doubtful to me whether it can. (1) Moore in his **"Reply to My Critics"** neither accepts nor rejects Malcolm's suggestion; indeed he does not mention it, and it very much looks as if Malcolm's idea was quite new to him, and one which he needed time to consider. (2) Moore (loc. cit.) makes a distinction (in effect) between my Example 1 and my Example 3 (this is the qualification I mentioned earlier). He allows that one can *prove* that material objects exist by holding up one's hands and saying "Here is one hand and here is another"; but he does not allow that one can *prove* that one sometimes knows for certain the truth of statements about material things from such a premise as "Both of us know for certain that there are chairs in this room." In his view, to say "We know for certain that there are chairs in this room, so sometimes one knows for certain the truth of propositions about material things" is to give not a "proof" but a "good argument" in favor of knowledge about material things; it is a good argument but (he says) some further argument is called for, and in this case the need for further argument is said to be connected with the fact that many more philosophers have asserted that *nobody knows* that there are material things than have said that there are no material things. Now I find it very difficult to see how Moore can successfully maintain that Example 1 gives a proof of the existence of material things and yet that Example 3 does not give a proof of our knowledge of material things. (Can he deny that his three requirements for a rigorous proof are satisfied in this case?) But this is not the point I am concerned with here. What I wish to suggest is that for Moore's technique to be properly represented as being in all cases a concealed appeal to ordinary language, he would surely have had to have treated Example 1 and Example 3 alike, for the denial of knowledge about material things does not go against ordinary language any less than the denial of the existence of material things. It might well be, of course, that no satisfactory and comprehensive account can be given of Moore's procedure, and that an account in terms of the appeal to ordinary language fits what he is doing most of the time, and so perhaps shows what he was (more or less unconsciously) getting at or feeling after. But to say this is different from saying outright that the applications of his technique are appeals to ordinary language.

One or two passages in *Some Main Problems in Philosophy* indicate a different (or at any rate apparently different) procedure. I shall try to present, in connection with a particular example, a somewhat free version of the position suggested by the passages I have in mind. Some philosophers have advanced the (paradoxical) thesis that we never know for certain that any inductive generalization is true, that inductive generalizations can at best be only probably true. Their acceptance of this thesis will be found to rest on a principle, in this case maybe some such principle as that for a proposition to be known with certainty to be true, it must either be a necessary truth or a matter of "direct experience" (in some sense) or be logically derivable from propositions of one or the other of the first two kinds. But inductive generalizations do not fall under any of these heads, so they cannot be known with certainty to be true. The sort of maneuver Moore would make in response to such a thesis (e.g. "But of course we know for certain that the offspring of two human beings is always another human being") might be represented as having the following force: "The principle on which your thesis depends is not self-evident, that is, it requires some justification; and since it is *general* in form, its acceptability will have to depend on consideration of the particular cases to which it applies; that is, the principle that all knowledge is of certain specified kinds will be refuted if there can be found a case of knowledge which is *not* of any of the specified kinds, and will be confirmed if after suitably careful consideration, no such counterexample is forthcoming. But I have just produced a counterexample, a case of knowledge which is not of any of the specified kinds, and which, furthermore, is an inductive generalization. You cannot, without cheating, *use* the principle to discredit my counterexample, i.e. to argue that my specimen is not really a case of knowledge; if the principle depends on consideration of the character of the particular cases of knowledge, then it cannot be invoked to ensure that apparent counterexamples are not after all to be counted as cases of knowledge. If you are to discredit my counterexample it must be by some other method, and there is no other method." This line of attack could, of course, be applied mutatis mutandis, to other paradoxical philosophical theses.

I have a good deal of sympathy with the idea I have just outlined; in particular, it seems to me to bring out the way in which, primarily at least, I think philosophical theses should be tested, namely by the search for counterexamples. Moreover, I think it might prove effective, in some cases, against the upholders of paradoxes. But I doubt whether a really determined paradox-propounder would be satisfied. He might reply: "I agree that my principle that all knowledge is of one or another specified kind is not self-evident, but I do not have to justify it by the method you suggest, that of looking for possible counterexamples. I can justify it by a careful consideration of the nature of knowledge, and of the relation between knowledge and other linked concepts. Since I can do this, I can, without begging the question, use my principle to discredit your supposed counterexamples." The paradox-propounder might seek also to turn the tables on his opponent by adding, "You, too, are operating with a philosophical principle, namely a principle about how philosophical theses are to be tested; but the acceptability of your principle, too, will (in your view) have to depend on whether or not my own thesis about knowledge constitutes a counterexample; and to determine this question, you will have to investigate independently of your principle the legitimacy of the grounds upon which I rely." To meet this reply, I would have to anticipate the latter part of my paper; and in any case I suspect that in meeting it, I should exhibit the rationale of Moore's procedure as being after all only a particular version of the "appeal to ordinary language." So I shall pass on to discuss the efficacy of this way of dealing with paradoxes, without explicit reference to Moore's work.

I can distinguish two different types of procedure in the face of a philosopher's paradox, each of which might count as being, in some sense, an appeal to ordinary language. Procedure 1 would seek to refute or dispose of paradoxes without taking into account what the paradox-propounders would say in elaboration or defense of their theses; these theses would simply be rebutted by the charge that they went against ordinary language, and this would be held sufficient to show the theses to be untenable, though of course a philosopher might well be required to do more than merely show the theses to be untenable. Procedure 2, on the other hand, would take into account what the paradox-propounder would say, or could be forced to say, in support of his thesis, and would aim at finding some common and at the same time objectionable feature in the positions of those who advance such paradoxes. Procedure 2, unlike Procedure 1, would not involve the claim that the fact that a thesis "went against" ordinary language was, by itself, sufficient to condemn it; I propose now to consider two versions of Procedure 1, to argue that at least as they stand, they are not adequate to silence a wide-awake opponent, or even to extract from him the reaction, "I see that you must be right, and yet . . . ," and finally to consider Procedure 2.

My first version is drawn from Malcolm. In the form in which I state it, this procedure applies only against nonempirically based paradoxes; indeed, Malcolm does not make any distinction between different types of paradox and in effect seems to treat all philosophical paradoxes as if they were of the nonempirically based kind. The kernel of Malcolm's position seems to be as follows. The propounder of a paradox is committed to holding that the ordinary use of certain expressions (e.g. "Decapitation was the cause of Charles I's death") is (a) incorrect and (b) self-contradictory or absurd. But this contention is itself self-contradictory or absurd. For if an expression is an ordinary expression, that is, "has an ordinary (or accepted) use"—that is to say, if it is an expression which "would be used to describe situations of a certain sort if such situations existed or were believed to exist"—then it cannot be self-contradictory (or absurd). For a self-contradictory expression is one which would never be used to describe any situation, and so has *no* descriptive use. Moreover, if an expression which *would* be used to describe situations of a certain sort (etc.) is in fact on a given occasion used to describe that sort of situation, then it is on that occasion correctly used, for correct use is just standard use. It will be seen that Malcolm's charge against the paradoxes is that they go against ordinary language not by misdescribing its use (to do that would be merely to utter falsehoods, not absurdities) nor by misusing it (that would be merely eccentric or misleading) nor by ill-advisedly proposing to change it (that would be merely giving bad advice), but by *flouting* it, that is, admitting a use of language to be ordinary and yet calling it incorrect or absurd. Furthermore, it will be seen that he attempts to substantiate his charge by consideration of what he takes to be the interrelation between the concepts of (a) ordinary use, (b) self-contradiction, and (c) correctness.

This version of Procedure 1 has three difficulties:

(1) The word "would," as it occurs in the phrase "expression which would be used to describe situations of a certain sort, if such situations existed or were believed to exist," seems to me to give rise to some trouble. The phrase I have just quoted might be taken as roughly equivalent to "expression which, given that a certain sort of situation had to be described, would be used." But this cannot be what Malcolm means; it is just not true that always or usually, when called upon to describe such a situation as a man's having lost his money, one would say "he has become a pauper." There are all sorts of things one would be more likely to say; yet presumably "he has become a pauper" is to be counted as an ordinary expression. It would be clearer perhaps to substitute, for the quoted phrase, the phrase "expression of which it would not be true to say that it would not be used to describe . . ." or more shortly "expression which *might be* used to describe . . ." Let us then take the original phrase in this sense. Now what about the sentence "Sometimes the ordinary use of language is incorrect" (which Malcolm says is self-contradictory)? This sentence (or some other sentence to the same effect) no doubt has been uttered seriously by paradox-propounders, and it might well seem that they *have* used it to describe the situation they believed to obtain with regard to the use of ordinary language. Does it not then follow that this sentence is one of which it is untrue to say that it would *not* be used to describe a certain sort of situation, or more simply, that this sentence is one which might be used to describe a certain sort of situation; that is, the sentence is *not* self-contradictory? If we can combine "has been used to describe" with "would not be used to describe" (and perhaps we can), then, at least, the sense of "would not be used" seems to demand scrutiny. I suspect, however, that Malcolm himself would not admit the legitimacy of the combination. He would rather say that the sentence in question has been uttered seriously, even perhaps has been "used," but has not been used to describe a certain sort of situation (just because it commits an absurdity); and so there is no difficulty in going on to say that it would not be used to describe any sort of situation, that is, is self-contradictory (and so nonordinary). This points the way to what seems to me a fundamental difficulty.

(2) I think Malcolm's opponent might legitimately complain that the question has been begged against him. For he might well admit that the expressions of which he complains are ordinary expressions, and even that they would be used to describe certain sorts of situations which the speaker believed to exist, but go on to say that the situations in question are (logically) impossible. This being so, the expressions are both ordinary *and* absurd. If he is ready in the first place to claim that an ordinary expression may be absurd, why should he jib at saying that an ordinary expression may be used to describe an *impossible* situation which the speaker mistakenly believes to exist? Malcolm's argument can be made to work only if we assume that no situation which a sentence would ordinarily be used to describe would be an impossible situation, and to assume this is to assume the falsity of the paradox-propounder's position.

Alternatively, the paradox-propounder might agree that an ordinary expression of the kind which he is assailing (e.g. "Decapitation was the cause of Charles I's death") would be used to describe such a situation as that actually obtaining at Charles I's death (i.e., it would be used to describe an *actual* situation and not merely an *impossible* situation); but then he might add that the user of such an expression would not *merely* be describing this situation but also be committing himself to an absurd gloss on the situation (e.g. that Charles's decapitation willed his death), or again (much the same thing) that the user would indeed be merely describing this situation, but would be doing so in terms which committed him to an absurdity. And to meet this rejoinder by redefinition would again be to beg the question in Malcolm's favor.

The paradox-prounder might even concede that an expression which would be used to describe a certain sort of situation would be correctly used to describe a situation of that sort, provided that all that is implied is that it is common form to use this expression in this sort of situation; but nevertheless maintaining that the correctness of use (in this sense) would not guarantee freedom from contradiction or absurdity.

Put summarily, my main point is that *either* Malcolm must allow that, in order to satisfy ourselves that an expression is "ordinary," we must first satisfy ourselves that it is free from absurdity (in which case it is not yet established that such an expression as "Decapitation caused Charles I's death" *is* an ordinary one), or he must use the word "ordinary" in such a way that the sentence I have just mentioned is undoubtedly an ordinary expression, in which case the link between being ordinary and being free from absurdity is open to question.

(3) Is it in fact true that an ordinary use of language cannot be self-contradictory, unless the "ordinary use of language" is *defined* by stipulation as non-self-contradictory, in which case, of course, Malcolm's version of the appeal to ordinary language becomes useless against the philosopher's paradox? The following examples would seem to involve nothing but an ordinary use of language by any standard but that of freedom from absurdity. They are not, so far as I can see, technical, philosophical, poetic, figurative, or strained; they are examples of the sorts of things which have been said and meant by num-

bers of actual persons. Yet each is open, I think, at least to the suspicion of self-contradictoriness, absurdity, or some other kind of meaninglessness. And in this context suspicion is perhaps all one needs.

(a) "He is a lucky person" ("lucky" being understood as dispositional). This might on occasion turn out to be a way of saying "He is a person to whom what is unlikely to happen is likely to happen."

(b) "Departed spirits walk along this road on their way to Paradise" (it being understood that departed spirits are supposed to be bodiless and imperceptible).

(c) "I wish that I had been Napoleon" (which does not mean the same as "I wish I were like Napoleon"). "I wish that I had lived not in the XXth century but in the XVIIIth century."

(d) "As far as I know, there are infinitely many stars."

Of course, I do not wish to suggest that these examples are likely in the end to prove of much assistance to the propounder of paradoxes. All I wish to suggest is that the principle "The ordinary use of language cannot be absurd" is either trivial or needs justification.

Another, possibly less ambitious version of Procedure 1 might be represented as being roughly as follows. Every paradox comes down to the claim that a certain word or phrase (or type of word or phrase) cannot without linguistic impropriety or absurdity be incorporated (in a specified way) in a certain sort of sentence T. For example, bearing in mind Berkeley, one might object to the appearance of the word "cause" as the main verb in an affirmative sentence the subject of which refers to some entity other than a spirit. The paradox-propounder will however have to admit that, if we were called on to explain the use of W to someone who was ignorant of it, we should not in fact hesitate to select certain exemplary sentences of type T which incorporated W, and indicate ostensively or by description typical sorts of circumstances in which such sentences would express truths. Now if it be admitted that such a mode of explanation of W's use is one we should naturally adopt, then it must also be admitted that it is a proper mode of explanation; and if it is a proper mode of explanation, how can a speaker who uses such an exemplary sentence, believing the prevailing circumstances to be of the typical kind, be guilty of linguistic impropriety or absurdity? You cannot obey the rules, and yet not obey them.

The paradox-propounder's reply might run on some such lines as these. If it were true that we always supposed the typical sorts of circumstances, to which reference is made in such an explanation of the meaning of a word, to be as they really are, and as observation or experience would entitle us to suppose, then the paradox would fall. But it may be that in the case of some words (such as possibly "cause") for some reason (perhaps because of a Hume-like natural disposition) we have a tendency to read more

into the indicated typical situation than is really there, or than observation would entitle us to suppose to be there. Furthermore, the addition we make may be an absurdity. For instance, we might have a tendency to read into what the common sense philosopher would regard as typical causal transactions between natural objects or events the mistaken and absurd idea that something is *willing* something else to happen. If we do do this (and how is it shown that we do not?), then even though we use the word "cause" in just the kinds of situations indicated by model explanations of the word's meaning, we shall still have imported into our use of the word "cause" an implication which will make objectionable the application of the word to natural events. Whenever we so apply the word "cause," what we say will imply an absurdity.

Let us ask how a philosophical paradox is standardly supported. One standard procedure (and this is the only one I shall consider, though there may be other quite different methods) is to produce one or more alleged entailments or equivalences which, if accepted, would commit one to the paradox. For example, the philosopher who maintains that only spirits can be causes might try to persuade us as follows: if there is a cause, then there is action; if there is action, then there is an agent; if there is an agent, then there is a spirit at work; and there we are. This particular string of alleged entailments is not perhaps very appetizing, but obviously in other cases something more alluring can be provided. Now if we ask how the propounder of the paradox supposes it to be determined whether or not his entailments or equivalences hold, we obviously cannot reply that the question is to be decided in the light of the circumstances in which we apply the terms involved, for it is obvious that we do not restrict our application of the word "cause" to spirits, and if we did, then all suspicion of paradox would disappear. The paradox-propounder seemingly must attach special weight to what we say, or what we can be got to say, about the meaning or implication of such a word as "cause." In effect he asks us what we mean by "cause" or "know" (giving us some help) and then insists that our answers show what we *do* mean.

Leaving on one side for the moment the question why he does this and with what justification, let us consider the fact that the interpretation which he gives of such a word as "mean" seems to differ from the interpretation of that word which would be given by his opponent. To differentiate between the two interpretations, let us use "mean1" as a label for the sense that the paradox-propounder attributes to the word "mean" (in which what a man says he means by a word is paramount in determining what he in fact does mean), and let us use "mean2" as a label for the sense which the opponent of the paradox-propounder would attribute to the word "mean" (in which what a man means is, roughly speaking, determined by the way in which he applies the word). The paradox-propounder would say "'Cause' means (that is, means1) so and so," and his opponent would say "'Cause' means (that is, means2) such and such." Now it seems that the dispute between them cannot be settled without settling the divergence between them with regard to the word "mean." Can this divergence be settled? It seems to be difficult, for if the paradox-propounder claims that "mean" means (that is, "mean1") and his opponent claims that "mean" means (that is, "mean2"), then we seem to have reached an impasse. And it is likely that this would in fact be the situation between them.

But then we might reflect that the dispute between them, in becoming unsettlable, has evaporated. For the paradox-propounder is going to say "Certain ordinary utterances are absurd because what (in certain circumstances) we say that we mean by them is absurd, but these can be replaced by harmless utterances which eradicate this absurdity, and the job of philosophical analysis is to find these replacements," while his opponent is going to say "No ordinary utterances are absurd, though sometimes what we say we mean by them is absurd, and the job of philosophical analysis is to explain what we really do mean by them." Does it matter which way we talk? The facts are the same.

I do not feel inclined to rest with this situation, and fortunately there seem to be two ways out of it, in spite of the apparent deadlock:

(1) I suspect that some philosophers have assumed or believed that "mean" means "mean," (that what a man says he means is paramount in determining what he does mean) because they have thought of "meaning so and so" as being the name of an introspectible experience. They have thought a person's statements about what he means have just the same kind of incorrigible status as a person's statements about his current sensations, or about the color that something seems to him to have at the moment. It seems to me that there are certainly some occasions when what a speaker says he means is treated as specially authoritative. Consider the following possible conversations between myself and a pupil:

> *Myself:* "I want you to bring me a paper tomorrow."
>
> *Pupil:* "Do you mean that you want a newspaper or that you want a piece of written work?"
>
> *Myself:* "I mean 'a piece of written work.'"

It would be absurd at this point for the pupil to say "Perhaps you only think, mistakenly, that you mean 'a piece of written work,' whereas really you mean 'a newspaper.'" And this absurdity seems like the absurdity of suggesting to someone who says he has a pain in his arm that perhaps he is mistaken (unless the suggestion is to be taken as saying that perhaps there is nothing physically wrong with him, however his arm feels). It is important to notice that although there is this point of analogy between meaning something and having a pain, there are striking differences. A pain may start and stop at specifiable times; equally something may begin to look red to one at 2:00 P.M. and cease to look red to one at 2:05 P.M. But it would be absurd for my pupil (in the preceding example) to say to me "When did you begin to mean

that?" or "Have you stopped meaning it yet?" Again there is no *logical* objection to a pain arising in any set of concomitant sentences; but it is surely absurd to suppose that I might find myself meaning that it is raining when I say "I want a paper"; indeed, it is odd to speak at all of "my finding myself meaning so and so," though it is not odd to speak of my finding myself suffering from a pain. At best, only *very* special circumstances (if any) could enable me to say "I want a paper," meaning thereby that it is raining. In view of these differences, we may perhaps prefer to label such statements as "I mean a piece of written work" (in the conversation with my pupil) as "declarations" rather than as "introspection reports." Such statements as these are perhaps like declarations of intention, which also have an authoritative status in some ways like and in some ways unlike that of a statement about one's own current pains.

But the immediately relevant point with regard to such statements about meaning as the one I have just been discussing is that, insofar as they have the authoritative status which they seem to have, they are not statements which the speaker could have come to accept as the result of an investigation or of a train of argumentation. To revert to the conversation with my pupil, when I say "I mean a piece of written work," it would be quite inappropriate for my pupil to say "How did you discover that you meant that?" or "Who or what convinced you that you meant that?" And I think we can see why a "meaning" statement cannot be both specially authoritative and also the conclusion of an argument or an investigation. If a statement is accepted on the strength of an argument or an investigation, it always makes sense (though it may be foolish) to suggest that the argument is unsound or that the investigation has been improperly conducted; and if this is conceivable, then the statement maker *may* be mistaken, in which case, of course, his statement has not got the authoritative character which I have mentioned. But the paradox-propounder who relies on the type of argumentation I have been considering requires *both* that a speaker's statement about what he means should be specially authoritative *and* that it should be established by argumentation. But this combination is impossible.

(2) A further difficulty for the paradox-propounder is one which is linked with the previous point. There is, I hope, a fairly obvious distinction (though also a connection) between (a) what a given expression means (in general), or what a particular person means *in general* by a given expression, and (b) what a particular speaker means, or meant, by that expression on a particular occasion; (a) and (b) may clearly diverge. I shall give examples of the ways in which such divergence may occur. (1) The sentence "I have run out of fuel" means in general (roughly) that the speaker has no material left with which to propel some vehicle which is in his charge; but a particular speaker on a particular occasion (given a suitable context) may be speaking figuratively and may mean by this sentence that he can think of nothing more to say. (2) "Jones is a fine fellow" means in general that Jones has a number of excellences (either without qualification or

perhaps with respect to some contextually indicated region of conduct or performance); but a particular speaker, speaking ironically, may mean by this sentence that Jones is a scoundrel. In neither of these examples would the particular speaker be giving any unusual sense to any of the words in the sentences; he would rather be using each sentence in a special way, and a proper understanding of what he says involves knowing the *standard* use of the sentence in question. (3) A speaker might mean, on a particular occasion, by the sentence "It is hailing" what would standardly be expressed by the sentence "It is snowing" *either* if he had mislearned the use of the word "hailing" *or* if he thought (rightly or wrongly) that his addressee (perhaps because of some family joke) was accustomed to giving a private significance to the word "hailing." In either of these cases, of course, the speaker will be using some particular word in a special nonstandard sense.

These trivial examples are enough, I hope, to indicate the possibility of divergence between (a) and (b). But (a) and (b) are also connected. It is, I think, approximately true to say that what a particular speaker means by a particular utterance (of a statement-making character) on a particular occasion is to be identified with what he intends by means of the utterance to get his audience to believe (a full treatment would require a number of qualifications which I do not propose to go into now). It is also, I think, approximately true to say that what a sentence means in general is to be identified with what would *standardly* be meant by the sentence by particular speakers on particular occasions; and what renders a particular way of using a sentence *standard* may be different for different sentences. For example, in the case of sentences which do not contain technical terms it is, I think, roughly speaking, a matter of general practice on nonspecial occasions; such sentences mean in *general* what people of some particular group would normally mean by using them on particular occasions (this is, of course, oversimplified). If this outline of an elucidation of the distinction is on the right lines, then two links may be found between (a) and (b). First, if I am to mean something by a statement-making utterance on a particular occasion—that is, if I intend by means of my utterance to get my audience to believe something—I must think that there is some chance that my audience will recognize from my utterance what it is they are supposed to believe; and it seems fairly clear that the audience will not be able to do this unless it knows what the general practice, or what my practice, is as regards the use of this type of utterance (or unless I give it a supplementary explanation of my meaning on this occasion). Second (and obviously), for a sentence of a nontechnical character to have a certain meaning in general, it must be the case that a certain group of people do (or would) use it with that meaning on particular occasions.

I think we can confront my paradox-propounder with a further difficulty (which I hope will in the end prove fatal). When he suggests that to say "x (a natural event) caused y" means (wholly or in part) "x willed y," does he

intend to suggest that particular speakers use the sentence "x caused y" on particular occasions to mean (wholly or in part) "x willed y" (that this is what they are telling their audience, that this is what they intend their audience to think)? If he is suggesting this, he is suggesting something that he must admit to be false. For part of his purpose in getting his victim to admit "x caused y" means (in part at least) "x willed y" to get his victim to admit that he should not (strictly) go on saying such things as that "x caused y" just because of the obvious falsity or absurdity of part of what it is supposed to mean; and he is relying on his victim's *not* intending to induce beliefs in obvious falsehoods or absurdities. However, if he is suggesting that "x caused y" means *in general* (at least in part) "x willed y," even though no particular speaker ever means this by it (or would mean this by it) on a particular occasion, then he is accepting just such a divorce between the *general* meaning of a sentence and its *particular* meaning on particular occasions as that which I have been maintaining to be inadmissible.

In conclusion, I should like to remind you very briefly what in this paper I have been trying to do. I have tried to indicate a particular class of statements which have been not unknown in the history of philosophy, and which may be described as being (in a particular sense) paradoxes. I have considered a number of attempts to find a general principle which would serve to eliminate all such statements, independently of consideration of the type of method by which they would be supported by their propounders. I have suggested that it is difficult to find any principle which will satisfactorily perform this task, though I would not care to insist that no such principle can be found, nor to deny that further elaboration might render satisfactory one or another of the principles which have been mentioned. I have considered a specimen of what I suspect is one characteristic method in which a paradox-propounder may support his thesis (though this may not be the *only* method which paradox-propounders have used); and finally I have tried to show that the use of this method involves its user in serious (indeed I hope fatal) difficulties.

NOTES

[1] Malcolm, "Moore and Ordinary Language," in *The Philosophy of G. E. Moore*, ed. Schlipp.

[2] *Contemporary British Philosophy*, vol. 2.

Bernard Harrison (essay date 1991)

SOURCE: "Forster and Moore," in *Inconvenient Fictions: Literature and the Limits of Theory*, Yale University Press, 1991, pp. 98-122.

[*In the following excerpt, Harrison examines the influence of Moore's philosophy on the writings of Bloomsbury author E. M. Forster.*]

I

The influence of Moore on the young Forster is vouched for by Leonard Woolf: 'That is the point: under the surface all six of us, Desmond, Lytton, Saxon, Morgan, Maynard and I, had been permanently inoculated with Moore and Moorism. . . .'[1] The search for traces of Moorism in the novels, however, has turned up relatively little. P. N. Furbank in his *Life* (1977) is skeptical about even the likelihood of literary gold in these bleak philosophical uplands: 'Too much has been made of the influence of G. E. Moore on him, for he never read Moore; but the epigraph to Moore's **Principia Ethica,** "Everything is what it is, and not another thing", hits off his own idea of the Cambridge "truth".'[2] Respect for truth and for Reality—for the hardness and solidity of the actual—are certainly to be gained from reading Moore, and no doubt these things are part of what Forster and his friends did gain from him. Woolf again: 'The main things which Moore instilled deep into our minds and characters were his peculiar passion for truth, for clarity and common sense, and a passionate belief in certain values.'[3] But these admirable if rather generalized virtues might be imbibed from any number of philosophers of stature. Did none of Moore's peculiar and characteristic doctrines exert any permanent influence on those 'inoculated with Moore and Moorism'?

S. P. Rosenbaum, in an interesting and ingenious article,[4] argues for the direct influence on *The Longest Journey* of some of Moore's epistemological doctrines—those expressed in his famous article **'The Refutation of Idealism'.** Moore claims there *inter alia* that there is an irreducible difference between what is perceived and the perceiving of it, and Rosenbaum connects this kind of Realism with the ethical kind which consists in distinguishing carefully between the ideas we are tempted to form of others and what they are, and are like really. There is something in this, and Rosenbaum is sustained not only by the fact that Realism was of the essence of the revolution in philosophy wrought by Moore and Russell in the Cambridge of Forster's youth, but by Forster's own account of the influences that went into the novel: 'There was the metaphysical idea of Reality ("the cow is there"): there was the ethical idea that reality must be faced (Rickie won't face Stephen). . . .'[5]

But the connection thus established between metaphysical and ethical Realism seems more curious than fruitful; it is not clear in the end how much it can be made to contribute to our reading of the novel. Rosenbaum himself sees the problem: 'It is, of course, not necessary to know anything about Moore's "The Refutation of Idealism" to see that *The Longest Journey* is a novel about appearance and reality. What an awareness of Moore's philosophy can do for criticism of the novel is to help it avoid misinterpretations.'[6]

Unfortunately the 'misinterpretation' which Rosenbaum offers as a test of his reading is the generally accepted reading which makes Ansell as nearly the embodiment of truth as critical rigour, force of intellect and sound human sympathies can make a man. If Forster was at the time of writing the novel the consistent Moorean Realist that Rosenbaum wishes to make of him, then this cannot be, for Ansell fails to get his fellowship because he has read too much Hegel, and is in other ways tainted with Idealism. Rosenbaum's way around this is to treat Ansell as a flawed character whose 'sense of reality' needs to be 'corrected and completed by Stephen Wonham'. I find this unconvincing, as does Furbank: 'the trouble with this is that, whenever Ansell's philosophical inconsistencies are noted in the novel, Forster's tone suggests that they do not matter in the least—Ansell's position, humanly speaking, is absolutely sound.'[7]

The effect of this is to relegate 'the metaphysical idea of Reality' to Forster's 'quarry': to the status of an idea which influenced the shape of the novel rather than one which figures in it. What matters *in* the novel is merely that 'sense of reality' of which, as Russell once observed, philosophers, stand in more need than ordinary men; not the kind of metaphysical grounding for Realism which some philosophers, including Moore, have seen as the special function of their subject to provide. The technical machinery, the *arguments,* which make up the substance of Moore's contribution to epistemology have no place in *The Longest Journey,* nor is it easy to see how they could have, unless Forster had chosen to make his characters merely mouthpieces for metaphysical disputation—as those in, say, Berkeley's *Three Dialogues.*

For all that, however, I do not think that the effect on Forster of being 'inoculated with Moore and Moorism' did lie merely in the acquisition of a respect for truth. There is profit to be gained from reading Forster with some awareness of the more abstruse technicalities of Moore's philosophy. But to this enterprise a number of preliminary caveats are necessary. First, I think the technicalities in question are more likely to be those associated with Moore's ethics than those associated with his epistemology. Here again I am in agreement with Furbank:

> Rosenbaum persuades me that I have underestimated Moore's influence on E. M. Forster. However, the influence that I now think I see is of a slightly different kind from what he suggests, and certainly much less direct. It was, as we know, characteristic of Moore that he should approach Ethics by way of a survey of 'intrinsic' goods or things that are good in themselves. . . . And this was so much Forster's own attitude to life and ethics—he so explicitly repudiated the 'Wilcox' approach, which concerned itself with things merely as means and with the use they could be put to; and he attached so much importance to the discrimination of the various intrinsic goods offered by the universe—that I would suspect we can detect in him the general climate of thought of Moore's Cambridge.[8]

Second, and again following Furbank, I do not think that Forster's engagement with Moore was a direct one. He encountered Moore's work not as a body of philosophical arguments, but as a body of effects which those arguments were having on the minds of his contemporaries. We have confirmation of this from Forster himself: 'I did not receive Moore's influence direct—I was not up to that and have never read *Principia Ethica.* It came to me at a remove, through those who knew the Master. The seed fell on fertile, if inferior, soil, and I began to think for myself.'[9] Hence in what follows I shall be concerned as much with J. M. Keynes's account, in 'My Early Beliefs', of the impact of *Principia Ethica* at Cambridge as with that work itself.

Third, and here I depart from both Rosenbaum and Furbank, I doubt if Moore's effect upon Forster was, in the ordinary sense, wholly a case of 'influence'. The term suggests a simple transfer of ideas or ideals from one writer to another who receives them with conscious or unconscious complaisance and proceeds to embody them in his work. The supposition that the relationship between Moore and Forster fits this pattern seems to me to underestimate the power and seriousness of the latter's work. Forster, already as Keynes drily puts it 'the elusive colt of a dark horse',[10] was not simply a complaisant publicist for the Moore-inspired outlook which he encountered among his friends at Cambridge. Some things he took from it; in other respects he was, like Keynes, a severe and searching critic.

This must, though, raise the question of how one can make critical headway against a philosophy by writing a novel. Novels, as I have just been arguing myself, do not—unless their characters are just animated metaphysical positions like Hylas and Philonous—contain any *arguments.* How then can a novel engage with the technicalities of a subject which consists of nothing but arguments?

The answer is, I take it, that a philosophy isn't *just* a body of arguments. A philosophy establishes itself by arguments, certainly; the question is, though, what exactly is being established? Thomas Nagel has distinguished between claims about reality which are 'objective' in the sense that they embody no reference to any particular point of view, and claims which, while they may correctly pick out some real aspect of things, pick it out in a way which is inherently tied to some special point of view.[11] Boyle's Law would be an example of the first kind of claim; examples of the second kind would include claims about what it is like, say, to be a bat, or to see colours as human beings see them. Philosophical claims for the most part, it seems to me, fall squarely into the second of Nagel's categories. What philosophical argument tries to establish, that is to say, is the intellectual credentials of some special point of view or other. Philosophy thus has a dual status: it exists on the one hand as sets of arguments, and on the other hand as the points of view such bodies of argument tend to establish. Professional philosophers tend to perceive their subject under the first of these aspects: they are more interested in the technical detail of the arguments than in the viewpoints the arguments are meant to establish. They tend to see these latter merely as motives for attempting to argue in a given direction: as mere starting points or limiting conditions for the subject, and thus as things lacking in interesting internal complexity. Another way of putting the same point would be to say that, for the professional philosopher, the internal complexity of a philosophical point of view *is* simply that of the body of arguments for and against it.

To the non-philosopher, on the other hand, the positions attacked and defended by philosophers are complex in their own right, and the complexity they exhibit is not identical with that of the technical arguments for or against them, though these will generally need to be taken into account to some extent if we are to say what such a position *is:* what its content consists in. To the non-philosopher a philosophical position is simply a rather abstract way of representing an outlook on life: a point of view which ordinary, actual persons may adopt, and even try seriously to live by. From this direction the complexity of a philosophical position is a matter of what it does for, and to, people who adopt it in that way. It is in this way that philosophy comes to be of interest to the novel; for one of the things in which novelists are professionally interested is the question of how far our intellectual and moral ambitions—our more grandiose and general theories about life, and the feelings, impulses and acts which go with them—can be made to cohere with, to stand up to, the predicaments and experiences forced on us by life.

Novels, in short, can chart the pitfalls which confront the intellectually confident holder of a philosophical position when he or she moves from argument to commitment and from commitment to action. If it is objected that the resulting critique does not engage directly with philosophy under its aspect as argument, the answer is that this is not the only aspect, nor even finally, perhaps, the most important one, under which philosophy presents itself to us.

It is in this sense, at any rate, that I want to claim Forster is a critic, as well as a disciple, of 'Moorism'. Before getting on with the argument, however, there remains a fourth and final caveat, and a further respect in which what I have to say here will depart from the paths trodden by the small amount of recent discussion of Forster's relationship to Moore. This is that I do not think the place to look for Forster's settling of accounts with Cambridge and 'Moorism' is necessarily, or at any rate primarily, the obvious one. Most critics have looked for the influence of Cambridge philosophizing in *The Longest Journey,* because that novel is partly set in undergraduate Cambridge, opens with a philosophical discussion redolent of the Cambridge Apostles, and contains one character who is an embryonic philosopher. I think it may prove more fruitful, at least at the outset, to look instead at the work closest in date of publication to Forster's Cambridge years: *Where Angels Fear to Tread.*

II

Moore's ethics is a version of utilitarianism. It retains the most striking feature of utilitarianism, and the one which makes many ordinary unphilosophical people uncomfortable with it, once they have grasped its implications; namely, its consequentialism. The consequentialist holds that whether an action is morally right or wrong depends solely on its consequences: on the nature of the state of affairs which it brings into being. This differs sharply from the common view that the rightness or wrongness of actions depends on what one might call their *moral constitution;* that what matters is whether a given action *constitutes* the keeping of a promise, *constitutes* a betrayal, *constitutes* a kindness or a piece of cruelty: that, in short, it is the nature of the act and not its consequences which makes the difference morally. Consequentialists of course have ways of squaring their position with this commonly held view of the matter. The most usual is to argue that society trains us to feel that acts having a given moral constitution are right or wrong in virtue of having that constitution, for the very good reason that *in the general run of cases* the moral constitution of an act is a reliable guide to the utility or disutility of its consequences. But, or so consequentialists from Mill onward have argued, these ingrained nonconsequentialist intuitions are liable in certain circumstances to lead us seriously astray morally, either because they conflict with one another, or because under certain extreme conditions refusing to act because of the moral constitution of the act demanded of one may require one to accept very bad consequences indeed. In such cases, the consequentialist argues, our everyday intuitions about the moral constitution of acts must yield to consequentialist considerations, which shows that such considerations are, after all, the nerve of morality.

None of this commits the utilitarian to any disrespect for ordinary moral rules in the general course of everyday life, for it is part of the utilitarian's position that in the general run of cases respect for the generally accepted rules can be relied upon to produce the best possible consequences. But it does set him apart from the ordinary, unenlightened person, whose respect for the commonly accepted dictates of morality is automatic, unthinking and unconditional in a way in which the utilitarian's can never be. The latter's theory places him under a moral obligation to decide for himself, by appealing to his own estimate of the relative weights of the competing utilities, in which cases ordinary moral considerations should be respected and in which they should not.[12] Utilitarianism as a moral outlook is thus of a piece with that peculiarly Protestant, peculiarly English form of individualism which consists in demanding for oneself as an individual not the right to do as one pleases but, more subtly and more dangerously, the right to decide for oneself, in the last analysis, what is Right. In *Where Angels Fear to Tread* Harriet most obviously represents the Evangelical form of this tendency, but it is one to which all the English characters, in one way or another, ultimately subscribe.

Utilitarianism so characterized might seem to exemplify what Furbank calls 'the "Wilcox" approach' to life: an approach concerned more with the practical consequences of action than with ultimate questions of value. This would be a misunderstanding. Merely in order to define his notion of utility, the utilitarian has to give some account of what sorts of things are ultimately worthy to be brought into being. This is where Moore's philosophy comes into its own. Bentham, the father of the theory, held that the only intrinsically valuable thing is pleasure. This is open to a great many objections, of which only two need concern us here. The first is that it commits the utilitarian, implausibly, to the claim that the only things which ultimately have value are mental states. The second—Moore's objection—is that it forces the utilitarian to deny what seems to be a truth of logic: that even if it is granted that no state of affairs could have any value if it contained no pleasure, it does not follow that the value of a state of affairs is proportional to the quantity of pleasure it contains. A given quantity of pleasure derived from having grasped just such a logical truth, for instance, may possess more value—more worthiness-to-be-brought-into-being—than the same quantity of pleasure derived from imagining some hideous revenge, even though the revenge in question remains unacted. Earlier utilitarians failed to notice this logical gap, Moore argues, because they tacitly, and mistakenly, assumed the *non-natural* property *goodness* to be simply identical with whatever *natural* property it is—the property of *being pleasant,* for instance—that confers value upon states of affairs. Moore baptized this error, if error it be, 'the Naturalistic Fallacy'.

Moore's own account of intrinsic value is founded upon the rejection of ethical naturalism. Its fundamental claim is that the property *goodness* is not identical with any of the natural properties which confer goodness (value; worthiness-to-be-brought-into-being) upon states of affairs. (This is the point of Moore's Butlerian epigraph, *Everything is what it is, and not another thing.*) The enquiry into what is of ultimate or intrinsic value thus divides into two distinct questions. First, there is the question of what natural properties of things do in fact confer value upon the situations in which they occur. Moore's answer to this question is well known: among the most important intrinsic sources of value in life are friendship and the contemplation of beauty. Second, there is the question of how much value these natural features of things confer, in each case, upon specific states of affairs. Answers to both questions, Moore argues, are to be sought by a common method. The method involves carefully comparing, in imagination, one thing with another, leaving out of account any causal consequences or antecedents that either may have, and considering each simply for what it is in itself. In answering questions of the second type, what have to be compared are states of affairs, taken as internally related 'organic wholes' whose intrinsically valuable and non-intrinsically valuable elements work together to yield whatever value the state of affairs possesses, in such a way that there is no possible mode of further analysis which would allow one to assign responsibility for the resultant sum of value to one element of the total situation rather than another.

Moore's account of intrinsic value might appear to constitute, technically speaking, no more than a minor, though interesting and important, adjustment to utilitarian theory. Moore himself called his theory 'Ideal Utilitarianism'. But we are interested in its impact on young, literate readers who were not technical philosophers. What attracts such readers to philosophical theories of ethics is, I suspect, the light they expect such theories to throw on the nature of the moral life. They want, like most people but more especially young people, to know how to live. What they look for in a philosopher, therefore, is some clear and arresting statement about what it is to be moral: about what it is that specifically characterizes the moral standpoint.

Now, the account of what is characteristic of the moral standpoint to be gleaned from Moore's 'Ideal Utilitarianism' is markedly different from that to be gleaned from most other forms of the doctrine. The impression one gains from most versions of utilitarianism is that the moral standpoint is pre-eminently a practical one, in which the energies of the virtuous mind are more or less wholly given over to assessing the consequences of actions or policies with a view to selecting those most productive of some reasonably straightforwardly and uncontroversially defined good labelled 'general happiness', or 'welfare'. This is not the impression one gains from *Principia Ethica.* The focus of the entire book is on the question of how we are to determine what things are intrinsically valuable: worthy to be sought for their own sake alone. Inevitably, as we read the book, this comes to seem the central issue which we confront as *moral* beings; and questions about how we are to achieve the realization of intrinsic goods, once we have determined which those are, seem to relegate themselves naturally to the subordinate status of '*merely* practical' questions: questions, that is, whose solution requires no peculiarly *moral* insight, but merely empirical knowledge and everyday practical nous.

The (fairly extraordinary) claim that moral consciousness, strictly defined as such, excludes the practical from its sphere is not, one supposes, one which Moore would have accepted, let alone one which he would have wished to defend. The fact remains that the impression left by an enthusiastic reading of *Principia Ethica,* especially one which dwells lovingly on chapter VI, is that the moral standpoint is a quasi-aesthetic one, consisting largely in the possession and exercise of informed connoisseurship with regard to the discrimination of intrinsic value.

If we are to trust J. M. Keynes, this is very much the way in which Forster's young contemporaries read Moore:

> Now what we got from Moore was by no means exactly what he offered us. He had one foot on the threshold of the new heaven, but the other foot in Sidgwick and the Benthamite calculus and the general rules of correct behaviour. There was one chapter in the *Principia* of which we took not the slightest notice. We accepted Moore's religion, so to speak, and discarded his morals. Indeed, in our opinion, one of the greatest advantages of his religion was that it made morals unnecessary—

meaning by 'religion' one's attitude towards oneself and the ultimate and by 'morals' one's attitude towards the outside world and the intermediate. To the consequence of having a religion and no morals I return later.

(p. 82)

A little later Keynes describes the content of 'the religion' as follows:

> Nothing mattered except states of mind, our own and other people's of course, but chiefly our own. These states of mind were not associated with action or achievement or with consequences. They consisted in timeless, passionate states of contemplation and communion, largely unattached to 'before' and 'after'. Their value depended, in accordance with the principle of organic unity, on the state of affairs as a whole which could not be usefully analysed into parts. For example, the value of the state of mind of being in love did not depend merely on the nature of one's own emotions, but also on the worth of their object and on the reciprocity and nature of the object's emotions; but it did not depend much on what happened, or how one felt about it, a year later, though I myself was always an advocate of a principle of organic unity through time, which still seems to me only sensible.

(p. 83)

It will now perhaps become clear why I see *Where Angels Fear to Tread* as something more than a black social comedy about national character and suburban class pretensions. Though it would be false to the book and to Forster to read it with solemnity, nevertheless the novel has a serious as well as a black side to it. It is in part an exploration of what is liable to happen to people who attempt to live, as Keynes puts it, with 'a religion and no morals'.

Before pursuing this, however, we should pay attention to one final, methodological, feature of Moore's moral philosophy: its intuitionism. As Keynes indicates, Moore's way of settling questions of intrinsic value involved holding a given state of affairs before the mind, in the shadowless light of consciousness, and asking oneself whether one could, or could not, will to bring *that* into being. The essence of the method is that one has to put both the causal antecedents and the consequences of the state of affairs entirely out of one's mind, and consider it simply in itself. The acquisition of moral knowledge, in other words, is conceived as analogous to the acquisition of knowledge through sensory perception. Just as I know with simple, immediate certainty that *this* is my hand, so I know with simple, immediate certainty that *this* (love, say, or the contemplation of beauty) is intrinsically valuable.

One has, I think, to get into a rather special state of intellectual exaltation to find plausible the suggestion that knowledge of ultimate good and evil is as easily accessible as this, and accessible on such a purely private and intellectual level. Common sense tells us that the difference between right and wrong, good and evil, is only to be learned by slower and more painful means; means which intrinsically involve relationships with others, much experience, many nasty shocks to the system, and above all the passage of time: that, in short, such knowledge is taught not in the singing school of the soul, but only in the school of hard knocks. Experience teaches us, moreover, that our views about what is ultimately good and bad are liable to change as a result of experience.

Moore's deeply Cartesian methodology makes no allowance for any of this. It proceeds on the assumption that the final truth about what is to be valued in life is already, timelessly, settled; and that we can come to know what is it merely by directing the inward eye of consciousness in the right sort of way upon sufficiently carefully specified objects. Seen from this angle, Moore's ethics partakes of the *logocentrism* which Jacques Derrida regards as the most enduring and characteristic feature of the Western metaphysical tradition. This is apparent from Moore's treatment of the two predicates 'is good' and 'is yellow' as analogous in respect of being unanalysable and ultimate in our conceptual scheme. Just as the meaning of 'yellow' is an object—a property— directly accessible to consciousness in sensory experience, so the meaning of 'good' is a property directly accessible to consciousness through the peculiar species of thought-experiment by which we assess the intrinsic value attaching to an organic whole. The task of the philospher *as writer*—of Moore's celebrated sixth chapter, for instance—is merely to transcribe the truths about intrinsic value which consciousness so directed reveals.

The Cartesianism of Moore's view comes out in another, closely related way. His moral epistemology, like Descartes's general epistemology, makes the acquisition of knowledge, in this case moral knowledge, at least in its most adequate and ultimate form, the outcome of processes of reflection internal to the individual mind. 'Moorism' about intrinsic value thus provides a further way of intellectually articulating that distinctively English, distinctively Protestant strain of individualism I mentioned earlier, which reserves to the individual mind the right and the power to determine for itself, by the excercise of an inner light proper to it, what is Right.

III

Where Angels Fear to Tread is on the face of it a tragi-comedy of manners, about a raw English suburb and an ancient Italian town, neither of which comes out of the book particularly well. The English characters include Mrs Herriton, a wealthy Sawston widow, her fiercely Evangelical daughter Harriet, and her lawyer son Philip. The values with which Philip enters the novel are clearly meant to embody a version of Cambridge 'Moorism'. 'By far the most valuable things, which we know or can imagine,' Moore has written, 'are certain states of consciousness, which may be roughly described as the pleasure of human intercourse and the enjoyment of beautiful ob-

jects.'[13] Philip, weak on the first of these moral absolutes, is strong on the second, which he opposes to what he sees as the philistine rule-worship practised by Sawston in general and his sister Harriet in particular. 'At twenty-two he went to Italy with some cousins, and there he absorbed into one aesthetic whole olive trees, blue sky, frescoes, country inns, saints, peasants, mosaics, statues, beggars. He came back with the air of a prophet who would either remodel Sawston or reject it. All the energies and enthusiasms of a rather friendless life had passed into the championship of beauty' (p. 61).[14]

Given the obsessive discussion of the moral properties of organic wholes recorded by Keynes among the Cambridge Apostles, I doubt if Forster's choice of the phrase 'into one aesthetic whole' is accidental. And if it is not, it is certainly satirical in intent. An organic whole, to be the seat of a moral absolute, should be, one feels, more coherent than Philip's hodgepodge.

Loosely connected to the Herriton clan is Mrs Herriton's daughter-in-law, Lilia Theobald, left widowed and socially, if not entirely financially, dependent on the Herritons by another son, Charles. There are also Irma, Lilia's daughter, and Caroline Abbott, a friend of the family, on whose shifts of moral position much hangs.

Lilia is a vulgar, bouncy woman of a type uncongenial to the Herritons, whose unsuitability consists in part in a tendency to encourage unsuitable suitors. As the novel opens she is being packed off at Philip's suggestion for an extended tour of Italy in the company of Caroline Abbott, with the object, from the Herritons' point of view, of getting her away from the latest of these suitors. Philip's hopes for the tour nicely catch the way in which moral and aesthetic considerations freely interpenetrate one another in his mind.

> 'I admit she is a Philistine, appallingly ignorant, and her taste in art is false. Still, to have any taste at all is something. And I do believe that Italy really purifies and ennobles all who visit her. She is the school as well as the playground of the world. . . .'

> He found the situation full of whimsical romance: there was something half-attractive, half-repellent in the thought of this vulgar woman journeying to places he loved and revered. Why should she not be transfigured? The same had happened to the Goths.
>
> (p. 9)

Solicitous for Lilia's aesthetico-moral redemption, Philip advises the pair to spend some time in the ancient and beautiful Tuscan hill town of Monteriano. There Lilia meets and falls in love with her most unsuitable suitor yet: an Italian dentist's son by the name of Gino Carella. Gino is twenty-one, Lilia considerably older. Miss Abbott, whom the Herritons know as a prim young spinster devoted to Church causes and the care of an elderly father, might have been expected to discourage such a rash attachment. But alas, Caroline Abbott turns out to have a romantic streak of her own, and sees in it Lilia's last chance of freedom and happiness. The news reaches the Herritons in a cautiously worded letter from old Mrs Theobald announcing Lilia's engagement, in which Gino, thanks to the remoter ramifications of his extended family, has been transmogrified into a member of the Italian nobility. Mrs Herriton is quite able to read between lines as far apart as these, and Philip is dispatched by the night train to put a stop to the engagement. He arrives too late: Lilia and Gino are already married. Lilia tells him exactly what she thinks of the Herritons' attempts over twelve years to train her into conformity with Herriton ideas of propriety, and Gino laughs at him and ends what should have been a serious interview by pushing him over backward. Philip returns much discomfited to Sawston, and Mrs Herriton duly severs relationships with Lilia, refusing even to let her write to Irma.

There matters might have rested. But in Monteriano Lilia discovers the disagreeable side of marriage to an Italian. The social circle to which she has access is extremely limited; it is thought improper for her to continue her English habit of going for long walks alone. She is virtually confined to home and church. Finally, to cap it all, she discovers that Gino is unfaithful to her. She makes various hopeless attempts at escape, then after a long illness dies in childbirth, leaving Gino a son.

Reactions in Sawston to this news are various. For Philip it constitutes a spiritual crisis.

> . . . Lilia's marriage toppled contentment down forever. Italy, the land of beauty, was ruined for him. She had no power to change men and things who dwelt in her. She, too, could produce avarice, brutality, stupidity—and what was worse, vulgarity. It was on her soil and through her influence that a silly woman had married a cad. He hated Gino, the betrayer of his life's ideal, and now that the sordid tragedy had come, it filled him with pangs, not of sympathy, but of final disillusion.
>
> (p. 62)

Mrs Herriton's impulse, and Harriet's, is to let sleeping dogs lie, and keep the existence of a Herriton baby in Monteriano a secret, especially from Irma. It is Caroline Abbott who once again troubles the waters. She reveals to Philip how much she is responsible for Lilia's second marriage: how she had felt about Lilia's treatment by the Herritons over the years, and how she said to Lilia one warm night in a hotel bedroom in Monteriano, 'Why don't you marry him if you think you'll be happy' (p. 66). Not surprisingly Caroline now feels guilty and responsible for Lilia's child. She has the impertinence to ask Mrs Herriton 'what is to be done' about it, and threatens to take an interest in any expedition to rescue it. This is too much for Mrs Herriton. A letter is sent to Gino offering to adopt the child; when this fails, Philip is sent off once more to Monteriano, this time with Harriet in tow to see that weakness does not get the better of him.

Before Philip and Harriet have got far into Italy, they are quarrelling in the heat, and Philip's spiritual malaise has begun to pass off, leaving in its place a renewed pleasure in Italy and renewed doubts about the moral credentials of Sawston.

> 'Because he was unfaithful to his wife, it doesn't follow that in every way he's absolutely vile.' He looked at the city. It seemed to approve his remark.
>
> 'It's the supreme test. The man who is unchivalrous to a woman—'
>
> 'Oh stow it! Take it to the Back Kitchen. It's no more a supreme test than anything else. The Italians never were chivalrous from the first. If you condemn him for that, you'll condemn the whole lot.'
>
> 'I condemn the whole lot.'
>
> 'And the French as well?'
>
> 'And the French as well.'
>
> 'Things aren't so jolly easy,' said Philip, more to himself than to her.
>
> (pp. 86-7)

In Monteriano, nothing goes according to plan. Caroline Abbott is there before them, but Gino is out of town. Caroline, who has already met Gino, conveys to Philip his apologies and sorrow for having treated Philip so rudely the previous year. This completes Philip's re-conversion to Italy, and he proposes that the ill-assorted party fill in the time on its hands with a visit to the Monteriano opera house. There, in the course of an evening which deeply scandalizes Harriet, he meets Gino in the company of some other young Italian bloods, and they carry him off to the café with them, thus completing the ruin of his intention to 'rescue' the child from Gino.

Caroline Abbott spends an uneasy night, however, and in the morning goes to visit Gino. While she is waiting for him, he returns, and puts her completely off her stroke by his charm, his inconsequentiality and, as will appear, his masculinity. While she is still reeling, he tells her of his plan to marry again so that the baby will be properly cared for, and draws her into the protracted business of giving it a bath, something he will no longer trust the servant Perfetta to do because she 'is too rough', and to do which he has cheerfully torn himself away from the café. Caroline Abbott is entirely unmanned by this display of maternal instinct, and is still seated in the loggia with the dripping baby on her knee when Philip arrives, to perceive the scene as 'the Virgin and child, with Donor', by Bellini.

Philip stays to proceed, quite unsuccessfully, with the negotiations for the adoption of the child by the Herritons. Caroline Abbott leaves, in turmoil. The issue, as she puts it to Philip in the church of Santa Deodata later that day, is clear to her: ' . . . I do expect you to settle what is right and to follow that. Do you want the child to stop with his father, who loves him and will bring him up badly, or do you want him to come to Sawston, where no-one loves him, but where he will be brought up well.'

She repents again, this time of ever having goaded the Herritons into interfering with the child's future, and wants Philip to be decisive and call off Harriet. But Philip is in no state to be decisive. Exercising the same genial tolerance towards Harriet as towards Gino, he goes off for one final attempt, in the Caffé Garibaldi, to persuade the latter to part with the child, and when that fails he prepares to leave Monteriano. Harriet, however, will not give up so easily. She makes mysterious arrangements with Philip for the carriage to pick her up not at the hotel, but at the Siena gate near Gino's house; and when she enters the carriage she is carrying the baby. On the way down the hill of Monteriano in a sudden thunderstorm the carriage overturns and the baby is killed.

Philip, who has broken his arm, goes to take the news to Gino, who is both inconsolable and violent, and who tortures Philip by grinding the broken bones of his arm together until Caroline Abbott puts a stop to it. But this is the end of the enmity between Philip and Gino, who has 'the southern knack of friendship', and to whom Philip is soon 'bound by ties of almost alarming intimacy' (p. 152). With Caroline Abbott he is not so lucky. When he proposes to her on the train ascending from Italy towards the St. Gotthard tunnel, she reveals that she is in love, sexually and physically in love, with Gino, but that nevertheless she is going back to Sawston to resume her loveless life there.

IV

In *Where Angels Fear to Tread,* as in other Forster novels, it is not altogether easy to say whose side Forster is on. One inviting way of reading the novel is to take it as a satire on the prosaic, hypocritical and selfish values of Sawston, conducted from the standpoint of Romance, represented by Philip Herriton, Caroline Abbott, and Monteriano. Thus Norman Kelvin suggests that of the two main themes of the novel, the first is that engagements between people can also be engagements with 'culture and history', while the second is 'that romance, reserved for a few, easily confused with a "spurious sentiment" superficially resembling it, is paradoxically in the light of its élitist connotations, essential for all life.'[15]

There are many difficulties with this. First, Sawston and its representatives are not unrelievedly condemned in the book. To Caroline, passing a sleepless night after the opera, it is revealed as Poggibonsi, from whose rule Monteriano emancipated itself in the twelfth century, 'a joyless, straggling place, full of people who pretended'. But that is Caroline's vision, not Forster's; whereas it *is* the authorial voice of the novel which ends Harriet's quarrel with Philip in the hot, dusty train like this: 'She kept her promise, and never opened her lips all the rest

of the way. But her eyes glowed with anger and resolution. For she was a straight, brave woman, as well as a peevish one' (p. 87). That same voice also tells us that when Harriet vanishes just before the final departure from Monteriano with the baby, she leaves her prayer book on her bed open at the words, 'Blessed be the Lord my God who teacheth my hands to war and my fingers to fight'. We are reminded sharply, if we are prepared to be reminded, that Harriet is on her way to rescue a child for whom, however belatedly, she has assumed responsibility, from a man she considers, not without evidence, to be a brute and a lecher. Harriet, in short, is a figure of some moral substance, not just a figure of fun. For that matter Sawston itself, seen through the remorseful Lilia's tears, resembles an earthly paradise:

> One evening, when [Gino] had gone out thus, Lilia could stand it no longer. It was September. Sawston would be just filling up after the summer holidays. People would be running in and out of each other's houses all along the road. There were bicycle gymkhanas, and on the 30th Mrs Herriton would be holding the annual bazaar in her garden for the C. M. S. It seemed impossible that such a free happy life could exist.
>
> (p. 55)

I see no reason at all why we should take this Betjemanesque idyll as merely the expression of Lilia's jaundiced view of Monteriano. For one thing, Lilia's view of Monteriano is by this point in the novel understandably jaundiced. For another, Forster expends quite as much loving care in depicting the warts of Monteriano as in depicting those of Sawston, from the absurd superstition of its cult of Santa Deodata to the opera house 'thoroughly done up, in the tints of the beetroot and the tomato', from the 'horrible sighings and bubblings' of the dumb idiot who brings Harriet's message requesting Philip to meet her at the Siena gate to Gino's friend Spiridione's chilling advice on how best to settle Lilia down into her new role:

> 'Is she a Catholic?'
>
> 'No.'
>
> 'That is a pity. She must be persuaded. It will be a great solace to her when she is alone.'
>
> (p. 47)

Then again, just as the novel resists our efforts to turn Harriet into a figure of unrelieved bigotry, so it resists our efforts to turn Philip Herriton into a convincing hero or Caroline Abbott into a convincing heroine. Certainly both in different ways stand for Romance, in opposition to the values of Sawston; but just because those two are its representatives it is not easy to construe the function of Romance in the book as anything but that of a principle of comic disorder. Philip's romantic aesthetico-moralizings are what send Lilia to Italy in the first place. Later, the revival of his romantic vision of Italy contributes to his nervelessness in the face of Caroline Abbott's appeal to him to be decisive about the fate of Gino's child. Caroline really does not do much better. It is her moment of romantic enthusiasm at somebody else's expense which assists Lilia up the flowery path to her appalling marriage with Gino; and the later feelings of guilt which lead to Caroline's prodding the Herritons into doing something about the child are, while in one way honourable, in another thoroughly sentimental and self-regarding. Caroline's claim to be the real heroine of the novel rests, of course, on her belated honesty: her capacity in the final pinch to put aside all sentimental moralizing in the face of a real human encounter. This is a serious claim: the episode in which she and Gino bathe the baby clearly is the moral centre of the novel. But her unsentimental acceptance of the reality before her eyes, and of her own solidly physical reaction to it, is the opposite of the romantic, 'aestheticizing' moral sensibility she partly shares with Philip. And though she rises to this occasion, she does not rise far enough.

In short, I cannot find any textual grounds in the novel for regarding Romance as a principle of life. On the contrary, as the plot unfolds, Romance consistently lights the way to graves as fine and private as any dug in Sawston.

Why, then, should Forster have chosen to construct the novel around the contrast between Sawston and Monteriano? It is here, I think, that Moore and Keynes can help us. From Keynes's account we know that Forster found dominant among his Cambridge friends a way of taking Moore's version of utilitarianism which exalted knowledge of the intrinsic values of things into a religion, and tended rather to look down on 'morality', meaning by that, as Keynes puts it, 'one's attitude towards the outside world and the intermediate'. I have suggested that there are links at the level of theory between this outlook and the long tradition of English puritanism and moral individualism. Keynes confirms those links at the level of feeling: 'Our religion closely followed the English puritan tradition of being chiefly concerned with the salvation of our own souls. The divine resided within a closed circle. There was not a very intimate connection between "being good" and "doing good"; and we had a feeling that there was some risk that in practice the latter might interfere with the former.' ('My Early Beliefs', p. 84)

The basic comic situation in *Where Angels Fear to Tread* consists, I take it, in the juxtaposition of Philip Herriton, who believes, in the style of the Cambridge Apostles, that he has a far keener insight into the intrinsic values of things than the dull souls around him, with the suburban, puritan rule-morality which he affects to despise. The comedy arises from the evident fact that Philip's values are not only no sounder than those of his family, but are in crucial respects the same values. What I have in mind here is not merely Philip's tendency throughout the early part of the novel to relapse at any moment of stress into attitudes characteristic of the average young Englishman of his class and period. More importantly, Philip shares with his mother and Harriet a certain coldness. For all

three of them morality is primarily an inward condition—a matter of inner fidelity to high and commanding abstractions: in Philip's case, Italy and Beauty; in Harriet's, the requirements of Low-Church rectitude; in Mrs Herriton's, those of social order and respectability. The common feature linking all the English characters in the book is that none of them, with the sole exception of Caroline Abbott, ever feels the need to set his or her own values aside in order to respond directly to the needs and condition of another. Examples of the refusal to make the least move outward from an entrenched moral position abound in the book, not least in the Herritons' unsympathetic treatment of the unfortunate Lilia. But Philip is as prone to this as the rest: when news of Lilia's 'sordid tragedy' reaches him, 'it filled him with pangs, not of sympathy, but of final disillusion.' Even Lilia runs her life more in response to her inward dreams and fantasies than in response to what is actually going on around her, and from this comes her downfall, when she chooses to treat Gino not as another human being, with desires and values of his own, but as a pretty Italian boy whom she can fascinate and control. One of the running ironies of the book, I take it, is that Philip's own inner condition, as revealed in action, is not half as remote from Lilia's as he thinks it is. This shows, for instance, in his response to the baby-bathing episode, which leaves Caroline morally disturbed in her purpose, but which Philip simply assimilates wholesale to his dream of Italy:

> There she sat, with twenty miles of view behind her, and he placed the dripping baby on her knee. . . . For a time Gino contemplated them standing. Then, to get a better view, he knelt by the side of the chair, with his hands clasped before him.
>
> So they were when Philip entered, and saw, to all intents and purposes, the Virgin and the Child, with Donor. 'Hallo!' he exclaimed; for he was glad to find things in such cheerful trim.
>
> (p. 122)

If the negative pole of the novel is the moral self-absorption of English puritanism, whether in the form of commonplace suburban philistinism or in the intellectualized mandarin form represented by 'Moorism' in one of its aspects, what is its positive pole? Its positive pole, I take it, is Friendship, that most Moorean as well as most Forsterian of values. So far as Philip makes any spiritual progress at all (and even then it is hardly to be described as growth, more as an involuntary pitchforking at the hands of life from one state to another) it is progress in the direction of friendship. He begins unpromisingly: 'All the energies and enthusiasm of a rather friendless life had passed into the championship of beauty' (pp. 61-2). But he ends 'bound by ties of almost alarming intimacy' to Gino; and he even manages to hear out Caroline Abbott's confession of her feelings for Gino and take well her 'You're my friend forever, Mr Herriton, I think'. It looks, oddly, as if Philip has simply passed from championship of one of Moore's two 'most valuable things', to, if not exactly championship of, at least forcible immersion in the other.

No doubt the young Forster did draw sustenance from Moore's elevation of friendship to the status of one of the two most valuable things 'which we know or can imagine'. Nevertheless, Forster's idea of friendship is not quite the same as Moore's. Moore's 'most valuable things' are described by him as 'certain states of consciousness', one sub-set of which 'may be roughly described as the pleasures of human intercourse'. This way of putting it, because it invites us to think of the enjoyment of a friendship as the enjoyment of *states of consciousness* resulting from it, does suggest rather strongly that friendship is nothing more than a cultivated amenity, a refined and purely mental gratification offering no serious threat to the integrity of the self. And, once again, Keynes can be called to testify that the young men of Forster's Cambridge generation read Moore this way. 'Nothing mattered except states of mind . . . timeless, passionate states of contemplation and communion.'

It is a noticeable feature of *Where Angels Fear to Tread* that friendship in the book is not treated in quite this light. Friendship with Gino, or for that matter any unguarded and direct encounter with him, tears apart all three of the English characters who come into contact with him. In Philip's friendship with Miss Abbott as well there is as much pain as pleasure, as much loss as gain. What is lost for both, and for Lilia as well, is the firm complacent hold, with which each sets out, upon a system of largely theoretical but quite unquestioned and untested moral values and assumptions in terms of which each defines his or her self. Friendship breaks the defensive crust of inwardly generated values, sets the still waters of the self in motion towards change or towards destruction. Forster's point, I take it, is that friendship is not just an amenity, a refined gratification, because it is not ultimately controllable in its effects upon them by those who enter into it; and that it is not controllable because it is not purely mental in its nature, not just a matter of *states of consciousness*. It reaches into the physical side of our being: into the facts of our embodiment which both puritanism, in its drive towards perfect purity and integrity of the self, and Cartesian philosophy endeavour to deny.

Keynes, looking back on Moore and 'Moorism', finds it a blend of seriousness and comedy: impressive in its philosophical detachment and its concern with ultimate goods, absurd in its capacity for *ad hoc* armchair moralizing:

> It was a purer, sweeter air by far than Freud cum Marx. It is still my religion under the surface. I read again last week Moore's famous chapter on 'The Ideal'. It is remarkable how wholly oblivious he managed to be of the qualities of the life of action and also of the pattern of life as a whole. He was existing in a timeless ecstasy. His way of translating his own particular emotions of the moment into the language of generalized abstraction is a charming and beautiful comedy.
>
> ('My Early Beliefs', p. 92)

It would be difficult to find better words to describe the mental condition in which the younger English characters in *Where Angels Fear to Tread* approach the world beyond their native shores. Like Moore, but without his seriousness, they 'exist in a timeless ecstasy'; that is to say, they endeavour sedulously to ignore the concrete, the physical and the temporal aspects of life. Like him, but without his innocence, they display a suspicious facility in 'translating [their] own particular emotions into the language of generalized abstraction'. They want, above all things, to be moral, but they want morality to remain confined to the realm of thought and talk.

Monteriano and Gino possess the at times almost grotesque physicality which Forster bestows upon them because, I take it, they are meant to stand in comic contrast to the fastidious Manichaean refinement with which the four English characters approach their respective Italian Waterloos. The crucial moments of the novel all draw their moral energy from the intensity with which they confront their English protagonists with the concrete physical facts of life, and the inescapable interplay of mind and body. Gino's absurd half-assault on Philip in the hotel room; the 'great clods of earth, large and hard as rocks', over which Lilia stumbles in her attempt to catch the *legno* and escape; the baby's body lying in the rut in rain and darkness; Gino's torture of Philip, and the gesture with which he drinks the warmed milk intended for the dead child and 'either by accident or in some spasm of pain', breaks the jug to pieces, all come to mind as examples. The terms in which Caroline Abbott invites Philip to consider whether the baby is to be loved and badly brought up in Monteriano or well brought up and unloved in Sawston are not without significance here. She says to him, 'Settle it. Settle which side you are to fight on' (p. 130). Meaning: settle it for yourself, settle it *in your mind.* But Caroline has not 'settled' it for herself, by any process of thought—it has been settled for her by the physical, tangible presence of Gino's love for the child in the bathing episode, reinforced no doubt by the equally physical attraction she feels towards Gino.

From this point of view we can make sense of something which has puzzled some critics of the novel: Forster's ironic moral approval of Philip's readiness to be flattered into altogether abandoning his moral condemnation of Gino at the first hint of an apology from the latter.

> What did the baby matter when the world was suddenly the right way up? Philip smiled, and was shocked at himself for smiling, and smiled again. For romance had come back to Italy; there were no cads in her; she was beautiful, courteous, lovable, as of old. And Miss Abbott—she, too, was beautiful in her way, for all her gaucheness and conventionality. She really cared about life, and tried to live it properly. And Harriet—even Harriet tried.
>
> This admirable change in Philip proceeds from nothing admirable, and may therefore provoke the gibes of the cynical. But angels and other practical people will accept it reverently, and write it down as good.
>
> (pp. 97-8)

Norman Kelvin suggests that Forster is here allowing his own approval of Philip's easygoing attitude to the situation to stand in contradiction to Caroline Abbott's well-founded condemnation of it and that this constitutes a failure in the moral coherence of the novel.[16] I see no incoherence. The whole drift of the book is that redeeming impulses do not come from conscious moralizing, which is as often as not self-interested, but from concretely and directly encountering others in ways which bring into play aspects of ourselves which our reflective consciousness can neither wholly grasp nor wholly control. Philip is being betrayed out of his previous rather pompous stance towards Gino by just this kind of impulse. And it does lead him towards a more adequate, a more realistic perception of how things stand. It jerks him out of the absurd disillusionment with his former values into which the failure of Lilia's marriage plunged him, and it does not simply reconstitute those values. If it leaves him something of a moral relativist, able to look down with amused tolerance on the values of both Sawston and Monteriano without accepting either, well, it is also preparing the overthrow of the cheery moral agnosticism which constitutes the second phase of Philip's reaction to the loss of his Moorish faith in the virtual identity of aesthetic and moral sensibility, since it is preparing him for friendship with Gino.

v

Philip's anthropological relativism, the new-found belief upon which he lectures Harriet in the train to the effect that what is a mark of vileness in Sawston is not necessarily so in Monteriano, brings me back in conclusion to the issue of Forster's 'Realism'. Rosenbaum's claim is that Forster's interest in 'the ethical idea that reality must be faced' derived directly from the metaphysical Realism of Moore. The conclusion towards which I have been arguing is that, on the contrary, it developed from Forster's uneasiness about certain aspects of the Moorean ethical Realism which so impressed his Cambridge contemporaries. The worry is the one which most philosophers nowadays would cite as their reason for relegating Moore's doctrine of intrinsic value to the status of a historical curiosity, and on which Keynes unerringly puts his finger forty years on: 'How did we know which states of mind were good? This was a matter of direct inspection, of direct unanalysable intuition about which it was useless and impossible to argue. In that case who was right when there was a difference of opinion?' ('My Early Beliefs', p. 84)

There is, of course, no answer to this one, and Keynes goes on amusingly to detail the various ruses by which members of the Apostles strove to veil the embarrassing outlines of this unfortunate fact: 'In practice, victory was with those who could speak with the greatest appearance of clear, undoubting conviction. . . . Moore at this time was a master of this method—greeting one's remarks with a gasp of incredulity—*Do* you *really* think *that,* an expression of face as if to hear such a thing said reduced him to a state of wonder verging on imbecility, . . . *Oh!*

he would say, goggling at you as if either you or he must be mad: and no reply was possible' (p. 85). Such, in all seriousness, is the degree of moral certainty upon which it is good form to presume in Sawston; and it is precisely the effortless English assumption of the immediate evidence of at least some ultimate moral propositions to all but the manifestly mad or wicked (though some difference of opinion over which these are may be tolerated, if not exactly welcomed) which meets its Waterloo in Monteriano. God knows what truths about the nature of the good Caroline Abbott would have discovered had she applied Moore's method before meeting Gino, but it seems doubtful whether they would have included the proposition that love between father and child morally trumps all considerations of upbringing.

The conclusion towards which Forster's narrative seems to be leading us is that what appears to trump what is morally very much a matter of where we happen to be standing. There is nothing particularly Realist about this conclusion; indeed, it is rampantly Idealistic. We must, however, distinguish between two types of Idealism. There is, on the one hand, the Absolute or Dialectical kind which goes in for degrees of truth. One negative thesis associated with that kind of Idealism says that there is no standpoint from which we can finally, absolutely, grasp and write about the realities of our situation. This thought is present in Forster's work from the beginning, it seems to me. It accounts, indeed, for the occurrence of motifs drawn from Oriental religion long before *A Passage to India,* for example, the mandala in *The Longest Journey,* of which Rickie asks whether it is real, to be told by Ansell that only the undrawable, ungraspable centre is. If I am correct about the working out in *Where Angels Fear to Tread* of the thought that we cannot view our existential situation from a standpoint external to it, then we should not be at all surprised that Ansell, who has the root of the matter in him, should have read Hegel, or imagine that Forster nodded to or displayed his ignorance of Cambridge philosophy in making him so, when in fact the way Forster chooses to draw Ansell shows that Forster was ignorant neither of philosophy nor Cambridge. Finally, of course, the notion that we cannot get outside our situation has a good claim to be regarded as the ur-thought of Modernism; and I think Forster's interest in it may account for the feeling many readers have that despite the scrupulously pre-Modernist form of his fiction, it is in some not easily definable way engaged with Modernist themes and problems.

On the other hand, however, there is Idealism of the other, Berkeleyan kind, which identifies being with appearing and which yawns invitingly at the feet of anyone who dabbles in Idealism of the first kind. If *Where Angels Fear to Tread* can be read as I have suggested, that possibility yawns at Forster's. In philosophical terms, the alternative to intuitionism of the type defended by Moore is generally thought to be some form of non-cognitivism. And although gallant efforts have been made in some quarters to base a belief in the objectivity of moral judgements upon purely logical foundations, it remains hard to see how a non-cognitivist can avoid some version of moral relativism: the doctrine that moral judgement is wholly relative to the customs and expectations of a particular society or social group. This is the position into which Philip, showing an impressive capacity to anticipate the direction to be taken by academic philosophy over the coming half-century, has settled by the time we find him lecturing Harriet on the historical absurdity of condemning an Italian for unchivalrousness. We need, I think, to understand Philip's subsequent behaviour in Monteriano in the light of this earlier passage: not simply as *frivolity* (for which there is no particular warrant elsewhere in the novel), but as issuing from a new-found conviction that one cannot judge one society by the lights of another—that what separates people of different moral outlook is not *error* about the topography of a moral landscape accessible to both, but simply empty space. One can imagine an equally amusing, though slighter, version of the novel being written with this as its central thesis. But clearly it is not the central thesis of the book we have: Philip's moral relativism is not the last word.

What Forster is out to demonstrate in the book, it seems to me, is that even if relativism should happen to have the last word on the level of theorizing about morality, what has the last word at the level of moral commitment and change of outlook is not theory but relationship. Two remarks of Furbank seem to me of particular value here. The first concerns 'the extraordinary precipitateness and swiftness of transformation of his [Forster's] narrative. . . . Hardly any characters exchange two sentences before they have changed in relation to each other, and also changed in themselves, often for ever.'[17] The second is Furbank's observation that for Forster 'what supremely mattered was human relationships . . . people mattered, but only relatively, for people are inevitably in a ceaseless state of flux and dissolution; the thing which may contain more reality and permanence is found in *relationships* between people.'[18]

Why does relationship have the power to change people 'in themselves'? The answer, I take it, lies in the way in which the confident moral conclusions which we derive from solitary, inward reflection are apt to die on our lips when we measure them against the acts and words of the alien Other. The moral objectivities we encounter on such occasions are admittedly of a rather negative, not to say Popperian, kind—they afford us knowledge only of what Will Not Wash, morally speaking, not of what will—but that does not make them any the less objectivities. And they afford us as much in the way of moral objectivity as we are ever likely to obtain. Of course, if we are to enjoy even this much grasp on moral objectivity, it is essential above all things that we do not falsify the Other. It is primarily for this reason, it seems to me, that Forster wanted to insist upon the importance of 'the ethical idea that reality must be faced'. In so far as he was a Realist, he was a Realist about personal relationship; not, or not primarily, about cows or tables. And this, of course, is how it comes about that the bathing of Gino's little son can provide *Where Angels Fear to Tread*

with a moral centre which has the power to transcend, and through Caroline Abbott to rebuke, Philip's moral relativism. In that episode both Caroline Abbott and the reader are forced to reckon with the physical, undeniable presence of a love to which Gino has cheerfully sacrificed the pleasures of the café that morning, and to which he manifestly intends to go ahead and sacrifice those of the single state. As Caroline discovers, there is not much arguing with that. It has indeed, as Rosenbaum suggests, something of the blank Reality of Moore's two hands, though, as I have tried to suggest, the workings of Forster's mind in the novel are perhaps a little more complicated than that.

NOTES

[1] Leonard Woolf, *Beginning Again: An Autobiography of the Years 1911-1918* (London, 1972), p. 24.

[2] P. N. Furbank, *E. M. Forster: A Life* (London, 1977), I. 49.

[3] Woolf, *Beginning Again*, p. 24.

[4] S. P. Rosenbaum, 'The Longest Journey: E. M. Forster's Refutation of Idealism', in *E. M. Forster: A Human Exploration*, ed. G. K. Das and John Beers (London, 1979), pp. 32-54.

[5] E. M. Forster, Introduction to the World's Classics edn. of *The Longest Journey,* cited in Rosenbaum, p. 34.

[6] Rosenbaum, *'The Longest Journey'*, p. 41.

[7] P. N. Furbank, 'The Philosophy of E. M. Forster', in *E. M. Forster, Centenary Revaluations*, ed. Judith Scherer Herz and Robert K. Martin (London, 1982), p. 46.

[8] Ibid., p. 47.

[9] E. M. Forster, 'How I Lost My Faith', *The Humanist* 78, no. 9 (Sept. 1963), 263.

[10] J. M. Keynes, 'My Early Beliefs', in *Two Memoirs* (London, 1949), p. 81; subsequent page references in the text are to this edn.

[11] Thomas Nagel, 'What It Is Like To Be a Bat', *Philosophical Review* 83 (1974), 435-51.

[12] See R. M. Hare, *Moral Thinking* (Oxford, 1981), pp. 25-43, for a clear and trenchant defence of this aspect of utilitarianism. Chapter 5 of John Stuart Mill's essay 'Utilitarianism' is one *locus classicus* for the view.

[13] G. E. Moore, *Principia Ethica,* chap. VI, 113.

[14] Page references are to the Penguin edn.: E. M. Forster, *Where Angels Fear to Tread* (London, 1959).

[15] Norman Kelvin, *E. M. Forster* (Carbondale, Ill., 1967), p. 43.

[16] Ibid., p. 48.

[17] Furbank, 'Philosophy of Forster', p. 39.

[18] Ibid., p. 43.

Kent Linville and Merrill Ring (essay date 1991)

SOURCE: "Moore's Paradox Revisited," in *Synthese*, Vol. 87, No. 1, April, 1991, pp. 295-309.

[*In the following essay, Linville and Ring apply Ludwig Wittgenstein's principles to Moore's paradox.*]

Wittgenstein "once remarked that the only work of Moore's that greatly impressed him was his discovery of the peculiar kind of nonsense involved in such a sentence as, e.g., 'It is raining but I don't believe it'".[1] Present practice is to refer to the difficulties generated by sentences of this form, as well as to sentences of the form "I believe that p but not p", as "Moore's paradox".[2] Despite Wittgenstein's great reputation and regard for the importance of Moore's "discovery", little interest has been generated in the topic. And yet, central issues in epistemology and the philosophy of language are involved in the resolution of this paradox. Since this is not generally appreciated, we begin our discussion by establishing what some of those important issues are, thereby crediting Wittgenstein's assessment of the importance of the paradox. Then, we develop an account of the aberrant nature of Moore's sentences (hereafter labelled "MS") that is indebted to Wittgenstein, and which challenges the assumptions that motivate the standard form of discussion of these sentences initiated by Moore.

Moore says "such a thing as 'I went to the pictures last Tuesday, but I don't believe that I did' is a perfectly absurd thing to say [i.e., assert], although what is asserted is something perfectly possible logically".[3] Moore makes two claims here (besides stating the basic fact that MS would be absurd to assert), claims which have become canonical in subsequent literature. First, the peculiarity or absurdity of MS cannot reside in the sentence itself, since it is not self-contradictory, and second, that its absurdity (therefore) arises only in speech (expressing, as it apparently does, a possibility in thought). So what puzzles Moore and his followers is why the assertion of MS should be absurd, when "what it asserts" might be true.

Explanations offered of that absurdity, with the exception of Wittgenstein's,[4] rest on one or another version of the doctrine that saying or asserting implies believing.[5] To say "not-p", according to this view, is to imply that one doesn't believe that p; this implied "I don't believe that p" conflicts with one saying "I believe that p", thereby generating the absurdity of such an assertion. And because "I don't believe that p" is only (non-deductively) implied and not entailed, the assumed non-self-contradictory character of MS is maintained.

Wittgenstein, on the other hand, gives a quite different account of the absurdity of MS. On his view, "'I believe that this is the case' is used like the assertion 'This is the case'";[6] that is, "I believe that p" is a form of the assertion that p. Hence, MS conjoins a form of the assertion that p and an assertion that not p and its absurdity arises from *that* conflict.

Now that we have described these two competing accounts of how the clauses of MS come into conflict, it is obvious each results from a different interpretation of the function of "I believe". In Moorean accounts, that belief phrase is assumed to be self-referential—to say something about, be descriptive of, the speaker. Thus they see the paradox to be that of explaining how a statement such as "I believe it is raining" (understood to be "about the speaker") *can* conflict with the other clause of MS, since it is clearly about some other (logically-independent) subject matter—the weather. Because their response to MS is guided by *that* question, the explanations they produce involve the prior assumption that "I believe" *is* self-referential; and that unexamined thought gives rise, in turn, to the other two staples in Moorean discussion: the ideas that MS is not self-contradictory and (therefore) that its absurdity arises only in speech.

Our discussion, following Wittgenstein's lead, argues that the three ideas we have identified as guiding Moorean solutions of the paradox are muddled, so our study, if successful, "dissolves" Moore's paradox by showing it to be the outgrowth of misunderstandings.[7] And since our criticisms aim to show that the philosophical requirements which prompt Moorean invocations of the doctrine that saying implies believing result from antecedent confusion, direct criticism of that doctrine will be ancilliary to our overall strategy, which is designed to show that "I believe it is raining but it's not", for example, is absurd because it consists of two contradictory assertions about the weather.

We begin by locating the ideas motivating standard discussions of Moore's paradox in a different, and undeniable important, philosophical setting.

Wittgenstein hints at the historical significance of the primitive idea in Moorean discussions of MS (that "I believe" is self-referential) in the following remark:

> The significance of such possibilities of transformation, for example of turning all statements into sentences beginning 'I think' or 'I believe' (and thus, as it were, into descriptions of my inner life) will become clearer in another place. (Solipsism)[8]

The paradigmatic statement of solipsism is of course found at the conclusion of Descartes's "First Meditation", where he vows "resolute attachment" to the thought that I, "having no hands, no eyes, no flesh, no blood, nor any senses, . . . [nonetheless] falsely believe myself to possess all these things".[9] And this is the genesis of the philosophical heritage which informs Moorean sensibilities. For the assumed meaning of "I believe", around which standard discussion of Moore's paradox turns, is also at the heart of the Cartesian enterprise in the *Meditations.* Indeed, both the skepticism of the "First Meditation" and the *cogito* of the "Second Meditation" depend upon a self-referential construal of those words. For consider, since Descartes's skeptical hypothesis is intended to immunize him from error, providing an antidote to the threat posed by the *malin génie,* the "doubt" expressed in the resolution to "consider myself falsely believing" *cannot* involve full-bodied disbelief; to disbelieve a proposition ("I have hands, eyes . . . ," for example) is to believe its contradictory ("I believe that it is not the case I have hands, eyes . . . ."), and that would leave Descartes equally exposed to error.

So what Descartes's maneuver comes to, what his "hypothesis" requires, is detaching belief from truth. This non-epistemic rendering of "I believe" is spelled out in the *Principles,* where, explaining the *cogito,* he characterizes judgments involving perception as though they functioned to describe inner-experience rather than to assert "representational content":

> [I]f I say I see, or I walk, I therefore am, and if by seeing and walking I mean the action of my eyes or my legs . . . my conclusion is not absolutely certain; because it may be that, as often happens in sleep, I think I see or I walk, although I never open my eyes or move from my place. . . . But if I mean only to talk of my . . . consciously seeming to see or to walk, it becomes quite true because my assertion now refers only to my mind, which alone is concerned with my feeling or *thinking that I see* and I walk.[10]

Now we can tie these thoughts of Descartes's directly to the issue at stake in the resolution of Moore's paradox, by imagining an "Eighth Set of Objections" to the *Meditations,* opening with the following question:

> Dear Descartes, in your *Meditations* you take 'I am seated here by a fire' or 'This is a hand' to be dubitable; whereas statements such as 'I think (believe/doubt) that this is a hand' you hold to be indubitable. Now you apparently understand this epistemological difference to reflect a semantic contrast, a difference in what is asserted in the two cases. The former assertions go beyond reports of one's experience, claiming to report an independently existing reality; while the latter assertions, when carefully considered, are seen to be nothing but descriptions of one's own states of mind, and so they are, according to the *cogito,* indubitable. But then, why can't we assert such a thing as 'I believe I have hands, but I don't'? Surely it would be perfectly absurd to assert such a thing, although I can't see that it should be, if you are correct in your understanding of what its conjuncts actually say.

So Descartes, too, might have been called upon to explain the oddness of MS. And with this historical perspective in view, we now return to standard discussions

of Moore's paradox, to consider the related claims they make that MS is impeccable in thought, and that it becomes marred only when embodied in speech. For unless the entire thrust of Wittgenstein's later philosophy is fundamentally misguided, it will turn out that precisely because Mooreans are correct in claiming MS is absurd in speech (on permanent holiday, if you will), they are wrong in maintaining its intelligibility in thought. For the claim that an expression's meaning is a function of its having a place, and the place it has in speech and communication is at the center of Wittgenstein's later philosophy. Among the numerous examples we might cite as reminders of this, the following, though long, is especially apt, since it relates that theme directly to Moore's paradox:

> How would it be, if a soldier produced military communiqués which were justified on grounds of observation; but he adds that he believes they are incorrect. . . . The communiqué is a language-game with these words. It would produce confusion if we were to say: the words of the communiqué— the proposition communicated—have a definite sense, and the giving of it, the 'assertion' supplies something additional. As if the sentence, spoken by a gramophone, belonged to pure logic; as if here it had the pure logical sense; as if here we had before us the object logicians get hold of and consider—while the sentence as asserted, communicated, is what it is in *business.* As one may say: the botanist considers a rose *as a plant,* not as an ornament for a dress or room or as a delicate attention. The sentence, I want to say, has no sense outside the language-game. This hangs together with its not being a kind of *name.* As though one might say ' "I believe . . ."—*that's how it is'* pointing (as it were inwardly) at what gives the sentence its meaning.[11]

So the Fregean distinction between assumption and assertion, and the idea of a "pure logical sense", which formal logic is to catch in abstraction from the empirical settings of assertion, is a myth, or so Wittgenstein maintains. Meaning is inextricably scenic: "Words have their meaning only in the flow of life".[12]

Bringing this theme to bear on the useless sentences here at issue, we begin by pressing for a precise characterization of the phenomenology implied by the Moorean claim that "what it [MS] asserts" is a perfectly possible, thinkable state of affairs. Taking "thinkability" literally invites the following question: Can we have the thought "I believe it's raining but it's not" without absurdity? Surely not. If we try to think that MS is so, that strikes us as being every bit as ludicrous as trying to imagine its public declaration; passing it through our head produces the same sense of absurdity as passing it through our lips.

The Moorean response to this will no doubt be that the intelligibility being claimed for MS is not based on the grounds that we can think *it,* but rather, that it is possible to imagine (or "entertain" the thought of) oneself believing it is raining, say, *and* that it's not raining. And this, our objector insists, shows that what MS asserts is perfectly possible logically.

Among traditional philosophers who assume meaning and understanding either are or essentially involve mental states or processes, such appeals are common fare. As a reminder of that, we recall two important examples, the first from Hume, the second from Wittgenstein's *Tractatus*:

> Suppose a person present with me, who advances propositions to which I do not assent, *that* Caesar *dy'd in his bed, that silver is more fusible than lead, or mercury heavier than gold;* 'tis evident, that notwithstanding my incredulity, I clearly understand his meaning, and form all the same ideas, which he forms. My imagination is endow'd with the same powers as his.[13]

> 'A state of affairs is thinkable': what this means is that we can picture it to ourselves.[14]

Of course the *Investigations* argues that whether or not a sentence has sense and what sense it has is not determined by the products of the imagination:

> It is no more essential to the understanding of a proposition that one should imagine anything in connection with it, than that one should make a sketch from it.[15]

Nor are such items sufficient to secure understanding; pictures, whether images or sketches, public or private, are themselves signs which can be variously interpreted, so they *require* rather than produce *understanding:*

> Imagine a picture representing a boxer in a particular stance. Now this picture can be used to tell someone how he should stand, should hold himself; or how he should not hold himself; or how a particular man did stand in such-and-such a place, and so on.[16]

But this general and rather abstract discussion will most likely not do to correct the sense that we do have a successful appeal to the imagination in connection with MS, that here "a picture is conjured up which . . . [does] fix the sense *unambiguously;* . . . a picture . . . which seems to make the sense of the expression *unmistakable*".[17] Exposing this apparition of sense to be the result of confusion requires more detailed discussion.

Our beliefs are where we stand cognitively, so to speak; indeed, though this analogy is weak it is not overworked by noting that the verisimilitude of *any* representation of *oneself* falsely believing will be limited in a manner akin to a drawing picturing where one *is standing:*

> A painter does not draw the spot where he is standing. But in looking at his picture I can deduce his position by relation to the things drawn. On the other hand, if he puts himself into his picture I know for certain that the place where he shows himself is not the place where he is.[18]

Analogously, the person pictured to exhibit what MS asserts is, perforce, a surrogate for "I" in "I believe", and so is subject to its logic. Therefore, if we imagine the person depicted to be believing falsely, we can "deduce" one is not then thinking from within that picture, i.e., from within the "logical space" of "I believe"; for when belief is thus identified ("I believe . . ."), one cannot (logically) proceed to indicate that the belief *is* false—one's current beliefs *are* one's representation(s) of reality. When we envisage ourselves from afar, as Hume was wont to say, we observe both belief and contrary reality, and so the relevant belief words are *observational;* but of course "I believe" is not observational. We do not say "I believe it's raining" because we have taken note of ourselves grabbing a raincoat or our saying "I believe it's raining"; even more absurd is the thought that we base those words on what we imagine ourselves to be saying and doing.

This criticism of the Moorean appeal to the imagination—where they assume we find or may produce an exhibit of what MS allegedly asserts—may be thought to mistake epistemological for semantical differences; that is, a Moorean may object that, of course, "I believe" is not ascribed on the basis of observation, but that's because such ("intentional") states are "known directly", rather than by inference from behavioral symptoms, as in the case of "You (He) believe(s)". So although it is correct that non-first-person belief words are required to articulate the Moorean thought experiment, still, that in no way shows the thought is not cogent. For making the required correction (substituting the second- or third-person form of words) does not alter the "propositional content" of one's thought.

That something along these lines would be Moore's response is clear in his following comment:

> 'I went to the pictures last Tuesday, but I don't believe that I did' is absurd to say, although *what is asserted is something which is perfectly possible logically: it is perfectly possible that you did go to the picture and yet you do not believe that you did.[19]

Of course Moore is not alone in his unself-conscious assumption that changes in pronoun make mere grammatical rather than logical alterations in what is said or asserted (given the "indexicals" are understood to "identify the same referent"). For example, the still widely used canonical "A believes that *p*" is also employed on the assumption it has the same truth-value, expresses the same proposition, no matter what we substitute for "A". And, the assimilation underlying this practice takes us to an important conceptual source of the thought we earlier identified as basic or primitive in both Descartes's thinking and Moorean accounts of MS, namely, that "I believe" is self-referential. No one will deny that prefixing "You (or He) believe(s)" to a simple assertion such as "It is raining" *does* change its subject matter—transforming a proposition about the weather into one about the person's belief. And, the assimilation of the first-person to those other forms of the verb leads one to think a similar transformation is effected there, and thus, to suppose those words are self-referential.

In opposition to the assimilation guiding such thinking, Wittgenstein enjoins:

> Don't look at it as a matter of course, but as a most remarkable thing, that the verbs 'believe', 'wish', 'will' display all the inflexions possessed by 'cut', 'chew', 'run'.[20]

But before we consider how "believes" actually functions in our language, it is important to appreciate the general nature, and thus the full significance, of the presuppositions shaping the "matter of course" (*a priori*) thinking Wittgenstein warns against. As is made clear by the following questions which he poses in opening the *Investigations*'s discussion of Moore's paradox, those presuppositions are manifestations of the very picture of language his later philosophy labors to show is at the bottom of philosophical perplexity generally:

> How did we ever come to use such an expression as 'I believe . . .'? Did we at some time become aware of a phenomenon (of belief)?
>
> Did we observe ourselves and other people and so discover belief?[21]

The conception of language, of reality, and of the relation between them that comes with affirmative answers to Wittgenstein's questions is familiar to readers of the *Investigations,* which of course opens with a quotation from Augustine illustrating that philosophically bedeviling picture of language. The offending "primitive idea of the way language functions"[22] is, in outline, this: words are names, language functions to report the existence of what is named; and since words only name what is there to be named, the nature of things is independent of and prior to the ways in which we use language to talk about them. Learning the meaning of "believe(s)", then, is learning to identify the phenomenon of human experience it names—belief. "I believe" is the form of words we have for identifying the presence of the phenomenon in oneself; "You" and "He believes" are words and phrases which identify that phenomenon in others. Moreover, when gripped by this model we are inclined to think of sentences as names, too (perhaps along Fregean lines, as a kind of complex proper name). Therefore, since we assume "I believe it is raining" and "It is raining", for example, *must* name different processes, when one is affirmed and the other denied (as in MS), we think that that *can't* be a contradiction.

Discussion of the philosophical conception of language and companion metaphysics, we have pointed out in the background of Moorean discussions, is beyond the purview of this brief study. However, there is a direct and untoward consequence of those ideas for first-person belief talk which is perhaps sufficiently jarring to loosen their grip. This consequence is remarked by Wittgenstein in the following comment:

> A: 'I believe it's raining'.—B: 'I don't believe so'. Now they are not contradicting each other; each one is simply saying something about himself.[23]

Standard discussions of Moore's paradox are focused on the phrases "I believe" or "I don't believe" nested in a single sentence, and thus in one mouth, and so such discussions fail to reveal the implausible consequence which their construal of those words has for an understanding of their role in contexts of *interpersonal* disagreement in belief. But as Wittgenstein's above remark calls to attention, the Moorean construal of those phrases effectively elides that role, rendering such remarks bits of autobiography: A: "I feel anxious"—B: "I don't". However, if I say "I believe the Prime Minister will soon fall from office", and an interlocutor responds "I don't believe that he will", there is disagreement.

Once we turn from the monolithic view of meaning and reference which arises from a "name-thing" ("'Fido'-Fido") conception of language, we see quite clearly "I believe" and "He believes" do not have the same function. Wittgenstein expresses their salient difference this way: "'I believe that this is the case' is used like the assertion 'This is the case'; and yet the *hypothesis* that I believe this is the case is not used like the hypothesis that this is the case".[24] That is, "I believe that the Prime Minister will fall from power" takes a position on, makes a truth-claim about, the Prime Minister; whereas "He believes that the Prime Minister will fall from power" takes no such stand (as witnessed by the fact "He believes the Prime Minister will fall from power, but he won't" is an impeccable assertion).

Wittgenstein brings out the conceptual difference in those belief phrases from yet another angle, by asking the following:

> I say of someone else 'He seems to believe. . . .' and other people say it of me. Now, why do I never say it of myself, not even when others rightly say it of me? —Do I myself not see and hear myself, then? . . . [25]

The short answer is "seeing and hearing myself" is irrelevant, because "I believe that *p*" announces a verdict about the truth-value of *p,* not the condition of the person rendering that verdict;[26] and others can say of me that I seem to believe because their words—"He seems to believe that *p*" (said of me)—do form a hypothesis about me, not a verdict about *p.*

In sum then, "I believe" and "He believes" are different instruments which perform functions as distinct as that made familiar by John Austin between "I promise" and "He promises". "I believe", rather than altering the subject matter of assertions, attenuates or otherwise modifies statements. One form this takes is brought out in Urmson's classic article "Parenthetical Verbs", in which he compares "I believe that *p*" to "It is probable that *p*".[27] Though again, one sometimes offers up a proposition on the platter of "I believe" as a matter of conversational form, thereby acknowledging that *p* is controversial (that others may doubt or deny it), though nonetheless, certain of it oneself. In neither case, though, is one adverting to a state or condition of the speaker; as Wittgenstein cautions: "Don't regard a hesitant assertion as an assertion of hesitancy".[28]

We must now anticipate and defend against various objections to our account of "I believe", objections motivated by the thought that in saying "I believe" surely something gets said about the speaker. Such criticisms can be developed in numerous ways. We concentrate here on central examples, leaving it to the reader to adapt the principle guiding our responses to those further cases. The error in all such objections is the same: recognizing that information about the speaker is made available by his speaking, the attempt is made to locate that information in his words "I believe", whereas properly it should be assigned elsewhere.

Starting with a simple case, of course a person can be saying something about himself when using "I believe". "Can you run a mile in six minutes?"—"Yes, I believe I can". But that this remark is about the speaker is not a function of the words "I believe", but of the second occurrence of the pronoun. Or again, we answer questions like "Do you believe Gorbachev will succeed in reforming the Soviet economy?" by saying "Yes, I believe he will", or "No, I don't believe he will". Don't such answers show we are saying something about ourselves? The erroneous assumption here is that the question is about the respondent. But surely the question is *about Gorbachev*, though of course *addressed* to the respondent. Again: "If you say 'I believe he's happy', inferences about your behavior are possible. Doesn't that show something gets said about the assertor?" No, inferences about my behavior can also be made on the basis of my saying "He's happy", but it doesn't follow that *that* assertion is about the speaker. Of course if you assert "I believe . . .", that is *your* assertion and inferences about you are possible. But that you have spoken and thereby opened up the possibility of inferences being made about yourself is not the same thing as asserting something about yourself.

Similar kinds of confusion arise from projecting features of the context of utterance onto the use of "I believe". Someone applying for Conscientious Objector status, for example, may well say to officials, "I believe violence is evil". But it is not that his words are about himself, rather *he* is the object of inquiry, an inquiry in which the authorities are interested in the person. Their pursuing the question of whether violence *is* evil, even had the applicant said straight off "Violence is evil", would be out of place in such proceedings. The following observation of Wittgenstein's helps clarify what is at issue here, which is how words that are about some other subject matter can, nonetheless, be spoken to provide information about oneself:

> The language-game of reporting can be given such a turn that a report is not meant to inform the hearer about its subject matter but about the person making the report.
>
> It is so when, for instance, a teacher examines a pupil. (You can measure to test the ruler.)[29]

In asking, "Who discovered America?" the teacher is seeking to learn something about the pupil. Yet the student can only perform successfully by using words which are not about himself, by saying, for example, "Columbus, I believe".

Finally, further occasion for the misinterpretation of the logic of assertions arises when traditional talk of truth conditions is applied to propositions modified by "epistemic verbs". This kind of difficulty is illustrated by David Lewis, when he states:

> If someone says "I declare that the Earth is flat" (sincerely, not play-acting, etc.) I claim that he has spoken truly: he does indeed so declare. I claim this not only for the sake of my theory but as a point of common sense. Yet one might be tempted to say that he has spoken falsely, because the sentence embedded in his performative—the content of his declaration, the belief he avows—is false. Hence I do not propose to take ordinary declaratives as paraphrased performatives . . . because that would get their truth conditions wrong.[30]

Applying Lewis's reasoning to Moore's sentences of course inclines one to hold that the assignment of conflicting truth values to its clauses poses no problem of logical consistency. But this inclination and Lewis's claim, that it is supported by common sense, are clearly wrong. The truth is, rather, to the contrary, as George Lakoff observes:

> Note that in statements it is the propositional content, not the entire sentence, that will be true or false. For example, if I say to you 'I state that I am innocent', and you reply 'That's false', you are denying that I am innocent, not that I made the statement. That is, in sentences where there is an overt performative verb of saying or stating or asserting, the propositional content, which is true or false, is not given by the sentence as a whole.[31]

Of course "believe" is not a performative verb, but Lakoff's point holds there, too. Lewis is confusing sincerity conditions with truth conditions, conflating questions of truth with questions of truthfulness; these are two *different* language-games or modes of assessment, both of which can be engaged in with respect to "I declare", "I state", or "I believe" statements, unlike "I have pain" statements, for example.

Before we conclude with a final criticism of standard treatments of Moore's paradox, we should make note of one implication of this study for studies of belief. Our account of the uselessness of MS, if correct, inverts orthodox treatments of belief. This reorientation requires independent development, of course, but we can sketch how the developed story would parallel Wittgenstein's well-known "reversals" of the traditionally held primacy of appearance language over physical object language,[32] or of doubt over belief.[33] On the account of believing developed here, belief is not, as traditionally assumed, the source of assertions (a mental reservoir, a neural network, or whatever from which assertions flow); rather, belief is itself "a new joint in", an elaboration or modification of, the concept of assertion.

To this point in our discussion, our criticism of the standard account of the absurdity of Moore's sentences has attacked the ideas which motivate it; we have said nothing about the Moorean solution itself, about their saying-implies-believing doctrine. We close by showing why that doctrine, though perhaps true,[34] does not explain the infelicity of MS.

Those who maintain that saying implies believing gloss "implies" in terms of what might be called the associated rights of "givings" and "takings" in communication. Moore writes in explanation, "If we hear a man say . . . , we should all take it that . . .".[35] Toulmin claims that a forecaster's "It will rain" is about the weather and only "implies, or gives people to understand" what his beliefs are.[36] Again, Nowell-Smith develops a notion of contextual implication, which he explains in terms of justified takings: "A statement *p* contextually implies a statement *q* if anyone . . . would be entitled to infer *q* from *p* in the context in which they occur".[37] In sum, the idea that there is an implication relation between saying and believing is explained as amounting to the claim that there is an inference ticket from asserting to a state of the assertor.

As a principle of inference, however, the doctrine saying-implies-believing is not something that a person can employ about himself. We do not infer what we ourselves believe from what we say; we cannot say "I said '*p*', therefore (*ceteris paribus*), 'I believe *p*'". Saying does not imply believing, it implies "He believes": "'He said *p*', so (*ceteris paribus*) he believes *p*". To make the principle here relevant to MS, one must stretch it to include our taking the same interest in our own words as another can. But when one works out that possibility, the data which the principle is being invoked to explain (viz., the absurdity of asserting MS) disappears:

> If I listened to the words of my mouth, I might say someone else was speaking out of my mouth.
>
> 'Judging from what I say, *this* is what I believe.' Now, it is possible to think out circumstances in which these words would make sense.
>
> And then it would also be possible for someone to say 'It is raining and I don't believe it'. or 'It seems to me that my ego believes this, but it isn't true.' One would have to fill out the picture with behaviour indicating that two people were speaking through my mouth.[38]

NOTES

[1] Norman Malcolm: 1958, *Ludwig Wittgenstein: A Memoir,* London, p. 177.

[2] This practice probably derives from Wittgenstein; cf. his discussion of these sentences in Ludwig Wittgenstein: 1968, *Philosophical Investigations,* 3rd ed., trans. G. E. M. Anscombe, New York, Part II, pp. 190-92.

[3] G. E. Moore: 1942, "A Reply to My Critics", *The Philosophy of G. E. Moore,* ed. P. A. Schilpp, Evanston, pp. 542-43.

[4] In addition to Wittgenstein's extensive discussion of the paradox, both in the *Investigations* and elsewhere (cited below, note 11), this discussion draws on Kent Linville and Mervill Ring: 1972, "Moore's Paradox: Assertions and Implication", *Behaviorism* I, pp. 87-102.

[5] For an extensive bibliography of the major writings on Moore's paradox, see Jaakko Hintikka: 1962, *Knowledge and Belief,* Ithaca, p. 64, footnote. To that, add Hintikka's own work in that book, pp. 64-76; J. L. Austin: 1962, *How to do Things with Words,* Cambridge, pp. 48-49; Norman Malcolm: 1963, *Knowledge and Certainty,* Englewood Cliffs, pp. 16-17; P. H. Nowell-Smith: 1954, *Ethics,* London, pp. 80-81; B. C. van Fraassen: 1984, "Belief and the Will", *Journal of Philosophy* 81, pp. 235-56; and Bernard Williams: 1973, *The Problems of the Self,* Cambridge, p. 137. Considerations of length lead us to only assert the basic sameness of these accounts, leaving verification to the reader.

[6] Wittgenstein, op. cit., p. 190. Cp.: "The sentence 'I want some wine to drink' has roughly the same sense as 'Wine over here'!" Ludwig Wittgenstein: 1980, *Remarks on the Philosophy of Psychology,* trans. G. E. M. Anscombe, eds. G. E. M. Anscombe and G. H. von Wright, Chicago, vol. I, section 469.

[7] "Something surprising, a paradox, is a paradox only in a particular, as it were, defective, surrounding. One needs to complete this surrounding in such a way that what looked like a paradox no longer seems one". Ludwig Wittgenstein: 1978, *Remarks on the Foundations of Mathematics,* 3d ed., Oxford, section VII, no. 43.

[8] Wittgenstein, *Investigations,* Part I, p. 24.

[9] René Descartes: 1967, *The Philosophical Works of Descartes,* trans. Haldane and Ross. Cambridge, vol. I, p. 148.

[10] Ibid., p. 222, emphasis added.

[11] Wittgenstein, *Remarks on the Philosophy of Psychology,* vol. I, sec. 487-88.

[12] Ludwig Wittgenstein: 1980, *Remarks on the Philosophy of Psychology,* trans. C. G. Luckhardt and A. E. Aue, eds. G. H. von Wright and Neikki Nyman, Chicago, vol. II. sec. 687.

[13] David Hume: 1967, *A Treatise of Human Nature,* ed. Selby-Biggs, Oxford, p. 95.

[14] Ludwig Wittgenstein: 1963, *Tractatus Logico-Philosophicus,* trans. D. Pears and B. McGuinness, London, 3.001.

[15] Wittgenstein, *Investigations,* Part I, p. 396.

[16] Ibid., note p. 11.

[17] Ibid., pp. 426, 352.

[18] Simone Weil: 1970, *First and Last Notebooks,* trans. Richard Rees, London, p. 146.

[19] Moore, op. cit., p. 542.

[20] Wittgenstein, *Investigations,* p. 190. Cp.: "Must the verb 'I believe' have a past tense form? Well, if instead of 'I believe he's coming' we always said 'He could be coming' (or the like), but nevertheless said 'I believed . . .' —in this way the verb 'I believe' would have no *present.* It is characteristic of the way in which we are apt to regard language, that we believe that there must after all in the last instance be uniformity, symmetry: instead of holding on the contrary that it doesn't *have* to exist". Wittgenstein, *Remarks on the Philosophy of Psychology,* vol. I, sec. 907.

[21] Wittgenstein, *Investigations,* p. 190.

[22] Ibid., Part I, p. 2.

[23] Wittgenstein, *Remarks on the Philosophy of Psychology,* vol. II, sec. 419.

[24] Wittgenstein, *Investigations,* p. 190.

[25] Ibid., p. 191.

[26] "That he believes such and such, *we* gather from observation of his person, but *he* does not make the statement 'I believe . . .' on the grounds of observation of himself. And *that* is why 'I believe p' may be equivalent to the assertion of *p.* And the question 'Is it so?' to 'I'd like to know if it is so?'". Wittgenstein, *Remarks on the Philosophy of Psychology,* vol. I. sec. 504.

[27] J. O. Urmson: 1952, "Parenthetical Verbs", *Mind* LXI, reprinted in *Essays in Conceptual Analysis,* ed. A. Flew (London, 1956).

[28] Wittgenstein, *Investigations,* p. 192.

[29] Ibid., pp. 190-91.

[30] From David Lewis: 1972, "General Semantics", in Harman and Davidson, eds. *Semantics for Natural Language,* Dordrecht, p. 210, as quoted in George Lakoff: 1975, "Pragmatics in Natural Logic", in E. L. Keenan, ed., *Formal Semantics of Natural Language,* Cambridge, p. 256.

[31] Ibid., p. 257.

[32] Ludwig Wittgenstein: 1967, *Zettel,* eds. G. E. M. Anscombe and G. H. von Wright, trans. G. E. M. Anscombe, Oxford, sec. 413-26.

[33] Ludwig Wittgenstein: 1969, *On Certainty,* eds. G. E. M. Anscombe and G. H. von Wright, trans. Denis Paul and G. E. M. Anscombe, Oxford, sec. 115, 160.

[34] We use "perhaps true" advisedly; cf. Henry A. Alexander Jr.: 1967, "Comments on Saying and Believing", in *Epistemology: New Essays in the Theory of Knowledge,* ed. Avrum Stroll, New York, pp. 159-78.

[35] Moore op. cit., p. 543.

[36] Toulmin, op. cit., pp. 52, 85.

[37] Nowell-Smith, loc. cit.

[38] Wittgenstein, *Investigations,* p. 192.

Thomas Leddy (essay date 1991)

SOURCE: "Moore and Shusterman on Organic Wholes," in *The Journal of Aesthetics and Art Criticism,* Vol. 49, No. 1, Winter, 1991, pp. 63-73.

[*In the following essay, Leddy examines Moore's refutation of idealism in light of the contemporary debate between analytic philosophy and deconstruction.*]

It is natural in periods of crisis in a paradigm to turn back to the founders in an effort to think carefully through the reasons for the founding of the movement. The origins of analytic philosophy can be found partly in G. E. Moore's objections to the idealism of the British Hegelians, e.g., Bradley and McTaggart. The debate between Moore and these idealists is particularly interesting when we consider recent comparisons that have been drawn by Rorty and others between 19th century idealism and 20th century textualism.[1] Richard Shusterman has recently reopened the debate by considering the opposing views of such continental philosophers as Derrida and Nehamas and analytic philosophers concerning the concept of organic unity.[2] He has made the interesting observation that although Derrida has opposed organic unity as a principle of aesthetic value he is committed to a more radical form of organic unity that asserts the interconnectedness of everything in the world. Shusterman also attributes this more radical organicism to Nehamas and, through Nehamas's interpretation of Nietzsche, to Nietzsche. On this Nietzschean view, things have no characters independent of their interrelations with other things—and, directly or indirectly, everything is interrelated with everything else. Things are also relative to interpretations—different interpretations produce different things. On this view all properties are equally essential; thus the distinction between essence and accident dissolves.[3]

Shusterman believes that Moore's arguments against the radical or Hegelian conception of organic unity can also be directed against this Nietzschean position. Shusterman recognizes that these arguments are based on a concept of "stable part" which is open to deconstruction. In light of the disadvantages of deconstruction and analysis he turns to pragmatism as a mediation between the two. The pragmatist, along with the deconstructionist, sees things in the world as interpretations—but the pragmatist takes such interpretations to be so deeply entrenched in our actual thinking as to have the status of facts. The pragmatist also values the distinction between understanding and interpretation which is undercut by the deconstructionist. The pragmatist does not see the world either as all logical atoms or all integrated interrelations, but as "partly joined and partly disjoined."[4]

In an earlier paper Shusterman used Moore's arguments concerning organic wholes to criticize some of Harold Osborne's views. More recently, however, he has, I think wisely, distanced himself from Moore's position. Although he still takes Moore's arguments to be powerful, he thinks that Moore did not sufficiently take into account the "temporal, vitalistic, developmental sense of organic unity" promoted by the romantics.[5] Shusterman suggests that what counts as a part may change with time; parts can be differently constituted by different interpretations.[6]

I am sympathetic to Shusterman's attempts to mediate the debate between analytic philosophy and deconstruction by way of a non-foundationalist pragmatism, and with his recognition of the force of the romantic position on organic wholes. In this paper I want to suggest how this new skepticism concerning Moore's position can be used to defend Osborne's organicism against Shusterman's earlier arguments. In short, I will show that we cannot prove that a part of a painting does *not* partake essentially in the emergent properties of the whole. Second, I will draw on Nietzsche's perspectivism to criticize Moore's arguments against radical organicism. Finally, I will argue for retention of the idea that there are essences, albeit relativized to interpretation or world-version.

I. MEANS, PARTS AND EMERGENT PROPERTIES

Unlike some later writers in the analytic tradition Moore refused to reject all internal relations in favor of a world of externally related logical atoms. He saw himself as mediating between idealism at one extreme and mechanistic materialism at the other. His position on organic relations was essential to this mediation. A mechanistic materialist would assume that the value of a whole must be determinable by summing up the values of its parts (assuming that the very concept of "value" is allowed.) But Moore denied this. For him "The value of a whole must not be assumed to be the same as the sum of the value of its parts" (p. 28).

Discussion of organic wholes comes at the end of the first chapter of *Principia Ethica* when Moore considers the different degrees in which things have the indefinable property of "good." He believes that certain wholes may possess this property in a way that cannot be accounted for by summing up the degree to which the parts possess it (p. 36). The example he first uses to describe this kind of whole is the same sort of example he uses in **"The Refutation of Idealism."** There he argues that contemporary idealism is based on the principle that *esse* is *percipi* which in turn rests on the idea that consciousness of any object, for instance yellow, is an organic whole such that each part "would not be what it is *apart from its relation to the other.*"[7] Consciousness of yellow was indeed a whole but one consisting in distinct parts, consciousness and yellow. These parts may be separated or abstracted without changing their natures.

In *Principia Ethica* the paradigm of the organic whole is consciousness of a beautiful object. Moore insists that this "single instance" will adequately illustrate the kind of relation that is to be found between parts and organic wholes. He argues that although consciousness by itself seems to have neutral value, and although a beautiful object of which no one has consciousness would seem to have very little value, consciousness of a beautiful object has great intrinsic value. Thus consciousness of a beautiful object is a whole which has greater value than the sum of its constituent parts.

Consciousness of a beautiful object is not entirely satisfactory as an example of an organic whole. As Moore admits, it is difficult to distinguish consciousness from its objects.[8] He *could* have drawn his example from traditional organic wholes such as the human body or the work of art. In fact he soon shifts to these sorts of examples in his discussion.

The reason why he picked the same type of example as he used in his refutation of idealism is that although he advocates organic wholes he cannot advocate wholes whose parts are essentially connected with the whole. The Hegelians see consciousness and the object of consciousness as interanimating each other so that the consciousness is different when the object of consciousness is different. Moore requires strict separation between consciousness and the object of consciousness. Thus, for Moore, consciousness is *externally* related to the object of consciousness. This is important when considering a supposed debate between Moore and the deconstructionists, since although the deconstructionist would not speak of consciousness, they *would* stress that the world interpreted cannot be radically separated from the act of interpretation. Moreover, since his "single instance" turns out to be an instance of external relation it is likely that he does not really believe that other organic wholes have internal relations. For him, the relationship between parts of organic wholes is mechanistic, although there is a mysterious surge of value when the parts are combined.

II. TWO OF MOORE'S ASSUMPTIONS

Because of his desire to avoid materialism Moore insists on a distinction between two kinds of necessity: the natural necessity of the means/end relation, and the logical necessity of the part/whole relation. A part of an organic whole is a necessary condition for the good of the whole, but in a different way than the means is a necessary condition for that good as an end. The latter is merely a causal or natural necessity (p. 29).

The distinction between means and part is not always as sharp as Moore believes it to be. Think of Georgia O'Keefe painting one of her Santa Fe mountain scenes. What was needed in order to finish the painting? What were the means? Many things may be listed depending on our concerns. We may begin with objects used in the painting. An initial answer might be "paints and paintbrushes." But perhaps the hills themselves are means. What about the train ticket she purchased to go to Santa Fe? We also think of techniques as means. Should we include all of her acts with respect to the finished product as means? In order to paint the scene she had to go to the place, she had to use certain brush strokes, she had to make brush stroke number 256, etc.

Now consider how we would separate means from parts. The railroad ticket and the act of going to Santa Fe are clearly not parts of the work. On the other hand the paints she used as means are also parts of the work. What about brush-stroke number 256? The term "brush-stroke" is interestingly ambiguous. It might be said that the brush-stroke *as act* is a means whereas the brush-stroke *as configuration* is a part. Yet the action painters of the 1960s have clearly shown us that the relationship between the brush-stroke as act and the brush-stroke as part of the work is intimate. It could be argued that the brush-stroke as configuration has a meaning which is at least partially a function of the intentionally funded brush-stroke as act. If so, can a thing's reality be radically separated from its meaning? Can artwork-as-process be radically separated from artwork as product?

Moore insists that the necessity of the means/end relation is "merely a natural or causal necessity" (p. 29). He takes this to mean in part that the annihilation of the means "would leave the value of that which it is now necessary to secure entirely unchanged" (p. 29). But how do we go about annihilating the brush-stroke as necessary means without at the same time annihilating the brush-stroke as end? This would pose problems even if time travel were possible!

The second fundamental premise in Moore's argument against the Hegelians is that "The part of a valuable whole retains exactly the same value when it is, as when it is not, a part of that whole" (p. 30). On this view the emergent value lies entirely in the whole. But, how can we measure the value of the part in the two cases? Moore assumes, and Shusterman does not question this, that if the part has little or no intrinsic value when separated from the whole then it will have the same value when it is part of the whole. It will only *appear* to have more value insofar as it will reflect the increased emergent value of the whole.[9]

The problem with this premise is that one can argue that isolation of the part from the whole transforms the part into something different. Moore thinks this argument forces his opponents into holding that the part both is and is not the same. This raises a nest of difficult metaphysical problems that go back to Parmenides. One can hold with Parmenides that something cannot both be itself *and* change. But this leads to believing that nothing ever changes. Until we resolve this problem it may be safest to assume that it is not contradictory to say that something can be transformed into something else.

Moore could have argued that the Hegelian must agree with the logical atomist that the value of the whole is equal to the sum of its parts. However the Hegelian has two other options. It could be admitted that the value of the whole *is* equal to the value of the sum of the parts but *only* on the condition that we do not see the parts as isolated units and that we do not interpret "the sum of the parts" literally in terms of adding units. Or it could be argued that although the parts have emergent value, the whole has value which is emergent *upon* the sum of these emergent values.

All this is highly speculative. It is likely that it is undecidable whether the emergent property really resides in the part, the whole, or both. Moore says that if the part no longer displays the emergent property when it is isolated then the property is not essential to the part. His opponents say that if the part is isolated so that it no longer displays the emergent property then it is no longer the same part. The problem is that we can never know the nature of the non-isolated part. Generally when we seek to know things we isolate them, and one cannot isolate the non-isolated part.

Another problem with Moore's position is that it is doubtful whether organic wholes have any absolutely intrinsic parts. Parts are constituted *as* parts. Consider, for example, the very act of painting. Think of O'Keefe painting a landscape. Prior to the act of painting the landscape the bits of brown paint which are now in the landscape were in a paint-tube. But it would be odd to say that they were *parts* of the content of O'Keefe's paint-tube. They were constituted as parts in the act of painting.

The process of painting begins with breaking up the paint into parts by squeezing the tube so that dabs of paint appear on the pallet. Each dab is at that point (and not before) constituted as what used to be a part of the contents of the tube. Another re-constitution of parts occurs when the painter uses a brush to place parts of these dabs onto the painting surface. Whatever is a part on the painting surface is relative to what is being expressed, and that, in turn is relative to an ongoing interpretation which accompanies the creative process. The initial expression is generally followed by a process of revision and re-working—a mixing and re-creation of parts on the painting surface. Seldom is the identity of the parts of paint in the original pallet dabs retained on the surface of the painting.

How do we establish the parts of the surface of the painting? This can be done in different ways. A traditional way is to point at a part and describe it by referring to pictorial content, e.g., "that dog over there" or "the blue line above the yellow triangle." But since the late 19th century we have been able to designate a part by photographing it. This is also a new way of *constituting* a part. In the old method the viewer is called upon to individuate the part according to conventional conceptions of boundaries between object and non-object. By contrast, breaking the painting into parts through photographing "details" is generally a matter of producing new rectangular pictures which include a bit more or less than what the viewer would include in traditional part individuation. For instance the detail might include some of the background. Or it might fail to include all of a figure—for example the tail of a dog. When the part is indicated and individuated by gesture and description, the viewer may keep the rest of the painting in mind as a kind of background. Thus the two methods of indicating and constituting parts treat the background differently. The method of individuating by photographic detail retains *some* of the background with specificity as exact as the photograph allows. But it loses the rest of the background completely. The method of pointing and description retains *all* of the rest of the painting as background, but without exact specificity. In the case of photographic reproduction the detail can take on its own meaning, as when a postcard of a detail becomes a decoration in a house or an element in a collage.[10]

Another way that parts can be individuated is simply to cut away the part. Imagine a vandal doing this. If the police "discover the missing part" the museum conservator can reintegrate it into the painting. Similarly, a collage artist may take a cheap painting and cut off a patch. No matter how randomly this is done, the patch is now constituted as a part or, more precisely, formerly a part of the whole to which it once belonged. Of course collage artists generally cut away at photographs of works rather than at the works themselves. This process points out another feature of the constitution of parts. Just as photographing a detail is a way of constituting a part so too is cutting away part of the photograph. The newly constituted part now plays a role as a part or element in a new organic whole—the new work being created by the collage artist. Prior to the act of cutting the painting or photograph the newly constituted part was not, strictly speaking, a part of a whole. The collage artist treats the photograph of other artworks in much the same way as the painter treats the paint in the tube. We should distinguish between the act of constituting a part primarily as a part of the original work and constituting it primarily as a part of a future work.

III. DETACHED ARMS AND PAINTED SMILES

Moore thought that the reason we mistake means for parts may be found in the following kind of case. Since an arm which is part of a body differs from a dead arm we think: "The arm which is a part of the body would not be what it is, if it were not such a part" (p. 34). Yet he took this to be a contradiction—presumably since it assumes that something could not be the same as itself.

In fact, according to Moore, the dead arm was never a part of the body—"it is only *partially* identical with the living arm" (p. 34). By "partially identical" he means that some of the parts of the dead arm are identical with parts of the living arm, and some are not. If some parts are identical then the same thing *can* at one time form a part and at another time not form a part of an organic whole.

Moore also holds that the living arm has some properties or parts (he does not seem to distinguish the two) which the dead arm does not have. These properties or parts are causally dependent on other parts of the body but would still retain their character if they *could* be detached from the body—it is not *analytically* true that they are parts of the body (p. 35).

Moore's unexplained shift from talk of parts to talk of properties indicates a confusion between parts and properties and a resultant equivocation. It is not clear that any *part* (for example, finger, bone, or cell) is unaffected by the act of detaching the arm from the living body. A finger on the dead arm is not the same as it was when the arm was living. For instance, it no longer has the property of "being moveable by me in the way I used to move it." Losing a very specific property, namely "being part of the body," caused it to lose other properties. It probably gained some, mostly negative, properties as well.

There is no question that the dead arm also shares some properties with the living arm: for example, "having history X prior to the accident" and "having five fingers." This is why Moore thought that the two arms are partially identical. But although some properties of a part may remain unchanged after the part is detached from the whole there is no reason to believe that parts themselves can.

We think the dead arm is the same (in one sense of "same") as the live arm because of their shared history—i.e., the spatial-temporal continuity with the live arm. Shared history, however, is not sufficient for even this sense of sameness. A cremated arm does not seem to be the same arm because it doesn't seem to be any arm at all. I may say, with respect to my friend's cremated arm, "*That* is Arthur's arm"—but only with great irony (the irony is greater the less the heap of ash looks like an arm).

Sameness seems relative to purposes. Rather than saying that the dead arm is partially identical to the living arm we need only to say that under certain circumstances we *take it* as identical to the living arm. This isn't arbitrary—the "taking" must serve our purposes, fit the situation, and accord with our major presuppositions.

Moore offers the following argument. Assume that the arm is detached but still living. (We can imagine that it "lives" in a vat.) It is possible that this arm will have no intrinsic value. It is also possible that the whole body would have greater intrinsic value *with* than *without* the arm. We might believe that *as* a part it has great value but *by itself* it has none, and that therefore its importance lies in its relation to the whole. But, Moore argues, the value does not belong to *it,* for to "have value merely as a part is equivalent to having no value at all, but merely being a part of that which has it" (p. 35).

We have already explored some of the problems with this sort of argument. Shusterman, however, finds it attractive. He uses an example from art to support this position. He argues that we may point to a line in a picture of a face and assert that this part is a silly smile, but only because of the arrangement of the other lines of the face. As he puts it: "the silliness . . . of the smile is a property of the whole face, not just of the single line."[11]

He would allow Osborne's claim that the emergent properties are reflected back onto the parts, but insists that, for Moore (and himself), strictly speaking, what displays or expresses emergent properties is not a particular part, or even that part in conjunction with other parts, but the whole itself.[12] I take Shusterman to mean that, e.g., the aspect of a painting that expresses the gracefulness of a horse's neck is not a particular line in conjunction with other lines but the entire painting. The particular line is not really graceful. Descriptions relating to parts serve only to focus our attention on the aesthetic whole so that its emergent properties may be perceived.[13]

When I first read these arguments I was surprised. It seemed to me that we value parts of works of art as well as the wholes. Even though the value of the part depends on the properties of the whole we can still appreciate it as a value of the part. Examples from temporal arts come readily to mind: in literature we may appreciate a chapter without appreciating the novel as a whole. Painting is a difficult case because generally when we are looking at a painting we are looking at the whole, although exceptions include the act of standing close to a painting or the act of looking at a very large mural. It might still be the case that we can truly appreciate the smile on the Mona Lisa without necessarily appreciating the painting as a whole. This may be true even if, as I shall argue later, a deep appreciation of the smile requires situating it within a larger context.

I then asked how we can *know* that the silliness is a property of the face alone or of the line alone. The line would not necessarily be silly if it were taken out of that context and placed in a new context. But then it would not be the same line—unless we simply define "sameness of line" in terms of geometrical coordinates. Perhaps the question is whether the essence of the line is in its geometrical coordinates or in its meaning. But when I appreciate the line surely I appreciate it for its meaning not for its geometrical coordinates.

It also seemed that the same argument that denied silliness to the line and located it in the face can be used to deny silliness in the face and locate it in the painting as a whole. But we do not say that a painting with a silly smile is a silly painting. Indeed, we can even imagine a face with a silly smile which is not a silly face—which in fact is very serious. For example, Velasquez's portrait of a court jester titled *Don Juan de Austria.* These factors led me to prefer the theory that the property is emergent from the smile at least as much as it is from the face.

The force of Shusterman's argument seems to hang on peculiarities of faces as wholes. For instance, it is often said that a smile is not simply a function of the lips but of changes in the entire face. We speak of some people as having smiling faces. Perhaps Velasquez's achievement was to violate some of these expectations by painting a silly smile on a serious face. Perhaps the smiles on some faces are properties more of the region around the mouth than of the face as a whole.

IV. SAVING THE ORGANIC WHOLE

Moore thinks that Hegelians believe that organic wholes have three properties: (1) the parts are related to one another and to the whole as means to ends, (2), the parts have no meaning or significance apart from the whole, and (3) the whole has a value which is greater than the value of the sum of the parts. He also attributes to them the belief that these three properties are identical or at least necessarily connected (p. 31). Moore accepts the third of these properties and limits his own use of the term "organic" to this sense. He has two main objections to the combination view. First, believing that (1) is identical to (3) is to confuse the means/end relationship with the relationship between parts and wholes in organic wholes. We have already discussed this point. Second, the point expressed in (2) is self-contradictory. We will now turn to this criticism.

Although Moore believes that the Hegelians hold the combination view, he identifies their position most strongly with (2). He interprets the idea that the part has "no meaning or significance apart from the whole" in terms of the phrase "the part is no distinct object of thought," which he then interprets to mean that "the whole, of which it is a part, is in its turn a part of it" (p. 33). He holds this supposition to be self-contradictory. He admits that the part has one predicate that it would not otherwise have—that it is "a part of the whole." But he denies that this predicate "alters the nature or enters into the definition of the thing which has it" (p. 33). His argument for the claim that this position is self-contradictory is: to say that the part has the predicate "is part of the whole" is to assume that it is distinct from the whole. Thus "no part contains analytically the whole to which it belongs" and "The relation of part to whole is *not* the same as that of whole to part" (p. 33). He concludes that the Hegelian view implies the absurd idea that "the whole is always a part of its part" (p. 34). The Hegelians believe that "if you want to know the truth about a part . . . you must consider *not* the part, but . . . the whole" (p. 34). They must therefore believe that "*nothing* is true of the part but only of the whole" (p. 34). But when we say that a part is part of its whole "we do *not* merely mean that the whole is a part of itself." The Hegelian position implies the contradictory view that the statement "this is a part of that whole" has no meaning since the subject and predicate would not have distinct meanings.

I do not want to defend the Hegelian position here. However, I suspect that Moore's opponents are more sophisticated than he makes them out to be. Even if we accept Moore's reconstruction of their position we can see that although some of the claims are clearly false *on one interpretation* they may be true *on another.* For example, in one sense it is clearly false that the part has no meaning or significance apart from the organic whole. If we cut a patch out of a painting and hang it as a separate work it will still have meaning and value even though it is detached from the whole to which it previously belonged. It could even have *greater* value than the original whole! (As an amateur collage artist I have long been interested in the way that appropriated segments of advertisements or of kitsch art can have more aesthetic value than the originals.)

On the other hand the Hegelian could be interpreted as right in two ways. First, the part does not have significance apart from, *any* organic whole since even if it is hung separately it still might be considered part of a new organic whole which is a work of art that is *made out of* a part of another work. Those fragments of Greek sculptures which retain meaning and intrinsic value apart from their original wholes may do so simply because they are reconstituted as organic wholes. Second, although the detached part takes on a new life it is still arguable that *as a part* of the original whole it had its meaning and value through its relation to that whole.

It is equally ambiguous to say that the part is "no distinct object of thought." It is true, as Moore says, that we can think of a part without necessarily thinking of the organic whole to which it belongs. We can think of Mona Lisa's smile without necessarily thinking about the painting as a whole. We can, as I suggested above, value a part independently from our evaluation of the whole. At the same time, if we wish to have a deeper and more appreciative understanding of the part we will generally have to think of it in relation to some relevant organic whole. This would ordinarily be the work itself, although other organic wholes might also be relevant: for example the corpus of Da Vinci, Renaissance painting in general, or the cultural life of Florence. In short, although the part *can* be a distinct object of thought it is not distinct from its context when it is the object of a deeper analysis. This implies that whether or not the part is a distinct object of thought is relative to our concerns. Yet this gives us no reason to doubt the Hegelian view that to understand the part in all of its complexity one must understand its relations to other parts and to all the relevant organic wholes to which it belongs—even though this task is probably an unreachable ideal.

Moore believes that the sentence "the part is no distinct object of thought" means that "the whole, of which it is

a part, is in turn a part of it." The correct inference is that the whole is *the same* as the part—although this would not be any less damaging to the Hegelian case. Shusterman helpfully restates Moore's argument in this way: "while P is originally identified as being distinct from W, as being a mere part of W, it is then contradictorily taken as analytically including W as part of itself, since it itself is constituted by the whole set of W's interrelations of parts."[14]

I have a Nietzschean suggestion which may help here— one that derives from another, perhaps more central aspect of his thought, his perspectivism. Granted, it is not the case that thinking of the whole and thinking of the part are the same. Yet it still may be true that the part is internally related to the whole and cannot remain the same if it is detached from the whole. The part and the whole are not the same object of thought, but only in the following sense: when thinking primarily of the part we think of the whole only in relation to the part, and when thinking primarily of the whole we think of the part only in its relation to the whole.

Consider how we perceive when we focus on the part or on the whole. When we focus on the part the whole of which it is a part becomes a background to the part and is interpreted *in terms of* the part. But when we focus on the whole we see the part from the perspective of the whole. Now if Nietzsche is right that reality itself is perspectival and that it is not possible to fully separate perception and discourse from the objects of perception and discourse (a point that Moore implicitly denies in **"The Refutation"**) then it can be said that, when we focus on the part, the world is constituted from the perspective of the part, and that, when we focus on the whole, the world is constituted from the perspective of the whole. It can be said that in one perspective some features are highlighted whereas in the other perspective other features are highlighted.

Such metaphors as "perspective" and "highlighting" should not mislead us. It is not as though the same domain of objects is depicted from different angles according to the same system of perspective. There is no neutral non-interpreted or pre-interpreted domain of objects. Nor is it as though the same items are subject to being seen differently because of accidental conditions of lighting. Objects take on a different character insofar as they are constituted differently within our experienced world. On this view the part is certainly *not* constituted "by the whole set of W's interrelations of parts" for that would assume that the whole/part relation is not perspectival in this sense of "perspective."

This sense of "perspective" can be understood partly in terms of the Lakoff/Johnson/Turner idea of conceptual metaphor.[15] When the whole is seen from the perspective of the part we have an instance of the conceptual metaphor WHOLES ARE THEIR PARTS. The whole is seen in terms of its fictional identity with the part. Characteristics of the part are attributed to the whole. Similarly we can see parts in terms of their wholes. The conceptual metaphor here is parts are their wholes. These are two different conceptual metaphors. Fictional identity does not allow for reversal of the terms in the way that ordinary identity does. Their difference can be seen in the fact that the whole is "contained in" the part in a very different sense than the part is "contained in" the whole.

Given all of this, it is perfectly correct for Moore to say that "The relation of part to whole is *not* the same as that of whole to part." Also one must agree with his assertion that the claims "if you want to know the truth about a part . . . you must consider *not* the part, but . . . the whole" and "nothing is true of the part" are false. Nonetheless it is still true that if you want to know the truth about the part you must consider the whole *as well as* the part, and no truth about the part is completely understood apart form understanding the whole.

V. DERRIDEAN CONSEQUENCES?

Moore's criticism of radical organicism ultimately fails because (1) he cannot prove that consciousness is radically distinguished from the object of consciousness, (2) he cannot prove that *means* towards the creation of organic wholes can be radically distinguished from the *parts* of organic wholes, (3) he cannot prove that parts have meanings and values that are unchanged when they are detached from organic wholes, and (4) he cannot prove that the emergent properties of organic wholes take the place of emergent properties of the parts of such wholes. I have tried to show that these points are particularly evident when we are discussing such things as paintings.

Does it then follow that everything is just a Derridean play of difference? Shusterman thinks it might—and this is perhaps the reason why he is reluctant to abandon Moore's arguments altogether. The problem, as he sees it, is that if parts are a function of their interrelation with other parts and of interpretation then there is no way to secure identity of parts.

Shusterman sees Derrida's *différance* as essentially the same as the Hegelian organicism which Moore "put into question."[16] On the Saussurian view, the linguistic system is a function of differences between elements. Derrida accepts this and adds that our world is mediated by language. He then concludes that there are no foundations or essences beyond this differential framework. Things depend for their identity and meaning on these differential interrelations. Thus, as with radical organicism, individuals or parts depend for their identity and meaning on the larger whole.

We need to ask whether the organicist position of the Hegelians (and that of Nietzsche when he implies that everything is interrelated to everything else in a worldwide organic whole) is as close to Derrida's as Shusterman makes it out to be. The first thing that comes to mind, which is recognized by Shusterman, is that Derrida makes a point of *denying* that the differential

framework forms an organic whole.[17] There are strong reasons to take this denial as authentic. It is certainly consistent with the rest of Derrida's position, for instance his rejection of Hegel's absolutism. The Hegelians believe that organic wholes are parts of larger organic wholes which ultimately are part of the universe as an organic whole. As Hegel says, "Everything that exists stands in correlation, and this correlation is the veritable nature of every existence. The existent thing in this way has no being of its own, but only in something else."[18] But this is where post-moderns like Derrida differ from the Hegelians. For the post-moderns there is no ultimate organic whole at the end. There is a great difference between saying that identity of a part is a function of the difference between that part and other parts and saying that its identity is a function of its relation to the whole.

This leads to my second point. Organicist Hegelians will not simply stress the *difference* between entities in organic wholes. They will also stress *sameness*. Shusterman quotes Hegel as saying "The existent thing . . . has no being of its own, but only in something else" but neglects to add the rest of the sentence: "in this other however it is self-relation; and correlation is the unity of the self-relation and relation-to-others."[19] As I have argued, there is at least a fictional identity between parts and whole and between parts and other parts. It is plausible that what is meant by the thesis that the essence of the part is in its relation to the whole and the other parts is that the part is fictionally identical to the whole and to the other parts. I suspect that there is a close relation between essence and fictional identity, although this is a subject for another paper. We may note that essence is more a matter of sameness than of difference. Insofar as Derrida rejects essences he must also reject the Hegelian notion of organic whole.

The best way to respond to this debate is simply to drop the most problematic aspects of the Derridean and Hegelian positions. As suggested above, we should abandon the idea that a complete account of identity can be based simply on the concept of difference. There is no more reason to abandon sameness in favor of difference then to abandon difference in favor of sameness. We should also abandon the idea that the world is some sort of ultimate organic whole. Nietzsche's idea that all things are interconnected goes beyond the bounds of what we can know. There is no reason to believe that organic wholes function as parts of greater organic wholes up to the universe as a whole. It is even arguable that Nietzsche's move was inconsistent with his own perspectivism.[20] Two different perspectives do not only constitute the world differently—they transform the elements. Elements which are in the foreground in one perspective are reinterpreted, thrown into the background, made irrelevant, or annihilated in another perspective. Why should we perspectivists agree with Nietzsche that "everything is bound to and conditioned by everything else?"[21] This can only be true insofar as "everything else" is relative to the world version (to use Goodman's term).[22] The perspectivist holds that there are many world versions. So it doesn't make sense to say that everything is related to everything else in some version-transcendent sense of "everything else." Perspectivism blocks the move to an ultimate organic whole.

Perspectivism, contrary to what is generally assumed, does not require the elimination of essences.[23] Granted, there are no fixed version-independent or perspective-independent essences. But we may still speak of something called "essence" which exists relative to perspective. We *take* things as essential. Essences, in this sense, are created as much as they are discovered. In fact, it is this practice of creating/discovering essences that makes it possible to speak of separate perspectives. For versions and perspectives are organic wholes, and organic wholes are the entities for which the term "essence" is most appropriate. Essences are not independent of the experienced world, nor the interpreted world—they are to be found within those worlds. Things do not have intrinsic natures absolutely or in relation to everything else but in relation to relevant frameworks. To say, as Nehamas believes Nietzsche would say, that "all properties are equally essential to their subjects and thus that there is ultimately no distinction to be drawn between essential and accidental properties at all" is to assume the standpoint of some version-independent reality—a standpoint which the true perspectivist denies.[24]

Shusterman considers three possible analytic arguments against *differance* and radical organicism. Two of these arguments are answered by Shusterman. The third may be answered by the more consistent perspectivism offered here. It is argued that the notion of differences presupposes entities differentiated.[25] But, as Shusterman notes, all that is needed is identity according to a particular interpretation. It is argued that the radical organicist position would make individuating reference and language itself impossible. But, as Shusterman argues, there can still be shared normative regularities which are not "based on any unchanging ontological referent outside a culture's social practices, and in fact themselves admit of some change and divergence without necessarily incurring a breakdown in communication."[26] Finally, it is argued that without interpretational atoms we end up in an infinite regress or circle of interpretations.[27] In his essay on Nietzsche and Nehamas, Shusterman leaves this objection unanswered, implying that it cannot be answered. In his more recent essay on analysis and deconstruction he imagines Derrida replying that this obsession with infinite regress and logical atoms is ensnared in the will to metaphysics. His answer is that Derrida himself is ensnared in metaphysics through his commitment to radical organic unity—a point which I have questioned. Another answer to the infinite regress argument is simply that real life is not a matter of infinite regresses. What actually happens is that in a particular situation such-and-such is constituted as the stopping point *for our purposes*. For instance two competing literary theorists may choose to agree on certain "interpretational atoms" *for the sake of argument*. The interpretational atoms are relative to a version—in this case a version constituted as a domain of conflict between two competing versions. In short, the various analytic arguments against radical organicism fail to be decisive when radical organicism is understood in a fully perspectivist way.[28]

NOTES

[1] G. E. Moore, *Principia Ethica* (1903; reprint, Cambridge University Press, 1968), I shall simply use page numbers to refer to this text; G. E. Moore, "The Refutation of Idealism" in *Philosophical Studies* (1903; reprint, Totowa, N.J.: Littlefield, Adams, 1968), pp. 1-30; Richard Rorty, "Nineteenth-Century Idealism and Twentieth-Century Textualism" in *Consequences of Pragmatism* (University of Minnesota Press, 1982), pp. 139-159.

Something needs to be said about the term "Hegelian." Moore saw himself as opposed to philosophers who "profess to have derived great benefit from the writings of Hegel" (p. 30). It is these authors who use the terms "organic whole" and "organic relation" in a way that Moore rejects. The authors he has in mind are Bradley and McTaggart. Whether or not Hegel himself held Bradley's view that all relations are internal relations or McTaggart's view that parts *must* be what they are is open to interpretation. One of this journal's readers has observed that some of Hegel's remarks indicate that he recognized the existence of fully contingent events. If so then Hegel would not agree with Bradley that all relations are internal relations. My main concern here is not to interpret Hegel, Bradley, or McTaggart but to assess arguments raised by Moore and Shusterman against a particular position which has been called Hegelian. When I use the term "Hegelian" I am mainly thinking of the position that (1) not all relations are external, and internal or organic relations are fundamental, (2) consciousness and the object of consciousness interanimate, and (3) organic wholes are such that their parts would not be the same if abstracted from them.

[2] Richard Shusterman, "Nietzsche and Nehamas on Organic Unity," *The Southern Journal of Philosophy* 26 (1988): 379-392; Shusterman, "Organic Unity: Analysis and Deconstruction" in *Redrawing the Lines: Analytic Philosophy, Deconstruction, and Literary Theory,* ed. Reed Way Dasenbrock (University of Minnesota Press, 1989).

Shusterman's "Osborne and Moore on Organic Unity," *British Journal of Aesthetics* 23 (1983): 352-359 is also relevant to this paper. It was directed against Harold Osborne's "Aesthetic and Other Forms of Order," *British Journal of Aesthetics* 22 (1982): 3-16. For Osborne there is a special aesthetic form of order unique to works of art. Drawing from McTaggart's conception of organic unity, Osborne argues that works of art are organic unities such that "no part . . . could have *existed* unless all the other parts had existed and had stood to each other in the relations in which they did in fact stand" (p. 12). By this he means that "If you isolate the elements or parts of a work of art, they become something other than what they were as elements or parts of the work of art" and not that they cease to exist altogether (p. 15). As long as the parts remain parts of the aesthetic whole they "reflect" its emergent properties. When they are detached from the whole they lose their aesthetic properties and retain only their natural properties. Although I cannot accept Osborne's radical disjunction between natural and aesthetic properties, preferring a more Deweyan sense of continuity between the natural and the aesthetic, and I believe that Osborne's use of the term "reflect" is unfortunate, I do think that the parts of aesthetic wholes are organically related to the wholes in *something* like his sense—and this is precisely what Shusterman uses Moore's arguments to reject.

A classical discussion of wholes and parts is to be found in Plato's *Theaetetus.* See especially 203e-205c, although the entire last part of the dialogue is relevant. Aristotle also addresses this issue in *Metaphysics* 1041b. Osborne reviews this history briefly in his article.

[3] Friedrich Nietzsche, *The Will to Power,* trans. Walter Kaufmann and R. J. Hollingdale (New York: Vintage Books, 1967); Alexander Nehamas, *Nietzsche: Life as Literature* (Harvard University Press, 1985). Shusterman and Nehamas interpret Nietzsche as a radical organicist. As Shusterman puts it, "The principle of organic unity constitutes the very core of Nietzsche's doctrine of the universal will to power" ("Nietzsche and Nehamas on Organic Unity," p. 379). This interpretation is based on claims by Nietzsche that "every atom affects the whole of being" (*Will to Power,* #634) and that nothing has a character of its own independent of its interrelations with others (ibid., #551).

[4] Shusterman, "Organic Unity: Analysis and Deconstruction," p. 110.

[5] Ibid., p. 99.

[6] Ibid., p. 100.

[7] Moore, "The Refutation of Idealism," p. 15.

[8] Ibid., p. 20.

[9] Shusterman, "Osborne and Moore on Organic Unity," p. 357.

[10] I am thinking here of the first film in John Berger's 1960s television series, "Ways of Seeing." In one sequence Berger discusses how a museum postcard can take on a new significance in the context of child's bulletin board. This film acknowledges the influence of Walter Benjamin's "The Work of Art in the Age of Mechanical Reproduction" in *Illuminations* (New York: Schocken Books, 1955).

[11] Shusterman, "Organic Unity: Analysis and Deconstruction," p. 98.

[12] Shusterman, "Osborne and Moore on Organic Unity," p. 355.

[13] Ibid., p. 356.

[14] Shusterman, "Nietzsche and Nehamas on Organic Unity," p. 383.

[15] George Lakoff and Mark Johnson, *Metaphors We Live By* (University of Chicago Press, 1980). See also George Lakoff and Mark Turner, *More than Cool Reason: A Field Guide to Poetic Metaphor* (The University of Chicago Press, 1989).

[16] Shusterman, "Organic Unity: Analysis and Deconstruction," p. 100.

[17] Ibid., pp. 108, 110.

[18] Hegel, *Hegel's Logic,* trans. William Wallace (Oxford University Press, 1975), p. 191.

[19] Ibid. Shusterman seems to hold that difference and identity presuppose each other and that this co-reliance is consistent with a rejection of foundational self-identical substances through the notion of "identity according to a particular interpretation" ("Organic Unity: Analysis and Deconstruction," p. 107). I agree with this view.

[20] It is arguable that Nehamas's and Shusterman's interpretation of Nietzsche as a radical organicist is itself undercut by the inconsistency of this position with Nietzsche's perspectivism.

[21] Nietzsche, *The Will to Power,* p. 316 (#584).

[22] Nelson Goodman, *Ways of Worldmaking* (Indianapolis: Hackett Publishing, 1978), see especially chapter one.

[23] In "Postmodernism and the Aesthetic Turn," *Poetics Today* 10 [forthcoming]: 604-622, Shusterman takes a view which is similar to mine: "If there are no logical necessities, there remain probabilities that constitute practical certainty; if there are no foundational essences, there remain historical norms (alterable and contestable as they are) which structure and regulate linguistic and other social practices, serving, so to speak, as relative, historicized essences" (p. 619). See my "Gardens in an Expanded Field," *British Journal of Aesthetics* 28 (1988) for an application of this view of essences to a particular problem in aesthetics.

[24] Nehamas, *Nietzsche: Life as Literature,* p. 155.

[25] Shusterman, "Nietzsche and Nehamas on Organic Unity," p. 384.

[26] Ibid., p. 391.

[27] Ibid., p. 384.

[28] I would like to thank John Gilmour and Richard Shusterman for comments they made on earlier drafts of this paper, and San Jose State University for granting me a sabbatical in order to work on these problems.

Sally A. Jacobsen (essay date 1993)

SOURCE: "Bloomsbury Revisited: Flipping through the Albums," in *Virginia Woolf: Themes and Variations,* Pace University Press, 1993, pp. 329-37.

[*In the following essay, Jacobsen examines Virginia Woolf's Moorean analysis in her letters and diaries of love and friendship, based on the Bloomsbury Group's understanding of Moore's* Principia Ethica.]

I discuss here primarily Virginia Woolf's 1918-1919 *Diary,* but her *Letters* led me to look into whether she practiced a conscious ethic of friendship growing out of the philosophy of G. E. Moore. Virginia's letters are prized for the affection and attention shown the writers and artists of Bloomsbury. Woolf wittily sustains Lytton Strachey in the bleak years of writer's block. She helps organize a fund to enable T. S. Eliot to quit work at Lloyd's Bank. She supports the value alike of the painting and nurturing motherhood of Vanessa Bell, and affirms the specialness of each nephew and niece from the moment they go away to school through affectionate private jokes. Woolf confirms the value of the personalities and serious work of writer Vita Sackville-West and elderly composer Ethel Smyth, teasing them about how passionately she desires their presences long after her romances with them have waned.

G. E. Moore's *Principia Ethica* in 1903 codified an ethic which placed on friendship a premium unusual in formal ethical systems. Bloomsbury recognized that the book's principles had been arrived at through two generations' discussions of the "Cambridge Apostles," an intellectual society of Cambridge men including Bertrand Russell, Desmond MacCarthy, and G. E. Moore—Russell and Moore already philosophy dons at Trinity by the time the next generation were elected—Leonard Woolf, Saxon Sydney-Turner, J. Maynard Keynes, and Lytton Strachey. The Apostles, led in the latter generation by G. E. Moore, discussed "those 'goods' which were ends in themselves, . . . the search for truth, aesthetic emotions and personal relations—love and friendship" (Desmond MacCarthy, quoted in Gadd 21-22). Leonard Woolf calls Moore "the only really great man whom I have ever . . . known" (145), saying, "Moore and the Society were the focus of my existence . . . at Cambridge. They dominated me intellectually and emotionally" (171).

"Bloomsbury" as we know it began with the younger Cambridge friends plus Desmond MacCarthy of the older Apostles attending the "Thursday Evenings" of Thoby Stephen (not himself an Apostle) in 1905. A "central core" of the group—MacCarthy, Strachey, Sydney-Turner, and Leonard Woolf—are described by Quentin Bell as sitting "around the discreet shrine of G. E. Moore" (100-101). To what extent can Virginia Woolf, through her participation in the Thursday discussions and reading of Moore, together with her intellectual closeness to Leonard, be said to be an "apostle" of G. E. Moore? Turning to Virginia's *Diary,* we find evidence that both

the Woolfs habitually practiced Moore's and the Apostles' mode of questioning oneself as to one's sense of value.

The *Principia Ethica* blended Platonic ideal "goods" with what Leonard Woolf calls "the divine voice of plain common sense" (162), from nineteenth-century realism (Rosenbaum, "Virginia" 14-17). Leonard emphasizes that the appeal of Moore's approach lay in his practicality in the formation of an ethic (148-51, 161-64), in Chapter Five of the *Principia.* Moore rejected the idea of "absolute good" and insisted that each person inquire into what seems to him "intrinsically good" in order to form his own ethic (Regan 159-60). An authority's declaration that something is "good" ought not to be viewed as a "command," but as a proposition to be proved by each person's experience or intuition (Regan 157, 159).

Virginia's *Diary* records conversational enquiries in Moore's vein. When Ray Strachey visited in June, 1918, Woolf writes, "We discussed the moral eminence of Moore, comparable to that of Christ or Socrates, so R[ay] & L[eonard] held. They challenged me to match him in that respect by any of my friends. I claimed for Nessa Duncan Lytton & Desmond something different but of equal value" (1:55). Not only is Moore the subject of the conversation, but Virginia's distinction, "something different but of equal value," is consistent with Moore's own kind of distinctions. The next month, on 29 July 1918, Virginia reports taking Ottoline down a peg when she corrects Ott's conception of love with a loftier definition: "I said that love meant a great many different things; & that to confine it to romantic love was absurd. I also maintained that one could love groups of people, & landscapes. Unluckily this remarked Ott. to . . . look longingly at a wheatfield" (*D* 1:175). The nature of love was a favorite topic with the Apostles—Maynard Keynes says that it "came a long way first" (53).

In Chapter Six of the *Principia Ethica,* "The Ideal," Moore examines the workings of friendship and "affection" as supreme goods, as part of his concept of "organic unities"—Ideal "goods" containing components which are less than beautiful, good, or ideal: "A whole composed of two great goods, even though one of these be obviously inferior to the other, may yet be . . . decidedly superior to either by itself" (186).

Virginia's *Letters* suggest that with the Moore-inspired Apostles, she practiced a conscious ethic of friendship. Woolf nurtured her friends through a huge correspondence—Joanne Trautmann Banks notes that Woolf's letters give "back a reflection of the other person" (Introduction), always "with the person's character and needs in mind" ("VW as Letter-Writer"). It might be argued that role-modeling on Julia Stephen's example, Virginia had developed her letter writing to the point that it was self-rewarding: it was fun, it was a way of being attentive that she was good at—and that G. E. Moore had little to do with it. Yet, given the vagaries of some of her friends—Clive Bell with his series of mistresses, often embroiling Virginia in his gossip; the profound silences of Saxon Sydney-Turner (*MB* 167-68; L. Woolf 116-19); the importunities of Ethel Smyth—it would require a conscious belief in the superior value of love in friendship, transcending the imperfections and even occasional lapses of affection in the friend, as Moore describes love, to justify the energy spent in her correspondence.

Virginia begins her *Diary* for 1919 with a writing project in friendship and appears to follow the Apostles' mode of inquiry into the "good," modeled on Moore. She resolves "to spend the evenings of this week . . . in making out an account of my friendships & their present condition, with some account of my friends characters; & to add an estimate of their work, & a forecast of their future works" (20 January; 1:234). The next day she writes to Saxon Sydney-Turner, the Apostle whom her brother Thoby had viewed as the most "brilliant" in Moore's style of cutting to the truth, and speaks of her "projected work on friendship," with a view towards which she is going through a box of old letters from Clive Bell and Saxon himself (*L* 2:317). The following day she asks herself, using Moore's Socratic method, "How many friends have I got?" and enumerates most of Bloomsbury, along with their qualities she most values and those she is willing to tolerate in order to enjoy what she values. She continues this examination of the "good" she finds in her friends on 24 January (*D* 1:234-36). In the intervening two and a half weeks before Sydney-Turner replies to her January 21 letter, she has given or sent him (with a missing letter?) "three large pages," asking the silent Saxon's advice about representing the difficulty of establishing an intimate friendship (Rosenbaum, *Bloomsbury* 21). It is likely that Woolf abstracted her *Diary* project into essay form for Saxon. Saxon replies, "I should like that chapter (?with illustrations) on the difficulty of getting in touch" (21).

The idea of analyzing her friendships seems to have been an outgrowth of a sticky situation in October of 1918 involving Clive Bell and Mary Hutchinson, his mistress, in which Virginia felt distinctly ill-used and hurt by her supposedly good friend Clive. Mark Gertler had told Clive and Mary that Virginia had said that Vanessa "disliked" Mary. "Disastrous results" could have befallen Vanessa, since she was already in the delicate situation with respect to Clive of being about to bear Duncan Grant's child, who would carry Clive's surname. Whereas by the following January Virginia takes the philosophical high road in anatomizing her friends, in October she is stung and hurt by the accusation. She writes Vanessa, "It's quite plain that it's hopeless for us to try and know each other's friends, and in future I shall try and steer clear of Gertler, . . . Mary, Jack [Mary's husband], Clive and all the rest of that set" (*L* 2:286-87). Similarly, in the *Diary* entry for 26 October Virginia concludes "that friendships maintained in this atmosphere are altogether too sharp, brittle, & painful" (1:208). She is hurt that Clive would lapse in affection and trust in believing a falsehood from an "outsider": "If I could have letters from Mary and Clive"—of apology, she must mean—"I should feel myself rewarded" (208). Shared

perceptions are of crucial importance to the value of love in friendship for G. E. Moore (196-204), and Virginia has discovered for herself through this episode a psychological truth articulated by Moore in discussing love: "The truth of what we believe is . . . important as preventing the pains of disappointment. . . . A misdirected attachment [is] unfortunate solely . . . [because] it leads us to count upon results, which the real nature of the object is not of a kind to ensure" (Moore 195).

The pain of this episode may well have precipitated Virginia's 1919 project of examining friendship as a value, perhaps after analyzing her feelings in conversation with Leonard, in Moorean fashion. When first listing her friends on 22 January 1919, Lytton, Desmond, and Saxon come first, "connected with Thoby." But Clive, who shares that connection and was as close to her as Lytton in 1905, in 1919 she puts "a little aside," to define her relationship to later, along with Ottoline Morrell and Roger Fry—all three ultimately counted among her serious friends, using what seems to be Moore's "organic" method of determining value, allowing for imperfections (*D* 1:234-35).

Virginia had participated enthusiastically in the Apostle sort of discussions, inspired by Moore, in Bloomsbury between 1905 and 1914. In her talk given before the Memoir Club in 1921 or 1922, "Old Bloomsbury," she records the gratification she felt at having her and Vanessa's ideas taken seriously:

> Never have I listened so intently to . . . an argument. Never have I been at such pains to sharpen and launch my own little dart. . . . No praise pleased me more than Saxon's saying . . . I had argued my case very cleverly. . . .
>
> Vanessa and I got probably much the same pleasure that under-graduates get. . . . In the world of [Hyde Park Gate] we were not asked to use our brains much. Here we used nothing else. . . . The young men . . . criticised our arguments as severely as their own. (*MB* 168-69)

Virginia finally actually read the ***Principia Ethica*** in August of 1908. She wrote Clive that she was splitting her "head over Moore every night, feeling ideas travelling to the remotest part of my brain, and setting up a feeble disturbance, hardly to be called thought" (19 Aug. 1908; *Congenial* 47). Clive, of course, is not one of the "worshipful" Apostles and can be counted on to appreciate her satire of Moore's tortuous fine distinctions. (It is possible for Virginia to parody Moore's style of philosophizing and at the same time hold his views.)

When she took up her inquiry into friendship in 1919, Virginia would not have been eager to repeat the "head-splitting" of following Moore through his fine distinctions. Rather, I think that she and Leonard continued the habit of Apostolic inquiry in conversation so enjoyable to Leonard at Cambridge and to Virginia in Bloomsbury before their marriage. One of the reasons Virginia decided to marry him, despite her lack of "vehement" feeling for him, was that he declared her magnificent in "intelligence" and "directness," as well as in wit and beauty (Leonard to Virginia, 12 Jan. 1912; Bell 1:181). Candor and directness in saying what one truly thought were supreme virtues among the Apostles, a point Virginia makes amusingly in "Old Bloomsbury" in reporting her misunderstanding of why Thoby found the silent Saxon "brilliant" (*MB* 167). In his 12 January 1912 proposal letter, Leonard argues the rightness of their match in the Apostle vein: "We like the same kinds of things & people, & above all it is realities which we understand & which are important to us" (Q. Bell 1:181).

In her *Diary* project on friendship, Virginia takes up Lytton Strachey's character first, and acknowledges that her portrayal of him is harsh:

> Stracheys [are] a prosaic race, lacking in magnanimity, shorn of atmosphere. . . . All the unpleasantness that I wish to introduce into my portrait of Lytton is contained [therein]— . . . a lack of physical warmth, lack of creative power, a failure of vitality warning him . . . to eke out his gifts parsimoniously. . . . Mentally of course it produces that metallic & conventionally brilliant style which prevents his writing from reaching, in my judgment, the first rate. (24 January 1919. *D* 1:235-36)

On 31 January Virginia tries to "square her disparaging remarks" with the fact that Lytton dominated "a generation at Cambridge" (1:238). She decides, "if I underrate, . . . the main cause is that while I admire, . . . I'm not interested in what he writes. Thomas Hardy has what I call an interesting mind; . . . but not Lytton" (*D* 1:238). Lacking warmth or passion, Lytton needs more than his ineffable scintillating style to earn Virginia's respect. She guards against valuing him uncritically, perhaps because their gifts are similar, and she aims higher aesthetically and morally (in warmth) than what she could achieve depending merely upon her cleverness. Besides the longstandingness of their friendship, this similarity in their temperaments accounts for Virginia keeping him among the foremost of her friends. Lytton is an object lesson for her of the need to take on serious aesthetic projects. On 25 May, she mentions their "clear perception of the other's meaning" as a value (1:277). Intimate, complete understanding with someone in Moore's system of Organic Unities would transcend defects in personal warmth or greatness of achievement.

On the 18 of February Woolf takes up Desmond MacCarthy in her disquisition on friendship, "& how I find him sympathetic compared to the Stracheys": "I dont think that he possesses any faults as a friend. He is not an heroic character. He finds pleasure too pleasant, . . . dallying too seductive" (1:241). Above all, "Desmond is faithful," a quality that distinguishes the friendship of Saxon Sydney-Turner, too, whom she considers on the same day. With Saxon, one is aware, even after two hours of tepid & almost entire silence, that he is strictly true,

genuine, unalloyed" (1:242). Thus, Woolf views a "faithful" affection one can *trust* as equally important with a capacity for profound honesty and goals one can respect.

Virginia's delineation of the value and weaknesses she finds in her friends continues intermittently through March 1919. In the months following, she considers the broader subject of happiness, of which love, friendships and accomplishments were construed as components among Moore's followers. Moore draws distinctions between "Happiness" and mere "pleasure" in "Hedonism," Chapter Three of the *Principia Ethica.* A little more than a month later, just back from Asheham, Virginia reports that Leonard's and her satisfactions "were mainly of a spiritual nature requiring some subtlety to relate." She then asks herself, "Happiness—what, I wonder constitutes happiness?" (1:269) She concludes that "the most important element is work," but the question follows immediately upon her contemplation of their satisfying spiritual communion at Asheham. Biographers have neglected conversational stimulation in the bond between these two very cerebral marriage partners. Even though Spater and Parsons, for example, use *The Marriage of True Minds* as a title, they focus more on Leonard's husbandly solicitousness than on their exchange of ideas (69-71). Virginia's *Diary* is evidence that the Woolfs practiced the Apostolic ideal of "passionate contemplation and communion with a beloved person" (Keynes 53).

WORKS CITED

Bell Quentin. *Virginia Woolf: A Biography.* New York: Harcourt Brace Jovanovich, 1972.

Gadd, David. *The Loving Friends: A Portrait of Bloomsbury.* New York: Harcourt Brace Jovanovich, 1974.

Keynes, John Maynard. *My Early Beliefs.* In *The Bloomsbury Group: A Collection of Memoirs, Commentary and Criticism,* ed. S. P. Rosenbaum. Toronto: Univ. Toronto Press, 1975. 48-64.

Moore, G. E. *Principia Ethica* (1903). Cambridge: Cambridge UP, 1968.

Regan, Tom. *Bloomsbury's Prophet: G. E. Moore and the Development of his Moral Philosophy.* Philadelphia: Temple UP, 1986.

Rosenbaum, S. P., ed. *The Bloomsbury Group: A Collection of Memoirs, Commentary and Criticism.* Toronto: Univ. Toronto P, 1975.

———. "Virginia Woolf and the Intellectual Origins of Bloomsbury." *Virginia Woolf: Centennial Essays,* ed. Elaine K. Ginsberg and Laura Moss Gottlieb. Troy, NY: Whitson, 1983. 11-26.

Spater, George, and Ian Parsons. *A Marriage of True Minds: An Intimate Portrait of Leonard and Virginia Woolf.* New York: Harcourt Brace Jovanovich, 1977.

Trautmann Banks, Joanne. Introduction and Notes to *Congenial Spirits: The Selected Letters of Virginia Woolf.* New York: Harcourt Brace Jovanovich, 1989.

—————. "Virginia Woolf as Letter Writer: A Reflection of the Other Person." Typescript of draft introduction to *Congenial Spirits.* circa. 1987.

Woolf, Leonard. *Sowing: An Autobiography of the Years 1880 to 1904.* New York: Harcourt Brace Jovanovich, 1960.

Woolf, Virginia. *Congenial Spirits: The Selected Letters of Virginia Woolf.* Ed. Joanne Trautmann Banks. New York: Harcourt Brace Jovanovich, 1989.

—————. *The Diary of Virginia Woolf. Volume One: 1915-1919.* Ed. Anne Olivier Bell. New York: Harcourt Brace Jovanovich, 1977.

—————. *The Letters of Virginia Woolf.* Ed. Nigel Nicolson and Joanne Trautmann. 6 vols. New York: Harcourt Brace Jovanovich, 1975-1980.

—————. *Moments of Being: Unpublished Autobiographical Writings.* Ed. Jeanne Schulking. New York: Harcourt Brace Jovanovich, 1976.

Jane Heal (essay date 1994)

SOURCE: "Moore's Paradox: A Wittgensteinian Approach," in *Mind,* Vol. 103, No. 409, January, 1994, pp. 5-24.

[*In the following essay, Heal advances the thesis that Moore's paradox makes more sense when approached with Wittgenstein's theory.*]

I

"I believe that it is raining but it isn't." It would be perfectly absurd, claimed Moore, to say this or its like. But why? After all, it is clearly *possible* that I should believe that it is raining when it is not, that others should realise and remark on the error I make. Why should my doing so myself be somehow absurd?

My aim in this paper is to suggest that Wittgenstein's approach to this issue has much to recommend it and that seeing its attraction might provide an entry point to understanding the nature of Wittgenstein's later philosophy of mind. A proper account of that is clearly beyond the scope of this paper and moreover could not be given without treating those issues of meaning and metaphysics which Wittgenstein discusses in the early part of the *Investigations,* before he moves on to reflect on psychological concepts. So my object is to consider some features of the paradox in detail but only to gesture in the direction of the larger topics, in a way that may at least make it seem worthwhile to look into them further.[1]

The next section outlines the paradox slightly more fully and suggests two conditions which a satisfactory solution should meet. It sketches two possible approaches to the matter, the Wittgensteinian (which at this point will not look at all attractive) and the more familiar one initiated by Moore himself. III examines this second approach in more detail and suggests that it cannot meet the two conditions. IV and V consider the question of how the paradox could be treated in the framework of a functionalist theory of belief. IV argues that on certain particular versions of functionalism the oddness of the Moorean utterances disappears. We do not get an explanation of why they are absurd; rather we get a view on which there is no absurdity to be explained. V suggests that this disappearance of the paradox is likely to be a feature of all versions of functionalism and is, moreover, a serious defect in them. The upshot of this discussion is to put us in a better position to appreciate the attractions of the Wittgensteinian strategy, which is briefly outlined in the final VI.

II

So what is Moore's paradox? An initial point to note is that there are really two paradoxes, one having to do with sentences of the form "I believe that *p* but not *p*" and the other with sentences of the form "I don't believe that *p* but *p*". One of Moore's discussions of the issue deals with the first and the other with the second, but it looks as if he did not notice that there might be a significant difference. Wittgenstein also makes no explicit differentiation. His actual discussion is however mainly centred on the first.[2] I shall endeavour to say something about both.

Moore himself describes what is paradoxical in terms of assertion. What is to be explained is why it would be so strange to (attempt to) make some public and informative statement with this sort of content. Why cannot I do so, given that others clearly can make such assertions (given appropriate changes of pronouns etc.) and that I can state such things of myself in the past or future?

However, this stress on assertion overlooks the fact that there is something equally strange about the idea that someone realises the sentences to be true of him or herself, i.e. makes the sort of judgment which they express, whether overtly communicated to another or not.[3] We have just the same reasons as in the case of assertion—that others can have the thought of me, that I can think it of myself in the past or future—to suppose that it ought to be possible.

This yields the first condition on a solution, namely that it must be of adequate generality to explain the oddness of both thought and assertion. So any proposal which calls essentially on features which are found only in communication and have no relevant analogue in thought will not fit the bill.

A second condition is this: the solution must identify a contradiction, or something contradiction-like, in the

Moorean claims. It will not do, for example, to show that they are odd merely in that they depict situations which we take to be empirically extremely unlikely. The oddness is conceptual: there is some kind of tension or incompatibility between the two parts of the claims, and it is this which needs to be elucidated.

Let us now sketch briefly the two possible lines of approach to a solution. Consider the first paradox, namely "I believe that *p* but not *p*". Here we have two potentially contradictory elements, namely "*p*" and "not *p*". But the one is insulated from the other by the operator "I believe that". We could then try to generate a contradiction or tension by, somehow, neutralising or removing the "I believe that". This is Wittgenstein's line:

> One may say the following queer thing: "I believe it is going to rain" means something like "It is going to rain" . . . Moore's paradox may be expressed like *this:* "I believe *p*" says roughly the same as "*p*" but "Suppose I believe that *p*" does not say roughly the same as "Suppose *p*". (1980, pp. 91, 92)

How can this be? Is it that I have so much confidence in my own judgment that I can present, to others and to myself, the fact that I believe something as strong or conclusive evidence that it is so? Do I make the inference (and expect others to as well) "I/she believe(s) that *p*; so *p*"? The solution has the virtue of satisfying our two conditions. This, however, is about all that can be said for it. The cost of adopting it is to represent the thinker (and his or her potential audience) as willing to overlook the very feature of belief—namely its acknowledged fallibility—which generated the paradox in the first place. The thought was "Everybody knows that belief is a state of the person—a feeling, disposition to behave or what not—which is independent of how it is outside. Why therefore may a person not self ascribe such a belief state while acknowledging its falsehood?" The currently proposed "solution" seems just to ignore the central point, the very one which generates the puzzle.

Another serious weakness of this solution is that is difficult to apply it to the second paradox. It is true that we sometimes use "I do not believe that *p*" as a way of expressing disbelief. Where this is the case, then the second paradox is merely an alternative wording for the first. But where "I do not believe that *p*" is taken as a self ascription of ignorance as to whether *p*, then we do have a genuinely different conceptual structure. We could get some equivalence between "I do not believe that *p*" and the claim that not *p* only by imagining our thinker or speaker to take him or herself to be omniscient. ("What I am not aware of, is not there to be thought of.") This looks several degrees madder even than a claim of infallibility.

So this whole approach looks very unattractive. I shall suggest in VI that it is not in fact the only way of getting "*p*" out of "I believe that *p*" (for the first paradox). Wittgenstein discusses and implicitly criticises the particular solution just discussed (1980 p. 92) and it is distinct from the view he wishes to recommend. But for the moment we may find it difficult to see in what other way this skeletal first strategy could be fleshed out. So let us turn to the other and more familiar line. This is, of course, the reverse, namely to expand the "not *p*" into an "I do not believe that *p*" (for the first paradox) and the "*p*" into "I believe that *p*" (for the second) and to generate a tension at this level. Most discussions assume that this is the line we need to pursue for both paradoxes. But let us bear in mind that we might need one line for the first and a different one for the second. For the moment, however, we shall consider attempts to apply the second strategy across the board.

III

It is clear that the contents "*p*" or "not *p*" alone will not suffice to do the job of generating the propositions "I believe that *p*" or "I do not believe that *p*". Whatever it is which supplies us with these claims, in such a way that they can be in some kind of tension with the claims in the other halves of the Moorean judgments, the propositions by themselves cannot do it. *Qua* propositions they carry only whatever the logical implications are of "*p*" or "not *p*", which do not in general include anything about people thinking or not thinking. So, it seems, it must be the occurrence of some event (or state) which has the proposition "*p*" or "not *p*" as content which brings with it the idea we need.

Many discussions, starting with Moore's own, take the event in question to be that of my (apparently sincerely) asserting that *p* or that not *p*. This event does the job by, somehow, implying that I do (or do not) believe that *p*. A number of different stories could be told about how the new proposition gets brought to our attention. We could say that it was merely a matter of inductive generalisation: those who assert that *p* (or not *p*) usually do believe that *p* (or do not believe that *p*): hence the new proposition enters the scene in virtue of hearers making such inductive inferences. This (very crudely) is Moore's own approach.

More subtly, one could say that it is a matter of how the speech act of assertion works. Thus Baldwin writes:

> The implication [of belief or non belief by assertion] must arise from the intention, constitutive of the speech act of assertion, of providing one's audience with information through their recognition that this is one's intention. For since one cannot be understood as intending to inform someone that *p* unless one is believed by them to believe that *p*, the intention to be thus understood includes the intention to be taken to believe what one asserts. (1990 p. 228)

Suppose that this is correct. Then when I say "I don't believe that *p* but *p*" it seems that, by the first part of my utterance I intend to induce the belief that I do not believe that *p* (because that is the content of that bit of the assertion) while by the second part I intend to induce belief that I believe that *p* (in virtue of the principle stated in the last sentence of the quotation). So I intend to produce contradictory beliefs. Thus it looks as if, by this sort of unpacking, we could reveal some contradiction or contradiction-like phenomenon in the Moorean claim.

The above sort of story works best for the second paradox. In order to account for the oddness of the first Moorean claim (viz. "I believe that *p* but not *p*"), we have to go through more elaborate manoeuvres. That I say "not *p*" somehow carries with it (in virtue of truths about the workings of assertion, or whatever) the idea that I believe that not *p*. This is the first step. But we can get from that to the idea that I do not believe that *p* only if we assume that I am rational and so do not have contradictory beliefs. So I, as a speaker, seem to be committed to inducing the (quite coherent) belief that *I* have contradictory beliefs. But I will be committed further to inducing contradictory beliefs *in my hearer* only if I assume that he or she will take me to be rational and I intend him or her to make the extra step.[4]

It is worth noting that more work needs to be done to make these arguments really cogent.[5] For example, one difficulty is this. The original Gricean account, which seems to be invoked, says that in asserting that *q* I reveal to my audience my intention that she believe that *q* and intend her to have this knowledge as her reason for believing that *q*. It is true that I cannot achieve my intended goal by this route (in normal circumstances) unless my audience also takes it that I intend her to have a true belief and that I am myself well informed as to whether or not *q*. So, if all goes as planned, my audience will after the utterance be in possession of information from which she can infer that I believe that *q*. But we cannot without calling on further principles of epistemic logic and the logic of intention derive from this that I must intend my audience to believe that I believe that *q*. If on the other hand we take the later Gricean account (on which when I assert that *q* I intend my audience to believe that I believe that *q*) we run into other snags. I shall not pursue these matters in detail since it is not part of my case that this general line of explication of the absurdity of the Moorean assertion does definitely work, although it seems plausible that something of this general sort can be made defensible. But if this is not so and the sort of account sketched above ultimately fails, because contradiction or some contradiction-like phenomenon can be derived only by calling on further invalid principles, then this strengthens the case for thinking that we should look elsewhere for a solution.[6]

Let us however concede, for the sake of the argument, that the above approach can be developed persuasively and the act of uttering either of the Moorean sentences in an attempted sincere assertion can thus be shown to be bizarre and (in one case at least) to involve an attempt to induce contradictory beliefs. The question remains of whether these reflections say all there is to be said. And the central reason for thinking that they do not is that

they fail to meet the first condition on a solution of the paradoxes. They tell us what would be odd about asserting a Moorean claim but say nothing about why it might be odd to think it. If there is no public and communicatively intended utterance, these strategies of solution can get no grip.

But can they be extended? Can we find some interior analogue? Baldwin (1990 pp. 229-32) argues that we can. And he suggests further that reflection on the parallel will show us something of Wittgenstein's purposes in discussing the paradox which, as Baldwin remarks, clearly have little to do with Gricean ideas about the structure of acts of assertion. Baldwin holds that a rational thinker will not consciously hold a Moorean belief "for much the same reason that a rational speaker will not consciously assert a Moorean sentence". Clearly when I consciously make some judgment I do not put on some inner performance with the intention of convincing myself of something. But the fact that the belief is *conscious* (where a "conscious" state is understood as one accompanied by awareness of itself) will do some similar work, in making the fact of my belief do double duty as also a sort of claim that it itself exists. So let us suppose that I consciously believe "I believe that *p* but not *p*". Now let us also take it that holding a conjunctive belief (whether consciously or otherwise) implies belief (whether consciously or otherwise) in each of the conjuncts. Then it follows that I consciously believe that I believe that *p* and I consciously believe that not *p*. So now, because of this second belief and in virtue of the consciousness, I believe that I believe not *p*. So I (consciously) believe that I believe *p* and I believe that I believe not *p*. If we are further allowed to take it that any two beliefs (even if one is conscious and the other not) yield a belief in the conjunction of their contents, then I believe that I believe *p* and that I believe not *p*. So I believe that I have a contradictory belief.

In the case of the second paradox a suitably adapted chain of similar manoeuvres (which I shall not spell out in detail) can yield the conclusion that I believe of myself both that I do not believe that *p* and that also that I do believe that *p*. So here we get the outcome that I actually have a contradictory belief about myself if I consciously believe the second Moorean claim.

It is again important to note how much work is being done here by principles of epistemic logic. But let us waive this point. And let us grant also what Baldwin claims, namely that the two resultant beliefs can neither of them be held by a conscious rational thinker. The interesting question is what significance this has.

Wittgenstein concentrates on the first paradox (absurdity of self attribution of particular error). What the paradoxicality of this shows, Baldwin claims, is that an individual cannot hold apart her conception of the world as it is and her conception of the world as she takes it to be. The subject of belief cannot appear in the world as the subject of belief. Baldwin (1990 p. 231) suggests that this is as far as Wittgenstein goes explicitly in his later discussions but that what is implicit in it is a Tractarian view of the subject. "Wittgenstein's view is that the way to come to terms with Moore's paradox is through a metaphysical conception of the subject. The reason that there are truths about me which I cannot believe is that because these are truths about me as a metaphysical subject they cannot appear in my world."

I would like to suggest that this is not a mandatory reading of the later Wittgenstein on this topic. One reason for uneasiness with it is that postulation of a metaphysical subject seems very likely to lead to solipsism and thus to a strong form of first/third person asymmetry in the meaning of psychological terms. But there seem to be many indications that these are views that Wittgenstein is struggling against in his later writings. Other people are in the world, as embodied fallible subjects, and so am I. Arguably this "I" (the embodied, fallible, one among many) is the only sort of subject or person the later Wittgenstein wants us to recognise. If this is right then his problem is to explain the phenomena—i.e. Moore's paradoxes—in a way which precisely does not tempt us back to the Tractarian non-worldly "limit" subject.

Another reason for worry is that further thought suggests that we have not, in the above reflections on conscious belief, fully satisfied the second condition on a solution for the first paradox; we have not yet found something contradiction-like in the thought "I believe that p but not p". Let us remind ourselves again of exactly what absurdity or tension enters the scene in the would-be Moorean thoughts. There is an important asymmetry here. In the case of the second paradox what we would have without consciousness is a complex thought event, the occurrence of the second element of which necessarily falsifies the content of the first. The addition of consciousness gives me the further thought "I believe that p". So I end up believing a contradiction about my own psychological state. We can certainly agree with Baldwin that a rational thinker will not make this judgment, since doing so is itself a manifestation of irrationality. The contradictoriness is right there in the judgment which is made. Thus as far as the second paradox goes, this line of solution seems satisfactory.

When we consider the first paradox things are less clear. If I have the thought "I believe that p but not p" without consciousness there exists a complex thought event, the second element in which can occur without falsifying the content of the first, provided that I have contradictory beliefs. And I can have such beliefs. This is what prevents us disentangling the first paradox with the apparatus we used for the second. When consciousness is added, I come to be aware that I believe not p and so to be aware that I have contradictory beliefs. But having this thought itself is not (in any obvious way) a manifestation of irrationality. The original claim—believing that p—is one item and my recognising that it is false—my realising that I believe that p but not p—is another. Now all I am doing, in the current third judgment, is, perfectly rationally and properly, recognising the consequences of

these other states. Certainly I cannot recognise the error of a belief and at the same time have it persist without ending up with contradictory beliefs. And so, we may say, this will not happen to me unless I am irrational. I am irrational because my recognition of the error of a belief has failed to eradicate that belief in me. This is bad cognitive functioning in me. If this is how things are (and we have no account yet which shows that it could not be so with me) how could it be irrational or contradictory to recognise that it is so? On this representation of the structure of the thoughts the error and its recognition and the consequent contradictoriness are all *outside* the content of the conscious Moorean thought I am now having. But intuitively this is extremely unconvincing. "I believe that p but not p" (as a conscious thought) is in itself contradictory and tension-ridden, in at least as strong a way as "I do not believe that p but p". Someone who thinks it seems to be thinking contradictorily in that very judgment, not merely to be committed to recognising difficulty elsewhere. Our problem is to explain why it is absurd to think "I believe that p but not p". But all we have succeeded in doing is showing that if I were able to think it I would then be committed to recognising that my thoughts were contradictory. We have no explanation of why this should be something absurd for me to do, any more than we have an explanation for why it should be absurd to recognise the original error.

We might try saying that it is conceptually impossible to think that p and that not p consciously at the same time. The Moorean claim would inherit this conceptual absurdity precisely because it seems to countenance such a possibility. But this move is unsatisfactory. It is acknowledged on all hands that a person may have contradictory beliefs. How does the addition of consciousness guarantee removal of our liability to such error? One may say that consciousness brings the two beliefs together and hence makes it extremely likely that rationality will operate in noticing the clash and removing one or both. But "extremely likely" is not "conceptually certain". We may insist by fiat that it is necessary, but it would remain mysterious why we should be entitled to do so. Consciousness is being invoked as a *deus ex machina*, but the explanation we have of its nature (as involving second order thought) does not show how it could have the postulated powers. If we admit that, however unlikely, it is nevertheless an empirical possibility that a person should (thoroughly irrationally of course) believe p and not p consciously at the same time, then we invite the response that if this happens to someone then the right coherent thing for him to do is to acknowledge it in a Moorean judgment.

The object of this section was to examine the second strategy for dealing with the paradoxes, namely that of expanding the "p" or "not p" into some claim about my beliefs and thus generating a contradiction. The suggestion I wish to make is that it may work for the second paradox but is far from satisfactory in dealing with the first, for the reasons just outlined. I also wished to suggest that, although Baldwin is quite right in emphasising that the contradictoriness of Moore's first paradoxical remark (if and when we do get it explained) connects closely with the impossibility of prising apart the conception of the world and the conception of what we believe the world to be, talk of a metaphysical conception of the subject may not be either the later Wittgenstein's reaction or the best reaction to the phenomenon.

IV

It is natural at this point to think that we might get help with our problem by looking more closely into the meaning of the word "believe". If we set out in more detail what the state of belief is then perhaps the nature and source of the Moorean oddity would become apparent to us. Let us therefore consider functionalism and its implications for our question.[7] What I shall suggest is that, far from being helped to track the source of the contradiction, what we find is that the oddness of the Moorean claim seems to evaporate.

We start from what is common to all versions of functionalism, broadly construed, namely this: to say that someone believes that p is to say roughly "He or she is in a state which, together with his or her desires, will normally cause behaviour which satisfies those desires only if p". This general view is compatible with a whole variety of further detailed views, on how "normal" is to be captured, on how desires are to be identified, on whether further conditions on normal causal origins should be imposed, etc. My aim is simply to gesture in the direction of those accounts of belief which are offered when, recoiling from Cartesian introspectionism, we insist that psychological notions have as their central role a causal/explanatory task vis-à-vis behaviour and we stress that psychological states are attributed on the basis of observed patterns and dispositions in behaviour. Let us summarise these views by saying that they equate having a belief that p with being in a state apt to cause behaviour appropriate to its being the case that p.

It is very important to functionalism that the meaning of "believe" is uniform and is given by some such account whether I attribute belief to myself or another. The functionalist may admit that I do not observe my own patterns of behaviour in order to see what I believe. Perhaps, he will say, I have some internal, pre-consciously operating, self-scanning device which delivers to me usually true judgments about my beliefs. This operates in a way which enables me to short-cut any need for self observation. All the same, the functionalist will say, what I mean when I say "I believe . . ." is fully captured by the mention of causes of behaviour etc. There is, and could be, no more than this, namely the facts about truth conditions and the descriptive meaning of "believe", to be said about the role of the word in the language.

Now consider the following case. We are familiar with the Mueller-Lyer illusion where the visual appearance of one item being longer than the other is not dissipated by the discovery that it is in reality equal or even shorter.

Suppose such a case to involve some objects A and B, say sticks and not merely lines, and suppose that A looks, and continues to look, longer than B, while the reality is that B is very slightly longer than A. Suppose further that, in my particular case, it is not only visual impressions which fail to fall into line with increased information, but also a considerable part of my bodily behaviour. For example, if I want the longer of the two sticks then I find my hand reaching out towards A rather than B; if someone asks me to point to the longer, I point to A and so forth.

Is this quite absurd and unimaginable? It would be rash to rule it out on a priori grounds. Moreover, phenomena do exist which somewhat resemble what has been described and which give some hint of what it might be like to experience it. For example, when watching a film taken from a roller coaster people sway and clutch their seats. Despite their knowledge that they are not moving, the visual input carries such vivid messages of plunging and swooping that the appropriate bodily behaviour is difficult to restrain.

The account of belief sketched above mandates us to say in such an extended Mueller-Lyer case: "I believe that A is longer than B, but B is longer than A". That is, we can believe and assert of ourselves, with perfect intelligibility and propriety, the Moorean sentence. There is some state in me (viz. the illusion with its extended powers) which is causing me to behave in a way which will be successful in fulfilling my desires only if A is longer than B; but A is not longer than B, as I have realised and stated in the other part of my utterance. The question which set us off brooding on the paradox was this: to say "I believe that p" is just to say that things are a certain way with me, without commitment to how it is with the rest of the world; so why can I not discover that things are that way with me while also remarking that in the world outside not p? What we have done with the thought experiment is to flesh this out with a particular account (the functionalist one) of what has to be the case with me when I believe. And we have discovered that when belief is so construed, the oddness vanishes.

Here is another case. I embark upon a certain course of action, entering a competitive examination for a job, exhibiting many signs of cheerfulness and confidence; I am jaunty and smiling; I say "I'm going to win this one"; I make no arrangements for alternative jobs. At the same time I do other things which are appropriate preparations for the treatment of a person who has received a horrible and unexpected (let me stress that) shock. For example, I collect herbs and brew a potion, the peculiar and sole virtue of which is to console for the frightful pangs associated with unanticipated misfortune. It is clear from when I brew the liquid and where I stow it that I am the intended recipient and that the day it is to be taken is the day of the announcement of the examination result. I am aware of what I am doing and say "I believe that I am going to fail and more, I believe that I believe falsely that I shall succeed. But of course I shall succeed!"

The case makes essentially the same point as the extended Mueller-Lyer. Both seem to licence the straightforward making of the Moorean claim. The second case, however, shows additionally that we can also licence on the basis of non-linguistic behaviour ascription of the belief "I believe falsely that *p*".

What should we conclude from these cases? One move would be to take them at their face value and, accepting functionalism, to say that they show that there is no paradox; there is really no oddness in Moorean claims, hence no problem in explaining why there should be oddness; we have been led into the mistaken idea that there was some oddness simply by lack of imagination and by the rareness of the cases; Moorean claims are not conceptually quasi-contradictory but merely extremely unlikely to be true.

A way of avoiding this somewhat unwelcome and implausible collapse of our whole problem would be to say that there are faults in the so far rather vague functionalist story we have been telling. It is clear, it might be said, that not all my behaviour, in the extended Mueller-Lyer, is appropriate to A's being longer than B. After all, I intentionally produce, in the second part of the utterance, a verbal account of how things are. This action is under the control of some other representation of the world than the one which is directing the movement of my limbs. Similar remarks are clearly appropriate in the examination case. Perhaps we should so formulate our functionalist account that a belief can be attributed only if *all* behaviour is unified under the control of one representation?

But this is clearly too strong a demand. People do have contradictory beliefs, and each of such a pair will manifest itself in a different area of behaviour. In general when we become aware of such contradictions after reflection one belief or the other or both disappear. What is undoubtedly unusual about the cases imagined is that the person has contradictory beliefs, and knows it, but that both persist—one controlling one part of behaviour, e.g. limb movement, and the other some different part, e.g. vocalisation. This is doubtless all very unfortunate for the person who is its subject and (in some sense) irrational. But to acknowledge that it is regrettable and irrational is very different from supposing that it could not happen or could not be quite straightforwardly described if it did happen. Nothing in the functionalist story seems to entitle us to rule out the persistence of contradictory beliefs in the imagined cases, even when the subject is aware of them as contradictory. So we seem driven back to the conjecture that the whole idea of a paradox was a mistake. Is this acceptable?

In setting up these cases I have helped myself to the whole normal background of human life, behaviour and speech. I have helped myself to the idea that the Moorean utterance as a whole (if made sincerely) expresses a belief which I have, and consequently that its second part expresses my belief that not *p*. It is clearly presupposed in setting up the paradox that the "I" spoken of in the explicit self description is the same as the person whose belief is expressed in the utterance as a whole and that the "belief" explicitly spoken of is the same as the belief expressed, viz. belief in the ordinary sense. (If "I" meant "this rabbit" and "believe that *p*" meant "eats grass" of course there would be no paradox.) In toying with the idea that there is really no paradox we have assumed these presuppositions to be fulfilled—namely that the "I" spoken of and the "I" who speaks are the same and that the functional account of belief is the one and only one, which captures not only the sense of the explicit self description but also what could be said of me about my relation to the whole proposition expressed by the Moorean sentence.

Are these assumptions right? One fact to note is that it is extremely natural to fall into some kind of contrastive emphasis and/or verbal elaboration in reporting the imagined cases. For example one might well be tempted to say "This body believes that *p* but not *p*" or (bringing out the fact that the second part expresses a belief) "*This body* believes that *p* but *I* believe that not *p*". Another formulation might also seem apt: "I believe in a bodily way that *p* but not *p*" or "I believe in *a bodily way* that *p*, but I *really* believe that not *p*". The impulse to produce this kind of contrastive description suggests that there may be something wrong in the assumptions that the sense of belief and/or the postulated subject of belief are uniform. The impulse behind the reformulations is to allow me to distance myself from the explicitly ascribed belief, either by assigning it to another subject or by denying that it is full belief. But if it is right to do either of these things then we will be wrong to think that we have discovered the nonexistence of the paradox. If the subject of belief or the sense of "believe" are not the same, we may find when we bring them into line again that the paradox has reappeared.

Which of the two moves, if either, is likely to be the more defensible? Distinguishing between "me" and "this body" is plausible at the level of sense or mode of presentation but highly controversial at the level of reference. It would seem rash to embark on a defence of dualism. The alternative, distinguishing kinds of belief, has no such obvious drawbacks and does seem to provide a way of expressing something which needs saying, namely that my relations to the proposition that *p* and to the proposition that not *p* are importantly different in the imagined case. For example, as far as conversation and further personal interaction with me is concerned (debating what is really the case, making plans for the future, sharing a joke, being outraged at my flippancy, blaming me, encouraging me, condoling with me, etc.) you will treat me as one who believes not *p*; it is on the basis of this that all your moves will be premised. This is part of what we understand in grasping that normal human life is proceeding as the background to the strange events. The regrettable fact that in certain respects I carry on as if I believed that *p*, i.e. that my limbs from time to time execute various manoeuvres, is something that you and I will plan to change or circumvent.

Let us then use "believe" in the clear understanding that we are speaking of a particular relation to a proposition, namely the one which I have when I "really" believe it. Now suppose I say "I believe not *p*—as our conversations, plans etc. rightly assume—but in fact *p*"? The paradox has reappeared, since this utterance is extremely odd, as is equally the idea that I should make this judgment about myself. All the old flavour of contradictoriness is detectable.

What we found earlier was that we had a worrying disappearance of the paradox on our original functionalist account of belief. We first considered avoiding this by reformulating functionalism to rule out contradictory beliefs and found that unsatisfactory. Can we now explain the reappearance of the paradox by pointing to some further modified and enriched functionalist account of belief? If so, we can preserve both functionalism and our intuition that the paradox is central to the nature of belief. This would seem to be rather a satisfactory outcome. So perhaps we should try something like this, as an elucidation of the sense of "believe" I have been gesturing at with this talk of conversation and normal human life: "A believes that *p*" means "A behaves, including behaviour in deliberation and vocalisation, in a way which will be desire-fulfilling if and only if *p*". (Making this move might also satisfy the impulse to insist that what has gone wrong so far is that we have not considered specifically conscious belief. On the account suggested earlier, conscious belief is belief accompanied by belief in itself. And this latter will on the current approach consist in dispositions to behaviour appropriate to the first level belief, e.g. among other things in explicit deliberative and vocal behaviour.)

This formulation does not provide the stable resting place we might hope. Instead it invites the imagination of further bizarre cases. Suppose, for example, that under the influence of certain drugs or tiredness the extended Mueller-Lyer case extends itself even further, so that I find not merely my bodily behaviour but also some chains of images and representation and some vocalisations taking off under the control of the belief that A is longer than B. In other words, I find that I cannot stop ideas of what would be the case if A were longer than B coming into my mind and when they get there they exert the same control over bodily behaviour as the original erroneous belief; and I find myself uttering out these new conclusions, even though, in some sense, I wish to repudiate them. I still, however, have enough control of my voice, when I try, to say "I believe that A is longer than B but B is longer than A".

It is clear that if this happens to me I am in even worse case than when my limbs alone are carrying on bizarrely. But, to reiterate the earlier point, to remark that something would be a grave misfortune to a person is quite a different thing from supposing that it cannot happen or be recognised and described by him or her. On the current hypothesis about the meaning of "believe" an entirely straightforward form of words is instantly available, to be

used quite literally and unparadoxically, to describe my unfortunate state, viz. "I believe that *p* but not *p*". So we have again mislaid the strange nature of the Moorean claim and the revised functionalist story does not, after all, quite capture that apparent sense of "believe" we meant to gesture at when we talked of normal human life and conversation.

v

What conclusions should we draw from the discussion of the last section? I wish now to suggest that there are general reasons for thinking that any functionalist approach must run into the same troubles as the versions we have examined and so must fail to account for the idea that there is something contradictory about the Moorean claim. I shall further urge that this is a serious problem for functionalism.

The first point to note is that functionalism is formulated within a (natural and attractive) metaphysical view. On this view the world contains a variety of phenomena which people may come across and of which they may form some conception (cf. Wittgenstein 1953, p. 190). Among these are states of themselves, including beliefs. They come across these either by introspection (although this idea would more naturally go with a Humean or Cartesian view than with a functionalist one) or in seeking to explain, in proto scientific folk-psychology, the behaviour of themselves and those around them. The linguistic behaviour of the word "believe" is to be explained by unpacking the truth conditions of claims about beliefs; these in turn are explained by pointing to the conception people have of the phenomenon they have come across, a conception which will more or less accurately capture the nature of the pre-existing phenomenon. (Lurking behind this commonsensical-seeming account are further pictures e.g. of the world as already sliced by nature at the joints and awaiting only labelling from us, of empiricism as the right account of concept acquisition and of the correspondence theory of truth.)

The second point to remark is the particular content of the conception of belief with which functionalism fills out this general schema. Belief is something which goes on within a person (and has the kind of properties such internal or intrinsic states could have, e.g. experiential character or causal power vis-à-vis bodily behaviour) but is independent of how things are outside him or her. What we "come across" when we come across belief is something which has a representational character, but where what is represented may either exist or not.

Given this general conception, it is difficult to see how any functionalist account could discover contradiction in a Moorean claim. By its second element, functionalism has been set up to give maximum force to the thoughts that make it appear that the Moorean claim should not be absurd. But also, by its first element, it has deprived itself of any materials from metaphysics or theory of meaning which it could use to extract itself from this difficulty. The second element says that when I ascribe a belief to myself I say that I am in such and such an inner state, which is independent of how things are in the world. The first element says that we must talk only of truth conditions in explaining semantic features of sentences. (Thus talk of language games or deep "grammatical" first/third person asymmetries or any such waffly stuff is ruled out.) So if there is a contradiction it must come from the truth conditions. But the truth conditions have been set up precisely to rule out the possibility of such contradiction.

This is not a tight proof that something recognisably functionalist cannot deliver the goods, and we may if we choose try yet more elaborate versions of the kinds of accounts examined in the last section. But it is possible to be sceptical of success in exhibiting any contradictoriness in the Moorean claim by this route. Suppose this scepticism is well founded. Should we nevertheless stay with the idea that some functionalist story (such as the more elaborate one considered at the end of the last section) does give the right account of belief? And should we in consequence say that there is no contradiction in the Moorean claim? Philosophers, in thinking that there is, have perhaps merely overreacted to the fact that the claim describes a very unusual situation, or to the fact that there is some kind of pragmatic oddity in the Moorean utterance, or to the fact that there is contradictory belief somewhere in the psyche of the person who makes the Moorean claim.

There is a problem of principle with this proposal, which provides some backing for the feeling that we should not just dismiss the apparent contradictory character of Moorean claims as a mass delusion among philosophers. When we consider the unfortunate people enmeshed in the extended Mueller-Lyer situations, it is clear that the particular functionalist account of the end of IV does *not* capture the ordinary sense of "believe". We may agree that the use of the word "believe" is not totally inappropriate. Someone who found him or herself in such a situation might well say "It is as if I believed that *p*". But such a person would not say straightforwardly "I believe that *p*"—as the functionalist story demands. What is true of this version of functionalism will (I suggest) be true of any other version which fails to deliver a contradiction in the Moorean utterance, for the following reason. If there is no contradiction then the subject may coherently acknowledge the supposed belief that *p* while at the same time affirming that in reality not *p*. And if the subject does thus affirm that not *p* (while coherently acknowledging also the going on of the supposed functionalist belief that *p*) we will surely want to say that this affirmation is what expresses his or her "real" belief and hence that whatever was captured by the functionalist story is not (contrary to hypothesis) real belief. In summary, if functionalism does not deliver a contradiction we can have the subject acknowledging the supposed "belief" but also disowning it. And then the functionalist story has not captured the ordinary sense of "believe". My challenge to the functionalist, in brief, is to show how what happened

to the definitions proposed in IV could be avoided by any other proposed definition which satisfies the functionalist overall demands. Putting these thoughts together in sequence we have this: a deep seated metaphysical picture motivates functionalism; but functionalism cannot deliver the contradiction; in failing to deliver a contradiction it undermines its claim to capture the normal sense of "believe".

The thrust of the argument is to suggest that the source of the muddle we find ourselves in is the metaphysical picture which dictates the shape of the functionalist account. The next section pursues that thought. Other options are available at this point. I do not claim to have conclusive proof that no version of functionalism can reveal the Moorean claim as contradictory. Nor have we proof that we must retain the idea of the contradictoriness. The considerations urged on both these issues were suggestive rather than fully cogent. Hence two options at least are to look to further versions of functionalism or to the defensibility of abandoning the paradoxes. A third quite different possibility would be to suggest that we should look to the epistemology of belief to find a solution. It has been suggested (following Wittgenstein) that usually when a person self-ascribes the belief that *p* he or she does so on grounds which are the same as his or her grounds for judging that *p*. Thus if I am asked "Do you believe that *p*?" I do not think about myself. Rather I ask "*p?*" And if the answer is "yes" then I say "I believe that *p*". If this is the standard route to self ascriptions of belief then perhaps some contradictory character appears in "I believe that *p* but not *p*" when said in circumstances where the presumption is of the normal epistemology.[8] (I shall not examine the details of what contradiction would emerge or exactly how.) On this scenario it is not the metaphysics behind functionalism nor yet its particular account of the meaning of "believe" which leads to our inability to elucidate the paradox but rather our blindness about the distinctive epistemology of "believe".

Investigation of this proposal would require more space than we have here. So I simply note it and turn to ask how things might go if we did not like the look of any of these options and chose instead to question functionalism and its framework.

VI

What alternative could there be to using the word "believe" as a label for some phenomenon, some internal state of people, which people come across in themselves or others? A possible answer is that it is a phenomenon which comes into existence *together with* certain practices of ascribing it. The full phenomenon of belief, the kind of belief which people have, only exists when creatures like ourselves engage in practices of belief ascription—where those practices do *not* have the shape which the metaphysical picture underlying functionalism demands. Someone being trained to use the word "believe" in his or her first language is not simply being taught to connect the word with a pre-existing something of which he or she is aware; rather such a learner is being educated into being a believer. Let me try to make this less schematic by outlining what I suggest to be a Wittgensteinian account of belief ascription, together with how it accounts for the contradictoriness of Moorean claims.

The proposal may be put like this. We have a practice with the word "believe" which combines a number of features. The first, (A), is that beliefs are often attributed to people on the basis of observed patterns in behaviour. So the sort of third personal criteria which the functionalist emphasises are indeed connected to the concept. It is no mistake to think that they are. But there is much more to be said than this. A second feature, (B), is that a person learning the language is also trained to say "I believe that *p*" sometimes as a substitute for the plain assertion "*p*". This training, of its very nature, makes the trained person's utterance of "I believe that *p*" very often occur without his or her checking any criteria. In particular the trained person does not check up on his or her behaviour. If any evidence is looked at it is evidence as to whether *p*. But often, of course, if a person has already settled that *p* then he or she does not check anything before saying "*p*" and in these cases he or she would likewise not check anything before saying "I believe that *p*".[9]

If we stopped at this point and considered only (B) we would have an extremely direct solution to Moore's problem. "I believe that *p*" is merely (as far as (B) alone goes) an alternative way of saying "*p*". So of course one who says "I believe that *p* but not *p*" contradicts him or herself. In effect what has been said is "*p* but not *p*". This is, in essence, the solution we shall continue to defend. All the same, we cannot stop at this point, for this would leave the two uses of "believe" (the third person behaviour-based one and the first person present tense one just described) unconnected with each other. However, there is a third feature, (C), of the practice with "believe" which knits them together. It is that these first person utterances—produced criterionlessly as sketched above—are taken as self descriptions in which the speaker presents him or herself as satisfying the behavioural conditions for belief mentioned in (A). Not only are such utterances taken as self descriptions; they are also taken as authoritative, provided they are sincere. So the non-existence of appropriate behaviour is grounds for questioning the truth of a self-ascription of belief and at the same time grounds for questioning its sincerity.

Suppose that we want to hold that these three features are all elements of the one unified concept of belief and we want to say that the notion thus defined, in virtue of feature (B), helps to show why Moorean utterances are paradoxical; then we are faced with a problem. How can we retain the rough equation of "I believe that *p*" with "*p*" when (C) becomes part of the package? Isn't it much more sensible at this point to say that the lack of explicit attention to one's own behaviour (which everyone acknowledges to be a feature of self ascription of belief) is the result of our having some unconsciously operating

self-scanning mechanism? Should we not at the same time play down the idea that a subject is really authoritative about his or her own beliefs? Perhaps all that is involved in our uneasiness in attributing error to the sincere self-ascriber is our having got used to relying on what people say about themselves because it is generally true. This way lies a return to the familiar functionalist story, and thus loss of the equation hinted at by (B) and loss of ability to explain the paradox.

Let us try another tack. There is a way to hold on both to the rough equation (of "I believe that *p*" with "*p*" suggested by (B)) and also to the authoritativeness of (C). It is to shift from thinking of this authority as epistemological to thinking of it as constitutive. To put matters in another idiom, judging that one believes that *p* has a sort of performative character. I do *not* mean by this that any element of choice is in question. A person does not choose his or her beliefs. Relatedly the proposal is not that saying "I belive that *p*" (which is a voluntary action) constitutes belief that *p*. The authoritativeness built into our practices with "believe" is authoritativeness only for *sincere* first person pronouncements; we build into the practice that questioning truth must also be questioning sincerity. The constitutive link which we can then see the practice as embodying is one which ties thinking that I believe that *p* (i.e. what the sincerity of my remark consists in) to believing that *p*. So the proposal is of "performativeness" only in the sense that the abstract feature we are familiar with from consideration of performatives is present in this case too, namely that the occurrence of a representation of a state of affairs is itself what constitutes that state of affairs. The representation we are here speaking of is my thinking that I believe that *p*. In summary, I am entitled to pronounce on my beliefs not because I have some privileged epistemological access to an independent state but because when I come to think that I believe that *p* then I do, in virtue of that very thought, believe that *p*. It is however important to remember that, as with any performative, certain background conditions must be present which render the claim "happy", in Austin's terms.[10] Thus we do not give the subject *carte blanche* to pronounce on his or her beliefs, even when tired, deranged, under stress, under the influence of drugs etc.

If we are prepared to make this radical move, then we can hang on to something like the simple solution of the paradox. Suppose I say sincerely "I believe that *p*" and thereby express my belief that I believe that *p*. This belief, namely that I believe that *p*, itself constitutes in me a belief that *p*. So my utterance "I believe that *p*" also expresses belief that *p*. In doing this it is, from one perspective, just an alternative form of assertion that *p*. So if I now add "but not *p*" then I have contradicted myself.

Thus we have in "I believe that *p*" an utterance which is, at one and the same time, a member of two different classes. On the one hand it is a self description of me as a believer and as such it has all the possibilities of grammatical transformation, entry into inference and possibility of incompatibility with behavioural evidence which that involves. On the other hand it is an expression of belief that *p*, an alternative way of voicing out what could also be voiced out as *"p"*. When we sense the contradiction in the Moorean utterance we hear "I believe that *p*" in this second role. When we become puzzled about why the utterance is contradictory we hear it in the first role.[11]

The remarks of the last paragraph bear on the oddness of the overt Moorean assertion. But what of the Moorean thought? Clearly a closely analogous solution can be offered. As we have already stressed, what is central to the proposal is not that the utterance "I believe that *p*" constitutes belief but that its sincerity does so. If our concept of belief does indeed work like this then the same dual character to be found in the utterance "I believe that *p*" will also be found in the thought with that content. When we contemplate someone having this thought we take him or her to have a representation which is at the same time about the self and about the world. It is both a belief that he or she believes that *p* and a belief that *p*. One and the same state enters into two sets of inferential, evidence responsive, etc. relations. We have the troublesome sense that the Moorean thought is both coherent and incoherent as we concentrate now on one and now on another of the patterns in which its first element sits.

Functionalism is not entirely wrong. The third personal behavioural criteria which it stresses are genuinely part of the notion of belief.[12] But, to put things metaphorically, it captures only one dimension of a notion which has a type of complexity or depth not envisaged within the metaphysical and linguistic picture of which functionalism is a part. The real shape of the concept is one in which criterionless first person ascription and behaviourally based third person ascription are inseparably linked.

> Even in the hypothesis the pattern is not what you think. When you say "Suppose I believe" you are presupposing the whole grammar of the word "to believe", the ordinary use, of which you are master. (Wittgenstein 1980, p. 192)

So in ascribing belief to another one may make the ascription on the basis of behaviour but will take for granted the ability of the subject to make criterionless self ascription. In self-ascribing criterionlessly one will take for granted appropriate behaviour. If psychological notions did not have this complexity of shape then our normal human interactions with each other would be impossible.

We are strongly inclined to say that one utterance—"I believe that *p*"—cannot be univocal and also combine the two roles of which I have spoken. Relatedly we shall protest that a supposedly descriptive concept defined by the joint presence of features (A), (B) and (C) is misbegotten and impossible. There will perhaps be pressure to divide usage up into a proper descriptive element (behavioural criteria again) and something else (i.e. the aberrant first person present tense use) which is given an expressive or speech act account. But what entitles us to

do this or necessitates it? Can't we have concepts of whatever shape we like, governed by whatever patterns of ascription rules we like, if they do good work for us? Clearly we could not set up the practice I have just sketched, and operate the notion of "belief" which it defines, unless various contingencies obtained, most strikingly that people's sincere criterionless self ascriptions do, almost invariably, pass the test of acceptability by behavioural criteria. The practice with the word "believe" is erected on a substructure of facts about our social nature, ability to respond to certain training, brain workings and so forth. But is this any criticism of the concept or proof that it does not have the nature sketched? To answer this question would involve tackling large issues to do with concepts, meaning, truth and fact and would take us beyond the remit of this paper.[13]

NOTES

[1] For a related approach see Linville and Ring 1991. I have found much thought provoking material in Gombay 1988. Pears 1991 is also helpful. Baldwin 1990 has much of interest, although I disagree with him for reasons sketched later. Moore's discussions are found in Moore 1942, pp. 540-3 and 1944, p. 204. Wittgenstein's remarks are scattered at various places in his writings, but the central material is in 1953, pp. 190-2 and 1980, pp. 90-6. I would like to thank D. H. Mellor, two anonymous referees for *Mind* and the Editor of *Mind* for helpful comments on earlier drafts of this paper.

[2] The discussion in Wittgenstein 1953 is quite explicitly, barring one passage on p. 192, about the first paradox and since this represents his most considered statement on that matter we must give it considerable weight in attributing a focus of interest to Wittgenstein. The kinds of cases considered in Wittgenstein 1980 range more widely and at pp. 93, 94 and 96 we find wording which suggests that the second paradox is being dealt with. But even here, close attention to the content suggests that in some of the cases it is the first paradox which concerns him.

[3] The point is made by Linville and Ring and by Baldwin. It is also emphasised by Sorensen in an interesting discussion in his 1988 differing substantially in approach both from the Wittgensteinian one explored here and the Moorean one. Sorensen's book contains much useful material on earlier writing on the paradoxes.

[4] See Jones 1991 for some more reflections on this and on how bringing in the conception of assertion as conveying knowledge might strengthen the account.

[5] I am grateful to the Editor and referees of *Mind* for calling these points and their implications to my attention.

[6] For further helpful discussion of the pitfalls of employing epistemic logic in attempted solutions of the paradoxes see Sorensen, pp. 19 ff.

[7] I have focused here on a functionalist account of belief because it is the most likely to seem plausible to a modern reader. But a line of argument similar to the one about to be developed could, I think, be produced if we had started instead with a Humean feeling-based account or a Cartesian inner act view.

[8] I am grateful to one of the referees for drawing this possibility to my attention.

[9] Here the practice which is the basis for the distinctive epistemology alluded to at the end of the last section appears, but placed as an element in an overall account of a non-functionalist character. There is clearly a parallel between what is suggested here about "believe" and Wittgenstein's views about how "It hurts" or "I am in pain" are introduced as replacements for non-linguistic pain behaviour. It seems highly probable that it was the possibility of linking Moore's paradox with these strands of his thought which aroused the enthusiasm Wittgenstein expresses in his 1944 letter to Moore, quoted in Gombay, p. 192.

[10] See Austin 1962 for the classic account of performative utterances. The proposal just outlined here has something in common with that suggested by C. Wright in some recent papers and ascribed by him to Wittgenstein. But it differs from Wright's in continuing to give a central role to behavioural criteria. On Wright's view the treatment of psychological states is parallel to a familiar treatment of secondary qualities, namely (to put it crudely) that they lie in the eye of the beholder. In my view this does not accurately represent Wittgenstein's approach.

[11] Let me briefly contrast this account of the matter with the best that we would be able to come up with if we were to take the authoritativeness of self attributions of belief as epistemological. Here we allow in traditional style infallible access to one's own mental states, which are nevertheless conceived of as distinct from the states of knowledge to which they give rise. On this story one who sincerely asserts "I believe that *p*" will indeed believe that *p*. If we add the other part of the Moorean claim, also sincere, we clearly have a person who believes *p* and also believes not *p*. So contradictory beliefs are implicit in this story, but the utterance itself is not directly expressive of a contradiction. Thus this account loses the contradiction again. Moreover, it lands us with the problem of explaining how there can be this sort of infallible knowledge of anything.

[12] I would like to suggest here that what we mean by "behaviour" needs close scrutiny and that the range of "behaviour" we recognise and the kinds of descriptions of it we are willing to offer may be different for creatures who can have the full personal kind of belief sketched here and ones which cannot. Thus it is possible that the first and third personal are woven together in further ways than those indicated here.

[13] For some discussion of why willingness to introduce considerations about the presuppositions of concepts and

to talk of the "language games" they are linked with need not undermine ideas of truth and realism, see Heal 1989 especially Ch. 8.

REFERENCES

Austin, J. L. 1962: *How to Do Things with Words.* Oxford: Oxford University Press.

Baldwin, T. 1990: *G. E. Moore.* London and New York: Routledge.

Gombay, A. 1988: "Some Paradoxes of Counterprivacy". *Philosophy,* 63, pp. 191-210.

Heal, B. J. 1989: *Fact and Meaning.* Oxford: Basil Blackwell.

Jones, O. R. 1991: "Moore's Paradox, Assertion and Knowledge". *Analysis,* 51, pp. 183-6.

Linville, K. and Ring, M. 1991: "Moore's Paradox Revisited". *Synthese,* 87, pp. 295-309.

Moore, G. E. 1942: "Reply to My Critics" in P. Schilpp ed. *The Philosophy of G. E. Moore.* La Salle, Illinois: Open Court.

————. 1944: "Russell's Theory of Descriptions" in P. Schilpp ed. *The Philosophy of Bertrand Russell.* La Salle, Illinois: Open Court.

Pears, D. 1991: "Wittgenstein's Account of Rule Following". *Synthese,* 87, pp. 273-83.

Sorensen, R. 1988: *Blindspots.* Oxford: Oxford University Press.

Wittgenstein, L. 1953: *Philosophical Investigations.* Oxford: Basil Blackwell.

————. 1980: *Remarks on the Philosophy of Psychology,* Vol. I. Oxford: Basil Blackwell.

Wright, C. 1989: "Wittgenstein's Later Philosophy of Mind". *Journal of Philosophy,* 86, pp. 622-34.

————. 1989: "Wittgenstein's Rule-following Considerations and the Central Project of Theoretical Linguistics" in A. George ed. *Reflections on Chomsky.* Oxford: Basil Blackwell, pp. 233-64.

FURTHER READING

Bibliography

Gilcher, Edwin. *Supplement to a Bibliography of George Moore.* Westport, Conn.: Meckler, 1987, 95 p.

Corrects errors from the 1971 Moore bibliography and includes articles and books published since 1970.

Langenfeld, Robert. *George Moore: An Annotated Secondary Bibliography of Writings about Him.* New York: AMS Press, 1987, 531 p.
  Contains detailed annotations of Moore's letters and articles.

Biography

Levy, Paul. *Moore: G. E. Moore and the Cambridge Apostles.* London: Weidenfeld and Nicolson, 1979, 335 p.
  Focuses on Moore's development as a philosopher and his early years at Cambridge.

Criticism

Baldwin, Thomas. *G. E. Moore.* London and New York: Routledge, 1990, 337 p.
  Overview of Moore's early philosophy and lengthy analysis of his later writings, contrasting Moore's ideas with the philosophical teachings of Bertrand Russell.

Hill, John. *The Ethics of G. E. Moore: A New Interpretation.* The Netherlands: Van Gorcum 1976, 144 p.
  Draws a connection between morality and Moore's writings on ethics, claiming that Moore brought the two concepts together in his famous explanation of the undefinable "good."

Klemke, E. D. *The Epistemology of G. E. Moore.* Evanston, Ill.: Northwestern University Press, 1969, 205 p.
  Discusses Moore's concepts of common sense, ordinary language, semantics, and analytical philosophy, as well as epistemological issues.

Moore, G. E. *The Elements of Ethics.* Tom Regan, ed. Philadelphia: Temple University Press, 1991, 200 p.
  Introduction by Regan analyzes Moore's lectures to the London School of Ethics and Social Philosophy and argues that Moore's *Principia Ethica* is a much better-reasoned philosophical work.

O'Conner, David. *The Metaphysics of G. E. Moore.* London: D. Reidel Publishing Company, 1982, 180 p.
  Examines Moore's writings on metaphysics, finding the philosopher unable to construct a precise system that might include all of his beliefs.

Regan, Tom. *Bloomsbury's Prophet: G. E. Moore and the Development of His Moral Philosophy.* Philadelphia: Temple University Press, 1986, 307 p.
  Explores the themes of individuality and personal ethics in Moore's philosophy and relates his influence on such Bloomsbury figures as Lytton Strachey, John Maynard Keyes, and Desmond McCarthy.

Sylvester, Robert Peter. *The Moral Philosophy of G. E. Moore.* Philadelphia: Temple University Press, 1990, 231 p.
  Attempts to elucidate Moore's system of ethical thought by examining his writings on metaphysics.

Frederic Remington

1861-1909

(Full name Frederic Sackrider Remington) American artist, essayist, sculptor, novelist, and short story writer.

INTRODUCTION

Remington is considered the premiere artist of the turn-of-the-century American West. His works include thousands of esteemed paintings and drawings of Western life, as well as twenty-five bronze sculptures, including his best-known piece *The Bronco-Buster*. As a writer, Remington is noted for the essays he wrote to accompany his illustrations, his short story collections, and his principal novel *John Ermine of the Yellowstone*. In his works, both visual and narrative, Remington attempted to capture the ideals of the Old West and decried their rapid passing in the late nineteenth century. More successful as a visual artist than a writer, Remington began to explore the techniques of the European Impressionists late in life, and is considered one of the progenitors of Impressionism in North America.

Biographical Information

Remington was born in Canton, New York on 4 October 1861. Though he would later adopt the Western United States as the subject of his art and writing, he maintained close ties to the Northeast throughout his life. Remington enrolled at the Yale University School of Fine Arts in 1878. After his father's death in 1880 he refused to return to Yale. Instead, in August of the following year, he traveled west to Montana where he recorded what he saw in sketches and prose. Remington sold his first illustration to *Harper's Weekly* in early 1882, and over the next several years published his drawings of Western scenes and short articles in various periodicals, including *Century* and *Outing*. In 1885 he took up sculpture while continuing with his literary and other artistic pursuits. Remington enrolled at the Art Student League of New York in 1886 and attended briefly. Meanwhile, his paintings, sculptures, and drawings had earned him great distinction as a popular artist. He illustrated Theodore Roosevelt's *Ranch Life and the Hunting Trail* along with several other works by well-known authors, including Henry Wadsworth Longfellow's *Song of Hiawatha* and Francis Parkman's *Oregon Trail*. Remington's later work as an illustrator and war correspondent took him across America, to Cuba during the Spanish-American War, and to Europe and Asia. He published his first novel, *John Ermine of the Yellowstone*, in 1902. His second novel, *The Way of an Indian*, appeared in serialized form, but the work failed to achieve the same popular success as *John Ermine*. For the next three years Remington focused on painting. He died on December 26, 1909 at his home near Ridgefield, Connecticut.

Major Works

In addition to his documentary-style paintings, illustrations, and bronze sculptures of scenes from the American West at the turn of the twentieth century, Remington produced a series of articles, short fiction, and novels that complement these works. His first collection of essays, illustrations, and stories, *Pony Tracks* records his early travels, notably his visits to northern Mexico and the desert Southwest. Remington's second collection, *Crooked Trails,* offers his assessments of compelling figures of the Old West, among them Texan Big-Foot Wallace, a professional hunter and Indian fighter. The eponymous hero of Remington's short story collection *Sundown Leflare* is a half-Indian and half-white drifter who remains alienated from both Native American and white culture. In these five dialect stories set on the high plains, Remington dramatizes his principal theme: the steady passing of the old Western way of life. Remington's novel *John Ermine of the Yellowstone* plays out a related theme: John Ermine, a white man raised by Crow Indians, falls in love with Katherine Searleses, a beautiful Easterner. *The Way of an Indian*, Remington's final work of fiction, recounts the story of White Otter, an alienated Cheyenne warrior who becomes tribal chief after surviving a series of violent encounters with white men and hostile Indians.

Critical Reception

Overall, Remington's paintings and sculpture are more highly esteemed by critics than are his literary works. While his novel *John Ermine of the Yellowstone* was popular at the time of its first publication and went through several printings, it is now considered to be of minor consequence. Contemporary critics of his writing have tended to view Remington as a skilled local colorist, who faithfully evoked the rapidly passing age of the American West in his fiction and journalistic essays. His detractors, however, have observed that Remington's works are frequently marred by sentimentality, and even racism. Remington is also thought to have had a sizable influence on his friend, the writer Owen Wister, whose finest cowboy novel *The Virginian* was published only shortly before *John Ermine*. The Remington-Wister correspondence has also proven of interest to critics of the works of these two men who were instrumental in creating and promoting the myth of the Old West.

PRINCIPAL WORKS

Pony Tracks (essays, illustrations, and short stories) 1895
Crooked Trails (essays, illustrations, and short stories) 1898

Sundown Leflare (short stories) 1899
John Ermine of the Yellowstone (novel) 1902
The Way of an Indian (novel) 1906
My Dear Wister: The Frederic Remington-Owen Wister Letters [edited by Ben Merchant Vorpahl] (letters) 1972
The Collected Writings of Frederic Remington [edited by Peggy and Harold Samuels] (essays, short stories, and novels) 1979

CRITICISM

J. Frank Dobie (essay date 1961)

SOURCE: "A Summary Introduction to Frederick Remington," in *Prefaces*, Little, Brown and Company, 1961, pp. 175-86.

[*In the following essay, originally published in 1961, Dobie describes Remington's life and praises his writing and the power of his visual art.*]

Frederic Remington worked for only about twenty-five years. During the half-century that has raced by since he died just past his forty-eighth birthday—still in the Horse Age—his fame as depictor of the Old West has not perceptibly diminished. Yet no adequate life of him has been published. The one considerable piece of writing on his life and work worthy of respect by people entitled to an opinion is the chapter "Remington in Kansas" (pages 194-211, plus a wealth of notes, pages 355-363) in *Artists and Illustrators of the Old West*, 1850-1900, by the late Robert Taft, of the University of Kansas, published by Charles Scribner's Sons, New York, 1953. The present essay owes far more to this noble work of vast knowledge, all ordered and evaluated, and of quiet power than to all other sources.

Frederic Remington, Artist of the Old West, by Harold McCracken, 1947, contains a useful bibliography of Remington's writings, books illustrated by him, appearances in periodicals, and his bronzes.

Remington's own writings—all illustrated—are the best sources for facts and understanding about him, but many of them in magazines antedating his death—including the autobiographical sketch in *Collier's Weekly* (New York, March 18, 1905)—are available in only a few libraries.

The most knowledgeable person alive on Remington is probably Miss Helen L. Card, proprietor of the Latendorf Bookshop (containing more art than books), 714 Madison Avenue, New York. She does not publish enough, but her two pamphlets, privately printed at Woonsocket, Rhode Island, 1946, on *A Collector's Remington* (I. "Notes on Him; Books Illustrated by Him; and Books Which Gossip About Him." II. "The Story of His Bronzes, with a Complete Descriptive List") contain as much concentrated protein as wheat germ.

Frederic Sackrider Remington was born of parents strong of body and character in Canton, New York, October 1, 1861. His father owned and edited the local newspaper but left it to fight for the Union. Frederic, an only child, early learned to swim, fish, and play Indian in the woods. He hung around the Canton fire station in order to associate with the horses. He drew them and other forms of life on margins of schoolbooks and in albums. From high school he was sent to a military academy, against which he rebelled, at the same time filling a sketchbook with pictures of cavalrymen battling horseback Indians. At home on vacation, he improvised a studio in an uncle's barn. His models were horses—not only carriage horses but several Western ponies belonging to town people.

In the fall of 1878 he went to Yale University, playing football and studying in the Yale Art School. The one other member of his art class was Poultney Bigelow, who became editor of *Outing* magazine and, in 1886, discovered in some pictures offered him "the real thing, the unspoiled, native genius dealing with Mexican ponies, cowboys, cactus, lariats, and sombreros." The artist turned out to be Remington of Yale.

In 1880, Remington's father died and Frederic inherited a few thousand dollars. He refused to return to Yale but seems not to have known what he wanted until he made a trip to Montana in August of 1881. In 1882, *Harper's Weekly* (February 25) published a picture entitled "Cowboys of Arizona: Roused by a Scout." According to the credit line it was "drawn by W. A. Rogers from a sketch by Frederic Remington."

Young Frederic had been corresponding with a Yale friend named Robert Camp (B.A., 1882) of Milwaukee who had gone to Butler County, Kansas, where he was trying his hand at sheep raising. By the end of 1882 he owned a section of land and 900 sheep. In March, 1883, Remington joined him and bought a quarter section (160 acres) not far from Camp's for $3,400. It had a three-room frame house, a well, a corral, and two barns on it. Shortly thereafter he bought an adjoining quarter section for $1,250. He bought horses before he bought sheep. The one he rode was a dun mare from Texas that would not have been ridden by any self-respecting range man in Texas—solely because she was a mare: such was the etiquette of the times. But she suited Remington and he named her Terra Cotta. He hired a hand named Bill, who by his talk was an authority on horses. They built a sheep shed. Remington then bought several hundred sheep, which Bill left him to herd until he hired a neighboring boy and thus bought his own freedom. He was still chief cook and bottle washer on his own ranch.

At that time sheep were as respectable as mules or cattle. As Robert Taft shows, up to 1885 no conflict in Kansas existed between sheepmen and cowmen. Remington did not become an artist of sheep, though he made a drawing of his own flock. Inside one of his barns he carved on the wooden wall the picture of a cowboy roping a steer. He was depicting the conventional rather than what he saw.

His post office was Peabody, Kansas. Under date of May 11, 1883, he wrote a "legal friend" in Canton, New York: "Papers came all right—are the cheese—man just shot down the street—must go." Robert Taft made full examination of files of Peabody newspapers, interviewed many people, including Robert Camp, Remington's ranching *compadre,* but found no evidence whatsoever of "man just shot down the street." To tell the truth, Remington carried on the shooting most of his life.

Of his practice in drawing during his Kansas sojourn, Robert Taft wrote:

> He spent considerable time with his sketch book. He sketched his ranch, his sheep, his neighbors and their activities. He went to Plum Grove and sketched the preacher who visited the schoolhouse on Sundays and the sketch was then passed around the audience. A neighbor bought a trotting horse and Remington drew the horse. Bob Camp's cook was greatly pleased when Remington drew for him on rough wrapping paper a sketch of a cow defending her calf from the attack of a wolf. Many evenings a crowd would gather at the Remington ranch and Remington would sketch the individuals as they "chinned" with one another or as they boxed, for boxing was a favorite sport of the young ranchers. Few cared to put on the gloves with Remington.

In the spring of 1884 he rode horseback to Dodge City, then the "cowboy capital of the world," and other points in the cow country. Back with his sheep, he learned that Terra Cotta could not outdodge a jackrabbit. Then he learned that a mare "looking old and decrepit," owned by a stranger looking still older and more decrepit, could outrun two horses that his friends and his hired man Bill had spent days and nights extolling. He lost Terra Cotta on a bet. He wrote and illustrated the jackrabbit and horse races for *Outing* magazine (New York, May, 1887), under title of **"Coursing Rabbits on the Plains."**

On Christmas Eve at a schoolhouse party, Remington and his gay friends got so prankish that they were ejected. In a justice of the peace court he paid the costs for his bunch. He did not like dipping sheep, or helping with lambing, or shearing, or any other drudgery. The market for wool was away down before his first clip sold. In May, 1884, after sheep-ranching for two months over a year, he sold out to become a professional artist. Robert Taft points out that his brief ranching experience was essentially contemporaneous with similarly brief ranching experiences of Theodore Roosevelt, Owen Wister, and Emerson Hough. He came to illustrate both Wister and Roosevelt and to know them well. Hough, in sarcasm, later called Buffalo Bill, Ned Buntline, and Frederic Remington "the tripartite" creators of the American West. The Kansas year set him on his course.

In October, 1884, Remington married the girl who had been waiting for him—Eva Caten, of Gloversville, New York, not far from his own home town. They went to Kansas City to live, but Remington's pictures were not finding a buyer and before long Eva returned to the boun-

teous table of her people, while Frederic rode horseback for Arizona and the Apaches. When he got to New York the next year he found, as has been told, a market in *Outing,* edited by his Yale friend Poultney Bigelow. That same year he broke into *Harper's Weekly.* Eva now joined him in New York and thenceforth they lived together, childless, in reasonable harmony so far as the world knows.

By 1888 he was illustrating Roosevelt's *Ranch Life and the Hunting Trail* and other books and was moving up into the *Century* and other superior magazines. He did a great deal of writing and illustrating for *Harper's Monthly,* beginning in 1889, but did not hit the big pay that *Collier's* provided until 1898. His nonfiction books are made up mostly of materials first used in magazines.

For years after his pictures—with writings—came into demand, Remington alternated pretty much between trips westward for copy, ideas, knowledge, all sorts of notes and sketches and work in his studio. The contents of **Pony Tracks,** both writing and pictures, illustrate the kind of experiences to the West and South that Remington transmuted into what makes him remembered. In December, 1932, at the Piedra Blanca hacienda, in northern Coahuila, Mexico, I encountered an old, stove-up American cowhand who had ridden with Remington across unfenced ranges of that country. He said that nobody had to wait for the stout man, but that he had to have an extra-stout horse under him. A few years later I came to know Montague Stevens, of New Mexico, with whom Remington went on a grizzly hunt that he put into *Harper's Monthly* and later into **Pony Tracks.** General Nelson Miles was on that hunt also, and in his book *Meet Mr. Grizzly*—excellent on hounds, on sense of smell, and on the Trinity College, Cambridge—author Montague Stevens pays a lot more attention to the general than to the artist. The artist in his account pays lively attention to the bear, to hounds and cow horses, and to "a big Texan" who'd been shot by a forty-five, who cooked for the camp and could read sign.

About 1892, Remington bought a house in New Rochelle, not far out of New York City, and established a studio there. In that year, also, he illustrated Parkman's *The Oregon Trail*—one of his outstanding achievements. In 1898 he bought Ingleneuk, a five-acre island in the St. Lawrence River, enlarged the house on it, and built a studio. For another decade, however, New Rochelle was to remain home for the Remingtons.

He could toil terribly, habitually rising at six, breakfasting at seven (half a dozen chops "and other knick knacks" as Mr. Pickwick would say), then working in the studio until midafternoon, often returning in the evening. For a long time he struggled to keep his weight down. At sixteen he described himself as 5 feet 8 inches high, weighing 180 pounds. He was mighty proud of the way he rode up with General Nelson Miles and other seasoned soldiers during their chasing around after Sioux in the year 1890. At that time Remington weighed 215 pounds.

In 1894, age thirty-three, he recorded: "Without a drink in three weeks. Did 15 miles a day on foot and am down to 210 pounds." In 1897, age thirty-six, he wrote a friend: "Have been catching trout, killing deer—feel bully—absolutely on the water wagon, but it don't agree with me. I am at 240 pounds and nothing can stop me but an incurable disease." He had only eleven years left before the incurable disease would strike him down. Long before the end he had grown too fleshy to mount a horse or do much walking, but not to keep on drawing and painting and writing.

In 1894 the sculptor Ruckstull set up a tent on a vacant lot in New Rochelle, and there other art people of the community watched him model an equestrian statue for some military hero, whose name is unimportant, to be erected in front of the state capitol of Pennsylvania. Remington was eager to learn the sculptor's technique, and Ruckstull seems to have been just as eager to teach him. Augustus Thomas, the playwright whose *Arizona* had been proposed by Remington, noticed that Remington had "the sculptor's angle of vision" and encouraged him to strike out in that field. Here I'm following Helen Card. In 1895, Remington achieved his first and perhaps his best statue, "The Bronco Buster," which is only two feet high. In years that followed he achieved twenty-three other bronzes. Numerous sculptors have made numerous cowboys and range horses but "The Bronco Buster" was the first in the field. To quote Helen Card again, "Subject was everything to Remington, and with him techniques and theories were properly only means to help him tell his story. . . . Rodin's remark was that if you are unconscious of the technique, but are moved to the soul [by the result] then you may be quite certain that the technique is all there."

In May 1909 the Remingtons moved to an expensive house and studio on a plot of ground they had bought near Ridgefield, Connecticut. Remington had burned many pictures with which he was dissatisfied. Although he could not ride horseback in the West any more, he was settling down to put on canvas things that wanted to come out of himself. He had said more than once that he wanted his epitaph to be: HE KNEW THE HORSE. On Christmas Day of that year (1909) he was very ill. The next day he died, forty-eight years, two months, and twenty-six days old.

One cannot be absolute on the numbers, but according to one statement, Remington had completed more than 2,700 paintings and drawings, had illustrated 142 books, and had furnished illustrations for 41 different magazines. He is not being judged now by quantity, and will not be judged by quantity. He knew the horse, all right, and he knew the West—but more as a reporter than as a part of it. At times he was a superb reporter. I would say that in "The Sioux Outbreak in South Dakota," a chapter in *Pony Tracks,* he is a better reporter on cavalrymen than sentimental and loved Ernie Pyle was on American soldiers in World War II.

He knew cavalry horses and cavalrymen better than he knew cows, cow horses, and cowboys. On board a battle-ship off the Cuban coast during the Spanish-American War, he wrote in an article for *Harper's Weekly:* "I want to hear a shave-tail bawl; I want to get some dust in my throat, kick dewy grass, see a sentry in the moonlight, and talk the language of my tribe."

As well as he pictured and wrote about "my tribe," if what he said in combined mediums be compared with Captain John G. Bourke's *On the Border with Crook,* Remington diminishes in amplitude, in richness of knowledge, in ease and familiarity with land, frontiersmen, soldiers, Indians, and in nobility of outlook.

In the fourteenth edition of the *Encyclopaedia Britannica,* Rembrandt has six pages and Remington has one-sixth of one page. I guess the proportions are about right. Evaluations of Remington will not be right unless the evaluers keep perspective and proportion. Now and then a writer's best, an artist's best—for some imaginers at least—is something untypical, though not unrepresentative—something that has smouldered long in him and is near to him but would hardly be wanted by his rut-following editors, publishers, and public. "The Fight for the Waterhole" is near the climax of Remington's paintings of violence. Placed next to it in a little-known album of reproductions is a picture entitled "A Prayer to the Gray Wolf." It shows an Indian standing with one foot on the head of a dead buffalo partly consumed by wolves while a second Indian stands out on the bleak prairie, maybe ten steps away, his shortened shadow on the ground, arms and hands spread downward, his whole body in an attitude of supplication. He is brother to a wolf trotting around rather near while two of his mates stand away out yonder beyond rifle range. The quietness of everything, the at-oneness between man and beasts (both the quick and the dead) and the earth (including sparse clumps of grass)—this is not the Remington many times iterating "man-just-shot-down-the-street."

It is not necessary to run down good Bourbon in order to enjoy good Scotch, and I trust I am not doing that when I say that Remington toiled too furiously trying to satisfy the demand for naked action to linger and let things soak into him. He knew more than he understood. In this respect he is not the equal of Charles M. Russell, although he may have had some advantage in craftsmanship. I cannot say. As a reporter through eye and ear, through drawing, painting, and writing, Remington habitually got and gave the right words, but less frequently the right tune. Sometimes even his soldiers seem to me clever imitations of Kipling's.

In ripeness, the right tempo is always present. I think of two drawings by Charlie Russell. One of them is "The Trail Boss." He is sidling over in the saddle, resting his knees, while his horse rests on three feet. The two repose on a slight elevation of ground, the herd moseying by, and you may be sure the boss is not looking at the steers in general but in particular. He knows every one in that long, strung-out herd, the drag so far behind that only the dust it raises can be seen. No honest trail boss ever wanted any stampede; but if one should occur in the middle of the night, this boss and the bony cow horse would leap into action—in order to restore quiet.

In my mind's eye I often recall a black-and-white vignette of Russell's, one among forty illustrations he did for *The Virginian*. A cowboy on herd, the fat steers lazily grazing, is prone, asleep, his head in the shade of his horse, the only shade there is. The horse is not used to a man stretched out on the ground under him and is not contented. Russell made "dead man's prices" painting action for calendars and for rich purchasers of Western culture. He also was a sculptor. No bronze he made is more permeated with the beautiful, the spiritual, and with understanding of Indian nature than one called "Secrets of the Night." It is of a medicine man, cunning and mysterious, with an owl, wings spread, beak at the listener's ear.

Well, Frederic Remington reported aright much that nobody can ever again see or hear. If his illustrations for Longfellow's *Hiawatha* are made on somewhat the same principle that an interior decorator chooses pictures, it is to be remembered that he understood the crouch of a panther, the howl of the coyote, and the gesture of the medicine man. If few secrets of the invisible passed into him, he translated the drama of the visible into an astounding variety of pictures that do not fade in interest or power.

John Seelye (review date 1972)

SOURCE: "When West Was Wister," in *The New Republic,* Vol. 167, No. 8, September 2, 1972, pp. 28-33.

[*In the following review of* My Dear Wister: The Frederic Remington-Owen Wister Letters, *Seelye examines the relationship between these two artists and illuminates their views of the American West.*]

When Huck Finn declared that he was going to light out for the Territory, he was speaking of the area beyond Arkansas and Missouri, the present states of Oklahoma and Kansas, as it existed in the 1840s. He was expressing the wanderlust of all Americans, for whom the westering urge had held, like the trade winds, for more than two centuries, but he was expressing in particular Mark Twain's own discontent with "civilization," the strictures and structure of the eastern establishment as opposed to the open, untrammeled spaces and freedom of the western territories. *The Adventures of Huckleberry Finn* is set in the 1840s, but it was written in the '70s and '80s, and the meaning of that final declaration gains a certain dimension thereby, for the frontier was fast closing in and closing down as well. And Mark Twain was not alone in his nostalgic reaction to the complexities of emerging Modern America. Even as it closed, the western frontier was sought by an avid trio which was to create the popular image of what the West was all about, a compound of cowboys, cavalry, and cussed Injuns: Owen Wister, Frederic Remington and Theodore Roosevelt.

The Adventures of Huckleberry Finn was published in 1885, and it was in that same year that young Owen Wister took a train trip to the Wyoming Territory for his health. The son of Philadelphia gentry and the grandson of Fanny Kemble, Wister had graduated from Harvard with hopes of a career in music. He had been encouraged in this ambition by the praise of Franz Liszt during a postgraduate tour of Europe, but family pressure had forced him into a business career and the study of law. Freud would have recognized the "nervous ailment" which resulted in Wister's trip west: like Huck Finn, he had sickened of civilization and lit out for the only remaining territory. His first western journey eventually led to Wister's writing the book that has become, with all its faults, the "classic" western novel—*The Virginian*.

It was in 1885 also that Frederic Remington made a decisive trip to the Far West. A native of upstate New York who had attended Yale until family reversals made him withdraw, Remington like Wister had artistic ambitions. But art as she was taught (in a basement) at Yale in the late 19th century did not satisfy him, and as Wister enjoyed the Harvard curriculum less than club life and amateur theatricals (while graduating *magna cum laude*), so the burly Remington got his greatest satisfaction from playing on the Yale football team captained by Walter Camp. Entering college the same year as Wister, he lasted only a year. His father's death and his mother's displeasure with his artistic leanings were but two of several reasons, but the result was a restless period of wandering about from job to job. By 1882, when Wister was touring Europe and enjoying Wagner's operas, Remington had drifted as far west as Peabody, Kan. He bought a mule ranch with some of the money left him by his father, but soon found that ranching was pretty much like any other business and to hell with it. He sold his ranch in 1884 and headed "somewhere else," this time to the Southwest. He apparently had no definite plan, but he did a considerable amount of sketching in the field, amateurish but energetic drawings which contain all the essentials but none of the craft of his later work. Returning to Kansas City, Remington was able to sell some of the paintings based on his sketches, and though he was swindled out of his patrimony by owners of a saloon he had invested in, the loss was less a setback than the cutting of familial apron strings. He returned to New York only long enough to marry the girl who was waiting for him, and then headed west again to Arizona.

Though Remington and Wister both went west in 1885, they went separately, in more ways than one. Of the two, it was Remington who most resembled Huck Finn, whose personality was most easily accommodated to the western mood, and who, early on, had determined that his future would be tied up with an artistic record of the last frontier. Wister, on the other hand, went west for his health, not for material, and had no idea of becoming a "western" writer. It would be hard to think of a less likely candidate for that office than the dilettantish dude who was escorted to Wyoming by two maiden aunts in 1885. Still, his daily journal (edited in part by his daughter and published in 1958 as *Owen Wister Out West*) recorded a surprisingly positive reaction: the scenery struck him as monotonous but "beautiful," and reminded him "of the northern part of Spain," and a nighttime scene recalled "*Die Walküre*—this which is much more than my most romantic dream could have hoped." He wasn't at all surprised, he wrote, that "a man never comes back after he has once been here for a few years." Yet he only stayed a couple of months himself, and when he returned to Boston, he went back to Harvard Law School as well, and though he began to have some success at writing, his pieces in the *Atlantic* were on "The Greek Play" and "Republican Opera."

Wister went west again in the summer of 1887, but once again returned to law school in Philadelphia. In 1888, he took another western vacation, and returned home to finish his degree and set up a law practice. He also worked on an opera about Montezuma, a subject only remotely connected with Wyoming, but when another bout of bad health sent him west in the fall of 1889, he returned with notes for the stories which were to make him famous, and his next trip in the summer of 1891 was, like Remington's journey in 1885, with the stated intention "to jot down all shreds of local colour and all conversations and anecdotes decent or otherwise that strike me as native wild flowers. After a while I shall write a great fat book about the whole thing." The "fat book" eluded him for the time being, and the "whole thing" seems never to have come within his grasp, but that fall his first western stories, "Hank's Woman" and "How Lin McLean Went East," were published by *Harper's*. They established him quickly as a western writer, but as their titles suggest, Wister's West (like that of Bret Harte) was from the very beginning an extension of eastern attitudes. Wister noted with relief in his earliest journals that "every man, woman, and cowboy I see comes from the East—and generally from New England, thank goodness." Lin McLean was just such a cowboy, and though his trip back home ended in disgust over eastern narrowness, the cycle of his western adventures (published as *Lin McLean* in 1895) ended in a proper marriage, symbol of western accommodation to eastern ideals of order.

Considering the importance of marriage to the ending of *The Virginian*, Wister in a number of his short stories betrays a surprising element of misogyny, and there are other signs that his use of the marriage theme was the result of mixed motives. Molly Stark, the heroine of *The Virginian*, took her first name from that of Wister's own bride, and the idyllic honeymoon in the novel was based on Wister's also. The largely feminine readership of *Harper's* (where Wister's books were serialized) was another factor, as was the blue pencil of its editor, Henry Mills Alden, but perhaps the greatest influence shaping Wister's West, responsible for the taming process by which his realistic journal entries became romantic fiction, was Wister's good friend and fellow Harvard graduate, Theodore Roosevelt. Wister was not always comfortable with Roosevelt's progressive politics (and lived long enough to die loathing the even more progressive

Roosevelt of the '30s), but the old school tie was strong and his respect for the man was great. Though he didn't always follow Roosevelt's literary advice, he accepted it, and was affected likewise by the sheer magnetism of the man. What Howells was to Mark Twain, Roosevelt was to Wister, not so much a literary censor as a moral mentor, whose force of personality shaped the final bias of the other man's work.

Roosevelt, like Andrew Jackson, William Henry Harrison, Ulysses S. Grant and a score of sundry other Indian killers and filibusterers, had made political capital out of his own wilderness campaign, and not a little literary capital also. Having graduated from Harvard three years before Wister, he preceded him west as well, following a sequence of personal and political disasters. From 1883 to 1887 he raised beef and his own muscles in Dakota Territory, affecting a legendary transformation and fixing a useful political image. Though his western enterprise ended in the disastrous winter of 1886-87, the books he wrote upon returning east, along with his complementary philosophy of "the strenuous life," promoted a popular idea of the West as a perpetual preserve of high-minded adventure. Even before he became Wister's literary adviser, Roosevelt's *Ranch Life and the Hunting Trail* (1891) helped to create an eastern market for the western idea—so long as that idea was suitable to eastern tastes.

Roosevelt's book was illustrated by Remington, whose fortunes were on the rise by the early '90s, and when Wister's "Hank's Woman" appeared in *Harper's Weekly*, the same issue carried part of a series by Remington on the Sioux uprising which resulted in the Battle of Wounded Knee, and it was only a matter of time before Alden would assign him to illustrate one of Wister's stories. This was "Balaam and Pedro," first printed in 1893 and one of the early stories which were to be transformed into the narrative of *The Virginian*. It was this story, with its eye-gouging incident, which provided the first occasion of a real difference of opinion between Roosevelt and Wister, one in which Roosevelt finally persevered— a decisive victory. Remington and Wister met while the story was still in press, and though Wister at first was reluctant to accept Remington's offers to collaborate, a circumstantial incident convinced him that the success of his story was due in large part to the illustration. The result was nearly a decade of teamwork, a partnership which also had its effect on the direction of Wister's writing.

In the triangular relationship of Roosevelt-Remington-Wister, the artist seems to have been the odd man out. Roosevelt and Remington never had more than a casual, professional acquaintance, and though the politician admired the artist's work and commissioned the famous (and fictitious) picture of the storming of San Juan Hill, Roosevelt would have found the earthy Remington a trifle too coarse for his tastes. Wister too seems to have kept his collaborator out of his personal life, yet Remington, through his illustrations, linked his name firmly to those two good friends. And though all three contributed their share to the crystallization of the popular idea of the cowboy, the greatest of all American folk heroes, it was Remington's paintings and statues which were the pictorial harbinger of that medium responsible for our present-day notions of the West, a West singularly deficient in just those qualities of moral decency which Roosevelt and Wister together promoted. There are no women save squaws in Remington's paintings, and the only marriage he ever celebrated was that hybrid union of beast and man which produced the celibate centaur of our national mythology. Like Virgil, Remington portrayed arms and the man, and his themes were always violent.

Several years ago, G. Edward White wrote a penetrating study of the efforts of Roosevelt and Wister to establish a synthesis between western rugged independence and eastern habits of order, a "consensus" West that had as its twin paradigms the Rough Riders and *The Virginian*. The coming together in a heroic bond in Cuba of eastern dudes and western cowboys showed that Americans *were* Americans, for all o' that, and when the Virginian married a daughter of New England in the Far West and then went on to make a fortune from his coal lands, why that was reassuring also. Frederick Jackson Turner once wrote that the Captain of Industry was the Old Frontiersman in new guise, and he may very well have had *The Virginian* in mind; but in any event Turner was an important spokesman for the idea of consensus, of the ultimate good to come from the marriage of East and West. Not so Remington, for whom the East and the West were unreconcilable opposites. Instead of viewing the West as a transforming arena, he regarded it as an evanescent phenomenon, like the great desert itself, rugged in appearance but as delicate an ecostructure as a frail cactus flower. The West and the East he saw as worlds apart, and the invasion of the one by the other spelt doom for the last territory of freedom. Alone of the eastern trio, in this as in all other ways, Remington seems to have escaped his heritage almost completely. Perhaps because he came from the upstate New York area which produced Leatherstocking, a country still woodsy enough to evoke a wilderness, Remington was actually able to make the psychic leap proposed by Huckleberry Finn. Lighting out for the vanishing territory of 1885, in a sense he never came back, and his early death in 1909 was as symbolic as Wister's bitter, alienated old age.

Given these psychological and cultural antagonisms, the relationship between Remington and Wister could only have been a sort of uneasy truce, producing a collaborative tension which was suggested but not spelled out in White's study of the three men. Ben Merchant Vorpahl has now written a book which does spell it out, a study which is central to an understanding of what the West, as a literary idea, is all about. Vorpahl occasionally snarls his interweaving relationships (it is not always easy to determine who was doing what when and where), and to my mind he is guilty of occasional overstatements in the service of his thesis. But I say this only to emphasize the positive, because I have not had the pleasure of reading such a well-written, graceful, and even witty treatment of popular culture—which often attracts jargon-laden sociological silliness—in a long time.

Vorpahl is clearly up to as well as on to his subject, and the real subject of his book is Frederic Remington, who comes across in his letters to Wister as a slangy, profane, earthy, gourmandizing, woman-fearing, fat American boy—a 300-pound Huckleberry. Toward the end of this book, I began to sorrow that Remington was never called upon to illustrate Mark Twain's classic. His habits of mind, even his wry turn of phrase, constantly bring Twain to mind, and it seems a shame that somewhere along the way the two great nostalgists did not collaborate. It is clear that they belong to the same camp, the Red Man tribe as opposed to the White Man club which both Philip Rahv and Leslie Fiedler (for different reasons) have defined as the chief split of sensibility in American literature.

Wister, of course, belonged to the White Men, and Vorpahl's study suggests that the relationship between the two men resembled that uneasy friendship between Hawthorne and Melville. Though Remington's artistry was essentially flawed by his mixed motives, and though Wister's craft was similarly marred by commercial and cultural considerations, both men did have ambitions to excel in their chosen fields. The eventual fate of their relationship therefore leads us to consider the fate of American literature as well as the fate of the American West, and such a consideration leads us to the inescapable conclusion that the fate of American literature *was* the fate of the American West, at least so far as the 19th century is concerned. Vorpahl's book is therefore an important additional chapter to Edwin Fussell's *Frontier* and Henry Nash Smith's *Virgin Land*.

As his hyphenated subtitle indicates, Vorpahl relies heavily on the Remington-Wister correspondence preserved in the Wister archive in the Library of Congress, which hyphenate should read "Remington-to-Wister," because the correspondence is decidedly one-sided. While Wister had a strong sense of his importance and saved all his received correspondence, his manuscripts and related documents, Remington like Melville was a "burner," and even went so far in his last, reclusive years as to destroy many of his most famous canvases. Few if any letters from Wister to him survive, and Vorpahl has had to rely on Wister's letters to his mother (he wrote regularly to her as long as she lived), to his other associates, and on his western journals for material with which to balance the account. Moreover, Remington was a terse even cryptic though exuberant correspondent, and Vorpahl has had to do a painstaking job of research to determine, often, just what in hell he was talking about in his letters. What Remington did not say is often more important than what he discussed, and the resemblance to Melville's correspondence to Hawthorne is more than superficial.

Like Melville, Remington was the one who did most of the pushing, again and again extending futile invitations to Wister to come "up" for a visit. But this one-sidedness took a sudden reversal once Remington began to cast his future fame in bronze and think of abandoning illustration and painting forever. It seems quite clear that Remington's interest in Wister was dictated by professional not personal considerations, that Wister's stories created opportunities for illustration and income. Throughout, Remington indulges in heavy-handed kidding about Wister's unlikely role as western writer, and his remarks about the ephemeral nature of print and paper were similarly pointed. Wister, for his part, seems to have remained rather condescending toward his partner, regarding him as a "mere" illustrator, until that talk about bronze and immortality began. Wister then turned suitor, but it was too late. By then certain troublesome matters of collaboration had gone awry, and the never more than imperfect sympathies between two thin-skinned artists quickly soured.

The partnership ended virtually on the eve of the publication of *The Virginian*, and Remington did not illustrate Wister's famous book. He had, however, illustrated a number of the stories from which the novel was derived, and Vorpahl makes it abundantly clear that Wister's slow drift (under the genteel influence of what Remington called "upholstery of a library chair," referring to eastern editors) toward an easternized, school-marmalade West contributed greatly to the estrangement. Like Roosevelt, Wister was from the beginning a latter-day Parkman, a romantic historian of the West, who knew better than he wrote and used his journal material to structure a consensus West—a territory of the mind. Remington, though at the outset a realist, became increasingly withdrawn and mystical as the West that he had known disappeared. *His* West, that is to say, became a territory of the heart.

But until this drift separated the two men, there was nearly a decade of often intense collaboration of artist and writer, one which transcended the usual relationship. If Roosevelt held Wister in a thrall of personality, Remington too had his attractions, and though it was Remington who paid court to Wister, it was the writer who seems to have been the chief beneficiary of the arrangement. The main purpose of Vorpahl's study is to demonstrate the deeper literary aspects of the Remington-Wister partnership, aspects which have hitherto been unknown, and what emerges is, like the correspondence, one-sided. First, there is the extent of Wister's indebtedness to Remington for "material," for like Wister's journal, Remington was crammed full of firsthand western experience. Thus Wister's early and important essay, "The Evolution of the Cowboy," is shown to have been indebted to the artist for far more than its illustrations. Secondly, Vorpahl demonstrates that Wister had an ideational (ideological might be a better word) debt as well. Not only the facts and anecdotes in "The Evolution of the Cowboy" were borrowed from Remington, but the main thesis as well, a thesis which was twisted out of a Remington essay, **"The Horse of the Plains,"** and which became the main ontological support of *The Virginian*.

It was Wister's idea, an early manifestation of his chauvinistic Anglophilia, that the cowboy was a last avatar of the old Anglo-Saxon spirit, a veritable knight of the prairie. That the real cowboy was as often Negro or Irish or Swedish as English in his origins did not hinder Wister, any more than the presence of two black regiments in the Cuban campaign darkened Roosevelt's white-on-white "consensus." The posterity of Wister and Roosevelt is necessarily clouded by the outright bigotry of the one and the politically veiled but undeniable racist notions of the other. Remington was even more guilty in this regard, and his letters are filled with "hebes" and "dagos" and "niggers," nor did he ever take the opportunity to celebrate the passing of the black cowboy. But so far as "The Evolution" is concerned, Wister's indebtedness to him concerns an essay in which Remington's racism is, if anything, sublimated. The point of **"The Horse of the Plains"** was that the animal that made the cowboy such a significant figure was essentially the horse of the Spanish conquistadores, the Arabian Barbary, or "Barb." Conquistadore, vaquero, Indian, cowboy—all western men rode the same mount, and Remington's illustrations supposedly demonstrated this neohippean nongenesis.

As Wister begged and borrowed cowboy etymologies and like data from Remington, so did he pirate his Barbary thesis, for his theory of the "pure" Anglo-Saxon cowboy was obviously derived from the thesis about the "pure" Barbary strain—that is, he substituted the Anglo-Saxon knight for the Arabian horse. Remington knew that Wister's thesis was so much wishful thinking, but since their partnership had just begun and was important to him, he kept quiet and did the illustrations required of him—even a mawkish "The Last Cavalier," which shows a cowboy riding along against a ghostly backdrop of knightly, Anglo-Saxon predecessors. So antithetical was this subject to Remington's own conceptions and techniques (his skies, as Vorpahl points out, are western: big and empty) that it is clearly an inferior picture, and yet its original seems to have been the only recorded acquisition of Remington's work by Wister. Though it was untypical of the painter, the subject matter was endemic to the writer's view of history; it helped provide the subsequent rationale for the distortions of form and fact that went into the writing of *The Virginian*.

Still, the evolution of Wister's ultimate cowboy was a slow, ten-year metamorphosis. His earliest stories, the ones which Remington illustrated, were among his most realistic, and so long as Wister stuck fairly close to his journals and his recollections, Remington was delighted to illustrate them. But as the character of the Virginian gradually began to evolve from a slangy, simple, even comic cowpoke to a version of flowering knighthood, Remington became less comfortable. In time he grew resentful of having to depict a West and a cowboy which had become a creation of an eastern sensibility. At about this point in their joint career, Remington began to write short stories himself, and though he may have been Wister's inferior in this regard, there is no doubt but that the West he wrote about was the tragic and evanescent ground of his not Wister's imagination. Vorpahl demonstrates, in fact, that Remington's stories are a tacit argument, a quiet rebuttal.

Like Wister, Remington began by writing a series of short stories concerning one character, "Sundown LeFlare," a half-breed cowboy and scout who tells his stories in a heavy dialect to the narrator, a convention which Wister relied on also. But where all of Wister's white heroes make their separate peace with the regulating, marriage-and-business-oriented spirit of the East, Sundown LeFlare is at heart a renegade, a picaro, an illiterate "breed." Wister also wrote admiringly of the Indian, but as the title of his first collection of stories, *Red Men and White,* suggests, the union for him was never more than conterminous. For Remington, the mixture of bloods was catalytic and fated, and Vorpahl makes clear enough the antagonisms—between East and West and Wister and Remington—which went into the creation of Sundown LeFlare.

These antagonisms are even more obvious in Remington's novel, **John Ermine of the Yellowstone,** published late in the same year that *The Virginian* appeared, and obviously written as a response to that book. **John Ermine** is a minor work of art but a major indeed initiatory stage in an important subliterary genre, the latter-day recrudescence of noble savagery with a distinctly Nietzschean twist which resulted in such disparate novels as Jack London's *Call of the Wild,* Ernest Thompson Seton's *Two Little Savages* and Cyrus Townsend Brady's *The Island of Regeneration,* and which is epitomized by Burroughs' *Tarzan of the Apes.* Vorpahl does not discuss the possibility of this genesis, but surely the story of a noble and titled Englishman who is orphaned in the jungle but survives to rule over all animate nature red in tooth and claw, and who returns eventually to England to resume the station and duties which he has inherited (only to return finally to the jungle), though containing obvious suggestions of Wister's Anglo-Saxon cowboy thesis, is actually closer to **John Ermine.**

Where Tarzan is adopted by "anthropoid apes," Ermine is kidnapped by Indians, and grows up in savage surroundings. Eventually he is reclaimed by a hermit of the mountains, a white recluse who takes it upon himself to teach the young boy the ways of his people. Growing to young manhood, John Ermine goes to live among other white men, as a scout for a cavalry troop. There he meets and falls in love with a daughter of one of the senior officers, the consensual theme. But though he is white, handsome and as blonde as a Viking, John Ermine is a savage at heart, not an English gentleman, and his rejection by the girl results in a vengeful finale which ends with his death—by the hand of an Indian he insulted. By means of his fable, Remington hoped to disprove Wister's thesis, deny the consensus interpretation, and lay to rest that old romantic trope of a noble-blooded hero in rags. It was a large order, and as the popularity of *The Virginian* and *Tarzan* suggests, he was not successful in carrying it out.

Though **John Ermine** was well received and went through several printings, it never matched the éclat of *The Virginian.* Even Henry James admired Wister's novel, though with a few telling reservations. James praised the characters and setting of *The Virginian,* but did not much like the ending. In his stories of Americans abroad, James had revealed his own disinclination to arrive at consensus. He refused to provide the marriage in *The American* which Howells begged him to include, and in *Daisy Miller* he gave his rustic little heroine a tragic death in Rome. James wanted Wister's hero to have the same fate: "I should have made him perish in his flower and in some splendid and somber way." Though James did not read and perhaps could not have read Remington's novel, he certainly would have found there an ending to his liking.

For James and Remington, in their far different ways, both belong to that odd fraternity founded by Cooper and continued by Melville and Mark Twain, that tradition in American literature which regards innocence and savagery as not permanent and enduring but fragile and fleeting qualities. If **John Ermine** throws a different perspective on *The Virginian,* it likewise illuminates the western implications of Billy Budd (who also "perishes in his flower") and suggests what might have happened had Huck Finn managed to get West and have those wild adventures amongst the Injuns. For all its faults, **John Ermine** is one of the missing links of American literature, and Ben Vorpahl is to be thanked for providing us with the details of its genesis.

Fred Erisman (essay date 1974-75)

SOURCE: "Frederick Remington: The Artist as Local Colorist," in *South Dakota Review,* Vol. 12, No. 4, Winter, 1974-75, pp. 76-88.

[*In the following essay, Erisman considers Remington's written works, seeing them primarily as examples of local color fiction that occasionally supersede this designation.*]

Frederic Remington (1861-1909), American painter and sculptor, needs no introduction; Frederic Remington, American author, is virtually unknown. No one having the sketchiest acquaintance with the American West can fail to recognize either a Remington bronze or a Remington oil. "The Bronco Buster," for example, or "Coming Through the Rye," with its four carousing cowboys, is as familiar as "The Fight for the Waterhole," "Dash for the Timber," or "A Cavalryman's Breakfast on the Plains." All are commonplaces. By contrast, the very titles of Remington's books are unfamiliar, and the number of persons who can claim a first-hand acquaintance with **Sundown Leflare** (1899), **John Ermine of the Yellowstone** (1902), or **The Way of an Indian** (1906) is infinitesimal.

That Remington's writings, fictional and non-fictional, are largely overshadowed by his paintings and sculptures is not surprising, but unfortunate. It is unfortunate because his fiction, and, to a lesser extent, his journalism, complements his pictorial vision of the West. In his writings, as in his pictorial works, Remington portrays the region as seen through the eyes of a dedicated local colorist. If his writings are largely free from the exploitation of sentimentality and the picturesque that blights the works of a Bret Harte, they nevertheless contain other, essential qualities of local color writing: a sincere regard for the typical inhabitants of an area, an understanding of the significance of the past and the present, and an awareness that life in a particular time and place has a uniqueness distinguishing it from the national life of which it is a part.

Of the several traits that identify local color in literature, the most obvious is the author's consistent attention to typical character types. Bret Harte makes good use of the technique in his stories of the mining camps, but it remains for Hamlin Garland to give it its most extended theoretical statement. In *Crumbling Idols* (1894), he calls for a truly localized literature, one dealing with "the heroism of labor, the comradeship of man,—a drama of average types of character, infinitely varied, but always characteristic." This literature, he goes on to say, will use the speech as well as the lives of the ordinary populace: "We propose to use the speech of living men and women. We are to use actual speech as we hear it and to record its changes. We are to treat of the town and city as well as of the farm, each in its place and through the medium of characteristic speech."[1] Local color writing, for Garland and others, is a literature of the average person.[2]

Remington's emphasis upon western types in his artistic works was recognized early. Owen Wister, introducing **Done In The Open** (1902), a book-length collection of his pictures, writes: "As the historian Green wrote what he called a history of the English *people,* so Remington is drawing his contemporary history of the most picturesque of the American *people.* . . . No artist until Remington has undertaken to draw so clearly the history of the people."[3] This opinion is echoed by Royal Cortissoz, the art critic, in *American Artists* (1923). Referring to Remington as a "painter of life", Cortissoz goes on to remark: "It is impossible to reflect upon his art without thinking of the merely human element that went to its making, the close contacts with men and with the soil in a part of our country where indeed the atmosphere of the studio is simply unthinkable. . . . His men and his horses are emphatically of the practical, modern world, a world of rough living, frank speech, and sincere action."[4] The point seems clear. Remington, in his paintings, chooses for subjects the basic types of the region that he is striving to depict.

The same characters who move through Remington's paintings appear in his writings. He concentrates, not surprisingly, upon the obvious—the Indian, as in **"The Story of the Dry Leaves"** (1899); the cowboy, as in **"In the Sierra Madre with the Punchers"** (1894); or the soldier, as in *John Ermine of the Yellowstone.* Equally typical, but perhaps less obvious, are those characters who indirectly reflect the impact of the white man upon the West—bartenders, gamblers, and half-breeds. His novel-length collection of short tales, **Sundown Leflare,** gives convenient access to some of these. Its hero, Laflare, is himself a half-breed—"cross-bred," Remington says, "red and white, so he never got mentally in sympathy with either strain of his progenitors. He knew about half as much concerning Indians as they did themselves, while his knowledge of white men was in the same proportion." Leflare, in turn, goes on to describe the professional gambler who eventually strips him of his money: "All time dar weare a leetle white man what was hang roun' de log house un shuffle de card. He know how shuffle dose card, I tell you. He was all time fool wid de card. He wear de store clothes, un he was not help us bran' de horse-ban', 'cause he sais, 'Dam de pony!'"[5] Remington is clearly working along the lines set down by Garland; not only does he include a variety of character types, but he attempts to capture the flavor of their idiom as well.

Additional evidence of Remington's desire to present typical characters appears in his delineation of women. His neglect of women in his painting is well-known;[6] in his writings, however, women abound, in a gallery of carefully drawn females spanning the full range from Indian squaws, as in **The Way of an Indian,** to officers' ladies and their frigidly Easternized daughters, as in **John Ermine of the Yellowstone.** He does not, to be sure, deal explicitly with saloon girls, those professionally friendly fixtures of the frontier, but he alludes to them often enough to establish their presence. No one would be surprised had Remington confined himself to writing about the military, Indians, or cowboys; these are the persons with whom he was most closely associated during his sojourns in the West. That he goes beyond these, however, to include a wide variety of character types, suggests that he, like the local colorists, is attempting to give a full-scale, comprehensive picture of Western life. He looks to the typical, at every level and in every setting.

A second characteristic of local color writing, somewhat less obvious than a concentration upon typical characters, is the author's tendency to deal with times gone by. This tendency, combined with the general geographic remoteness of the area being described, creates an aura of romantic nostalgia, from which the irretrievable past emerges as somehow better, or more noble, than the inescapable present.[7] Thus, for example, Harte's tales of the gold-mining camps of the 1850s or Sarah Orne Jewett's accounts of the fading New England fishing villages of the 1880s benefit from the remoteness of their subjects in space and time.

Admirers of Remington's art works recognized quite early that he, too, was memorializing a vanishing past. Francis Parkman, for example, commenting upon Remington's illustrations for the 1892 edition of *The Oregon Trail,* writes: "The Wild West is tamed and its savage charms have withered. If this book can help to keep their memory alive, it will have done its part. It has found a powerful helper in the pencil of Mr. Remington, whose pictures are as full of truth as of spirit, for they are the work of one who knew the prairies and the mountains before irresistible commonplace had subdued them."[8] It is apparent to the historian that Remington's pictures document the passing of the West.

Equally apparent is Remington's own consciousness of the West's demise and his role in documenting it. In 1900, writing to Owen Wister about the projected *Done In The Open,* he remarks: "I am as you know working on a big picture book—of the West and I want you to write a preface. I want a lala too no d——newspaper puff . . . but telling the d——public that this is the real old thing—step up and buy a copy—last chance—ain't going to be any more West etc."[9] More restrained but no less explicit is his public statement of 1905, published in an issue of *Collier's* devoted to his work:

> I knew [as early as 1881] the railroad was coming—I saw men already swarming into the land. I knew the derby hat, the smoking chimneys, the cord-binder, and the thirty-day note were upon us in a resistless surge. I knew the wild riders and the vacant land were about to vanish forever, and the more I considered the subject the bigger the Forever loomed. . . . I saw the living, breathing end of three American centuries of smoke and dust and sweat, and I now see quite another thing where it all took place, but it does not appeal to me.[10]

Remington makes his goal quite clear. He intends, as G. Edward White elsewhere notes, to raise the realities of the American West to "the level of history and romance."[11]

Since Remington, the artist, is devoted to invoking the spirit of the West's passing, it is not expected to find Remington, the author, equally devoted to the task. In his writings, his fond regard for times past is as explicit as his skepticism what his own time considers progress. Writing in *Crooked Trails* (1898) of Big-Foot Wallace, the Texas adventurer, for example, he says: "Wallace was a professional hunter, who fought Indians and hated 'greasers'; he belongs to the past, and has been 'outspanned' under a civilization in which he has no place." Later in the book he presents the military in the same light. Referring to Sergeant Carter Johnson of the Third Cavalry, he remarks: "He was thumped and bucked and pounded into what was in the seventies considered a proper frontier soldier, for in those days the nursery idea had not been lugged into the army."[12] Both passages carry the same message: life was livelier and sturdier in the past.

The theme reappears in Remington's stories of Sundown Leflare, the half-breed. Here, though, it is less blatant, tempered by the author's developing sense of an encroaching technology and its effect upon traditional ways. In speaking of his standing in the Indian community, Leflare says: "I was all same Enjun—fringe, bead, long hair—but I was wear de hat. I was hab' de bes' pony

een de country, un I was hab de firs' breech-loadair een de country. Ah, I was reech!" Though very much a part of the Indian world, he has already adopted the white man's hat, and measures his wealth with the white man's armament. The last story of the collection, which deals explicitly with the conflict of cultures, makes even clearer the degree of his contamination by progress. Subtle cultural tensions permeate the story, between Leflare and the narrator and the medicine man and the priest. Their most memorable expression, however, comes in Leflare's own actions—although a firm believer in the power of his medicine bag to strengthen his scouting ability, he nonetheless gains a tactical edge over his opponents with a pair of government-issue binoculars.[13]

Consistently though he laments the passing of the West and its way in his writings, Remington makes his most extended and sustained statement of the theme in his novel, *John Ermine of the Yellowstone.* The novel's East-meets-West theme is obvious throughout, as Ermine, the Indian-reared white scout, meets and falls in love with Katherine Searles, the product of an Eastern finishing school. As he unfolds the story of Ermine's inexorable downfall, Remington over and over refers to the scout's ties with the past. His ancestry, for example, predates American civilization: "Any white man could see at a glance that White Weasel was evolved from a race which, however remote from him, got its yellow hair, fair skin, and blue eyes amid the fjords, forests, rocks, and ice-floes of the north of Europe." Descendant of an ancient people though he may be, Ermine is still an integral part of the Western scene. He belongs, but must die; in contrast, the Katherine Searleses, though strangers to the West, will prevail. Remington speaks to this as he describes Ermine and a fellow scout on the trail: "These two figures, crawling, sliding, turning, and twisting through the sunlight on the rugged mountains, were grotesque but harmonious. America will never produce their like again. Her wheels will turn and her chimneys smoke, and the things she makes will be carried round the world in ships, but she never can make two figures which will bear even a remote resemblance to Wolf-Voice and John Ermine. The wheels and chimneys and the white men have crowded them off the earth."[14] There is no longer room for Western man.

Working well within the traditions of local color writing, Remington skillfully evokes romantic nostalgia in describing the West of an earlier day. He is not, however, satisfied with a sentimental lament for the end of a way of life. Instead, he goes on, stressing (as in the passage from *John Ermine* just cited) that the way of life that has ended is one organically suited to the time and place. It is natural. The way of life that replaces it is artificial, and will work to the detriment of human worth. His sense of the organic rightness of things, growing perhaps from his painter's vision, makes him more than just another local colorist.

Of the several qualities that define local color writing, the most significant is the writer's concern with giving a detailed presentation of the locale of the story, and a corresponding concern with the ways in which this locale can influence the actions of its inhabitants.[15] These concerns give local color writing its characteristic flavor; they also give it its importance. Locale, obviously, can be described in a variety of ways: "place (including climate, natural resources, and topography); time; cultural tradition; national, racial, or religious inheritance; mode of self-support; and remoteness, whether spatial or cultural, from other communities."[16] As the local colorist suggests to his readers the particular combinations of these elements to be found in a specific place, he also suggests what makes that place unique.

Accompanying this broadly based sense of local uniqueness is an awareness that the location of an event affects—and at times almost determines—the outcome of that event. The characters in a local color work, Donald A. Dike points out, "are deeply rooted in their environment, and their behavior depends on what it has made of them."[17] These characters, in short, and the events in which they take part, are molded by the circumstances in which they live; the resources available to them shape the ways in which they respond to life.

Well developed though his sense of place is, Remington's artistic goal is not so much the accurate portrayal of a specific site as the portrayal of a specific region—the "West". From his earliest drawings, as Ben M. Vorpahl remarks, he strives to capture the peculiar sense of the West, a spaciousness of landscape and spirit that emerges in his letters as an inarticulate "it".[18] As his art matures, his sense of place follows suit, until, as Royal Cortissoz writes, "Under a burning sun he [works] out an impression of his own. Baked dusty plains lead in his pictures to bare, flat-topped hills, shading from yellow into violet beneath cloudless skies which hold no soft tints of pearl or rose, but are fiercely blue when they do not vibrate into tones of green."[19] Impressionism it may be, but it is also a statement of the physical environment of the American West, revealing Remington's powerful response to setting.

A similar response appears in his writings, as he puts into words much the same vision that he expresses in oils. He gives no real specifics, concentrating instead upon the West's total impact. His remarks upon the desert sun are typical: "The sun is no detail out in the arid country. It does more things than blister your nose. It is the despair of the painter as it colors the minarets of the Bad Lands which abound around Adobe, and it dries up the company gardens if they don't watch the *acequias* mighty sharp."[20] More extended are his remarks in **Sundown Leflare**. Here he comments upon the geographical contrariness of the West, with its blending of monotony and variety. "The high plains," he begins, "do things in such a set way, so far as weather is concerned, and it is a day's march before you change views. I began to long for a few rocks . . . a pool of water with some reflections—in short, anything but the horizontal monotony of our surroundings." Monotony soon gives way to diversity, though, in

the vastness of the West and the shifting vistas that it contains: "If one has never seen [the Western landscape], words will hardly tell him how it stretches away, red, yellow, blue, in a prismatic way, shaded by cloud forms and ending among them—a sort of topographical map. I can think of nothing else, except that it is an unreal thing to look at."[21] This passage, as much as any in Remington's works, captures the essence of his reaction to the West. It is, for him, an area: vast, beautiful, and elemental. That is may also be Arizona, Montana, or the Dakotas is irrelevant. It is simply the West, and that is enough.

Concerned though he is with communicating the physical nature of the West, Remington tries also to communicate the far-reaching effects of the West upon all who live there. He unhesitatingly accepts the realities of Western life, recognizing that it is a continual struggle against superior forces—a recognition that appears in his paintings from the very beginning.[22] The forces can be literal, as in "The Fight For the Water Hole," with its five plainsmen surrounded by Indians, or figurative, as in "The Fall of the Cowboy," depicting the inexorable segmenting of the range by barbed wire. Whatever form they take, though, they are formidable, and leave their mark upon the individuals who encounter them.

Remington's grasp of Western reality contributed to the early acceptance of his work. His thorough delineation of the effects of range life upon the cowboy, for example, was instrumental in his receiving a major commission from *Outing Magazine* in 1886. When presented with a portfolio of drawings, the *Outing* editor, Poultney Bigelow, responded immediately: "No stage heroes these; no careful pomaded hair and neatly tied cravats; these were the men of the real rodeo, parched in alkali dust, blinking out from barely opened eyes under the furious rays of the Arizona sun. I had been there and my innermost corpuscle vibrated at the truth before me."[23] The same quality, more subtly stated, appears in Remington's 1893 illustrations for Owen Wister's "Balaam and Pedro". Here, in a single drawing, he combines the spaciousness of the West with the realities of human existence.[24]

Although evident in his paintings, Remington's sense of the organicism of Western life becomes even more evident in his writings. Perhaps because he is working in a different medium, he makes many explicit references to the effects of locale in his writings, until, as in his paintings, he conveys the totality of Western experience. "It is possible," G. Edward White writes, "to see emerging . . . a sense on Remington's part that the climatological and topographical diversity of his West did not preclude its having an environmental sameness. The characters and settings vary, but for Remington the process through which an individual confronts the world about him has a fundamental similarity. It is this process of confrontation, the result of an interaction between a certain kind of environment and, for all his sizes and shapes, a certain kind of individual, which Remington came to see as uniquely Western."[25] He sees, in short, that place works directly upon all living things, producing forms and patterns of life peculiar to the region.

The interaction of life and environment permeates Remington's writings. As early in 1889, in **"Horses of the Plains,"** he describes the Western bronco as a unique product of the region:

> He graces the Western landscape, not because he reminds us of the equine ideal, but because he comes of the soil, and has borne the heat and burden and the vicissitudes of all that pale of romance which will cling about the Western frontier. As we see him hitched to the plow or the wagon he seems a living protest against utilitarianism; but, unlike his red master, he will not go. He has borne the Moor, the Spanish conqueror, the red Indian, the mountain-man, and the vaquero through all the glories of their careers; but they will soon be gone, with all their heritage of gallant deeds.[26]

The bronco is for Remington the emblem of a vanished era because he "comes of the soil," having evolved to accommodate a specific set of regional requirements.

The effects of place take other forms, as well. In **Crooked Trails,** Remington writes in the *persona* of Joshua Goodenough, scout with Rogers' Rangers during the French and Indian War, remarking in passing on the general adaptations of life brought about by the conditions of the North Woods.[27] In **Pony Tracks** (1895), he comments upon the development of the Western saddle, which he sees as caused by the exigencies of Western life: "For a smooth road and a trotting horse, the European riding-master was right [about the English saddle]; but when you put a man in the dust or smoke, over the rocks and cut banks, on the 'bucking' horse, or where he must handle his weapons or his *vieta,* he must have a seat on his mount as tight as a stamp on an envelope, and not go washing around like a shot in a bottle."[28] Wherever man lives, the place affects his institutions, great and small.

Just as Remington uses his novel, **John Ermine,** to convey his most explicit statement of the West's passing, so, too, he uses it to speak most explicitly of the way in which location molds life. Ermine, as has been pointed out, is a white man of Scandinavian descent, who is reared from childhood by a tribe of Crow Indians. His genetic inheritance is European. His cultural inheritance, however, is Indian. When the crisis of the story is upon him, precipitated by his proposal of marriage to Katherine Searles, he reverts, not to genetic type, but to cultural type. His civilization vanishes, and he becomes an Indian: "Good-by, good-by, white men," he says, "and good-by, white woman; the frost is in your hearts, and your blood runs like the melting snow from the hills. When you smile, you only skin your fangs; and when you laugh, your eyes do not laugh with you." Ermine's reversion, implied by the language of this passage, Remington confirms as the book draws to an end: "All the patient

training of Crooked Bear [Ermine's white mentor], all the humanizing influence of white association, all softening moods of the pensive face in [Katherine's] photograph, were blown from the fugitive as though carried on a wind; he was a shellfish-eating cave-dweller, with a Springfield, a knife, and a revolver. He had ceased to think in English, and muttered to himself in Absaroke."[29] The Indian traits, ingrained within him by his upbringing and reinforced by the life he has led in the West, prove stronger than his racial ties. The Indian way of life, influenced and molded at every turning by the imperious demands of the Western environment, proves too strong for Ermine. His white skin cannot save him. He is an Indian, a product of the West, and he dies because of it.

Frederic Remington, writing of the landscape of the West as he painted it, makes clear its physical uniqueness, and the effects of this uniqueness upon life. Recognizing, as Lewis Mumford has said, that "the place does not determine human institutions; but it sets certain conditions," he goes on to explore the ways in which those conditions affect the life that develops under them.[30] The effect, whether in something so comparatively trivial as the style of a saddle or in something so profound as a human life, is inescapable.

Throughout Remington's writings, one finds widespread evidence of the techniques of the local colorists. Remington, like the local color writers, attempts to present the typical characters of a specific area; he emphasizes, sometimes subtly, sometimes blatantly, his sense of the passing of a way of life; and he leaves no doubt of his recognition that the environmental characteristics of a given locale influence the life lived in that locale. Unlike the local colorists, however, he frequently goes beyond the bare-bones definition of local color writing to give an intense statement of his sense of time and place. In this may lie his true literary achievement.

Bret Harte, like Remington an Easterner who went West as a young man, knew well the importance of local materials to the American writer. In 1899, looking back over his own career, Harte observes that the seeds of the American literature of the future reside in the short works of the present, those works that treat "characteristic American life, with absolute knowledge of its peculiarities and sympathy with its methods; with no fastidious ignoring of its habitual expression, or the inchoate poetry that may be found even hidden in its slang; with no moral determination except that which may be the legitimate outcome of the story itself; with no more elimination than may be necessary of the artistic conception, and never from the fear of the 'fetish' of conventionalism."[31] Harte states here the ideal. He recognizes that he has fallen short of it in his own work, but, knowing the goal for which he was striving, he sets it down for others to achieve.

Within his limits, geographic and artistic, Remington comes close to Harte's ideal, just as he also approximates Hamlin Garland's theories of local color. Determining early in his career to concentrate upon a few essential subjects—the Indian, the military, the West—he goes on to describe them with a thorough, often arrogant knowledge for their details. (His impatience with apparent inaccuracies in the works of others is legend.[32]) He attempts to capture the rhythms and inflections of Western speech, whether in the broken English of Sundown Leflare or in the only slightly tidied-up vernacular of the military encampment. He presents, as in his paintings, a selective picture of the American West, eliminating extraneous elements, and he concerns himself less with the telling of a conventionalized story than with the creation of a sense of place and character.

In his lifetime, Remington was widely acclaimed as an innovator in the realm of pictorial art. "He is," an editorial in *The Craftsman* announced in 1901, "one of the few men in this country who has created new conditions in our art; and must be reckoned with as one of the revolutionary figures in our art history."[33] Even as he was creating new conditions for American art, however, he was quietly advancing the cause of American literature. He will undoubtedly be remembered as a painter and sculptor; this is as it should be, for his paintings and bronzes are major achievements. He also deserves, however, to be recognized as a significant, although minor, author. By bringing the life of the American West in vivid and accurate detail to the readers of the genteel East, he contributes to the nineteenth century's growing sense of national unity;[34] by bringing to well-established local color writing the artist's vision, he contributes color and authenticity to the further development of the genre, moving it still further toward truly regional writing. His artistic achievements are major; but his literary achievements are far from negligible.

NOTES

[1] Hamlin Garland, *Crumbling Idols,* ed. Jane Johnson (1894; rpt. Cambridge: Belknap-Harvard, 1960), pp. 25, 132.

[2] Donald A. Dike, "Notes on Local Color and Its Relation to Realism," *College English,* 14 (November, 1952), 84.

[3] Owen Wister, "Introduction," in Frederic Remington, *Done In The Open* (New York: P. F. Collier & Sons, 1903), unpaged.

[4] Royal Cortissoz, *American Artists* (1923; rpt. Freeport, N. Y.: Books for Libraries Press, 1970), pp. 235, 229, 237.

[5] Frederic Remington, "The Great Medicine-Horse," *Sundown Leflare* (New York: Harper & Bros., 1899), p. 3; "Sundown Leflare's Money," *Sundown Leflare,* p. 79.

[6] Harold McCracken, *Frederic Remington: Artist of the Old West* (Philadelphia and New York: J. B. Lippincott, 1947), pp. 80-81.

[7] Claude M. Simpson, "Introduction," *The Local Colorists: American Short Stories, 1857-1900,* (New York: Harper & Bros., 1960), p. 6.

[8] Francis Parkman, "Preface to the Edition of 1892," *The Oregon Trail* (1892; rpt. New York: The Modern Library, 1949), p. xvi.

[9] Frederic Remington to Owen Wister, May, 1900, in Ben Merchant Vorpahl, *My Dear Wister—The Frederic Remington—Owen Wister Letters* (Palo Alto, Calif.: American West Publishing Co., 1972), p. 287.

[10] Frederic Remington, "A Few Words from Mr. Remington," *Collier's,* 34 (18 March 1905), 16.

[11] G. Edward White, *The Eastern Establishment and the Western Experience* (New Haven and London: Yale University Press, 1968), p. 121.

[12] Frederic Remington, "How the Law Got Into the Chaparral," *Crooked Trails* (1898; rpt. Freeport, N. Y.: Books for Libraries Press, 1969), p. 13; "A Sergeant of the Orphan Troop," *Crooked Trails,* p. 34.

[13] Remington, "Sundown Leflare's Warm Spot," *Sundown Leflare,* p. 56; "Sundown's Higher Self," *Sundown Leflare,* pp. 113-115.

[14] Frederic Remington, *John Ermine of the Yellowstone* (1902; rpt. Ridgewood, N. J.: The Gregg Press, 1968), pp. 22, 87-88.

[15] Simpson, pp. 12-13.

[16] Dike, p. 82.

[17] Dike, p. 83.

[18] Vorpahl, p. 118.

[19] Cortissoz, p. 239.

[20] Remington, "The Essentials at Fort Adobe," *Crooked Trails* pp. 68-69.

[21] Remington, "Sundown Leflare's Warm Spot," *Sundown Leflare,* p. 50; "Sundown's Higher Self," *Sundown Leflare,* pp. 107-108.

[22] Judith Alter, "Frederic Remington's Major Novel: *John Ermine,*" *Southwestern American Literature,* 2 (Spring, 1972), 44.

[23] Poultney Bigelow, quoted in McCracken, pp. 50-52.

[24] Vorpahl, p. 33.

[25] White, p. 104.

[26] Frederic Remington, "Horses of the Plains," *Century Magazine,* 37 (January, 1899), 343.

[27] Remington, "Joshua Goodenough's Old Letter," *Crooked Trails,* pp. 92-115, passim.

[28] Frederic Remington, "Chasing a Major-General," *Pony Tracks* (1895; rpt. Norman: University of Oklahoma Press, 1961), p. 11.

[29] Remington, *John Ermine*, pp. 244-245, 268-269.

[30] Lewis Mumford, "Regionalism and Irregionalism," *Sociological Review*, 19 (October, 1927), 285.

[31] Bret Harte, "The Rise of the 'Short Story,'" *Cornhill Magazine*, N. S. 7 (July, 1899), 8.

[32] Robert Taft, *Artists and Illustrators of the Old West, 1850-1900* (New York: Charles Scribner's Sons, 1953), pp. 228-230.

[33] Quoted in McCracken, p. 118.

[34] Simpson, pp. 5-7.

Christine Bold (essay date 1982)

SOURCE: "How the Western Ends: Fenimore Cooper to Frederic Remington," in *Western American Literature*, Vol. XVII, No. 2, Summer, 1982, pp. 117-35.

[*In the following essay, Bold analyzes Remington's* Sundown Leflare, John Ermine of the Yellowstone, *and* The Way of an Indian *as they build upon the narrative tradition of James Fenimore Cooper's* Leatherstocking Tales.]

> *Come back—do the 4 volume novel about a South Western Natty Bumpo [sic]—Believe me, I know.*
> Remington to Wister, Dec. 1899[1]

When Frederic Remington gave that advice to his defecting colleague, he did not acknowledge that he had already produced his own version of the *Leatherstocking Tales*. During 1897 and 1898, he had been writing the five short stories about Sundown that were collected in 1899 as *Sundown Leflare*.[2] That volume has a cyclical form and a central theme which are reminiscent of the Leatherstocking series' design. Its tone is different, however: the main figure remains more comical and grotesque than Natty; and the cycle is presented by a first-person narrator, a visiting eastern artist, who is always casual about the situation and its implications. Remington's fiction is not as obviously important as Fenimore Cooper's, but its similarities to the *Leatherstocking Tales* endow it with a considerable significance within the popular western genre. Like a great deal of western fiction, Remington's works begin with the model created by Cooper; but Remington developed from that paradigm increasingly melancholy stories, which are unlike the narratives of other popular western authors and yet are true to the vision of the Leatherstocking myth. His fiction constitutes an important offshoot to the main evolution of Westerns, but one which was fated to wither and die. As a publishing venture, *Sundown Leflare* was disastrous. It was not widely

reviewed or noticed or sold and by 1907, when he had to list his books for Perriton Maxwell, the art critic, Remington silently expunged both it and *John Ermine*, his novel, from the record of his achievements. He was denying his most interesting forays into fiction.

Remington, an artist before an author and a journalist before a novelist, came to fiction by degrees, and hesitantly. He looked for qualifying devices which would mark clearly the point where reportage ended and invention began. Thus, when his first attempt at fiction, **"The Affair of the - th of July,"** appeared among the journalistic treatments of current and recent events which were collected as *Pony Tracks* (1895), it was the only piece not to be told straightforwardly by the first-person narrator who inhabits the other reports. The story is based on an actual event, the 1894 Pullman riots of Chicago, and it expands that incident into a furor of carnage and death as soldiers and anarchists clash in an imaginary, apocalyptic fury. The fantasy is conveyed in a letter written by a military aide-de-camp present at the rioting; the epistolary device serves as an obvious demarcation between happening and report, actuality and fantasy. The division between these two categories is emphasized further in the clumsy ending: "Of course, my dear friend, all this never really happened, but it might very easily have happened if the mob had continued to monkey with the military buzz-saw."[3]

In his first uniformly fictive collection, *Sundown Leflare*, Remington hedged the delivery of the fiction around with even more qualificatory devices. The first story opens, as usual, with the first-person narrator, but his voice is only the last in the line of narrators. Old Paint, an Indian, is telling a legend which he heard from his father, who was told it by the grandfather. That legend, spoken in the Crow language, is being translated and interpreted by Sundown, a half-breed, to the white narrator, who passes it on to the reader. "Our" narrator's comment—"the problem in this case was how to eliminate 'Sundown' from 'Paint.' So much for interpreters." (p. 4)—must rebound on every participant in the chain of narrative, including himself. The origin of the story is obscured and the unreliability of the tale forefronted. Of course, the last figure in the line of narrators is Remington himself. He was demonstrating an unease with the fictionality of fiction. The further he moved from a verifiable event, the more voices he interposed between himself and the account and the more convoluted his story-telling became. From **"The Affair"** to **"The Spirit of Mahongui"** (1898), Remington's letter-writing voice became increasingly obscure and archaic, and the Sundown stories are told in a pidgin dialect which contorts gender, tense and syntactical sequence.

It is not immediately obvious that *Sundown Leflare* is anything more than a series of picaresque adventures, told in a bizarre dialect. It may have been that the author's discomfort with fiction caused him to articulate innovations in characterization and narrative time only through the story-telling voices; certainly, the whimsical tone adopted by both Sundown and the white narrator camouflages the work's experimentation. The connection with the Leatherstocking cycle is evident in the theme of the man caught between two races and two times. Neither red nor truly white, Natty mediates between the two sides and, though he exists in an age of progress, he adheres to past ways of life. Sundown is also introduced as a mediator between Indian and white man, but the cross in his blood is revealed much more casually: "Sundown was crossbred, red and white, so he never got mentally in sympathy with either strain of his progenitors. He knew about half as much concerning Indians as they did themselves, while his knowledge of white men was in the same proportion." (p. 3) He is an anachronistic, garrulous figure whose role is to translate the myth of a medicine-horse which Paint tells; but he insists on acting as interpreter and commentator as well. Remington's imagination, like Cooper's, was fired by his marginal frontiersman and, after the first story, Sundown takes over the centre of the stage, telling the white narrator about adventures from further and further into his past.

Although it emerges that Sundown is an alien whose present situation is potentially tragic (he has just been abandoned by his wife; he is old, penniless, alone), none of the pathos is allowed to have force. Because Sundown's reminiscences move toward the past, attention is increasingly directed away from his present circumstances until, in the last story, he appears as a young medicine-man, beginning a prestigious career inside an Indian tribe. In the order in which the autobiographical anecdotes first appeared in *Harper's Monthly*, Sundown describes himself at each stage of a progression from white to red: he talks about himself, firstly, as a buckskinned government scout; then he becomes a "breed" who steals horses; next, he describes himself, "I was all same Enjun . . . but I was wear de hat" (p. 56); and finally he is a medicine-man for the Piegans.

Each step of his transformation to youth is robbed of its possible heroism. The first epithet applied to Sundown recalls the introduction of Chingachgook in *The Pioneers*. However, whereas Fenimore Cooper explains the ceremonial import of the name "Big Snake," Remington's narrator reduces the metaphor to a reproach: "Oh, you reptile! will you never mind this thinking—it is fatal." (p. 18) In the final episode, Sundown explains his baptism. Like Natty and Chingachgook, he wins his name because of extraordinary abilities (he can see unnaturally far at sun-set), but in this case, the christening is based on trickery (he has secretly acquired a pair of binoculars and uses them under cover of twilight). Sundown is always incipiently heroic and romantic, in his delivery of an army order through murderous weather conditions or in his duel over an Indian woman, but he perpetually undercuts that impression in his telling of heroic deeds. In **"How Order No. 6 Went Through,"** it is his cowardice and common sense which he stresses; after the tale of the joust, he mentions that three years later he sold the squaw for a hundred dollars to a white man. But if the mood of the text is self-parody, Remington's illustrations create the opposite impression. The frontispiece shows Sundown in the present, as a half-breed in white man's clothing, a rumpled, unhandsome, vaguely clownish figure. The pictures become more stylized in lay-out and Sundown himself more Indianized, until, in the last illustrations, he is portrayed as a full Indian with a magnificent physique, splendid in his savage costume. The engravings follow the time-scheme of Sundown's tales, showing him as increasingly young and increasingly red. Remington provided one version of his central figure, the comic, in his writing and another, the heroic, in his illustration.

Sundown undergoes an experience akin to that of Natty and Chingachgook, who slough off the layers of age until they achieve the primal innocence of *The Deerslayer*. He is participating in the familiar American myth. While he is involved in straightforward *chronos*, in his developing relationship with the white narrator, during that relationship he articulates *kairos*,[4] when he presents himself in moments from the past. Because of the patterning of time, which is central to the collection's structure, since only that element orders the disparate conversations, this half-comic, half-romantic hero shares Natty's immortality. Although Natty ostensibly dies at the end of *The Prairie*, his death has no force, since it is implied that, setting with the sun, he will surely rise again with it. Indeed, Cooper brought him back to manhood thirteen years later in *The Pathfinder*.

Sundown articulates in his own language the sense of circular repetition which results from the interweaving of the two time-schemes. He always uses a mongrel verb construction, made up of present, imperfect and infinitive forms. Since he seems to not know the perfect tense, all his verbs are in the present, whose main use is the description of habitual acts, and the imperfect, which describes continuous actions without definite time limits. He has a vocabulary only for the on-going present and the unfinished past; he does not verbalize finitude and ending any more than he experiences them. Remington's conclusion is a more extreme version of Cooper's: both their heroes are eternally displaced and disjunct from the rules of human time. Both are assigned to a cycle which can perpetually repeat, but never proceed.

. . . . .

And when this man breaks from his static isolation, and makes a new move, then look out, something will be happening.
D. H. Lawrence on Natty Bumppo[5]

John Ermine of the Yellowstone (1902)[6] has none of the narrative devices of ***Sundown Leflare***. In the earlier work, Remington was tortuous and creative simultaneously, reflecting his neophytic experiments with long fiction and his desire to keep those experiments at one or more removes from the authorial voice. ***John Ermine*** is a more homogeneous work, which can openly express the tensions of the situation which it presents; in this maturer fiction, the author sloughed off all the first-person narrators and narrowed down his hero's alternatives to two. It is Remington's only fully-worked novel and a story which, while it explores the same theme as *Sundown Leflare,* has more in common, structurally and tonally, with the *Leatherstocking Tales.* Remington was not copying Cooper; in fact, he went beyond him. Both Natty and Sundown are part of self-engendering cycles, but Natty is much less versatile, because he is locked into a pattern of dualism which denies him the different guises and perspectives which his comic counterpart enjoys. In *John Ermine,* Remington again developed circumstances like those in the Leatherstocking series and he worked them through to their logical consequences, breaking through the indeterminacy of Cooper's conclusions.

Cooper worked to a dualistic design when he brought together the historical romance and the frontier saga to create his innovative western fiction; and he repeated the principles of counterpoint and opposition at every level of his work: in theme, characterization, plot, scene and even syntax. When he dramatized the meeting of savagery and civilization which entrap the frontiersman between them, he would punctuate the story with visual translations of the pattern, creating tableaux of three figures, arranged as two elements with a third as the axis which balances, conjoins or distinguishes them. Such are the scenes which open and close the main action of *The Last of the Mohicans:* when we meet Natty and Chingachgook, they are awaiting and discussing Uncas; the final scene is of the two older men standing on either side of the grave of the younger.

While Cooper established the dualistic pattern at every level of his text, he never exploited either of the consequences suggested by the condition he constructed: that is, he neither involved his wilderness hero in a sentimental reconciliation with either of the two environments, nor did he develop the potential for tragedy or self-destruction. He froze one hero into unresolvable stasis in plot, theme, imagery and structure; he also ended each novel with the conventional wedding of the romantic hero and heroine. Thus his conclusion embraced both the irreconcilable polarities which trap the frontiersman and the harmonious resolution of the romantic couple. All subsequent writers inherited the predicament of problematic duality, but none, until Remington, took further the implications of polarization.

Some authors echoed Cooper's conclusion unchanged. Most immediately, Robert Montgomery Bird wrote *Nick of the Woods* (1835) as a denial of Cooper's vision of the wilderness. He maintained, however, Cooper's unresolved ending: his Indian fighter, a schizophrenic who embodies more savagely than Natty the tensions of his dualistic experience, wanders farther into the wilderness with his dog at the end of the novel, having saved the heroine from captivity and enabled her to marry the romantic hero. That conclusion is repeated in a modern Western like *Shane,* in which the eponymous hero reunites husband and wife, ranchers and nesters, then disappears into the sunset on his horse.

More usually, the authors of popular Westerns exploited Cooper's gesture towards sentimental reconciliation. The thousands of dime novels which dominated the period from Cooper and Bird to the twentieth-century Western, centered the western hero and conventionalized the happy ending. Their collective achievement was to devise ingenious ways in which the western hero could take part in battles, rescues and escapes, kill villains and display wilderness craft, and yet end in harmony with a lover. Their methods were superficial: the most convenient strategy was disguise, which enables heroes like Seth Jones and Deadwood Dick to play various roles and keep them separate. In the tamer, turn-of-the-century dime novels, games were substituted for disguise, to create the impression that the hero is never involved in genuine destruction and can remain genteel and romantic at the end of his adventures. Both these methods produced simulated conflict and facile resolution, therefore the element of genuine difficulty was lost and the motivation for action became arbitrary.

It took Owen Wister to achieve something more truly synthetic. His western hero was the first to encompass capacities for civilization and wilderness within his own personality, rather than by artificial means. The apotheosis of sentimental reconciliation is understood to have occurred at the end of *The Virginian* (1902), where the western cowboy and an eastern schoolmistress marry.

These denouements obviously relate uniformly to the tendencies in Cooper toward sentimentalism. But, in the end, the *Leatherstocking Tales* tend more towards bleakness and hopelessness. Natty clearly cannot be absorbed by white society in the way of the Virginian, nor can he transgress his bloodright to join the Indians. That the intervening fiction should so invariably ignore the connotations of that situation, emphasizes the uniqueness of Remington's work. Using the same types of the savage and noble Indians and the innocent frontiersman, *John Ermine* makes explicit that which remains implicit and partly glossed-over in the Leatherstocking cycle: at the center of the novel are circumstances like Natty's, but they are taken to their extreme consequences.

As in *The Virginian,* the romantic interest in *John Ermine* is much more central than in any of Cooper's tales. It is not a sub-plot or a strategy to acknowledge the dictates of conventional romance, for the encounter of western hero and eastern heroine determines the course of the narrative. *John Ermine* tells of a white boy who has been brought up by Crow Indians. In his adolescence he is handed over to a white hermit who is venerated by the Indians and who re-educates Ermine in the ways of white men. In time, Ermine re-enters white society, by way of an army outpost in the West which he, with his half-breed companion, Wolf-Voice, joins as a scout. There he encounters Major Searle's daughter. He falls in love with her, proposes marriage and is rejected with horror. After shooting her successful (eastern) lover in the arm, he is hounded by the cavalry. Outlawed, he retreats briefly to the hermit's cave, but returns to the army post, intending to murder Katherine's fiancé. Instead, he is killed by a Crow scout, who bears an old grudge. Ermine's thwarted proposal stems from the same misapprehension as Natty's in *The Pathfinder*: both men, having proved their natural gentility by superior behavior in military service, approach a woman of higher social rank to their own. Natty's disappointment leads to his return to his previous circumstances: celibacy and wilderness life. Ermine's rebuff directly causes his death.

The comparison between their fates suggests itself the more keenly because of the similarities in their make-up. They are both isolated wilderness men who stand somewhere between Red and White: celibates and orphans who, while functioning as translators and mediators, stress their disjunction from both sides in their appearance and speech. John Ermine can be read as a more volatile Natty Bumppo, who breaks out of a repetitive cycle, confronts the contradictions in his circumstances and suffers the consequences.

Ermine's career involves some repetition in that it is made up of alternating alienation and reconciliation, as different groups try to remake him to their ideal. Initially taken from the Indians by white miners, to be their "Gold Nugget," he is recaptured by the tribe who consider him, as White Weasel, a promising warrior. He comes to notice the physical difference between himself and his Indian friends and when he is taken to Crooked-Bear, the old hermit exploits the differences, nurturing his hereditary, white instincts. Crooked-Bear also introduces the death-note, both in his meditations on the boy—"Weasel was more beautiful than he would ever be again" (p. 46)—and in his rebaptismal ritual, by which Weasel becomes John Ermine when the hermit gives him his first gun and he shoots a panther. When Ermine is sent from his mentor to seek a new community in the army camp, the ritual is repeated. A Captain refurbishes him with a new gun and uniform, admiring the sight "as though he had created it." (p. 109) Again, Ermine's appearance, particularly his hair, evokes the language of death—"You will fall dead when you see it." (p. 110) In each of these new arenas, he changes from outsider to insider and then becomes a stranger again, as he moves on to his next field of action. The pattern partly masks his accelerating progression towards an increasingly complete isolation. That development is charted closely. At first Ermine asserts that, "I have no relations anywhere on the earth, but I have friends." (p. 146) After the shooting in the last chapter ("The End of All Things"), he discovers that the Crows shun him; he abandons Crooked-Bear as mentor; he mistreats his last ally, his pony. Finally, "he had one friend left, just one; it is always the last friend such a one has,—the Night." (p. 269) This "friend" enables him to enter the army camp, where he dies, utterly alone and without having seen his assailant.

Ermine never has an impulse towards reconciliation, once he recognizes white men and Indians as distinct races. In his role as mediator in the army camp, he means to bring two sides together only, not to reconcile them. The resultant clash causes his death.

He had thought out the proposition that the Indians were just as strange to the white people as the white people were to them, consequently he saw a social opening. He would mix these people up so that they could stare at each other in mutual perplexity . . . (p. 153).

When he brings the Major's daughter and a Crow scout face to face, he intervenes to protect Katherine from the Indian's touch. Having insulted the Crow thus, he is eventually killed by him. His mixture of red and white sensibilities causes agonizing conflict within Ermine. He has two names, at times he is referred to as two separate characters and he prays to two gods. In his final despair he appeals to them both: "O Sak-a-war-te, why did you not take the snake's gaze out of her eyes, and not let poor Ermine sit like a gopher to be swallowed? God, God, have you deserted me?" (p. 246) Ermine understands two-sidedness to be at the root of his tragedy, but he ascribes that characteristic to the white soldiers. Whereas he apprehends vaguely a possible unity behind his beliefs—"Sak-a-war-te and the God of the white men—he did not know whether they were one or two" (p. 133)—he unreservedly identifies duality with the white attitude and blames that as the cause of his humiliation. He accuses the officers, "I tell you now that I do not understand such men as you are. You have two hearts: one is red and the other is blue; and you feel with the one that best suits you at the time." (p. 236) And he tells his hermit friend savagely, "The white men in the camp are two-sided; they pat you with a hand that is always ready to strike." (p. 264)

Ermine is articulating his predicament with a vocabulary and syntax which underline the dualism of his condition. In this, his language is reminiscent of Cooper's. Remington also insists on polarization in his arrangement of significant scenes, such as the meeting between the Indians and the visitors from the East, or in Ermine's death-scene, where the body is discovered flanked by the appurtenances of the red and white races; the blanket on one side, the rifle on the other. The picture echoes Natty's death scene, but it is a dehumanized and brutal version.

However, Remington diverges from Cooper's pattern of clear counterpoint to emphasize the ultimate contrast which his work presents—that is, the difference between this novel and the conventional western romance. At first, it is the novel's resemblance to the conventional model, rather than its difference, which is obvious. It has a typical cast and seems, initially, to follow a typical plot: Ermine's success in the white world suggests his continued happiness; there is a possibility of his victory as suitor; and the Western's convention leads the reader to anticipate a happy ending. But Remington raises the reader's expectations only to thwart them the more forcefully. One of his characters, talking of love, says, "I don't see how men write novels or plays about that old story; all they can do is to invent new fortifications for Mr. Hero to carry before she names the day." (p. 182) Of course, Remington's hero does not end his love quest like this; his experience is not just another old story, but something more anguished and unique. Situations which superficially seem to be similar are actually importantly different. The author builds up, within his tale, a pattern of apparent similarities which regularly turn out to be less important than the differences which they obscure. For example, Remington suggests resemblances between Wolf-Voice and John Ermine or Ermine and Lieutenant Butler, only to show that these likenesses are irrelevant when compared to the contrasts between the men. These more incidental feints towards similarity become formal devices which underline the impression that the novel as a whole, however much it appears a conventional romance, is something far different. The author is revealing, now much more subtly, his former unease about fiction. He insists on the fact that what he tells, though it occurs within fiction, does not restrict its force to an artistic fancy. "Then like the raising of a curtain, which reveals the play, the hermit saw suddenly that it was heavy and solemn—that he was to see a tragedy, and this was not a play; it was real, it was his boy, and he did not want to see a tragedy." (p. 263)

Crooked-Bear continues his reflections, suggesting not only that the ending is truer than fiction, but that it fits into a larger pattern. "I do not understand why men should be so afflicted in this world as Ermine and I have been, but doubtless it is the working of a great law, and possibly of a good one." (p. 267) The hermit acknowledges both the inevitability of the ending and its aptness and, again, the tale creates formal patterns to support that conclusion. Hints of inevitability are embedded in the prophecies which are communicated through repeated clusters of vocabulary. Thus, talk of death around Ermine prefigures his own death. Similarly, when he first encounters Katherine, he "tripped and stumbled, fell down, and crawled over answers to her questions." (p. 154) Those words are echoed in his final descent to death: he stumbles through the dark, crawls through the hills, finally to fall dead on the ground. There are other declensions which contribute to an accumulative impression of irrevocability. One is Ermine's increasing isolation, and that is accompanied by the sense of his shrinking future. A boy with "infinite possibilities" (p. 46), he is deflected into a more limited channel by a photograph and the woman whom it depicts. These idols are agents of confinement: the photograph in its very make-up; and the woman because of her restricting dress, her inhibited manners and her outlook which would cage Indians and put Ermine inside a picture frame. Certainly they restrict John Ermine's ambitions; he stays within his tent, dreaming. At last, Ermine is a man with no future, excluded even by the Indians, as they dream their futile dreams, each under his own tightly-drawn blanket. The pattern of decline is endorsed by the authorial voice, which recognizes the entire movement as the death of a type and a way of life, not just of an individual.

The internal construction of the novel attests to the idea that the ending is fitting and truthful to the situation proposed by the fiction. Beyond that, there is an impression that Remington has conformed most truthfully to the

implications of the Western's origins, because he developed Cooper's suggestion of tragic duality, rather than his portrayal of sentimental resolution. That wider sense of *John Ermine* enacting a valid trend in western material, is corroborated by Wister's novel, which appeared earlier the same year and which ostensibly celebrates the opposite inclination.

By 1902, Remington and Wister were no longer steady friends and they had lost confidence in each other's artistic abilities. While both were enthusiastic about the frontier, Remington believed that the wild West was irrevocably gone, where Wister thought that it could be revived as a corrective to contemporary social and political degeneration. Wister began to criticize Remington in private letters[7] and Remington can be seen to carry his disapprobation into his fiction. *The Virginian*[8] contains various relationships and many adventures, but its closing stages and its ending in particular have to do with the reconciliation of opposites. While first setting out the contrasts between East and West, heroine and hero, Wister proceeded to show the Virginian overcome all Molly's objections, and the two come together in marriage, thus uniting geography, social mores and literary types. In *John Ermine*, Remington gestured towards *The Virginian*, implying a direct contradiction of Wister's conclusion. The synopsis of the "old story" neatly summarizes the love-plot of *The Virginian* and the names "Molly" and "Mrs. Taylor" are introduced peripherally, but during crucial courtship scenes, in connection with Katherine and her mother. In his proposal to Katherine, Ermine invites her to "come to the mountains with me. I will make you a good camp." (p. 223) This is precisely where the Virginian takes Molly after their wedding and the two spend an idyllic month in primal isolation. Katherine, on the other hand, derides Ermine, accuses him of trying to turn her into a squaw and runs screaming into the house. Where Wister ends his novel on a note of peaceful reconciliation, Remington's closing scene is of Katherine shaking hands with the Crow who has killed Ermine. The Crow is called "her malevolent friend" (p. 271) and in that phrase is implied the travesty of reconciliation which has been effected by Ermine's death.

Yet Wister's novel is not as homogenous as it appears at first sight. There is a perceptible disjunction between the story and its ending. It is not only Remington who contradicts Wister, for Wister himself can be seen to be denying, subliminally, that which occurs at the most obvious level of his text.

The Virginian constructs its own set of symbols. The trauma of the rustlers' hanging, the Virginian's reaction and his subsequent injury by Indians are linked intimately with the scenes in which they occur and the feelings which they provoke. Thereafter, cottonwoods, mountains and woods, or cerebral activity and childishness, recur as intimations of evil. Therefore, in the moments before the final duel, the sight of cottonwoods reinforces an atmosphere of danger, and abstract conception divorced from concrete observation is a prime sin of Dr. MacBride's. In the last chapter, after the wedding, the significance of these symbols is inverted as hero and heroine sport in their isolated Eden. They camp among trees in the mountains, a double imprisonment, and the scene repeats a mental picture which the Virginian has forethought. In established western typology, the setting sun represents eternal life. The change which marriage brings to the Virginian is "like a sunrise." (p. 357) He seems to be regressing to a childhood state. Molly wonders, "Was this dreamy boy the man of two days ago? . . . his face changed by her to a boy's, and she leavened with him." (p. 357) Although the narrative has joined Molly and the Virginian in harmony, there remains a structural recognition of their irreconcilability. Dualistic tableaux are set up to establish the polarity of contrasts involved in the beginning, and Wister conveys the power of synthesis by uniting these polarities. But his dualisms remain: when the husband and wife swim in opposite pools with the island between them, they are echoing the configuration of an earlier scene, when they sat on either side of a table—"The inkstand stood between them" (p. 263)—to write letters to the East. The display of union is not convincing at any but the plot level, for the validity of the cowboy's adaptation to the East, the modern West and marriage is undercut by the network of inappropriate imagery and ambiguous statement on which it rests. Wister's novel, coherent in symbolism and structure in only thirty-five of the thirty-six chapters, represents the apotheosis of reconciliation for the western genre; therefore its failure is telling. It is prophetic of the further compromises and incapacities which would be shown by the novel which tells this story again and again—the popular Western. Writers like Ernest Haycox, who had none of the dime novelists' superficiality, strained to duplicate the happy ending, although it became increasingly inappropriate to novels which developed nihilistic and naturalistic themes.

The rupture in *The Virginian*'s design indicates the importance of **John Ermine's** overt recognition that the Westerner inevitably failed to integrate with society. That such a central work should betray the same concerns, in stifled form, suggests that, although Remington was the first and—until the advent of the anti-Western—last western writer to dramatize this irreversible conflict, he had realized a crucial aspect of the genre, which had been present, but muted, since Fenimore Cooper.

Remington's vision never became popular: while Wister created a divided novel about ultimate harmony, Remington produced a uniform expression of rupture. The ending was almost immediately reversed. When **John Ermine** was dramatized in 1903, by Louis Evans Shipman, Remington was persuaded to help with the revision of the script. The revised ending ran: Ermine shoots Katherine's fiancé dead. He is accused of murder, but successfully defends his action as self-defense and eventually wins Katherine as his bride.

. . . . .

art is a process of elimination . . .
                    Remington, March 1903[9]

John Ermine did not attract any imitators; it did not even retain its plot in its own dramatization; and Remington never repeated the dualistic structure. His artistic vision was becoming bleaker. His next work has no vivid interplay between contending forces, only an insistence on the futile gestures of the wild West's last inhabitants. Although **The Way of an Indian** (1906)[10] does not seem to fit the patterns of the *Leatherstocking Tales*, **Sundown Leflare** and **John Ermine**, it represents a comprehensible development within Remington's work. Sundown is the alien who passes through multiple perspectives and is destined to repeat forever that fluctuation, since he cannot affiliate himself permanently with any one type. John Ermine, who has allegiances to two races, is unable to maintain the same balancing act and is destroyed by the discordances between his two cultures. The hero of **The Way of an Indian** is never exposed to more than one racial experience and that is one which is already doomed to extinction. **The Way of an Indian** is Remington's last written work and it seems to represent the end-point in his vision of shrinking possibilities.

The hero is no man caught between two races, but a full-blooded Indian who only ever encounters white men as enemies. The book dramatizes his initiation to fighting manhood, his successful abduction of an Indian squaw, his victories and defeats in battle and, finally, his death as a Cheyenne chief. In his younger days, White Otter—variously rechristened as "the Bat" and "Fire Eater"—undergoes the same delusion as Sundown about the longevity of Indians and the temporality of the white man. This Indian, however, cannot create an alternative mythic time-scheme for himself. Because he is unable to reverse time, he cannot combat the effects of chronology and his delusion can never be transformed into vision. Once he understands the truth, despite his various battles with Whites, there is never any question but that he is a red man who belongs to a doomed race. "Old Big Hair, who sat blinking, knew that the inevitable was going to happen, but he said no word." (p. 36) Neither does Remington say a word to reverse, fictively, historical inevitability. There is no sense of duality in the text because there is never any doubt about the outcome. The author had settled on a fixed perspective and a single-faceted experience. In his account of the tribe's final massacre, he seems to be paralleling, from the opposite perspective, Custer's report of the "battle" at the Washita in 1868.[11] Telling one side of the story, Remington concentrated on the hopelessness of the Indian cause, in a tone that is elegiac rather than angry. When *Cosmopolitan* serialized the story (from November 1905), its editor felt it necessary to supply the alternative perspective that Remington no longer articulated. The magazine prefaced his installments with a synopsis of the action, written from a viewpoint antagonistic to that of the Indian. Remington continued to be involved in a contrapuntal pattern, although he was trying, now, for the opposite effect.

From its opening scene, **The Way of an Indian** is concerned with isolation and death. White Otter begins where John Ermine ended—alone and with a bad heart. He is worrying about his lack of protection from evil spirits and his consequent exclusion from the after-life. He ends in exactly the same posture—alone on a hillside, thinking about the after-life, but now an old man who is prepared to surrender to the evil spirits. Although there is a progression from chapter to chapter, as White Otter gains maturity, the thrust of the book is towards circularity and lack of achievement. The Cheyenne's life represents an accumulation of victories, but the reader is allowed to see their pettiness. His individual acts of combat are always against a helpless victim, one who does not realize that he is threatened until he is attacked (once from the rear) and therefore does not defend himself. Even the attack by an Indian band against three white trappers, in which the hero wins his new name, Fire Eater, is won only because the trappers die of thirst. The author presents the warriors as vultures, prepared to lay siege to the beaver-men, but too afraid to attack them directly. It is immediately after this unheroic event that Fire Eater kills a Shoshone by stabbing him in the back. He wins great renown for his performance in these confrontations, but his grandeur is tempered by the author's comment that, "the Fire Eater grew to be a great man in the little world of the Chis-chis-chash, though his affairs proportionately were as the 'Battles of the Kites and the Crows.'" (p. 152)

There is much death in the stories. Like John Ermine, this hero wins new names through his encounters with death, but his experiences are more passive. He achieves his first rebaptism by killing an unsuspecting Crow who thinks the intruder is his lover, and he is renamed Fire Eater for breaching the trappers' gunpowder flames, rather than for slaying any of the enemy. His last rebirth is a deception. Beaten by white traders, he declares himself dead and simulates a resurrection. In his final confrontation with death, the only rebirth which he desires is one into the after-life. White Otter is recurrently isolated and in darkness, prefiguring his death fearfully in his own mind, so his final demise is only the last act in a cycle which has much more to do with death than rebirth. That the cycle will not support any renewal of itself is underlined in the death of the chief's grandchild, which precedes his own. Fire Eater is the last of his line: the baby's death seals off the future; the present is a barren emptiness; the chief can imagine happiness only in death. The most memorable image of the work occurs when the chief takes his grandson to show him a dead white soldier, before the final defeat. The baby, soon to freeze to death himself, stabs the dead corpse.

> Pulling his great knife from its buckskin sheath, [Fire Eater] curled the fat little hand around its shaft and led him to the white body. . . . Comprehending the idea, the infant drew up and drove down, doing his best to obey the instructions, but his arm was far too weak to make the knife penetrate. The fun of the thing made him scream with pleasure, and the old Fire Eater chuckled at the idea of his little warrior's first *coup*. (p. 205)

The text never has the fertility of *Sundown Leflare* or *John Ermine.* The hero is a savage, stoic actor, with

whom the reader cannot identify. He seems a bloodless cipher in a text full of ritual, signs and tracks. The symbols tend to be inanimate or dead—for example, the hero's good medicine comes from a dead bat and a spider which he kills to discover its prophecy. Scenes are described in terms of the patterns and forms they adopt. These, also, are very often infertile or self-destructive; a circle easily changes from defense to trap. Fire Eater's band makes a late and ill-planned attack on white traders. They retreat to a waterhole, packing themselves in with a rigid formation which simply enables the surrounding Whites to close in the more quickly and massacre the group. This is a local instance of the absence of choice or fluidity which permeates the book. It is the play of alternatives which substantiates the meaning in Remington's other long fictions; the nature of the alternatives gives Sundown his humour and endows John Ermine with tragic force. There is none of that in *The Way of an Indian*; in fact, there is so much about death that the story is ended almost as soon as it begins, since the reader is constantly aware of the necessary outcome (especially if he has read *John Ermine* and *Sundown Leflare,* both of which refer to the downfall of the Cheyenne tribe).

Just before the serialization of *The Way of an Indian,* Remington had written, "My own pictures, if at all successful, are finished before they are begun . . ."[12] Strangely, he thought this last work his most successful fiction and it seems an example of that method translated into literature. There are no false possibilities suggested in this story and little sense of protest. The narrative is inevitable, predictable; in a sense it is all ending, a logical enough development for a writer who had already tried the never-ending circularity of *Sundown Leflare,* then the tragic and unexpected finality which is conveyed in the conclusion of *John Ermine.* Remington's theme of displacement had reached its climax in his last work, in its subject and technique. His fiction could progress no further.

Fenimore Cooper's major innovations and his most accomplished inventions were, of course, his subject-matter and his mythology. Yet he also left an important heritage in the details of his narrative technique, in his manipulation of narrative time and in the very incompleteness of his theme. He did not provide a final answer to his problematic proposition; Henry Nash Smith said, "if he had been able—as he was not—to explore to the end the contradiction in his ideas and emotions, the Leatherstocking series might have become a major work of art."[13] For over fifty years, none of the writers who took up Cooper's types and scenes developed further the darker and more resonant side of his fiction. Remington was interested in similar narrative patterns and he wrought them to more insistent extremes; and he became the first author to explore fully the contradictions in the image of the wilderness man at the disappearing frontier. He acted on impulses prefigured but not exhausted by Cooper and, despite the clumsiness of his fiction, it conveys powerful and convincing movements. *John Ermine,* especially, seems a more substantial model than *The Virginian* for the further development of the Western. Popular western fiction may have lost some better alternatives when Remington's design ended with him.

NOTES

[1] Quoted in Ben Merchant Vorpahl, *My dear Wister: The Frederic Remington-Owen Wister Letters* (Palo Alto, CA: American West Publishing Co., 1972), p. 283.

[2] *Sundown Leflare* (N.Y.: Harper & Brothers, 1899). Page numbers in parentheses in the text refer to this edition.

[3] *Pony Tracks* (1895; rpt. Norman: University of Oklahoma Press, 1961), p. 144.

[4] I am more concerned with the co-existence of two kinds of narrative time than with the most precise definitions of these terms. I am basing my usage on Frank Kermode's discussion of time in *The Sense of an Ending* (1967; rpt. N.Y.: Oxford University Press, 1979). He talks of *chronos* as "simple chronicity" (p. 46). *Kairos* refers to time which encompasses more than mere successiveness: it is time made significant through its relation to the end. "The *kairos* transforms the past . . . establishes concord with origins as well as ends" (p. 48). In his tale-telling, Sundown creates an alternative time-scheme which is significant because it starts at his ending and proceeds to his beginning. *Kairos* harmonizes his end and his beginning: as he grows older chronologically, he becomes younger mythologically.

[5] *Studies in Classic American Literature* (1924; rpt. G.B.: Penguin, 1971), p. 69.

[6] *John Ermine of the Yellowstone* (1902; rpt. N.Y.: Grosset & Dunlap, 1908). Page references are to this edition.

[7] Vorpahl, p. 309.

[8] *The Virginian* (1902; rpt. N.Y.: Pocket Books, 1977). Page references are to this edition.

[9] Quoted in Edwin Wildman, "Frederic Remington, the Man," *Outing, the Magazine,* 41, No. 6 (March 1903), 712.

[10] *The Way of an Indian* (London: Gay & Bird, 1906). Page references are to this edition.

[11] This is suggested in Peggy and Harold Samuels, eds., *The Collected Writings of Frederic Remington* (N.Y.: Doubleday, 1979), p. 626. I have culled much of my information on *The Way of an Indian* from the "Notes" to this edition.

[12] Frederic Remington, "A Few Words from Mr. Remington," *Collier's,* 18 (March 1905), 16.

[13] *Virgin Land: The American West as Symbol and Myth* (Cambridge, Mass.: Harvard University Press, 1950), p. 61.

FURTHER READING

Biography

Allen, Douglas. *Frederic Remington and the Spanish-American War.* New York: Crown Publishers, Inc., 1971, 178 p.
    Biography of Remington that particularly focuses on his attraction to all things military.

Erisman, Fred. *Frederic Remington.* Idaho: Boise State University, 1975, 44 p.
    Brief biography that includes a bibliography of books, stories, and articles by Remington as well as secondary sources on the artist.

Manley, Atwood and Margaret Manley Mangum. *Frederic Remington and the North Country.* New York: E. P. Dutton, 1988, 272 p.
    Explores Remington's life and career within "the familial, geographical, and cultural context of upstate New York."

McCracken, Harold. *Frederic Remington: Artist of the Old West.* J. B. Lippincott Company, 1947, 157 p.
    Biography of Remington as the exceptional artist of the American West.

Samuels, Peggy and Harold. *Frederic Remington: A Biography.* Garden City, N. Y.: Doubleday & Company, Inc., 1982, 537 p.
    Comprehensive study of Remington's life and influence on North American art.

Criticism

Buscombe, Edward. "Painting the Legend: Frederic Remington and the Western." *Cinema Journal* 23, No. 4 (Summer 1984): 12-27.
    Probes the relationship between Remington's pictorial art and the Western film genre.

Hassrick, Peter H. *Frederic Remington: Paintings, Drawings, and Sculpture in the Amon Carter Museum and the Sid W. Richardson Foundation Collections.* New York: Harry N. Abrams, Inc., 1973, 218 p.
    Features photographs of Remington's art preceded by an introduction on the artist and his celebration of Western life.

Hine, Robert V. Review of *My Dear Wister: The Frederic Remington-Owen Wister Letters.* *The Journal of American History* LIX, No. 4 (March 1973): 1016.
    Discusses the Remington-Wister correspondence and the development of the cowboy-hero figure.

Nemerov, Alexander. *Frederic Remington & Turn-of-the-Century America.* New Haven, Conn.: Yale University Press, 1995, 244 p.
    Offers formal, psychoanalytic, and cultural interpretations of Remington's art.

Review of *The Collected Writings of Frederic Remington.*
The New Yorker 55 (April 9, 1979): 158-59.
> Regards Remington's writing as "forthright,
> accomplished, and tinged with the sentimentalities of
> his period."

White, G. Edward. *The Eastern Establishment and the
Western Experience: The West of Frederic Remington,
Theodore Roosevelt, and Owen Wister.* New Haven,
Conn.: Yale University Press, 1968, 238 p.
> Considers the Eastern idea of the American West through
> the eyes of the artist (Remington), president (Roosevelt),
> and writer (Wister) who helped shaped it.

The following sources published by Gale contain further information on
Remington's life and work: *Contemporary Authors*, Vol. 108; *Dictionary of
Literary Biography*, Vols. 12, 186, 188; *Something about the Author*, Vol. 41.

M. Carey Thomas

1857-1935

(Full name Martha Carey Thomas) American educator and essayist.

INTRODUCTION

Thomas was one of the most influential advocates of a woman's right to higher education. A prominent American educator, Thomas served as president of Bryn Mawr College between 1894 and 1922. Her collected writings, including her *Education of Women,* contain her insights on the intellectual equality of women and men, and powerful arguments for the continued expansion of educational opportunities to women. A feminist and progressive, Thomas is also remembered as an active member of the women's suffrage movement in the United States.

Biographical Information

Thomas was born on 2 January 1857 in Baltimore, Maryland, the eldest of ten children in the Quaker family of James Carey Thomas and Mary Whitall Thomas. At the age of seven she was severely burned in an accident at her parents' home, an incident that led Thomas to question the existence of a benevolent God and moved her along the path to secularism. During her recovery, she embarked on a wide program of reading, which she details in her early journals. Thomas was educated at Quaker schools, including the Howland Institute near Ithaca, New York. After graduation she determined to attend college, an unusual desire for a women of that era. Defying her father, Thomas enrolled at Cornell University in 1875. While there she dropped her first name, preferring Carey Thomas, and earned her bachelor's degree in 1877. Thomas continued to pursue her education at Johns Hopkins University; however, she was barred from attending classes with male students and chose to withdraw within a year. Thomas later traveled to Europe in 1879 with hopes of earning an advanced degree in philology. She enrolled at the University of Leipzig in Germany, but because of her gender was refused a doctorate. She moved to Switzerland, and in 1882 obtained her Ph.D. from the University of Zurich, graduating *summa cum laude.* Following her return to the United States, Thomas received an appointment as first dean of Bryn Mawr College for Women in 1884. She was later named the school's second president in 1894. Thomas published her *Education of Women* in pamphlet form in 1899. Its reprinting the following year as part of the *Monographs on Education in the United States* series positioned her as the leading proponent of women's access to higher education. Following two decades of vocal activism on behalf of her belief in the equality of men and women, Thomas retired from her position as president of Bryn Mawr in 1922. She died on 2 December 1935 of heart failure.

Major Works

Aside from her abundant personal diaries and correspondence, which were collected in *The Making of a Feminist: Early Journals and Letters of M. Carey Thomas,* Thomas wrote a series of essays on the education of women in the United States. In these writings, Thomas outlines her thoughts on the equality of women and men. A firm believer in Darwinian ideas as they relate to society, she eschewed intellectual segregation based on sex. She argued instead that women should be allowed to compete with their male counterparts on the plane of higher education, rather than be limited to instruction in social niceties, such as etiquette and music, duties of parenthood and child-rearing. Over the course of her career as president of Bryn Mawr College, Thomas also presented her view of the future of women's education and asked women to make a choice to devote their lives to the advancement of human knowledge "to make it possible for the few women of creative and constructive genius born in any generation to join the few men of genius in their generation in the service of their common race." Scholars recognize Thomas's early essay *Education of Women* among her most dynamic statements of these beliefs. During her career she also wrote on other, generally social, topics. Thomas's 1924 essay *How to Get into the League of Nations* demonstrates her support of the League of Nations as a mechanism to ensure international peace.

Critical Reception

That Thomas was an integral part of the women's progressive movement in the early twentieth century is of little doubt to modern critics. Contemporary scholarship, therefore, has typically focused on other issues related to her cultural influence. Of particular interest has been Thomas's passionate devotion to reading. Using the records offered by her journals, critics have interpreted Thomas's youthful pursuit of literature as a means of transcending the limits placed upon her as a woman in Victorian America. Elucidating this process, Helen Lefkowitz Horowitz and Barbara Sicherman have both studied Thomas's capacity to imaginatively "create" herself through reading and related this propensity to significant cultural shifts in America during the late nineteenth and early twentieth centuries.

PRINCIPAL WORKS

Education of Women (essay) 1899
Dr. Thomas on Woman's Ballot (essay) 1907
How to Get into the League of Nations (essay) 1924
The Making of a Feminist: Early Journals and Letters of M. Carey Thomas [edited by M. H. Dobkin] (journals and letters) 1979

CRITICISM

M. Carey Thomas (essay date 1901)

SOURCE: "Education for Women and Men," in *The Educated Woman in America: Selected Writings of Catharine Beecher, Margaret Fuller, and M. Carey Thomas,* edited by Barbara M. Cross, Teachers College Press, 1901, pp. 145-54.

[*In the following essay, originally published in 1901, Thomas presents arguments for equality in the higher education of women and men.*]

A subject like this fairly bristles with possibilities of misunderstanding. To get a firm grip of it we must resolutely turn our minds from all side issues and endeavor to put the question in so precise a form as to make sure that we at least mean the same thing. Stripped of its non-essentials we shall find that the real question at issue has very seldom been seriously argued. Not, of course, because of its unimportance—it is all-important—but because its approaches are set round about with our dearest prejudices, especially if we are men. Logical pitfalls lie on all sides of us; controversies past and present darken the air; our path leads us thru hard-won battlefields. If we are women, our almost irresistible impulse is to slay again the slain; if we are men, the graves of our dead comrades provoke an equally irresistible desire to send a scattering volley into some weak side-encampment of the enemy instead of lining up squarely for the last logical trial of arms. I have contrasted men and women advisedly, because this is one of the very few questions on which most educated men and women are to be found in opposite sides of the camp. If it were possible to discuss it dispassionately, I believe men and women could reach substantial agreement.

I will try, first of all, to state the subject of discussion so that there may be no possibility of our misunderstanding each other in regard to it; next, I will make an attempt to clear the way of prejudices and prejudgments that have really nothing at all to do with the argument; and finally, I will address myself to the argument itself. Higher education means generally any education above the high-school grade; that is, the education given in the technical and professional school as well as in the college.

In regard to technical and professional education there should, it seems to me, be little, if any, serious difference of opinion, and I shall therefore begin with that. We may differ as to whether it is desirable for a college course to precede, and be presupposed in, the course of a technical or professional school, but we cannot think that men students of law or medicine or architecture, for example, should be college-bred, while women students of law, medicine, or architecture should not. Personally I am confident that in ten years' time after graduation, physicians, and lawyers, and architects, whether men or women, whose parents have been able to send them to college, will be found to have outstripped their non-college-bred competitors both in reputation and in income. But, however we decide this matter, it must be decided in the same way for men and women. Sex cannot affect the question of the best preliminary preparation for professional and technical study.

So also with professional and technical courses themselves. Once granted that women are to compete with men for self-support as physicians or lawyers, whether wisely or unwisely does not now concern us, being merely one of the many side issues that have in the past so obscured our judgment of the main argument; indeed, if women are not to compete there will be, of course, no women in medical schools and law schools and no reason for argument at all—the question is simply, what is the best attainable training for the physician or the lawyer, man or woman? There is no reason to believe that typhoid or scarlet fever or phthisis can be successfully treated by a woman physician in one way and by a man physician in another way. There is indeed every reason to believe that unless treated in the best way the patient may die, the sex of the doctor affecting the result less even than the sex of the patient. The question needs only to be put for us to feel irrevocably sure that there is no special woman's way of dealing with disease. And so in law, in architecture, in electricity, in bridge-building, in all mechanic arts and technical sciences, our effort must be for the most scientific instruction, the broadest basis of training that will enable men and women students to attain the highest possible proficiency in their chosen profession. Given two bridge-builders, a man and a woman, given a certain bridge to be built, and given as always the unchangeable laws of mechanics in accordance with which this special bridge and all other bridges must be built, it is simply inconceivable that the preliminary instruction given to the two bridge-builders should differ in quantity, quality, or method of presentation because while the bridge is building one will wear knickerbockers and the other a rainy-day skirt. You may say you do not think that God intended a woman to be a bridge-builder. You have, of course, a right to this prejudice; but as you live in America, and not in the interior of Asia or Africa, you will probably not be able to impose it on women who wish to build bridges. You may say that women's minds are such that they cannot build good bridges. If you are right in this opinion you need concern yourselves no further—bridges built by women will, on the whole, tend to fall down, and the competition of men who can build good bridges will force women out of the profession. Both of these opinions of yours are side issues, and, however they may be decided hereafter, do not in the remotest degree affect the main question of a common curriculum for men and women in technical and professional schools. But you may say that men and women should study bridge-building and medicine and law in separate schools, and not together. You may be foolish enough, and wasteful enough, to think that all the expensive equipment of our technical and professional schools should be duplicated for women, when experience and practice have failed to bring forward a single valid objection to professional coeducation, and when the present trend of public opinion is overwhelmingly against you; and for the sake of argument let us grant that beside every such school for men is to be founded a similar school for women. But this duplication of professional schools for women leaves us just where we were in regard to the curriculum of professional study to be taught in such women's schools. So long as men and women are to compete together, and associate together, in their professional life, women's preparation for the same profession cannot safely differ from men's. If men's preparation is better, women, who are less well prepared, will be left behind in the race; if women's is better, men will suffer in competition with women. What is best in medical training for men will be best in medical training for women; what has bad results in medical training for men will be found to have the same bad results in women's medical training. Whatever we may think of women's right to gain a livelihood in any given occupation, we

must all agree that, if they are to compete successfully with men engaged in this same occupation, they must receive as thoro and prolonged a preparation for it as men. Even if we hold that women's minds differ from men's, this too is a side issue, for we must all recognize that for the purposes of successful competition it is desirable to minimize this difference by giving the *same* and not a different preparation. The greater the natural mental difference between the sexes the greater the need of a men's curriculum for professional women, if they are to hold their own in professional life after leaving the university.

The above argument applies with equal force to the training given by the university graduate school of arts and sciences. Statistics indicate that an overwhelmingly large majority of men and women graduate students are fitting themselves for the profession of higher teaching, that over one-third of all graduate students in the United States are women, and that the annual increase of women graduate students is greater than that of men. In the lower grades of teaching men have almost ceased to compete with women; in the higher grade, that is, in college teaching, women are just beginning to compete with men, and this competition is beset with the bitterest professional jealousy that women have ever had to meet, except perhaps in medicine. There are in the United States only eleven independent colleges for women of at all the same grade as the three hundred and thirty-six coeducational colleges where women and men are taught together, yet only in these separate colleges for women have women an opportunity of competing with men for professors' chairs. It is very rare indeed for coeducational colleges to employ any women instructors, and even then only so many women are as a rule employed as are needed to look after the discipline or home life of the women students. Where women are teaching in coeducational colleges side by side with men their success is regarded by men teachers with profound dislike, and on account of this sex jealousy college presidents and boards of trustees (all of whom are, as a rule, men) cannot, even if they would, materially add to the number of women teachers or advance them. The working of the elective system, however, permits us to see that men students show no such jealousy, but recognize the able teaching of women by overcrowding their classes. Women have succeeded so brilliantly, on the whole so much better than men, as primary and secondary teachers, that they will undoubtedly repeat this success in their college teaching so soon as artifical restrictions are removed. No one could seriously maintain that, handicapped as women now are by prejudice in the highest branches of a profession peculiarly their own, they should be further hampered by a professional training different from men's. Indeed, one-half of the pupils to be taught by them in schools and in colleges, if they succeed in gaining admission on an equal footing into college faculties, are boys or men who should, according to this theory, receive a training different from that of their teachers. And, further, unless we could prove that in future all women students will be taught in separate women's colleges in a different way from men students and only by differently trained women professors, we should deprive women professors who were trained differently from men in the graduate school of the power to compete successfully with men, even for chairs in women's colleges. As in medicine, law, and bridge-building, so in arts and sciences the professional work of the graduate school must from the very nature of the case be the same for men and women. Science and literature and philology are what they are and inalterable, and the objects of competition are one and the same for both men and women—instructorships and professors' chairs, scholarly fame, and power to advance, however little, the outposts of knowledge.

We have, I think, then reached substantial agreement as to the subdivision of higher education that concerns itself with professional and technical training. We are prepared to admit that when women are to compete with men in the practice of the same trade or profession, there should be as little difference as possible in their preliminary education. Further than this, I think most of us will agree that coeducation in professional and technical schools is the only economical and feasible method of educating women.

But this line of reasoning will be incomplete unless we ask ourselves whether there are not some subjects peculiar to women in which we must maintain special women's technical schools. There are certainly three professional schools where women students already largely outnumber men: normal schools, including normal departments of universities, schools of nursing, and schools for library study. If cooking and domestic service ever become lucrative professions, and more especially if men of wealth ever come to choose their wives for culinary and sanitary lore instead as at present for social and intellectual charm, such schools will tend to spring up and, like normal schools, will undoubtedly be attended almost exclusively by women. They will beyond question be taught exactly in the same way·as if they were to be attended exclusively by men. The method of teaching cooking is one and the same and does not depend on the sex of the cooks. In this sense even the higher education of women in cooking will not differ from that of men. There are, however, not enough elements of intellectual growth in cooking or housekeeping to furnish a very serious or profound course of training for really intelligent women. Likewise I do not think highly of the acumen of those people who predict the coming of schools of professional training for wifehood or motherhood. What requires the harmonious balance of all our human faculties can scarcely be taught in a professional school, nor is the intellectual side sufficiently prominent to be made the subject of prolonged training.

The burden of proof is with those who believe that the college education of men and women should differ. For thirty years it has been as nearly as possible the same, with brilliantly satisfactory results, so far as concerns women. College women have married as generally as their non-college-bred sisters, and have as a rule married better than their sisters, because they have chosen a larger proportion of professional men; they have not died in childbirth, as was predicted; they have borne their proper proportion of children, and have brought up more than the usual proportion of those born; they have made efficient housekeepers and wives as well as mothers; their success as teachers has been so astonishingly great that already they are driving non-college-bred women teachers out of the field. There is, in short, not a word to be said against the success and efficiency and healthfulness of these women educated by men's curriculum.

Indeed, except practice on the piano and violin and banjo and other musical instruments, which we might have believed that women would wish in a college course, (altho most happily they do not), let us ask ourselves what other subjects peculiar to women could be introduced in a college curriculum? I have never heard more than three suggested: infant psychology, to which there is no special objection as an elective in a college curriculum (I believe, however, that as many men as women will be foolish enough—I am expressing my own point of view—to elect it, and, after all, as many college men will become fathers as college women will become mothers); chemistry with special reference to cooking, and food values and domestic science generally, which is already introduced in some coeducational colleges and will never, in my opinion, be largely elected because it lacks the wider outlook of the more general sciences and belongs rather in the technical school; and physiology with special reference to motherhood and wifehood, which is never likely to be elected voluntarily by women college students who do not know whether they will marry; nor is it, in my opinion, desirable that it should be elected. It would certainly lead to much unhappiness in married life if such courses were elected by women and not by the men they marry also. These subjects, even if we grant (which I do not) that they are especially desirable for women to study in college, would not constitute a woman's curriculum. They would simply form three electives out of many to be introduced as occasion serves into such colleges as are open to women.

Undoubtedly the life of most women after leaving college will differ from that of men. About one-half will marry in a rather deliberate fashion, choosing carefully, and on the whole living very happily a life of comparative leisure, not of self-support; about one-third will become professional teachers, probably for life; and the greater part of the remainder will lead useful and helpful lives as unmarried women of leisure. And just because after leaving college only one-third, and that in the peculiarly limited profession of teaching, are to get the wider training of affairs that educates men engaged in business and in the professions all their lives thru, women while in college ought to have the broadest possible education. This college education should be the same as men's, not only because there is, I believe, but one best education, but because men and women are to live and work together as comrades and dear friends and married friends and lovers, and because their effectiveness and happiness and the welfare of the generation to come after them will be vastly increased if their college education has given them the same intellectual training and the same scholarly and moral ideals.

M. Carey Thomas (essay date 1908)

SOURCE: "Motives and Future of the Educated Woman," in *The Educated Woman in America: Selected Writings of Catharine Beecher, Margaret Fuller, and M. Carey Thomas,* edited by Barbara M. Cross, Teachers College Press, 1965. pp. 158-69.

[*In the following essay, originally published in 1908, Thomas observes the state of women's education at the time and makes recommendations for its future.*]

The passionate desire of women of my generation for higher education was accompanied thruout its course by the awful doubt, felt by women themselves as well as by men, as to whether women as a sex were physically and mentally fit for it. I think I can best make this clear to you if I refer briefly to my own experience. I cannot remember the time when I was not sure that studying and going to college were the things above all others which I wished to do. I was always wondering whether it could be really true, as every one thought, that boys were cleverer than girls. Indeed, I cared so much that I never dared to ask any grown-up person the direct question, not even my father or mother, because I feared to hear the reply. I remember often praying about it, and begging God that if it were true that because I was a girl I could not successfully master Greek and go to college and understand things to kill me at once, as I could not bear to live in such an unjust world. When I was a little older I read the Bible entirely thru with passionate eagerness because I had heard it said that it proved that women were inferior to men. Those were not the days of the higher criticism. I can remember weeping over the account of Adam and Eve because it seemed to me that the curse pronounced on Eve might imperil girls' going to college; and to this day I can never read many parts of the Pauline epistles without feeling again the sinking of the heart with which I used to hurry over the verses referring to women's keeping silence in the churches and asking their husbands at home. I searched not only the Bible, but all other books I could get for light on the woman question. I read Milton with rage and indignation. Even as a child I knew him for the woman hater he was. The splendor of Shakspere was obscured to me then by the lack of intellectual power in his greatest women characters. Even now it seems to me that only Isabella in *Measure for Measure* thinks greatly, and weighs her actions greatly, like a Hamlet or a Brutus.

I can well remember one endless scorching summer's day when sitting in a hammock under the trees with a French dictionary, blinded by tears more burning than the July sun, I translated the most indecent book I have ever read, Michelet's famous—were it not now forgotten, I should be able to say infamous—book on woman, *La femme.* I was beside myself with terror lest it might prove true that I myself was so vile and pathological a thing. Between that summer's day in 1874 and a certain day in the autumn in 1904, thirty years had elapsed. Altho during these thirty years I had read in every language every book on women that I could obtain, I had never chanced again upon a book that seemed to me so to degrade me in my womanhood as the seventh and seventeenth chapters on women and women's education, of President Stanley Hall's *Adolescence.* Michelet's sickening sentimentality and horrible over-sexuality seemed to me to breathe again from every pseudoscientific page. But how vast the difference between then and now in my feelings, and in the feelings of every woman who has had to do with the education of girls! Then I was terror-struck lest I, and every other woman with me, were doomed to live as pathological invalids in a universe merciless to women as a sex. Now we know that it is not we, but the man who believes such things about us, who is himself pathological, blinded by neurotic mists of sex, unable to see that women form one-half of the kindly race of normal, healthy human creatures in the world; that women, like men, are quickened and inspired by the same study of the great traditions of their race, by the same love of learning, the same love of science, the same love of abstract truth; that women, like men, are immeasurably benefited, physically, mentally and morally, and are made vastly better mothers, as men are made vastly better fathers, by subordinating the distracting instincts of sex to the simple human fellowship of similar education and similar intellectual and social ideals.

It was not to be wondered at that we were uncertain in those old days as to the ultimate result of women's education. Before I myself went to college I had never seen but one college woman. I had heard that such a woman was staying at the house of an acquaintance. I went to see her with fear. Even if she had appeared in hoofs and horns I was determined to go to college all the same. But it was a relief to find this Vassar graduate tall and handsome and dressed like other women. When, five years later, I went to Leipzig to study after I had been graduated from Cornell, my mother used to write me that my name was never mentioned to her by the women of her acquaintance. I was thought by them to be as much of a disgrace to my family as if I had eloped with the coachman. Now, women who have been to college are as plentiful as blackberries on summer hedges. Even my native city of Baltimore is full of them, and women who have in addition studied in Germany are regarded with becoming deference by the very Baltimore women who disapproved of me.

During the quarter of the century of the existence of the Association of Collegiate Alumnae two generations of college women have reached mature life, and the older generation is now just passing off the stage. We are therefore better prepared than ever before to give an account of what has been definitely accomplished, and to predict what will be the tendencies of women's college and university education in the future.

The curriculum of our women's colleges has steadily stiffened. Women, both in separate, and in coeducational colleges, seem to prefer the old-fashioned, so-called disciplinary studies. They disregard the so-called accomplishments. I believe that to-day more women than men are receiving a thoro college education, even altho in most cases they are receiving it sitting side by side with men in the same college lecture rooms.

The old type of untrained woman teacher has practically disappeared from women's colleges. Her place is being taken by ardent young women scholars who have qualified themselves by long years of graduate study for advanced teaching. Even the old-fashioned untrained matron, or house-mother, is swiftly being replaced in girls' schools, as well as in women's colleges, by the college-bred warden or director.

We did not know when we began whether women's health could stand the strain of college education. We were haunted in those early days by the clanging chains of that gloomy little specter, Dr. Edward H. Clarke's *Sex in Education.* With trepidation of spirit I made my mother read it, and was much cheered by her remark that, as neither she, nor any of the women she knew, had ever seen girls or women of the kind described in Dr. Clarke's book, we might as well act as if they did not exist. Still, we did not *know* whether colleges might not produce a crop of just such invalids. Doctors insisted that they would. We women could not be sure until we had tried the experiment. Now we have tried it, and tried it for more than a generation, and we know that college women are not only not invalids, but that they are better physically than other women in their own class of life. We know that girls are growing stronger and more athletic. Girls enter college each year in better physical condition. For the past four years I have myself questioned closely all our entering classes, and often their mothers as well. I find that an average of sixty percent enter college absolutely and in every respect well, and that less than thirty percent make, or need to make, any periodic difference whatever in exercise, or study, from year's end to year's end. This result is very different from that obtained by physicians and others writing in recent magazines and medical journals. These alarmists give grewsome statistics from high schools and women's colleges, which they are very careful not to name. Probably they are investigating girls whose general hygienic conditions are bad. The brothers of such girls would undoubtedly make as poor a showing physically when compared to Harvard and Yale men, or the boys of Groton or St. Paul's, as their sisters make when compared to Bryn Mawr students. Certainly their sisters who have not been to high school or college would in all probability be even more invalided and abnormal. Seventy percent of the Bryn Mawr students come from private schools and from homes where the nutrition and sanitary conditions are excellent. They have undoubtedly been subjected up to the age of nearly nineteen to strenuous and prolonged college preparation, yet their physical condition is far above that of the girls of these other investigations. One

investigation yields the shocking result that sixty-six percent of college freshmen are practically invalids during certain times in each month, and another that seventy-three percent of high school girls are in similar condition. If such results are to be credited, the explanation must be found, as I have said, in the general mal-nutrition and unsanitary life of such girls. Here, as so often when women are investigated, causes which would produce ill-health in boys are not excluded. Surely the Bryn Mawr students approach much more nearly to the normal type. Those other girls are horribly abnormal.

We are now living in the midst of great and, I believe on the whole beneficent, social changes which are preparing the way for the coming economic independence of women. Like the closely allied diminishing birth rate, but unlike the higher education of women, this great change in opinion and practise seems to have come about almost without our knowledge, certainly without our conscious coöperation. The passionate desire of the women of my generation for a college education seems, as we study it now in the light of coming events, to have been a part of this greater movement.

In order to prepare for this economic independence, we should expect to see what is now taking place. Colleges for women and college departments of coeducational universities are attended by ever-increasing numbers of women students. In seven of the largest western universities women already outnumber men in the college departments.

A liberal college course prepares women for their great profession of teaching. College women have proved to be such admirably efficient teachers that they are driving other women out of the field. Until other means of self-support are as easy for women as teaching, more and more women who intend to teach will go to college. Such women will elect first of all the subjects taught by women in the high schools, such as Latin, history, and the languages. They will avoid chemistry, physics, and other sciences which are usually taught by men. Until all women become self-supporting, more women than men will go to college for culture, especially in the west, and such women will tend to elect the great disciplinary studies which men neglect because they are intrinsically more difficult and seem at first sight less practical. For these obvious reasons certain college courses are therefore already crowded by women and almost deserted by men in many of the coeducational universities.

And just because women have shown such an aptitude for a true college education and such delight in it, we must be careful to maintain it for them in its integrity. We must see to it that its disciplinary quality is not lowered by the insertion of so-called practical courses which are falsely supposed to prepare for life. Women are rapidly coming to control women's college education. It rests with us to decide whether we shall barter for a mess of pottage the inheritance of the girls of this generation which the girls of my generation agonized to obtain for themselves and for other girls.

We know now that college women marry in about the same proportion, and have about the same number of children as their sisters and cousins who have not been to college. We know also that no one nowadays has more than about two children per marriage—neither college men, nor college women, nor the brothers or sisters of college men and women who have not been to college, nor native white American families, nor American immigrant families in the second generation. This great diminution in the birth rate has taken place notably in the United States, France, Great Britain, and Australia, and is manifesting itself in lesser, but ever increasing degrees, in all other civilized countries. In bringing about this great social change college women have borne no appreciable part. Indeed, only one-half a college woman in every 1000 women is married, the ratio of college women to other women being as 1 to 1000. Although this diminishing birth rate is wholly independent of women's college education, it can not fail to effect it greatly. If it is true, as it seems to be, that college women who marry will have on an average only two children apiece, they could not, if they wished, spend all their time in caring for these two rapidly growing up children, who, moreover, after ten years will be at school, unless they perform also the actual manual labor of their households. In such cases women will presumably prefer to do other work in order to be able to pay wages to have this manual labor done for them. No college-bred man would be willing day after day to shovel coal in his cellar, or to curry and harness his horses, if by more intellectual and interesting labor he could earn enough to pay to have it done for him. Nor will college women be willing to do household drudgery if it can be avoided. Such married women must, therefore, also be prepared for self-support. Likewise the increasingly small proportion of the married fifty percent who will marry men able to support them and their two children in comfort will not wish to be idle. They too must be prepared for some form of public service. Of course, the fifty percent of college women who do not marry, that is, all except the very few who will inherit fortunes large enough to live on thruout life, must be prepared for self-support.

It seems, therefore, self-evident that practically all women, like practically all men, must look forward after leaving college to some form of public service, whether paid, as it will be for the great majority of both men and women, or unpaid, does not matter. Why should not women, like liberally educated men, fit themselves after college for their special work? When their life-work is more or less determined, let those women who expect to marry and keep their own houses (after all, the women householders will be only about half even of those who marry, say twenty-five percent of all college women) study domestic and sanitary science. But it is as unreasonable to compel all women to study it irrespective of their future work as it would be to compel all men to study dentistry or medicine. It is the same with child-study and all other specialized studies. They belong, one and all, in the graduate professional school.

I believe also that every women's college ought to maintain not only a graduate school of philosophy of the highest grade, but also for holders of the bachelor's degree only a purely graduate school of education connected with a small practise school like the famous practise school of the University of Jena. Only so can we make true and inspired teachers of this vast throng of women going out of our women's colleges into the schoolrooms of the country. The fate of the next generation of children is in their eager hands. It is our mission to see to it that they are as enlightened and as truly wise as they are eager. I know of no way except by teaching them in our graduate schools to reverence abstract truth.

But there is still another and, as it seems to me, more cogent reason for our women's colleges maintaining graduate schools of philosophy. The highest service which colleges can render to their time is to discover and foster imaginative and constructive genius. Such genius unquestionably needs opportunity for its highest development. This is peculiarly the case with women students. As I watch their gallant struggles I sometimes think that the very stars in their courses are conspiring against them. Women scholars can assist women students, as men can not, to tide over the first discouragements of a life of intellectual renunciation. Ability of the kind I am speaking of is, of course, very rare, but for this reason it is precious beyond all other human products. If the graduate schools of women's colleges could develop one single woman of Galton's "X" type—say a Madame Curié, or a Madame Kovalewsky born under a happier star—they would have done more for human advancement than if they had turned out thousands of ordinary college graduates.

The time has now come for those of us who are in control of women's education to bend ourselves to the task of creating academic conditions favorable for the development of this kind of creative ability. We should at once begin to found research chairs for women at all our women's colleges, with three or four hours a week research teaching and the rest of the time free for independent investigation. We should reserve all the traveling fellowships in our gift for women who have given evidence, however slight, of power to do research work. We should bring pressure on our state universities to give such women opportunities to compete for professors' chairs. In the four woman suffrage states this can be accomplished in the twinkling of an eye: it will only be necessary for women's organizations to vote for university regents with proper opinions. The Johns Hopkins University situated in conservative Baltimore has two women on its academic staff who are lecturing to men. Why can not all chairs in the arts departments of universities, that is, in the college and school of philosophy, be thrown open to the competition of women? This is the next advance to be made in women's education—the last and greatest battle to be won.

Only women know how true it is that in the development of the highest scientific and scholarly qualifications women have today far less favorable conditions than even men in Mississippi.

Mr. Havelock Ellis found that in Great Britain women of genius formed only one-twentieth of the whole number. Professor Odin found that in France women of talent were in precisely the same proportion, only one-twentieth of the whole number, but that women furnished 29 percent of eminent actors, and 20 percent of all prose writers of distinction. In Great Britain likewise 53 percent of all women of genius were authors, and 30 percent actors. The explanation is clear. Women of genius and talent had more opportunity to come to the surface in these two professions. In all probability the same proportion of women of genius and talent were born with aptitude for scientific research, but were crushed by their unfavorable environment.

It seems to me then to rest with us, the college women of this generation, to see to it that the girls of the next generation are given favorable conditions for this higher kind of scholarly development. To advance the bounds of human knowledge, however little, is to exercise our highest human faculty. There is no more altruistic satisfaction, no purer delight. I am convinced that we can do no more useful work than this—to make it possible for the few women of creative and constructive genius born in any generation to join the few men of genius in their generation in the service of their common race.

Roberta Frankfort (essay date 1977)

SOURCE: "Martha Carey Thomas: The Scholarly Ideal and Bryn Mawr Woman," in *Collegiate Women: Domesticity and Career in Turn-of-the-Century America,* New York University Press, 1977, pp. 26-40.

[*In the following essay, Frankfort describes the evolution of Thomas's vision of the educated woman.*]

When in 1899 Martha Carey Thomas, the young and spirited president of Bryn Mawr College, accused the venerated president of Harvard University, Charles Eliot, of having "sun spots" on his brain, the account was carried in newspapers across the country. Her presumption was a rarity among even educated women whose preoccupation with conflicts between womanliness and intellect often necessitated withdrawal from issues that would bring the ambiguity to the surface. But Martha Carey Thomas took a firm stand in favor of the intellect, and her fierce rhetoric attests to her willingness—even eagerness—to confront those who argued that the feminine nature stood in opposition to rigorous intellectual training.

In pitting herself against Charles Eliot, Thomas confronted the anti-feminist argument in highly articulate, well-reasoned form. In his early speeches and writings, Eliot had claimed that women had neither the intelligence nor the need to study the great traditions of learning in-

herited from the past. Although he eventually changed his mind about women's innate abilities, he never wavered from the conviction that different groups served separate and distinct functions and should be educated accordingly. He was "vividly aware of the importance Darwinism attached to individual variation,"[1] and believed that the natural and fitting duties of groups would complement each other. Eliot claimed that the value of an occupation was to be judged by its product, and that the result of these normal or natural duties would contribute to the progress of the human race—progress toward public justice and happiness, the chief ends of mankind.[2]

The natural duties of women consisted, according to Eliot, in making family life more productive; the products of a serviceable woman's care—dutiful, thoughtful, loving children—would confirm the great importance of her natural occupation for the progress of humanity. Eliot wrote that "the prime motive of the higher education of women should be recognized as the development in women of the capacities and powers which will fit them to make family life and social life more intelligent, more enjoyable, happier, and more productive—more productive in every sense, physically, mentally, and spiritually."[3]

It was inevitable, perhaps, said Eliot, that ambitious women leaders should have tried to direct the higher education of women toward bringing them into new occupations, particularly into the professions as men have made them. "But wiser ways and methods will come into play, because it is not the chief happiness or the chief end of women, as a whole, to enter these new occupations, or to pursue them through life. They enter many which they soon abandon, and that is well—particularly the abandonment!"[4] Certainly, Eliot considered Thomas to be one of those ambitious leaders who, in her desire to bring women into new professions, was undermining public justice and happiness.

Carey Thomas never answered Eliot's contentions in a systematic, logical fashion. Rather, her rhetoric was often rambling and too "energetically unreflective"[5] to be always consistent and concise. In her zeal to provide educated women with sufficient armor to combat stultifying domestic lives, she spoke with forceful metaphors. Her responses to Eliot were not meted out on a philosophical plane; rather, she attacked and confronted on a very personal level while picking out those points that she could, with her dramatic images, attempt to reduce to absurdity. Thus, after Eliot had given a speech welcoming a new president of Wellesley College in which he said that liberal arts curricula of women's colleges were too imitative of those of men's colleges, President Thomas used her opening address at Bryn Mawr College in 1899 to reply:

> As progressive as one may be in education or in other things there may be in our minds some dark spot of mediaevalism, and clearly in President Eliot's otherwise luminous intelligence women's education is this dark spot. He might as well have told the president of Wellesley to invent a new Christian religion for Wellesley or new symphonies

and operas, a new Beethoven and Wagner, new statues and pictures, a new Phidias and a new Titian, new tennis, new golf, a new way to swim, skate and run, new food, and new drink. It would be easier to do all this than to create for women a new science of geography, a new Greek Tragedies, new chemistry, new philosophies, in short a new intellectual heavens and earth.[6]

Eliot's opinions on women were derived from a view of the world that disavowed uniformity of group functions. Carey Thomas, however, did not operate from a comprehensive image of the world. Her arena was much less encompassing, and it consisted primarily of well-educated men and women. But for her, these groups were not to function as static units performing complementary, unchanging functions whose value would be judged by their products. Instead of complementary functions she envisioned the struggle for superiority. The process of this competition and not the product of "natural" occupations was, for Thomas, the basic component of progress. If Eliot employed Darwinian theory to justify the status quo for women, Carey Thomas used his notion of competition and struggle to urge women out of the home and into the "battlefield": "in the higher grade, that is in college teaching, women are just beginning to compete with men, and this competition is beset with the bitterest professional jealousy that women have ever had to meet, except perhaps in medicine. . . . Women have succeeded so brilliantly, on the whole so much better than men, as primary and secondary teachers, that they will undoubtedly repeat this success in their college teaching as soon as artificial restrictions are removed."[7]

It is clear that Martha Carey Thomas did not, at least early in her life, make concessions to domesticity as Alice Palmer and Elizabeth Peabody did. Her disagreements with Eliot were indicative of her rejection of the woman's role as submissive and passive even if her servility would be extended to those who needed her outside of the home. Thomas wished to prove women's equal—if not superior—abilities, and, in order to do this, men and women had to compete in the same arenas. It was in the area of academics and research that Carey Thomas believed women would best be able to demonstrate their strength.

Her choice of scholarship as a proving ground for women—with its concomitant elements of graduate work and university teaching[8]—stemmed, in part, from what she referred to as a natural disposition that had its origins in her childhood. She spoke of her younger years as preparation for these "higher pursuits" in the same passionate, effusive language with which she chided her critics; the almost unidimensional way in which she pictured her early life as paving the way for her later interests is evidence that image making was very important to her. It is clearly true, though, that she had a rebellious nature and that she was resentful of limitations placed upon her because of her sex and beliefs about women's intellectual inferiority. She wrote of begging God to kill her if it were indeed true that she could never master Greek and go to college. She claimed to have wept over the account of Adam and Eve, fearing that Eve's curse might imperil girls' attending college. She wrote:

> I can well remember one endless scorching summer's day when sitting in a hammock under the trees with a French dictionary, blinded by tears more burning than the July sun, I translated the most indecent book I have ever read, Michelet's famous—were it not now forgotten, I should say infamous—book on women, *La femme*. I was beside myself with terror lest it might prove true that I myself was so vile and pathological a thing.[9]

Despite the difficulty in sorting exaggerations from reality in Thomas's writing, it is evident that she did attach a special significance to scholarly pursuits early in her life. She seemed to see scholarship as serious and significant enough to be an antidote to women's frivolity, which she claimed to witness in her own family. Thomas's parents were prominent Quakers who consistently indulged Martha, their oldest child, born in 1857. She had always been "bent on pre-eminence, and she resented the privileges granted her four younger brothers, her father, and the masculine sex in general."[10] Yet her father was a doctor and a scholar, and it was his life rather than that of her mother that she sought to emulate. Her mother's preoccupations with upper-class parties and philanthropies bored and even appalled her: "I ain't going to get married and I don't want to teach school. I can't imagine anything worse than living a regular young lady's life. . . . I don't care if everybody would cut me."[11] Martha Carey Thomas pictured her mother's life as wasteful, and she saw no way of coming to terms with "the frivolities of a society girl and the servitude of the matron"[12] except by rejecting the whole way of life.

The choice of academia as the vehicle for escape was not unprecedented for women who had never achieved prominence in other fields reserved for men such as law, medicine, or finance. There were notable women intellects both in Europe and America whose notoriety was perhaps more visible to the surrounding societies than their intellectual achievements. The mocking eighteenth-century term "bluestocking," used to describe educated or literary women, testifies to their presence. Margaret Fuller, who a generation before had proclaimed her faith in the freed intelligence, was certainly a precursor. Yet the differences in the way Fuller and Thomas viewed the intellect are significant. Fuller had in the 1830s and 1840s proclaimed her faith in the emancipated intellect, not only as an end in itself but as a way of releasing women from domestic servitude. Her image was of mindless, bored matrons becoming attuned to their inner energies which longed to be released. Fuller's means of release was a process which, although containing similar elements for all women, was a highly individualized one. Self-education was the key, for she saw the traditional classical education as sterile and monotonous with its emphasis upon rote and rhetoric. It was this process—rather than any emerging society that might result from it—that was essential to Fuller. Fifty years later, Carey

Thomas also saw the intellect as providing liberation for women. But the process—as well as the end result—was to be highly controlled. Higher education provided a vehicle for this discipline; institutional settings would tame the intellect. The "liberation" itself was restricted, for Thomas chose the particular areas that she wanted women to pursue. And, indeed, it was not individual liberation that mattered as much as the advancement of women in general and their ability to compete with men. Thomas insisted upon women's achievement, but she did not, as did Fuller, insist upon the companion ideas of initiative and individuality. Her agenda was not for the individual but for the group—and she believed that the female college would help her to carry through that agenda.

Thomas herself attended educational institutions. A college education was available in 1874, and Carey Thomas, unlike other upper-class girls, chose to go to college rather than to spend several years abroad acquiring a taste for Old World culture. Despite her family's interest in education, they resisted her attempts to attend college, for it was not considered the role of a socially prominent young lady to go to college. A college education was more suitable to daughters of upper-middle-class and middle-class families who could afford the tuition and who were not obeisant to high society's image of the woman who was cultivated yet decidedly not a bookworm.[13] Thomas was warned that a college education might scare away prospective husbands. "According to her cousin Logan Pearsall Smith, the Baltimore clan found her desire for a college education as shocking a choice as a life of prostitution."[14] However, she did go to Cornell in 1874.

She chose Cornell primarily for the same reason that Alice Freeman Palmer chose the University of Michigan: women's colleges were not yet academically respected and thus did not offer an alternative to established coeducational institutions. Thomas spurned Vassar as "an advanced female seminary."[15] Before going to Cornell, Thomas had herself attended a female seminary—the Howland Institute, a school near Ithaca, New York. It was founded and run by the Howland family who were Quakers and knew the Thomases. Thus, Carey Thomas's attendance at Cornell—a short distance from Howland and founded also by a Quaker, Ezra Cornell—was not surprising. Certainly, the interconnection of family and religious ties was comforting to families who were sending their daughters away to school.

At Cornell Thomas was disappointed by the "frivolity of the women students."[16] She must also have been disappointed by—or certainly keenly aware of—the Cornell tradition of "anticoedism." Her later associations with Cornell as a trustee and an eminent alumna made her an apologist for Cornell, and she did not dwell upon undergraduate experiences that might have been disturbing. Andrew D. White, president of the university from 1866 to 1885, favored coeducation, and in a defense of girls' attendance he wrote:

Strong men, in adversity and perplexity, have often found that the "partners of their joys and sorrows" give no more real strength than would Nuremberg dolls. Under this theory, as thus worked out, the aid and counsel and solace fail just when they are most needed. In their stead the man is likely to find some scraps of philosophy begun in boarding-schools and developed in kitchens and drawing rooms.[17]

White's attitude toward women's learning was more enlightened than that of his fellow president, Charles Eliot, who had not yet even accepted any need for female higher education. Yet White's defense was less than radical: he would have women become intelligent and cultivated marriage partners, able to offer their husbands astute advice instead of "fetishisms and superstitions." Many of Cornell's students, though, plainly resented the presence of women. Whether from their feeling that women deflected any pretense of Ivy League status or from a general acceptance of a common belief that college was no place for women, the "cold-shouldering of the females by the males existed from the first" and continued at least until the First World War.[18] This reaction must surely have strengthened rather than diminished Thomas's competitiveness; it most likely, too, encouraged her belief that coeducation was a phenomenon that might only flourish in the future. Given the attitudes of resistance on the part of academic men, Thomas, even more directly than Palmer, saw the female college as a place where women's convictions and intellect might be strengthened without the interference of hostile forces.

But Thomas did not loiter at Cornell for "reconsiderations." With a fixity of purpose that left family and friends in awe of her, she left for the University of Leipzig to confront the rigors of a German university. She found the culture of Europe exhilarating, labored at philology, and dismissed the male students as dull.[19] But since Leipzig did not give the doctorate to women, Carey Thomas left for Zurich, and received the degree *summa cum laude* for her dissertation entitled "Sir Gawayne and the Green Knight." Interestingly, she found the study grueling and seemed to think of the many hours of research as boring and tedious. It becomes even more apparent from this personal experience that her interest was not in the scholarship itself but in the products or rewards of that scholarship, which would prove her triumph as a woman. When she talked to others about the joys of renouncing other preoccupations for the intellectual life— or, as she called it, "intellectual renunciation"—her words seem hollow, for it was the dignity of women and not the rigor of research that she was promoting.

Once at Bryn Mawr she hoped to prevent frivolity as she sought to fashion and perfect "the type of Bryn Mawr woman which will, we hope, become as well known and universally admired a type as the Oxford and Cambridge man or the graduate of the great English public schools."[20] Such a woman, she hoped, would be equipped to take up the gauntlet and enter a "gallant struggle" where "pitfalls lie on all sides of us; controversies past and present darken the air: our path leads us thru hard-won battlefields."[21] She would also be capable of enduring a life of intellectual renunciation. Her priorities were staunch:

> The highest service which colleges can render to their time is to discover and foster imaginative and constructive genius. Such genius unquestionably needs opportunity for its highest development.... Ability of the kind I am speaking of is, of course, very rare, but for this reason it is precious beyond all other human products.... It seems to me then to rest with us, the college women of this generation, to see to it that the girls of the next generation are given favorable conditions for this higher kind of scholarly development.[22]

During her first several decades at Bryn Mawr, Carey Thomas was intent on producing this mission-oriented woman whose sense of purpose would be strong enough to subdue feelings of loneliness and occasional discouragement. Knowing that other women were pursuing a scholarly life might also be of great comfort. "Sex solidarity," according to Thomas, was becoming a very compelling force in the world. She wrote: "As I watch their gallant struggles I sometimes think that the very stars in their courses are conspiring against them. Women scholars can assist women students, as men can not, to tide over the first discouragements of a life of intellectual renunciation."[23]

Ideas of competition between the sexes, lives of intellectual renunciation, and sex solidarity were, of course, inconsistent with the acceptance of marriage as an alternative—particularly for Carey Thomas's idealized scholars. In a widely quoted passage she strongly affirmed her belief that ambitious careers and marriage were diametrical opposites: "Women scholars have another and still more cruel handicap. They have spent half a lifetime in fitting themselves for their chosen work and then may be asked to choose between it and marriage. No one can estimate the number of women who remain unmarried in revolt before such a horrible alternative."[24] Carey Thomas herself, of course, remained unmarried. Her emphasis on sex solidarity coupled with occasional statements predicting women's natural but as yet unblossomed superiority—particularly in the areas of academics and college teaching—reveal a definite elitism and separatism in her thinking. She was an isolationist with respect to men, living most of her adult life with close women friends[25] surrounded by a college filled with women students.

She did realize, however, that not all women graduates—not even all of those from Bryn Mawr—would become Madame Curies or even outstanding scholars. She recognized and seemed to accept the inevitable fact that some women college graduates "will marry in a rather deliberate fashion."[26] She even publicly subscribed to the rather popular defense of women's higher education which rested on the premise that a college education increased the probability that both men and women would "live and work together as comrades and dear friends and married

friends and lovers."[27] But she added a less popular qualifier: "their effectiveness and happiness and the welfare of the generation to come after them will be vastly increased if their college education has given them the same intellectual training and the same scholarly and moral ideas."[28] It was crucial, according to Thomas, that this education be the same for both sexes. She told those men who claimed that a woman's college education should make provisions for the wifely and motherly roles to "begin by educating their own college men to be husbands."[29]

Her abrupt retorts left no doubt that, despite statements sentimentalizing the love and respect between college men and women, the separatist strain in her thinking as well as her basic distrust of men's motives ran deep. She believed that an isolated women's institution would best be able to mold the woman whose mind would not be tainted by thoughts of sex, marriage, and children—all of which interfered with women's achievements: "It is undesirable to have the problems of love and marriage presented for decision to a young girl during the four years when she ought to devote her energies to profiting by the only systematic intellectual training she is likely to receive during her life."[30] She occasionally, however, deferred to the benefits of a coeducational institution, for at least, she said, it assured women of equal educational opportunity which some of the more compromising institutions for women did not supply. Also, coeducation might provide the ambitious woman with "the priceless associations of college life."[31]

But regardless of whether a woman attended a coeducational institution or whether she was predisposed to marriage, Carey Thomas was adamant in her insistence that all women should prepare for self-support. She loathed images of complacent, submissive wives and mothers and felt that college women who married would presumably prefer to do other work in order to be able to pay wages to have what she considered household drudgery done for them. And, characteristically employing the same standards for men as for women, she wrote: "No college-bred man would be willing day after day to shovel coal in his cellar, or to curry and harness his horses, if by more intellectual and interesting labor he could earn enough to pay to have it done for him."[32] One Bryn Mawr woman, having repeatedly been warned by President Thomas against the greatest evil—complacent wifehood—wrote in a book of reminiscences published by her class that "just to prove that though married, I am not a useless frivolous creature—I am Reader in German at the Central High School." Another graduate wrote: "Next year I will be one more added to Miss Thomas' notable list of those married *and* employed."[33]

But most notable to Thomas were her beloved scholars to whom she did not even sanction the option of marriage. At Bryn Mawr commencements she reserved her highest praise for those women who planned to continue their studies in graduate schools. She particularly lauded those who would travel abroad, sacrificing all personal pleasures that might await them in America for a chance to study with a revered professor in a well-known European university. Her speeches to Bryn Mawr students reiterated again and again the altruistic satisfactions they would receive in sacrificing their lives to advancing "the bounds of human knowledge," not to mention the bounds of women's achievements. Her writings and talks stressing equality and congeniality between the sexes that would be spurred by women's higher education were saved mainly for the world outside Bryn Mawr College, for she had wished to encourage as many of her students as possible to lead lives of "intellectual renunciation" and "sex solidarity."

Thomas's belief that Bryn Mawr College would remain an isolated training ground for a new breed of woman reveals her faith in the power of the collegiate experience to mold lifetime careers and ambitions. She saw herself as capable of producing a new female specialty which would have the strength to compete successfully with men in a controlled arena. Yet, in trying to carve a sphere for women's excellence, she ignored—and would have her students ignore—the larger social context that was the source of the inequality. The limitations both of collegiate instruction and the insularity Thomas insisted upon would inevitably become clear to her. She could never make a connection with the outside world without some conflict and dissonance resulting; she could not expect her students to maintain her posture. Inevitably, Thomas's orthodoxy deteriorated, largely under the pressure of outside opinion which insisted upon female specialites that were in tune with domesticity. It would take more than one institution standing alone to make such alternative actions possible.

By about 1910 her rhetoric began to change, and she was telling her students that it might indeed be possible for women to successfully combine marriage and an academic career: "The next advance in women's education is then to throw open to the competition of women scholars the rewards and prizes of a scholar's life and to allow women professors like men professors to marry, or not, as they see fit."[34] "Allowing" her venerated women scholars to marry and "join the few men of genius in their generation in the service of their common race"[35] was, for Thomas, a major revision in her professed beliefs.

But of even more significance was her increasing deemphasis on the scholar as the most "precious beyond all other human products."[36] In more and more speeches after 1910 she spoke nostalgically of intellectual preoccupations as if they were remnants of another generation—a generation that she felt part of. She reminisced about long afternoons and evenings that students would devote to "voracious and limitless reading of poetry and unending discussions of abstract questions among themselves."[37] The poets and popular novelists in her day—Wordsworth, Shelley, Keats, Browning, George Eliot, and Balzac—seemed unacceptable to a generation who admired Kipling and Tolstoi. She wrote: "The students of today are interested in what they believe to be very mod-

ern and practical studies, apparently without regard to the relative teaching ability of the professors. Students often say to me that they wish to study these subjects because, as they say, they will help them to deal with life, and it is dealing with life that they are eager for."[38]

Carey Thomas, who had never before considered introducing so-called practical and modern courses into the staunchly classical and rigorous Bryn Mawr curriculum, was now forced to reevaluate the programs of study as well as her own ideals about the model Bryn Mawr graduate. By 1910 a whole new generation of students was entering women's colleges—students for whom the college experience was not unique. The mission-oriented student who, convinced of her specialness, came to Bryn Mawr prepared to be swayed by Thomas's calls to advance the dignity of women through careers in research and academia was largely replaced by students who were impatient with the irrelevance of academic life. They looked outward to find rewarding relationships and to seek careers that would not be so isolating.

And, by 1910, new careers for college women were very much the topic of discussion in such forums as the Association of Collegiate Alumnae (later known as the American Association of University Women) and in the colleges themselves. As more and more women attended college, they saw their collective experience as providing ways of solving problems about occupations and life styles rather than as supplying them with already defined alternatives. Students entering college must certainly have been aware of talk about careers for women in social work and domestic economy, which, because of the new technological emphasis, were given applied scientific status. Such areas as sanitary science, domestic science, and hygiene began to appear as courses of study in some women's colleges. Careers in social reform for women were not new; women such as Alice Palmer had urged students to pursue charitable work thirty years before. But her notions about this work were vague; she seemed to see women scurrying from one cause to another, aiding in whatever capacity they were needed. Now, however, careers became more clearly defined and professionalized. Entering Bryn Mawr students, who saw no evidence of these courses and emphases in their curriculum, must surely have begun to pressure Carey Thomas to awaken to the new phenomena.[39]

Thomas, however, always sensitive to the possible degradation of women, must have feared that these new careers were merely an attempt to professionalize traditional areas of acceptability for women. Therefore, in responding to demands for change, she tried to incorporate some of these new concerns without sacrificing too much of the intellectual rigor. Courses in social work were introduced on the graduate level—although undergraduates could elect some of them—and the emphasis was more on sociology than on applied science. In addition, through her speeches, she tried to remove the shroud of feminine gentility so often associated with social work and asked her students to march boldly to the rescue, confronting the "stupendous weight of crime and misery."[40] She also stressed that social reform should be the task of both men and women, who must join together to fight injustice.

By about 1910 Carey Thomas had retreated from extolling sex solidarity and had begun to advocate congeniality between the sexes. Furthermore, she shifted from promoting isolating scholarly pursuits to praising careers aimed at "social reconstruction and human betterment."[41] Much of the vehemence that she had displayed in lauding scholarly careers was now transferred to careers in social reform. In dramatic language, previously reserved exclusively for prospective scholars, she proclaimed to graduating Bryn Mawr students:

> You are the children of your generation, the generation on whom will rest the heavy civic responsibilities which our generation turned aside. We confidently believe that your Bryn Mawr education will have fitted you to meet them. The hope of social reform lies with the young men and women leaving college to enter into active life. As I have tried to show in my address, a thousand voices are calling you to this great work—We bid you God's speed.[42]

Thomas's rhetoric changed over time; her struggle for women's dignity became less solitary as she brought it outside of academia and Bryn Mawr into the social realm of men and women. Her own life seemed to be altered, for she began to look beyond the academic world of Bryn Mawr and gave vigorous support to the suffrage, prohibition, and international peace movements. Yet she berated those women—and men—who saw social reform as being inherently suitable for women with their more refined moral sensibilities, and continued to call for women's educational circumstances to be the same as those for men. She remained adamant about the necessity that women refuse to bow to subservience, and she urged them to become both economically and psychologically independent.

NOTES

[1] Hugh Hawkins, *Between Harvard and America: The Educational Leadership of Charles W. Eliot* (New York, 1972), p. 289.

[2] Charles W. Eliot, *The Man and His Beliefs* (New York, 1923), p. 575.

[3] Ibid., p. 167.

[4] Ibid.

[5] Laurence R. Veysey, "Martha Carey Thomas," in *Notable American Women*, ed. Edward T. James, vol. 3 (Cambridge, Mass., 1971), p. 448. Veysey's succinct account of Thomas is a very insightful, balanced portrait that contrasts to most posthumous writing on Thomas—which is overwhelmingly positive and sees her as *the* pioneer of women's higher education.

[6] Martha Carey Thomas, "Notes for the Opening Address at Bryn Mawr College," Bryn Mawr College Archives, 1899. This address is unusual, for she did not often use the Bryn Mawr College forum for such vehement and specific attacks.

[7] Martha Carey Thomas, "Should the Higher Education of Women Differ from That of Men?" *Educational Review* 21 (1901): 5.

[8] See Martha Carey Thomas, "The Future of Women in Independent Study and Research," Publications of the Association of Collegiate Alumnae, Series 3, Number 6 (February 1903). Although she most often spoke of the value of independent research, she realized that most women would need further means of support and, therefore, advocated university teaching as well.

[9] Quoted in Edith Finch, *Carey Thomas of Bryn Mawr* (New York, 1947), p. 87. There is some rich material on Thomas's early life in this biography, but the end tends to deteriorate into an apology for Thomas's administration at Bryn Mawr.

[10] Barbara Cross, *The Educated Woman in America* (New York, 1965), p. 31. The primary source material on Thomas that Cross presents is very illustrative of the change in her rhetoric which is discussed later in this chapter.

[11] Quoted in Finch, p. 36.

[12] Cross, p. 32.

[13] It is difficult to provide a social class analysis of women college students of this period without knowing fathers' occupations. There are some indications, though, that most students came from middle- to upper middle-class families—probably daughters of professionals or business people. Tuition with room and board was high in comparison to average salaries of the time. At Bryn Mawr, families paid $350 a year in 1885; by 1889 the fee had gone up to $400. If, in 1885, a well-paid high school principal made $2500 a year, he would have to scrimp and save to send his daughter to college. Scholarships were offered, but in the early years of low endowments not too many students had an opportunity to attend at a reduced rate. College did not become fashionable for upper-class women until well into the twentieth century. Most often, as is indicated here, they would be trooped off to Europe to become sufficiently cultivated marriage partners. Too much classical education was not deemed to be womanly. The European tour was made by many young American women—among them Jane Addams whose stepmother, who was responsible for the trip, was of a prominent family. Addams, of course, was not a typical "neurasthenic" woman (to use Christopher Lasch's phrase). She graduated from a seminary which had officially become a college at the time of her graduation and she would use the European junket for quite different purposes than most. See Jane Addams, *Twenty Years at Hull House.* (New York, 1910)—especially the

chapter entitled "The Snare of Preparation." See also Allen F. Davis, *American Heroine, The Life and Legend of Jane Addams* (New York, 1971), ch. 2.

[14] Cross, p. 34. See also Logan Pearsall Smith's *Unforgotten Years* (Boston, 1938).

[15] Ibid.

[16] Ibid.

[17] Quoted in Morris Bishop, *A History of Cornell* (Ithaca, New York, 1962), p. 147.

[18] Ibid., p. 151.

[19] Finch, p. 87.

[20] Thomas, "Notes for the Opening Address at Bryn Mawr College."

[21] Thomas, "Should the Higher Education of Women Differ from That of Men?," p. 1.

[22] Thomas, "Present Tendencies in Women's College and University Education," *Educational Review* 25 (1908): 83.

[23] Ibid.

[24] Martha Carey Thomas, "The Future of Women's Higher Education," *Mount Holyoke College: The Seventy-fifth Anniversary* (South Hadley, Mass., 1913), pp. 100-104.

[25] The issue of whether Thomas's relationships with close women friends assumed a sexual character is the subject of part of a recent rather gossipy history of the Seven Sister schools—Elaine Kendall, *Peculiar Institutions: An Informal History of the Seven Sister Colleges* (New York, 1975, 1976). The obsession with this issue dwells on the irrelevant; what is important is the way her notion of sex separation became translated to students and to college policy.

[26] Thomas, "Should the Higher Education . . . ," p. 10.

[27] Ibid.

[28] Ibid.

[29] Martha Carey Thomas, "The College Women of the Present and Future," 1901, Bryn Mawr College Archives.

[30] Martha Carey Thomas, "Education of Women," in *Monographs on Education in the United States,* ed. Nicholas Murray Butler (New York, 1899), p. 358.

[31] Ibid.

[32] Thomas, "Present Tendencies . . . ," p. 82.

[33] Bulletins of the Class of 1916, comments by Zelda Branch Cramer and Marion Brown, Bryn Mawr College Archives.

[34] Thomas, "The Future of Women's Higher Education," p. 102.

[35] Thomas, "Present Tendencies . . . ," p. 85.

[36] Ibid.

[37] Martha Carey Thomas, "Notes for Commencement Address at Bryn Mawr College, June 6, 1907," Bryn Mawr College Archives.

[38] Ibid. These words sound all too familiar and are, indeed, part of the progressive rhetoric. As much recent scholarship on progressivism has shown, the "life adjustment" movement often was a catchword for social control; and conservative purposes were evident in some of the most radical-sounding ideals. See Christopher Lasch, *The New Radicalism in America* (New York, 1965), pp. 13-14 for a discussion of this idea in reference to Jane Addams. It is clear that women's turn toward social work careers—at least on a rhetorical level—was part of this whole mentality. See Chapter VI.

[39] For evidence of this see Bryn Mawr College Bulletins, Class of 1916, Bryn Mawr College Archives, especially the statement of Isabel Vincent Harper.

[40] Thomas, "Notes for Commencement Address . . . ,"

[41] Ibid.

[42] Ibid.

Helen Lefkowitz Horowitz (essay date 1992)

SOURCE: "Nous Autres: Reading, Passion, and the Creation of M. Carey Thomas," in *The Journal of American History,* Vol. 79, No. 1, June, 1992, pp. 68-95.

[*In the following essay, Horowitz explores the ways in which Thomas "created herself" through her reading of romantic literature, and in so doing challenged accepted ideas of a woman's private identity and same-sex love.*]

What does it mean to read? Does an author fill readers with a text, etching impressions on the blank slates of their minds? Or do readers shape a text, giving it content and meaning to suit their bents and instincts? As reader-response theorists engage in this new version of the philosophical debate between John Locke and Immanuel Kant, something critical is being lost. Although reading is a varied activity taking different forms on different occasions, some reading can be as dynamic as personal conflict. Texts are not infinitely plastic, capable of being molded in any form by readers. Texts have hard edges; they pose challenges and riddles to be unraveled. Reading can be a no-holds-barred tussle between reader and author.

I have looked at the reading of M. Carey Thomas, a prominent American educator and feminist of the late nineteenth and early twentieth centuries.[1] In her youth, reading was an intensely active experience that evoked her deepest emotions. An inheritor of the romantic tradition, she asked works of imaginative literature to speak directly to her. Questioning the faith of her parents, she sought in books answers to her most profound questions of life and love. As she matured and read with friends, the reading of poetry and fiction became part of her most intimate relationships: passionate words merged with passionate acts. She discovered works that changed her and works that confirmed those parts of herself that found no resonance in the lives of her parents and community. Through reading she shaped an identity that, although forced under cover by the demands of a religiously conservative segment of society, nonetheless guided her personal relationships for the rest of her life. Through reading, M. Carey Thomas created herself.[2]

It has not been easy to see this. Thomas was a formidable public figure who sheathed herself in the conventions of her era. She is remembered for her achievements as an educator. She was the founding dean and second president of Bryn Mawr College and the leading advocate of higher education for women in the early twentieth century. Educated at the Howland School in upstate New York and at Cornell University, she received her B.A. in 1877. She was one of the first women in the United States to obtain a graduate education. She entered Johns Hopkins University but withdrew after one year. Although granted the formal right to take a second degree, she was denied the ability to participate in graduate seminars, and working on her own proved demoralizing. In 1879 she went to the University of Leipzig and in 1882 was the first woman to receive a Ph.D. *summa cum laude* from the University of Zürich. At age twenty-five she proposed herself as president of the new college that was to become Bryn Mawr. The position of dean was created that she might fill it. Determined to turn what was endowed as a Quaker college for women into a center of cosmopolitan scholarship, she set entrance standards high, established a graduate school, and recruited an outstanding faculty trained abroad and at Johns Hopkins. Modeled after the University of Leipzig and Johns Hopkins, Bryn Mawr aspired to offer the highest-quality education to its undergraduate and graduate female students. In 1894, Thomas became Bryn Mawr College's second president and served until her retirement in 1922.

Thomas also moved to the broader stage. With the collaboration of female friends, she created the Bryn Mawr School, a college-preparatory secondary school for girls in Baltimore. These same friends united in a successful effort to endow the Johns Hopkins Medical School as a coeducational graduate medical school. She was one of the founders of the Naples Table, which offered a scientific research position in Italy for American women, and

of the Athens Hostel for students in Classics, which assured graduate men and women a safe and comfortable residence. In the first decades of the twentieth century, she lectured extensively on women and higher education.

An ardent feminist, she joined actively in the suffrage movement and headed the Collegiate Equal Suffrage League. In the years of her retirement, she gave her support to the Equal Rights Amendment, the peace movement, and the efforts at immigration restriction that led to the National Origins Act of 1924.

Scholars and students in women's history and women's studies have been interested in the Thomas of the early years.[3] A child and young woman of strong will and vibrant personality, she broke through conventions that bound many others of her sex. Knowing that marriage would end her autonomy, she forced herself to dampen her attraction to men and turned to women for her life's loves. Her intimate relations with Mamie Gwinn and Mary Garrett have intrigued contemporary researchers because of what they might suggest about women's sexuality and same-sex love in the late nineteenth century.

Thomas has proved to be a baffling subject because she had to hide so much of herself from public view. She began her public activity within the context of a Quaker college for women, headed by a board of trustees of thirteen conservative Quaker men who included her father, her uncle, and several cousins. Her female friendships were well accepted within this world because they were misunderstood. But her agnosticism and her aestheticism were dangerous and would have ended her career at Bryn Mawr had they been known. Her behavior in public had to accord with nineteenth-century orthodox Quaker codes, which condemned most imaginative and artistic expression. She could not attend theater or opera or frequent art museums where she might be seen; she largely reserved the satisfaction of her cultural tastes to European summers. To negotiate the boundaries between private and public required Thomas to develop a complex persona in which her religious doubt and her aesthetic passions were kept from view.

Perhaps unwittingly, Thomas left for historians a collection of papers that permit a reconstruction of hidden elements of her experience. Her mother kept a journal of her daughter from her birth. As a child, Minnie, as she was nicknamed, began her own diary, which she kept, with some lapses, throughout her life. In it she recorded the most important and anguished thoughts of her adolescent years. In her extended absences from home for education, daughter wrote to mother, and mother answered. Letters were a record and were saved. As a woman, Carey, as she called herself, wrote to friends and family members. Her letters were preserved and ultimately returned to her. In addition, she kept a running list of what she read. These materials are preserved in the Bryn Mawr College Archives.

At a crucial moment I decided to read what Thomas read, and I turned to her own writing for guidance. I began to weave back and forth from Thomas's letters and diary to works of poetry and fiction. What I found astonished me. I had known of nineteenth-century British poets only from the sanitized collections of my own youth or from their diminished late twentieth-century reputations. A completely different literature of high romanticism and early decadence opened before me, and with it I was able to understand M. Carey Thomas for the first time. Through poetry and fiction, Thomas learned that passion lay at the core of her being.

The critical clue came in a letter of August 12, 1880, to her mother. Carey Thomas was twenty-three and attending lectures in literature and philology at the University of Leipzig. She had been abroad for almost a year studying and traveling with Mamie Gwinn. Her mother, Mary Whitall Thomas, was a prominent Baltimore Quaker and moral reformer. In the letter, Carey argued for the right to publish an article about art in Rome as she had written it. For propriety's sake, Mary had urged Carey to delete references to the body. After presenting her case, Carey then paid her mother a compliment. She reported that when Mamie had learned of Mary Thomas's broad appreciation of literature, she had exclaimed, "Why I did'nt know any one who did not belong to *us* . . . believed that." Carey explained that by us, she and Mamie meant "*nous autres*—the Gautier, Rossetti school."[4]

"Us," "nous autres," "the Gautier, Rossetti school": these are remarkable phrases for a Quaker daughter from Baltimore to relay in 1880 to a mother whose life was infused with religious and moral enthusiasm. Although it was a throwaway line in a letter devoted to other purposes, as with many such gestures, it had a major underlying import. After pages of argument about her right to publish her own words, Carey Thomas was attempting to establish a bond of connection with her mother. She and Mamie imagined themselves linked to the French novelist Théophile Gautier and the British Pre-Raphaelites. In a gesture of magnanimity, Carey reached out to compliment her mother for having aesthetic tastes broad enough to meet her own. If Mary Thomas understood the meaning of her daughter's words, however, she would have realized the unbridgeable gap between the generations.

In the famous preface to his novel *Mademoiselle de Maupin*, published in 1835, Gautier set out the principles that would govern all his writing. "Nothing is really beautiful unless it is useless," he declared. It was a declaration of aesthetic independence. Art is not a tool of politics, religion, or philosophy; the aim of art is the exploration of ideal beauty. Heady words when they were first published, they still had power in 1880. They proclaimed the supremacy of art and beauty against the claims of family and Quaker Meeting. What is more, as we shall consider, they prefaced a book of special import.[5]

And Rossetti? Carey Thomas's conjunction of Gautier with Dante Gabriel Rossetti, the British poet and painter, is curious, and it is one that would not ordinarily have

been made in 1880. Although Carey enjoyed Rossetti's poems and responded powerfully to his paintings when she saw them two years later, in the 1880 aside to her mother, Rossetti was probably a stand-in for the far more controversial poet Algernon Charles Swinburne. Very soon after the letter to her mother, Carey wrote Mary Garrett a long letter about her dreams of art. Mamie was then reading a Swinburne chorus aloud to her, and Carey wrote, "It is lovelier than even my remembrance of it— I do not think any one of the past generation can realize the *rapture and fire* which this new pre-Raphaelite school strikes to our hearts." When writing to her mother about art, even when the comment was an aside, Carey found Rossetti, the leading Pre-Raphaelite, a safer choice than her true artistic passion, Swinburne. More than any of his English contemporaries, Swinburne had insisted on the utter independence of art from standards outside itself, on the necessity that art be free of service to religion and morality. The paganism and eroticism of his poems scandalized the English-speaking public.[6]

For Carey Thomas to accept Mamie Gwinn's identification with Gautier and Rossetti/Swinburne as one of the "nous autres" was to say a great deal about herself—far more, perhaps, than she intended. Her sentence holds a key to her consciousness. Moreover it opens an understanding of how a Quaker daughter born in the constricted world of mid-nineteenth-century Baltimore could emerge by her early twenties as a free-thinking woman capable of pursuing an independent course in Europe to attain the Ph.D. and of passionately loving another woman. In the most fundamental way, M. Carey Thomas refashioned herself through reading. As she read, she traveled beyond her immediate milieu into the intense world of the imagination. Reading gave her the materials with which to fabricate a new self.

Her mother, Mary Thomas, was a deeply religious member of the Society of Friends. The daughter of prosperous and pious Philadelphia Quakers, she married James Carey Thomas, a Baltimore doctor and Quaker minister. Minnie was the eldest of their ten children, eight of whom survived into adulthood. Mary was recognized as a leader in the Women's Meeting and a minister to women. By 1880 she was a powerful force in the Woman's Christian Temperance Union of Maryland. She regarded her marriage as a happy and successful one, but she often said that her primary affections went out to other women, especially her sisters and daughters.[7]

Mary Thomas is an example of the world captured so tellingly in Carroll Smith-Rosenberg's landmark article, "The Female World of Love and Ritual." She was, it seems, a mid-nineteenth-century woman who loved other women sororally and unselfconsciously. When Smith-Rosenberg examined the correspondence of such women, she found that as they moved from the mother-daughter bond to the peer world of friendships, they brought expectations of emotional and physical closeness. Women were each other's most important intimate friends, sustaining each other through the crises of the life cycle.

Although such women had fathers and may have married and had sons, their emotional world was peopled most intensely by other women.[8]

Born in Baltimore in 1857, Minnie received much from her mother but would fail her in a critical respect. As the firstborn, she was the special object of Mary's deep love and solicitude. From her earliest moments, Mary watched for signs of Minnie's "new heart," her rebirth in Christ. But it never came. At age seven, Minnie received a life-threatening burn. Mary recorded in the journal that she kept of her daughter that Minnie had "said she did not see why Heavenly Father was not with her then, He was with Shadrach, Meshach, & Abednego in the fiery furnace, and she thought He might have been with her." Although Mary's attention was already divided among her growing brood, her need to care for Minnie during the long recovery restored their earlier closeness. The daughter that emerged from convalescence remained for a time within the Quaker fold, but the experience of saving grace eluded her.[9]

By her early teens, Minnie Thomas's energy and imagination began to open new possibilities to her. Her lively spirit searched the social and cultural world about her for confirmation. In a Quaker family, theater and music could not be enjoyed, but books there were in abundance. Minnie Thomas had the advantage of intelligent parents and an extraordinary aunt, the renowned spiritual writer Hannah Whitall Smith, who offered unusual companionship and conversation; but the family circle insisted on the literal word of Scripture, conformity to Christian ways of thinking, and personal faith. Alone and with a book, however, Minnie Thomas could think her own thoughts.

One can look at many forces in the shaping of a life. In M. Carey Thomas's biography, a compelling case can be made for the influence of an unusual family, the childhood burn, and educational advantages. But these were all enabling factors, necessary but not sufficient. The critical element that gave substance and direction to her life was her reading.

Loving parents had encouraged Minnie to read the Bible, poetry, and mythology. As she matured, she gradually took hold of her own choices and formed her own judgments. As she was exposed to adult conversation, lectures, and discussion about controversial issues, Minnie reached out to the intellectual world. Living away from home at seminary and college opened her to new thought and the influences of friends. Increasingly, her reading took place within the shared world of peers. Heretical texts challenged Quaker creed. She read poetry within her most intimate relationships. Literature and love became conflated. In the years of her schooling, these new influences were in an unstable equilibrium with the demands of family and Quaker Meeting. But once she went abroad with Mamie Gwinn, Carey Thomas was able to consolidate the self that her reading had inspired. She searched out texts and sites that confirmed her identity, along with that of Mamie Gwinn, as one of "nous autres."

Thomas's reading took her in two directions. Both began with the poetry of Percy Bysshe Shelley. The first path— not our central concern here—led from Shelley to Herbert Spencer. By her early twenties, Thomas rejected Christianity and believed in positivist science. When she sought graduate training in Germany, it was as a philologist, a scientist of literature. She created Bryn Mawr as a graduate school and college that would bring German scholarship to the United States. That scientific truth and the most advanced learning were to be brought to women students was a particular source of satisfaction to her.

The second path forms the subject of this study. It led from Shelley to the poetry of Swinburne and the fiction of Gautier. By August 1880, as she aligned herself with "*nous autres*—the Gautier, Rossetti school," Carey Thomas defined herself in a way that took her far beyond Baltimore, Quaker Meeting, and the sentimental consciousness of the women of her mother's generation.

As a young child she had memorized Shelley's shorter poems; as a seventeen-year-old, she read his longer works. In her retirement, M. Carey Thomas wrote a list of "the great liberal influences" that led to "her emancipation": "first of all came Notes to Queen Mab." *Queen Mab* is an early Shelley poem, suppressed when it was published in 1813 as a revolutionary work. It offers an indictment of past and present society and a vision of a just and democratic order. The poem is searingly anti-Christian, going beyond anticlericalism to hold up to ridicule and ignominy the sacred myths of the Judeo-Christian tradition. Shelley's extensive notes to his poem address a range of issues: the necessity of political justice (citing William Godwin, the political philosopher whose daughter by Mary Wollstonecraft became Mary Shelley), opposition to marriage, and belief in a universe governed by necessity—all of which would inform the young Minnie Thomas. Most dramatically, the notes declared, "There is no God!"—at least in the Christian sense—and submitted proofs that belief in God was a passion contrary to reason.[10]

Shelley proved to be a powerful stimulant to Minnie Thomas. She wrote in her journal the year before she went to Cornell, "How well I remember my half distressed delight when I read the first infidel views I ever met with in the raving of Shelley—yet such thoughts are very familiar now." A few years later she wrote to a friend, "You know I have Shelley to thank and thru him Godwin, for almost all the light I walk by."[11]

Shelley was a step to one of the most important influences in Carey Thomas's life, Swinburne. In the summer before she entered college, Minnie met Francis Gummere and Richard Cadbury, lively Germantown Quaker youths a little older then herself who fancied themselves aesthetes and who read, memorized, and imitated the poetry of Shelley and Swinburne. At Cornell, Professor H. H. Boyesen, a published writer of fiction as well as a scholar, became both mentor and intellectual companion. Relations between some of the female co-eds and the younger male professors were informal and involved elements of courtship. In the fall of her first year at Cornell, Carey—as she called herself beginning in the fall of 1875—wrote home that Professor Boyesen had asked her to waltz with him but that she had refused, having just told one of her male classmates that she did not know how. Boyesen, she wrote, "flushed crimson but I do not think he was angry for he sat down and talked very interestingly about Swinburne, Rossetti, etc." He lent her a volume of Swinburne's poetry. They had long talks about literature. Boyesen guided much of the extracurricular reading that fundamentally shaped her sense of herself and the world.[12]

Although Carey studied literature intensively at Cornell, her reading of Swinburne took place outside of class. At Cornell she formed a romantic friendship with Margaret Hicks. She did learn to waltz, a violation of Quaker mores. When she wrote of waltzing with Margaret, her mother was appalled but was reassured that at least Carey waltzed only with members of her own sex. The two co-eds began to read Swinburne together in the evening. Carey wrote to a close friend, "Well I have been and gone and done it." She and Margaret had fallen in love. "It was dancing and Swinburne that did it." Miss Hicks had taught her how to waltz "and we waltzed and waltzed together." They would study and then "about half past nine we would finish studying and she would undress and put on her trailing wrapper and come in to my bed room and we would lie there and read." One evening as they were lying together reading Swinburne, "I made an unguarded remark and was perfectly astonished at the way she responded."[13]

In her diary, Carey constructed a slightly different narrative. The two were reading Swinburne's *Atalanta in Calydon* together. "Miss Hicks would come in her wrapper after I was in bed and we would read it out loud and we learned several of the choruses. One night we had stopped reading later than usual and obeying a sudden impulse I turned to her and asked 'do you love me?' She threw her arms around me and whispered 'I love you passionately' She did not go home that night and we talked and talked. She told me she had been praying that I might care for her." Carey's diary version fit the conventions of the romantic novels she knew so well, except for the same sex of the two lovers.[14]

That Carey's love during her years at Cornell was a woman never struck her as other than natural. And her mother accepted it in the same vein. Mary Thomas consistently supported her daughter's involvement in special friendships. To a woman of Mary Thomas's era, the love of women for women was an essential part of life, although she mistakenly assumed that Carey shared her generation's construction of sentimental friendship. More threatening to both mother and daughter was the possibility that Carey might fall in love with a man. In fact, during her Cornell years Carey was secretly enamored of Francis Gummere.

Carey had met Frank Gummere when she was at Howland, but her real interest in him grew the summer before she attended Cornell when she was visiting at the country home of her close friend Anna Shipley. Frank had accompanied his friend Richard Cadbury, who was in love with Anna. Carey found herself often in Frank's company, and the two talked about their religious doubt and poetry. For example, two years later Carey recalled in her journal that one day when they were together Frank spoke about Shelley's *The Cenci*. His reference to the scandalous dramatic poem of incest shocked Carey. That evening after the four played a game and talked, they recited poems. Carey and Anna failed at William Wordsworth's "Intimations of Immortality." Carey got embarrassed as she attempted a poem by Robert Browning. Frank recited two Swinburne poems, "The Garden of Proserpine" and "Hymn to Proserpine." Carey recalled in her journal that those poems "haunted me for two years until I found them last year in 'Laus Veneris.'" At such moments, as earlier when she and Margaret Hicks fell in love, the language of Swinburne's poetry was the language of courtship.[15]

But for Carey Thomas it was clearly more. In these years she was breaking with the forms and the content of traditional religion, which in her pious family had shaped the rhythms and terms of life. Science and poetry came to take the place of religion: while scientific speculation became her theology, reciting poems was her ritual. The poems of Swinburne were a powerful substitute for Quaker Meeting.

In her college years, Carey read Swinburne's long narrative poems. *Atalanta in Calydon* presented a theme from Greek mythology in the manner of ancient Greek drama. It is a poem of vengeance, of a mother's rage, not her love. Since Carey was pursuing studies in Greek literature, she would have appreciated the poem's faithfulness to both Greek narrative and form. Given the state of her religious uncertainty, she would have been interested in its stark paganism. The virgin huntress Atalanta would have appealed as a model of chaste power. The poems that Frank Gummere recited were Swinburne's presentation of the Proserpine myth. In "Hymn to Proserpine," a Roman worshipper of the goddess of the underworld bewails that Proserpine has been displaced by the mother of Christ. The cult of the Galilean has conquered Rome, bringing its gray shadows, its pale virgin, and its martyred saints to replace the intense colors and sensuous delights surrounding the old Roman gods. As he awaits death, the Roman refuses to accept the new faith: "I kneel not, neither adore you, but standing, look to the end." "The Garden of Proserpine" celebrates death, a death that is an end, a "sleep eternal / In an eternal night." It contains some of Swinburne's most-quoted lines, asserting a pre-Christian Roman vision:

> From too much love of living,
>   From hope and fear set free,
> We thank with brief thanksgiving
>   Whatever gods may be
> That no life lives for ever;
> That dead men rise up never;
> That even the weariest river
>   Winds somewhere safe to sea.[16]

These two poems were published in 1866 in England in Swinburne's *Songs and Ballads.* We know from Carey's journal entry that she first learned of the poems in 1875 when she heard Frank Gummere recite them. Only in 1877 did she find them in *Laus Veneris,* an American edition of *Songs and Ballads* that highlighted the poem of that title. Both in England and in the United States, the poems of *Songs and Ballads* created a scandal. Unlike Shelley, Swinburne did not write treatises in verse. He presented his poems not as testaments of his own beliefs, but as experiments with the verse forms and mentalities of other ages. However, the poems' celebration of paganism—an outrage to Christianity—and their intense, unconventional eroticism shocked many readers.

In poetry and life, Swinburne crossed boundaries and deliberately sought the perverse. Many of the best known poems in the volume—"Anactoria," "Faustine," "Laus Veneris," "Dolores"—link love and pain. The pleasure of pain and the pain of pleasure were to be Swinburne's most enduring themes. In "Anactoria" Swinburne recasts a poem of Sappho, the Greek poet of the seventh century B.C. In the poem Sappho rages against her beloved female disciple, who has turned to another. In Swinburne's version, anguish is mixed with lust, and in over three hundred lines the Greek poet reaps her imagined vengeance:

> That I could drink thy veins as wine, and eat
> Thy breasts like honey! . . .
>
> . . . . .
>
> . . . oh that I
> Durst crush thee out of life with love, and die,—
> Die of thy pain and my delight, and be
> Mixed with thy blood and molten into thee![17]

In "Anactoria" and other poems Swinburne portrays a world of sexual ambiguity and same-sex love. The poem "Hermaphroditus" was suggested by the statue in the Louvre of the Greek mythological figure, the son of Hermes and Aphrodite, who became united in one body with a nymph, one of the mythological female nature spirits. Swinburne plays with the way that male and female are blended in the god, evoking longings that cannot be satisfied:

> Love stands upon thy left hand and thy right,
> Yet by no sunset and by no moonrise
> Shall make thee man and ease a woman's sighs,
> Or make thee woman for a man's delight.
> To what strange end hath some strange god made
>   fair
> The double blossom of two fruitless flowers?[18]

"Sapphics" is based on the legend of Sappho and her school of women disciples devoted to the worship of Aphrodite. Swinburne tells of Aphrodite's reluctant flight from the island of Lesbos, her "hair unbound" and her "feet unsandalled." Sappho, the tenth muse, sang a song for her. Sappho did not see Aphrodite, shaken and weeping, as she left, but

> Saw the Lesbians kissing across their smitten

> Lutes with lips more sweet than the sound of lute-
>   strings
> Mouth to mouth and hand upon hand, her chosen
>   Fairer than all men

Above them soared her song:

> Newly fledged, her visible song, a marvel,
> Made of perfect sound and exceeding passion,
> Sweetly shapen, terrible, full of thunders,
> Clothed with the wind's wings.

"Such a song was that song" that the other muses and gods, "All reluctant, all with fresh repulsion," fled from her and Lesbos, leaving the land "barren / Full of fruitless women and music only," singing "Songs that break the heart of the earth with pity."[19]

Songs and Ballads opened to Carey Thomas a poetic world of vivid images, an often pagan world in which Swinburne explored and exploded conventional boundaries between desire and pain, men and women. To one familiar with Greek mythology and medieval lore, as Carey Thomas was, nothing in the poems is arcane or obscure. To Carey, searching for moorings and for a way of understanding her emotions, Swinburne's poetry could offer confirmation not only of her religious doubt but also of her passionate feelings toward women as well as men.

It was in a journal entry of March 1878 that Carey noted that she had found Swinburne's *Laus Veneris,* the American edition of *Songs and Ballads.* Her list of books read does not include it; however, it lists many of Swinburne's other works in prose and poetry read during the two years that she spent in Baltimore after she graduated from Cornell. This was the most terrible time in her life. She was locked in linked crises of faith, commitment to work, and love that put her in conflict with her parents, made her unable to study in a sustained fashion, and drew her alternately to Francis Gummere, Mamie Gwinn, and Mary Garrett. Love for a man posed a danger to her dream of independence and a life of scholarship. Frank Gummere was handsome, intelligent, ambitious to become a scholar, and poetic, and he was from an impeccable Quaker family. Carey was deeply attracted to him. But for Carey Thomas to contemplate marriage in the late 1870s was to foresee giving up her "soul life" for a vicarious existence serving a husband and children. Carey cooled Frank's interest and forced herself to give him up. He quickly became engaged to another. Carey refocused her affections on Mamie and Mary, two young Baltimore women she had met on her return home after Cornell. As women, neither Mamie nor Mary threatened her independent future.[20]

Swinburne was in her mind much of the time. In June 1878, she wrote to Mary that her last week had been "almost transfigured" by reading Swinburne's new book of poems, the *Poems and Ballads, Second Series.* "The high water mark of his poetry is reached in the 'Last Oracle' and 'the deserted Garden' and 'Ave Atque Vale' are inexpressibly beautiful." She recommended them to Mary as perfect for her voyage to Europe. "It is just the thing to read on the deck with the 'rose red sea weed' and the 'cruel and bitter sea' that he is forever immortalizing before you." Swinburne's poems were deeply connected to her loss of Christian faith: "Oh Mary it is all so sweet, so sad, so absolutely hopeless—and for me I see nothing better."[21]

In July 1878, Mamie came to visit Carey at the family summer cottage. They "talked and read Swinburne." One day at sunset they read his "Hymn of Man," from *Songs before Sunrise*. Written to promote Italian unification, these poems followed the Shelleyan tradition of interlinked atheism and political radicalism, portraying a world made right by human action. Carey wrote in her journal, "It is a paean of triumph over the vanishing of the Christian religion. To Mamie it was elixir to me poison: though I could not help the bewildering beauty of it carrying me away." Again Carey confronted both the loss of religious faith and the reawakening of love, this time for Mamie.[22]

In August 1879, her personal crisis was suddenly over. Her parents agreed to allow her to go abroad to study for a higher degree, if she could find a companion to live with her. Mamie Gwinn convinced her own mother to let her go. Carey and Mamie went to live abroad together for four years.[23]

The two settled in Leipzig, Germany, where the university allowed women to attend lectures. Carey Thomas began serious preparation for a degree while Mamie Gwinn, who had not had formal secondary schooling in Baltimore, continued to read more eclectically. They avoided socializing with men and found the women students beneath their notice. With the exception of letters and visits from family and friends, for Carey and Mamie, their social world abroad was each other.

Carey's friends included both Francis Gummere, also studying in Leipzig, and Richard Cadbury, who was in Paris writing a long dramatic poem. Engaged to be married, Frank had shifted in Carey's mind from being the object of love to being one of imitation and competition. Richard proved to be an important catalyst for Carey's thoughts on art and life. When he was courting Anna Shipley, he had spent time with Carey; and in the June before they left for Europe, they enjoyed an afternoon together, rowing and getting soaked in a thunderstorm. Richard got Carey's permission to establish a friendly correspondence.

In her letters to Richard, Carey wrote of her reactions to the glories of European art and her desire to be a writer. These letters are filled with the intensity of her aesthetic experiences. To Richard, she denied that scholarship mattered to her in any inner sense. What she wrote about were her aspirations to create. At Cornell, her academic work was separate from her intellectual interests. This continued in exaggerated fashion in her two Baltimore

years when she had tried unsuccessfully to study Greek. By the time of her study abroad, Carey had constructed a hierarchy of ambition in which artistic (in her case poetic) creation was most valued, followed by interpretation, and then service to others. Despite the stimulating professors at Leipzig and the excitement of the new science of philology, Carey sustained her earlier belief in the conflict between creative work and scholarship.[24]

To Richard, she distanced herself from Germany, which she likened to "Scholastic Europe in the Middle Ages," although she admitted, "It may be I shall be drawn in and race with the rest." The real joy was poetry. The meaning of Europe was the inspiration that it allowed. In Carey's understanding, the subject of poetry was the European landscape and its history. Americans knew it only through literature, but the sojourner in Europe could experience it firsthand. She wrote to Richard that in a Gothic cathedral she "*felt* what sent men on the Crusades . . . to *feel* a thing is far beyond knowledge." In her new enthusiasm she asserted that Swinburne, Rossetti, Gautier, Alfred, Lord Tennyson, William Morris, and Charles-Pierre Baudelaire "have not felt strongly enough, have not put themselves—their impassioned ecstacy and agony into their work—perhaps because they could not— that their works are 'cheap show.'" She was setting her sights on Greece and Rome and Venice where she would store up her impressions for poetry. "Don't you think that thoughts come from every new sensation?" Late at night, after Mamie fell asleep, she tried to compose. Her poems were as yet unworthy, "mere spelling, putting word and word together." In somewhat the same vein, Carey wrote to Mary Garrett. She felt that her reading of Swinburne was inspiring her efforts at poetry: "I feel as if my daimon had broken out of his bottle." She had sketched out her dramatic lyric, its scene set in Venice.[25]

Richard's efforts to write a poem in the Swinburne manner made Carey envious. She criticized it carefully and promised to send him in return anything that she wrote. As early as her first November abroad, however, she knew the prospects were not good. "My experiments or rather the experiments I hoped to try here have come to an abrupt close." She needed all her time to study and to soak up impressions. She was clearly daunted by the examples before her. She wrote to Richard about Swinburne's poems: "Atalanta is modern in the best sense but Erechtheus. . . . is truly *Greek*. If one has the lyrical power that form is a wonderful one but one which only Shelley and Swinburne have thus far been able to use. Ergo I cannot send you any samples of my work I have done nothing since I wrote you."[26]

As she attempted to deal with the counterclaims of art and scholarship, Carey Thomas made a pact with herself. During the term she would pursue scholarship, as diligently as any German man in the university. But in the four months of university vacation each year she would travel, storing up impressions that she would later turn into the material of poetry and fiction. In early spring of her first year abroad, she wrote to Richard, "I have decided now to make comparative literature my center—one might call it my circumference and therein is its charm—travel all vacations—4 months of the year—take time for writing-practice—and take a degree at the end—well because I'm a woman Father and Mother are willing to extend the time to 4 years if needful."[27]

Carey's letters to Richard and Mary are misleading, for they tend to emphasize only one side of what was for her a less-balanced debate. In Leipzig she was working very hard as a university student, attending lectures, reading, mastering the elements of philology. To be a good letter, a letter to an intimate friend could not be about work; it had to be about her inner life. Poetry was the medium of feeling as well as a creative pursuit to which Carey aspired. Letters are moreover deceptive in that they are written to those who are absent. Carey was trying to win both Richard and Mary; thus she never referred to the one who meant the most to her and was shaping all her thinking—Mamie Gwinn.

Mamie was four years younger than Carey, eighteen when she went with her to Europe. Anglican, raised in wealth, she was the daughter of Maryland's attorney general, a prominent lawyer whose clients included the late Johns Hopkins. Members of Mamie's family were, as were Carey's, university trustees. Mamie was brilliant, elusive, and precocious—moody, restless, not easily satisfied. And she was beautiful, with a languid beauty, set off by pale skin and soft dark hair. In Baltimore, Carey had fallen in love with her in the familiar way: "We talked and read Swinburne." Mamie was intensely literary. She knew English poetry well and wrote poems that Carey admired. Carey, in her work mode, feared Mamie as "a terrible temptation. . . . She represents all that side of my nature I am trying to suppress—the roving through literature and study seeking out whatever the bent of my fancy leads to and, the dilettante spirit, the complete contradiction to the steady working spirit I am endeavoring to summon."[28]

It was Mamie's influence above all that drew Carey to imagine herself as an artist and to think of living abroad as cultivating aesthetic sensibility. Mamie chafed under the restrictions of the academic year. Whenever Mamie or Carey was sick or had time free from work, they read poetry to each other. Mamie insisted that all their vacations be spent in travel.

Their first trip was Italy. How Carey reveled in it! As the train neared Rome she wept with joy.[29] Rome was all that she dreamed. She and Mamie dedicated themselves to art, visiting and revisiting the papal palace and the Sistine Chapel. To Carey every ruin was imbued with artistic and historic meaning. This first trip was a lover of literature's visit. Carey and Mamie searched out the places described by Virgil and the tombs of poets. As they visited the Borghese Gardens, Nathaniel Hawthorne's *The Marble Faun* was in their minds. Carey made "a pilgrimage to Shelley's grave." Something deeply personal happened to Carey in her years abroad,

something she particularly identified with Italy. At times she expressed it as "tropical life in ones veins," "mellowing," and "faun life." Carey dreamed that Italy would be the wellspring of great poems that would bring her fame. Poetry remained a private avocation, but Italy was forever associated with leisure, Mamie, and the pleasure of their life together.[30]

Before going abroad, Carey had written in her diary in reference to Mamie, "There is a passionate devotion between girls I feel sure." In Leipzig, the two shared a suite of rooms. They ate three meals a day together. After lectures, they usually changed to their wrappers and read in the same room. Mamie might put her head in Carey's lap. They nursed each other in sickness, reading poetry to each other. They accompanied each other to medical examinations. They crawled into the same bed during a storm. They kissed each other on the lips each morning and night.[31]

As Carey came to comprehend her love for Mamie, she could draw on her mother's world, so tenderly evoked by Smith-Rosenberg. The notion that women loved women best of all was embedded in her family—her mother's closeness to her own sisters, her mother's and aunt's special affection for their female children and their nieces. In her family, such love for women was sustained even as young women fulfilled the biblical injunction and society's expectation in marriage and motherhood. As a typical young woman reached early maturity, the women of her family would prepare her for courtship and marriage. But as Carey went to Cornell and then abroad, her own ambition and commitment to women's advancement coupled with her parents' fears about a potential marriage outside Quaker circles broke this pattern. In the years after Cornell, she herself, without confiding in her mother, silenced her attraction to Francis Gummere because marriage would end her dream of scholarship and power.

As Carey fell in love with Mamie, she, as in her girlhood, turned to focus on a special female friend. No one around her suggested that this was inappropriate or wrong. In fact, because her family insisted that their daughter have proper companionship abroad, the opposite message was delivered. Only when Mamie was allowed to go with her to Germany could Carey's parents countenance her study abroad.

But Carey Thomas was a woman with energies and consciousness very different from those of her mother. Shelley and Swinburne were shaping her sensibility. Through Swinburne she was learning of the intensity of sapphic love. Works of fiction, especially Gautier's *Mademoiselle de Maupin,* were opening to her a sensuous world of eroticism between women.

From childhood Thomas was a reader of fiction. Although in moralistic flights as an adolescent she had condemned novel reading, she read novels and romances voraciously. As she matured, she regarded fiction as a pleasure for off-hours or as a path to aesthetic knowledge. After college, as Carey dreamed of becoming a poet or a writer, she turned to the popular writers of the day. Much of what she read contained endless variations on the marriage plot, in which a beautiful young woman overcame the obstacles to true love. Many of these books confirmed the heterosexual prescriptions embedded in Western culture—many, but not all. In some French novels, male writers described women's erotic feelings toward each other. They did not enter empathetically into a woman's world for women's enlightenment but offered titillation to their male readers. Just as brothels staged spectacles of women making love to each other to arouse male patrons as a prelude to heterosexual embrace, so novels paired women to provoke men. But a woman who loved another woman might read such a book in a different spirit.

Mademoiselle de Maupin was a text that could enhance a woman's knowledge of her sexual responses to a woman. In this novel, the heroine of the title dresses as a man to learn of men's ways. As Theodore de Serenne, she rides, fights, drinks, and dines with men and learns of their crudity and utter contempt for the women they profess to love. Rosette, the sister of one of Theodore's companions, falls in love with her, as does Rosette's lover, the poet d'Albert. The male poet suffers sharp feelings of self-loathing before he learns that the man he has fallen in love with is a woman. However, for Maupin/Theodore and Rosette, there is no such pain. In one scene, narrated by Maupin, Rosette lures her to a rural retreat where they partake of wine and sweets. Rosette sits in her lap, "her arms round my neck, her hands interlaced behind my head, and her lips pressed to mine in a maddened kiss. I felt her half-naked and insurgent breasts leap against my breast and her fingers tighten about my hair. A thrill ran right through my body and the nipples of my breasts grew hard." The only regret that Maupin feels is that she is physically unable to consummate this love.[32]

In addition to Rosette, Maupin wins the love of Ninon, a girl just entering puberty, and spirits her away from a vicious mother. Ninon, dressed as a boy, serves Theodore as her page. Ninon, in her innocence, thinks she is Theodore's mistress. "Her illusion was made perfectly complete by the kisses I gave her," Maupin recalls. To the erotic play among adult women is thus added that of an older woman with a girl, one "so diaphanous, so slender, so light, of so delicate and exquisite a nature" that she made even the beardless, effeminate Maupin/Theodore seem masculine by comparison. Theodore took "a malicious pleasure" in keeping Ninon "from the rapacity of men. . . . Only a woman could love her delicately and tenderly enough."[33]

To d'Albert, Maupin/Theodore's passionate embrace of women makes her all the more desirable. Nothing in her past is understood by him as casting a shadow over her future as his perfect mistress. She comes to him pure, declaring herself "as virgin as the Himalayan snows."[34] In his pursuit of her, d'Albert applies well the vast sexual

experience that many of the earlier sections of the novel graphically describe. Their single night of repeated lovemaking is the passionate climax of the novel. What writers write, however, is not what readers necessarily read. While Gautier's masculine audience may have been satisfied by the book's outcome, certain of his female readers may have read the book for its earlier descriptions of female-female embrace.

Carey Thomas read *Mademoiselle de Maupin* in Baltimore in December 1878. Her letters and diary entries of the time make no mention of it, but a letter to her mother written abroad reveals its importance. In the fall of 1881, Carey and Mamie received an extended visit from Gertrude Mead, a friend of Mary Garrett, who was traveling after graduation from Vassar College. During this visit Gertrude made a play for Carey, trying to take her away from Mamie, something Mamie never forgave. (Many years later, Carey described Gertrude as having made "the wildest sort of love" to her on that visit.) Carey enjoyed Gertrude very much and the attention that she bestowed. After Gertrude left, Carey wrote home to ask her mother to send to Gertrude her copy of *Mademoiselle de Maupin*. Carey was never a neat person, and she often did not know where her immediate possessions were. Yet, after more than two years away from home, she could tell her mother just where the book was located. By recalling where she had placed the book and by having it sent to Gertrude after her visit, Carey signaled its special importance. In autobiographical notes penned late in her life, Thomas left a short list labeled "Youth" and "Sex." *Mademoiselle de Maupin* is one of its four entries.[35]

Much was still to come after Carey Thomas's revealing letter of August 1880 to her mother. In the three years that Carey and Mamie remained abroad, they consolidated their relationship into a secure and satisfying intimacy. In letters home Carey argued for the right of women to choose women as their "life's loves," and she suggested that she regarded Mamie as linked to her as in a marriage.[36] Poetry was the retreat of their life together; Italy, the location of their vacations. During the term Carey put away her artistic dreams and concentrated her energy only on scholarship. After two years in Leipzig, she prepared for her Ph.D. at the University of Zürich, the only European university that allowed women to take a degree. She wrote two theses: one on the legends of Sir Gawain and the Green Knight; the other, written with Mamie's direct help and possibly with many of her words, on the poetry of Swinburne. She passed her examinations *summa cum laude*. After Carey took her degree, Carey and Mamie traveled to England to see an exhibition of Rossetti's paintings. They ventured to the Jersey coast to experience the site of some of Swinburne's most notable poems. And they spent a good part of a year in Paris, intentionally living for a time near Gautier's haunts and studying the very paintings that he admired.

Gautier and Swinburne opened up an intense and passionate world to Carey Thomas, a world that in her leisure with Mamie she sought to make her own. In 1883 that world took on a visual dimension at the exhibit of Rossetti's paintings in London. Carey wrote to Mary Garrett that for three weeks she sat "before them day after day and absorbed as one can imagine a sponge thrown into an ocean of depth and colour gradually expanding till every cell is full of light." She was fascinated with the woman's face repeated in many of Rossetti's important paintings, "with its sensuous mouth and intellectual forehead. . . . the same wonderful eyes and more than wonderful neck, which curves and undulates and upbears the 'small head of flowerlike.'" This figure, modeled after the wife of William Morris, reappeared in many of Rossetti's paintings of women. The repeated figure was to Carey an inhabitant "of a land of dreams." The beauty of the paintings was revealed only to those who brought "the desire" of their "hearts. . . . It was our desire, and it is quite impossible for me to talk about the pictures calmly." Mamie was sending Mary the catalog. From it Mary would see "how many and how desirable they were for those of us who care for dreamers of dreams, and seers of visions." The Rossetti figure stayed with Carey for the rest of her life, as the image of ideal beauty. It has been called "androgynous" by modern critics. Carey saw it as exotic, provocative, cerebral, desirable. Rossetti's friendship with Swinburne, especially during the period in which Swinburne wrote his early lyrics, linked Rossetti's paintings to Swinburne's highly charged, erotic images. Long afterward in writing Mamie about an actress she had seen in a London play, Carey described her as "such a beautiful Rossetti-Swinburne woman."[37]

As Carey set her sights on the new Quaker college for women that Joseph Wright Taylor was establishing in Bryn Mawr, Pennsylvania, she began to assume the mantle of conventional public behavior necessary for a woman seeking the trust of conservative Quaker men. But an important part of herself remained with Mamie the "nous autres" of 1880. Gautier and Swinburne/Rossetti were the stars of her firmament that set the course of her emotional life. She had moved far beyond her mother's world, beyond Baltimore, beyond even Cornell. Through her reading she had entered an alternative realm that allowed her remarkable personal freedom. No longer bound by Christianity, its theology or its moral strictures, she had the possibility of imagining herself as a being exempt from the boundaries of traditional womanhood. In Gautier's fiction, ideal beauty and the responses it evoked were neither male nor female. In Swinburne's poetry, life and death, pain and joy, lovers who knew not male and female swirled in passionate embrace. At age 23, Carey sealed her identity as one of "*nous autres—the* Gautier, Rossetti school."

This self-definition would stay with her always. In time, Mary Garrett would replace Mamie Gwinn as the center of her passionate life. In the 1890s Carey Thomas would pay close attention to the Oscar Wilde trial and read the medical literature on sexuality. But what she learned from the sexologists would only be added to a more fun-

damental identity formed during her young womanhood. By her early maturity, identifying deeply with Swinburne and Gautier, Carey Thomas could believe that her love for another woman was passionate in its nature. "Passionate" to her meant full of "rapture and fire" like the Pre-Raphaelite poems she loved.

Carey Thomas was an unusual woman, but she did not exist in a cultural vacuum. She shared her aestheticism with her male and female friends at Cornell and in Baltimore and Philadelphia. They read and chanted Swinburne's poems to each other. *Atalanta in Calydon* and "The Garden of Proserpine" formed the matter of courtship and intimacy. *Mademoiselle de Maupin* was passed among female friends.

As other historians probe the lives of M. Carey Thomas's female contemporaries and their interrelationships in the 1870s and 1880s, they should be alert to a new possibility. After the sentimentalism of the mid-nineteenth century and before the lesbian consciousness that emerged at the turn of the century, there may have existed a mentality that defined itself as passionate.

Since 1975, when Smith-Rosenberg first framed it, historians of women have been working with a specific chronology of same-sex love. A number of writers, including Jeffrey Weeks, George Chauncey, and Jane Caplan, have focused on the social construction of homosexuality as it emerged at the end of the nineteenth century. Smith-Rosenberg summarized this literature and connected it explicitly to the attack on women's higher education in "The New Woman as Androgyne," published in 1985. These studies have established that, at the end of the nineteenth century, male scientific practitioners began to tell women that they were sexual beings. The most important texts were Richard von Krafft-Ebing's *Psychopathia Sexualis,* first published in Stuttgart in 1886 and translated into English in 1908, and Havelock Ellis's articles, which began appearing in the mid-1890s. These male sexologists drew a distinction between the sexual feelings and behavior between women and men that they called "normal" and those they labeled "abnormal." They defined the "Mannish Lesbian" as a woman who imitated men intellectually, professionally, and sexually. Through their detailed case studies, they informed women about themselves.[38]

Basic to this conceptualization of the change from sentimental friendship to lesbianism is the understanding that nineteenth-century, white, middle-class women were taught to deny their sexual feelings. The prescriptive literature insisted on the woman's fundamental innocence before being sexually awakened by a man. In an era that valued men's consistent labor and women's domestic authority, commitment to premarital chastity and postmarital restraint provided powerful sources of control.[39]

Other historians have questioned these critical assumptions about nineteenth-century culture. In *At Odds,* Carl

N. Degler challenged historians to explore the difference between prescription and behavior and presented significant anecdotal evidence of women's willing engagement in sexual activity. Ellen K. Rothman strengthened Degler's case with her emphasis on emotional and sexual intimacy between men and women. In her new book, *Searching the Heart,* Karen Lystra has pushed the argument for sexual expressiveness even further. She argues that by the 1830s the American middle class was committed to the ideal of romantic love. Nineteenth-century, middle-class individuals "fell in love." The two selves merged, and as they did they expressed their love in sexual language and behavior. In drawing a sharp distinction between public and private behavior, they enhanced the eroticism behind closed doors.[40]

Lystra's work makes it clear that it is not enough to juxtapose prescriptive literature with behavior. It is not only what one does that is important; it is the construction one places on it. Moreover, the understanding that one gives to one's acts turns back to shape what one does. Lystra demonstrates that nineteenth-century letter writers fell in love using their era's language of romance and feeling. Although she discounts the influence of etiquette-book models on actual love letters, many of those she cites suggest that their authors may have taken their cues from fiction.[41]

As we revise our notions of love and sexual expressiveness between women and men in the nineteenth century, we must rethink the question of women's love for other women. We should return to Smith-Rosenberg's exploration of the letters women wrote each other to see the way in which Anglo-American poetry and fiction helped shape the way that women defined their relationships. My own intensive look at one woman's reading forces us to question the prevailing paradigm of women's same-sex love. Carey Thomas and the women of her circle were not part of either the world of sentimental friendship or that of lesbianism. They did not take their primary cues from prescriptive literature. They were not passive victims of male definitions. They sought out and read works of fiction and poetry, written largely by men, that opened them to a sensuous world of eroticism between women. They actively and willingly chose the passionate sensibility of "nous autres."[42]

In turning away from prescriptive literature as the primary guide to personal awareness in the late nineteenth century and toward the works of poets and novelists, we need to explore the insights of reader-response theory. What happens when a piece of literature written by a man for men is read by a woman? We have generally assumed that nineteenth-century female readers responded directly to the misogyny of male writers. What if some women readers simply ignored any negative messages being sent and received from the text positive signals? If this is possible, where might such a female reader place herself in the text? What lessons might she take from a poem or a novel? What knowledge might she glean about herself from the characters? Such questions are the more pressing when we realize that readers such as Carey Thomas, unleashed from the moorings of organized religion, were looking to literature for answers to their essential questions about life and love.[43]

At the same time, we must insist that the text itself, if it has been freely chosen, has a content capable of stirring the imagination and emotions of a reader. Reading a poem, discussing it, making love to its stanzas can force a reader to think and feel anew. The reader and the text confront each other, and neither may be the same after the encounter.

It was from the works of Swinburne and Gautier that Carey Thomas, as a young woman, learned about herself. She never forgot. Her ambitions required her to hide this private self from the world outside. From her return to the United States in 1883 until her retirement from Bryn Mawr College in 1922, she had to maintain public conformity to Quaker codes and to avoid offending Quaker taste. Although Bryn Mawr's Jacobean Gothic architecture and certain English courses in the curriculum gave outward expression to Thomas's aesthetic, the trustees did not have the knowledge necessary to read these traces.[44]

M. Carey Thomas came to wear a protective mantle of Quaker usage, but underneath it she was a woman of heady passions who lived in the intensely romantic and erotic universe of Swinburne's poetry, Gautier's fiction, and Rossetti's paintings. In 1884 she wrote an untitled poem for Mary Garrett, meant for her eyes alone. In it Carey imagined the Ideal as the woman of a Rossetti painting sending thoughts from "some far land of passion":

> These many years within the sanctuary
> Which is my heart, alone I break and eat
> The bread and wine of dreams. I hear the beat
> Of hurrying thoughts, that wing from over sea
> From some far land of passion crying to me
> Until at morn or eve I go—and meet
> Mid dreams and thoughts made manifest her feet
> Mid many hearts her heart's deep mystery.
>
> For in that hour, afar or near at hand,
> When I shall pass beyond her eyes and know
> The very dreaming heart of her to grow
> One with my thought and splendid, understand
> Why I have loved her silence, I shall go
> Content, nor lonely, in the passionate land.[45]

No single expression better captures Carey Thomas's consciousness. She imagines herself, severed from religious belief, as living within the "sanctuary" of the heart, taking communion with art, breaking and eating "the bread and wine of dreams." God is absent; but the Ideal—Rossetti's compelling woman—calls from the land "from over sea." Death—passing "beyond her eyes"—will bring Carey union with her. Carey then will "know the very dreaming heart of her to grow one with my thought," and joined with the Ideal, she will go "content, nor lonely, in the passionate land."

In the decades that followed, Carey continued to express this side of herself to Mary and Mamie, especially in her intense reactions to opera and theater. At times, however, Carey revealed her private, passionate self in a mere phrase or an image. One example from an 1899 letter to Mary allows a fleeting glimpse into Carey's consciousness, kept shielded by her public persona. M. Carey Thomas, now a college president and a leading spokeswoman for women's higher education, took the public stand for Prohibition expected of a prominent Quaker. Mary kept an apartment in New York for their use but was traveling abroad at the time the letter was written. "Ah," wrote Carey, "if we could have some champagne and sandwiches and a talk in our pretty bedroom under the Rossetti and the Ariadne!"[46]

To one familiar only with the public persona of M. Carey Thomas in 1899, this image of her—drinking champagne under a Rossetti painting in the bedroom she shared with Mary Garrett in a New York City apartment—defies belief. To us, aware of the young woman who envisioned herself as one of "nous autres," it recalls Carey Thomas's private identity as a passionate woman who reveled in aesthetic delights and formed intense, loving commitments to other women.

Carey Thomas created this self through her reading. Within a shared world of intimate friendships, she found in the poetry of Swinburne and the fiction of Gautier works that guided her for the rest of her life. Underneath the thick layers of protective convention that came to encase her, a part of Carey Thomas always remained linked with "the Gautier, Rossetti school."

Our recovery of Thomas's private identity through her reading has led us to rethink the way we have understood women, sexuality, and same-sex love in the 1870s and 1880s. Ultimately it has forced us to think about reading itself, both as a private act and as a social experience, a charged encounter with words capable of evoking intense emotions and of changing a person forever.

NOTES

[1] This article is part of a larger study of the life of M. Carey Thomas, to be published by Alfred A. Knopf in 1994. Biographical information has been gleaned from the principal repository of Thomas material: the M. Carey Thomas Papers (Bryn Mawr College Archives, Bryn Mawr, Pa.). The bulk of the collection has been published on microfilm: Lucy Fisher West, ed., *The Papers of M. Carey Thomas* (microfilm, 217 reels, Woodbridge, Conn., 1982). Biographical studies of Thomas are Laurence R. Veysey, "Martha Carey Thomas," *Notable American Women, 1607-1950: A Biographical Dictionary,* ed. Edward T. James (3 vols., Cambridge, Mass., 1971), III, 446-50; Edith Finch, *Carey Thomas of Bryn Mawr* (New York, 1947); and Marjorie Housepian Dobkin, ed., *The Making of a Feminist: Early Journals and Letters of M. Carey Thomas* (Kent, Ohio, 1979), 1-27.

A note about the use of names. When I use the full name M. Carey Thomas, it is to refer to the biographical subject and adult woman who became the college president. She was never addressed by her first name, Martha. Minnie is the name she used as a child, although close friends and family continued to use it long afterward. She assumed the name Carey when she went to Cornell University in 1875. When I refer to her as a child I call her Minnie Thomas or Minnie. When I refer to her as an adult in her personal capacity, I call her either Carey Thomas or Carey. In referring to her in professional capacity, I call her Thomas. Because this piece centers on her personal life, I normally do not refer to her as Thomas, except when confusion between her two first names requires it.

[2] Barbara Sicherman first alerted me to the importance of reading in shaping the consciousness of late nineteenth-century educated women. Her paper on women's reading at the June 1987 Berkshire Conference in Women's History at Wellesley College has recently been published: Barbara Sicherman, "Sense and Sensibility: A Case Study of Women's Reading in Late-Victorian America," in *Reading in America: Literature & Social History,* ed. Cathy N. Davidson (Baltimore, 1989), 201-25. My thinking and research have been stimulated by Barbara Sicherman, "Engaging Texts: Stories of Reading of the Progressive Generation of Women," paper delivered at the annual meeting of the Organization of American Historians, St. Louis, April 1986 (in Barbara Sicherman's possession).

[3] Dobkin, ed., *The Making of a Feminist;* Carroll Smith-Rosenberg, "The New Woman as Androgyne: Social Disorder and Gender Crisis, 1870-1936," in Carroll Smith-Rosenberg, *Disorderly Conduct: Visions of Gender in Victorian America* (New York, 1985), 245-96.

[4] M. Carey Thomas to Mary Whitall Thomas, Aug. 12, 1880, West, ed., *Papers of M. Carey Thomas,* frame 413, reel 31. Here, as elsewhere, I note the frame on which the letter begins. Throughout I have corrected Thomas's spelling and have spelled out the words that she abbreviated.

[5] Théophile Gautier, *Mademoiselle de Maupin,* trans. Joanna Richardson (Harmondsworth, Eng., 1981), 39.

[6] M. Carey Thomas to Mary Garrett, Nov. 11, 1880, West, ed., *Papers of M. Carey Thomas,* frame 222, reel 15. The emphasis is mine.

[7] James Thomas Flexner, *An American Saga: The Story of Helen Thomas & Simon Flexner* (Boston, 1984), 92-99, 174-76. See, for example, Mary Whitall Thomas to M. Carey Thomas, Aug. 19, 1876, West, ed., *Papers of M. Carey Thomas,* frame 316, reel 61.

[8] Carroll Smith-Rosenberg, "The Female World of Love and Ritual: Relations between Women in Nineteenth Century America," *Signs,* 1 (Autumn 1975), 1-29.

[9] Mary Whithall Thomas Journal, vol. 2, Jan.-Oct. 1864, West, ed., *Papers of M. Carey Thomas,* frame 141, reel 1.

[10] M. Carey Thomas to Elizabeth S. Sergeant, June 17, 1927, *ibid.,* frame 1088, reel 28; Percy Bysshe Shelley, *Queen Mab,* in *The Complete Works of Percy Bysshe Shelley,* ed. Roger Ingpen and Walter E. Peck (10 vols., New York, 1926-1930), I, 55-165, esp. 146.

[11] M. Carey Thomas Journal, vol. 11, Thanksgiving 1874, West, ed., *Papers of M. Carey Thomas,* frame 516, reel 1; M. Carey Thomas to Richard Cadbury, April 7, 1880, *ibid.,* frame 235, reel 13.

[12] M. Carey Thomas to Mary Whitall Thomas and James Carey Thomas, [Fall 1875], *ibid.,* frame 143, reel 31.

[13] Mary Whitall Thomas to M. Carey Thomas, Oct. 23, 1875, *ibid.,* frame 358, reel 61; M. Carey Thomas to Anna Shipley, Nov. 21, 1875, *ibid.,* frame 166, reel 29.

[14] M. Carey Thomas Journal, vol. 11, June 12, 1877, *ibid.,* frame 524, reel 1.

[15] M. Carey Thomas Journal, vol. 22, March 24, 1878, *ibid.,* frame 879, reel 2.

[16] Algernon Charles Swinburne, *Laus Veneris, and Other Poems and Ballads* (New York, 1867), 75-81, esp. 78, 189-92, esp. 192.

[17] *Ibid.,* 68.

[18] *Ibid.,* 90.

[19] *Ibid.,* 228-29.

[20] M. Carey Thomas Journal, vol. 12, "List of books read, 1873-82," West, ed., *Papers of M. Carey Thomas,* frames 555-62, reel 1; *ibid.,* vol. 22, Feb. 22, 1878, frame 875, reel 2; *ibid.,* Feb. 13, 1878, frame 872, reel 2.

[21] M. Carey Thomas to Garrett, June 14, 1878, *ibid.,* frame 15, reel 15.

[22] M. Carey Thomas Journal, vol. 22, March 24, 1878, *ibid.,* frame 879, reel 2; *ibid.,* Aug. 25, 1878, frame 894, reel 2.

[23] M. Carey Thomas to Mary Whitall Thomas, [Aug. 29, 1879], *ibid.,* frame 202, reel 31.

[24] M. Carey Thomas to Cadbury, Nov. 2, 1879, *ibid.,* frame 225, reel 13; M. Carey Thomas to Cadbury, Nov. 10, 1881, *ibid.,* frame 253, reel 13; M. Carey Thomas to Cadbury, Feb. 10, 1881, *ibid.,* frame 257, reel 13.

[25] M. Carey Thomas to Cadbury, Nov. 2, 1879, *ibid.,* frame 225, reel 13; M. Carey Thomas to Garrett, Nov. 11, 1880, *ibid.,* frame 222, reel 15.

[26] M. Carey Thomas to Cadbury, Nov. 26, 1879, *ibid.,* frame 229, reel 13; M. Carey Thomas to Cadbury, [Feb. 10, 1881 on envelope], *ibid.,* frame 257, reel 13.

[27] M. Carey Thomas to Cadbury, April 7, 1880, *ibid.,* frame 233, reel 13.

[28] M. Carey Thomas Journal, vol. 22, March 24, 1878, *ibid.,* frame 879, reel 2; *ibid.,* Nov. 12, 1878, frame 901, reel 2; *ibid.,* March 24, 1878, frame 879, reel 2; *ibid.,* March 18, 1878, frame 875, reel 2. Outside of scattered manuscript sources, there is no known biographical material on Mamie Gwinn.

[29] M. Carey Thomas to Mary Whitall Thomas, March 7, 1880, *ibid.,* frame 312, reel 31.

[30] M. Carey Thomas to Cadbury, April 7, 1880, *ibid.,* frame 233, reel 13; M. Carey Thomas to Cadbury, Oct. 14, 1880, *ibid.,* frame 242, reel 13; M. Carey Thomas to Cadbury, Nov. 23, 1880, *ibid.,* frame 247, reel 13.

[31] M. Carey Thomas Journal, vol. 22, Oct. 12, 1878, *ibid.,* frame 901, reel 2. What Carey Thomas understood as passion in 1878 is conveyed by her section of a never-published joint novel she wrote with her friends during her years in Baltimore. A young male character, Percy, suggested by the poet Shelley, draws a woman toward him, and the narrator sees in his glance "deep love, & reality of passion in his eyes." An older woman tells the narrator that Percy is "sensitive to the least influence, passionate, sensuous—Pleasure is now his only rule." Vol. 123, *ibid.,* reel 2. Letters from M. Carey Thomas to her mother from 1879 to 1881 convey something of the life that Carey and Mamie led in Leipzig, but the clearest sense is gained from Mamie Gwinn to M. Carey Thomas, [March 1882], *ibid.,* esp. frame 41, reel 53.

[32] Théophile Gautier, *Mademoiselle de Maupin,* trans. R. Powys Mathers and E. Powys Mathers (London, 1948), 222.

[33] *Ibid.,* 264, 265.

[34] *Ibid.,* 277.

[35] M. Carey Thomas Journal, vol. 12, "List of books read, 1873-82," Dec. 1878, West, ed., *Papers of M. Carey Thomas,* frame 561, reel 1; M. Carey Thomas to Garrett, Oct. 18, 1896, *ibid.,* frame 79, reel 20; M. Carey Thomas to Mary Whitall Thomas, Dec. 28, 1881, *ibid.,* frame 798, reel 31; Manuscript fragment, Autobiographical Materials, *ibid.,* [no frame numbers], reel 74.

[36] M. Carey Thomas to Mary Whitall Thomas, Nov. 13, 1880, *ibid.,* frame 560, reel 31. In February 1882, as she schemed to get away from work for an excursion, Carey wrote to her mother that she and Mamie hoped for "some cheap little journey of a week or two some where—'a wedding trip up side down' as Mamie says." M. Carey

Thomas to Mary Whitall Thomas, Feb. 12, 1882, *ibid.*, frame 37, reel 32.

[37] M. Carey Thomas to Garrett, March 18, 1883, *ibid.*, frame 314, reel 15; M. Carey Thomas to Mamie Gwinn, July 1, 1898, Alfred Hodder Papers (unprocessed collection, Princeton University Archives, Princeton, New Jersey).

[38] Although these writers differ significantly in their interpretations, especially on the weight to give to the sexologists' influence, they accept an essentially two-stage chronology. See Jeffrey Weeks, "Havelock Ellis and the Politics of Sex Reform," in *Socialism and the New Life: The Personal and Sexual Politics of Edward Carpenter and Havelock Ellis,* ed. Sheila Rowbotham and Jeffrey Weeks (London, 1977), 139-92; George Chauncey, "From Sexual Inversion to Homosexuality: The Changing Medical Conceptualization of Female 'Deviance,'" in *Passion and Power: Sexuality in History,* ed. Kathy Peiss and Christina Simmons (Philadelphia, 1989), 87-117; Jane Caplan, "Sexuality and Homosexuality," in *Women in Society: Interdisciplinary Essays,* ed. Cambridge Women's Studies Group (London, 1981), 149-67; Smith-Rosenberg, "The New Woman as Androgyne," 245-96. Women's historians have judged much of the sexologists' impact to be negative, for in telling women that they could be homosexual, they made intense woman-to-woman friendship suspect, a source of loss for those women who defined themselves as heterosexual. They labeled and stigmatized lesbian relationships. However, they provided lesbians with a definition of their emotions as sexual, which—when rephrased in an accepting era—could lead lesbians to positive understanding and enhanced experience.

[39] Nancy F. Cott, "Passionlessness: An Interpretation of Victorian Sexual Ideology, 1790-1850," *Signs,* 4 (Winter 1978), 219-36; Daniel Scott Smith, "Family Limitation, Sexual Control, and Domestic Feminism in Victorian America," *Feminist Studies,* 1 (Winter-Spring 1973), 40-57; Ben Barker-Benfield, "The Spermatic Economy: A Nineteenth Century View of Sexuality," *Feminist Studies,* 1 (Summer 1972), 45-74.

[40] Carl N. Degler, *At Odds: Women and the Family in America from the Revolution to the Present* (New York, 1980); Ellen K. Rothman, *Hands and Hearts: A History of Courtship in America* (New York, 1984); Karen Lystra, *Searching the Heart: Women, Men, and Romantic Love in Nineteenth-Century America* (New York, 1989).

[41] See, for example, the correspondence between Robert Burdette and Clara Baker. Lystra, *Searching the Heart,* 92-100.

[42] I have avoided two words in describing the acts and feelings of M. Carey Thomas in the 1870s and 1880s: *lesbian* and *sexual.* I have done so quite consciously. Only when she read the sexologists in the mid-1890s was Carey Thomas told that women's passionate feeling for each other had a sexual basis.

[43] For an excellent selection of this literature, introduced by an informative essay, see Jane P. Tomkins, ed., *Reader-Response Criticism: From Formalism to Post-Structuralism* (Baltimore, 1980), esp. ix-xxvi. For important examples of the range of possibilities in applying reader-response critical approaches to contemporary American subjects, see Janice A. Radway, *Reading the Romance: Women, Patriarchy, and Popular Literature* (Chapel Hill, 1984). For a telling example of how Madame de Staël, Madame Roland, and George Sand found inspiration in the works of Jean-Jacques Rousseau, works understood as profoundly antifeminist by today's readers, see Gita May, "Rousseau's 'Antifeminism' Reconsidered," in Samia I. Spencer, *French Women and the Age of Enlightenment* (Bloomington, 1984), 309-17. I am grateful to Barbara Sicherman, whose work helped provoke these questions.

[44] I have written extensively about Thomas and Bryn Mawr College architecture in Helen Lefkowitz Horowitz, *Alma Mater: Design and Experience in the Women's Colleges from their Nineteenth-Century Beginnings to the 1930s* (New York, 1984), 105-33. One delightful example of a Thomas misstep comes from the Bryn Mawr College Oral History Project. An alumna recalled a moment from 1904, her freshman year: "We were sitting in chapel. The poet Swinburne had died—she always gave these little talks before daily chapel—and she gave her recollections of hearing his poetry. . . . she was absolutely carried away. Evidently Dr. Barton, the poor, learned Quaker who always was there at the same time for the religious part of the service that we had—evidently he told her it wasn't the proper thing to show such enthusiasm for Swinburne before young ladies. The next day she made an absolutely deadpan speech about Swinburne's less commendable qualities." Agnes Goldman Sanborn interview by Florence Newman Trefethen, Nov. 18, 1987, typescript, p. 140, Bryn Mawr College Oral History Project (Bryn Mawr College Archives).

[45] M. Carey Thomas to Garrett, July 3, 1884, West, ed., *Papers of M. Carey Thomas,* frame 471, reel 15.

[46] M. Carey Thomas to Garrett, Dec. 21, 1899, *ibid.*, frame 816, reel 22.

Barbara Sicherman (essay date 1993)

SOURCE: "Reading and Ambition: M. Carey Thomas and Female Heroism," in *American Quarterly,* Vol. 45, No. 1, March, 1993, pp. 73-103.

[*In the following essay, Sicherman analyzes Thomas's reading and its relation to expanding social roles for women in the late nineteenth century.*]

"[T]he fact is," fourteen-year-old Minnie Thomas declared in 1871: "I don't care much for any thing except dreaming about being grand & noble & famous but that

I can never be." She did become famous as M. Carey Thomas, president of Bryn Mawr College, where she provided a model and an environment that promoted ambition in other female dreamers. As an adolescent she hoped to show "that the woman who has fought all the battles of olden time over again whilest reading the spirited pages of Homer Vergil Heroditus . . . been carried away by Carlyle & 'mildly enchanted by Emerson' . . . is not any less like what God really intended a woman to be than the trifling ballroom butterfly than the ignorant wax doll baby which *they* admire." The passage reveals persistent themes of Thomas's adolescence: her passionate absorption in books, the possibilities for female heroism she found in classic texts, a feminist outlook that sought to erase rather than highlight sexual difference, and a belief that intellectual endeavor, even the sort usually gendered "male," need not unsex a woman. It also demonstrates a reciprocal relation between Thomas's reading and her ambition, continuing: "my greatest hope & ambition is to be an author an essayist an historian to write hearty earnest true books that may do their part towards elevating the human race."[1] The woman who could read herself into books might grow up to write them.

Thomas left an unusually full record of her reading: taken together, her teenage diary, letters, booklists, and later autobiographical musings make it possible to reconstruct a reading profile of her early years. This study of reading in a particular time and place focuses on reading as a behavior rather than as the elucidation of texts traditionally practiced by literary critics. Reader-response criticism, by denying that texts have a universal meaning, in theory grants substantial interpretive authority to readers. For the most part, however, it has produced readings within the academic community and has had little to say about how historically situated readers have responded to texts or what reading as an *activity* has meant to them. A striking exception is Janice Radway who, in her pioneering study of twentieth-century romance readers, views reading as "a complex intervention in the ongoing social life of actual social subjects." By listening to her respondents, Radway discovered not only their reading preferences but also what the *event* of reading meant to them— in this instance, a "declaration of independence" from their families.[2]

Extrapolating from a welter of fugitive comments, it becomes clear that, for Thomas, reading constituted a complex system of cultural and social practices and a source of personal meaning. In this paper, I will concentrate on the connections between reading and female ambition, a subject that cuts across the entire spectrum of Thomas's reading behavior. Three aspects of her interactions with books are especially relevant. A seeker after culture from an early age, Thomas found in reading access to such formerly male bastions as the classics, the higher "thought life," and honorable employment, then opening up for single women of the comfortable classes. Reading was also a social activity and a focal point for Thomas's romantic friendships with women. Finally, reading was a source of emotional gratification, providing "comfort"

and relief from loneliness, "inexpressible joy" and healing pain. These modes of reading—for self-improvement, for sociability, and for emotional sustenance—were all integral to women's reading culture in late-Victorian America. Although analytically separable, together they gave reading an unusual salience for young women of Thomas's generation.[3]

Thomas's lofty ambitions and passion for reading were common among white, middle- and upper-middle class women growing up in Gilded-Age America; like Thomas, they expressed even in their teens a passionate desire to "make something of themselves." Far from being idle dreamers, some grew up to become the influential Progressive generation, attaining eminence in public life, in academe, in science and medicine, in social welfare and reform. A self-conscious vanguard who often thought of themselves collectively as the "first" generation of college women, they were, in Jane Addams's view, "this special generation," in Vida Scudder's, women who could "make ourselves significant if we will." For privileged women of Thomas's generation, dreams of glory often came from books.[4]

At a time when culture was replacing religion as the supreme source of values, books were revered objects, repositories of what Matthew Arnold designated "the best which has been thought and said in the world." Middle-class girls as well as boys were inducted into a culture of reading that valorized books and learning. They cut their teeth on the new secular children's books and magazines that flourished in the postbellum era before moving on to the "standard" works of English fiction and history; most also had access to a wide range of fiction, including some they considered "trash," a category with highly permeable boundaries. This straining after culture had its elitist side, a desire to acquire what Bourdieu calls "cultural capital."[5] But for women like Thomas, engagement with books was more than the prescribed behavior of a cultural elite: it was the key to education, employment, and empowerment.

As with all pleasures, young women sometimes experienced conflict over their reading. Traditional warnings against fiction as the royal road to seduction, addiction, and housewifely neglect had diminished by the late-Victorian era, but some of the negative connotations of women and reading lingered. Novel reading remained a trope for female idleness, daydreaming, and lack of purpose, particularly during adolescence. At fourteen, Thomas explained her desire for a vocation: "I can[']t stand being dependent on any body even Mother & Father & I want to do something else besides eating reading & dressing." At times she chided herself for her propensity to build "aircastles," a state often occasioned by reading. But even when adolescents struggled to read less "trash" and keep their "obsession" in bounds, like Thomas most kept on reading.[6]

Reading was dangerous because, as with Radway's romance readers, it opened up imaginative space that permitted women to bracket some of the conventions of Victorian life and enter a world of fantasy of their own choosing and subject at least in part to their own control. The term "escapism," with its connotations of uselessness or worse, is inadequate for understanding this process. For ambitious female adolescents of the Progressive generation, reading could be escape *to* as well as escape *from:* in their (day)dreams began possibilities. In a society that expected women to be selfless, even the desire to have a self was subversive.

Studies of the relationships among fantasy, cognition, and reading offer clues to how the process worked. In contrast to psychoanalysis, which privileges unconscious desires as the driving force of human behavior, cognitive psychologists highlight the importance of conscious processes. To Jerome Singer, daydreaming is "conscious fantasy behavior" and thus a cognitive skill rather than a sign of social inadequacy or repressed libido. Along with other stimuli of fantasy like books and movies, daydreaming is a form of internalized play that encourages "a more flexible and *playful* approach to one's own thought processes," thereby promoting growth and self-mastery. In this view, fantasy-prone individuals are often highly creative and self-directing. Because daydreaming permits the individual to pay attention to inner processes, "to produce images, to rework the unpleasant, or to contemplate the future in the complete privacy of one's mind," it is of special importance during adolescence, a time of doubt about achievement, the future, and sexuality.[7]

Other psychologists explicitly connect reading with dreaming and relate both to changes in consciousness: "Books are the dreams we would most like to have, and, like dreams, they have the power to change consciousness." By shifting the focus of attention away from the self, books carry the reader "off into other worlds," sometimes with a concentration so intense that reading may be said to "transfigur[e] both book and reader." Like daydreaming, reading frees individuals from the need to act and permits them to become spectators. This spectator role is not one of detached aloofness. Reading stimulates desire rather than pacifying it: something happens to readers that becomes imperative for them to understand. By permitting readers to remove themselves temporarily from the necessity to act, the spectator role enables them to use this freedom "to *evaluate* more broadly, more amply" and thus to "modify categories according to 'the way [one] feel[s] about things.'"[8] The heightened imaginative capacity and sense of vicarious participation associated with reading can help individuals to evaluate, clarify, and alter feelings.

Books could not create a desire for female heroism where no tendency existed in the reader. Class position, family support, and expanding vocational opportunities all nurtured ambition and put some women in a favorable position to *realize* their goals. But, in conjunction with a supportive family culture and a network of friends that encouraged female aspiration, reading could *stimulate* worldly ambition by providing the occasion for perceiv-

ing one's inmost needs and wants—desires that might later be acted upon. Particularly during the impressionable preadolescent and adolescent years, reading opened up in imagination a range of possibilities not otherwise available to women.

Reading was thus not so much a "cause" of female ambition as a vehicle for articulating and, consequently, intensifying desires. Thomas noted more than once the excitement—and fear—she experienced on seeing her own thoughts expressed by someone else: "[S]ometimes when I have been reading a book . . . that has made a difference in me, whether it lie in me or in the book or poem I can never tell (I think perhaps it is a habit of th[ough]'t which blindly works on behind a veil until some sentence on the pages of a book or in the mouth of a person rends it & with a passion of appropriation the thought is mine.)." Appropriation is the key word. It suggests both a reciprocal relationship between reader and text and the reader's ability to make her own meaning. Seeing a thought on the printed page enables the reader to perceive what until then had existed only "blindly . . . behind a veil." The articulation of a half-formed thought or hidden desire, its exposure to consciousness, makes it available for further reflection and elaboration, and thus for the development of even more novel thoughts. In Thomas's view: "As one grows older the book or the th[ough]'t become the real life, and reaching thus horizon after horizon the land becomes in time a *new* land upon whose possession we must enter."[9]

In the process of articulating desires and appropriating meanings, women tried out a variety of selves, some of them at odds with the "true women" they were expected to become. Jane Addams, for example, confessed to a fondness for a character representing a new, and freer, persona. Claiming that her favorite childhood story was Undine, Addams compared the water sprite to Scott's White Lady in *The Monastery* (1820), who "has a peculiar attraction for me, there is something glorious to me in the idea of being without a soul, doing what you please without being responsible to yourself." The idea of Addams without a soul is arresting, for it was her soulfulness that most struck those who knew her as an adult, and even as a child she was solemn. Addams's persona was self-consciously playful, a momentary diversion. Books also offered inspiring models against which to measure oneself. Emily Greene Balch recalled with pleasure the stories of Maria Edgeworth and Charlotte Yonge which "were largely built around a heroine who had a mission," while Agnes Hamilton found in the heroine of Yonge's *The Daisy Chain* (1856) a model for her own efforts to establish a church in the poor section of Fort Wayne.[10]

Altogether, the middle-class literature of the era was conducive to dreams of heroism outside family life. The very reticence that made Victorian a byword for prudery encouraged such aspirations. As Martha Vicinus has shown, the downplaying of sexuality and the marriage plot in girls' biographies encouraged fantasies about other sources of fulfillment, including those that gave women a large public role. Because women have been traditionally figured as readers of sentimental romances, it has been assumed that they identify solely or primarily with heroines in search of a romantic hero. But in their diaries and autobiographies, middle-class women of the Progressive generation often expressed greater interest in female heroism than in prince charmings. It was quest rather than romance plots that engaged them.[11]

In the opening passage of her memoir, Mary White Ovington suggests multiple origins for her later career as a leader of the NAACP: "Every imaginative child who has access to books or hears tales of a romantic past— and the past grows romantic in the telling—has a gallery of heroes upon which he loves to brood." Her heroes included Robert Bruce and Erling the Bold; "but the pictures that stirred me most and that I turned to oftenest were those of fugitive slaves. I saw Eliza crossing the ice on the last lap in her course to freedom . . . Anthony Burns incredibly escaping to Boston to be incredibly returned to slavery; and Frederick Douglass—most dramatic because he wrote his own story."[12] Here Ovington, who was white, mixes real heroes, black and white, with a fictional heroine—Eliza of *Uncle Tom's Cabin*—in a way that suggests the capaciousness of imagination. For Ovington the quest plot *was* romantic.

Women not only read themselves into texts, they also playacted favorite parts. These enactments started early, in childhood games of the siege of Troy and Robin Hood and in home theatricals. Women tried on aspects of favorite characters, working and reworking them in imagination. Especially during early adolescence, reading became a staging ground for rehearsing future selves. In the late-Victorian era, more than in our own, these rehearsals were often shared. Despite claims by historians of the book that reading had shifted from a public to a private practice, reading remained for women a social and collective as well as individual endeavor, one firmly rooted in relationships. Rehearsing their fantasies with sympathetic family members and with female friends and schoolmates, middle-class women found peer sanction for their desire to make themselves significant. The female culture of reading, with its attendant rituals that fostered friendship and love, healing and learning, reinforced individual efforts at self-creation and at reading against the grain. By encouraging one another to pursue in life at least some of their dreams, ambitious women of the Progressive generation together developed a new sense of female destiny.

. . . . .

Thomas's parents were orthodox Quakers active in the Baltimore Society of Friends, James Carey Thomas as a preacher, Mary Whitall Thomas as clerk of the Women's Meeting; both conducted Bible classes. Though well off—Thomas's father was a prominent physician and her mother came from a wealthy family—her parents were not typical bourgeois consumers of culture: Quakers forbade theater, music, and novels. They permitted poetry,

however, and "a complete set of 'British Poets'"—the only secular literature in the house—launched Thomas on a lifelong love of verse. Although religious concerns came first, the elder Thomases were not personally severe and sometimes bent the rules: they had a piano which they hid when grandmother Whitall visited.[13]

Thomas's youthful reading sometimes alarmed her parents, what she read and the way she read it. Dismayed by her daughter's "wildly excited" appearance on listening to Macaulay's "Ivry," Thomas's mother warned: "[R]emember that 'it was nothing but poetry'"; and, in a scene of unusual violence, her father "snatched" a copy of Byron's *Don Juan* from her and threw it into the fire. But despite Quaker scruples and some monitoring of her reading, Thomas had the run of an uncle's library where she had access to "all the English prose classics." Retrospectively she emphasized her responsiveness to the poetry and fiction usually designated as "high culture," but contemporary sources record her eagerness to read whatever she could. At thirteen, the year she began her journal, she was reading "Ruskin on arcitecture," *Tom Brown at Oxford,* and *The Green-Mountain Girls,* a "trashy" novel borrowed from the Mercantile Library. She had recently begun to study Greek. By her mid-teens, G. H. Lewes's *Life of Goethe* and Emerson's *Representative Men* appeared on her reading list, as did romances by E. Marlitt.[14]

In autobiographical reminiscences, Thomas linked reading to her evolving sense of self. Titles listed under the headings "Childhood" and "Girlhood" suggest that she defined herself by what she read. Discussing the near-fatal burn that confined her to inactivity for eighteen months shortly after her seventh birthday, she observed: "I got up a romantic Victorian. I think that the change would have come in any case but probably more slowly. . . . And then I began to read for myself and my education began and changed my childish world."[15] Thomas here identifies herself with a group of writers and a mode of reading that fostered self-discovery. The romantic poets' emphasis on the ego and self-creation appealed to one eager to find new ways for women to live. Shelley, the exemplar of the misunderstood intellectual and radical critic of society, was an early and lifelong favorite.

Thomas's engagement with literature was intense and active. Between the ages of thirteen and fifteen, when she went away to boarding school, she engaged in a wide variety of literary activities. In addition to writing poetry and starting a journal, she kept a commonplace book and compiled lists of favorite poems and books. She also wrote poetry and short stories and sent one of each to *Harper's;* both were rejected.[16]

The links between Thomas's ambition and her mode of reading can be traced in her responses to two favorites in early adolescence, *Little Women* (1868-69) and Carlyle's *On Heroes, Hero-Worship, and the Heroic in History* (1841). These seem an unlikely pairing, but in Thomas's feminist readings, both promoted dreams of glory, especially literary glory. Both books were also favorites of other ambitious women of Thomas's generation. Fifteen-year-old Jane Addams observed: "I have read and re-read 'Little Women' and *it* never seems to grow old." More surprising is the appeal of Carlyle, a schoolgirl favorite well into the century. Four years later, after completing a heroic biography of Michelangelo, Addams claimed she had enjoyed it "more than anything which I have read since Carlyle's Hero Worship."[17]

When Thomas began her journal in 1870, she did so in the persona of Jo March, the tomboy heroine of *Little Women*. "Ain't going to be sentimental / 'No no not for Jo' (not Joe)," she proclaimed. Emulating a literary character was a common practice among young diarists as they attempted to establish their own personal and literary identities. But there were compelling reasons for Thomas to choose Jo. In the first half of the novel, Jo rejects not only sentimentality but also traditional femininity, as did Thomas; in the same entry she referred sarcastically to being a *"young lady,"* a state she was resisting despite her father's admonitions. Jo was both a "bookworm" and ambitious: like Thomas, she wanted to do something "splendid." Most important, she was a successful author who was paid for her writing. Alcott's heroine appealed because as "Jo (not Joe)" she demonstrated that women could be writers and in other ways aspire.[18]

Thomas's emulation of Jo exemplifies the ways in which women used reading to act out fantasies of achievement, first in early adolescent role-playing, later, given the right circumstances, in life. For a time, *Little Women* loomed large in her relations with her closest friends, Franklin Whitall Smith and Bessie King, both cousins. Thomas assumed the persona of "Jo" in 1868, the year Alcott's heroine first flashed across the literary landscape; Frank took the part of "Laurie." These sobriquets coexisted for a time with earlier literary nicknames, Minnehaha and Hiawatha. Thomas's incarnation as Longfellow's Indian princess was more a play on her childhood name—Minnie—than a serious persona. It was different with Jo March. Bessie King, who had evidently accepted the secondary role of Oweenee in the earlier fantasy, made an unsuccessful bid to become Jo, the only acceptable heroine of *Little Women*. Frank insisted that Bessie decide what "she *would* like to be called, if she won't be Jo 2., or Meg, or Beth, or Amy; or Daisy, or anybody besides Jo 1. since *thou will* be the latter." Rather than play second fiddle, Bessie decided to be Polly, heroine of a new Alcott novel, *An Old-Fashioned Girl*. In 1879, as Thomas started graduate study in Germany, King acknowledged the importance of this childhood play: "Somehow today I went back to those early days when our horizon was so limited yet so full of light & our path lay as plain before us. It all came of reading over Miss Alcott's books now the quintescence of Philistinism then a Bible. . . . Doesn't thee remember when to turn out a 'Jo' was the height of ambition"? With *Little Women*, then, we are dealing with a key text in the formation of Thomas's subjectivity and with a fantasy that was shared rather than simply private.[19]

It has been suggested that Alcott's classic has been mis-read as a story of female independence when it is really a tale of "restraint, resignation, and endurance"; in this version Jo becomes only a moderately adventurous hero-ine who learns to govern her passions and settles for domesticity.[20] Whatever the case today, Jo March, the most frequently cited heroine in the autobiographies, dia-ries, and letters I have consulted, was not read in this way in the late-Victorian era; of some two dozen women who mention her, none does so as a symbol of resignation. Disclaiming sentimentality, like other "schoolgirl non-sense," serious-minded youngsters rejected "good-goody" Sunday school girls and found excessively good heroines unrealistic, for example, Esther in *Bleak House*—"a character to forever be admired and extolled, *but are* there any such?" When set against fictional pre-cursors, like Ellen Montgomery of *The Wide, Wide World* (1850), or even her contemporary Elsie Dinsmore, char-acters from whom stringent forms of obedience are ex-acted, Jo presents a *new* model of girlhood, one that extended what Hans Robert Jauss calls the reader's "ho-rizon of expectations."[21]

Framed by the quest of Christian in *The Pilgrim's Progress* to reach the celestial city, *Little Women* is a story of women seekers. Under their mother's tutelage and with Christian as a model, the March sisters strive to perfect their characters. But the novel is also a quest for female vocation. In a chapter titled "Castles in the Air," each sister reveals her deepest desires. Jo's is "to do something splendid . . . something heroic, or wonder-ful . . . I think I shall write books, and get rich and famous." Amy wants to "be the best artist in the whole world," while Meg desires to be mistress of a "lovely house" and to "do good, and make every one love me dearly." Only Beth has no ambition, other than "to stay at home safe with father and mother, and help take care of the family." Beth dies because she can find no way of growing up: "I'm not like the rest of you; I never made any plans about what I'd do when I grew up; I never thought of being married, as you all did. I couldn't seem to imagine myself anything but stupid little Beth, trotting about at home, of no use anywhere but there. I never wanted to go away." Her mysterious illness thus results from a failure of imagination, an inability to build castles in the air. In its loving depictions of the young women's struggles to attain their goals, *Little Women* succeeds in authorizing female vocation and individuality. If Alcott capitulated to popular sentiment in marrying off Jo, she resisted pairing her with the romantic Laurie, a hero with whom a love plot would have been more compelling than it was with the rumpled Professor Bhaer. Nor did Alcott rule out the possibility of future artistic creativity: al-though married and managing a large household and school, Jo has not entirely given up her literary dreams, nor Amy her artistic ones.[22]

Little Women was the exemplary female text of the era, Jo March—virtually a contemporary of Thomas's—the exemplary adolescent heroine.[23] The realistic plot, right down to the amateur theatricals and the reading of *The*

Pilgrim's Progress, resonated with the experiences of middle-class girls; even young men found the book appealing for its realism. The book's everyday and "slangy" style also made it easy for girls to read and rewrite Alcott to their own liking.[24] Finally, Jo's status as an author was an important—and attainable—goal.

As Thomas's interactions with *Little Women* suggest, reading and writing were not discrete activities but existed on a continuum. Reading stimulated a desire to write as well as to read, as the diaries and letters of Thomas and her contemporaries indicate; some succeeded in publishing poems and stories, especially in the popular new secular magazines for children.[25] In these ambitions, they could look to a tradition of female authorship that included not only "geniuses" like George Eliot and the Brontës, but also the host of "scribbling women" who earned their livelihoods with their pens.[26] In the late nineteenth century, women's organizations had substantial cultural authority and played an important role in validating women's literary output, conditions that did not go unmarked by aspiring young writers.[27]

In her early teens Thomas had a penchant for romancing that *Little Women* could not satisfy. These grander visions were of the sort traditionally enacted by male heroes. Critics as diverse as Rachel Brownstein, Jonathan Culler, Judith Fetterley, and Patrocinio Schweickart have assumed that women read themselves only into female parts or that reading "as a man" is necessarily harmful, or both. Such a perspective would restrict women readers largely to passive roles or at best that of a sprightly female heroine. It is much too limited in view of the imaginative possibilities opened up by reading, particularly to women like Thomas who had access to a wide range of literature.[28]

Cora Kaplan's claim that novels can provide women readers with multiple and shifting identifications, with heroes as well as heroines, offers a sounder starting point. Defining fantasy "as 'daydream,' as a conscious, written narrative construction, or as an historical account of the gendered imagination," Kaplan maintains that women's romantic fantasies—usually considered regressive in feminist scenarios—can be more than scenes of subordination. Drawing on psychoanalytic studies that suggest that subjects participate in fantasies without occupying a fixed position, she analyzes her own experiences reading historical novels in which "the female reader [is invited] to identify across sexual difference and to engage with narrative fantasy from a variety of subject positions and at various levels." She suggests that a novel like Colleen McCullough's *The Thorn Birds*, which "allows a very free movement between masculine and feminine positions," permits women to read themselves as subjects rather than "see themselves narcissistically through the eyes of men" as objects.[29]

Thomas read herself into male as well as female plots, into nonfictional as well as fictional characters, and into the lives of authors as well. The quest tales of knighthood

(which she and Frank Smith invoked in discussions of their vocational plans), the classics, and Carlyle's *On Heroes* provided Thomas with material for her daydreams. At fourteen, she declared that *On Heroes* "has interested me more than any book I ever read almost." In a copybook dated 1871-1872, quotations from Carlyle predominate under "Selections From Prose Writers." Years later, Bessie King sent her a copy of Froude's life of Carlyle, "for the sake of old times when he was a prophet to us—thee must spare time to look over it."[30]

Carlyle's cranky rhetoric is difficult to read today, but it stirred his contemporaries and remained a favorite of young people into the 1890s. From its ringing opening declaration—"Universal History, the history of what man has accomplished in this world, is at bottom the History of the Great Men who have worked here"—*On Heroes* endorses individual action in ways calculated to inspire idealistic young people not only to admire but also to cultivate heroic genius. The influence of Carlyle, for whom the "Man-of-Letters Hero . . . [is] our most important modern person. . . . What he teaches, the whole world will do and make," is apparent in Thomas's desire, at the peak of adolescent romanticism, to write "hearty earnest true books that may do their part towards elevating the human race." Long after Carlyle had ceased to be a prophet, his prose echoes in her assertion, at twenty-four: "Hero worship, or rather genius worship is one manifestation of the religious insti[n]ct in wh[ich]. one can pour heart & soul."[31]

Carlyle's models—the hero as divinity, prophet, poet, priest, man of letters, and king—are all male. Why then did they appeal to Thomas? When she read Carlyle, she was already a feminist determined to prove women the intellectual equals of men, a project she later fulfilled at Bryn Mawr: "[H]ow *unjust—how narrow-minded*—how *utterly uncomprehensible* to deny that women ought to be educated & worse than all to deny that they have equal powers of mind. If I ever live & grow up my *one* aim & consentrated [sic] purpose *shall* be & is to show that a woman *can learn can reason can compete* with man in the grand fields of literature & science & conjecture that opens before the 19 century that a woman can be a woman & a *true* one with out having all her time engrossed by dress & society." Given such an outlook, Thomas would not have made a prophet of Carlyle if she had read him as excluding her.[32]

Instead, she inserted herself into the text, reading the generic masculine as in- rather than exclusive. Her copybook contains a feminist passage from *Jane Eyre*: "women feel just as men feel . . . they suffer from too rigid a restraint, too absolute a stagnation, precisely as men would suffer." Thomas was more eager to minimize sexual difference than most of her contemporaries. But she was not alone in reading herself into male parts, as the example of Mary White Ovington suggests. The lesser self-consciousness of a pre-Freudian age encouraged such generic readings. Despite the polarized gender ideology of the era, there was considerable tolerance of tomboys, at least prior to adolescence: girls read "boys' books," engaged in boisterous play with male relatives or on their own, and in other ways participated in activities usually gendered male. Tales of knighthood were popular among female questers: Thomas and Addams were among those who invoked the figure of the knight as they sought their life missions.[33]

As they matured, women often found contemporary fictional heroines wanting in the requisite qualities of heroism. Katharine Lee Bates, a Wellesley College senior in 1879, wrote of the heroine of William Dean Howells's *The Lady of the Aroostook:* "We deny that Lydia Blood is a sample of our best national girlhood, much less the boasted American heroine, for the predominant stamp of heroism must be activity, visible or invisible, and this girl is as passive as a wooden angel, or a wax rose, with neither thorns nor fragrance." Women writers offered more promising models, and young women admired, read, and read about Elizabeth Barrett Browning and George Eliot; they also read about queens and reformers of various stripes. For those seeking adventure, male heroes, fictional and real, offered intriguing possibilities if not exclusive models.[34]

There was even some cultural encouragement for young women to read the generic "he" as inclusive. About the time Thomas was reading Carlyle, Victoria Woodhull and other feminists were claiming that because women were "persons" they were already enfranchised under the terms of the fourteenth and fifteenth amendments.[35] Some Victorian writers explicitly made room for women within their definitions of heroism. And, although Carlyle's heroes were all male, as were Emerson's "representative men," the era's pervasive worship of genius extended to both sexes. In a college essay on "Some of the Representative Men of the Present Time," Thomas unself-consciously proclaimed George Eliot the "representative" novelist.[36]

Three years earlier, at the age of fifteen, Thomas had acted out another fantasy of female literary achievement with Bessie King. The focal point was "a library with all the splendid books with a bright wood fire always burning dark crimson curtains & furniture, great big easy chairs where we could sit lost in books for days together." Far from being idle dreamers, the companions were authors and laboratory scientists of whom people would say: "'Their example arouses me, their books enoble [sic] me, their deeds inspire me & behold they are women'!" Thus did Thomas transform the image of reading as a passive activity of school girl dependence into one of adult purposefulness. Gender symbolism permeates this vision: the masculine accountrements of the library accompanied the appropriation of names that were masculine or ambiguous as to gender. Thomas and King were, respectively, Rush and Rex, the latter a play on King's name which, Thomas explained, meant Queen. Here, as elsewhere in her role-playing, Thomas seems to have regendered the male hero as female; she also imagined a future that transcended gender.[37]

The fantasy prefigured Thomas's life at Bryn Mawr: the decor, the intellectual ethos, and the feminist life ventures with women. Here the fifteen-year-old "[wrote] her own life in advance of living it," in Carolyn Heilbrun's telling phrase. It was a life in which Thomas was to inspire other women by her ideals and example and ennoble them by her books. It is less important that she did not gain fame as a writer than that books were the touchstone for a fantasy—again a shared one—in which Thomas imagined herself a (female) Carlylean hero.[38]

. . . . .

From an early age Thomas understood that to fulfill any of her ambitions she must claim an education; her intense desire and persistent efforts to achieve this goal constitute major themes of her journal. Despite some initial resistance from her father, she attended Cornell and earned a B.A. in 1877. She subsequently pursued graduate study, at Johns Hopkins, the University of Leipzig, and the University of Zurich, from which she received her Ph.D., in philology in 1882—summa cum laude. On informing her mother of her triumph her first words were: "'Hail the conquering hero comes.'"[39]

It was one thing to imagine oneself a hero, another for a woman "to be somebody" in Gilded-Age America. After graduating from Cornell, Thomas found authorization for her dreams from members of a Baltimore literary circle. Formed in the winter of 1877-78, the "Friday Night" combined self-conscious literary intellectualism with friendship, love, and female sociability of a more traditional sort. In addition to Bessie King, the group included Mary E. Garrett, wealthy daughter of the president of the Baltimore and Ohio Railroad, Garrett's close friend Julia Rogers, and Mamie Gwinn, the youngest and most intellectually daring. At the time, Thomas was studying at Hopkins; King, despite serious illness, hoped to become an artist; and Garrett and Rogers were preparing to take the Harvard entrance examinations.[40]

The women were drawn together by mutual literary interests and their sense of being modern women. These qualities were evident even in their teens, when Garrett, King, Rogers, and Thomas insisted on studying Greek, still the ultimate (male) marker of intellectual status. At sixteen Garrett talked back to John Ruskin who in his popular essay "Lilies," subtitled "Of Queens' Gardens," maintained that women should have "nearly" the same education as men but should not study as deeply. Garrett pronounced the essay "perfectly beautiful," but repudiated Ruskin's admonition "that woman's knowledge should merely be elementary . . . just so that she may be able to help her husband. . . . No! 'Knowledge . . . is power' and I, for one, am going to do my best to gain it."[41]

By the late 1870s, the five women were aspiring intellectuals who felt "mortified" by a gap in literary knowledge. Their understanding of the world had been shaped in large measure by their reading; Thomas, for example, claimed that her eyes had been opened "to the great world of passion" by a professor's reading of Tennyson's "Maud." Rejecting anything that smacked of "philistinism," they had a shared disdain for the ordinary, including the common lot of women. Books kept Thomas and her circle neither "tranquil" nor "pacified."[42]

The Friday Night met fortnightly at one of the women's homes; according to Thomas they wrote "2 chapt[ers] of a novel & an essay or two each night." Their shared dreams of literary glory culminated in a collective novel, with members writing alternating chapters; several, including Thomas, embarked on novels of their own.[43] In addition to their formal activities, members engaged in joint study: two or three read German or learned Greek together. All kept up with the latest English and American literary magazines and talked and wrote endlessly about books that moved them. Some of the reading rituals indulged in by members seem more congruent with traditional female roles than with their image as an avant garde. Reading was also an occasion of love and of healing: they read poetry to one another to cure headaches.[44] Through their literary activities and personal friendships, the group forged a collective identity that valorized female intellect and independence.

Taken together the activities of the Friday Night reveal the multiple possibilities of reading in promoting female agency. In particular, the social nature of their reading, with its potent blend of intellectual challenge and emotional sustenance, provided a setting in which vocational plans flourished. Meeting at a critical time, when women's ambitions often fell victim to marriage, illness, or the care of ailing relatives, the Friday Night demonstrated the importance of like-minded peers in helping women sustain an often precarious vision. For aspiring writers, the emphasis on writing and on reading each others' literary compositions had practical potential as well. After formal meetings ceased, members continued to pursue their literary interests. Rogers was working simultaneously on five articles in September 1880, by which time Thomas had already published a brief, unsigned piece in *The Nation* and several in *The Quaker Alumnus*, a shortlived publication with which she was affiliated.[45]

The Friday Night also constituted a forum for exploring avant garde ideas on marriage, religion, and literature. Gravitating to writers they considered transgressive, the women considered themselves an advanced set, "our chosen few" in King's words, *"nous autres"* in Thomas's.[46] Thomas had early been drawn to Shelley, whose "infidel views" she read with "half distressed delight." Under Gwinn's influence, she now claimed William Godwin as a mentor. The greatest influence on Thomas at this time was Swinburne. She became a devotee during her Cornell years, responding to his poetry with "rapture & fire." Through Swinburne she was drawn to aestheticism, to Dante Gabriel Rossetti, Théophile Gautier, and others who sought to *épater les bourgeois.* Enlisting under the banner of "art for art's sake," the young women enjoyed

shocking others by acknowledging that they read French novels; they also felt constrained at times to justify their actions by claiming they were improving their French.[47]

If the women rejected orthodox Christianity and endorsed the radical artistic currents of the day, their attitudes toward sexuality were in some respects more traditional than modern. Despite their desire to shock, all but Gwinn rejected Godwin's endorsement of free love.[48] When—evidently for the first time—Thomas and other group members read up on the facts of life in her father's medical books and *What Women Should Know* (1873) by social purity reformer Eliza Duffey, she "went to bed sick, absolutely"; she was twenty-one. Influenced by admonitions from her mother and her aunt Hannah Whitall Smith, leaders in the Maryland WCTU and social purity movements respectively, Thomas retained a deeply Victorian suspicion of male sexuality and a belief in female asexuality and moral superiority. These essential components of the paradigm of "passionlessness" ran counter to her stated commitment to gender equality.[49]

Above all, members of the Friday Night admired and cultivated female independence. In King's view: "There is no doubt that the feeling which is silently growing among women for independent life, apart from their relations to men[,] is the motive power for the revolution we hope for." Endlessly debating "the woman question," they considered it difficult if not impossible for a married woman to fulfill her potential and kept a close watch whenever a suitor appeared. Thomas, who considered family life hampering to male as well as female genius, did not rule out marriage in theory and urged a recently engaged friend to stick with her work. Nevertheless, during the period of the Friday Night, Thomas fled from a man she thought she loved on the grounds that marriage would interfere with her career. "If it were only possible for women to elect women as well as men for a 'lives [sic] love,'" she wrote her mother, "all reason for an intellectual woman['s] marriage w[oul]d be gone." Throughout her life, Thomas was attracted to women. What was an "if" became a reality: she lived first with Mamie Gwinn and, after Gwinn's marriage, with Mary Garrett.[50]

On the threshold of adulthood, Thomas still invoked the old theme: "I do not care for anything except to try for the realization of some of my dreams." In her twenties, however, her dreams led in different, and conflicting, directions. On the one hand, she sought to inspire young women and to ensure that they would not have to struggle as she had: "Study . . . & influence are the two things I care about." But even while preparing for a scholarly career and doing everything she could to be named president of the new Quaker college that would become Bryn Mawr, she expressed deep ambivalence about scholarship.[51]

Projecting a "lyrical love drama" in blank verse in her early twenties, Thomas held on to a Carlylean vision of the supremacy of the writer, together with the romantic view of writing as an act of inspired genius. Here

Thomas's choice of male literary mentors may have been inhibiting. It was harder for a woman to write when she had before her the model of male "genius" rather than "female scribbler." Setting her literary sights by the canons of high culture, she wrote of women poets in the gendered terms of male critics: Elizabeth Barrett Browning had *"passion capital"* but "executes in the most contemptibly, careless feminine way." Moreover, the license claimed by her literary heroes ran counter to the norms of female respectability. When she asked her parents to forward an article she had written to *Harper's,* they objected because of "indelicate" allusions to "the models' naked female backs & thighs & knees."[52]

Thomas's idealization of high culture and her championing of aestheticism posed serious problems for her feminist goals. The aesthetic movement undermined the Carlylean view of literature as a source of moral influence and of the writer as the supreme moral agent. Its proponents set themselves apart not only from the masses but also from the middle class, the philistines who could not appreciate genuine culture. For a woman who sought to influence her times, in particular to advance the cause of women, this was treacherous ground.[53]

Thomas employed the language of possession about both her reading and her ambition. While struggling with issues of career choice and professional training, intimacy and independence, at times she found her passion for reading troublesome, a threat rather than a stimulus to ambition. "Every thing seems secondary to my desire to read," she wrote in her journal, "it has come as I imagine possession of some demoniacal force came upon those old seers in the wilderness." Believing that novels, like other pleasures including female friendships, were a distraction from study, she gave them up for several weeks in June 1878. The subsequent "longing for a novel" and "visions" of titles "dancing before" her suggest a breaking through of repressed desire, the pleasure principle that Thomas associated with youth and passion: "[A]s Christ said the life of his followers must be a 'dying daily,' so a thought life requires many renunciations & crucifixions. Novels & lounging & daydreaming before sunsets . . . are inexpressibly pleasant, but if we girls are to accomplish anything we must give them up."[54]

Thomas's strenuous efforts to control her reading in her early twenties came at a time of considerable stress.[55] But, taken together with subsequent comments, her struggles suggest that there may be something of a natural life cycle to women's reading. Thomas herself linked intense reading experiences with youth. At the advanced age of twenty-three, she was surprised to weep over Robert Browning's "A Blot in the 'Scutcheon," "as I used to in the *Sturm & Drang Periode* over Keats or Shelley." She hoped the Friday Night "w[oul]d . . . be reborn," but thought it unlikely once members began to pursue their interests: "It is much easier to meet when each has an untried enthusiasm." It is unlikely that reading, whether individual or social, has its greatest significance during a period of prolonged adolescence. A time of dreaming and planning, of "untried enthusiasms," it is a stage of life when reading retains an intensity less often found among adults, for whom, presumably, doing replaces dreaming.[56]

Thomas's intuition that the Friday Night would not meet again proved accurate. But each of its members found ways to fulfill at least some of her "enthusiasms." All supported feminist causes. Thomas, whose family was less well off than those of her friends, was the only full-time professional. In 1885 she became the first dean and professor of English at Bryn Mawr College, opening a new chapter not only in her own life but also in the history of higher education in the United States. Mamie Gwinn helped Thomas establish Bryn Mawr's rigorous intellectual standards and later taught there; Elizabeth King (Ellicott) became a leader in the women's club and suffrage movements in Maryland; Julia Rogers was active in volunteer activities in Baltimore, particularly those promoting women's higher education, and published articles on cultural topics in *The Atlantic Monthly* and *The Nation;* and Mary Garrett became a prominent suffragist and philanthropist. Before they fell out in the 1890s, the women created two lasting legacies. They founded the Bryn Mawr School in Baltimore, a rigorous college preparatory school for girls (1885), and successfully campaigned for the admission of women to the Johns Hopkins Medical School, at its opening in 1893 the premier medical institution in the United States. The stunning success at Hopkins depended on the close relationship of several of the women's fathers to the University and Medical School and on Garrett's sizable fortune. But these triumphal ventures also exemplify the collective nature of feminist endeavor which, in this case, began in the private and collective dreams of five young women seeking to fulfill the potential of their sex, dreams reinforced by their encounters with print.[57]

Thomas remained true to her youthful literary heroes. Carlyle's *On Heroes* was required reading at the Bryn Mawr School. In her two-year survey of English language and literature, required of all Bryn Mawr College students, she lavished praise not only on Shelley but also on the pre-Raphaelites and Swinburne long after they had fallen out of favor. She often claimed that reading was more satisfying than people and told Bryn Mawr College students that she had never passed a day without reading an hour or more in bed. In adulthood, reading may have been more a refuge from life's unfinished business than a spur to action. But it remained an invitation to pleasure; in her seventies, she declared books her "supreme delight," a temptation that kept her from writing her autobiography.[58]

. . . . .

In this study of M. Carey Thomas I have identified a distinctively female culture of reading. I am not suggesting that all bourgeois women read in the same way or with the same intensity, or that Thomas was entirely typical of readers of her class. Inspired by Shelley and the

Romantic poets, with their emphasis on the ego and self-creation, she may have read herself more easily into grandly heroic roles. Her equalitarian feminism did not, for the most part, recognize different spheres for men and women, the more common model among her contemporaries. Where Thomas championed Swinburne and the pre-Raphaelites, others had a penchant for the literature of social protest, for Tolstoy and Walter Besant, the Ruskin of *Unto This Last.*" Nevertheless, shared modes of reading and interpretive conventions permitted many middle-and upper-middle class women to read in self-authorizing ways. Whether stimulated by families, boarding-school and college life, an older tradition of homosocial bonding, or all three, young women often found in reading space to imagine themselves in new ways and to "talk back" to even the most acclaimed authors.

Does this mean that readers, or audiences, have unlimited freedom in interpreting texts? Janice Radway has recently raised this question, citing approvingly a critic who claims: "'there is no overall intrinsic message or meaning in the work.'" Radway goes on to observe: "whatever the theoretical possibility of an infinite number of readings, in fact, there are patterns or regularities to what viewers and readers bring to texts in large part because they acquire specific cultural competencies as a consequence of their particular social location."[59]

Thomas's ability to read herself into texts in empowering ways hinged on her social location in the upper-middle class. Bourgeois women of the Progressive generation, by seizing the authorizing ideology of their class—individualism, formerly for men only—dreamed and read their way into history. Theirs was no Horatio Alger rags-to-riches story, or even one of rags to respectability: women of their class were by definition both respectable and outside the calculus of the market. For women, ambition took the form of entering history as subjects rather than as objects. What was a traditional aspiration for men became for women a novel dream. Such subversive appropriations were not envisioned by critics who believed in the stabilizing force of culture.

An astonishing number of women of the Progressive generation also *wrote* their way into history. In autobiographies that charted their pilgrimages and their progress, they found ways of understanding and constructing themselves far removed from the ideal of self-sacrificing womanhood advanced in their youth by evangelical Protestantism and other sources of authority. Raised on what Victorians considered the "best" books and the belief that writers were the supreme moral authorities, they moved easily from reading to writing. They looked to female as well as male models and to a tradition of female authorship and cultural authority that lasted throughout the century. In their later years, women autobiographers thought they had accomplished enough to make their own stories worth telling, perhaps even inspiring, to others. That they constructed themselves around work rather than personal life underscores their achievement. Women had too long been relegated to private life; at last, they could claim a public one.[60]

Preliminary research on men's autobiographies of the era reveals considerably less attention to reading. The exceptions seem to be mainly those who felt marginal in some way. For the rest, only an occasional man highlights reading, mainly those who later had a professional interest in books. Such differences may be due in part to the conventions of men's and women's autobiographies. But they also point to disparities in upbringing and to men's greater opportunities for other sorts of expression. Expected to be more active and having role models close at hand, men had less need of books to define themselves. Perhaps that explains men's lesser passion for reading, whether measured by autobiographical attributions or by twentieth-century surveys, which consistently find women the predominant readers of fiction.[61]

Evidence from working-class women underscores the class basis of Thomas's ability to read herself into quest plots. Dorothy Richardson, a middle-class writer temporarily employed in a paper-box factory, contrasts her love of *Little Women,* which her co-workers dismissed as "'no story—that's just everyday happenings,'" with their preference for Laura Jean Libbey's *Little Rosebud's Lovers,* a tale of a working-class woman's triumph over all sorts of adversity, including two villainous lovers. Expectations shaped by class as well as educational levels help account for reading preferences. Reading themselves into quest plots may have required too great a leap for most working-class women, whereas romance, particularly in its "Cinderella" version, offered the possibility of pleasurable release: from tiring work, from poverty, from sordidness. By contrast, for middle-class women, heterosexual romance would almost certainly put an end to ambition of other than the domestic sort. Working-class traditions were also less likely to foster an individualistic outlook. British working-class autobiographers, for example, tended to construct an identity around membership in their class, as "'social atoms'" rather than as highly "individuated 'ego[s].'"[62]

In its emphasis on reading as an ongoing part of the lives of individuals, this study, like Radway's work, challenges the tendency of some literary critics to privilege texts and to ascribe to them a universal meaning and absolute prescriptive power. As Roger Chartier has noted, "reading is not simply submission to textual machinery." Gender, class, and historical era are just a few of the variables that influence how books are read and interpreted and the meaning of reading during the course of a life. Historians seeking to understand past experiences of reading will look more to "interpretive communities" than to the "intended" or "inferred" readers hypothesized by some reader-response critics.[63] Bourgeois women of the Progressive generation read many genres, not a single one; they read history, criticism, the classics, and devotional literature as well as fiction; they read more English than American novels. It is less likely that such diverse works contained identical messages than that they were read through lenses fashioned in a particular time and place. Much of what the Progressive generation read was no doubt intended to instill conventional wisdom about gender arrangements. But women's interpretive conventions and social mode of reading often encouraged subversive appropriations.[64] Belief in the possibility of self-creation was a product of a particular class and historical moment. Nevertheless it was a belief that inspired women of the comfortable classes to re-create—through their reading—not only themselves but also the texts they considered their own.

NOTES

This essay is part of a larger study on reading and gender in the late-Victorian era; portions were presented earlier: "Engaging Texts: Stories of Reading of the Progressive Generation of Women," Organization of American Historians, Apr. 8, 1989; "Reading the Self: Books and Identity Among Progressive Women," Rutgers Center for Historical Analysis, Oct. 17, 1989; and "Reading and Female Ambition: M. Carey Thomas and the Heroic Self," American Studies Association, Nov. 2, 1991. Joan Jacobs Brumberg, Mary Kelley, Linda K. Kerber, Dolores Kreisman, Louise L. Stevenson, the participants in the Rutgers Center for Historical Analysis, 1989-1990, and members of my feminist writing group all made helpful suggestions. Special thanks go to Joan Hedrick, Janice Radway, and Martha Vicinus for thoughtful and generous readings that went beyond the call of sisterhood; Janice Radway's intellectual work has been indispensable. I also want to thank Janet Thurman Murphy for research assistance, Caroline Rittenhouse, Bryn Mawr College Archivist, for help with the M. Carey Thomas Papers, the Rutgers Center for Historical Analysis for a stimulating year, Trinity College for a research leave, and the William R. Kenan, Jr., Professorship of American Institutions and Values for research funds. Helen Lefkowitz Horowitz, "'Nous Autres': Reading, Passion, and the Creation of M. Carey Thomas," *Journal of American History* 79 (June 1992): 68-95, appeared after I completed this essay.

[1] M. Carey Thomas Journal, Nov. 10, Feb. 26 [1871], *The Papers of M. Carey Thomas in the Bryn Mawr College Archives,* ed. Lucy Fisher West (Woodbridge, Conn., 1982), reel 1; microfilm edition (hereafter MCTP). Youthful misspellings have been retained. Mournful school essays in early adolescence reveal Thomas's fear that she would fail to fulfill her aspirations. See, for example, "The History of a Pin," MCTP, reel 74, frames 1084-87; her teacher commented on "all the *intensity* of feeling & unsatisfied desire" expressed in the story.

[2] *Reading the Romance: Women, Patriarchy, and Popular Literature* (Chapel Hill, 1984); the quotation is from the preface to the 1991 edition, 7. For a critical review of reader-response criticism, see Jonathan Rose, "Rereading the English Common Reader: A Preface to a History of Audiences," *Journal of the History of Ideas* 53 (Jan.-Mar. 19 92): 47-70.

[3] A complete study of Thomas's reading would treat more fully her intellectual development, her move from religion to aestheticism, her infatuation with Greek, and the emotional intensity of her reading.

[4] Addams, "Woman's Special Training for Peacemaking," *Proceedings of the Second National Peace Congress, Chicago, May 2-5, 1909* (1909): 252; Scudder quoted in Arthur Mann, *Yankee Reformers in the Urban Age: Social Reform in Boston, 1880-1900* (Chicago, 1954), 201. I use the designation "Progressive" more in a generational than in a political sense, for those born roughly between 1855 and 1875. For recent approaches, see *Gender, Class, Race, and Reform in the Progressive Era,* ed. Noralee Frankel and Nancy S. Dye (Lexington, Ky., 1991). Generalizations about women readers are based on research in the diaries, letters, and autobiographies of several dozen white women, including Jane Addams, Florence Kelley, Grace and Edith Abbott, Charlotte Perkins Gilman, Mary Austin, Mary Richmond, Theodate Pope Riddle, and Ida Tarbell. This article is part of a larger project on gender and reading in the late nineteenth century that will include material on African-American and immigrant women. Barbara Sicherman, "Sense and Sensibility: A Case Study of Women's Reading in Late-Victorian America," *Reading in America: Literature and Social History,* ed. Cathy N. Davidson (Baltimore, 1989), 201-25, considers the uses of reading in the mainly female Hamilton family and the reasons reading was so empowering for women at this time.

[5] Pierre Bourdieu, *Distinction: A Social Critique of the Judgement of Taste,* trans. Richard Nice (Cambridge, Mass., 1984).

[6] MCTP Journal, June 20 [1871], MCTP, reel 1. Beatrice Webb, too, "admonished herself for the egoism of romantic fantasy and the egoism of ambition"; even at the age of eleven, she concluded that novels stimulated these propensities. Deborah Epstein Nord, *The Apprenticeship of Beatrice Webb* (Ithaca, N.Y., 1985), 89. Useful discussions of the discourse on women readers and women's reading behavior include: Cathy N. Davidson, *Revolution and the Word: The Rise of the Novel in America* (New York, 1986) and Linda K. Kerber, *Women of the Republic: Intellect and Ideology in Revolutionary America* (Chapel Hill, 1980), ch. 8. Louise L. Stevenson discusses reading advice literature in *The Victorian Homefront: American Thought and Culture, 1860-1880* (New York, 1991), ch. 2.

[7] Jerome L. Singer, *Daydreaming: An Introduction to the Experimental Study of Inner Experience* (New York, 1966), 211, 173, and 143-52. Singer analyzes several of his own recurrent adolescent fantasies—some stimulated by books—which revolved around heroic figures bound for great success, 15-28. Among his subjects, daydreaming peaked between ages fourteen and seventeen, 172.

[8] Victor Nell, *Lost in a Book: The Psychology of Reading for Pleasure* (New Haven, 1988), 2, 9; James Britton, *Language and Learning* (London, 1970), 109. Nell's analysis of reading builds on Johan Huizinga's definition

of play as "a stepping out of 'real' life into a temporary sphere of activity with a disposition all of its own," in *Homo Ludens: A Study of the Play-Element in Culture* (1938; 2d ed., Boston, 1955), 8.

[9] MCT to Mary E. Garrett, Wednesday evening, [July 30, 1884], MCTP, reel 15.

[10] Addams to Ellen Gates Starr, Aug. 11, 1879, reel 1, The Jane Addams Papers, ed. Mary Lynn McCree Bryan (Ann Arbor, 1984); microfilm edition (hereafter JAP); Mercedes M. Randall, *Improper Bostonian: Emily Greene Balch* (New York, 1964), 45; Sicherman, "Sense and Sensibility," 212. *Undine* (1811), by the German romantic Friedrich de La Motte Fouqué, was popular with American girls.

[11] "What Makes a Heroine?: Nineteenth-Century Girls' Biographies," *Genre* 20 (Summer 1987): 171-88. In a stimulating analysis, Rachel Blau DuPlessis, *Writing beyond the Ending: Narrative Strategies of Twentieth-Century Women Writers* (Bloomington, 1985), maintains that in nineteenth-century fiction, quest (Bildung) and romance "could not coexist and be integrated for the heroine at the resolution," 3.

[12] *The Walls Came Tumbling Down* (1947; 2d ed., New York, 1969), 3-4. Ovington links these literary associations to the family culture, noting that the stories she heard from her abolitionist grandmother also fueled her imagination: "I did not get all the material for my dreams from books."

[13] MCTP, "Autobiographical Materials," reel 74, frame 860; Helen Thomas Flexner, *A Quaker Childhood* (New Haven, 1940), 11. These sources contain biographical material on Thomas and her family, as do *The Making of a Feminist, Early Journals and Letters of M. Carey Thomas,* ed. Majorie Housepian Dobkin (n.p., Kent State University Press, 1979), James Thomas Flexner, *An American Saga: The Story of Helen Thomas and Simon Flexner* (Boston, 1984), and Edith Finch, *Carey Thomas of Bryn Mawr* (New York, 1947). Thomas's claim that her parents' interest in religion was so intense that it precluded other types of reading is contradicted by contemporary evidence.

[14] "Autobiographical Materials," MCTP, reel 74, frames 551-52, 868, 858, and MCT Journal, Nov. 12, and Nov. 19 [1870], reel 1. Thomas kept lists of her reading from 1873 to 1883, ibid., frames 541-72. In the early years, her categories were: books she wanted to buy, those she "got some new thoughts from!," those that were "utterly worthless!," and those she liked, frame 541. Despite Thomas's formulaic remonstrances about reading trash, she seems to have been little troubled by the secular nature of her reading, a matter of considerable concern to her closest male cousin. See [Hannah Whitall Smith], *The Record of a Happy Life: Being Memorials of Franklin Whitall Smith, A Student of Princeton College. By His Mother* (Philadelphia, 1873), 182-87.

[15] "Autobiographical Materials," MCTP, reel 74, frames 857-58. Thomas called the period of her illness a time of "enforced quiet" and passivity. As an active child, she must have found the passivity of invalidism unbearable even though it brought greater attention from her beloved mother; she must also have learned to live intensely in imagination. Thomas claimed that the years between her recovery and boarding school were occupied mainly by reading (reel 74, frame 497).

[16] On the submissions to *Harper's,* see MCT Journal, Jan. 2, 1872, MCTP, reel 1; the poem was "The Lovers," in "My Poetical Effusions," reel 1, frames 351-52. Earlier, an aunt mailed a poem, "Snowflakes," to *The Leisure Moments,* a Quaker publication; it may have been published. MCT Journal, Jan. 9, 1871, reel 1; Finch, *Thomas,* 23.

[17] Addams to Vallie Beck, Mar. 16, 1876 and Addams to Ellen Gates Starr, May 15, 1880, JAP, reel 1. See also Addams to Starr, Aug. 11, 1879, ibid.: "there is something in Carlyle that just suits me as no one else does."

[18] MCT Journal, June 20, 1870, MCTP, reel 1; there is an earlier, fragmentary journal. As a model for diary keeping, Jo was a transitional figure; by 1872 Thomas kept the journal in her own name only. On adolescent diary keeping, a predominantly female activity, see Jane H. Hunter, "Inscribing the Self in the Heart of the Family: Diaries and Girlhood in Late-Victorian America," *American Quarterly* 44 (Mar. 1992): 51-81 and Joan Jacobs Brumberg, "'Dear Diary': Continuity and Change in the Voices of Adolescent Girls," unpublished paper.

[19] Franklin Whitall Smith to MCT, Feb. 20, 1870, MCTP, reel 58; Elizabeth King Ellicott to MCT, Nov. 23 [1879], reel 39. Thomas and Smith addressed one another in letters as Laurie and Jo and also signed in these personae.

[20] Linda K. Kerber, "Can a Woman Be an Individual?: The Limits of Puritan Tradition in the Early Republic," *Texas Studies in Literature and Language* 25 (Spring, 1983): 166. Alcott criticism is extensive; useful introductions are Alma J. Payne, *Louisa May Alcott: A Reference Guide* (Boston, 1980) and Madeleine B. Stern, ed., *Critical Essays on Louisa May Alcott* (Boston, 1984). See also Sarah Elbert, *A Hunger for Home: Louisa May Alcott and "Little Women"* (Philadelphia, 1984).

[21] Vallie Beck to Jane Addams, Aug. 10, 1877, JAP, reel 1; see also MCT Journal, passim. The domestic fiction of an earlier era does not seem to have played an important part in the formation of female adolescent identity for Thomas's generation, except perhaps negatively. In "Literary History as a Challenge to Literary Theory, *New Directions in Literary History,* ed. Ralph Cohen (Baltimore, 1974), 11-41, Jauss maintains that in literature (as distinct from historical life) the horizon of expectations "not only preserves real experiences but also anticipates unrealized possibilities, widens the limited range of social behavior by new wishes, demands, and goals, and thereby opens avenues for future experience," 37.

[22] *Little Women* (New York: The Modern Library, 1983), 178, 177, 460, 601. My reading of the novel was stimulated by a conversation with Lauren Berlant.

[23] Despite initial doubts by Alcott and her publisher, the first volume (1868) sold well and the publisher demanded a sequel, which appeared in 1869. See *The Journals of Louisa May Alcott,* ed. Joel Myerson and Daniel Shealy, with Madeleine B. Stern (Boston, 1989); *The Selected Letters of Louisa May Alcott,* ed. Joel Myerson and Daniel Shealy, with Madeleine B. Stern (Boston, 1987); and *Louisa May Alcott: Her Life, Letters and Journals,* ed. Ednah D. Cheney (1889; 2d ed., Boston, 1890).

[24] On the cleaning up of Alcott's prose between the 1868-69 edition and the 1880 version, on which the modern text is based, see Elaine Showalter, "*Little Women:* The American Female Myth," in *Sister's Choice: Tradition and Change in American Women's Writing* (Oxford, 1991), 55-57. Even before reading Alcott's *Rose in Bloom,* Jane Addams wanted to finish "the story to suit [her]self"; Addams to Vallie Beck, May 3, 1877, JAP, reel 1. To Frank Smith, the appeal of *Little Women* was enhanced by its autobiographical status, although he had the "real" Jo marrying Laurie; Smith to MCT, Mar. 6, 1870, MCTP, reel 58. Years later, an aspiring poet wrote Thomas: "Do you know what I've been reading with great delight? 'Little Women,' & I tell you they're more genuine art creations, narrow, vulgar, petty though they be, than even George Eliot's complicated creatures. And why because they're wrought from within outwardly." Richard Cadbury to MCT, Aug. 4, 1880, reel 37. Alcott was one of the few authors of "girls' books" mentioned by male autobiographers, among them Theodore Roosevelt.

[25] Thomas and her cousin Bessie King had a home publication, which may have been modelled on "The Pickwick Portfolio" in *Little Women.* Radway notes that many romance writers were originally romance readers; *Reading the Romance,* 2nd ed., 17.

[26] Jane Addams's notes for an American literature course at Rockford College indicate that the canon included school texts and domestic literature as well as *belles lettres* which later dominated the field. Emma Willard appears along with Harriet Beecher Stowe, as do pertinent biographical facts from which an aspiring writer might take heart—such as publication of a first poem at fifteen. "American Literature," [1878-1879], JAP, reel 27, frames 239-95. On women authors, see Nina Baym, *Woman's Fiction: A Guide to Novels by and about Women in America, 1820-1870* (Ithaca, N.Y., 1978); Mary Kelley, *Private Woman, Public Stage: Literary Domesticity in Nineteenth-Century America* (New York, 1984); and Susan Coultrap-McQuin, *Doing Literary Business: American Women Writers in the Nineteenth Century* (Chapel Hill, 1990). See also Theodora Penny Martin, *The Sound of Our Own Voices: Women's Study Clubs, 1860-1910* (Boston, 1987).

[27] On changing sources of cultural authority, see Paul Lauter, "Race and Gender in the Shaping of the American Literary Canon: A Case Study from the Twenties," *Feminist Studies* 9 (Fall 1983): 435-63; Joan Shelley Rubin, "Self, Culture, and Self-Culture in Modern America: The Early History of the Book-of-the-Month Club," *Journal of American History* 71 (Mar. 1985): 782-806; Lawrence W. Levine, *High Brow/Low Brow: The Emergence of Cultural Hierarchy in America* (Cambridge, Mass., 1988); and Janice Radway, "The Scandal of the Middlebrow: The Book-of-the-Month Club, Class Fracture, and Cultural Authority," *South Atlantic Quarterly* 89 (Fall 1990): 259-84.

[28] These seem to me to be the implications of works as diverse as Rachel M. Brownstein, *Becoming a Heroine: Reading about Women in Novels* (New York, 1984 [1982]); Jonathan Culler, *On Deconstruction: Theory and Criticism after Structuralism* (Ithaca, N.Y., 1982), 43-64; Judith Fetterley, *The Resisting Reader: A Feminist Approach to American Fiction* (Bloomington, Ind., 1978); Patrocinio P. Schweickart, "Reading Ourselves: Toward a Feminist Theory of Reading," *Gender and Reading: Essays on Readers, Texts, and Contexts,* ed. Elizabeth A. Flynn and Patrocinio P. Schweickart (Baltimore, 1986), 31-62.

[29] Cora Kaplan, "*The Thorn Birds:* Fiction, Fantasy, Femininity," in *Sea Changes: Feminism and Culture* (London, 1986), 125, 120, 134, 123.

[30] MCT Journal, Mar. 12 [1871], MCTP, reel 1 (see also supra, 73); the prose selections include Mahomet, Dante, and Luther from *On Heroes,* one from *Sartor Resartus,* and a biographical entry about Carlyle, MCTP, reel 1, frames 417 ff.; Elizabeth King Ellicott to MCT, May 14 [1882], reel 39.

[31] *On Heroes, Hero-Worship, and the Heroic in History. Six Lectures. Reported, with Emendations and Additions* (New York, 1841), 1, 178; MCT to Mary E. Garrett, June 10 [1881], reel 15. A taste for Carlyle seems to have marked a stage for men as well as women. Sociologist Edward Alsworth Ross claimed that he was "a thrall of Carlyle" at twenty but outgrew hero worship and "Carlylese" two years later. *Seventy Years of It: An Autobiography* (New York, 1936), 21, 30.

[32] MCT Journal, Feb. 26 [1871], MCTP, reel 1.

[33] "Selections From Prose Writers," MCTP, reel 1, frame 435; Sharon O'Brien, "Tomboyism and Adolescent Conflict: Three Nineteenth-Century Case Studies," in *Woman's Being, Woman's Place: Female Identity and Vocation in American History,* ed. Mary Kelley (Boston, 1979), 351-72 (Alcott is one of O'Brien's examples). For a powerful reading experience in which Thomas identifies with a Christian knight, see MCT Journal, Nov. 16, 1874, MCTP, reel 1, frames 513, 515-16.

[34] Klee, "The American Heroine," *Evening Transcript,* July 21, 1879, in Katharine Lee Bates Papers, Scrapbook

of Writings (1876-1885), Wellesley College Archives. I am grateful to Patricia Palmieri for calling this reference to my attention and to Wilma Slaight for providing a copy.

[35] I am grateful to Joan Hedrick for suggesting this connection.

[36] "Some of the Representative Men of the Present Time" [1875], "Autobiographical Materials," MCTP, reel 74, frames 1091-96; Thomas's representative "men" were all writers. See also Charles Kingsley, "Heroism," *Sanitary and Social Lectures and Essays* (London, 1889), 225-54; the essay was first published in 1874.

[37] MCT Journal, Mar. 14, 1872, MCTP, reel 1. See also MCT to Franklin Whitall Smith, "I put no date," reel 29, frame 483, and [May 4, 1872], frames 430-44, which includes a poem, "Rex & Rush," written on the occasion of this fantasy, and Smith to MCT, Mar. 7, 1872, reel 58. Before starting Cornell in 1875, Thomas exchanged her childhood nickname, Minnie, for the grownup and more ambiguous Carey. In her early twenties, Thomas continued to assert the essential similarity of the sexes. Favoring an androgynous ideal that allowed for tenderness in men and strength in women, she sought to remove gendered labels from these traits and to redefine them as human. See, for example, MCT to Richard Cadbury [1880-81], reel 13, frames 260-61, and MCT to Mary Whitall Thomas, Feb. 27 [1881], reel 31, MCTP.

[38] Carolyn G. Heilburn, *Writing a Woman's Life* (New York, 1988), 11. Heilbrun assumes that this writing occurs "unconsciously, and without [the woman's] recognizing or naming the process." But Thomas and many of her contemporaries consciously wrote their lives in advance. On Thomas and Bryn Mawr, see Helen Lefkowitz Horowitz, *Alma Mater: Design and Experience in the Women's Colleges from Their Nineteenth-Century Beginnings to the 1930s* (New York, 1984), 105-33.

[39] MCT to Mary Whitall Thomas, Nov. 25, 1882, MCTP, reel 32. Thomas's mother and aunt Hannah Whitall Smith, a Quaker preacher and religious writer, encouraged her ambitions.

[40] Although Thomas was admitted to Hopkins as a graduate student, she was not allowed to attend classes and resigned the following year. The fullest account of the Friday Night is Barbara Landis Chase, "M. Carey Thomas and the 'Friday Night': A Case Study in Female Social Networks and Personal Growth," M.A. thesis, Johns Hopkins University, 1990. I am grateful to Barbara Chase for sending a copy of her thesis. There are articles on Elizabeth King Ellicott, Mary Elizabeth Garrett, and Julia R. Rogers in *Notable Maryland Women,* ed. Winifred G. Helmes (Cambridge, Md., 1977). See also Hugh Hawkins, "Mary Elizabeth Garrett," *Notable American Women, 1607-1950,* ed. Edward T. James, Janet Wilson James, and Paul S. Boyer (Cambridge, Mass., 1971), II: 21-22; "Autobiographical Materials"

(on Garrett), MCTP, reel 75, frames 551-672; and "In Memoriam Mary Gwinn Hodder," *Bryn Mawr Alumnae Bulletin* (Jan. 1941), 19. Biographical data on group members was also obtained from Bryn Mawr College, the Enoch Pratt Free Library, the Maryland Historical Society, and Goucher College.

[41] Mary E. Garrett Diary, Tuesday [June 14, 1870], Mary E. Garrett Papers, Bryn Mawr College Archives. Garrett also rejected Ruskin's strictures against studying theology. *Sesame and Lilies. Three Lectures* (New York, 1865 2d ed., New York, 1890). Garrett was studying Greek despite her father's disapproval. At about the same time, Garrett, Rogers, and King participated in an informal reading group. Thomas was invited to join, but it is not clear whether she did. Garrett Diary, Sat. [June 11, 1870] and Friday [June 17, 1870], Garrett Papers.

[42] MCT to Mary E. Garrett, [postmarked July 24, 1879], MCTP, reel 15; Elizabeth King Ellicott to MCT, Dec. 16 [1880], reel 39. Garrett thought it degrading that Jane Austen's characters did not aspire beyond the "commonplace." Garrett to MCT, July 15, 1879, reel 42.

[43] MCT Journal, Feb. 2 [1878], MCTP, reel 2; the collective novel is in MCTP, ibid., frames 914-78. Gwinn recalled later that Garrett, Rogers, and King "had been projecting a small club of the like-minded, to convene at one another's houses fortnightly and read to one another bookish papers." Mary Mackall Gwinn Hodder to Logan Pearsall Smith, 17 Feb. 1938, Mary Mackall Gwinn Faculty File, Bryn Mawr College Archives. An essay by Gwinn on seven Bolognese women intellectuals from the fourteenth through eighteenth centuries reveals both a conscious search for role models and recognition of the difficulties under which they labored. Mary Mackall Gwinn Hodder, "The Friday Night, 1878-1879," MCTP, reel 71, frames 5-14. For the generative influence of the heterosocial parlor on women's literary careers, see Joan D. Hedrick, "Parlor Literature: Harriet Beecher Stowe and the Question of 'Great Women Artists,'" *Signs* 17 (Winter 1992): 275-303.

[44] In Germany, Thomas and Gwinn made a practice of reading novels during their periods, the time physicians deemed women most liable to injure themselves by studying. Indulging themselves in a pleasure they sometimes denied themselves, they turned a negative image of women reading to their own purposes—while also hedging their bets. MCT to Mary E. Garrett, Nov. 30 [1880], MCTP, reel 15.

[45] See untitled entry on statues recently excavated at Pergamus, then on display in Berlin, in the "Notes" section, *The Nation* No. 765 (Feb. 26, 1880): 156, and articles on education in *The Quaker Alumnus* I (1879): 36-37, 57-58, and 64; for a time Thomas's and King's names appeared on the masthead.

[46] Elizabeth King Ellicott to MCT, [May 1880], MCTP, reel 39; MCT to Mary Whitall Thomas, [July 12, 1880],

reel 31. Thomas defined *"nous autres"* as "the Gautier, Rossetti school"; in the context of the letter (a reply to one from her mother probably dated June 22, 1880, reel 61) she seems to be referring principally to the group's commitment to literary excellence rather than to sexual transgression. Helen Lefkowitz Horowitz in "'Nous Autres'" emphasizes the importance of Thomas's reading in creating an identity based on acknowledged "passion" for women. She views this identity, which she links especially to Thomas's reading of Swinburne and Théophile Gautier's *Mademoiselle de Maupin,* as falling in time and nature between the sentimental friendships of "the female world of love and ritual" described by Carroll Smith-Rosenberg and a full-fledged twentieth-century lesbian identity. My argument does not hinge on the question of Thomas's sexual identity, but see supra, 90.

[47] MCT Journal, Thanksgiving 1874, MCTP, reel 1, frame 516; MCT to Garrett, Nov. 10, [1880], reel 15. Cf. Elizabeth King Ellicott to MCT, Oct. 9 [1881], reel 39. Of "a true type of a *'literary smash'*" with a female friend at Cornell, Thomas said: "It was dancing & Swinburne that did it." MCT to Anna Shipley, Jan. 30, 1876, Nov. 21 [1875], reel 29; the poem was *Atalanta in Calydon.* Although Swinburne's scandalous reputation seems to have abated among literary critics by the mid-1870s, Thomas felt obliged to defend her favorite to a young Quaker friend, ibid. For a discussion of Swinburne's challenge to religion and conventional sexual norms, see Thaïs E. Morgan, "Swinburne's Dramatic Monologues: Sex and Ideology," *Victorian Poetry* 22 (Summer 1984): 175-95. Other influences in Thomas's move away from orthodoxy were Matthew Arnold's *Religion and Dogma* and Herbert Spencer. Still struggling with the question of belief, she read Spencer's attack on religion "almost choking with anger," but felt compelled to accept him because she could find "no flaw in his logic." MCT to Mary E. Garrett, July 7, 1878, MCTP, reel 15.

[48] MCT Journal, Feb. 2 [1878], MCTP, reel 2. Gwinn later claimed she had never believed in free love. Gwinn Hodder to Logan Pearsall Smith, 17 Feb. 1938, Bryn Mawr College Archives.

[49] MCT Journal, Apr. 6, 1878, MCTP, reel 2. See also MCT to Mary Whitall Thomas, dated "first day 8th mo. 25th," but probably July 25, 1880, reel 31; Nancy F. Cott, "Passionlessness: An Interpretation of Victorian Sexual Ideology, 1790-1850," *Signs* 4 (Winter 1978): 219-36.

[50] Elizabeth King Ellicott to MCT, Saturday [1884], reel 39; MCT to Margaret Hicks Volkmann, [Aug. 30, 1880], reel 32; MCT to Mary Whitall Thomas, Nov. 13, 1880, reel 31, all MCTP. See also MCT Journal, Mar. 24 [1878], reel 2. On Thomas's sexual identity, see Horowitz, "'Nous Autres'"; Lillian Faderman, *Odd Girls and Twilight Lovers: A History of Lesbian Life in Twentieth-Century America* (New York, 1991), 28-31, 37; Carroll Smith-Rosenberg, "The New Woman as An-

drogyne: Social Disorder and Gender Crisis, 1870-1936," *Disorderly Conduct: Visions of Gender in Victorian America* (New York, 1985), esp. 273-74; and Dobkin, *The Making of a Feminist,* esp. 77-87.

[51] MCT to Mary E. Garrett, New Year's Eve 1880, MCTP, reel 15; MCT to Mary Whitall Thomas, Feb. 7, 1880, reel 31. See also MCT to Richard Cadbury, June 26 [1880], reel 13; all MCTP. Thomas's family connections did not hurt her career options: her father and an uncle were trustees of the new college.

[52] MCT to Mary E. Garrett, Nov. 2 [1880], reel 15; Mary Whitall Thomas to MCT, June 28, 1880, reel 61, MCTP. Thomas also described Christina Rossetti as having "her broken woman['s] heart in her hand"; MCT to Richard Cadbury, undated [1880-81], reel 13, frame 259. Despite such disparaging remarks. Thomas was genuinely interested in women writers of her era, liked some of their work, and must have envied them. She wrote self-consciously of waiting for her "daimon" and of finding it "a profanation" to write "in cold blood"; see, for example, MCT to Cadbury, Nov. 23, 1880, reel 13.

[53] I wish to thank Martha Vicinus for elucidating these points.

[54] MCT Journal, Mar. 24, July 6, [1878], MCTP, reel 2; MCT to Mary E. Garrett, July 7, 1878, reel 15. Thomas described going to the circulating library and getting out novels "almost without meaning to." The theme of self-renunciation and a 'dying daily' recurred. See Journal, June 26 [1878], reel 2. See also Journal, Aug. 23 [1878], reel 2, in which Thomas describes overcoming a momentary impulse to commit suicide; she attributes a literary reflection on Shelley with resolving her religious doubts and saving her. The passage reads like an account out of romantic literature, with its vogue for youthful suicide.

[55] In mid-1878, Thomas felt distracted by a relationship with a prospective suitor; she was distressed by Johns Hopkins's failure to treat her as a regular student; and she was still troubled about religion.

[56] MCT to Mary E. Garrett, Nov. 2 [1880] and Oct. 15 [1881], MCTP, reel 15. Cf. Julia Rogers to Garrett, [Sept. 10, 1880], reel 71; noting that she could hardly make herself put down *Bleak House,* Rogers thought it was "rather late in life . . . to be absorbed in this way by such books." On reading and prolonged adolescence, see Sicherman, "Sense and Sensibility." In the twentieth century, at least, book and magazine reading decreased with age; married women also read less. See Carl F. Kaestle et al., *Literacy in the United States: Readers and Reading since 1880* (New Haven, 1991), 190, 201.

[57] The story is told in part in Alan M. Chesney, *The Johns Hopkins Hospital and The Johns Hopkins University School of Medicine: A Chronicle,* I (Baltimore, 1943), and Hugh Hawkins, *Pioneer: A History of the Johns Hopkins University, 1874-1889* (Ithaca, N.Y., 1960). On

the Bryn Mawr School, see Rosamond Randall Beirne, *Let's Pick the Daisies: The History of the Bryn Mawr School, 1885-1967* (Baltimore, 1970).

[58] Flexner, *A Quaker Childhood,* 302; Millicent Carey McIntosh, "Foreword," in Dobkin, *Making of a Feminist,* x. Thomas's course notes are in MCTP, reel 4; see esp. frames 879-85 and 900. On reading as a temptation, see "Autobiographical Materials," reel 74, frame 497.

[59] Quotations are from the new introduction to *Reading the Romance* (1991), 8.

[60] For this reason, I find Patricia Meyer Spacks's criticism of women autobiographers for presenting "selves in hiding" somewhat misplaced; "Selves in Hiding," in *Women's Autobiography: Essays in Criticism,* ed. Estelle C. Jelinek (Bloomington, 1980), 112-32. Men's autobiographies of the period were also constructed around work; see Robert F. Sayre, "The Proper Study—Autobiographies in American Studies," *American Quarterly* 29 (1977): 254-55. Informative essays appear in *Interpreting Women's Lives: Feminist Theory and Personal Narratives,* ed. The Personal Narratives Group (Bloomington, 1989); *The Private Self: Theory and Practice of Women's Autobiographical Writings,* ed. Shari Benstock (Chapel Hill, 1988); and *Life/Lines: Theorizing Women's Autobiography,* ed. Bella Brodzki and Celeste Schenck (Ithaca, N.Y., 1988). See also Heilbrun, *Writing a Woman's Life.* Despite years of effort and masses of assembled notes, Thomas never wrote her autobiography. For whatever reason, at the end of her life she was unable to cast herself as the hero—or heroine—of her own story.

[61] Women autobiographers attribute a great deal to reading (the choice of a vocation, the loss of faith), but the emphasis on ambition as such is mine.

[62] Dorothy Richardson, *The Long Day: The Story of a New York Working Girl* (1905; 2d ed., Chicago, 1972), 75-86, quotation, 86; Michael Denning, *Mechanic Accents: Dime Novels and Working-Class Culture in America* (London and New York, 1987), 197-200, ana-lyzes *Little Rosebud's Lovers* as a "Cinderella story"; Regenia Gagnier, "Social Atoms: Working-Class Autobiography, Subjectivity, and Gender," *Victorian Studies* 30 (Spring 1987): 335-63. See also Mary Jo Maynes, "Gender and Narrative Form in French and German Working-Class Autobiographies," *Interpreting Women's Lives,* 103-17. By focusing on class differences here, I do not mean to suggest that there was no overlap either in reading tastes or in ambition. There was. But social location influences interpretation. For several Jewish immigrant autobiographers, for example, *Little Women* was their first "real" American novel. As such, they found it liberating, but for different reasons than Thomas did.

[63] Roger Chartier, "Texts, Printing, Readings," *The New Cultural History,* ed. Lynn Hunt (Berkeley and Los Angeles, 1989), 156. The classic statement on interpretive communities is Stanley Fish, *Is There a Text in This Class?: The Authority of Interpretive Communities* (Cambridge, Mass., 1980), 167-73.

[64] Chartier highlights reading as "appropriation," in "Texts, Printing, Readings," 173. As noted, Thomas also used the term.

FURTHER READING

Biography

Horowitz, Helen Lefkowitz. *The Power and Passion of M. Carey Thomas.* New York: Alfred A. Knopf, 1994, 526 p.
    Comprehensive critical biography of Thomas.

Meigs, Cornelia. "Martha Carey Thomas." In *What Makes a College? A History of Bryn Mawr,* pp. 65-120. New York: The Macmillan Company, 1956.
    Studies Thomas's considerable influence as president of Bryn Mawr College between 1894 and 1922.

Ben Ames Williams

1889-1953

American novelist and short story writer.

INTRODUCTION

Williams was one of the best-known American writers of magazine fiction and novels of the first half of the twentieth century. A frequent contributor to the *Saturday Evening Post* and other popular periodicals of the 1920s and 1930s, Williams published more than 400 short stories, essays, and serialized novels. He also produced more than thirty books of fiction in a variety of subgenres, including adventures, mysteries, and historical novels. Over the course of his career, Williams came to be associated with rural Maine, where many of his stories, including those collected in *Fraternity Village,* were set. In these and other works Williams sought "to interweave fact and fiction," as evidenced by the meticulous research he generally conducted before writing. Primarily considered a popular author, Williams is nonetheless valued as a skilled realist and craftsman of the short story form; his historical novel *House Divided* is viewed among his finest achievements.

Biographical Information

Williams was born in Macon, Mississippi on 7 March 1889. He spent his youth in Jackson, Ohio, where his father Daniel Webster Williams was editor and owner of the local newspaper. Williams received his primary education in Jackson, and later attended the Allen School in West Newton, Massachusetts and was privately tutored for a time while living with his family in Cardiff, Wales. He entered Dartmouth College in 1906 and upon graduation in 1910 moved to Ohio to run the *Standard Journal*, his father's paper. In September of that year he returned to the Northeast. Williams took a job as a reporter at the *Boston American* and began to write short fiction. During the course of four years, over eighty of his stories were rejected for publication by various periodicals; he waited four years before one of his pieces, "The Wings of Lias," was accepted for publication in *Smith's Magazine*. By 1916, increased sales of his writing allowed Williams to leave the *American* and concentrate on fiction writing. Between 1917 and 1941, 179 of his stories, essays, and serials appeared in the *Saturday Evening Post,* and others were published in competing periodicals. In 1918 Williams visited the small town of Searsmont, Maine where he purchased a summer home. He continued to return to Searsmont for the remainder of his life, fictionalizing the village as Fraternity, Maine in an extended series of short stories. Williams's first unserialized novel, *Splendor,* appeared in 1927. Over the next several decades he published short fiction and 35 more novels, many of them best-sellers. Williams died on 4 February 1953 of a heart attack.

Major Works

During the course of his career, Williams wrote several adventure and mystery novels including *The Silver Forest, The Dreadful Night,* and *Leave Her to Heaven.* It is for his realistic short stories and historical novels that he is primarily distinguished. *Splendor* details the life of a Boston journalist, Henry Beeker, in the years 1872 to 1916. *Come Spring* describes the circumstances of Joel Adam after returning to Maine's wilderness frontier following the close of the American Revolutionary War. Williams's sprawling Civil War novel *House Divided* analyzes the impact of war on an aristocratic Southern family, and is filled with historical detail uncovered by considerable research. Set in southern Ohio during the 1890s, *Owen Glen* recounts the life of a young Welsh-American boy growing up in a small mining town. Representative of his early short fiction, "They Grind Exceedingly Small," an ironic parable, appeared in the *Saturday Evening Post* in 1919 and later earned Williams the O. Henry Memorial Award. Among his other short works, the stories of *Fraternity Village* epitomize many of Williams's detailed, character-driven pieces. These tales frequently featured the amusing, idyllic anecdotes of Chet McAusland or the thrill of adventure, as in "Another Man's Poison," a tale of two escaped convicts who invade the otherwise bucolic town of Fraternity.

Critical Reception

Extremely popular in their day, many of Williams's novels appeared at the top of best-seller lists. Beyond popular appreciation, the balance of criticism at the time came from generally positive reviewers and Williams himself, who admitted that he consciously emulated the style of such writers as Guy de Maupassant, O. Henry, and Bret Harte. Early in his career, Williams also acknowledged that the work of translating Georges Polti's *Thirty-Six Dramatic Situations* had provided him with fodder for the plotlines of his stories. Since his death, critical appreciation of Williams's fiction has failed to match his earlier, popular success. Nevertheless he has been praised for his realism, use of detail and irony, directness, and skill as a storyteller.

PRINCIPAL WORKS

All the Brothers Were Valiant (novel) 1919
The Sea Bride (novel) 1919
The Great Accident (novel) 1920
Evered (novel) 1921
Black Pawl (novel) 1922
Audacity (novel) 1923
Sangsue (novel) 1923
Thrifty Stock, and Other Stories (short stories) 1923
The Rational Hind (novel) 1925
The Silver Forest (novel) 1926
Immortal Longings (novel) 1927
Splendor (novel) 1927
The Dreadful Night (novel) 1928
Death on Scurvy Street [also published as *The Bellmer Mystery*] (novel) 1929
Great Oaks (novel) 1930
Touchstone (novel) 1930
An End to Mirth (novel) 1931
Pirate's Purchase (novel) 1931
Honeyflow (novel) 1932
Money Musk [republished as *Lady in Peril*] (novel) 1932
Mischief (novel) 1933
Pascal's Mill (novel) 1933
Hostile Valley [republished as *Valley Vixen*] (novel) 1934
Small Town Girl (novel) 1935
Crucible (novel) 1937
The Strumpet Sea [republished as *Once Aboard the Whaler*] (novel) 1938
The Happy End (short stories) 1939
Thread of Scarlet (novel) 1939
Come Spring (novel) 1940

The Strange Woman (novel) 1941
Time of Peace (novel) 1942
Leave Her to Heaven (novel) 1944
It's a Free Country (novel) 1945
House Divided (novel) 1947
Fraternity Village (short stories) 1949
Owen Glen (novel) 1950
The Unconquered (novel) 1953

CRITICISM

Charles C. Baldwin (essay date 1925)

SOURCE: "Ben Ames Williams," in *The Men Who Make Our Novels,* revised edition, Dodd, Mead and Company, 1925, pp. 578-83.

[*In the following essay, Baldwin evaluates Williams as a storyteller.*]

We live and learn, we do; and there's no place for learning like an American college. Take Dartmouth—if you can. When Ben Ames Williams entered Dartmouth in 1906 he was told that he had no faintest conception of what good English was or ought to be. Four years later, on graduation, the same prof—remembered as the caster of that first slur—openly hailed Mr. Williams as one of only two men in his class capable of producing true literary English.

However, true literary English is a drug on the market; and Williams' learning brought him little or nothing. During six years as reporter (and latterly as a re-write man) on the Boston *American,* eighty-two short stories by Mr. Williams were refused before one, in 1914, was accepted—and in 1912 he had married an old sweetheart, the daughter of a long line of sea-captains familiar with the China trade. It was a desperate business, but it explains, in part, Mr. Williams' austerity. It proves his courage, if proof were necessary. It attests the hard discipline he underwent before winning to his present success.

There is in every line he writes a history of that long bout with the editors. Soon or late he would force them to accept him. But the ordeal made him old as it made him impatient of irrelevance. He has none of the amateur knowingness of Chambers or Vance and none of the sheer fatuity of Arthur Stringer. He is a magazine author, true; but with Hergesheimer, he always gives of his best—he is serious. He writes because he is a born writer, and not because some editor or other has taken a fancy to his writings.

II

Though born in Macon, Mississippi, March 7, 1889, Mr. Williams spent his youth in Jackson, Ohio, where his father was (and is) the editor of a country weekly, one of the most amusing and likable of Ohio's thousand and one editors, recently a candidate for governor in the primaries, running against Donahey.

William Dean Howells was the son of an Ohio editor; and Howells got his learning (what little it was) of Latin and Greek from browsing among his father's books. So too, with Williams. The house was like a library; and until he went East to school, at fifteen, his chief delight had been in listening to his mother read from one or another of his father's books. Indeed, until he entered Dartmouth, he had little formal education, for he had scarcely begun at his Eastern preparatory school when his father was made consul at Cardiff, in Wales, and the family transferred to Britain. There he studied Latin with a tutor until he found himself reading it for pleasure; from then on most of his preparation for college was done alone.

III

It was in 1916 that Mr. Williams was discovered by Bob Davis of *Munsey's*, the most enterprising and generous editor in America—possibly (now) excepting H. L. Mencken. Encouraged by Mr. Davis, Williams resigned from the Boston *American* and settled down to an author's life. He took a house at Newtonville in Massachusetts and spent his summers at a camp near Belfast in Maine. One place or the other he works, fishes, shoots, plays with his two growing boys, and drives a Ford station-wagon, locally known as the Yellow Peril.

IV

Mr. Williams is first, last and all the time a storyteller. It is the story that matters to him. And so his characters are forced, are created and designed, to fit the patterns of his plots. Yet because his plots have something of the diffuseness, the irony and inevitability of life, his characters, at times, grip the heart. I say "at times" because I am more often amazed by the skill of Mr. Williams than touched by the humanness of his people. It is the sorry scheme of things rather than the sorry plight of men and women caught in the tangle of that scheme that is brought out and emphasized in Mr. Williams' books.

Evered is a case in point. Evered is a farmer in New England, morose and lonely, with a great reputation for temper and strength. There is a tale of his having killed a neighbor, in self-defense, when that neighbor disputed his way of slaughtering hogs. Evered marries (for his second wife) a Mary whom he loves. She knows he loves her and he knows it; yet such is his inability, his want of understanding, his alone-ness, he cannot express that love and so assure her (and himself) of it. Evered is the owner of a huge red bull, a bull gone wild, a bull that is the central character of the story, the peg from which everything hangs. This bull breaks loose from the bull-pen, to go on a rampage. Evered takes his gun and starts out in search of the bull. In the pasture he comes upon his wife

in whispered conversation with a man, in intimate conversation. He stops. He watches them. He notes the way they lean together, how considerate they are, one of the other. He is certain that they are lovers. The world goes black before him. He is consumed with rage and jealousy, his lips are hot with hate. Just then the bull comes into the pasture.

It is a fault (I am sure) in this type of story that you know that Evered, in his madness, allows the bull to kill his wife; and that later, repenting of his folly, coming to see that he has been an idle accomplice in murder, he will go out and with his bare hands duel with that bull, under a clear moon, to the death. It is a fault that is ever-present in the too careful plotting of romance. It may be like life but it is not fine art. Here we scheme our ways or drift to our conclusions; but in art there is a wider vision, more of the divinely unexpected, less of calculation.

V

Black Pawl is like *Evered* in its slow moving toward an appointed goal. It has the directness and simplicity of Greek tragedy, the pity and the irony of the Greeks. You realize that these people cannot escape their fate. But in that realization you lose something of the joy of surprise. You feel that there is no help for them and so you sit back; you do not join with them in their adventures; you are the audience pure and simple, an onlooker.

Black Pawl is the name of a whaling captain, so named to distinguish him from his son, Red Pawl—the one having black and the other a pawl of red hair. The mother of Red had deserted them, running away with a seaman while the boy was on his first voyage to the South Pacific with his father; and Black Pawl raises his son in hatred of all love, of all gentle and good and lovely things. It is the consummation of that hate, its final flowering and destruction, when the good that is in the Captain comes to death grips with the evil in the son, that makes the book.

Not that this is all the good that is in the story. There is the sea—and the clear stars of a tropic night—a missionary—and the captain's daughter who had been born to the runaway wife eight months after Black Pawl set out on the whaling expedition that was to separate them forever. There is talk of God and a man's way with his woman, of murder and vengeance and retribution. There are three or four titanic battles. And there is death to top it all.

VI

Mr. Williams is not an easy writer; he is not facile or slipshod or merely sensational. Again and again his sentences come like periods to a full stop, ending all debate in the just and only appropriate word. They have finality. They are convincing. Indeed I believe that Mr. Williams will take that place in our literature that should have been Hergesheimer's—had Mr. Hergesheimer been a little less anxious to see his name in print and a little more honest with his readers, giving us something for nothing, life in the trappings of a dream.

Mr. Williams is the author of *All the Brothers Were Valiant,* 1919; *The Sea Bride,* 1919; *The Great Accident,* 1920; *Evered,* 1921; *Black Pawl,* 1922; *Audacity,* 1923; *Thrifty Stock and Other Stories,* 1923.

Walter Jerrold (review date 1929)

SOURCE: "Four Against Ennui," in *The Bookman,* London, Vol. LXXV, No. 449, February, 1929, pp. 287-88.

[In the following review, Jerrold describes Williams's thriller The Dreadful Night.*]*

Mr. Ben Ames Williams has . . . provided us with a "thriller," but one of simpler and more customary kind as his title, *The Dreadful Night,* may be said to indicate. The setting is provided by a lake on the islets of which prosperous Bostonians have built themselves lordly pleasure houses for summer rustication. Molly Sockford has sent her children home to the city and is awaiting her husband, that they may close up for the winter. He is unaccountably delayed; she is joined by a girl friend and later by a newspaper man who comes with a tale of horrid tragedy from a neighbouring island, where he has been to interview a celebrated singer. And then the dreadfulness threatens them—for Mrs. Sockford possesses the sinister emerald! The author succeeds in imparting an appropriate sense of the eerie to a lively narrative.

Robert van Gelder with Ben Ames Williams (interview date 1943)

SOURCE: "An Interview with Ben Ames Williams," in *Writers and Writing,* Charles Scribner's Sons, 1946, pp. 339-42.

[In the following interview, originally conducted in 1943, Williams reveals to van Gelder his method of writing.]

"One of the tough problems of a writer," said Ben Ames Williams, an extremely likable man who has been established as a writer for twenty-seven years, "is rarely talked about. But it is a problem that always has bothered me. It is this: what to do with yourself in the afternoons. I've tried just about everything—golf, bridge, backgammon, mah jong, a couple of hookers of whisky and the movies. You see, there's this need for anything that will give your brain just a little to do, just enough action to get the work out of it, so that you can go to sleep at night. Otherwise, you're working endlessly.

"We spend about six months each year on our farm in Maine—go to bed before sunset and get up before sunrise—and there we have an elaborate croquet game that sometimes is good for five hours in the afternoon—the way we work that is, the ball never is out of bounds; you wander all over the countryside. That's good, but hardly a complete solution. Now Ken Roberts (author of "Northwest Passage") works in the mornings, then carves wood. He also manages his place, which is a fairly large one. However, at night he works for an hour just before dinner. Well, as you can see—no cocktails. And if it were me I'd be all steamed up again, would rush through dinner and keep right on working afterward. My system is to work for three or four hours very hard in the morning—only the first two hours are any good, but I never realize that I'm getting tired and make a lot of extra work for myself by continuing on beyond the time when I should quit."

Probably in the minds of most of his readers Mr. Williams is stamped as a Maine man. His imaginary Maine village of "Fraternity" was the background of many of his most popular stories. Actually he was born in Mississippi—a grandnephew of the Confederate General Longstreet—grew up in Ohio, and was schooled in Massachusetts, in Cardiff, Wales—where his father was United States Consul—and at Dartmouth College in New Hampshire.

"My wife comes from a Maine family—but she was born in China and lived there until she was thirteen. It was more or less of an accident that we went to Maine, but there I met A. L. McCorrison, the Bert McAusland of my stories, and we—well, we hit it off. Through Bert I got the feel of his country and so I used it often as a setting. Place means a lot to me—it is the conditions of life that make people—and I learned the conditions of life there. Then Bert died in 1931, willing us his farm. We spend a lot of time on the farm, but I haven't used a Maine setting much in these last twelve years—a lot of the sting went out of the countryside with Bert.

"Of course, what it all comes down to—the meaning must be there for you, that's the first need when you sit down to write anything. When I was younger I suppose I was hardier when it came to accepting meanings—my first story that managed to get between book covers was written in ten days in 1919, and it came out of a glance through Polti's 'Thirty-six Dramatic Situations.' The situation was that of enmity between brothers. With only that to start, and some knowledge of whaling, I wrote *All the Brothers Were Valiant*—which apparently still is read because I still get letters about it. In other words, I found the meaning after the start had been made. But usually the meaning, feeling whatever it is, comes first.

"One foggy night years ago I rowed a boat out to a bell buoy and sat alone, the bell clanging beside me—nothing but the sound, the water, the night, the fog—and smoked a pipe. Well, to me that situation meant a lot, it stirred my imagination, and at least a dozen—probably more—of my stories have come out of those few minutes by the bell buoy, though the bell buoy never has been in one of them. There's no explaining it. It's just that the moment had meaning for me."

Mr. Williams said that he had had proof early that he had no inborn ability as a writer. "Starting in 1910, I worked as a newspaperman for four years, and every night through those four years I spent two to three hours trying to write short stories, and the four years were up before one of my stories sold. Well, a man who works that hard and doesn't get anywhere for that long is no born writer. I finally taught myself enough to get along and since then have sold going on 400 short stories and serials. Yes, I used Polti—in fact I'm his translator. I learned what a short story must be. But I don't write them any more."

"Why did you stop?"

"Partly because I lost my respect for money back in the depression when I became overanxious and couldn't sell the stories that I wrote. And partly because they weren't fun any more.

"Four times in my life I've turned my back on easy money because I knew that for me easy money wasn't any good. When my stories were selling in the top markets, when the movies were snapping them up—I'd reverse my field and feel better when I'd turned out stuff that was different and that I thought was good, even if the editors didn't think so. You see, if you go along playing up to the standard you've set just because that standard happens to be popular, you get into a formula—and for you the formula inevitably wears out. It's too much like digging ditches when you're hired out to dig them. Some one else is telling you to dig here and dig there, and then go back and dig a little deeper where you dug before. There's no more fun in it. I repeat myself enough on my own when I go my own way.

"The last time I turned away from short-story writing it wasn't because I wanted to—I had lost the touch. Stories are becoming shorter and shorter as the big weeklies more and more imitate the picture magazines. They'll all be down to one word on a page one of these days.

"I can't turn around in those short lengths, and, anyway, I enjoy writing novels. For in them I can take the space I need, can say the things I want to say, can enjoy the work of writing, can be—completely—my own man, not hired out to any one."

Mr. Williams said that he does an enormous amount of preliminary blocking out of characters before he really settles into the work of a novel.

"For example, before writing *The Strange Woman*—which is having a rebirth that astonishes me but makes me fairly happy, too, as it is selling well enough so that it is not necessary for me to rush on the books that I have in the works now—I wrote about 100,000 words of biographies of the main characters before I started the story.

"In most of my novels you'll find good-sized chunks of characterization as a new person is introduced. These usually represent a good many thousand words that I wrote when I was thinking out the person.

"I always write at length, getting it all down. I write rapidly and not too critically and revise slowly and with pains. I rewrote one chapter in *Time of Peace*—my latest book—thirteen times.

"I'm happy writing books—it is unfortunate that I didn't start as a novelist instead of a short-story writer. But I had no choice. There was so much respect in my family for books that—well, the idea that I could write anything so impressive as a book did not occur to me until I was well along in my thirties. It was only after publishers had been putting hard covers on my stories for a number of years that I decided to make a try as a novelist."

Florence Talpey Williams (essay date 1963)

SOURCE: "About Ben Ames Williams," in *Colby Library Quarterly,* Vol. VI, No. 7, September, 1963, pp. 263-77.

[*In the following excerpt, Williams's wife offers a sketch of her husband's life and career.*]

[*Ben-Ames—he dropped the hyphen while still a schoolboy—was born in Macon, Mississippi, on March 7, 1889, to Sarah Marshall Ames and Daniel Webster Williams.*] This is what his father wrote in his diary of this event: "Ben Ames was a child of very mature grandfathers, and one very mature grandmother, while the other grandmother and his parents were no longer children. This maturity of ancestors is supposed to be one condition that produces a genius. He was born at 11:30 A.M. after we had become much alarmed. He was a large child with a very large head. He had large limbs and body and promised to be a large man, like his grandfather Ames and my Williams cousins."

[*Williams had a congenital handicap which few readers, allured by his detailed and vivid descriptions, would suspect.*] Occasionally the family took a drive out into the country in a carriage hired from a livery stable in Jackson. On one of these drives, Ben's parents saw a huge clump of fire pinks by the roadside and said to him: "Oh, see those flowers, Ben-Ames! You hop out and pick a few of them, will you?" Ben got out cheerfully enough, then stood hesitantly by the roadside. "Well, where are the flowers?" he asked. Said his father, "Don't be so obstinate, Ben-Ames, don't you see those bright red flowers right where you're standing?" "What flowers?" asked Ben, and when they continued to point at them, he leaned over and gathered a few. But he picked more foliage than flowers, and it was then that they realized for the first time that he was red-green color blind.

[*Williams came early to love language and insist upon proper usage. In grade school he willingly risked banishment for criticizing a provincial principal who pro-*]

nounced "peonies" as "pineys."] One day his teacher said: "Now children, you can leave your pencils lay on your desks." Ben put up his hand and corrected her grammar. He was promptly sent to the principal of the school, who sided with the teacher! [*He did not easily outgrow this perfectionist zeal. Under his photograph in the graduation class yearbook at Dartmouth, his colleagues thus characterized him*]:

> He knows,
> He knows that he knows.
> He knows that he knows that he knows.

[*The positive side of Williams' nature had another early outcropping. In the era when Lord Fauntleroy suits and long golden curls were* de rigueur *for all proper little boys, Ben's mother tricked him out regally and sent him off to the birthday party of a neighborhood girl.*] When Ben came home his mother asked him about the party: had he remembered to say "How do you do" politely; had he said "Happy Birthday" to his little hostess and given her the birthday present? Oh, yes. "And what did she say?" asked his mother. "Oh, she took the present and told me to go home because she didn't want me at her party." "Oh, dear!" exclaimed his horrified mother. "What did you do then?" "Oh, nothing much. I just slapped her face and stayed."

[*Keats was inspired to verse upon first looking into Chapman's Homer. Ben's initial literary effort came after first looking at an electric automobile, when he was eleven. Poetic license is subjected to severe strain at several points, to say nothing of the fact that the Williamses had no cow.*]

> Oh, what would I give for an automobile
> Instead of wild horses that run.
> For to ride in one makes me happy feel.
> Everyone thinks it is fun.
> For in it, I could go for the cow,
> I'm sure it would go too slow.
> When Mother says, "You'd better go now,"
> I won't say a word but just go.
> Whenever I want it to stop
> All I have to do is to check
> The current and then out I drop
> But suppose there should happen a wreck?

[*Ben attributed his insatiable appetite for books to his parents' habit of reading to him from his very youngest days.*] One day he came into the room where his mother was reading to herself, and he said, "Read to me?" His mother replied that she would as soon as she finished the chapter she was reading. "Oh, read me what you are reading now," he urged. "You wouldn't be interested in this. It's a novel by Dickens and it's grown-up reading." "Well, I want you to read it to me just the same," he persisted, so his mother started to read aloud. Ben sat quietly for a while, then got restless. His mother continued to read. Presently he got up and walked slowly to the door. "Well, I guess I'll go out and play. I never did like Dickens," he said, as he walked out of the room. [*It is an amusing corollary that, when asked to name his list of*

ten favorite books many years later, he listed A Tale of Two Cities *as alternate to Fielding's* Tom Jones.]

[*Williams the boy was as determined an achiever as Williams the man. He was the tallest and heaviest boy at prep school and made up his mind to play center on the football team.*] He wrote home jubilantly of this prospect, only to receive a shattering reply—*absolutely no football!* His mother had heard all about the terrible injuries inflicted on football players, especially centers, and he must promise not to play. Eventually, a compromise was reached. Reluctantly his mother wrote that she still forbade Ben to be on the team, but she did not object to his *practicing* with the boys. Result: he often practiced all afternoon as virtually a one-man opposition to the team. He received quite a battering on the field, but if he was hurt his mother had no cause to worry, because he wasn't playing football, just practicing!

[*Call it drive or tenacity or perversity, Williams knew what he wanted and let nothing bar his way to it.*] When he finished freshman year at Dartmouth his English professor told Ben that he hadn't the slightest idea how to write the English language. Ben continued to elect a lot of English courses, and at the end of senior year the same professor told him he was one of the few men in his class capable of writing literary English. In telling this Ben used to say: "One sure way to make me do a thing was to tell me I was incapable of it."

[*God moves in mysterious ways His wonders to perform. It seems probable, from hindsight, that Williams would have become a writer of fiction no matter what job he had taken after leaving college. But when one considers that practically every other teacher or professor of English is an author* manqué *who surrendered ambition in favor of a regular salary, the following verbal lapse assumes portentous weight.*] Through the college office, Ben was recommended as a teacher of English at a top-ranking school for boys in Connecticut—Hotchkiss. He immediately sent a wire to his father: "I have been offered a job teaching shall I accept?" When the telegram was delivered to his father it read: "I have been offered a job traveling shall I accept?" The idea of their son's being a traveling salesman was definitely abhorrent to his parents, and the prompt reply was "No!" Ben used to say that the telegraph company unwittingly changed the whole course of his life with one word.

[*Deciding upon a career as newspaper reporter, Williams made a discouraging circuit of the Boston offices, garnering only a flimsy "Come around in two or three weeks" from Jim Reardon, managing editor of the* American. *In the interim, Ben acquired a nasty gash on his forehead from diving into shallow water, and sported a "cocoon dressing" over the several required stitches. At the expiration of the waiting period he presented himself again at the* American.] "You told me to come back in two or three weeks, Mr. Reardon, and said you might have a job for me." Well, Mr. Reardon wasn't quite sure, and talked vaguely of a possible opening in two or three weeks and kept looking at the cocoon dressing on Ben's forehead. That seems to have irritated Ben beyond endurance, and he looked Mr. Reardon in the eye and barked: "Look here, Mr. Reardon, you've been putting me off all summer. *Do* you want me, or *don't* you want me? *This is* your last chance!" "Come in Monday morning," said Mr. Reardon quietly. He told Ben later that he was so surprised he couldn't think of anything else to say. Ben had landed his first job.

[*In the fall of 1911 Williams was sharing a room in the South End with Peter Webb Elliott, a reporter on the Boston* Traveler. *At that time the drama critic on that paper was Earl Derr Biggers, who was later to create Charlie Chan. Williams describes by what a roundabout route he came to write his first short story.*] "Through Earl's influence Pete was trying to write fiction. Since I was diligently engaged in saving money—to get married—I could not afford to waste my substance in riotous living; and since Pete spent his evenings pounding out short stories on a rented typewriter, I could not entice him into a game of cribbage or into any other pastime to kill the hours before we went to bed. His industry infected me, and I rented a typewriter and set it up at the other end of the room, and wrote my first fiction story. It was called **"Getting a Job."** This story, like the four score which followed it, completely failed to interest anyone except myself. Yet I continued to write, and by the time of our marriage I had settled down to a steady routine."

[*The Williamses were married on September 4, 1912, after which Ben returned to writing for the newspaper during the day and at fiction in the evening. His record for non-sales remained intact.*] On the seventh of March, 1914, Ben's 25th birthday, he records that I gave him a leather-bound account book with "Ben Ames Williams" embossed in gold on the cover. I still have this account book, and you can all read what he wrote on the first page: "This book is the embodiment of Faith, Hope, and Charity. For three years I have been trying to write fiction—with little encouragement and no emoluments. Yet I have faith and hope and pray for charity and so on this seventh day of March, 1914, my twenty-fifth birthday—open an account of expenses and possible receipts from freelance writing. The book itself is Florence's answer to my request for an account book: it is worthy of Shakespeare. But I have vowed that if five years shows no real success at writing, I will lock this book in my deepest drawer and forget it. B. A. Williams."

[*For three years rejection slips had been a major fact of Williams' life. Little daunted, he said*]: "I wrote and wrote, encouraged by Florence's unshakeable certainty that the stories I wrote were good ones, and were better all the time, and that the editors who rejected them were a lot of idiots! I don't recall that the possibility of earning a large sum of money by my writing entered into my thoughts at all. I wrote because I had set out to learn to write; and a stubborn persistence and a certain blind faith in myself, have always been part of my equipment."

[*With the inception of his five-year plan, however, his fortune took a sharp turn. After rejecting several of Ben's stories, Charles Agnew McLean, editor of the Street and Smith magazines, bought for $50 a tale based on Williams' Mississippi background,* **"Wings of 'Lias."** *It was published in* Smith's Magazine *for July 1915.*]

[*This was the opening wedge. Thereafter Ben appeared with fair regularity in the periodicals, largely through the interest of Robert H. Davis, editor for the Munsey string of magazines. But all was not unadulterated attar.*] We had two sons, aged three and one, and had moved to a larger house. There Ben set up his typewriter and kept on writing, and it was six months before he definitely decided to resign from the paper. With a wife and two sons to support, it was only natural that Ben should hesitate to take such a momentous step. His mother made it possible by offering to make up the difference between what his salary had been and what he earned by writing stories. Ben wrote at this time: "I recognized the fact that a lifetime of dashing off short stories to meet bills would be sheer drudgery, and that there must be somewhere in the back of my mind, a clear idea of what my aim was to be."

[*In his record book appears this passage, dated October 26, 1916*]: "Here is what I want to do with my life. In the first place, to love and to be loved, worthily, not alone by my wife and my children and my mother and father and sister, but by the world, or so much of it as I encounter. In the second place, to build myself into a writer not only with a popular appeal but with a claim to real rank among those who were worth while. In the third place, to hold some post in public life where I can help to right some wrongs. Whether that post be official or unofficial does not matter, and perhaps the eye and the pen can do more than public office. In the fourth place, to lift those who are mine to so much of wealth as is necessary to allow us all to get the most—and the best—from ourselves." [*The order of emphasis in this credo is revelatory of Williams' values. First and foremost, despite the drain that writing and subsequent popularity put on his time, he remained the family man enormously devoted to his wife and children.*]

[*By 1919 Williams was well launched in the short story field but reacted ecstatically when informed by Macmillan that they would publish* **All the Brothers Were Valiant** *in book form: "I walked on air! This was to be a book, and there was for me a magic in the words!" His second book of record is* **The Sea Bride,** *also published by Macmillan in 1919. As a matter of fact, however, his third book was really his first in point of conception*]: "**The Great Accident** was the first thing I had written which was planned and executed with book publication primarily in mind; **All the Brothers Were Valiant** and **The Sea Bride** were written after **The Great Accident** was begun, and before it was finished." [*Nevertheless, all three appeared first as magazine serials.*]

[*Early in the game Williams became disillusioned about the authenticity of professional criticism. He released* *this wry observation following reviews of **The Great Accident** (1920), which unfolds around Jackson, Ohio, where he had spent his boyhood*]: "One American critic, superlatively wise, wrote that after making a real success with **All the Brothers Were Valiant** I had rushed into print with **The Sea Bride,** another whaling story. Now, he said, I had abandoned the field with which I was familiar and had attempted to write a novel of life in a small midwestern town where I was completely at a loss. Since I had spent a dozen years or more in that small midwestern town, while on the other hand I had never seen a whaling vessel, this review awoke in me a doubt of the infallibility of critics from which I have not yet recovered."

[*Before long Williams became an outstanding contributor to the* Saturday Evening Post, Collier's, Country Gentleman, Maclean's, *and other periodicals of large circulation. And he learned, the hard way, that readers could be as caustic as critics.*] In choosing names for unattractive characters, I have usually tried to select a name so commonplace that it was unlikely to be found in life. One such instance brought me some amusing correspondence. In a Fraternity story there were to be three ruffians. I thought of one of them as a foreigner, which suggested Polack, but since racial nicknames seem to me in poor taste, I changed the name to Pollock. But I remembered Clem Pollock (an older reporter on the Boston *American*) so I changed the initial consonant to K, quite sure there were no Kollocks in the world. When the story appeared I had irate letters from two sisters in New Jersey who assured me that there was a General Kollock on Washington's staff, that another had served on the Supreme Court bench, and that, in short, I had slandered an old and honored family. Another member of the family wrote in a more humorous vein that all the Kollocks must be turning in their graves at my profanation."

[*The female of the species proved more virulent than the male.*] "Since I wrote **The Strange Woman** and **Leave Her to Heaven,**" grumbled Williams, "Florence has suffered much from the asininity of readers. The vocal minority are convinced that I have learned to know women by living a life of debauchery or that Florence was at least to some degree the model for the vicious characters I drew. Florence and I fell in love with each other over forty years ago and we have been married thirty-four years and neither of us has ever regretted it." [*Mrs. Williams chose to accent the lighter side.*] Ben was so exasperated by some of the letters that he turned them over to me to answer. I recall with amusement one letter from a woman who wrote to say that she could tell him the story of her life that far transcended the lives of his two heroines, and suggested that she come to live with him a little while, so that she could tell him all about it!

[*Williams' integrity and his pride of craftsmanship always outranked the almighty dollar in his estimation. After **Evered** (1921) was published, he was offered "dizzyingly high prices" for his stories by motion picture studios. At a conference with Samuel Goldwyn he agreed* to sign a contract to deliver four stories a year. Then he returned to Boston and started to write a serial.*] "I found myself thinking constantly of the moving picture possibility of the story I was writing. The experience was sufficient to convince me that in agreeing to sign the contract I had made a mistake. I wrote Mr. Goldwyn, told him my feeling and said I was sure the contract, if signed, would hurt my work. I said I was willing to sign it, if he wished me to do so, but that if he would call off the whole arrangement I would appreciate it. He very generously agreed to do so. I have always been grateful for the understanding attitude he took at that time."

[*Not all aspects of Hollywood appeared as sane, however. In 1929 Williams was brought out to the movie metropolis to write a story for Will Rogers, who had made a great success in* Jubilo. *Williams ran into "the institution called 'a story conference,'" usually fatal to a writer's sense of humor, but he managed to escape with some of his feathers.*] "The experience was a trying one. After six weeks, the original story had been torn to shreds, patched, mended, darned, and torn to shreds again until it lost not only all resemblance to its original form, but also all vitality and usefulness. My weeks in the studio were from the studio's point of view completely unprofitable. Except for a few scenes which I wrote and which were used in retakes on one picture, nothing I did for them has, as far as I know, ever seen the light." [*One of his assignments during this period was to write a sequel for the O. Henry story which had been filmed as* In Old Arizona.*] "The story was to deal with the building of the first transcontinental railway. There must be a part in the picture for a Swedish-dialect comedian. There must be another part for a boy who had done well in another picture, and also for an ingenue. There was to be a herd of buffalo which stampeded and almost killed the heroine. There was to be an attack by Indians and a rescue by the United States Cavalry. And just about the time I was ready to begin work, a cablegram came from Mr. Sheehan saying that he had seen a 'grandeur' short subject of Niagara Falls, and that water photographed beautifully on the new film, and that I must accordingly put into the picture some rapids, and if possible some waterfalls!" [*Despite this mad mishmash of effects, Williams wrote the scenario and—maddest of all—"the 'grandeur' film and the stock market collapsed together, and the picture has never been made."*]

[*The absurdities of Hollywood tickled Williams' risibility but they also struck him hard enough to spin him around. He had been contemplating, not without glee, the heady size of his income.*] "But of that 1920 income about seventy per cent came from the moving picture studios; and that definitely alarmed me. I deliberately changed my style and the structure of my tales, deliberately sought to write stories that would move at a more leisurely pace, and that would depend more on character and less on action. I tried to appraise my situation. In a book from the Sunday School library which I read as a boy, a mother, dying, gave her son as his inheritance one piece of advice. 'Every day of your life,' she said, 'I want you to go away quietly by yourself and think for an hour.' That advice has always seemed to me sound; and I remembered it. I began to write less and think more. The first beginning of an understanding of myself had an immediate and tangible result. I decided to write a novel that should be simply the life of an ordinary man. I knew I was not yet competent to do what I had in mind to do, but I began to prepare for it. In my weekly record of work done, there appears this notation: 'Week ending March 20, 1921, Thoughts on Splendor.'" [*Splendor was published in November 1927.*]

[*Williams' library of background and reference books, now at Colby College, attests to his sincerity and indefatigability when in pursuit of authoritative data or atmosphere for his stories. Entries in his diary and notebooks reveal that for* **Splendor** *he "must read the Boston papers from 1877 to date" (1922), and that before he was through he "had read the newspaper history of Boston over a period of forty years."*] In further preparation for **Splendor,** Ben began a program of novel reading. Thomas Hardy's novels interested him and he noted: "Hardy has a singular capacity for inventing interesting— though often outlandish—incident. The appeal of his books for me lies largely in this mosaic of incident with which he develops his characters." He began to reread Dickens' novels. . . . Ben turned to Knut Hansen's *Growth of the Soil,* and said of it, "A wonderful book, of the sort I would like **Splendor** to be." Ben continued his reading with Balzac's *Eugenie Grandet;* he read Samuel Pepys' diaries "with keen pleasure." Then he plunged into *War and Peace,* finding "pages enough of this that need never have been written." Years later he was to write: "**House Divided** runs to almost three thousand typed pages, but will not equal *War and Peace* and its two thousand in print. I may add that in later readings my opinion of *War and Peace* changed decidedly!" After *War and Peace* he turned to *Anna Karenina, Madame Bovary, The Brothers Karamazov, Crime and Punishment,* half a dozen novels by Balzac, *Tom Jones,* and *Vanity Fair.* He read American biography, such as Albert Bigelow Paine's *Life of Mark Twain,* Ida Tarbell's *Lincoln,* and Grant's *Memoirs.* And he was also reading Cellini and Boswell.

[*Williams' quest combined curiosity, synthesis, and esthetic morality. His appetite for improvement was unappeasable.*] "I was seeking to discover, in these novels admitted to be great, a common denominator toward which I might strive. It seemed to me that they had gusto. I thought I could work for that. But they had another point in common. They dealt in each case with vice; with vicious men or women, with vicious society, or with vicious aspects of society. I did not want to write about vice and degradation. Probably I was a prude."

"Since the above was written, two of my novels have dealt with vicious women; and at least one of them, **The Strange Woman,** has been considered by some people to be an 'immoral' book. I do not agree. It seems to me not only a sound psychological study but also 'moral' in the

highest sense; for certainly, though vice is portrayed in its pages, that portrayal is not calculated to inspire emulation. It explores the vicious aspects of a woman's character; but the reader abhors the woman herself and feels pity rather than esteem."

[*When one asks a writer what his principal aim is or which of his own works he likes best, the answer is likely to contain lofty circumlocution or unconscious rationalization. The following anecdote by Mrs. Williams is both frolic and revelatory.*] To Ben it was a never-failing source of satisfaction to discover someone crying over something he had written. I used to try to control my weeping, sometimes with difficulty, I admit, just to avoid his interrupting me to ask with a certain relish: "What are you reading—what part are you reading now?" [*Was Williams more concerned with the undertones of human pathos and tragedy than he was with his major melody of broad good humor?*]

[*How scrupulously Williams implemented even his slightest short story is revealed by these remarks in one of his notebooks*]: "In fact it is seldom possible to write even a short story without some investigation of the factual background of the subject with which the author wishes to deal. It has been necessary for me at various times to study a wide range of subjects; I have to know something about detective methods, about surgery, about law and its practices, about navigation, about the training of race horses, and of baseball players and fighting dogs and hunting dogs and boxers, about architecture, about the physical geography of cities and regions which I never saw and never expect to see, and about a thousand other subjects. Research is a routine part of a professional writer's job, and it includes everything from asking a blacksmith to show how he makes a horseshoe to a study of the tribal customs of the aboriginal Indians in Florida." [*Williams' publication of over four hundred titles required knowledge in all of these areas, and more. In his introduction to* **The Happy End** *Kenneth Roberts, a remarkably fastidious researcher himself, records his profound respect "for Mr. Williams' accuracy as a chronicler of fact."*]

[*Williams and Roberts became acquainted when, as young reporters, they were covering the same murder trial for different Boston newspapers. Peeved at the "extremely large" person "who sat mountainously between me and the witness stand, moving restlessly," Roberts leaned over and asked Williams to shift position. A brawny friendship developed between them over the years: they hunted, fished, and trekked together, they sought each other out when depressed, they took gay junkets in the Caribbean islands with their wives, they labored over each other's manuscripts in disregard of their own current projects, and they signalized each other's successes fittingly. At the end of January 1953 Williams had completed work on* **The Unconquered** *and Roberts on The Seventh Sense. This called for commemoration and they naturally selected each other for company. Mrs. Williams describes their last memorable*] *weekend.*] Ben picked me up at Symphony Hall after the concert on Friday and we headed for Maine. It wasn't long before Ben asked me to drive, as he hated to drive in the dark, and he also admitted he felt tired. The let-down after a long period of work was always depressing and I was glad that the warm hospitality at Rocky Pasture lay ahead.

What a weekend that was! Never had Anna [Mrs. Roberts] and I seen our two writing men in a gayer mood. They were like two youngsters suddenly released from their school books, and never had they laughed more together.

[*After more than three decades of unparalleled success as a writer and of undeviating robust health, Williams noted: "Heart turning somersaults at bedtime." He confessed to unaccustomed fatigue and devised some ideas for a new novel "with no conviction." What he buoyantly dismissed as "the heart stuff" persisted, without incapacitating him, for some three years. A tone of dire premonition invests his diary entry for November 14, 1952: "Woke at four, profoundly depressed. I had been up at 1:20, a curious feeling as I left my bed that I was saying good-by to it." Williams was avid about the sport of curling, and with his physician's permission was participating in a tournament at The Country Club in Brookline on February 4, 1953.*] The match went well, and Ben prepared to make his last shot. He leaned over to deliver his curling stone, looked up to see it make the winning shot, and then suddenly fell on the ice. There were two doctors on Ben's rink within ten steps of where he lay. They could feel no pulse. His great heart had stopped beating.

[*Williams chose to be buried in Maine rather than in Mississippi, where he was born; in Ohio, where he grew up; or in Massachusetts, where he spent much of his adulthood. Like many a writer before and after him, Williams fell in love with Maine and adopted it as his own. When he was fifteen his parents sent him to a lakeside summer boys' camp in the Pine Tree State. Mrs. Williams' family was old-line Maine; Ben frequently hunted and fished in its woods; they honeymooned on one of its islands; and they both enjoyed to the hilt their numerous visits with the Robertses at Kennebunkport. And then there was Bert McCorrison, the Chet McAusland of the Fraternity stories. Ben came to know Bert in 1918; day by day thereafter their mutual affection and respect deepened. When Bert died in 1931 he bequeathed his farm, Hardscrabble, in Searsmont, Maine, to Ben. For better than two decades Williams used Hardscrabble as his writing base all summer and part of the spring and fall.*] The knoll, two hundred or so yards behind the barn at Hardscrabble, with Levenseller Mountain beyond, was in many ways Ben's favorite earth spot. Whenever we were at the farm we never missed walking out there after our early evening meal, to watch the sunset. The view to the west was often spectacular—all crimson and gold—but the afterglow on Levenseller to the east and the clouds above it thrilled him even more. There was always birdsong around us, and we spoke sparingly. The ring of hills was forever changing in color as the sun sank lower, and Ben often quoted from his favorite psalm: "I will lift up mine eyes unto the hills from whence cometh my help."

The knoll came to be the focal point of Hardscrabble life. Before its rough stone fireplace at the picnic table we had our family parties, and sat far into the evening in the firelight telling stories and singing.

Ben had expressed the wish to have his ashes at the farm, and the knoll was there to welcome them. We rolled a big boulder from across the road, placed it on the knoll facing Levenseller, and had his name carved on it. We love to go for a picnic on the knoll with the rock only a few yards away. Ben seems very near to us.

[*Ben Ames Williams was a man of direct motivation. He made up his mind to learn to write—and for a quarter-century was as popular as anyone writing in his time. Of this he was manifestly proud, but he drew more intense satisfaction from another accomplishment. The comment he made while reviewing his credo of 1916 is the measure of a man.*] "Not all the things I sought have been achieved; but the thing I wanted most—the love and trust of my family—is mine. In that certainty today I am strong." [*Fit epitaph for a consummate human being.*]

Joseph B. Yokelson (essay date 1963)

SOURCE: "Ben Ames Williams: Pastoral Moralist," in *Colby Library Quarterly*, Vol. VI, No. 7, September, 1963, pp. 278-93.

[*In the following essay, Yokelson discusses the pastoral mode of Williams's fiction.*]

I

In statements about his books Ben Ames Williams consistently stressed his desire to give pleasure or simply to tell a good story. Authorial practice varies: to D. H. Lawrence fiction was a vehicle for a prophetic vision, to some writers it may be no more than a mechanical variation of the boy-meets-girl formula. But that a writer aims to entertain does not preclude his maturest judgments and deepest feelings from finding their way into his work. Thus a reading of even a sampling of Ben Ames Williams' fiction reveals a concatenation of ideas, assumptions, and biases which should perhaps not be labelled a philosophy but which nevertheless cohere into a sort of pastoral myth. It is this myth which raises the rustics in his local color stories above mere eccentric types, makes a historical novel like *Come Spring* far more than a chronicle, and gives point to a psychological shocker like *Leave Her to Heaven.* In fact, given the explicitness with which Williams sometimes uses the pastoral point of view, one might call him a pastoral moralist.

The pastoral myth appears in its nearly pure form in an early story, **"Thrifty Stock."** More a sermon than a story, perhaps, **"Thrifty Stock"** dramatizes not a conflict between full-fledged characters but a conversion to the pastoral way of life. Shackled to a small store in the city and hungering for the soil which his father worked, Mr. Moore buys a farm with a run-down orchard in "Fraternity," Maine. His daughter Lucia, who is almost emaciatedly thin and who makes up heavily, swears, smokes, and calls herself a "fellow," at first resents the move to the country. Soon after her arrival she discovers her neighbor, Johnny Dree, who runs a prosperous apple orchard, and with his acquaintance a change begins for the Moore family. Not without sense, Lucia suggests to her father, who is going increasingly into debt, that he might raise apples like Johnny. When the father complains that he has poor trees, Lucia recites what she has learned from Johnny—that one must take care of a tree and also that the Moore trees are "good, thrifty stock." When Mr. Moore points out weakly that it takes years to make an orchard, Lucia scolds him into talking with Johnny.

Responding in a neighborly fashion, Johnny introduces Moore to the mysteries of pomiculture and advises him to hire help only when he has to. During the long winter Lucia is convinced that she cannot bear the drudgery of farm life, but at times she forgets to be unhappy and even finds pleasure in the "ordered simplicity" of the life. By the end of the winter she is stronger, her figure is rounding out, and her color is natural. In the spring she and her father diligently attend the apple trees, but after a tremendous burst of bloom, the crop is destroyed by a frost. Lucia, nearly hysterical with disappointment, is tamed into silence by Johnny, to the astonishment of Mr. Moore. The "stoic patience" of the farmer carries Johnny and the Moores through the coming months. Lucia and Johnny achieve a deeper understanding: she teaches him how to relax; he cures her of smoking and swearing. When Johnny's mother dies and Lucia goes to comfort him, Johnny in his quiet way proposes.

The following year the orchards yield enormously and prices are up because of a poor crop elsewhere. When Moore gratefully comments on the improvement in his life, Johnny moralizes:

> "I've said to Lucy some times, you can learn a lot from an apple tree. If it's got grass and weeds around its roots, they starve it for water; and the scale and the aphis and the borer hurt it; and the suckers waste its strength. You were kind of like that when you came up here. You'd been crowded in with a lot of other folks—grass and weeds around you, cutting off the air and the good things you needed. And the way you lived, there were all sorts of things hurting you; no exercise, and no time to yourself, and Lucy's dancing all night, and smoking, and your inside work and all, the way the bugs hurt a tree."

Mr. Moore agrees that he feels new and strong like the trees, with all the "suckers and bugs and all the wasteful things trimmed out of our lives," and he adds that he is no longer worried about Lucia, or Lucy, who has come to like her more humble name. Gazing at his wife, "full with

the promise of the greatest fruition of all," Johnny affirms: "Aye, Lucy's like the trees. She's come to bearing now."

II

The image of Lucy "come to bearing" like the apple trees is a significant one for Williams; it epitomizes his feeling about the right or "natural" relationship between men and women, about the love that should rule between them. To this relationship Williams was to return repeatedly. It is the chief subject of **Honeyflow** (1932), *The Strange Woman* (1941), and *Leave Her to Heaven* (1944), and an important strand in *Come Spring* (1940).

In the first three books, the central female character in some way violates the right relationship, is alienated from the natural. Mima Robbins, in *Come Spring,* can be seen as the full exemplar of the attitude adumbrated in the pregnancy of Lucy Moore. Mima's healthiness is revealed early in the book as she muses on the problem of immortality:

> To bestow that life [in oneself] was the only certain way to preserve it. The preachers spoke of immortality as though it were as far away as the stars; but was it not immortality to pass on a part of your life to make another one? Yet before your life was fit to be passed on, it must be kept fine and clean.

Later, watching her sister nurse her baby, Mima feels herself "tingling with a fierce desire" for motherhood. Just as apple trees bear fruit and seeds to perpetuate the stock, so Mima, attuned to the drives in nature, will find fulfillment in perpetuating the race. Her love for Joel Adams, though tenacious, is that of one bearer of the life force for another, not the selfish desire for a passion which excludes the rest of the world. "I want to have Joel's babies," Mima declares, "even if I hated him, or if he hated me, I'd want that just the same." At times Mima's blind vitalism merges with her faith in the American dream of material and spiritual bounty. She and Joel will breed fine children who will not simply preserve the stock but "harness the continent," "put their mark" on it.

Strangely, perhaps, in a time not many generations removed from the Puritans, Mima and her family allow the demands of the life force to override conventional morality. With her mother's applause, Mima installs herself as housekeeper in Joel Adams' cabin, and in the spring, stirred by the mating calls of the pigeons in the forest, she gives herself to Joel. When it becomes apparent a few months later that Mima is pregnant, Mr. and Mrs. Robbins calmly accept the situation. Joel momentarily feels trapped, but the life force impels him as strongly as it does Mima, and he gives up his dreams of freedom for the responsibilities of fatherhood.

Honeyflow is Williams' first and perhaps most explicit study of a woman's unhealthy relationship to the male and hence of her deviation from nature. Sophie Randle, the central character of the book, spends most of her childhood repressed and unloved in an orphanage, her only consolation being the long hours she spends alone singing to herself. Adopted by her uncle, a Maine farmer, she learns to delight in the hills and woodlands around Fraternity. In the course of her wanderings she meets and is befriended by Margaret Dale, who has bought an old mansion where she may nurse her sister, the burnt-out opera star, Tullia D'Aragon. When Tullia discovers that Sophie has a beautiful voice, she determines to make her an instrument through which she can relive her past triumphs, and she persuades her former manager, Hammel, to finance a year of lessons for Sophie. Sophie responds with an equal determination to become famous but to avoid burning herself out by feeling too much. She rejects the love of Hammel's son and dedicates herself to learning the fundamentals of her art. When Tullia is killed by an old lover, Hammel, judging Sophie's singing to lack emotion, tries to send her back to Maine; but in the crisis Sophie brings a mysterious seductiveness to the aid of her ambition and departs for Italy with Hammel.

In the next ten years, Sophie develops a great voice and, bestowing herself "with calculation," uses a succession of lovers to further her career. She makes her debut at the Metropolitan in the opera *Lilith,* which has been created for her by one of her lovers, Johann Rossbach, the greatest composer of the day.

The story of Lilith is symbolic of Sophie's fate as a woman of genius. Written at the height of the suffrage movement, the opera expresses Rossbach's belief that "woman belongs at home" and that "only grief and tragic regret can come from her insistence on equality and independence." Tired of his nomad existence in the forest and wishing to settle down and raise a family, Adam breaks with Lilith, who leaves him to wander from Eden by herself. She is wooed by Eblis, the Prince of Darkness, and promises to yield if Adam has forgotten her. Returning to Eden, Lilith and Eblis find Adam a husbandman with wife and child. Lilith musters her seductive powers and is about to win Adam away from dreary domesticity when Eve reminds Adam of their child and curses Lilith. Adam turns back to Eve, and Lilith, crushed, bids farewell to Eden and disappears with Eblis, hopelessly longing for the things forever denied her: "a hut of boughs with a dull mortal for a husband, and a human child."

Margaret Dale, now married and the mother of several children, attends Sophie's debut at the Met. Margaret warns Sophie that there are payments still to be made, and the second half of the novel shows these payments coming due. With no further conquests to make, Sophie becomes restless and sings more than she should. Frightened by the realization that her voice is not inexhaustible and that she is growing old, Sophie for the first time falls violently in love—with Alex Austin, a callow young man—and hastily marries. Williams draws the parallel between man and nature:

> An apple tree, its roots attacked, the end of life

and therefore of productiveness at hand, will bear most richly, as though it were a sentient thing striving to perpetuate the life within it while there still is time. Thus the life force in woman, too long denied, may like a damned stream burst its bonds and sweep her blindly forward along the road till now refused.

Unfortunately, all of Sophie's mature splendor cannot hold Alec, who is drawn to a young rival of Sophie's. And it is Alec himself who suggests to Sophie the lesson of nature. Describing to her the "honeyflow," the period when the nectar of a plant flows strongly and attracts the bees, he remarks that the honeyflow of fall flowers is like Indian summer—"sweet, but soon gone." Sophie is quick to grasp the instruction:

> Suppose there grew a single blossom which could distill nectar as she chose, so that she was besought by many bees, and glorying in her power rebuffed them all, until suddenly her sweets were gone. Her sister blooms would have ripened long before to fruitfulness; there must come to her a time when her beauty without fragrance would become a mockery. Sophie thought that such a blossom would be very lonely, at the approach of fall.

If Mima is Williams' saint and Sophie, a sinner, Jenny Hager in *The Strange Woman* and Ellen Berent in *Leave Her to Heaven* are like the lurid, inhuman figures in a demonology. For them love is the opposite of what it is for Mima—exclusive, inward-turning, and ultimately destructive.

Jenny Hager, who lives in Bangor between the war of 1812 and the Civil War, devotes herself to such causes as total abstinence and abolitionism and maintains the reputation of a saint; but in her private life she is a sadist who destroys three men. First, though but a teen-ager, she deliberately arouses her father, Tim Hager, who blames himself and goes to pieces under the constant poundings of self-accusation. Married to old Isaiah Poster, to whom she has fled to escape one of her father's beatings, she methodically sets about ruining Poster's son Ephraim by luring him into adultery and at the same time inciting him to murder his father. She threatens to expose the adulterous relationship if Ephraim does not do away with the old man. By the time Ephraim accidentally kills Isaiah, Jenny has no further use for him and turns him away to sink his shame in dissipation.

Before he dies of the delirium tremens, Ephraim disgorges the story of his ordeal to his college friend, John Evered; but when Evered saves Jenny's life after a shipwreck, Ephraim's incredible story is wiped from his mind and he marries Jenny. Their life is at first "richly happy," and Jenny produces four sons. But unlike Mima, Jenny is not content to pass life on, to create new independent existences: she seeks complete dominance over her children. One day John discovers her brutally whipping one of them. With a "malicious mirth" she reminds him of Ephraim's story—whereupon John forsakes Jenny's bed. Barely daunted, Jenny takes as a lover Elder Pittridge, a temperance crusader and a good friend of the family. After a few months, however, Jenny discards him and sends him, as she did Ephraim, to disintegrate in the riverfront taverns. On the night of the great flood of '46, after discovering that Jenny has given birth to his child in a house of prostitution, Pittridge disappears.

For the rest of her life, Jenny exercises her viciousness within the family. Two of her sons, unable to bear her cruelty, go off and settle in the South; and when the Civil War starts, she enjoins the remaining sons to kill their brothers mercilessly. During these years, the corruption in Jenny's soul attacks her exterior and she gradually wastes away with an unspecified illness. Her son Dan, back from the war after losing a foot at Gettysburg, shrinks from her as a man might from a serpent. When Jenny dies, John marries the wholesome Margaret Pawl, who loved him even before he met Jenny.

Williams chivalrously suggests that Jenny, recurringly visited by uncontrollable impulses, is two women. If Jenny reminds one of a victim of demonic possession, there is no mitigation for Ellen Berent: in her opposition to the life force she is pure, unmotivated diabolism. After the death of her father, whom she has totally dominated, Ellen fastens herself to Richard Harland, attracted by his resemblance to her father. She employs no mere lover's hyperbole when, shortly after the marriage, she announces that Richard must think of no one but her, not even of his crippled younger brother Danny, to whom he is devoted. She even resolves to herself never to have children. Perceiving soon that she will never have all of Richard while Danny lives, Ellen lets the boy drown while he is swimming in a Maine lake; then when she understands that her husband has seen all from their cabin, she tries to bind him to her by announcing that she is pregnant. The lie succeeds, and in a few weeks Ellen makes it good. But ignorant—symbolically perhaps—of the mysteries of gestation and fearful that Richard will discover her deception, she gets rid of the hated child by throwing herself down a flight of stairs while pretending to be sleep walking.

With the death of the child dies Richard's remaining tenderness for Ellen. Unable to win Richard back by threat or seduction, Ellen poisons herself with arsenic. Richard marries Ellen's truly womanly sister Ruth shortly afterwards. But Ellen once told Richard that she would never let him go, and now her malice reaches from beyond the grave. She has arranged her suicide to look like a murder, and by a provision of her will Ruth is to be charged with the deed if she ever marries Richard. Ruth is exonerated only when Richard reveals that Ellen is capable of murder and thereby confesses his own complicity in Danny's death. After two years in prison Richard is reunited with Ruth at a retreat in the Maine woods.

III

When Johnny Dree in **"Thrifty Stock"** advises Mr. Moore not to hire outside help to cultivate his orchard, he is not simply conforming to the stereotype of the niggardly Yankee: he is expressing rather one of the axioms of Williams' pastoral morality.

For Williams nature is not only a model or a source of instruction; it is an instrument by means of which one is enabled to surpass nature and become truly human. Erich Fromm has written: *"In the process of work, that is, the molding and changing of nature outside himself, man molds and changes himself.* He emerges from nature by mastering her; he develops his powers of co-operation, of reason, his sense of beauty. . . . The more his work develops the more his individuality develops."* Fromm is here describing work as it was carried on, ideally at least, in pre-industrial societies, when one could love the necessity of struggling with nature because of the satisfactions that necessity created. There is something more than mere nostalgia for the picturesque horsedrawn plough or than a belated expression of the Puritan ethic in Williams' idealization of the individual farmer working his own land: the pastoral myth adds an implicit criticism of modern technological society which neo-Freudian psychoanalysis criticizes explicitly.

The Robbins family in **Come Spring** voices most eloquently the pastoral gospel of work. Mima sets the theme early in the book, before the family has reached its uncleared tract north of Thomaston: "Here's a new country everywhere, and it's not the King's anymore. We've said it's ours; but it's not ours just for the saying. We have to use it before it's ours; clear the land and make it bear." Two satisfactions obtained from work meet in the word "ours"; rootedness,—or being able to call something one's own—, and the differentiation of the self. After a few years of making his farm, Mr. Robbins, confessing that he once disliked work, declares that he "wouldn't give a damn for a world with no chance in it to work up a good lather of sweat every day"; and in an exalted, if unorthodox, moment he even sees his labor as uniting him with the universe, "Maybe God and the world He made are the same thing. Maybe when you clear a field and bring it to bearing you're taking care of Him." The characters' words are supported throughout **Come Spring** by accounts of felling trees, ploughing, and raising shelters—accounts which, because they convey the arduousness of mastering the land, convince one of the joy and pride derived from doing the job.

One of Williams' most poignant stories, **"Road Discontinued,"** deals with a family, the Pattens, which, taking the opposite way from the Moores, loses sight of the satisfactions of work and abandons the land for the deracinated life of the city. Contrasted with the Pattens is an immigrant family, which makes the land its own by causing it to bear.

As a child Beth Patten spends her summers in the old farmhouse on Patten Road in Fraternity. She loves to hear gran'ther (her great-grandfather) tell how the original Pattens built the house with native timber, cut the road, and laid out their farms along it. But, as gran'ther ruefully relates, people left or died off and only cellar holes and lilac bushes remain of the old farms. "It takes work to make a farm, Beth," he declares, "and work to keep one going. Most things a man wants, it takes work to get them and work to keep them." Gran'ther alone seems to retain the true spirit of the original Pattens: he lives at the farm all winter, doing the chores himself. When Grandpa Patten renovates the farmhouse and hires men to run the farm which he writes off on his income tax, Gran'ther grumbles: "You can't hire a man to keep up a farm. . . . You've got to put your own sweat into it."

When both her great-grandfather and grandfather are dead and she is ten, Beth, out riding one day, comes across a somewhat older boy tending a fresh grave—that of his mother, who has died in childbirth, the boy explains. The boy's name is Nikky Karonen. When Beth asks whether he lives on the Freeman place, a farm which the first Patten had given to his daughter as a wedding present, Nikky in his inarticulate way echoes Mima's pronouncement that one owns the land by working it: "It ain't anybody's place. It's our own land." He defends the fittingness of not burying his mother in a cemetery with the same words: "It's our land." Remembering that her ancestors were buried in their own land, Beth feels a bond with Nikky and when her parents express outrage at the crude burial, she reminds them of the practice of the original Pattens, of pieties which they no longer understand.

Williams' depiction of Beth's father is bitter. When the stock market collapses, Mr. Pattern tries to make the farm pay but fails. He rejects brusquely his wife's suggestion that she and Beth might help out to cut down expenses; and he dismisses her remark that the Karonens, working the way the old Pattens did, have made their fields bear miraculously: "They don't know any better. . . . It takes two or three generations for foreigners to understand our American ways." Finally, in true American fashion, Mr. Patten sells the farm to the government, which is buying up "submarginal" land, and over the protests of Beth, who has come to love Nikky, the family removes to Boston. For a while Beth and Nikky correspond, but gradually the letters stop.

Two years later, now a sophomore in college and going with a law student who reminds her of Nikky, Beth drives over from Camden to see the old farmhouse. She finds Patten Road much deteriorated and the house so decayed that she cannot bear to look at it. When she fetches Nikky to pull her car out of a mudhole and sees him tall and brown behind his plough, Beth realizes that she can have happiness only with him. But Nikky has married a local girl and is awaiting his first child. As Beth emerges from the Patten Road onto the main highway she finds her alienation from the happy, productive pastoral life symbolized by a newly posted sign: "Road Discontinued. By Order of the Town."

IV

The late frost which ruins Mr. Moore's first apple crop is not an exception to Williams' picture of nature. His pas-

toral myth imagines no Golden Age or luxurious Garden of Eden. Nature can be tough and hard. On the abandoned farms around Fraternity the land goes swiftly back to alder and birch. In *Come Spring* black flies and mosquitoes attack the pioneers clearing their tracts; frosts blast the crops they need to get through the winter; deep snows isolate them. Mima hears about a woman, marooned forty days along the Kennebec, whose baby starved to death, and for a moment she contemplates a wilderness "impersonal and pitiless, . . . willing to dawdle forty days over the business of killing a little child."

If the toughness and hardness of nature create tragedy, they also stimulate in response pride and courage, which the pioneers in *Come Spring* amply exhibit. Further, in direct confrontation of a demanding nature men learn how they must order their lives if they are to survive. They perceive the necessities, the essentials of existence, and they throw overboard the superficial baggage of urban man. How far this simplification may be carried is shown in *Come Spring*: I'm Davis, the hermit, constructs a comfortable hovel between two ledges, using elm and birch bark and rushes. Even in the coldest weather, Davis reports, he is "as warm as mice. . . . I do good." Life in Fraternity, though far from so primitive, is still comparatively frugal. Lucia Moore at first resents it as barren, but gradually comes to love it for its order and simplicity and to see in it a sort of wisdom.

Although Williams acknowledges the hardness of nature and its value, as it were, for "soul-making," his emphasis is ultimately on faith and hope.

> I know that winter death has never tried
> The earth but it has failed—

he might be said to hold with Robert Frost. Johnny Dree, with the farmer's "stoic patience," knows that nature does not betray, that the good years outnumber the bad. Though the frost destroys the apple crop one spring, he can assure Mr. Moore that apple trees are "like money in the bank." In **"The Sunrise Side,"** old Jeff Arthur, reputed to have the largest orchard in the state, castigates those who try to take short-cuts with nature:

> "Man that sets out to start an orchard, he can't take no short cuts. He's got to be willing to wait nine-ten years . . . before his first pay day comes around. . . . You've heard folks say that you hadn't ought to put a thing off till tomorrow; but I tell you it's a sight better to wait till tomorrow than it is to take some fool short cut so's you'll get there today. My experience is, there allus does come another day. I never see a day yet that another one didn't come along the very next morning!"

Applying his philosophy to economic and social problems, Arthur scornfully refers to those people who complain about hard times as "sunset-siders," who concentrate on the end of things rather than on the new day. "Me, I raise apples," he declares. "If folks want to eat them, they can buy 'em. And there allus has been, yes and allus will be, enough folks want to eat apples so it'll pay in the long run." The title *Come Spring* derives from the refrain which laces the novel together, a refrain which asserts the cyclical triumph over "winter death" both in nature and in human affairs: The pond will sparkle once again, the leaves will shoot, the alewives will run. Joel may realize that he loves Mima, his broken leg will mend, come spring.

To those who front it properly, nature can be benevolent and bountiful. One must work, but one must limit one's demands to the essentials. Williams says of the towns around Fraternity that "life in them flows easily," but if it does so, it is because "there is no great striving after more things than one can use":

> The men are content to get their gardening quickly done so that they may trail the brooks for trout; they hurry with their winter's wood to find free time for woodcock and pa'tridge; and when the snow lies, they go into the woods with trap for mink or hound for fox.

In some stories, where Williams seems to be condoning laziness, he is indirectly pointing out the bounty of nature by exposing the foolishness of unnecessary toil. Even Johnny Dree, it will be recalled, has to learn to relax. Dave Burley, in **"Lazybones,"** is the laziest man in Fraternity. He likes only to hunt and fish and talk. His wife is an energetic type who prides herself on her family's industry. When Mr. Covert, who represents the owners, puts the local store up for sale, Mrs. Burley longs to buy it. Angered by her husband's indifference, she sends him to clean up the attic, which has been untouched—rightly, Dave thinks—for thirty years. Among the old trash Dave finds a letter from his wife's uncle which shows that the uncle was too lazy to learn to spell correctly. Equipped with this silencer, Dave knocks off for the afternoon and when his wife berates him a few days later, he produces the letter. Mr. Covert recognizes the stamp on it as a rare one and pays Burley enough for it so that he can buy the store. Burley asks: "If I'd cleaned out the attic first time ma told me, I'd have burned them old letters, stamps and all; and then when we needed a few thousand dollars, where'd we ha' been?" And he concludes: "I always did say work'll git you in trouble if you do too much of it. It's the man that's got sense enough to know when not to work that gits along."

In one of his best stories, **"The Eftest Way,"** Williams presents the most outspoken and persuasive version of Dave Burley's credo. Although there is no mention of urban society, the implicit comparison between country and city life that one finds in all of Williams' pastoral tales emerges very strongly. Whereas the city dweller is cramped and budgeted, engages in a thousand "visions and revisions," dares not eat a peach, Uncle Joe Deal takes no thought for tomorrow, enjoys his hunting and fishing, drinks and eats as he pleases. He has no visible occupation. "On the whole, no doubt," Williams comments on Uncle Joe's story, "a highly immoral tale, daring to suggest that sober and ascetic virtue may be, after

all, but the weakness of a coward." Even as he grows older, as his eyes go bad and his legs give way, Uncle Joe refuses to become sober and ascetic. "Set ten years in a chair! I'd ruther gun one day and let the chair rock in the wind the next," he tells Chet McAusland. And one fine Indian summer day, when the woodcocks are so tame that one can almost touch them, Uncle Joe, while making a beautiful double shot, dies of a heart attack.

Uncle Joe and Chet McAusland of the Fraternity stories and Leick Thorne and Sime Verity in *Leave Her to Heaven* are the characters who bear Williams' ideals. Joel Adams in *Come Spring* is on the way to becoming such a person. These are all "good men"—faithful, modest, competent. Hunters or farmers, they love the land they gun or work. Some, like Chet McAusland, love their dogs, who come of good stock and, like Reck in **"Mine Enemy's Dog,"** are incorruptible. These men live in poor or declining areas; they appear to have been left behind by the progress of civilization. But Williams shows that to be left behind is almost a badge of superiority. The city people, busy making money and achieving status, are actually inferior. They may exert the power in the world, but they have not the moral excellence of the farmer or hunter who by remaining on the land has kept in touch with the perduring values. And though power may be exercised by the outsider, the pastoral characters form a fraternity of men with standards which will not be violated. Scratch an eccentricity and there you will find a standard. Brad Miller in **"The Piano"** sends to his death a burglar who in his search for money foolishly wrecks the piano that Brad has bought to honor his wife's memory. Even one of the meanest of the Fraternity characters, Andy Wattles in **"Another Man's Poison,"** becomes a terror when two escaped convicts rob him of supplies belonging to the store which he works in and loves.

Although Williams makes excursions into the glamorous territory of public figures, as in *Honeyflow,* his characteristic and best work concerns itself with the lives of ordinary and insignificant persons like Brad Miller. In *Come Spring,* a historical novel, he concentrates on the clearing of the wilderness by the Robbins family and relegates the major historical events and personages of the Revolutionary War to the background. In a postscript to the novel he writes:

> The historical novel usually concerns itself with persons who have made a major imprint on their times . . . with generals and statesmen and kings and queens. But for every general there were ten thousand soldiers, and for every king there were subjects. An historical novel may as justly deal with the lives of people who were important not individually but in the mass.

Williams' feeling for the common man (preferably rural) appears in his accurate rendering of colloquial diction and in what may be called the folk-tale quality of many of his Fraternity stories. These have the air of history slipping into legend. They are about extraordinary dogs like Tantrybogus who lived to an advanced age and, though blind and lame, followed his master to the field to make a final point. Or they are about transformations like that of Andy Wattles from a lusterless youth to the single-handed conqueror of two hardened criminals. Or there is the heroic death of the hunter, Uncle Joe, who in the manner of a Hemingway hero gets off two perfect shots as he is stricken fatally. Although the inhabitants of Fraternity, both human and animal, are obscure, they have in them the stuff of legend: they are the best of shots, the wisest of dogs, even, as in **"Jeshurun Waxed Fat,"** the stingiest and slothfulest of men. These are the tales that, retold at the post office and general store, create a sustaining sense of continuity with the past and with the land, the site of the extraordinary deeds.

V

Although he was a contemporary of Faulkner, Hemingway, and Dos Passos, Williams virtually eschewed their formal experiments and adhered to traditional story-telling techniques. His first novel, *All the Brothers Were Valiant,* shows the influence of Conrad in certain incidents, and *Victory* is mentioned in *Leave Her to Heaven*; but Williams appears not to have been influenced by Conrad's manipulations of time except in *Leave Her to Heaven,* where events are given from two perspectives. He does not use the stream of consciousness, counterpoint structure, or the Camera Eye. His stories do not begin *in medias res* like some of Hemingway's but generally introduce the main character, discuss him in a leisurely fashion, then present him in a significant incident. The emphasis, as he himself points out, is on local color and character. Williams' style, too, remains well within the canons of tradition. In his diction, indeed, one finds a strain of the archaic: "Be it recorded . . ." or "yet is there always some new thing in Fraternity." Only in his point of view perhaps does Williams join the mainstream of twentieth-century experimentation. In later works, like **"Road Discontinued"** and *Come Spring,* the action is seen almost entirely through the eyes of the central character.

The pastoral outlook is a conservative one. "Where I am, and the people I love, is all the world I want," Mima tells Joel. And since the truths of life are few and simple, new ideas, new ways of doing things are not embraced simply because of the newness. It is not surprising that this conservatism is reflected in the formal aspects of Williams' works.

Nevertheless, Williams' fiction is relevant to our times. Dealing with origins in a historical novel like *Come Spring,* Williams seeks to give us who live among disintegrative forces a feeling of connectedness, the sense of being not simply an isolated phenomenon without past or future but part of a historical process. At the same time the novel makes us aware of our loss of the satisfactions—and perhaps virtues—of the Robbins family. The Fraternity stories may at first reinforce the impression of loss: the society of farmers and hunters in Fraternity is a shrinking one, and we seem to gaze at it from an increasing distance. The recurring descriptions of the landscape,

however, tend to reassure us that our loss is not final: the blue hills, the woods, the meadows, and the streams remain; nature waits only to give instruction and to be cultivated like the "thrifty stock" of Mr. Moore. Williams the pastoral moralist is not convinced that we must follow the lead of the Pattens; the way of Nikky Karonen is also open.

Richard Cary (essay date 1963)

SOURCE: "Ben Ames Williams and Robert H. Davis: The Seedling in the Sun," in *Colby Library Quarterly,* Vol. VI, No. 7, September, 1963, pp. 302-25.

[*In the following essay, Cary recounts the friendship of Williams and his editor Robert H. Davis.*]

When the stout and florid Editor first saw the Tyro and his wife, he grinned genially, extended his hand, and said, "I'm Bob Davis." Years later he roared with laughter as he recalled the scene. "I found myself facing the youngest, the most frightened pair of kids I had ever seen, and, so help me, they were holding hands!"[1] His impression of the eager, uncertain, emergent author, "weighing 280 on the hoof and broad as a roll-top desk,"[2] was one he never let Ben Ames Williams forget.

Born twenty years and a thousand miles apart (Robert Hobart Davis on March 23, 1869, in Brownville, Nebraska; Ben Ames Williams in Macon, Mississippi, on March 7, 1889), their lives traced dissimilar route-lines before, inevitably, they conjoined in a publishing office in New York City on June 19, 1916. It was a fertile meeting for both men: the novice whose reading audience was to become the widest of his time in America and the veteran whose knowledge and influence were the widest in the field of popular magazine fiction.

From the two hundred and fifty Davis letters to Williams, now at Colby College, and the eighty Williams letters to Davis in the collection of his papers at the New York Public Library,[3] it has been possible to recreate the evolution of their professional relationship and to chart the pulse of their personal reactions to each other. Davis's letters range from 1914 to 1941, Williams' from 1919 to 1941. A diminution of frequency occurs after 1923, but it is not until the Thirties that they failed to communicate several times during any given year. Of the two, Williams was the more conservative of phrase and sentiment. They began with the formalistic "Mr.," soon dropping this salutation in favor of "Dear Ben" and "Dear Bob." In this mode Williams continued without variance. Davis shifted playfully to Williams' two front initials, to the full "Benjamin" (which was *not* his name), and sometimes to the nepotal "Benji." The tenor of their expression was in accord with these respective propensities. Their gathered letters constitute a vital chronicle of two men parallel in principles but diverse in demeanor.

I

Bob Davis came by his dramatic flair honestly. He was the son of a New England minister who went west as a missionary among the Indians and eventually counted Sitting Bull as one of his parishioners. Bob was desultorily educated in the public schools of Carson City, Nevada, later became a compositor on the local *Appeal.* In the Mark Twain tradition, he moved farther west and in time served as reporter for all three of San Francisco's major dailies. Then as now New York City was the cynosure of all enterprising newspapermen. At 26 Davis arrived in the metropolis. He made his mark in a succession of journalistic coups, the most spectacular of which were his exposé of the so-called Beef Trust which was shipping putrefied meat to our soldiers in the Spanish-American War and his graphic recital of the Corbett-Fitzsimmons heavy-weight championship fight. In less than ten years, after passing employment on three other papers, he was appointed managing editor of the *Sunday News.* At such a high plateau most men would have been content to solidify a reputable career. Not so Bob Davis.

His public triumphs and his influential position brought him happiness enough, for he was irrevocably gregarious. But it must have been during his stint on the *Sunday World* in 1903 that he caught a glimpse of his native vocation. It was then that he met O. Henry, then that he savored the fascination of discovering unfledged writers and encouraging them to accomplishments beyond their own dreams. In the following year Davis, now editor-in-chief of the Munsey magazines,[4] signed footloose O. Henry to a life-saving five-year contract.

O. Henry was one in a long chain of writers Davis recognized initially or rescued from the doldrums. To skirt the risk of tedium, herewith is only a partial list of those who acknowledged Bob Davis as their literary godfather: Edgar Rice Burroughs, Zane Grey, Edison Marshall, Mary Roberts Rinehart, Octavus Roy Cohen, Max Brand, Fannie Hurst, Israel Zangwill, Dorothy Canfield Fisher, Sophie Kerr, Frank L. Packard, Montague Glass, Arthur Somers Roche, Faith Baldwin, James Oliver Curwood, Rex Beach, Louis Joseph Vance, Charles Van Loan, and Ben Ames Williams. On one of his trips to London in search of publishable novels Davis induced Joseph Conrad to rewrite a script which he later printed in *Munsey's* as "Victory." Sam Hellman, another Davis protégé, could think of no editor who had "graduated more writers from pulp to prominent pay." More than sixty authors dedicated books to him.

For years Bob Davis read an estimated million words per week and thought of himself as a conduit for American fiction. But Arnold Bennett cherished him for more than that. After their first meeting, Bennett spoke of Davis as an "immense personal magnetic force," and rated him, to boot, as "certainly one of the most dramatic and enthralling letter writers alive."[5] It took no special perceptivity on Bennett's part to make these statements; both are indisputable. Mary Roberts Rinehart carefully preserved "those brilliant and sometimes incredibly funny letters," while Max Brand vowed that Davis letters "always make me happy, because even if the news is disastrous you put such a punch behind the words that you make a fellow glad to be a living human."

As to Davis's "force," it had two salient strands: first, his philosophy of friendship; second, his tremendous versatility. Making friends was his principal hobby; "Know lots of people" his favorite slogan. He was intrigued by the potentialities in human relationships and the values accruing therefrom. He felt that "Every important advancement you ever made was . . . due to some acquaintance,"[6] and he wasn't talking about opportunism. Because his own capacity to give was inexhaustible he believed that everyone had within him the spark to brighten derelict spirits or to ignite lagging talents. In this respect he was generous to a fault, though it must not be presumed that he was "a male wandering Pollyanna." Upon "the corrupt, the prurient, the bogus" he heaped the "blistering language of Fisherman's Wharf." He was "plain as an old shoe" to his biographer, and the New York *Sun* obituarist recalled him as "never jaded, satirical, highbrow or radical." Davis harbored no stainless illusions about himself. To an interviewer he declared, "I do not object to the truth."

The aptitudes of Bob Davis were astonishingly multilateral. He wrote successfully in disparate genres of verse, fiction, and drama. He composed songs and subtle photographic studies. A famed gourmet and a prizefight promoter, he also reveled in his reputation as a fisherman (Sam Blythe called him "the Compleatest Angler"). As a journalist he scaled several Everests, none loftier, however, than his panegyric, "I Am the Printing Press." A Biblical recitative in form and tone, it appeared in some sixteen hundred newspapers, was printed separately in millions of copies, paraphrased over two thousand times, translated in every civilized enclave of the world, and ultimately cast in bronze. "No novelist could hope for such a circulation or such permanency," sighed Arnold Bennett. Towering above even this was his expertise as an editor, the facet of greatest import to this account.

Much of what is relevant about Ben Ames Williams before he became aware of Bob Davis has already been told by Mrs. Williams in the first pages of this issue and need not be repeated here. Suffice it to observe that Williams lived at his Mississippi birthplace for a year and a half, was moved to Jackson, Ohio (where his father was editor of the *Standard-Journal*), then came east to school in Massachusetts, spent a year in Cardiff (where his father was U. S. Consul), attended Dartmouth College, went to work on the Boston *American,* married, and settled in the environs of the Hub.

By 1910 he was bending over a typewriter almost every night, tirelessly turning reams of blank sheets into short stories which, as he said, "failed to interest anyone but myself." There was a stubborn streak in Williams. Disregarding the gale of rejection slips, he persisted for four rewardless years. Calmly he assayed his situation. "I had early proof that I possessed no inborn ability as a writer. . . . A man who works that hard and doesn't get anywhere for that long is no born writer."[7] Quite as calmly he laid out his future course. On his twenty-fifth birthday Mrs. Williams gave him a notebook in which to record his daily progress as an author. On the first page he wrote: "I have vowed that if five years shows no real success at writing I will lock this book in my deepest drawer and forget it."

Before the first year of this pentad elapsed, however, Charles Agnew McLean accepted "Wings of 'Lias" for *Smith's Magazine,* paying Williams $50 for this story based on his southern background. There were explosions of joy back at the homestead, but Williams pondered the news with sad ambivalence. It seemed "a small recompense for the more or less back-breaking work which I had crowded into my so-called leisure hours over the preceding three years. And the worst of it was that I recognized even in that moment, that the incident was closed. . . . There is nothing so completely in the past as a story after it is sold."[8] In the order of writing, this was his eighty-fourth story. He was assuredly entitled to his psychic frustration, the sense of flabby revulsion which afflicts every creative artist when his creature no longer is *his*.

There were other rejections and other acceptances before Bob Davis rose as a dominant factor in Williams' literary fortunes. From the point of view of calendar and map they had meandered along converging sides of a scalene triangle, the tip of which they now approached.

II

Williams tried for at least fourteen months to land a story in one of the Munsey magazines. Davis read all his contributions and refused all of them with jolly aplomb—not, however, without furnishing incisive comments about their shortcomings. In his first letter of record (December 10, 1914), he returned **"Cell Number 6"** with the decree that it "seems to be a much-ado-about-nothing story. . . . Sorry, Colonel Williams, but you are reaching out an endless arm to seize coincidence." By now Williams had written over a hundred stories and had met almost as many rebuffs. But this was not just another routine rejection. The man had taken time to diagnose, and there were twinkling implications in that "Colonel."[9] Williams sent him more.

On December 28 Davis demonstrated the sensitivity to public taste which had sustained him for a decade in his current position. He found **"A Police Petruchio"** rather funny, but declared, "I am afraid it would create adverse criticism. No matter how offensive the spud-throwing female happened to be, there is no reason why Tim should have pinched her. Everybody isn't as broadminded about these matters as authors and editors." To soften the negation he added, "I expect to be forgiven for sending this story back." Ben Ames Williams, struggling toward a formula which would not leave "the people cold," could only be grateful.

Bob Davis sometimes enheartened new writers by buying their stories with no intent to publish them. There is no indication that he favored Williams with such largesse. He continued to revert the stream of manuscripts to its

source with unmitigated frankness. In January 1915 he said of **"The Squealer"**: "You go too far in this story. It is sordid and repellant." In November: "The son of the major [in **'The Rutherford Shows'**] is an almost impossible person, and I am afraid he will not get by with the reading public."[10] Williams began to feel that his "deadly facility" of writing eight to ten thousand words a day, acquired through reportorial exigencies, was a distinct handicap.

Abruptly the tide turned. On February 12, 1916, Davis wrote: "I can use **'Glissez, M'Sieu Kellee, Glissez'** at $50.00." On March 9: "Your nautical bronco-buster [**'The Whale Buster'**] is rather an agreeable person. I will send you a check next week." On April 5 he expressed some reservations about **"Worth a Leg"**—"compared with your whaling yarn, it doesn't start"—but he bought it for a slightly lower price. Precisely two months after first acceptance by Davis, Williams was electrified by his offer of $350 for **"In the Redbrush."** The letters of May 4 and 15, however, sharply reminded him that authorship is at best a chameleon profession. Said Davis in the old vein: "Even if [**'The Fluctuating Woodlot'**] were not puzzling and unconvincing, it would fall down on the fact that you can't sympathize with any of the characters." He condemned **"The Sob Story"** as "pretty obvious. . . . We have had an overdose of old reporters, bright managing editors and sobarines lately."

The most crucial dilemma of Williams' career arose when Davis paid a stately sum for the next story submitted, a serial called **"The Whaler."** Should Williams resign his job and wager everything on fiction? Could he earn enough to support his wife and two sons? His editor at the Boston *American* predicted he would go far as a newspaperman and advised caution. But the lure of the muse was such that it impelled Williams to seek more accordant ears. He decided to go to New York and consult with Davis. The editor was delighted. He invited the Williamses to a lunch of "some perfectly well-cooked grub . . . served by a waiter who doesn't speak German," at which they could discuss literature "as a business, as an art, as a pastime, and as a scourge."

They met at his office, broke the ice, and then—in Mrs. Williams' words: "We walked to a restaurant, the Beaux Arts, for lunch, and we were not only awed by the tall buildings and the broad avenues of New York but by the fact that Mr. Davis seemed to know everybody. Instead of the crowding and hurrying of today, our progress was leisurely, and Mr. Davis had a charming way of pointing things out to us and saluting his acquaintances, making us feel that we really did this every day. And at lunch he talked and talked, and we sat and listened, and I drank only half of the first cocktail I had ever seen! He advised Ben to quit the paper and write fiction, and when I timidly asked him how I could help the most, he exclaimed, 'Spend the rest of your life letting this overgrown pup have his own way!' And he turned to Ben and said, 'You look big and strong and healthy! I think you ought to be able to write!'"[11] That was all the mandate Ben Ames Williams needed.

He hurried back to his tranquil Boston suburb and engaged his typewriter with renewed intensity. If he assumed that Davis's personal approval would lead to any softening of his crisp impeachments, he was quickly disabused. Within the year following their meeting Davis shot these barbs at him:

> July 7, 1916: Regarding **"Received Payment"**—It's well written, and although it has a lesson and a moral, neither of them leads anywhere in particular.

> July 13, 1916: Regarding **"Eastward into Eden"**—Seems to me to have all the characteristics of a woodpile. . . . It isn't worthy of you, and you're throwing good time away, into the bargain. . . . I think these bad breaks of yours are the result of inexperience.

> September 18, 1916: Regarding **"Lese Majesty of the Law"**—My Gawd man! This isn't a story. . . . It is entirely too durn rough. . . . Go back to your old style.

> March 13, 1917: Permit me to intimate, my fat Welsh friend, that 85,000 words a month is too much for any man to write. I don't care how strong a man he is. I will lecture you a little more violently to your face.

> June 19, 1917: Yes, I do like **"Where Your Treasure Is,"** but the first 67 pages don't develop very much except gas.

Had he not known his man, Williams might well have desisted thereupon. Fortunately he saw behind Davis's screen of punitive quips the deft mentor guiding him past inconspicuous pitfalls. In the middle of this beleaguered period, reassured by a subsidy from his mother, Williams resigned from the *American.* Davis interposed needed moral sanction. "I am glad you are going into the fiction game. I'll do everything I can to make your experiment a success. . . . My best wishes to Mrs. Williams. Tell her that she is a noble and brave woman to encourage you in the legitimate occupation of writing for a living, and I don't think she will regret it."

Shortly, a new note gained ascendency in Davis's critiques. Although he continued to castigate with his old zest (of **"Deeds, Not Words"** he wrote: "I had scheduled this story to open the *Railroad Man's Magazine* as a weekly, but, honestly, I haven't the nerve to hand it to them"), he began to qualify the harshness. Words of approbation appeared more and more frequently. The first hint of this new tune came on July 13, 1916: "When I slang your suggestions, I do it with a double purpose. First, and back of it all, is a real interest in you. If I didn't feel sure of your stroke, I wouldn't ask you to take an oar. But I like you and believe in you, and I am quite sure that you and the little wife will some day forgive me what in this instance will seem to be unwarranted violence."

Thereafter the harmonic of praise, instigation, and augury dilated perceptibly:

> October 15, 1917: I have no fault to find with your fiction. It is satisfactory to me in every way, and if the public fails to write as many letters as it ought to, disregard their indifference because in time you will arrive at the top. Have no fear about that. I will bet money that Ben Ames Williams will be as well known as any writer in this country in three years; and then of course I will lose you but I will not cease to admire you.

> January 31, 1918: I want you to always feel that you have got a quick market here, and I will go a long ways off the beaten path to be of service to you. But what's the use; you know that.

> June 12, 1918: As I said before, it hurts me to write this letter, . . . I don't want you to mistake me for a moody, temperamental old man who doesn't know his mind. . . . If anything in this letter irritates you, forgive me. I don't mean to do that. . . . I have no diplomacy. I prefer the plain truth all the time. I think it is better for both of us.

> April 10, 1919: As I said before, Benjamin, I never make mistakes in the prophecy business—well, hardly ever. And never in relation to you.

> February 17, 1920: I didn't take a chance when I prophesied your future.

> May 11, 1920: I'm not a prophet; but I do know a writing guy when I see him and when I announce that a new star is rising in the east, by the jumpin' gods of war, a new star *is* rising in the east.

Davis's usefulness to Williams was not confined to such tonic generalities. Notwithstanding the strain of his multiple responsibilities, Davis took time to read each of Williams' manuscripts attentively and assess it minutely. Most notable are his extended suggestions for revision of plot, characterization, tone, and length of **"After His Own Heart,"** and his three-page, single-spaced typewritten analysis of **"Deeds, Not Words."** He steered Williams away from gauche, oblique, or divulgent titles, warning him that they would repel readers or betray his dénouement. (He rejected, for instance, "Deep Waters," "Spindrift," "Sea Wrack," "Salt of the Sea," "Wrack of the Sea," and "The Harsh Salt" as possible titles for ***The Sea Bride,*** the final name of Williams' second published book.) He prodded Williams about atmosphere and continuity in **"The Whaler,"** the derivative quality of **"A Monstrous Little Voice,"** the lack of dramatic pace in **"Where Your Treasure Is."** On March 7, 1922, he expostulated against themes regarded as verboten by the American public. "Ben, the whole thing is a fine and magnificent piece of writing, but you might just as well throw kerosene on a black cat, touch a match to him and turn him loose among the tenement houses as to hurl this story into the pages of a magazine. . . . You can bet your sweet socks I would print it in one minute if I had the nerve." No other publisher on this side of the Atlantic dared either. *Sangsue,* a then "dangerous" treatment of miscegenation, achieved only an English edition.

More often than not Williams accepted Davis's judgments and instituted proposed changes. Wisely, Davis tempered his objections with comedy and consideration. "It is entirely up to you," he would say; or, "Yell 'no!' and I will subside and slap it to press as she is writ"; or, "I don't want to force a title upon you that's not agreeable"; or, "Will you 'stand aside, sir' and let me sail this ship out of the harbor? . . . My whole heart is wrapped up in it." Out of unlike temperaments they had evolved an amalgam of understanding and mutual respect, the younger man earnestly assimilating the injunctions of superior experience.

Very early in the game Davis sensed that he would lose Williams to the "high class periodicals." And here emerged the elemental generosity of spirit which made him friend as well as editor to so large and contrastive an assortment of personalities. He was clearly reluctant ("I hate to let one of your manuscripts out of this office"), but by September 1916 he was already telling Williams that one of his stories was "sure-fire" for the *Pictorial Review, Woman's Home Companion, Delineator,* or *Ladies' Home Journal,* "so take my tip and shoot it to one of them." When Williams sold his first story to the *Saturday Evening Post*[12] Davis wrote with lucent sincerity: "Yes, I do congratulate you with all my heart. . . . I am not surprised at your success. I guess it is good-bye Ben so far as I am concerned. . . . Well, old sport, you have my blessing." After decrying and returning "The Squealer," Davis nevertheless cheered when Williams rewrote the story and placed it with *Collier's.*

There are many comparable instances but that of ***The Great Accident*** eclipses all others as an illustration. Late in 1917 Williams broached it as a serial. Davis responded ardently, "You bet your life I want a crack at [it], but I won't be irritated if you sell it to another high priced editor for a boxcar full of money. . . . When prosperity comes to you I shall not be depressed." He persevered on the same high scale after reading the first installment. Subsequently it turned out rather too long and wound up in another precinct. Two paragraphs by Bob Davis attest the reciprocity of confidence, the unsubtle loyalty of each man for the other. The first is from his letter of May 19, 1919:

> You need not feel a bit sorry about ***The Great Accident.*** I knew the moment I read it that if the right editor could be found, you would get some real money for it. My offer was a guarantee of faith and while I saw in your eye a willingness to accept right then and there, I made up my mind I wouldn't let you accept it, although I wanted the story just as bad as Lorimer wants it. I couldn't however print it serially in a monthly magazine. It would have taken twelve numbers to get it to press, and only an absolute, downright, blown-in-the-bottle ass would have had the nerve to cut it. Its appearance in the *Post* will give you national fame. From now on your reputation is made. Nobody can stop you. All the editors in Christendom cannot retard you another day.

On the editorial page of the New York *Sun* (November 26, 1932) he summarized the incident in "Recollections as to the Behavior of the Writer Folk":

> Thirteen years ago Ben Ames Williams brought me a manuscript of a novel entitled ***The Great Accident.*** I told him that for my purpose it was too long by 30,000 words, but that if he would cut it down I would pay $2000 for the first serial rights, volunteering the information, however, that it was worth more in its original form and should be offered to one of the weeklies. He insisted upon making the cuts and closing the deal. "Try it on one first-class weekly," I urged, "and if it comes back it's mine." Reluctantly, but with no assurance of success, he took my advice. Inside of two weeks ***The Great Accident*** had been read and accepted by the first weekly editor to get his hands on it, and Ben was richer by exactly $6000.

They exulted together over Williams' rapid rise through the economic strata of periodical publication. He told Davis about the *Saturday Evening Post*'s offer of ten cents per word for serials and, although it meant that Williams was irretrievably lost to the "pulps" thereafter, Davis retorted: "Don't put lead in your shoes, Ben—let yourself go up in the air where you can soar around and look down on the 5c a word squads." Adding impishly, "Don't forget I am holding out some of your best stuff to spring later on when you get famous. I am a cagy Welshman." Seven months later the new rate was doubled. Williams wrote happily (May 9, 1920): "You're a great man; and I am beginning to think you're a prophet."

Only two slight swirls marred the surface of their deep-running friendliness in these pristine days. In the case of Williams' second appearance in the *Post* (November 24, 1917) Davis's pique was directed at himself. "I will be honest with you, Ben—I am not going to read '**Steve Scaevola.**' I haven't the time. I lost the lobster originally, and now he can go to hell." The second case bore a faint accusation of benefits forgot. Davis had asked to read a newly completed story and was informed that the *Post* had already purchased it. "If '**The Road of Casualty**' is to appear in the *Post* I will read it there. Don't bother Paul to send me the manuscript." Williams' agent, Paul Reynolds, nevertheless sent it. In due time Davis returned it, remarking with understandable grumpiness, "Why don't you offer me a story as good as this once in a while?"

In 1920 Davis established his own agency for sale and distribution of fiction, plays, and motion picture rights. In this capacity he pushed Williams toward lusher pastures, opening up prospects for publication of his novels while delicately avoiding conflict with Williams' regular representative—"I think I can get very fine terms for you, but I don't want to appear to be butting in, and I shall not butt in." He also multiplied opportunities for movie contracts, after having conscientiously forewarned Williams: "Don't let your mind dwell on the motion picture end of the business of writing or your work will suffer. . . . Do one thing or the other—a moving picture king or a literary guy—one of the two. Don't try to be both at the same time." Williams had of course to learn this lesson on his own. After one thirteen-week stretch as a Hollywood scenario writer in 1929 he saw the sagacity of Davis's dictum.

One might pause here to recite the saga of Davis, Williams, and Samuel Goldwyn, but the details of their negotiations—so complex and irresolute—demand a chapter of their own. There is room only to note that this interchange did not terminate in typical Hollywood style, with all parties heartily reviling each other. After the breakdown of expectations Goldwyn wrote Davis, "I appreciate your position and am wholly in sympathy with you"; Davis wrote Williams, "A noble, kindly, big-hearted, generous performance"; Williams wrote Davis about Goldwyn, "He's a good fellow. May his tribe increase."

Long after they had severed professional relations and Williams had made an unshakeable place for himself, Davis maintained his role of chief chider and laudator. In his diary for 1924 Williams observed: "Bob Davis says I no longer write good stories, that I am a slave to my interest in character." This he excused as being "deliberate on my part." In 1927 he sent Davis a copy of *Splendor* with the bantering entreaty that "If you are not pleased with it tell me; if you are, tell the world!" On December 7 Davis dispatched a lengthy audit of the novel, visibly striving not to be captious, and concluding ambiguously: "*Splendor* will not sell many copies because the few people who understand the excellence of the book borrow—and keep—the literature that appeals to them." Williams rejoined on the 12th: "I must confess that from your letter I can not tell whether you enjoyed *Splendor* or not. I am inclined to think that you did not, which will always be a source of regret to me." Davis complained about *Come Spring* (1940) being somewhat "long in starting" and scored the epilogue as "the worst anti-climax that ever came under my eye." Yet he pronounced the book in toto "the swellest prerevolutionary record ever penned." In the midst of reading *The Strange Woman* (1941) Davis effused, "It's the liveliest thing you've produced."

Williams was no longer psychically dependent upon Davis. He altered approved objectives *deliberately*; he questioned dispraise. Change what might, however, the influence was indelible, the gratitude unfaltering, the homage instinctive. To Davis's reproof of *Come Spring* he conceded: "I was myself in some doubt about the postscript." And, inversely, he was elated over Davis's acclaim of *The Strange Woman*: "There's no one from whom I would rather have had it." The seedling had sprouted foliage of its own but could never forget the sun that had graced the spring of its time.

III

Davis and Williams were brought together by their ruling concern with the formulation of fiction. Without delay they discovered in each other affinities of character and avocations which admitted access of feelings far more profound than those usual in business. They were both born in the month of March, a fact which Davis cited owlishly. Both were totally devoted to their wives, who inveterately accompanied them on their long-ranging travels. (Mrs. Davis saw all the exotic ports and quarters depicted in his many volumes; the Williamses stopped in every one of the forty-eight states over the course of five motor trips and had planned to visit Alaska and Hawaii upon their admission to the union.) Williams was addicted to his children, and the childless Davis often romped with them, taught them to fish, remembered their birthdays, wrote them letters.

Two traits in particular Davis seized upon and continuously joggled at Williams with the assurance of a friend who can say anything with impunity. The first was their national patrimony—both were of Welsh descent. Davis was sometimes serious on this score. "Having descended from an imaginative race, you shouldn't weaken the structure of your future by dealing in the obvious present. . . . The fact that you come from a nation which remains to this day unconquered does not mean that it's inadvisable to conquer yourself. Get away from those old plots" (July 13, 1916). In the next year (July 19) he said to Mrs. Williams: "Ben is Welsh; so am I. And for that reason I can write frankly to him." At other times he chaffed—"Don't forget to tell your son that a certain well known editor is a Welsh gentleman" (December 28, 1916)—or prefaced his designation of "Welshman" with a scurrilous adjective. In his staider way Williams fended off these thrusts with talk about Welsh memorabilia, and blithely defined his tormentor as "darganfyddodd Robert H. Davis, Golygydd y Munsey Magazines" (February 2, 1919).

The second trait which Davis airily expounded was their physical similitude—both were on the portly side. Here Davis minced no words, addressing Williams as "fatty," "Mr. Fat Man," "you big fat Welsher." (Neither, however, combined the two attributes to suggest that they were both sons of W[h]ales.) "A fat man like you lying around in low temperatures," jibed Davis in September 1918, "has got about as much chance of surviving as a pumpkin in a corn furrow." At their first meeting he charged Williams with "weighing 280 on the hoof," later compressing his estimate to 260. Williams disowned marginal quantities of this embonpoint, describing himself coolly as "about thirty-five per cent above the normal weight for age and height." Once he groaned: "One of my friends here says he saw [Irvin S. Cobb] in Washington recently, and that Irv is getting thin. Have you noticed it? Ask him to send me his prescription. I've gained three pounds" (January 19, 1923).

They had a common passion for sports and games, at which both were highly proficient. Adopting the elaborate ritual of men who value each other's skill, each bragged unconscionably about his own prowess and pretended that the other was completely inept. As usual, Davis was the more emotive.

Bridge appealed, but games of greater virility enslaved them. Boxing they enjoyed as a spectator sport. After gleefully predicting that Georges Carpentier would anni-hilate Jack Dempsey, they sat in the stands and watched the reverse take place. Archly they notified each other of long drives and low scores in golf. Following an oppres-sive accident in 1930 Davis prattled with characteristic grit and humor: "The leg is just as good as new and I can whack off thirty-six holes without halting. There is no sign of the hitch or hike in my step. Moreover, I am now dancing. My next imitation is to go into the lion taming business and the running high jump."

Curling, however, stirred him only to profanity. Williams was an adept, having participated in several international matches. When he tried to inveigle Davis with accounts of astounding performances, Davis merely sniffed, "As for curling, I enclose a column showing what I think of the God damn game." The kindliest comparison he mus-tered therein was: "A curler who begins to tighten up in the larynx and lose his powers of articulation is worse off than a gigolo stricken by hardening of the arteries."[13]

Hunting and fishing were their paramount diversions. In letter after letter they forsook matters of basic business for the fascinating minutiae of trout and moose and guns and rods and lures. They swapped audacious stories about the weight of bass and the span of antlers which had fallen to their wiles, none of which either seemed to put much stock in. "Ben looks upon me only as a fisher-man and, confidentially, a bad fisherman at that," com-plained Davis to Mrs. Williams (May 6, 1918). "He never believes anything I tell him. When I talk about trout and bass Ben looks out of the window and smiles." Fishing, most effectually, released the lurking boyishness in both men. Temporarily removed from the frenetic de-mands of daily occupation, Williams would recall the days before he was ten, "walking open-eyed in the out-of-doors" under his father's tutelage, shooting his first feathered game in Mississippi, catching his first fish in a southern Ohio creek. Davis would detonate alliteratively at the prospect of some good Maine angling. "Oh, boy! wait until you see me bashing the bass up in the Belfast backwaters."

For the most part Davis camouflaged their infatuation with woods and waters by pulling Williams' leg. He ex-pressed sadness over Williams' primal ignorance about fishing and declared it was he who had initiated the Williams boys in the art. "Any attempt on your part to pose as the pater-familias piscatore will be met with a lawsuit." With deadpan benevolence he wrote out in-volved instructions about elementary procedures, con-cluding: "Ben, you will be the death of me. I have tried to make an outdoors man of you but you haven't an eye for it." He challenged his veracity: "I expect you to do a little lying, but not much"; "You're either stalking an elephant or a whale all the time. There's no twilight zone, no minimum with you. Maximum room only." And when Williams sent photographs to substantiate his alleged fantasies, Davis hooted: "I told [Mrs. Davis] those fish were taken out of a hatchery, gassed, laid out on a small plank and photographed for the mere purpose of deceiv-ing the populace. I told her I couldn't understand how Mrs. Williams, the mother of two fine big boys, could live with a man who caught such little fish." Once in a while, for a trice, he stepped out from behind the mask of Thalia. "Even if the fishing in Lakeport appears to be indifferent, I'd rather spend a week with you in a flat-bottom boat than any other living guy; hot or cold, fat or lean" (August 11, 1927). When all was said, external nature was only a canal to the inner man.

All this badinage Williams parried according to his lights. Casually he catalogued his hits and misses in for-est and stream. With controlled bliss he descanted upon the incomparable gunning or fishing that was to be had in Belfast and Searsmont, Maine, in Lakeport, New Hamp-shire, in Nova Scotia, dropping invitations for Davis to join him—which Davis did, often enough. Once Williams went off on an hilarious tack, but the joke was on him-self; he had shot a duck decoy.

Davis liked to organize rod and rifle junkets or to include Williams in parties organized by others. Two of these had instant literary consequence for Williams. In the summer of 1922 Davis suggested "a ten-day trout and bass trip" up the Allagash River in Maine, with Irving S. Cobb and two other cronies. After some confusion about local nomenclature was dispelled (Davis snorted, "Most of the names of the lakes up there look as though they were devised entirely by drunks"), the expedition was led to its destination by a seasoned game warden, David Brown. During their stay at the wilderness camp Brown told Will-iams a tale about the murder of a warden while in pursuit of poachers. On his return Williams wrote **"The Road of Casualty,"** basing the plot on this episode. By weird coin-cidence Brown disappeared on the very day the first install-ment of the story was published.[14] His body was discovered in a pond the following spring. Although no evidence of foul play was adduced, Williams felt "all cut up and blue as indigo," as Davis put it. "I wouldn't be disturbed by the suggestion of prophecy in your story," he consoled Will-iams. "It only shows that you sense in advance the things about which you write. It is a great gift. Don't deplore it."

The second jaunt engendered no melodrama but more copy. It began with Davis's note of November 5, 1928: "A convention of the world's leading intellects will be held at Sea Island Beach, Georgia. The party will be made up of magazine editors, publishers and distinguished authors. The group cannot be complete without you. . . . All kinds of game, salt and fresh water fishing, to say nothing of wild turkeys, and politicians upon whom the law goes off No-vember 6th. Come and kill a candidate." Williams went and was captivated by the atmosphere of palm trees, oaks, and Spanish moss. He spent "from one to four months of each of the next six years in that region" with his family. The impact upon his creative consciousness resulted in two books with Georgian setting, *Great Oaks* in 1930 and *Pirate's Purchase* in 1931.

A fine paradox inheres in outdoor sports: they contain just enough crudity and egotism to permit a man to demonstrate affection toward another man without appearing to be effeminate or sentimental. Fishing and hunting were routes by which Williams and Davis approached levels of deepest understanding. While Davis was baldly ironic in his utterances, Williams inclined toward connotation:

> He plays golf in two languages and catches bass in three. He's the only man in the United States who knows why a bull bass tries to eat a four inch wooden plug painted blue and white. . . . He will stop a game of golf at the seventeenth green, with the score all even, to go catch a bass; he will stop fishing with a seven-pound bass hooked and dancing a fandango about the boat, to go ashore and eat dinner. He will leave the finest dinner uneaten to go into the kitchen and cook; and his idea of heaven is a spotless kitchen full of onions, garlic, chives and capers, in which he is permitted to cook as much as he pleases.[15]

Tone to the contrary, they were saying the same thing: "My friend, you're priceless."

IV

From the beginning they fortified each other's souls. In 1919 Davis asserted that "[I was] twenty years ahead of you, and now I am a thousand years behind you." Later he told Williams: "Do whatever you think right, Benny, always; and do it with the full conviction that I ratify, applaud, and approve everything you do and the way you do it. . . . Nothing is going to make any difference between you and me"; and "I am yours to command, order about, kick, maltreat and abuse. Nothing you can do will make me love you less—or even more." When Williams effectuated a lucrative movie sale and was promoted to a higher per-word scale by the *Saturday Evening Post,* he turned instantaneously to Davis. "Do you mind my blowing about these things to you? I've got to blow to somebody; and I've a notion I can count on your sympathy. Sympathy is the word. I feel as though you and I were about the only sane men left in the business of letters."[16] At the request of a magazinist, Williams drew this portrait: "Davis is a wonderful companion and a devoted friend. . . . He is as wise as a serpent, as simple as a child, as profane as a mule-driver, as gentle as the old family doctor, as loyal as a wife, and as understanding as a mother."[17]

They exhibited devotion in many other concrete ways. When either published a book he sent a copy to the other, duly inscribed. Davis's comment upon receipt of Williams' second novel typified his response. "Any book from your hand to mine is sufficient dedication for all time. . . . *The Sea Bride* which comes from your pen is one aspect of your power. Those things which come from your heart, the which I hold closest, are all the rest" (October 18, 1919). Williams proffered Davis the compliment supreme on his last book, *Hawaii, U.S.A.* "Your books more than those of any writer I know carry in every line the flavor of the author, and to anyone who knows the author, that is sufficient recommendation" (October 20, 1941).

Although Williams published forty volumes, he was extremely chary about formal dedications, confining these to his father and mother, his wife and daughter. He made only one departure from his immediate family. *Thrifty Stock* (1923) was chastely assigned "To Robert H. Davis." Davis, recipient of some threescore dedications, "was very much touched. . . . All we need now is a conversation in Welsh."

They exchanged ideas freely and donated plots to one another. After bandying the manuscript of **"Deeds, Not Words"** between them for several months in 1918, Williams, wearied of revisions, volunteered to release his right to it. "I wouldn't think of giving the plot to any one else," answered Davis. "I gave it to you first and it is yours to have and to hold and whatever revenues you gather are yours likewise." Eleven years later, wearing the shoe himself this time, Davis rhapsodized: "Wait till you see what I have done with the story of the mother who lugged her son under the freight train. Good God, that is a beaut, Ben! . . . With you, no man can talk without receiving some benefit."

With decent constraint they purveyed each other to the public. Davis included a Williams photograph in *Man Makes His Own Mask* (1932),[18] reprinted a Williams anecdote in *The More I Admire Dogs* (1936), "biographed" him in the *Saturday Evening Post* for April 3, 1920, and gave him liberal space in several of his New York *Sun* columns. Williams featured Davis in a number of his sports articles, prepared special commentary for Wainwright Evans's interview, but most distinctly verified his feeling for Davis in the spring of 1930 when the latter sustained an excruciating mishap. En route from Florida after recording his impressions of that area for the *Sun,* Davis broke his ankle and twisted his knee while trying to avoid a fall. Congestion set in and what at first seemed a run of the mill injury veered perilously close to a fatality. Badly incapacitated, Davis had to forego all writing for a spell.

Swiftly his brigade of friends moved into the breach. Fannie Hurst sent a flurry of telegrams soliciting essays to fill Davis's thrice a week space in the *Sun.* Williams immediately pledged "at least one column of stuff," as did everyone who was asked.

The first of twenty-four guest columns appeared on June 3, entitled "Fannie Hurst Recalls." Irvin S. Cobb, Mary Roberts Rinehart, Rex Beach, Booth Tarkington, George Ade, William Lyon Phelps, Ring Lardner, Dorothy Canfield Fisher, H. L. Mencken, Albert Payson Terhune, and other devotees of Davis followed. Topics ranged from Fisher's irrelevant plaint on the difficulties of a translator's task to Mencken's irreverent recollections of Davis as a gastronomic prodigy. Williams' piece came out on June 10, a sensitive exposition leading from Davis's bosom qualities to his overt demeanor. Nicely apportioning sentiment, sincerity, and wit, Williams described Davis's "rich gusto" in word and act, his "Gargantuan capacity for enjoyment," and his "positive and unequivocal" opinions. Merging statement into illustration, Williams deftly climaxed his column with accounts of Davis's first fishing venture in a Maine lake ("the most contemptible body of water in the northern hemisphere" with "the most timorous, weak-witted, supine and flabby of all fishes"), and his celebrated fishing escapade with Williams' son Chuck on Penobscot Bay, about which Davis wrote this quatrain in "Feeding the Fishes":

> In all my days of angling,
> My keenest single joy
> Was handing clams to cunners—
> With Ben Ames Williams' boy.[19]

Despite the glittering competition, Williams' screed excited highest appreciation from Davis. On June 16 and again on September 24 he avowed in effect that "nobody can ever write a better column than you wrote for me in the Pinch Hitters contest. Everybody I know speaks about it." Moreover, while Davis recuperated, Williams amplified the length and frequency of his letters, one of them the most loquacious and diverting in his entire correspondence.

Bob Davis took immense satisfaction in the epithet Fannie Hurst coined for him—Christopher Columbus of American Letters. About so many authors, including Williams, he could rightfully say, "I pulled your frying fat out of the burning before you became carbon," and he put a strict premium on gratitude. Once, after twenty-seven years, their friendship teetered on this uncertain wire. Apropos Williams' **The Happy End** Davis wrote on June 12, 1941: "I can't say that I am crazy about the last paragraph on page 10, being as how I helped in a small way to keep alive your confidence in yourself. . . ." He reminded him of "the reorganization in hopes and fears that took place in my office one afternoon when I told you to chuck journalism and come with me." Then he cited with some bitterness the defection of another writer he had discovered, but before the end of his letter he was contritely imploring Williams not to "be cross with me."

The offending paragraph referred fleetingly to Williams' resignation from newspaper work "without serious misgivings." Surprised that this should be taken as a slight, Williams hastened to answer the following day: "I'm . . . sorry to hear you expected me, in the space of a short introduction, to do justice to your part in my doings. In my as yet unpublished (and uncompleted) autobiography, you're down in black and white to the tune of several pages, with quotes from various of your letters and other specifications." Williams did indeed give Davis full credit in at least two places in this manuscript, as he did intermittently in letters, in Edward J. O'Brien's *Best Short Stories of 1918* ("Like a good many others, I owe a debt to Robert H. Davis of *Munsey's* for the encouragement that kept me going"), and in Kunitz & Haycraft's *Twentieth Century Authors* (1942). No alienation developed. Davis soon regained his equilibrium and by October 21 was again crowing over the fact that "years ago I picked a man from an obscure Boston newspaper who could write so great a book [**The Strange Woman**]."

v

Roads fork. No two people of congruent ability persist in identical paths together unless one forfeits faith in himself and merely tags along. Neither Davis nor Williams was by nature a vassal. It was inevitable, therefore, that their possessive interests should propel them into separate ways. As Davis settled pleasurably into his niche in the *Sun,* the copious correspondence of the first dozen years slackened. By this time Davis was busily ferreting out dramatic slices of life in every colorful corner of the world and Williams had fixed his sights on history and the novel. There was less occasion, less opportunity now. In the Thirties more letters began with "In the absence of Mr. Davis . . ." and were signed by his secretaries. By 1936 the exchange trickled down to three letters, two of them Christmas notes:

> *Williams, December 21:* Our paths cross not very often; but our thoughts cross constantly; and your place in my contemplations has been a big one now for twenty years. I only wish it were bigger.

> *Davis, December 23:* Despite the long intervals of silence between us, there has never been any wavering of our affection for you, Florence or the kids. . . . I suppose when I am an old man with white whiskers and your kids have all got long beards, that we will run into each other some day.

There is no record of another letter until three years later.

An elegiac note pervades their sentiments hereafter. Caught in the spiral of *tempus fugit,* they strove to revoke the painful finality of Robert Frost's "Yet knowing how way leads on to way, / I doubted if I should ever come back." They tried to touch the dormant strings to music again. "As Irv Cobb would say, [we'd] tear our pants to have a glimpse of you," wrote Williams. Davis answered in kind. "Recently I saw a portrait of you in the act of wearing a mustache. What are you trying to hide?" But in the same letter he fretted, "Ben, you make me homesick. Despite my long life of touring, I am allergic to wandering." They proposed meetings which were abrogated by Davis's having to dash off to India or Los Angeles or Puerto Rico or Honolulu. On May 5, 1941, Davis jubilantly informed Williams that he would be in the Bucksport, Maine, region on an assignment—wasn't this ideal for a nostalgic reunion? Conflicts and commitments on both sides nearly wrecked this plan too, but Mrs. Williams confirms that it was consummated to their infinite gratification. On June 12 Davis murmured fervently, "Pray God we all meet again."

This was not to be. Davis died sixteen months to the day without seeing the Williamses again. Termed "the most lovable figure in American literature today" at an honorific luncheon attended by such as Sinclair Lewis and Theodore Dreiser, Davis had grappled a legion of friends to his soul with unceasing goodwill. Mrs. Williams commemorates his "colorful, beloved, picturesque" image and his unrepayable service to young writers. The sun gone down, Williams intoned with soft reserve: "His death left sincere and lasting grief in the hearts of hundreds of people," not the least of whom was Ben Ames Williams.

NOTES

[1] Florence Talpey Williams, *All About Da* (Portland, Me., privately published, 1962), 72. This is Mrs. Williams' informal biography of her husband, "written for my grandchildren."

[2] Fred S. Mathias, *The Amazing Bob Davis* (New York, 1944), 7.

[3] The Davis letters are a recent gift to the College by Mrs. Williams. Quotations from both sets of letters are made through the kindness of Mrs. Williams and Mrs. Madge Lee Davis, and the cooperation of the Manuscript Division of the New York Public Library.

[4] Frank A. Munsey, born in Mercer, Maine, created an empire of newspapers and popular magazines around the turn of the century which rivaled Hearst's for a couple of decades. Davis not only controlled *Munsey's Magazine* and *Argosy* but also launched and edited seven other Munsey periodicals. In 1926 he became a columnist on the New York *Sun*, a Munsey newspaper.

[5] Arnold Bennett, "Robert H. Davis," *American Magazine*, LXXVI (August 1913), 34, 36.

[6] Fred C. Kelly, "Be Sociable," *American Magazine*, LXXXI (March 1916), 33.

[7] New York *Times* (February 5, 1953), 23.

[8] *All About Da*, 69.

[9] Williams wrote apropos this letter: "Here was something new. A letter with a real criticism, and a real suggestion. . . . And this was the first time any editor ever told me, in words of one syllable that I could understand, why my story had failed to sell. This was the first of a series of letters, all specific, all definite." In Wainwright Evans, "Bob Davis—Maker of Literary Geniuses," *National Pictorial Brain Power Monthly*, I (November 1921), 54.

[10] "Busy as he was, he always had time to help along young people who were trying to break into the fiction field. He would give them plain talk, so plain that even the most obtuse could get its import. But it was helpful and encouraging." New York *Times* (October 12, 1942), 17.

[11] *All About Da*, 72.

[12] "The Mate of the Susie Oakes," CLXXXIX (April 14, 1917), 71.

[13] The letter was written on March 21, 1940; the column, "Bob Davis Reveals," appeared in the editorial page of the New York *Sun*, February 19, 1935.

[14] *Saturday Evening Post*, CXCV (November 11 & November 18, 1922).

[15] Evans, 54.

[16] The two Davis quotations are from his letters of June 21 and December 22, 1921; Williams' from his letter of October 28, 1919.

[17] Evans, 54.

[18] Davis took great pride in his camera character studies. Expectably, Williams belittled his accomplishments. On May 6, 1919, Davis said to Mrs. Williams: "Once I told him I was a good photographer. That upset him completely. He burst into laughter." Davis thus describes a photo he had sent her: "The side view shows Ben in an Ibsenian mood. The shock of hair, the strong, firm chin, the eagle eye, the vast jowl, are Benjamin at his best." This might well have served as caption to the portrait of Williams which Davis used in *Man Makes His Own Mask*, a volume of his "psychographs" of 130 celebrities. On unnumbered page 231 is a profile of the right side of Williams' face. (On May 1, 1931, Davis had written him: "I am quite aware that you wish beautification and not realism. But I do want your notorious mug in my book.") On facing page 230 is a brief biographical sketch in which Davis iterated his perennial jests about Williams' size ("He is more than twice the weight of his wife."), his penchant for "dashing through the spruce jungles" with his annually discarded flivvers, his clumsiness, his gentility, his love of sports outdoor and in, and his Welshness.

[19] An inscribed copy of these verses (*Field and Stream, May 1920*), framed with a photograph of Davis and Chuck Williams fishing from a rowboat, hangs in Williams' studio at Hardscrabble Farm.

Richard Cary (essay date 1972)

SOURCE: "Ben Ames Williams: The Apprentice Years," in *Colby Library Quarterly*, Vol. IX, No. 11, September, 1972, pp. 586-99.

[*In the following essay, Cary explores the early portion of Williams's literary career to 1920.*]

Fate, or whatever it is that impels a man's life in one direction rather than another at crucial crossroads, was particularly whimsical on the day in January 1910 when Ben Ames Williams (1889-1953) was preparing for final examinations prior to graduation from Dartmouth College. "Through a series of circumstances of which I have no recollection, a boys' school in Connecticut, which needed someone to start in February as a teacher in English, offered me a job. I telegraphed Father: 'Have been offered a job teaching. Shall I accept?' My handwriting has always been difficult and as delivered to Father, the telegram read: 'Have been offered a job travelling. Shall I accept?' Father told me years afterward that if the telegram had read 'teaching' he would have told me to take the job, but he had no desire to see me become a travelling man."[1] Since the advent of handwriting, men have pored and cursed over cacography. For Williams it proved to be the ineluctable boon, diverting him from a purgatory of grading endless, immature English "themes" and thrusting him toward a career as one of the most popular storytellers of his time.

Williams could easily have gone the professional route. "My mother had always a devotion to the best things in literature. . . . Before I was six years old I loved the roll of words; by the time I was ten I was a voracious reader."[2] But the paternal factor, this time through long implantation instead of accidental distortion, drew Williams into the trajectory of his future work: "Probably the predisposing influence was that my father was an editor."[3] The senior Williams owned and ran the Jackson (Ohio) *Standard Journal,* and here Ben Ames plied before and after school hours and all day Saturdays. He ran as printer's devil, swept floors, washed forms, set type, and fed the presses. As it did Franklin, Whitman, Twain, and Howells (not too long ago or far away in Ohio) "writing an occasional item that found print" infected Williams with the *virus scribendi.* In the summer of 1908 he did a stint as reporter for the Oklahoma City *Times,* and from February to June 1910 worked as editor "and the entire editorial staff" for the *Standard Journal* in place of his father, who had been elected to the Ohio State Senate. So it was in the nature of a psychological avoidance for him to declare, "It was more by drift than by decision that I sought a newspaper"[4] when he grasped his diploma and trended to Boston in search of a job.

He pounded the streets vainly that summer of 1910 until, out of frustration, he faced down the managing editor of the Boston *American:* "Look here, Mr. Reardon, you've been putting me off all summer. *Do* you want me, or *don't* you want me? *This* is your last chance!" So surprised he could think of nothing else to say, Reardon muttered, "Come in Monday morning."[5] Williams had his foot in the door.

Before long he was rooming on the South End with Peter Webb Elliott, a reporter for the Boston *Traveler.* The example of the drama critic on that paper, Earl Derr Biggers (*Seven Keys to Baldpate,* Charlie Chan), had infused in Elliott the desire to turn out saleable magazine fiction, a task he tackled every evening with grim zeal. As Williams tells it, he wanted to get married, so he was saving eight dollars a week out of his salary of fifteen, and eschewing the night life of Boston, even in the winter of 1910-1911 too expensive for his budget. When his efforts to inveigle Elliott into a game of cribbage to fill the hours from supper to bedtime failed, Williams adopted Elliott's expedient. "I hired a typewriter, bought a ream of paper, and wrote a short story called **'Getting a Job.'** Editors who saw that manuscript unanimously agreed that it was wasted effort, but I wrote another story, and another, and another, till the total ran to dozens, and then to scores. Each story I sent to an editor, and when the manuscript was rejected, to another editor, and another, and another."[6]

Piqued rather than disheartened by this barrage of rejection slips, Williams dug in his heels—he was going to learn to write. He read assiduously essays on style and dramatic construction; he studied Stevenson's short stories, and Maupassant's and Kipling's and O. Henry's and Balzac's and Bret Harte's; he wrote in emulation of Stevenson, of Dickens, then "ran through several authors. Nothing sold, nevertheless."[7] The only "literary" fruits of his extracurricular activity were "three highly inflammatory rhymes" advocating conquest of Mexico, which the *American* printed. By blows at best, Williams remanded them to Gehenna. "These I did not preserve," he commented dryly.[8]

In September 1912 Williams married Florence Talpey. Bolstered by the "unshakable certainty" of his young bride and "a stubborn persistence and a certain blind faith in myself," he continued reporting by day and writing fiction by night. On his 25th birthday in 1914 his wife presented him a leather-bound account book with his name embossed in gold on the cover. Across the first page he wrote: "This book is the embodiment of Faith, Hope, and Charity. For three years I have been trying to write fiction—with little encouragement and no emoluments. Yet I have faith and hope and pray for charity . . ."[9] Three decades later he told an interviewer that through those arid years "I spent two or three hours trying to write short stories, and the four years were up before one of my stories sold." If nothing else, the experience provided a wary self-assessment. "Well, a man who works that hard and doesn't get anywhere for that long is no born writer."[10] Time and again he was to advise tyros, "I learned how to write by writing." For the editor of *The Editor* he elaborated: "Inspiration, there's no such animal. No, it's not extinct—it never existed. Writing stories is not done with rolling eyes, and fiction material is not plucked in frenzy from the void. Writing stories is the result of patiently and persistently applying intelligence to a given task, like anything else. . . . You can't practice medicine without your training—well, neither can you write stories without apprenticeship."[11] Against such volition, what walls could resist for how long?

As authors go, Williams kept meticulous records of his output, work in progress, in the mail, in print; but as authors go, he was wont to omit, to duplicate, or to contradict. Thus, at various points he stated that his first published story was as early as the 80th and as late as the 88th in order of writing, an impressive tribute to his stamina in either case. His contemporary, thereby most reliable recollection places it as number 84. Except for a short sentence lauding his ability to render local color in **"Getting a Job,"** the rejection slips received by Williams distressed him with their curt impersonality. In 1913 *Good Housekeeping* turned him down while admitting that his story had "some mighty good points" and that the "boy and girl are so human," and the *Metropolitan* gentled its formal repulse by suggesting in a postscript that the *Outlook* might be interested. The first real rift in the greyness did not occur until July 14, 1914, when Charles Agnew MacLean (for *Popular Magazine*) sent a critique of some 350 words in tandem with his rejection of Williams' novel-length **"The Impudent Lady's Maid."**

Shrewdly presuming a novice, MacLean put a sure finger on Williams' misaligned emphasis at this stage:

> I don't remember to have read anything of yours before, but I am curious to know whether or not fiction is a new thing to you. You write, it seems to me, at times very well indeed, but this story is so unconvincing that I am afraid very few of our readers would be satisfied with it. There are short passages that have a good deal of charm and reality but incident seems to follow incident in a bewildering sort of a way. I would say that this story revolves very rapidly on its own axis rather than progresses. A successful narrative ought to have plenty of action and incident, but the action ought to carry one forward and there ought to be some logical reason for everything in the story. I have kept this with me for a short time wondering if I might not be able to advise you as to how to rewrite it, but I have given the idea up. The story is too bewildering and there is not enough of real meaning to the plot.

He added consolingly: "I would be very interested indeed to hear from you again, and will always be extremely interested in anything you are good enough to submit to me."[12]

Williams "immediately wrote him at length about myself" and aimed a stream of stories at MacLean in the next three months, all of which he refused "almost with apologies." Such consistent negation from so sympathetic a source persuaded Williams to take a hard look at his tactics so far. "I had tried to sell stories on plot, to sell them on description, to sell them on incident, to sell them on style; and had failed. This time I set out to sell them on characterization."[13] Having decided that his characters had been one-dimensional, he imbued those in his next story with distinctive utterance: "my hero stuttered, the heroine talked normally, an old Negro spoke broad dialect, one spinster aunt talked prunes and prisms, and the other used what I hoped was the language of an ardent horsewoman."[14] With an access of new hope in his new procedure, he dispatched the story to MacLean. *Wunderbar!* On the last day of November 1914 MacLean wrote that he would buy it—on condition. "The condition was that I cut out the young man's stuttering, the suffragist's horseyness, the other aunt's primness, and temper the dialect of the darky. I *did*." The irony: "When I was through, you couldn't tell one character from another." The miracle: "But he took the story, and printed it, too."[15]

After Williams conformed with another specification, to cut out a thousand words, **"Wings of 'Lias"** appeared in

Smith's Magazine, July 1915. His first emergence in print, and the concomitant cash he received, should have elicited a degree of jubilation and high celebration. The reverse was true. Morosely he calculated that in three years he had spent $80.94 for typewriter rental, paper, pencils, envelopes, postage, and express; in rebate, the story brought only $50. Into this equation he added the outlay of two hours per day at the writing. "So by that first appearance, and by the eventual check, I was profoundly depressed." He reconsidered his indefatigable experiments ("I had in the course of these three years tried a dozen ways to write. I had cultivated first a simple style and then a flowery one; I had been staccato and I had been wordy"). He contemplated his extraordinary industry, painfully translating Georges Polti's *Thirty-Six Dramatic Situations* with only the help of his college French. "So much labor," he mourned, "so many hopes; was this all?"[16]

One short story published seemed such minimal recompense. In his account book he had vowed "that if five years shows no real success at writing I will lock this book in my deepest drawer and—forget it." Well, when all was said, he *had* succeeded in getting printed. Not much, perhaps, but well within his self-decreed deadline. Williams "rallied from that depression sufficiently" to reassert his determination. With the New Year, he destroyed all but three of the eighty-five stories he had on hand and started afresh.

Williams finished twenty-one stories in this first year of his renascence and sold five, four of them to the Street and Smith magazines of which MacLean was general editor. He returned **"The Impudent Lady's Maid"** again in January, pleading "the opportunity of seeing more of your work . . . something that will 'fit'"; by November he found it acceptable "in its present form." He returned **"The Little Tike"** because it strained probability too much but offered to take it if Williams could "think up some malady, or accident, a little less fantastic"; within a week Williams had fixed it up to suit. MacLean also took **"Marker's Hobbies"** late in November. Although *American Magazine* sent back **"Deep Stuff"** because "there is not enough happening," MacLean urged Williams to "cut this 800 words and tone down the slang a little. I want it. Hurry it back." The editor of *Short Stories* was glad to use **"The Taming of Nips Blaas"** though he turned down the much-traveled **"Impudent Lady's Maid"** and two others. *Adventure* objected to the old plot and obtrusive point of view in **"Received Payment,"** yet invited Williams to "Come again."

Looking back at 1915 Williams had considerably less cause for year-end gloom. Four of his stories had been published, with two others contracted for and on schedule. He had earned $245 from his moonlighting, not of course munificent, but indicative of the potential. Charles MacLean was imploring material. Better still, Bob Davis was beginning to take notice.

Robert Hobart Davis (1869-1942) came out of the West to become editor in chief of the Munsey chain of magazines, a cut above the Street and Smith line.[17] During his regime he introduced or developed a scintillating host of taletellers: Edgar Rice Burroughs, Zane Grey, O. Henry, Mary Roberts Rinehart, Max Brand, Rex Beach, Israel Zangwill, Fannie Hurst, to name only the most popular. It took Williams more than fourteen months to get a story past Davis' basilisk eye. At the time it constituted a hazard fraught with disappointments for Williams, but in retrospect he cited Davis as the most salutary force in his life as a professional writer.

On the 10th of December 1914 Davis discounted **"Cell Number 6"** as "a much-ado-about-nothing story"; on the 28th he decried the "offensive" elements in **"A Police Petruchio."** Although he declined both stories, he softened the blow by bantering Williams as "Colonel" in the first instance and expecting "to be forgiven for sending this story back" in the second. Davis' evident qualities of honesty, broad humor, and spontaneous humanity matched precisely those of Ben Ames Williams and explains why they became cordial friends and remained so until Davis died. But affinity is one thing, editorial judgment another. The whole of 1915 rolled by without a single acceptance by Davis. "Very unpleasant," he labeled one story; "too sordid and repellant," he said of another which *Collier's* less fastidiously bought and brought out shortly after. "Puzzling and unconvincing," "pretty obvious," he damned two more. Not until Lincoln's Birthday in 1916 did Davis descry something to his taste. He blustered about the title, **"Glissez, M'Sieu Kellee, Glissez,"**—"which is a dead giveaway"—was bound he would change it, but didn't. It ran in *All-Story Weekly* for July 1. In quick succession Davis acquired **"The Whale Buster," "Worth a Leg," "The Sure Thing," "In the Redbrush,"** and **"Once Aboard the Whaler."** In the first half of his third productive year Williams' income vaulted to an unprecedented $910. The barrier that had so effectively confounded him seemed ready to be breached now.

The $400 check Williams received for **"Once Aboard the Whaler"** in June 1916 churned to the surface a notion that had lurked deep in his mind for five years. Early in July he journeyed to New York City for a conference with Davis, the theme being: "Do you think I can make a living writing fiction?" Davis' answer was a vociferous yes. With a wife, two small sons, and a large house to sustain, Williams was understandably hesitant about leaving a steady job. His mother's offer to make up the difference between what his salary had been and what he earned by writing stories clinched his decision. On December 23 he resigned from the *American*. He had, as he wrote then, "passed a sort of landmark."

The second half of 1916 was auspicious. Williams sold five more stories, three to the Munsey magazines, one each to *American Boy* and *St. Nicholas*. While still dominated by Davis, his market was starting to spread. But all was not roses in this climacteric year. Davis spurned **"Eastward to Eden"** as having "all the characteristics of a wood pile"; over **"Lese Majesty of the Law"** he ex-

ploded, "My Gawd man! This isn't a story." Other editors were no less blunt. The *Metropolitan* turned back one story because it already had "on hand an overdose of the gruesome." *Pictorial Review* found **"The Eccentric Miss X"** overly long. Two stories eventually sold were originally passed up as not "worth the space it covers" and "too juvenile." These point up a trait which becomes more manifest as Williams proceeds into a wider field of competition: his willingness and astonishing agility to revise and revise and revise a story until it satisfies him and, not incidentally, the implicated editor.

From the vantage of eight years' hindsight Williams pondered his productivity during the period 1910 through 1916. "In the course of that time I not infrequently wrote eight to ten thousand words a day. This deadly facility has always since been a handicap to me."[18] As 1916 came to a close and Williams began to attract notice from Hollywood, Davis laid down an amiable caveat in parallel vein. "Don't let your mind dwell on the motion picture end of the business of writing or your work will suffer. It will become a series of dramatic incidents more or less unrelated and quite impossible to follow. Do one thing or the other—a moving picture king or a literary guy—one of the two. Don't try to be both at the same time." Williams wisely did not succumb to the call of pelf.

In his first month of emancipation from the *American* Williams completed and sold to Davis a four-part serial, **"Three in a Thousand."** He also decided to hire an agent, although later he wrote: "I do not recommend an agent for a beginner, because the best agents cannot bother with the work of beginners; it is not sufficiently sure of its market. But as soon as you can show an agent that your work sells, and if you don't like the bother of marketing it yourself, why, then employ one by all means."[19] The man he took on was Paul R. Reynolds. At first Reynolds simply sent Williams' stories on to Davis. Soon he varied his program. On March 9, 1917 he notified Williams that the *Saturday Evening Post* had bought **"The Mate of the Susie Oakes."** Breaking into the *Post*, "the goal of most of the aspiring young authors of the day, was another milestone on the road to learning how to write."[20] Joy in the Williams' home was unconfined. The news came as a slightly belated gift for Williams, whose 28th birthday had occurred on the 7th. "We celebrated two birthdays."

Davis was one of the first to commend Williams on his accession to the *Post*. "Yes, I do congratulate you with all my heart. . . . I am not surprised at your success. I guess it is good-bye so far as I am concerned. I lose them all sooner or later. Well, old sport, you have my blessing." No other event in 1917 could conceivably outshine this entry. Meanwhile the ordinary vicissitudes of authorship persisted. Davis accepted two more of Williams' stories and, this time, made good his threat to change their titles. A third story he liked but complained that "the first 67 pages don't develop very much except gas." Additionally, he rode Williams for his self-acknowledged excess: "Permit me to intimate, my fat Welsh friend, that 85,000 words a month is too much for any man to write."

Then, the second thunderclap of the year—on September 27 the *Post* purchased **"Steve Scaevola."** On being apprised, Davis countered jocularly: "You ought to be ashamed of yourself to throw the *Saturday Evening Post* in my face. They take a story occasionally; I take everything you write. . . . Regards to your wife. *She's* a lady, anyhow." A week later, seriously: "I will bet money that Ben Ames Williams will be as well known as any writer in this country in three years." There was a touch of rue in his tone, as when a maestro perceives a fond protégé rising inexorably out of his ken.[21] John M. Siddall, editor of the *American Magazine,* wrote what may stand as a model of many letters Williams now began to receive: "I want to congratulate you on your last *Saturday Evening Post* story 'Steve Scaevola.' It is a splendid piece of work and makes me wish very much you would give us a chance at something of yours when you can."

All told, Williams published ten titles during 1917: *All-Story* (7), *Post* (2), *Collier's* (1). In his account book he set down this register of his first year as a free lance:

Wrote during year	25 short stories 10 novelettes 1 essay parts of two novels
Wrote during year	586,000 words
Sold during year	388,000 words
Sold during year	5 short stories 8 novelettes

These figures may strike less hardy practitioners as formidable, or even incredible, but Williams was to supersede every one of them in sequent years. There was no need to apply for his mother's subsidy.

The writing of fiction for popular consumption was now sturdily established as both a means of expression and a source of livelihood. Williams reviewed his situation, took steps to systematize his approach to the problem of viable materials. He initiated a scrapbook in which he pasted newspaper items suggestive of plots, characters, or themes. He ruminated about process and technique.

> Some of my stories grow out of incidents observed or imagined; some are transcribed almost literally from experiences related to me; some grow up around a character, or an apt title, or a trait of character; some are built up as a play is built up, to put forward a definite dramatic situation; some put in the form of fiction a philosophic or religious idea which has appealed to me; some are merely whimsical studies in contrast. . . .
>
> Save in one or two rare cases, I have always outlined my stories in advance. The exceptions were novelettes in which I knew in a general way what I wanted to do—a trend of character—and let this trend develop as I went along. I write from the beginning to the end. The end is usually as clearly in mind as though it were already written,

before I begin to write. I revise until I can no longer discover ways to improve the story. . . .

> The most important single element of technique seems to me to be the introduction at every opportunity of commonplace details of daily life. . . . These things lend, I think, a similitude of life. . . .[22]

He would suffer several changes of heart in his prescriptions for writing superior fiction, but these remained salient guides in his methodology for the balance of his career.

The pattern of one acceptance to every four or five rejections set in 1917 prevailed through the following year. The *Post* printed nothing at all by Williams. Davis carried over as the paramount power, but Williams' presence overflowed into broader territory. *All-Story* featured five of his twelve publications in 1918, *Country Gentleman* two, and each of the other five found separate haven in *Farmer's Wife, Bellman, Detective Story Magazine, Railroad Man's Magazine,* and—ah—*Snappy Stories* with a rather unrepresentative piece, **"The Pacifist."** Davis gave Williams a particularly hard time over his title "The Perfect Ways," snubbing such variants as "Deep Waters," "Spindrift," "Sea Wrack," "Salt of the Sea," "The Harsh Salt," preferring his own invention, ***The Sea Bride.*** He won his point, ran the story under that name in *Munsey's* (March-August 1919), and it was issued in book form later that year by Macmillan. Astute as ever, MacLean announced to Paul Reynolds in October 1918 regarding **"Storming John"**: "It is not as good as I expected from Mr. Williams. I am buying the stuff now for the stuff he is going to write in the future." Alas for grand strategy, he, like Davis, was scheduled to slide into eclipse before very long. That year Williams wrote 608,000 words, sold 336,000.

Insofar as Williams' stories are concerned, the death knell of the pulps sounded on June 7, 1919. Starting on that date, the *Saturday Evening Post* presented its readers three of his short stories and two serials within the space of six months. Prior to and following this period, Williams published fifteen other titles during the year, mostly to magazines of lower station. With this new ingress, however, the direction of his efforts shifted perceptibly toward altitudes previously inaccessible. The *American Magazine, Pictorial Review,* and *People's Home Journal* clamored for his byline, the latter abject over some small misunderstanding in the past. *Everybody's,* which had published ***All the Brothers Were Valiant*** (Williams' first serial to reappear as a book) and two shorter narratives early in the year, regretted his refusal to let them "order" stories, declaring they would rather have them from him than "almost anyone" they knew. The editor of *Leslie's,* attracted by Williams' work in *Everybody's,* asked for stories of modern setting, "genuine heart interest . . . virile . . . clean and wholesome," but there is no evidence that Williams tried to accommodate him. Moffatt, Yard & Company, book publishers, invited him to drop by and talk over a prospect. Ditto Small, Maynard & Company, Brentano's, and Marshall Jones Company, a young, enterprising firm. Little, Brown & Company, exceedingly desirous of publishing **The Sea Bride,** was edged out by Macmillan, who also opened negotiations for **The Great Accident** (Williams' third book). The American Play Company inquired about the dramatic rights to that story. Half a dozen motion picture producers sent heroic propositions. And to cap all, Edward J. O'Brien pinned three stars on "The Right Whale's Flukes" and included a biographical sketch of Williams in *The Best Short Stories of 1918.*

Davis was of course privy to all this and bowed to the inevitable with becoming grace. "I am glad other people are beginning to realize that you can write, but don't forget that your wife and I 'knew you when.'" By his own audit, Williams sold approximately 75,000 words more than he wrote in 1919, demand outstripping yield for the first time. In this heady year he marketed eight short stories, seven novelettes, one novel, and three titles to the movies. The *Post,* as might be expected, paid him the largest sum to date (excepting movie rights) for the three-part **"Jubilo"**—$1500. Undeniably, Ben Ames was out of the woods in terms of professional repute and remuneration.

Williams published twenty times in 1919, only eleven in 1920. The qualitative rise amply compensated for the quantitative slump. Besides the *Post* (3 appearances) and *Collier's* (4), *Cosmopolitan, Good Housekeeping,* the *Red Book,* and *Munsey's* (1 each) welcomed him to their pages. The *American Magazine,* as well as *Harper's* and *Century,* pressed him for publishable new fictions. The International Press Bureau offered to syndicate some of his earlier unsold items, either short or serial, "nothing of the sophisticated type." Page Company, Penn Publishing Company, and Harcourt, Brace joined the ranks of book producers eager to admit his name to their lists; Mills & Boon, Ltd. expressed delight with its arrangement to issue his first three novels in England. **"They Grind Exceedingly Small"** was included in the *O. Henry Memorial Award Prize Stories of 1919.* In January 1920 Blanche Colton Williams, chairman of the Award Committee, notified him that **"The Field of Honor"** had also been selected to appear as one of the thirty best stories in the forthcoming volume. In March she had to retract because "no publishing house could be found which would print in book form more than a part of them." Williams had made his way into singularly good company. Others on this élite list were James Branch Cabell, Edna Ferber, Ben Hecht, Joseph Hergesheimer, Rupert Hughes, Fannie Hurst, Melville D. Post, and Wilbur Daniel Steele—only Steele, Anne D. Sedgwick, and Williams winning multiple mention. The prefatory text stated unequivocally that *all* the titles recorded were "worthy of preservation under covers." As if in instant reparation, **"Sheener"** was chosen by O'Brien for his 1920 best-of-the-year anthology.

Williams wound up eight short stories and three novelettes (by which he meant serials) in 1920 and sold ten of them, not exceptional statistics for him any longer. The prime characteristic of his success was the climb to periodicals of higher editorial standards, with some pretensions to literary quality. Popular, yes, but not vulgar in the best Latin sense of the words. It was as much as Williams aspired to at this juncture. He had set out to learn to write, and he had learned to write sufficient unto his purpose. "I don't believe either Mrs. Williams or myself had in this connection any dream of fame and/or fortune. The fact was simply that I liked to write—and that she liked to see me enjoy myself."[23] The *Saturday Evening Post* represented an Olympus of a sort to him and his contemporaries. To be gathered into its pantheon of authors, to be accepted three or five or eight (and eventually twenty-one) times in a year constituted a seal of approval and a personal vindication. In the forties and early fifties Williams elevated himself beyond the *Post* but remained staunchly loyal to its memory as it foundered and faded. It had been the rope he grasped to pull himself upward. It had, by its severer demands, compelled him to beget a better product. It had put an end to his apprentice years.

Williams' awareness of his own deficiencies and his attention to the strictures of editors and critics served him well, for they enabled him before he was through to create such authentic mirror-worlds as **Owen Glen, Come Spring,** and **House Divided.** From the beginning he applied himself with relentless dedication. "I read," he said, "and thought and studied and tried."[24] Even when the advisories were starkly diametric—one chiding him for too much plot, another for not enough; one, too gruesome, another, too bland—he strove unsparingly to reconcile, reaching all the while for a style and idiom entirely his own. He had not attained the mark by 1920, but he was well on his way.

Any overview of Williams' first phase as author would be wanting if it did not embody—would in fact be tangential if it did not *conclude* with Robert Davis' two ebullient cheers as Williams broke out of his pulp cocoon. The first: "The pore fellow wrote more than eighty stories and three novelettes and didn't get no encouragement a tall. But by gosh he had intestines, that fellow had!—and he, now, *stayed;* and dod-gast my eyes, danged if he didn't ketch on." The second: "I'm not a prophet; but I do know a writing guy when I see him and when I announce that a new star is rising in the east, by the jumpin' gods of war, a new star *is* rising in the east."

Selah.

NOTES

[1] Ben Ames Williams, *American Notes* (unpublished autobiography), 267-268.

[2] "Ben Ames Williams," *Saturday Evening Post,* CXCVII (October 18, 1924), 54.

[3] Ben Ames Williams, *Now I'll Tell One* (unpublished autobiography), 164.

[4] *Ibid.* With utter guilelessness he added, "the Jackson *Standard Journal* was, during my boyhood, very much a part of my life."

[5] Florence Talpey Williams, *All About Da* (privately published, Chestnut Hill, Mass., 1962), 58.

[6] *American Notes*, 103.

[7] John Mason Potter, "Not Worth the Effort," Boston *Post Magazine* (February 3, 1952), 9.

[8] *American Notes*, 273; *Now I'll Tell One*, 211.

[9] *All About Da*, 67.

[10] Robert van Gelder, "An Interview With Mr. Ben Ames Williams," New York *Times Book Review* (February 14, 1943), 2.

[11] Ben Ames Williams, "Authorial Ideals and Beliefs," *The Editor* (October 6, 1928), 7.

[12] This letter and others quoted in this essay are now part of the Williams collection in Colby College Library.

[13] "Ben Ames Williams," in Gelett Burgess, editor, *My Maiden Effort* (Garden City, N. Y., 1921), 269.

[14] *American Notes*, 104.

[15] *My Maiden Effort*, 270.

[16] *American Notes*, 104-105; *Now I'll Tell One*, 197.

[17] For a detailed account of the Williams-Davis relationship, see Richard Cary, "Ben Ames Williams and Robert H. Davis: The Seedling in the Sun." *Colby Library Quarterly*, VI (September 1963), 302-325.

[18] *Saturday Evening Post*, 54.

[19] *The Editor*, 8.

[20] *All About Da*, 74.

[21] Nevertheless, at one point Davis did release a shaft of editorial irascibility. On November 24, 1917 he said to Williams: "I will be honest with you, Ben—I am not going to read 'Steve Scaevola.' I haven't the time. I lost the lobster originally, and now he can go to hell."

[22] Arthur Sullivant Hoffman, *Fiction Writers on Fiction Writing* (Indianapolis, 1923), 41, 83-84, 310.

[23] *American Notes*, 275.

[24] *Ibid.*, 198.

Ben Ames Williams, Jr. (essay date 1973)

SOURCE: "House United," in *Colby Library Quarterly*, Vol. X, No. 4, December, 1973, pp. 179-90.

[*In the following essay, Ben Ames Williams, Jr. presents a biographical remembrance of his father.*]

Whenever my father wrote a story in which there was a disagreeable woman, he would get many letters from female readers offering him the joys of their friendship, because they assumed he was using his wife as a model. And Mother would receive an almost equal number of scolding letters. Then in one of his books a boy who was at Dartmouth got a girl "in trouble." Both my brother and I, having gone to Dartmouth, got many an askance glance from acquaintances for several weeks after publication.

Yet in answer to the often-asked question: "What is it like to be in the family of a famous author?" our answer has always been—"Wonderful." Then, if the questioner would hold still, we would happily enlarge on how fine it was to live with him, to share his exciting life, to be stimulated by his vital mind and be guided by his great spirit and wisdom. Because that's how it was—wonderful!

When Professor Cary asked me to write about my father for the *Quarterly*, I accepted the opportunity with pleasure. What to say about him becomes more difficult. Perhaps if I just start at the beginning.

My first recollection must go back to when I was four or five. We lived then in Newtonville, Massachusetts, and I remember that my bed was in a sort of alcove. I was in bed, asleep, but cold. My father came in from the hall, silhouetted large against the lighted door—he was a big man—carrying his bathrobe. It was made of a wonderfully heavy woolen material, soft but thick. He spread it over me gently and looked at me, but didn't touch me. I woke, but didn't speak—I was happy to have him there. He went out and closed the door, and I remember with a feeling of great comfort even now that the bathrobe had his smell on it and it was all around me.

That is a fair way to express our life with my father—he was all around us. Supporting us, guiding, loving, leading, challenging—a very strong force. I'm sure my mother, older brother and younger sister all felt some different things about him than I did, but I am also sure that for all of us he was a superb source of life and strength to grow.

During the years when we were young, Dad had an office in town, with a secretary, and he worked a full day, often early morning to mid-afternoon. But his evenings were for family and friends, so I am sure we were together more than other families where "business obligations" might take some time. And we were able to spend our summers in the country—New Hampshire or Maine—and take long trips together—the Southwest, Newfoundland—because we were not tied to any scheduled vacation of his, and he could work anywhere.

I remember once we went to Newfoundland salmon fishing, by train and boat. On the way home on the train Dad wrote a story and he later told me that he sold it for enough to pay for that not inexpensive trip for four of us. Perhaps that is one reason I always thought I would be a writer when I grew up.

One of the last times I was with Dad before he died in February of 1953, we had a long talk about my livelihood—banking—and I remember that in that penultimate talk he finally conceded a point that we had many times discussed in good humor, that it did sound as though it might be interesting.

To fill in the canvas a little, I would tell you where Dad came from. His mother was Sarah Marshall Ames, of Macon, Mississippi. (Many years later, I acquired a beloved mother-in-law: Jessie Ames Marshall, and there were probably remote ties through the two families.) Sarah must have been a very early co-ed, going from Macon to college at Ohio University (Athens, Ohio) in about 1880. There she met Daniel Webster Williams, my grandfather, who learned Welsh as early as he learned the alien English in the southern Ohio Welsh community of Oak Hill.

Like so many of those early towns, Oak Hill started out as a cooperative, and my great-grandfather is alleged to have suggested at the first full town meeting that since their iron mine operated at a loss, while the town's bull showed a profit, they should liquidate the mine and buy another bull.

Sarah Ames Marshall and Daniel married, and in due course my father was born, 1889, in Macon, Mississippi. They lived then in Jackson, Ohio, but of course Grandmother went home to Macon where it would be "safer to have the baby."

Dad grew up in Jackson, but always had close ties with his mother's home and a certain loyalty to the South was always a strong part of him. My grandfather was many things—historian, schoolteacher, editor, and finally owner-publisher of the Jackson *Sun Journal.* So Dad early-on was in the fourth estate, and naturally enough his first job after college was on a newspaper, in Boston. (As was mine, and my brother was in the newspaper business for twelve years.)

But most of all, my grandfather was an observer of the world around him, the people, flora and fauna, foibles and follies, and beauties of the world. Dad often told me that a walk with him was like a week in a good school.

To begin to close the circle, Mother and Dad met when she was 14 and he 15 at the school in West Newton, Massachusetts, where he was preparing for Dartmouth and she was visiting a step-relation who taught arithmetic. Mother arrived in West Newton by way of her birthplace in Tientsin, China, where she was born of an American father and an English mother: Clipper ship captain Henry Talpey and his lovely wife, Constance Mary Beatrice (Fryer). My grandfather died when my mother was thirteen, and my grandmother brought her small family, including my mother, to Dorchester, Mass.

After a proper interval and proper courtship, my grandmother married Josiah Chase of York, Maine, and travelers up the Maine Turnpike now pass under the bridge of Chase Pond Road. (Josiah was always frustrated that it was known as Chase *Pond,* when to his proprietary eye it was clearly a *Lake.* To this day, Chase Pond provides the water supply for much of the coastal area of York County, and is the lake on whose furthest shore my father built a lean-to to which he took my mother by canoe after their wedding.)

Dad was graduated from Dartmouth in 1910, Mother from Wellesley in 1912, and they were married on September 4, 1912. I sometimes wonder at people who refer to our great mobility today when within my next two older generations people from England, Wales, China, Mississippi, and Ohio somehow contrived to produce a young newspaperman and his wife living in Newton Highlands, Massachusetts!

Dad worked at night as a reporter on the old Boston *American* for six years, and during the day he began writing fiction at home.

The transition from part-time writing to full-time was aided by my grandmother who prompted Dad to quit the paper and write by pledging to pay him any difference between his newspaper salary and his story sales. The first year she paid him $200, and that was all. There was not much money, enough, but no extra as my brother and I came along. Dad wrote over eighty stories before he sold the first one, a fact he sometimes used to quiet the young gushing student writers who would say to him, "Of course, with your natural genius, Mr. Williams, you wouldn't understand how hard it is to *learn* to write."

He learned, with no teachers except observation and the occasional editor who would take the trouble to say *why* they were rejecting a submission. Robert H. Davis, editor of the old *Munsey's Magazine,* was one of these and they became great friends. Bob Davis helped Dad in major ways. Once he rejected a story and told Dad the characters were not clearly delineated, so Dad rewrote the story with no change except to give every character an accent—Southern, French, or State-of-Maine—and the story sold.

Dad was fond of telling young writers, with whom he would always visit (and often talked at Boulder and other schools of writing) that what was needed for a successful writing career was paper, pencil, desk, chair, strong glue and strong trousers, plus a desire to write. In his lifetime, Dad sold approximately 435 short stories and thirty-five novels, some of which were first published as serials. How many more stories were unfinished or abandoned we don't know, but in the thirty-seven years he devoted wholly to writing after he quit the newspaper, he produced prodigiously, yet with ever-improving quality. He never ceased being a student of his own craft.

We have notebooks containing plots, characters, sketches, floor plans, battlefield maps, physical descriptions, and endless pieces of ideas all put down for future use. When he was doing research for what I consider his greatest book, **House Divided,** Dad went to Gettysburg before doing the battle chapters, and sat on stone walls, and leaned against trees his characters later used. One of the reasons that Dad and Kenneth Roberts were such friends was that they shared a reverence for reality and accuracy.

Many of his earlier stories were about whaling, and while Dad had never sailed on a whaler, he had read the books, the journals, *Moby-Dick*; and crawled all over the retired ships in Mystic and other ports. And he *had* been on the ocean. His father was American consul to Wales the year before Dad went to college, so he spent the summer there. Dad and his father took a walking trip in the summer of 1906 over Snowden from the Royal Goat hotel in Beddgaelert. In the summer of 1937 I took the same trip and was able to see my father's handwriting in the hotel register of 1906. I slept in the same room, and, along toward morning. I began to suspect, the same bed. In 1951, my mother and my sister also visited Beddgaelert and saw both our names in the register!

Having grown children of my own now, and a grandchild, I can appreciate my father as a *father* even more than I did when I lived in his house. He was great. I never felt any lack of love and support from him, but I always felt a gentle urging. He wanted us above all to be honest with ourselves. He used to say that you cannot successfully fool yourself. He wanted us to achieve, not for money or acclaim, but because any slob could be a non-achiever. He wanted us to think independently and always urged us to read the whole story, not just the headlines. Having sat on the city desk of a newspaper, he knew the limitations of headlines. And I remember when World War II started he told us to watch the battle lines on the maps, not just read the communiqués. (World War II was tough to watch on the maps for a long time!)

Perhaps a key day in my full awareness of my father was when I first realized he could be wrong in a matter of factual reasoning. I was twenty-three. Thus he was a foundation for me to build myself upon. I finally learned that he had the odd shortcoming, thank goodness, because no one could be as right and true as I saw him when I was a boy.

When I would ask a question, he would always answer, but not until he had made me try to figure it out for myself. He would explain new things, and then ask us to go back over them to be sure we had understood, and that he had said it right.

I remember once he and my brother and I had been out in a marsh while Dad tried for a black duck. Driving home after dark, we three in the front seat, I in the middle—eight or nine years old I suppose—he decided the time had come to tell us the facts of life. Dad was a good man, shy and I am sure steadfast in the Puritan ethic, so it was not easy for him to tell all to us. But he did, and he used to love to recount the sequence of events later.

After laboring his way through, with some fear and trembling but in keeping with his practice, he said, "Now do you understand? Do you have any questions?"

Apparently, I replied somewhat aggressively, "Yes, I do."

"What is it?" hesitantly.

"I want to know what makes all those black spots inside street light reflectors?"—proving the wisdom of the modern child psychologists who advise against premature disclosure of the mysteries.

But Dad was always there. I remember on more than one occasion when I did wrong, clearly, palpably wrong, he would do nothing just then. Often later when I might see the error of my ways and perhaps even admit to it, he would say something like, "Yes, I wasn't sure that what you did was the right way, but I thought you might figure it out."

Punishment, when deserved, was delivered strongly, not harshly, and immediately. But then no grudges, no long periods of being in disgrace.

Once in Newtonville, when I was eight or nine, I was fully clothed in a blue serge suit, knickers. My brother was deep in the bath tub. I did something calling for immediate reaction on my father's part—I have no recollection of it—so he picked me up and lowered me into my brother's bath. I remember no particular feeling of having been chastised, but a great and lasting impression of how skinny my brother looked, naked, as I landed on top of him. In retrospect, it was my mother who got the "punishment."

Dad's insistence on the doctrine of "think for yourself" guided his own life as well as ours, and was responsible for many interesting variables in our lives. When I was ten and my brother twelve, Dad found absurdity in some of the things we were taught at school, so he hired an MIT graduate student to tutor us at home. For three years we got what turned out to be a good lesson in how to learn, and enough raw material to stay even with our contemporaries. But we also forewent some of the social education that goes with school, and when my brother went to boarding school at fifteen and I to day school, we had some catching up to do on how to get along with a group. However, we had been to more different parts of our country, learned more about certain important things like partridge, and perhaps spent more time in adult company than many of our classmates. On balance, I believe it was a good experience for us, and Dad no longer fretted under what he deemed to be pointless pedagogy.

During the years when we were away at boarding school and college, and my sister was controllably quiet around the house, Dad began to write at home, and to write novels of greater scope. *The Strumpet Sea* in 1938, *Thread of Scarlet* in 1939, *Come Spring* in 1940, *The Strange Woman* in 1941, *Time of Peace* 1942, *Ama-*

teurs at War 1943, *Leave Her to Heaven* 1944, *It's a Free Country* 1945, and finally, but not the last, *House Divided* in 1947.

Each of those a major, serious book. Most with an attention to the American civilian during America's wars which was in some ways a basic concept of the majority of Dad's late books. But observe the volume. One a year, if you count the 2-volume *House Divided* as two.

Dad had his first bad heart attack in 1938 and we often felt, in his books after that, he was trying to get all of himself and his philosophy into the record before trouble came again. *Come Spring* particularly is full of my father as a man, a husband, and a father. It is a great book, and a great personal legacy for all of us. One would get a clear picture of my father only by reading *Come Spring.* This is a book about good people doing what they thought was right. They had their weaknesses and their failures, but they did found a town in Maine (Union) and clear the wilderness and reproduce themselves. I have often thought that Dad wished he could have lived back then, and been Joel of *Come Spring.*

In Dad's workroom in the Barn at our farm in Searsmont, Maine—inherited from Bert McCorrison who was the model for "Chet McAusland" in a hundred-odd **"Fraternity Village"** stories—there is a large desk. Behind the desk a photograph on the wall shows four piles of manuscript, ranged in front of an old, high-silhouette typewriter. The piles are medium, smaller, larger, and medium. And they are labelled, successively:

1) First draft, Longhand, 895 Pages
2) New material added, 401 Pages
3) Copied after Revision, 1564 Pages
4) Final typed manuscript, 1185 pages.

In the third pile are many tortured pages, with dozens of revisions, each one seeking the right way to say it. My father was a craftsman—and if that is different from being an artist, so be it—and he was interested in his craft. He left us many examples of his plans for stories. And he left many records of his care.

On the wall of the loft in the Barn in Searsmont there is a tide table showing the ebb and flow of the tide through Robinson's Hole, between Buzzard's Bay and Vineyard Sound, between Naushon Island and Pasque, in the year 1811. This had to do with research for *Thread of Scarlet* and Dad was not content to have the tide come and go. If his characters were to be in those waters at four a.m., he wanted the current forces to be authentic. He was not a stickler, he just knew that to make things real they had best be realistic.

I was writing a book once and asked my father to read a passage describing a night-time stalk down a trail to a river's edge. I described the action well enough, but when Dad finished reading he handed it back and said, to this effect, "Have him smell something? Did his feet feel something through his moccasins? Did a cobweb cling stickily to his face? Could he hear anything, his own heart, or night sounds? Involve his senses, and your reader's senses—don't just tell what happened."

That is as good a way as I know to describe Dad's approach to writing. Care, industry, craftsmanship. He always said the story was the easy part. Polti's *Thirty-Six Dramatic Situations* (in which all possible plots are outlined and subdivided) was on his shelves, and he gave copies to his children as we majored in English. The story part is easy; the hard part is to involve the senses and emotions of your reader and make it real.

I once saw Dad perform as the "speaker" at a family night at our country club. He was to be unrehearsed and "tell a story" about some object picked by a lady in the audience. So one dear person shyly named her own, vintage black hat. Dad told one of Polti's stories—perhaps, "A man betrayed by his brother (mother, father, sister, friend)" about the black hat. It could have been told about anything picked by anyone in the audience.

This may not be what you wanted, Dick Cary, but I had better stop because I could go on forever with great pleasure. To remember my father and reflect upon his life and way of life is for me a privilege. He did it very well.

Perhaps readers of the *Quarterly* would like to share one of our Lares and Penates.

My mother, who died in November 1970, seventeen years after Dad, wrote a book about him for the family, called *All About Da.* Dadcu ("Dah-kee") is Welsh for Grandfather, and that's what I called my grandfather. Our children and my brother's and sister's worked out the easier "Da." It is a delightful thing for us to have and after she tells about his death, on the Curling Rink at The Country Club in Brookline, she wrote:

EPILOGUE

The knoll, two hundred or so yards behind the barn at Hardscrabble, with Levenseller Mountain beyond, was in many ways Da's favorite earth spot. Whenever we were at the farm we never missed walking out there after our early evening meal, to watch the sunset. The view to the west was often spectacular—all crimson and gold—but the afterglow on Levenseller to the east and the clouds above it thrilled him even more. There was always a birdsong around us, and we spoke sparingly. The ring of hills was forever changing in color as the sun sank lower, and Da often quoted from his favorite psalm: "I will lift up mine eyes unto the hills from whence cometh my help."

The knoll came to be the focal point of Hardscrabble life. Before its rough stone fireplace at the picnic table we had our family parties, and sat far into the evening in the firelight telling stories and singing.

Da had expressed the wish to have his ashes at the farm, and the knoll was there to welcome them. We rolled a big boulder from across the road, placed it on the knoll facing Levenseller, and had his name carved on it. You grandchildren know it as "Da's rock." We love to go for a picnic on the knoll with the rock only a few yards away. Da seems very near us.

Here is part of a letter I received from Bob Bradley last summer. He and I always exchange letters on our birthdays in August and this is what Bob wrote:

> My memory returns to an evening when we were discussing Hamlet. I had mentioned some lines that especially appealed to me. Uncle Ben said in turn that he liked best of all Hamlet's words just before death to Horatio:
>
> "If thou didst ever hold me in thy heart
> Absent thee from felicity awhile
> And in this harsh world draw thy breath in pain
> To tell my story."
>
> He especially relished the phrase "absent thee from felicity." And you remember how he could relish a phrase, as well as a view, a game, laughter, Old Fashioneds, roast woodcock and grouse, and fiddleheads. No one enjoyed his enjoyment more than he. Of course my thoughts are rich in memories of him, for he did much to shape my outlook and my thinking.

Da said many wise things and here are two I think you will want to remember:

> Freedom is worthy of the name only when the mind is free, and the mind which permits its thinking to be done for it, which takes its opinions in predigested forms, is a mind enslaved.

And he said this:

> Life is the acceptance of responsibilities or their evasion; it is a business of meeting obligations or avoiding them. To every man the choice is continually being offered, and by the manner of his choosing you may fairly measure him.

And this is what Da said about himself:

> I have liked many people, disliked few. It is true that many people bore me. Mediocrity coupled with complacent self-assurance always repels me; but on the other hand, to feel that a person is unhappy has always attracted me to that person. I have been most profoundly moved by the deep bravery in man which enables him to endure the many petty torments that are apt to be so much more harassing than the great crises in our lives. It is easy enough to face death, but it is not easy to face a wretched life with a high head. I have found men almost unbelievably honest, slow to take an unfair advantage, and stout to fulfill their obligations. It seems to me that honesty and an enduring courage are the most nearly universal human attributes.

> When I was beginning to consider leaving the Boston *American,* I wrote in one of my notebooks

this paragraph:

> "Here is what I want to do with my life. In the first place to love and to be loved, worthily, not alone by my wife and by my mother and father and sister, but by the world, or so much of it as I encounter. In the second place to build myself into a writer not only with a popular appeal but with a claim to real rank among those who were worthwhile. In the third place, to hold some post in the public life where I can help to right some wrongs. Whether that post be official does not matter, and perhaps the eye and the pen can do more than public office. In the fourth place, to lift those who are mine to so much of wealth as is necessary to allow us all to get the most—and the best—from ourselves.

> Not all the things I sought have been achieved; but the thing I wanted most—the love and trust of my family—is mine. In that certainty today I am strong."

The love and trust of his family grow with the years, and in them Da is stronger than ever. The rock on the knoll, looking out to the hills, is a symbol of our love. I am glad I have been able to absent me from felicity awhile to tell his story.

Richard Cary (essay date 1973)

SOURCE: "Ben Ames Williams and 'The Saturday Evening Post'," in *Colby Library Quarterly,* Vol. X, No. 4, December, 1973, pp. 190-222.

[*In the following essay, Cary examines Williams's decades-long contribution of short stories and serialized novels to the* Saturday Evening Post.]

Ben Ames Williams (1889-1953) wrote eighty-four stories before he sold one. For five years, while working full time as a reporter for the Boston *American,* he applied two or three of his off hours daily to turning out narratives which he hoped would appeal to editors of popular fiction magazines. The steady downpour of rejection slips, which dampened his spirits not one whit, was finally stayed by Charles Agnew MacLean, who printed **"The Wings of 'Lias"** in *Smith's Magazine* of July 1915. In that year Williams published three more stories in the so-called pulps, and seemed well launched toward a career as purveyor of gratifying adventure and romance. When in the following year Robert H. Davis, editor in chief of the Munsey magazines, embraced him as both friend and frequent contributor to *All-Story Weekly,* Williams' level and direction as a writer appeared to be defined.[1]

Williams' entry into authorship had been prompted by a desire to capitalize his restless energies, to "kill time," he once said offhandedly. However, the more he wrote, the more he became intrigued by the mysteries of his craft. As he acquired degrees of professional competence, he paid increasing attention to his own emergent creative guidelines. He harked gratefully to Davis' monitory counsels, yet began to navigate his own course. And he lifted his eyes toward a higher plane.

After he raised his rate of publication to six stories for the year, Williams resigned his newspaper job in December 1916 in order to funnel all his vitality into the writing of successful fiction. His confidence (now and later) in the efficacy of literary agents was, to say most, inconsequential:

> Can an agent sell a story which an author could not sell? Roughly, no.
>
> Can an agent tell an author why his story did not sell? Roughly, no.
>
> Can an agent teach a writer how to write saleably? Roughly, no.[2]

"Until a writer is able to sell stories, he has no need of an agent," he concluded. Nevertheless, he hired one at this point, an established operator named Paul R. Reynolds. When at first Reynolds merely relayed most of the stories to Bob Davis, Williams felt his lack of faith absolved. "I could have done that myself," he grunted. But he hung on, reluctant to tie up his time with business details and perversely certain "that Reynolds would widen my market and raise my prices more quickly than I could."[3] Soon he would have reason to applaud his sagacity.

Williams' first recorded refusal from the *Saturday Evening Post* is dated January 29, 1917, addressed to him, and signed "The Editors." They turned down **"The Squealer"**—which Davis had found "sordid and repellent" in 1915 and which *Collier's* printed, revised, in September 1917—but the corporate frigidity of the *Post* signature was somewhat relaxed by a warming comment: "Its workmanship is interesting and we would be glad to read any manuscript that you care to submit."[4] Late in February he completed a tale about whalers and sent it on to his agent. While in the midst of another, dealing with the Golden Candlestick of the Temple at Jerusalem, Williams received news from Reynolds that he had sold **"The Mate of the Susie Oakes"** to the *Post*. Jubilation was rife in the Williams household. As Mrs. Williams put it: "The word of the sale . . . came on the ninth of March, and as [Ben's] birthday is on the seventh, it proved to be a fine birthday present . . . we celebrated two birthdays."[5]

For Williams, this was a momentous initiation—"my first sale to one of the 'slick' magazines." Overshadowing that distinction, "The *Saturday Evening Post* was then . . . the magazine which to the beginning writer represented the ultimate goal."[6] At the helm since 1899, George Horace Lorimer (1867-1937) had steered an "elderly and indisposed" periodical to first place in circulation and prestige among those catering to that wide swath of readers designated "the general public." This leadership it retained until halfway through the thirties. As strongly entrenched

in the American cultus as hamburger and Santa Claus, its only rival in the five-cent field was the unrestricted ride in the New York City subway. To see one's name introduced into the *Post*'s notable roll of authors was to feel oneself entering a special galaxy. Williams' rose-colored reaction is thereby understandable. "Since I had 'broken into the *Post*,' it seemed to me the future was secure."[7] More so, in fact, than he could have dreamed.

"Lorimer was the *Post* and the *Post* was Lorimer," says his biographer. A species of benevolent despot, strong but not hard, Lorimer was with rare exception "Mr. Lorimer" to his writer and editors, and "The Boss" among themselves. A tough taskmaster over himself, he expected from them a comparable devotion to duty. Basically gregarious and sentimental, he kept a tight lid on his emotions and intimate relationships to a minimum. He usually entertained authors at lunch in the company's Philadelphia headquarters, bringing them together with editors, charting the *Post* while he ate. What made the *Post* particularly attractive to writers, over and above the honorific status, was its promptitude of decision, its generous scale of payment, and its regard for authorial sensibility. After Lorimer died, Williams reflected on their association of twenty years.

> Although I was to sell many stories to the *Post* during the years that followed, I never came to know Mr. Lorimer except over the luncheon table and in such semi-formal ways. He protected himself against many people. This had perhaps been forced upon him by the fact that so many men and women who sought to know him better had their own interests in mind. . . . Mr. Lorimer always treated me with the utmost consideration; and on the one occasion when he asked me to make a change in a story, he yielded to my opinion that the story was better as it stood than it would be if the change he had suggested were made. There is among many critics and among literary folk in general a disposition to accuse the *Post* of tempting writers into evil ways by dangling the Golden Fleece before their eyes. That may in some cases be true. I do not know. But I know it was not true in mine. I wrote what I pleased, and of my work that was shown them the *Post* bought what they pleased. . . . [Lorimer] was a positive personality and so was I, and it is possible that that lack of tact for which I have always been distinguished would have made impossible any real friendship between us; but I have always regretted that such a relationship did not develop (*NITO*, 213-214).

The attitude on both sides was clearly self-protective, the wariness of two headstrong men with mutual respect avoiding direct confrontation. Williams was never offered a contract, for Lorimer preferred the free-lance approach, but all of his best work was for years shown first to the *Post*.

Exigencies of space compelled Lorimer to cut **"The Mate of the Susie Oakes"** slightly, without consultation. Williams, in full glow of admission to the palace, did not protest. He concentrated instead on placing another story therein. On September 27, 1917 Reynolds notified him that Lorimer had taken **"Steve Scaevola."** Williams published eight other stories that year, the sum of which impressed him less than the two that made the *Post*. Novice offshoots, they nonetheless caught Lorimer's eye. In 1918 he wrote Williams about the aims of the National War Saving Committee "to sell thrift, savings, solidity to the country," asking his help "to bring this home to the American people in stories and articles or in whatever way you find easiest and nearest at hand." Williams says nothing about his response to this solicitation. He either did not try or did not satisfy. Neither did he succeed with any other theme. Of the twelve stories he published in seven different magazines during 1918 not one turned up in the *Post*.

In a variety of ways, 1919 proved an *annus mirabilis* for Williams. Twenty of his titles were presented in magazines; four serials were converted into books; five were produced as movies; three of his short stories and two serials appeared in the *Post*; one of the former (**"They Grind Exceeding Small"**) became the darling of a dozen anthologies, was reproduced in the *O. Henry Memorial Award Prize Stories of 1919*; **"The Field of Honor"** (*American Magazine*) was also certified "as worthy of preservation under covers" by the volume's editor, Blanche Colton Williams (no kin). In number, quality, and revenue Williams had truly achieved a breakthrough. One external factor favoring his ascent was the business recovery of postwar 1919. Circulation of the *Post* climbed back to two million copies and advertisements multiplied commensurately, enabling purchase of a greater number of scripts. *The Great Accident,* one of the lengthiest serials ever run in the *Post* (some 150,000 words), would no doubt have been resisted in bleaker times. Lorimer was pleased by the "steady improvement" of Williams' work. He opined that the story "would be better for serial use if it were not quite so leisurely in its movement, but I think by running extra long instalments we can overcome this handicap." Bob Davis, who had been trying to lure *The Great Accident* away from Williams since 1917, surrendered handsomely: "I wanted the story just as bad as Lorimer wants it. I couldn't however print it serially in a monthly magazine. It would have taken twelve numbers to get it to press, and only an absolute, downright, blown-in-the-bottle ass would have had the nerve to cut it. Its appearance in the *Post* will give you national fame. From now on your reputation is made. Nobody can stop you."

Williams developed **"They Grind Exceeding Small,"** an exemplum of poetic retribution, from a slim anecdote told him by a friend. He rated it "not a particularly good story" and was undisturbed over its being "published inconspicuously in the *Post*."[8] Conversely, editor Churchill Williams (no kin) prodded him for more such "good" stories, wondering wistfully "what the chances are for this!" Ben Ames himself eventually came to esteem its adoption by so many anthologists.

"Jubilo," the first of Williams' serials printed by the *Post* and one of his most popular over the years, opened the way to acquaintance with Will Rogers. It also inspired a puckish footnote on the fine art of filmmaking.

> He [Rogers] had made a number of moving pictures in the days before speech reached the screen, but of these only one was a success. It happened that that one was made from a story of mine called **"Jubilo,"** and this had led to my meeting Will Rogers in New York while he was playing in the *Follies,* and on other occasions. He once told me that when they were preparing to make **"Jubilo,"** the story, which had been published in the *Saturday Evening Post,* was turned over to a scenario writer to be converted into moving picture form. The writer, according to Will, ran into distractions; with the result that on the day they were to begin shooting the picture, neither the scenario nor the writer could be found. The location had been chosen and the company and the director were ready; so the director took the copies of the *Post* in which **"Jubilo"** had appeared, and shot the picture from them without waiting for a scenario.

> As far as Will knew, and as far as I have been able to discover, that was the only time a moving picture was ever made direct from a story in this way (*NITO,* 337-338).

The decade of the twenties, with its conic spiral of socio-economic boom and bust, was for Williams a period of widening market and literary growth. Alarmed by the flood of easy movie money (his income soared 500% in 1919 and more than doubled again in 1920), he faced down the threat of creeping superficiality. "I deliberately changed my style and the structure of my tales, deliberately sought to write stories that would move at a more leisurely pace, and that would depend more on character and less on action."[9] A courageous decision and one he adhered to despite a 50% drop in revenue during 1921. Lorimer was not partial to "introspective" stories, "stories in which one looks within and finds nothing,"[10] and he had already faulted Williams for being too "leisurely." In that year he bought precisely one title for the *Post,* a serial, **"Miching Mallecho."** Nevertheless, Williams had by now made his mark on a substantial percentage of the *Post*'s readership. Adelaide Neall, for twenty-seven years Lorimer's "right-hand man," had in fact asked Williams for an autobiographical sketch to insert in the "Who's Who" section to give these readers "the opportunity to get better acquainted" with him. He instead prevailed on Robert H. Davis, who came through with a typically whimsical portrait, "A Biography Written Backward," featured on April 3, 1920.

Just as Charles MacLean and Bob Davis dominated and shaped Williams' first aspect as author, so did Lorimer and Thomas B. Costain (1885-1965) his second. The advent of Costain to the *Post* in 1920 coincided with Williams' altered course, and Costain's presence indubitably turned the tide in Williams' favor. A vigorous, imaginative, efficient editor, Costain soon established himself as Lorimer's heir apparent. He journeyed up to Boston to induce more contributions from Williams, and they hit it off immediately. In the next two decades they spent pleasant weekends at each others' winter and summer homes, compared notes on their growing children, and—bridge enthusiasts both—often played in tournaments together and discussed the game's intricacies at length, orally and on paper. Most important, Costain took the chill off Williams' contact with the *Post* by assuming direct communication with him in the matter of his submissions, acting as an emollient between two frictional spirits.

In the summer of 1918 Williams started fishing with Bert McCorrison, who owned Hardscrabble Farm in the rural Maine region of Searsmont. Taken by the people and the setting, Williams conceived a series of stories based upon recurring characters and a single locality, because "I came to believe that a background familiar to the reader makes a story richer."[11] With actual towns in the vicinity of Searsmont named Union, Unity, Liberty, Hope, Freedom, and Friendship, Williams almost inevitably dubbed his fictional counterpart Fraternity.[12] His chief hazard was managing an authentic transcription of the Maine dialect, "the subtle intonations of a Maine farmer" which, when "translated into print . . . become caricatures." He surmounted this plight, as did Synge in the Aran Isles, "by catching from the common talk distinctive phrases" and shading them into the larger context.[13] His first two stories about Fraternity were picked up by *Collier's,* which presented them in December 1919 and January 1920.

Lorimer hovered between two stools in regard to the Fraternity construct. He appreciated the appeal of microcosm, the built-in continuity and habituation of such series, and in his time he sponsored Tugboat Annie, Mr. Tutt, Glencannon, Potash and Perlmutter, and Ring Lardner's "Busher," to name only five. They were mostly fast-moving and funny; Williams' was slow-paced and cursory, depending upon muted accumulation for effects. When Williams offered "Evered," a serial about a homicidal bull, Lorimer capitulated. He printed it in three installments beginning February 21, 1920, and in addition took "Old Tantrybogus" for March 6. They were the vanguard of some threescore to appear in the *Post,* many on Costain's instigation. Williams planned several as a series within a series, a septology structured on the Seven Deadly Sins. In his presentation copy of *Hostile Valley* to Kenneth Roberts, he wrote: "*Evered* was anger, *The Rational Hind* was pride, *Mischief* was envy, '**A Man of Plot**' was covetousness, and this was a try at lust. Gluttony and Sloth were never written." (Elsewhere he joked, "because they came too close to home.") In another instance, he attempted to hang a Fraternity tale on the thread of *Hamlet* but abandoned the idea when too many influences from the original kept forcing themselves into his revival.

Costain's first letters to Williams were models of discretionary and strategic praise. Suggesting a change in text, always potentially explosive, he exhibited utmost deference to Williams' judgment; soliciting a story with politi-

cal motif, he carefully appended, "We understand, of course, that you prefer to follow your own bent and write whatever story happens to be in the front of your mind"; relating to *Pascal's Mill,* "We all feel that it is perhaps the best work you have done. Certainly, in some respects, it surpasses any of your previous stories." In May 1921 Williams broached to Lorimer a series of short stories treating each of the commandments in the Decalogue, and here Costain best illustrated his function as buffer for The Boss.

After Lorimer had read and reacted to Williams' projection of the Decalogue series, Costain took over. First the agreeable angle. Lorimer, he reported, "was tremendously impressed with the magnitude of the idea." Then the onerous view, which he took upon himself. "I hope you are going to find it possible to treat these stories as a serial and complete them all before offering them for publication." Williams sent in the first five stories, and Costain delicately straddled Lorimer's explicit disapproval and Williams' possible indignation. "I think it would be better to say frankly that Mr. Lorimer feels that the stories are uneven." One he thought was "handled with great strength," two others "sound" but not up to his "highest mark," the fourth "too sketchy" and allegorical, the last "not on a level" with the rest. "It would be necessary therefore to do considerable rewriting." Once again he pressed the issue of employing "a single character throughout" or "a common narrator," this time under Lorimer's aegis. Having exposed the iron, he now donned the velvet. "We hope that you will not misunderstand our viewpoint or misinterpret our purpose." He hoped the series when completed would be published in the *Post.* In a postscript he further softened Lorimer's censures. "By the way, if you don't see your way clear to following Mr. Lorimer's suggestion, could you meet it by laying each story in the same locality?" Williams did not see his way clear. Costain cheered him for pursuing his own plan, which "seems to be the best one." The series went to *Collier's.* In this instance the catalyst failed to mollify the active elements.

In the next four years Williams' appearances in the *Post* reached their numerical peak, specifically, eight titles in 1923, sixteen in 1924, twelve in 1925, and twenty-one (his highest overall total) in 1926. Skepticism over his expanding vogue and concern over his literary integrity marked the first half of this period. It struck Williams as ironic that "In the year since I had determined to write stories that would not sell, every story I wrote had sold, and the price the *Post* paid me for short stories had doubled!"[14] He reasoned that "If the editors thought too well of my stories, there must be something wrong with them. I re-read a dozen or so, decided that their interest depended too much on plot, and began to reduce plot to a minimum. Mr. Lorimer of the *Post* objected, and his objections could not be taken lightly; but I continued to write what I chose, and found a decided satisfaction in producing an occasional almost plotless story so good that Mr. Lorimer felt constrained to buy it."[15] But gloating was not enough. "Just as in 1920 I had changed the character of my work in order to avoid what seemed to me a dangerous popularity with the moving picture studios, so now I deliberately put into effect another change in order to avoid what seemed to me a dangerous popularity with magazine editors."[16] He agonized over the plotlessness of *The Rational Hind,* the dullness of **"The Ancient Landmark,"** the slowness of *Immortal Longings* and **"The Eftest Way,"** sure no one would buy them.[17] But the *Post* took them all, two of the titles were later issued as books, and one collected in the anthology, *Classics of the American Shooting Field.*

Bob Davis, his action-oriented mentor of the past, told Williams he no longer wrote good stories, he was a slave to his interest in character. As though in direct repudiation, Williams enunciated these three points of his new literary creed in the *Post* of October 18, 1924 (p. 54):

> I have tried for some years to hang all my stories on at least two pegs: The one, character; and the other, drama in the eternal sense of the word. It seems to me thus possible to approach most closely to a recognizable portrait of life.
>
> I cannot help feeling that since continued popularity is immortality, so present popularity, unless it demonstrably results from unworthy causes, creates at least a presumption of merit. I would rather write a best seller which the critics scorned than a story which they applauded but which left the people cold.
>
> But I would rather write a story which seemed good to me, whatever others thought of it, than any other sort at all; and by that rule I run.

He was categorically devoted to "experimental work of one kind or another" now, and reconciled to popularity—from a worthy cause.

Williams acceded less testily to requests that he cut his texts, agreeing, for example, that two pages of exposition about a worm farm were dispensable in a short story. Costain turned just a trifle tougher in criteria during the middle twenties but stayed flexible and commendatory in language. He told Williams The Boss considered one of his mystery stories "a bear" and chimed in that the method of telling was "absolutely new." He urged Williams to diminish Reynolds' intermediation by letting the *Post* see *all* his stories first—"We generally find that an agent who makes up his mind as to what we want and what we don't want is wrong four times out of five." By the end of the year he was complimenting Williams on the "grand lot of fiction" he had provided. "I imagine you have broken nearly all records in 1924." Over and above the twelve short stories and four serials in the *Post,* Williams had published nine short stories, two serials, and an article in *Collier's, Ladies' Home Journal, Country Gentleman, Liberty, Good Housekeeping, Woman's Home Companion,* and *Outdoor America.*

1925-1926 were highwater years for the *Post* in respect to growth and prosperity, as they were emphatically for Williams. His reputation spread to the point where he began to be the target for con men and impersonators. He received one letter, in care of the *Post,* from an irate Southerner demanding that he return and marry his jilted daughter; he was reported killed in New Mexico, also working incognito as a farmhand in the Midwest; he was dunned for his son's alleged nonpayment of rent in New York City (Ben Jr. was eight years old at the time). In both years Costain, obviously fronting for Lorimer, attempted to dissuade Williams from his casual line of storytelling. Admitting that there had been no slackening of reader interest in the Fraternity stories, and that there was no question about the value in the Fraternity location, he nonetheless carped on how "continuously" Williams had been writing them, and that "a change of base might be advisable for a time." He allayed the stricture by assuring Williams that the *Post* always got the "best kind" of response from Fraternity stories, and that he could go back to them anytime later on, "of course."

Costain also nibbled at Williams' stories outside the Fraternity fold. Along with rejecting "The Question Puller" in May 1926 (taken by the *Elks Magazine*), Costain said:

> You like to write stories around a single situation or idea; and although we like to have them in the *Post,* slender stories of the kind are not ideal for our purpose. There can be no doubt that the more plotty or substantial story goes better with the general reader. You have written three or four slender stories for us recently, and we felt that the list would not stand more of the kind.
>
> We like to have you go your own gait, but perhaps you will pardon a suggestion this time. Give us a few plotty stories now. . . .

Williams evidently concurred, for in the next week Costain purred: "We are never anxious to dictate the direction of an author's work, and we hope you will understand. . . . Glad to note . . . that you have some good plotty stories ready to sprout."

The meridian of 1926 was attained on October 9. In that issue of the *Post* appeared **"Coconuts,"** a story fabricated around a mathematical problem for which Williams gave no solution. He later recalled that "The day after the story was published in the *Post,* letters and telegrams poured in on them in Philadelphia and on me. I had so many inquiries that I considered preparing a mimeographed reply." On the 11th Lorimer ejaculated happily, "Hell's apopping down here." On the 14th Miss Neall entered the picture, diverting to Williams epistles from agitated readers, at first in ones and twos, then in packets. "Say something soothing to Mr.———," she begged. Merritt Hurlburd, a staff editor, appealed for a few statistics—number of letters received, extremes of time spent in solving the puzzler, et cetera, which he wanted for public relations purposes. A month following the fateful debut, Miss Neall wrote: "We here in the office have about reached the stage where the very word 'coconuts' gives us an attack of nerves." Williams, to boot, continued getting letters on the subject for the next quarter-century. The furore left him modestly untouched. "Of course that flood of letters did not prove that the story was a particularly good one. It merely suggested that many people are interested in mathematical puzzles."[18] He undoubtedly was more gratified by the selection of **"The Nurse"** (in *Harper's*) as one of the *O. Henry Memorial Award Prize Stories of 1926.*[19]

The back side of the twenties witnessed Williams' undeterred climb to higher apices with the *Post.* Although acceptances declined in quantity, the prices now paid him set a record for monetary return in 1928. Pleasant encounters outnumbered the abrasive, but a perceptible difference of opinion developed during this era, a presage of future rift. Among the amiable incidents: **"Old Loving-Kindness"** (April 2, 1927) drew if not more letters than **"Coconuts,"** at least "more letters of appreciation" than any short story Williams ever wrote; Lorimer, who had instituted a department of "Americana" in the *Post* to rebut the contention of H. L. Mencken and George Jean Nathan in the *American Mercury* that "everybody and everything in America [was] rotten," warmed to Williams' forthright support; he declared "Letters From Fraternity," written by Bert McCorrison and edited by Williams, "good Americana" and published it in six installments; on the closing day of 1928 Lorimer said to Williams, "I am glad to be on the list of those that you number among your friends. We have a long list of writers and a shorter list of those who are both writers and good friends, and you qualify near the top"; **"Protect-Your-Men"** (March 12, 1927) was collected in *The Best Short Stories of the World War*; Costain informed Williams that "a number of people around here" believed him to be "some new sort of machine with the capacity of turning out perfect copy."

The debits, however, effectively balanced the account. For one, Costain became more assertive. He changed the title of one story seemingly on his own, and in another exacted a change in characterization—"which we believe you could undertake without hampering your literary conscience or anything of that kind"—not without a pinch of deprecation. He objected to Williams' basal mode: "The descriptive episodes are always one of the best features of a Ben Ames Williams story, but the first galley is all description even now." And in May 1928 he said it straight out to Williams, eyeball to eyeball: "We have been taking fewer stories the last three or four months and it has been due entirely to one thing. Your interest has been for the time being in psychological reactions and the story has been very slender. We like some stories of that kind but the number we can publish is necessarily limited."

Williams tilted with Lorimer by proxy over **"The Wild Ones,"** a short story in which the character of the protagonist emerges through a discontinuous sequence of offhand revelations and a culminating analogy with wild natural creatures. All things being equal, Costain explained, Lorimer preferred direct narration. Williams

stuck to his gun, convinced that the "thematic idea" was "more forcibly expressed" from the first-person stance. Shortly, the rumbling in the rear having subsided, Costain acquiesced, and the story was printed as originally cast. On the evidence of hundreds of letters between Williams and his editors, it must be said that he was a reasonable man, amenable to suggestion and quick to revise when criticism seemed legitimate. Yet he could turn adamant when his esthetic principles were affronted. Rather than argue, his usual recourse was to sell to another outlet, of which there was now an eager legion.

The first truly scarifying disappointment Williams suffered from the *Post* came in the spring of 1927 with its decision not to serialize **Splendor.** His work-journal entries disclose that he thought initially about this book in March 1921. Then he saturated himself in relevant authors (Hardy, Samuel Hopkins Adams, Herbert Quick, Dickens, Jack London, Balzac, Pepys, St. Teresa, Tolstoi), collected reams of preparatory notes, projected innumerable lines of narrative and sketches of characters, and expended inordinate stores of energy in the final composition. The project took on the nature of a totem for him: "It was my first attempt to express for publication the ideas which I was beginning to formulate." So, when Costain sent the negative news, it did not matter that he placatingly called the script "a big piece of work." Nor did it matter that Dutton snapped it up immediately and published it as a book. Williams looked to the *Post* as his lodestar. Now some of the light had expired.

Twice more in 1929 the *Post* saw fit to turn away long works by Williams. The ineligibility of **Touchstone,** a mystery yarn, did not appear to affect him markedly; he disposed of it as a serial to the *Ladies' Home Journal* and as a book to Dutton. He had brighter expectations for **Great Oaks,** a group of six associated tales about a Georgia island, in which he propounded a favorite thesis—the primacy of environmental over hereditary influence in the development of human psyche.

> If there be an underlying theme in the tales I write it is most definitely expressed in this book; for I believe in the potency of place and the impotency of man. In my stories the physical background is usually stressed, because it seems to me usually to explain the character of the actors. The New Englander is as much the product of his rock acres and his bitter winters as is the southerner the result of his calm and pleasant land. . . . I believe that a wise eye, looking across a certain countryside, can with some certainty predict what manner of men he will find dwelling there.[20]

Not strictly scientific, to be sure, but what today is called gut reaction—which makes for headier writers, like Hemingway as against, say, Spilhaus.

The trend of negotiations over **Great Oaks** was somewhat Florentine. In April Costain twice professed his and Lorimer's ardor for "the idea," which kept "looking better to us all the time." Whatever form the series took in

Williams' mind, he insisted, would be entirely satisfactory to them. "If a story refused to tell itself in anything less than two or three part length, it must be given its head." After several intermediary exchanges on the subject, Williams mailed the completed series to Lorimer on July 12. The same day, Costain reported from Williams' camp on Lake Winnipesaukee in New Hampshire: "I have read it, and feel that it comes pretty close to being Mr. Williams' best work. . . . I am quite keen about this story personally." Ten days later, on the contrary, Lorimer returned it to Williams with more praise and apologetics than was his wont. "It has had four readings here in the office," he went on, "and we are all in agreement that it will not serialize." Where Costain stood in this final adjudication, the correspondence does not make clear. In a roundabout way Williams learned that Lorimer decried the script as "too dull for utterance." That the book was instantly distributed by Dutton in America and Stanley Paul in England, and that it proved one of his better sellers were bittersweet victories for Williams.

Most of the residue of resentment was flushed away when in October 1929 Costain inquired desirously about Fraternity—"we are beginning to get letters from readers who would like more." Now Williams was solidly ensconced in his own creative predilections, so the *Post*'s editorial ambivalence toward these easygoing stories no longer jolted him. He had ready patrons for them elsewhere. Notwithstanding, the stories had got their impetus and achieved household fame through the *Post,* and he preferred to place them there. He was unquestionably pleased to see their early resumption.

An event of prime significance to Williams' future occurred as the twenties closed out. Reynolds severed his partnership with Harold Ober, and Williams chose to go along with Ober as his agent on a trial basis. Ober (who handled F. Scott Fitzgerald, among others) promptly demonstrated his aptitude through the duple sale of **Great Oaks.** He became and remained Williams' author representative for the rest of his life. At the outset Williams ruled unequivocally that he would deal directly with Curtis Publishing Company magazines—the *Post, Ladies' Home Journal,* and *Country Gentleman.* On his side, Ober started indoctrinating Williams toward two major shifts in *modus operandi*: 1) "It will be a good thing for you, and the *Saturday Evening Post* as well, to have stories of yours appearing in other magazines"; 2) "I don't think any editor is apt to buy a difficult story when he feels quite sure that the moment he declines a story that he will get another offered to him." A compound of astute business tactics with sure advantages for agent as for client, and a beneficial brake on Williams' hyperabundance if acted upon. Ober's advices reformed Williams' procedures less than did his own drive toward newer objectives in the writing of fiction. At any rate, Ober guided him expertly through one of the most trying periods of American history, the Great Depression of the thirties.

The full impact of the stock market crash of 1929 did not rattle the world of the *Saturday Evening Post* until well past the middle of 1930. Receipts in the first six months showed a drop of some 5% from the corresponding half in the previous year, but a successful campaign of newspaper advertising staved off any tendency to panic. Oddly, of all topics to come to the fore at this time, the question of a raise in rates consumed the attention of Williams and the top command at the *Post* for four months.

On May 8 Costain put it to Williams plainly: "I have talked to Mr. Lorimer about price. Although he feels that this is a bad time to consider increases in view of the uncertainty of business conditions, he is going to tilt the ante some." Then began a protracted interchange of proposals, agreements, reconsiderations, concessions, withdrawals, conciliations and, finally, tacit compromise. Williams simply expressed hope that the raise for short stories be "a substantial one." Lorimer did not want Williams to be dissatisfied. Costain mentioned a figure 50% higher than Williams' current price, though injecting the proviso that Williams send more stories of "the plotty type" and fewer on "character development." He added candidly that the latter were "not worth the larger price." If Williams "could square it with [his] literary conscience . . . we would be only too delighted to put the increase into effect on the next story." Williams acknowledged this dichotomy in his work. In defense he cited one of his character stories taken by the *Post* which was superior to one of his action stories also taken by the *Post*. He suggested they pay the full increase for stories they "like" and only half the increase for those they did not like "quite so well." Lorimer, through Costain, allowed that this was the "most practical" solution, "so we will leave it at that." As it turned out, no short story ever rated the full increase. Williams, who had left himself more or less on the mercy of the court throughout (I "have no inclination to bargain or haggle"), raised no commotion. With an audible sigh of relief, Costain nudged the subject into limbo. "You are certainly taking a most fair attitude about this matter of price and I can tell you we appreciate it. We are getting rather hardened to the other method—the wailing and gnashing of teeth."

During the twenties Williams contributed eighty-one short stories, twenty-six serials, an autobiographical sketch, and the edition of McCorrison's letters to the *Post*. The decade of the thirties witnessed a sharp quantitative drop: forty-eight short stories, six serials, and seven articles. Two forces largely determined this diminution: the contracting economy and Williams' expanding vision. As the number of solvent banks in the nation shrank, so did the size of the *Post*. From a longtime average of over two hundred pages per issue, by 1933 some comprised only sixty pages, with twelve to fifteen given over to advertisements. Profits dwindled proportionately. When Williams grumbled about the price paid him for an article, the *Post* righteously took a hard stand: "The literary market is distinctly bearish at the present time. Some of the magazines have been rather hard hit and are not buying. The result is that prices are showing a tendency to come down for the first time since the dizzy climb began about six years ago. This is natural enough, and fair enough." Costain twice paraphrased Lorimer to the effect that the *Post* was being generous, considering the state of things. Despite the stark reversal of circumstance, Lorimer obdurately held to prior principles which had exalted the *Post* as "the biggest nickel's worth in the country."

The seven predominantly autobiographical articles by Williams in 1930 and 1933 signaled a definite transition in his literary aims. The metamorphosis of his method of turning out a script aptly defines the ultimate direction his writing took. At the very beginning he used a typewriter; his sentences were too short.[21] He next experimented with dictation; his sentences were too long. "Now," he told a reporter for the Utica *Observer Dispatch* in 1941, "I do it in longhand and each sentence is about the right length." Translated to conceptual terms: his first method resulted in the great spate of short stories that stamped his presence in the field; his second method produced the swarm of two-parters against whose awkward length the *Post* and other periodicals so strenuously inveighed; his third method proved ideal for the cluster of novels milling in the back of his head as the thirties advanced. The scenario is unfolded too neatly here, of course, but Williams' maturation as a writer did intrinsically follow these broad lines from his novitiate **"The Wings of 'Lias"** (1915) to his posthumous *The Unconquered* (1953).[22]

Until Costain's departure from the *Post* in 1934, the mixture as before prevailed. Costain continued to congratulate Williams on his "plotty" stories and reprove him for the "character" pieces. Williams submitted some forty titles as possibilities for one of his sea yarns, among them **"Pirate's Purchase."** Lorimer settled on one of the drabbest, **"Make-Believe,"** for *Post* publication. When Dutton brought out the book as *Pirate's Purchase,* Williams enjoyed another of his tiny triumphs. The *Post* decreed that *Honeyflow* had no prospects as a serial; Dutton thereupon launched it as a book. Score one more for Williams. His reminder about the full pay raise for short stories ("hard times or no hard times") roused Lorimer to asperity: "Costain has passed the buck and your letter . . . to me. Speaking purely from the economic point of view, let me say that I believe writers are today the most fortunate class in America. . . . Now, though we are not planning to reduce prices, we certainly can see no basis for increasing them at this time. . . . I like your work and I value you as a contributor, but, as you will appreciate, I have to watch both sides of the scales."

Williams proliferated ideas for stories at the start of the 30s decade—a David Harum character in Fraternity, a murder mystery in Fraternity, a Utopian tale, a serial à la d'Artagnan, a crook story, a projected novel on a modern Napoleon, an adventure yarn about a mendacious Maine guide. All very well, but Costain warned him that the *Post* was "pretty well loaded up" with material and was "buying only those that hit us pretty hard." The rate of rejection began a long and steady surge. "These are tough

times" became the slightly variable dirge. The summer numbers of 1931 were drastically reduced in bulk, with "some sweeping cuts in prices" to authors. For three of the first four years in this period Williams managed to swim unchecked against the current, faltering a bit in 1932, regaining his wind in 1933. Indicatively, four of his ten acceptances that year were non-fiction. He tried to recapture the exhilarating reader response to **"Coconuts"** through a similar mental teaser based on the algebraic fallacy that 1 equals 2. Costain advised him to trim out the algebra and beef up the plot, which Williams did, to no avail. He changed the title and sold **"The Meddler"** to a lesser source several years later. However, Williams did attract bales of sentimental mail by his *Post* story at this time, **"The Shape of Fear,"** wherein a dog attacks and kills his master.

Williams wrangled with Lorimer over both the price and the length of **"The Crutile."** After first palming off the dispute to Costain, Lorimer set his foot down firmly: "You are under a misapprehension with regard to the two-part story," he wrote Williams. "It is our *bête noire,* and I should be glad never to print another one, as it falls between two stools. It fails to satisfy the part of our constituency that reads only short stories, or the confirmed serial readers who apparently want something that will carry them along for four, five or six issues." Having classified it as neither fish nor fowl, he nevertheless printed it in the *Post* as a two-parter, at his original figure. Ironically, Carolyn Wells sought it out for her annual anthology, *The Best American Mystery Stories of the Year.*

Behind the scenes, Ober kept up a drumming obbligato of admonitions and proposals. Patently, the *Post* was "heavily stocked," so why persist in thrusting stories at it only to be rejected? He assured Williams that Lorimer might resent his authors defecting to *Collier's* which he viewed as a direct rival, but not to *Liberty* or *Cosmopolitan* or others, which he did not. Despite occasional scuffles and rebuffs, the *Post* still ranked at the top in Williams' estimation. Following some months of contemplative silence, he explained that "When I have finished a story which seems to me good *Post* stuff, and when I know that if they like it the whole transaction will be cleaned up within a week," then he'd rather let the *Post* have "first shot."[23] When Ober faced him with a request from *Redbook,* Williams retorted that he would be glad to sell it a story, but not one "potentially good enough for the *Post,* unless the bargain was . . . at least equal to that which the *Post* would give me." For an obverse instance, about a bridge serial returned by a number of magazines as "too technical," he expressed himself "reasonably sure that it could readily be revised and made saleable to the *Post.*" The image of the *Post* which he had formulated as an aspirant to its inner circle and which he had embellished over fifteen years as a favored contributor refused to disintegrate under the blasts of a new reality.

Conditions in the publishing business worsened decidedly as the thirties proceeded. Advertising rates fell, postal rates rose; the *Post* became "quite thin" by past standards, its copy list bloated; Curtis dividends were cut, as were authors' prices—Williams no exception. Stories came back from the *Post* faster and more frequently, one for being "almost in article form," a second for weakness in "trade lingo," and more and more because of the pervading "full list." Although Costain undoubtedly meant to be helpful, his summation in April 1932 had an aura of the moribund about it: "We would like to see stories every so often . . . it would be fairer to you if we did not ask to see everything that you do in short length. My suggestion would be that you do some short stories with the *Journal* and the *Gent* in mind as alternative markets." In June he notified Williams of a 20% cutback in the rate he had been receiving, simultaneously slicing an additional 20% from the price for **"The Sedative"** ("a little thing in story interest") and a total 60% below the usual level for **"Chet McAusland of Fraternity"** ("not in reality a story"). To all this Williams reacted as to a grand equestrian abruptly unhorsed. "Of course I am glad to play along in any way I can. I think you know that I've always preferred to sell to you people." If it would help, he said, he would accept part payment in Curtis stock, an arrangement not possible under the company's financial setup.

In his **American Notes** (pp. 107-108) Williams reviewed these parlous events with a blend of puzzlement and subdued umbrage. "My chief satisfaction for some years had come from writing stories which the editors accepted under protest, but I suddenly found myself unable to write stories which the editors would buy at all. . . . I wrote . . . more and more; but I sold less and less." He worked out a strategy and revealed it to Ober. He would curtail offerings to the *Post,* stockpile some for the future, and send others to Ober. "Of course if you happen to make any sales, even at reduced prices, I shall be pleased." Decisions by the *Post* in 1933 were mostly adverse. He rerouted a number of short stories to other magazines, and Dutton published **Hostile Valley,** a novel about Fraternity.

Actuated by the phenomenal popularity of Earl Derr Biggers' Charlie Chan and Sax Rohmer's Fu Manchu, Costain tried to incite Williams to emulation. "The public just naturally like stories in which an Oriental character appears." Williams mulled over briefly his past efforts at intermittent serials (Inspector Tope, the Headmaster, Fraternity) and concluded that, except for the last, work in such vein did not suit his temperament. "Frankly," he wrote back to Costain, "I don't believe I'm up to the job," giving as major reasons his incapacity to handle oriental character or to invent orient sayings (never having known a Chinese or Japanese national), and his misdoubt that "the mere presence of a Chinaman as a leading figure in a story has quite as much selling power as you think." That was Costain's last editorial impulse to Williams as a staff member of the *Post.* For the remainder of 1934 the necessity to reject ran so high that Costain resumed his early tack of telling Williams, whenever he could accept a story, "It is one of the best you

have sent us in quite a long while." At the end of August he announced he was leaving the *Post* for a position with Fox Films.

Lorimer and Costain had never really learned to live with each other in fourteen years of propinquity. Their relationship was subliminally taut. To Costain, Lorimer represented retardation, a bar to the top; to Lorimer, Costain seemed inordinately eager to take command. Lorimer respected Costain's proficiency and left the *Post* in his hands while he was away, not however without sheets of itemized instructions, nor without keeping in constant contact, once cabling Adelaide Neall, "Is anybody dead have we discontinued publication?" Costain, who all along knew his own strength, chafed under such stringency, had once before resigned in a huff but retracted on Lorimer's entreaty. Now he left for Hollywood, later inaugurated the *American Cavalcade* monthly, then became an editor at Doubleday, Doran & Co. In all these capacities he regularly solicited Williams for viable materials. Their correspondence petered out in the forties when Costain renounced the editorial yoke to free himself for the more lucrative writing of historical romances, soon taking his place in the front row of bestsellers with *The Black Rose, The Moneyman,* and *The Silver Chalice.*

With Costain's exodus from the *Post,* Williams fell into the jurisdiction of editors Wesley W. Stout, Erdmann Brandt, and Lorimer's son Graeme. After several rejections by the first two, of stories too "thin" and "lacking action," Graeme principally assumed the duty of handling Williams' scripts. His letters are a chronicle of diminishing acceptances, which he conveyed with deference (due Williams as an old hand) and finality (due the magazine as a canted vessel). Before 1934 was out he reported unfavorably on eight stories—because of retroactive viewpoint, too obvious conclusion, too late for the football season, unconvincing motivation, lack of love interest—before one caught hold. George Lorimer, whose opinions Graeme adverted to more than once, came to the fore in October and again in December to dulcify Williams after rejection of a Fraternity piece. "There is no reason why you should not write an occasional Fraternity story," he urged, "provided you have a good strong plot for it. Atmosphere and background were a help to the earlier stories, but we have so thoroughly covered the ground round Fraternity that I think in future stories the dependence will have to be on the story itself." He was rubbing directly against the grain of Williams' intent in these deliberately lyrical tales. Lorimer must have thought he made amends by buying **"The Idolator"** as the year ended.

To Ober, Williams confessed complete frustration and some sadness over his impaired situation with the magazine: "I have quit trying to guess what the *Post* will or will not do," he wrote. "They are sometimes pretty slow in deciding on a story now, and it has worked out for the last year or so that I seldom offer them more than two stories a month." Matters improved a trifle in 1935 (seven acceptances) and remained virtually stagnant in

1936 (six). Not yet ready to forsake the field, Williams condensed and revised stories voted down by the *Post* and sent them to Ober, with occasionally a script not seen by the *Post*.[24] His market, dominated for a dozen years by the *Post*, dilated again to include more frequently *Collier's, Country Gentleman, Redbook, Ladies' Home Journal, Women's Pictorial, Woman's Home Companion, Bridge World, Progressive Farmer, The Writer,* New York *Sunday News*, Portland *Sunday Telegram,* and the Boston *Traveller.* Ober found it expedient now and again to sell at somewhat lower prices but he took precaution that these decrements did not hurt Williams' rates "in other quarters."

Graeme Lorimer, always specific about grounds for rejection ("you once said that you preferred reasons to polite evasions . . . so I'm taking you at your word"), explained that improbabilities of plot and two-dimensional characterizations in **Crucible** enjoined it for *Post* usage; Houghton Mifflin issued it as a novel. When Graeme was occupied elsewhere, it befell Brandt to pass the *Post*'s judgments along to Williams. Two clichés earmarked his letters: 1) "In Mr. Graeme Lorimer's absence it is my unpleasant duty to return this story"; 2) "Needless to say, we appreciate having had the opportunity of reading it." Repeated *ad nauseam,* they must have irritated Williams more acutely than the routine declination. The one silver note among all this dissonance was struck by Adelaide Neall, who wrote nostalgically about **"Coconuts"**: "I still receive six or eight letters a year from persons who have turned their hair gray, puzzling over this thing."

Still in the fullness of his vigor, George Horace Lorimer announced his retirement from the *Post* in a signed editorial on December 26, 1936. Privy to this news before public release, Williams sent him a three-page, single-spaced letter, most of which merits reproduction here for overtones revelatory of both men's natures.

December 21, 1936

Dear Mr. Lorimer:

I suspect that you and I just now have one feeling in common; the feeling that something which has been for a great many years apparently permanent and unshakable is about to end. Even though your withdrawal from the editorship of the *Post* is by choice, I suspect you must have, in advance of the fact, a sense of loss, a feeling that a great part of yourself is gone forever. . . .

I first became acquainted with the *Saturday Evening Post* so long ago that I do not remember whether it was before or after 1900. My Grandfather Williams lived in a little town named Oak Hill, Ohio; and my father, and his brother, and his four sisters were all pretty avid readers. . . . I remember discovering once when I spent a summer at my grandfather's home—in the disused attic, what seems to me in retrospect to have been a great heap of magazines, and most of those magazines were either *Lippincott's* or the *Saturday Evening Post.* My recollection of the latter may be faulty, but I remember it as not much more than a large leaflet, in which I nevertheless found a great many things the reading of which gave me pleasure.

From the time of my marriage in 1912, until we built our present home in 1923, I bought and kept at least one copy of every issue of the *Saturday Evening Post*; and in our house in Newtonville they were all arranged in order on shelves built for their accommodation. . . .

I'm not sure how long ago it was that I began to identify you with the *Post,* or the *Post* with you. Mr. Reynolds sold you one of my stories for the first time in 1917, and I remember what a kick I had from that sale. The story was called **"The Mate of the Susie Oakes,"** and had to do with the whale fisheries. It may have been sold to you in the latter part of 1916, but I remember that it was published in April 1917, because I found it in a copy of the *Post* which I bought on the way home from Ohio, just after the United States entered the War. It was hidden away in the back part of the magazine in a sort of apologetic manner; and, as I recall it, a paragraph or two, either at the end or the beginning, had been dropped out bodily for "make-up" reasons.

A good many years later, I used the word "tremorous" in a story, and the proof reader queried it and suggested "tremulous" instead. I was quite aware that there was no such word in the dictionary as "tremorous," and yet it seemed to me then— and does now—a good word in the spot where I used it. So I crossed out the "tremulous" on the proofs. However, when the story appeared, "tremulous" it was.

On another occasion, I described in one of my stories a cribbage game at the climactic point involving a matter of pegging out; and for some reason—presumably a question of space—two paragraphs were condensed into one in the story, by someone in your office, with the result that the dealer of that particular hand was said in the story to have failed to score a single point. Every cribbage player knows that the dealer must always peg at least one point, and probably a dozen people wrote me to complain about the mistake I had made.

I think those three occasions are the only ones upon which any change in one of my stories has been made in the *Post* office. Certainly they are the only ones I have ever noticed. Which is one of the reasons why writers, during your many years as Editor there, have preferred publication in the *Post* above other magazines.

This letter set out simply to offer you and Mrs. Lorimer and Graeme the Compliments of the Season, and I apologize for writing at such length! But I could not resist expressing the sense of personal loss I feel in anticipation of your retirement, and the regret I have always felt that, in spite of our numerous professional contacts, I have not had an opportunity to know you personally more intimately. I have always felt that you and I have fundamentally the same point of view toward the fundamental things in human life. It may be that I acquired it from you. Certainly it has been a part of my own character for many years. . . .

Cordially yours,

Ben Ames Williams

The tensility of their long relationship is easily inferred. To the end they addressed each other by their last names.

On the last day of that year Lorimer answered graciously: "I, too, have many pleasant memories of our long association, and I shall look forward to seeing you from time to time in the future, as when I return from my vacation I shall have a little more leisure and a chance to circulate more freely." There is no record that they did indeed meet again. When Lorimer died in October 1937, Williams dipped into his great store of affective humanity and characterized the editor appreciatively for Mrs. Lorimer:

I never knew him so well as I wished to, but I never saw him without feeling for days afterward a definite and stimulating reaction from that contact.

Each of us is apt to discover in the individuals we meet some particular trait which may or may not really exist; but it always seemed to me that the fundamental thing in Mr. Lorimer was that he was shy, that he had the embarrassed simplicity of a boy. Probably this is largely my imagination, but I always felt it very strongly in talking with him; and certainly it was never his stature as a man which impressed me so much as what seemed to me his simplicity. . . . It always seemed to me that his strength lay in the fact that the magnificent dimensions of his own life and career had never distorted his sense of proportion in the least degree.

At the *Post* a new era was taking shape. Lorimer had designated Wesley Winans Stout to take his place as editor in chief, and he had been duly installed. Unlike his predecessor, from whom all decision flowed, Stout leaned to a collective, consultative approach with his associate editors Graeme Lorimer, Erdmann Brandt, Richard Thruelson, Martin Sommers, W. Thornton Martin for art, and Miss Neall. Despite Brandt's suasive remarks ("our readers have missed you in the book. . . . Nothing would give us more pleasure than to have you back. . . . Personally, I have a hunch it won't be long"), Williams fared dismally under the new system. In all of 1937 he placed precisely one short story with the *Post* (low mark since 1921), and a total of eight short stories and one two-parter in the remaining four years of Stout's regime. This anecdote recounted by Williams in his *American Notes* (p. 108) adroitly exhumes the strains of failure, chagrin, *idée fixe,* and illusory desire that wracked his mind at that time.

In 1937, I finished a long serial called *Crucible.* No magazine would buy it, but Houghton Mifflin agreed to publish it as a book. I was summoned to a "sales conference" and Ferris Greenslet asked:

"Mr. Williams, your latest serial was published in the *Post* when?"

"In 1933."

"And what have you been doing since then!"

"Trying," I told him, "to write another serial which the *Post* would buy."

When his fiction fell on barren ground, Williams tried to sell non-fiction to the *Post* with as little success. Discovery of a bona fide first edition of Poe's *Tamerlane* in a Skowhegan, Maine, attic jogged a comprehensive essay on its history out of him. The original and two recasts were turned down. He next based a short story upon actual incidence. Brandt sent back the verdict: overlong, anticlimactic. Williams inserted a variant ending ("I have already tried a dozen different ways to wind up this story") which the *Post* group approved, and so **"Come-Uppance,"** a neo-Flying Dutchman experience, made the grade. He wondered if the *Post* would be interested in an article about curling, a Scottish game then gaining some currency in Canada and New England, which he had taken up zealously. No, the *Post* would not, but had he considered its possibilities as a background for fiction? Yes, he had, and proceeded to incorporate it into a story. The *Post* returned it. Stout asked Williams if he had any "present-day, non-mystery" serials fermenting. Williams quickly provided a two-page synopsis about a bitch-wife and mother who ruins the lives of her husband and four daughters, and as quickly withdrew it when it did not "seem to write." He proposed another, which eventuated as *Time of Peace;* it too never took root in the pages of the *Post.*

Two matters of lateral importance overhung the months of July and August 1939. The first revolved around the *Post*'s desire to publish a biography of Will Rogers by his widow. She consented to do it without collaborator but soon learned that she needed help. She asked for Williams, whom she had met in Hollywood during her husband's filming of Williams' **"Jubilo."** Followed now a protracted, labyrinthian series of negotiations and maneuvers between Mrs. Rogers and the *Post,* and the *Post* and Williams, rather reminiscent of last year's Howard Hughes cabal without the smear of fraud. The *Post* opted for a full-scale, formal biography; Mrs. Rogers held out for a selective, anecdotal frame. The *Post* arranged meetings between her and Williams; she turned skittish and avoided them. The *Post* offered Williams a stated sum in payment; Mrs. Rogers felt it would detract from her own total. Telegrams flew back and forth. Subsidiary rights were questioned. Her indecision deepened. She now stipulated that her collaborator not be a "name." Williams bowed out after a couple of fruitless trips in midsummer to New York and Philadelphia. "Uncle Clem's Boy" by Betty Blake Rogers finally appeared in the *Post* in eight parts (October-November 1940) pretty much in form, point of view, and idiom as she had specified, no collaborator cited.

The second episode bristled with potentials for serious legal altercation but Williams' affable attitude rendered it small potatoes. Stout informed him that a story called "Wooden Nickels" in the Chicago *Daily News* was a manifest piracy of Williams' **"Nutmeg Burley"** in the *Post* of November 12, 1938. Did he wish the *Post* to write or would he take action himself? Williams agreed that copying had been done, "However, I don't feel particularly indignant about it." He knew a chap who wrote daily short stories for a Boston paper for a pittance, and under such pressure "it seems to me not surprising that ethical considerations might occasionally be forgotten." In any case, since the *Post* owned the serial rights, it was their affair. Stout did admonish the *Daily News,* though less about the "shoplifting" than the probable low pay to the poor hack. So died a tempest in a teacup.

Williams appeared in the *Post* only three times in 1939, the third story portentously titled **"Times Have Changed."** The next year was drearier, rejections numbering at least twenty-two, with only one acceptance. After prolonged haggling over reductions in length (Williams made three), numerous "perhaps minor changes," and "unnecessary sex implications," Brandt announced that the entire staff was now in accord over **"My Grandmother's Leg."** Williams took time out to recapitulate. He had started off by writing short stories, intentionally concentrating in the genre because he usually earned more for a story than for a book. As he grew older, however, he tended to write longer and longer stories; he had more to say and he wished to do more with his characters. Often he would begin a short story and wind up with a serial. Editors, on the other hand, were demanding shorter and shorter stories. "The big weeklies more and more imitate the picture magazines. They'll all be down to one word on a page one of these days," Williams grumbled to an interviewer. He attributed his loss of love for the short story partly to over-anxiety when he could not sell them during the depression, partly to his having "lost the touch," and partly to their not being "fun any more."[25] To another newspaperman he explained his disaffection in another way. He had become extremely "tired of the necessary cutting for a short story—so I gave up short story writing and let myself go with novels."[26]

For decades Williams had circumvented the concept of writing a novel initially as a book. His first eleven books were reprints of ten magazine serials and one collection of previously published short stories. *Splendor* (1927) was his first pristine volume to the public, although it too had been intended as a serial. The same pattern held for his next sixteen books. Not until *Come Spring* (1940) did he consciously envision a novel as a unit. "There was so much respect in my family for books," he told van Gelder (p. 26), "that—well, the idea that I could write anything so impressive as a book did not occur to me until I was

well along in my thirties. It was only after publishers had been putting hard covers on my stories for a number of years that I decided to make a try as a novelist." This was his admissible fraction of the motivation. The other— 1941 was his apocalyptic year with the *Post.* His final story, with the wryly prophetic title of **"Road Discontinued,"** appeared in the magazine on February 8. Once or twice yearly until 1950 he half-heartedly turned out a tale for other periodicals, but with his severance from the *Post* Williams' days as a writer of short stories consequentially ended.

The doleful last words were left for Adelaide Neall to intone. In three letters from June to September she tiptoed exquisitely over his feelings (she had been with him from the beginning, twenty-five years back), setting forth in excusatory phrases the several reasons his fiction no longer suited the *Post,* now desperately reaching for a new readership in times of headlong socio-cultural change. She pinpointed length as his premier handicap, also competition from the largely pictorial *Life* magazine, the expanding attraction of radio, and the frenetic pace induced by imminent war. "I still believe sincerely that you are going to write stories for us and I know you can," she assured, at the next breath having to concur with "the rest of the staff" that his stuff was inadequate to the newer needs. Into his private journal Williams impressed his own thoughts at year end: "Except for the May-June spree in recoil from *The Strange Woman*—I wrote no magazine fiction. . . . I am now bent on writing books, novels, rather than stories, and see no immediate likelihood that I will write another short story." His face was to the wind now and he sped resolutely in his chosen direction. In the remaining thirteen years of his life he produced nine books, including his best known—*The Strange Woman, Leave Her to Heaven*—and his best— *House Divided, Owen Glen, The Unconquered.*

It is arguable that the determining vector in Williams' life as a writer was the *Saturday Evening Post.* He had commenced writing fiction without preconceptions or pretensions, assertedly to fill in wasteful hours and turn an honest dollar. He might have hunkered down smugly in the mystery-romance-adventure formulae favored by pulp magazines, his first haven. The *Post's* higher requirements forced him to upgrade his standards; its literate, middle-American audience bestirred him to search inward for a medium personally truthful and publicly responsive. Dreading the stereotype, he scrupulously reversed his field when his fiction sold too readily. The *Post* nurtured his natural andante style, exemplified in the Fraternity stories. Most important, Williams uncovered the core of his own sensibility in the ethos of the *Post.*

Williams was a large, amiable, decent, optimistic, meat-and-potatoes man, wary of sophistication or posture. He would have said of writers what Lorimer said of editors, that their prime qualification "is being an ordinary man." Williams did write to this effect: "I never lived in New York where writers like to foregather; and the number of members of my profession with whom I have had more than the most casual acquaintance is small. The men I have known best have been doctors, lawyers, architects, newspapermen, men of business, farmers, guides, and woodsmen. I am at ease with them." He proceeded solidly on this basis of a world he knew. "My stories have been for the most part manufactured out of things I have seen and heard and read and thought."[27] **"Jubilo"** is about a flivver and dishwashing, he told an interviewer.

The philosophical, the ostentatiously intellectual angles of creative writing he eschewed for the same pragmatic reason. Asked if he had ever taken a course in story-telling, Williams rejoined with a stout *no*. "I once read a book on it. It helped me not at all."[28] Yet he developed an eclectic set of theories wholly operable within the frame of his endowment: the arch function of art is "to stimulate emotion"; "discords between persons bound together by blood ties" constitute the most dramatic human situation; if a story is to succeed it must embody a necessary harmony "between the reader's preconception of what should happen and the fictional version." Williams' immense reverence for the great books drew him back to "the old Greeks." From Aristotle he extracted the meditations on pity-and-terror and the tragic flaw. "I have repeatedly tried to write stories on the general theme that a man's mistakes or misdeeds do in later life rise up to confound and sometimes destroy him. . . . I try to follow the logic of character, regardless of whether the ending is happy or unhappy."[29] And a subtler apperception of the happy ending, so often a sore point between him and the *Post:*

> Now, there can be beauty in tragedy. There can be happiness in tragedy; and there is no reason in the world why a short story which has a tragic conclusion cannot at the same time have a happy ending. Even death is often the happiest thing that can happen to a man at a given time . . . a story should end in such a way that the reader, if he voices his thoughts, will say to himself: "Well, there! That's the best thing that could have happened to him!"[30]

In these days of rampant Mailers, Capotes, and other televised prima donnas, Williams' modest appraisement of his gifts, methods, aims, and accomplishments comes as a refreshing breeze from the slopes of Helicon:

> I have been a professional writer, working at my trade, for some twenty-five years. I make no claims to genius or even to talent. I learned to write by hard work, and I have worked hard at writing—and enjoyed it.

> To have worked hard at writing fiction, without any pretense to inspiration, is held by some to be vaguely contemptible. I do not agree with this point of view. I find nothing despicable in having liked to write, nor in having written a great deal—some of it very poor—nor in having sold as much as possible of what I have written.

. . . . .

> Certainly I am not conceited about my work. Occasionally I write something which seems to me good of its kind, and I have always tried to write short stories and novels as well as I could. But I have rarely persuaded myself that they were good. . . . So, though critics have compared my work favorably with that of authors as various as Thomas Hardy and de Maupassant, as William Dean Howells and Dumas, as Sigrid Undset and Bret Harte, I have not been deceived (*NITO*, 408-409; 10-11).

Nor did he deal in other forms of self-delusion. He purposively bucked the tide of editor-approval in the twenties, inverting his style when it appeared to him too slick and his stories selling too readily. Truth of self-expression meant more to him than a glut of bylines. In the forties, he resisted the hectic new temper of the times, amplifying rather than dehydrating his product.[31] As a writer, Williams underwent progressive exfoliation in three stages: first, he shed the pulps; second, he transcended the *Post;* finally, he forged for himself, as any right artist must inevitably do. But for the *Post*, which brought him out frequently against its own inclination, Williams might never have achieved his ultimate proportion.

NOTES

[1] For detailed accounts of this period in Williams' life as author, see Richard Cary, "Ben Ames Williams: The Apprentice Years," *Colby Library Quarterly*, IX (September 1972), 586-599; and Richard Cary, "Ben Ames Williams and Robert H. Davis: The Seedling in the Sun," *CLQ*, VI (September 1963), 302-325.

[2] Ben Ames Williams, "The Function of the Agent," in William Dorsey Kennedy, editor, *The Free-Lance Writer's Handbook* (Cambridge, Mass., 1926), 214-217.

[3] Ben Ames Williams, *Now I'll Tell One* (unpublished autobiography), 212.

[4] This letter and others quoted in this essay are now part of the Williams collection in Colby College Library.

[5] Florence Talpey Williams, *All About Da* (privately published, Chestnut Hill, Mass., 1962), 75.

[6] *Now I'll Tell One*, 213.

[7] *Ibid.*, 214.

[8] Ben Ames Williams, "Authorial Ideals and Beliefs," *The Editor* (October 6, 1928), 7; *Now I'll Tell One*, 307-308.

[9] *Now I'll Tell One*, 262.

[10] John Tebbel, *George Horace Lorimer and The Saturday Evening Post* (Garden City, N. Y., 1948), 241.

[11] "Ben Ames Williams," *Saturday Evening Post*, CXCVII (October 18, 1924), 54.

[12] Two comments by Williams on this score are noteworthy. In the preface to his *Thrifty Stock and Other Stories* (New York, 1923): "The village called Fraternity is an actual one; and the surrounding countryside has a beauty which grows with long acquaintance. It is perhaps unnecessary to say that the characters are—with one exception—fictitious. The exception is Mr. A. L. McCorrison, better known as Bert. . . . He appears in some of the stories, under the name of Chet McAusland." In a letter to Richard Thruelson, an editor of the *Post,* July 27, 1938: "The town of Fraternity, since you inquire, is bounded by Montville on the northwest, Morrill and Belmont on the northeast, Lincolnville on the southeast, and Appleton and Hope on the southwest. In other words, in these Fraternity stories I have used the town of Searsmont, Maine, and the immediately surrounding locale."

[13] *Now I'll Tell One,* 258.

[14] *Ibid.,* 310.

[15] Ben Ames Williams, *American Notes* (unpublished autobiography), 107.

[16] *All About Da,* 110.

[17] About this unavoidable catch of authorship he wrote: "My judgment of my own stories from the point of view of salability has always been bad. Of all my short stories, readers have seemed to prefer "Homework," "Old Loving-Kindness," "Sheener," and "Solitude." In each case, I kept the stories on hand for a long time after I had written them. . . . In each case I refrained from offering these stories because I thought them probably unsalable. They pleased me as stories, but I did not expect them to please editors. Once the stories had been published, however, I was not surprised that readers liked them" (*Now I'll Tell One,* 306).

[18] *Ibid.,* 306-b.

[19] He derived additional satisfaction when "Scapegoat," in the *Post* on November 7, 1925, was included in John Clair Minot's *The Best College Stories I Know* (Boston, 1931), and the following year in Grantland Rice's *The Omnibus of Sport* (New York).

[20] Stanley J. Kunitz, *Authors Today and Yesterday* (New York, 1933), 699.

[21] In this connection, an anecdote related by Tebbel (p. 73) richly illustrates the hypersensitive relationship between Lorimer and Williams. Lorimer had an aversion to stories he thought were too short. "Nobody can really tell a story in less than three thousand words," he remarked. "De Maupassant did," Williams reminded him. "De Maupassant's dead," retorted Lorimer curtly.

[22] A lesser factor operating in Williams' swing away from short stories was purely practical: "the work involved in writing eight short stories is certainly much greater than that in writing one serial," he told Costain. At current rates, it was better business to concentrate on longer fiction.

[23] Without its knowledge, the *Post* underwent a poetic irony. Having had first refusal of Williams' stories for years, in 1932 it bought "The Sedative" after *Cosmopolitan* had rejected it.

[24] Ober, ever ardent about extending Williams' territory, responded with alacrity: "I think it would be a good thing for the *Post* to occasionally see a story in another magazine, which they have not seen. If they know that they are seeing absolutely everything of yours first, they may be a little too casual about declining stories."

[25] Robert van Gelder, "An Interview With Mr. Ben Ames Williams," New York *Times Book Review* (February 14, 1943), 2, 26.

[26] William H. Clark, "Ben Ames Williams Hides Away at Dawn to Write His Books," Boston *Sunday Globe* (November 12, 1944), 3.

[27] Tebbel, 209; *Now I'll Tell One,* 9-a; David Noel, "Ben Ames Williams," *Scholastic,* VI (April 4, 1925), 5; *Now I'll Tell One,* 408.

[28] Arthur Sullivant Hoffman, *Fiction Writers on Fiction Writing* (Indianapolis, 1923), 263.

[29] Hoffman, 388; *Now I'll Tell One,* 410; Ben Ames Williams, "Fiction Harmony," *The Writer,* XLIX (March 1936), 67; Herbert Edwards, "Ben Ames Williams at Hardscrabble Farm," *Down East,* XV (April 1969), 38.

[30] Ben Ames Williams, "The Happy Ending," *The Writer,* LIV (October 1940), 292. A member of the Editorial Board, Williams contributed to this magazine a number of articles on the practical and conceptual facets of short-story writing.

[31] The germ of Williams' penchant for the longer form of fiction unquestionably languished in the deep recesses of his mind for many years before he allowed it to emerge. As early as 1923 he made these discerning observations in his epilogue "Note" to *Thrifty Stock,* a collection of his short stories:

"The novel, obviously enough, depends for its interest upon delineation and development of character, and presents a comprehensive picture of some phase, large or small, of the social system. There need be no plot; there is usually merely a chronology. The story, on the other hand whatever its length, depends for its interest primarily upon incident and situation; it deals with conflicts and contrasts, with sacrifices and surrenders, with achievements and acquirements, with penalties and punishments, with sorrow and rescue, prosperity and disaster, and all the torment of obstructed passion. In short, with drama. There need be no social background; there need not even be any characters, in the strict sense of the word" (p. 347).

" . . . it is obviously much more difficult to write a great story than it is to write a great novel" (p. 347).

"It is probably fair to say that a short story is harder to write, in proportion to its length, than any other form of fiction. . . . It is infinitely easier to tell a story in ten or fifteen thousand words than it is to tell the same story in five thousand" (p. 349).

"A novel may be written in a blind, leisurely, chronological fashion, a page at a time, the end never very definitely in view. . . . The writer of a great short story conceives his story, not as a beginning, nor as a middle, but as a whole" (p. 351).

FURTHER READING

Bibliography

Cary, Richard. "Ben Ames Williams in Books." *Colby Library Quarterly* VI, No. 7 (September 1963): 293-302.
 Bibliography of Williams's novels and anthologized short stories.

———. "Ben Ames Williams in Periodicals and Newspapers." *Colby Library Quarterly* IX, No. 11 (September 1972): 599-615.
 Chronological bibliography of the periodical publication of Williams's short stories.

———. "Ben Ames Williams in the *Saturday Evening Post*." *Colby Library Quarterly* X, No. 4 (December 1973): 223-30.
 Bibliography of the short stories Williams contributed to the *Saturday Evening Post* between 14 April 1917 and 8 February 1941.

Criticism

Phelps, William Lyon. Review of *Black Pawl. Scribner's Magazine* LXXIII, No. 1 (January 1923): 118-19.
 Features a positive assessment of the missionary-hero of Williams's *Black Pawl*.

———. Review of *The Rational Hind. Scribner's Magazine* LXXVIII, No. 4 (October 1925): 436.
 Calls Williams's *The Rational Hind* "an admirable story of Maine farmers."

Review of *The Great Accident. The Dial* LXIX (August 1920): 211.
 Describes *The Great Accident* as "an American novel pulsing with democracy."

Review of *Owen Glen. College English* 12, No. 2 (November 1950): 126.
 Characterizes *Owen Glen* as a "rewarding and enlightening" novel of coal-mining and small-town life.

The following source published by Gale contains further information on Williams's life and work: *Dictionary of Literary Biography*, Vol. 102

Twentieth-Century
Literary Criticism

Cumulative Indexes
Volumes 1-89

How to Use This Index

Alcott, Amos Bronson 1799-1888 .... **NCLC 1**
See also DLB 1
Alcott, Louisa May 1832-1888. **NCLC 6, 58;
DA; DAB; DAC; DAM MST, NOV; SSC
27; WLC**
See also AAYA 20; CDALB 1865-1917; CLR
1, 38; DLB 1, 42, 79; DLBD 14; JRDA;
MAICYA; SATA 100; YABC 1
Aldanov, M. A.
See Aldanov, Mark (Alexandrovich)
Aldanov, Mark (Alexandrovich) 1886(?)-1957
TCLC 23
See also CA 118
Aldington, Richard 1892-1962 .... **CLC 49**
See also CA 85-88; CANR 45; DLB 20, 36, 100,
149
Aldiss, Brian W(ilson) 1925- . **CLC 5, 14, 40;
DAM NOV**
See also CA 5-8R; CAAS 2; CANR 5, 28, 64;
DLB 14; MTCW 1; SATA 34
Alegria, Claribel 1924-**CLC 75; DAM MULT**
See also CA 131; CAAS 15; CANR 66; DLB
145; HW
Alegria, Fernando 1918- .... **CLC 57**
See also CA 9-12R; CANR 5, 32, 72; HW
Aleichem, Sholom .... **TCLC 1, 35; SSC 33**
See also Rabinovitch, Sholem
Aleixandre, Vicente 1898-1984 ... **CLC 9, 36;
DAM POET; PC 15**
See also CA 85-88; 114; CANR 26; DLB 108;
HW; MTCW 1
Alepoudelis, Odysseus
See Elytis, Odysseus
Aleshkovsky, Joseph 1929-
See Aleshkovsky, Yuz
See also CA 121; 128
Aleshkovsky, Yuz .... **CLC 44**
See also Aleshkovsky, Joseph
Alexander, Lloyd (Chudley) 1924- ... **CLC 35**
See also AAYA 1, 27; CA 1-4R; CANR 1, 24,
38, 55; CLR 1, 5, 48; DLB 52; JRDA;
MAICYA; MTCW 1; SAAS 19; SATA 3, 49,
81
Alexander, Samuel 1859-1938 .... **TCLC 77**
Alexie, Sherman (Joseph, Jr.) 1966-**CLC 96;
DAM MULT**
See also CA 138; CANR 65; DLB 175, 206;
NNAL
Alfau, Felipe 1902- .... **CLC 66**
See also CA 137
Alger, Horatio, Jr. 1832-1899 .... **NCLC 8**
See also DLB 42; SATA 16
Algren, Nelson 1909-1981**CLC 4, 10, 33; SSC
33**
See also CA 13-16R; 103; CANR 20, 61;
CDALB 1941-1968; DLB 9; DLBY 81, 82;
MTCW 1
Ali, Ahmed 1910- .... **CLC 69**
See also CA 25-28R; CANR 15, 34
Alighieri, Dante
See Dante
Allan, John B.
See Westlake, Donald E(dwin)
Allan, Sidney
See Hartmann, Sadakichi
Allan, Sydney
See Hartmann, Sadakichi
Allen, Edward 1948- .... **CLC 59**
Allen, Fred 1894-1956 .... **TCLC 87**
Allen, Paula Gunn 1939- .... **CLC 84; DAM
MULT**
See also CA 112; 143; CANR 63; DLB 175;
NNAL
Allen, Roland
See Ayckbourn, Alan
Allen, Sarah A.
See Hopkins, Pauline Elizabeth

Allen, Sidney H.
See Hartmann, Sadakichi
Allen, Woody 1935- **CLC 16, 52; DAM POP**
See also AAYA 10; CA 33-36R; CANR 27, 38,
63; DLB 44; MTCW 1
Allende, Isabel 1942- . **CLC 39, 57, 97; DAM
MULT, NOV; HLC; WLCS**
See also AAYA 18; CA 125; 130; CANR 51,
74; DLB 145; HW; INT 130; MTCW 1
Alleyn, Ellen
See Rossetti, Christina (Georgina)
Allingham, Margery (Louise) 1904-1966**CLC
19**
See also CA 5-8R; 25-28R; CANR 4, 58; DLB
77; MTCW 1
Allingham, William 1824-1889 ...... **NCLC 25**
See also DLB 35
Allison, Dorothy E. 1949- .... **CLC 78**
See also CA 140; CANR 66
Allston, Washington 1779-1843 .... **NCLC 2**
See also DLB 1
Almedingen, E. M. .... **CLC 12**
See also Almedingen, Martha Edith von
See also SATA 3
Almedingen, Martha Edith von 1898-1971
See Almedingen, E. M.
See also CA 1-4R; CANR 1
Almodovar, Pedro 1949(?)- .... **CLC 114**
See also CA 133; CANR 72
Almqvist, Carl Jonas Love 1793-1866 **N C L C
42**
Alonso, Damaso 1898-1990 .... **CLC 14**
See also CA 110; 131; 130; CANR 72; DLB
108; HW
Alov
See Gogol, Nikolai (Vasilyevich)
Alta 1942- .... **CLC 19**
See also CA 57-60
Alter, Robert B(ernard) 1935- .... **CLC 34**
See also CA 49-52; CANR 1, 47
Alther, Lisa 1944- .... **CLC 7, 41**
See also CA 65-68; CAAS 30; CANR 12, 30,
51; MTCW 1
Althusser, L.
See Althusser, Louis
Althusser, Louis 1918-1990 .... **CLC 106**
See also CA 131; 132
Altman, Robert 1925- .... **CLC 16, 116**
See also CA 73-76; CANR 43
Alvarez, A(lfred) 1929- .... **CLC 5, 13**
See also CA 1-4R; CANR 3, 33, 63; DLB 14,
40
Alvarez, Alejandro Rodriguez 1903-1965
See Casona, Alejandro
See also CA 131; 93-96; HW
Alvarez, Julia 1950- .... **CLC 93**
See also AAYA 25; CA 147; CANR 69
Alvaro, Corrado 1896-1956 .... **TCLC 60**
See also CA 163
Amado, Jorge 1912- **CLC 13, 40, 106; DAM
MULT, NOV; HLC**
See also CA 77-80; CANR 35, 74; DLB 113;
MTCW 1
Ambler, Eric 1909-1998 .... **CLC 4, 6, 9**
See also CA 9-12R; 171; CANR 7, 38, 74; DLB
77; MTCW 1
Amichai, Yehuda 1924- ... **CLC 9, 22, 57, 116**
See also CA 85-88; CANR 46, 60; MTCW 1
Amichai, Yehudah
See Amichai, Yehuda
Amiel, Henri Frederic 1821-1881 .... **NCLC 4**
Amis, Kingsley (William) 1922-1995**CLC 1, 2,
3, 5, 8, 13, 40, 44; DA; DAB; DAC; DAM
MST, NOV**
See also AITN 2; CA 9-12R; 150; CANR 8, 28,
54; CDBLB 1945-1960; DLB 15, 27, 100,
139; DLBY 96; INT CANR-8; MTCW 1

Amis, Martin (Louis) 1949-**CLC 4, 9, 38, 62,
101**
See also BEST 90:3; CA 65-68; CANR 8, 27,
54, 73; DLB 14, 194; INT CANR-27
Ammons, A(rchie) R(andolph) 1926-**CLC 2, 3,
5, 8, 9, 25, 57, 108; DAM POET; PC 16**
See also AITN 1; CA 9-12R; CANR 6, 36, 51,
73; DLB 5, 165; MTCW 1
Amo, Tauraatua i
See Adams, Henry (Brooks)
Amory, Thomas 1691(?)-1788 .... **LC 48**
Anand, Mulk Raj 1905- .. **CLC 23, 93; DAM
NOV**
See also CA 65-68; CANR 32, 64; MTCW 1
Anatol
See Schnitzler, Arthur
Anaximander c. 610B.C.-c. 546B.C.**CMLC 22**
Anaya, Rudolfo A(lfonso) 1937- ..... **CLC 23;
DAM MULT, NOV; HLC**
See also AAYA 20; CA 45-48; CAAS 4; CANR
1, 32, 51; DLB 82, 206; HW 1; MTCW 1
Andersen, Hans Christian 1805-1875**NCLC 7;
DA; DAB; DAC; DAM MST, POP; SSC
6; WLC**
See also CLR 6; MAICYA; SATA 100; YABC
1
Anderson, C. Farley
See Mencken, H(enry) L(ouis); Nathan, George
Jean
Anderson, Jessica (Margaret) Queale 1916-
CLC 37
See also CA 9-12R; CANR 4, 62
Anderson, Jon (Victor) 1940-.. **CLC 9; DAM
POET**
See also CA 25-28R; CANR 20
Anderson, Lindsay (Gordon) 1923-1994**C L C
20**
See also CA 125; 128; 146
Anderson, Maxwell 1888-1959**TCLC 2; DAM
DRAM**
See also CA 105; 152; DLB 7
Anderson, Poul (William) 1926- .... **CLC 15**
See also AAYA 5; CA 1-4R; CAAS 2; CANR
2, 15, 34, 64; DLB 8; INT CANR-15; MTCW
1; SATA 90; SATA-Brief 39
Anderson, Robert (Woodruff) 1917-**CLC 23;
DAM DRAM**
See also AITN 1; CA 21-24R; CANR 32; DLB
7
Anderson, Sherwood 1876-1941**TCLC 1, 10,
24; DA; DAB; DAC; DAM MST, NOV;
SSC 1; WLC**
See also CA 104; 121; CANR 61; CDALB
1917-1929; DLB 4, 9, 86; DLBD 1; MTCW
1
Andier, Pierre
See Desnos, Robert
Andouard
See Giraudoux, (Hippolyte) Jean
Andrade, Carlos Drummond de .... **CLC 18**
See also Drummond de Andrade, Carlos
Andrade, Mario de 1893-1945 .... **TCLC 43**
Andreae, Johann V(alentin) 1586-1654**LC 32**
See also DLB 164
Andreas-Salome, Lou 1861-1937 ... **TCLC 56**
See also DLB 66
Andress, Lesley
See Sanders, Lawrence
Andrewes, Lancelot 1555-1626 .... **LC 5**
See also DLB 151, 172
Andrews, Cicily Fairfield
See West, Rebecca
Andrews, Elton V.
See Pohl, Frederik
Andreyev, Leonid (Nikolaevich) 1871-1919
TCLC 3
See also CA 104

Andric, Ivo 1892-1975 .... **CLC 8**
See also CA 81-84; 57-60; CANR 43, 60; DLB 147; MTCW 1

Androvar
See Prado (Calvo), Pedro

Angelique, Pierre
See Bataille, Georges

Angell, Roger 1920- .... **CLC 26**
See also CA 57-60; CANR 13, 44, 70; DLB 171, 185

Angelou, Maya 1928-**CLC 12, 35, 64, 77; BLC 1; DA; DAB; DAC; DAM MST, MULT, POET, POP; WLCS**
See also AAYA 7, 20; BW 2; CA 65-68; CANR 19, 42, 65; CLR 53; DLB 38; MTCW 1; SATA 49

Anna Comnena 1083-1153 .... **CMLC 25**

Annensky, Innokenty (Fyodorovich) 1856-1909 **TCLC 14**
See also CA 110; 155

Annunzio, Gabriele d'
See D'Annunzio, Gabriele

Anodos
See Coleridge, Mary E(lizabeth)

Anon, Charles Robert
See Pessoa, Fernando (Antonio Nogueira)

Anouilh, Jean (Marie Lucien Pierre) 1910-1987 **CLC 1, 3, 8, 13, 40, 50; DAM DRAM; DC 8**
See also CA 17-20R; 123; CANR 32; MTCW 1

Anthony, Florence
See Ai

Anthony, John
See Ciardi, John (Anthony)

Anthony, Peter
See Shaffer, Anthony (Joshua); Shaffer, Peter (Levin)

Anthony, Piers 1934- .... **CLC 35; DAM POP**
See also AAYA 11; CA 21-24R; CANR 28, 56, 73; DLB 8; MTCW 1; SAAS 22; SATA 84

Anthony, Susan B(rownell) 1916-1991 **T C L C 84**
See also CA 89-92; 134

Antoine, Marc
See Proust, (Valentin-Louis-George-Eugene-) Marcel

Antoninus, Brother
See Everson, William (Oliver)

Antonioni, Michelangelo 1912- .... **CLC 20**
See also CA 73-76; CANR 45

Antschel, Paul 1920-1970
See Celan, Paul
See also CA 85-88; CANR 33, 61; MTCW 1

Anwar, Chairil 1922-1949 .... **TCLC 22**
See also CA 121

Apess, William 1798-1839(?)**NCLC 73; DAM MULT**
See also DLB 175; NNAL

Apollinaire, Guillaume 1880-1918**TCLC 3, 8, 51; DAM POET; PC 7**
See also Kostrowitzki, Wilhelm Apollinaris de
See also CA 152

Appelfeld, Aharon 1932- .... **CLC 23, 47**
See also CA 112; 133

Apple, Max (Isaac) 1941- .... **CLC 9, 33**
See also CA 81-84; CANR 19, 54; DLB 130

Appleman, Philip (Dean) 1926- .... **CLC 51**
See also CA 13-16R; CAAS 18; CANR 6, 29, 56

Appleton, Lawrence
See Lovecraft, H(oward) P(hillips)

Apteryx
See Eliot, T(homas) S(tearns)

Apuleius, (Lucius Madaurensis) 125(?)-175(?) **CMLC 1**

Aquin, Hubert 1929-1977 .... **CLC 15**
See also CA 105; DLB 53

Aquinas, Thomas 1224(?)-1274 ..... **CMLC 33**
See also DLB 115

Aragon, Louis 1897-1982 .. **CLC 3, 22; DAM NOV, POET**
See also CA 69-72; 108; CANR 28, 71; DLB 72; MTCW 1

Arany, Janos 1817-1882 .... **NCLC 34**

Aranyos, Kakay
See Mikszath, Kalman

Arbuthnot, John 1667-1735 .... **LC 1**
See also DLB 101

Archer, Herbert Winslow
See Mencken, H(enry) L(ouis)

Archer, Jeffrey (Howard) 1940- ..... **CLC 28; DAM POP**
See also AAYA 16; BEST 89:3; CA 77-80; CANR 22, 52; INT CANR-22

Archer, Jules 1915- .... **CLC 12**
See also CA 9-12R; CANR 6, 69; SAAS 5; SATA 4, 85

Archer, Lee
See Ellison, Harlan (Jay)

Arden, John 1930-**CLC 6, 13, 15; DAM DRAM**
See also CA 13-16R; CAAS 4; CANR 31, 65, 67; DLB 13; MTCW 1

Arenas, Reinaldo 1943-1990 . **CLC 41; DAM MULT; HLC**
See also CA 124; 128; 133; CANR 73; DLB 145; HW

Arendt, Hannah 1906-1975 .... **CLC 66, 98**
See also CA 17-20R; 61-64; CANR 26, 60; MTCW 1

Aretino, Pietro 1492-1556 .... **LC 12**

Arghezi, Tudor 1880-1967 .... **CLC 80**
See also Theodorescu, Ion N.
See also CA 167

Arguedas, Jose Maria 1911-1969 **CLC 10, 18**
See also CA 89-92; CANR 73; DLB 113; HW

Argueta, Manlio 1936- .... **CLC 31**
See also CA 131; CANR 73; DLB 145; HW

Ariosto, Ludovico 1474-1533 .... **LC 6**

Aristides
See Epstein, Joseph

Aristophanes 450B.C.-385B.C.**CMLC 4; DA; DAB; DAC; DAM DRAM, MST; DC 2; WLCS**
See also DLB 176

Aristotle 384B.C.-322B.C. ... **CMLC 31; DA; DAB; DAC; DAM MST; WLCS**
See also DLB 176

Arlt, Roberto (Godofredo Christophersen) 1900-1942
TCLC 29; DAM MULT; HLC
See also CA 123; 131; CANR 67; HW

Armah, Ayi Kwei 1939- . **CLC 5, 33; BLC 1; DAM MULT, POET**
See also BW 1; CA 61-64; CANR 21, 64; DLB 117; MTCW 1

Armatrading, Joan 1950- .... **CLC 17**
See also CA 114

Arnette, Robert
See Silverberg, Robert

Arnim, Achim von (Ludwig Joachim von Arnim) 1781-1831 ...... **NCLC 5; SSC 29**
See also DLB 90

Arnim, Bettina von 1785-1859 .... **NCLC 38**
See also DLB 90

Arnold, Matthew 1822-1888**NCLC 6, 29; DA; DAB; DAC; DAM MST, POET; PC 5; WLC**
See also CDBLB 1832-1890; DLB 32, 57

Arnold, Thomas 1795-1842 .... **NCLC 18**
See also DLB 55

Arnow, Harriette (Louisa) Simpson 1908-1986 **CLC 2, 7, 18**
See also CA 9-12R; 118; CANR 14; DLB 6; MTCW 1; SATA 42; SATA-Obit 47

Arouet, Francois-Marie
See Voltaire

Arp, Hans
See Arp, Jean

Arp, Jean 1887-1966 .... **CLC 5**
See also CA 81-84; 25-28R; CANR 42

Arrabal, Fernando
See Arrabal, Fernando

Arrabal, Fernando 1932-.... **CLC 2, 9, 18, 58**
See also CA 9-12R; CANR 15

Arrick, Fran .... **CLC 30**
See also Gaberman, Judie Angell

Artaud, Antonin (Marie Joseph) 1896-1948 **TCLC 3, 36; DAM DRAM**
See also CA 104; 149

Arthur, Ruth M(abel) 1905-1979 ...... **CLC 12**
See also CA 9-12R; 85-88; CANR 4; SATA 7, 26

Artsybashev, Mikhail (Petrovich) 1878-1927 **TCLC 31**
See also CA 170

Arundel, Honor (Morfydd) 1919-1973**CLC 17**
See also CA 21-22; 41-44R; CAP 2; CLR 35; SATA 4; SATA-Obit 24

Arzner, Dorothy 1897-1979 .... **CLC 98**

Asch, Sholem 1880-1957 .... **TCLC 3**
See also CA 105

Ash, Shalom
See Asch, Sholem

Ashbery, John (Lawrence) 1927-**CLC 2, 3, 4, 6, 9, 13, 15, 25, 41, 77; DAM POET**
See also CA 5-8R; CANR 9, 37, 66; DLB 5, 165; DLBY 81; INT CANR-9; MTCW 1

Ashdown, Clifford
See Freeman, R(ichard) Austin

Ashe, Gordon
See Creasey, John

Ashton-Warner, Sylvia (Constance) 1908-1984 **CLC 19**
See also CA 69-72; 112; CANR 29; MTCW 1

Asimov, Isaac 1920-1992 **CLC 1, 3, 9, 19, 26, 76, 92; DAM POP**
See also AAYA 13; BEST 90:2; CA 1-4R; 137; CANR 2, 19, 36, 60; CLR 12; DLB 8; DLBY 92; INT CANR-19; JRDA; MAICYA; MTCW 1; SATA 1, 26, 74

Assis, Joaquim Maria Machado de
See Machado de Assis, Joaquim Maria

Astley, Thea (Beatrice May) 1925-... **CLC 41**
See also CA 65-68; CANR 11, 43

Aston, James
See White, T(erence) H(anbury)

Asturias, Miguel Angel 1899-1974 **CLC 3, 8, 13; DAM MULT, NOV; HLC**
See also CA 25-28; 49-52; CANR 32; CAP 2; DLB 113; HW; MTCW 1

Atares, Carlos Saura
See Saura (Atares), Carlos

Atheling, William
See Pound, Ezra (Weston Loomis)

Atheling, William, Jr.
See Blish, James (Benjamin)

Atherton, Gertrude (Franklin Horn) 1857-1948 **TCLC 2**
See also CA 104; 155; DLB 9, 78, 186

Atherton, Lucius
See Masters, Edgar Lee

Atkins, Jack
See Harris, Mark

Atkinson, Kate .... **CLC 99**
See also CA 166

Attaway, William (Alexander) 1911-1986 **CLC 92; BLC 1; DAM MULT**
See also BW 2; CA 143; DLB 76

Atticus
See Fleming, Ian (Lancaster); Wilson, (Thomas) Woodrow

See Moorcock, Michael (John)

Barea, Arturo 1897-1957 .... **TCLC 14**
See also CA 111

Barfoot, Joan 1946- .... **CLC 18**
See also CA 105

Baring, Maurice 1874-1945 .... **TCLC 8**
See also CA 105; 168; DLB 34

Baring-Gould, Sabine 1834-1924 .. **TCLC 88**
See also DLB 156, 190

Barker, Clive 1952- .... **CLC 52; DAM POP**
See also AAYA 10; BEST 90:3; CA 121; 129;
CANR 71; INT 129; MTCW 1

Barker, George Granville 1913-1991 **CLC 8,
48; DAM POET**
See also CA 9-12R; 135; CANR 7, 38; DLB
20; MTCW 1

Barker, Harley Granville
See Granville-Barker, Harley
See also DLB 10

Barker, Howard 1946- .... **CLC 37**
See also CA 102; DLB 13

Barker, Jane 1652-1732 .... **LC 42**

Barker, Pat(ricia) 1943- .... **CLC 32, 94**
See also CA 117; 122; CANR 50; INT 122

Barlach, Ernst 1870-1938 .... **TCLC 84**
See also DLB 56, 118

Barlow, Joel 1754-1812 .... **NCLC 23**
See also DLB 37

Barnard, Mary (Ethel) 1909- .... **CLC 48**
See also CA 21-22; CAP 2

Barnes, Djuna 1892-1982 **CLC 3, 4, 8, 11, 29;
SSC 3**
See also CA 9-12R; 107; CANR 16, 55; DLB
4, 9, 45; MTCW 1

Barnes, Julian (Patrick) 1946- **CLC 42; DAB**
See also CA 102; CANR 19, 54; DLB 194;
DLBY 93

Barnes, Peter 1931- .... **CLC 5, 56**
See also CA 65-68; CAAS 12; CANR 33, 34,
64; DLB 13; MTCW 1

Barnes, William 1801-1886 .... **NCLC 75**
See also DLB 32

Baroja (y Nessi), Pio 1872-1956 **TCLC 8; HLC**
See also CA 104

Baron, David
See Pinter, Harold

Baron Corvo
See Rolfe, Frederick (William Serafino Austin
Lewis Mary)

Barondess, Sue K(aufman) 1926-1977 **CLC 8**
See Kaufman, Sue
See also CA 1-4R; 69-72; CANR 1

Baron de Teive
See Pessoa, Fernando (Antonio Nogueira)

Baroness Von S.
See Zangwill, Israel

Barres, (Auguste-) Maurice 1862-1923 **T C L C
47**
See also CA 164; DLB 123

Barreto, Afonso Henrique de Lima
See Lima Barreto, Afonso Henrique de

Barrett, (Roger) Syd 1946- .... **CLC 35**

Barrett, William (Christopher) 1913-1992
CLC 27
See also CA 13-16R; 139; CANR 11, 67; INT
CANR-11

Barrie, J(ames) M(atthew) 1860-1937 **T C L C
2; DAB; DAM DRAM**
See also CA 104; 136; CDBLB 1890-1914;
CLR 16; DLB 10, 141, 156; MAICYA; SATA
100; YABC 1

Barrington, Michael
See Moorcock, Michael (John)

Barrol, Grady
See Bograd, Larry

Barry, Mike
See Malzberg, Barry N(athaniel)

Barry, Philip 1896-1949 .... **TCLC 11**
See also CA 109; DLB 7

Bart, Andre Schwarz
See Schwarz-Bart, Andre

Barth, John (Simmons) 1930- **CLC 1, 2, 3, 5, 7,
9, 10, 14, 27, 51, 89; DAM NOV; SSC 10**
See also AITN 1, 2; CA 1-4R; CABS 1; CANR
5, 23, 49, 64; DLB 2; MTCW 1

Barthelme, Donald 1931-1989 **CLC 1, 2, 3, 5, 6,
8, 13, 23, 46, 59, 115; DAM NOV; SSC 2**
See also CA 21-24R; 129; CANR 20, 58; DLB
2; DLBY 80, 89; MTCW 1; SATA 7; SATA-
Obit 62

Barthelme, Frederick 1943- ...... **CLC 36, 117**
See also CA 114; 122; DLBY 85; INT 122

Barthes, Roland (Gerard) 1915-1980 **CLC 24,
83**
See also CA 130; 97-100; CANR 66; MTCW 1

Barzun, Jacques (Martin) 1907- .... **CLC 51**
See also CA 61-64; CANR 22

Bashevis, Isaac
See Singer, Isaac Bashevis

Bashkirtseff, Marie 1859-1884 ...... **NCLC 27**

Basho
See Matsuo Basho

Bass, Kingsley B., Jr.
See Bullins, Ed

Bass, Rick 1958- .... **CLC 79**
See also CA 126; CANR 53

Bassani, Giorgio 1916- .... **CLC 9**
See also CA 65-68; CANR 33; DLB 128, 177;
MTCW 1

Bastos, Augusto (Antonio) Roa
See Roa Bastos, Augusto (Antonio)

Bataille, Georges 1897-1962 .... **CLC 29**
See also CA 101; 89-92

Bates, H(erbert) E(rnest) 1905-1974 **CLC 46;
DAB; DAM POP; SSC 10**
See also CA 93-96; 45-48; CANR 34; DLB 162,
191; MTCW 1

Bauchart
See Camus, Albert

Baudelaire, Charles 1821-1867 .**NCLC 6, 29,
55; DA; DAB; DAC; DAM MST, POET;
PC 1; SSC 18; WLC**

Baudrillard, Jean 1929- .... **CLC 60**

Baum, L(yman) Frank 1856-1919 ... **TCLC 7**
See also CA 108; 133; CLR 15; DLB 22; JRDA;
MAICYA; MTCW 1; SATA 18, 100

Baum, Louis F.
See Baum, L(yman) Frank

Baumbach, Jonathan 1933- .... **CLC 6, 23**
See also CA 13-16R; CAAS 5; CANR 12, 66;
DLBY 80; INT CANR-12; MTCW 1

Bausch, Richard (Carl) 1945- .... **CLC 51**
See also CA 101; CAAS 14; CANR 43, 61; DLB
130

Baxter, Charles (Morley) 1947- **CLC 45, 78;
DAM POP**
See also CA 57-60; CANR 40, 64; DLB 130

Baxter, George Owen
See Faust, Frederick (Schiller)

Baxter, James K(eir) 1926-1972 .... **CLC 14**
See also CA 77-80

Baxter, John
See Hunt, E(verette) Howard, (Jr.)

Bayer, Sylvia
See Glassco, John

Baynton, Barbara 1857-1929 .... **TCLC 57**

Beagle, Peter S(oyer) 1939- .... **CLC 7, 104**
See also CA 9-12R; CANR 4, 51, 73; DLBY
80; INT CANR-4; SATA 60

Bean, Normal
See Burroughs, Edgar Rice

Beard, Charles A(ustin) 1874-1948 **TCLC 15**
See also CA 115; DLB 17; SATA 18

Beardsley, Aubrey 1872-1898 .... **NCLC 6**

Beattie, Ann 1947- **CLC 8, 13, 18, 40, 63; DAM
NOV, POP; SSC 11**
See also BEST 90:2; CA 81-84; CANR 53, 73;
DLBY 82; MTCW 1

Beattie, James 1735-1803 .... **NCLC 25**
See also DLB 109

Beauchamp, Kathleen Mansfield 1888-1923
See Mansfield, Katherine
See also CA 104; 134; DA; DAC; DAM MST

Beaumarchais, Pierre-Augustin Caron de 1732-
1799 .... **DC 4**
See also DAM DRAM

Beaumont, Francis 1584(?)-1616 **LC 33; DC 6**
See also CDBLB Before 1660; DLB 58, 121

**Beauvoir, Simone (Lucie Ernestine Marie
Bertrand) de** 1908-1986 **CLC 1, 2, 4, 8,
14, 31, 44, 50, 71; DA; DAB; DAC; DAM
MST, NOV; WLC**
See also CA 9-12R; 118; CANR 28, 61; DLB
72; DLBY 86; MTCW 1

Becker, Carl (Lotus) 1873-1945 ..... **TCLC 63**
See also CA 157; DLB 17

Becker, Jurek 1937-1997 ....**CLC 7, 19**
See also CA 85-88; 157; CANR 60; DLB 75

Becker, Walter 1950- .... **CLC 26**

Beckett, Samuel (Barclay) 1906-1989 **CLC 1,
2, 3, 4, 6, 9, 10, 11, 14, 18, 29, 57, 59, 83;
DA; DAB; DAC; DAM DRAM, MST,
NOV; SSC 16; WLC**
See also CA 5-8R; 130; CANR 33, 61; CDBLB
1945-1960; DLB 13, 15; DLBY 90; MTCW
1

Beckford, William 1760-1844 .... **NCLC 16**
See also DLB 39

Beckman, Gunnel 1910- .... **CLC 26**
See also CA 33-36R; CANR 15; CLR 25;
MAICYA; SAAS 9; SATA 6

Becque, Henri 1837-1899 .... **NCLC 3**
See also DLB 192

Beddoes, Thomas Lovell 1803-1849 **NCLC 3**
See also DLB 96

Bede c. 673-735 .... **CMLC 20**
See also DLB 146

Bedford, Donald F.
See Fearing, Kenneth (Flexner)

Beecher, Catharine Esther 1800-1878 **N C L C
30**
See also DLB 1

Beecher, John 1904-1980 .... **CLC 6**
See also AITN 1; CA 5-8R; 105; CANR 8

Beer, Johann 1655-1700 .... **LC 5**
See also DLB 168

Beer, Patricia 1924- .... **CLC 58**
See also CA 61-64; CANR 13, 46; DLB 40

Beerbohm, Max
See Beerbohm, (Henry) Max(imilian)

Beerbohm, (Henry) Max(imilian) 1872-1956
TCLC 1, 24
See also CA 104; 154; DLB 34, 100

Beer-Hofmann, Richard 1866-1945 **TCLC 60**
See also CA 160; DLB 81

Begiebing, Robert J(ohn) 1946- .... **CLC 70**
See also CA 122; CANR 40

Behan, Brendan 1923-1964 **CLC 1, 8, 11, 15,
79; DAM DRAM**
See also CA 73-76; CANR 33; CDBLB 1945-
1960; DLB 13; MTCW 1

Behn, Aphra 1640(?)-1689 **LC 1, 30, 42; DA;
DAB; DAC; DAM DRAM, MST, NOV,
POET; DC 4; PC 13; WLC**
See also DLB 39, 80, 131

Behrman, S(amuel) N(athaniel) 1893-1973
CLC 40
See also CA 13-16; 45-48; CAP 1; DLB 7, 44

Belasco, David 1853-1931 .... **TCLC 3**
See also CA 104; 168; DLB 7

Belcheva, Elisaveta 1893- .... **CLC 10**

See also Bagryana, Elisaveta
Beldone, Phil "Cheech"
  See Ellison, Harlan (Jay)
Beleno
  See Azuela, Mariano
Belinski, Vissarion Grigoryevich 1811-1848
  NCLC 5
  See also DLB 198
Belitt, Ben 1911- .... **CLC 22**
  See also CA 13-16R; CAAS 4; CANR 7; DLB
  5
Bell, Gertrude (Margaret Lowthian) 1868-1926
  TCLC 67
  See also CA 167; DLB 174
Bell, J. Freeman
  See Zangwill, Israel
Bell, James Madison 1826-1902 ... **TCLC 43;**
  BLC 1; DAM MULT
  See also BW 1; CA 122; 124; DLB 50
Bell, Madison Smartt 1957- ..... **CLC 41, 102**
  See also CA 111; CANR 28, 54, 73
Bell, Marvin (Hartley) 1937-**CLC 8, 31; DAM**
  POET
  See also CA 21-24R; CAAS 14; CANR 59; DLB
  5; MTCW 1
Bell, W. L. D.
  See Mencken, H(enry) L(ouis)
Bellamy, Atwood C.
  See Mencken, H(enry) L(ouis)
Bellamy, Edward 1850-1898 .... **NCLC 4**
  See also DLB 12
Bellin, Edward J.
  See Kuttner, Henry
Belloc, (Joseph) Hilaire (Pierre Sebastien Rene
  Swanton) 1870-1953 **TCLC 7, 18; DAM**
  POET; PC 24
  See also CA 106; 152; DLB 19, 100, 141, 174;
  YABC 1
Belloc, Joseph Peter Rene Hilaire
  See Belloc, (Joseph) Hilaire (Pierre Sebastien
  Rene Swanton)
Belloc, Joseph Pierre Hilaire
  See Belloc, (Joseph) Hilaire (Pierre Sebastien
  Rene Swanton)
Belloc, M. A.
  See Lowndes, Marie Adelaide (Belloc)
Bellow, Saul 1915-**CLC 1, 2, 3, 6, 8, 10, 13, 15,**
  25, 33, 34, 63, 79; DA; DAB; DAC; DAM
  MST, NOV, POP; SSC 14; WLC
  See also AITN 2; BEST 89:3; CA 5-8R; CABS
  1; CANR 29, 53; CDALB 1941-1968; DLB
  2, 28; DLBD 3; DLBY 82; MTCW 1
Belser, Reimond Karel Maria de 1929-
  See Ruyslinck, Ward
  See also CA 152
Bely, Andrey .... **TCLC 7; PC 11**
  See also Bugayev, Boris Nikolayevich
Belyi, Andrei
  See Bugayev, Boris Nikolayevich
Benary, Margot
  See Benary-Isbert, Margot
Benary-Isbert, Margot 1889-1979 .... **CLC 12**
  See also CA 5-8R; 89-92; CANR 4, 72; CLR
  12; MAICYA; SATA 2; SATA-Obit 21
Benavente (y Martinez), Jacinto 1866-1954
  TCLC 3; DAM DRAM, MULT
  See also CA 106; 131; HW; MTCW 1
Benchley, Peter (Bradford) 1940- **CLC 4, 8;**
  DAM NOV, POP
  See also AAYA 14; AITN 2; CA 17-20R; CANR
  12, 35, 66; MTCW 1; SATA 3, 89
Benchley, Robert (Charles) 1889-1945**TCLC**
  1, 55
  See also CA 105; 153; DLB 11
Benda, Julien 1867-1956 .... **TCLC 60**
  See also CA 120; 154
Benedict, Ruth (Fulton) 1887-1948 **TCLC 60**

See also CA 158
Benedict, Saint c. 480-c. 547 .... **CMLC 29**
Benedikt, Michael 1935- .... **CLC 4, 14**
  See also CA 13-16R; CANR 7; DLB 5
Benet, Juan 1927- .... **CLC 28**
  See also CA 143
Benet, Stephen Vincent 1898-1943 . **TCLC 7;**
  DAM POET; SSC 10
  See also CA 104; 152; DLB 4, 48, 102; DLBY
  97; YABC 1
Benet, William Rose 1886-1950 .... **TCLC 28;**
  DAM POET
  See also CA 118; 152; DLB 45
Benford, Gregory (Albert) 1941- ..... **CLC 52**
  See also CA 69-72; CAAS 27; CANR 12, 24,
  49; DLBY 82
Bengtsson, Frans (Gunnar) 1894-1954**T C L C**
  48
  See also CA 170
Benjamin, David
  See Slavitt, David R(ytman)
Benjamin, Lois
  See Gould, Lois
Benjamin, Walter 1892-1940 .... **TCLC 39**
  See also CA 164
Benn, Gottfried 1886-1956 .... **TCLC 3**
  See also CA 106; 153; DLB 56
Bennett, Alan 1934-**CLC 45, 77; DAB; DAM**
  MST
  See also CA 103; CANR 35, 55; MTCW 1
Bennett, (Enoch) Arnold 1867-1931**TCLC 5,**
  20
  See also CA 106; 155; CDBLB 1890-1914;
  DLB 10, 34, 98, 135
Bennett, Elizabeth
  See Mitchell, Margaret (Munnerlyn)
Bennett, George Harold 1930-
  See Bennett, Hal
  See also BW 1; CA 97-100
Bennett, Hal .... **CLC 5**
  See also Bennett, George Harold
  See also DLB 33
Bennett, Jay 1912- .... **CLC 35**
  See also AAYA 10; CA 69-72; CANR 11, 42;
  JRDA; SAAS 4; SATA 41, 87; SATA-Brief
  27
Bennett, Louise (Simone) 1919-**CLC 28; BLC**
  1; DAM MULT
  See also BW 2; CA 151; DLB 117
Benson, E(dward) F(rederic) 1867-1940
  TCLC 27
  See also CA 114; 157; DLB 135, 153
Benson, Jackson J. 1930- .... **CLC 34**
  See also CA 25-28R; DLB 111
Benson, Sally 1900-1972 .... **CLC 17**
  See also CA 19-20; 37-40R; CAP 1; SATA 1,
  35; SATA-Obit 27
Benson, Stella 1892-1933 .... **TCLC 17**
  See also CA 117; 155; DLB 36, 162
Bentham, Jeremy 1748-1832 .... **NCLC 38**
  See also DLB 107, 158
Bentley, E(dmund) C(lerihew) 1875-1956
  TCLC 12
  See also CA 108; DLB 70
Bentley, Eric (Russell) 1916- .... **CLC 24**
  See also CA 5-8R; CANR 6, 67; INT CANR-6
Beranger, Pierre Jean de 1780-1857**NCLC 34**
Berdyaev, Nicolas
  See Berdyaev, Nikolai (Aleksandrovich)
Berdyaev, Nikolai (Aleksandrovich) 1874-1948
  TCLC 67
  See also CA 120; 157
Berdyayev, Nikolai (Aleksandrovich)
  See Berdyaev, Nikolai (Aleksandrovich)
Berendt, John (Lawrence) 1939- ...... **CLC 86**
  See also CA 146; CANR 75
Beresford, J(ohn) D(avys) 1873-1947 **T C L C**

81
  See also CA 112; 155; DLB 162, 178, 197
Bergelson, David 1884-1952 .... **TCLC 81**
Berger, Colonel
  See Malraux, (Georges-)Andre
Berger, John (Peter) 1926- ....**CLC 2, 19**
  See also CA 81-84; CANR 51; DLB 14, 207
Berger, Melvin H. 1927-................... **CLC 12**
  See also CA 5-8R; CANR 4; CLR 32; SAAS 2;
  SATA 5, 88
Berger, Thomas (Louis) 1924-**CLC 3, 5, 8, 11,**
  18, 38; DAM NOV
  See also CA 1-4R; CANR 5, 28, 51; DLB 2;
  DLBY 80; INT CANR-28; MTCW 1
Bergman, (Ernst) Ingmar 1918- **CLC 16, 72**
  See also CA 81-84; CANR 33, 70
Bergson, Henri(-Louis) 1859-1941 **TCLC 32**
  See also CA 164
Bergstein, Eleanor 1938- .... **CLC 4**
  See also CA 53-56; CANR 5
Berkoff, Steven 1937- .... **CLC 56**
  See also CA 104; CANR 72
Bermant, Chaim (Icyk) 1929- .... **CLC 40**
  See also CA 57-60; CANR 6, 31, 57
Bern, Victoria
  See Fisher, M(ary) F(rances) K(ennedy)
Bernanos, (Paul Louis) Georges 1888-1948
  TCLC 3
  See also CA 104; 130; DLB 72
Bernard, April 1956- .... **CLC 59**
  See also CA 131
Berne, Victoria
  See Fisher, M(ary) F(rances) K(ennedy)
Bernhard, Thomas 1931-1989 **CLC 3, 32, 61**
  See also CA 85-88; 127; CANR 32, 57; DLB
  85, 124; MTCW 1
Bernhardt, Sarah (Henriette Rosine) 1844-1923
  TCLC 75
  See also CA 157
Berriault, Gina 1926- . **CLC 54, 109; SSC 30**
  See also CA 116; 129; CANR 66; DLB 130
Berrigan, Daniel 1921- .... **CLC 4**
  See also CA 33-36R; CAAS 1; CANR 11, 43;
  DLB 5
Berrigan, Edmund Joseph Michael, Jr. 1934-
  1983
  See Berrigan, Ted
  See also CA 61-64; 110; CANR 14
Berrigan, Ted .... **CLC 37**
  See also Berrigan, Edmund Joseph Michael, Jr.
  See also DLB 5, 169
Berry, Charles Edward Anderson 1931-
  See Berry, Chuck
  See also CA 115
Berry, Chuck .... **CLC 17**
  See also Berry, Charles Edward Anderson
Berry, Jonas
  See Ashbery, John (Lawrence)
Berry, Wendell (Erdman) 1934- **CLC 4, 6, 8,**
  27, 46; DAM POET
  See also AITN 1; CA 73-76; CANR 50, 73; DLB
  5, 6
Berryman, John 1914-1972**CLC 1, 2, 3, 4, 6, 8,**
  10, 13, 25, 62; DAM POET
  See also CA 13-16; 33-36R; CABS 2; CANR
  35; CAP 1; CDALB 1941-1968; DLB 48;
  MTCW 1
Bertolucci, Bernardo 1940- .... **CLC 16**
  See also CA 106
Berton, Pierre (Francis Demarigny) 1920-
  CLC 104
  See also CA 1-4R; CANR 2, 56; DLB 68; SATA
  99
Bertrand, Aloysius 1807-1841 .... **NCLC 31**
Bertran de Born c. 1140-1215 .... **CMLC 5**
Besant, Annie (Wood) 1847-1933 .... **TCLC 9**
  See also CA 105

See Stendhal

Bomkauf
See Kaufman, Bob (Garnell)

Bonaventura .... **NCLC 35**
See also DLB 90

Bond, Edward 1934- **CLC 4, 6, 13, 23; DAM DRAM**
See also CA 25-28R; CANR 38, 67; DLB 13; MTCW 1

Bonham, Frank 1914-1989 .... **CLC 12**
See also AAYA 1; CA 9-12R; CANR 4, 36; JRDA; MAICYA; SAAS 3; SATA 1, 49; SATA-Obit 62

Bonnefoy, Yves 1923- ... **CLC 9, 15, 58; DAM MST, POET**
See also CA 85-88; CANR 33, 75; MTCW 1

Bontemps, Arna(ud Wendell) 1902-1973 **C L C 1, 18; BLC 1; DAM MULT, NOV, POET**
See also BW 1; CA 1-4R; 41-44R; CANR 4, 35; CLR 6; DLB 48, 51; JRDA; MAICYA; MTCW 1; SATA 2, 44; SATA-Obit 24

Booth, Martin 1944- .... **CLC 13**
See also CA 93-96; CAAS 2

Booth, Philip 1925- .... **CLC 23**
See also CA 5-8R; CANR 5; DLBY 82

Booth, Wayne C(layson) 1921- .... **CLC 24**
See also CA 1-4R; CAAS 5; CANR 3, 43; DLB 67

Borchert, Wolfgang 1921-1947 .... **TCLC 5**
See also CA 104; DLB 69, 124

Borel, Petrus 1809-1859 .... **NCLC 41**

Borges, Jorge Luis 1899-1986 **CLC 1, 2, 3, 4, 6, 8, 9, 10, 13, 19, 44, 48, 83; DA; DAB; DAC; DAM MST, MULT; HLC; PC 22; SSC 4; WLC**
See also AAYA 26; CA 21-24R; CANR 19, 33, 75; DLB 113; DLBY 86; HW; MTCW 1

Borowski, Tadeusz 1922-1951 .... **TCLC 9**
See also CA 106; 154

Borrow, George (Henry) 1803-1881 **NCLC 9**
See also DLB 21, 55, 166

Bosman, Herman Charles 1905-1951 **T C L C 49**
See also Malan, Herman
See also CA 160

Bosschere, Jean de 1878(?)-1953 ... **TCLC 19**
See also CA 115

Boswell, James 1740-1795 . **LC 4; DA; DAB; DAC; DAM MST; WLC**
See also CDBLB 1660-1789; DLB 104, 142

Bottoms, David 1949- .... **CLC 53**
See also CA 105; CANR 22; DLB 120; DLBY 83

Boucicault, Dion 1820-1890 .... **NCLC 41**

Boucolon, Maryse 1937(?)-
See Conde, Maryse
See also CA 110; CANR 30, 53, 76

Bourget, Paul (Charles Joseph) 1852-1935 **TCLC 12**
See also CA 107; DLB 123

Bourjaily, Vance (Nye) 1922- .... **CLC 8, 62**
See also CA 1-4R; CAAS 1; CANR 2, 72; DLB 2, 143

Bourne, Randolph S(illiman) 1886-1918 **TCLC 16**
See also CA 117; 155; DLB 63

Bova, Ben(jamin William) 1932- ...... **CLC 45**
See also AAYA 16; CA 5-8R; CAAS 18; CANR 11, 56; CLR 3; DLBY 81; INT CANR-11; MAICYA; MTCW 1; SATA 6, 68

Bowen, Elizabeth (Dorothea Cole) 1899-1973 **CLC 1, 3, 6, 11, 15, 22, 118; DAM NOV; SSC 3, 28**
See also CA 17-18; 41-44R; CANR 35; CAP 2; CDBLB 1945-1960; DLB 15, 162; MTCW 1

Bowering, George 1935- .... **CLC 15, 47**

See also CA 21-24R; CAAS 16; CANR 10; DLB 53

Bowering, Marilyn R(uthe) 1949- .... **CLC 32**
See also CA 101; CANR 49

Bowers, Edgar 1924- .... **CLC 9**
See also CA 5-8R; CANR 24; DLB 5

Bowie, David .... **CLC 17**
See also Jones, David Robert

Bowles, Jane (Sydney) 1917-1973 **CLC 3, 68**
See also CA 19-20; 41-44R; CAP 2

Bowles, Paul (Frederick) 1910- **CLC 1, 2, 19, 53; SSC 3**
See also CA 1-4R; CAAS 1; CANR 1, 19, 50, 75; DLB 5, 6; MTCW 1

Box, Edgar
See Vidal, Gore

Boyd, Nancy
See Millay, Edna St. Vincent

Boyd, William 1952- .... **CLC 28, 53, 70**
See also CA 114; 120; CANR 51, 71

Boyle, Kay 1902-1992 **CLC 1, 5, 19, 58; SSC 5**
See also CA 13-16R; 140; CAAS 1; CANR 29, 61; DLB 4, 9, 48, 86; DLBY 93; MTCW 1

Boyle, Mark
See Kienzle, William X(avier)

Boyle, Patrick 1905-1982 .... **CLC 19**
See also CA 127

Boyle, T. C. 1948-
See Boyle, T(homas) Coraghessan

Boyle, T(homas) Coraghessan 1948- **CLC 36, 55, 90; DAM POP; SSC 16**
See also BEST 90:4; CA 120; CANR 44, 76; DLBY 86

Boz
See Dickens, Charles (John Huffam)

Brackenridge, Hugh Henry 1748-1816 **N C L C 7**
See also DLB 11, 37

Bradbury, Edward P.
See Moorcock, Michael (John)

Bradbury, Malcolm (Stanley) 1932- **CLC 32, 61; DAM NOV**
See also CA 1-4R; CANR 1, 33; DLB 14, 207; MTCW 1

Bradbury, Ray (Douglas) 1920- **CLC 1, 3, 10, 15, 42, 98; DA; DAB; DAC; DAM MST, NOV, POP; SSC 29; WLC**
See also AAYA 15; AITN 1, 2; CA 1-4R; CANR 2, 30, 75; CDALB 1968-1988; DLB 2, 8; MTCW 1; SATA 11, 64

Bradford, Gamaliel 1863-1932 ...... **TCLC 36**
See also CA 160; DLB 17

Bradley, David (Henry), Jr. 1950- ...**CLC 23, 118; BLC 1; DAM MULT**
See also BW 1; CA 104; CANR 26; DLB 33

Bradley, John Ed(mund, Jr.) 1958- .. **CLC 55**
See also CA 139

Bradley, Marion Zimmer 1930- **CLC 30; DAM POP**
See also AAYA 9; CA 57-60; CAAS 10; CANR 7, 31, 51, 75; DLB 8; MTCW 1; SATA 90

Bradstreet, Anne 1612(?)-1672 **LC 4, 30; DA; DAC; DAM MST, POET; PC 10**
See also CDALB 1640-1865; DLB 24

Brady, Joan 1939- .... **CLC 86**
See also CA 141

Bragg, Melvyn 1939- .... **CLC 10**
See also BEST 89:3; CA 57-60; CANR 10, 48; DLB 14

Brahe, Tycho 1546-1601 .... **LC 45**

Braine, John (Gerard) 1922-1986 **CLC 1, 3, 41**
See also CA 1-4R; 120; CANR 1, 33; CDBLB 1945-1960; DLB 15; DLBY 86; MTCW 1

Bramah, Ernest 1868-1942 .... **TCLC 72**
See also CA 156; DLB 70

Brammer, William 1930(?)-1978 .... **CLC 31**
See also CA 77-80

Brancati, Vitaliano 1907-1954 .... **TCLC 12**
See also CA 109

Brancato, Robin F(idler) 1936- .... **CLC 35**
See also AAYA 9; CA 69-72; CANR 11, 45; CLR 32; JRDA; SAAS 9; SATA 97

Brand, Max
See Faust, Frederick (Schiller)

Brand, Millen 1906-1980 .... **CLC 7**
See also CA 21-24R; 97-100; CANR 72

Branden, Barbara .... **CLC 44**
See also CA 148

Brandes, Georg (Morris Cohen) 1842-1927 **TCLC 10**
See also CA 105

Brandys, Kazimierz 1916- .... **CLC 62**

Branley, Franklyn M(ansfield) 1915- **CLC 21**
See also CA 33-36R; CANR 14, 39; CLR 13; MAICYA; SAAS 16; SATA 4, 68

Brathwaite, Edward Kamau 1930- . **CLC 11; BLCS; DAM POET**
See also BW 2; CA 25-28R; CANR 11, 26, 47; DLB 125

Brautigan, Richard (Gary) 1935-1984 **CLC 1, 3, 5, 9, 12, 34, 42; DAM NOV**
See also CA 53-56; 113; CANR 34; DLB 2, 5, 206; DLBY 80, 84; MTCW 1; SATA 56

Brave Bird, Mary 1953-
See Crow Dog, Mary (Ellen)
See also NNAL

Braverman, Kate 1950- .... **CLC 67**
See also CA 89-92

Brecht, (Eugen) Bertolt (Friedrich) 1898-1956 **TCLC 1, 6, 13, 35; DA; DAB; DAC; DAM DRAM, MST; DC 3; WLC**
See also CA 104; 133; CANR 62; DLB 56, 124; MTCW 1

Brecht, Eugen Berthold Friedrich
See Brecht, (Eugen) Bertolt (Friedrich)

Bremer, Fredrika 1801-1865 .... **NCLC 11**

Brennan, Christopher John 1870-1932 **T C L C 17**
See also CA 117

Brennan, Maeve 1917-1993 .... **CLC 5**
See also CA 81-84; CANR 72

Brent, Linda
See Jacobs, Harriet A(nn)

Brentano, Clemens (Maria) 1778-1842 **N C L C 1**
See also DLB 90

Brent of Bin Bin
See Franklin, (Stella Maria Sarah) Miles (Lampe)

Brenton, Howard 1942- .... **CLC 31**
See also CA 69-72; CANR 33, 67; DLB 13; MTCW 1

Breslin, James 1930-1996
See Breslin, Jimmy
See also CA 73-76; CANR 31, 75; DAM NOV; MTCW 1

Breslin, Jimmy .... **CLC 4, 43**
See also Breslin, James
See also AITN 1; DLB 185

Bresson, Robert 1901- .... **CLC 16**
See also CA 110; CANR 49

Breton, Andre 1896-1966 **CLC 2, 9, 15, 54; PC 15**
See also CA 19-20; 25-28R; CANR 40, 60; CAP 2; DLB 65; MTCW 1

Breytenbach, Breyten 1939(?)- . **CLC 23, 37; DAM POET**
See also CA 113; 129; CANR 61

Bridgers, Sue Ellen 1942- .... **CLC 26**
See also AAYA 8; CA 65-68; CANR 11, 36; CLR 18; DLB 52; JRDA; MAICYA; SAAS 1; SATA 22, 90

Bridges, Robert (Seymour) 1844-1930 **T C L C 1; DAM POET**

See also CA 104; 152; CDBLB 1890-1914; DLB 19, 98

Bridie, James .... **TCLC 3**
See also Mavor, Osborne Henry
See also DLB 10

Brin, David 1950- .... **CLC 34**
See also AAYA 21; CA 102; CANR 24, 70; INT CANR-24; SATA 65

Brink, Andre (Philippus) 1935- **CLC 18, 36, 106**
See also CA 104; CANR 39, 62; INT 103; MTCW 1

Brinsmead, H(esba) F(ay) 1922- ...... **CLC 21**
See also CA 21-24R; CANR 10; CLR 47; MAICYA; SAAS 5; SATA 18, 78

Brittain, Vera (Mary) 1893(?)-1970 . **CLC 23**
See also CA 13-16; 25-28R; CANR 58; CAP 1; DLB 191; MTCW 1

Broch, Hermann 1886-1951 .... **TCLC 20**
See also CA 117; DLB 85, 124

Brock, Rose
See Hansen, Joseph

Brodkey, Harold (Roy) 1930-1996 .... **CLC 56**
See also CA 111; 151; CANR 71; DLB 130

Brodskii, Iosif
See Brodsky, Joseph

Brodsky, Iosif Alexandrovich 1940-1996
See Brodsky, Joseph
See also AITN 1; CA 41-44R; 151; CANR 37; DAM POET; MTCW 1

Brodsky, Joseph 1940-1996 CLC **4, 6, 13, 36, 100; PC 9**
See also Brodskii, Iosif; Brodsky, Iosif Alexandrovich

Brodsky, Michael (Mark) 1948- .... **CLC 19**
See also CA 102; CANR 18, 41, 58

Bromell, Henry 1947- .... **CLC 5**
See also CA 53-56; CANR 9

Bromfield, Louis (Brucker) 1896-1956 **T C L C 11**
See also CA 107; 155; DLB 4, 9, 86

Broner, E(sther) M(asserman) 1930- **CLC 19**
See also CA 17-20R; CANR 8, 25, 72; DLB 28

Bronk, William 1918- .... **CLC 10**
See also CA 89-92; CANR 23; DLB 165

Bronstein, Lev Davidovich
See Trotsky, Leon

Bronte, Anne 1820-1849 .... **NCLC 71**
See also DLB 21, 199

Bronte, Charlotte 1816-1855 **NCLC 3, 8, 33, 58; DA; DAB; DAC; DAM MST, NOV; WLC**
See also AAYA 17; CDBLB 1832-1890; DLB 21, 159, 199

Bronte, Emily (Jane) 1818-1848 **NCLC 16, 35; DA; DAB; DAC; DAM MST, NOV, POET; PC 8; WLC**
See also AAYA 17; CDBLB 1832-1890; DLB 21, 32, 199

Brooke, Frances 1724-1789 .... **LC 6, 48**
See also DLB 39, 99

Brooke, Henry 1703(?)-1783 .... **LC 1**
See also DLB 39

Brooke, Rupert (Chawner) 1887-1915 **T C L C 2, 7; DA; DAB; DAC; DAM MST, POET; PC 24; WLC**
See also CA 104; 132; CANR 61; CDBLB 1914-1945; DLB 19; MTCW 1

Brooke-Haven, P.
See Wodehouse, P(elham) G(renville)

Brooke-Rose, Christine 1926(?)- .... **CLC 40**
See also CA 13-16R; CANR 58; DLB 14

Brookner, Anita 1928- **CLC 32, 34, 51; DAB; DAM POP**
See also CA 114; 120; CANR 37, 56; DLB 194; DLBY 87; MTCW 1

Brooks, Cleanth 1906-1994 **CLC 24, 86, 110**

See also CA 17-20R; 145; CANR 33, 35; DLB 63; DLBY 94; INT CANR-35; MTCW 1

Brooks, George
See Baum, L(yman) Frank

Brooks, Gwendolyn 1917- **CLC 1, 2, 4, 5, 15, 49; BLC 1; DA; DAC; DAM MST, MULT, POET; PC 7; WLC**
See also AAYA 20; AITN 1; BW 2; CA 1-4R; CANR 1, 27, 52, 75; CDALB 1941-1968; CLR 27; DLB 5, 76, 165; MTCW 1; SATA 6

Brooks, Mel .... **CLC 12**
See also Kaminsky, Melvin
See also AAYA 13; DLB 26

Brooks, Peter 1938- .... **CLC 34**
See also CA 45-48; CANR 1

Brooks, Van Wyck 1886-1963 .... **CLC 29**
See also CA 1-4R; CANR 6; DLB 45, 63, 103

Brophy, Brigid (Antonia) 1929-1995 **CLC 6, 11, 29, 105**
See also CA 5-8R; 149; CAAS 4; CANR 25, 53; DLB 14; MTCW 1

Brosman, Catharine Savage 1934- ..... **CLC 9**
See also CA 61-64; CANR 21, 46

Brossard, Nicole 1943- .... **CLC 115**
See also CA 122; CAAS 16; DLB 53

Brother Antoninus
See Everson, William (Oliver)

The Brothers Quay
See Quay, Stephen; Quay, Timothy

Broughton, T(homas) Alan 1936- ..... **CLC 19**
See also CA 45-48; CANR 2, 23, 48

Broumas, Olga 1949- .... **CLC 10, 73**
See also CA 85-88; CANR 20, 69

Brown, Alan 1950- .... **CLC 99**
See also CA 156

Brown, Charles Brockden 1771-1810 **N C L C 22, 74**
See also CDALB 1640-1865; DLB 37, 59, 73

Brown, Christy 1932-1981 .... **CLC 63**
See also CA 105; 104; CANR 72; DLB 14

Brown, Claude 1937- **CLC 30; BLC 1; DAM MULT**
See also AAYA 7; BW 1; CA 73-76

Brown, Dee (Alexander) 1908- ... **CLC 18, 47; DAM POP**
See also CA 13-16R; CAAS 6; CANR 11, 45, 60; DLBY 80; MTCW 1; SATA 5

Brown, George
See Wertmueller, Lina

Brown, George Douglas 1869-1902 **TCLC 28**
See also CA 162

Brown, George Mackay 1921-1996 **CLC 5, 48, 100**
See also CA 21-24R; 151; CAAS 6; CANR 12, 37, 67; DLB 14, 27, 139; MTCW 1; SATA 35

Brown, (William) Larry 1951- .... **CLC 73**
See also CA 130; 134; INT 133

Brown, Moses
See Barrett, William (Christopher)

Brown, Rita Mae 1944- **CLC 18, 43, 79; DAM NOV, POP**
See also CA 45-48; CANR 2, 11, 35, 62; INT CANR-11; MTCW 1

Brown, Roderick (Langmere) Haig-
See Haig-Brown, Roderick (Langmere)

Brown, Rosellen 1939- .... **CLC 32**
See also CA 77-80; CAAS 10; CANR 14, 44

Brown, Sterling Allen 1901-1989 **CLC 1, 23, 59; BLC 1; DAM MULT, POET**
See also BW 1; CA 85-88; 127; CANR 26, 74; DLB 48, 51, 63; MTCW 1

Brown, Will
See Ainsworth, William Harrison

Brown, William Wells 1813-1884 ... **NCLC 2; BLC 1; DAM MULT; DC 1**
See also DLB 3, 50

Browne, (Clyde) Jackson 1948(?)- .... **CLC 21**
See also CA 120

Browning, Elizabeth Barrett 1806-1861 **NCLC 1, 16, 61, 66; DA; DAB; DAC; DAM MST, POET; PC 6; WLC**
See also CDBLB 1832-1890; DLB 32, 199

Browning, Robert 1812-1889 **NCLC 19; DA; DAB; DAC; DAM MST, POET; PC 2; WLCS**
See also CDBLB 1832-1890; DLB 32, 163; YABC 1

Browning, Tod 1882-1962 .... **CLC 16**
See also CA 141; 117

Brownson, Orestes Augustus 1803-1876 **NCLC 50**
See also DLB 1, 59, 73

Bruccoli, Matthew J(oseph) 1931- ... **CLC 34**
See also CA 9-12R; CANR 7; DLB 103

Bruce, Lenny .... **CLC 21**
See also Schneider, Leonard Alfred

Bruin, John
See Brutus, Dennis

Brulard, Henri
See Stendhal

Brulls, Christian
See Simenon, Georges (Jacques Christian)

Brunner, John (Kilian Houston) 1934-1995 **CLC 8, 10; DAM POP**
See also CA 1-4R; 149; CAAS 8; CANR 2, 37; MTCW 1

Bruno, Giordano 1548-1600 .... **LC 27**

Brutus, Dennis 1924- **CLC 43; BLC 1; DAM MULT, POET; PC 24**
See also BW 2; CA 49-52; CAAS 14; CANR 2, 27, 42; DLB 117

Bryan, C(ourtlandt) D(ixon) B(arnes) 1936- **CLC 29**
See also CA 73-76; CANR 13, 68; DLB 185; INT CANR-13

Bryan, Michael
See Moore, Brian

Bryant, William Cullen 1794-1878 . **NCLC 6, 46; DA; DAB; DAC; DAM MST, POET; PC 20**
See also CDALB 1640-1865; DLB 3, 43, 59, 189

Bryusov, Valery Yakovlevich 1873-1924 **TCLC 10**
See also CA 107; 155

Buchan, John 1875-1940 ..... **TCLC 41; DAB; DAM POP**
See also CA 108; 145; DLB 34, 70, 156; YABC 2

Buchanan, George 1506-1582 .... **LC 4**
See also DLB 152

Buchheim, Lothar-Guenther 1918- .... **CLC 6**
See also CA 85-88

Buchner, (Karl) Georg 1813-1837 . **NCLC 26**

Buchwald, Art(hur) 1925- .... **CLC 33**
See also AITN 1; CA 5-8R; CANR 21, 67; MTCW 1; SATA 10

Buck, Pearl S(ydenstricker) 1892-1973 **CLC 7, 11, 18; DA; DAB; DAM MST, NOV**
See also AITN 1; CA 1-4R; 41-44R; CANR 1, 34; DLB 9, 102; MTCW 1; SATA 1, 25

Buckler, Ernest 1908-1984 .... **CLC 13; DAC; DAM MST**
See also CA 11-12; 114; CAP 1; DLB 68; SATA 47

Buckley, Vincent (Thomas) 1925-1988 **CLC 57**
See also CA 101

Buckley, William F(rank), Jr. 1925- **CLC 7, 18, 37; DAM POP**
See also AITN 1; CA 1-4R; CANR 1, 24, 53; DLB 137; DLBY 80; INT CANR-24; MTCW 1

Buechner, (Carl) Frederick 1926- **CLC 2, 4, 6,**

13, 77; MTCW 1; SATA 36
Christie, (Ann) Philippa
See Pearce, Philippa
See also CA 5-8R; CANR 4
Christine de Pizan 1365(?)-1431(?) .... **LC 9**
See also DLB 208
Chubb, Elmer
See Masters, Edgar Lee
Chulkov, Mikhail Dmitrievich 1743-1792**LC 2**
See also DLB 150
Churchill, Caryl 1938- ..... **CLC 31, 55; DC 5**
See also CA 102; CANR 22, 46; DLB 13;
MTCW 1
Churchill, Charles 1731-1764 .... **LC 3**
See also DLB 109
Chute, Carolyn 1947- .... **CLC 39**
See also CA 123
Ciardi, John (Anthony) 1916-1986 . **CLC 10,
40, 44; DAM POET**
See also CA 5-8R; 118; CAAS 2; CANR 5, 33;
CLR 19; DLB 5; DLBY 86; INT CANR-5;
MAICYA; MTCW 1; SAAS 26; SATA 1, 65;
SATA-Obit 46
Cicero, Marcus Tullius 106B.C.-43B.C.
CMLC 3
Cimino, Michael 1943- .... **CLC 16**
See also CA 105
Cioran, E(mil) M. 1911-1995 .... **CLC 64**
See also CA 25-28R; 149
Cisneros, Sandra 1954- . **CLC 69, 118; DAM
MULT; HLC; SSC 32**
See also AAYA 9; CA 131; CANR 64; DLB 122,
152; HW
Cixous, Helene 1937- .... **CLC 92**
See also CA 126; CANR 55; DLB 83; MTCW
1
Clair, Rene .... **CLC 20**
See also Chomette, Rene Lucien
Clampitt, Amy 1920-1994 ..... **CLC 32; PC 19**
See also CA 110; 146; CANR 29; DLB 105
Clancy, Thomas L., Jr. 1947-
See Clancy, Tom
See also CA 125; 131; CANR 62; INT 131;
MTCW 1
Clancy, Tom ..**CLC 45, 112; DAM NOV, POP**
See also Clancy, Thomas L., Jr.
See also AAYA 9; BEST 89:1, 90:1
Clare, John 1793-1864 **NCLC 9; DAB; DAM
POET; PC 23**
See also DLB 55, 96
Clarin
See Alas (y Urena), Leopoldo (Enrique Garcia)
Clark, Al C.
See Goines, Donald
Clark, (Robert) Brian 1932- .... **CLC 29**
See also CA 41-44R; CANR 67
Clark, Curt
See Westlake, Donald E(dwin)
Clark, Eleanor 1913-1996 .... **CLC 5, 19**
See also CA 9-12R; 151; CANR 41; DLB 6
Clark, J. P.
See Clark, John Pepper
See also DLB 117
Clark, John Pepper 1935-.. **CLC 38; BLC 1;
DAM DRAM, MULT; DC 5**
See also Clark, J. P.
See also BW 1; CA 65-68; CANR 16, 72
Clark, M. R.
See Clark, Mavis Thorpe
Clark, Mavis Thorpe 1909- .... **CLC 12**
See also CA 57-60; CANR 8, 37; CLR 30;
MAICYA; SAAS 5; SATA 8, 74
Clark, Walter Van Tilburg 1909-1971**CLC 28**
See also CA 9-12R; 33-36R; CANR 63; DLB
9, 206; SATA 8
Clark Bekederemo, J(ohnson) P(epper)
See Clark, John Pepper

Clarke, Arthur C(harles) 1917-**CLC 1, 4, 13,
18, 35; DAM POP; SSC 3**
See also AAYA 4; CA 1-4R; CANR 2, 28, 55,
74; JRDA; MAICYA; MTCW 1; SATA 13,
70
Clarke, Austin 1896-1974 .... **CLC 6, 9; DAM
POET**
See also CA 29-32; 49-52; CAP 2; DLB 10, 20
Clarke, Austin C(hesterfield) 1934-**CLC 8, 53;
BLC 1; DAC; DAM MULT**
See also BW 1; CA 25-28R; CAAS 16; CANR
14, 32, 68; DLB 53, 125
Clarke, Gillian 1937- .... **CLC 61**
See also CA 106; DLB 40
Clarke, Marcus (Andrew Hislop) 1846-1881
NCLC 19
Clarke, Shirley 1925- .... **CLC 16**
Clash, The
See Headon, (Nicky) Topper; Jones, Mick;
Simonon, Paul; Strummer, Joe
Claudel, Paul (Louis Charles Marie) 1868-1955
TCLC 2, 10
See also CA 104; 165; DLB 192
Claudius, Matthias 1740-1815 .... **NCLC 75**
See also DLB 97
Clavell, James (duMaresq) 1925-1994**CLC 6,
25, 87; DAM NOV, POP**
See also CA 25-28R; 146; CANR 26, 48;
MTCW 1
Cleaver, (Leroy) Eldridge 1935-1998**CLC 30;
BLC 1; DAM MULT**
See also BW 1; CA 21-24R; 167; CANR 16, 75
Cleese, John (Marwood) 1939- .... **CLC 21**
See also Monty Python
See also CA 112; 116; CANR 35; MTCW 1
Cleishbotham, Jebediah
See Scott, Walter
Cleland, John 1710-1789 .... **LC 2, 48**
See also DLB 39
Clemens, Samuel Langhorne 1835-1910
See Twain, Mark
See also CA 104; 135; CDALB 1865-1917; DA;
DAB; DAC; DAM MST, NOV; DLB 11, 12,
23, 64, 74, 186, 189; JRDA; MAICYA; SATA
100; YABC 2
Cleophil
See Congreve, William
Clerihew, E.
See Bentley, E(dmund) C(lerihew)
Clerk, N. W.
See Lewis, C(live) S(taples)
Cliff, Jimmy .... **CLC 21**
See also Chambers, James
Clifton, (Thelma) Lucille 1936- **CLC 19, 66;
BLC 1; DAM MULT, POET; PC 17**
See also BW 2; CA 49-52; CANR 2, 24, 42,
76; CLR 5; DLB 5, 41; MAICYA; MTCW 1;
SATA 20, 69
Clinton, Dirk
See Silverberg, Robert
Clough, Arthur Hugh 1819-1861 ... **NCLC 27**
See also DLB 32
Clutha, Janet Paterson Frame 1924-
See Frame, Janet
See also CA 1-4R; CANR 2, 36, 76; MTCW 1
Clyne, Terence
See Blatty, William Peter
Cobalt, Martin
See Mayne, William (James Carter)
Cobb, Irvin S. 1876-1944 .... **TCLC 77**
See also DLB 11, 25, 86
Cobbett, William 1763-1835 .... **NCLC 49**
See also DLB 43, 107, 158
Coburn, D(onald) L(ee) 1938- .... **CLC 10**
See also CA 89-92
Cocteau, Jean (Maurice Eugene Clement) 1889-
1963 ....

**CLC 1, 8, 15, 16, 43; DA; DAB; DAC; DAM
DRAM, MST, NOV; WLC**
See also CA 25-28; CANR 40; CAP 2; DLB
65; MTCW 1
Codrescu, Andrei 1946-**CLC 46; DAM POET**
See also CA 33-36R; CAAS 19; CANR 13, 34,
53, 76
Coe, Max
See Bourne, Randolph S(illiman)
Coe, Tucker
See Westlake, Donald E(dwin)
Coen, Ethan 1958- .... **CLC 108**
See also CA 126
Coen, Joel 1955- .... **CLC 108**
See also CA 126
The Coen Brothers
See Coen, Ethan; Coen, Joel
Coetzee, J(ohn) M(ichael) 1940- **CLC 23, 33,
66, 117; DAM NOV**
See also CA 77-80; CANR 41, 54, 74; MTCW
1
Coffey, Brian
See Koontz, Dean R(ay)
Cohan, George M(ichael) 1878-1942**TCLC 60**
See also CA 157
Cohen, Arthur A(llen) 1928-1986 . **CLC 7, 31**
See also CA 1-4R; 120; CANR 1, 17, 42; DLB
28
Cohen, Leonard (Norman) 1934- **CLC 3, 38;
DAC; DAM MST**
See also CA 21-24R; CANR 14, 69; DLB 53;
MTCW 1
Cohen, Matt 1942- .... **CLC 19; DAC**
See also CA 61-64; CAAS 18; CANR 40; DLB
53
Cohen-Solal, Annie 19(?)- .... **CLC 50**
Colegate, Isabel 1931- .... **CLC 36**
See also CA 17-20R; CANR 8, 22, 74; DLB
14; INT CANR-22; MTCW 1
Coleman, Emmett
See Reed, Ishmael
Coleridge, M. E.
See Coleridge, Mary E(lizabeth)
Coleridge, Mary E(lizabeth) 1861-1907**TCLC
73**
See also CA 116; 166; DLB 19, 98
Coleridge, Samuel Taylor 1772-1834**NCLC 9,
54; DA; DAB; DAC; DAM MST, POET;
PC 11; WLC**
See also CDBLB 1789-1832; DLB 93, 107
Coleridge, Sara 1802-1852 .... **NCLC 31**
See also DLB 199
Coles, Don 1928- .... **CLC 46**
See also CA 115; CANR 38
Coles, Robert (Martin) 1929- .... **CLC 108**
See also CA 45-48; CANR 3, 32, 66, 70; INT
CANR-32; SATA 23
Colette, (Sidonie-Gabrielle) 1873-1954**T C L C
1, 5, 16; DAM NOV; SSC 10**
See also CA 104; 131; DLB 65; MTCW 1
Collett, (Jacobine) Camilla (Wergeland) 1813-
1895 ....
NCLC 22
Collier, Christopher 1930- .... **CLC 30**
See also AAYA 13; CA 33-36R; CANR 13, 33;
JRDA; MAICYA; SATA 16, 70
Collier, James L(incoln) 1928-**CLC 30; DAM
POP**
See also AAYA 13; CA 9-12R; CANR 4, 33,
60; CLR 3; JRDA; MAICYA; SAAS 21;
SATA 8, 70
Collier, Jeremy 1650-1726 .... **LC 6**
Collier, John 1901-1980 .... **SSC 19**
See also CA 65-68; 97-100; CANR 10; DLB
77
Collingwood, R(obin) G(eorge) 1889(?)-1943
TCLC 67

See also CA 117; 155
Collins, Hunt
See Hunter, Evan
Collins, Linda 1931- ....CLC 44
See also CA 125
Collins, (William) Wilkie 1824-1889NCLC 1, 18
See also CDBLB 1832-1890; DLB 18, 70, 159
Collins, William 1721-1759 . LC 4, 40; DAM POET
See also DLB 109
Collodi, Carlo 1826-1890 .... NCLC 54
See also Lorenzini, Carlo
See also CLR 5
Colman, George 1732-1794
See Glassco, John
Colt, Winchester Remington
See Hubbard, L(afayette) Ron(ald)
Colter, Cyrus 1910- .... CLC 58
See also BW 1; CA 65-68; CANR 10, 66; DLB 33
Colton, James
See Hansen, Joseph
Colum, Padraic 1881-1972 .... CLC 28
See also CA 73-76; 33-36R; CANR 35; CLR 36; MAICYA; MTCW 1; SATA 15
Colvin, James
See Moorcock, Michael (John)
Colwin, Laurie (E.) 1944-1992CLC 5, 13, 23, 84
See also CA 89-92; 139; CANR 20, 46; DLBY 80; MTCW 1
Comfort, Alex(ander) 1920-CLC 7; DAM POP
See also CA 1-4R; CANR 1, 45
Comfort, Montgomery
See Campbell, (John) Ramsey
Compton-Burnett, I(vy) 1884(?)-1969CLC 1, 3, 10, 15, 34; DAM NOV
See also CA 1-4R; 25-28R; CANR 4; DLB 36; MTCW 1
Comstock, Anthony 1844-1915 ...... TCLC 13
See also CA 110; 169
Comte, Auguste 1798-1857 .... NCLC 54
Conan Doyle, Arthur
See Doyle, Arthur Conan
Conde, Maryse 1937- .... CLC 52, 92; BLCS; DAM MULT
See also Boucolon, Maryse
See also BW 2
Condillac, Etienne Bonnot de 1714-1780 L C 26
Condon, Richard (Thomas) 1915-1996CLC 4, 6, 8, 10, 45, 100; DAM NOV
See also BEST 90:3; CA 1-4R; 151; CAAS 1; CANR 2, 23; INT CANR-23; MTCW 1
Confucius 551B.C.-479B.C. .. CMLC 19; DA; DAB; DAC; DAM MST; WLCS
Congreve, William 1670-1729 LC 5, 21; DA; DAB; DAC; DAM DRAM, MST, POET; DC 2; WLC
See also CDBLB 1660-1789; DLB 39, 84
Connell, Evan S(helby), Jr. 1924-CLC 4, 6, 45; DAM NOV
See also AAYA 7; CA 1-4R; CAAS 2; CANR 2, 39, 76; DLB 2; DLBY 81; MTCW 1
Connelly, Marc(us Cook) 1890-1980 .. CLC 7
See also CA 85-88; 102; CANR 30; DLB 7; DLBY 80; SATA-Obit 25
Connor, Ralph .... TCLC 31
See also Gordon, Charles William
See also DLB 92
Conrad, Joseph 1857-1924TCLC 1, 6, 13, 25, 43, 57; DA; DAB; DAC; DAM MST, NOV; SSC 9; WLC
See also AAYA 26; CA 104; 131; CANR 60; CDBLB 1890-1914; DLB 10, 34, 98, 156; MTCW 1; SATA 27

Conrad, Robert Arnold
See Hart, Moss
Conroy, Pat
See Conroy, (Donald) Pat(rick)
Conroy, (Donald) Pat(rick) 1945-CLC 30, 74; DAM NOV, POP
See also AAYA 8; AITN 1; CA 85-88; CANR 24, 53; DLB 6; MTCW 1
Constant (de Rebecque), (Henri) Benjamin 1767-1830 ....
NCLC 6
See also DLB 119
Conybeare, Charles Augustus
See Eliot, T(homas) S(tearns)
Cook, Michael 1933- .... CLC 58
See also CA 93-96; CANR 68; DLB 53
Cook, Robin 1940- .... CLC 14; DAM POP
See also BEST 90:2; CA 108; 111; CANR 41; INT 111
Cook, Roy
See Silverberg, Robert
Cooke, Elizabeth 1948- .... CLC 55
See also CA 129
Cooke, John Esten 1830-1886 .... NCLC 5
See also DLB 3
Cooke, John Estes
See Baum, L(yman) Frank
Cooke, M. E.
See Creasey, John
Cooke, Margaret
See Creasey, John
Cook-Lynn, Elizabeth 1930-.. CLC 93; DAM MULT
See also CA 133; DLB 175; NNAL
Cooney, Ray .... CLC 62
Cooper, Douglas 1960- .... CLC 86
Cooper, Henry St. John
See Creasey, John
Cooper, J(oan) California .... CLC 56; DAM MULT
See also AAYA 12; BW 1; CA 125; CANR 55
Cooper, James Fenimore 1789-1851NCLC 1, 27, 54
See also AAYA 22; CDALB 1640-1865; DLB 3; SATA 19
Coover, Robert (Lowell) 1932- CLC 3, 7, 15, 32, 46, 87; DAM NOV; SSC 15
See also CA 45-48; CANR 3, 37, 58; DLB 2; DLBY 81; MTCW 1
Copeland, Stewart (Armstrong) 1952-CLC 26
Copernicus, Nicolaus 1473-1543 .... LC 45
Coppard, A(lfred) E(dgar) 1878-1957 T C L C 5; SSC 21
See also CA 114; 167; DLB 162; YABC 1
Coppee, Francois 1842-1908 .... TCLC 25
See also CA 170
Coppola, Francis Ford 1939- .... CLC 16
See also CA 77-80; CANR 40; DLB 44
Corbiere, Tristan 1845-1875 .... NCLC 43
Corcoran, Barbara 1911- .... CLC 17
See also AAYA 14; CA 21-24R; CAAS 2; CANR 11, 28, 48; CLR 50; DLB 52; JRDA; SAAS 20; SATA 3, 77
Cordelier, Maurice
See Giraudoux, (Hippolyte) Jean
Corelli, Marie 1855-1924 .... TCLC 51
See also Mackay, Mary
See also DLB 34, 156
Corman, Cid 1924- .... CLC 9
See also Corman, Sidney
See also CAAS 2; DLB 5, 193
Corman, Sidney 1924-
See Corman, Cid
See also CA 85-88; CANR 44; DAM POET
Cormier, Robert (Edmund) 1925-CLC 12, 30; DA; DAB; DAC; DAM MST, NOV
See also AAYA 3, 19; CA 1-4R; CANR 5, 23,

76; CDALB 1968-1988; CLR 12, 55; DLB 52; INT CANR-23; JRDA; MAICYA; MTCW 1; SATA 10, 45, 83
Corn, Alfred (DeWitt III) 1943- .... CLC 33
See also CA 104; CAAS 25; CANR 44; DLB 120; DLBY 80
Corneille, Pierre 1606-1684 .... LC 28; DAB; DAM MST
Cornwell, David (John Moore) 1931-CLC 9, 15; DAM POP
See also le Carre, John
See also CA 5-8R; CANR 13, 33, 59; MTCW 1
Corso, (Nunzio) Gregory 1930- .... CLC 1, 11
See also CA 5-8R; CANR 41, 76; DLB 5, 16; MTCW 1
Cortazar, Julio 1914-1984CLC 2, 3, 5, 10, 13, 15, 33, 34, 92; DAM MULT, NOV; HLC; SSC 7
See also CA 21-24R; CANR 12, 32; DLB 113; HW; MTCW 1
CORTES, HERNAN 1484-1547 .... LC 31
Corvinus, Jakob
See Raabe, Wilhelm (Karl)
Corwin, Cecil
See Kornbluth, C(yril) M.
Cosic, Dobrica 1921- .... CLC 14
See also CA 122; 138; DLB 181
Costain, Thomas B(ertram) 1885-1965 C L C 30
See also CA 5-8R; 25-28R; DLB 9
Costantini, Humberto 1924(?)-1987 . CLC 49
See also CA 131; 122; HW
Costello, Elvis 1955- .... CLC 21
Cotes, Cecil V.
See Duncan, Sara Jeannette
Cotter, Joseph Seamon Sr. 1861-1949 T C L C 28; BLC 1; DAM MULT
See also BW 1; CA 124; DLB 50
Couch, Arthur Thomas Quiller
See Quiller-Couch, SirArthur (Thomas)
Coulton, James
See Hansen, Joseph
Couperus, Louis (Marie Anne) 1863-1923
TCLC 15
See also CA 115
Coupland, Douglas 1961-CLC 85; DAC; DAM POP
See also CA 142; CANR 57
Court, Wesli
See Turco, Lewis (Putnam)
Courtenay, Bryce 1933- .... CLC 59
See also CA 138
Courtney, Robert
See Ellison, Harlan (Jay)
Cousteau, Jacques-Yves 1910-1997 .. CLC 30
See also CA 65-68; 159; CANR 15, 67; MTCW 1; SATA 38, 98
Coventry, Francis 1725-1754 .... LC 46
Cowan, Peter (Walkinshaw) 1914- .... SSC 28
See also CA 21-24R; CANR 9, 25, 50
Coward, Noel (Peirce) 1899-1973CLC 1, 9, 29, 51; DAM DRAM
See also AITN 1; CA 17-18; 41-44R; CANR 35; CAP 2; CDBLB 1914-1945; DLB 10; MTCW 1
Cowley, Abraham 1618-1667 .... LC 43
See also DLB 131, 151
Cowley, Malcolm 1898-1989 .... CLC 39
See also CA 5-8R; 128; CANR 3, 55; DLB 4, 48; DLBY 81, 89; MTCW 1
Cowper, William 1731-1800 . NCLC 8; DAM POET
See also DLB 104, 109
Cox, William Trevor 1928- .... CLC 9, 14, 71; DAM NOV
See also Trevor, William
See also CA 9-12R; CANR 4, 37, 55, 76; DLB

14; INT CANR-37; MTCW 1
Coyne, P. J.
  See Masters, Hilary
Cozzens, James Gould 1903-1978**CLC 1, 4, 11, 92**
  See also CA 9-12R; 81-84; CANR 19; CDALB 1941-1968; DLB 9; DLBD 2; DLBY 84, 97; MTCW 1
Crabbe, George 1754-1832 .... **NCLC 26**
  See also DLB 93
Craddock, Charles Egbert
  See Murfree, Mary Noailles
Craig, A. A.
  See Anderson, Poul (William)
Craik, Dinah Maria (Mulock) 1826-1887 **NCLC 38**
  See also DLB 35, 163; MAICYA; SATA 34
Cram, Ralph Adams 1863-1942 ..... **TCLC 45**
  See also CA 160
Crane, (Harold) Hart 1899-1932 **TCLC 2, 5, 80; DA; DAB; DAC; DAM MST, POET; PC 3; WLC**
  See also CA 104; 127; CDALB 1917-1929; DLB 4, 48; MTCW 1
Crane, R(onald) S(almon) 1886-1967**CLC 27**
  See also CA 85-88; DLB 63
Crane, Stephen (Townley) 1871-1900 **TCLC 11, 17, 32; DA; DAB; DAC; DAM MST, NOV, POET; SSC 7; WLC**
  See also AAYA 21; CA 109; 140; CDALB 1865-1917; DLB 12, 54, 78; YABC 2
Cranshaw, Stanley
  See Fisher, Dorothy (Frances) Canfield
Crase, Douglas 1944- .... **CLC 58**
  See also CA 106
Crashaw, Richard 1612(?)-1649 .... **LC 24**
  See also DLB 126
Craven, Margaret 1901-1980 . **CLC 17; DAC**
  See also CA 103
Crawford, F(rancis) Marion 1854-1909**TCLC 10**
  See also CA 107; 168; DLB 71
Crawford, Isabella Valancy 1850-1887**NCLC 12**
  See also DLB 92
Crayon, Geoffrey
  See Irving, Washington
Creasey, John 1908-1973 .... **CLC 11**
  See also CA 5-8R; 41-44R; CANR 8, 59; DLB 77; MTCW 1
Crebillon, Claude Prosper Jolyot de (fils) 1707-1777 .... **LC 1, 28**
Credo
  See Creasey, John
Credo, Alvaro J. de
  See Prado (Calvo), Pedro
Creeley, Robert (White) 1926-**CLC 1, 2, 4, 8, 11, 15, 36, 78; DAM POET**
  See also CA 1-4R; CAAS 10; CANR 23, 43; DLB 5, 16, 169; DLBD 17; MTCW 1
Crews, Harry (Eugene) 1935- **CLC 6, 23, 49**
  See also AITN 1; CA 25-28R; CANR 20, 57; DLB 6, 143, 185; MTCW 1
Crichton, (John) Michael 1942-**CLC 2, 6, 54, 90; DAM NOV, POP**
  See also AAYA 10; AITN 2; CA 25-28R; CANR 13, 40, 54, 76; DLBY 81; INT CANR-13; JRDA; MTCW 1; SATA 9, 88
Crispin, Edmund .... **CLC 22**
  See also Montgomery, (Robert) Bruce
  See also DLB 87
Cristofer, Michael 1945(?)- .... **CLC 28; DAM DRAM**
  See also CA 110; 152; DLB 7
Croce, Benedetto 1866-1952 .... **TCLC 37**
  See also CA 120; 155
Crockett, David 1786-1836 .... **NCLC 8**

See also DLB 3, 11
Crockett, Davy
  See Crockett, David
Crofts, Freeman Wills 1879-1957 .. **TCLC 55**
  See also CA 115; DLB 77
Croker, John Wilson 1780-1857 .... **NCLC 10**
  See also DLB 110
Crommelynck, Fernand 1885-1970 ..**CLC 75**
  See also CA 89-92
Cromwell, Oliver 1599-1658 .... **LC 43**
Cronin, A(rchibald) J(oseph) 1896-1981**CLC 32**
  See also CA 1-4R; 102; CANR 5; DLB 191; SATA 47; SATA-Obit 25
Cross, Amanda
  See Heilbrun, Carolyn G(old)
Crothers, Rachel 1878(?)-1958 ...... **TCLC 19**
  See also CA 113; DLB 7
Croves, Hal
  See Traven, B.
Crow Dog, Mary (Ellen) (?)- .... **CLC 93**
  See also Brave Bird, Mary
  See also CA 154
Crowfield, Christopher
  See Stowe, Harriet (Elizabeth) Beecher
Crowley, Aleister .... **TCLC 7**
  See also Crowley, Edward Alexander
Crowley, Edward Alexander 1875-1947
  See Crowley, Aleister
  See also CA 104
Crowley, John 1942- .... **CLC 57**
  See also CA 61-64; CANR 43; DLBY 82; SATA 65
Crud
  See Crumb, R(obert)
Crumarums
  See Crumb, R(obert)
Crumb, R(obert) 1943- .... **CLC 17**
  See also CA 106
Crumbum
  See Crumb, R(obert)
Crumski
  See Crumb, R(obert)
Crum the Bum
  See Crumb, R(obert)
Crunk
  See Crumb, R(obert)
Crustt
  See Crumb, R(obert)
Cryer, Gretchen (Kiger) 1935- .... **CLC 21**
  See also CA 114; 123
Csath, Geza 1887-1919 .... **TCLC 13**
  See also CA 111
Cudlip, David 1933- .... **CLC 34**
Cullen, Countee 1903-1946**TCLC 4, 37; BLC 1; DA; DAC; DAM MST, MULT, POET; PC 20; WLCS**
  See also BW 1; CA 108; 124; CDALB 1917-1929; DLB 4, 48, 51; MTCW 1; SATA 18
Cum, R.
  See Crumb, R(obert)
Cummings, Bruce F(rederick) 1889-1919
  See Barbellion, W. N. P.
  See also CA 123
Cummings, E(dward) E(stlin) 1894-1962**CLC 1, 3, 8, 12, 15, 68; DA; DAB; DAC; DAM MST, POET; PC 5; WLC**
  See also CA 73-76; CANR 31; CDALB 1929-1941; DLB 4, 48; MTCW 1
Cunha, Euclides (Rodrigues Pimenta) da 1866-1909 ....**TCLC 24**
  See also CA 123
Cunningham, E. V.
  See Fast, Howard (Melvin)
Cunningham, J(ames) V(incent) 1911-1985 **CLC 3, 31**

See also CA 1-4R; 115; CANR 1, 72; DLB 5
Cunningham, Julia (Woolfolk) 1916-**CLC 12**
  See also CA 9-12R; CANR 4, 19, 36; JRDA; MAICYA; SAAS 2; SATA 1, 26
Cunningham, Michael 1952- .... **CLC 34**
  See also CA 136
Cunninghame Graham, R(obert) B(ontine) 1852-1936 ....
TCLC 19
  See also Graham, R(obert) B(ontine) Cunninghame
  See also CA 119; DLB 98
Currie, Ellen 19(?)- .... **CLC 44**
Curtin, Philip
  See Lowndes, Marie Adelaide (Belloc)
Curtis, Price
  See Ellison, Harlan (Jay)
Cutrate, Joe
  See Spiegelman, Art
Cynewulf c. 770-c. 840 .... **CMLC 23**
Czaczkes, Shmuel Yosef
  See Agnon, S(hmuel) Y(osef Halevi)
Dabrowska, Maria (Szumska) 1889-1965**CLC 15**
  See also CA 106
Dabydeen, David 1955- .... **CLC 34**
  See also BW 1; CA 125; CANR 56
Dacey, Philip 1939- .... **CLC 51**
  See also CA 37-40R; CAAS 17; CANR 14, 32, 64; DLB 105
Dagerman, Stig (Halvard) 1923-1954 **TCLC 17**
  See also CA 117; 155
Dahl, Roald 1916-1990**CLC 1, 6, 18, 79; DAB; DAC; DAM MST, NOV, POP**
  See also AAYA 15; CA 1-4R; 133; CANR 6, 32, 37, 62; CLR 1, 7, 41; DLB 139; JRDA; MAICYA; MTCW 1; SATA 1, 26, 73; SATA-Obit 65
Dahlberg, Edward 1900-1977 .. **CLC 1, 7, 14**
  See also CA 9-12R; 69-72; CANR 31, 62; DLB 48; MTCW 1
Daitch, Susan 1954- .... **CLC 103**
  See also CA 161
Dale, Colin .... **TCLC 18**
  See also Lawrence, T(homas) E(dward)
Dale, George E.
  See Asimov, Isaac
Daly, Elizabeth 1878-1967 .... **CLC 52**
  See also CA 23-24; 25-28R; CANR 60; CAP 2
Daly, Maureen 1921- .... **CLC 17**
  See also AAYA 5; CANR 37; JRDA; MAICYA; SAAS 1; SATA 2
Damas, Leon-Gontran 1912-1978 .... **CLC 84**
  See also BW 1; CA 125; 73-76
Dana, Richard Henry Sr. 1787-1879**NCLC 53**
Daniel, Samuel 1562(?)-1619 .... **LC 24**
  See also DLB 62
Daniels, Brett
  See Adler, Renata
Dannay, Frederic 1905-1982 . **CLC 11; DAM POP**
  See also Queen, Ellery
  See also CA 1-4R; 107; CANR 1, 39; DLB 137; MTCW 1
D'Annunzio, Gabriele 1863-1938**TCLC 6, 40**
  See also CA 104; 155
Danois, N. le
  See Gourmont, Remy (-Marie-Charles) de
Dante 1265-1321 .... **CMLC 3, 18; DA; DAB; DAC; DAM MST, POET; PC 21; WLCS**
d'Antibes, Germain
  See Simenon, Georges (Jacques Christian)
Danticat, Edwidge 1969- .... **CLC 94**
  See also CA 152; CANR 73
Danvers, Dennis 1947- .... **CLC 70**
Danziger, Paula 1944- .... **CLC 21**

See also AAYA 4; CA 112; 115; CANR 37; CLR 20; JRDA; MAICYA; SATA 36, 63, 102; SATA-Brief 30

Da Ponte, Lorenzo 1749-1838 .... **NCLC 50**

Dario, Ruben 1867-1916 .... **TCLC 4; DAM MULT; HLC; PC 15**
See also CA 131; HW; MTCW 1

Darley, George 1795-1846 .... **NCLC 2**
See also DLB 96

Darrow, Clarence (Seward) 1857-1938**T C L C 81**
See also CA 164

Darwin, Charles 1809-1882 .... **NCLC 57**
See also DLB 57, 166

Daryush, Elizabeth 1887-1977 ...... **CLC 6, 19**
See also CA 49-52; CANR 3; DLB 20

Dasgupta, Surendranath 1887-1952**TCLC 81**
See also CA 157

Dashwood, Edmee Elizabeth Monica de la Pasture 1890-1943
See Delafield, E. M.
See also CA 119; 154

Daudet, (Louis Marie) Alphonse 1840-1897 **NCLC 1**
See also DLB 123

Daumal, Rene 1908-1944 .... **TCLC 14**
See also CA 114

Davenant, William 1606-1668 .... **LC 13**
See also DLB 58, 126

Davenport, Guy (Mattison, Jr.) 1927-**CLC 6, 14, 38; SSC 16**
See also CA 33-36R; CANR 23, 73; DLB 130

Davidson, Avram 1923-1993
See Queen, Ellery
See also CA 101; 171; CANR 26; DLB 8

Davidson, Donald (Grady) 1893-1968**CLC 2, 13, 19**
See also CA 5-8R; 25-28R; CANR 4; DLB 45

Davidson, Hugh
See Hamilton, Edmond

Davidson, John 1857-1909 .... **TCLC 24**
See also CA 118; DLB 19

Davidson, Sara 1943- .... **CLC 9**
See also CA 81-84; CANR 44, 68; DLB 185

Davie, Donald (Alfred) 1922-1995 . **CLC 5, 8, 10, 31**
See also CA 1-4R; 149; CAAS 3; CANR 1, 44; DLB 27; MTCW 1

Davies, Ray(mond Douglas) 1944- ... **CLC 21**
See also CA 116; 146

Davies, Rhys 1901-1978 .... **CLC 23**
See also CA 9-12R; 81-84; CANR 4; DLB 139, 191

Davies, (William) Robertson 1913-1995 **C L C 2, 7, 13, 25, 42, 75, 91; DA; DAB; DAC; DAM MST, NOV, POP; WLC**
See also BEST 89:2; CA 33-36R; 150; CANR 17, 42; DLB 68; INT CANR-17; MTCW 1

Davies, W(illiam) H(enry) 1871-1940**TCLC 5**
See also CA 104; DLB 19, 174

Davies, Walter C.
See Kornbluth, C(yril) M.

Davis, Angela (Yvonne) 1944- **CLC 77; DAM MULT**
See also BW 2; CA 57-60; CANR 10

Davis, B. Lynch
See Bioy Casares, Adolfo; Borges, Jorge Luis

Davis, Harold Lenoir 1894-1960 ...... **CLC 49**
See also CA 89-92; DLB 9, 206

Davis, Rebecca (Blaine) Harding 1831-1910 **TCLC 6**
See also CA 104; DLB 74

Davis, Richard Harding 1864-1916**TCLC 24**
See also CA 114; DLB 12, 23, 78, 79, 189; DLBD 13

Davison, Frank Dalby 1893-1970 ..... **CLC 15**
See also CA 116

Davison, Lawrence H.
See Lawrence, D(avid) H(erbert Richards)

Davison, Peter (Hubert) 1928- .... **CLC 28**
See also CA 9-12R; CAAS 4; CANR 3, 43; DLB 5

Davys, Mary 1674-1732 .... **LC 1, 46**
See also DLB 39

Dawson, Fielding 1930- .... **CLC 6**
See also CA 85-88; DLB 130

Dawson, Peter
See Faust, Frederick (Schiller)

Day, Clarence (Shepard, Jr.) 1874-1935 **TCLC 25**
See also CA 108; DLB 11

Day, Thomas 1748-1789 .... **LC 1**
See also DLB 39; YABC 1

Day Lewis, C(ecil) 1904-1972 . **CLC 1, 6, 10; DAM POET; PC 11**
See also Blake, Nicholas
See also CA 13-16; 33-36R; CANR 34; CAP 1; DLB 15, 20; MTCW 1

Dazai Osamu 1909-1948 .... **TCLC 11**
See also Tsushima, Shuji
See also CA 164; DLB 182

de Andrade, Carlos Drummond
See Drummond de Andrade, Carlos

Deane, Norman
See Creasey, John

de Beauvoir, Simone (Lucie Ernestine Marie Bertrand)
See Beauvoir, Simone (Lucie Ernestine Marie Bertrand) de

de Beer, P.
See Bosman, Herman Charles

de Brissac, Malcolm
See Dickinson, Peter (Malcolm)

de Chardin, Pierre Teilhard
See Teilhard de Chardin, (Marie Joseph) Pierre

Dee, John 1527-1608 .... **LC 20**

Deer, Sandra 1940- .... **CLC 45**

De Ferrari, Gabriella 1941- .... **CLC 65**
See also CA 146

Defoe, Daniel 1660(?)-1731 ..... **LC 1, 42; DA; DAB; DAC; DAM MST, NOV; WLC**
See also AAYA 27; CDBLB 1660-1789; DLB 39, 95, 101; JRDA; MAICYA; SATA 22

de Gourmont, Remy(-Marie-Charles)
See Gourmont, Remy (-Marie-Charles) de

de Hartog, Jan 1914- .... **CLC 19**
See also CA 1-4R; CANR 1

de Hostos, E. M.
See Hostos (y Bonilla), Eugenio Maria de

de Hostos, Eugenio M.
See Hostos (y Bonilla), Eugenio Maria de

Deighton, Len .... **CLC 4, 7, 22, 46**
See also Deighton, Leonard Cyril
See also AAYA 6; BEST 89:2; CDBLB 1960 to Present; DLB 87

Deighton, Leonard Cyril 1929-
See Deighton, Len
See also CA 9-12R; CANR 19, 33, 68; DAM NOV, POP; MTCW 1

Dekker, Thomas 1572(?)-1632 .. **LC 22; DAM DRAM**
See also CDBLB Before 1660; DLB 62, 172

Delafield, E. M. 1890-1943 .... **TCLC 61**
See also Dashwood, Edmee Elizabeth Monica de la Pasture
See also DLB 34

de la Mare, Walter (John) 1873-1956**TCLC 4, 53; DAB; DAC; DAM MST, POET; SSC 14; WLC**
See also CA 163; CDBLB 1914-1945; CLR 23; DLB 162; SATA 16

Delaney, Franey
See O'Hara, John (Henry)

Delaney, Shelagh 1939-**CLC 29; DAM DRAM**

See also CA 17-20R; CANR 30, 67; CDBLB 1960 to Present; DLB 13; MTCW 1

Delany, Mary (Granville Pendarves) 1700-1788 **LC 12**

Delany, Samuel R(ay, Jr.) 1942-**CLC 8, 14, 38; BLC 1; DAM MULT**
See also AAYA 24; BW 2; CA 81-84; CANR 27, 43; DLB 8, 33; MTCW 1

De La Ramee, (Marie) Louise 1839-1908
See Ouida
See also SATA 20

de la Roche, Mazo 1879-1961 .... **CLC 14**
See also CA 85-88; CANR 30; DLB 68; SATA 64

De La Salle, Innocent
See Hartmann, Sadakichi

Delbanco, Nicholas (Franklin) 1942- **CLC 6, 13**
See also CA 17-20R; CAAS 2; CANR 29, 55; DLB 6

del Castillo, Michel 1933- .... **CLC 38**
See also CA 109

Deledda, Grazia (Cosima) 1875(?)-1936 **TCLC 23**
See also CA 123

Delibes, Miguel .... **CLC 8, 18**
See also Delibes Setien, Miguel

Delibes Setien, Miguel 1920-
See Delibes, Miguel
See also CA 45-48; CANR 1, 32; HW; MTCW 1

DeLillo, Don 1936- **CLC 8, 10, 13, 27, 39, 54, 76; DAM NOV, POP**
See also BEST 89:1; CA 81-84; CANR 21, 76; DLB 6, 173; MTCW 1

de Lisser, H. G.
See De Lisser, H(erbert) G(eorge)
See also DLB 117

De Lisser, H(erbert) G(eorge) 1878-1944 **TCLC 12**
See also de Lisser, H. G.
See also BW 2; CA 109; 152

Deloney, Thomas 1560(?)-1600 .... **LC 41**
See also DLB 167

Deloria, Vine (Victor), Jr. 1933- ..... **CLC 21; DAM MULT**
See also CA 53-56; CANR 5, 20, 48; DLB 175; MTCW 1; NNAL; SATA 21

Del Vecchio, John M(ichael) 1947- ... **CLC 29**
See also CA 110; DLBD 9

de Man, Paul (Adolph Michel) 1919-1983 **CLC 55**
See also CA 128; 111; CANR 61; DLB 67; MTCW 1

De Marinis, Rick 1934- .... **CLC 54**
See also CA 57-60; CAAS 24; CANR 9, 25, 50

Dembry, R. Emmet
See Murfree, Mary Noailles

Demby, William 1922-**CLC 53; BLC 1; DAM MULT**
See also BW 1; CA 81-84; DLB 33

de Menton, Francisco
See Chin, Frank (Chew, Jr.)

Demijohn, Thom
See Disch, Thomas M(ichael)

de Montherlant, Henry (Milon)
See Montherlant, Henry (Milon) de

Demosthenes 384B.C.-322B.C. ...... **CMLC 13**
See also DLB 176

de Natale, Francine
See Malzberg, Barry N(athaniel)

Denby, Edwin (Orr) 1903-1983 .... **CLC 48**
See also CA 138; 110

Denis, Julio
See Cortazar, Julio

Denmark, Harrison
See Zelazny, Roger (Joseph)

Dennis, John 1658-1734 .... **LC 11**
See also DLB 101
Dennis, Nigel (Forbes) 1912-1989 ...... **CLC 8**
See also CA 25-28R; 129; DLB 13, 15; MTCW
1
Dent, Lester 1904(?)-1959 .... **TCLC 72**
See also CA 112; 161
De Palma, Brian (Russell) 1940- .... **CLC 20**
See also CA 109
De Quincey, Thomas 1785-1859 ...... **NCLC 4**
See also CDBLB 1789-1832; DLB 110; 144
Deren, Eleanora 1908(?)-1961
See Deren, Maya
See also CA 111
Deren, Maya 1917-1961 .... **CLC 16, 102**
See also Deren, Eleanora
Derleth, August (William) 1909-1971 **CLC 31**
See also CA 1-4R; 29-32R; CANR 4; DLB 9;
DLBD 17; SATA 5
Der Nister 1884-1950 .... **TCLC 56**
de Routisie, Albert
See Aragon, Louis
Derrida, Jacques 1930- .... **CLC 24, 87**
See also CA 124; 127; CANR 76
Derry Down Derry
See Lear, Edward
Dersonnes, Jacques
See Simenon, Georges (Jacques Christian)
Desai, Anita 1937- **CLC 19, 37, 97; DAB; DAM
NOV**
See also CA 81-84; CANR 33, 53; MTCW 1;
SATA 63
de Saint-Luc, Jean
See Glassco, John
de Saint Roman, Arnaud
See Aragon, Louis
Descartes, Rene 1596-1650 .... **LC 20, 35**
De Sica, Vittorio 1901(?)-1974 .... **CLC 20**
See also CA 117
Desnos, Robert 1900-1945 .... **TCLC 22**
See also CA 121; 151
Destouches, Louis-Ferdinand 1894-1961 **C L C
9, 15**
See also Celine, Louis-Ferdinand
See also CA 85-88; CANR 28; MTCW 1
de Tolignac, Gaston
See Griffith, D(avid Lewelyn) W(ark)
Deutsch, Babette 1895-1982 .... **CLC 18**
See also CA 1-4R; 108; CANR 4; DLB 45;
SATA 1; SATA-Obit 33
Devenant, William 1606-1649 .... **LC 13**
Devkota, Laxmiprasad 1909-1959 . **TCLC 23**
See also CA 123
De Voto, Bernard (Augustine) 1897-1955
TCLC 29
See also CA 113; 160; DLB 9
De Vries, Peter 1910-1993 **CLC 1, 2, 3, 7, 10,
28, 46; DAM NOV**
See also CA 17-20R; 142; CANR 41; DLB 6;
DLBY 82; MTCW 1
Dexter, John
See Bradley, Marion Zimmer
Dexter, Martin
See Faust, Frederick (Schiller)
Dexter, Pete 1943- ... **CLC 34, 55; DAM POP**
See also BEST 89:2; CA 127; 131; INT 131;
MTCW 1
Diamano, Silmang
See Senghor, Leopold Sedar
Diamond, Neil 1941- .... **CLC 30**
See also CA 108
Diaz del Castillo, Bernal 1496-1584 .... **LC 31**
di Bassetto, Corno
See Shaw, George Bernard
Dick, Philip K(indred) 1928-1982 **CLC 10, 30,
72; DAM NOV, POP**
See also AAYA 24; CA 49-52; 106; CANR 2,

16; DLB 8; MTCW 1
Dickens, Charles (John Huffam) 1812-1870
**NCLC 3, 8, 18, 26, 37, 50; DA; DAB; DAC;
DAM MST, NOV; SSC 17; WLC**
See also AAYA 23; CDBLB 1832-1890; DLB
21, 55, 70, 159, 166; JRDA; MAICYA; SATA
15
Dickey, James (Lafayette) 1923-1997 **CLC 1,
2, 4, 7, 10, 15, 47, 109; DAM NOV, POET,
POP**
See also AITN 1, 2; CA 9-12R; 156; CABS 2;
CANR 10, 48, 61; CDALB 1968-1988; DLB
5, 193; DLBD 7; DLBY 82, 93, 96, 97; INT
CANR-10; MTCW 1
Dickey, William 1928-1994 .... **CLC 3, 28**
See also CA 9-12R; 145; CANR 24; DLB 5
Dickinson, Charles 1951- .... **CLC 49**
See also CA 128
Dickinson, Emily (Elizabeth) 1830-1886
**NCLC 21; DA; DAB; DAC; DAM MST,
POET; PC 1; WLC**
See also AAYA 22; CDALB 1865-1917; DLB
1; SATA 29
Dickinson, Peter (Malcolm) 1927- **CLC 12, 35**
See also AAYA 9; CA 41-44R; CANR 31, 58;
CLR 29; DLB 87, 161; JRDA; MAICYA;
SATA 5, 62, 95
Dickson, Carr
See Carr, John Dickson
Dickson, Carter
See Carr, John Dickson
Diderot, Denis 1713-1784 .... **LC 26**
Didion, Joan 1934- **CLC 1, 3, 8, 14, 32; DAM
NOV**
See also AITN 1; CA 5-8R; CANR 14, 52, 76;
CDALB 1968-1988; DLB 2, 173, 185;
DLBY 81, 86; MTCW 1
Dietrich, Robert
See Hunt, E(verette) Howard, (Jr.)
Difusa, Pati
See Almodovar, Pedro
Dillard, Annie 1945- ... **CLC 9, 60, 115; DAM
NOV**
See also AAYA 6; CA 49-52; CANR 3, 43, 62;
DLBY 80; MTCW 1; SATA 10
Dillard, R(ichard) H(enry) W(ilde) 1937-
CLC 5
See also CA 21-24R; CAAS 7; CANR 10; DLB
5
Dillon, Eilis 1920-1994 .... **CLC 17**
See also CA 9-12R; 147; CAAS 3; CANR 4,
38; CLR 26; MAICYA; SATA 2, 74; SATA-
Essay 105; SATA-Obit 83
Dimont, Penelope
See Mortimer, Penelope (Ruth)
Dinesen, Isak .... **CLC 10, 29, 95; SSC 7**
See also Blixen, Karen (Christentze Dinesen)
Ding Ling .... **CLC 68**
See also Chiang, Pin-chin
Diphusa, Patty
See Almodovar, Pedro
Disch, Thomas M(ichael) 1940- .... **CLC 7, 36**
See also AAYA 17; CA 21-24R; CAAS 4;
CANR 17, 36, 54; CLR 18; DLB 8;
MAICYA; MTCW 1; SAAS 15; SATA 92
Disch, Tom
See Disch, Thomas M(ichael)
d'Isly, Georges
See Simenon, Georges (Jacques Christian)
Disraeli, Benjamin 1804-1881 .... **NCLC 2, 39**
See also DLB 21, 55
Ditcum, Steve
See Crumb, R(obert)
Dixon, Paige
See Corcoran, Barbara
Dixon, Stephen 1936- .... **CLC 52; SSC 16**
See also CA 89-92; CANR 17, 40, 54; DLB 130

Doak, Annie
See Dillard, Annie
Dobell, Sydney Thompson 1824-1874 **N C L C
43**
See also DLB 32
Doblin, Alfred .... **TCLC 13**
See also Doeblin, Alfred
Dobrolyubov, Nikolai Alexandrovich 1836-1861
NCLC 5
Dobson, Austin 1840-1921 .... **TCLC 79**
See also DLB 35; 144
Dobyns, Stephen 1941- .... **CLC 37**
See also CA 45-48; CANR 2, 18
Doctorow, E(dgar) L(aurence) 1931- **CLC 6,
11, 15, 18, 37, 44, 65, 113; DAM NOV, POP**
See also AAYA 22; AITN 2; BEST 89:3; CA
45-48; CANR 2, 33, 51, 76; CDALB 1968-
1988; DLB 2, 28, 173; DLBY 80; MTCW 1
Dodgson, Charles Lutwidge 1832-1898
See Carroll, Lewis
See also CLR 2; DA; DAB; DAC; DAM MST,
NOV, POET; MAICYA; SATA 100; YABC 2
Dodson, Owen (Vincent) 1914-1983 **CLC 79;
BLC 1; DAM MULT**
See also BW 1; CA 65-68; 110; CANR 24; DLB
76
Doeblin, Alfred 1878-1957 .... **TCLC 13**
See also Doblin, Alfred
See also CA 110; 141; DLB 66
Doerr, Harriet 1910- .... **CLC 34**
See also CA 117; 122; CANR 47; INT 122
Domecq, H(onorio) Bustos
See Bioy Casares, Adolfo; Borges, Jorge Luis
Domini, Rey
See Lorde, Audre (Geraldine)
Dominique
See Proust, (Valentin-Louis-George-Eugene-)
Marcel
Don, A
See Stephen, SirLeslie
Donaldson, Stephen R. 1947- **CLC 46; DAM
POP**
See also CA 89-92; CANR 13, 55; INT CANR-
13
Donleavy, J(ames) P(atrick) 1926- **CLC 1, 4, 6,
10, 45**
See also AITN 2; CA 9-12R; CANR 24; 49, 62;
DLB 6, 173; INT CANR-24; MTCW 1
Donne, John 1572-1631 **LC 10, 24; DA; DAB;
DAC; DAM MST, POET; PC 1; WLC**
See also CDBLB Before 1660; DLB 121, 151
Donnell, David 1939(?)- .... **CLC 34**
Donoghue, P. S.
See Hunt, E(verette) Howard, (Jr.)
Donoso (Yanez), Jose 1924-1996 **CLC 4, 8, 11,
32, 99; DAM MULT; HLC**
See also CA 81-84; 155; CANR 32, 73; DLB
113; HW; MTCW 1
Donovan, John 1928-1992 .... **CLC 35**
See also AAYA 20; CA 97-100; 137; CLR 3;
MAICYA; SATA 72; SATA-Brief 29
Don Roberto
See Cunninghame Graham, R(obert) B(ontine)
Doolittle, Hilda 1886-1961 **CLC 3, 8, 14, 31, 34,
73; DA; DAC; DAM MST, POET; PC 5;
WLC**
See also H. D.
See also CA 97-100; CANR 35; DLB 4, 45;
MTCW 1
Dorfman, Ariel 1942- ...... **CLC 48, 77; DAM
MULT; HLC**
See also CA 124; 130; CANR 67, 70; HW; INT
130
Dorn, Edward (Merton) 1929- ... **CLC 10, 18**
See also CA 93-96; CANR 42; DLB 5; INT 93-
96
Dorris, Michael (Anthony) 1945-1997 .. **C L C**

Farrell, James T(homas) 1904-1979**CLC 1, 4, 8, 11, 66; SSC 28**
See also CA 5-8R; 89-92; CANR 9, 61; DLB 4, 9, 86; DLBD 2; MTCW 1
Farren, Richard J.
See Betjeman, John
Farren, Richard M.
See Betjeman, John
Fassbinder, Rainer Werner 1946-1982**CLC 20**
See also CA 93-96; 106; CANR 31
Fast, Howard (Melvin) 1914- **CLC 23; DAM NOV**
See also AAYA 16; CA 1-4R; CAAS 18; CANR 1, 33, 54, 75; DLB 9; INT CANR-33; SATA 7
Faulcon, Robert
See Holdstock, Robert P.
Faulkner, William (Cuthbert) 1897-1962**CLC 1, 3, 6, 8, 9, 11, 14, 18, 28, 52, 68; DA; DAB; DAC; DAM MST, NOV; SSC 1; WLC**
See also AAYA 7; CA 81-84; CANR 33; CDALB 1929-1941; DLB 9, 11, 44, 102; DLBD 2; DLBY 86, 97; MTCW 1
Fauset, Jessie Redmon 1884(?)-1961**CLC 19, 54; BLC 2; DAM MULT**
See also BW 1; CA 109; DLB 51
Faust, Frederick (Schiller) 1892-1944(?) **TCLC 49; DAM POP**
See also CA 108; 152
Faust, Irvin 1924- .... **CLC 8**
See also CA 33-36R; CANR 28, 67; DLB 2, 28; DLBY 80
Fawkes, Guy
See Benchley, Robert (Charles)
Fearing, Kenneth (Flexner) 1902-1961 . **CLC 51**
See also CA 93-96; CANR 59; DLB 9
Fecamps, Elise
See Creasey, John
Federman, Raymond 1928- .... **CLC 6, 47**
See also CA 17-20R; CAAS 8; CANR 10, 43; DLBY 80
Federspiel, J(uerg) F. 1931- .... **CLC 42**
See also CA 146
Feiffer, Jules (Ralph) 1929- ..... **CLC 2, 8, 64; DAM DRAM**
See also AAYA 3; CA 17-20R; CANR 30, 59; DLB 7, 44; INT CANR-30; MTCW 1; SATA 8, 61
Feige, Hermann Albert Otto Maximilian
See Traven, B.
Feinberg, David B. 1956-1994 .... **CLC 59**
See also CA 135; 147
Feinstein, Elaine 1930- .... **CLC 36**
See also CA 69-72; CAAS 1; CANR 31, 68; DLB 14, 40; MTCW 1
Feldman, Irving (Mordecai) 1928- ..... **CLC 7**
See also CA 1-4R; CANR 1; DLB 169
Felix-Tchicaya, Gerald
See Tchicaya, Gerald Felix
Fellini, Federico 1920-1993 .... **CLC 16, 85**
See also CA 65-68; 143; CANR 33
Felsen, Henry Gregor 1916- .... **CLC 17**
See also CA 1-4R; CANR 1; SAAS 2; SATA 1
Fenno, Jack
See Calisher, Hortense
Fenollosa, Ernest (Francisco) 1853-1908 **TCLC 91**
Fenton, James Martin 1949- .... **CLC 32**
See also CA 102; DLB 40
Ferber, Edna 1887-1968 .... **CLC 18, 93**
See also AITN 1; CA 5-8R; 25-28R; CANR 68; DLB 9, 28, 86; MTCW 1; SATA 7
Ferguson, Helen
See Kavan, Anna
Ferguson, Samuel 1810-1886 .... **NCLC 33**
See also DLB 32

Fergusson, Robert 1750-1774 .... **LC 29**
See also DLB 109
Ferling, Lawrence
See Ferlinghetti, Lawrence (Monsanto)
Ferlinghetti, Lawrence (Monsanto) 1919(?)- **CLC 2, 6, 10, 27, 111; DAM POET; PC 1**
See also CA 5-8R; CANR 3, 41, 73; CDALB 1941-1968; DLB 5, 16; MTCW 1
Fernandez, Vicente Garcia Huidobro
See Huidobro Fernandez, Vicente Garcia
Ferrer, Gabriel (Francisco Victor) Miro
See Miro (Ferrer), Gabriel (Francisco Victor)
Ferrier, Susan (Edmonstone) 1782-1854 **NCLC 8**
See also DLB 116
Ferrigno, Robert 1948(?)- .... **CLC 65**
See also CA 140
Ferron, Jacques 1921-1985 .... **CLC 94; DAC**
See also CA 117; 129; DLB 60
Feuchtwanger, Lion 1884-1958 .... **TCLC 3**
See also CA 104; DLB 66
Feuillet, Octave 1821-1890 .... **NCLC 45**
See also DLB 192
Feydeau, Georges (Leon Jules Marie) 1862-1921 .... **TCLC 22; DAM DRAM**
See also CA 113; 152; DLB 192
Fichte, Johann Gottlieb 1762-1814**NCLC 62**
See also DLB 90
Ficino, Marsilio 1433-1499 .... **LC 12**
Fiedeler, Hans
See Doeblin, Alfred
Fiedler, Leslie A(aron) 1917- . **CLC 4, 13, 24**
See also CA 9-12R; CANR 7, 63; DLB 28, 67; MTCW 1
Field, Andrew 1938- .... **CLC 44**
See also CA 97-100; CANR 25
Field, Eugene 1850-1895 .... **NCLC 3**
See also DLB 23, 42, 140; DLBD 13; MAICYA; SATA 16
Field, Gans T.
See Wellman, Manly Wade
Field, Michael 1915-1971 .... **TCLC 43**
See also CA 29-32R
Field, Peter
See Hobson, Laura Z(ametkin)
Fielding, Henry 1707-1754 ..... **LC 1, 46; DA; DAB; DAC; DAM DRAM, MST, NOV; WLC**
See also CDBLB 1660-1789; DLB 39, 84, 101
Fielding, Sarah 1710-1768 .... **LC 1, 44**
See also DLB 39
Fields, W. C. 1880-1946 .... **TCLC 80**
See also DLB 44
Fierstein, Harvey (Forbes) 1954- ... **CLC 33; DAM DRAM, POP**
See also CA 123; 129
Figes, Eva 1932- .... **CLC 31**
See also CA 53-56; CANR 4, 44; DLB 14
Finch, Anne 1661-1720 .... **LC 3; PC 21**
See also DLB 95
Finch, Robert (Duer Claydon) 1900- **CLC 18**
See also CA 57-60; CANR 9, 24, 49; DLB 88
Findley, Timothy 1930- . **CLC 27, 102; DAC; DAM MST**
See also CA 25-28R; CANR 12, 42, 69; DLB 53
Fink, William
See Mencken, H(enry) L(ouis)
Firbank, Louis 1942-
See Reed, Lou
See also CA 117
Firbank, (Arthur Annesley) Ronald 1886-1926 **TCLC 1**
See also CA 104; DLB 36
Fisher, Dorothy (Frances) Canfield 1879-1958 **TCLC 87**
See also CA 114; 136; DLB 9, 102; MAICYA;

YABC 1
Fisher, M(ary) F(rances) K(ennedy) 1908-1992 **CLC 76, 87**
See also CA 77-80; 138; CANR 44
Fisher, Roy 1930- .... **CLC 25**
See also CA 81-84; CAAS 10; CANR 16; DLB 40
Fisher, Rudolph 1897-1934**TCLC 11; BLC 2; DAM MULT; SSC 25**
See also BW 1; CA 107; 124; DLB 51, 102
Fisher, Vardis (Alvero) 1895-1968 ...... **CLC 7**
See also CA 5-8R; 25-28R; CANR 68; DLB 9, 206
Fiske, Tarleton
See Bloch, Robert (Albert)
Fitch, Clarke
See Sinclair, Upton (Beall)
Fitch, John IV
See Cormier, Robert (Edmund)
Fitzgerald, Captain Hugh
See Baum, L(yman) Frank
FitzGerald, Edward 1809-1883 .... **NCLC 9**
See also DLB 32
Fitzgerald, F(rancis) Scott (Key) 1896-1940 **TCLC 1, 6, 14, 28, 55; DA; DAB; DAC; DAM MST, NOV; SSC 6, 31; WLC**
See also AAYA 24; AITN 1; CA 110; 123; CDALB 1917-1929; DLB 4, 9, 86; DLBD 1, 15, 16; DLBY 81, 96; MTCW 1
Fitzgerald, Penelope 1916- ... **CLC 19, 51, 61**
See also CA 85-88; CAAS 10; CANR 56; DLB 14, 194
Fitzgerald, Robert (Stuart) 1910-1985**CLC 39**
See also CA 1-4R; 114; CANR 1; DLBY 80
FitzGerald, Robert D(avid) 1902-1987**CLC 19**
See also CA 17-20R
Fitzgerald, Zelda (Sayre) 1900-1948**TCLC 52**
See also CA 117; 126; DLBY 84
Flanagan, Thomas (James Bonner) 1923- **CLC 25, 52**
See also CA 108; CANR 55; DLBY 80; INT 108; MTCW 1
Flaubert, Gustave 1821-1880**NCLC 2, 10, 19, 62, 66; DA; DAB; DAC; DAM MST, NOV; SSC 11; WLC**
See also DLB 119
Flecker, Herman Elroy
See Flecker, (Herman) James Elroy
Flecker, (Herman) James Elroy 1884-1915 **TCLC 43**
See also CA 109; 150; DLB 10, 19
Fleming, Ian (Lancaster) 1908-1964 . **CLC 3, 30; DAM POP**
See also AAYA 26; CA 5-8R; CANR 59; CDBLB 1945-1960; DLB 87, 201; MTCW 1; SATA 9
Fleming, Thomas (James) 1927- .... **CLC 37**
See also CA 5-8R; CANR 10; INT CANR-10; SATA 8
Fletcher, John 1579-1625 .... **LC 33; DC 6**
See also CDBLB Before 1660; DLB 58
Fletcher, John Gould 1886-1950 .... **TCLC 35**
See also CA 107; 167; DLB 4, 45
Fleur, Paul
See Pohl, Frederik
Flooglebuckle, Al
See Spiegelman, Art
Flying Officer X
See Bates, H(erbert) E(rnest)
Fo, Dario 1926- **CLC 32, 109; DAM DRAM; DC 10**
See also CA 116; 128; CANR 68; DLBY 97; MTCW 1
Fogarty, Jonathan Titulescu Esq.
See Farrell, James T(homas)
Folke, Will
See Bloch, Robert (Albert)

74; DLB 13; MTCW 1; SATA 66

Frye, (Herman) Northrop 1912-1991 **CLC 24, 70**
See also CA 5-8R; 133; CANR 8, 37; DLB 67, 68; MTCW 1

Fuchs, Daniel 1909-1993 .... **CLC 8, 22**
See also CA 81-84; 142; CAAS 5; CANR 40; DLB 9, 26, 28; DLBY 93

Fuchs, Daniel 1934- .... **CLC 34**
See also CA 37-40R; CANR 14, 48

Fuentes, Carlos 1928- **CLC 3, 8, 10, 13, 22, 41, 60, 113; DA; DAB; DAC; DAM MST, MULT, NOV; HLC; SSC 24; WLC**
See also AAYA 4; AITN 2; CA 69-72; CANR 10, 32, 68; DLB 113; HW; MTCW 1

Fuentes, Gregorio Lopez y
See Lopez y Fuentes, Gregorio

Fugard, (Harold) Athol 1932- **CLC 5, 9, 14, 25, 40, 80; DAM DRAM; DC 3**
See also AAYA 17; CA 85-88; CANR 32, 54; MTCW 1

Fugard, Sheila 1932- .... **CLC 48**
See also CA 125

Fuller, Charles (H., Jr.) 1939- **CLC 25; BLC 2; DAM DRAM, MULT; DC 1**
See also BW 2; CA 108; 112; DLB 38; INT 112; MTCW 1

Fuller, John (Leopold) 1937- .... **CLC 62**
See also CA 21-24R; CANR 9, 44; DLB 40

Fuller, Margaret .... **NCLC 5, 50**
See also Ossoli, Sarah Margaret (Fuller marchesa d')

Fuller, Roy (Broadbent) 1912-1991 **CLC 4, 28**
See also CA 5-8R; 135; CAAS 10; CANR 53; DLB 15, 20; SATA 87

Fulton, Alice 1952- .... **CLC 52**
See also CA 116; CANR 57; DLB 193

Furphy, Joseph 1843-1912 .... **TCLC 25**
See also CA 163

Fussell, Paul 1924- .... **CLC 74**
See also BEST 90:1; CA 17-20R; CANR 8, 21, 35, 69; INT CANR-21; MTCW 1

Futabatei, Shimei 1864-1909 .... **TCLC 44**
See also CA 162; DLB 180

Futrelle, Jacques 1875-1912 .... **TCLC 19**
See also CA 113; 155

Gaboriau, Emile 1835-1873 .... **NCLC 14**

Gadda, Carlo Emilio 1893-1973 .... **CLC 11**
See also CA 89-92; DLB 177

Gaddis, William 1922-1998 **CLC 1, 3, 6, 8, 10, 19, 43, 86**
See also CA 17-20R; 172; CANR 21, 48; DLB 2; MTCW 1

Gage, Walter
See Inge, William (Motter)

Gaines, Ernest J(ames) 1933- **CLC 3, 11, 18, 86; BLC 2; DAM MULT**
See also AAYA 18; AITN 1; BW 2; CA 9-12R; CANR 6, 24, 42, 75; CDALB 1968-1988; DLB 2, 33, 152; DLBY 80; MTCW 1; SATA 86

Gaitskill, Mary 1954- .... **CLC 69**
See also CA 128; CANR 61

Galdos, Benito Perez
See Perez Galdos, Benito

Gale, Zona 1874-1938 **TCLC 7; DAM DRAM**
See also CA 105; 153; DLB 9, 78

Galeano, Eduardo (Hughes) 1940- ... **CLC 72**
See also CA 29-32R; CANR 13, 32; HW

Galiano, Juan Valera y Alcala
See Valera y Alcala-Galiano, Juan

Galilei, Galileo 1546-1642 .... **LC 45**

Gallagher, Tess 1943- ...... **CLC 18, 63; DAM POET; PC 9**
See also CA 106; DLB 120

Gallant, Mavis 1922- ... **CLC 7, 18, 38; DAC; DAM MST; SSC 5**

See also CA 69-72; CANR 29, 69; DLB 53; MTCW 1

Gallant, Roy A(rthur) 1924- .... **CLC 17**
See also CA 5-8R; CANR 4, 29, 54; CLR 30; MAICYA; SATA 4, 68

Gallico, Paul (William) 1897-1976 ..... **CLC 2**
See also AITN 1; CA 5-8R; 69-72; CANR 23; DLB 9, 171; MAICYA; SATA 13

Gallo, Max Louis 1932- .... **CLC 95**
See also CA 85-88

Gallois, Lucien
See Desnos, Robert

Gallup, Ralph
See Whitemore, Hugh (John)

Galsworthy, John 1867-1933 **TCLC 1, 45; DA; DAB; DAC; DAM DRAM, MST, NOV; SSC 22; WLC**
See also CA 104; 141; CANR 75; CDBLB 1890-1914; DLB 10, 34, 98, 162; DLBD 16

Galt, John 1779-1839 .... **NCLC 1**
See also DLB 99, 116, 159

Galvin, James 1951- .... **CLC 38**
See also CA 108; CANR 26

Gamboa, Federico 1864-1939 .... **TCLC 36**
See also CA 167

Gandhi, M. K.
See Gandhi, Mohandas Karamchand

Gandhi, Mahatma
See Gandhi, Mohandas Karamchand

Gandhi, Mohandas Karamchand 1869-1948 **TCLC 59; DAM MULT**
See also CA 121; 132; MTCW 1

Gann, Ernest Kellogg 1910-1991 ...... **CLC 23**
See also AITN 1; CA 1-4R; 136; CANR 1

Garcia, Cristina 1958- .... **CLC 76**
See also CA 141; CANR 73

Garcia Lorca, Federico 1898-1936 **TCLC 1, 7, 49; DA; DAB; DAC; DAM DRAM, MST, MULT, POET; DC 2; HLC; PC 3; WLC**
See also CA 104; 131; DLB 108; HW; MTCW 1

Garcia Marquez, Gabriel (Jose) 1928- **CLC 2, 3, 8, 10, 15, 27, 47, 55, 68; DA; DAB; DAC; DAM MST, MULT, NOV, POP; HLC; SSC 8; WLC**
See also AAYA 3; BEST 89:1, 90:4; CA 33-36R; CANR 10, 28, 50, 75; DLB 113; HW; MTCW 1

Gard, Janice
See Latham, Jean Lee

Gard, Roger Martin du
See Martin du Gard, Roger

Gardam, Jane 1928- .... **CLC 43**
See also CA 49-52; CANR 2, 18, 33, 54; CLR 12; DLB 14, 161; MAICYA; MTCW 1; SAAS 9; SATA 39, 76; SATA-Brief 28

Gardner, Herb(ert) 1934- .... **CLC 44**
See also CA 149

Gardner, John (Champlin), Jr. 1933-1982 **CLC 2, 3, 5, 7, 8, 10, 18, 28, 34; DAM NOV, POP; SSC 7**
See also AITN 1; CA 65-68; 107; CANR 33, 73; DLB 2; DLBY 82; MTCW 1; SATA 40; SATA-Obit 31

Gardner, John (Edmund) 1926- **CLC 30; DAM POP**
See also CA 103; CANR 15, 69; MTCW 1

Gardner, Miriam
See Bradley, Marion Zimmer

Gardner, Noel
See Kuttner, Henry

Gardons, S. S.
See Snodgrass, W(illiam) D(e Witt)

Garfield, Leon 1921-1996 .... **CLC 12**
See also AAYA 8; CA 17-20R; 152; CANR 38, 41; CLR 21; DLB 161; JRDA; MAICYA; SATA 1, 32, 76; SATA-Obit 90

Garland, (Hannibal) Hamlin 1860-1940 **TCLC 3; SSC 18**
See also CA 104; DLB 12, 71, 78, 186

Garneau, (Hector de) Saint-Denys 1912-1943 **TCLC 13**
See also CA 111; DLB 88

Garner, Alan 1934- **CLC 17; DAB; DAM POP**
See also AAYA 18; CA 73-76; CANR 15, 64; CLR 20; DLB 161; MAICYA; MTCW 1; SATA 18, 69

Garner, Hugh 1913-1979 .... **CLC 13**
See also CA 69-72; CANR 31; DLB 68

Garnett, David 1892-1981 .... **CLC 3**
See also CA 5-8R; 103; CANR 17; DLB 34

Garos, Stephanie
See Katz, Steve

Garrett, George (Palmer) 1929- **CLC 3, 11, 51; SSC 30**
See also CA 1-4R; CAAS 5; CANR 1, 42, 67; DLB 2, 5, 130, 152; DLBY 83

Garrick, David 1717-1779 .... **LC 15; DAM DRAM**
See also DLB 84

Garrigue, Jean 1914-1972 .... **CLC 2, 8**
See also CA 5-8R; 37-40R; CANR 20

Garrison, Frederick
See Sinclair, Upton (Beall)

Garth, Will
See Hamilton, Edmond; Kuttner, Henry

Garvey, Marcus (Moziah, Jr.) 1887-1940 **TCLC 41; BLC 2; DAM MULT**
See also BW 1; CA 120; 124

Gary, Romain .... **CLC 25**
See also Kacew, Romain
See also DLB 83

Gascar, Pierre .... **CLC 11**
See also Fournier, Pierre

Gascoyne, David (Emery) 1916- .... **CLC 45**
See also CA 65-68; CANR 10, 28, 54; DLB 20; MTCW 1

Gaskell, Elizabeth Cleghorn 1810-1865 **NCLC 70; DAB; DAM MST; SSC 25**
See also CDBLB 1832-1890; DLB 21, 144, 159

Gass, William H(oward) 1924- **CLC 1, 2, 8, 11, 15, 39; SSC 12**
See also CA 17-20R; CANR 30, 71; DLB 2; MTCW 1

Gasset, Jose Ortega y
See Ortega y Gasset, Jose

Gates, Henry Louis, Jr. 1950- **CLC 65; BLCS; DAM MULT**
See also BW 2; CA 109; CANR 25, 53, 75; DLB 67

Gautier, Theophile 1811-1872 .. **NCLC 1, 59; DAM POET; PC 18; SSC 20**
See also DLB 119

Gawsworth, John
See Bates, H(erbert) E(rnest)

Gay, John 1685-1732 .... **LC 49**

Gay, Oliver
See Gogarty, Oliver St. John

Gaye, Marvin (Penze) 1939-1984 ..... **CLC 26**
See also CA 112

Gebler, Carlo (Ernest) 1954- .... **CLC 39**
See also CA 119; 133

Gee, Maggie (Mary) 1948- .... **CLC 57**
See also CA 130; DLB 207

Gee, Maurice (Gough) 1931- .... **CLC 29**
See also CA 97-100; CANR 67; SATA 46, 101

Gelbart, Larry (Simon) 1923- .... **CLC 21, 61**
See also CA 73-76; CANR 45

Gelber, Jack 1932- .... **CLC 1, 6, 14, 79**
See also CA 1-4R; CANR 2; DLB 7

Gellhorn, Martha (Ellis) 1908-1998 **CLC 14, 60**
See also CA 77-80; 164; CANR 44; DLBY 82

Genet, Jean 1910-1986 **CLC 1, 2, 5, 10, 14, 44,**

Hailey, Arthur 1920-CLC **5; DAM NOV, POP**
See also AITN 2; BEST 90:3; CA 1-4R; CANR 2, 36, 75; DLB 88; DLBY 82; MTCW 1

Hailey, Elizabeth Forsythe 1938- ..... **CLC 40**
See also CA 93-96; CAAS 1; CANR 15, 48; INT CANR-15

Haines, John (Meade) 1924-.............. **CLC 58**
See also CA 17-20R; CANR 13, 34; DLB 5

Hakluyt, Richard 1552-1616 .... **LC 31**

Haldeman, Joe (William) 1943- .... **CLC 61**
See also CA 53-56; CAAS 25; CANR 6, 70, 72; DLB 8; INT CANR-6

Hale, Sarah Josepha (Buell) 1788-1879NCLC **75**
See also DLB 1, 42, 73

Haley, Alex(ander Murray Palmer) 1921-1992 CLC **8, 12, 76; BLC 2; DA; DAB; DAC; DAM MST, MULT, POP**
See also AAYA 26; BW 2; CA 77-80; 136; CANR 61; DLB 38; MTCW 1

Haliburton, Thomas Chandler 1796-1865 **NCLC 15**
See also DLB 11, 99

Hall, Donald (Andrew, Jr.) 1928- CLC **1, 13, 37, 59; DAM POET**
See also CA 5-8R; CAAS 7; CANR 2, 44, 64; DLB 5; SATA 23, 97

Hall, Frederic Sauser
See Sauser-Hall, Frederic

Hall, James
See Kuttner, Henry

Hall, James Norman 1887-1951 ..... **TCLC 23**
See also CA 123; SATA 21

Hall, Radclyffe
See Hall, (Marguerite) Radclyffe

Hall, (Marguerite) Radclyffe 1886-1943 **TCLC 12**
See also CA 110; 150; DLB 191

Hall, Rodney 1935-.......................... **CLC 51**
See also CA 109; CANR 69

Halleck, Fitz-Greene 1790-1867 .... **NCLC 47**
See also DLB 3

Halliday, Michael
See Creasey, John

Halpern, Daniel 1945- .... **CLC 14**
See also CA 33-36R

Hamburger, Michael (Peter Leopold) 1924-CLC **5, 14**
See also CA 5-8R; CAAS 4; CANR 2, 47; DLB 27

Hamill, Pete 1935- .... **CLC 10**
See also CA 25-28R; CANR 18, 71

Hamilton, Alexander 1755(?)-1804 **NCLC 49**
See also DLB 37

Hamilton, Clive
See Lewis, C(live) S(taples)

Hamilton, Edmond 1904-1977 .... **CLC 1**
See also CA 1-4R; CANR 3; DLB 8

Hamilton, Eugene (Jacob) Lee
See Lee-Hamilton, Eugene (Jacob)

Hamilton, Franklin
See Silverberg, Robert

Hamilton, Gail
See Corcoran, Barbara

Hamilton, Mollie
See Kaye, M(ary) M(argaret)

Hamilton, (Anthony Walter) Patrick 1904-1962 **CLC 51**
See also CA 113; DLB 191

Hamilton, Virginia 1936-....... **CLC 26; DAM MULT**
See also AAYA 2, 21; BW 2; CA 25-28R; CANR 20, 37, 73; CLR 1, 11, 40; DLB 33, 52; INT CANR-20; JRDA; MAICYA; MTCW 1; SATA 4, 56, 79

Hammett, (Samuel) Dashiell 1894-1961 **C L C 3, 5, 10, 19, 47; SSC 17**

See also AITN 1; CA 81-84; CANR 42; CDALB 1929-1941; DLBD 6; DLBY 96; MTCW 1

Hammon, Jupiter 1711(?)-1800(?) ..**NCLC 5; BLC 2; DAM MULT, POET; PC 16**
See also DLB 31, 50

Hammond, Keith
See Kuttner, Henry

Hamner, Earl (Henry), Jr. 1923- ...... **CLC 12**
See also AITN 2; CA 73-76; DLB 6

Hampton, Christopher (James) 1946- CLC **4**
See also CA 25-28R; DLB 13; MTCW 1

Hamsun, Knut .... **TCLC 2, 14, 49**
See also Pedersen, Knut

Handke, Peter 1942-CLC **5, 8, 10, 15, 38; DAM DRAM, NOV**
See also CA 77-80; CANR 33, 75; DLB 85, 124; MTCW 1

Hanley, James 1901-1985 ..... CLC **3, 5, 8, 13**
See also CA 73-76; 117; CANR 36; DLB 191; MTCW 1

Hannah, Barry 1942- .... **CLC 23, 38, 90**
See also CA 108; 110; CANR 43, 68; DLB 6; INT 110; MTCW 1

Hannon, Ezra
See Hunter, Evan

Hansberry, Lorraine (Vivian) 1930-1965CLC **17, 62; BLC 2; DA; DAB; DAC; DAM DRAM, MST, MULT; DC 2**
See also AAYA 25; BW 1; CA 109; 25-28R; CABS 3; CANR 58; CDALB 1941-1968; DLB 7, 38; MTCW 1

Hansen, Joseph 1923-......................... **CLC 38**
See also CA 29-32R; CAAS 17; CANR 16, 44, 66; INT CANR-16

Hansen, Martin A(lfred) 1909-1955**TCLC 32**
See also CA 167

Hanson, Kenneth O(stlin) 1922- .... **CLC 13**
See also CA 53-56; CANR 7

Hardwick, Elizabeth (Bruce) 1916- CLC **13; DAM NOV**
See also CA 5-8R; CANR 3, 32, 70; DLB 6; MTCW 1

Hardy, Thomas 1840-1928**TCLC 4, 10, 18, 32, 48, 53, 72; DA; DAB; DAC; DAM MST, NOV, POET; PC 8; SSC 2; WLC**
See also CA 104; 123; CDBLB 1890-1914; DLB 18, 19, 135; MTCW 1

Hare, David 1947-........................ CLC **29, 58**
See also CA 97-100; CANR 39; DLB 13; MTCW 1

Harewood, John
See Van Druten, John (William)

Harford, Henry
See Hudson, W(illiam) H(enry)

Hargrave, Leonie
See Disch, Thomas M(ichael)

Harjo, Joy 1951- .... **CLC 83; DAM MULT**
See also CA 114; CANR 35, 67; DLB 120, 175; NNAL

Harlan, Louis R(udolph) 1922- .... **CLC 34**
See also CA 21-24R; CANR 25, 55

Harling, Robert 1951(?)- .... **CLC 53**
See also CA 147

Harmon, William (Ruth) 1938- .... **CLC 38**
See also CA 33-36R; CANR 14, 32, 35; SATA 65

Harper, F. E. W.
See Harper, Frances Ellen Watkins

Harper, Frances E. W.
See Harper, Frances Ellen Watkins

Harper, Frances E. Watkins
See Harper, Frances Ellen Watkins

Harper, Frances Ellen
See Harper, Frances Ellen Watkins

Harper, Frances Ellen Watkins 1825-1911 **TCLC 14; BLC 2; DAM MULT, POET; PC 21**

See also BW 1; CA 111; 125; DLB 50

Harper, Michael S(teven) 1938- .... CLC **7, 22**
See also BW 1; CA 33-36R; CANR 24; DLB 41

Harper, Mrs. F. E. W.
See Harper, Frances Ellen Watkins

Harris, Christie (Lucy) Irwin 1907- **CLC 12**
See also CA 5-8R; CANR 6; CLR 47; DLB 88; JRDA; MAICYA; SAAS 10; SATA 6, 74

Harris, Frank 1856-1931 .... **TCLC 24**
See also CA 109; 150; DLB 156, 197

Harris, George Washington 1814-1869**NCLC 23**
See also DLB 3, 11

Harris, Joel Chandler 1848-1908 ... **TCLC 2; SSC 19**
See also CA 104; 137; CLR 49; DLB 11, 23, 42, 78, 91; MAICYA; SATA 100; YABC 1

Harris, John (Wyndham Parkes Lucas) Beynon 1903-1969
See Wyndham, John
See also CA 102; 89-92

Harris, MacDonald .... **CLC 9**
See also Heiney, Donald (William)

Harris, Mark 1922- .... **CLC 19**
See also CA 5-8R; CAAS 3; CANR 2, 55; DLB 2; DLBY 80

Harris, (Theodore) Wilson 1921- ..... **CLC 25**
See also BW 2; CA 65-68; CAAS 16; CANR 11, 27, 69; DLB 117; MTCW 1

Harrison, Elizabeth Cavanna 1909-
See Cavanna, Betty
See also CA 9-12R; CANR 6, 27

Harrison, Harry (Max) 1925- .... **CLC 42**
See also CA 1-4R; CANR 5, 21; DLB 8; SATA 4

Harrison, James (Thomas) 1937- CLC **6, 14, 33, 66; SSC 19**
See also CA 13-16R; CANR 8, 51; DLBY 82; INT CANR-8

Harrison, Jim
See Harrison, James (Thomas)

Harrison, Kathryn 1961- .... **CLC 70**
See also CA 144; CANR 68

Harrison, Tony 1937- .... **CLC 43**
See also CA 65-68; CANR 44; DLB 40; MTCW 1

Harriss, Will(ard Irvin) 1922- .... **CLC 34**
See also CA 111

Harson, Sley
See Ellison, Harlan (Jay)

Hart, Ellis
See Ellison, Harlan (Jay)

Hart, Josephine 1942(?)-CLC **70; DAM POP**
See also CA 138; CANR 70

Hart, Moss 1904-1961**CLC 66; DAM DRAM**
See also CA 109; 89-92; DLB 7

Harte, (Francis) Bret(t) 1836(?)-1902**TCLC 1, 25; DA; DAC; DAM MST; SSC 8; WLC**
See also CA 104; 140; CDALB 1865-1917; DLB 12, 64, 74, 79, 186; SATA 26

Hartley, L(eslie) P(oles) 1895-1972**CLC 2, 22**
See also CA 45-48; 37-40R; CANR 33; DLB 15, 139; MTCW 1

Hartman, Geoffrey H. 1929-............. **CLC 27**
See also CA 117; 125; DLB 67

Hartmann, Sadakichi 1867-1944 ... **TCLC 73**
See also CA 157; DLB 54

Hartmann von Aue c. 1160-c. 1205**CMLC 15**
See also DLB 138

Hartmann von Aue 1170-1210 ...... **CMLC 15**

Haruf, Kent 1943-............................. **CLC 34**
See also CA 149

Harwood, Ronald 1934-......... **CLC 32; DAM DRAM, MST**
See also CA 1-4R; CANR 4, 55; DLB 13

Hasegawa Tatsunosuke

See also CA 114; DLB 207

Hollis, Jim
See Summers, Hollis (Spurgeon, Jr.)

Holly, Buddy 1936-1959 .... TCLC 65

Holmes, Gordon
See Shiel, M(atthew) P(hipps)

Holmes, John
See Souster, (Holmes) Raymond

Holmes, John Clellon 1926-1988 ...... CLC 56
See also CA 9-12R; 125; CANR 4; DLB 16

Holmes, Oliver Wendell, Jr. 1841-1935 T C L C 77
See also CA 114

Holmes, Oliver Wendell 1809-1894 NCLC 14
See also CDALB 1640-1865; DLB 1, 189;
SATA 34

Holmes, Raymond
See Souster, (Holmes) Raymond

Holt, Victoria
See Hibbert, Eleanor Alice Burford

Holub, Miroslav 1923-1998 .... CLC 4
See also CA 21-24R; 169; CANR 10

Homer c. 8th cent. B.C.- ... CMLC 1, 16; DA;
DAB; DAC; DAM MST, POET; PC 23;
WLCS
See also DLB 176

Hongo, Garrett Kaoru 1951- .... PC 23
See also CA 133; CAAS 22; DLB 120

Honig, Edwin 1919-............................ CLC 33
See also CA 5-8R; CAAS 8; CANR 4, 45; DLB 5

Hood, Hugh (John Blagdon) 1928-CLC 15, 28
See also CA 49-52; CAAS 17; CANR 1, 33;
DLB 53

Hood, Thomas 1799-1845 .... NCLC 16
See also DLB 96

Hooker, (Peter) Jeremy 1941- .... CLC 43
See also CA 77-80; CANR 22; DLB 40

hooks, bell .... CLC 94; BLCS
See also Watkins, Gloria

Hope, A(lec) D(erwent) 1907- ...... CLC 3, 51
See also CA 21-24R; CANR 33, 74; MTCW 1

Hope, Anthony 1863-1933 .... TCLC 83
See also CA 157; DLB 153, 156

Hope, Brian
See Creasey, John

Hope, Christopher (David Tully) 1944- C L C 52
See also CA 106; CANR 47; SATA 62

Hopkins, Gerard Manley 1844-1889 .. N C L C 17; DA; DAB; DAC; DAM MST, POET;
PC 15; WLC
See also CDBLB 1890-1914; DLB 35, 57

Hopkins, John (Richard) 1931-1998 ..CLC 4
See also CA 85-88; 169

Hopkins, Pauline Elizabeth 1859-1930T C L C 28; BLC 2; DAM MULT
See also BW 2; CA 141; DLB 50

Hopkinson, Francis 1737-1791 .... LC 25
See also DLB 31

Hopley-Woolrich, Cornell George 1903-1968
See Woolrich, Cornell
See also CA 13-14; CANR 58; CAP 1

Horatio
See Proust, (Valentin-Louis-George-Eugene-)
Marcel

Horgan, Paul (George Vincent O'Shaughnessy)
1903-1995 .... CLC 9, 53; DAM NOV
See also CA 13-16R; 147; CANR 9, 35; DLB
102; DLBY 85; INT CANR-9; MTCW 1;
SATA 13; SATA-Obit 84

Horn, Peter
See Kuttner, Henry

Hornem, Horace Esq.
See Byron, George Gordon (Noel)

Horney, Karen (Clementine Theodore Danielsen) 1885-1952 .... TCLC 71

See also CA 114; 165

Hornung, E(rnest) W(illiam) 1866-1921
TCLC 59
See also CA 108; 160; DLB 70

Horovitz, Israel (Arthur) 1939-CLC 56; DAM DRAM
See also CA 33-36R; CANR 46, 59; DLB 7

Horvath, Odon von
See Horvath, Oedoen von
See also DLB 85, 124

Horvath, Oedoen von 1901-1938 ... TCLC 45
See also Horvath, Odon von
See also CA 118

Horwitz, Julius 1920-1986 .... CLC 14
See also CA 9-12R; 119; CANR 12

Hospital, Janette Turner 1942- .... CLC 42
See also CA 108; CANR 48

Hostos, E. M. de
See Hostos (y Bonilla), Eugenio Maria de

Hostos, Eugenio M. de
See Hostos (y Bonilla), Eugenio Maria de

Hostos, Eugenio Maria
See Hostos (y Bonilla), Eugenio Maria de

Hostos (y Bonilla), Eugenio Maria de 1839-1903
TCLC 24
See also CA 123; 131; HW

Houdini
See Lovecraft, H(oward) P(hillips)

Hougan, Carolyn 1943- .... CLC 34
See also CA 139

Household, Geoffrey (Edward West) 1900-1988
CLC 11
See also CA 77-80; 126; CANR 58; DLB 87;
SATA 14; SATA-Obit 59

Housman, A(lfred) E(dward) 1859-1936
TCLC 1, 10; DA; DAB; DAC; DAM MST,
POET; PC 2; WLCS
See also CA 104; 125; DLB 19; MTCW 1

Housman, Laurence 1865-1959 .... TCLC 7
See also CA 106; 155; DLB 10; SATA 25

Howard, Elizabeth Jane 1923- ..... CLC 7, 29
See also CA 5-8R; CANR 8, 62

Howard, Maureen 1930- .... CLC 5, 14, 46
See also CA 53-56; CANR 31, 75; DLBY 83;
INT CANR-31; MTCW 1

Howard, Richard 1929- .... CLC 7, 10, 47
See also AITN 1; CA 85-88; CANR 25; DLB 5;
INT CANR-25

Howard, Robert E(rvin) 1906-1936 TCLC 8
See also CA 105; 157

Howard, Warren F.
See Pohl, Frederik

Howe, Fanny (Quincy) 1940- .... CLC 47
See also CA 117; CAAS 27; CANR 70; SATA-
Brief 52

Howe, Irving 1920-1993 .... CLC 85
See also CA 9-12R; 141; CANR 21, 50; DLB
67; MTCW 1

Howe, Julia Ward 1819-1910 .... TCLC 21
See also CA 117; DLB 1, 189

Howe, Susan 1937- .... CLC 72
See also CA 160; DLB 120

Howe, Tina 1937- .... CLC 48
See also CA 109

Howell, James 1594(?)-1666 .... LC 13
See also DLB 151

Howell, W. D.
See Howells, William Dean

Howells, William D.
See Howells, William Dean

Howells, William Dean 1837-1920TCLC 7, 17,
41
See also CA 104; 134; CDALB 1865-1917;
DLB 12, 64, 74, 79, 189

Howes, Barbara 1914-1996 .... CLC 15
See also CA 9-12R; 151; CAAS 3; CANR 53;
SATA 5

Hrabal, Bohumil 1914-1997 .... CLC 13, 67
See also CA 106; 156; CAAS 12; CANR 57

Hroswitha of Gandersheim c. 935-c. 1002
CMLC 29
See also DLB 148

Hsun, Lu
See Lu Hsun

Hubbard, L(afayette) Ron(ald) 1911-1986
CLC 43; DAM POP
See also CA 77-80; 118; CANR 52

Huch, Ricarda (Octavia) 1864-1947TCLC 13
See also CA 111; DLB 66

Huddle, David 1942-........................... CLC 49
See also CA 57-60; CAAS 20; DLB 130

Hudson, Jeffrey
See Crichton, (John) Michael

Hudson, W(illiam) H(enry) 1841-1922T C L C 29
See also CA 115; DLB 98, 153, 174; SATA 35

Hueffer, Ford Madox
See Ford, Ford Madox

Hughart, Barry 1934- .... CLC 39
See also CA 137

Hughes, Colin
See Creasey, John

Hughes, David (John) 1930-............. CLC 48
See also CA 116; 129; DLB 14

Hughes, Edward James
See Hughes, Ted
See also DAM MST, POET

Hughes, (James) Langston 1902-1967CLC 1,
5, 10, 15, 35, 44, 108; BLC 2; DA; DAB;
DAC; DAM DRAM, MST, MULT, POET;
DC 3; PC 1; SSC 6; WLC
See also AAYA 12; BW 1; CA 1-4R; 25-28R;
CANR 1, 34; CDALB 1929-1941; CLR 17;
DLB 4, 7, 48, 51, 86; JRDA; MAICYA;
MTCW 1; SATA 4, 33

Hughes, Richard (Arthur Warren) 1900-1976
CLC 1, 11; DAM NOV
See also CA 5-8R; 65-68; CANR 4; DLB 15,
161; MTCW 1; SATA 8; SATA-Obit 25

Hughes, Ted 1930-1998 . CLC 2, 4, 9, 14, 37;
DAB; DAC; PC 7
See also Hughes, Edward James
See also CA 1-4R; 171; CANR 1, 33, 66; CLR
3; DLB 40, 161; MAICYA; MTCW 1; SATA
49; SATA-Brief 27

Hugo, Richard F(ranklin) 1923-1982 CLC 6,
18, 32; DAM POET
See also CA 49-52; 108; CANR 3; DLB 5, 206

Hugo, Victor (Marie) 1802-1885NCLC 3, 10,
21; DA; DAB; DAC; DAM DRAM, MST,
NOV, POET; PC 17; WLC
See also DLB 119, 192; SATA 47

Huidobro, Vicente
See Huidobro Fernandez, Vicente Garcia

Huidobro Fernandez, Vicente Garcia 1893-
1948 .... TCLC 31
See also CA 131; HW

Hulme, Keri 1947- .... CLC 39
See also CA 125; CANR 69; INT 125

Hulme, T(homas) E(rnest) 1883-1917 T C L C 21
See also CA 117; DLB 19

Hume, David 1711-1776 .... LC 7
See also DLB 104

Humphrey, William 1924-1997 .... CLC 45
See also CA 77-80; 160; CANR 68; DLB 6

Humphreys, Emyr Owen 1919-......... CLC 47
See also CA 5-8R; CANR 3, 24; DLB 15

Humphreys, Josephine 1945- ..... CLC 34, 57
See also CA 121; 127; INT 127

Huneker, James Gibbons 1857-1921TCLC 65
See also DLB 71

Hungerford, Pixie
See Brinsmead, H(esba) F(ay)

Jorgensen, Ivar
    See Ellison, Harlan (Jay)
Jorgenson, Ivar
    See Silverberg, Robert
Josephus, Flavius c. 37-100 .... **CMLC 13**
Josipovici, Gabriel 1940- .... **CLC 6, 43**
    See also CA 37-40R; CAAS 8; CANR 47; DLB
        14
Joubert, Joseph 1754-1824 .... **NCLC 9**
Jouve, Pierre Jean 1887-1976 .... **CLC 47**
    See also CA 65-68
Jovine, Francesco 1902-1950 .... **TCLC 79**
Joyce, James (Augustine Aloysius) 1882-1941
        **TCLC 3, 8, 16, 35, 52; DA; DAB; DAC;
        DAM MST, NOV, POET; PC 22; SSC 3,
        26; WLC**
    See also CA 104; 126; CDBLB 1914-1945;
        DLB 10, 19, 36, 162; MTCW 1
Jozsef, Attila 1905-1937 .... **TCLC 22**
    See also CA 116
Juana Ines de la Cruz 1651(?)-1695**LC 5; PC
        24**
Judd, Cyril
    See Kornbluth, C(yril) M.; Pohl, Frederik
Julian of Norwich 1342(?)-1416(?) .... **LC 6**
    See also DLB 146
Junger, Sebastian 1962- .... **CLC 109**
    See also CA 165
Juniper, Alex
    See Hospital, Janette Turner
Junius
    See Luxemburg, Rosa
Just, Ward (Swift) 1935- .... **CLC 4, 27**
    See also CA 25-28R; CANR 32; INT CANR-
        32
Justice, Donald (Rodney) 1925- .. **CLC 6, 19,
        102; DAM POET**
    See also CA 5-8R; CANR 26, 54, 74; DLBY
        83; INT CANR-26
Juvenal .... **CMLC 8**
    See also Juvenalis, Decimus Junius
Juvenalis, Decimus Junius 55(?)-c. 127(?)
    See Juvenal
Juvenis
    See Bourne, Randolph S(illiman)
Kacew, Romain 1914-1980
    See Gary, Romain
    See also CA 108; 102
Kadare, Ismail 1936- .... **CLC 52**
    See also CA 161
Kadohata, Cynthia .... **CLC 59**
    See also CA 140
Kafka, Franz 1883-1924**TCLC 2, 6, 13, 29, 47,
        53; DA; DAB; DAC; DAM MST, NOV;
        SSC 5, 29; WLC**
    See also CA 105; 126; DLB 81; MTCW 1
Kahanovitsch, Pinkhes
    See Der Nister
Kahn, Roger 1927- .... **CLC 30**
    See also CA 25-28R; CANR 44, 69; DLB 171;
        SATA 37
Kain, Saul
    See Sassoon, Siegfried (Lorraine)
Kaiser, Georg 1878-1945 .... **TCLC 9**
    See also CA 106; DLB 124
Kaletski, Alexander 1946- .... **CLC 39**
    See also CA 118; 143
Kalidasa fl. c. 400- .... **CMLC 9; PC 22**
Kallman, Chester (Simon) 1921-1975 **CLC 2**
    See also CA 45-48; 53-56; CANR 3
Kaminsky, Melvin 1926-
    See Brooks, Mel
    See also CA 65-68; CANR 16
Kaminsky, Stuart M(elvin) 1934- ..... **CLC 59**
    See also CA 73-76; CANR 29, 53
Kane, Francis
    See Robbins, Harold

Kane, Paul
    See Simon, Paul (Frederick)
Kane, Wilson
    See Bloch, Robert (Albert)
Kanin, Garson 1912- .... **CLC 22**
    See also AITN 1; CA 5-8R; CANR 7; DLB 7
Kaniuk, Yoram 1930- .... **CLC 19**
    See also CA 134
Kant, Immanuel 1724-1804 ...... **NCLC 27, 67**
    See also DLB 94
Kantor, MacKinlay 1904-1977 .... **CLC 7**
    See also CA 61-64; 73-76; CANR 60, 63; DLB
        9, 102
Kaplan, David Michael 1946- .... **CLC 50**
Kaplan, James 1951- .... **CLC 59**
    See also CA 135
Karageorge, Michael
    See Anderson, Poul (William)
Karamzin, Nikolai Mikhailovich 1766-1826
        NCLC 3
    See also DLB 150
Karapanou, Margarita 1946- .... **CLC 13**
    See also CA 101
Karinthy, Frigyes 1887-1938 .... **TCLC 47**
    See also CA 170
Karl, Frederick R(obert) 1927- .... **CLC 34**
    See also CA 5-8R; CANR 3, 44
Kastel, Warren
    See Silverberg, Robert
Kataev, Evgeny Petrovich 1903-1942
    See Petrov, Evgeny
    See also CA 120
Kataphusin
    See Ruskin, John
Katz, Steve 1935- .... **CLC 47**
    See also CA 25-28R; CAAS 14, 64; CANR 12;
        DLBY 83
Kauffman, Janet 1945- .... **CLC 42**
    See also CA 117; CANR 43; DLBY 86
Kaufman, Bob (Garnell) 1925-1986 . **CLC 49**
    See also BW 1; CA 41-44R; 118; CANR 22;
        DLB 16, 41
Kaufman, George S. 1889-1961**CLC 38; DAM
        DRAM**
    See also CA 108; 93-96; DLB 7; INT 108
Kaufman, Sue .... **CLC 3, 8**
    See also Barondess, Sue K(aufman)
Kavafis, Konstantinos Petrou 1863-1933
    See Cavafy, C(onstantine) P(eter)
    See also CA 104
Kavan, Anna 1901-1968 .... **CLC 5, 13, 82**
    See also CA 5-8R; CANR 6, 57; MTCW 1
Kavanagh, Dan
    See Barnes, Julian (Patrick)
Kavanagh, Patrick (Joseph) 1904-1967 **C L C
        22**
    See also CA 123; 25-28R; DLB 15, 20; MTCW
        1
Kawabata, Yasunari 1899-1972 **CLC 2, 5, 9,
        18, 107; DAM MULT; SSC 17**
    See also CA 93-96; 33-36R; DLB 180
Kaye, M(ary) M(argaret) 1909- .... **CLC 28**
    See also CA 89-92; CANR 24, 60; MTCW 1;
        SATA 62
Kaye, Mollie
    See Kaye, M(ary) M(argaret)
Kaye-Smith, Sheila 1887-1956 .... **TCLC 20**
    See also CA 118; DLB 36
Kaymor, Patrice Maguilene
    See Senghor, Leopold Sedar
Kazan, Elia 1909- .... **CLC 6, 16, 63**
    See also CA 21-24R; CANR 32
Kazantzakis, Nikos 1883(?)-1957 **TCLC 2, 5,
        33**
    See also CA 105; 132; MTCW 1
Kazin, Alfred 1915- .... **CLC 34, 38**
    See also CA 1-4R; CAAS 7; CANR 1, 45; DLB

        67
Keane, Mary Nesta (Skrine) 1904-1996
    See Keane, Molly
    See also CA 108; 114; 151
Keane, Molly .... **CLC 31**
    See also Keane, Mary Nesta (Skrine)
    See also INT 114
Keates, Jonathan 1946(?)- .... **CLC 34**
    See also CA 163
Keaton, Buster 1895-1966 .... **CLC 20**
Keats, John 1795-1821**NCLC 8, 73; DA; DAB;
        DAC; DAM MST, POET; PC 1; WLC**
    See also CDBLB 1789-1832; DLB 96, 110
Keene, Donald 1922- .... **CLC 34**
    See also CA 1-4R; CANR 5
Keillor, Garrison .... **CLC 40, 115**
    See also Keillor, Gary (Edward)
    See also AAYA 2; BEST 89:3; DLBY 87; SATA
        58
Keillor, Gary (Edward) 1942-
    See Keillor, Garrison
    See also CA 111; 117; CANR 36, 59; DAM
        POP; MTCW 1
Keith, Michael
    See Hubbard, L(afayette) Ron(ald)
Keller, Gottfried 1819-1890**NCLC 2; SSC 26**
    See also DLB 129
Keller, Nora Okja .... **CLC 109**
Kellerman, Jonathan 1949- ... **CLC 44; DAM
        POP**
    See also BEST 90:1; CA 106; CANR 29, 51;
        INT CANR-29
Kelley, William Melvin 1937- .... **CLC 22**
    See also BW 1; CA 77-80; CANR 27; DLB 33
Kellogg, Marjorie 1922- .... **CLC 2**
    See also CA 81-84
Kellow, Kathleen
    See Hibbert, Eleanor Alice Burford
Kelly, M(ilton) T(erry) 1947- .... **CLC 55**
    See also CA 97-100; CAAS 22; CANR 19, 43
Kelman, James 1946- .... **CLC 58, 86**
    See also CA 148; DLB 194
Kemal, Yashar 1923- .... **CLC 14, 29**
    See also CA 89-92; CANR 44
Kemble, Fanny 1809-1893 .... **NCLC 18**
    See also DLB 32
Kemelman, Harry 1908-1996 .... **CLC 2**
    See also AITN 1; CA 9-12R; 155; CANR 6, 71;
        DLB 28
Kempe, Margery 1373(?)-1440(?) .... **LC 6**
    See also DLB 146
Kempis, Thomas a 1380-1471 .... **LC 11**
Kendall, Henry 1839-1882 .... **NCLC 12**
Keneally, Thomas (Michael) 1935- **CLC 5, 8,
        10, 14, 19, 27, 43, 117; DAM NOV**
    See also CA 85-88; CANR 10, 50, 74; MTCW
        1
Kennedy, Adrienne (Lita) 1931-**CLC 66; BLC
        2; DAM MULT; DC 5**
    See also BW 2; CA 103; CAAS 20; CABS 3;
        CANR 26, 53; DLB 38
Kennedy, John Pendleton 1795-1870**NCLC 2**
    See also DLB 3
Kennedy, Joseph Charles 1929-
    See Kennedy, X. J.
    See also CA 1-4R; CANR 4, 30, 40; SATA 14,
        86
Kennedy, William 1928- .. **CLC 6, 28, 34, 53;
        DAM NOV**
    See also AAYA 1; CA 85-88; CANR 14, 31,
        76; DLB 143; DLBY 85; INT CANR-31;
        MTCW 1; SATA 57
Kennedy, X. J. .... **CLC 8, 42**
    See also Kennedy, Joseph Charles
    See also CAAS 9; CLR 27; DLB 5; SAAS 22
Kenny, Maurice (Francis) 1929- ..... **CLC 87;
        DAM MULT**

Kogawa, Joy Nozomi 1935-.. **CLC 78; DAC; DAM MST, MULT**
See also CA 101; CANR 19, 62; SATA 99

Kohout, Pavel 1928- .... **CLC 13**
See also CA 45-48; CANR 3

Koizumi, Yakumo
See Hearn, (Patricio) Lafcadio (Tessima Carlos)

Kolmar, Gertrud 1894-1943 .... **TCLC 40**
See also CA 167

Komunyakaa, Yusef 1947-**CLC 86, 94; BLCS**
See also CA 147; DLB 120

Konrad, George
See Konrad, Gyoergy

Konrad, Gyoergy 1933- .... **CLC 4, 10, 73**
See also CA 85-88

Konwicki, Tadeusz 1926- **CLC 8, 28, 54, 117**
See also CA 101; CAAS 9; CANR 39, 59;
MTCW 1

Koontz, Dean R(ay) 1945- ..... **CLC 78; DAM NOV, POP**
See also AAYA 9; BEST 89:3, 90:2; CA 108;
CANR 19, 36, 52; MTCW 1; SATA 92

Kopernik, Mikolaj
See Copernicus, Nicolaus

Kopit, Arthur (Lee) 1937-**CLC 1, 18, 33; DAM DRAM**
See also AITN 1; CA 81-84; CABS 3; DLB 7;
MTCW 1

Kops, Bernard 1926- .... **CLC 4**
See also CA 5-8R; DLB 13

Kornbluth, C(yril) M. 1923-1958 .... **TCLC 8**
See also CA 105; 160; DLB 8

Korolenko, V. G.
See Korolenko, Vladimir Galaktionovich

Korolenko, Vladimir
See Korolenko, Vladimir Galaktionovich

Korolenko, Vladimir G.
See Korolenko, Vladimir Galaktionovich

Korolenko, Vladimir Galaktionovich 1853-1921 .... **TCLC 22**
See also CA 121

Korzybski, Alfred (Habdank Skarbek) 1879-1950 .... **TCLC 61**
See also CA 123; 160

Kosinski, Jerzy (Nikodem) 1933-1991**CLC 1, 2, 3, 6, 10, 15, 53, 70; DAM NOV**
See also CA 17-20R; 134; CANR 9, 46; DLB 2; DLBY 82; MTCW 1

Kostelanetz, Richard (Cory) 1940- .. **CLC 28**
See also CA 13-16R; CAAS 8; CANR 38

Kostrowitzki, Wilhelm Apollinaris de 1880-1918
See Apollinaire, Guillaume
See also CA 104

Kotlowitz, Robert 1924- .... **CLC 4**
See also CA 33-36R; CANR 36

Kotzebue, August (Friedrich Ferdinand) von 1761-1819 ....
NCLC 25
See also DLB 94

Kotzwinkle, William 1938- ..... **CLC 5, 14, 35**
See also CA 45-48; CANR 3, 44; CLR 6; DLB 173; MAICYA; SATA 24, 70

Kowna, Stancy
See Szymborska, Wislawa

Kozol, Jonathan 1936- .... **CLC 17**
See also CA 61-64; CANR 16, 45

Kozoll, Michael 1940(?)- .... **CLC 35**

Kramer, Kathryn 19(?)- .... **CLC 34**

Kramer, Larry 1935-**CLC 42; DAM POP; DC 8**
See also CA 124; 126; CANR 60

Krasicki, Ignacy 1735-1801 .... **NCLC 8**

Krasinski, Zygmunt 1812-1859 .... **NCLC 4**

Kraus, Karl 1874-1936 .... **TCLC 5**
See also CA 104; DLB 118

Kreve (Mickevicius), Vincas 1882-1954**TCLC**
27
See also CA 170

Kristeva, Julia 1941- .... **CLC 77**
See also CA 154

Kristofferson, Kris 1936-..................... **CLC 26**
See also CA 104

Krizanc, John 1956- .... **CLC 57**

Krleza, Miroslav 1893-1981 .... **CLC 8, 114**
See also CA 97-100; 105; CANR 50; DLB 147

Kroetsch, Robert 1927-**CLC 5, 23, 57; DAC; DAM POET**
See also CA 17-20R; CANR 8, 38; DLB 53;
MTCW 1

Kroetz, Franz
See Kroetz, Franz Xaver

Kroetz, Franz Xaver 1946- .... **CLC 41**
See also CA 130

Kroker, Arthur (W.) 1945-................. **CLC 77**
See also CA 161

Kropotkin, Peter (Aleksieevich) 1842-1921
TCLC 36
See also CA 119

Krotkov, Yuri 1917- .... **CLC 19**
See also CA 102

Krumb
See Crumb, R(obert)

Krumgold, Joseph (Quincy) 1908-1980 **C L C 12**
See also CA 9-12R; 101; CANR 7; MAICYA;
SATA 1, 48; SATA-Obit 23

Krumwitz
See Crumb, R(obert)

Krutch, Joseph Wood 1893-1970 ...... **CLC 24**
See also CA 1-4R; 25-28R; CANR 4; DLB 63, 206

Krutzch, Gus
See Eliot, T(homas) S(tearns)

Krylov, Ivan Andreevich 1768(?)-1844**N C L C 1**
See also DLB 150

Kubin, Alfred (Leopold Isidor) 1877-1959
TCLC 23
See also CA 112; 149; DLB 81

Kubrick, Stanley 1928- .... **CLC 16**
See also CA 81-84; CANR 33; DLB 26

Kumin, Maxine (Winokur) 1925- **CLC 5, 13, 28; DAM POET; PC 15**
See also AITN 2; CA 1-4R; CAAS 8; CANR 1, 21, 69; DLB 5; MTCW 1; SATA 12

Kundera, Milan 1929- **CLC 4, 9, 19, 32, 68, 115; DAM NOV; SSC 24**
See also AAYA 2; CA 85-88; CANR 19, 52, 74; MTCW 1

Kunene, Mazisi (Raymond) 1930- .... **CLC 85**
See also BW 1; CA 125; DLB 117

Kunitz, Stanley (Jasspon) 1905-**CLC 6, 11, 14; PC 19**
See also CA 41-44R; CANR 26, 57; DLB 48;
INT CANR-26; MTCW 1

Kunze, Reiner 1933- .... **CLC 10**
See also CA 93-96; DLB 75

Kuprin, Aleksandr Ivanovich 1870-1938
TCLC 5
See also CA 104

Kureishi, Hanif 1954(?)- .... **CLC 64**
See also CA 139; DLB 194

Kurosawa, Akira 1910-1998 . **CLC 16; DAM MULT**
See also AAYA 11; CA 101; 170; CANR 46

Kushner, Tony 1957(?)-**CLC 81; DAM DRAM; DC 10**
See also CA 144; CANR 74

Kuttner, Henry 1915-1958 .... **TCLC 10**
See also Vance, Jack
See also CA 107; 157; DLB 8

Kuzma, Greg 1944-............................ **CLC 7**
See also CA 33-36R; CANR 70

Kuzmin, Mikhail 1872(?)-1936 ...... **TCLC 40**
See also CA 170

Kyd, Thomas 1558-1594**LC 22; DAM DRAM; DC 3**
See also DLB 62

Kyprianos, Iossif
See Samarakis, Antonis

La Bruyere, Jean de 1645-1696 .... **LC 17**

Lacan, Jacques (Marie Emile) 1901-1981
CLC 75
See also CA 121; 104

Laclos, Pierre Ambroise Francois Choderlos de 1741-1803 .... **NCLC 4**

Lacolere, Francois
See Aragon, Louis

La Colere, Francois
See Aragon, Louis

La Deshabilleuse
See Simenon, Georges (Jacques Christian)

Lady Gregory
See Gregory, Isabella Augusta (Persse)

Lady of Quality, A
See Bagnold, Enid

La Fayette, Marie (Madelaine Pioche de la Vergne Comtes 1634-1693 .... **LC 2**

Lafayette, Rene
See Hubbard, L(afayette) Ron(ald)

Laforgue, Jules 1860-1887**NCLC 5, 53; PC 14; SSC 20**

Lagerkvist, Paer (Fabian) 1891-1974 **CLC 7, 10, 13, 54; DAM DRAM, NOV**
See also Lagerkvist, Par
See also CA 85-88; 49-52; MTCW 1

Lagerkvist, Par .... **SSC 12**
See also Lagerkvist, Paer (Fabian)

Lagerloef, Selma (Ottiliana Lovisa) 1858-1940
TCLC 4, 36
See also Lagerlof, Selma (Ottiliana Lovisa)
See also CA 108; SATA 15

Lagerlof, Selma (Ottiliana Lovisa)
See Lagerloef, Selma (Ottiliana Lovisa)
See also CLR 7; SATA 15

La Guma, (Justin) Alex(ander) 1925-1985
CLC 19; BLCS; DAM NOV
See also BW 1; CA 49-52; 118; CANR 25; DLB 117; MTCW 1

Laidlaw, A. K.
See Grieve, C(hristopher) M(urray)

Lainez, Manuel Mujica
See Mujica Lainez, Manuel
See also HW

Laing, R(onald) D(avid) 1927-1989 . **CLC 95**
See also CA 107; 129; CANR 34; MTCW 1

Lamartine, Alphonse (Marie Louis Prat) de 1790-1869 ....
NCLC 11; DAM POET; PC 16

Lamb, Charles 1775-1834 ..... **NCLC 10; DA; DAB; DAC; DAM MST; WLC**
See also CDBLB 1789-1832; DLB 93, 107, 163;
SATA 17

Lamb, Lady Caroline 1785-1828 ... **NCLC 38**
See also DLB 116

Lamming, George (William) 1927- **CLC 2, 4, 66; BLC 2; DAM MULT**
See also BW 2; CA 85-88; CANR 26, 76; DLB 125; MTCW 1

L'Amour, Louis (Dearborn) 1908-1988 **C L C 25, 55; DAM NOV, POP**
See also AAYA 16; AITN 2; BEST 89:2; CA 1-4R; 125; CANR 3, 25, 40; DLB 207; DLBY 80; MTCW 1

Lampedusa, Giuseppe (Tomasi) di 1896-1957
TCLC 13
See also Tomasi di Lampedusa, Giuseppe
See also CA 164; DLB 177

Lampman, Archibald 1861-1899 ... **NCLC 25**
See also DLB 92

Lee, Shelton Jackson 1957(?)- .... **CLC 105;**
BLCS; DAM MULT
See also Lee, Spike
See also BW 2; CA 125; CANR 42
Lee, Spike
See Lee, Shelton Jackson
See also AAYA 4
Lee, Stan 1922- .... **CLC 17**
See also AAYA 5; CA 108; 111; INT 111
Lee, Tanith 1947- .... **CLC 46**
See also AAYA 15; CA 37-40R; CANR 53;
SATA 8, 88
Lee, Vernon .... **TCLC 5; SSC 33**
See also Paget, Violet
See also DLB 57, 153, 156, 174, 178
Lee, William
See Burroughs, William S(eward)
Lee, Willy
See Burroughs, William S(eward)
Lee-Hamilton, Eugene (Jacob) 1845-1907
TCLC 22
See also CA 117
Leet, Judith 1935- .... **CLC 11**
Le Fanu, Joseph Sheridan 1814-1873NCLC 9,
58; DAM POP; SSC 14
See also DLB 21, 70, 159, 178
Leffland, Ella 1931- .... **CLC 19**
See also CA 29-32R; CANR 35; DLBY 84; INT
CANR-35; SATA 65
Leger, Alexis
See Leger, (Marie-Rene Auguste) Alexis Saint-
Leger
Leger, (Marie-Rene Auguste) Alexis Saint-
Leger 1887-1975 . **CLC 4, 11, 46; DAM**
POET; PC 23
See also CA 13-16R; 61-64; CANR 43; MTCW
1
Leger, Saintleger
See Leger, (Marie-Rene Auguste) Alexis Saint-
Leger
Le Guin, Ursula K(roeber) 1929- **CLC 8, 13,**
22, 45, 71; DAB; DAC; DAM MST, POP;
SSC 12
See also AAYA 9, 27; AITN 1; CA 21-24R;
CANR 9, 32, 52, 74; CDALB 1968-1988;
CLR 3, 28; DLB 8, 52; INT CANR-32;
JRDA; MAICYA; MTCW 1; SATA 4, 52, 99
Lehmann, Rosamond (Nina) 1901-1990CLC 5
See also CA 77-80; 131; CANR 8, 73; DLB 15
Leiber, Fritz (Reuter, Jr.) 1910-1992 CLC 25
See also CA 45-48; 139; CANR 2, 40; DLB 8;
MTCW 1; SATA 45; SATA-Obit 73
Leibniz, Gottfried Wilhelm von 1646-1716LC
35
See also DLB 168
Leimbach, Martha 1963-
See Leimbach, Marti
See also CA 130
Leimbach, Marti .... **CLC 65**
See also Leimbach, Martha
Leino, Eino .... **TCLC 24**
See also Loennbohm, Armas Eino Leopold
Leiris, Michel (Julien) 1901-1990 ..... **CLC 61**
See also CA 119; 128; 132
Leithauser, Brad 1953- .... **CLC 27**
See also CA 107; CANR 27; DLB 120
Lelchuk, Alan 1938- .... **CLC 5**
See also CA 45-48; CAAS 20; CANR 1, 70
Lem, Stanislaw 1921- .... **CLC 8, 15, 40**
See also CA 105; CAAS 1; CANR 32; MTCW
1
Lemann, Nancy 1956- .... **CLC 39**
See also CA 118; 136
Lemonnier, (Antoine Louis) Camille 1844-1913
TCLC 22
See also CA 121
Lenau, Nikolaus 1802-1850 .... **NCLC 16**

L'Engle, Madeleine (Camp Franklin) 1918-
CLC 12; DAM POP
See also AAYA 1; AITN 2; CA 1-4R; CANR 3,
21, 39, 66; CLR 1, 14; DLB 52; JRDA;
MAICYA; MTCW 1; SAAS 15; SATA 1, 27,
75
Lengyel, Jozsef 1896-1975 .... **CLC 7**
See also CA 85-88; 57-60; CANR 71
Lenin 1870-1924
See Lenin, V. I.
See also CA 121; 168
Lenin, V. I. .... **TCLC 67**
See also Lenin
Lennon, John (Ono) 1940-1980 . **CLC 12, 35**
See also CA 102
Lennox, Charlotte Ramsay 1729(?)-1804
NCLC 23
See also DLB 39
Lentricchia, Frank (Jr.) 1940- .... **CLC 34**
See also CA 25-28R; CANR 19
Lenz, Siegfried 1926- .... **CLC 27; SSC 33**
See also CA 89-92; DLB 75
Leonard, Elmore (John, Jr.) 1925-CLC 28, 34,
71; DAM POP
See also AAYA 22; AITN 1; BEST 89:1, 90:4;
CA 81-84; CANR 12, 28, 53, 76; DLB 173;
INT CANR-28; MTCW 1
Leonard, Hugh .... **CLC 19**
See also Byrne, John Keyes
See also DLB 13
Leonov, Leonid (Maximovich) 1899-1994
CLC 92; DAM NOV
See also CA 129; CANR 74, 76; MTCW 1
Leopardi, (Conte) Giacomo 1798-1837N C L C
22
Le Reveler
See Artaud, Antonin (Marie Joseph)
Lerman, Eleanor 1952- .... **CLC 9**
See also CA 85-88; CANR 69
Lerman, Rhoda 1936- .... **CLC 56**
See also CA 49-52; CANR 70
Lermontov, Mikhail Yuryevich 1814-1841
NCLC 47; PC 18
See also DLB 205
Leroux, Gaston 1868-1927 .... **TCLC 25**
See also CA 108; 136; CANR 69; SATA 65
Lesage, Alain-Rene 1668-1747 .... **LC 2, 28**
Leskov, Nikolai (Semyonovich) 1831-1895
NCLC 25
Lessing, Doris (May) 1919-CLC 1, 2, 3, 6, 10,
15, 22, 40, 94; DA; DAB; DAC; DAM MST,
NOV; SSC 6; WLCS
See also CA 9-12R; CAAS 14; CANR 33, 54,
76; CDBLB 1960 to Present; DLB 15, 139;
DLBY 85; MTCW 1
Lessing, Gotthold Ephraim 1729-1781 . **LC 8**
See also DLB 97
Lester, Richard 1932- .... **CLC 20**
Lever, Charles (James) 1806-1872 **NCLC 23**
See also DLB 21
Leverson, Ada 1865(?)-1936(?) ...... **TCLC 18**
See also Elaine
See also CA 117; DLB 153
Levertov, Denise 1923-1997CLC 1, 2, 3, 5, 8,
15, 28, 66; DAM POET; PC 11
See also CA 1-4R; 163; CAAS 19; CANR 3,
29, 50; DLB 5, 165; INT CANR-29; MTCW
1
Levi, Jonathan .... **CLC 76**
Levi, Peter (Chad Tigar) 1931- .... **CLC 41**
See also CA 5-8R; CANR 34; DLB 40
Levi, Primo 1919-1987 . **CLC 37, 50; SSC 12**
See also CA 13-16R; 122; CANR 12, 33, 61,
70; DLB 177; MTCW 1
Levin, Ira 1929- .... **CLC 3, 6; DAM POP**
See also CA 21-24R; CANR 17, 44, 74; MTCW
1; SATA 66

Levin, Meyer 1905-1981 . **CLC 7; DAM POP**
See also AITN 1; CA 9-12R; 104; CANR 15;
DLB 9, 28; DLBY 81; SATA 21; SATA-Obit
27
Levine, Norman 1924- .... **CLC 54**
See also CA 73-76; CAAS 23; CANR 14, 70;
DLB 88
Levine, Philip 1928-CLC 2, 4, 5, 9, 14, 33, 118;
DAM POET; PC 22
See also CA 9-12R; CANR 9, 37, 52; DLB 5
Levinson, Deirdre 1931- .... **CLC 49**
See also CA 73-76; CANR 70
Levi-Strauss, Claude 1908- .... **CLC 38**
See also CA 1-4R; CANR 6, 32, 57; MTCW 1
Levitin, Sonia (Wolff) 1934- .... **CLC 17**
See also AAYA 13; CA 29-32R; CANR 14, 32;
CLR 53; JRDA; MAICYA; SAAS 2; SATA
4, 68
Levon, O. U.
See Kesey, Ken (Elton)
Levy, Amy 1861-1889 .... **NCLC 59**
See also DLB 156
Lewes, George Henry 1817-1878 ... **NCLC 25**
See also DLB 55, 144
Lewis, Alun 1915-1944 .... **TCLC 3**
See also CA 104; DLB 20, 162
Lewis, C. Day
See Day Lewis, C(ecil)
Lewis, C(live) S(taples) 1898-1963CLC 1, 3, 6,
14, 27; DA; DAB; DAC; DAM MST, NOV,
POP; WLC
See also AAYA 3; CA 81-84; CANR 33, 71;
CDBLB 1945-1960; CLR 3, 27; DLB 15,
100, 160; JRDA; MAICYA; MTCW 1; SATA
13, 100
Lewis, Janet 1899-1998 .... **CLC 41**
See also Winters, Janet Lewis
See also CA 9-12R; 172; CANR 29, 63; CAP
1; DLBY 87
Lewis, Matthew Gregory 1775-1818NCLC 11,
62
See also DLB 39, 158, 178
Lewis, (Harry) Sinclair 1885-1951 . **TCLC 4,**
13, 23, 39; DA; DAB; DAC; DAM MST,
NOV; WLC
See also CA 104; 133; CDALB 1917-1929;
DLB 9, 102; DLBD 1; MTCW 1
Lewis, (Percy) Wyndham 1882(?)-1957TCLC
2, 9
See also CA 104; 157; DLB 15
Lewisohn, Ludwig 1883-1955 .... **TCLC 19**
See also CA 107; DLB 4, 9, 28, 102
Lewton, Val 1904-1951 .... **TCLC 76**
Leyner, Mark 1956- .... **CLC 92**
See also CA 110; CANR 28, 53
Lezama Lima, Jose 1910-1976CLC 4, 10, 101;
DAM MULT
See also CA 77-80; CANR 71; DLB 113; HW
L'Heureux, John (Clarke) 1934- .... **CLC 52**
See also CA 13-16R; CANR 23, 45
Liddell, C. H.
See Kuttner, Henry
Lie, Jonas (Lauritz Idemil) 1833-1908(?)
TCLC 5
See also CA 115
Lieber, Joel 1937-1971 .... **CLC 6**
See also CA 73-76; 29-32R
Lieber, Stanley Martin
See Lee, Stan
Lieberman, Laurence (James) 1935- CLC 4,
36
See also CA 17-20R; CANR 8, 36
Lieh Tzu fl. 7th cent. B.C.-5th cent. B.C.
CMLC 27
Lieksman, Anders
See Haavikko, Paavo Juhani
Li Fei-kan 1904-

Martineau, Harriet 1802-1876 .... **NCLC 26**
See also DLB 21, 55, 159, 163, 166, 190; YABC 2

Martines, Julia
See O'Faolain, Julia

Martinez, Enrique Gonzalez
See Gonzalez Martinez, Enrique

Martinez, Jacinto Benavente y
See Benavente (y Martinez), Jacinto

Martinez Ruiz, Jose 1873-1967
See Azorin; Ruiz, Jose Martinez
See also CA 93-96; HW

Martinez Sierra, Gregorio 1881-1947**TCLC 6**
See also CA 115

Martinez Sierra, Maria (de la O'LeJarraga) 1874-1974 ....
TCLC 6
See also CA 115

Martinsen, Martin
See Follett, Ken(neth Martin)

Martinson, Harry (Edmund) 1904-1978**C L C 14**
See also CA 77-80; CANR 34

Marut, Ret
See Traven, B.

Marut, Robert
See Traven, B.

Marvell, Andrew 1621-1678 ... **LC 4, 43; DA; DAB; DAC; DAM MST, POET; PC 10; WLC**
See also CDBLB 1660-1789; DLB 131

Marx, Karl (Heinrich) 1818-1883 . **NCLC 17**
See also DLB 129

Masaoka Shiki .... **TCLC 18**
See also Masaoka Tsunenori

Masaoka Tsunenori 1867-1902
See Masaoka Shiki
See also CA 117

Masefield, John (Edward) 1878-1967**CLC 11, 47; DAM POET**
See also CA 19-20; 25-28R; CANR 33; CAP 2; CDBLB 1890-1914; DLB 10, 19, 153, 160; MTCW 1; SATA 19

Maso, Carole 19(?)- .... **CLC 44**
See also CA 170

Mason, Bobbie Ann 1940-**CLC 28, 43, 82; SSC 4**
See also AAYA 5; CA 53-56; CANR 11, 31, 58; DLB 173; DLBY 87; INT CANR-31; MTCW 1

Mason, Ernst
See Pohl, Frederik

Mason, Lee W.
See Malzberg, Barry N(athaniel)

Mason, Nick 1945- .... **CLC 35**

Mason, Tally
See Derleth, August (William)

Mass, William
See Gibson, William

Master Lao
See Lao Tzu

Masters, Edgar Lee 1868-1950 **TCLC 2, 25; DA; DAC; DAM MST, POET; PC 1; WLCS**
See also CA 104; 133; CDALB 1865-1917; DLB 54; MTCW 1

Masters, Hilary 1928- .... **CLC 48**
See also CA 25-28R; CANR 13, 47

Mastrosimone, William 19(?)- .... **CLC 36**

Mathe, Albert
See Camus, Albert

Mather, Cotton 1663-1728 .... **LC 38**
See also CDALB 1640-1865; DLB 24, 30, 140

Mather, Increase 1639-1723 .... **LC 38**
See also DLB 24

Matheson, Richard Burton 1926- ..... **CLC 37**
See also CA 97-100; DLB 8, 44; INT 97-100

Mathews, Harry 1930- .... **CLC 6, 52**
See also CA 21-24R; CAAS 6; CANR 18, 40

Mathews, John Joseph 1894-1979 .. **CLC 84; DAM MULT**
See also CA 19-20; 142; CANR 45; CAP 2; DLB 175; NNAL

Mathias, Roland (Glyn) 1915- .... **CLC 45**
See also CA 97-100; CANR 19, 41; DLB 27

Matsuo Basho 1644-1694 .... **PC 3**
See also DAM POET

Mattheson, Rodney
See Creasey, John

Matthews, Greg 1949- .... **CLC 45**
See also CA 135

Matthews, William (Procter, III) 1942-1997 **CLC 40**
See also CA 29-32R; 162; CAAS 18; CANR 12, 57; DLB 5

Matthias, John (Edward) 1941- .... **CLC 9**
See also CA 33-36R; CANR 56

Matthiessen, Peter 1927-**CLC 5, 7, 11, 32, 64; DAM NOV**
See also AAYA 6; BEST 90:4; CA 9-12R; CANR 21, 50, 73; DLB 6, 173; MTCW 1; SATA 27

Maturin, Charles Robert 1780(?)-1824**NCLC 6**
See also DLB 178

Matute (Ausejo), Ana Maria 1925- .. **CLC 11**
See also CA 89-92; MTCW 1

Maugham, W. S.
See Maugham, W(illiam) Somerset

Maugham, W(illiam) Somerset 1874-1965 **CLC 1, 11, 15, 67, 93; DA; DAB; DAC; DAM DRAM, MST, NOV; SSC 8; WLC**
See also CA 5-8R; 25-28R; CANR 40; CDBLB 1914-1945; DLB 10, 36, 77, 100, 162, 195; MTCW 1; SATA 54

Maugham, William Somerset
See Maugham, W(illiam) Somerset

Maupassant, (Henri Rene Albert) Guy de 1850-1893 ....
NCLC 1, 42; DA; DAB; DAC; DAM MST; SSC 1; WLC
See also DLB 123

Maupin, Armistead 1944-**CLC 95; DAM POP**
See also CA 125; 130; CANR 58; INT 130

Maurhut, Richard
See Traven, B.

Mauriac, Claude 1914-1996 .... **CLC 9**
See also CA 89-92; 152; DLB 83

Mauriac, Francois (Charles) 1885-1970**C L C 4, 9, 56; SSC 24**
See also CA 25-28; CAP 2; DLB 65; MTCW 1

Mavor, Osborne Henry 1888-1951
See Bridie, James
See also CA 104

Maxwell, William (Keepers, Jr.) 1908-**CLC 19**
See also CA 93-96; CANR 54; DLBY 80; INT 93-96

May, Elaine 1932- .... **CLC 16**
See also CA 124; 142; DLB 44

Mayakovski, Vladimir (Vladimirovich) 1893-1930 .... **TCLC 4, 18**
See also CA 104; 158

Mayhew, Henry 1812-1887 .... **NCLC 31**
See also DLB 18, 55, 190

Mayle, Peter 1939(?)- .... **CLC 89**
See also CA 139; CANR 64

Maynard, Joyce 1953- .... **CLC 23**
See also CA 111; 129; CANR 64

Mayne, William (James Carter) 1928-**CLC 12**
See also AAYA 20; CA 9-12R; CANR 37; CLR 25; JRDA; MAICYA; SAAS 11; SATA 6, 68

Mayo, Jim
See L'Amour, Louis (Dearborn)

Maysles, Albert 1926- .... **CLC 16**
See also CA 29-32R

Maysles, David 1932- .... **CLC 16**

Mazer, Norma Fox 1931- .... **CLC 26**
See also AAYA 5; CA 69-72; CANR 12, 32, 66; CLR 23; JRDA; MAICYA; SAAS 1; SATA 24, 67, 105

Mazzini, Guiseppe 1805-1872 .... **NCLC 34**

McAuley, James Phillip 1917-1976 .. **CLC 45**
See also CA 97-100

McBain, Ed
See Hunter, Evan

McBrien, William Augustine 1930- .. **CLC 44**
See also CA 107

McCaffrey, Anne (Inez) 1926-**CLC 17; DAM NOV, POP**
See also AAYA 6; AITN 2; BEST 89:2; CA 25-28R; CANR 15, 35, 55; CLR 49; DLB 8; JRDA; MAICYA; MTCW 1; SAAS 11; SATA 8, 70

McCall, Nathan 1955(?)- .... **CLC 86**
See also CA 146

McCann, Arthur
See Campbell, John W(ood, Jr.)

McCann, Edson
See Pohl, Frederik

McCarthy, Charles, Jr. 1933-
See McCarthy, Cormac
See also CANR 42, 69; DAM POP

McCarthy, Cormac 1933- **CLC 4, 57, 59, 101**
See also McCarthy, Charles, Jr.
See also DLB 6, 143

McCarthy, Mary (Therese) 1912-1989**CLC 1, 3, 5, 14, 24, 39, 59; SSC 24**
See also CA 5-8R; 129; CANR 16, 50, 64; DLB 2; DLBY 81; INT CANR-16; MTCW 1

McCartney, (James) Paul 1942- **CLC 12, 35**
See also CA 146

McCauley, Stephen (D.) 1955- .... **CLC 50**
See also CA 141

McClure, Michael (Thomas) 1932-**CLC 6, 10**
See also CA 21-24R; CANR 17, 46; DLB 16

McCorkle, Jill (Collins) 1958- .... **CLC 51**
See also CA 121; DLBY 87

McCourt, Frank 1930- .... **CLC 109**
See also CA 157

McCourt, James 1941- .... **CLC 5**
See also CA 57-60

McCoy, Horace (Stanley) 1897-1955**TCLC 28**
See also CA 108; 155; DLB 9

McCrae, John 1872-1918 .... **TCLC 12**
See also CA 109; DLB 92

McCreigh, James
See Pohl, Frederik

McCullers, (Lula) Carson (Smith) 1917-1967 **CLC 1, 4, 10, 12, 48, 100; DA; DAB; DAC; DAM MST, NOV; SSC 9, 24; WLC**
See also AAYA 21; CA 5-8R; 25-28R; CABS 1, 3; CANR 18; CDALB 1941-1968; DLB 2, 7, 173; MTCW 1; SATA 27

McCulloch, John Tyler
See Burroughs, Edgar Rice

McCullough, Colleen 1938(?)- **CLC 27, 107; DAM NOV, POP**
See also CA 81-84; CANR 17, 46, 67; MTCW 1

McDermott, Alice 1953- ....: **CLC 90**
See also CA 109; CANR 40

McElroy, Joseph 1930- .... **CLC 5, 47**
See also CA 17-20R

McEwan, Ian (Russell) 1948- .... **CLC 13, 66; DAM NOV**
See also BEST 90:4; CA 61-64; CANR 14, 41, 69; DLB 14, 194; MTCW 1

McFadden, David 1940- .... **CLC 48**
See also CA 104; DLB 60; INT 104

McFarland, Dennis 1950- .... **CLC 65**
See also CA 165

See Chekhov, Anton (Pavlovich)
Myers, L(eopold) H(amilton) 1881-1944
TCLC 59
See also CA 157; DLB 15
Myers, Walter Dean 1937-. **CLC 35; BLC 3;
DAM MULT, NOV**
See also AAYA 4, 23; BW 2; CA 33-36R;
CANR 20, 42, 67; CLR 4, 16, 35; DLB 33;
INT CANR-20; JRDA; MAICYA; SAAS 2;
SATA 41, 71; SATA-Brief 27
Myers, Walter M.
See Myers, Walter Dean
Myles, Symon
See Follett, Ken(neth Martin)
Nabokov, Vladimir (Vladimirovich) 1899-1977
**CLC 1, 2, 3, 6, 8, 11, 15, 23, 44, 46, 64;
DA; DAB; DAC; DAM MST, NOV; SSC
11; WLC**
See also CA 5-8R; 69-72; CANR 20; CDALB
1941-1968; DLB 2; DLBD 3; DLBY 80, 91;
MTCW 1
Nagai Kafu 1879-1959 .... **TCLC 51**
See also Nagai Sokichi
See also DLB 180
Nagai Sokichi 1879-1959
See Nagai Kafu
See also CA 117
Nagy, Laszlo 1925-1978 .... **CLC 7**
See also CA 129; 112
Naidu, Sarojini 1879-1943 .... **TCLC 80**
Naipaul, Shiva(dhar Srinivasa) 1945-1985
CLC 32, 39; DAM NOV
See also CA 110; 112; 116; CANR 33; DLB
157; DLBY 85; MTCW 1
Naipaul, V(idiadhar) S(urajprasad) 1932-
**CLC 4, 7, 9, 13, 18, 37, 105; DAB; DAC;
DAM MST, NOV**
See also CA 1-4R; CANR 1, 33, 51; CDBLB
1960 to Present; DLB 125, 204, 206; DLBY
85; MTCW 1
Nakos, Lilika 1899(?)- .... **CLC 29**
Narayan, R(asipuram) K(rishnaswami) 1906-
CLC 7, 28, 47; DAM NOV; SSC 25
See also CA 81-84; CANR 33, 61; MTCW 1;
SATA 62
Nash, (Frediric) Ogden 1902-1971 . **CLC 23;
DAM POET; PC 21**
See also CA 13-14; 29-32R; CANR 34, 61; CAP
1; DLB 11; MAICYA; MTCW 1; SATA 2,
46
Nashe, Thomas 1567-1601(?) .... **LC 41**
See also DLB 167
Nashe, Thomas 1567-1601 .... **LC 41**
Nathan, Daniel
See Dannay, Frederic
Nathan, George Jean 1882-1958 ... **TCLC 18**
See also Hatteras, Owen
See also CA 114; 169; DLB 137
Natsume, Kinnosuke 1867-1916
See Natsume, Soseki
See also CA 104
Natsume, Soseki 1867-1916 .... **TCLC 2, 10**
See also Natsume, Kinnosuke
See also DLB 180
Natti, (Mary) Lee 1919-
See Kingman, Lee
See also CA 5-8R; CANR 2
Naylor, Gloria 1950-**CLC 28, 52; BLC 3; DA;
DAC; DAM MST, MULT, NOV, POP;
WLCS**
See also AAYA 6; BW 2; CA 107; CANR 27,
51, 74; DLB 173; MTCW 1
Neihardt, John Gneisenau 1881-1973**CLC 32**
See also CA 13-14; CANR 65; CAP 1; DLB 9,
54
Nekrasov, Nikolai Alekseevich 1821-1878
NCLC 11

Nelligan, Emile 1879-1941 .... **TCLC 14**
See also CA 114; DLB 92
Nelson, Willie 1933- .... **CLC 17**
See also CA 107
Nemerov, Howard (Stanley) 1920-1991**CLC 2,
6, 9, 36; DAM POET; PC 24**
See also CA 1-4R; 134; CABS 2; CANR 1, 27,
53; DLB 5, 6; DLBY 83; INT CANR-27;
MTCW 1
Neruda, Pablo 1904-1973**CLC 1, 2, 5, 7, 9, 28,
62; DA; DAB; DAC; DAM MST, MULT,
POET; HLC; PC 4; WLC**
See also CA 19-20; 45-48; CAP 2; HW; MTCW
1
Nerval, Gerard de 1808-1855**NCLC 1, 67; PC
13; SSC 18**
Nervo, (Jose) Amado (Ruiz de) 1870-1919
TCLC 11
See also CA 109; 131; HW
Nessi, Pio Baroja y
See Baroja (y Nessi), Pio
Nestroy, Johann 1801-1862 .... **NCLC 42**
See also DLB 133
Netterville, Luke
See O'Grady, Standish (James)
Neufeld, John (Arthur) 1938- .... **CLC 17**
See also AAYA 11; CA 25-28R; CANR 11, 37,
56; CLR 52; MAICYA; SAAS 3; SATA 6,
81
Neville, Emily Cheney 1919- .... **CLC 12**
See also CA 5-8R; CANR 3, 37; JRDA;
MAICYA; SAAS 2; SATA 1
Newbound, Bernard Slade 1930-
See Slade, Bernard
See also CA 81-84; CANR 49; DAM DRAM
Newby, P(ercy) H(oward) 1918-1997 **CLC 2,
13; DAM NOV**
See also CA 5-8R; 161; CANR 32, 67; DLB
15; MTCW 1
Newlove, Donald 1928- .... **CLC 6**
See also CA 29-32R; CANR 25
Newlove, John (Herbert) 1938- .... **CLC 14**
See also CA 21-24R; CANR 9, 25
Newman, Charles 1938- .... **CLC 2, 8**
See also CA 21-24R
Newman, Edwin (Harold) 1919- .... **CLC 14**
See also AITN 1; CA 69-72; CANR 5
Newman, John Henry 1801-1890 .. **NCLC 38**
See also DLB 18, 32, 55
Newton, (Sir)Isaac 1642-1727 .... **LC 35**
Newton, Suzanne 1936- .... **CLC 35**
See also CA 41-44R; CANR 14; JRDA; SATA
5, 77
Nexo, Martin Andersen 1869-1954 **TCLC 43**
Nezval, Vitezslav 1900-1958 .... **TCLC 44**
See also CA 123
Ng, Fae Myenne 1957(?)- .... **CLC 81**
See also CA 146
Ngema, Mbongeni 1955- .... **CLC 57**
See also BW 2; CA 143
Ngugi, James T(hiong'o) .... **CLC 3, 7, 13**
See also Ngugi wa Thiong'o
Ngugi wa Thiong'o 1938- .. **CLC 36; BLC 3;
DAM MULT, NOV**
See also Ngugi, James T(hiong'o)
See also BW 2; CA 81-84; CANR 27, 58; DLB
125; MTCW 1
Nichol, B(arrie) P(hillip) 1944-1988 **CLC 18**
See also CA 53-56; DLB 53; SATA 66
Nichols, John (Treadwell) 1940- .... **CLC 38**
See also CA 9-12R; CAAS 2; CANR 6, 70;
DLBY 82
Nichols, Leigh
See Koontz, Dean R(ay)
Nichols, Peter (Richard) 1927-**CLC 5, 36, 65**
See also CA 104; CANR 33; DLB 13; MTCW
1

Nicolas, F. R. E.
See Freeling, Nicolas
Niedecker, Lorine 1903-1970 .... **CLC 10, 42;
DAM POET**
See also CA 25-28; CAP 2; DLB 48
Nietzsche, Friedrich (Wilhelm) 1844-1900
TCLC 10, 18, 55
See also CA 107; 121; DLB 129
Nievo, Ippolito 1831-1861 .... **NCLC 22**
Nightingale, Anne Redmon 1943-
See Redmon, Anne
See also CA 103
Nightingale, Florence 1820-1910 ... **TCLC 85**
See also DLB 166
Nik. T. O.
See Annensky, Innokenty (Fyodorovich)
Nin, Anais 1903-1977**CLC 1, 4, 8, 11, 14, 60;
DAM NOV, POP; SSC 10**
See also AITN 2; CA 13-16R; 69-72; CANR
22, 53; DLB 2, 4, 152; MTCW 1
Nishida, Kitaro 1870-1945 .... **TCLC 83**
Nishiwaki, Junzaburo 1894-1982 .... **PC 15**
See also CA 107
Nissenson, Hugh 1933- .... **CLC 4, 9**
See also CA 17-20R; CANR 27; DLB 28
Niven, Larry .... **CLC 8**
See also Niven, Laurence Van Cott
See also AAYA 27; DLB 8
Niven, Laurence Van Cott 1938-
See Niven, Larry
See also CA 21-24R; CAAS 12; CANR 14, 44,
66; DAM POP; MTCW 1; SATA 95
Nixon, Agnes Eckhardt 1927- .... **CLC 21**
See also CA 110
Nizan, Paul 1905-1940 .... **TCLC 40**
See also CA 161; DLB 72
Nkosi, Lewis 1936- .... **CLC 45; BLC 3; DAM
MULT**
See also BW 1; CA 65-68; CANR 27; DLB 157
Nodier, (Jean) Charles (Emmanuel) 1780-1844
NCLC 19
See also DLB 119
Noguchi, Yone 1875-1947 .... **TCLC 80**
Nolan, Christopher 1965- .... **CLC 58**
See also CA 111
Noon, Jeff 1957- .... **CLC 91**
See also CA 148
Norden, Charles
See Durrell, Lawrence (George)
Nordhoff, Charles (Bernard) 1887-1947
TCLC 23
See also CA 108; DLB 9; SATA 23
Norfolk, Lawrence 1963- .... **CLC 76**
See also CA 144
Norman, Marsha 1947-**CLC 28; DAM DRAM;
DC 8**
See also CA 105; CABS 3; CANR 41; DLBY
84
Normyx
See Douglas, (George) Norman
Norris, Frank 1870-1902 .... **SSC 28**
See also Norris, (Benjamin) Frank(lin, Jr.)
See also CDALB 1865-1917; DLB 12, 71, 186
Norris, (Benjamin) Frank(lin, Jr.) 1870-1902
TCLC 24
See also Norris, Frank
See also CA 110; 160
Norris, Leslie 1921- .... **CLC 14**
See also CA 11-12; CANR 14; CAP 1; DLB 27
North, Andrew
See Norton, Andre
North, Anthony
See Koontz, Dean R(ay)
North, Captain George
See Stevenson, Robert Louis (Balfour)
North, Milou
See Erdrich, Louise

DLB 9, 22, 102; DLBD 17; JRDA; MAICYA;
SATA 100; YABC 1
Ray, Satyajit 1921-1992 .. **CLC 16, 76; DAM
MULT**
See also CA 114; 137
Read, Herbert Edward 1893-1968 ..... **CLC 4**
See also CA 85-88; 25-28R; DLB 20, 149
Read, Piers Paul 1941- .... **CLC 4, 10, 25**
See also CA 21-24R; CANR 38; DLB 14; SATA
21
Reade, Charles 1814-1884 .... **NCLC 2, 74**
See also DLB 21
Reade, Hamish
See Gray, Simon (James Holliday)
Reading, Peter 1946- .... **CLC 47**
See also CA 103; CANR 46; DLB 40
Reaney, James 1926- .. **CLC 13; DAC; DAM
MST**
See also CA 41-44R; CAAS 15; CANR 42; DLB
68; SATA 43
Rebreanu, Liviu 1885-1944 .... **TCLC 28**
See also CA 165
Rechy, John (Francisco) 1934- **CLC 1, 7, 14,
18, 107; DAM MULT; HLC**
See also CA 5-8R; CAAS 4; CANR 6, 32, 64;
DLB 122; DLBY 82; HW; INT CANR-6
Redcam, Tom 1870-1933 .... **TCLC 25**
Reddin, Keith .... **CLC 67**
Redgrove, Peter (William) 1932- .. **CLC 6, 41**
See also CA 1-4R; CANR 3, 39; DLB 40
Redmon, Anne .... **CLC 22**
See also Nightingale, Anne Redmon
See also DLBY 86,
Reed, Eliot
See Ambler, Eric
Reed, Ishmael 1938- **CLC 2, 3, 5, 6, 13, 32, 60;
BLC 3; DAM MULT**
See also BW 2; CA 21-24R; CANR 25, 48, 74;
DLB 2, 5, 33, 169; DLBD 8; MTCW 1
Reed, John (Silas) 1887-1920 .... **TCLC 9**
See also CA 106
Reed, Lou .... **CLC 21**
See also Firbank, Louis
Reeve, Clara 1729-1807 .... **NCLC 19**
See also DLB 39
Reich, Wilhelm 1897-1957 .... **TCLC 57**
Reid, Christopher (John) 1949- .... **CLC 33**
See also CA 140; DLB 40
Reid, Desmond
See Moorcock, Michael (John)
Reid Banks, Lynne 1929-
See Banks, Lynne Reid
See also CA 1-4R; CANR 6, 22, 38; CLR 24;
JRDA; MAICYA; SATA 22, 75
Reilly, William K.
See Creasey, John
Reiner, Max
See Caldwell, (Janet Miriam) Taylor (Holland)
Reis, Ricardo
See Pessoa, Fernando (Antonio Nogueira)
Remarque, Erich Maria 1898-1970 **CLC 21;
DA; DAB; DAC; DAM MST, NOV**
See also AAYA 27; CA 77-80; 29-32R; DLB
56; MTCW 1
Remington, Frederic 1861-1909 .... **TCLC 89**
See also CA 108; 169; DLB 12, 186, 188; SATA
41
Remizov, A.
See Remizov, Aleksei (Mikhailovich)
Remizov, A. M.
See Remizov, Aleksei (Mikhailovich)
Remizov, Aleksei (Mikhailovich) 1877-1957
TCLC 27
See also CA 125; 133
Renan, Joseph Ernest 1823-1892 .. **NCLC 26**
Renard, Jules 1864-1910 .... **TCLC 17**
See also CA 117

Renault, Mary .... **CLC 3, 11, 17**
See also Challans, Mary
See also DLBY 83
Rendell, Ruth (Barbara) 1930- . **CLC 28, 48;
DAM POP**
See also Vine, Barbara
See also CA 109; CANR 32, 52, 74; DLB 87;
INT CANR-32; MTCW 1
Renoir, Jean 1894-1979 .... **CLC 20**
See also CA 129; 85-88
Resnais, Alain 1922- .... **CLC 16**
Reverdy, Pierre 1889-1960 .... **CLC 53**
See also CA 97-100; 89-92
Rexroth, Kenneth 1905-1982 **CLC 1, 2, 6, 11,
22, 49, 112; DAM POET; PC 20**
See also CA 5-8R; 107; CANR 14, 34, 63;
CDALB 1941-1968; DLB 16, 48, 165;
DLBY 82; INT CANR-14; MTCW 1
Reyes, Alfonso 1889-1959 .... **TCLC 33**
See also CA 131; HW
Reyes y Basoalto, Ricardo Eliecer Neftali
See Neruda, Pablo
Reymont, Wladyslaw (Stanislaw) 1868(?)-1925
TCLC 5
See also CA 104
Reynolds, Jonathan 1942- .... **CLC 6, 38**
See also CA 65-68; CANR 28
Reynolds, Joshua 1723-1792 .... **LC 15**
See also DLB 104
Reynolds, Michael Shane 1937- .... **CLC 44**
See also CA 65-68; CANR 9
Reznikoff, Charles 1894-1976 .... **CLC 9**
See also CA 33-36; 61-64; CAP 2; DLB 28, 45
Rezzori (d'Arezzo), Gregor von 1914-1998
CLC 25
See also CA 122; 136; 167
Rhine, Richard
See Silverstein, Alvin
Rhodes, Eugene Manlove 1869-1934 **TCLC 53**
Rhodius, Apollonius c. 3rd cent. B.C.- **C M L C
28**
See also DLB 176
R'hoone
See Balzac, Honore de
Rhys, Jean 1890(?)-1979 **CLC 2, 4, 6, 14, 19,
51; DAM NOV; SSC 21**
See also CA 25-28R; 85-88; CANR 35, 62;
CDBLB 1945-1960; DLB 36, 117, 162;
MTCW 1
Ribeiro, Darcy 1922-1997 .... **CLC 34**
See also CA 33-36R; 156
Ribeiro, Joao Ubaldo (Osorio Pimentel) 1941-
CLC 10, 67
See also CA 81-84
Ribman, Ronald (Burt) 1932- .... **CLC 7**
See also CA 21-24R; CANR 46
Ricci, Nino 1959- .... **CLC 70**
See also CA 137
Rice, Anne 1941- .... **CLC 41; DAM POP**
See also AAYA 9; BEST 89:2; CA 65-68; CANR
12, 36, 53, 74
Rice, Elmer (Leopold) 1892-1967 **CLC 7, 49;
DAM DRAM**
See also CA 21-22; 25-28R; CAP 2; DLB 4, 7;
MTCW 1
Rice, Tim(othy Miles Bindon) 1944- **CLC 21**
See also CA 103; CANR 46
Rich, Adrienne (Cecile) 1929- **CLC 3, 6, 7, 11,
18, 36, 73, 76; DAM POET; PC 5**
See also CA 9-12R; CANR 20, 53, 74; DLB 5,
67; MTCW 1
Rich, Barbara
See Graves, Robert (von Ranke)
Rich, Robert
See Trumbo, Dalton
Richard, Keith .... **CLC 17**
See also Richards, Keith

Richards, David Adams 1950- **CLC 59; DAC**
See also CA 93-96; CANR 60; DLB 53
Richards, I(vor) A(rmstrong) 1893-1979 **C L C
14, 24**
See also CA 41-44R; 89-92; CANR 34, 74; DLB
27
Richards, Keith 1943-
See Richard, Keith
See also CA 107
Richardson, Anne
See Roiphe, Anne (Richardson)
Richardson, Dorothy Miller 1873-1957 **TCLC
3**
See also CA 104; DLB 36
Richardson, Ethel Florence (Lindesay) 1870-
1946
See Richardson, Henry Handel
See also CA 105
Richardson, Henry Handel .... **TCLC 4**
See also Richardson, Ethel Florence (Lindesay)
See also DLB 197
Richardson, John 1796-1852 **NCLC 55; DAC**
See also DLB 99
Richardson, Samuel 1689-1761 **LC 1, 44; DA;
DAB; DAC; DAM MST, NOV; WLC**
See also CDBLB 1660-1789; DLB 39
Richler, Mordecai 1931- **CLC 3, 5, 9, 13, 18, 46,
70; DAC; DAM MST, NOV**
See also AITN 1; CA 65-68; CANR 31, 62; CLR
17; DLB 53; MAICYA; MTCW 1; SATA 44,
98; SATA-Brief 27
Richter, Conrad (Michael) 1890-1968 **CLC 30**
See also AAYA 21; CA 5-8R; 25-28R; CANR
23; DLB 9; MTCW 1; SATA 3
Ricostranza, Tom
See Ellis, Trey
Riddell, Charlotte 1832-1906 .... **TCLC 40**
See also CA 165; DLB 156
Riding, Laura .... **CLC 3, 7**
See also Jackson, Laura (Riding)
Riefenstahl, Berta Helene Amalia 1902-
See Riefenstahl, Leni
See also CA 108
Riefenstahl, Leni .... **CLC 16**
See also Riefenstahl, Berta Helene Amalia
Riffe, Ernest
See Bergman, (Ernst) Ingmar
Riggs, (Rolla) Lynn 1899-1954 ..... **TCLC 56;
DAM MULT**
See also CA 144; DLB 175; NNAL
Riis, Jacob A(ugust) 1849-1914 ..... **TCLC 80**
See also CA 113; 168; DLB 23
Riley, James Whitcomb 1849-1916 **TCLC 51;
DAM POET**
See also CA 118; 137; MAICYA; SATA 17
Riley, Tex
See Creasey, John
Rilke, Rainer Maria 1875-1926 **TCLC 1, 6, 19;
DAM POET; PC 2**
See also CA 104; 132; CANR 62; DLB 81;
MTCW 1
Rimbaud, (Jean Nicolas) Arthur 1854-1891
**NCLC 4, 35; DA; DAB; DAC; DAM MST,
POET; PC 3; WLC**
Rinehart, Mary Roberts 1876-1958 **TCLC 52**
See also CA 108; 166
Ringmaster, The
See Mencken, H(enry) L(ouis)
Ringwood, Gwen(dolyn Margaret) Pharis
1910-1984 .... **CLC 48**
See also CA 148; 112; DLB 88
Rio, Michel 19(?)- .... **CLC 43**
Ritsos, Giannes
See Ritsos, Yannis
Ritsos, Yannis 1909-1990 .... **CLC 6, 13, 31**
See also CA 77-80; 133; CANR 39, 61; MTCW
1

See Lovecraft, H(oward) P(hillips)
Rowson, Susanna Haswell 1762(?)-1824
NCLC 5, 69
See also DLB 37, 200
Roy, Arundhati 1960(?)- .... **CLC 109**
See also CA 163; DLBY 97
Roy, Gabrielle 1909-1983 **CLC 10, 14; DAB;**
DAC; DAM MST
See also CA 53-56; 110; CANR 5, 61; DLB 68;
MTCW 1; SATA 104
Royko, Mike 1932-1997 .... **CLC 109**
See also CA 89-92; 157; CANR 26
Rozewicz, Tadeusz 1921- .. **CLC 9, 23; DAM**
POET
See also CA 108; CANR 36, 66; MTCW 1
Ruark, Gibbons 1941- .... **CLC 3**
See also CA 33-36R; CAAS 23; CANR 14, 31,
57; DLB 120
Rubens, Bernice (Ruth) 1923-.... **CLC 19, 31**
See also CA 25-28R; CANR 33, 65; DLB 14,
207; MTCW 1
Rubin, Harold
See Robbins, Harold
Rudkin, (James) David 1936- .... **CLC 14**
See also CA 89-92; DLB 13
Rudnik, Raphael 1933- .... **CLC 7**
See also CA 29-32R
Ruffian, M.
See Hasek, Jaroslav (Matej Frantisek)
Ruiz, Jose Martinez .... **CLC 11**
See also Martinez Ruiz, Jose
Rukeyser, Muriel 1913-1980**CLC 6, 10, 15, 27;**
DAM POET; PC 12
See also CA 5-8R; 93-96; CANR 26, 60; DLB
48; MTCW 1; SATA-Obit 22
Rule, Jane (Vance) 1931- .... **CLC 27**
See also CA 25-28R; CAAS 18; CANR 12; DLB
60
Rulfo, Juan 1918-1986 ...... **CLC 8, 80; DAM**
MULT; HLC; SSC 25
See also CA 85-88; 118; CANR 26; DLB 113;
HW; MTCW 1
Rumi, Jalal al-Din 1297-1373 .... **CMLC 20**
Runeberg, Johan 1804-1877 .... **NCLC 41**
Runyon, (Alfred) Damon 1884(?)-1946**T C L C**
10
See also CA 107; 165; DLB 11, 86, 171
Rush, Norman 1933- .... **CLC 44**
See also CA 121; 126; INT 126
Rushdie, (Ahmed) Salman 1947-**CLC 23, 31,**
55, 100; DAB; DAC; DAM MST, NOV,
POP; WLCS
See also BEST 89:3; CA 108; 111; CANR 33,
56; DLB 194; INT 111; MTCW 1
Rushforth, Peter (Scott) 1945- .... **CLC 19**
See also CA 101
Ruskin, John 1819-1900 .... **TCLC 63**
See also CA 114; 129; CDBLB 1832-1890;
DLB 55, 163, 190; SATA 24
Russ, Joanna 1937- .... **CLC 15**
See also CANR 11, 31, 65; DLB 8; MTCW 1
Russell, George William 1867-1935
See Baker, Jean H.
See also CA 104; 153; CDBLB 1890-1914;
DAM POET
Russell, (Henry) Ken(neth Alfred) 1927-**C L C**
16
See also CA 105
Russell, William Martin 1947- .... **CLC 60**
See also CA 164
Rutherford, Mark .... **TCLC 25**
See also White, William Hale
See also DLB 18
Ruyslinck, Ward 1929- .... **CLC 14**
See also Belser, Reimond Karel Maria de
Ryan, Cornelius (John) 1920-1974 ..... **CLC 7**
See also CA 69-72; 53-56; CANR 38

Ryan, Michael 1946- .... **CLC 65**
See also CA 49-52; DLBY 82
Ryan, Tim
See Dent, Lester
Rybakov, Anatoli (Naumovich) 1911-1998
CLC 23, 53
See also CA 126; 135; 172; SATA 79
Ryder, Jonathan
See Ludlum, Robert
Ryga, George 1932-1987**CLC 14; DAC; DAM**
MST
See also CA 101; 124; CANR 43; DLB 60
S. H.
See Hartmann, Sadakichi
S. S.
See Sassoon, Siegfried (Lorraine)
Saba, Umberto 1883-1957 .... **TCLC 33**
See also CA 144; DLB 114
Sabatini, Rafael 1875-1950 .... **TCLC 47**
See also CA 162
Sabato, Ernesto (R.) 1911-**CLC 10, 23; DAM**
MULT; HLC
See also CA 97-100; CANR 32, 65; DLB 145;
HW; MTCW 1
Sa-Carniero, Mario de 1890-1916 . **TCLC 83**
Sacastru, Martin
See Bioy Casares, Adolfo
Sacher-Masoch, Leopold von 1836(?)-1895
NCLC 31
Sachs, Marilyn (Stickle) 1927- .... **CLC 35**
See also AAYA 2; CA 17-20R; CANR 13, 47;
CLR 2; JRDA; MAICYA; SAAS 2; SATA 3,
68
Sachs, Nelly 1891-1970 .... **CLC 14, 98**
See also CA 17-18; 25-28R; CAP 2
Sackler, Howard (Oliver) 1929-1982 **CLC 14**
See also CA 61-64; 108; CANR 30; DLB 7
Sacks, Oliver (Wolf) 1933- .... **CLC 67**
See also CA 53-56; CANR 28, 50, 76; INT
CANR-28; MTCW 1
Sadakichi
See Hartmann, Sadakichi
Sade, Donatien Alphonse Francois, Comte de
1740-1814 ....
NCLC 47
Sadoff, Ira 1945- .... **CLC 9**
See also CA 53-56; CANR 5, 21; DLB 120
Saetone
See Camus, Albert
Safire, William 1929- .... **CLC 10**
See also CA 17-20R; CANR 31, 54
Sagan, Carl (Edward) 1934-1996**CLC 30, 112**
See also AAYA 2; CA 25-28R; 155; CANR 11,
36, 74; MTCW 1; SATA 58; SATA-Obit 94
Sagan, Francoise .... **CLC 3, 6, 9, 17, 36**
See also Quoirez, Francoise
See also DLB 83
Sahgal, Nayantara (Pandit) 1927- .... **CLC 41**
See also CA 9-12R; CANR 11
Saint, H(arry) F. 1941- .... **CLC 50**
See also CA 127
St. Aubin de Teran, Lisa 1953-
See Teran, Lisa St. Aubin de
See also CA 118; 126; INT 126
Saint Birgitta of Sweden c. 1303-1373**C M L C**
24
Sainte-Beuve, Charles Augustin 1804-1869
NCLC 5
Saint-Exupery, Antoine (Jean Baptiste Marie
Roger) de 1900-1944**TCLC 2, 56; DAM**
NOV; WLC
See also CA 108; 132; CLR 10; DLB 72;
MAICYA; MTCW 1; SATA 20
St. John, David
See Hunt, E(verette) Howard, (Jr.)
Saint-John Perse
See Leger, (Marie-Rene Auguste) Alexis Saint-

Leger
Saintsbury, George (Edward Bateman) 1845-
1933 .... **TCLC 31**
See also CA 160; DLB 57, 149
Sait Faik .... **TCLC 23**
See also Abasiyanik, Sait Faik
Saki .... **TCLC 3; SSC 12**
See also Munro, H(ector) H(ugh)
Sala, George Augustus .... **NCLC 46**
Salama, Hannu 1936- .... **CLC 18**
Salamanca, J(ack) R(ichard) 1922-**CLC 4, 15**
See also CA 25-28R
Sale, J. Kirkpatrick
See Sale, Kirkpatrick
Sale, Kirkpatrick 1937- .... **CLC 68**
See also CA 13-16R; CANR 10
Salinas, Luis Omar 1937- ...... **CLC 90; DAM**
MULT; HLC
See also CA 131; DLB 82; HW
Salinas (y Serrano), Pedro 1891(?)-1951
TCLC 17
See also CA 117; DLB 134
Salinger, J(erome) D(avid) 1919-**CLC 1, 3, 8,**
12, 55, 56; DA; DAB; DAC; DAM MST,
NOV, POP; SSC 2, 28; WLC
See also AAYA 2; CA 5-8R; CANR 39; CDALB
1941-1968; CLR 18; DLB 2, 102, 173;
MAICYA; MTCW 1; SATA 67
Salisbury, John
See Caute, (John) David
Salter, James 1925- .... **CLC 7, 52, 59**
See also CA 73-76; DLB 130
Saltus, Edgar (Everton) 1855-1921 . **TCLC 8**
See also CA 105; DLB 202
Saltykov, Mikhail Evgrafovich 1826-1889
NCLC 16
Samarakis, Antonis 1919- .... **CLC 5**
See also CA 25-28R; CAAS 16; CANR 36
Sanchez, Florencio 1875-1910........ **TCLC 37**
See also CA 153; HW
Sanchez, Luis Rafael 1936- .... **CLC 23**
See also CA 128; DLB 145; HW
Sanchez, Sonia 1934-.... **CLC 5, 116; BLC 3;**
DAM MULT; PC 9
See also BW 2; CA 33-36R; CANR 24, 49, 74;
CLR 18; DLB 41; DLBD 8; MAICYA;
MTCW 1; SATA 22
Sand, George 1804-1876**NCLC 2, 42, 57; DA;**
DAB; DAC; DAM MST, NOV; WLC
See also DLB 119, 192
Sandburg, Carl (August) 1878-1967**CLC 1, 4,**
10, 15, 35; DA; DAB; DAC; DAM MST,
POET; PC 2; WLC
See also AAYA 24; CA 5-8R; 25-28R; CANR
35; CDALB 1865-1917; DLB 17, 54;
MAICYA; MTCW 1; SATA 8
Sandburg, Charles
See Sandburg, Carl (August)
Sandburg, Charles A.
See Sandburg, Carl (August)
Sanders, (James) Ed(ward) 1939- .. **CLC 53;**
DAM POET
See also CA 13-16R; CAAS 21; CANR 13, 44;
DLB 16
Sanders, Lawrence 1920-1998**CLC 41; DAM**
POP
See also BEST 89:4; CA 81-84; 165; CANR
33, 62; MTCW 1
Sanders, Noah
See Blount, Roy (Alton), Jr.
Sanders, Winston P.
See Anderson, Poul (William)
Sandoz, Mari(e Susette) 1896-1966 .. **CLC 28**
See also CA 1-4R; 25-28R; CANR 17, 64; DLB
9; MTCW 1; SATA 5
Saner, Reg(inald Anthony) 1931- .... **CLC 9**
See also CA 65-68

Tate, (John Orley) Allen 1899-1979 **CLC 2, 4, 6, 9, 11, 14, 24**
See also CA 5-8R; 85-88; CANR 32; DLB 4, 45, 63; DLBD 17; MTCW 1

Tate, Ellalice
See Hibbert, Eleanor Alice Burford

Tate, James (Vincent) 1943- ..... **CLC 2, 6, 25**
See also CA 21-24R; CANR 29, 57; DLB 5, 169

Tavel, Ronald 1940- .... **CLC 6**
See also CA 21-24R; CANR 33

Taylor, C(ecil) P(hilip) 1929-1981 .... **CLC 27**
See also CA 25-28R; 105; CANR 47

Taylor, Edward 1642(?)-1729 ..... **LC 11; DA; DAB; DAC; DAM MST, POET**
See also DLB 24

Taylor, Eleanor Ross 1920- .... **CLC 5**
See also CA 81-84; CANR 70

Taylor, Elizabeth 1912-1975 ..... **CLC 2, 4, 29**
See also CA 13-16R; CANR 9, 70; DLB 139; MTCW 1; SATA 13

Taylor, Frederick Winslow 1856-1915 **T C L C 76**

Taylor, Henry (Splawn) 1942- .... **CLC 44**
See also CA 33-36R; CAAS 7; CANR 31; DLB 5

Taylor, Kamala (Purnaiya) 1924-
See Markandaya, Kamala
See also CA 77-80

Taylor, Mildred D. .... **CLC 21**
See also AAYA 10; BW 1; CA 85-88; CANR 25; CLR 9; DLB 52; JRDA; MAICYA; SAAS 5; SATA 15, 70

Taylor, Peter (Hillsman) 1917-1994 **CLC 1, 4, 18, 37, 44, 50, 71; SSC 10**
See also CA 13-16R; 147; CANR 9, 50; DLBY 81, 94; INT CANR-9; MTCW 1

Taylor, Robert Lewis 1912-1998 .... **CLC 14**
See also CA 1-4R; 170; CANR 3, 64; SATA 10

Tchekhov, Anton
See Chekhov, Anton (Pavlovich)

Tchicaya, Gerald Felix 1931-1988 .. **CLC 101**
See also CA 129; 125

Tchicaya U Tam'si
See Tchicaya, Gerald Felix

Teasdale, Sara 1884-1933 .... **TCLC 4**
See also CA 104; 163; DLB 45; SATA 32

Tegner, Esaias 1782-1846 .... **NCLC 2**

Teilhard de Chardin, (Marie Joseph) Pierre 1881-1955 ....
TCLC 9
See also CA 105

Temple, Ann
See Mortimer, Penelope (Ruth)

Tennant, Emma (Christina) 1937- **CLC 13, 52**
See also CA 65-68; CAAS 9; CANR 10, 38, 59; DLB 14

Tenneshaw, S. M.
See Silverberg, Robert

Tennyson, Alfred 1809-1892 ... **NCLC 30, 65; DA; DAB; DAC; DAM MST, POET; PC 6; WLC**
See also CDBLB 1832-1890; DLB 32

Teran, Lisa St. Aubin de .... **CLC 36**
See also St. Aubin de Teran, Lisa

Terence 195(?)B.C.-159B.C. **CMLC 14; DC 7**

Teresa de Jesus, St. 1515-1582 .... **LC 18**

Terkel, Louis 1912-
See Terkel, Studs
See also CA 57-60; CANR 18, 45, 67; MTCW 1

Terkel, Studs .... **CLC 38**
See also Terkel, Louis
See also AITN 1

Terry, C. V.
See Slaughter, Frank G(ill)

Terry, Megan 1932- .... **CLC 19**

See also CA 77-80; CABS 3; CANR 43; DLB 7

Tertullian c. 155-c. 245 .... **CMLC 29**

Tertz, Abram
See Sinyavsky, Andrei (Donatevich)

Tesich, Steve 1943(?)-1996 .... **CLC 40, 69**
See also CA 105; 152; DLBY 83

Tesla, Nikola 1856-1943 .... **TCLC 88**

Teternikov, Fyodor Kuzmich 1863-1927
See Sologub, Fyodor
See also CA 104

Tevis, Walter 1928-1984 .... **CLC 42**
See also CA 113

Tey, Josephine .... **TCLC 14**
See also Mackintosh, Elizabeth
See also DLB 77

Thackeray, William Makepeace 1811-1863 **NCLC 5, 14, 22, 43; DA; DAB; DAC; DAM MST, NOV; WLC**
See also CDBLB 1832-1890; DLB 21, 55, 159, 163; SATA 23

Thakura, Ravindranatha
See Tagore, Rabindranath

Tharoor, Shashi 1956- .... **CLC 70**
See also CA 141

Thelwell, Michael Miles 1939- .... **CLC 22**
See also BW 2; CA 101

Theobald, Lewis, Jr.
See Lovecraft, H(oward) P(hillips)

Theodorescu, Ion N. 1880-1967
See Arghezi, Tudor
See also CA 116

Theriault, Yves 1915-1983 .... **CLC 79; DAC; DAM MST**
See also CA 102; DLB 88

Theroux, Alexander (Louis) 1939- **CLC 2, 25**
See also CA 85-88; CANR 20, 63

Theroux, Paul (Edward) 1941- **CLC 5, 8, 11, 15, 28, 46; DAM POP**
See also BEST 89:4; CA 33-36R; CANR 20, 45, 74; DLB 2; MTCW 1; SATA 44

Thesen, Sharon 1946- .... **CLC 56**
See also CA 163

Thevenin, Denis
See Duhamel, Georges

Thibault, Jacques Anatole Francois 1844-1924
See France, Anatole
See also CA 106; 127; DAM NOV; MTCW 1

Thiele, Colin (Milton) 1920- .... **CLC 17**
See also CA 29-32R; CANR 12, 28, 53; CLR 27; MAICYA; SAAS 2; SATA 14, 72

Thomas, Audrey (Callahan) 1935- **CLC 7, 13, 37, 107; SSC 20**
See also AITN 2; CA 21-24R; CAAS 19; CANR 36, 58; DLB 60; MTCW 1

Thomas, D(onald) M(ichael) 1935- . **CLC 13, 22, 31**
See also CA 61-64; CAAS 11; CANR 17, 45, 75; CDBLB 1960 to Present; DLB 40, 207; INT CANR-17; MTCW 1

Thomas, Dylan (Marlais) 1914-1953 **TCLC 1, 8, 45; DA; DAB; DAC; DAM DRAM, MST, POET; PC 2; SSC 3; WLC**
See also CA 104; 120; CANR 65; CDBLB 1945-1960; DLB 13, 20, 139; MTCW 1; SATA 60

Thomas, (Philip) Edward 1878-1917 . **T C L C 10; DAM POET**
See also CA 106; 153; DLB 98

Thomas, Joyce Carol 1938- .... **CLC 35**
See also AAYA 12; BW 2; CA 113; 116; CANR 48; CLR 19; DLB 33; INT 116; JRDA; MAICYA; MTCW 1; SAAS 7; SATA 40, 78

Thomas, Lewis 1913-1993 .... **CLC 35**
See also CA 85-88; 143; CANR 38, 60; MTCW 1

Thomas, M. Carey 1857-1935 .... **TCLC 89**

Thomas, Paul

See Mann, (Paul) Thomas

Thomas, Piri 1928- .... **CLC 17**
See also CA 73-76; HW

Thomas, R(onald) S(tuart) 1913- **CLC 6, 13, 48; DAB; DAM POET**
See also CA 89-92; CAAS 4; CANR 30; CDBLB 1960 to Present; DLB 27; MTCW 1

Thomas, Ross (Elmore) 1926-1995 ... **CLC 39**
See also CA 33-36R; 150; CANR 22, 63

Thompson, Francis Clegg
See Mencken, H(enry) L(ouis)

Thompson, Francis Joseph 1859-1907 **TCLC 4**
See also CA 104; CDBLB 1890-1914; DLB 19

Thompson, Hunter S(tockton) 1939- **CLC 9, 17, 40, 104; DAM POP**
See also BEST 89:1; CA 17-20R; CANR 23, 46, 74; DLB 185; MTCW 1

Thompson, James Myers
See Thompson, Jim (Myers)

Thompson, Jim (Myers) 1906-1977(?) **CLC 69**
See also CA 140

Thompson, Judith .... **CLC 39**

Thomson, James 1700-1748 ... **LC 16, 29, 40; DAM POET**
See also DLB 95

Thomson, James 1834-1882 **NCLC 18; DAM POET**
See also DLB 35

Thoreau, Henry David 1817-1862 **NCLC 7, 21, 61; DA; DAB; DAC; DAM MST; WLC**
See also CDALB 1640-1865; DLB 1

Thornton, Hall
See Silverberg, Robert

Thucydides c. 455B.C.-399B.C. .... **CMLC 17**
See also DLB 176

Thurber, James (Grover) 1894-1961 . **CLC 5, 11, 25; DA; DAB; DAC; DAM DRAM, MST, NOV; SSC 1**
See also CA 73-76; CANR 17, 39; CDALB 1929-1941; DLB 4, 11, 22, 102; MAICYA; MTCW 1; SATA 13

Thurman, Wallace (Henry) 1902-1934 **T C L C 6; BLC 3; DAM MULT**
See also BW 1; CA 104; 124; DLB 51

Ticheburn, Cheviot
See Ainsworth, William Harrison

Tieck, (Johann) Ludwig 1773-1853 **NCLC 5, 46; SSC 31**
See also DLB 90

Tiger, Derry
See Ellison, Harlan (Jay)

Tilghman, Christopher 1948(?)- .... **CLC 65**
See also CA 159

Tillinghast, Richard (Williford) 1940- **CLC 29**
See also CA 29-32R; CAAS 23; CANR 26, 51

Timrod, Henry 1828-1867 .... **NCLC 25**
See also DLB 3

Tindall, Gillian (Elizabeth) 1938- ...... **CLC 7**
See also CA 21-24R; CANR 11, 65

Tiptree, James, Jr. .... **CLC 48, 50**
See also Sheldon, Alice Hastings Bradley
See also DLB 8

Titmarsh, Michael Angelo
See Thackeray, William Makepeace

Tocqueville, Alexis (Charles Henri Maurice Clerel, Comte) de 1805-1859 **NCLC 7, 63**

Tolkien, J(ohn) R(onald) R(euel) 1892-1973 **CLC 1, 2, 3, 8, 12, 38; DA; DAB; DAC; DAM MST, NOV, POP; WLC**
See also AAYA 10; AITN 1; CA 17-18; 45-48; CANR 36; CAP 2; CDBLB 1914-1945; DLB 15, 160; JRDA; MAICYA; MTCW 1; SATA 2, 32, 100; SATA-Obit 24

Toller, Ernst 1893-1939 .... **TCLC 10**
See also CA 107; DLB 124

Tolson, M. B.
See Tolson, Melvin B(eaunorus)

Tolson, Melvin B(eaunorus) 1898(?)-1966
    CLC 36, 105; BLC 3; DAM MULT, POET
    See also BW 1; CA 124; 89-92; DLB 48, 76
Tolstoi, Aleksei Nikolaevich
    See Tolstoy, Alexey Nikolaevich
Tolstoy, Alexey Nikolaevich 1882-1945**T C L C
    18**
    See also CA 107; 158
Tolstoy, Count Leo
    See Tolstoy, Leo (Nikolaevich)
Tolstoy, Leo (Nikolaevich) 1828-1910**TCLC 4,
    11, 17, 28, 44, 79; DA; DAB; DAC; DAM
    MST, NOV; SSC 9, 30; WLC**
    See also CA 104; 123; SATA 26
Tomasi di Lampedusa, Giuseppe 1896-1957
    See Lampedusa, Giuseppe (Tomasi) di
    See also CA 111
Tomlin, Lily .... **CLC 17**
    See also Tomlin, Mary Jean
Tomlin, Mary Jean 1939(?)-
    See Tomlin, Lily
    See also CA 117
Tomlinson, (Alfred) Charles 1927-**CLC 2, 4, 6,
    13, 45; DAM POET; PC 17**
    See also CA 5-8R; CANR 33; DLB 40
Tomlinson, H(enry) M(ajor) 1873-1958**TCLC
    71**
    See also CA 118; 161; DLB 36, 100, 195
Tonson, Jacob
    See Bennett, (Enoch) Arnold
Toole, John Kennedy 1937-1969 **CLC 19, 64**
    See also CA 104; DLBY 81
Toomer, Jean 1894-1967**CLC 1, 4, 13, 22; BLC
    3; DAM MULT; PC 7; SSC 1; WLCS**
    See also BW 1; CA 85-88; CDALB 1917-1929;
    DLB 45, 51; MTCW 1
Torley, Luke
    See Blish, James (Benjamin)
Tornimparte, Alessandra
    See Ginzburg, Natalia
Torre, Raoul della
    See Mencken, H(enry) L(ouis)
Torrey, E(dwin) Fuller 1937- .... **CLC 34**
    See also CA 119; CANR 71
Torsvan, Ben Traven
    See Traven, B.
Torsvan, Benno Traven
    See Traven, B.
Torsvan, Berick Traven
    See Traven, B.
Torsvan, Berwick Traven
    See Traven, B.
Torsvan, Bruno Traven
    See Traven, B.
Torsvan, Traven
    See Traven, B.
Tournier, Michel (Edouard) 1924-**CLC 6, 23,
    36, 95**
    See also CA 49-52; CANR 3, 36, 74; DLB 83;
    MTCW 1; SATA 23
Tournimparte, Alessandra
    See Ginzburg, Natalia
Towers, Ivar
    See Kornbluth, C(yril) M.
Towne, Robert (Burton) 1936(?)- ..... **CLC 87**
    See also CA 108; DLB 44
Townsend, Sue .... **CLC 61**
    See also Townsend, Susan Elaine
    See also SATA 55, 93; SATA-Brief 48
Townsend, Susan Elaine 1946-
    See Townsend, Sue
    See also CA 119; 127; CANR 65; DAB; DAC;
    DAM MST
Townshend, Peter (Dennis Blandford) 1945-
    CLC 17, 42
    See also CA 107
Tozzi, Federigo 1883-1920 .... **TCLC 31**

See also CA 160
Traill, Catharine Parr 1802-1899 .. **NCLC 31**
    See also DLB 99
Trakl, Georg 1887-1914 .... **TCLC 5; PC 20**
    See also CA 104; 165
Transtroemer, Tomas (Goesta) 1931-**CLC 52,
    65; DAM POET**
    See also CA 117; 129; CAAS 17
Transtromer, Tomas Gosta
    See Transtroemer, Tomas (Goesta)
Traven, B. (?)-1969 .... **CLC 8, 11**
    See also CA 19-20; 25-28R; CAP 2; DLB 9,
    56; MTCW 1
Treitel, Jonathan 1959- .... **CLC 70**
Tremain, Rose 1943- .... **CLC 42**
    See also CA 97-100; CANR 44; DLB 14
Tremblay, Michel 1942- **CLC 29, 102; DAC;
    DAM MST**
    See also CA 116; 128; DLB 60; MTCW 1
Trevanian .... **CLC 29**
    See also Whitaker, Rod(ney)
Trevor, Glen
    See Hilton, James
Trevor, William 1928-**CLC 7, 9, 14, 25, 71, 116;
    SSC 21**
    See also Cox, William Trevor
    See also DLB 14, 139
Trifonov, Yuri (Valentinovich) 1925-1981
    CLC 45
    See also CA 126; 103; MTCW 1
Trilling, Lionel 1905-1975 ...... **CLC 9, 11, 24**
    See also CA 9-12R; 61-64; CANR 10; DLB 28,
    63; INT CANR-10; MTCW 1
Trimball, W. H.
    See Mencken, H(enry) L(ouis)
Tristan
    See Gomez de la Serna, Ramon
Tristram
    See Housman, A(lfred) E(dward)
Trogdon, William (Lewis) 1939-
    See Heat-Moon, William Least
    See also CA 115; 119; CANR 47; INT 119
Trollope, Anthony 1815-1882**NCLC 6, 33; DA;
    DAB; DAC; DAM MST, NOV; SSC 28;
    WLC**
    See also CDBLB 1832-1890; DLB 21, 57, 159;
    SATA 22
Trollope, Frances 1779-1863 .... **NCLC 30**
    See also DLB 21, 166
Trotsky, Leon 1879-1940 .... **TCLC 22**
    See also CA 118; 167
Trotter (Cockburn), Catharine 1679-1749**L C
    8**
    See also DLB 84
Trout, Kilgore
    See Farmer, Philip Jose
Trow, George W. S. 1943- .... **CLC 52**
    See also CA 126
Troyat, Henri 1911- .... **CLC 23**
    See also CA 45-48; CANR 2, 33, 67; MTCW 1
Trudeau, G(arretson) B(eekman) 1948-
    See Trudeau, Garry B.
    See also CA 81-84; CANR 31; SATA 35
Trudeau, Garry B. .... **CLC 12**
    See also Trudeau, G(arretson) B(eekman)
    See also AAYA 10; AITN 2
Truffaut, Francois 1932-1984 .. **CLC 20, 101**
    See also CA 81-84; 113; CANR 34
Trumbo, Dalton 1905-1976 .... **CLC 19**
    See also CA 21-24R; 69-72; CANR 10; DLB
    26
Trumbull, John 1750-1831 .... **NCLC 30**
    See also DLB 31
Trundlett, Helen B.
    See Eliot, T(homas) S(tearns)
Tryon, Thomas 1926-1991 . **CLC 3, 11; DAM
    POP**

See also AITN 1; CA 29-32R; 135; CANR 32;
    MTCW 1
Tryon, Tom
    See Tryon, Thomas
Ts'ao Hsueh-ch'in 1715(?)-1763 .... **LC 1**
Tsushima, Shuji 1909-1948
    See Dazai Osamu
    See also CA 107
Tsvetaeva (Efron), Marina (Ivanovna) 1892-
    1941 .... **TCLC 7, 35; PC 14**
    See also CA 104; 128; CANR 73; MTCW 1
Tuck, Lily 1938- .... **CLC 70**
    See also CA 139
Tu Fu 712-770 .... **PC 9**
    See also DAM MULT
Tunis, John R(oberts) 1889-1975 ...... **CLC 12**
    See also CA 61-64; CANR 62; DLB 22, 171;
    JRDA; MAICYA; SATA 37; SATA-Brief 30
Tuohy, Frank .... **CLC 37**
    See also Tuohy, John Francis
    See also DLB 14, 139
Tuohy, John Francis 1925-
    See Tuohy, Frank
    See also CA 5-8R; CANR 3, 47
Turco, Lewis (Putnam) 1934- ...... **CLC 11, 63**
    See also CA 13-16R; CAAS 22; CANR 24, 51;
    DLBY 84
Turgenev, Ivan 1818-1883 .... **NCLC 21; DA;
    DAB; DAC; DAM MST, NOV; DC 7; SSC
    7; WLC**
Turgot, Anne-Robert-Jacques 1727-1781 **L C
    26**
Turner, Frederick 1943- .... **CLC 48**
    See also CA 73-76; CAAS 10; CANR 12, 30,
    56; DLB 40
Tutu, Desmond M(pilo) 1931-**CLC 80; BLC 3;
    DAM MULT**
    See also BW 1; CA 125; CANR 67
Tutuola, Amos 1920-1997**CLC 5, 14, 29; BLC
    3; DAM MULT**
    See also BW 2; CA 9-12R; 159; CANR 27, 66;
    DLB 125; MTCW 1
Twain, Mark**TCLC 6, 12, 19, 36, 48, 59; SSC 6,
    26; WLC**
    See also Clemens, Samuel Langhorne
    See also AAYA 20; DLB 11, 12, 23, 64, 74
Tyler, Anne 1941- . **CLC 7, 11, 18, 28, 44, 59,
    103; DAM NOV, POP**
    See also AAYA 18; BEST 89:1; CA 9-12R;
    CANR 11, 33, 53; DLB 6, 143; DLBY 82;
    MTCW 1; SATA 7, 90
Tyler, Royall 1757-1826 .... **NCLC 3**
    See also DLB 37
Tynan, Katharine 1861-1931 .... **TCLC 3**
    See also CA 104; 167; DLB 153
Tyutchev, Fyodor 1803-1873 .... **NCLC 34**
Tzara, Tristan 1896-1963 ...... **CLC 47; DAM
    POET**
    See also CA 153; 89-92
Uhry, Alfred 1936- ... **CLC 55; DAM DRAM,
    POP**
    See also CA 127; 133; INT 133
Ulf, Haerved
    See Strindberg, (Johan) August
Ulf, Harved
    See Strindberg, (Johan) August
Ulibarri, Sabine R(eyes) 1919-**CLC 83; DAM
    MULT**
    See also CA 131; DLB 82; HW
Unamuno (y Jugo), Miguel de 1864-1936
    **TCLC 2, 9; DAM MULT, NOV; HLC; SSC
    11**
    See also CA 104; 131; DLB 108; HW; MTCW
    1
Undercliffe, Errol
    See Campbell, (John) Ramsey
Underwood, Miles

See also CA 13-16R; CAAS 22; CANR 5, 21, 44, 67; DLB 175; NNAL

Vizinczey, Stephen 1933- .... **CLC 40**
See also CA 128; INT 128

Vliet, R(ussell) G(ordon) 1929-1984 **CLC 22**
See also CA 37-40R; 112; CANR 18

Vogau, Boris Andreyevich 1894-1937(?)
See Pilnyak, Boris
See also CA 123

Vogel, Paula A(nne) 1951- .... **CLC 76**
See also CA 108

Voigt, Cynthia 1942- .... **CLC 30**
See also AAYA 3; CA 106; CANR 18, 37, 40; CLR 13, 48; INT CANR-18; JRDA; MAICYA; SATA 48, 79; SATA-Brief 33

Voigt, Ellen Bryant 1943- .... **CLC 54**
See also CA 69-72; CANR 11, 29, 55; DLB 120

Voinovich, Vladimir (Nikolaevich) 1932-**CLC 10, 49**
See also CA 81-84; CAAS 12; CANR 33, 67; MTCW 1

Vollmann, William T. 1959- .. **CLC 89; DAM NOV, POP**
See also CA 134; CANR 67

Voloshinov, V. N.
See Bakhtin, Mikhail Mikhailovich

Voltaire 1694-1778 . **LC 14; DA; DAB; DAC; DAM DRAM, MST; SSC 12; WLC**

von Aschendrof, BaronIgnatz
See Ford, Ford Madox

von Daeniken, Erich 1935- .... **CLC 30**
See also AITN 1; CA 37-40R; CANR 17, 44

von Daniken, Erich
See von Daeniken, Erich

von Heidenstam, (Carl Gustaf) Verner
See Heidenstam, (Carl Gustaf) Verner von

von Heyse, Paul (Johann Ludwig)
See Heyse, Paul (Johann Ludwig von)

von Hofmannsthal, Hugo
See Hofmannsthal, Hugo von

von Horvath, Odon
See Horvath, Oedoen von

von Horvath, Oedoen
See Horvath, Oedoen von

von Liliencron, (Friedrich Adolf Axel) Detlev
See Liliencron, (Friedrich Adolf Axel) Detlev von

Vonnegut, Kurt, Jr. 1922-**CLC 1, 2, 3, 4, 5, 8, 12, 22, 40, 60, 111; DA; DAB; DAC; DAM MST, NOV, POP; SSC 8; WLC**
See also AAYA 6; AITN 1; BEST 90:4; CA 1-4R; CANR 1, 25, 49, 75; CDALB 1968-1988; DLB 2, 8, 152; DLBD 3; DLBY 80; MTCW 1

Von Rachen, Kurt
See Hubbard, L(afayette) Ron(ald)

von Rezzori (d'Arezzo), Gregor
See Rezzori (d'Arezzo), Gregor von

von Sternberg, Josef
See Sternberg, Josef von

Vorster, Gordon 1924- .... **CLC 34**
See also CA 133

Vosce, Trudie
See Ozick, Cynthia

Voznesensky, Andrei (Andreievich) 1933-**CLC 1, 15, 57; DAM POET**
See also CA 89-92; CANR 37; MTCW 1

Waddington, Miriam 1917- .... **CLC 28**
See also CA 21-24R; CANR 12, 30; DLB 68

Wagman, Fredrica 1937- .... **CLC 7**
See also CA 97-100; INT 97-100

Wagner, Linda W.
See Wagner-Martin, Linda (C.)

Wagner, Linda Welshimer
See Wagner-Martin, Linda (C.)

Wagner, Richard 1813-1883 .... **NCLC 9**
See also DLB 129

Wagner-Martin, Linda (C.) 1936- .... **CLC 50**
See also CA 159

Wagoner, David (Russell) 1926- **CLC 3, 5, 15**
See also CA 1-4R; CAAS 3; CANR 2, 71; DLB 5; SATA 14

Wah, Fred(erick James) 1939- .... **CLC 44**
See also CA 107; 141; DLB 60

Wahloo, Per 1926-1975 .... **CLC 7**
See also CA 61-64; CANR 73

Wahloo, Peter
See Wahloo, Per

Wain, John (Barrington) 1925-1994 . **CLC 2, 11, 15, 46**
See also CA 5-8R; 145; CAAS 4; CANR 23, 54; CDBLB 1960 to Present; DLB 15, 27, 139, 155; MTCW 1

Wajda, Andrzej 1926- .... **CLC 16**
See also CA 102

Wakefield, Dan 1932- .... **CLC 7**
See also CA 21-24R; CAAS 7

Wakoski, Diane 1937- **CLC 2, 4, 7, 9, 11, 40; DAM POET; PC 15**
See also CA 13-16R; CAAS 1; CANR 9, 60; DLB 5; INT CANR-9

Wakoski-Sherbell, Diane
See Wakoski, Diane

Walcott, Derek (Alton) 1930-**CLC 2, 4, 9, 14, 25, 42, 67, 76; BLC 3; DA; DAB; DAC; DAM MST, MULT, POET; DC 7**
See also BW 2; CA 89-92; CANR 26, 47, 75; DLB 117; DLBY 81; MTCW 1

Waldman, Anne (Lesley) 1945- .... **CLC 7**
See also CA 37-40R; CAAS 17; CANR 34, 69; DLB 16

Waldo, E. Hunter
See Sturgeon, Theodore (Hamilton)

Waldo, Edward Hamilton
See Sturgeon, Theodore (Hamilton)

Walker, Alice (Malsenior) 1944- **CLC 5, 6, 9, 19, 27, 46, 58, 103; BLC 3; DA; DAB; DAC; DAM MST, MULT, NOV, POET, POP; SSC 5; WLCS**
See also AAYA 3; BEST 89:4; BW 2; CA 37-40R; CANR 9, 27, 49, 66; CDALB 1968-1988; DLB 6, 33, 143; INT CANR-27; MTCW 1; SATA 31

Walker, David Harry 1911-1992 .... **CLC 14**
See also CA 1-4R; 137; CANR 1; SATA 8; SATA-Obit 71

Walker, Edward Joseph 1934-
See Walker, Ted
See also CA 21-24R; CANR 12, 28, 53

Walker, George F. 1947- . **CLC 44, 61; DAB; DAC; DAM MST**
See also CA 103; CANR 21, 43, 59; DLB 60

Walker, Joseph A. 1935- .... **CLC 19; DAM DRAM, MST**
See also BW 1; CA 89-92; CANR 26; DLB 38

Walker, Margaret (Abigail) 1915-1998**CLC 1, 6; BLC; DAM MULT; PC 20**
See also BW 2; CA 73-76; 172; CANR 26, 54, 76; DLB 76, 152; MTCW 1

Walker, Ted .... **CLC 13**
See also Walker, Edward Joseph
See also DLB 40

Wallace, David Foster 1962- ..... **CLC 50, 114**
See also CA 132; CANR 59

Wallace, Dexter
See Masters, Edgar Lee

Wallace, (Richard Horatio) Edgar 1875-1932 **TCLC 57**
See also CA 115; DLB 70

Wallace, Irving 1916-1990 **CLC 7, 13; DAM NOV, POP**
See also AITN 1; CA 1-4R; 132; CAAS 1; CANR 1, 27; INT CANR-27; MTCW 1

Wallant, Edward Lewis 1926-1962**CLC 5, 10**

See also CA 1-4R; CANR 22; DLB 2, 28, 143; MTCW 1

Wallas, Graham 1858-1932 .... **TCLC 91**

Walley, Byron
See Card, Orson Scott

Walpole, Horace 1717-1797 .... **LC 49**
See also DLB 39, 104

Walpole, Hugh (Seymour) 1884-1941**TCLC 5**
See also CA 104; 165; DLB 34

Walser, Martin 1927- .... **CLC 27**
See also CA 57-60; CANR 8, 46; DLB 75, 124

Walser, Robert 1878-1956 **TCLC 18; SSC 20**
See also CA 118; 165; DLB 66

Walsh, Jill Paton .... **CLC 35**
See also Paton Walsh, Gillian
See also AAYA 11; CLR 2; DLB 161; SAAS 3

Walter, Villiam Christian
See Andersen, Hans Christian

Wambaugh, Joseph (Aloysius, Jr.) 1937-**CLC 3, 18; DAM NOV, POP**
See also AITN 1; BEST 89:3; CA 33-36R; CANR 42, 65; DLB 6; DLBY 83; MTCW 1

Wang Wei 699(?)-761(?) .... **PC 18**

Ward, Arthur Henry Sarsfield 1883-1959
See Rohmer, Sax
See also CA 108

Ward, Douglas Turner 1930- .... **CLC 19**
See also BW 1; CA 81-84; CANR 27; DLB 7, 38

Ward, Mary Augusta
See Ward, Mrs. Humphry

Ward, Mrs. Humphry 1851-1920 .. **TCLC 55**
See also DLB 18

Ward, Peter
See Faust, Frederick (Schiller)

Warhol, Andy 1928(?)-1987 .... **CLC 20**
See also AAYA 12; BEST 89:4; CA 89-92; 121; CANR 34

Warner, Francis (Robert le Plastrier) 1937-**CLC 14**
See also CA 53-56; CANR 11

Warner, Marina 1946- .... **CLC 59**
See also CA 65-68; CANR 21, 55; DLB 194

Warner, Rex (Ernest) 1905-1986 ...... **CLC 45**
See also CA 89-92; 119; DLB 15

Warner, Susan (Bogert) 1819-1885 **NCLC 31**
See also DLB 3, 42

Warner, Sylvia (Constance) Ashton
See Ashton-Warner, Sylvia (Constance)

Warner, Sylvia Townsend 1893-1978 **CLC 7, 19; SSC 23**
See also CA 61-64; 77-80; CANR 16, 60; DLB 34, 139; MTCW 1

Warren, Mercy Otis 1728-1814 ..... **NCLC 13**
See also DLB 31, 200

Warren, Robert Penn 1905-1989**CLC 1, 4, 6, 8, 10, 13, 18, 39, 53, 59; DA; DAB; DAC; DAM MST, NOV, POET; SSC 4; WLC**
See also AITN 1; CA 13-16R; 129; CANR 10, 47; CDALB 1968-1988; DLB 2, 48, 152; DLBY 80, 89; INT CANR-10; MTCW 1; SATA 46; SATA-Obit 63

Warshofsky, Isaac
See Singer, Isaac Bashevis

Warton, Thomas 1728-1790 .....**LC 15; DAM POET**
See also DLB 104, 109

Waruk, Kona
See Harris, (Theodore) Wilson

Warung, Price 1855-1911 .... **TCLC 45**

Warwick, Jarvis
See Garner, Hugh

Washington, Alex
See Harris, Mark

Washington, Booker T(aliaferro) 1856-1915 **TCLC 10; BLC 3; DAM MULT**
See also BW 1; CA 114; 125; SATA 28

Wilson, Robert M. 1944- .... **CLC 7, 9**
See also CA 49-52; CANR 2, 41; MTCW 1
Wilson, Robert McLiam 1964- .... **CLC 59**
See also CA 132
Wilson, Sloan 1920- .... **CLC 32**
See also CA 1-4R; CANR 1, 44
Wilson, Snoo 1948- .... **CLC 33**
See also CA 69-72
Wilson, William S(mith) 1932- .... **CLC 49**
See also CA 81-84
Wilson, (Thomas) Woodrow 1856-1924 **TCLC 79**
See also CA 166; DLB 47
Winchilsea, Anne (Kingsmill) Finch Counte 1661-1720
See Finch, Anne
Windham, Basil
See Wodehouse, P(elham) G(renville)
Wingrove, David (John) 1954- .... **CLC 68**
See also CA 133
Wintergreen, Jane
See Duncan, Sara Jeannette
Winters, Janet Lewis .... **CLC 41**
See Lewis, Janet
See also DLBY 87
Winters, (Arthur) Yvor 1900-1968 **CLC 4, 8, 32**
See also CA 11-12; 25-28R; CAP 1; DLB 48; MTCW 1
Winterson, Jeanette 1959- **CLC 64; DAM POP**
See also CA 136; CANR 58; DLB 207
Winthrop, John 1588-1649 .... **LC 31**
See also DLB 24, 30
Wiseman, Frederick 1930- .... **CLC 20**
See also CA 159
Wister, Owen 1860-1938 .... **TCLC 21**
See also CA 108; 162; DLB 9, 78, 186; SATA 62
Witkacy
See Witkiewicz, Stanislaw Ignacy
Witkiewicz, Stanislaw Ignacy 1885-1939 **TCLC 8**
See also CA 105; 162
Wittgenstein, Ludwig (Josef Johann) 1889-1951 **TCLC 59**
See also CA 113; 164
Wittig, Monique 1935(?)- .... **CLC 22**
See also CA 116; 135; DLB 83
Wittlin, Jozef 1896-1976 .... **CLC 25**
See also CA 49-52; 65-68; CANR 3
Wodehouse, P(elham) G(renville) 1881-1975 **CLC 1, 2, 5, 10, 22; DAB; DAC; DAM NOV; SSC 2**
See also AITN 2; CA 45-48; 57-60; CANR 3, 33; CDBLB 1914-1945; DLB 34, 162; MTCW 1; SATA 22
Woiwode, L.
See Woiwode, Larry (Alfred)
Woiwode, Larry (Alfred) 1941- .... **CLC 6, 10**
See also CA 73-76; CANR 16; DLB 6; INT CANR-16
Wojciechowska, Maia (Teresa) 1927- **CLC 26**
See also AAYA 8; CA 9-12R; CANR 4, 41; CLR 1; JRDA; MAICYA; SAAS 1; SATA 1, 28, 83; SATA-Essay 104
Wolf, Christa 1929- .... **CLC 14, 29, 58**
See also CA 85-88; CANR 45; DLB 75; MTCW 1
Wolfe, Gene (Rodman) 1931- **CLC 25; DAM POP**
See also CA 57-60; CAAS 9; CANR 6, 32, 60; DLB 8
Wolfe, George C. 1954- .... **CLC 49; BLCS**
See also CA 149
Wolfe, Thomas (Clayton) 1900-1938 **TCLC 4, 13, 29, 61; DA; DAB; DAC; DAM MST, NOV; SSC 33; WLC**

See also CA 104; 132; CDALB 1929-1941; DLB 9, 102; DLBD 2, 16; DLBY 85, 97; MTCW 1
Wolfe, Thomas Kennerly, Jr. 1930-
See Wolfe, Tom
See also CA 13-16R; CANR 9, 33, 70; DAM POP; DLB 185; INT CANR-9; MTCW 1
Wolfe, Tom .... **CLC 1, 2, 9, 15, 35, 51**
See also Wolfe, Thomas Kennerly, Jr.
See also AAYA 8; AITN 2; BEST 89:1; DLB 152
Wolff, Geoffrey (Ansell) 1937- .... **CLC 41**
See also CA 29-32R; CANR 29, 43
Wolff, Sonia
See Levitin, Sonia (Wolff)
Wolff, Tobias (Jonathan Ansell) 1945- . **C L C 39, 64**
See also AAYA 16; BEST 90:2; CA 114; 117; CAAS 22; CANR 54, 76; DLB 130; INT 117
Wolfram von Eschenbach c. 1170-c. 1220 **CMLC 5**
See also DLB 138
Wolitzer, Hilma 1930- .... **CLC 17**
See also CA 65-68; CANR 18, 40; INT CANR-18; SATA 31
Wollstonecraft, Mary 1759-1797 .... **LC 5**
See also CDBLB 1789-1832; DLB 39, 104, 158
Wonder, Stevie .... **CLC 12**
See also Morris, Steveland Judkins
Wong, Jade Snow 1922- .... **CLC 17**
See also CA 109
Woodberry, George Edward 1855-1930 **TCLC 73**
See also CA 165; DLB 71, 103
Woodcott, Keith
See Brunner, John (Kilian Houston)
Woodruff, Robert W.
See Mencken, H(enry) L(ouis)
Woolf, (Adeline) Virginia 1882-1941 **TCLC 1, 5, 20, 43, 56; DA; DAB; DAC; DAM MST, NOV; SSC 7; WLC**
See also CA 104; 130; CANR 64; CDBLB 1914-1945; DLB 36, 100, 162; DLBD 10; MTCW 1
Woolf, Virginia Adeline
See Woolf, (Adeline) Virginia
Woollcott, Alexander (Humphreys) 1887-1943 **TCLC 5**
See also CA 105; 161; DLB 29
Woolrich, Cornell 1903-1968 .... **CLC 77**
See also Hopley-Woolrich, Cornell George
Wordsworth, Dorothy 1771-1855 .. **NCLC 25**
See also DLB 107
Wordsworth, William 1770-1850 .. **NCLC 12, 38; DA; DAB; DAC; DAM MST, POET; PC 4; WLC**
See also CDBLB 1789-1832; DLB 93, 107
Wouk, Herman 1915- **CLC 1, 9, 38; DAM NOV, POP**
See also CA 5-8R; CANR 6, 33, 67; DLBY 82; INT CANR-6; MTCW 1
Wright, Charles (Penzel, Jr.) 1935- **CLC 6, 13, 28**
See also CA 29-32R; CAAS 7; CANR 23, 36, 62; DLB 165; DLBY 82; MTCW 1
Wright, Charles Stevenson 1932- ... **CLC 49; BLC 3; DAM MULT, POET**
See also BW 1; CA 9-12R; CANR 26; DLB 33
Wright, Frances 1795-1852 .... **NCLC 74**
See also DLB 73
Wright, Jack R.
See Harris, Mark
Wright, James (Arlington) 1927-1980 **CLC 3, 5, 10, 28; DAM POET**
See also AITN 2; CA 49-52; 97-100; CANR 4, 34, 64; DLB 5, 169; MTCW 1
Wright, Judith (Arandell) 1915- **CLC 11, 53;**

PC 14
See also CA 13-16R; CANR 31, 76; MTCW 1; SATA 14
Wright, L(aurali) R. 1939- .... **CLC 44**
See also CA 138
Wright, Richard (Nathaniel) 1908-1960 **C L C 1, 3, 4, 9, 14, 21, 48, 74; BLC 3; DA; DAB; DAC; DAM MST, MULT, NOV; SSC 2; WLC**
See also AAYA 5; BW 1; CA 108; CANR 64; CDALB 1929-1941; DLB 76, 102; DLBD 2; MTCW 1
Wright, Richard B(ruce) 1937- .... **CLC 6**
See also CA 85-88; DLB 53
Wright, Rick 1945- .... **CLC 35**
Wright, Rowland
See Wells, Carolyn
Wright, Stephen 1946- .... **CLC 33**
Wright, Willard Huntington 1888-1939
See Van Dine, S. S.
See also CA 115; DLBD 16
Wright, William 1930- .... **CLC 44**
See also CA 53-56; CANR 7, 23
Wroth, LadyMary 1587-1653(?) .... **LC 30**
See also DLB 121
Wu Ch'eng-en 1500(?)-1582(?) .... **LC 7**
Wu Ching-tzu 1701-1754 .... **LC 2**
Wurlitzer, Rudolph 1938(?)- .... **CLC 2, 4, 15**
See also CA 85-88; DLB 173
Wycherley, William 1641-1715 **LC 8, 21; DAM DRAM**
See also CDBLB 1660-1789; DLB 80
Wylie, Elinor (Morton Hoyt) 1885-1928 **TCLC 8; PC 23**
See also CA 105; 162; DLB 9, 45
Wylie, Philip (Gordon) 1902-1971 ... **CLC 43**
See also CA 21-22; 33-36R; CAP 2; DLB 9
Wyndham, John .... **CLC 19**
See also Harris, John (Wyndham Parkes Lucas) Beynon
Wyss, Johann David Von 1743-1818 **NCLC 10**
See also JRDA; MAICYA; SATA 29; SATA-Brief 27
Xenophon c. 430B.C.-c. 354B.C. ... **CMLC 17**
See also DLB 176
Yakumo Koizumi
See Hearn, (Patricio) Lafcadio (Tessima Carlos)
Yanez, Jose Donoso
See Donoso (Yanez), Jose
Yanovsky, Basile S.
See Yanovsky, V(assily) S(emenovich)
Yanovsky, V(assily) S(emenovich) 1906-1989 **CLC 2, 18**
See also CA 97-100; 129
Yates, Richard 1926-1992 .... **CLC 7, 8, 23**
See also CA 5-8R; 139; CANR 10, 43; DLB 2; DLBY 81, 92; INT CANR-10
Yeats, W. B.
See Yeats, William Butler
Yeats, William Butler 1865-1939 **TCLC 1, 11, 18, 31; DA; DAB; DAC; DAM DRAM, MST, POET; PC 20; WLC**
See also CA 104; 127; CANR 45; CDBLB 1890-1914; DLB 10, 19, 98, 156; MTCW 1
Yehoshua, A(braham) B. 1936- ... **CLC 13, 31**
See also CA 33-36R; CANR 43
Yep, Laurence Michael 1948- .... **CLC 35**
See also AAYA 5; CA 49-52; CANR 1, 46; CLR 3, 17, 54; DLB 52; JRDA; MAICYA; SATA 7, 69
Yerby, Frank G(arvin) 1916-1991 . **CLC 1, 7, 22; BLC 3; DAM MULT**
See also BW 1; CA 9-12R; 136; CANR 16, 52; DLB 76; INT CANR-16; MTCW 1
Yesenin, Sergei Alexandrovich
See Esenin, Sergei (Alexandrovich)
Yevtushenko, Yevgeny (Alexandrovich) 1933-

Literary Criticism Series
Cumulative Topic Index

This index lists all topic entries in Gale's *Classical and Medieval Literature Criticism, Contemporary Literary Criticism, Literature Criticism from 1400 to 1800, Nineteenth-Century Literature Criticism,* and *Twentieth-Century Literary Criticism.*

Topic Index

Topic Index

Twentieth-Century Literary Criticism
Cumulative Nationality Index

Nationality Index

Hardy, Thomas **4, 10, 18, 32, 48, 53, 72**
Henley, William Ernest **8**
Hilton, James **21**
Hodgson, William Hope **13**
Hope, Anthony **83**
Housman, A(lfred) E(dward) **1, 10**
Housman, Laurence **7**
Hudson, W(illiam) H(enry) **29**
Hulme, T(homas) E(rnest) **21**
Hunt, Violet **53**
Jacobs, W(illiam) W(ymark) **22**
James, Montague (Rhodes) **6**
Jerome, Jerome K(lapka) **23**
Johnson, Lionel (Pigot) **19**
Kaye-Smith, Sheila **20**
Keynes, John Maynard **64**
Kipling, (Joseph) Rudyard **8, 17**
Laski, Harold **79**
Lawrence, D(avid) H(erbert Richards) **2, 9, 16, 33, 48, 61**
Lawrence, T(homas) E(dward) **18**
Lee, Vernon **5**
Lee-Hamilton, Eugene (Jacob) **22**
Leverson, Ada **18**
Lewis, (Percy) Wyndham **2, 9**
Lindsay, David **15**
Lowndes, Marie Adelaide (Belloc) **12**
Lowry, (Clarence) Malcolm **6, 40**
Lucas, E(dward) V(errall) **73**
Macaulay, Rose **7, 44**
MacCarthy, (Charles Otto) Desmond **36**
Maitland, Frederic **65**
Manning, Frederic **25**
Meredith, George **17, 43**
Mew, Charlotte (Mary) **8**
Meynell, Alice (Christina Gertrude Thompson) **6**
Middleton, Richard (Barham) **56**
Milne, A(lan) A(lexander) **6, 88**
Moore, G. E. **89**
Morrison, Arthur **72**
Murry, John Middleton **16**
Nightingale, Florence **85**
Noyes, Alfred **7**
Oppenheim, E(dward) Phillips **45**
Orwell, George **2, 6, 15, 31, 51**
Ouida **43**
Owen, Wilfred (Edward Salter) **5, 27**
Pinero, Arthur Wing **32**
Powys, T(heodore) F(rancis) **9**
Quiller-Couch, Arthur (Thomas) **53**
Richardson, Dorothy Miller **3**
Rohmer, Sax **28**
Rolfe, Frederick (William Serafino Austin Lewis Mary) **12**
Rosenberg, Isaac **12**
Ruskin, John **20**
Rutherford, Mark **25**
Sabatini, Rafael **47**
Saintsbury, George (Edward Bateman) **31**
Saki **3**
Sapper **44**
Sayers, Dorothy L(eigh) **2, 15**
Shiel, M(atthew) P(hipps) **8**
Sinclair, May **3, 11**
Stapledon, (William) Olaf **22**
Stead, William Thomas **48**
Stephen, Leslie **23**
Strachey, (Giles) Lytton **12**
Summers, (Alphonsus Joseph-Mary Augustus) Montague **16**
Sutro, Alfred **6**
Swinburne, Algernon Charles **8, 36**
Symons, Arthur **11**

Thomas, (Philip) Edward **10**
Thompson, Francis Joseph **4**
Tomlinson, H(enry) M(ajor) **71**
Upward, Allen **85**
Van Druten, John (William) **2**
Wallace, (Richard Horatio) Edgar **57**
Wallas, Graham **91**
Walpole, Hugh (Seymour) **5**
Ward, Mrs. Humphry **55**
Warung, Price **45**
Webb, (Martha) Beatrice (Potter) **22**
Webb, Mary (Gladys Meredith) **24**
Webb, Sidney (James) **22**
Welch, (Maurice) Denton **22**
Wells, H(erbert) G(eorge) **6, 12, 19**
Williams, Charles (Walter Stansby) **1, 11**
Woolf, (Adeline) Virginia **1, 5, 20, 43, 56**
Yonge, Charlotte (Mary) **48**
Zangwill, Israel **16**

ESTONIAN
Talvik, Heiti **87**
Tammsaare, A(nton) H(ansen) **27**

FINNISH
Leino, Eino **24**
Soedergran, Edith (Irene) **31**
Westermarck, Edward **87**

FRENCH
Alain **41**
Alain-Fournier **6**
Apollinaire, Guillaume **3, 8, 51**
Artaud, Antonin (Marie Joseph) **3, 36**
Barbusse, Henri **5**
Barres, (Auguste-) Maurice **47**
Benda, Julien **60**
Bergson, Henri(-Louis) **32**
Bernanos, (Paul Louis) Georges **3**
Bernhardt, Sarah (Henriette Rosine) **75**
Bloy, Leon **22**
Bourget, Paul (Charles Joseph) **12**
Claudel, Paul (Louis Charles Marie) **2, 10**
Colette, (Sidonie-Gabrielle) **1, 5, 16**
Coppee, Francois **25**
Daumal, Rene **14**
Desnos, Robert **22**
Drieu la Rochelle, Pierre(-Eugene) **21**
Dujardin, Edouard (Emile Louis) **13**
Durkheim, Emile **55**
Eluard, Paul **7, 41**
Fargue, Leon-Paul **11**
Feydeau, Georges (Leon Jules Marie) **22**
France, Anatole **9**
Gide, Andre (Paul Guillaume) **5, 12, 36**
Giraudoux, (Hippolyte) Jean **2, 7**
Gourmont, Remy (-Marie-Charles) de **17**
Huysmans, Joris-Karl **7, 69**
Jacob, (Cyprien-)Max **6**
Jammes, Francis **75**
Jarry, Alfred **2, 14**
Larbaud, Valery (Nicolas) **9**
Leautaud, Paul **83**
Leblanc, Maurice (Marie Emile) **49**
Leroux, Gaston **25**
Loti, Pierre **11**
Martin du Gard, Roger **24**
Melies, Georges **81**
Mirbeau, Octave **55**
Mistral, Frederic **51**
Moreas, Jean **18**
Nizan, Paul **40**
Peguy, Charles Pierre **10**

Peret, Benjamin **20**
Proust, (Valentin-Louis-George-Eugene-) Marcel **7, 13, 33**
Rachilde **67**
Radiguet, Raymond **29**
Renard, Jules **17**
Rolland, Romain **23**
Rostand, Edmond (Eugene Alexis) **6, 37**
Roussel, Raymond **20**
Saint-Exupery, Antoine (Jean Baptiste Marie Roger) de **2, 56**
Schwob, Marcel (Mayer Andre) **20**
Sorel, Georges **91**
Sully Prudhomme **31**
Teilhard de Chardin, (Marie Joseph) Pierre **9**
Valery, (Ambroise) Paul (Toussaint Jules) **4, 15**
Verne, Jules (Gabriel) **6, 52**
Vian, Boris **9**
Weil, Simone (Adolphine) **23**
Zola, Emile (Edouard Charles Antoine) **1, 6, 21, 41**

GERMAN
Andreas-Salome, Lou **56**
Auerbach, Erich **43**
Barlach, Ernst **84**
Benjamin, Walter **39**
Benn, Gottfried **3**
Borchert, Wolfgang **5**
Brecht, (Eugen) Bertolt (Friedrich) **1, 6, 13, 35**
Carossa, Hans **48**
Cassirer, Ernst **61**
Doblin, Alfred **13**
Doeblin, Alfred **13**
Einstein, Albert **65**
Ewers, Hanns Heinz **12**
Feuchtwanger, Lion **3**
Frank, Bruno **81**
George, Stefan (Anton) **2, 14**
Goebbels, (Paul) Joseph **68**
Haeckel, Ernst Heinrich (Philipp August) **83**
Hauptmann, Gerhart (Johann Robert) **4**
Heym, Georg (Theodor Franz Arthur) **9**
Heyse, Paul (Johann Ludwig von) **8**
Hitler, Adolf **53**
Horney, Karen (Clementine Theodore Danielsen) **71**
Huch, Ricarda (Octavia) **13**
Kaiser, Georg **9**
Klabund **44**
Kolmar, Gertrud **40**
Lasker-Schueler, Else **57**
Liliencron, (Friedrich Adolf Axel) Detlev von **18**
Luxemburg, Rosa **63**
Mann, (Luiz) Heinrich **9**
Mann, (Paul) Thomas **2, 8, 14, 21, 35, 44, 60**
Mannheim, Karl **65**
Michels, Robert **88**
Morgenstern, Christian **8**
Nietzsche, Friedrich (Wilhelm) **10, 18, 55**
Ophuls, Max **79**
Otto, Rudolf **85**
Plumpe, Friedrich Wilhelm **53**
Raabe, Wilhelm (Karl) **45**
Rilke, Rainer Maria **1, 6, 19**
Simmel, Georg **64**
Spengler, Oswald (Arnold Gottfried) **25**
Sternheim, (William Adolf) Carl **8**
Sudermann, Hermann **15**
Toller, Ernst **10**
Vaihinger, Hans **71**
Wassermann, (Karl) Jakob **6**
Weber, Max **69**

Wedekind, (Benjamin) Frank(lin) 7
Wiene, Robert 56

GHANIAN
Casely-Hayford, J(oseph) E(phraim) 24

GREEK
Cavafy, C(onstantine) P(eter) 2, 7
Kazantzakis, Nikos 2, 5, 33
Palamas, Kostes 5
Papadiamantis, Alexandros 29
Sikelianos, Angelos 39

HAITIAN
Roumain, Jacques (Jean Baptiste) 19

HUNGARIAN
Ady, Endre 11
Babits, Mihaly 14
Csath, Geza 13
Herzl, Theodor 36
Horvath, Oedoen von 45
Jozsef, Attila 22
Karinthy, Frigyes 47
Mikszath, Kalman 31
Molnar, Ferenc 20
Moricz, Zsigmond 33
Radnoti, Miklos 16

ICELANDIC
Sigurjonsson, Johann 27

INDIAN
Chatterji, Saratchandra 13
Dasgupta, Surendranath 81
Gandhi, Mohandas Karamchand 59
Ghose, Aurabinda 63
Iqbal, Muhammad 28
Naidu, Sarojini 80
Premchand 21
Ramana Maharshi 84
Tagore, Rabindranath 3, 53
Vivekananda, Swami 88

INDONESIAN
Anwar, Chairil 22

IRANIAN
Hedayat, Sadeq 21

IRISH
A.E. 3, 10
Baker, Jean H. 3, 10
Cary, (Arthur) Joyce (Lunel) 1, 29
Dunsany, Lord 2, 59
Gogarty, Oliver St. John 15
Gregory, Isabella Augusta (Persse) 1
Harris, Frank 24
Joyce, James (Augustine Aloysius) 3, 8, 16,
   35, 52
Ledwidge, Francis 23
Martin, Violet Florence 51
Moore, George Augustus 7
O'Grady, Standish (James) 5
Shaw, Bernard 45
Shaw, George Bernard 3, 9, 21
Somerville, Edith 51
Stephens, James 4
Stoker, Bram 8
Synge, (Edmund) J(ohn) M(illington) 6, 37
Tynan, Katharine 3
Wilde, Oscar 1, 8, 23, 41
Yeats, William Butler 1, 11, 18, 31

ITALIAN
Alvaro, Corrado 60
Betti, Ugo 5
Brancati, Vitaliano 12
Campana, Dino 20
Carducci, Giosue (Alessandro Giuseppe) 32
Croce, Benedetto 37
D'Annunzio, Gabriele 6, 40
Deledda, Grazia (Cosima) 23
Giacosa, Giuseppe 7
Jovine, Francesco 79
Lampedusa, Giuseppe (Tomasi) di 13
Malaparte, Curzio 52
Marinetti, Filippo Tommaso 10
Mosca, Gaetano 75
Papini, Giovanni 22
Pareto, Vilfredo 69
Pascoli, Giovanni 45
Pavese, Cesare 3
Pirandello, Luigi 4, 29
Saba, Umberto 33
Svevo, Italo 2, 35
Tozzi, Federigo 31
Verga, Giovanni (Carmelo) 3

JAMAICAN
De Lisser, H(erbert) G(eorge) 12
Garvey, Marcus (Moziah Jr.) 41
Mais, Roger 8
McKay, Claude 7, 41
Redcam, Tom 25

JAPANESE
Akutagawa, Ryunosuke 16
Dazai Osamu 11
Futabatei, Shimei 44
Hagiwara Sakutaro 60
Hayashi, Fumiko 27
Ishikawa, Takuboku 15
Masaoka Shiki 18
Miyamoto, Yuriko 37
Miyazawa, Kenji 76
Mizoguchi, Kenji 72
Nagai Kafu 51
Natsume, Soseki 2, 10
Nishida, Kitaro 83
Noguchi, Yone 80
Rohan, Koda 22
Santoka, Taneda 72
Shimazaki Toson 5
Yokomitsu Riichi 47
Yosano Akiko 59

LATVIAN
Rainis, Janis 29

LEBANESE
Gibran, Kahlil 1, 9

LESOTHAN
Mofolo, Thomas (Mokopu) 22

LITHUANIAN
Kreve (Mickevicius), Vincas 27

MEXICAN
Azuela, Mariano 3
Gamboa, Federico 36
Gonzalez Martinez, Enrique 72
Nervo, (Jose) Amado (Ruiz de) 11
Reyes, Alfonso 33
Romero, Jose Ruben 14
Villaurrutia, Xavier 80

NEPALI
Devkota, Laxmiprasad 23

NEW ZEALANDER
Mander, (Mary) Jane 31
Mansfield, Katherine 2, 8, 39

NICARAGUAN
Dario, Ruben 4

NORWEGIAN
Bjoernson, Bjoernstjerne (Martinius) 7, 37
Bojer, Johan 64
Grieg, (Johan) Nordahl (Brun) 10
Hamsun, Knut 2, 14, 49
Ibsen, Henrik (Johan) 2, 8, 16, 37, 52
Kielland, Alexander Lange 5
Lie, Jonas (Lauritz Idemil) 5
Obstfelder, Sigbjoern 23
Skram, Amalie (Bertha) 25
Undset, Sigrid 3

PAKISTANI
Iqbal, Muhammad 28

PERUVIAN
Palma, Ricardo 29
Vallejo, Cesar (Abraham) 3, 56

POLISH
Asch, Sholem 3
Borowski, Tadeusz 9
Conrad, Joseph 1, 6, 13, 25, 43, 57
Peretz, Isaac Loeb 16
Prus, Boleslaw 48
Przybyszewski, Stanislaw 36
Reymont, Wladyslaw (Stanislaw) 5
Schulz, Bruno 5, 51
Sienkiewicz, Henryk (Adam Alexander Pius) 3
Singer, Israel Joshua 33
Witkiewicz, Stanislaw Ignacy 8

PORTUGUESE
Pessoa, Fernando (Antonio Nogueira) 27
Sa-Carniero, Mario de 83

PUERTO RICAN
Hostos (y Bonilla), Eugenio Maria de 24

ROMANIAN
Bacovia, George 24
Caragiale, Ion Luca 76
Rebreanu, Liviu 28

RUSSIAN
Aldanov, Mark (Alexandrovich) 23
Andreyev, Leonid (Nikolaevich) 3
Annensky, Innokenty (Fyodorovich) 14
Artsybashev, Mikhail (Petrovich) 31
Babel, Isaak (Emmanuilovich) 2, 13
Bagritsky, Eduard 60
Balmont, Konstantin (Dmitriyevich) 11
Bely, Andrey 7
Berdyaev, Nikolai (Aleksandrovich) 67
Bergelson, David 81
Blok, Alexander (Alexandrovich) 5
Bryusov, Valery Yakovlevich 10
Bulgakov, Mikhail (Afanas'evich) 2, 16
Bulgya, Alexander Alexandrovich 53
Bunin, Ivan Alexeyevich 6
Chekhov, Anton (Pavlovich) 3, 10, 31, 55
Der Nister 56
Eisenstein, Sergei (Mikhailovich) 57